Longman Companion
to Twentieth Century Literature
Second Edition

Longman Companion
to Twentieth Century Literature

Second Edition

A. C. Ward

Book Club Associates
London

Longman Group Limited
London
Associated companies, branches and representatives
throughout the world

This edition © Longman Group Ltd 1970, 1975

This edition published 1975 by
Book Club Associates
by arrangement with Longman Group Limited

Printed in Great Britain at the University Press, Oxford

Preface

This *Companion* is designed as much for personal possession as a guide to home reading as for consultation in schools and colleges, public and institutional libraries and offices, and by journalists and other professional workers.

Arranged alphabetically throughout and fully cross-referenced, the contents comprise:

Biographical and bibliographical entries on the great and many lesser writers of the present century, mainly English and Scottish but including also those Commonwealth (Australian, Canadian, Caribbean, New Zealand), African, American, French, German, Spanish and Russian writers with an international reputation whose books have appeared in English editions.

Articles on literary categories: Autobiography, Biography, Criticism, Drama, Essays, Fiction, Poetry.

Summaries of outstanding novels, plays, and other literary works.

Fictional characters described and related to the books or plays in which they appear.

Authors' pseudonyms.

Literary terms, topical phrases, and references and allusions to persons, institutions, and matters likely to arouse curiosity in the course of general reading.

Advice for authors on the preparation and publication of manuscripts.

Articles on Censorship, Copyright, Literary Societies, and other organizations.

Each biographical entry appears under the writer's pseudonym or preferred name, immediately followed by the full birthname and cross-referenced under the surname, thus enabling any author to be traced quickly in library and other catalogues.

Marriages and family detail are noted only when pertinent. Inherited and conferred titles are given, but not other state honours or institutional awards, the increasing number of which diminishes their significance as pointers to merit. But the distinction still attaching to the Nobel Prize and the Order of Merit is marked by the composite entries under those headings (pp. 386, 398).

Fictional characters appear under the name most often used for them in the novel or play and also under the full name.

A few exceptions are made to the principle that only authors who lived into the present century qualify for inclusion. For example, though Gerard Manley Hopkins died in 1889 his work is of twentieth-century adoption. Where an author's works were substantially divided between this century and the last, only those published since 1900/01 are included: thus Thomas Hardy's poetry is noted but not his fiction, and only the final novels of Henry James. A few isolated works of earlier date appear if they have some topical interest.

Many authors are included whose works have given widespread pleasure, as well as those intellectually exacting and academically approved. The preferences and rights both of Aunt Edna and of her dissenting nieces and nephews are recognized.

Individual works summarized include (*a*) some that have established themselves on a long-term valuation as classics; (*b*) some neglected or part-forgotten books which appear to merit revaluation; (*c*) some that made a strong impact – social or other – on their generation, not necessarily or exclusively by literary quality; (*d*) some to which I am happy to repay a debt of gratitude for particular pleasure or enlightenment.

Within the limits of available space, exclusions are inevitable. By the 1970s British publishers were bringing out an average of ninety new books for every day of the year, plus reprints and new editions of older books, figures which indicate the need for a guide through the literary forest and also the certainty of rebuke on account of names missing from the following pages.

For dates and other factual information I have drawn in varying degree on the sources listed under the heading Reference Books (p. 444). I am indebted to Colin Rickards, who provided material on which the Caribbean entries are based; to Janet Paul for help with New Zealand entries; to Dorothy Harris for typing several thousand cards with calm efficiency; and, above all, to the provider of the daily sustenance and seclusion which made this book possible.

A.C.W.

Note to second edition

I am indebted to friends and reviewers who drew attention to errors and oversights which the call for a new edition has enabled me to correct. Dates for deaths recorded from 1970 to January 1975 have been inserted, notable publications during the same period added, and necessary adjustments made where new biographical or other information has become available. A number of writers more prominent now than at the time of original compilation are included and, to accommodate these, some passages of diminished interest have been deleted.

The Appendix, on certain present-day trends, is new.

A.C.W.

An asterisk (*) preceding a word indicates that an individual entry appears alphabetically under that word.

A.A. *See* Anthony *Armstrong.

Aaron's Rod. Novel by D. H. *Lawrence published in 1922. Aaron Sisson, secretary to the Miners' Union for a colliery in the English midlands, leaves his wife and children and becomes a flautist in the orchestra of a London opera house. Later he follows an acquaintance he had made there to Italy, and in Florence becomes the lover of the Marchesa del Torre, but fails to find in her the release from the isolation of soul which he both dreads and cherishes. He continues to be fundamentally held to the wife he deserted, and much of the novel consists in conversation, typically Laurentian, on woman's impulse in marriage to use love as a means of forcing man into subjection and service. His flute (symbolically 'Aaron's rod') is smashed in an anarchist bomb explosion at the end of the book.

Abbey Theatre, Dublin. The building acquired in 1904 by Miss A. E. F. *Horniman for the *Irish Players. Plays by W. B. *Yeats, Lady *Gregory, J. M. *Synge, Lennox *Robinson, St John *Ervine, Sean *O'Casey and many other Irish playwrights were performed there. The original building was partially destroyed by fire in 1951, but with aid from the Eire government its work continued.

Abbott, Caroline. Lilia Herriton's friend and her companion during Italian travel in E. M. Forster's *Where Angels Fear to Tread* (1905).

Abercrombie, Lascelles (1881-1938). Born at Ashton-on-Mersey, Cheshire; educated at Malvern and Victoria University, Manchester; held lectureships in literature and the fine arts and became Professor of English Literature in the University of Leeds (1922-29) and in the University of London (1929-35). A collected edition of his verse was included in the Oxford Poets series in 1930, but his most notable poem *The Sale of St Thomas* appeared later (1931). He also wrote several volumes on poetics, including *The Theory of Poetry* (1924) and *The Idea of Great Poetry* (1925), and a critical study, *Thomas Hardy* (1912).

Abercrombie, Patrick (Sir Leslie Patrick Abercrombie, 1879-1957; knighted 1945). Professor of Town Planning in the University of London, 1935-46; was consultant on reconstruction of areas in Bath, etc., destroyed by German bombing in World War II, and drew up the Greater London Plan in 1944.

Abinger Harvest. A collection of essays by E. M. *Forster published in 1936. Divided into four parts: Part I, *The Present*, includes 'Notes on the English Character', and articles on Mrs Grundy, Roger *Fry, 'Liberty in England', etc. Part II, *Books*, discusses *Ibsen, T. S. *Eliot, *Proust, *Firbank, *Conrad, T. E. *Lawrence and others. In Part III, *The Past*, Voltaire, Gibbon, Coleridge and Hannah More appear, with papers on other topics, ancient and modern. Part IV, *The East*, begins with 'Salute to the Orient', and has sections on India (where Forster worked for some years) and essays on Marco Polo and Rabindranath *Tagore among others. The book is named from the Surrey village, Abinger Hammer, where the author lived at the time.

Able, Mr. In W. H. Hudson's *Green Mansions* (1904) the shortened name preferred by Abel Guevez de Argensola, the narrator in love with Rima.

Abraham Lincoln. Play in six scenes and a prologue by John *Drinkwater first performed at the Birmingham Repertory Theatre on 12 October 1918. Written in the form of an episodic chronicle drama, the scenes proceed from early 1860, with the invitation to Lincoln to stand for President, to 14 April 1865, the evening of his murder in the theatre. The intermediate scenes treat of Lincoln's ideals, motives, and conflicts facing and conducting the Civil War to prevent the Southern States from seceding on the slavery abolition issue. After the entry of America into World War I, the historical Lincoln became an heroic symbol of high-principled action, and the success of Drinkwater's play was due to its timeliness, though its combination of idealism, comedy, and effective character-drawing made the success merited. Two Chroniclers who speak the Prologue antiphonally and comment between scenes act as Chorus.

Absent-minded Beggar, The. Verses by Rudyard *Kipling, published in the *Daily Mail* on 31 October 1899, and set to music by Sir Arthur Sullivan. Both poet and composer forewent any payment on condition that all fees due for the use of the words and/or the tune should go to a fund for the dependents of the troops engaged in the Boer War in South Africa. The Absent-minded Beggar Fund eventually reached £250,000, justifying a production which, in the author's own opinion, 'had some elements of direct appeal but lacked poetry'.

Abstract Art. Painting and sculpture which confines itself to forms and shapes in mass, line, and colour, and eschews emotional or intellectual content associated with subject or narrative or living objects. It became a dominant mode in the 20th century.

Absurd, The. See The *Theatre of the Absurd.

Académie Française, L'. See *French Academy.

Academy, The. Founded in 1869 as a literary, scientific, and art monthly, *The Academy* was published fortnightly from 1871 and weekly from 1874 to 1922 when it merged with the *English Review*. Matthew Arnold was among those who wrote for it, and its contributors included numerous present-century notable men of letters.

Academy, British. See *British Academy.

Academy, Royal. See *Royal Academy of Arts.

Achebe, Chinua. See *African Writers.

Achillas. General of Ptolemy's troops in *Caesar and Cleopatra* by Bernard Shaw.

Acis. In the fifth and final part of *Back to Methuselah* by Bernard Shaw, the youth with whom Amaryllis falls in love on the day she is born.

Ackerley, J. R. (Joe Randolph Ackerley, 1896-1967). Born in London; educated at Rossall School and (after war service, 1914-18) at Cambridge, where he studied law. He then went to India as private secretary and tutor in a maharaja's household, an experience that produced *Hindoo Holiday* (1932). For nearly a quarter of a century he was literary editor of *The Listener* (B.B.C.). He also wrote a play, *Prisoners of War* (1925); a novel, *We Think the World of You* (1960); *My Dog Tulip*, about his Alsatian (1956); and compiled an anthology, *Escapers All* (1932). His autobiography, *My Father and Myself*, was published posthumously (1968).

Ackland, Rodney (1908-). Born and educated in London; studied for the stage and acted from 1924 for many years in London and the provinces. Author of *Improper People* (1929), *Strange Orchestra* (1932) and other plays, as well as many adaptations of novels by other writers. *The Celluloid Mistress* (autobiography, 1954).

Action Française, L'. Founded in Paris in 1899 as the organ of a political group notorious for antisemitic and fascist tendencies. It ceased publication in 1944.

Action Painting. Term applied to a type of painting in vogue in the U.S. and elsewhere after *c*. 1940. Paint is thrown, splashed, dribbled, on to the canvas or other surface, 'on the theory that colour, line, form, and texture, used freely in informal combination, have greater power of expression and visual excitement'. The idea is related to Surrealism and other derivatives of the unconscious.

Acton, Lord (Sir John Emerich Edward Dalberg, 1834-1902; 8th baronet; 1st Baron Acton, 1869). Regius Professor of Modern History in the University of Cambridge, 1895-1902; helped to plan the *English Historical Review* (1886; still continuing) and the *Cambridge Modern History*. Most of his work was published posthumously: *Lectures on Modern History* (1906), *The History of Freedom* (1907), *Lectures on the French Revolution* (1910)—all of value to scholars and students. By a wider public he is best known as the author of a comment which assumed more significance in the middle decades of the twentieth century: 'Power tends to corrupt, and absolute power corrupts absolutely. Great men are almost always bad men . . .' (in a letter to Mandell Creighton, April 1887, printed in Creighton's *Life and Letters* by Louise Creighton, 1904, vol. i, p. 372).

Adam. Appears as a character in Part I of *Back to Methuselah* by Bernard Shaw.

Adamastor. Volume of poems by Roy *Campbell published in 1930. It included a number of the author's most notable pieces, among them 'The Zulu Girl', 'The Zebras', 'The Sisters', 'Horses on the Camargue'.

Adam Smith, Janet (Janet Buchanan Adam Smith, 1905- ; Mrs Michael *Roberts). Born in Aberdeen, daughter of the Principal of the University Sir George Adam Smith; educated at Cheltenham and Oxford. Literary Editor of the *New Statesman*, 1952-60. Author of *R. L. Stevenson* (1937), *Mountain Holidays* (1946), *Life Among the Scots* (1946), *John Buchan* (1965).

Adams, Henry (Henry Brooks Adams, 1838-1918). A descendant of the Adams family, prominent in the United States since John Adams became the second President in 1796,

Henry Adams was primarily a historian, but is remembered in literature for the humanism and fine prose of his *Mont-Saint-Michel and Chartres: a study of thirteenth-century unity* (1904; 1913) and *The Education of Henry Adams: a study of twentieth-century multiplicity* (1907; 1918). Each of these was privately circulated on the first of the dates given, and published later.

Adcock, St John (Arthur St John Adcock, 1864-1930). Wrote novels, short stories, poems, essays, and books on London, including *London from the Top of a 'Bus* (1906) and *The Booklover's London* (1913); *Collected Poems* (1929); Editor of *The *Bookman* from 1923.

Adding Machine, The. Play in seven scenes by Elmer *Rice, produced in New York in 1923 by the Theatre Guild. The chief characters are Mr and Mrs Zero; others are Mr and Mrs One, Two, Three, Four, Five, and Six, Daisy Diana Dorothea Devore, and The Boss. A product of *Expressionism, the theme exposes Zero and his like as slave creatures doomed to an everlasting cycle of mentally and emotionally starved existences. As a contemporary document the play is an indictment of commercialized social organization reducing men and women to soulless automata.

Adelphi. An area in London between the Strand and the Thames built in the 18th century by the brothers Robert and James Adam. It was one of their most notable and ambitious architectural achievements and embraced one of London's finest groups of private residences. The main part was demolished in the 1930s and replaced by office blocks. Among notable writers who lived in Adelphi before the demolition were Bernard *Shaw and J. M. *Barrie.

Adler, Alfred (1870-1937). Born near Vienna. He practised as an eye specialist from 1897, but his later world-repute developed from studies in neurology and psychoanalysis. He associated with Sigmund *Freud from 1906, until the increasing divergence of their opinions led to a permanent break five years later. Adler opposed his own theory of the *inferiority complex* to Freud's emphasis on sexual repression, as the key to understanding psychical problems and neuroses. Despite fundamental disagreements, Freud, Adler, and Carl *Jung were the founding fathers of the study and practice of psychiatry.

Among Adler's writings are *The Practice and Theory of Individual Psychology* (1924), *Understanding Human Nature* (1927), *The Pattern of Life* (1931).

Admirable Bashville, The, or Constancy Rewarded, 'being the Novel of *Cashel Byron's Profession* done into a Stage Play in three Acts and in Blank Verse', by Bernard *Shaw. The novel having been piratically dramatized in America, Shaw had to secure English copyright by quickly making his own stage version. He chose blank verse because, he explained, it 'is so childishly easy and expeditious' that he was able to do in a week what would have taken him a month in prose. Lydia Carey, a rich landowner, falls in love with Cashel Byron who has rented a lodge on her estate, not disclosing that it is to be his training quarters. Lydia is not aware that he is a pugilist until her footman, Bashville, reads her a newspaper report of a contest won by Cashel. Because he has kept his profession secret from her, Lydia declines to receive him when he visits her house in London, but she relents after Bashville has knocked him down. They all go to another fight at Islington which ends in a riot. Bashville, who is in love with Lydia, renounces his aspirations and is taken in hand by Cashel, who sees in him the makings of a champion boxer. The blank verse largely parodies lines from Shakespeare. The first professional performance was in London in 1903 and the piece was first published in 1909, being later included in the volume *Translations and Tomfooleries* (1930).

Admirable Crichton, The. Comedy in four acts by J. M. *Barrie, performed in London in 1902. The Earl of Loam, a peer with democratic ideals, compels his Society-conscious daughters Lady Mary Lasenby and her younger sisters Lady Catherine and Lady Agatha to entertain the household staff as equals at a tea-party once a month. These gatherings embarrass both the family and the staff, who insist on entering in the strict order of precedence ordained by servants'-hall etiquette. Lord Loam plans a yachting cruise for himself, his daughters, his nephew, and the young man to whom Lady Mary is engaged. The party is completed by Crichton the butler and Tweeny the kitchen maid. The yacht is wrecked and all on board are stranded on a desert island. When Crichton, the one competent person among them shows signs of insubordination, the rest move to another part of the island, but soon return hungry. Two years later a log house has been built and Crichton accepted as leader. Lady Mary has become infatuated by him, but when she tells him that he is the best man among them he replies 'On an island, my lady, perhaps; but in England, no' and decides to leave Lord Loam's service. The title of the play is from an account by Sir Thomas Urquhart (c. 1611-60) of the varied accomplishments of James Crichton (1560-82), called 'the admirable Crichton' by Urquhart.

Adventure, An. First published in 1911 as by 'Miss Morison' and 'Miss Lamont', this account of how 'two women of the twentieth century found themselves walking together in the Trianon (at Versailles) of 1789, and, there, coming upon figure after figure (including Marie Antoinette) unaccountably risen from that unfamiliar past', was at first dismissed by some critics as an hallucination, and received by others as acceptable evidence of a unique psychical experience. The book was occasionally reprinted during the next twenty years, but received a new and stronger impetus in the 1930s as a confirmation of the space–time theory developed from the relativity principle of *Einstein. The authors of *An Adventure* were by that time known to be Miss Anne *Moberly and Miss Eleanor *Jourdain, successively Principals of St Hugh's College, Oxford, and the 1931 edition of their book included a note by J. W. *Dunne, whose *Experiment with Time* had produced widespread acceptance of the view that 'past', 'present', and 'future' are simultaneous features of 'now'. Dunne's note to *An Adventure* points out that 'if Einstein is right, the contents of time are just as "real" as the contents of space. Marie Antoinette—body and brain—is sitting in the Trianon garden now . . . . It is a *four*-dimensional "now", such as would be employed by a super-mind which could perceive Marie Antoinette and you (who are reading this) as equally present to perception.'

Adventure Story. Chronicle play in a prologue, two acts, and an epilogue by Terence *Rattigan, performed in London in March 1949. The ten central scenes pass (336-323 B.C.) from Delphi, where Alexander the Great attempts unsuccessfully to consult the Oracle, to Babylon, Issus, Gaugemela,

Parthia, Bactria, and Alexandria-at-the-end-of-the-world, representing stages in Alexander's defeat of the Persians under Darius III, who is assassinated in Act II sc. i by Prince Bessus of Bactria, one of his allies. Darius's mother, wife, and daughter are captured, Alexander treats the Queen-Mother as his own mother, and marries Roxana, daughter of a defeated chieftain. In the last scene of Act II Alexander and his Greek forces are on the eve of the expedition into India, a further stage in his purpose of becoming Master of the World, ruling a world state: 'No more war. No more oppression . . . . A universal peace, blessed by the Almighty Gods.' The prologue and epilogue frame the main action and show Alexander dying of fever after the failure of the Indian enterprise and being urged to name his successor. He replies: 'Who is to be Master of the World? . . . Who shall I condemn to death? No one. This will be my last act of mercy. Let them fight it out for themselves. . . . The adventure is over.'

Adventures of the Black Girl in Her Search for God, The. A parable by Bernard *Shaw published in 1932. In reply to the question 'Where is God?' the white woman missionary who had converted the black girl replies 'He has said "Seek and ye shall find me."'' The girl goes into the African forest in search of God, encountering in turn Noah's God, Job's God, and then Koheleth (Ecclesiastes the preacher), the prophet Micah, Pavlov, the discoverer of conditioned reflexes, Jesus, St Peter, a party of explorers ('the Caravan of the Curious'), Mahomet, a sculptor (image-maker, carving crucifixes as well as statuettes of Venus), Voltaire, and finally a redhaired Irishman whom she marries, settling down with him and their coffee-coloured children. Her search had confused her with conflicting and irreconcilable presentations of the nature of God and opinions as to his existence or non-existence. In a section following the tale, Shaw notes that he wrote it in Africa, proceeds to discuss the Bible and its uses, points to the black girl's conclusion 'that it is wiser to take Voltaire's advice by cultivating her garden and bringing up her piccaninnies than to spend her life imagining that she can find a complete explanation of the universe', and ends with a reference to his 'curious and sudden inspiration to write this tale' instead of a play as he intended.

AE. (pseudonym of George William Russell, 1867-1935). Born in County Armagh of Protestant parents; educated in Dublin, where he started work at a brewery in 1884 and then from 1890 was for six years a draper's clerk. Meanwhile he had met W. B. *Yeats while studying at art school, and through him became associated with the Irish Agricultural Organization Society and edited its *Irish Homestead* from 1906 to 1923; then it merged with the *Irish Statesman*, which he edited from 1923 to 1930. As AE he had published *Homeward: Songs by the Way* (1894), and he continued to write verse, regarding it as his most important activity, notwithstanding his effective participation in Irish agrarian and political affairs. He was not a convinced separatist, since he believed interdependence was economically important for both Ireland and England. At the beginning of their long friendship Yeats had interested Russell in theosophy and it continued to be an important factor in his religious philosophy, upon which he discoursed in *The Candle of Vision* (1918). Two fantasies—*Song and Its Fountains* (1932) and *The Avatars* (1933)— express his idealistic political views; these are most directly stated in *Cooperation and Nationality* (1912) and *The National Being: some thoughts on an Irish policy* (1917). He published numerous books of verse, among them *The Divine Vision* (1904), *Lyrical Poems, Old and New* (1906), *Deirdre: A Drama* (1907), *Gods of War* (1915). *Collected Poems* (1913; enlarged edition 1926) preceded *Enchantment* (1930), *Vale* (1931), *The House of the Titans* (1934). *Deirdre* (1907) is a prose drama. His pseudonym was arrived at accidentally when AE was all that a printer's reader could make of his intended pen-name AEon. There is much about him in George Moore's *Hail and Farewell*.

Aesthetic Movement. Associated especially with the 1890s, those in the movement propagated the theory that art has no moral obligations but is concerned only with beauty or 'exquisite moments'. Though the principle of 'art for art's sake' to which the movement was devoted had earlier exponents, its modern manifestation is frequently attributed to misapplication of certain tenets in the final chapter of *Studies in the History of the Renaissance* (1873) by Walter Pater (1839-94). The movement, with its extravagances of attitude and dress, was ridiculed in *Patience* (1881), a Gilbert and Sullivan comic opera, and was for several decades regarded as discredited by the downfall of Oscar *Wilde, its leading figure, while Aubrey Beardsley's amoral drawings were generally considered obscene and were, indeed, condemned by a Scottish court as late as 1967. Arthur *Symons, Lionel *Johnson, and John *Davidson were among the lesser associates of the movement, which is analysed minutely in *The Eighteen Nineties* (1913) by Holbrook *Jackson.

Aesthetics. The philosophy and science of the fine arts—poetry, music, painting and sculpture. See *Introduction to Aesthetics* (1949) by E. F. *Carritt.

Affable Hawk. Pseudonym used by Desmond *MacCarthy for literary articles in the *New Statesman*.

Affair, The. Novel by C. P. *Snow, published in 1960, a volume in the *Strangers and Brothers* sequence, in which Lewis Eliot is a leading character. The 'affair' is the case of a young research Fellow, Donald Howard, at an imaginary Cambridge college who is accused of a scientific fraud, and after investigation by the Court of Seniors is deprived of his Fellowship. Largely through the importunity of his wife, Laura, though also because some of the Fellows believe him innocent, the case is twice reopened, the second time with Lewis Eliot and another barrister representing the opposing sides before the Court of Seniors, and Howard is somewhat ungenerously reinstated. The impact of college politics on human relationships is a main theme, with the friendships and animosities of dons and dons' wives in the foreground, and the graceless character of Howard himself as an obstacle to the claims of justice.

Affluent Society, The. By J. K. *Galbraith, published in 1958. An analytical study of economics considered historically and in relation to the change from a state of society in which poverty was a majority problem to one in which for most Western nations it has since become a minority problem. 'Conventional wisdom' (the clinging to 'acceptable ideas' no longer valid) is attacked as having been undermined and rendered obsolete by the march of events, which demands some fundamental rethinking about work, leisure, happiness and social harmony.

African Queen, The. Novel by C. S. *Forester published in 1935. Rose Sayer, thirty-three, sister of an ascetic English missionary whose sole helper and utterly dedicated admirer she had been for ten years in German Central Africa, is left alone when he dies at the beginning of World War I, after the local German commander has conscripted all the people of the mission station and commandeered their food and possessions. On the day of the Rev. Samuel Sayer's death she is visited by Charles Allnutt, a cockney mining engineer from the Belgian Congo, whose native workers have deserted and left him with the *African Queen* (laden with supplies and explosives for the mines), a small river steam-launch in an advanced state of disrepair. Rose's Christian convictions are overborne by a determination to be revenged on the Germans for raiding the mission, and she induces the reluctant Allnutt to embark with her on the launch with the purpose of destroying the German gunboat *Königin Luise* which controls Lake Wittelsbach and prevents Allied invasion from the Congo. The *African Queen* makes a perilous voyage along the river Ulanga, negotiating rapids, escaping attack from a German post, and inching a passage along narrow junglebound mudclogged channels. The dangers, which include repeated severe attacks of malaria, draw Rose and Allnutt together as they fight their way through, he keeping the half-derelict engine working and carrying out repairs to the propellor shaft and blades, she controlling the tiller. They have their most testing experience on reaching the mangrove swamp in the delta where the river joins the lake. Having observed the gunboat, they prepare the launch for a suicide attack on the *Königin Luise,* using the explosives they have on board. Their plan is frustrated by a tropical storm which sinks the *African Queen.* They are rescued and captured, but are released before the *Luise* is sunk by two British armed fast motor boats brought overland to the lake, and decide to marry.

African Witch, The. Novel by Joyce *Cary published in 1936. Louis Aladai, an Oxford-educated Nigerian, on returning to his own country claims to be the next heir to the Emirate of his province, Rimi, with a native population of a million and a small number of British traders and officials headed by the Resident, J. O. Burwash. Accustomed to treatment as an equal at the university and befriended there by Judith Coote, a history don, Aladai is bewildered and incensed by the whites' social discrimination in his own country. Miss Coote, who has come to Nigeria as the fiancée of Captain Rackham, assistant police commissioner, incurs disapproval by continuing to regard Louis as a friend. The young man's sister, Elizabeth Aladai, untouched by European education, is a *ju-ju* priestess with great influence. She holds witch trials and, believing herself possessed of magical gifts of detection, condemns to imprisonment and torture innocent victims accused of witchcraft, though herself exercising the power of an arch-witch. She disposes of husbands she is tired of, and has taken Akande Tom, a young and handsome negro, as her latest favourite. Among the whites, Rackham becomes infatuated with Dryas Honeywood, a new arrival, younger and prettier than Judith. She also behaves courteously to Louis Aladai, arousing Rackham's anger and leading him to strike the young Nigerian, who is knocked into the river in the ensuing fight. Meanwhile the Resident has seemed to favour a rival claimant to the Emirate, and this, coupled with Rackham's attack, drives Aladai to rebel and abandon European clothing. The native village women's clubs combine to make war on the whites, and further trouble is caused by a crazed mulatto preacher, Selah Coker, whose gospel is a bastard combination of Christianity and blood sacrifice. Aladai relapses into savagery under Coker's malign oratory, and both are killed by local troops sent to quell the disturbances, during which Dryas Honeywood disappears, presumed murdered. Rackham resigns and returns to England, his engagement to Judith ended. Akande Tom tries to break with Elizabeth Aladai, but she silently bewitches him and he worms snakelike to her feet 'a flattened, boneless mass'.

African Writers. The two-word heading of this entry is intended to relate only to Black African authors, excluding all those of European origin, however remote, who were born or settled and have written in Africa. Those appear under their individual names elsewhere in this book. But the removal of Europeans from consideration does little to clear the field, for Black African writings in European languages, mainly English, come from no fewer than fifteen countries within the continent of Africa: Angola, Cameroun, Congo, Dahomey, Gambia, Ghana, Guinea, Ivory Coast, Kenya, Moçambique, Nigeria, Ruanda, Senegal, Sierra Leone, South Africa. In selecting poems and prose passages from these countries for the anthology *African Writing Today* (Penguin Books, 1967), the editor, Ezekiel Mphahlele, drew upon forty-two writers. He says in the Introduction: 'We like to think that Africans outside South Africa will soon feel the need to talk to their own immediate human environment, in their art, when the white-man-listen theme has exhausted itself.' Even from among those books in which 'the white-man-listen theme' might be supposed present, few have so far been published in England, since an English public for literature from Africa has still to be cultivated. Following is a selected reading-list of London-published editions. Chinua Achebe (1930-): novels— *Things Fall Apart* (1958), *No Longer at Ease* (1960), *Arrow of God* (1964), *A Man of the People* (1966). John Pepper Clark: *Three Plays* (1966; Song of a Goat, The Masquerade, The Raft), *A Reed in the Tide* (poems; 1965). Sarif Easmon: *Dear Parent and Ogre* (play; 1964), *The New Patriots* (play; 1965), *The Burnt-out Marriage* (novel; 1967). Cyprian Ekwensi: novels— *Jagua Nana* (1961), *Burning Grass* (1962), *Beautiful Feathers* (1963), *People of the City* (1963), *Iska* (1966). Camara Laye: novels— *The African Child* (1959), *The Radiance of the King* (1965). Ezekiel Mphahlele: *Down Second Avenue* (autobiography; 1959), *The African Image* (essays; 1962). Onuora Nzekwu: novels—*Wand of the Noble Wood* (1961), *Blade Among the Boys* (1962). Lenrie Peters: *The Second Round* (novel; 1966). Wole Soyinka: plays—*A Dance of the Forests* (1963), *The Lion and the Jewel* (1963), *The Road* (1965); *The Interpreters* (novel; 1965). Amos Tutuola: novels— *The Palm-Wine Drunkard* (1952), *My Life in the Bush of Ghosts* (1954), *The Brave African Huntress* (1958); *Feather Woman of the Jungle* (short stories; 1962). ANTHOLOGIES: Ed. Neville Denny, *Pan-African Short Stories* (1965); Ed. Paul Edwards, *Modern African Narrative* (1966); John Reed and Clive Wake, *A Book of African Verse* (1964); Richard Rive, *Modern African Prose* (1964). PERIODICAL: *Black Orpheus*. CRITICISM: Oladele Taiwo: *An Introduction to West African Literature* (1967). *Introduction to African Literature* (Critical Writing from *Black Orpheus*) ed. by Ulli Bier (1967).

After Many a Summer. Novel by Aldous *Huxley, published in 1939. Engaged by telegram, Jeremy Pordage, a middle-aged English graduate of Trinity College, Cambridge, arrives in Los Angeles, where a coloured chauffeur waits to drive him to the home of his millionaire employer, Jo Stoyte, whose recent purchase of the Hauberk Papers Jeremy is to catalogue. On the way to 'Mr Stoyte's place', a mock castle with medieval appurtenances, the chauffeur displays the millionaire's other possessions, including 'Beverly Pantheon, the Personality Cemetery' ornamented with numerous nude statues, coloured fountains, miniature reproductions of Shakespeare's tomb and the Taj Mahal, while a Perpetual Wurlitzer broadcasts day and night organ music. Living in the castle, besides the sixty-year-old Stoyte, are his twenty-two-year-old mistress, Virginia Maunciple, his 'house physician', Dr Sigmund Obispo, who is also seeking to discover a specific for longevity, and Obispo's young assistant, Peter Boone. A bungalow nearby is occupied by elderly William Propter, author of *Short Studies in the Counter Reformation,* who compensates Stoyte's brutal exploitation of the poor whites employed as casuals in his orange groves by practical measures for their welfare. In discussions with Jeremy and Peter, Propter advocates a way of life freed from 'time and craving . . . the raw material of evil'. At once comic and ironic, philosophic, religious, and erotic, and in its development both tragic and horrific, the narrative leads—by way of the 18th-century manuscript journal of the 5th Earl of Gonister found by Jeremy among the Hauberk Papers—to a conclusive anticipation of Stoyte and Obispo's search for the elixir of life. The title is part of a line from Tennyson's 'Tithonus'.

After Strange Gods. Subtitled 'A Primer of Modern Heresy', this book (published 1934) contains the three Page-Barbour Lectures delivered by T. S. *Eliot at the University of Virginia in the previous year. *Tradition* and *orthodoxy* considered as desirably complementary in literature form the main theme, provoked by the author's conviction that 'In an age of unsettled beliefs and enfeebled tradition the man of letters, the poet, and the novelist are in a situation dangerous for themselves and for their readers'.

Agate, James (James Evershed Agate, 1877-1947). Dramatic critic on the *Sunday Times* and other papers. He collected several volumes of his articles, and his extensive autobiography was published in successive volumes as *Ego* (1935) to *Ego 9* (issued posthumously in 1948).

Age of Anxiety, The. A six-part work in varied verse forms and occasional prose by W. H. *Auden, published in 1948. Subtitled 'A Baroque Eclogue' it has been described as 'a modernistic morality in often elusive language on the ageless theme of the world's need of a saviour', with a wide range of allusiveness 'which stretches from myth and ancient history to sad and silly little tunes and "hot numbers" from a juke box'.

Agony column. Colloquial name for the Personal Column of *The Times*, containing miscellaneous small advertisements sometimes used as a medium for more or less cryptic pseudonymous communications relating to emotional crises or other personal distresses.

Ah King. Volume of six short stories by W. Somerset *Maugham published in 1933 and containing some of his best work in this medium: 'Footprints in the Jungle', 'The Book-Bag', 'The Vessel of Wrath', 'The Door of Opportunity', 'The Back of Beyond', 'Neil Macadam'.

Ah, Wilderness! Comedy in four acts by Eugene *O'Neill written in 1933. The scene is mainly the sitting room in the Millers' house in 'a large small-town' in Connecticut. Nat and Essie Miller, parents of three sons (Arthur, Richard, Tommy), and a daughter (Muriel) have living with them Sid Davis (Essie's brother, a good-hearted joker, but an incorrigible drunk) and Lily Miller (Nat's sister, forty-two, an unmarried school teacher, who is in love with Sid but refuses to marry him because of his habits). Arthur is a college football type; Richard is in the stage of adolescent revolutionary priggishness and given to quoting Swinburne, Oscar Wilde, Bernard Shaw, Ibsen. The father of his girl friend, Muriel McComber, calls to complain that Richard is corrupting the girl by introducing her to such writings, and brings a letter in which Muriel repudiates

Richard. The boy is induced by his elder brother's college friend, Wint Selby, to join him in dating 'a couple of swift babies from New Haven', and Richard returns maudlin-drunk, having been thrown out of the bar when he fails to respond to the 'typical college "tart" of the period' with whom Selby has involved him. The following morning his sister brings Richard another letter from Muriel explaining that she was compelled by her father to write the previous letter, and the two are reconciled. *Ah, Wilderness!* is O'Neill's only domestic comedy. The title is from a line in Fitzgerald's translation of the *Rubaiyat of Omar Khayyam*.

Aidé, Hamilton (Charles Hamilton Aidé, 1826-1906). Poet, novelist, playwright, and amateur painter. The bulk of his work belongs to the 19th century, but a volume of poems, *Past and Present* appeared in 1903, a novel *The Chivalry of Harold* in 1907, and *We are Seven: Half Hours on the Stage* in 1902. Irving played Philip in Aidé's play with that title (1874), dealing with Count Philip de Miraflore and based on Balzac's story *La Grande Bretèche*.

Aiken, Conrad (Conrad Potter Aiken, 1889-1973). American poet, novelist, short-story writer and critic; born at Savannah, Georgia. Educated at Concord and Harvard. Professor of Poetry at the Library of Congress, 1950-52. His writings show a marked interest in psychoanalysis and in (then) new literary techniques. Novels include *Great Circle* (1933) and *King Coffin* (1935). *Collected Poems* (1953); *Collected Criticism* (1958); *Collected Short Stories* (1960).

Ainger, Alfred (1837-1904). Educated at London and Cambridge universities; ordained in the Anglican Church (1860); Canon of Bristol (1887-1903); Court chaplain. Edited Charles Lamb's works, and wrote a biography of him (1882) and of George Crabbe (1903), besides much literary journalism. *Lectures and Essays* (2 vols, 1905) were collected posthumously.

Air-conditioned Nightmare, The. By Henry *Miller, published in 1945. After long expatriation the author returns from Europe and makes a journey across the United States, feeling the need to effect a reconciliation with his native land. He finds that a great change has come over America and is distressed by the evidences of soulless materialism: 'The lack of resilience, the feeling of hopelessness' and over it all a 'veneer of fatuous optimism'. He meets with many sorts of people and his pessimism concerning the state of the nation is lightened by contacts with artists and others who share his ideals.

Aisgill, Alice. See *Alice Aisgill.

Akhmatova, Anna. Pseudonym of Anna Andreyevna Gorenko (1889-1966). Born near Odessa; lived mainly in Leningrad. Her poet husband was accused of counter-revolutionary activity and shot in 1921. She came to be ranked as Russia's greatest woman poet and received honours from universities abroad, including Oxford, though in her own country her staunch Christian convictions led to periods of ostracism. She published *Evening* (1912), *The White Flock* (1917); much later, *Requiem,* a poem provoked by the Stalin persecutions, and a considerable body of other poetical work, as well as studies of Pushkin.

A la recherche du temps perdu. Novel by Marcel *Proust, in eight sections, published 1913-28; translated into English (1923-32) in twelve volumes collectively entitled *Remembrance of Things Past,* all but the last volume by *Scott-Moncrieff; Stephen *Hudson completed the series, but his translation was superseded by that of Andreas Mayor (1970) based on the 1954 definitive French text.

Alain-Fournier (*né* Henri Alban Fournier, 1886-1914). Born near Bourges; educated at a village school and at Brest. Visited England in 1905, studying the works of the 19th-century Pre-Raphaelite painters. Killed early in World War I. His novel *Le Grand Meaulnes* (translated as *The Lost Domain* in 1959), first published in France in 1912, has become established as a classic dreamlike story of 'coiled surprises and wavering colours', 'suffused in the kind of romanticism which is associated with names like Novalis and Keats' (Alan Pryce-Jones, introduction to The World's Classics edition).

Alan, A. J. (pseudonym of Leslie Harrison Lambert, 1883-1940). Though the stories told by A. J. Alan were one of the most popular of all B.B.C. broadcasts, his identity was unknown to the public (and even to many of the B.B.C. staff) until after his death, when his name, his age, and that he was a senior Foreign Office executive were the sum total of the biographical information divulged. Notwithstanding that his first broadcast on 31 January 1924 was on his part a diffident amateur experiment, he immediately displayed complete mastery of apparently impromptu storytelling, his pauses and hesitations appearing spontaneous, though they were painstakingly rehearsed. Recognizing that the success of his 'turn' might be lessened by frequency, he would accept no more than three engagements a year. Selections of his stories were published as *Good Evening, Everyone!* (1928), *A. J. Alan's Second Book* (1933), and *The Best of A. J. Alan* (edited by Kenelm Foss, 1954).

Albanesi, Madame (*née* Effie Maria Henderson, 1859-1936; married Chevalier Carlo Albanesi, Professor of Music, who died 1926). Author of more than seventy popular romantic novels: e.g. *Peter a Parasite* (1901), *Susannah and One Elder* (1903), *The Sunlit Hills* (1915), *The House that Jane Built* (1921), *The Moon through Glass* (1928), *An Unframed Portrait* (1935). *Sister Anne* (1908) was produced in a dramatized version with Marion Terry in the cast. Madame Albanesi's biography of her daughter *Meggie Albanesi* (1928) told the story of the tragically brief life of an accomplished young actress who died at the age of twenty-four after excellent performances in plays by Galsworthy *(The *Skin Game),* Clemence Dane *(A *Bill of Divorcement),* and others. In addition to writings under her own name, Madame Albanesi wrote even more prolifically under the pseudonym Effie Adelaide Rowlands, producing over 120 romantic novels.

Albee, Edward (1928-). Born in Washington, D.C.; educated at Columbia University. Author of *The American Dream* (1960), *The Death of Bessie Smith* (1962), *The Zoo Story* (1963), *Who's Afraid of Virginia Woolf?* (1964), *Tiny Alice* (1964), *All Over* (1972) and other plays.

Albertine. A leading character in *A la recherche du temps perdu by Marcel Proust; full name, Albertine Simonet. The narrator meets her first in Balbec, takes her to Paris as his mistress, and is torn between love and jealousy on account of her lesbian associations. She is killed in a riding accident.

Alden, Isabella Macdonald. *See* Pansy.

Alden, Roberta. *See* *Roberta Alden.

Aldine. Name given to printing type designed by the Venetian printer Aldus Manutius (1450-1515). He was the inventor of italic type.

Aldington, Richard (1892-1962). Born in Hampshire; educated at Dover College and London University. He was shell-shocked in World War I. Before the war he had begun to publish poetry and married (in 1913) the American Imagist poet Hilda *Doolittle, from whom he was divorced in 1937. In 1915 they published *Images, Old and New;* his *Collected Poems* appeared in 1928. He became widely known with *Death of a Hero* (1929), one of the outstanding novels of World War I. As a friend of D. H. *Lawrence he wrote *Portrait of a Genius, But . . .* (1950), taking the title from the phrase often applied to Lawrence by those who took a qualified view of him; Aldington also compiled an anthology of Lawrence's prose, *The Spirit of Place* (1935). Among his other works are *All Men are Enemies* (novel, 1933), *Wellington* (biography, 1946); later books of verse include *A Dream in the Luxembourg* (1930). His controversial *Lawrence of Arabia: A Biographical Enquiry* (1955), opposed a different interpretation of T. E. *Lawrence's character and achievements to those commonly accepted. He also translated Julien *Benda's *La Trahison des Clercs,* as *The Great Betrayal* (1928). Autobiography: *Life for Life's Sake* (1940).

Aldiss, Brian (1925-   ). Author of *The Brightfount Diaries* (1955) and many later volumes, including *Brian Aldiss Omnibus I* (1969), *II* (1971). Received award as best contemporary writer of science fiction, of which he wrote a history (*Billion Year Spree,* 1973).

Aleichem, Shalom (pseudonym of Solomon J. Rabinowitz, 1859-1916). Born in Russia; settled in America, with an interval of several years in Italy. Became well known internationally with his stories and novels of Jewish life, written in Yiddish and mostly set in villages of the Ukraine; a number of these were dramatized, and he also wrote a few other plays.

Alexander, George (Sir George Alexander, 1858-1918; knighted 1911). A leading actor of his period, noted for his distinguished bearing and his civilized management of the St James's Theatre from 1890-1918, during which he continuously encouraged contemporary British playwrights, including Stephen *Phillips *(Paolo and Francesca)* and Oscar *Wilde, in whose *The *Importance of Being Earnest* he had one of his greatest successes as John Worthing.

Alexander, Mrs (pseudonym of Annie French, later Mrs Alexander Hector, 1825-1902). Popular novelist from 1866 until her death. Her best known book was *The Wooing o't* (1873) and her last *Kitty Costello* (1904).

Alexander, Samuel (1859-1938). Born in Sydney, N.S.W. Educated at Melbourne and Oxford, and became the first Jewish scholar to hold a Fellowship in the University of Oxford, where he remained until his appointment as Professor of Philosophy in the University of Manchester in 1893, holding that Chair until 1924. He was acknowledged as one of the foremost modern philosophers, and though primarily a metaphysician his mind was open to the influences of contemporary science. A prose stylist, his writings include *Beauty and Other Forms of Value* (1933), but his most important work is *Space, Time, and Deity* (2 vols, 1920).

Alexandria Quartet, The. A series of four novels by Lawrence *Durrell: *Justine* (1957), *Balthazar* (1958), *Mountolive* (1958), *Clea* (1960). A complex narrative with intertwining love, political, and religious themes and a large company of characters both serious and comic, the whole work is especially notable for its projection of the atmosphere and the best and worst aspects of the city of Alexandria, ancient and modern.

Alice Aisgill. Joe Lampton's mistress in John Braine's *Room at the Top* (1957). After he tells her that he is to marry Susan Brown she crashes her car and dies next day from dreadful injuries.

Alington, Adrian (Adrian Richard Alington, 1895-1958). Born at Oxford; educated at Marlborough and Oxford. Wrote numerous novels, including *Slowbags and Arethusa* (1930) and *The Career of Julian Stanley-Williams* (1931).

Alington, Cyril (Very Rev. Cyril Argentine Alington, 1872-1955). Born at Candlesby,

Lincs; educated at Marlborough and Oxford. Headmaster of Eton, 1916-33; Dean of Durham, 1933-51. Author of novels, biographies, reminiscences, and biblical and other religious works.

All God's Chillun Got Wings. Play by Eugene *O'Neill, produced in New York in 1924. The chief characters—Jim Harris, a coloured man, and a white girl, Ella Downey—are brought up in a New York slum. Through race prejudice she rejects him until she has been deserted by a scoundrelly white, Mickey, by whom she has an illegitimate child which dies. Ella then marries Jim, and after living in France for a short time they settle in New York, where he becomes a law student, but his wife's race antagonism revives and she becomes insane. He fails in his examinations, but remains with Ella who, in her madness, imagines they are children again.

All Men are Brothers. English title of an early Chinese novel translated (1933) by Pearl *Buck. Probably a cumulative narrative evolved during a long period, it is mainly concerned with the doings of a large company of outlaws.

All Men are Enemies. Novel by Richard *Aldington published in 1933. Antony Clarendon, born and brought up in a 17th-century mansion, is entranced by a brief idyll with his cousin Evelyn in adolescence, and carries his memory of it into adult life, though on his next meeting with her, in middle age, he finds that she has undergone a 'strange and repellent metamorphosis' after years in India as the wife of a civil servant. Antony in the intervening period has travelled in Italy and elsewhere on the Continent, his intention of training as an architect being frustrated by World War I, in which he is wounded. He has had sexual relations with Margaret, a friend of earlier years, and also an overwhelmingly passionate love affair with an Austrian girl, Katharine, whom he endeavours to reach when the war is over. After much hampering by passport officials he gets to Austria, but failing to find Katha he returns to England, reluctantly marries Margaret, and goes into business as a company director. Finding his marriage and his business both dead-ends, he resigns the directorship, realizes his capital, goes abroad again and resumes the search for Katha, discovering

her at length where they first met, in the Mediterranean isle of Aeaea, ill-fed and poorly clothed after near-starvation in postwar Austria. The way is cleared for their marriage when Margaret writes that she is divorcing Antony. Though its subtitle describes the book as 'a romance', much space is given to discussions on social conditions, the State, socialism, democracy, war, the General Strike in 1926, and the widespread disillusion of the post-1918 period.

All Our Yesterdays. Novel by H. M. *Tomlinson published in 1930. One of the outstanding novels of World War I, it gives a quasi-historical view of British affairs from 1900, when the South African war was in progress, to the Armistice in 1919. The view is from the domestic angle of the working-class Bolt family, the father, Tom Bolt, being a shipwright with a Thames-side firm building warships; and from the Fleet Street angle of special correspondents and of war correspondents in France and Belgium. Among the highlights are an account of the hysterical and destructive London crowd celebration of the relief of Mafeking; a journey in a typical pre-1914 African colony; a lengthy and moving record of the miseries and tragedies of trench warfare, endured by the fighting men and creating problems beyond the capacity of generals to solve. Tomlinson's own experiences as a newspaper man and war correspondent give authority to the narrative. The title is from *Macbeth* V.v. 22-3: 'all our yesterdays have lighted fools the way to dusty death'.

All Passion Spent. Novel by V. *Sackville-West, published in 1931. Following the death at the age of ninety-four of Henry Lyulph Holland, 1st Earl of Slane, sometime Viceroy of India, the sons and daughter decide that their eighty-eight-year-old mother shall henceforward divide her time between the four who have suitable households. Lady Slane is determined, however, to live apart with only her old French maid, Genoux, as housekeeper and companion. She rents a small house she had coveted many years before at Hampstead, where the eccentric owner-agent, Gervase Bucktrout, 'a safely old gentleman' befriends her, aided by his builder and decorator, Mr Gosheron. Happily installed and keeping her children at arm's length, except for occasional visits by her youngest son Kay, a bachelor and collector of globes, compasses and astrolabes, she sits in the sun and reviews her past life, weighing years of duty and devotion to her statesman-husband against the sacrifice of her early desire for an independent career as a painter. She is visited by her son Kay's old friend, Mr FitzGeorge, an octogenarian millionaire with an immensely valuable collection of antiques and works of art. He reveals that he first saw Lady Slane in India half a century before, fell in love with her, and remained unmarried. She was unaware of this and only with difficulty recalled the meeting. FitzGeorge becomes a regular visitor and friend until his sudden death, leaving £80,000 a year and his collection worth £2 million to Lady Slane, who, to the disgust of her avaricious family, immediately passes the money to hospitals and the collection to the nation. She is shortly visited unannounced by her great-granddaughter Deborah, who comes to thank her for renouncing the fortune and thus freeing Deborah from being a wealthy heiress and enabling her to escape marriage to a duke's son. The girl wishes to be a musician, as her great-grandmother had wished to be a painter. Deborah leaves, 'profoundly lulled and happy' because of the approval of Lady Slane, whom Genoux finds dead in her chair an hour later. The title of the book is from the final words of Milton's *Samson Agonistes*.

All Quiet on the Western Front. Anti-war novel by Erich Maria *Remarque. Originally in German it was translated into many languages (English, 1929) and was one of the most acclaimed protest books resulting from World War I, and had further currency as a film. The title is an ironic reproduction of a phrase repeatedly used in official communiqués relating to operations in France and Flanders.

All Souls. A post-graduate college of Oxford University, its Warden and Fellows elected in part from persons eminent in academic and public life. It has sometimes been criticized for its supposed undercover influence in political and state affairs. Founded in 1438, with its Fellows then limited to forty.

Allaby, Christina. In Samuel Butler's *The *Way of All Flesh* (1903), daughter of the Rev. Mr Allaby. Married Theobald Pontifex

and bore Ernest (the central character), Joseph and Charlotte.

Allan, Maud (1883-1956). Born in Toronto of English-Irish-Scottish descent; educated in San Francisco; studied music in Berlin intending to be a pianist, but turned to classical dancing, making her début in Vienna in 1903. Thereafter she toured the world, earning fame for her 'exquisite grace and almost perfect technique . . . as the greatest living exponent of the poetry of motion', and notoriety among the puritanical who objected to barefoot dancing in diaphanous costumes. Her performance in *Salome* by Oscar *Wilde in April 1918 involved her in a *cause célèbre* for libel against Pemberton *Billing. She wrote *My Life and Dancing* (1908).

Allegory. A narrative in verse or prose with a secondary meaning—usually a moral or spiritual one—beneath the overt one. In English literature the outstanding allegories are Spenser's *Faerie Queene* and Bunyan's *Pilgrim's .Progress*. A present-century example is *Animal Farm* by George Orwell.

Allegory of Love, The. A Study in Medieval Tradition, by C. S. *Lewis, published in 1936. Centred on the theme of courtly love which appeared 'quite suddenly at the end of the eleventh century' in France, this study examines the characteristics of a highly specialized sentiment whose rules embraced 'Humility, Courtesy, Adultery, and the Religion of Love'. The new feeling arose in the princely courts, and the beloved, invariably a married lady, was accepted as the feudal superior of the obedient lover, however noble his rank. Romantic passion found its only channel of expression in this relationship, since marriages 'had nothing to do with love', being solely 'matches of interest'. Lewis discusses the classical precursors of Allegory, which became the dominant form in the literature of courtly love, and he then devotes liberal space to chapters on *The Romance of the Rose;* Chaucer; Gower and Thomas Usk; and *The Faerie Queene*.

Allègre, Henry. Millionaire collector and amateur painter in Joseph Conrad's *The *Arrow of Gold* (1919). He introduces the Basque peasant girl Rita to Paris society and leaves his wealth and possessions to her.

Allen, C. K. (Sir Carleton Kemp Allen, 1887-1966; knighted 1952). Born in Sydney,

Australia; educated there and (as a *Rhodes Scholar) in England at Oxford, where he became Professor of Jurisprudence (1929-31) and Warden of Rhodes House (1931-52). Author of *Law in the Making* (1927), *Bureaucracy Triumphant* (1931), *The Queen's Peace* (1953), and other works on law and administration; a novel *(The Judgement of Paris*, 1924), and short stories and miscellaneous writings.

Allen, George (1832-1907), pupil of Ruskin, for whom he acted as publisher from 1871, a connection from which the firm of George Allen & Unwin sprang. Allen was trained as an engraver and executed illustrations for Ruskin's *Modern Painters. See also* Stanley *Unwin.

Allen, Hervey (William Hervey Allen, 1889-1949). Born at Pittsburg; educated there and at Harvard. Wrote several books of verse, a biography of Edgar Allan Poe *(Israfel*, 1926), an autobiographical novel of World War I *(Toward the Flame*, 1926), and had his chief success with *Anthony Adverse* (1933), a long novel set in the period of the Napoleonic wars.

Allen, James Lane (1849-1925). Born in Kentucky; educated at Transylvania University. After school-teaching in his home state he devoted himself to writing fiction and essays concerned with the same region. *A Kentucky Cardinal* (1894), a love story centred on nature themes, and *The Choir Invisible* (1897), an idealistic romance of unfulfilled love, were the most widely read of his novels.

Allen, Walter (Walter Ernest Allen, 1911-   ). Born in Birmingham; educated there at King Edward's Grammar School and at the University. Schoolmaster in Birmingham and visiting lecturer and Professor at American universities. In addition to journalism and broadcasting, wrote novels *(Innocence is Drowned*, 1938; *Living Space*, 1940; *Rogue Elephant*, 1946; *All in a Lifetime*, 1962); and several volumes of literary history and criticism, including *The English Novel*, 1954; *Six Great Novelists*, 1955.

Alleyn, Roderick. Chief Detective Inspector (later Superintendent), of the Criminal Investigation Department, Scotland Yard, a principal character in crime novels by Ngaio *Marsh. He married Agatha Troy,

painter, whom he had previously cleared of a murder charge.

Allingham, Margery (Margery Louise Allingham, 1904-1966; Mrs Philip Youngman Carter). Educated at the Perse High School for Girls, Cambridge. She became an outstanding crime novelist, with Albert Campion as the bland and humorous amateur detective, who first appeared in *The Crime at Black Dudley* (1928). Of her numerous other novels in this category *Death of a Ghost* (1934), *Flowers for the Judge* (1936), *More Work for the Undertaker* (1949), *The Tiger in the Smoke* (1952) are among the best. *The Oaken Heart* (1941) is about an English village in wartime.

Alliteration. A literary device used consistently in Anglo-Saxon poetry and frequently in later writings, especially in the works of Swinburne (who also parodied the practice in *Nephelidia*). Employed originally with a structural purpose, alliteration in modern times has become chiefly a means (sometimes facetious) of aural decoration.

Allnutt. The cockney mining engineer in C. S. Forester's *The *African Queen* (1935).

Almayer's Folly. A Story of an Eastern River. Joseph *Conrad's first novel, published in 1895. Kaspar Almayer, though virtually down-and-out after twenty years in a decaying trading station on the Pantai river in Borneo, is sustained by visions of grandeur arising from his belief that he will eventually find treasure in the interior of the country. In anticipation of wealth he builds a new house which visiting Dutch naval officers derisively name 'Almayer's Folly'. Married to a slatternly and shrewish native woman, all his affection and ambition are concentrated on their daughter Nina. She falls in love with Dain Maroola, a rajah's son from Bali, who becomes a fugitive when an illicit load of gunpowder in the brig he owns explodes and kills Dutch sailors. Nina escapes to Bali with him, abandoning her father, who swears never to forgive her, but to forget her utterly. Finding it impossible to forget, he burns down the house, which is crowded with memories of her, and goes to live in the empty Folly where he takes to opium smoking and one morning is found dead, having 'that serene look' which 'testified silently . . . that the man lying there under the gaze of indifferent eyes had been permitted to forget before he died'. There are impressive descriptions of river and forest and memorable secondary characters, among them the Siamese slave girl Taminah, and Babalatchi, the local Sultan's 'prime minister'.

Almedingen, E. M. (*née* Martha Edith von Almedingen, 1898-1971). Born and educated in St Petersburg. Lecturer on English Medieval History and Literature, Petrograd University, 1920-22; Lecturer on Russian Literature, Oxford University, 1951. Settled in England from 1923. Author of poetry (*Rus*, 1939; *Out of Seir*, 1943), a verse play (*Storm at Westminster*, 1952), novels (*Frossia*, 1943; *Dasha*, 1944; *The Inmost Heart*, 1948; *The Scarlet Goose*, 1957; etc.), autobiographical books (*Tomorrow Will Come*, 1941; *The Almond Tree*, 1947; *Within the Harbour*, 1950), and biographies of Paul I of Russia (*So Dark a Stream*, 1959) and *The Empress Alexandra*, *1872-1918* (1961); *Charlemagne* (1968), etc.

Alpha of the Plough. *See* A. G. *Gardiner.

Alroy Kear. *See* Kear, Alroy.

Altamira. The site near Santander in northern Spain where a number of the world's finest prehistoric cave-paintings were discovered in 1879 by a child while her father was engaged in archaeological work nearby. The discovery made little impression until the end of the century, when further interest was aroused and the paintings examined by experts. Since the publication of *La Caverne d'Altamira* by E. Cartailhac and H. *Breuil in 1906, they have been much visited and studied. The paintings depict various animals—wild boars, horses, and bison—with considerable realism and artistic skill, the modelling in shades oi red and brown with the addition of black showing an advanced stage of aesthetic development. That such paintings had also some ritual significance is probable.

Altiora Bailey. *See* Bailey, Altiora.

Alvarez Quintero, Serafin and **Joaquin.** *See* Quintero.

Amanda. The Postmistress General in *The *Apple Cart* by Bernard Shaw. She captures her audiences at political meetings by singing comic songs.

Amanda. Married to Victor Prynne after divorce from Elyot Chase in Noel Coward's *Private Lives* (1930).

Amaryllis. *See* Acis.

Ambassadors, The. Novel by Henry *James published in 1903. Lewis Lambert Strether of Woollet, Massachusetts is sent to Europe by the rich middle-aged widow to whom he is engaged, to induce her son, Chadwick Newsome, to return from Paris and enter the family business. Chad has written no letters in his long absence and is assumed to be infatuated by some 'bad woman'. While passing through England Strether becomes friendly with Maria Gostrey, a mature American spinster, who conducts him around in London and Paris together with his straitlaced Connecticut lawyer companion Waymarsh. Later she becomes a wise and farseeing confidante. Astonished to find Chad transformed in Paris from the unpleasant youth he had known at home, Strether recognizes on meeting her that the change is due to the civilizing influence of Mme de Vionnet. Convinced, from the tone of his letters, that Strether's mission has failed, Mrs Newsome sends her married daughter Sarah Pocock with her husband and young sister-in-law as further ambassadors to Paris. But Sarah also fails and retires, frustrated and angry. By accident it is later revealed that Chad and Mme de Vionnet are lovers; but, satisfied that the relationship is fundamentally good, Strether (now estranged from Mrs Newsome) leaves for America after impressing on Chad that it would be infamous to forsake his mistress.

Ambiguity. After the publication in 1930 of *Seven Types of Ambiguity* by William *Empson, the word became a critical and academic cliché for the double or multiple meanings that may be intended by (or read into or imposed upon) words and phrases in poetry. Though a reader's alertness to the overtones and undertones of language may increase both pleasure and mental profit it may also with less advantage induce a cryptogrammatic attitude to literature.

Ambivalence. Simultaneous opposing emotional or intellectual attitudes towards a person or object or matter, wavering feelings or thoughts. It became an academic vogue word in the 1950s and hardened into a cliché when more generally adopted.

Ambler, Eric (1909-   ). Born and educated in London. Apprenticed as an engineer, but turned to advertisement copywriting before settling as a professional writer from 1936, producing mystery novels (including *Epitaph for a Spy*, 1938; *The Mask of Dimitrios*, 1939; *Journey into Fear*, 1940) and many film scripts.

American Dream, The. One-act comedy by Edward *Albee, first performed in 1961. Set in the living-room of a middle-class apartment, with Mommy, Daddy, and Grandma as leading characters, the humour arises from the inconsequence of the dialogue and the spells of self-contradictory conversation. Of the two remaining characters, Mrs Baker has been asked to call but no one knows why; while the Young Man stands for 'the American Dream', 'clean-cut, midwest farm-boy type, almost insultingly good-looking in a typically American way. Good profile, straight nose, honest eyes, wonderful smile . . .' Superficially nonsensical but fundamentally ironical, its deliberate irrationality connects it with the contemporary *Theatre of the Absurd, while the symbolical dismemberment of 'the bumble' links it with the *Theatre of Cruelty.

American Language, The. A valuable work by H. L. *Mencken, distinguishing differences in the development and usage of English in the United States. The first edition was published in 1920; revised editions and supplementary volumes appeared at later dates.

American Tragedy, An. Novel by Theodore *Dreiser published in 1925. After working as a hotel bellboy, Clyde Griffiths, born poor in Kansas City, is taken up by his rich uncle, in whose New York factory he is attracted by Roberta Alden, who becomes pregnant by him. He then falls in love with Sondra Finchley and determines to kill Roberta. He takes her on a lake in a rowing boat which overturns and the girl is drowned. Though it is not certain that the capsizing of the boat was not accidental, Griffiths is tried, condemned and executed. The novel is massive in its proportions and develops with a sense of inevitability.

American Writers. In the main, the United States at the beginning of the twentieth century was still a province of European culture. The New England tradition was dominant from the time of the Pilgrim Fathers until the nineteenth century passed, while the vast and varied influx of immi-grants from Ireland and the Continent had not yet been welded into a nation with a distinctive American voice and outlook capable of creating an independent literature. A lonely few—notably Herman Melville (1819-91), Walt Whitman (1819-92), and Mark Twain (1835-1910)—had diverged from the Emerson–Longfellow–Lowell path, which remained European in all essentials even when the material they chose had a native gloss, as in Longfellow's *Hiawatha*. Emerson probed to the root of the matter when he said, as early as 1837 in his oration on *The American Scholar,* 'Our day of dependence, our long apprenticeship to the learning of other lands, draws to a close. The millions that around us are rushing into life, cannot always be fed on the sere remains of foreign harvests', but the best part of a century went by before the European obsession was overcome. Then, ironically, it was renewed firsthand contact with Europe that severed the cultural link. Nothing but speculation is possible about what the history of modern American literature might have been without the impact of World War I, and it may be coincidence that the dawn of widespread awareness of a new wave in American writing can be dated 1919 with the publication of Eugene *O'Neill's first plays and H. L. *Mencken's *The American Language* and the first collection of *Prejudices*, his forcibly iconoclastic essays. These portents were followed in the next year by Sinclair *Lewis's *Main Street* and in 1922 by his *Babbitt*. The satire of Mencken and Lewis struck home with the more force since there had been little previous sign that America would be ready to have its social and cultural entrails exposed to ridicule, though the more solemn and severe 'muckraking' campaign of the 1900s had uncovered many nests of corruption and other evils in the nation's government and business (see *The Octopus*, 1901, and *The Pit*, 1903, both by Frank *Norris; *The *Jungle*, 1906, by Upton *Sinclair; *Susan Lenox: Her Fall and Rise,* 1917, by David Graham *Phillips; and the *Autobiography* (1931) of Lincoln *Steffens, a leader of the campaign). But while the literature of protest arouses intense immediate interest, its life is rarely long. Before the postwar renaissance of American literature, some of those to be associated with it had begun to publish. Theodore *Dreiser's *Sister Carrie* appeared in 1900, a quarter of a century before his masterpiece *An *American Tragedy* (1925). Robert *Frost's first poems *A Boy's Will* (1913) heralded the half-century of fame he experienced in his lifetime and the enduring classic rank which seems certain. Though it is only one of Edgar Lee *Masters's many books of verse, the *Spoon River Anthology* (1915) alone has survived and is unique in form and content. In 1916 two writers who were to be more prominent in the 1920s and after, Sherwood *Anderson and Carl *Sandburg, published their first books; Anderson established himself as a master of the short story with *Winesburg, Ohio* (1919), while Sandburg went on to publish his *Complete Poems* (1950) and much prose, including a monumental biography of Abraham Lincoln (6 vols, 1926, 1939). Few of the newer writers aimed to be valued as literary stylists. Urgencies of matter rather than elegancies of manner were to the fore, and some reputations—such as those of Theodore Dreiser and later of Thomas *Wolfe—were gained in spite of much turgid prose. Among those contemporaries to whom writing continued to be an art, Willa *Cather had published *O Pioneers!* (1913) and other novels before her place in American literature became assured with **My Ántonia* (1918), *The *Lost Lady* (1923), and **Death Comes for the Archbishop* (1927). What has been called 'her graceful Vergilian style' keeps on the safe side of mannerism, as does that of Thornton *Wilder in *The *Bridge of San Luis Rey* (1927) and *The *Ides of March* (1948). On the other hand, as its title might suggest, gracefulness of style tends towards excessive fragility in Elinor *Wylie's *The Venetian Glass Nephew* (1925). The toughness which was to make a deep mark on the American novel is a particular legacy from Ernest *Hemingway, as the cult of dissipation is from Scott *Fitzgerald, whose novels remain as a memorial of the 1920s, the jazz age. America's one playwright of world rank is still Eugene O'Neill, with Elmer *Rice, Maxwell *Anderson, Robert *Sherwood, Clifford *Odets, Arthur *Miller, and Tennessee *Williams as successors on varying levels. The distinctive tradition of American humour has been carried on in the twentieth century by Don *Marquis, Ogden *Nash, Dorothy *Parker, Damon *Runyon, James *Thurber and many others. Modern American poetry exercised a potent

influence internationally through Ezra *Pound and T. S. *Eliot, both expatriates like Gertrude *Stein, whose experiments with language in both verse and prose astonished many but were comprehended by few. Born before the last quarter of the nineteenth century, Edwin Arlington *Robinson and Amy *Lowell each wrote distinguished poetry in the new century, as did the somewhat younger Wallace *Stevens, William Carlos *Williams, Marianne *Moore, and Robinson *Jeffers. The next generation had Archibald *MacLeish, Hart *Crane, Allen *Tate. Increasingly, poetry became material for academic study and verbal analysis, largely under the authority of the New Criticism, with I. A. *Richards (an English scholar domiciled in America), Pound, Eliot, Cleanth *Brooks, J. C. *Ransom (author of *The *New Criticism*, 1941), Yvor *Winters and others, though the last-named developed a more liberal and sardonic approach. Though she died in the 1880s, Emily *Dickinson's poetry, found a devoted audience only in the 20th century, to which she belongs more in spirit than to her own time. Since their name is legion, the contemporary American writers cannot here be named without a multitude of omissions, though most of the notable ones have entries under their individual names, whether noted in the present article or not. Three further groups require brief mention, however. A new dimension was given to detective novels by Raymond *Chandler and Dashiell *Hammett. The South (mainly the Confederate States who sought to secede from the Union at the time of the Civil War) has produced an abundant literary harvest in this century in the works of William *Faulkner, Robert Penn *Warren, Truman *Capote, Carson *McCullers, Eudora *Welty, Tennessee *Williams, Thomas *Wolfe, and many others including the phenomenal one-book woman Margaret *Mitchell whose *Gone with the Wind* (1936) is not to be despised merely on the ground of its unprecedented popularity in print and on the screen. Inasmuch as it has its ultimate roots in the slave States, the third group to be mentioned here, Negro literature, is also of the South, though the setting may vary from book to book. Booker T. *Washington, author of *Up from Slavery* (1901) and a pioneer of Negro education, was later berated by younger compatriots as an ameliorist, and the protest novels of Richard *Wright and James *Baldwin received more attention and praise when the Civil Rights campaign was in motion in the 1950s-1960s.

Amerigo, Prince. In Henry James's *The *Golden Bowl* (1904), an impoverished Italian who marries an American millionaire's daughter, Maggie Verver; her friend Charlotte Stant is his secret mistress.

Amery, L. S. (Leopold Stennett Amery, 1873-1955). Statesman and author. Born in India; educated at Harrow and Oxford. On the editorial staff of *The Times*, 1899-1909. After holding junior ministerial posts, became First Lord of the Admiralty in 1922, and later Secretary for the Colonies, for the Dominions, and for India and Burma. He wrote on many political topics from 1906 onward; *Thoughts on the Constitution* (1947); and a three-volume autobiography, *My Political Life* (1953, 1954, 1955).

Ames, Jennifer. See Maysie *Greig.

Amis, Kingsley (1922-   ). Born in Clapham; educated at City of London School and Oxford; after service in World War II became Lecturer in English at the University College of Swansea in 1949. A volume of poems (*A Frame of Mind*, 1953) was followed by *Lucky Jim* (1954) which was immediately adopted by critics and journalists as the type-novel of its generation and widely read as a work of humour. Later novels: *That Uncertain Feeling*, (1955); *I Like it Here*, (1958); *Take a Girl Like You*, (1960); *Ending Up*, (1974), etc.

Amory Blaine. Chief character in Scott Fitzgerald's *This Side of Paradise* (1920).

Amphitryon 38. Comedy in a Prologue and three acts by S. N. *Behrman, adapted (1937) from the French of Jean *Giraudoux, who wrote the play in 1929 and gave it the title on the ground that the Greek legend on which it is based had been used thirty-seven times by earlier playwrights, Plautus, Dryden and Molière among them. The chief characters are Jupiter, Mercury, Alkmena, Amphitryon (Alkmena's husband), and Leda, Queen of Sparta. The story is of Jupiter's assumption of Amphitryon's shape in order to visit and embrace Alkmena, but a new twist is given in the play to the classical myth, in that Alkmena at the end persuades Jupiter that friendship is finer

than love as he conceives it. The charm of the play lies, however, in its wit and delicate humour.

-ana. Literary or other material on the fringes of biography or central studies of a person's life and work; or of matters relating to a place or period. Thus, collections of anecdotes, casual reminiscences, workroom fragments, and other trivia bearing upon, say, Bernard Shaw are described as Shaviana; miscellaneous notes on say, Bristol as Bristoliana; on the Victorian period, Victoriana.

Ana de Ulloa, Doña. Appearing first as the Old Woman in Act III (the Don Juan in Hell scene) of *Man and Superman* by Bernard Shaw, she is shortly transformed into a young and handsome woman 'magnificently attired' and resembling Ann Whitefield, her counterpart in the rest of the play. Doña Ana 'vanishes into the void' at the end of the scene, crying 'I believe in the Life to Come. A father! a father for the Superman!'.

Anastasia Vulliamy. The orphan who applies to the Lord Chamberlain for a husband in *The Fascinating Foundling* by Bernard Shaw.

Anatol. A series of seven short plays concerning the amorous exploits of the character so named, by Arthur *Schnitzler.

Anatomist, The. A Lamentable Comedy of Knox, Burke and Hare and the West Port Murders. Play in three acts by James *Bridie, produced in Edinburgh in 1930. An Author's Note prefixed to the printed text relates the play to an actual situation in 1828, at which time 'the demand for anatomy subjects far exceeded the supply' and so-called 'resurrection men' rifled graves, or, in such cases as that of Burke and Hare, used murder as a means of providing corpses for the medical schools. The scene is Edinburgh in 1828 and the chief characters are: Robert Knox, M.D., a middle-aged lecturer in anatomy; Augustus Raby, one of his students; Walter Anderson, a demonstrator in anatomy; Mary Paterson, a prostitute; Amelia Dishart, and her sister Mary Belle with whom Anderson is in love; William Burke and William Hare. Mary Belle refuses to marry Anderson unless he abandons surgical dissection. Knox backs Anderson, saying that 'The comparative anatomist . . . institutes a divine search for facts . . . his facts will be collected and their sum will be the Truth.' Anderson gets drunk in a low tavern, where Mary Paterson takes care of him when he falls into a drunken sleep. Burke and Hare deliver a tea chest to Knox's rooms. When it is opened Anderson recognizes the body of Mary Paterson, but his horror that the girl has been murdered is not shared by Knox, who says 'your friend will be improving the minds of the youth of the town in place of corrupting their morals'. On the morning of Burke's execution (Hare having turned King's evidence) there is a riot in the streets, with the mob crying out against Knox, evidence at the trial having proved the delivery of Mary Paterson's body to him. Knox is stoned by the mob. As the rioters are about to break in, a group of Knox's students drive them away. Knox says he will continue his lectures and begins a discourse on 'The Heart of the Rhinoceros' as the play ends.

Ancients, The. The He-Ancient and the She-Ancient in Part V of *Back to Methuselah* by Bernard Shaw. The period is A.D. 31,920. The Ancients have lived for hundreds of years, have outgrown human pleasures and desires while still tied to 'this tyrannous body', but are destined to an immortality in which 'there will be no people, only thought'.

And Even Now. Volume of twenty essays by Max *Beerbohm, published in 1922. Dedicated to his wife, it contains several of the best of his mature shorter writings including 'No 1 The Pines', an intensely funny yet kindly account of his visit as a young man to the joint home of Swinburne and *Watts-Dunton at Putney; 'William and Mary', a moving account of his return to a country cottage, now unoccupied and dilapidated, where an Oxford friend and his wife, who both died young, lived during their brief happiness; 'The Golden Drugget'; 'Servants'; 'Quia Imperfectum'; 'Something Defeasible', on the prospect of Demos triumphant; 'A Clergyman', on a passage in Boswell's *Johnson*; 'Laughter'.

Anderson, Alexander (1845-1909). Born in southern Scotland, at Kirkconnel; educated at a village school; worked as a quarryman and on the railway; taught himself to read in several languages and went abroad by favour of a Glasgow patron. In 1880 became

assistant Librarian at Edinburgh University and in 1904 acting Chief Librarian until he died. From boyhood he wrote verse, much of it published under the pseudonym 'Surfaceman': e.g. *A Song of Labour, and other Poems* (1873), *Songs of the Rail* (1878), *Ballads and Sonnets* (1879), *Later Poems* (with a biographical sketch by Alexander Brown, 1912).

Anderson, Anthony. The Christian minister in *The *Devil's Disciple* by Bernard Shaw.

Anderson, Maxwell (1888-1959). American playwright; born at Atlantic, Pennsylvania; worked as a journalist before sharing considerable success with *What Price Glory* (1924) a play provoked by recollections of World War I and written in collaboration with Laurence Stallings. Many plays by his own hand followed, and he was particularly acclaimed for the literary and dramatic merit of such verse plays as *Elizabeth the Queen* (1930), *Mary of Scotland* (1933), *Winterset* (1935), *The Masque of Kings* (1936); among his other plays are *Joan of Lorraine* (1947), *Anne of the Thousand Days* (i.e. Anne Boleyn; 1948), *The Bad Seed* (1955).

Anderson, Sherwood (1876-1941). American novelist, short-story writer and essayist; his fiction was largely concerned with the less prosperous classes in the Middle West; outstanding among the novels is *Poor White* (1920) and among the short-story collections *Winesburg, Ohio* (1919).

Andrade, E. N. da C. (Edward Neville da Costa Andrade, 1887-1971). Born in London; educated at London, Heidelburg, Cambridge, and Manchester Universities. Professor of Physics in the University of London, 1928-50. Author of numerous writings on Physics, including *The Structure of the Atom* (1923; 3rd edn. 1927); *The Mechanism of Nature* (1930; revised 1936); *The Atom and its Energy* (1947); *An Approach to Modern Physics* (1956). He also wrote verse: *Poems and Songs* (1949).

Andrewes, For Lancelot. See *For Lancelot Andrewes*.

Andreyev, Leonid Nikolaevich (1871-1919). Russian novelist and playwright. Born at Orel; studied law at St Petersburg and Moscow Universities, but turned to painting, journalism, and the writing of fiction, receiving praise for his short stories from

Maxim Gorky. Smarting under violent attacks from others, who found his works morbid and obscene, he withdrew to permanent residence in Finland and became an implacable opponent of the Soviet revolution. Of his numerous writings, English translations gave British and American currency to *The Seven Who Were Hanged* (1909), *Confessions of a Little Man During Great Days* (1917), and to the play *He Who Gets Slapped* (1916).

Andrézel, Pierre. *See* Karen *Blixen.

Androcles and the Lion. A fable play in a prologue and two acts by Bernard *Shaw, performed in London in 1913. Androcles is 'a small, thin, ridiculous little man' with a shrewish wife, Megaera. They have been turned out of their home because he has become a Christian. On their way to Rome they encounter a limping lion in the jungle and Androcles, an animal lover, removes a thorn from its paw. The scene changes to a gate outside Rome where a group of Christian prisoners in charge of a Centurion are resting before being committed to the arena. Among the Christians are Lavinia, a young woman of higher social standing than the others; Spinthio, 'the wreck of a good-looking man gone hopelessly to the bad'; Ferrovius, 'powerful and violent'; and Androcles. The Captain of the Roman guard rebukes the Christians for their obstinacy in refusing to drop incense on the altar of the gods and alleges that they are thereby committing suicide, not being persecuted. Lavinia replies that it would be physically and spiritually impossible for her to make the prescribed gesture: 'My body would be true to my faith even if you could corrupt my mind.' In the arena before the Emperor, Spinthio rushes to save himself but lands instead in a lion's cage and is killed; Ferrovius kills six of the gladiators and joins the Praetorian Guard; Androcles is recognized by the lion he succoured and goes off with him to a job in the royal menagerie. Ferrovius' feat leads the Emperor to pardon all the assembled Christians, among whom Lavinia declares that she will 'strive for the coming of the God who is not yet' but agrees that the 'handsome Captain' may come and argue with her occasionally.

Angel Pavement. Novel by J. B. *Priestley, published in 1930. Reaching London on a cargo steamer from the Baltic, Mr Golspie, bulky and middle-aged, calls on the firm of Twigg & Dersingham in Angel Pavement 'a typical City side-street near St Paul's'. The firm, dealers in veneers and inlays, are in decline, and the coming of Golspie with an exclusive agency for the importation of such materials at a price which will enable them to undersell their competitors, promises a return of prosperity. Within this framework the story follows the surviving director, Dersingham, and the office staff into their several homes and personal relationships: Mr Smeeth, office manager; Turgis, the clerk; Miss Matfield, secretary-typist; and Stanley Poole, office boy. Mr Smeeth is wholly devoted to his work; Turgis falls tragically in love with Golspie's flirtatiously heartless daughter, Lena; Miss Matfield, sick of life in a women's hostel, is taken out expensively by Golspie; Stanley, embryonic detective, busies himself with 'shaddering' imaginary criminals. Twigg & Dersingham's revival under Golspie's influence turns to disaster when he disappears to South America, having committed them to heavy purchases at much higher prices than those at which they had contracted to sell to their customers.

Angell, Sir Norman (pseudonym of Ralph Norman Angell Lane, 1872-1967; knighted 1931). Born in Lincolnshire; educated in France and Switzerland. Went to America 1891-8, working first on a cattle ranch and subsequently as a journalist, a profession he continued on returning to Europe, becoming (1905-14) editor and general manager of the *Continental Daily Mail*. In 1910 he published *The Great Illusion* (based on his privately circulated *Europe's Optical Illusion,* 1909), a work which became immediately and lastingly famous throughout the world in over twenty translations (new edition 1933). Its argument, that war could not pay under modern conditions and must be ruinous to victors as well as to the defeated, while it did not prevent the two greatest wars in history, has been disastrously justified. He became Labour M.P. for North Bradford in 1929, but retired in 1931 to devote himself to writing and lecturing on international questions. His less influential later works include *The Economic Chaos and the Peace Treaty* (1919), *Let the People Know* (1943), *The Steep Places* (1947). *After All* (1951) is his autobiography.

Angels. In the popular language of the theatre, wealthy persons who put up money to enable plays to be staged.

Angels of Mons, The. Among the popular legends of World War I was that a host of heavenly angels hovered protectively above the British Army during the retreat from Mons in 1914. It grew from a fictional story by Arthur *Machen with that title published in an evening paper and reprinted in *The Bowmen and Other Legends* (1915).

Anglo-Saxon Attitudes. Novel by Angus *Wilson published in 1956. A phallic idol in the stone coffin of the 7th-century missionary bishop Eorpwald, excavated in East Anglia, dismays Christians to whom it appears as evidence that a long-revered Father of the Church had secretly apostatized and relapsed to pagan worship. The discovery is authenticated by the Rev. Reginald Portway, Secretary of the local Antiquarian Association, and by Lionel Stokesay, Regius Professor of English History, but doubt lingers for many years in the mind of Gerald Middleton, who by the time the novel begins is an internationally respected sixty-four-year-old Professor Emeritus of Early Medieval History. His delayed quest and discovery of the truth about Eorpwald's tomb is the main thread of a narrative concerned also with the varied personalities of other members of the Historical Association and, especially, with his own family. His Danish wife, Ingeborg, a sentimental idealist with a perverse inattention to facts is besotted by blind devotion to her son Johnnie, who gives up his seat in parliament and becomes a self-humbugging television champion of 'the little man' opposed by 'State tyranny'. The title is a phrase from Lewis Carroll's *Through the Looking Glass*.

Angry Young Man. An autobiography by Leslie *Paul published in 1951. The phrase which became a journalistic and colloquial cliché, 'angry young men', did not gain widespread currency until *Look Back in Anger* by John Osborne was regarded as pioneering a new type of drama. Though it was hard to find any who acknowledged themselves to be 'angry young men', the title was popularly attached to social misfits reacting to the self-recognition of their own personal inadequacy, though also to those who united in opposition to nuclear armaments. The other writers brought under this label, usually in spite of their own protests, included Kingsley *Amis, John *Wain, and John *Braine. In so far as there was group anger it arose largely among those of working-class parentage who, having received university education from the state, found themselves thereafter socially stateless, out of contact and frequently out of sympathy with their family environment, yet unqualified by upbringing and temperament to be at ease on a different social level. Though the newspapers became tired of the label, it could in practice be applied to the revolting university students of the late 1960s. For an American counterpart see *Beat Generation.

Angst. The German word became familiar through its use as a Freudian term for 'a combination of apprehensions, uncertainty and fear' producing anxiety-melancholia or anxiety-neurosis, displayed in more or less continuous depression or in morbid and unfounded dread. Though such conditions may be genuinely psychopathic through inner disturbance, *Angst* appears sometimes to be an imitative state induced in readers by literary references or implications—as in the writings of Sören *Kierkegaard.

Animal Farm. A short prose satire by George *Orwell published in 1945. In the form of an allegory or fable it tells of a group of farm animals who revolt against their human masters and organize to run the farm themselves on equalitarian principles. Idealistic intentions are progressively undermined by the assumption of total authority by the pigs, who treacherously distort the high-minded slogans of the revolution, which is at length betrayed by a rapprochement with the original masters. *Animal Farm* represents Orwell's final disillusionment with Soviet Russia in the Stalin period. It is chiefly remembered by the pigs' epigram, 'All animals are equal, but some animals are more equal than others.' The book became extremely popular and was early hailed as a classic. It had, however, been rejected for publication by T. S. Eliot for reasons assigned in his letter of 13 June 1944, which Mrs Eliot made available in *The Times* dated 6 January 1969.

Animula. Poem by T. S. *Eliot published in 1929. Beginning with the line (printed by the author as a quotation), 'Issues from the hand of God, the simple soul', it describes by implication the human passage from infancy onward till the soul 'issues from the hand of time. . . . Irresolute and selfish, misshapen, lame'. Its theme is developed from lines in the *Purgatorio* of Dante (Canto XVI).

Ann Pornick. Arthur Kipps's girl friend and later his wife in H. G. Wells's *Kipps* (1905). They cut a sixpence in half and share it as 'a Token' when they fall in love. *Half a Sixpence* is the title of a play based on it in the 1960s.

Ann Veronica. Novel by H. G. Wells published in 1909. The youngest of five children and left motherless at thirteen, Ann Veronica Stanley at twenty-one reaches the climax of her struggle to break free from the restrictive control of her solicitor father and of his sister who took charge after Mrs Stanley's death. Forbidden to go with friends to an art-school fancy-dress dance, or to change from the limitations of a science course at a minor women's college to more exacting study at Imperial College, she runs away from home, rents a room in London, borrows money (from an acquaintance of her father who later tries to seduce her), and enrols as a biology student at the Central Imperial College. Under the influence of a Miss Miniver, Ann Veronica joins the women's suffrage movement and takes part in a raid on the House of Commons which leads to her arrest and a month in prison. She decides to compromise and return home when her sentence is served, but continues her biology course. Mr Manning, a senior civil servant prominent in local society at home and long her admirer, proposes marriage. She accepts, but breaks the engagement when she realizes that she is in love with Godwin Capes, laboratory demonstrator at the College, who is married but separated from his wife. Though he has scruples, Ann Veronica sweeps them aside and they elope to Switzerland. When he is free they marry and are reconciled with her family, Capes having meanwhile become a successful playwright (pseudonymously as Thomas More) and ingratiated himself with Mr Stanley. Regarded in its day as advanced and immoral, the novel was quickly outpaced in practice by the sexual liberation it adumbrated.

Ann Vickers. Novel by Sinclair *Lewis published in 1933. Born in the small town of Waubanakee in Illinois, the daughter of a Superintendent of Schools whose wife died when the child was ten, Ann Vickers proceeds by way of the local school and a women's college to become after graduation an organizer at suffrage headquarters at Clateburn, Ohio. During intervening years she had rejected Christianity, fallen in and out of love, and regretted shrinking from the amorous advances of her male history teacher at the college. At a riotous suffrage meeting Ann is among those arrested, and a short spell in prison preludes her moving to New York to take up work as a resident teacher in a Settlement House. When she is twenty-six and America has entered World War I, she becomes the mistress of Captain Lafayette Resnick, having declined his offer of marriage before he leaves for camp. At an accidental encounter in a restaurant some weeks later she finds him with another girl, soon after discovering herself pregnant. She has an abortion, and returns to settlement work for a time, resigning to visit Europe. On her return she takes up moral rescue and prison work, and as educational director and chief clerk at a women's prison witnesses the horrors, cruelty and depravity of American penal methods. She subsequently becomes a nationally famous reformer as superintendent of the Stuyvesant Industrial Home for Women in New York, marries, but has a son by another man with whom she finally settles.

Ann Whitefield. *See* *Whitefield, Ann.

Anna. Tobit's wife, and mother of Tobias, in *Tobias and the Angel* by James Bridie.

Anna Christie. Play in four acts by Eugene *O'Neill performed in 1921, published in 1922. Christopher Christopherson, about fifty, ashore from the coal barge of which he is now captain after years as bosun of a sailing ship, is drinking in a New York bar with Marthy Owen, who lives with him on the barge, when he is handed a letter from his daughter Anna, whom he last saw as a child in Sweden fifteen years before. Her mother, now dead, brought her to America, where Anna lived on a cousin's farm in Minnesota, her father being determined to keep her away from 'dat ole davil sea'. She runs away from the farm and gets a job as a children's nurse, which the letter her father receives says she is leaving to visit him. The address of the New York bar is the only one she has as a place to get in touch with her father, who is out getting food when she arrives. He has always thought of her as a pretty and innocent girl, but in conversation with Marthy she describes her actual life since she ran away from the farm after being seduced at sixteen. From nurse-maiding she became a prostitute in a brothel, and when that was raided by the police she was given a month in prison, where she became ill and was sent to hospital. She has come to her father expecting he will provide her with a room and meals. He, meanwhile, remains ignorant of her past, and she soon grows to enjoy voyaging on his barge. When they rescue a boatload of shipwrecked sailors, Anna and Mat Burke, an Irish stoker, fall in love. She refuses to marry him and tells Mat and her father the true story of her previous life. Burke curses her and leaves, but he returns after a two-day debauch, and is reconciled after she has sworn on a crucifix that he is the only man she has ever felt love for. Unknown to each other Christopherson signs on as bosun and Burke as stoker on the same ship.

Anna Livia Plurabelle. A section of *Finnegans Wake* by James Joyce, first published separately in 1928.

Anna of the Five Towns. Novel by Arnold *Bennett published in 1901. Anna Tellwright, daughter of the wealthy but miserly Ephraim Tellwright, is given to understand by her father on her twenty-first birthday that she is to assume control of the fortune of nearly £50,000 amassed from money left to her at her mother's death years earlier. Tellwright, however, continues to dominate Anna, and forces her to demand the payment of rent owed by Titus Price and his son Willie, the near-bankrupt owners of a local pottery manufactory. To stave off the immediate payment the Prices forge a bill of exchange in the name of a rich celebrity of the town (Bursley), expecting to redeem the bill with money due to them from a London firm. On the failure of that firm Titus hangs himself, fearing discovery and prosecution. Although Anna at length recognizes that she loves the unfortunate Willie, her tyrannous parent will not let her forgo the debt, and she carries out her earlier promise to marry the successful

Henry Mynors. Although Willie had decided to emigrate to Australia, on learning that his father had also embezzled church funds he throws himself into a disused pitshaft, his suicide remaining undiscovered. In addition to its merit as a study of human character, the novel has a documentary interest in its firsthand glimpses of life in a provincial Wesleyan community where a sewing meeting, a school treat, and a religious revival campaign are highlights. See also *Five Towns.

Annajanska, the Bolshevik Empress. A Revolutionary Romancelet. Play in one act by Bernard *Shaw, first performed in London in January 1918; published as one of the 'Playlets of the War' in the *Heartbreak House* volume (1919). The original title was *Annajanska, the Wild Grand Duchess* and purported to be 'from the Russian of Gregory Blessipoff'. Set in General Strammfest's office in a military station in Beotia after a revolution in which he has been made Commander-in-Chief by his own solicitor, the General wishes only to restore his previous royal master whom his family had served for seven centuries. News comes that the royal Grand Duchess Annajanska has joined the revolution, but having been taken prisoner she is brought before General Strammfest 'enveloped from head to foot by a fur-lined cloak' which temporarily hides the Hussar uniform revealed after she has shown herself to be a woman of martial spirit who supports the revolution because it is led by an 'energetic minority' who will govern the people incompetent to govern themselves. When Strammfest sees her commandingly in uniform he hails her as 'The Bolshevik Empress'.

Annals of Innocence and Experience. Autobiography by Sir Herbert *Read, published in 1941.

Annan, Lord (Noel Gilroy Annan, 1916-   ; life peer 1965). Educated at Stowe and Cambridge, where he became Provost of King's College in 1956, having been University Lecturer in Politics since 1948. Provost of University College, London, from 1966. Author of *Leslie Stephen: His Thought and Character in Relation to his Time* (1951); *The Curious Strength of Positivism in English Political Thought* (1959).

Annotation. The critical or editorial function of providing explanatory notes to a literary work; or the making of marginal comments in a book or manuscript.

Annual Register, The. The oldest periodical publication in the United Kingdom, first issued in 1758 on the initiative of Edmund Burke, who became its first editor. The 1958 issue contained a preface by Asa Briggs surveying the history of the *Register* during two hundred years of unbroken publication. Its annual issues provide a summary of current history by regional divisions, and sections on Religion, Science, Law, Economics, and the Arts and Literature in the United Kingdom.

Annunzio, Gabriele d'. *See* Gabriele *d'Annunzio.

Anouilh, Jean (1910-). Born in Bordeaux; educated at a Paris school and in the University there. Began to write plays while still a schoolboy; studied law; then worked as an advertisement copy-writer. After World War II he became a prolific and successful playwright, and already, during the German occupation, his *Antigone* (1944) had been produced in Paris, despite its relevance to the prevailing tyranny. A number of his plays were produced with marked success in London after the war, translated by various hands: *Antigone, Ring Round the Moon, Colombe, Becket, The Rehearsal.* In France, collections of his plays were published as *Pièces roses* (1945 and later volumes) and *Pièces noires* (1945 and later).

Anstey, F. (pseudonym of Thomas Anstey Guthrie, 1856-1934). Humorous writer whose greatest success was *Vice Versa* (1882) a farcical novel in which a father and son interchange ages and personalities. He was for years a regular contributor to *Punch* and also had successes in the theatre with plays adapted from his novels.

Anstruther, Joyce. *See* Jan *Struther.

Anthologies. Collections of poetry and/or prose selected from the writings of various authors, usually by an editor who may or may not contribute biographical notes and comment. The word (from the Greek *anthos* and *logia*—flower collection) was first applied in the present sense to the ancient *Greek Anthology*, but the most notable English anthology is *The Golden Treasury* compiled by Francis Turner Palgrave (1824-97) with Tennyson's help and published in 1861. Sir Arthur *Quiller-Couch's *Oxford Book of English Verse* (1900) also had a prolonged success, though the editor's level of taste and standards of textual procedure were later to be severely judged. Countless anthologies followed—became, indeed, a publishing habit—but none has borne so lasting an impress of the editor's mind and authority as *The Golden Treasury,* though its range is narrower than that of a multitude•of its successors. Robert Bridges's *The Spirit of Man* (1915), Walter *de la Mare's *Come Hither* (1923) and Lord Wavell's *Other Men's Flowers* (1944) are outstanding personal selections. The *New Oxford Book of English Verse 1250-1950,* edited by Helen *Gardner, which superseded in 1972 Quiller-Couch's book (mentioned above), conformed textually to scholarly standards and ranged beyond the lyrical and more popular field preferred by Q.

Anthony Adverse. A long novel by Hervey *Allen, published 1933; set in the period of the Napoleonic wars.

Anthony, C. L. Pseudonym of Dodie *Smith under which she wrote several successful plays: *Autumn Crocus* (1930), *Theatre Royal* (1934), and others. From 1935 she wrote under her own name.

Anthony, Captain. Master of the *Ferndale* in Joseph Conrad's *Chance* (1914); 'son of Carleon Anthony, the poet'; marries Flora de Barral.

Anthony, John. Chairman of the Trenartha Tin Plate Company in John Galsworthy's *Strife* (1909); resigns after fifty years on the Board when he is outvoted on the settlement of a prolonged strike.

Anthony, Michael (1932-). Born and educated in Trinidad; worked in the oil industry there before going to England in 1954, where he took employment in factories, and for British Railways and the Post Office, later becoming a sub-editor for Reuters. Settled in Brazil. Author of short stories: *The Games Were Coming* (1963), *The Year in San Fernando* (1965), *Green Days by the River* (1967).

Antibiotics. Chemical substances (*penicillin, streptomycin, and others) which destroy bacteria and are used in the treatment of a variety of diseases.

Antic Hay. Novel by Aldous *Huxley, published in 1923. Theodore Gumbril, uncomfortable on his hard oaken seat during chapel service at the school where he is a master, mentally invents trousers with an inflatable seat. Having resigned his post, he gets Bojanus, his tailor, to make a pair of the pneumatic trousers, and markets the invention as Gumbril's Patent Small-Clothes, driving a profitable deal with Boldero, the capitalist who is to exploit it. Theodore, having overcome inborn diffidence by wearing an artificial beard which gives him confidence as 'the Complete Man', embarks upon temporary amorous adventures with Rosie Shearwater and 'Mrs Emily X', but has a more complex relationship with Myra Viveash, who has been 'dead inside' since Tony Lamb was killed in World War I. The novel is notable for the conversation pieces which border the main narrative, e.g. between Theodore and Bojanus on Liberty, and between Theodore and Boldero on advertising methods; for the architect Gumbril senior's monologue while displaying his immense model of London rebuilt on an ideal plan; and for discussions and meditations on art, music, and other topics, involving Lippiat the painter, Shearwater the physiologist, etc. The title is from lines in Marlowe's *Edward II*.

Anticipations of the Reaction of Mechanical and Scientific Progress upon Human Life and Thought. Essays by H. G. *Wells published in 1902: I. Locomotion in the Twentieth Century; II. The Probable Diffusion of Great Cities; III. Developing Social Elements; IV. Certain Social Reactions; V. The Life-History of Democracy; VI. War in the Twentieth Century; VII. The Conflict of Languages; VIII. The Larger Synthesis; IX. Faith, Morals, and Public Policy in the Twentieth Century. The book aimed to bring together 'the material for a picture of the human community somewhere towards the year 2000'. As an early product of the speculative and prophetic Wells, it is noteworthy both for its total misses and for its hits near the centre of the target.

Anticlimax. Descent (sometimes sudden) from a high or serious level to one that is mean or trivial. Anything that arouses hope or expectation which it disappoints. Used as a literary device it serves to shock attention or to provide comic contrast. See Bathos.

Antigone. A play by Jean *Anouilh first performed in France in 1942. Intended as an allegory of France during the German occupation, its purpose was unperceived by the enemy.

Anti-hero. In the second half of the 19th century, novelists' heroes approximated more and more nearly to 'ordinary' people and shed more and more of the qualities associated with traditional heroes in fiction. This tendency became common practice in such early 20th-century novels as those of H. G. *Wells and Arnold *Bennett, but they and their contemporaries introduced non-heroes rather than anti-heroes. It was after World War II that the anti-hero became a predominant character in fiction and stage plays written by, e.g. Kingsley *Amis (in *Lucky Jim*), John *Wain (*Hurry on Down*), John *Osborne (*Look Back in Anger*), John Braine (*Room at the Top*), Harold *Pinter (*The Caretaker*)—and many others. Anti-heroes reject standards of conduct or social behaviour formerly held to be essential in civilized society. Some deliberately revolt against those standards and regard the modern world as a jungle in which tooth and claw prevail; others are unaware of the existence of standards; others again, having been educated away from their early environment and become stranded intellectually and emotionally, turn sour and affect to despise what they cannot grasp; yet again others, such as Davies in *The Caretaker,* are inarticulate flotsam of humanity. Anti-heroes of another sort appear in the novels of Graham *Greene, where addiction to sin—mortal or merely shabby, but always unheroic—is the doorway to redemption. It became an academic fashion *c.* 1950-60 to search out 'anti-heroes' in earlier English writings, even in all the novels of Jane Austen.

Ántoine, André (1858-1943). Born in Limoges. After working as a clerk in Paris he became, via an amateur company, the leader of the advanced theatre in France, starting the Théâtre Libre in 1887 for the production of (mainly) realistic plays barred from the regular theatres. He ceased to direct the Théâtre Libre in 1895, but two years later founded the Théâtre Antoine, where he carried on similar work until 1906, when he became director of the government-controlled

Odéon. Antoine not only transformed the French theatre but also set an example followed by the *Independent Theatre promoted in London by J. T. *Grein.

Antoinette Cosway. Central character in Jean Rhys's *Wide Sargasso Sea* (1966). Intended to represent Mr Rochester's mad wife in *Jane Eyre*, her earlier life in the West Indies is presented and her subsequent confinement in Rochester's English home up to the time she appears in Charlotte Brontë's novel.

Antonia Shimerda. Central character in Willa Cather's *My Ántonia* (1918); daughter of Bohemian immigrants farming on poor land in Nebraska.

Anthroposophy. A development from theosophy, originated by Rudolf *Steiner, who founded the Anthroposophical Society in 1913.

Antrobus family. Central characters in Thornton Wilder's *The *Skin of Our Teeth* (1942): George, his wife Maggie, their children Henry and Gladys.

Anzac. The Australian and New Zealand Army Corps formed for active service in World War I. They fought in several zones but were particularly associated with the Dardanelles campaign against the Turkish army.

Apache. Generic title for the Paris hooligans and gangsters whom adolescent girls elsewhere viewed romantically in the 1920s; *apache* dances then became a vogue, as jiving did after World War II. Apache was originally the name of a North American Indian tribe.

Apes of God, The. Satirical novel by P. Wyndham *Lewis, published in 1930.

A.P.H. See A. P. *Herbert.

Aphorism. A saying which expresses in a few profound or witty words some truth or conviction. In *The Faber Book of Aphorisms* (1964) the editors distinguish between an epigram (which 'need only be true of a single case') and an aphorism (which 'is either universally true or true of every member of the class to which it refers').

Aphrodite in Aulis. Novel by George *Moore published in 1930. Kebren, son of a fishmonger in Athens, exasperates his father by his clumsiness in the business and by reading Homer's *Iliad* when he should be serving customers. He turns actor, but grows tired of being always cast as a messenger when he wants to play kings. Leaving the theatre, he becomes a travelling rhapsodist giving readings from the *Iliad*. One night he hears what it takes to be the voice of a god telling him to go to Aulis. He sets out on foot and on reaching Aulis is given hospitality in the house of Otanes, a shipowner and merchant who is a widower with one young daughter, Biote. She wearies of Kebren's Homeric readings and falls in love with him. They marry, and Kebren is soon immersed in Otanes's business and goes on long voyages, endeavouring to recapture the trade which formerly made Aulis a great and flourishing seaport. Biote bears two sons, Rhesos and Thrasillos, who break away from their parents as they grow up and take off for Athens, where Rhesos is accepted as a pupil by the famous sculptor, Phidias, and Thrasillos learns to be an architect, both assisting on the structure of the Parthenon. Later, back in Aulis, they are commissioned to erect a temple in honour of the goddess Aphrodite. Rhesos is unable to find inspiration for his statue of the goddess, until he sees the two daughters of his father's friend Mnasalcas, a prosperous sheepfarmer, swimming out of the sea. The two girls, Earine and Melissa, marry the brothers. When the temple is finished, Phidias and the dramatists Sophocles, Euripides, and Aristophanes attend the opening ceremony, and Aristophanes, satirizing a local celebrity, gives an impromptu synopsis of an unwritten play, *The Apes*. The book ends with the populace being admitted to the shrine of Aphrodite in Aulis.

Apjohn, Henry. The young poet in *How He Lied to Her Husband* by Bernard Shaw.

Apocalypse. An uncompleted essay by D. H. *Lawrence on the theme of Revelation, published posthumously in 1931.

Apollinaire, Guillaume (pseudonym of Wilhelm Apollinaris Kostrowitski, 1880-1918). Born in Rome of a Polish mother. Chiefly a poet (*Alcools*, 1913; *Calligrammes*, 1918), he also wrote novels, short stories and plays, which are in some degree a symbolistic presentation of the 'new spirit' he discerned in the life of his time. He was much involved also with contemporary art movements among *avant garde* painters, writing on the Cubists (*Les Peintres cubistes*, 1913) and for one of his novels (*La Femme assise*, 1920) using a title familiar through a painting by Picasso, though in subject they have nothing in common. His 'surrealist drama' *Les Mamelles de Tirésias* (1918) was used in 1944 by the French composer Francis Poulenc as the libretto for a one-act comic opera.

Apollodorus. The 'dashing . . . handsome and debonair' Sicilian carpet purveyor in *Caesar and Cleopatra* by Bernard Shaw.

Apostles, The. Title applied (at first facetiously) to a Conversazione Society formed by a group of young university men at Cambridge in 1820 for the discussion of literary, philosophical, and political topics. Among the members were Tennyson, Arthur Hallam, Frederick Maurice, Monckton Milnes and others who later became distinguished in their several fields. The Society continued and in the early years of the present century its strictly limited membership included Rupert *Brooke, as well as J. M. *Keynes, G. E. *Moore, and Lytton *Strachey, the last three afterwards associated with the *Bloomsbury Group.

Apple Cart, The. A Political Extravaganza in two acts and an interlude by Bernard *Shaw. First performed in Warsaw in 1929 and later in the same year in England at the Malvern Festival. While the two Private Secretaries of King Magnus are dealing with the morning's correspondence, Boanerges, President of the Board of Trade, arrives for an appointment with the king. When Magnus enters, the two discuss constitutional monarchy, the king dissenting from Boanerges's opinion that the royal function is to be 'an indiarubber stamp' giving formal approval to his ministers' decisions. Magnus and the secretaries leave just before the rest of the Cabinet arrive to discuss the crisis caused by the king's public speeches and inspired articles in the Press. They decide, after much squabbling, to present an ultimatum: either Magnus must refrain from unapproved speeches and sponsored articles or the Government will resign. When Magnus returns, he warns them of the consequences if they have a dumb king, and in a later meeting with the Cabinet in the afternoon he tells them that he will resign, dissolve Parliament, and become a candidate for the Royal Borough of Windsor at the ensuing general election. Dismayed by the certainty that he will be elected, the

Prime Minister declares that 'the crisis is a washout' and tears up the ultimatum. In the Interlude between the acts, the king's lady friend, Orinthia, fails to persuade him that a 'rose' like herself is preferable to his 'cabbage' of a wife as queen.

Appleby, Inspector (later **Sir John**). Scotland Yard detective in crime stories by Michael *Innes.

Après-midi d'un faune, L'. (The afternoon of a faun). Poem by Stéphane Mallarmé published in 1876. It inspired Debussy's tone poem *Prélude à l'Après-midi d'un faune* (1894), on which was founded a ballet made famous by Nijinsky's choreography and dancing in Diaghilev's company in 1912.

Apron Stage. A platform extending beyond the proscenium arch in modern theatres. It was derived from the Elizabethan stage with the intention of restoring intimacy between actors and audience which the 'picture frame' stage prevented. Later theatre architecture extended the stage still further into the auditorium, culminating in 'theatre in the round', which achieved total intimacy and abolished stage illusion and suspense.

Aragon, Louis (1897-   ). Born in Paris. His fiction was at first a literary counterpart of surrealism (as in the novel *Le Paysan de Paris*, 1926); later he wrote as a whole-hearted Communist (as in the poem translated as *The Red Front*, 1933) and produced much journalism for left-wing papers. Throughout he showed a mastery of style in both verse and prose.

Arabia Deserta, Travels in. Charles *Doughty's record of his life among the desert Arabs, published in 1888. Its length and the archaic style characteristic of its author made it known to few until T. E. *Lawrence's enthusiasm brought it to the notice of a larger public through a new edition and an abridgement (1920-21).

Arb, Violet. Widow of a successful Clerk of the Works; marries miserly Henry Earlforward in Arnold Bennett's *Riceyman Steps* (1923).

Arber, Edward (1836-1912). Professor of English in Birmingham (1881-94) after serving as an Admiralty clerk (1854-78), but remembered as the initiator and editor of Arber's Reprints, a series of 16th and

17th century works in verse, prose, and drama (Ascham, Bacon, John Earle, Latimer, Milton, More, Udall, Villiers, Thomas Watson, and others), not otherwise easily available at that time.

Archbishop of Rheims, The. The 'full-fed political prelate with nothing of the ecclesiastic about him except his imposing bearing' in *Saint Joan by Bernard Shaw.

Archbishop of York, The. In Part III of *Back to Methuselah by Bernard Shaw. He appears as the Rev. Bill Haslam in Part II, and is now 283 years old, having been in the meantime twice an Archbishop, a President, and a General.

Archer, William (1856-1924). Dramatic critic and playwright, born in Perth, settled in London. He was an ardent advocate of the new intellectual drama associated with *Ibsen, whose plays he translated with assistance from other members of his family. Bernard *Shaw was much indebted to him for a generous introduction to profitable journalism and also for suggestions which led to the first of Shaw's plays, *Widowers' Houses. The two men remained friends, and an essay 'How William Archer impressed Bernard Shaw' included in Three Plays by Archer (1927), ends 'I still feel that when he went he took a piece of me with him'. (Shaw reprinted this essay on Archer in Pen Portraits and Reviews, 1931.) Largely on account of his enthusiasm for Ibsen and of the austerity of his own prose style, Archer was widely regarded as 'a dour Scot', but Shaw emphasized that 'Archer was like myself, the victim of an unsleeping and incorrigible sense of humour'. Archer's The Old Drama and the New (1923) is a perceptive survey. Collections of his earlier writings as dramatic critic to The World (1893-7) were issued annually under the title The Theatrical World. With Shaw's Our Theatres in the Nineties they provide a valuable record of the contemporary stage. Four years before his death Archer became suddenly and surprisingly prosperous with The Green Goddess, a melodrama packed with entertaining improbabilities far removed from the intellectual realism of Ibsen.

Archer-Shee Case, The. See The *Winslow Boy.

Archers, The. A fictional country family whose farming and family affairs attracted a multitude of B.B.C. listeners for years after World War II. People of all classes became devotees of the programme, and the births, marriages, and deaths of Archers aroused interest and stirred emotion equivalent to the concern felt for living relatives and intimate friends.

Archetype. A word much used in psychology since it was given currency by C. G. *Jung, and thence extended to literary and art criticism in reference to any individual work or form or episode that prefigures or symbolizes a type or an experience—as, e.g., Job may be taken as the archetype of afflicted humanity. From the Greek arché (original) and typos (form).

archy and mehitabel: a cockroach and an alley-cat invented by the American Don *Marquis. Their adventures (combining satire and buoyant humour) are related by archy in free verse which employs no capital letters, for archy the cockroach uses a typewriter by jumping on the keys but lacks the weight required to work the shift-key. mehitabel's part is a scurrilous one, involving many kittens and an often proclaimed motto—'toujours gai'.

Arden, John (1930-   ). Born in Barnsley; educated at Sedbergh, Cambridge, and Edinburgh College of Art. Worked as an architect before turning to the theatre. Author of All Fall Down (1955), The Waters of Babylon (1957), *Live Like Pigs (1958), Sergeant Musgrave's Dance (1960), Armstrong's Last Goodnight (1964), The Ballygombeen Bequest (1972), and other plays.

Ardizzone, Edward (Edward Jeffrey Irving Ardizzone, 1900-   ). Best known as painter and illustrator, but is also the author of numerous children's books with his own pictures: e.g. Little Tim and the Brave Sea Captain (1936), Tim All Alone (1956), Diana and Her Rhinoceros (1964), The Young Ardizzone (autobiographical, 1970).

Ariadne. The former Ariadne (Addie) Shotover in *Heartbreak House by Bernard Shaw. She has married Sir Hastings Utterword before the play begins, and has become an arrogant snob.

Ariel. Title given by André *Maurois to his biographical study of Shelley (1923).

Arjillax. Sculptor of the Ancients in Part V of *Back to Methuselah by Bernard Shaw. He derides 'pretty-pretty' sculpture as mere 'confectionery' compared with the 'intensity of mind' he claims is stamped on his own work.

Arkell, Reginald (1882-1959). Born at Lechlade, Glos.; educated at Burford Grammar School. Wrote much for the stage (lyrics for revues, etc.), as well as books of light verse, humorous books on garden and country themes (*Green Fingers,* 1934, and its successors, all reissued in *Collected Green Fingers,* 1957); *A Cottage in the Country* (1934) and a study of *Richard Jefferies* (1933).

Arlen, Michael (pseudonym of Dikran Kouyoumdjian, 1895-1956). Born in Bulgaria of Armenian parents; educated in England at Malvern College; naturalized as a British subject 1922. After World War I he became a popular and fashionable short-story writer (*The Romantic Lady,* 1921; *These Charming People,* 1923; and other volumes), and novelist (*The Green Hat,* 1924; etc.). He continued tó write until his last novel, *Flying Dutchman,* was published in 1939, but his blend of cynicism and tart romanticism was particularly attuned to the mood of the 1920s.

Armageddon. The place so-named in The Revelation of St John the Divine (16: 14, 16) where the 'spirits of devils' were to 'go' forth unto the kings of the earth and of the whole world, to gather them to the battle of that great day of God Almighty'. The word was applied by journalists, preachers, and others to World War I.

Armistice Day. 11 November 1918, the day on which at 11 a.m. World War I ended with the capitulation of the Central Powers (Germany and her associates) to the Western Allies (France, the British Empire and the U.S.A.). Thereafter at 11 a.m. on each successive 11 November a five-minutes silence was kept in memory of the killed, and a ceremony held at the Cenotaph erected in Whitehall, London.

Arms and the Man. An Anti-Romantic Comedy. Play in three acts by Bernard *Shaw, performed in London in 1894. While pursued by advancing Bulgarians, Captain Bluntschli, a Swiss mercenary in the Serbian army defeated at Slivnitza in 1885, takes refuge in the bedroom of Raina Petkoff, daughter of a Bulgarian officer, Major Paul Petkoff, and engaged to Major Sergius Saranoff, who has distinguished himself at the head of a cavalry charge. Raina hides Bluntschli, though she is contemptuous when he confesses that he carries chocolate, not cartridges, in his ammunition pouches, because soldiers need food more than arms. He escapes next morning wearing one of her father's coats which she has given him. Later, after the war is over, he comes back to return the coat and, having solved a military problem which baffled Major Petkoff and Sergius, is invited to stay. In the pocket of the coat Petkoff finds a photograph of his daughter inscribed 'Raina, to her Chocolate Cream Soldier: a Souvenir'. Bluntschli proposes to Raina and is accepted, having established that as heir to a wealthy hotelier's business in Switzerland he is the social and financial equal of the Petkoffs. Sergius consoles himself with Louka, the maidservant.

Armstrong, Anthony (George Anthony Armstrong Willis, 1897-   ). Born at Esquimault, British Columbia; educated in England at Uppingham and Cambridge; served in France during World War I and afterwards, as 'A.A.', contributed humorous articles weekly to *Punch* from 1925 to 1933. His humorous novels, crime novels, and miscellaneous writings are extremely numerous, and he also wrote, collaborated in, or adapted many plays, having an outstanding success with the ingenious *Ten-Minute Alibi,* which ran in Lodnon for nearly 900 performances from January 1933 and was afterwards rewritten as a novel.

Armstrong, Martin (Martin Donisthorpe Armstrong, 1882-1974). Born near Newcastle upon Tyne; educated at Charterhouse and Cambridge. Worked in an architect's office before spending a year in Italy. Served in France during World War I, then took to journalism and the writing of novels and short stories, having already published verse before the war. His prose includes novels ranging from *The Goat and Compasses* (1925) to *The Snake in the Grass* (1938); short stories: *The Puppet Show* (1922), *Selected Stories* (1951); poetry: *Collected Poems* (1931). *The Paint Box* (1931) is an unexcelled introduction to the appreciation of pictures, written for children but helpful also tó adults.

Armstrong, Terence Ian Fytton. *See* John *Gawsworth.

Armstrong, Thomas (1899-   ). Born in Yorkshire; educated at Wakefield and the Royal Naval College, Keyham; after naval service in World War I settled to authorship, producing successful novels dealing with the English industrial north, *The Crowthers of Bankdam* (1940), *King Cotton* (1947), etc.

Arnim, Countess von. See *Elizabeth, pseudonym.

Arno, Peter (pseudonym of Curtis Arnoux Peters, jnr, 1906-1968). Educated in Connecticut and at Yale. Gained international repute as a humorous cartoonist with drawings regularly in *The New Yorker* from 1925, collected in *Peter Arno's Parade* (1930) and later volumes.

Arnold, Ida. See *Ida Arnold.

Arnold, Sir Edwin (1832-1904; knighted 1888). Educated at London and Oxford Universities; won the Newdigate Prize (1852). After a period in the Indian Education Service he joined the *Daily Telegraph* in London in 1861 and was editor from 1873 to 1889. Thereafter he travelled much in the East and wrote travel books on India, Japan, etc. His contemporary fame rested on *The Light of Asia* (1879) in which he attempted epical treatment of the life and doctrine of the Buddha.

Around Theatres. A selection from the dramatic criticism contributed by Max *Beerbohm to the *Saturday Review*, 28 May 1898-16 April 1910. Published in 2 vols, 1925; reprinted in 1 vol, 1953. Beerbohm became dramatic critic to the *Saturday Review* when Bernard *Shaw relinquished the post, having written the famous sequence of articles subsequently collected in *Our Theatres in the Nineties*.

Arrow of Gold, The. 'A Story Between Two Notes' by Joseph *Conrad published in 1919. The 'two Notes' frame the story of Doña Rita, born a peasant and in childhood a goat-herd in her native Basque country, but in adolescence taken up by Henry Allègre, a millionaire amateur painter and collector of art treasures— ivories, enamels, miniatures. He takes her abroad and at length to Paris, where her beauty and intelligence make her a centre of admiration. Allègre dies, leaving to Rita his fortune and collection, including several houses, one in the Street of the Consuls in Marseilles, where much of the novel is set. There the young man known as Monsieur George is drawn into the circle supporting the conspiracy to place the Pretender Don Carlos de Bourbon on the Spanish throne. Meanwhile Doña Rita has become a devoted Carlist, and—having been brought into her company by a Mr Mills ('a relation of Lord X') and J. K. Blunt whose two chief declarations are 'I live by my sword' and *'Je suis Américain, catholique et gentilhomme'*—Monsieur George is persuaded to undertake gun-running in 'a fast sailing craft' he buys, with his fearless Corsican friend Dominic as captain. After some successful expeditions the boat is sunk. George falls in love with Rita, who has rejected Blunt as a suitor, and following a frienzied attempt by José Ortega to force her to fulfil a childhood promise of marriage, she retires with George to a drystone cottage in the Maritime Alps, until he challenges Blunt to a duel on hearing that the American has slandered him. Blunt, dishonourably firing a second time, severely wounds George. Rita cares for him until he is out of danger, then goes out of his life leaving him only the jewelled arrow of gold she wore in her hair.

Arrowsmith. Novel by Sinclair *Lewis published in 1925. Starting as an unpaid boy-of-all-work to a drunken country doctor, Martin Arrowsmith proceeds to the midwestern University of Winnemac where he graduates in medicine and sets up in practice at Wheatsylvania, Dakota, the small-town home of Leora Tozer, whom he met as a probationer nurse and married. At the University he had become devoted to Max Gottlieb, Professor of Bacteriology, whose passion for scientific truth is accompanied by a sardonic estimate of human worth. Martin's practice brings small reward and he becomes assistant to Almus Pickerbaugh, Director of Public Health at Nautilus, Iowa, moving later to Chicago as pathologist at a private clinic, after Pickerbaugh's mountebank methods have sickened him and Martin himself has been ostracized when he refuses to kowtow to local commercial interests. The Rouncefield Clinic, which flourishes on fashionable surgery for wealthy patients, cramps Martin's research work, and at Gottlieb's invitation he joins the McGurk Institute of Biology in New York, where he is allotted a laboratory and promised at least a year of uninterrupted scientific investigation. Having discovered an unidentifiable 'chemical or germ' which destroys bacteria, he is sent as chief of a McGurk Commission to conduct a controlled experiment in a plague-stricken island in the West Indies. He fails to exercise strict scientific control and is unable to determine whether the passing of the epidemic is due to his inoculations or to other causes. His wife Leora dies of the disease. After returning to New York he marries Joyce Lanyon, a rich widow, whose society friends soon wear him down, and he joins a former McGurk colleague to follow a promising line of bacterial research in an isolated laboratory built in the Vermont woods.

Arsenic and Old Lace. See Joseph *Kesselring.

Art for Art's Sake. See *Aesthetic Movement.

Art Nouveau. A movement in Europe and America at the end of the 19th century which popularized a sinuous style in design and plant-forms applied to various objects and as decoration on furniture, etc. It died out in the new century, but interest revived in the 1960s and was reflected in exhibitions of *art nouveau* work.

Artaud, Antonin (1896-1948). Born in Marseilles. Worked as an actor prior to founding in collaboration with Roger *Vitrac the Théâtre Alfred Jarry in Paris in 1927. His volume of essays *Le Théâtre et son double* (1938; Eng. trans. by M. C. Richards: *The Theatre and its Double*, New York, 1958) enunciated theories which led in the international scene to others' plays to which the generic titles *Theatre of the Absurd and *Theatre of Cruelty became attached. Artaud travelled widely, to Mexico and elsewhere. He became a drug addict and mentally deranged.

Artemas (pseudonym of Arthur Telford Mason). Author of *The Book of Artemas: Concerning men, and the things that men did do at the time when there was a war* (1917) and later 'Artemas' books.

Arts Council of Great Britain. State-supported organization developed from the World War II CEMA (Council for the Encouragement of Music and the Arts) and granted a royal charter under its new title in 1946. It makes grants to approved bodies devoted to drama, opera, ballet, music, etc. and to selected individuals for literary work,

especially poetry. It also organizes art exhibitions and contributes to the cost of suitable exhibitions arranged by others. Similar work overseas is the concern of the *British Council.

Ascent of F6, The. Tragedy in two acts by W. H. *Auden and Christopher *Isherwood published in 1936. F6 is a (reputedly haunted) mountain standing on the frontier line which marks off British Sudoland from Ostrian Sudoland. Both nations claim the mountain as part of their colonial territory, and the natives declare that 'the white man who first reaches the summit of F6, will be lord over *both* the Sudolands, with his descendants, for a thousand years'. The British therefore send an expedition led by Michael Ransom to climb the mountain, but an avalanche overwhelms them. The play symbolized and allegorized political problems insistent in the 1930s.

Asch, Sholem (1880-1957). Born in Poland. His novels, short stories and plays in Yiddish were translated into various languages, and in Britain and America he became known by such novels as *Salvation* (1934), *The Nazarene* (1939), and *The Apostle* (1943), in which his aim was to reconcile Jewish and Christian beliefs.

Ash Wednesday. Poem by T. S. *Eliot published in 1930. Owing much to Dante, and closepacked with religious allegory and symbolism, it is explicable only in its own mystico-poetic language, though in the final section there are allusions to sea and coast which reflect the author's memories of his early New England upbringing.

Ashburnham, Edward and Leonora. Leading characters in Ford Madox Hueffer's *The *Good Soldier* (1915).

Ashe, Gordon. See John *Creasey.

Ashenden. The narrator in *Cakes and Ale* etc. by W. Somerset Maugham.

Ashenden, or The British Agent. Volume of short stories by W. Somerset *Maugham published in 1928, and based on the author's experiences as an Intelligence Officer during World War I in France, Switzerland, Italy, and Russia. Although written in the first person by 'Ashenden', his adventures and impressions are recorded with detachment and sardonic disillusion.

Ashford, Daisy (*née* Margaret Ashford,

1881-1972). Born at Petersham, Surrey, daughter of a War Office official; educated at Hayward's Heath; studied art at the Slade School, and lived for some time in Switzerland; married in 1920 and settled in Norfolk where her husband, James Devlin, became a market gardener after resigning his army commission. Like many other children she amused herself by writing stories, among them The *Young Visiters, written when she was nine. Nearly thirty years later it was read and recommended by Frank *Swinnerton and, published in 1919, was an immediate success. Described in an Introduction by J. M. *Barrie as a masterpiece, its unpremeditated comic view of the adult world aligns it with Jane Austen's juvenilia, notably Love and Freindship (first published in 1922). Daisy Ashford did not pursue a literary career, but a further gathering of childhood pieces appeared in Daisy Ashford: Her Book (1923).

Ashley Library. The extensive and valuable collection of first editions of notable 17th-century and later books made by Thomas J. *Wise and bought from him by the British Museum. He also compiled a printed catalogue in ten volumes which is of considerable bibliographical merit. The subsequent exposure of Wise as a forger of literary 'rarities' with only an imaginary ancestry had little bearing upon the authority of the Ashley Library, which contains very few suspect items, apart from such formerly imperfect copies as he had completed with pages extracted surreptitiously from the British Museum's own literary treasures.

Ashmolean Museum, Oxford. The oldest public museum in Britain, it was opened in 1683 to house the objects of antiquity bequeathed to the University at various dates in the 17th-century by Sir Thomas Bodley, John Selden, Lord Henry Howard, John Tradescant, and by Elias Ashmole who made it a condition that a suitable new building should be provided for the collection he left. Though the Museum was moved in 1845 from Broad Street to the present site in Beaumont Street, it still perpetuates Ashmole's name, though it has received important benefactions from later donors. In addition to Greek, Roman, Egyptian, and Indian sculptures, the collection has Eastern and European paintings, ceramics, bronzes, coins, tapestries, furniture, glassware, jewellery

(including the famous King Alfred's Jewel), and objects from the Palace of Knossos in Crete excavated by Sir Arthur *Evans.

Ashton, Helen (Helen Rosaline Ashton, 1891-1958). Born in London; educated there at the University, preparatory to taking a medical degree. Turned to writing, having her chief success with Dr Serocold (1930), a novel covering one day's experiences of an English country physician. Her later novels included one on the Wordsworths, William and Dorothy (1938), and another on Jane Austen, Parson Austen's Daughter (1949). A successful film, White Corridors, was based on her novel of hospital life, Yeoman's Hospital (1944).

Ashton, Winifred. See Clemence *Dane.

Ashton-Warner, Sylvia (pseudonym of Sylvia Henderson). She was born at Stratford, Taranaki, New Zealand; educated at Wairarana College and Auckland Teachers' Training College. Taught with her husband in Maori schools, where she developed her Creative Teaching Scheme. Author of Spinster (1958), Teacher (1963), Myself (1968), and other novels.

Aside. In a play, a brief remark spoken for the audience to hear, but conventionally supposed to be inaudible to other characters on the stage. It superseded the Elizabethan and Jacobean soliloquy as a common device in 18th-19th century drama, but has been discarded.

Asimov, Isaac (1920-   ). Born in Russia; settled in America; educated at Brooklyn High School and Columbia University. Became a research chemist and Associate Professor of Biochemistry at Boston University. Author of medical textbooks and works of popular science, including The Intelligent Man's Guide to Science (1960), but is more widely known as a writer of science fiction: I, Robot (1952), Foundation (1953), The Caves of Steel (1954), The Naked Sun (1958), The Martian Way (1964), Opus 100 (1969). In addition he wrote under the pseudonym Paul French.

Ask the Fellows Who Cut the Hay. A country chronicle by George Ewart Evans, published in 1956. Centred on the village of Blaxhall, a few miles from the east coast of Suffolk, it preserves memories of rural life and farming methods as recollected by older local inhabitants. Sheep tending and shearing; the growing and harvesting of crops; the purpose and employment of farm implements and machines, old and new; domestic crafts—breadmaking, bacon and ham curing, cheesemaking, beer brewing, clothes washing; all these occupations of the men's and women's working lives are treated within the framework of local life, which embraces churchgoing and campanology, education (and field work by the children), the inn as a social centre; smuggling, legends and common sayings. The author, while regretting the passing of old ways, recognizes the human benefits of the new, and suggests practical measures for reinvigorating village life through the influence of parish councils. The title is from a line of verse by Ezra *Pound.

Askwith, Betty (Hon. Betty Ellen Askwith, 1909-). Daughter of Baron Askwith. Author of poems (*First Poems*, 1928; *Poems*, 1933), novels (*The Admiral's Daughters*, 1947; *The Blossoming Tree*, 1954; etc.), and humorous books in collaboration with Theodora *Benson (*Lobster Quadrille*, 1930; *How to be Famous*, 1937; etc.). Also *Lady Dilke* (biography; 1969).

Aslib. The Association of Special Libraries and Information Bureaux. Founded in London in 1924 'to promote the establishment of special libraries and information services and to assist their development by means of publications, training, conferences, advisory and other services'.

Asmoday. The demon overcome by the Archangel in *Tobias and the Angel* by James Bridie.

Asphalt Jungle, The. See W. R. *Burnett.

Asquith, Cynthia (*née* Lady Cynthia Charteris, d. 1960; daughter of the 11th Earl of Wemyss; married Herbert *Asquith). Author and editor of numerous books, including *A Portrait of [J. M.] *Barrie*, whose secretary she was (1918-37); she was also an admired friend of D. H. *Lawrence, who appears in her autobiographical *Remember and Be Glad* (1952).

Asquith, Elizabeth. See Princess (Antoine) *Bibesco.

Asquith, Hon. Herbert (1881-1947; son of 1st Earl of Oxford and Asquith). Author of *Poems 1912-33* and of novels including *Orland* (1927).

Asquith, Margot (*née* Emma Alice Margaret Tennant, 1864-1945; married Herbert Henry Asquith, later Prime Minister and 1st Earl of Oxford and Asquith). The candour and wit that made her a Society luminary for many years also enlivened her *Autobiography of Margot Asquith* (1922), which provides an acute hostess's-eye-view of persons and contemporary politics. She was said to have been the model for the name character of E. F. *Benson's *Dodo*.

Asquith of Yarnbury, Baroness (*née* Helen Violet Asquith, 1887-1969). Daughter of Herbert Henry and Helen Asquith. Educated privately and in Dresden and Paris. Married in 1915 Sir Maurice Bonham Carter (died 1960). Created a Life Peeress 1964. Held numerous public appointments. A brilliant public speaker and of masterly intellect, she remained a stalwart advocate of the Liberal Party through its years of decline and was a formidable defender of her father's political reputation. Her *Winston Churchill as I Knew Him* (1965) records a long and mutually valued friendship.

Assingham, Fanny. American-born wife of an English colonel, Robert Assingham, in Henry James's *The *Golden Bowl* (1904). She views with concern the complications in the lives of her friends Maggie Verver, Prince Amerigo, and Charlotte Stant.

Assonance. Approximate rhyming of such words as (in *Strange Meeting* by Wilfred *Owen) 'moan . . . mourn', 'wild . . . world', 'hair' . . . 'hour' . . . 'here', etc. A device favoured by 20th century poets in reaction from the smooth melodious tone of traditional rhyming verse.

Aston, James. See T. H. *White.

Astor family. Of German-American origin, the Astors have taken an important place in English public life since William Waldorf Astor (1879-1952) was elected M.P. for Plymouth in 1910. When he became 2nd Viscount Astor in 1919, his wife, Viscountess Astor (*née* Nancy Witcher Langhorne, 1879-1964), became the first woman M.P. at Westminster on her election to her husband's vacant seat for Plymouth, which she represented continuously for a quarter of a century (1919-45). Her wit and impassioned advocacy of temperance and other causes involved her in much controversy, but also won affectionate admiration from multitudes who came to regard her as a true-born Englishwoman rather than as a Virginian. She wrote *My Two Countries* in 1923. In the 1930s, when the German Nazi menace was threatening, the Astors incurred some political odium through allegations that at Cliveden (Buckinghamshire), one of their residences, country-house parties of socially influential persons were seeking to exercise backstairs and behind-the-scenes influence on the government. Though these allegations were denied and the existence of a Cliveden Set was said to be a myth invented by political opponents, the impression persisted, in some measure because of the Astors' connection with such newspapers as *The Times* and the *Observer*. The founder of the family, John Jacob Astor (1763-1848), was born near Heidelberg, and migrated to the U.S., where he made an immense fortune in furs. His great-grandson, John Jacob II (1864-1912), was drowned in the sinking of the liner *Titanic* through collision with an iceberg; his son, William Waldorf (1848-1919) settled in England in 1892, became proprietor of the *Pall Mall Gazette* (1893-1916), and 1st Viscount Astor in 1917. John Jacob III (1886-1971), younger son of the 1st Viscount, became M.P. for Dover, Chairman of *The Times* Publishing Company 1922 and 1st Baron Astor of Hever in 1956. His son Gavin Astor became Director of *The Times* in 1952; and David Astor (1912-   ), son of the 2nd Viscount, editor of the *Observer* in 1948. The connection with *The Times* was materially affected when the paper came under the control of Lord Thomson in 1967.

At Swim-Two-Birds. *See* Brian *O'Nolan.

Atalanta in Calydon. A poetic drama in the classical Greek mode by Swinburne. The lyrical portions are most remembered, especially the chorus beginning 'When the Hounds of Spring are on Winter's traces'.

Ataturk. *See* Kemal.

Athelny family. In Somerset Maugham's *Of Human Bondage* (1915), **Thorpe** Athelny, journalist, **Betty** his wife, and their children, **Athelstan, Harold, Edward, Sally, Molly, Connie, Rosie,** and **Jane.** Thorpe Athelny is attended in hospital by Philip Carey, whom they afterwards befriend, and Sally marries Philip.

Athenaeum, The. A weekly review of literature

and art founded in 1828 and with many distinguished contributors throughout its long life. It was merged with *The Nation* in 1921, and the combined paper became one with *The New Statesman* in 1931.

Athenaeum Club. Founded in 1824 in Pall Mall, London. Its members are drawn mainly from literary, artistic, and clerical circles.

Athens, The Modern. Complimentary name applied to Edinburgh, which is also sometimes called The Athens of the North.

Atherton, Gertrude (*née* Gertrude Franklin Horn, 1857-1948). American novelist, notable for *The Conqueror* (1902) and *Black Oxen* (1923), the latter dealing with the rejuvenation of a New York social celebrity by means of a glandular operation. The former of these novels is based on the life of Alexander Hamilton.

Athlone Press. The official publishing organization of the University of London; so named from the Earl of Athlone, Chancellor of the University at the time the Press was instituted. The title 'University of London Press' was pre-empted years earlier to a commercial publishing house which at that time was the production and distribution channel for books sponsored by the University, and continues as a business independent of the University.

Atkins, Tommy. Generic colloquial name for the British private soldier. It originated in instructions printed in army pay-books, where the words Tommy Atkins were used as a substitute name in a formula to be copied by the holder of the pay-book when making his will.

Atlantic Charter, The. Statement of war aims and peace principles issued jointly by Winston Churchill as British Prime Minister and Franklin D. Roosevelt, President of the United States, on 14 August 1941. Besides declaring that neither of their nations desired to profit in any respect by the war, but wished all peoples to live under governments freely chosen by themselves, they advocated worldwide disarmament, general social security, and that men and women everywhere should be enabled to live free from fear and want. These principles were afterwards embodied in the charter of the United Nations.

Atlantic Monthly, The. Founded in Boston in

1857; contributed to by many of America's leading writers on literary and political subjects. It maintained its high reputation throughout several generations, and was the most influential American publication in its intellectual class until reading habits changed after World War I and the former large body of educated and cultured readers of magazines dwindled.

Attlee, Clement Richard (1883-1967; 1st Earl Attlee 1955). Born in Putney; educated at Haileybury and Oxford. Called to the Bar 1906; practised until 1909. Lecturer in Social Science at London School of Economics, 1913-23, apart from service in World War I. Entered Parliament as Labour M.P. for Limehouse in 1922 and remained its representative until 1950, when he transferred to the West Walthamstow constituency until he went to the House of Lords. After holding a number of lesser ministerial offices he became Deputy Prime Minster in Winston Churchill's administration 1942-45 and followed him as Prime Minister when the Labour government came to power in 1945. During his term of office until 1951 he presided over the measures (including nationalization of mines, transport, gas and electricity, and health services) which constituted the Labour Party's programme for establishing the Welfare State. He wrote several books on socialism and an autobiography *As it Happened* (1954).

Attwell, Mable Lucie (Mrs Harold Earnshaw, 1879-1964). Born in London; educated at Cooper's Company School. Dissenting from the methods of the art schools attended later, she turned to the making of illustrations and soon established a profitable connection despite initial discouragement from an agency. For half a century thereafter her pictures of small wellrounded children were immensely popular, notwithstanding changes in taste and the disapproval of critics who considered them slick in style and sentimental. The 'Mabel Attwell child' became an almost universal nursery favourite, appearing on infants' tableware, toys, and other juvenile objects, as well as in thousands of pictures large and small, often with words in prose or verse by the artist herself. Also in demand as a publishers' illustrator, she supplied drawings for editions of Grimm, Hans Andersen, *Alice in Wonderland*, *Peter Pan*, *The Water Babies;* and from 1922 to 1961 *Lucie Attwell's Annual* appeared regularly.

Aubade. A dawn song. See Edith Sitwell's 'Aubade' beginning 'Jane, Jane, /Tall as a crane,/ The morning light creaks down again', which is one of the best-known pieces in her Bucolic Comedies (1923).

Auden, W. H. (Wystan Hugh Auden, 1907-1973). Born in York; educated at Gresham's School, Holt, and at Oxford. After visiting Germany he was for a while a provincial schoolmaster before becoming established as a writer among a group in London which included Stephen *Spender, Cecil *Day-Lewis, Louis *MacNeice and others accepted as leaders of a new movement in poetry, though owing much in form and literary temper to T. S. *Eliot and G. M. *Hopkins. Unlike Eliot, however, they were at that time strongly leftward in their political tendencies and inclined their early verse in the same direction. In 1937 Auden drove an ambulance for the Republicans in Spain during the Civil War, and in 1939 went to the United States, became a naturalized American citizen and took up teaching in colleges and universities in that country. He received various literary awards in Britain and America, and in 1956 was elected Professor of Poetry at Oxford for the statutory five-year period. In his later development Auden grew less unorthodox in his opinions, while in politics continuing to be left of centre though less aggressive. With the ageing of Eliot and after the death of the meteoric Dylan *Thomas, he became the most publicized poet of the time. The original hope of his generation that their poetry could be made to speak acceptably to the common man was rarely fulfilled, for both in form and expression most of their work was within the comprehension of only sophisticated and intellectualized readers, though such a ballad as *The Night Mail* shows that a wider appeal was not outside Auden's range. In collaboration with his friend Christopher *Isherwood he wrote for performance *The Dog Beneath the Skin* (1935; a metaphysical satirical extravaganza in verse and pantomime doggerel), *The *Ascent of F6* (1936). and *On the Frontier* (1938); in collaboration with MacNeice, *Letters from Iceland* (1936). His own books of verse include *Poems* (1930), *The Orators* (in prose and verse;

1932), *The Dance of Death* (1933), *Look, Stranger* (1936), *Spain* (1937), *Another Time* (1940), *New Year Letter* (1941), *For the Time Being* (1945), *The *Age of Anxiety* (1948). A visit to China during the Sino-Japanese conflict produced *Journey to a War* (prose by Isherwood, sonnets and a verse commentary by Auden: 1939). In collaboration with an American, Chester Kallman, he wrote (1951) the libretto for Stravinsky's *The Rake's Progress*. Other works: *Nones* (1951), *The Shield of Achilles* (1956), *Homage to Clio* (1960), *The Dyer's Hand* (1963), *About the House* (1966). *Collected Shorter Poems 1927-57* (1966), *Collected Longer Poems* (1968), *City Without Walls* (1969), *Epistle to a Godson* (1972).

Audoux, Marguerite (1863-1937). French novelist. Orphaned in childhood, she was first employed as a farm-worker in the provinces and then in Paris as a seamstress. From spare-time writing she at length produced an autobiographical novel *Marie-Claire* (1910) which had an international circulation.

Aufklarung (*German,* Enlightenment). Applied to the Revival of Learning (14th-16th centuries) and to the 18th century movement for political liberation and scientific enlightenment.

Aufsteig, General. Described as 'the Emperor of Turania travelling incognito' in Part IV of **Back to Methuselah* by Bernard Shaw.

August, John. Pseudonym used by Bernard *De Voto for novels and detective stories: *Troubled Star* (1939), *Rain Before Seven* (1940), *Advance Agent* (1942).

Augustus Carp. *See* H. H. *Bashford.

Augustus Does His Bit. A True to Life Farce. Play in one act by Bernard *Shaw, first performed in London by the Stage Society in January 1917. Opening with a comic dialogue between Lord Augustus Highcastle and his elderly clerk, satirizing official wartime regulations, the scene continues with a telephone call from Augustus's brother at the War Office, warning him that an attempt will be made by a woman spy to steal from him a secret list of anti-aircraft emplacements. He is then visited by an attractive lady who says that her German sister-in-law has made a bet with Augustus's brother that she will get the list. While Augustus is searching for the list to put it in a safer place, the clerk returns bringing a paper found in the hotel coffee room. By subterfuge the lady obtains it—and wins the bet *she* has made with Augustus's brother.

Aumonier, Stacy (1887-1928). After beginnings as landscape painter and as interior decorator, he turned to performing his own character sketches in theatres, before serving in World War I. He found his true *métier* in the writing of short stories, mostly humorous but occasionally grim: *Three Bars Interval* (1917), *One After Another* (1920), *Miss Bracegirdle and Others* (1923), *Fifteen Tales* (1924).

Aunt Edna. A mythical but universal and immortal playgoer invented by Terence *Rattigan in the Preface to vol. 2 of his *Collected Plays* (1953). He pictures her as a 'middle-class, middle-aged, maiden lady, with time on her hands and the money to help her pass it'. She is 'a hopeless lowbrow' whom novelists, painters, composers can afford to ignore, but the playwright cannot. 'She, or her ghost, is, I believe, as strong a force in Moscow as in London; . . . and she has lived for over two thousand years': she sat on the stone seats at Athens laughing with Aristophanes, and in the Globe Theatre enjoying *As You Like It.* 'It was surely Aunt Edna that Shakespeare was addressing. He was right. It was indeed as she liked it. It is as she likes it now, and I am sure that it will continue to be as she likes it for the rest of her limitless life.'

Aunt Susan. *See* Ponderevo.

Auntie Hamps. *See* Mrs Clara *Hamps.

Aunt's Story, The. Novel by Patrick *White, published in 1948. Its three parts are set consecutively in Australia, Europe and America; the story of Theodora Goodman progresses from her 'apartness' as a child through stages of mental alienation until she is on the point of being put in care by American casual acquaintances. Intentionally avoiding any imposition of order on Theodora's confusion of time and place, illusion and actuality, the narrative is a modishly brilliant exercise in the higher incoherence.

Aunty Flo. The plump widowed landlady of the Potwell Inn in H. G. Wells's *The *History of Mr Polly* (1910); so called by her brutal thieving nephew Jim.

Austin, Alfred (1853-1913). Poet Laureate, 1896-1913. His appointment after a lapse of four years following the death of Tennyson was more a recognition of political sympathies than of poetic merit. He was a minor and prolific versifier, more apt as a prose writer on gardens. Any fame he has gained is due to a couplet attributed only doubtfully to him—'Along the wires the electric message came: /"He is no better, he is much the same" '—a reference to the illness of Edward VII when Prince of Wales.

Austin, J. L. (John Langshaw Austin, 1911-1960). Educated at Shrewsbury and Oxford. White's Professor of Moral Philosophy in the University of Oxford from 1952. Author of *Philosophical Papers* (1961), *Sense and Sensibilia* (1962), *How to do Things with Words* (1962), the two last named edited by others.

Australia Felix. The first volume (published in 1917) of Henry Handel Richardson's trilogy *The *Fortunes of Richard Mahony* (1930).

Australian Writers. An inevitably brief entry on Australian writing in the present century can attempt no more than name some of those whose books have reached publication in England and attracted either popular or critical attention there. With daunting masses of their own (and American) literature confronting them, English readers can scarcely be reproached if Henry Kingsley's *Geoffrey Hamlyn* (1859), Marcus Clarke's *For the Term of His Natural Life* (1874), and Rolf Boldrewood's *Robbery under Arms* (1888) still appear the unsuperseded classics of Australian life. Apart from bush ballads by A. B. *Paterson (1864-1941) and Henry *Lawson (1867-1922) there were few signs of a distinctively Australian literature until after World War I. The first important novel to make a strong impact in England was Henry Handel *Richardson's trilogy *The *Fortunes of Richard Mahony* (1917; 1925; 1929). No other Australian writer's work received as much attention in England until Patrick *White's *Voss* (1957) and his other novels appeared, though a more limited public was reached by the short stories and novels of Katharine Susannah Pritchard (1884-1969) and Vance Palmer (1885-1959) and the novels of Martin *Boyd (1893-   ). Among the playwrights only Ray Lawler's

Summer of the Seventeenth Doll (1957) has been successful on the London stage. Mainly through anthologies of verse circulating in England, the poems of Dame Mary *Gilmore (1865-1962), C. J. Dennis (1876-1938), Hugh McCrae (1876-1958), Louis Esson (1879-1943), Kenneth Slessor (1901-   ), Douglas Stewart (1913-   ), J. S. *Manifold (1915-   ) and, especially, Judith *Wright (1915-   ) among others have attracted attention. That those named here represent only a trickle from the broad stream is made plain by Cecil Hadgraft's *Australian Literature 1950-1962. And see* Samuel Alexander, Guy Boothby, C. H. Chambers, Dame Mary Gilmore, Maysie Greig, Richard Hillary, Norman Lindsay, Philip Lindsay, John Manifold, Frederic Manning, Alan Moorehead, A. B. Paterson, Henry Handel Richardson, Arthur Upfield, Patrick White, Judith Wright.

Authors, Advice for. Unless already commissioned by a publisher to write a specified book, an author with a manuscript in hand should make himself familiar with the kinds of books advertised by particular publishers or listed in their catalogues. Some are general publishers, open to consider books of many kinds, from novels to scientific and technical works; others are specialist publishers of, for example, medical books, or legal books, or school textbooks. An author wastes his time and postage money, and invites disappointment, if he submits the manuscript of, say, a novel to a publisher who does not trade in fiction. A reputable literary agent will relieve an author of the task of approaching a publisher if he considers a manuscript has merit; and he will deal with business matters—contracts, royalties, paperback and serial rights, etc.—if he succeeds in getting the manuscript accepted. The agent will, of course, charge a standard rate for his services. An inexperienced author who decides to deal with a publisher direct will do well to ensure that his manuscript is set out in an orderly manner. A carelessly prepared, untidy manuscript is severely handicapped from the start. Most publishers and printers adopt what is known as a 'house style' as a means of ensuring uniform practice in the printing of their books. Although there may be in particular instances some variations in detail, the suggestions which are set out below provide reliable guidelines, and if followed will reduce the number of untidy if not unpublishable manuscripts reaching publishers' offices. *An author should not take his manuscript personally to a publisher without an appointment; nor should he expect to be given an opinion or judgment while he waits.* Manuscripts have to be read (usually by more than one person) and reported on before a publisher is able to consider practical possibilities. N.B.—Some British publishers are adopting an American practice of refusing to consider any unsolicited manuscript.

PREPARATION OF MANUSCRIPTS

Manuscripts should be on white paper, typed in double spacing with a lefthand margin of not less than one inch. Since MSS inevitably undergo much handling during production, flimsy paper should be avoided, and the top copy should always be sent, not a carbon (except as an additional copy). *Dates.* These should be set out as 11 June 1919, with the month spelt out and no intermediate commas.

Figures. A consistent method should be adopted for numbers used in descriptive matter. Common practice varies between the use of words up to nine or ninety-nine, with figures for 10 (or 100) onward. In statistical matter figures should always be used. For percentages in descriptive matter figures should generally be used, followed by 'per cent'. The symbol % is used only in statistical material.

Commas are not needed after short phrases at the beginnings of sentences unless the following phrase or clause is enclosed in commas: eg. 'On 15 July the Prime Minister announced . . .' *but* 'On 15 July, when speaking in Parliament, the Prime Minister announced . . .'. Commas need not be inserted before 'and' in the enumeration of more than two things, except to avoid ambiguity.

Quotation marks. Single quotation marks (' ') should be used; double (" ") only for quotations within quotations.

Apostrophes. When a noun ending in 's' is used adjectivally the apostrophe is usually omitted: e.g. 'the Thirty Years' War', 'a United Nations meeting'; *but* 'a six weeks' sojourn'. Do not insert an apostrophe in plurals such as the 1880s, M.P.s, etc. The apostrophe should be inserted only when the contraction represents a genuine possessive, as in 'the M.P.'s house', 'the year

1940's events'.

Capitals. Capital initials should be used sparingly, but avoid ambiguity when words have both a particular and a common meaning: e.g. 'the rotary press has revolutionized the Press'; 'the Civil Service is proud to render civil service to the public'; 'the Post Office controls innumerable local post offices'.

Use capital initials for Act of Parliament; Bill (parliamentary); Cabinet; Church (when meaning a denominational body, but not when used of an individual building); Conservative Party (and other political parties when the name is given in full); Foreign Office (and other Government Departments); Note (from one Government to another); Prime Minister (and all holders of Ministerial and other senior public offices).

Italics. Use italics (indicated by single underlining in typescript) for names of books, plays, operas, newspapers, periodicals, and ships. But references to titles of articles in periodicals, to chapters (when titled) of books—and to individual poems, short stories, essays and articles in collective volumes—should be in roman within quotation marks. Do not use italics for i.e., e.g., viz.

Footnotes and references. References to authorities should be given in footnotes, not in the main text. Except when a detailed bibliography is provided elsewhere in the book, full particulars of the work referred to should be given in the first footnote reference to it: e.g. Jeremiah Smith, *History of Income Tax* (Grey & Brown, 1980), vi, 982. The first Christian name should always be given (not an initial only), for ease of location in library catalogues. When a reference is made to an article in a periodical it should specify the volume, date of individual issue in brackets, and pages. Except in mathematical works, figures (not asterisks or other symbols) should be used to mark the position in the text to which the correspondingly numbered footnotes relate. It is convenient for the printer to have footnotes typed in one numbered sequence on a separate set of sheets, whether they are to appear on pages or at the end of book or chapter. If necessary the printer will renumber notes page by page after galley proofs have been returned.

Scripture references. Use arabic numerals, dividing chapter and verse by a colon:

e.g. Genesis 2:14; Psalm 18:29; Luke 19:47; 2 Corinthians 4:8; Revelation 8:13. *Shakespeare references.* Act III, Scene ii, line 297, to appear as III. ii. 297.

Quotations. Prose quotations of more than six lines should be separated from the main narrative by being typed, indented, and without quotation marks at beginning and end (unless a passage of conversation is included). All quotations of poetry should be similarly treated, except when it is more appropriate to run a line into the text within single quotes. Brief passages of prose, run into the text and within single quotation marks, should have all the punctuation of the original within the quotes; but if a quotation is (or ends with) an incomplete sentence the following full point should be outside the quotation mark. Omissions following a completed sentence are shown by four full points (. . . .) including the closing full point of the sentence; omissions within a sentence by three full points.

Headings, subheadings, etc. The typescript should show headings and subheadings, etc., consistently marked to show relative importance.

Abbreviations. Omit full points after Dr, Mr, Mrs, Messrs, and others ending with the final letter of the word.

When in doubt. Helpful general guidance is given in the *Authors' and Printers' Dictionary,* by F. Howard Collins and others (Oxford University Press).

See *Proof corrections; and* Appendix.

Authors, The Society of. Founded in 1884 to protect the interests of its members in regard to copyright, contracts, fees, etc. and to provide legal advice. *The Author* is its official organ.

Autobiography. The growth of interest in both normal and morbid psychology in the 20th century, largely under the influence of *Freud and his followers, produced as a byproduct a much more extensive and intensive crop of autobiographies than in any preceding period. Earlier concentration on personal events—*what* people do—became challenged by concentration on personal motives—*why* people do what they do. But that this deflection of interest was born of the *zeitgeist* operating variously, and only in a particular emphasis through Freud and the professional psychiatrists, is suggested by the later 19th century novels of introspection, especially those from

Russia (Dostoievsky's in particular, but also the output of Tolstoy in his post-conversion phase), and by the writings of the Scandinavians, *Ibsen and *Strindberg. It is significant that the first English 20th century autobiography in the new mode of uninhibited frankness was by an early admirer of Ibsen, Edmund *Gosse, whose *Father and Son* (1907), its author's single enduring work, displayed his young self and his parents without subterfuge, and consequently earned immediate though temporary condemnation. In date of writing, however, Gosse was not the pioneer of son-and-parent realism. The *Way of All Flesh* by Samuel *Butler (published in 1903), commonly catalogued as a novel, is largely autobiographical, for while the later experiences of Ernest Pontifex have no resemblance to Butler's own, Ernest's early life with his parents is a rendering of that of the author, savagely presented and riddled with irony and satire. Compared with Gosse's delicate silverpoint engraving, Butler's book is energetically corrosive and in that respect the more remarkable, since it was written between 1872 and 1874, when the Victorian and biblical rule of filial obedience and respect was not openly murmured against. The *Private Papers of Henry Ryecroft* (1908), a book of a different character, presents George *Gissing in a more engaging aspect than anything else he wrote. If sincerity is an indispensable factor in autobiography, Oscar Wilde's *De Profundis* (1905; full edn. 1949) may be considered not to qualify under the present heading; but as a psychological document of self-exposure it surmounts the verbal artificiality which in Wilde was a paradoxical personal type of sincerity and naturalism, even when it appears in the guise of conscious attitudinizing. Attitudinizing of another sort is evident in *Hail and Farewell,* the three-volume autobiography of George *Moore—*Ave* (1911), *Salve* (1912), *Vale* (1914). Moore had published his *Confessions of a Young Man* in 1888, but though that remains a live book it is outmatched by the later trilogy, a masterpiece of often unconscious self-portraiture, with other references that angered more than a few of Moore's acquaintances. *The Memoirs of a Fox-Hunting Man* (1928), *The Memoirs of an Infantry Officer* (1930), and *Sherston's Progress* (1936) report several stages in the life of Siegfried *Sassoon. *Barbellion's

Journal of a Disappointed Man (1919) is
a unique and courageous record by a young
man aware of gradually approaching death.
H. G. *Wells revealed less of his essential
self in *Experiment in Autobiography* (2 vols,
1934) than can be gathered piecemeal from
his novels, and *Something Of Myself* (1937)
by Rudyard *Kipling is featureless. *The
Journals of Arnold *Bennett* (edited posthumously by Newman Flower, 3 vols,
1932-3) give an admirable living picture
of the man at large in his world. *The Mirror
of the Sea* (1906) and *A Personal Record*
(1912) are essential in the Joseph *Conrad
canon. *Sixteen Self-Sketches* (1948) by
Bernard *Shaw contains several indispensable personal fragments. *Left Hand Right
Hand* (5 vols, 1944-50) by Osbert *Sitwell is a
unique period portrait. Routine autobiographies by politicians and military leaders
are legion, and for the greater part are
source material to be sifted by future
historians rather than contributions to
literature. An exception is *My Early Life*
(1930) by Winston *Churchill (famous for
its account of his escape from the Boers),
whose later life is inseparable from the
history of his times as recorded in his *The
World Crisis* (4 vols, 1923-9) and the six
volumes of *The Second World War* (1948-54).
A humbler story, but one that nevertheless
has high claims to permanence both as
literature and as social history, is told in
Lark Rise to Candleford (1945) and *Still
Glides the Stream* (1948) by Flora
*Thompson. These recreate a phase of
English rural life which was materially
restrictive and hard; yet, as the author's
exquisitely unsentimentalized narrative
shows, more humanly satisfying than the
materialistic relative prosperity that replaced
it. Among innumerable later autobiographies, *Over the Bridge* (1955) by Richard
*Church was deservedly more highly
praised than its continuation *The Golden
Sovereign* (1957). Much directly autobiographical material inevitably appears in
personal letters, though the telephone and
the habit of dictating to a typist have gone
far towards killing the art of letter writing.
But such a collection as *The Letters of
T. E. *Lawrence* (1938) is a better key to
his puzzling temperament than any of his
public writings; and even though *Ellen
Terry and Bernard Shaw: A Correspondence*
(1931) deals with only a fragment of their
otherwise diverse lives, it is an invaluable

fragment. In fiction, the autobiographical
infusion is universal and beyond tracing.
The gibe against any novelist that 'he used
his friends for copy' could be extended to
most novelists, even the greatest, and to
none more certainly than to D. H.
*Lawrence, from whose fiction a more
revealing composite portrait of himself can
be pieced together than has been provided
by his many biographers and interpreters.
Compton *Mackenzie, Bertrand *Russell,
and Leonard *Woolf produced multi-
volume autobiographies and, like Harold
*Nicolson's *Diaries and Letters 1930-62,*
they portray the period as well as the authors.
And see Sackville-West, V.

Autobiography of a Super-tramp, The, by
W. H. *Davies. Published in 1908 with a
Preface by Bernard Shaw. Starting from
his birth, childhood and youth in the West
Country, where he was apprenticed to a
picture-frame maker, Davies devotes the
rest of his story to his experiences in the
United States, Canada, and England as a
beggar, pedlar, gridler (street singer), with
brief intervals of work as a fruit picker and
on transatlantic cattle-boats. Sleeping either
in the open air or (mainly) in cheap lodging-
houses for men, his one ambition is to
become recognized as a poet. He writes
innumerable verses wherever a table can
be found—in public libraries or in a dim
lodging-house corner—at first vainly offering
leaflets from house to house, until by
painfully slow means he saves the money
to pay for a volume of his poems to be
printed. He posts copies of the book to a
large number of prominent people, and
amid many disappointments receives
enough praise in press reviews to enable
him to end his wandering life and settle
to his subsequent successful literary career.
The autobiography has many word-portraits
of remarkable characters met on the roads
and in the doss-houses, as well as stories
of strange events, among which is the
central calamity . of a severed foot for
Davies while attempting to jump a fast-
moving train between Ottawa and Winnipeg,
resulting in an amputation from the knee
and a peg leg.

Autobiography of Alice B. Toklas. Though
purporting to be the story of her friend
Miss Toklas, this is in fact the autobiography
of Gertrude *Stein herself.

Avante-garde. Term applied to (or adopted by) innovators in the arts; the advance guard who react against traditional forms and standards.

Ave. The first volume of the autobiographical trilogy *Hail and Farewell* by George Moore. The individual titles of the second and third volumes are *Salve* and *Vale*.

Avellanos, Don José. Costaguanan patriot in Joseph Conrad's *Nostromo* (1904); sometime his country's Minister Plenipotentiary to the Court of St James, father of Antonia, in love with Martin Decoud.

Avery, Maurice. Michael Fane's friend in *Sinister Street* (1913) by Compton Mackenzie.

Axel Heyst. See Axel *Heyst.

Axel's Castle. A collection of essays by Edmund *Wilson published in 1931. Subtitled 'A Study of the Imaginative Literature of 1870-1930' it deals with (1) Symbolism (2) W. B. Yeats (3) Paul Valery (4) T. S. Eliot (5) Marcel Proust (6) James Joyce (7) Gertrude Stein (8) Axel and Rimbaud. An appendix gives an account of the beginnings of *Dada. The castle named in Wilson's title is an edifice in *Axël*, a symbolist drama (1890) by Villiers de l'Isle Adam.

Axis, The. Popular name for the pact between Hitler and Mussolini (Rome-Berlin Axis) made in 1936. It prepared the way for World War II and was joined by Japan (Rome-Berlin-Tokyo Axis).

Ayer, Sir Alfred Jules (1910-   ). Knighted 1970. Educated at Eton and Oxford. Professor of the Philosophy of Mind and Logic, University of London, 1946-59, Professor of Logic at Oxford from 1959. He became prominent as the chief advocate in Britain of the philosophical system known as Logical Positivism, propagating it in his *Language, Truth and Logic* (1936; revised edn. 1946), and in a composite volume *Logical Positivism* which he edited in 1960. His other works include *The Foundations of Empirical Knowledge* (1940), *Thinking and Meaning* (1947), *The Problem of Knowledge* (1956).

Aylwin. Novel of gipsy life in East Anglia by Theodore *Watts-Dunton published in 1898.

Aymé, Marcel (1902-1967). Born at Joigny on the river Yonne between Sens and Auxerre, the son of a blacksmith. Hating school and quickly abandoning plans for studying medicine, he strayed through miscellaneous occupations in Paris before settling to write novels, the earliest of these drawing upon his familiarity with peasant life while young. His most characteristic work, produced after World War II, is in satirical novels written with ironical detachment, and in others displaying amoral humour—e.g. *The Green Mare* (*La Jument Verte*, 1933). He also wrote children's books, *Les Contes du chat perché* (1939), etc.

Ayres, Ruby M. (Ruby Mildred Ayres, 1883-1953). Wrote numerous popular romantic novels, most of which were serialized in newspapers and magazines: *The Remembered Kiss* (1918), *The Man in her Life* (1935), *Sunrise for Georgie* (1941), *Steering by a Star* (1949), and many others.

Ayscough, Florence (*née* Wheelock, 1878-1942; married Francis Ayscough). Born in Shanghai; educated privately and in Boston. In collaboration with Amy *Lowell she produced free verse renderings of Chinese poems in *Fir-Flower Tablets* (1922) and wrote a number of books on oriental topics: *A Chinese Mirror* (1925), *Tu Fu: The Autobiography of a Chinese Poet* (1934), *Firecracker Land* (1932), etc.

Ayscough, John. Pseudonym of Francis Browning Drew Bickerstaffe-Drew (1858-1928). Born in Leeds; educated at Lichfield and Oxford; became a Roman Catholic in 1877 and entered the priesthood, becoming at length a private chamberlain to Pope Pius X and in 1909 a Papal Count. He wrote a number of novels with a religious purpose: *Dromina* (1909), *San Celestino* (1909), *Monksbridge* (1914), *Brogmersfield* (1924). *Pages from the Past* (1922) is autobiographical.

Aziz. Muslim doctor in E. M. Forster's *A *Passage to India* (1924). Accused by Adela Quested of making 'insulting advances' in a Marabar cave, but at his trial she withdrew the charge.

B.B. *See* Ralph Bloomfield *Bonington.

Babbitt. Novel by Sinclair *Lewis, published in 1922. Set in an imaginary but typical American Middle West town, Zenith, with George F. Babbitt a forty-six-year-old real-estate man as central character, it satirizes United States business and social life in the 1920s. Babbitt, a comic creation whose popularity did much to make English readers aware of contemporary American literature, is presented as a success by the common standards of his generation, but at the end he tells his son: 'I've never done a single thing I've wanted to do in my whole life!'

Babbitt, Irving (1865-1933). Born at Dayton, Ohio; educated at Harvard and in Paris. Spent most of his professional life as a university teacher, mainly at Harvard, where he was Professor of French Literature from 1912. Though he wrote several books on French literary and philosophical themes, his contemporary repute came chiefly from advocacy of a system of thought antagonistic to Romanticism. Though named Humanism it had nothing in common with Renaissance humanism, being rigidly austere and intellectualized. Though Babbitt and his philosophy were lauded while he was alive, his individual influence was hardly sustained, except in so far as it was in line with the *New Criticism propagated by writers of the next generation. His works include *The New Laokoön* (1910), *Rousseau and Romanticism* (1919), and *Democracy and Leadership* (1924), which expressed views of an authoritarian kind.

Babel, Isaac (Isaak Emmanuilovich Babel, 1894-1939/40). Born in a district of Odessa, he suffered, with his parents, the disabilities of Jews in Russia under the Tsarist régime, but acquired a university education and struggled to obtain literary work. At length, encouraged by Maxim Gorky, he became a distinguished writer of short stories with a reputation which spread beyond the U.S.S.R. Nevertheless he was arrested in 1937 on an unannounced charge, and died (from typhus or was shot) in a concentration camp in 1939 or 1940. His *Collected Stories* (including the volumes entitled *Red Cavalry* and *Tales of Odessa*) appeared in English translation in 1957.

Back-room boy. *See* Boffin.

Back to Methuselah: A Metabiological Pentateuch. Play in five Parts by Bernard *Shaw, first produced in New York in 1922; first English production in 1923 at the Birmingham Repertory Theatre. Act I of Part I, 'In the Beginning', is set in the Garden of Eden, 4004 B.C. Adam and Eve have their first intimation of death when they find a dead fawn. The Serpent speaks to Eve of death and birth, life and conception, imagination and will power, and declares they are not doomed to live for ever. Adam learns of love and jealousy, hope and happiness and marriage. Act II, in Mesopotamia 'a few centuries later', introduces Cain, the first murderer, who finds his greatest joy in fighting and destruction. Eve becomes disgusted both by Cain's ideal and by Adam's dull preoccupation with digging, and she aspires to 'something else' not yet known, 'but some day we shall find out'. Part II, 'The Gospel of the Brothers Barnabas', early 1920s, takes place in the Hampstead study of Franklyn Barnabas, who has written a book on longevity. He is visited by his brother Conrad, a professor of biology, and by Lubin, a rival politician. A general election is near and Barnabas, invited to address a meeting in Middlesbrough, causes consternation to Lubin and Burge by declaring that he will proclaim the gospel of the brothers Barnabas as 'Back to Methuselah' and a human life-span of 300 years. Part III, 'The Thing Happens', A.D. 2170, set in the official parlour of the President of the British Islands, who is Burge-Lubin looking 'as if Nature had made a composite photograph' of the two politicians in the preceding part. His Chief Secretary is a Chinese and his Minister of Health a Negress. A cinema film reveals that two supposed different archbishops, a president, and a general are all one man. Now in office as archbishop, he confesses that he is 283 years old, but since he retains a middle-aged appearance that caused him to be prosecuted for alleged false pretences when he applied for a retiring pension when he was over eighty, he has staged a series of spurious deaths by drowning in order to continue to draw a salary in successive guises. Other secret long-livers are revealed, and since the coloured minister of health and the white archbishop are convinced that the normal English are mentally immature, they decide to marry and produce interracial long-lived children. Part IV, 'The Tragedy of an Elderly Gentleman', A.D. 3000: Act I on Burrin Pier, Galway Bay. The gentleman, Joseph Popham Bolge Bluebin Barlow, O.M., has come from Baghdad, now the British Commonwealth capital, to Ireland on a pilgrimage to his ancestors' native land. He is discovered by an apparently young woman—Zoo, actually in her second century—and as he seems to need a nurse she puts him in charge of Zozim, a male of ninety-four. Barlow and an English Envoy, and others with them, plan to consult the Oracle at the Temple (Acts II and III). The Oracle is asked by the English Envoy for advice concerning a forthcoming election. There is thunder and lightning, following which the Oracle answers 'Go home, poor fool!' The Elderly Gentleman, left alone, is visited by the Oracle, whose hands he grasps; she 'looks steadily into his face' and he falls dead. Part V, 'As Far as Thought can Reach', A.D. 21920, A Sunlit Glade before a Temple, with an altar in the middle of the glade. Youths and girls are dancing. They seem about eighteen. Hatched fully-grown from eggs, their childhood lasts only until they are four, by the long-livers' time. After a new child of apparently about seventeen is born from an egg on the altar in the presence of a She Ancient, there is a discussion about art between two sculptors, Arjillax and Martellus, before Pygmalion comes in and lectures about artificial human beings he has made. Two of them appear. The male figure speaks in a stereotyped pseudo-biblical language; the female becomes quarrelsome and threatening. When Pygmalion restrains her she bites his hand and he falls dead. The Ancients destroy the two figures and warn the assembled company not to attempt to make living toys. The Ancients then talk of their past and of their ultimate destiny, to be immortal—'She: The day will come when there will be no people, only thought. He: And that will be life eternal.' The final speech is Lilith's famous monologue including the phrase 'Of Life only is there no end . . . .' The Preface to the play is headed 'The Infidel Half Century'. It attacks Darwinism and puts forward Shaw's belief in *Creative Evolution.

Back-scratching. *See* Log-rolling.

Baconian theory. Since the publication in 1857 of William Henry Smith's *Bacon and*

Shakespeare, a literature has grown up based on the supposition that the plays ascribed to Shakespeare could not have been written by anyone with no more learning than the Stratford grammar school could provide. In the search for authors presumed to be better qualified, Francis Bacon has had most advocates, and the presumption has been supported by ingenious means, including evidence drawn from cryptograms. Other claimants have also been put forward, including Edward de Vere (17th Earl of Oxford), William Stanley (6th Earl of Derby), and Christopher Marlowe. The faith of loyal Shakespearians remains unshaken, trust in the power of innate ability outweighing confidence in the utility of academic learning and social elevation. The controversy is critically surveyed in *The Shakespeare Claimants* by H. N. Gibson (1962).

Baden-Powell, Robert Stephenson Smyth (1857-1941; 1st Baron Baden-Powell, 1929). Born in London, son of the Rev. Baden Powell, Professor of Geometry in the University of Oxford. After a distinguished army career which included the defence of Mafeking, he devoted his life from about 1905 to the founding and direction of the Boy Scout movement, becoming Chief Scout in the worldwide organization from 1920 until he died. He wrote extensively on matters relating to Boy Scouts (*Scouting for Boys,* 1908; *The Wolf Cub's Handbook,* 1916, for the junior branch of the movement; *Rovering to Success,* 1922, for the Rover Scouts, a senior branch) but his earlier *Aids to Scouting* (1899), written for army training, first created interest among teachers of boys. His other books include *My Adventures as a Spy* (1915) and autobiographical works, *Indian Memories* (1915) and *Lessons from the 'Varsity of Life* (1933). The Girl Guides were founded by him in 1909.

Bagnold, Enid (1889-   ). Educated at Godalming and on the Continent; studied art until she turned to nursing during World War I, but displeased the hospital authorities by basing her *Diary Without Dates* (1917) upon her V.A.D. experiences. She then served with a French transport unit, which gave her material for a novel *The Happy Foreigner* (1920). In that year she married Sir Roderick Jones, wrote a successful novel, *Serena Blandish,* in 1925, and in

1935 *National Velvet,* which has become a classic story of a racehorse. Her later books include *The Loved and the Envied* (1951) and she also wrote successful plays, including *Lottie Dundass* (1941) and *The Chalk Garden* (1954). *Four Plays* (1969). *Autobiography* (1969).

Bailey (*née* Macvitie) **Altiora,** wife of Oscar Bailey in H. G. Wells's *The *New Machiavelli* (1911). She spoke 'of everybody as a "type"; she saw men as samples moving'. Oscar Bailey 'has a mind as orderly as a museum, and an invincible power over detail'. Wells was supposed to have modelled them on Beatrice and Sidney *Webb.

Bailey, H. C. (Henry Christopher Bailey, 1878-1961). Born in London; educated at the City of London School and Oxford; graduated with distinction in classics; on the staff of the *Daily Telegraph* 1901-46. As a writer he passed from an early group of historical novels to the numerous detective stories which won popularity. These centre around Reginald Fortune, amateur detective with a particular though lightly-borne knowledge of medicine and surgery, upon which he frequently acts as adviser to the police. A collective volume of the stories was published in 1942 as *Meet Mr Fortune.*

Bailey, John (John Cann Bailey, 1864-1931). Author of biographical and critical works including *Dr Johnson and his Circle* (1913), *Milton* (1915), *The Continuity of Letters* (1923), and *Shakespeare* (1929). As a lecturer, though not aurally attractive, he was illuminating, as in *Poetry and Commonplace* (1920), on Wordsworth.

Bain, Francis William (1863-1940), author of a series of 'Hindu' love stories beginning with *A Digit of the Moon* (1899), which he pretended to have translated from a Sanskrit manuscript.

Baines, Constance and **Sophia.** Sisters who are the outstanding women characters in *The *Old Wives' Tale* by Arnold Bennett. Constance marries Samuel Povey, draper's assistant, and remains contentedly in the shop at Bursley. Sophia marries a good-for-nothing commercial traveller, lives precariously, and is in Paris throughout the German siege of the city in 1870.

Baird, John Logie (1888-1946). Born at Helensburgh, Scotland; trained as an

electrical engineer, but in that profession and later in business he was frustrated by illness. From 1922, after a breakdown in health, he devoted himself to the invention and development of television, transmitting a first crude picture over a few feet in 1924 and giving the first practical demonstration (with homemade apparatus) in 1926. From that date he progressed rapidly, and the B.B.C. started an experimental service with his system in 1929, but employed a different method from 1937. Baird continued to experiment until his death, and succeeded in proving the possibility of colour and stereoscopic television.

Bairnsfather, Bruce (1888-1959). Born in India; educated at Westward Ho!; served in France in World War I and became Official War Cartoonist to the U.S. Army in Europe. He became famous through his invention of a Cockney soldier character he named Old Bill, whose face and comic sayings were a source of laughter among men in the trenches and people at home. Collections of the drawings and captions appeared as *Bullets and Billets* (1917), and the same character reappeared in *Old Bill Stands By* (1939) and *Old Bill Does It Again* (1940). His autobiography *Wide Canvas* appeared in 1939.

Baker, Frank (1908-). Born in London; educated at Winchester Cathedral School. Started as an insurance clerk but after a few years embarked on a varied career which included working as a village organist, cabaret pianist, broadcaster, and writing music, poetry, and fiction. His most successful novel, *Miss Hargreaves* (1940), was also popular in stage and radio adaptations.

Baker, G. P. (George Pierce Baker, 1866-1935). Born in Providence, Rhode Island; educated at Harvard, where he became Professor of English (1905-24) and started the famous 47 Workshop for the production of plays written by his students, among whom were Eugene *O'Neill and others who became prominent as dramatists, stage designers, and critics. In 1925 he moved to Yale as head of the new Department of Drama there. Among his own writings is *Dramatic Technique* (1919). He edited *Plays of the 47 Workshop* (4 vols, 1918-25).

Baker, Ray Stannard (1870-1946). First came into prominence as one of the journalists and publicists who in the period *c.* 1902-11 engaged in exposure of corruption in American politics and big business (*see* Muckrakers). Later he became an associate of President Woodrow Wilson whose *Life and Letters* he issued in 8 vols (1927-39). He achieved popular success with a series of essays written under the pseudonym David *Grayson.

Balchin, Nigel (Nigel Marlin Balchin, 1908-1970). Born in Wiltshire; educated there at Dauntsey's School and at Cambridge. Trained as a scientist, he engaged in scientific research and had industrial and business interests while writing as a leisure occupation. Several novels, including *Darkness Falls from the Air* (1942), preceded his outstanding success with *The Small Back Room* (1943), a story of wartime research and frustration with an exciting climax. Among his later novels *Mine Own Executioner* (1945) and *The Borgia Testament* (1948) are outstanding. Using the pseudonym Mark Spade, he wrote humorous pieces for *Punch,* collected in *How to Run a Bassoon Factory, or Business Explained* (1934), etc.

Balderston, J. L. (John Lloyd Balderston, 1889-1954). Born in Philadelphia; educated at Columbia University. Editor and journalist; Lecturer in Drama in the University of South Carolina from 1952. Wrote for the theatre and cinema, and shared the notable success of *Berkeley Square* (1928) a play (written in collaboration with J. C. *Squire) based on *A Sense of the Past* by Henry *James.

Baldwin, Faith (1893-   ). Born at New Rochelle, N.Y.; educated in Brooklyn and other schools. A prolific writer, her many romantic love stories had an extensive magazine circulation and equal success in volume form. Typical novels are *Mavis of Green Hill* (1921), *The Office Wife* (1930), *Rich Girl, Poor Girl* (1938), *Blue Horizons* (1942), *Marry for Money* (1948), *The Juniper Tree* (1952).

Baldwin, James (James Arthur Baldwin, 1924-   ). Born in Harlem, New York City; educated at high school in New York. Experienced religious conversion in early adolescence and did much preaching for a few years until he lost his faith. Then worked at odd jobs until he was twenty-one. Went to Paris in 1948 and remained in Europe until 1956, when he returned to his own country, having already published novels: *Go Tell It on the Mountain* (1953) and *Giovanni's Room* (1956) and written *The Amen Corner* (a play performed at Harvard 1955 and later in London). Other novels: *Another Country* (1962), *Going to Meet the Man* (1965); play: *Blues for Mr Charlie* (1964); essays: *Notes of a Native Son* (1955), *Nobody Knows My Name* (1961), *No Name in the Street* (1972).

Balestier, Wolcott (Charles Wolcott Balestier, 1861-1891). He wrote a number of novels and short stories, but is remembered as the collaborator with Rudyard *Kipling (who married Balestier's sister Caroline) in *The Nalauka* (1892), a novel set in India and California.

Balfour, A. J. (Arthur James Balfour, 1848-1930; first Earl of Balfour, 1922). Before achieving eminence as a statesman (he was Prime Minister from 1902 to 1905), Balfour had a reputation as philosopher based on his *Defence of Philosophic Doubt* (1879) and *Foundations of Belief* (1895). He also wrote *Criticism and Beauty* (1910), *Theism and Humanism* (1915), *Theism and Thought* (1923), *Essays Speculative and Political* (1920), and the incomplete *Chapters of Autobiography* (published posthumously, 1930).

Balfour Declaration. The announcement by the Foreign Secretary, A. J. *Balfour, in 1917 that the British Government supported the principle of Jewish settlement in Palestine to establish a national home there. It foreshadowed the independent State of Israel.

Ball, Sir Robert Stawell (1840-1913; knighted 1886). Professor of Astronomy, Dublin, 1874-92, Cambridge, 1893-1913. Author of numerous popular works on astronomy, including *The Story of the Heavens* (1886, and many later reprints). He was also a mathematician; works in that field: *The Theory of Screws* (1876), *A Treatise on the Theory of Screws* (1900), etc.

Ballad of East and West, The. Written in 1889 by Rudyard *Kipling; it begins with a line that became proverbial: 'Oh, East is East, and West is West, and never the twain shall meet'.

Ballantyne, David Watt (1924-   ). Born in Auckland, New Zealand; educated at

Gisborne. Worked as a journalist on New Zealand and London papers, 1943-65. Author of *The Cunninghams* (1948), *The Last Pioneer* (1963), *A Friend of the Family* (1966), and other novels; *And the Glory* (1963), short stories. See New Zealand Writers.

Bambi. See Felix *Salten.

Bancroft, G. P. (George Pleydell Bancroft, 1868-1956). Son of the famous stage players Sir Squire Bancroft and his wife (*née* Marie Wilton). Educated at Eton and Oxford; called to the Bar; Clerk of Assize for the Midland Circuit 1913-46. His play *The Ware Case* (1913) was a stage success, and he wrote his recollections as *Stage and Bar* (1939).

Banting, Sir Frederick Grant (1891-1941; knighted 1934). Born in Ontario, Canada, of Irish and Scottish forebears; trained for the ministry at Toronto University but transferred to the medical school there, and after service in World War I specialized as an orthopaedic surgeon. In 1921 he undertook, with others, the research which within a few months brought fame to himself and benefit to humanity—the preparation of insulin, a discovery that saved the lives of countless sufferers from diabetes. He proceeded with research into the treatment of other diseases up to the time of his death in an aeroplane crash in Newfoundland.

Barbara Undershaft. Salvation Army daughter of Andrew and Lady Britomart Undershaft in *Major Barbara* by Bernard Shaw.

Barbellion, W. N. P. (pseudonym of Bruce Frederick Cummings, 1889-1919). Born at Barnstaple, Devon; being of frail physique and an excessively shy nature, his early education was undertaken by his brother before he went to a private school in his home town. He developed an intense love of nature and many often lonely excursions and protracted watching of birds and animals led him to know 'more about North Devon and the wild creatures that inhabited its wide spaces than probably any other living person'. By the time he was fourteen he had determined to be a naturalist, and except for an interval as a reporter on the same local paper as his father, he studied continuously to achieve his purpose and in 1912 obtained a post at the British Museum (Natural History),

South Kensington. Soon his health deteriorated and he was found to be afflicted with disseminated sclerosis. After months of prostration he died at Gerrards Cross, Buckinghamshire, soon after the publication of his immediately acclaimed diary *The Journal of a Disappointed Man*.

Barber, Margaret Fairless. See Michael Fairless.

Barbusse, Henri (1874-1935). French journalist and realistic novelist. His *Le Feu* (1916; translated as *Under Fire*) was one of the most moving novels of World War I, dealing with life in the trenches and elsewhere among the lesser ranks of the French Army.

Barclay, Florence Louisa (*née* Charlesworth, 1862-1921). Born at Limpsfield, Surrey, daughter of a clergyman who moved to an east London parish, Limehouse, about 1870; there she married the Rev. Charles Barclay in 1881. She wrote about a dozen novels, and had more than a million circulation with *The Rosary* (1909). Though critics derided her novels for their 'silliness and sentimentality' they acknowledged her ability to tell an absorbing story.

Barea, Arturo (1897-   ). Born in Badajoz, Spain; educated in Madrid. After working as a clerk, Republican press censor and broadcaster, following service in the Spanish army he settled in England in 1939 and became well known with his novel *The Forge* (1941). This and other books—which include studies of *Lorca* (1944) and *Unamuno* (1952)—were translated by his wife. See Garcia *Lorca; Unamuno.

Baring, Maurice (1874-1945). Born in London of a family of bankers; educated at Eton and Cambridge; in the diplomatic service from 1898 to 1904; acted as foreign press correspondent for the *Morning Post* and *The Times*, 1904-12; in the Royal Flying Corps during World War I. He wrote novels (*Passing By*, 1921; *C.*, 1924; *Cat's Cradle*, 1925; *Daphne Adeane*, 1926; *The Lonely Lady of Dulwich*, 1934), plays (*The Black Prince*, 1902; *Gaston de Foix*, 1903; *Diminutive Dramas*, 1911); historical tales (*Robert Peckham*, 1930; *In the End is my Beginning*, 1931); his nonfiction books include *Landmarks in Russian Literature* (1910), *The Puppet Show of Memory* (autobiography), 1922), *Have You Anything to Declare* (anthology, 1936). Baring's writings are marked by liberal culture, humanism, subtlety of humour, and refinement of style, characteristics that won admiration and praise from a select audience.

Baring-Gould, Sabine (1834-1924). Born at Exeter; educated privately and at Cambridge; ordained in the Anglican Church in 1864, and held several livings, for his last forty years at Lew Trenchard in Devon. He wrote *The Lives of the Saints* in many volumes (1872-7) and other religious works; travel books, studies in folklore, and many novels; but he made a permanent mark as the author of *Onward Christian Soldiers*.

Barker, Sir Ernest (1874-1960; knighted 1944). Born in Cheshire; educated at Manchester Grammar School and Oxford, where he afterwards held various University appointments. Principal of King's College, London, 1920-27. Wrote prolifically on political thought and classical subjects; other works include *Britain and the British People* (1942) and an autobiography, *Age and Youth* (1953).

Barker, George (George Granville Barker, 1913-   ). Born at Loughton, Essex, of Anglo-Irish parentage; educated at a London County Council school in Chelsea, and at the Regent Street Polytechnic, until at fourteen he started work, tried various jobs, and earned little. A novel, *Alanna Autumnal*, published in 1933 and *Thirty Preliminary Poems* in the same year led to his receiving grants from various quarters, and in 1939 he became for a year visiting Professor of English Literature at the Imperial Tohoku University in Japan. From 1940 to 1943 he lived in the U.S. Critical opinion of his poetry has wavered between high praise of his lyrical talent and dislike of his verbal mannerisms and aggressive tone. His later poems include *Calamiterror* (1937), *Sacred and Secular Elegies* (1943), *Love Poems* (1947), *News of the World* (1950), *The True Confession of George Barker* (1950; revised edn 1957), *Dreams of a Summer Night* (1966), *Poems of Places and People* (1971).

Barker, H. Granville (1877-1946). Known as Harley Granville-Barker from 1918. Born in Kensington, London, son of an estate agent and of an Italian-descended mother, who performed both before and after marriage as a public reciter and bird-mimic. The boy travelled with his mother and appeared on the same platforms as a child reciter. When thirteen he began to train for the stage at Sarah Thorne's theatre-school at Margate and toured with her company for a few months before playing for the first time in London at the Comedy Theatre in May 1892. A few years later he was in Ben *Greet's Shakespeare Company and there met Lillah McCarthy whom he married in 1906. In the years between, he had much acting experience in London and the provinces, played Richard II under the direction of William *Poel, formed friendships with Gilbert *Murray, William *Archer, and Bernard *Shaw, and in 1900 began as play-producer at a *Stage Society performance. Also important, in view of the future, was his playing Eugene Marchbanks in Shaw's *Candida*, again for the Stage Society, in July 1900. He was also experimenting as a dramatist and his first notable play *The Marrying of Ann Leete* was performed by the Stage Society in 1902. It impressed the audience, though many found it baffling. In collaboration with William Archer he wrote *Scheme and Estimates for a National Theatre* (1904), and during the rest of his life he was a leading advocate in the National Theatre movement, which met with general indifference until the 1960s. A further edition of the Barker-Archer book appeared as *A National Theatre: Scheme and Estimates* (1907); and *The Exemplary Theatre* (1922) and *A National Theatre* (1930) were by Barker alone. The most fruitful of his practical services to the English stage began in 1904, when he joined as producer with J. E. *Vedrenne as manager in the famous *Court Theatre season that lasted for three years, during which Barker produced plays by Shaw, Gilbert Murray, St John *Hankin, *Galsworthy, *Masefield, W. B. *Yeats and others, as well as translations of *Maeterlinck, *Ibsen, and *Hauptmann. In addition, his own best play *The *Voysey Inheritance* was performed there in February 1905. As well as producing, he frequently acted during this season, and became recognized as the ideal performer of a number of Shaw's characters. A similar but much shorter season followed at the Savoy Theatre in the autumn of 1907, while at the Imperial in November Barker's *Waste* was given a private performance, the Censor having refused to license the play. His next engagement as producer was for Charles *Frohman's repertory season at the Duke of York's from March to May 1910, one of the new plays put on being his own

The *Madras House. Next to the Court season, the most important of his ventures as producer was under his own management at the Savoy (1911-14) with productions of *The Winter's Tale, Twelfth Night* and *A Midsummer Night's Dream.* These set a new standard in Shakespeare production, with scrupulous attention to the text and to the speaking of verse. Although he continued to act as producer from time to time, the Savoy season was his last important contribution to the English stage. Throughout he had had Lillah McCarthy as leading lady both before and after their marriage in 1906, but during a season in New York (1914-15) he fell in love with Mrs Helen Huntington, the wife of a millionaire, and after both had been divorced they married in London in 1918. Now furnished with ample wealth, Granville-Barker (the hyphen was adopted at this time) was led by his wife's aversion to stage people to separate himself from former associates, and for the remainder of his life he was occupied mainly as a writer on Shakespeare's plays and (in collaboration with his wife) as an adapter of plays from the Spanish of *Sierra and the brothers *Quintero. Two plays by himself, *The Secret Life* and *His Majesty* were published in 1923 and 1928 respectively. In 1923 he began to write introductions for a limited edition of single plays by Shakespeare, each play having colour plates by a leading contemporary artist. This 'Players' Shakespeare' ceased publication after eight plays had been issued, but it set Granville-Barker on the path of Shakespeare scholarship. To the eight Prefaces he added others, the whole appearing in five volumes as *Prefaces to Shakespeare* (1927, 1930, 1937, 1945, 1947). From 1937 to 1939 he was Director of the British Institute in Paris. Though the work of an actor and producer is commonly regarded as ephemeral, Barker's services to the theatre in these capacities was lasting through its influence on others, and in spite of the praise given to the Prefaces, his divorce from the stage was not compensated by the recruitment of one more to the host of Shakespeare commentators.

Barkley, Catherine. Nurse and a leading character in Ernest Hemingway's *A *Farewell to Arms* (1939).

Barnardo, Dr (Thomas John Barnardo, 1845-1905). Born in Dublin; educated there and began work as a wine-merchant's clerk before experiencing religious conversion. Moved to London in 1866, intending to train as a medical missionary for service in China, but determined instead to devote himself to the rescue and care of abandoned and destitute children. He qualified as a surgeon, but in the meantime had founded the East End Juvenile Mission (1867) and started in 1870 a boys' home in Stepney Causeway which was the seed from which the Dr Barnardo's Homes developed with many beneficent and far-spreading branches.

Barnes, Djuna (1892-). Born in New York county; educated at home. As well as journalism she wrote plays, verse, and fiction much praised by *avant-garde* critics and readers for distinction of style and psychopathological interest, though others found them turgid and obscure. T. S. Eliot's commendation in an introduction made *Nightwood* (1936) her most publicized novel; other writings by her include *The Book of Repulsive Women* (1915), *A Book* (*sic*, 1923), and *Ryder* (1928). She spent many years among American expatriates in Paris.

Baron, Alexander (1917-). Born in London; educated there, at Hackney Downs School. Worked as a local government clerk before becoming assistant editor of *The Tribune*, 1938-9; then served in World War II, was invalided from the army in 1946, and until 1949 was editor of *New Theatre*. His first novel (of war experiences) *From the City, From the Plough* (1948) marked him as outstanding among the new generation of writers. This was followed by *There's No Home* (1950), *Rosie Hogarth* (1951) and other novels on contemporary themes, before he turned to historical fiction with *The Golden Princess* (1954). Later books: *King Dido* (1969), *The In-Between Time* (1971).

Baroque. Applied first as a descriptive term to architecture, sculpture, and painting (mainly of the 17th and 18th centuries) in which emotion and sometimes religious ecstasy were conveyed by the representation of restless movement and grotesque forms (and in music by corresponding means); the word was afterwards loosely extended to such poetry and prose as is complex in meaning, elaborate or flamboyant and irregular in form, and possibly grotesque or ambiguous in imagery. The metaphysical writers of the 17th century and their latter-day disciples can be described as *baroque*.

Barrès, Maurice (1862-1923). Born in Lorraine; educated in Nancy and Paris. Beginning as a journalist, his interests throughout life were divided between literature and politics (he was a deputy in the French Chamber for many years). He wrote patriotic novels in an unfictional style (e.g. *Le Roman de l'energie nationale*, a trilogy, 1897-1902), and in general tendency was reactionary.

Barrett, Wilson (*née* William Henry Barrett, 1846-1904), actor and playwright, who had his most popular successes in *The Silver King* (1882) by Henry Arthur *Jones and Henry Herman, and in his own Christians-and-Romans melodrama *The Sign of the Cross* (1896).

Barretts of Wimpole Street, The. Comedy in four acts by Rudolf *Besier, first performed at the Malvern Festival in 1930. Dealing with the love story of the two poets, Elizabeth Barrett and Robert Browning, and set in Elizabeth's bed-sitting room at 50 Wimpole Street, London, the play also introduces her father, Edward Moulton-Barrett, his two other daughters and six sons, the *fiancés* of Elizabeth's two sisters Arabel and Henrietta, and minor characters. The enormous contemporary success of the play was due in part to the perennial interest of a love relationship which transformed a docile invalid woman into a courageous runaway bride and relatively robust wife, and in part to the representation of the widowed Mr Barrett as a tyrannical Victorian father with an ambiguous emotional attitude towards his famous daughter, a Freudian touch which attracted many who might have responded less readily to the comedy and sentiment.

Barrie, J. M. (Sir James Matthew Barrie, Bart, 1860-1937; baronet 1913). Born at Kirriemuir, Forfarshire, Scotland, the ninth in the family of ten of a handloom weaver; educated locally and at Dumfries Academy and Edinburgh University, though his most influential education had begun at home in childhood reading with his mother, whom he 'immortalized' under her maiden name in *Margaret Ogilvie* (1896). He had also begun to write stories by the time he first went to school, and while an undergraduate in Edinburgh he was contributing literary, dramatic, and music criticism to Scottish

papers, though he afterwards admitted that he was ignorant in musical matters. By the time he graduated in 1882 he was determined that his career should be in literature, towards which the first step was taken when he joined the staff of the *Nottingham Journal* early in 1883 as leader writer and general provider of reviews, literary articles, fiction, and whatever else might be required. When the Nottingham engagement ended in the autumn of 1884 he returned home, but already he had had articles accepted by London papers and in March 1885 he moved to London, occupying himself precariously as an unattached journalist. He published his first book at his own expense in 1887, after several publishers had refused it. Called *Better Dead* and intended as a novel, it satirized on an elementary level a large number of prominent politicians and other public figures. It made no stir, but in the next year he achieved the first of his many successes with *Auld Licht Idylls*, a collection of the sketches of Scottish life which he had contributed to the *St James's Gazette* and to a short-lived weekly, *Home Chimes*. This was followed by *When a Man's Single* (1888), *An Edinburgh Eleven: Pen Portraits from College Life* (1889), and in 1889 also by *A Window in Thrums*, the place-name he adopted in writing of his native Kirriemuir. With *The Little Minister* (1891) he started the sequence of books in which his personal brand of sentiment brought him contemporary popularity, but also unfavourable comment after his death, when critics who viewed his writings and personality through the lens of Freudian psychology saw him as a permanent adolescent emotionally stunted by a 'mother-fixation'. It is not certain that this view of Barrie will prevail, however, for *Sentimental Tommy* (1896) and the mother-devotion displayed in *Margaret Ogilvie*, may well undergo revaluation. Nevertheless, there is evidence in Barrie's writings that he shrank from realities of adult life and took refuge in such fantasies as *Peter Pan* (1904; published 1928), 'the boy who wouldn't grow up', *Dear Brutus* (1917; published 1923) with its 'wood of the second chance' and its phantom child, and *Mary Rose* (1920; published 1924) who vanishes on 'the island that likes to be visited'. It is impossible to know whether the persistent success of *Peter Pan* with generation after generation of children is due to some essential element of child nature distilled by Barrie or to a blight of whimsy. If Barrie was indeed an arrested adolescent, he was not unaware of the dangers of that state, for in *Tommy and Grizel* (1900), a sequel to *Sentimental Tommy*, he contemplates the situation tragically rather than whimsically. Peter Pan began life in stories Barrie told in Kensington Gardens to a friend's young boys and first appeared in print in *The Little White Bird* (1902). That was virtually the end of Barrie as a writer of non-dramatic prose, apart from *Peter and Wendy* (1911), a narrative version of the play, and *The Greenwood Hat* (privately printed 1930; published edition 1937), an autobiography. With the opening years of the 20th century he established his second and more successful career as a playwright. During the 1890s he had had some minor pieces produced—*Ibsen's Ghost* (1891), *Walker, London* (1892), *The Professor's Love Story* (1892), *The Little Minister* (1897)—all well received. But it was *Quality Street* (1902; published 1913) that made him a leading figure among contemporaries whose plays were regarded as belonging to literature as well as to the stage. From among his subsequent plays the most notable are *The *Admirable Crichton* (1902; published 1914), *What Every Woman Knows* (1908; published 1918), *Dear Brutus* and *Mary Rose*, besides *Peter Pan*. He also wrote what is probably the best of all one-act comedies *The Twelve-Pound Look* (1910; published 1914) and the mystifying *Shall We Join the Ladies* (1921; published 1927). After a prolonged silence he returned to the theatre with a biblical play *The Boy David* (1936; published 1938) which was a failure on the stage but has been rated by some critics as one of his best pieces. Barrie's personal life was shadowed by the failure of his marriage (in 1894 to Mary Ansell, an actress, whom he divorced in 1909 on learning of her association with Gilbert *Cannan) and by the death of one of his adopted sons (Michael Davies) in 1921. He was Rector of St Andrews University (1919) and of Edinburgh University (1930-37). A statue of Peter Pan by Sir George Frampton was set up in Kensington Gardens in 1912 and the bird-sanctuary island in the Serpentine there is popularly known as Peter Pan's Island.

Barrington, E. Pseudonym under which Eliza Louisa Moresby *Beck wrote historical novels.

Barrington, Maurice. *See* D. W. *Brogan.

Barrington-Ward, Robert McGowan (1891-1948). Born at Worcester; educated at Westminster and Oxford; joined the staff of *The Times*, 1913; assistant editor of *The Observer*, 1919-27; returned to *The Times* as assistant editor and chief writer of leading articles, 1927; deputy editor, 1934; editor 1941 until his death.

Barron, Oswald (1868-1939). Author (under the pseudonym 'The Londoner') of a series of short essays contributed during a period of twenty years to the *Evening News* and described by *The Times* as 'always urbane, generally whimsical, and sometimes learned'. A volume of selections from these was published as *Day In and Day Out* (1924). His essays were a by-product, for as Maltravers Herald of Arms Extraordinary he was the leading contemporary authority on Heraldry, author of the *Encyclopaedia Britannica* article on that subject and a contributor on genealogy and armoury to the *Victoria County History*.

Barrow Poets. A group founded in 1951 with the purpose of selling books of verse from street barrows in London during the Festival of Britain. Refused a licence for outdoor trading they turned to poetry readings and music recitals in public houses and other places of popular resort. By 1969 they had so far won wider acceptance as to give a lunch-time recital in Westminster Abbey, and with official and municipal encouragement to sell from their barrows in the Queen Elizabeth Hall on the South Bank of the Thames.

Barry, Sir Gerald (Gerald Reid Barry, 1898-1968; knighted 1951). Educated at Marlborough and Cambridge. Editor of the *Saturday Review*, 1924-30; founded and edited the *Week-end Review*, 1930-34; editor of the *News Chronicle*, 1936-47; Director-General, Festival of Britain, 1951. Edited *A Week-end Calendar* (1933), *This England* (1934); with Sir Francis Meynell, *The Week-end Book* (1955 edn).

Barry, Philip (1896-1949). Born in New Jersey; educated in his home town, Rochester, and at Yale. Spent a short time in the U.S. diplomatic service before entering Harvard as a drama student under Professor G. P. *Baker. He became from 1922, when his *You and I* was a success in New York, one of the leading contemporary American playwrights. *The Animal Kingdom* (1932) and *The Philadelphia Story* (1939) were most widely known.

Barrymore family. American actors of English origin: **Maurice** (1847-1905), *né* Herbert Blythe, born in India, educated at Cambridge; studied law but became a leading actor in London and New York under the name Barrymore. The three children of him and his actress wife (*née* Georgiana Drew, 1856-93) established the Barrymore stage hierarchy which led Edna *Ferber and George S. *Kaufman to collaborate in writing *The Royal Family* (1927; title in England, *Theatre Royal*), a successful play. The eldest of the three, **Lionel** Barrymore (1878-1954) became best known as a film actor; **Ethel** (1879-1959) played with distinction in Shakespeare, Ibsen, Barrie, Galsworthy, and many plays, both classic and modern; **John** (1882-1942) was an outstanding Hamlet and a stage genius hampered by eccentricities and indulgences.

Barsac, Louis. See Ernest James *Oldmeadow.

Barth, Karl (1886-1968). Born in Basle, Switzerland; educated in Bern, and at Berlin and other German universities. A Minister of the Reformed Church, first at Geneva. Professor of Theology at, successively, the universities of Göttingen, Münster, and Bonn, and became internationally famous when he refused to subject his Christian beliefs to the heretical demands of the Nazi régime. His theological writings had a wide circulation and met with strong dissent as well as ardent approval. Those translated into English include *The Word of God and the Word of Man* (1928), *The Church and the Political Problems of Our Day* (1939), *Church and State* (1939), *Against the Stream* (1954). His interest in music is shown in *Wolfgang Amadeus Mozart* (1956).

Bartimeus (pseudonym of Lewis Anselmo da Costa Ricci, 1886-1967; knighted as Sir Lewis Ritchie, 1947), who changed his name to Ritchie in 1941. He served in the British navy from 1901 to 1944, retiring with the rank of Captain, and wrote a large number of popular stories of naval life under his pseudonym: *Naval Occasions* (1914), *Seaways* (1923), *Under Sealed Orders* (1938), *East of Malta, West of Suez* (1943), etc., and *The Turn of the Road* (1946).

Bartlett, Charlotte. In E. M. Forster's *A *Room with a View* (1908), cousin of Lucy Honeychurch, and her chaperone in Italy.

Bartlett, John (1820-1905). Born at Plymouth, Massachusetts; educated locally. Started work at the University Book Store, Cambridge, Mass., in 1836 and became its owner from 1849. His name is well known as the compiler of valuable reference books which still circulate in revised editions: *Familiar Quotations* (1st edn 1855) and *Complete Concordance to Shakespeare* (1st edn 1894).

Bartlett, Vernon (1894-   ). Born at Westbury, Wiltshire; educated at Blundell's School, Devon. Travelled widely on the Continent; wounded and invalided in World War I; from 1916 worked for various British newspapers and for the League of Nations. He became widely known when he broadcast on foreign affairs for the B.B.C. from 1928 to 1934. M.P. for Bridgwater, Somerset, 1938-50. Author of books on politics and current affairs, a novel (*Calf Love*, 1929), and an autobiography, *This is My Life* (1938).

Bashford, H. H. (Sir Henry Howarth Bashford, 1880-1961; knighted 1938). Born at Bedford; educated there and at London Hospital, qualifying as a physician in 1904. He specialized in industrial medicine, especially in the service of the General Post Office for many years, eventually as Chief Medical Officer, 1933-43. In addition he wrote a number of novels from 1909 onward, but had more success with a volume of essays drawing upon his professional experiences, *At the Corner of Harley Street* (1927). *August Carp, Esq. by Himself. Being the Autobiography of a Really Good Man* (1924), published anonymously, was revealed as by Bashford in a 1966 reprint.

Bashville. Lydia Carey's footman in *The *Admirable Bashville* (1903) by Bernard Shaw.

Basic English. A form of language aiming at simplification for (especially non-English) learners by employing a standard limited vocabulary. Its originators were C. K. *Ogden and I. A. *Richards. Critics of the system objected that it frequently substituted roundabout phraseology for single words not in the prescribed vocabulary.

Bason, Fred (Frederick Thomas Bason,

1907-1973). Born in Southwark; educated at a Council school there; became and continued as a bookseller, branching out later as author, lecturer and broadcaster. Among his books on a variety of subjects from bibliography to fishing are the several volumes of *Fred Bason's Diary* (1951, 1952, 1955, 1960, each with an Introduction by a celebrated author) in which he expresses with gusto a humorous cockney view of his life and hard times.

Basso, Hamilton (1904-64). Born in New Orleans; educated at Tulane University. Author of *Cinnamon Seed* (1934), *Sun in Capricorn* (1942) and other novels of the Southern states. *See* Huey *Long.

Bast, Leonard. In E. M. Forster's *Howards End* (1910), insurance clerk; his cultural aspirations are encouraged by the Schlegel sisters; married to a sluttish wife, Jacky, he later becomes the father of Helen Schlegel's child.

Bastable family, The. *See* Edith *Nesbit.

Bates, H. E. (Herbert Ernest Bates, 1905-1974). Born at Rushden, Northamptonshire; educated at Kettering Grammar School. After brief periods as novelist and clerk he devoted himself to writing. From his farmer-grandfather's yarns he drew material for a number of his early short stories, in *Day's End* (1927) and other collections. During World War II, using the pseudonym Flying Officer X, he wrote short stories of the R.A.F. in *The Greatest People in the World* (1942) and *How Sleep the Brave* (1943). At the end of the war he found a larger public with such novels as *Fair Stood the Wind for France* (1944), *The Purple Plain* (1947), *Love for Lydia* (1954), and a sequence dealing with an unsophisticated English family at home and abroad.

Bates, Ralph (1899-   ). Born in Swindon; educated at the secondary school there. Served in World War I and afterwards worked in the railway factory in Swindon. Lived in Spain from 1930 to 1937 and fought in the Republican International Brigade during the Civil War. He settled in America in 1937 and in 1948 became Professor of Literature at New York University. He began to write while unemployed in Spain and published his first novel *Sierra* in 1933, following it with *Lean Men* (1934) and others dealing realistically with Spain and

Mexico as he experienced those countries. A later novel *Dolphin in the Wind* (1949) has an English village setting. He also wrote a biography, *Franz Schubert* (1934).

Bathos. In speech or writing, a sudden descent 'from the sublime to the ridiculous', either unawares or as an intentional device to produce a calculated effect by surprise or shock. A more emphatic form of anticlimax.

Battle of Britain. The aerial bombardment of Great Britain by the German air force in World War II. It caused much devastation and loss of life, but its ultimate failure caused the abandonment of invasion plans.

Battle of the Atlantic. The German submarine campaign against Allied shipping in World War II. It sank many merchant ships but was finally countered by defensive measures from sea and air.

Baudricourt, Captain Robert de. The 'military squire, handsome and physically energetic, but with no will of his own' in Bernard Shaw's *Saint Joan* (1923).

Bauhaus. A German school of art, architecture, industrial design, typography, etc., founded by Walter Gropius at Weimar in 1919. In 1925 it moved to Dessau, and in 1928 to Berlin until, under the Nazi régime, it was forced to close in 1933.

Baum, Lyman Frank (1856-1919). Born in New York state; educated at a military academy. He wrote a large number of children's books (some pseudonymously); the success of his *Mother Goose in Prose* (1897) and *Father Goose: His Book* (1899) was outstripped by that of *The Wonderful Wizard of Oz* (1900) which, after his death, delighted worldwide audiences through a film version. He continued the Oz adventures in numerous later books.

Baum, Vicki (1896-1960). Born in Vienna and educated there. Although trained for music she turned to writing and in 1930 had world success with her novel *Grand Hotel*, a story woven round a group of diverse personalities assembled in a Berlin hotel. A long succession of other novels followed at more or less yearly intervals, but though she remained an admirable story-teller her first wave of popularity was not repeated.

Bawcombe, Caleb. The old Wiltshire head-shepherd whose recollections provide basic material for W. H. Hudson's *A *Shepherd's Life* (1910).

Bax, Sir Arnold (Arnold Edward Trevor Bax, 1883-1953; knighted 1937). Born in London; educated privately and at the Royal Academy of Music. Composed much instrumental, choral and vocal music. Master of the King's Music from 1942 (Queen's Music from 1952) until his death. Stated his special interest in 'every aspect of Celtic life and history'; published *A Celtic Song-Cycle*. He spent some time in Ireland from 1902, became a friend of leaders of the revolutionary movement, and was considered an 'honorary Irishman'. Using the pseudonym Dermot O'Byrne, he wrote stories and sketches of Irish life—*Children of the Hills* (1913), *Wrack and other Stories* (1918)—verse (*Seafoam and Firelight*, 1909) and a play, *Red Owen* (1919). A volume of reminiscences, *Farewell, my Youth* (1943), appeared under his birth name.

Bax, Clifford (1886-1962). Educated privately and at the Slade School of Art. Turned from painting to writing, particularly plays: those produced including *The Poetasters of Ispahan* (1912), *Midsummer Madness* (1924), *Socrates* (1930), *The Venetian* (1931), *The Rose Without a Thorn* (1932), *The House of Borgia* (1935). Among a large number of other books are *Farewell, My Muse* (collected poems, 1932), *Inland Far* (autobiography, 1925), *Evenings in Albany* (1942), studies of *Leonardo da Vinci* (1932) and *W. G. Grace* (1952), and works of fiction and topography.

Bax, Ernest Belfort (1854-1926). Born at Leamington; educated privately in London and studied music and philosophy in Germany. Became active in British socialist politics from the 1880s and editor of *Justice*. Author of philosophical and historical works and, particularly, *Religion of Socialism* (1886), *Ethics of Socialism* (1889), *Socialism: Its Growth and Outcome* (in collaboration with William Morris, 1894), *Essays in Socialism* (1906), *Problems of Men, Mina and Morals* (1912). *Reminiscences and Reflections* (1918).

Baxter, Sir Beverley (Arthur Beverley Baxter, 1891-1964; knighted 1954). Born and educated in Canada. Migrated to England and entered journalism, becoming Editor-in-Chief of the *Daily Express* 1929-33. Elected as M.P. from 1935. Author of *The Parts Men Play* (1920) and some other fiction, *First Nights and Noises Off* (1949) and other collections of essays, and *Strange Street* (1935) his autobiography.

Baxter, James K. (James Keir Baxter, 1926-). Born in Dunedin, New Zealand; educated at universities in Otago and Wellington; worked as a teacher, journalist, and labourer. Author of *Beyond the Palisade* (1944). *Blow, Wind of Fruitfulness* (1948), *The Fallen House* (1953), *The Iron Breadboard* (parodies; 1957), *In Fires of No Return* (1958), *Pig Island Letters* (1966) and other verse collections; also critical works: *The Fire and the Anvil* (1954), *Aspects of Poetry in New Zealand* (1967).

Baylis, Lilian (Lilian Mary Baylis, 1874-1937). Manager of the *Old Vic from 1912 until her death. Though she had the reputation of being dictatorial, she gathered a loyal and devoted body of often eminent players and other helpers, and by combined efforts brought the Old Vic, and its later offshoot *Sadler's Wells, to a high level of theatrical achievement.

Bayly, Ada Ellen. See Edna *Lyall.

Baynes, Norman (Norman Hepburn Baynes, 1877-1961). Educated at Eastbourne and Oxford; Professor of Byzantine History in the University of London, 1931-42. Among his published works are *Israel among the Nations* (1927), *Byzantine Studies and Other Essays* (1955), and an edition of *Hitler's Speeches, 1922-39* (1942).

Bazin, Réné (1853-1922). Born in Angers; studied for the priesthood and then for the law, but eventually concentrated on writing, producing novels of French peasant life (e.g. *La Terre qui meurt*, 1899) and others dealing additionally with social problems (e.g. *Le Blé qui lève*, 1907).

Beach, Rex (Rex Ellingwood Beach, 1877-1949). Born in Michigan; educated in Florida and Chicago; studied law but led an active, hard and adventurous life which provided material for some of his many novels of rough outdoor life and robust masculinity, beginning with *Pardners* (1905) and shown representatively in *Alaskan Adventures* (1933, containing three previously published novels). Films based on his stories gave him additional popularity and wealth.

Beach, Sylvia (1887-1962). Born in Baltimore. Her family lived for a while in Paris during her girlhood, her father being a Presbyterian minister with duties there. She became devoted to France and in 1917 began associations with modern literature and its authors which led her in 1919 to start the soon-famous bookshop which she named *Shakespeare & Co., its most publicized venture being the production of James *Joyce's *Ulysses*. The bookshop became a rendezvous for many outstanding authors–British, American, and French–and the story of the enterprise was told by Sylvia Beach in *Shakespeare and Company* (1960).

Beachcomber. *See* D. B. Wyndham *Lewis and J. B. *Morton.

Beaglehole, J. C. (John Cawte Beaglehole, 1901-1971). Born and educated in New Zealand. Lecturer in History, Victoria University, 1936-48; Professor of British Commonwealth History there, 1963-66. Author of historical works including *The Exploration of the Pacific* (1934), *The Discovery of New Zealand* (1939; 2nd edn 1961). Edited *The Journals of Captain James Cook on his Voyages of Discovery* (3 vols 1955-67). Described by compatriots as 'probably our most distinguished scholar and one of the best prose writers of the twentieth century'.

Beale, Dorothea (1831-1906). Born in London; educated there and in Paris. Taught mathematics and Latin at Queen's College, London; head teacher, Clergy School, Casterton, Westmorland (the model for Lowood School in Charlotte Brontë's *Jane Eyre*); Principal of Cheltenham Ladies College, 1858-1906; founder of St Hilda's Hall, Oxford, 1893. She was one of the pioneers of higher education for women and her name is permanently associated with that of Frances Mary Buss (1827-94), founder of the North London Collegiate School for Ladies. Their single-minded austere devotion is memorialized in the squib: 'Miss Buss and Miss Beale/Cupid's darts do not feel;/How different from us/ Miss Beale and Miss Buss!'

Beard, Charles (Charles Austin Beard, 1874-1948). Born in Indiana; educated at De Pauw, Cornell, and Columbia universities and in England at Oxford, where he assisted in the founding of Ruskin College as a Labour educational institution. In his own country he was eminent as an economic historian, though his best-known work is

the more comprehensive *Rise of American Civilization* (2 vols, 1927), written in collaboration with his wife Mary Beard (*née* Ritter, 1876-1958), with whom he also wrote *America in Mid-Passage* (1939) and other works.

Beat Generation (or **Beatniks**). The name adopted by those adolescents, and some adults, who in the years following World War II repudiated 'respectability' and normal social behaviour and cultivated a deliberately rootless manner of living. The cult originated among young Americans of both sexes in California, and was manifested in literature in *On the Road* and other novels by Jack *Kerouac and in free verse by several writers including Allen *Ginsberg, whose *Howl!* was acclaimed by fellow beatniks. They used a distinctive slang, were devoted to jazz, and a minority became drug addicts in furtherance of their desire to contract-out from the materialistic and belligerent existence of the world they despised. What Americans had originated, adolescents in other countries imitated. In England they became known generally as *Angry Young Men, or as the Chelsea Set, though they were not confined to that London centre of art students and would-be artists. Recognizable often by an appearance of studied neglect in clothing and personal hygiene, and by a drooping and sagging posture, they were successors to those who after World War I had been named 'the lost generation'. The origin of the word 'beatnik' is in doubt. Though it has been assumed to derive from 'beaten' (in the sense of 'down and out') or from the persistent beat of jazz, an article by John Clellon Holmes in *Esquire* (Feb. 1958) attributed to Kerouac the view that 'The Beat Generation is basically a religious generation. . . . This includes anyone from fifteen to fifty-five who digs [enjoys; is excited by] *everything* . . . Beat means beatitude, not beat up.'

Beaton, Sir Cecil (Cecil Walter Hardy Beaton, 1904-   ). Knighted 1972. Educated at Harrow and Cambridge. Worked mainly as a photographer and designer of stage costumes and sets. As a writer he produced travel books etc. illustrated with his own photographs and drawings (e.g. *Cecil Beaton's New York*, 1939; *Near East*, 1943; *Far East*, 1945), *Photobiography* (1951), *The Glass of Fashion* (1954), *The Face of the*

c

World (1957), *The Wandering Years* (1961), *The Strenuous Years* (1973), etc.

Beauchamp, Kathleen Mansfield. Cousin of the following. See Katherine *Mansfield.

Beauchamp, Mary Annette. See *Elizabeth (Countess von Arnim).

Beauclerk, Helen (Mary Dorothea *née* Bellingham, 1892-1969; changed her name to that of a relative by whom she was adopted). Born at Cambridge; lived in France as a child and studied music there; worked as a journalist in London. Author of *The Green Lacquer Pavilion* (1926), *The Love of the Foolish Angel* (1929), *There Were Three Men* (1949), and other novels.

Beauvoir, Simone de (1908-). Born in Paris; educated at the University there, studying philosophy, a subject she then taught in various institutions from 1931 to 1943. She became a leading proponent of *Existentialism and co-editor with *Sartre of the existentialist periodical *Les Temps Moderne.* Her writings had a contemporary vogue in France and abroad, especially *Le Deuxième Sexe* (1949; translated as *The Second Sex,* 1953), an intemperate complaint against the status accorded to women, as seen from the standpoint of existentialism. Other books include: *L'Invitée* (novel, 1943), *Pour une morale de l'Ambiguité* (translated as *The Ethics of Ambiguity,* 1943), *Tous les Hommes sont mortels (All Men are Mortal,* novel, 1955), *All Said and Done* (1974).

Beaverbrook, Lord (William Maxwell Aitken, 1879-1964; 1st Baron Beaverbrook, 1917). Born at Maple, Ontario; educated at Newcastle, New Brunswick. In British House of Commons as M.P. for Ashton-under-Lyne, 1910-16; held various government appointments in World War II. He became a millionaire newspaper proprietor, owning the *Daily Express* and associated publications. His dynamic personality and idiosyncratic views made him a controversial figure, both warmly admired and severely criticized. Among his books, *Politicians and the Press* (1925), *Politicians and the War* (1928), and *Men and Power* (1956) have interest as contributions to contemporary history. *The Decline and Fall of Lloyd George* (1963).

Beazley, Sir John (John Davidson Beazley, 1885-1970; knighted 1949). Born in Glasgow;

educated at Christ's Hospital and Oxford. Professor of Classical Archaeology, University of Oxford, 1925-56. His early interest and impressive accomplishment in poetry was accompanied and eventually displaced by his passion for the study of Greek vase-painting, on which he became a world authority, writing in German and Italian as well as in impeccable English. Among the works in which his extensive knowledge is distilled are: *Attic Red-figure Vase-painters* (1942; 1963), *Potter and Painter in Ancient Athens* (1945), *Etruscan Vase-painting* (1947), *Attic Black-figure Vase-painters* (1956).

Beck, Eliza Louisa Moresby (-). Author of novels etc. under the pseudonyms E. *Barrington, Lily Adams *Beck, and Louis *Moresby.

Beck, Lily Adams. Pseudonym of Eliza Louisa Moresby Beck. Wrote on Buddhist themes, and studies of the occult.

Beckett, Samuel (1906-). Born in Dublin; educated at Portora Royal School and Trinity College, Dublin. Went to Paris as Lecturer in English, 1928-30; returned to Trinity College as Lecturer in French, 1930-32; thereafter lived mainly in Paris and was for a while secretary to James *Joyce. Author of poems (*Whoroscope,* 1930; *Echo's Bones,* 1936), short stories (*More Pricks than Kicks,* 1934), a critical study (*Proust,* 1931), novels (*Murphy,* 1938; *Watt,* 1944; *Molloy,* 1951; etc.), plays (*Waiting for Godot,* 1954; *End Game,* 1957; etc.). Most of his later writings were in French, some of which were translated into English by himself. The production of *Waiting for Godot* in London in 1955 was followed by prolonged controversy between those who found the play (and much of Beckett's other work) unintelligible, and those who accepted it as important and significantly symbolic of the futility and nothingness of human life, a pessimistic attitude which was currently fashionable. His plays are leading examples of the *Theatre of the Absurd cult.

Bedford. Bankrupt business man and would-be playwright in H. G. Wells's *The *First Men in the Moon* (1901). A friend of Cavor, he accompanies the inventor on the lunar flight and becomes narrator of their experiences.

Beecham, Sir Thomas (1897-1961; 2nd baronet; knighted 1916). Born at St Helens, Lancashire, eldest son of Sir Thomas Beecham, Bt, wealthy manufacturer of patent medicines, to whose title he succeeded in 1916 after having been himself knighted earlier in that year. He was educated at Rossall and Oxford, but his interests were almost exclusively musical, and at the age of twenty he founded an amateur orchestra and also in an emergency conducted the Hallé Orchestra at a concert arranged to inaugurate his father's term as Mayor of St Helens. Thereafter the younger Beecham's name was bound up with much that was outstanding in English musical history: he founded the New Symphony Orchestra and the Beecham Symphony Orchestra; brought the Diaghilev Russian Ballet to London for the first time in 1911 and a Russian opera company in 1913. With the Beecham Opera Company (later renamed the British National Opera Company) he did excellent work in the endeavour to establish modern grand opera as a popular art form, expending his private fortune. In 1932 he founded and as its conductor impressed his personality and high musical standards upon the London Philharmonic Orchestra. Beecham's range of taste and understanding in music was wide and often deep, but he was particularly gifted as an interpreter of French music— that of Berlioz perhaps most importantly— and he strove with only partial success to win over his countrymen to the music of his friend Frederick Delius. Although for years he scorned the gramophone and declined to have any part in providing 'tinned music', subsequent advances in recording technique converted him, and he became one of the most distinguished as well as one of the most popular conductors for records of classical music. Beecham, outspoken to the point of indiscretion, was no respecter of persons; yet in spite of idiosyncrasies which might on occasion pass the bounds of courtesy, and in his treatment of musical scores might distress musicologists, he was widely acknowledged as the one conductor of British birth who brought unique genius and personal magnetism to the direction of an orchestra. Music was his life. In *A Mingled Chime* (1944) he told something of his own story.

Beechcroft, T. O. (Thomas Owen Beechcroft, 1902-   ). Born in Bristol; educated at Clifton College and Oxford. Joined the staff of the B.B.C. *Collected Stories* (1946) and later volumes. Wrote a study of the short story and short-story writers, *The Modest Art* (1968).

Beeching, H. C. (Henry Charles Beeching, 1859-1919). Born in London; educated at the City of London School and at Oxford. He was ordained in 1882 and after holding a curacy in Liverpool became successively vicar of Yattendon in Berkshire, Canon of Westminster, and Dean of Norwich. Following books of verse to which he and two Oxford friends contributed he published independently *Love in a Garden and Other Poems* (1895), and *Pages from a Private Diary* (1898; first edition anonymous; 2nd edn 1903 under the pseudonym Urbanus Sylvan). Other writings included *Provincial Letters and Other Papers* (1906), *Religio Laici* (1902), *William Shakespeare: Player, Playmaker, and Poet* (1908).

Beeding, Francis. Joint pseudonym of John L. *Palmer and Hilary St George *Saunders.

Beerbohm, Sir Max (Henry Maxmilian Beerbohm, 1872-1956; knighted 1939). Born in Kensington, son of Julius Beerbohm, a corn-merchant from Memel who settled in London and founded trade papers. One of Julius's sons by his first wife became the famous actor-manager Sir Herbert Beerbohm Tree. Max, the youngest child of his father's second marriage, was educated at Charterhouse and Oxford, at both places showing signs of satirical talent as a caricaturist and writer. Apart from those in school and university publications, his first printed caricatures appeared in the *Strand Magazine* in 1892. Two years later *A Defence of Cosmetics* in the first number of *The *Yellow Book* started him on the career as essayist which was to make him a unique figure in contemporary literature for the remaining sixty years of his life. In 1896 his contributions to *The Yellow Book* and its successor *The Savoy* were collected in a small slim volume entitled with impudent humour *The Works of Max Beerbohm*. Elegantly printed as well as elegantly written, the book opened with the essay on *Dandies* which caused him for many years to be regarded as scarcely more than an apostle of dandyism, with its common implications of triviality and shallowness. In truth, as became slowly realized, his 'dandyism' was the hallmark of a scrupulous and impeccable style which extended from his dress to his prose and to his use of line in the satirical drawings he published at intervals from 1896 (*Caricatures of Twenty-Five Gentlemen*) to 1925 (*Observations*). The graphic brilliance of the drawings was almost invariably enhanced by the wit of the written captions either below or ballooning from the mouths of the persons. Though urbanity was pervasive in his satirical method, uncompromising direct attack occasionally broke through, as in the pictorial comments on World War I and its aftermath (in *A Survey*, 1921, and *Things New and Old*, 1923). In 1895 he accompanied his half-brother, Beerbohm Tree, on a theatrical tour in the U.S.; and after an interval of three years, during which he moved comprehensively among writers and artists in London and contributed (mostly drawings) to numerous periodicals, he followed Bernard *Shaw as dramatic critic to the *Saturday Review* from 1898 to 1910 (articles selected and revised in *Around Theatres*, vols I and II: limited edn 1924, reprinted in 1 vol, unlimited, 1953). During his years as dramatic critic he also published further volumes of essays: *More* (1899), and *Yet Again* (1909), as well as *The Happy Hypocrite: A Fairy Tale for Tired Men* (1897). He married an American actress, Florence Kahn, in 1910, and most of their happy life together (until she died in 1951) was spent at Rapallo, near Genoa, except when wars uprooted them. The peak of his achievements in sustained comic irony and satire was reached with *Zuleika Dobson, or An Oxford Love Story* (1911). In 1911 when he was forty, the publication of *A *Christmas Garland* added further to his literary reputation by ranking him with the few great parodists. *Seven Men* (1919), a series of imaginary portraits in prose, included 'Savonarola' Brown, with its unequalled parody of the worst extravagances of minor Elizabethan drama. *And Even Now* (1920) contained among its twenty essays the quickly famous account of a visit to Swinburne at *No. 2 The Pines*, Putney. *A Variety of Things* (1928), a miscellaneous collection of pieces, was headed by a story, *The Dreadful Dragon of Hay Hill*. This volume was the last published of his writings before he enlarged his audience from a fastidious limited company to a popular multitude, a surprising achievement which came through his broadcast

talks for the B.B.C. The first of these, on 29 December 1935, showed an immediate mastery of this channel of communication. While remaining 'the incomparable Max' and a withdrawn aristocrat of literature, he also displayed in a voice exquisitely modulated in tone and speed the ability to establish contact with all manner of listeners. *Mainly on the Air* (1946) prints a selection of these broadcasts. In his last years Max's undiminished sense of irony no doubt relished his elevation to the pedestal of a public monument, signalized by the knighthood conferred on him at the age of sixty-seven and by the formation in 1942 of the Maximilian Society.

Begbie, Harold (1871-1929). Born in Suffolk. Wrote many novels, biographies of William Booth and Sir Ernest Shackleton, but had his main success with popular religious books (*Broken Earthenware*, 1910; *In the Hand of the Potter*, 1911; etc.) published under the pseudonym A Gentleman with a Duster.

Behan, Brendan (1923-1964). Born and educated in Dublin. Served with the Irish Republican Army from 1937. Sentenced to a Borstal School in 1939, and to fourteen years by a Dublin military court in 1942 — facts publicized by himself. Author of plays (*The Quare Fellow*, 1956; *The Hostage*, 1959) and the autobiographical *Borstal Boy* (1958). The attention his writings received was buttressed by eccentric public behaviour; his chief declared recreations were drinking and talking.

Behaviorism. A system of psychology evolved by John B. *Watson.

Behrman, S. N. (Samuel Nathaniel Behrman, 1893-1973). Born in Worcester, Massachusetts; educated at Clark College, Harvard (where he studied drama at G. P. *Baker's 47 Workshop), and Columbia. He took various jobs while hoping during more than a decade to become an accepted playwright, and with *The Second Man* (1927) he achieved the first of the successes that made him one of America's leading writers of high comedy, reaching his peak with *Amphitryon 38* (1937), and *No Time for Comedy* (1939). He also wrote *Duveen* (1952), a biography of the millionaire art-dealer, and some recollections of his childhood in *The Worcester Account* (1954).

Beith, John Hay. *See* Ian *Hay.

Belaney, Archibald Stansfield. *See* *Grey Owl.

Belasco, David (1859-1931). Born in San Francisco; sent to a monastery school in Victoria, British Columbia, but ran away to join a circus and subsequently became an actor in travelling companies and at length a leading theatre manager and producer owning the Belasco Theatre in New York. He wrote numerous plays and adaptations, mostly spectacular sensational melodramas, of which only two have survived, and in another form, *Madame Butterfly* (adapted 1900, from a novel by John Luther Long) and *The Girl of the Golden West* (1905), utilized by Puccini as libretti for his operas *Madama Butterfly* (1904) and *La Fanciulla del West* (1910).

Bell, Adrian (Adrian Hanbury Bell, 1901-   ). Educated at Uppingham. Became a farmer in Suffolk and, as an offshoot of his practical experience on the land, wrote a series of engaging narratives of English country life without false romanticism: *Corduroy* (1930), *Silver Ley* (1931), *The Cherry Tree* (1932), *Folly Field* (1933), *Shepherd's Farm* (1939), *Apple Acre* (1942), *A Suffolk Harvest* (1956) and others; *Poems* (1935); *My Own Master* (autobiography, 1961).

Bell, Alexander Graham (1847-1922). Born in Edinburgh; educated there and in London; went first to Canada and then settled in the U.S. as teacher of 'vocal physiology' at Boston. Experiments in the conduction of speech by electricity led to his invention of the telephone in 1876. Other inventions included an early form of gramophone and a 'photophone' for the transmission of speech by light-waves. Founded the periodical *Science* in 1883.

Bell, C. F. Moberly (Charles Frederick Moberly Bell, 1847-1911). Born in Alexandria, Egypt; educated privately. Egyptian correspondent of *The Times* (1865 and later); became business manager of that paper in 1890 and in the endeavour to improve its financial situation he started various book publishing, bookselling, and subscription library schemes, including The Times Book Club. His plans for disposing of surplus library copies at much reduced prices soon after publication brought him into conflict with the publishing houses and bookshops, and led to the compact between publishers and booksellers known as the *Net Book Agreement. He also started in 1897 *Literature*, a weekly periodical replaced in 1901 by *The Times Literary Supplement*. On the formation of The Times Publishing Company in 1908 he became its managing director. Author of *Khedives and Pashas* (1884) and *Egyptian Finance* (1897).

Bell, Clive (Arthur Clive Howard Bell, 1881-1964). Born at East Shefford, Bedfordshire; educated at Marlborough and Cambridge; married Vanessa Stephen (Vanessa *Bell). Made a considerable reputation as an art critic, particularly with his invention of the term 'significant form'. Author of *Art* (1914), *Poems* (1921), *Since Cézanne* (1922), *Civilization* (1928), *Proust* (1929).

Bell, Gertrude (Gertrude Margaret Lowthian Bell, 1868-1926). Born in County Durham, educated at Queen's College (Harley Street, London) and Oxford. While still young she developed a passion for the East that was to lead her to undertake intrepid travels in Syria, Mesopotamia and particularly Arabia. These journeys produced *The Desert and the Sown* (1907) and *Amurath to Amurath* (1911), while her work for the British Government in the Arab lands during World War I produced *A Review of the Civil Administration of Mesopotamia* (1921). She was also an excellent letter-writer: *The Letters of Gertrude Bell* (1927), with lesser collections later.

Bell, J. J. (John Jay Bell, 1871-1934). A prolific writer of fiction and verse on Scottish themes; best known for a series of humorous stories beginning with *Wee Macgreegor* (1902) and continuing through several later volumes dealing with the same central character at ages from boyhood up; some episodes he adapted for the stage, and a volume of *Wee Macgreegor* with an introduction by the author appeared in the year of his death.

Bell, Joseph (1837-1911). Born in Edinburgh; educated there at the Academy and the University, qualifying in medicine and surgery. Starting as a dresser at the Edinburgh Royal Infirmary, he rose to be its senior surgeon and consulting surgeon and a member of the University Court. Edited the *Edinburgh Medical Journal*, 1873-96, and wrote textbooks on surgery. He was popularly believed to have been Conan *Doyle's model for some of the idiosyncrasies of Sherlock Holmes.

Bell, Neil (pseudonym of Stephen Southwold, 1887-1964). Born at Southwold, Suffolk; educated at village schools and St Mark's College, Chelsea. Though he tried journalism, teaching, drawing, and boat-building, as well as soldiering in World War I, his life was otherwise fully occupied as a prolific author. As Neil Bell he wrote *Precious Porcelain* (1931), *Bredon and Sons* (1934), *Pinkney's Garden* (1937), *Forgive Us Our Trespasses* (1947), *Flowers of the Forest* (1952), and more than a score of other novels, besides volumes of short stories. As Stephen Southwold he specialized in children's books, hardly less numerous. He also used other pseudonyms: Paul Martens (*Death Rocks the Cradle,* 1933; *The Truth About My Father,* 1934) and Miles (*The Seventh Bowe,* 1930).

Bell, Quentin (1910-   ). Son of Clive and Vanessa Bell; Slade Professor of Fine Art, Oxford, 1964-5, lecturer or professor of related art subjects at other universities from 1952. Author of *Ruskin* (1963), *Bloomsbury* (1968), and (chief among his other writings) the biography of his aunt *Virginia *Woolf* (1972).

Bell, Vanessa (*née* Vanessa Stephen, 1879-1961; married Clive *Bell in 1907). Born in London, the elder daughter of Sir Leslie *Stephen and sister of Virginia *Woolf; studied at the Ròyal Academy Schools, but soon rebelled against academic styles and became an adherent of the English *Post-Impressionist group led by Roger *Fry and centred on his *Omega Workshops. With her sister she became a figure in the *Bloomsbury Group. Her work as an artist included embroideries, interior decoration, designs for carpets and pottery, and book jackets.

Bell, Vicars (1904-   ). Educated at Reigate and University of London, schoolmaster and headmaster 1925-63. Author of *Little Gaddesden: The Story of an English Parish* (1949), *On Learning the English Tongue* (1953); and a number of detective novels including *Death Under the Stars* (1949), *Death and the Night Watches* (1954), *Death Walks by the River* (1959).

Belloc, Hilaire (Joseph Hilaire Pierre Belloc, 1870-1953). Born at La Celle St Cloud, near Paris, of a French barrister father and English mother (*née* Bessie Parkes, granddaughter of the eminent 18th-century scientist, Joseph Priestley). The siege of Paris in the Franco-Prussian War of 1870-1 caused the family to move to England. After their return to France, the father died in 1872 and Hilaire was brought back to England and educated at schools in Westminster and Hampstead before going to the Oratory School at Birmingham, where he acquired a love of the classics as well as further instruction in Roman Catholicism, the religion of his parents, to which he retained a lifelong devotion, clearly evident in his writings. After leaving the Oratory in 1887, he spent a brief period at a Catholic college in Paris, a few months on a farm in Sussex, flirted with architecture and with journalism in London and elsewhere, and then did a year's military service in the French artillery at Toul. In 1893 he went to Balliol College, Oxford, was President of the Union in the next year, gained First Class Honours in History in 1895, but failed to obtain a Fellowship at All Souls. A few years before, in London, he had fallen in love with Elodie Hogan, an American girl, and in 1896 married her in California. Belloc gave a number of lectures on historical subjects while in America and on returning to England became a University Extension lecturer, and also undertook private coaching at Oxford, where he settled with his wife until 1899. They then moved to Cheyne Walk in London, and Belloc became associated with a group of writers contributing to *The Speaker*, a political and literary weekly which had already printed essays, stories and verses by him. His earnings from lecturing and coaching were only very little increased by the publication of *Verses and Sonnets* (1895), *The Bad Child's Book of Beasts* (1896), *More Beasts for Worse Children* (1897) and *The Modern Traveller* (1898), but these books gave him some repute as a lyrical poet and as a comic and satirical versifier. Meanwhile he was furthering his study of the period and personalities of the French Revolution, which resulted in a succession of books: *Danton* (1899), *Robespierre* (1901), *Marie Antoinette* (1909), *The French Revolution* (1911), *The Last Days of the French Monarchy* (1916), and a historical novel *The Girondin* (1911). It was long before writing provided an adequate livelihood, and he contemplated, first, a career at the Bar, and, next, a political career. Nothing came of the former, but in January

1906 he was elected Liberal M.P. for South Salford. Although he made several notable speeches in the Commons on education and military matters, he was not an effective parliamentarian, mainly because he bitterly despised the party system, insisting that it represented no genuine differences on policy but was based on secret collusion between families sharing seats on both sides of the House. This led to his declining to stand as anything but an Independent in the second general election of 1910, and marked the end of his parliamentary career. As a sequel to this experience he wrote in collaboration with Cecil *Chesterton The Party System (1911). In support of the political views held by him and his friends, a weekly journal The Eye Witness was started in June 1912 with Belloc as editor, but he found the work irksome and resigned at the end of a year. His other political book at this stage, The Servile State (1912), has a prophetic interest since it foreshadowed the development which came a generation later in 'the Welfare State': 'It saw that men in modern industrial societies would willingly give up their freedom to secure sufficiency and security' (Robert Speaight, The Life of Hilaire Belloc, 1957, p. 317). From 1906 to 1909 he was Literary Editor of The Morning Post, his first regular salaried employment. The paper printed many of his best essays, and by the time his connection with it ended he was widely known and established as one of the half-dozen leading contemporary writers, no longer prone to complain that the dons at Oxford by denying him a Fellowship had condemned him to hardship. One of the most important events in his life was the first meeting with G. K. *Chesterton in 1900. Thereafter the two were very close friends, influencing one another deeply, and collaborating in several books for which Belloc provided the text and Chesterton the drawings (Emmanuel Burden, 1904, etc.). Bernard *Shaw analysed them as a composite creature 'The Chesterbelloc' (The New Age, 15 February 1908). Of the 150 books written by Belloc, few are likely to survive, for the majority were on matters of current controversy. In The Verse of Hilaire Belloc (1954), the definitive collection, are a number of lyrics with a good claim to remembrance; The *Path to Rome (1902) is among the best travel books and is a memorial to Belloc's prowess as a walker, as The Cruise of the 'Nona' (1925) is

to his love of sailing. If the familiar essay recovers the popularity it had in the first quarter of the 20th century, such volumes as Belloc's On Nothing (1908), On Everything (1909), On Anything (1910), On Something (1910) will be disinterred, and his writings on World War I will have a curious interest in the future. As a historian he wrote much on battles and warfare generally, as well as on the French Revolution particularly, in a vigorous picturesque style and with a faculty for projecting himself backward as an eyewitness of past events. Those who did not share his religious faith charged him with tendentious rewriting of history in the interests of his Church, though this alleged distortion will be as undetectable by those who share his beliefs as it will appear undisguisable to those of other beliefs and none. He became a naturalized British citizen in 1902. Such of his poems as 'The South Country' show his love of Sussex, where he settled in 1906 with his wife (who died in 1914) at King's Land, in the village of Slindon near Horsham, his home to the end of his life.

Belloc Lowndes, Mrs. See Mrs Belloc *Lowndes.

Bellow, Saul (1915-　). Born in Canada of Russian descent; educated at the University of Chicago and the Northwestern University, Illinois. Author of Dangling Man (1944), The Adventures of Augie March (1953), Henderson the Rain King (1959), Herzog (1964), other novels and The Last Analysis (1967) and other plays.

Beloff, Max (1913-　). Educated at St Paul's School and Oxford. Professor of Government and Public Administration, Oxford, from 1957. Author of The Foreign Policy of Soviet Russia (vol I, 1947; vol II, 1949), The Age of Absolutism 1660-1815 (1954), Foreign Policy and the Democratic Process (1955), The Balance of Power (1967), etc.

Bemelmans, Ludwig (1898-　). Born in the (then Austrian) Tyrol of a Belgian father and Bavarian mother; proving resistant to schooling, he was apprenticed to an hotel-owning uncle. Failing to accommodate himself to that also, he emigrated to the U.S. in 1914 and again worked in hotels, until America entered World War I, when he enlisted and found in army life material for My War With the United States (1937). He had previously written and illustrated children's books and produced others later, but his reputation was made as a humorist with a unique sense of fun often at odds with his recurrent intention to write serious satire. Though his individual brand of humour does not appeal to all, he achieved considerable popularity in both America and England with *Life Class* (1938), *Hotel Splendide* (1941), *I Love You, I Love You, I Love You* (1942), *How to Travel Incognito* (1952), and other books illustrated by himself.

Benavente y Martinez, Jacinto (1866-1954). Born and educated in Madrid, where he studied law but turned to playwriting and became one of the leading Spanish dramatists of his time. In English translation *Plays: 1st, 2nd, 3rd, and 4th Series* were published in 1917, 1919, 1923, and 1924.

Benchley, Robert (Robert Charles Benchley, 1889-1945). Born in Worcester, Massachusetts; educated at Harvard. Worked as contributor and departmental editor on several leading American magazines, including *Life* and the *New Yorker*. He excelled as a humorist, and as a writer of brilliant nonsense achieved an international reputation. *Love Conquers All* (1922), *The Treasurer's Report* (1930), *From Bed to Worse* (1934), *Inside Benchley* (1942), *Chips Off the Old Benchley* (1949) are characteristic volumes. He also appeared in films and as a broadcaster.

Benda, Julien (1867-1956). Born in Paris; educated at the Sorbonne. As a literary and philosophical critic he was mainly concerned to uphold reason and intellect against the emotional, sensational, or mystical approach. He was particularly antagonistic to the views of *Bergson, but among his numerous works it was *La Trahison des Clercs* (1927; trans. by Richard *Aldington as *The Great Betrayal*, 1928) that reached the widest audience. In it he charged philosophers, scholars, preachers, literary men and artists generally with forsaking their proper intellectual, spiritual and aesthetic realm in order to join in 'the game of political passions'. This 'upheaval in the moral behaviour of humanity' began at the end of the 19th century, he declared, and had since spread in ever-widening circles until all classes were drawn into the ambit of universal hatred.

Benét, Stephen Vincent (1898-1943). Born in Bethlehem, Pennsylvania, brother of the following; educated in California, Georgia, and at Yale and in Paris. His outstanding works are the long narrative poem of the American Civil War, *John Brown's Body* (1928), and in prose *The Devil and Daniel Webster* (a short story about a New Hampshire farmer who sells his soul to the devil but is saved by the pleading of a guest) included in *Thirteen O'Clock* (1937) and used for the libretto of a one-act opera with the same title (1939) and music by Douglas Moore, who used another of Benét's stories, *The Headless Horseman* for an operetta (1937).

Benét, William Rose (1886-1950). Brother of the preceding and sometime husband of Elinor *Wylie. He wrote much verse, including the autobiographical *The Dust Which is God* (1941), several novels and children's books, compiled anthologies and reference works, and was at various times on the staff of the *Century Magazine*, the *Saturday Review of Literature*, and other periodicals.

Benjamin, Lewis S. *See* Lewis *Melville.

Bennett, Arnold (Enoch Arnold Bennett, 1867-1931). Born at Hanley, Staffordshire, son of a solicitor; educated at Burslem and Newcastle-under-Lyme. Began work in his father's office at the age of eighteen, as preparation for a law degree; but although, three years later, he became a clerk in a London firm of solicitors, he did not complete his legal studies nor continue in his father's profession. Before he left Hanley— one of the *Five Towns in which the best of his novels were subsequently centred— his mind and temperament had been firmly and lastingly impressed by the beliefs, cultural interests, and industrial operations of the people among whom his early life was passed. Even though he diverged from the austere Wesleyanism of the family, he not only created lifelike pictures of chapelgoers and their religious activities in several novels, but was always himself unseparated from the ingrained effects of that early environment. In *The Truth About an Author*, published in 1903 when he was thirty-six, he speaks of his early love for the novels of *Ouida, with their 'scenes of gilded vice', and adds that he would never be able to satisfy the taste for 'liaisons made under pink lampshades' with which they inspired him, since his 'puritanical ancestry and upbringing' would always inhibit such longings. In the same book, while detailing the miseries of freelance journalism to which he committed himself after receiving his first 'pen-money', he avers that while the experience was degrading, the one bright aspect was that he 'wrote everything with a nice regard for English; I would lavish a night on a few paragraphs'. Thus the puritanism of his forebears, which he rejected, was exchanged in him for a puritanism of the written word, a hard-won 'dexterity in the handling of sentences': his craftsman's conscience was as active as their differently animated conscience. One of his biographers has said that Bennett's family in Hanley, 'although rigid Wesleyan Methodists', were 'uncommonly musical, artistic, and bookish', but he himself declared that until he took up his quarters 'in the abode of some artists in Chelsea' he had 'scarcely heard the word "beautiful" applied to anything whatever, save confections like Gounod's "There is a green hill far away". Modern oak sideboards were called handsome, and Christmas cards were called pretty; and that was about all.' Authors' quarrels with the circumstances of their early life usually ignore the vital factor that their works are rooted in those circumstances and conditioned by them. Bennett went to London when he was twenty-one with, he declared, no immediate object save to escape from an intellectual and artistic environment which had long been irksome; yet, though he never returned to live in the Midlands, his literary success and profit grew from the creative use of that irksome environment. Before migrating, he had been commissioned by the editor of a local paper to contribute a weekly column on the affairs of the town, and while working in the London solicitor's office he wrote for a popular periodical articles on legal topics. He then won a twenty-guinea prize for a humorous abridgement of a sensational serial, but when the same mass appeal publication rejected an original story as being below their literary standard, he succeeded in placing it in the most fastidiously aesthetic magazine of the day *The Yellow Book* (vol VI, July 1895). The story, entitled 'A Letter Home', is set in London among down-and-outs, one of whom, taken to hospital, writes a letter which never reaches his mother in the north, since he dies before completing the address. That success encouraged him to begin a novel in the realistic mode of the day, 'grey, sinister, and melancholy'. His models were mostly foreign – Zola, Flaubert, Maupassant, and others – and he was also an admirer of George *Moore who, as a disciple of Zola, was then regarded as the leader of the British realistic school. Bennett's first novel, originally to have been called *In the Shadow*, was published as *A Man from the North* in 1898. The profit to the author amounted to the price of a new hat. While the novel was being written, Bennett had been assistant editor (1893) and then editor (1896) of *Woman*, exchanging his lawyer's-office salary of £200 a year (in the 1890s an impressive income for a young man) for £150 for a halftime post. For *Woman* he wrote social paragraphs in 'Gwendolen's Column', polished the English of cookery recipes, and concocted 'anything, from a eulogy of a philanthropic duchess to a Paris fashion letter', and 'spent scores of ineffectual hours' trying with little success to instruct writing-women in the management of English syntax. He also served as the paper's literary and dramatic critic, and was meanwhile writing book reviews for other periodicals and giving lessons in journalism. These abundant outlets and the readiness of editors to print his work made Bennett conscious of his flair for word-spinning. It is impossible to decide whether, among the eighty books he had written by the end of his life, there would be a larger number of enduring ones if he had written less easily. If he was a facile journalist he was also an admirable one; and if much of his total output was ephemeral, all of it remains readable. When he reached London, there lay dormant in his mind all the Five Towns material that was to bring him fame, yet it was an Irishman from outside who was to provide the stimulus, and that, apparently, at second-hand. George Moore's novel *A Mummer's Wife* had been published as long before as 1884. In 1910 Bennett wrote that he had just read it for the third or fourth time, and in 1920 he told Moore that it was the first chapters of this novel 'which opened my eyes to the romantic nature of the district that I had blindly inhabited for over twenty years. You are indeed the father of all my Five Towns books'. Not until 1930 did Bennett learn that the basic material for those chapters had been requested by Moore from an older inhabitant of the Potteries district. Nevertheless, George Moore was one of the four writers named by Bennett as his favourite masters and models; and, like Moore, he was drawn to France. There he went in March 1903, having by then published several novels and such non-fiction as *Journalism for Women* (1898) and *How to Become an Author* (1903), as well as the autobiographical volume already mentioned. He had also written serials for a syndicate, calling them 'fantasias'. Among these was the still enjoyable and amusingly extravagant *Grand Babylon Hotel* (1902). Up to the time he departed for Paris, the most important of his writings was *Anna of the Five Towns* (1902). Two years after he left, came *Tales of the Five Towns* (1905), a collection of short stories, and a further collection called *The Grim Smile of the Five Towns* in 1907. But not until 1908 did he progress from being a successful writer of fiction to becoming a famous novelist certain of long remembrance in English literature. *The *Old Wives' Tale* published in that year is his peak achievement, and among his Five Towns books is equalled only by parts of *Clayhanger*, the first volume of a trilogy continued with *Hilda Lessways* (1911) and completed with *These Twain* (1916): reissued in one volume as The Clayhanger Family (1925). A series of short books to which the general title Pocket Philosophies was given later, began with *The Reasonable Life* (1907). *Fame and Fiction* (1901) and *Books and Persons* (1917) are collections of criticism and essays, the latter volume containing a selection from his writings in *The New Age* under the pen-name Jacob Tonson. Bennett lived in France, mainly in Paris and Fontainebleau, until 1912. He married Marguerite Soulie in 1907, an inharmonious union ended by their separation in 1921. *The Old Wives' Tale* proved to be at first a slow-selling masterpiece, and two years after it was published he still owed his literary agent nearly £1,000; yet mainly by sheer industry in the various literary kinds and by driving himself incessantly, his year's income in 1912 was £16,000. During the earlier part of World War I he wrote topical articles for the *Daily News* and other papers, and in its later stages worked for the Ministry of Information, becoming in the last month of the war Director of Propaganda. All his official work was unpaid and at the end of

1918 he declined a knighthood. When after the *Clayhanger* trilogy was finished he ceased to write of the Five Towns, it seemed that his genius was in decline. But *Riceyman Steps* (1923) revived his reputation, and was the last novel that would be admitted to the canon of his best works by most critics, though the political novel *Lord Raingo* (1926) has admirers. *Imperial Palace* (1930), published in the year before he died, is symptomatic of his delight in the spectacle of efficient organization on the grand scale and in the human relationships of the men and women who supply the motive power. In the postwar years Bennett ventured considerable sums in patronage of theatrical enterprises, and he lived on an opulent scale which strained his financial resources. He was often admonished for his delight in abundant living and by some was accused of vulgar ostentation. But it is fairer to see him as a man to whom niggardliness was impossible: he worked to the utmost and enjoyed to the utmost; and it is always to be remembered that as a literary craftsman, regarding authorship as honest work to be done conscientiously and assiduously, he has had no equal since Anthony Trollope. Among Bennett's disappointments was his relative lack of success as a dramatist, apart from *Milestones* (of which he was only part author) and *The Great Adventure* adapted from his underrated novel *Buried Alive* (1908). In addition to his public writings, Bennett kept a *Journal* from 1896 until shortly before his death. In more than a million words during thirty-four years, as the editor observes, he revealed his personality more closely than in all his novels, and 'in the manner of a modern Pepys' (*The Journals* of Arnold Bennett, edited by Newman Flower, 3 vols, 1932-3).

Bennett, H. S. (Henry Stanley Bennett, 1889-1972). Educated at Cambridge. Was for six years an elementary school teacher in London before returning to Cambridge, where he became University Reader in English, and Librarian of Emmanuel College. Author of *The Pastons and their England* (1922), *England from Chaucer to Caxton* (1928), *Life of Christopher Marlowe* (1931), *Life on the English Manor* (1937), *English Books and Readers, 1475-1557* (1955), etc.

Bennett, Joan (*née* Joan Frankau, 1896-   ;

married H. S. *Bennett, 1920). Educated at Wycombe Abbey, and at Cambridge where she became Lecturer in English. Author of *Four Metaphysical Poets* (1934), *Virginia Woolf: Her Art as a Novelist* (1945), *George Eliot: Her Mind and her Art* (1948), etc.

Benson, Arthur Christopher (1862-1925). Brother of the two following, born at Wellington College, son of the headmaster (afterwards Archbishop of Canterbury); educated at Eton and Cambridge, became a housemaster at Eton, and from 1915 was Master of Magdalene College, Cambridge. The popularity of his several volumes of urbane essays—*From a College Window* (1906), etc.—did not outlast his own lifetime, and the peculiar limitations of his outlook were penetratingly exposed in one of the parodies in *A *Christmas Garland* by Max Beerbohm. With Viscount Esher he edited several volumes of *The Letters of Queen Victoria* and wrote the words of *Land of Hope and Glory* (1897), the popular patriotic song set to music by Edward Elgar for the Diamond Jubilee celebrations of Queen Victoria.

Benson, Edward Frederic (1867-1940). Brother of the preceding and following; educated at Marlborough and Cambridge; employed at the British School of Archaeology in Athens, 1892-95. A successful career as novelist began with *Dodo* (1893), a frivolous satire on current Society, in which the name character was alleged to be a caricature of Margot Tennant (later Countess of Oxford and *Asquith). Other Dodo books followed, and were succeeded by novels of differing types, including school stories (*David Blaize*, 1915, etc.) and occult tales; and by biographies—*Charlotte Brontë* (1932), *Edward VII* (1933). His only works of enduring interest are the reminiscential volumes *As We Were* (1930), *As We Are* (1932), and *Final Edition* (1940), which give an engaging and authentic portrait of his forebears and contemporaries.

Benson, Robert Hugh (1871-1914). Brother of the two preceding; educated at Eton and Cambridge; after being ordained in the Anglican Church and holding a curacy in London he became a Roman Catholic and was subsequently an official at the Papal Court. As a writer he produced both historical and modern novels with a Roman Catholic emphasis—*The King's Achievement*

(1905), *The Queen's Tragedy* (1906), *The Sentimentalists* (1908), and many others.

Benson, Stella (Mrs James Carew Anderson, 1892-1933). Novelist and writer of travel books. Ill health took her to Switzerland, the West Indies, California, and China. She engaged in social work in Hoxton (London), taught in a mission school in Hong Kong, worked in a hospital X-ray department in Peking, and after her marriage in 1921 lived almost entirely in China. *The Little World* (1925) is an attractive and humorous product of her travels, and among her various other writings *Tobit Transplanted* (1931), a novel, is outstanding. She also wrote short stories and poems.

Benson, Theodora (Hon. Eleanor Theodora Roby Benson, 1906-1968; daughter of 1st Baron Charnwood). Author of novels (*Salad Days*, 1928; *Glass Houses*, 1929; *Façade*, 1933; *Concert Pitch*, 1934; etc.), travel books (*The Unambitious Journey*, 1935; etc.), short stories (*Best Stories of Theodora Benson*, 1940), and humorous books in collaboration with Betty *Askwith.

Bentley, E. C. (Edmund Clerihew Bentley, 1875-1956). Born at Shepherd's Bush, London; educated at St Paul's School and Oxford, afterwards studied law and was called to the Bar in 1902, but thereafter devoted himself to journalism, mainly for the *Daily News* until 1912 and then for the *Daily Telegraph*. In collaboration with his sometime schoolfellow and lifelong friend G. K. *Chesterton (as illustrator) he produced *Biography for Beginners* (1905), written in a form of four-line comic nonsense verses which he invented and which, known as Clerihews, had a contemporary vogue challenging that of *Limericks. The pattern was set by the opening specimen: 'The art of Biography/Is different from Geography./Geography is about maps,/Biography is about chaps.' Although the Sherlock Holmes stories by Conan *Doyle continued to be popular, Bentley's *Trent's Last Case* (1913) is a landmark in the history of the detective novel, for it had the effect of making crime fiction a recognized literary form among intellectuals and was thus largely responsible for the writing as well as the reading of such fiction by university dons and their equals. Two other Trent books produced late in the 1930s made little impression. *Those Days* (1940) is Bentley's autobiography.

Bentley, Nicolas Clerihew (1907-   ; son of the preceding). Born in Highgate, London; educated at University College School and the Heatherley School of Art. Author of humorous books illustrated by himself.

Bentley, Phyllis (Phyllis Eleanor Bentley, 1894-   ). Born at Halifax, Yorkshire; educated there and at Cheltenham College. After some schoolteaching, government secretarial work in World War I, and library cataloguing, she brought out her first novel, *Environment* (1922), in that and later books using her Yorkshire background. She had her first outstanding success with *Inheritance* (1932), a story set in Yorkshire at the time of the Industrial Revolution, followed by *A Modern Tragedy* (1934), dealing with the same county during the Great Depression of the 1930s. She wrote *Here is America* (1941), worked during the later part of World War II in the Ministry of Information (American Division), and continued to write afterwards—a study of her famous Yorkshire predecessors, *The Brontës* (1947), and further novels, including *The Rise of Henry Morcar* (1946), *Panorama* (1952), *Sheep May Safely Graze* (1972).

Berdyayev, Nikolai Aleksandrovich (1874-1948). Born at Kiev and educated at the University there. Although he was appointed Professor of Philosophy in the University of Moscow after the Revolution which he had foretold and welcomed, he was dismissed in 1922 on account of his continued religious beliefs. He then founded an Academy of the Philosophy of Religion in Berlin, remaining there until the coming of the Nazi régime, after which (in 1934) he moved to France and re-established his Academy at Clamart (near Paris), where he died. He discarded not only Marxism but also other secular beliefs on his road to the final acceptance of a personal interpretation of Christianity. His writings have had a considerable influence through various translations. Following works on Russian history and philosophy, he wrote *Freedom and the Spirit* (1935), *Slavery and Freedom* (1944), *The Beginning and the End* (1952), *Truth and Revelation* (1954), and an autobiography, *Dream and Reality* (1950).

Berenson, Bernard (1865-1959). Born in Lithuania; his family emigrated to Boston in 1875, where he was educated and (with aid from a wealthy patron) at Harvard and Oxford. Meanwhile a visit to Florence had fired an intense and enduring love of Italian paintings, on which he became the most learned scholar of his time, writing many authoritative works on the artists and their pictures. There is an autobiographical current in most of his writings on art, but this is overt in *Sketch for a Self-Portrait* (1945), *Rumour and Reflection* (1952), *The Passionate Sightseer* (1960; extracts from his diaries, 1947-56), and *One Year's Reading for Fun* (1960). He was admired and, by many, revered as a great personality—'timeless and serene'—as well as an incomparable connoisseur.

Beresford, J. D. (John Davys Beresford, 1873-1947). Born at Castor in Northamptonshire; educated at Oundle and Peterborough. Handicapped by lameness due to infantile paralysis, he turned to writing, after years as a draughtsman in architects' offices. *Jacob Stahl* (1911), his first novel, received high praise from critics who ranked him with other beginning novelists (Compton *Mackenzie, Frank *Swinnerton, Hugh *Walpole, and others) who at that time seemed to foreshadow a distinguished new age in English fiction. *Jacob Stahl* (1911) began a trilogy completed with *A Candidate for Truth* (1912) and *The Invisible Event* (1915). These, *Goslings* (1913), and *The House in Demetrius Road* (1914) preceded a long succession of novels, usually produced at the rate of one a year, which continued to find a public; but their sincere, solid, traditional and unspectacular qualities made little impression upon a new generation of critics. Beresford lived in France for several years, but died in Bath. *Writing Aloud* (1928) treats of his methods as an author.

Bergson, Henri (1859-1941). Born in Paris of Anglo-Jewish parentage; educated at the Lycée Condorcet and Ecole Normale in Paris. Held teaching appointments at various provincial and other institutions before becoming Professor of Greek philosophy and afterwards of Modern Philosophy at the Collège de France from 1900 to 1921. From the date of publication of *Essai sur les données immédiates de la conscience* (1889; translated as *Time and Free Will*, 1910) to that of *Les Deux sources de la morale et de la religion* (1932; *The Two Sources of Morality and Religion*, 1935) Bergson was both an international leader of serious thought and the unwilling centre of a fashionable cult. His first book challenged commonly accepted views of the nature of Time, and put forward arguments (since made familiar by others) distinguishing between conventional clock 'time' and variable human experience of duration, a subject returned to in *Durée et simultanéité* (1922). His principal work, *L'Evolution creatrice* (1907; *Creative Evolution*, 1911), postulates the existence in living creatures of an impulse or energy he named *l'élan vital* which accounts for the divergent processes of evolution in human and other developing organisms. This theory was popularized in English by Bernard *Shaw whose doctrine of the *Life Force owed a great deal to Bergson. Among his other philosophical works are *Matiêre et mémoire* (1896; *Matter and Memory*, 1911), and *Le Rire* (1900; *Laughter*, 1911). He diagnosed instinct, intelligence, and intuition as life's operative agencies. In his last years Bergson adopted a bravely defiant attitude towards the pro-German Vichy government, and insisted on sharing the humiliations and disabilities imposed upon his fellow Jews by anti-Semitic decrees.

Berkeley, Anthony. A pseudonym of Anthony Berkeley *Cox, under which he wrote many detective novels: *The Silk Stocking Murders* (1928), *Top Storey Murder* (1931), *Trial and Error* (1937), etc. Cox also used the name Francis *Iles.

Berkeley Square. Play in three acts by John L. *Balderston (in collaboration with J. C. *Squire), published in 1929. The plot was suggested by Henry *James's posthumous fragment *The Sense of the Past*. The action takes place in a Queen Anne house in Berkeley Square, and presents the love story of Helen Pettigrew and Peter Standish, who are transported backward in time from 1928 to 1784.

Berlin, Sir Isaiah (1909-   ; knighted 1957). Born in London; educated at St Paul's School and Oxford. Held British diplomatic appointments at Washington (1942-45) and Moscow (1945-46). Professor of Social and Political Theory, Oxford, 1957. President of Wolfson College from 1966. Author of *Karl Marx* (1939), *The Hedgehog and the Fox* (1953), *The Inevitability of History* (1954), *The Age of Enlightenment* (1956), *Two Concepts of Liberty* (1959), *Mr Churchill in 1940* (1964), *Fathers and Children* (1972).

Bernal, John Desmond (1901-1971). Born in Ireland; educated at Stonyhurst, Bedford, and Cambridge. Professor of Physics University of London from 1938. Author of *The World, the Flesh, and the Devil* (1929), *The Social Function of Science* (1939), *The Physical Basis of Life* (1951), *Marx and Science* (1952), *Science in History* (1954; new edn 1957).

Bernanos, Georges (1888-1948). Born in Paris; educated at the University and Catholic Institute there. From the late 1930s until 1945 he lived in Brazil, but then returned to France after having been an influential propagandist for General de Gaulle while in South America. His early royalist and right wing sympathies gave way to Christian convictions ardently and sometimes mystically expressed with an admixture of romantico-religious extravagance. He became known abroad mainly by the novels translated as *Diary of a Country Priest* (*Le Journal d'un curé de campagne*, 1936), and *The Star of Satan* (*Sous le soleil de Satan*, 1940).

Bernard, Jean Jacques (1888-1972). Born at Enghien-les-Bains, son of the following; educated in Paris. Author of plays, short stories, novels, and a description of life in a concentration camp for French Jews, *Le Camp de la mort lente: Compiègne 1941-1942* (1945). His most distinctive work was as a writer of plays in which an exquisite sensitiveness and depth of feeling are rendered in an atmosphere of stillness: *Martine* (1922; English translation 1927) and *L'Ame en peine* (1926; *The Unquiet Spirit*, 1932) are outstanding.

Bernard, Tristan (*né* Paul Bernard, 1866-1947). Father of the preceding. Born at Besançon. Author of plays and novels which had a great vogue in France, where he was chiefly noted as a humorist and wit.

Berners, Lord (Gerald Hugh Tyrwhitt-Wilson, 14th Baron Berners, 1883-1950). Born at Bridgnorth, Shropshire; educated at Eton; in the diplomatic service, 1909-19. Thereafter he followed his threefold interest in musical composition, writing, and painting, winning distinction in the first two. His ballets were produced by the Diaghilev company and by the Sadler's Wells and Covent Garden companies (*The Triumph of Neptune*, 1926; *A Wedding Bouquet*, 1937; *Cupid and Psyche* 1939; *Les Sirènes*,

1946), and he also wrote a variety of less-known instrumental pieces. Both as composer and as author he was a skilled parodist and a good-humoured satirist. Two autobiographical volumes give amusing glimpses of his early life, *First Childhood* (1934) and *A Distant Prospect* (1945); while among his satirico-humorous short novels are *The Camel* (1936), *Count Omega* (1941), and *The Romance of a Nose* (1941).

Bernhardt, Sarah. Stage name of Henriette Rosine Bernard (1844-1923). French actress with an international reputation as the greatest tragedienne of her time, an exceptionally lovely voice being among her gifts. She excelled in Racine's *Phèdre*, in plays by Victor Hugo, Dumas the younger, Sardou and Rostand, and essayed the name part in Shakespeare's *Hamlet* as well as Cordelia in *King Lear*. She performed frequently in England and the U.S. Her stage career continued even after the amputation of a leg when she was past seventy years old.

Bertillon, Alphonse (1853-1914). French anthropologist and police chief who developed a scientific system of identification of criminals based on the classification of physical measurements. Although he is sometimes popularly credited with the invention of the finger-print method of detection, this was in fact largely the work of Sir Francis Galton (1822-1911), who published *Finger Prints* (1893) and *Fingerprint Directory* (1895).

Besant, Mrs Annie (*née* Annie Wood, 1847-1933). Of Irish descent, she was privately educated, and rejected Christianity a few years after marrying (in 1867) the Rev. Frank Besant, from whom she separated in 1873. Thereafter she engaged in a succession of varied political, religious, and anti-religious activities which embraced atheism, socialism, Indian nationalism, and theosophy. Her link with contemporary literature was through Bernard *Shaw, being one of his early admirers and publishing two or three of his novels in small magazines which she controlled.

Besier, Rudolf (1878-1942). Born in Java; educated in Guernsey and Heidelberg. His early plays (e.g. *The Virgin Goddess*, 1908; *Don*, 1909; *Lady Patricia*, 1912) had a moderately good reception, but with *The *Barretts of Wimpole Street* (1930) he scored a huge success both in England and in America.

Best Seller. Publisher's term for a book which is bought in large numbers, usually soon after publication. Often the number sold is unspecified and the term may be only an advertising catchpenny appealing to those who reach for what 'everyone is reading'. The life of most such books is brief; the genuine best seller is one in steady demand for many years.

Besterman, Theodore (Theodore Deodatus Nathaniel Besterman, 1904-   ). Author of an extensive range of bibliographical works; books on psychical research—*The Mind of Annie Besant* (1928), *Mrs Annie Besant: A Modern Prophet* (1934); *Men against Women: A Study of Sexual Relations* (1934), *The Pilgrim Fathers* (1939); and various writings on Voltaire, including a ten-volume edition of his letters and a full-scale biography (1969). Director of the Institut et Musée Voltaire, Geneva.

Betham-Edwards, Matilda Barbara (1836-1919). Born at Westerfield, Sussex; travelled much, particularly in France; wrote *French Men, Women, and Books* (1910) and *Twentieth Century France* (1917); also verse and many novels, *The Lord of the Harvest* (1899) being the best of the latter.

Bethell, Mary Ursula (1874-1945). Born in Surrey; educated in England and New Zealand; studied music and painting. Social worker in London and Scotland, 1898-1902. Author of novels—*From a Garden in the Antipodes* (1929), *Time and Space* (1936), *Day and Night* (1939). *Collected Poems* (1950). *See* New Zealand Writers.

Betjeman, Sir John (1906-   ; knighted 1969). Educated at Marlborough and Oxford. He became widely known and popular as a radio broadcaster on architecture, and particularly as an advocate of English Victorian church architecture, which had long been derided by critics. Meanwhile he was issuing small books of poems—*Continual Dew* (1937), *New Bats in Old Belfries* (1940), *Old Lights for New Chancels* (1945), *A Few Late Chrysanthemums* (1954)—in which serious themes often appeared in apparently light verse in simple lyrical forms. His *Selected Poems* (1948) was acclaimed, but with the publication of *John Betjeman's Collected Poems* (1958) he had the rare experience for a poet of becoming a best-seller, 100,000 copies being sold in the original edition. This success, in which he was aided by the critics as well as the public, gave a fillip to his more ambitious and lengthy autobiographical poem, *Summoned by Bells* (1960). Poet Laureate, 1972.

Betteridge, Don. *See* Bernard *Newman.

Betti, Ugo (1892-1953). Born at Camerino, Italy; received a classical education at Parma and studied law, but his practice was interrupted by military service in World War I, during part of which he was a prisoner of war in Germany. Resuming practice afterwards, he was eventually a high court judge in Rome from 1930. He displayed a remarkable literary talent while still adolescent, and pursued a twofold career in literature and law, producing several volumes of poems and short stories, a novel, and over a score of plays. With the latter he achieved an international reputation rivalling that of *Pirandello. In *Three Plays* (1956) Henry Reed presented English translations of *La Regina e gli Insorti* (1949, *The Queen and the Rebels*), *Aiuola Bruciata* (1951-2, *The Burnt Flower-Bed*), and *Il Paesa delle Vacanza* (1937, *Summertime*). His translator describes Betti's plays as usually 'tragic in cast, and often violent, frightening or bizarre. . . . His subject is wickedness' and all his later plays are concerned with some aspect of 'men's fatal disregard or defiance of God'.

Between the Acts. Novel by Virginia *Woolf published in 1941.

Bevan, Edwyn Robert (1870-1943). Born in London; educated at Monkton Combe and Oxford; after losing inherited wealth in a financial crash he became Lecturer in Hellenistic History and Literature in the University of London, 1922-33. He wrote on religion and on classical subjects: *Symbolism and Belief* (1938), *Hellenism and Christianity* (1921), *The House of Seleucus* (on Hellenistic history; 1902), *Stoics and Sceptics* (1913), *The Land of the Two Rivers* (on Mesopotamia; 1917).

Beveridge, Lord (William Henry Beveridge, 1879-1963; knighted, 1919; 1st baron, 1946). Born at Rangpur, Bengal; educated at Charterhouse and Oxford. Leader-writer on *Morning Post* (1906-8), then held various civil service and government appointments concerned with employment, food supplies, etc. Director of the London School of

Economics 1919-37, meanwhile serving on statutory and other official committees on the coal industry, national insurance, and other social services. As Chairman of the Inter-Departmental Committee on Social Insurance and Allied Services (1941-42) he played an important part in planning for the postwar period (see *Beveridge and his Plan*, 1954, by his wife, Lady Beveridge, *née* Janet Philip) and must be regarded as one of the principal architects of the Welfare State. His many writings on public affairs include *Unemployment: A Problem of Industry* (1909; new edn 1930), *Insurance for All* (1924), *Changes in Family Life* (1932), *Planning under Socialism* (1936), *Pillars of Security* (1943), *Full Employment in a Free Society* (1944).

Bibesco (or Bibescu), **Princess** (*née* Elizabeth Charlotte Lucy Asquith, 1897-). Daughter of Herbert Henry and Margot Asquith. Married in 1919 Prince Antoine Bibesco (Bibescu), sometime Rumanian ambassador to the U.S. and Spain. She wrote novels—*The Fir and the Palm* (1923), *The Whole Story* (1925), *There is No Return* (1927), *Portrait of Caroline* (1931), *The Romantic* (1940); *Haven* (short stories etc., 1951, collected posthumously); and *I Have Only Myself to Blame* (1922). For close personal impressions of Prince Antoine *see* Enid *Bagnold's *Autobiography* (1969).

Bibesco, Princess (*née* Marthe Lucie Mahovary, 1887-1945; married Prince George Bibesco of Rumania in 1903). Born in Rumania; educated in France where most of her life was spent. Author of novels, biographies, and travel books, including a reminiscential volume on *Proust, many of which have been translated into English and other languages.

Bibliography. A loosely used word which may denote either (*a*) a short list of books setting down works by a particular author or on a stated subject; or (*b*) a minutely exhaustive description of the physical make-up, publishing history, etc. of an author's complete writings, or of writings by sundry authors purposely grouped. Bibliography of the latter type is both a science and an art demanding training and expertise. The Edinburgh Bibliographical Society was founded in 1890 and the Bibliographical Society in London in 1892.

Bickerstaffe-Drew, Francis Browning Drew. *See* John *Ayscough.

Bierce, Ambrose (Ambrose Gwinett Bierce, 1842-1914). Born in Ohio; mainly self-educated by reading at home, where his father was a farmer. After serving in the Civil War he was employed as a journalist in San Francisco before migrating to England from 1872 to 1876 where he worked on the staff of *Fun* and published collections of his satirical writings—*The Fiend's Delight* (1872) and others—under the pseudonym Dod Grile. Returning to America in 1876 he resumed journalism in San Francisco, and after much miscellaneous writing produced *Tales of Soldiers and Civilians* (1891; reissued in 1898 under its better-known title *In the Midst of Life*). This volume contains at least two pieces, 'A Horseman in the Sky' and 'An Occurrence at Owl Creek Bridge', which have placed him among the foremost masters of the short story. Though he wrote numerous later stories, sketches, and verses he did not again reach so high a level, for he had only an uncertain control of his literary weapons of irony, sardonic humour and disillusion. He finally turned his back on the society whose standards revolted him and went to Mexico during one of its civil wars. He never returned and the manner of his death is unknown. *Collected Works*, 12 vols, 1909-12; *Letters*, 1922.

Big Brother. The leader whose face is on all the posters captioned 'Big Brother is Watching You' in George Orwell's *Nineteen Eighty-Four* (1949).

Big Steamers. A poem written in World War I by Rudyard *Kipling to enforce attention to the service of the Merchant Navy. It ends: '. . . if any one hinders our coming you'll starve'.

Biggles. *See* W. E. *Johns.

Bill of Divorcement, A. Play in three acts by Clemence *Dane, produced at the St Martin's Theatre, London, on 14 March 1921. Set in the hall and the drawing room of 'a small house in the country'. It is assumed that 'the recommendations of the Majority Report of the Royal Commission on Divorce and Matrimonial Causes have become the law of the land' by the date on which the action takes place (Christmas Day 1933, i.e. twelve years ahead of the date of the first production). Hilary Fairfield, shell-shocked in the war and belonging to a family with an hereditary strain of insanity, returns home unannounced after escaping from the asylum in which he has been for fifteen years. He finds that his wife Margaret is about to marry Gray Meredith, having obtained a divorce under a new law which allows insanity as a ground for ending a marriage. Hilary's repeated hysterical pleas for her to receive him back as her husband at length break her down with pity, and she tells Meredith that she must withdraw her promise to marry him. But her young daughter Sydney brings her mother and Meredith together again, forswearing her intention to marry Kit Pumphrey lest any children they might have should inherit the taint of insanity. The play ends with Sydney's declaration to her father that she will remain with him and make their home together. Hester Fairfield, Sydney's bitter puritanical spinster aunt, and the Rev. Christopher Pumphrey, the local rector, who refuses to marry any divorced person, represent the spirit of intolerance against which Sydney as a representative of the younger generation is in (also intolerant) revolt.

Billing, Noel Pemberton (1880-1948). Journalist; M.P. 1916-21. He was the central figure in a notorious action brought against him by Maud *Allan in 1918. Posing as a super-patriot, he alleged that the Germans possessed a 'Black Book' in which they had entered the names of a large number of prominent persons whom in certain circumstances they could blackmail into treason. The case, brought before Mr Justice Darling, was scandalously misconducted, for Billing flouted all judicial principles while conducting his own defence. He defied the judge, and led one of his own witnesses to assert that Darling's own name was in the sinister but in all probability wholly fictitious Black Book. By invoking the still unrehabilitated ghost of Oscar *Wilde (in a performance of whose *Salome* Maud Allan had performed the Dance of the Seven Veils), and by hysterical innuendoes against men in high positions which played upon the patriotic fears of the jury at a critical stage of World War I, Billing won a case which the judge had allowed him to degrade to a rowdy melodrama.

Bindloss, Harold (1866-1945). Born in Liverpool, but did not settle permanently in England until 1896, after he had spent several years at sea and in Africa and Canada. He then became a journalist and from 1898 to 1940 the author of a large number of adventure novels, mainly in colonial settings: *A Wide Dominion* (1899), *The League of the Leopard* (1904), *The Secret of the Reef* (1915), *The Man from the Wilds* (1922), *The Lady of the Plain* (1935).

Bingham, John (John Michael Ward Bingham, 1908-1960; 7th Baron Clanmorris). Educated at Cheltenham and in France and Germany. Practised as a journalist in London and the provinces. Civil Assistant at War Office from 1950. Succeeded to the title 1960. Author of crime novels: *My Name is Michael Sibley* (1952), *Five Roundabouts to Heaven* (1953), *The Paton Street Case* (1955), *Night's Black Agent* (1961), and others.

Binyon, Laurence (Robert Laurence Binyon, 1893-1943). Educated at St Paul's School and Oxford, where he won the Newdigate Prize for a poem, *Persephone*. On the staff of the British Museum—in the Department of Printed Books, 1893-95, and the Department of Prints and Drawings, 1895-1933. He compiled a comprehensive official catalogue (4 vols, 1898-1907) of the Museum's collection of drawings, and in *Painting in the Far East* (1908) spoke authoritatively on Chinese and Japanese art, as he did also in lectures on that of India and Persia. In addition he published books on Botticelli, Blake, the English Water-Colour Painters and *Landscape in English Art and Poetry* (1931). From his student years he wrote poetry, issued at intervals in individual volumes and assembled in *Collected Poems* (1931), with later additions. Though he had no large public for the generality of his verse, a poem written in the early months of World War I—'For the Fallen'—made his name known throughout the English-speaking world. Lines from it are carved on the wall beside the entrance to the British Museum as a memorial to members of the staff who died in the War.

Biography (1). The practice of biography as a literary art has never flourished in England. Boswell's masterpiece owes its pre-eminence to personal devotion to its subject more than to any conscious purpose of literary creation; and of the few other biographies holding high rank by the beginning of the present century—such as Southey's *Nelson*, Lockhart's *Scott*, Mrs Gaskell's *Charlotte Brontë*—only the last-named is still actively esteemed. In this century, John Morley's *Gladstone* (1903) has not maintained its

early reputation, but Sir Edward Cook's *Florence Nightingale* (1913) has in some degree emerged from the shadow cast by Lytton *Strachey's essay in *Eminent Victorians* (1918)—in which it was nevertheless praised—and has withstood the competition of Cecil *Woodham-Smith's *Florence Nightingale* (1950). It is a melancholy fact that no contemporary poet, playwright or novelist has been made the subject of a biography that is itself notable as literature, though Michael Holroyd's *Lytton Strachey* (1967-8) has merits unobscured by its excessive length. Since the one-man temporary revolution in biographical writing effected by Strachey himself depended upon brevity and irony, it seems the inverted crown of irony that his own life story is extended to above 1200 pages in two volumes. The true verdict on his *Eminent Victorians* remains in suspense, for whereas the literary brilliance and the wit and irony are superb, the evident malice cannot be reconciled with the reasonable requirements of unslanted biography. But if the final verdict is in doubt, there is no question that Strachey's immediate influence on biographical writing in general was disastrous. The immense popular success of his *Eminent Victorians* and *Queen Victoria* (1921) made biography suddenly appear a profitable medium, and through the next decade or so there poured out a spate of biographies in which the genuine intellectual skill and literary distinction of Strachey were degraded to technical trickery and pert denigration: the debunking epidemic had set in and recovery was slow. But though such rogue productions are to be dismissed as vulgar fictionalizations, orthodox biography is handicapped by problems peculiar to itself. For every notable public figure, civil or military, a biography must needs be written within a measurable time after death as a historical necessity. But no such biography can be other than a partial portrait: too little information is available, the susceptibilities of relatives and friends hamper the biographer and may out of piety intentionally distort the portrait. Very rarely can an eminent person be as faithfully portrayed within little more than a decade of his death as was George V in 1952 by Harold *Nicolson. There the biographer's literary ability and practical experience in affairs of state met no untowardly imposed obstacles. In the majority of instances, however, there must be more or less of distancing between the biographer and his subject, as with David *Cecil's *The Stricken Deer* (1929) on William Cowper, Duff *Cooper's *Talleyrand* (1932), Noel *Annan's *Leslie Stephen* (1951), Roy Jenkins's *Sir Charles Dilke* (1958) and *Asquith* (1964). The eminence of the author as statesman gives special distinction to (Sir) Winston *Churchill's biographical writings —the life of his father (Lord) *Randolph Churchill* (1906) and that of his ancestor John Churchill, 1st Duke of Marlborough, *Marlborough* (1933-38). By the mid-century biographies had proliferated more as an industry than as an art, under the fostering influence of grants from philanthropic trusts, foundations, fellowships, etc., mainly American. Many such products were exhaustingly long, excessively documented, humorlessly annotated, and discouraging to readers as well as sometimes unserviceable to their human subjects.

Biography (2). Poem of 272 lines in rhyming couplets by John *Masefield, first printed in the *English Review* and included in *Philip the King and Other Poems* (1914). It surveys the author's sea-going experiences, friendships, wanderings in London (with J. M. *Synge) and other memories.

Biometrika. A quarterly journal for the statistical study of biological problems; founded in 1902 by Karl *Pearson and edited by him until 1930.

Bird, Cyril Kenneth. See Fougasse.

Bird in Hand. Comedy in three acts by John *Drinkwater first performed at the Birmingham Repertory Theatre on 3 September 1927. The scene is the country inn of the play's title, in Gloucestershire. The local squire's son, Gerald Arnwood, is unofficially courting Joan Greenleaf, only daughter of the innkeeper, who objects to the association on the traditional ground that social classes should not mix. Joan is defiant in continuing to meet Gerald, and her mother, believing them to be honestly in love, supports her. Thinking he has found them in a compromising situation, the innkeeper, Thomas Greenleaf, is prepared to take violent action, but in a comic night scene he is out-argued by three overnight visitors to the inn—Mr Blanquet (a sardine salesman), Cyril Beverley (idle son of a

titled yeast manufacturer), and Ambrose Godolphin K.C. Next morning Gerald's father, Sir Robert Arnwood, comes to visit Joan's father and by means of a verbal ruse inveigles him into agreeing to the marriage.

Birkenhead, 1st Earl of (Frederick Edwin Smith, 1872-1930; baronet, 1918; baron, 1919; viscount, 1921; earl, 1922). Born at Birkenhead; educated at the Grammar School there and at Oxford. Called to the Bar 1899 and quickly established himself as an outstandingly brilliant advocate. Entering the House of Commons as Conservative M.P. for a Liverpool constituency in 1906, he as quickly achieved a second reputation as political orator, witty and pugnacious, admired and hated. He became Attorney-General in 1915 and Lord Chancellor in 1919. Though he was a co-leader with Lord Carson in Ulster's plan *c.* 1913-14 for armed resistance if Irish Home Rule were imposed on the Northern Provinces, he took a leading part in the Irish settlement in 1921. He was Secretary of State for India, 1924-28, but subsequently left politics for directorships in the City of London. A sentence in his address as Rector of Glasgow University on 7 November 1923-'The world continues to offer glittering prizes to those who have stout hearts and sharp swords'—provoked a wave of antagonism from those who considered it an incitement to belligerency, even as an earlier speech (against the Disestablishment of the Welsh Church) provoked G. K. *Chesterton's verses 'Antichrist, or the Reunion of Christendom'. Birkenhead wrote valuable law books and, towards the end of his life, popular volumes such as *Contemporary Personalities* (1924), *Famous Trials of History* (1926), etc., and an autobiography, *Law, Life, and Letters* (1927).

Birkett, Lord (William Norman Birkett, 1883-1962; knighted 1951; baron 1958). Born at Ulverston, Lancashire; educated at Barrow-in-Furness and Cambridge. Called to the Bar, 1913, and became a successful defender in criminal trials. Entered Parliament as Liberal M.P. for a Nottingham constituency in 1923 but ceased to be a candidate after defeat in 1931. His legal successes were attained by quiet persuasion as contrasted with the emotional appeals of some contemporary advocates, and after his retirement from the Courts (he was a judge from 1941 to 1957) his scrupulous fairness enabled him to serve as a valuable intermediary, notably in averting the threatened printers' strike in 1951. As a man of liberal and humane interests he was an appropriate and well appreciated President of the *National Book League.

Birkin, Rupert. Inspector of Schools in D. H. Lawrence's *Women in Love* (1920); resigns and marries Ursula Brangwen.

Birmingham, George A. (pseudonym of James Owen Hannay, 1865-1950). Born in Belfast; educated at Haileybury and Trinity College, Dublin. He was ordained in the Protestant communion, held livings in Ireland and in England, and served as a chaplain in France during World War I and later at the British Embassy in Budapest. From such works as *The Spirit and Origin of Christian Monasticism* (1903) he turned to the writing of humorous novels and plays, having immediate success with *Spanish Gold* (1908) and in the London theatre with *General John Regan* (1913). His output of fiction was large and, over a long period, annual; but from time to time he wrote again on religion, was an admirable preacher, and served his parishioners with devotion.

Birmingham Repertory Theatre. Opened in 1913 by Barry Vincent Jackson (knighted 1925) who had for some years actively sponsored The Pilgrim Players, an amateur company with distinguished players and playwrights among its members. The new theatre quickly became an important centre, producing Shakespeare and other classics, English and foreign, as well as plays by Shaw, Galsworthy and other contemporaries.

Birney, Earle (Alfred Earle Birney, 1904-   ). Born in Calgary, Alberta; educated at Canadian universities and the Universities of California and London. Professor of English, University of British Columbia, 1946; Writer-in-residence, University of Toronto, 1965. Author of *David and other Poems* (1942), *Now is Time* (1945), *The Strait of Anian* (1952), *Selected Poems* (1966); a poetic drama, *Trial of a City* (1952); travel, *Ice Cold Bell or Stone* (1962), *Near False Creek Mouth* (1964); novels, *Turvey* (1949), *Down the Long Table* (1955); literary essays, *The Creative Writer* (1966).

Birrell, Augustine (1850-1933). Statesman, barrister, and essayist; born at Wavertree,

near Liverpool; educated at Caversham and Cambridge; called to the Bar, 1875; Professor of Law in the University of London, 1896-9; M.P. for West Fife, 1889-1900; for North Bristol, 1906-18; President of the Board of Education, 1905-7; Secretary of State for Ireland, 1907-16. Though he survived violent political storms centring on the Education measures of 1902 and 1906 and on the Home Rule for Ireland struggle, he was not by temperament a forceful politician. His reputation rests on the urbane essays published in *Obiter Dicta* (1st series 1884; 2nd series, 1887) and *More Obiter Dicta* (1924); his *Charlotte Brontë* (1887) was an unhackneyed contribution to Brontë studies.

Bitch-goddess. In a letter to H. G. *Wells in 1906, William *James wrote of 'the moral flabbiness born of the exclusive worship of the bitch-goddess Success'. The origination of the term has been mistakenly attributed to later writers.

Björnson, Björnstjerne (1832-1910). Born and educated in Norway. He worked as a newspaper editor and theatrical manager, as well as writing on politics and producing novels and plays. As a dramatist he was only less eminent in his time and country than *Ibsen his contemporary, but his plays had no equivalent success abroad. English translations have appeared (in Everyman's Library) of *Three Dramas* ('The Editor'; 'The Bankrupt'; 'The King') and *Three Comedies* ('The Newly-Married Couple'; 'Leonarda'; 'A Gauntlet').

Black. Cant term applied in industrial disputes to a firm, ship, etc. for or on which labour is prohibited during a strike.

Black and Tans. British auxiliaries in Ireland who fought unsuccessfully to quell the rebellion 1919-22. They were thus named locally on account of the colours of their uniform.

Black Book. An almost certainly mythical German secret-service compilation alleged by Noel Pemberton *Billing to contain the names of 47,000 British men and women supposed to be addicted to unspecified criminal practices and therefore susceptible to enemy blackmail in World War I. It was never produced, but the defendant's allegations made it the central feature in the libel action brought by Maud *Allan against Billing in 1918.

Black Comedy. Term applied to certain plays and novels in which humour is derived from the authors' sense of the absurdity or total meaninglessness of human existence— as in the works of Samuel *Beckett and Eugene *Ionesco—or, at its extreme, from horror or moral obliquity as in plays by Friedrich Durrenmatt and Jean Genet. It can be regarded as an aberrant product of postwar decivilization in which anti-art warred against art and traditional conceptions suffered inversion. See also *Sick humour.

Black Girl. See The *Adventures of the Black Girl in Her Search for God, by Bernard *Shaw.

Blackmur, Richard Palmer (1904-1965). Born in Massachusetts; educated there at Cambridge Latin School. Worked on editorial staffs of literary periodicals before becoming Professor of English at Princeton University from 1951 (with a year in England as visiting Pitt Professor at Cambridge, 1961-2). Although his collected volumes of verse (From Jordan's Delight, 1937; The Second World, 1942; The Good European, 1947) won him esteem as a poet, his influence as a critic was more marked. Since none of his writings aimed at ease of presentation or pure enjoyment of literature, he was attuned to the contemporary 'New Criticism' which gave priority to intensive textual scholarship, and it was this trend that brought him acclaim for The Expense of Greatness (1940), Language as Gesture (1952), The Lion and the Honeycombe (1955), Form and Value in Modern Poetry (1957).

Blackwood, Algernon (Algernon Henry Blackwood, 1869-1951). Born in Kent, educated at Wellington School and Edinburgh; worked in Canada for some time from about 1900, but later devoted himself to the writing of novels and short stories largely on occult themes, from among which John Silence (1908) made the most enduring impression. He also wrote children's books and an autobiography, Episodes Before Thirty (1923).

Blackwood's Edinburgh Magazine. Founded in 1817 by the Scottish publisher William Blackwood, originally as Edinburgh Monthly Magazine. Competing with the *Edinburgh Review and the *Quarterly Review it attracted many distinguished contributors and achieved lasting notoriety with its attack on the 'Cockney School of Poetry' including Keats. It became familiarly known as 'Maga'.

Bladesover. The mansion and estate where George Ponderevo's mother is housekeeper in H. G. Wells's *Tono Bungay (1909). Though there fictitiously named, it has actual existence as Uppark, near Petersfield in Sussex, now a National Trust property.

Blaine, Amory. See *Amory Blaine.

Blair, Eric Arthur. See George *Orwell.

Blake, George (1893-1961). Born in Glasgow; educated at Greenock Academy. His law studies were interrupted by World War I, during which he was severely wounded in Gallipoli. After the war he settled to journalism, being in turn book-reviewer and editor before becoming briefly a member of a publishing firm. His first novel was issued in 1923, but it was with Young Malcolm (1926) that he established himself as a novelist, gaining further repute with The Shipbuilders (1935), a subject with which he was well qualified to deal since his family were shipbuilders. In addition to numerous other novels, he wrote Down to the Sea (1937) and The Firth of Clyde (1952) both the outcome of his first-hand knowledge of the Scottish shipyards.

Blake, Nicholas. Pseudonym under which Cecil *Day-Lewis wrote detective novels: The Beast Must Die (1938), The Smiler With the Knife (1939), Malice in Wonderland (1940), The Case of the Abominable Snowman (1941), Head of a Traveller (1949), etc.

Blakeney, Sir Percy. 'The *Scarlet Pimpernel' in Baroness Orczy's novel with that title (1905). He married Marguerite St Just.

Blanche, Anthony. Flamboyant wit and aesthete in Evelyn Waugh's *Brideshead Revisited (1945).

Bland, Fabian. Pseudonym under which Hubert *Bland and Edith *Nesbit wrote The Prophet's Mantle (1888).

Bland, Hubert (1856-1914). A prominent member of the *Fabian Society; husband of Edith *Nesbit. Author of With the Eyes of a Man (essays; 1905), Letters to a Daughter (1906), The Happy Moralist (1907), Olivia's Latchkey (1913).

Bland, Mrs Hubert. See E. *Nesbit.

Blandamer, The Lords. Their coat of arms provides the title of J. Meade Falkner's novel The *Nebuly Coat (1903). The living claimant to the title is an impostor, but the fact remains unpublicized and his marriage to Anastasia, the daughter of the late rightful heir, restores the succession to the true line through their son. The claimant is killed when the tower of Cullerne Minster crashes.

Blast. See Wyndham *Lewis.

Blatchford, Robert (Robert Peel Glanville Blatchford, 1851-1943). Born at Maidstone of parents who were stage players. After having broken his apprenticeship to a brushmaker he joined the army and served from 1871 to 1878. To add to his insufficient wage as a timekeeper he turned to writing, and in 1885 became a writer of leading articles for the Sunday Chronicle, losing that connection when he turned Socialist in 1891. He then founded The Clarion as a socialist periodical, making it a success and contributing to it a series of articles published separately in 1893 as Merrie England and achieving an ultimate circulation estimated as over two million. After World War I, which Blatchford supported, he ran articles in The Clarion attacking orthodox religion, and for a time was denounced as a blasphemer. He became a freelance journalist after The Clarion failed, and in 1931 brought out his autobiography, My Eighty Years.

Blenkinsop, Dr. The honest, decent, almost penniless physician suffering from tuberculosis in Bernard Shaw's The *Doctor's Dilemma (1906).

Blimp, Colonel. Invented by David *Low in cartoons to represent a type of elderly Englishman with reactionary opinions and high blood-pressure.

Bliss, Judith. Retired glamorous actress and leading character in Noel Coward's *Hay Fever (1925). David her husband; Simon and Sorel their son and daughter.

Blithe Spirit. A comedy (1941) by Noel *Coward.

Blixen, Karen (née Karen Christence Dinesen, 1885-1962; married Baron Carl Frederick Blixen-Finecke, 1914). Born in Denmark; educated in Copenhagen, and studied painting there and in Paris and Rome. After marriage settled in Kenya and,

following her divorce from Baron Blixen, managed the coffee plantation there from 1921-31. She then returned to Denmark and wrote Seven Gothic Tales (1934), Out of Africa (1938), Winter Tales (1942), Last Tales (1957), Anecdotes of Destiny (1958) and Shadows on the Grass (1960). Though she used the pseudonym Isak Dinesen she was equally well known as Karen Blixen. During the Nazi occupation of her country in World War II she used the pseudonym Pierre Andrézel for a novel afterwards translated as The Angelic Avengers (1946), a symbolic satire on the invaders.

Blok, Alexander (Aleksander Aleksandrovich Blok, 1880-1921). Born in St Petersburg, son of a professor of law at the University of Warsaw; studied at the University of St Petersburg. Published his first poems (influenced by the symbolists) in 1904 (Verses to the Lady Beautiful). He early developed enthusiasm for the revolutionary movements in Russia and after the Bolshevik victory produced his masterpiece The Twelve (Dvenadtsat, 1918), generally regarded as the greatest poetic achievement in Soviet literature, followed by The Scythians (Skify, 1920).

Blom, Eric Walter (1888-1959). Author of many books on musical subjects and editor of the 5th edition of Grove's Dictionary of Music and Musicians.

Bloom, Leopold. Jewish advertisement canvasser in James Joyce's *Ulysses (1922).

Bloom, Molly. Wife of the central character in *Ulysses by James Joyce. Her prolonged *interior monologue in the final chapter is an outstanding example of the stream-of-consciousness method.

Bloomsbury Group, The. Name given to certain writers and painters who lived and met in that west-central district of London c. 1910-1940. They included Virginia and Leonard *Woolf, Lytton *Strachey, J. M. *Keynes; and, more occasionally, E. M. *Forster, Bertrand *Russell, and Desmond *MacCarthy. The artists included Douglas Grant, Vanessa *Bell (sister of Virginia Woolf), Roger *Fry and others. They achieved considerable distinction in their varied fields, but incurred some contemporary disapproval of their unorthodox principles and assumption of intellectual superiority. Though they denied being in any formal sense a 'group', they displayed strong communal interests and the title applied to them has persisted.

Blouet, Léon Paul. *See* Max *O'Rell.

Blow, Mrs Goliath. War-mongering rich woman in John Drinkwater's *Abraham Lincoln* (1918).

Blue Angel, The. *See* Heinrich *Mann.

Blue Moon, At the Sign of The. *See* D. B. Wyndham *Lewis.

Blue Review. *See Rhythm* (2).

Blumenfeld, R. D. (Ralph David Blumenfeld, 1864-1948). Born in Wisconsin of German-Danish parentage. After training in his father's printing works, he was engaged by the United Press to report Queen Victoria's 1887 jubilee, and on returning to America joined the *New York Herald*, became its London manager in 1890 and its New York superintendent in 1893. He left the *Herald* in the next year, and in 1900 was appointed news editor of the London *Daily Mail*. Four years later he went to the *Daily Express* as editor and remained until 1922, by which time the paper had come under the control of Lord *Beaverbrook, Blumenfeld having meanwhile carried a stage further the revolution in British journalism initiated by Alfred Harmsworth (Lord *Northcliffe).

Blundell, Mary E. *See* M. E. *Francis.

Blunden, Edmund (1896-1974). Born at Yalding in Kent, where his schooling began before he went to Christ's Hospital (the Bluecoat School), where Coleridge, Lamb, Leigh Hunt and others whom his own prose writings were to celebrate had been taught a century before. Distinguishing himself in Latin and Greek, he won a classics scholarship to Oxford early in 1914, but his time at the University was broken by army service in France during World War I. He returned to Oxford in 1919 but found the life there incongruous with that of the war years, and in 1920 he moved to London as assistant editor of *The Athenaeum*, which was absorbed by *The Nation* soon after. While still at school, Blunden had printed at his own expense two booklets of poems and followed them with two others similarly produced in 1916, the year in which his first London-published writings appeared in a series of 'Little Books of Georgian Verse'.

The editor's note to this small collection, *Pastorals*, commended it as revealing 'the private thoughts and feelings of a youth passing from college to camp in verse of unusual interest and accomplishment'. Blunden, however, is not among the self-revealing poets, for the dominant note in his verse and prose alike is reticence, notably in what may be, finally, his outstanding permanent contribution to English literature, *Undertones of War* (1928). In this, without minimizing the shockingness of the things endured, the masterly prose and interspersed poems make their profound impact through severe and ironical avoidance of over-emphasis. In the preceding years he had established a reputation as a nature poet, gifted in presenting the English countryside as well in its winter aspects as at the other seasons: *The Waggoner* (1922), *The Shepherd* (1922), *English Poems* (1925)–the first of these including 'Almswomen', by which he will probably continue to be known to the largest number of readers through its choice by many anthologists. The collected volume *Poems of Many Years* (1957). though by no means complete, shows the increasing complexity of the poet's thought and use of words 'for conveying some perception of the grace byond the facts'– a phrase in his Preface to the 1957 volume. After the war he went for his health's sake on a voyage to South America, which gave material for his first prose book *The Bon-adventure: A Random Journal of an Atlantic Holiday* (1922); and he produced in the next year *Christ's Hospital: A Retrospect*. From 1924 he spent periods as Professor of English Literature at Tokyo University and (from 1953) as Head of the English Department in the University of Hong Kong, having between whiles been a Fellow and Tutor of Merton College, Oxford, and a member of *The Times Literary Supplement* staff. Among his many works are studies of Leigh Hunt (1930), Charles Lamb (1933), Thomas Hardy (1941), Shelley (1946), and a classic of the national game and his own region of England, *Cricket Country* (1944). Through edited editions, he attracted a new audience to a number of earlier poets, including John Clare, Christopher Smart, and William Collins, as well as to his contemporaries, Wilfred *Owen and Ivor Gurney. He was elected Professor of Poetry at Oxford in 1966, but ill-health caused him to retire in 1968.

Blunt, J. K. Swashbuckling American supporter of the Carlists in Joseph Conrad's *The *Arrow of Gold* (1919).

Blunt, Wilfred Scawen (1840-1922). Born in Sussex; educated at Stonyhurst and Oscott; entered the Foreign Service, serving in various European capitals and at Buenos Aires. With his wife (an accomplished orientalist) he travelled in the Arab countries and India, became a violent propagandist in support of self-government for colonial countries, and developed an intense antagonism to the British. In addition to being a notable horseman and breeder of Arab horses, he was a poet (*Collected Poems*, 1914). A record of his ideas and experiences appears in *My Diaries* (1920).

Bluntschli, Captain. Swiss mercenary, hotelier, and 'chocolate soldier' in Bernard Shaw's *Arms and the Man* (1894).

Blurb. Publisher's short description of a book, usually printed on the jacket, but sometimes inside on a leaf preceding the title page, or in a press advertisement. The purpose of a blurb is to serve as a sales aid, and can be either soberly factual or consciously fanciful, according to the reputation of the publisher and/or author, either of whom may have written it.

Blythe, Herbert (Maurice Barrymore, 1847-1905). *See* Barrymore family.

Blyton, Enid (Enid Mary Blyton, died 1968). Her innumerable books for children had an unexampled contemporary popularity with young readers on all social levels, though some educationists complained that they were devoid of mental stimulus and persistently commonplace in matter and style. A psychologist's diagnosis, 'she thought as a child and she wrote as a child', is quoted and developed in *Enid Blyton* by Barbara Stoney (1974).

Boanerges, Bill. The Home Secretary in *The *Apple Cart* by Bernard Shaw.

Boas, F. S. (Frederick Samuel Boas, 1862-1957). Educated at Clifton and Oxford. Professor of History and English Literature, Queen's College, Belfast, 1901-5. L.C.C. Inspector, 1905-27. Author of *Shakespeare and his Predecessors* (1896; new edn 1940), *Tudor Drama* (1933), *Christopher Marlowe* (1940), *Queen Elizabeth in Drama* (1949), *Sir Philip Sidney* (1955), etc.

Bodleian Library. The University Library at Oxford founded in 1602 by Sir Thomas Bodley (1545-1613), sometime English diplomatic representative at The Hague. He endowed it liberally and it has since received important gifts of books and manuscripts from many sources. It receives or can demand under the Copyright Act a copy of every book and periodical published in the United Kingdom, a right given also to the British Museum, the Cambridge University Library, the National Library of Scotland, the National Library of Wales, and the Library of Trinity College, Dublin.

Boffin. Research scientist; 'back-room boy'. The word was of unrecorded popular origination during World War II and applied to those engaged on secret or 'hush-hush' jobs mainly in furtherance of military and naval plans.

Bohun, Q.C. Barrister son of William the waiter in Bernard Shaw's *You Never Can Tell* (1895).

Bodkin, Thomas (1887-1961). Born in Dublin; educated at Clongowes Wood College and the University of Ireland; studied law and was called to the Bar in 1911. Later he studied art on the Continent, and from 1927 to 1935 was Director of the National Gallery of Ireland. Appointed to Birmingham University in 1935 as Professor of Fine Arts and Director of the Barber Institute, he remained there until his retirement in 1953. He wrote a considerable number of books on art subjects (including *The Approach to Painting*, 1927; revised edn 1946) and an autobiographical volume *My Uncle Frank* (1941).

Bodley Head, The. Name given to a London publishing house founded by John *Lane, who used as a street sign and also in his books a representation of the head of Sir Thomas Bodley (1545-1613) to whom the *Bodleian Library at Oxford was mainly indebted.

Bojanus, Mr. Talkative tailor in Aldous Huxley's *Antic Hay* (1923). He makes the first pair of Gumbril's Patent Small-Clothes (pneumatic trousers).

Bojer, Johan (1872-1959). Born near Trondheim in Norway; worked as a journalist in Paris (1902-7) and lived for varying periods in Italy, Germany, Holland, Belgium, and

England. Among his novels, short stories, and plays, the deepest impression was made abroad by *The Power of a Lie* (1908) and *The Great Hunger* (1918). His novels expressed his own political and social ideas while also depicting the lives of ordinary people in Norway.

Boldero, Herbert. Financier who markets Gumbril's invention and discourses on advertising in Aldous Huxley's *Antic Hay* (1923).

Boldrewood, Rolf (pseudonym of Thomas Alexander Browne, 1826-1915). Born in London; taken as a young child to Australia, where his father became one of the founders of the city of Melbourne. The son grew up to be first a squatter in Victoria, then a sheep-farmer in New South Wales, and later a magistrate and goldfields commissioner. As a writer he produced what has come to be regarded as the first Australian classic novel, *Robbery Under Arms* (1888).

Bolfry. The self-styled 'Duke and General of Legions' summoned from hell in James Bridie's *Mr Bolfry* (1943).

Bolitho, Hector (Henry Hector Bolitho, 1898-1974). Born in New Zealand, travelled extensively in Africa, America, Australia, and Europe, and wrote many popular biographies, particularly of members of the British royal family, as well as novels and plays.

Bolitho, William (né William Bolitho Ryall, 1890-1920). His family having been made homeless during the Boer War, he did various menial jobs as a boy before starting his education at Rondesbosch and going on to Cape Town University. After serving and being wounded in France with the British army in World War I, he became a journalist in Paris and New York. Author of *Murder for Profit* (1926; studies of mass murder), *Twelve Against the Gods* (1929; biographical sketches), etc.

Bolsheviks. The majority wing (*Bolsheviki*) of the Russian Social Democratic Party, which split in 1903, the minority wing (Mensheviks, or *Mensheviki*) advocating gradualism and cooperation with other parties working towards socialism, whereas the Bolsheviks under the leadership of Lenin worked for immediate revolution and the Marxist doctrine of proletarian dictatorship.

Bolt, Robert (1925-). Born in Manchester;

educated at the Grammar School and the University there. Became a school teacher in Somerset, but left that profession when his play *The Flowering Cherry* (1957) had a long run in London, followed by other successes: *A Man for All Seasons* (1960), a dramatic study of Sir Thomas More, and *The Tiger and the Horse* (1960), etc.

Bolton, Guy (1884-). Born at Broxbourne, Hertfordshire; educated privately and in Paris. Practised for a while as an architect in New York but from 1913 was a prolific author of plays, mainly libretti for musical comedies, some in collaboration with P. G. *Wodehouse with whom he also wrote a joint autobiography, *Bring on the Girls* (1954). Also wrote novels.

Bolton, Isabel (pseudonym of Mary Britton Miller, 1883-). Born in Connecticut; educated in Massachusetts. Under her own name she published several books of verse (*Songs of Infancy*, 1928, etc.) and a novel (*In the Days of Thy Youth*, 1943), but had more success when she adopted a changed literary style and a nom-de-plume. As Isabel Bolton, author of *Do I Wake or Sleep* (1946), she was likened to Henry *James and Virginia *Woolf, and wrote other novels: *The Christmas Tree* (1949), *Many Mansions* (1952).

Bond, James. Secret agent and immoralist in novels by Ian *Fleming.

Bone, Sir David (David William Bone, 1874-1959; knighted 1946). Born in Glasgow. One of four brothers, of whom see also James and Muirhead, below. From the age of fifteen his life was spent at sea, first as an apprentice in a sailing ship and ultimately as Commodore of the Anchor Line. Author of seafaring books: *The Brassbounder* (1910), *The Lookoutman* (1923), *Landfall at Sunset* (1955; autobiographical), and others.

Bone, Gertrude (née Gertrude Helena Dodd; married Muirhead *Bone 1903). Born in Holyhead; educated at Southport. Author of poems, novels, *Children's Children* (1908), *Old Spain* (1936), *Days in Old Spain* (1938), *Came to Oxford* (1952), etc., some with illustrations by her husband and others with drawings by Stephen *Bone.

Bone, James (1872-1962). Born and educated in Glasgow where he began work in a shipping office before moving in 1901 to London; he spent the rest of his career up to 1945 on the *Manchester Guardian*, becoming its London Editor in 1912. His manifold interests enabled him to acquire an exceptional knowledge of the metropolis in its many aspects, knowledge he put to service in *The London Perambulator* (1925), an entertaining record in the prose of a fine literary craftsman. *See also* David Bone.

Bone, Sir Muirhead (1876-1953; knighted 1937). Born in Glasgow. As illustrator collaborated with his wife (see Gertrude *Bone) in *Old Spain*, *Days in Old Spain*, and *Came to Oxford*. *See also* David Bone.

Bone, Stephen (1904-1958; son of Muirhead *Bone). Born in London; educated at Bedales and the Slade School of Art. Mainly a painter and illustrator, but also wrote boys' books, *The British Weather* (1946), *England and the English* (1951), and *A Guide Book to the West Coast of Scotland* (new edn 1952).

Bonham Carter, Violet. *See* Baroness *Asquith of Yarnbury.

Bonington, Sir Ralph Bloomfield. Fashionable Harley Street consultant in Bernard Shaw's *The *Doctor's Dilemma* (1906). Known to his friends as B.B.

Bonner, Edmund. Rich merchant-draper in Sydney and principal sponsor of the explorer's journey across desert Australia in Patrick White's *Voss* (1957). His wife is the aunt of the chief woman character, Laura Trevelyan.

Book Clubs. Organizations which offer to members, at rates lower than the publication price of the original editions, selected contemporary books. The reduction is made possible by arrangement with the publishers, whose first publication costs are spread over printing numbers increased by the estimated requirements of book clubs; thus the cost per volume is lessened. The book club membership is in some cases very large, and authors may benefit from this increase in sales, even if the percentage royalty is on a reduced scale. A book club may be a separate commercial firm, or, now, under another name, a branch of a regular publishing house or a bookshop. Members of book clubs have to wait for varying periods, which may be up to two years, before they can get particular books, and their choice is limited to the range of titles offered. Book clubs are money-saving for readers

who are tolerant of dependence upon book-selection by others. The Times Book Club, a subscription library, now closed, was an exception (*see* *Net Book Agreement).

Book Collector, The. A bibliographical quarterly founded in 1952 by John *Hayward (editorial director), Ian *Fleming and P. H. Muir. In 1956 the Board was joined by John Carter who wrote a summary of the journal's achievements 'After Ten Years' for the 1961 Winter number.

Book League. *See* *National Book League.

Book reviews. As a branch of journalism, book reviewing is inevitably affected by press economics, by the vagaries of public taste and interest, and more rarely by the whims of editors and owners. Heavy casualties among the quarterly and weekly reviews and monthly magazines in the present century put an end to the literary essay type of review such as provided Macaulay and others with ample space for critical assessment, while 'book pages' in daily newspapers have either disappeared or become increasingly scrappy as more and more books compete for attention in shrinking space. It is not now generally apparent that a high standard of competence is required of reviewers by those who engage them. While scientific and technical works are necessarily committed to reviewers with the requisite specialized knowledge (though not always free from personal or professional bias), the ruck of literary publications is more perfunctorily treated. The literary editor of a periodical (e.g., the *New Statesman*) may not only himself write with critical authority but also delegate current books to appropriately qualified reviewers, which should mean those with a background knowledge of comparative literature and of the conditions of authorship, and also with some matured knowledge of life outside the restricted circles of professional writers and scholars. Not all these desirable qualifications are possessed by the host of young men and women from the universities who aim to become book-reviewers; nor by those novelists, versifiers, and other writers who supplement meagre royalties by fees for reviews. The purpose and usefulness of book reviews are problematical. Publishers regard them as a form of unpaid advertising, though the common view is that personal recommendation from reader to reader is a more valuable kind of publicity. Authors are actuated as much by vanity as by the prospect of more sales in hoping for praise in reviews. Publishers and experienced authors know that in the reviewing of most books favourable and unfavourable opinions cancel out: A's book, hailed by X as a masterpiece is hooted by Y as despicable. But though the experienced author is, ideally, neither puffed up by reviewers' praise nor downcast by their strictures, and though few writers are 'kill'd off by one critique' or 'snuff'd out by an article', even a writer as sure of her public as Virginia Woolf could be desolated by harsh reviews. Readers' comments on reviews vary little, and are mostly complaints: that the reviewer, not the book, is made the prominent feature; that the reader of the review receives little or no guidance as to the interest or value of the book for himself; that reviewer X or Y invariably praises the wrong books and condemns those deserving praise; that the reviewer deals with the book he considers the author ought to have written rather than the one actually before him. Members of Parliament are required to 'declare their interest' before speaking on certain matters; it would often be of assistance to readers if book-reviewers declared their political or religious interest. The practice of reprinting reviews in book form has dwindled. Among those so issued in the present century are: Arnold *Bennett: Books and Persons (1917); J. C. *Squire: Books in General (1918, 1920, 1921); Edmund *Gosse: Books on the Table (1921, 1923); Virginia *Woolf: The Common Reader (1925, 1932); Bernard *Shaw: Pen Portraits and Reviews (1931); Desmond *MacCarthy: Criticism (1932); Raymond *Mortimer: A Channel Packet (1942); V. S. *Pritchett: In My Good Books (1942). See also *Literary criticism.

Book Society, The. An organization which supplied its members with a 'book of the month' chosen by its committee from current publications. It offered 'alternative choices' and issued a literary news publication.

Bookman, The. 'A monthly journal for book-readers, bookbuyers and booksellers' founded in 1891, continuing until 1934 when it was incorporated with the *London Mercury. Edited by Robertson *Nicoll until his death,

its biographical and other articles and book reviews did much to encourage intelligent reading and literary appreciation beyond academic limits. St John *Adcock succeeded Nicoll as editor.

Book War, The. See *Net Book Agreement.

Booth, Charles (1840-1916). Born and educated in Liverpool; founded the Booth steamship line. Later he concentrated attention on problems of labour and the condition of the poor, producing influential works on these and related subjects which stirred others to action, among those who assisted him being Beatrice Potter (afterwards Mrs Sidney *Webb), a cousin of his wife. His chief publications were the seventeen volumes constituting Life and Labour of the People in London (1891-1903), and in much public speaking and writing he advocated Old Age Pensions.

Booth, John Bennion (1880-1961). Educated at Liverpool University; began as a solicitor before joining in 1905 the staff of The Sporting Times ('The Pink 'Un') with which he remained for many years, a period reflected and celebrated in Old Pink 'Un Days (1924) and similar books. His interest in the old music halls led to his editing Seventy Years of Song (1943).

Booth, William (1829-1912). Born in Nottingham; had little schooling and much experience of poverty. He became an ardent religious convert during adolescence, and had some practice as a lay preacher while working as a pawnbroker's assistant in London. Having married Catherine Mumford in 1855 and acted as a travelling Methodist preacher for several years, he and his wife started the non-denominational Christian Mission in east London in 1865 which became the Salvation Army in 1878. He collaborated with W. T. *Stead in writing In Darkest England and the Way Out (1890), published under Booth's name. Though the book was severely and often unfairly criticized it aroused public sympathy and support for the organization to which 'the General' and Catherine Booth devoted the remainder of their lives and made a worldwide force in religion.

Boothby, Guy (Guy Newell Boothby, 1867-1905). Australian novelist; though his novels dealing with life in his native country are outstanding, his considerable popular success was achieved with those introducing the sinister Dr Nikola, who first appeared in a volume of stories with that title published in 1896.

Boothe, Clare (née Ann Clare Boothe, 1903- ; married to her second husband Henry Robinson Luce, 1935). Born in New York; educated privately. After her first marriage in 1923 to George Tuttle Brokaw ended in 1929, she worked for *Vanity Fair* and became its managing editor in 1932. A novel, *Stuffed Shirts* (1931), and a play, *Abide with Me* (1935), were followed in 1937 by *The Women*, a corrosive satire on her sex and social class which had a long run on the New York stage. Later she entered politics, was elected to Congress in 1942 and in 1953 became United States Ambassador to Italy. H. R. Luce was the millionaire owner of *Time, Life,* and *Fortune.*

ooze-and-bash fiction. Term applicable to novels in which drunkenness and violence are prominent, as in numerous American crime novels, in the sex-and-spy fantasies of Ian *Fleming, and in a type of quasi-realistic novels in vogue after World War II, e.g. *Saturday Night and Sunday Morning* by Alan *Sillitoe.

ordeaux, Henri (1870-1963). Born in Haute-Savoie. Studied law and practised for ten years, but then started on his career as an indefatigable writer of novels-with-a-purpose based on traditional values of 'church, home, and fatherland', among them *La Peur de vivre* (1902; translated into English as *The Fear of Living*, 1913), *La Robe de laine* (1910; *The Woollen Dress*, 1912), *La Neige sur les pas* (1912; *Footprints Beneath the Snow*, 1913), *Celle qui n'était pas invitée* (1931; *Murder Party*, 1931). He also wrote several series of essays, a number of volumes on World War I, travel books, and collections of dramatic criticism.

orden, Mary (1886-1968; married Major General Sir Edward Spears, 1918). Born in Chicago; educated at Vassar; settled in England. Author of *Jane–Our Stranger* (1922), *Flamingo* (1927), *Mary of Nazareth* (1933), *The Black Virgin* (1937), *Margin of Error* (1954), and other novels. Her first two novels were published under the pseudonym Bridget *Maclagan.

orstal Boy. By Brendan *Behan, published in

1958. Sent from Dublin at the age of sixteen by the Irish Republican Army in the 1930s during their bombing campaign, the author is arrested in Liverpool while in possession of explosives. After being held on remand in prison he is sentenced to three years training in a Borstal Institution and transferred to southern England. His account of these experiences details the squalor of prison life and the brutalities of existence in cells and in workrooms where mailbags must be sewn four stitches to the inch precisely, and presents in contrast a description of Borstal life where work in garden and orchard and in building and other crafts is rational and productive. Though hating the English as a nation, he develops less embittered feelings for some among the prisoners and detainees and even among the warders and officers, while withholding no evidence of miseries and cruelties inflicted both by staff and by those in their charge. Any disgust aroused by the obscenities and blasphemies which form the staple of the recorded conversations is dulled by sheer monotony of repetition, familiar as commonplace small talk in army and factory no less than in the un-censored talk here set down. The narrative is interspersed by Irish political and other ballads, and lightened by accounts of a concert and of a nativity play by the boys under the direction of a Matron who wins their reluctant affection. The book ends with Behan's deportation to Ireland after two years of Borstal.

Bosanquet, Bernard (1848-1923). Professor of Moral Philosophy, St Andrews (1903-08); author of *Knowledge and Reality* (1885), *Logic, or the Morphology of Knowledge* (2 vols, 1888), *A History of Aesthetic* (1892), *The Philosophical Theory of the State* (1899), *The Principle of Individuality and Value* (1912), *Social and International Ideals: being Studies in Patriotism* (1917), *The Meeting of Extremes in Contemporary Philosophy* (1921).

Bosinney, Philip. Irene Forsyte's lover in Galsworthy's *The *Forsyte Saga* (1922).

Boss, Mrs. Employed by Samuel *Butler's cousin. See Mrs *Jupp.

Boswell, James (1740-1795). After Boswell (the biographer of Samuel Johnson) died his large collection of personal papers was lost sight of until boxes of unpublished MSS were discovered in Malahide Castle, near Dublin in 1925. Further collections were found there in the 1930s and many letters and other writings at Fettercairn House, near Aberdeen. Taken together, these manuscripts constituted the most important literary discovery of the 20th century, and the great mass of material was acquired in 1949 by Yale University. Publication began with Boswell's *London Journal* in 1958 and has continued. It was estimated that some fifty printed volumes would be needed to exhaust the collection, which includes material not in Boswell's published version of the Life of Johnson.

Botteghe Oscure. A cosmopolitan literary review founded in 1948 by Princess Marguerite *Caetani and published in Rome until it ceased in 1963. Its contributors included most of the leading writers of Europe, America, and other countries.

Bottome, Phyllis (1884-1963; married A. E. Forbes-Dennis, 1917). Born at Rochester, Kent, of American-English parentage. Taken while a child to the U.S., where her father held a church appointment on Long Island. Intended to become an actress, but tuberculosis compelled her to seek curative treatment in Switzerland, and there at the age of seventeen she wrote her first novel, which was quickly accepted for publication. She served in Belgium as a relief worker during World War I and afterwards lived for a period in Vienna with her husband. Among her many novels *The Mortal Storm* (1937) received most attention for its anti-Nazi theme. Her life was largely devoted to humanitarian causes in many countries, these and other personal concerns being reflected in her book on *Alfred Adler: Apostle of Freedom* (1939) and in the autobiographical *Search for a Soul* (1947).

Bottomley, Gordon (1874-1948) Born in Yorkshire; educated there and started a career as bank clerk, but ill-health compelled him to give up business and live in retirement. He wrote much poetry, collected in *Poems of Thirty Years* (1925), but his distinctive contribution to the literature of his time was in poetic drama, notably *King Lear's Wife* (1915) and *Gruach* (1921), though the somewhat Celtic imagination shown in these and other pieces was not accompanied by a sufficient knowledge of stagecraft to give him the stage success he ardently desired. A mutually encouraging correspondence conducted with the painter Paul Nash over a prolonged period, and published as *Poet and Painter* in 1955, provides an intimate study of both Bottomley and Nash.

Bottomley, Horatio William (1860-1933). Born in east London and brought up in an orphanage, from which he ran away when fourteen; he then worked in a solicitor's office and as a shorthand writer in the Law Courts before turning to printing and publishing and, in 1889, to the company-promoting which was to ruin many small investors and to lead after numerous skilful evasions to his own final exposure and imprisonment. As a popular journalist and editor of the weekly periodical he founded in 1906, *John Bull*, and as M.P. for South Hackney (1906-12; 1918-22), he became a powerful demagogue and self-styled 'tribune of the people', with a talent for mob oratory of the type perfected by foreign dictators after his death. He was a master of impudence in conducting his own defence successfully in the courts during the cases brought against him, but in 1922 he was convicted on twenty-three charges of fraudulent conversion and sentenced to seven years' penal servitude. He attempted after his release in 1926 to rehabilitate himself with his former gullible public, but his power had gone, and though he had been at one stage in his career a millionaire he died in near poverty. Bottomley contributed nothing to the welfare of his host of followers, but on the contrary robbed them with barefaced audacity. His life-story is one of the important cautionary tales of the 20th century. Biography by Julian *Symons (1957).

Bourget, Paul (Paul Charles Joseph Bourget, 1852-1935). Born at Amiens; studied classics, philology and medicine, but abandoned the intention of teaching in order to write. Starting with a volume of poems, he then became an original and influential literary critic, and from 1884 a fecund writer of realistic fiction, employing the resources of psychological analysis in novels with a moralistic trend, branching into social investigation and politics. He also wrote several travel books on England, Italy, and the United States.

Bourne, George (pseudonym of George Sturt, 1863-1927). Born and educated at Farnham, Surrey, where he was for a while a teacher until he inherited in 1884 the family wheelwright business in the same place and worked in it until 1900, when he turned to writing: *The Bettesworth Book* (1901), *Memoirs of a Surrey Labourer* (1907), his classic masterpiece, *The*Wheelwright's Shop* (1923), *Change in the Village* (1912), *A Farmer's Life* (1922).

Bowen, Elizabeth (Elizabeth Dorothea Cole Bowen, 1899-1973). Married Alan Cameron 1923. Born in Dublin, her father being the owner of Bowen's Court (which she inherited), built in the 18th century on an estate in County Cork granted by Cromwell to one of his officers, a Colonel Bowen of Welsh ancestry. Taken to live in England from an early age, she was educated at Downe House School in Kent, and afterwards lived for periods in Ireland, London, France, and Italy until her marriage. She began to write when she was twenty, and thereafter writing became her absorbing passion. In several volumes of short stories— *Encounters* (1923), *Ann Lee's* (1926), *Joining Charles* (1929), *The Cat Jumps* (1934), *Look at All Those Roses* (1941), *The Demon Lover* (1945)—and in her novels: *The Hotel* (1927), *The Last September* (1929), *Friends and Relations* (1931), *To the North* (1932), *The House in Paris* (1935), *The *Death of the Heart* (1938), *The Heat of the Day* (1949), she depicted scenes and places with swift impressionistic strokes, while also probing the motives and conduct of the characters with an almost surgical detachment in exposing the nerves and sinews involved in human relationships. This appearance of aloof observation, however, is an aspect not of heartlessness but of a firm artistic control of her medium as a writer. Her astringent prose draws from the reader an immediate and at moments almost painful response to the disturbed emotions and abraded nerves of the characters. In addition to fictional works, which include *Eva Trout* (1969), there is a fragment of autobiography, *Seven Winters* (1942); a history of her Irish home, *Bowen's Court* (1942); essays and criticism in *English Novelists* (1942) and *Collected Impressions* (1950).

Bowen, Marjorie. (One of the pseudonyms of Gabrielle Margaret Vere Campbell: Mrs Arthur L. Long, 1886-1952). Born on Hayling Island, Hampshire. She struggled through a childhood of poverty and parental disharmony and began during adolescence to write in order to support her family. Her first novel, *The Viper of Milan* (1906), made her a popular historical novelist from the age of sixteen, and its full-blooded, colourful, and exciting presentation of a fragment of Renaissance Italy was an impressive even if melodramatic achievement. For a while she studied art at the Slade School and in Paris, and in 1912 married a Sicilian, Zeffrino Emilio Constanzo, who died in 1916. A year later she married A. L. Long. The total number of her books is in doubt, for she used numerous pseudonyms, and it was for a long time unknown that two further reputations, as George R. Preedy and as Joseph Shearing, were hers. It is supposed that she produced at least 150 works, and her comparative neglect by the critics was largely a consequence of her fecundity. A few among her writings as Marjorie Bowen were *The Glen o' Weeping* (1907), *I Will Maintain* (1910), *Mr Washington* (1915), *William, By the Grace of God* (1916), and studies of Emma Lady Hamilton (*Patriotic Lady*, 1935), William Cobbett (*Peter Porcupine*, 1936), John Wesley (*Wrestling Jacob*, 1938), and others.

As **George R. Preedy**: *General Crack* (1928), *The Rocklitz* (1930), *Tumult in the North* (1931), *My Tattered Loving* (1937), and biographies of John Knox and others.

As **Joseph Shearing** (mostly crime stories): *Forget Me Not* (1932), *Moss Rose* (1934), *Mignonette* (1949), *To Bed at Noon* (1951). Under less well known pen-names: as **John Winch**, *Idler's Gate* (1932), etc; as **Robert Paye**, *The Devil's Jig* (1930), *Julia Roseingrave* (1933). Under her birth name, Margaret Campbell: an autobiography, *The Debate Continues* (1939).

Bower, B. M. (*née* Bertha Muzzy, 1871-1940; married Clayton J. Bower, 1890). Born at Cleveland, Minnesota. Her parents moved with her to Montana, where in girlhood she acquired the intimate knowledge of ranch life employed in a long succession of Western novels, beginning with *Chip of the Flying U* (1904).

Bowra, Sir Maurice (Cecil Maurice Bowra, 1908-1971; knighted 1951). Educated at Cheltenham and Oxford, where he afterwards taught in the University, becoming Warden of Wadham College from 1938 and Professor of Poetry (1946-51). Trained as a classical scholar, he shared in the compilation of *The Oxford Book of Greek Verse* (1930) and wrote *Tradition and Design in the Iliad* (1935), *Ancient Greek Literature* (1935), and

Sophoclean Tragedy (1944); but his interests extended to modern English and European literature: *The Heritage of Symbolism* (1943), *Edith Sitwell* (1947), *The Creative Experiment* (1949), *The Romantic Imagination* (1950), *Inspiration and Poetry* (1955), *The Greek Experience* (1957), *Primitive Song* (1962), *Poetry and Politics, 1900-1960* (1966).

Boy David, The. Biblical play in three acts by J. M. *Barrie, first performed in Edinburgh in 1936. It was his last play and one of the least popular.

Boy With a Cart, The. One-act play in verse and prose by Christopher *Fry, produced in 1937 (published 1939) in the village of Coleman's Hatch, Sussex, and concerned with a local saint, Cuthman, who sets out pulling a cart in which his mother rides, and comes at length to Steyning, where with miraculous aid he builds a church. A spoken chorus is provided throughout by The People of South England.

Boyd, Ernest (Ernest Augustus Boyd, 1887-1946). Born in Dublin; educated privately and in Switzerland and Germany. Worked for a few years as a journalist in Dublin before entering the British consular service, from which he resigned in 1920 and settled in the U.S., where he made a reputation as a literary critic and biographer with *The Contemporary Drama of Ireland* (1917), *Appreciations and Depreciations* (1918), *Portraits: Real and Imaginary* (1924), *Literary Blasphemies* (1927), and studies of H. L. *Mencken (1925) and Maupassant (1926).

Boyd, James (1888-1944). Born in Pennsylvania; educated at Princeton and Cambridge; badly wounded in World War I; settled in North Carolina and wrote a succession of novels dealing with American history: *Drums* (1925; War of Independence), *Marching On* (1927; Civil War), etc.

Boyd, Martin (Martin à Beckett Boyd, 1893-   ). Born in Switzerland of Australian parentage. Trained as an architect but turned novelist: *The Lemon Farm* (1935), *Lucinda Brayford* (1946), *When Blackbirds Sing* (1962) and others. *Day of My Delight* (autobiography, 1965).

Boyd, Nancy. Pseudonym used by Edna St Vincent *Millay for *Distressing Dialogues* (1924).

Boyd, Thomas (Thomas Alexander Boyd, 1898-

1935). Born in Ohio; served in World War I and wrote realistically of the conflict in his novel *Through the Wheat* (1923), to which he provided a sequel *In Time of Peace* (1935). Author also of historical novels (*Shadow of the Long Knives*, 1928; etc.) and biographies.

Boyle, 'Captain' Jack. The 'Paycock' in Sean O'Casey's *Juno and the Paycock* (1924; published 1925); sixty, with a head resembling a stone ball on top of a gate-post; walks with 'a slow, consequential strut'; husband of Juno Boyle.

Boyle, Kay (1903-   ). Born at St Paul, Minnesota. Lived much in European countries from her early years, with intervals of journalism and teaching in America. Her poems and fiction had an appreciative *avant-garde* audience, her most widely known prose works being *Plagued by the Nightingale* (1930) and *The White Horses of Vienna and other Stories* (1935). *Collected Poems* (1962).

Boyle, Mary. Twenty-two-year-old daughter of Jack and Juno Boyle in Sean O'Casey's *Juno and the Paycock* (1925); well-made and good-looking, she is caught between opposing forces: her speech and manners are degraded by her environment, the influence of the books she has read is pushing her forward.

Bracknell, Lady. John Worthing's Aunt Augusta in Oscar Wilde's *The Importance of Being Earnest* (1895).

Bradbury, Ray Douglas (1920-   ). Born in Illinois. After a high-school education and much reading of sensational fiction and comic papers, he began to contribute stories to *pulp magazines, graduating after a few years to better class periodicals and appearing in successive annual anthologies of *The Best American Short Stories*. Somewhat against his will, he became best known—and seriously regarded by intellectuals—as a writer of *science fiction with *The Martian Chronicles* (1950), *The Golden Apples of the Sun* (1953), *Fahrenheit 451* (1953), etc.

Bradby, Ann. See Ann *Ridler.

Bradby, G. F. (Godfrey Fox Bradby, 1863-1947). Educated at Rugby and Oxford; Assistant Master and Housemaster at Rugby, 1888-1920. Author of a famous school-story *The *Lanchester Tradition* (1913) and other novels; also wrote verse: *The Way*, 1921; *Parody and Dust-Shot*, 1931; *The Sage's Note Book*, 1934), and on literature, religion, and history.

Braddon, Miss (Mary Elizabeth Braddon, 1837-1915; married John Maxwell, publisher, in 1874). Born in London; educated privately. Before she was twenty she wrote for £10 a serial called *Three Times Dead; or The Secret of the Heath*, a title which gives a clue to the sensational nature of the writing she was to do in many of her later novels, the chief being the long-remembered *Lady Audley's Secret* (1862). *See also* W. B. *Maxwell (her son).

Bradford, Roark (1896-1948). Born in Tennessee; educated at rural schools before serving in the American army. He wrote many stories about Negroes, the most famous being *Ol Man Adam an' His Chillun* (1928), dramatized in 1929 by Marc *Connelly as *Green Pastures* and later filmed.

Bradley, A. C. (Andrew Cecil Bradley, 1851-1935). Born at Cheltenham, educated there and at Oxford; lectured in English and in philosophy at Balliol College, 1876-81; Professor of Literature and History at University College, Liverpool, 1882-90; Professor of English Language and Literature at Glasgow University 1890-1900; Professor of Poetry at Oxford, 1901-06. His *Shakespearean Tragedy* (1904) outlived the denigrations of a later generation of critics. His *Oxford Lectures on Poetry* (1909) attracted less attention. He also wrote on philosophical subjects and religion.

Bradley, F. H. (Francis Herbert Bradley, 1846-1924). Brother of the preceding; educated at Cheltenham, Marlborough, and Oxford; spent most of his life as a Fellow at Merton College, Oxford, devoting himself to philosophical studies and becoming eminent in that field. His most original and influential work is *Appearance and Reality* (1893); among his other writings *Ethical Studies* (1876), *The Principles of Logic* (1883), and *Essays on Truth and Reality* (1914) are outstanding.

Bradley, Helen (1900-   ). Lancashire born and bred; diverted from desired music career, married a textile designer; when over sixty, won international renown as painter of 'modern primitives' depicting wittily Lancashire places and people recollected from her childhood, many appearing in colour with her own amusing commentary in *Miss Carter Wore Pink* (1971), *Miss Carter Came With Us* (1973).

Bradley, Katharine Harris. *See* Michael *Field.

Bradley, Mrs (afterwards Dame Beatrice). Woman detective in crime novels by Gladys *Mitchell.

Bradshaw. The name by which *Bradshaw's Railway Time Table* was commonly known. First published as a small pocket volume in 1839 at 6d, it grew in more than a century of continuous monthly publication to a world transport guide of over a thousand pages in each issue. The ever-increasing cost of printing made it no longer possible to publish after May 1961.

Brahms, Caryl (-   ). Born in Surrey; educated privately and at the Royal Academy of Music. Contributed ballet and theatre criticism to various London papers. In collaboration with S. J. Simon wrote a succession of eccentric humorous novels: *A Bullet in the Ballet* (1937), *Don't Mr Disraeli* (1940), *No Bed for Bacon* (1941), *Away Went Polly* (1952), etc. Also a biographical study, *Robert Helpmann, Choreographer* (1943).

Brailsford, Henry Noel (1873-1958). Born at Mirfield, Yorkshire; educated at Glasgow University. Worked as leader writer on *Manchester Guardian* and other papers; editor of *The New Leader*, 1922-26. Author of books on socialism and other political topics, and on Shelley, Voltaire and Gandhi.

Braine, John (John Gerard Braine, 1922-   ). Born in Yorkshire; educated in Bradford. Worked in various trades and then as a librarian before the success of his novel *Room at the Top* (1957) enabled him to settle to writing. *Life at the Top* (1962) deals with some of the same characters in later years.

Brains Trust. A sound broadcast programme started by the B.B.C. in 1943 and extended to television from 1955. Devised by Howard Thomas, the procedure was to assemble at each (usually weekly) session a small group of experts qualified to answer, impromptu, selected questions sent in by listeners. At its peak the original 'sound' Brains Trust attracted an audience of some 13 million each session. The original panel of experts was C. E. M. *Joad, Julian *Huxley, and Commander A. B. Campbell, with Donald McCullough as question-master.

Braithwaite, E. R. (Eustace Edward Braithwaite, 1920-   ). Born in British Guiana;

educated in New York and at Cambridge. In the R.A.F. in World War II; became a teacher in a London East-end school 1950; L.C.C. welfare officer 1958-60. Ambassador of Guyana to Venezuela from 1969. His teaching experiences are related in *To Sir, with Love* (1957). Other books: *A Kind of Homecoming* (1952), *Paid Servant* (1962), etc.

Bramah, Ernest (pen-name of Ernest Bramah Smith, 1868-1942). He shunned publicity and details of his personal life are few, though he is said to have lived for a time in China, and another period was surveyed in his *English Farming: Why I Turned it in* (1894). His reputation rests upon his stories of an imaginative Chinese philosopher in *The Wallet of Kai Lung* (1900), which had a long-delayed popularity and intellectualist acclaim in the 1910s and 1920s, and was followed by *Kai Lung's Golden Hours* (1922) and other Kai Lung volumes. He also wrote stories of a blind detective in *Max Carrados* (1914) and *The Eyes of Max Carrados* (1923), and on another level *A Guide to the Varieties and Rarity of English Regal Copper Coins* (1929).

Brand, Max (pseudonym of Frederick Schiller Faust, 1892-1944). Born in Seattle; educated at the University of California. From 1918 he wrote a continuous stream of Western novels, the best known being *Destry Rides Again* (1930), which made one of the best films in its class. He was also the author of the Dr Kildare series. His private passion was said to lie in verse writing, though he published no poems. He was killed in Italy while serving as a correspondent in World War II.

Brandes, Georg (Georg Morris Cohen Brandes, 1842-1927). Born in Copenhagen; educated at the University there. During many years he held a high international scholarly reputation with his *William Shakespeare* (1898) and *Main Currents of Nineteenth Century Literature* (1901-1905). He also wrote on *Ibsen, Anatole *France, *Nietzsche, Lassalle, Aristotle, Caesar, Goethe, Voltaire; and, from the point of view of a lifelong atheist, *The Jesus Myth* (1926).

Brangwen family. In D. H. Lawrence's *The *Rainbow* (1915): **Tom** Brangwen, farmer, marries Lydia Lensky, Polish widow, with a young daughter, **Anna**, who becomes the wife of Tom's nephew, **Will** Brangwen, and bears six children, including **Ursula** and **Gudrun**. Ursula Brangwen becomes a school teacher and the mistress of Anton Skrebensky until his departure for India. In *Women in Love* (1921) Ursula marries Rupert Birkin, sometime Inspector of Schools. Gudrun Brangwen, art teacher and sculptor, takes as her lover Gerald Crich, mine manager and owner, who is killed accidentally in the Swiss Alps.

Brangwen, Ursula. Central woman character in D. H. Lawrence's *The *Rainbow* (1915) and *Women in Love* (1920).

Brant, Adam. Captain of the clipper *Flying Trades* in Eugene O'Neill's *Mourning Becomes Electra* (1931); illegitimate son of David Mannon and Marie Brantome, a French Canadian nursemaid employed by the Mannons. When found to be pregnant she is turned out of the house by David's father. Her son abbreviates her name and, as Brant, is set on avenging his mother's disgrace. Instead, he falls in love with Christine, wife of Ezra Mannon, provides her with poison to kill her husband, and after the murder is shot by Orin, son of Christine and Ezra.

Brasch, Charles (Charles Orwell Brasch, 1909-). Born in Dunedin, New Zealand; educated at Waitaki, and in England at Oxford; worked as an archaeologist in Egypt, and as a teacher and civil servant in England. Returned to New Zealand after World War II and in 1947 founded (and edited until 1966) *Landfall*, the most fruitful of the Dominion's periodicals, printing much of the best current verse and creative prose. Author of *The Land and the People* (1939), *Disputed Ground* (1948), *The Estate* (1957), *Ambulando* (1964), and other verse collections; also *The Quest* (words in verse for an allegorical mime; 1946). See also *New Zealand Writers.

Brassbound, Captain. Central character in Bernard Shaw's *Captain Brassbound's Conversion* (1900).

Brathwaite, Edward (1930-). Born in Barbados; educated in the West Indies and at Cambridge. Taught in Ghana, 1955-62; then returned to the University of the West Indies as Lecturer in History. Author of short plays for African children, including *Odale's Choice* (1966), and of a three-part narrative poem: *Rights of Passage* (1967),

Masks (1968), *Islands* (1969). *See* *Caribbean Writers.

Brave New World. Novel by Aldous *Huxley published in 1932. In the year 632 A.F. (After Ford–their patron saint), at the Central London Hatchery and Conditioning Centre embellished with the World State's motto 'Community, Identity, Stability', the Director conducts new students through the Fertilizing, Bottling, and Decanting Rooms, the Infant Nurseries, and other of the four thousand rooms where males, females, and freemartins (the structurally normal but sterile group) of the new race are laboratory-developed and conditioned in Alpha, Beta, Gamma, Delta, or Epsilon grades according to the intellectual, manual, or menial work the State will require of them. By Bokanovsky's Process 'standard men and women in uniform batches' can be produced from a single egg–scores of identical workers to operate identical machines. Mind-conditioning takes place during infancy by repetitive 'sleep-teaching' through electrical whispering devices under the children's pillows. A Savage from a Mexican Reservation interrogates the Controller in England, utilizing appropriate quotations from an old copy of Shakespeare he had found at home. He learns that in this 'brave new world' beauty, truth, and individuality are excluded; and in conformity with Henry Ford the American motor magnate's gospel–'History is bunk', the past is repudiated, and only the new is valued. Finding this creed repulsive, the Savage retreats to solitude in a deserted lighthouse, scourges himself penitentially, and, hounded by helicopters with prying journalists and trippers, hangs himself.

Brazil, Angela (1868-1947). Born at Preston, Lancashire; educated in Manchester; studied art before becoming a governess. She settled to the writing of girls' school stories early in the present century, after a period of extensive foreign travel. Her novels were read with delight by multitudes of schoolgirls, who were undeterred by the books' limitations of class and conduct imposed by refined boarding school standards. Characteristic of the fifty or so novels are *A Fourth Form Friendship* (1911), *The School by the Sea* (1914), *The Madcap of the School* (1917). *My Own Schooldays: An Autobiography* appeared in 1925.

Bread and circuses. From the Latin 'panem et circenses' in the Tenth Satire of the Roman poet Juvenal (A.D. 60-c. 130). The passage in which the phrase appears is to the effect that the people of Rome limited their longings to two things only–bread, and games at the circus. Juvenal's pessimistic observation is echoed by those who liken contemporary Britain to Rome in decline.

Breakages Limited. The firm denounced by Lysistrata, Powermistress Royal, in Act I of Bernard Shaw's *The *Apple Cart* (1929). In an impassioned speech to the king and cabinet she details Breakages' enormities as a suppressive and destructive force working against the industrial progress and economic efficiency of the nation.

Breasted, James Henry (1865-1935). Born in Illinois; educated there and in the universities of Chicago, Yale and Berlin. Devoting himself to archaeology and particularly to Egyptology, he held museum appointments in Europe and America, becoming in 1905 and until 1933 Professor of Egyptology and Oriental History in the University of Chicago. His name was known in most countries as the author of *Ancient Times: A History of the Early World* (1916; revised in 1926 as *The Conquest of Civilization*).

Brecht, Bertolt (Bertolt Euger Friedrich Brecht, 1898-1956). Born at Augsburg. During World War I he was conscripted for hospital duty, and after the end of hostilities studied medicine and philosophy at the universities of Munich and Berlin. His dominating interest, however, was in the theatre, and by his mid-twenties he had already made a notable mark as a playwright with *Trommeln in der Nacht*. From the first his writings were strongly infused with pacifist and Marxist principles, though his critical outlook was universal rather than partisan. In 1928 his *Dreigroschenoper* (*The Threepenny Opera*, an adaptation and transposition to a 19th-century London setting of John Gay's *The Beggar's Opera*) won him repute that had become worldwide by the time of his death. Music for *The Threepenny Opera* was written by Kurt Weill, who had already collaborated with Brecht in *Aufstieg und Fall der Stadt Mahogony* (*The Rise and Fall of the City of Mahagonny*), produced in 1927. Until the coming of the Nazi régime, Brecht was on the staff of Berlin theatres, producing plays by himself and others and training actors. He sought to establish epic

D

drama which would dispense with the customary artifices and emotional compulsions of the theatre and lead players and playgoers alike to view stage characters with detachment and critical observation. With the arrival of Hitler as political dictator, Brecht was forced into exile, and after several years of wandering he settled in the U.S. until 1948, when he returned to Germany as director in East Berlin of a company, the Berliner Ensemble, which quickly became internationally famous. Among his later plays, *Mother Courage, The Good Woman of Setzuan, The *Caucasian Chalk Circle*, and *Galileo* have been produced in England in translations. Although he has been described as 'perhaps Germany's greatest dramatist', Brecht's ultimate rank will fall to be reconsidered when the true quality of his plays can be assessed independently of political affiliations.

Brenan, Gerald (1894-   ). Born in Malta. Spent part of his childhood in South Africa, India and Ceylon, but was educated in England. At seventeen he began a prolonged period of wandering with a donkey and cart through France and Italy and in Bosnia. Wounded in World War I, he lived in Spain for several years after 1918 and wrote *The Spanish Labyrinth* (1943), *The Face of Spain* (1950), *The Literature of the Spanish People* (1951), *A Holiday by the Sea* (a novel, 1961), *A Life of One's Own* (1962), *The Lighthouse always says Yes* (1966).

Brennan, Captain. Of the Irish Citizen Army in Sean O'Casey's *The *Plough and the Stars* (1926); a chicken butcher when not on military duty.

Breton, André (1896-1966). Born in Normandy, studied medicine and psychiatry; became one of the leaders of *Surrealism and author of *Manifeste du surréalisme* (1924), *Second Manifeste du surréalisme* (1930), *Qu'est-ce que le surréalisme?* (1934; English translation *What is Surrealism?*, 1936).

Brett Young, Francis. *See* Francis Brett *Young.

Breuil, Abbé Henri (Henri Edouard Prosper Breuil, 1877-1961). He was ordained to the priesthood, but followed throughout the remainder of his life the interest in prehistory which dominated him from early years and made him pre-eminent in the study of European and African cave paintings, on which he wrote with scrupulous scholarship and infectious enthusiasm, notably in *Four Hundred Years of Cave Art* (1952).

Brian, James. *See* A. G. *Street.

Brideshead Revisited: The Sacred and Profane Memories of Captain Charles Ryder. Novel by Evelyn *Waugh published in 1945. In the author's Preface to the 1959 revised edition the theme of the novel is stated as 'the operation of divine grace on a group of diverse but closely connected characters'. Moving with his regiment during World War II to changed quarters, Ryder (in peacetime a successful architectural painter) is surprised by being deposited at Brideshead – the family seat of the Marquis of Marchmain – where he had been a frequent guest in past years as close friend of the younger son, Lord Sebastian Flyte, his contemporary at Oxford. Sebastian holds aloof from his Catholic family, despising his priggish elder brother the Earl of Brideshead, disconcerted by his father the Marquis's settling abroad with a mistress, and unable to share the religious fervour of his mother. At Oxford, where his chief companions are Ryder and Anthony Blanche, a flamboyantly witty aesthete, Sebastian drinks heavily, degenerates into dipsomania and, when sent abroad, evades Mr Samgrass, the tutor put in charge of him. After severe illnesses between drunken bouts, he ends his life as a menial in a North African monastery. Ryder has continued to visit Brideshead, where the elder daughter Julia becomes engaged to a coarse and thrusting politician, marrying him in a Protestant church when he sardonically fails to qualify as a Catholic convert. The Marquis returns to Brideshead after his wife's death, and when himself dying is restored to the Church. Witnessing her father's deathbed reconciliation, Julia returns to the faith and renounces her intention of marrying Ryder after divorce. Shaken by this, Ryder's agnosticism withers under Brideshead influence.

Bridge, Ann (pseudonym of Mary Dolling O'Malley, *née* Sanders, 1891-   ). Born at Bridgend, Surrey, of an English father and American mother; educated at home and at the London School of Economics. Married Sir Owen St Clair O'Malley, 1913. She lived in many countries, first with relatives in Italy as a child and afterwards with her diplomat husband in China, Dalmatia, Turkey and elsewhere, experiences she utilized with skill and taste in agreeable novels: *Peking Picnic* (1932), *Illyrian Spring* (1935; set in Yugoslavia), *The Singing Waters* (1946; Albania), *The Dark Moment* (1952; Turkey). Her other novels include *Ginger Griffin* (1934), *Enchanter's Nightshade* (1937), *Four-Part Setting* (1939), *Frontier Passage* (1942). *Facts and Fictions* (1969).

Bridge of San Luis Rey, The. Novel by Thornton *Wilder published in 1927. Woven by the Incas about the beginning of the 17th century, the bridge–'a mere ladder of thin slats swung out over the gorge, with handrails of dried vine'–was used for more than a hundred years by travellers on the road from Lima to Cuzco in Peru. In July 1714 it broke and threw five persons into the gorge. Brother Juniper, a Franciscan missionary from Italy, resolves to inquire into the private lives of the five, hoping to find a pattern that would account for their sudden and simultaneous destruction by 'a sheer act of God'. His researches lead him to a literary masterpiece, the Letters of the Marquesa de Montemayor to her adored daughter in Spain. The Marquesa's young companion, Pepita, an orphan from a convent and unhappy in her new home, writes an unfinished letter to the Abbess which the Marquesa unintendedly reads. Its pathos determines her to begin a new life and give her love to the child. Two days later while on a journey they both fall from the bridge. A third victim, Esteban, also brought up in the convent, is one of twin foundlings inseparably devoted, who become scribes. Manuel is engaged to write letters by La Perichole, a beautiful and famous actress, with whom he becomes hopelessly in love. The infatuation causes a rift between the brothers, before Manuel's death leaves Esteban desolate. He attempts suicide but is rescued and persuaded to go to sea. On his way to Lima he is killed at the bridge. The remaining victims are Uncle Pio, who had transformed La Perichole from an awkward young café singer into a great actress, and her son Jamie whom he is taking to Lima to educate after his mother's beauty has been destroyed by smallpox. Brother Juniper is unable to

find in the lives of the five any evidence that divine justice required their destruction by the breaking of the bridge. Both he and the book he writes are condemned as heretical and both are burned.

Bridges, Robert (Robert Seymour Bridges, 1844-1930). Born at Walmer of a long-established and prosperous landed family, he was educated at Eton and Oxford, trained in medicine at St Bartholomew's Hospital, where he served as a physician after qualifying in 1874. Ill health having forced his retirement from the medical profession, he travelled in Europe and the Middle East, and from 1882 to 1904 lived in Berkshire, at Yattendon, which gave its name to *The Yattendon Hymnal* (1895-9) in the production of which he collaborated. Five volumes of *Shorter Poems* (1873, 1879, 1880, 1890, 1893), published modestly from the private press of C. H. Daniel, made him known to a select audience as a melodious and scholarly lyrist, and more ambitious poems followed in *The Growth of Love* (as *XXIV Sonnets*, 1876; as *LXXIX Sonnets*, 1898), *Eros and Psyche* (1885), *New Poems* (1899), besides *Prometheus the Firegiver* (1883) and *Demeter* (1904), two masques in the classical mode. The eight plays–*Nero* (I and II); *Palicio*; *The Return of Ulysses*; *The Christian Captives*, *Achilles in Scyros*, *The Humours of the Court*, and *The Feast of Bacchus*–written between 1885 and 1893 stand only as a monument to their author's deficiency in dramatic talent, and they have also dropped from notice as poems to be read or studied. After Alfred *Austin's death in 1913 Bridges was appointed Poet Laureate. Little known to the public, and producing nothing in the way of popular ceremonial verse, the demagogic Horatio *Bottomley jeered at him as 'a dumb Laureate', but his voice was heard in the *Ode on the Tercentenary Commemoration of Shakespeare* (1916), matching the *Ode to Music* which he had written in 1895 for the Bicentenary Commemoration of Henry Purcell. During many years Bridges experimented with quantitative verse and published Poems in Classical Prosody at intervals from 1903, culminating in a remarkable work of his old age *The *Testament of Beauty*, a poem of over 4,000 lines published in 1929 when he was eighty-five. Its immediate success with the public and the critics was followed a few years later by the common process of denigration by younger writers, but it gave Bridges a greater measure of acclaim and reward in his last few months than he received in the rest of his long life. He wrote prose essays on Keats, Milton, Shakespeare, and other subjects and was active as a founder-member of the Society for Pure English. Spending his last years in his home on Boar's Hill, Oxford, a somewhat gruffly forbidding sage to chance acquaintances, Bridges was of set purpose out of the public eye: 'I have lain in the sun/I have toil'd as I might/I have thought as I would' he wrote in 'Fortunatus Nimium' (*New Poems*, 1920), an appropriate epitaph. A number of his lyrics ('Cheddar Pinks'; 'London Snow'; 'I heard a linnet courting', 'Whither, O splendid ship'; and others) have a secure place in anthologies, and if his rank among the English poets is ultimately secondary, it will be sure. For the immediate generations of the 1920s and after, his name was best known in connection with the first publication in 1918 of the poems of his friend Gerard Manley *Hopkins.

Bridie, James (pseudonym of Osborne Henry Mavor, 1888-1951). Born in the Pollok-shields district of Glasgow; educated at Glasgow Academy and Glasgow University; studied medicine and became a qualified physician in 1913. During World War I he served with the R.A.M.C. in France, Belgium, the Middle East and India, his experiences in the latter regions providing material for his first book, *Some Talk of Alexander* (1926). In 1919 he bought a medical practice in Glasgow, but his interests were increasingly in the theatre and in writing. While a student he had been one of the editors of the Glasgow University magazine, to which he contributed both verse and prose, and also wrote pieces for performance by undergraduates. He became a director of the Scottish National Theatre Society (founded in 1921), which produced in 1928 *The Sunlight Sonata* written under his first pseudonym, Mary Henderson. His actual name, Dr O. H. Mavor, did not appear on any of the plays, and after 1928 he adopted James Bridie as a regular pen-name. Although he was a chief pillar of the Scottish National Theatre Society and principal founder of its successor, the Glasgow Citizens' Theatre, his chief

stage successes were secured elsewhere. In 1930 *Tobias and the Angel*, produced in the Festival Theatre at Cambridge, established Bridie among the leading play-wrights of his period, though his ceaseless itch for experimentation was to make most of his later plays more notable for their gusts of genius in occasional scenes than for completeness of dramatic form. *Tobias* is one of the few works, if not the only one, in which some destructive quirk of tempera-ment was not an obstacle to technical craftsmanship and artistic unity. Among the forty or so other plays written by Bridie, these are outstanding: *The *Anato-mist* (1930), *Jonah and the Whale* (1932), *A Sleeping Clergyman* (1933), *The Black Eye* (1935), *Susannah and the Elders* (1937), *The King of Nowhere* (1938), *Mr Bolfry* (1943), *Dr Angelus* (1946), *Daphne Laureola* (1949), *Mr Gillie* (1950). He had a command of verbal eloquence amounting almost to a revival of classical rhetoric, a power of stage argument little below that of Bernard Shaw, and a rich sense of comedy which became invigoratingly bacchanalian in *The Forrigan Reel* (1944). *One Way of Living*, his autobiography, appeared in 1939.

Brieux, Eugene (1858-1932). Born in Paris of a poor family and had little formal schooling. But he profited by self-education and began in boyhood to write plays. Until his middle thirties he worked first as a clerk and then as a journalist, until (1892 onward) he became a regular and prolific dramatist. He was always an advocate and practitioner of realistic plays with a social purpose, and his reputation in English-speaking countries was established by Bernard *Shaw, who wrote a long introductory essay for *Three Plays by Brieux (Maternity; The Three Daughters of M.Dupont; Damaged Goods)* published in London in 1911.

Briffault, Robert (1876-1948). Born in London of French and Scottish parentage; educated abroad, qualified as a physician and surgeon, and practised in New Zealand. Disabled during active service with an English regiment in World War I, he then devoted himself to writing on anthropological subjects with a leftward bias, *The Mothers: A Study of the Origins of Sentiments and Institutions* (3 vols, 1927) being outstanding as a pioneer work. Other notable books in their period were *The Making of Humanity* (1919; rewritten as *Rational Evolution*,

1930), *Sin and Sex* (1931), *Breakdown: The Collapse of Traditional Civilization* (1932), *Decline and Fall of the British Empire* (1938). He also wrote several novels of lesser merit, *Europa* (1935), *Fandango* (1940), etc.

Briggs, Asa (1921-   ). Born at Keighley, Yorks; educated at the grammar school there and Cambridge. Served in the Intelligence Corps 1942-45 before entering his academic career. Professor of Modern History, Leeds University 1955-61; Professor of History at Sussex University 1961 and Vice-Chancellor there from 1967. His publications include *The Age of Improvement* (1959), and a multi-volume history of the B.B.C.

Brighouse, Harold (1882-1958). Born at Eccles, Lancashire. Worked first in the cotton trade and later as dramatic critic of the *Manchester Guardian*, becoming acquainted with Miss A. E. F. *Horniman, who was then nursing the Manchester Repertory Theatre to fame and encouraging the birth of a local school of playwrights. It was by Miss Horniman's company that his best full-length play, *Hobson's Choice,* was produced in 1916. The majority of his other plays were in one act, chief among them *Dealing in Futures* (1909), *Odd Man Out* (1912), *Garside's Career* (1914).

Bright, Mrs Mary Chavelita. See George *Egerton.

Brighton Rock. Novel by Graham *Greene, published in 1938. A story of gang warfare in Brighton. A seventeen-year-old Catholic degenerate called Pinkie plans the murder of Fred Hale, who has been instrumental in killing the former leader of the gang now headed by Pinkie. As members of the gang are about to strangle Hale, he dies of heart failure and a verdict of death from natural causes is recorded at the inquest. Pinkie learns that by miscalculation a vital clue has been left in a café, and when attempting to recover it he fears that Rose, a young waitress in the café, may become suspicious. He makes a date with her, and in order that, as his wife, she could not be compelled to testify against him, he goes through a form of marriage with her before a registrar, though since both are Catholics they regard the ceremony and its consummation as mortal sin. Meanwhile middle-aged Ida Arnold, who had been briefly acquainted

with Hale, suspects that he was murdered and determines to get at the truth. She tries unsuccessfully to persuade Rose to leave Pinkie, and he, fearing she may succeed, plans a suicide pact with Rose, intending that she shall shoot herself but leave him alive. At the crucial moment she flings the revolver away just as Ida reaches them with a constable. Pinkie attempts to throw the bottle of vitriol he customarily carries in his pocket, but the constable's truncheon smashes it and the acid blinds Pinkie himself. In agony he rushes away and falls from the cliff edge. Rose goes to confession and is told by the priest that 'a Catholic is more capable of evil than anyone' but that 'the Church does not demand that we believe any soul is cut off from mercy'.

Brinkmanship. The word applied by an American journalist to the diplomacy of the Secretary of State, John Foster Dulles, in his dealings with Russia *c.* 1957. Dulles ventured as far as the brink of war in his determination to resist Soviet dictation in foreign affairs. See also *Gamesmanship.

Briscoe, Lily. A principal character in Virginia Woolf's *To the Lighthouse* (1927).

Britannus. Caesar's British Secretary in Bernard Shaw's *Caesar and Cleopatra* (1900).

British Academy. A society formed in 1902 to further the study of subjects not embraced by natural science: e.g. history, philosophy, linguistics, literature, archaeology, law, etc. A Fellow of the British Academy is entitled to append the letters F.B.A. to his name.

British Council, The. Established in 1934, the British Council was granted a Royal Charter in 1940, defining its aims as the promotion of a wider knowledge of Britain and the English language abroad and the development of closer cultural relations with other countries. By the 1960s the Council was represented in seventy-nine countries, including twenty-eight in the Commonwealth, and it has increasingly concentrated on educational work in developing countries in Asia and Africa. It is also the body designated by the British government for cultural relations with the Soviet Union. The Council's educational work comprises English language teaching, the printed word, the development of personal contacts, and the arts. It maintains a corps of language specialists to advise and assist educational authorities overseas, particularly in the training of teachers, and is increasingly concerned in the training of overseas science teachers. The Council assists some two hundred libraries in more than eighty countries, and makes grants to public library development, mainly in East and West Africa. It issues publications intended primarily for overseas students and teachers: *Writers and their Work*, a series of literary surveys with bibliographies of classic and modern English authors; periodical surveys of the novel, music, and the drama in Britain; general booklets of educational interest, and booklists for libraries, students, and teachers; and journals—*British Book News*, *The British Medical Bulletin*, and *British Medical Book Lists*. The Council has also initiated and sponsored poetry and drama recordings of the complete works of Shakespeare and the Argo Book of Recorded Verse.

British Library, The. Following government vacillations over many years, a parliamentary White Paper (Cmd 4572) of January 1971 decreed the institution of The British Library, to embrace the British Museum Library (still to retain that title), The National Reference Library for Science and Invention, The National Central Library, The National Lending Library for Science and Technology, and the British National Bibliography. Economic stringency and political strategy prevailing, the Library may go to premises distant from the present British Museum.

British Museum Library. The historic name for the National Library in Bloomsbury, West-Central London (but the Newspaper Department is at Colindale, on the northern outskirts). The library has grown from several munificent eighteenth-century gifts of private collections of manuscripts and printed books, for the cost of housing which a public lottery was authorized by an Act of 1753. The present Reading Room, annexed to the main British Museum, was opened in 1857. Many books and periodicals were destroyed by enemy bombing in World War II. Under the Copyright Act, publishers are legally obliged to deliver to the Museum a copy of every printed book and paper.

British Museum Reading Room. *See* British Museum Library.

British Weekly, The. A penny 'Journal of Social and Christian Progress' founded in 1886 in the Nonconformist interest. It also made a wide appeal to non-denominational readers during the thirty years that Robertson *Nicoll contributed a weekly middle article under the heading 'Letters of Claudius Clear', frequently with a literary bent. His friend J. M. *Barrie was an occasional contributor.

Britomart Undershaft, Lady. A 'typical managing matron of the upper class', aged about fifty; daughter of the Earl of Stevenage; married to Andrew Undershaft in Bernard Shaw's *Major Barbara* (1905).

Brittain, Vera (Vera Mary Brittain, 1896-1970; married Professor George E. G. Catlin, 1925). Born at Newcastle-under-Lyme; educated at Kingswood and Oxford. Her experiences as a nurse in World War I are indicated in the autobiographical *Testament of Youth* (1933) which gave her prominence among contemporary writers. In addition to novels, her books include *Testament of Friendship* (1940) which portrays from a close personal angle the novelist Winifred *Holtby, and *Testament of Experience* (1957).

Broadbent, Thomas. Of the firm of Doyle and Broadbent, civil engineers, Westminster. He accompanies Doyle to Ireland in Bernard Shaw's *John Bull's Other Island* (1904).

Broadsheet. A single leaf, usually printed on one side only with popular verses or prose matter. Historically, broadsheets were sold for a penny or less by pedlars and hawkers, and were a feature at public executions as the alleged dying confession of the condemned criminal. In the present century there have been occasional revivals of broadsheets for genuine literary purposes, as e.g. by The *Poetry Bookshop in the 1910s.

Brod, Max (1884-1968). Born in Prague. Author of novels, among them *The Redemption of Tycho Brahe* (in German 1916; Eng. trans. 1928), *Reubeni, Prince of the Jews* (1925; 1928), *The Kingdom of Love* (1928; 1930). His essays include *Three Loves* (1921; 1929). He was a close friend of Franz *Kafka, and published *The Castle* and *The Trial* after the death of Kafka, who had instructed him to destroy the manuscripts. He also wrote a biography of Kafka (1937; Eng. trans. 1947).

Brogan, Colm (1902- ; brother of the following). Born and educated in Glasgow; worked there as teacher and journalist and afterwards as journalist and political writer in London. Taking a critical and satirical view of the Welfare State he wrote *Who are the People?* (1943), *Our New Masters* (1947); also *The Educational Revolution* (1955) and other books.

Brogan, Sir Denis (Denis William Brogan, 1900-1974; knighted 1963). Born at Rutherglen, Scotland, of Irish ancestry; educated at Glasgow, Oxford, and Harvard universities. Lecturer on American history in the University of London before becoming Professor of Political Science at Cambridge from 1939; known to a wider public through the encyclopaedic knowledge and phenomenal memory he displayed in B.B.C. radio broadcasts. In addition to books on American, French, and English history and politics, he wrote a detective novel *Stop on the Green Light!* under the pseudonym Maurice Barrington in 1941 (reissued under his own name in 1950).

Bromfield, Louis (1896-1956). Born at Mansfield, Ohio; educated at Cornell and Columbia universities. Worked as a journalist in his own country and abroad before succeeding as a novelist with *Early Autumn* (1926), *The Strange Case of Miss Annie Spragg* (1928), *The Rains Came* (1937) and many others.

Brontë family. An extensive literature has grown up around the three Brontë sisters, their brother Branwell, and their father the Rev. Patrick Brontë, much of it simply reproductive and repetitive. Among the more valuable contributions are: *The Brontës' Web of Childhood* by Fannie E. Ratchford (1941), an examination of the Angria and Gondal stories which prefigure much in the novels of the sisters' maturity; *The Complete Poems of Emily Jane Brontë* edited from the manuscripts by C. W. Hatfield (1941), clarifies certain previously vexing textual and other problems specified in Hatfield's Introduction; *The Brontë Story* by Margaret Lane (1953) added useful information to that provided in Mrs Gaskell's 1857 biography of Charlotte;

The Father of the Brontës by Annette B. Hopkins (1958) corrected previous misapprehensions concerning the Reverend Patrick; *Anne Brontë*, by Winifred Gerin (1959) does justice to the usually neglected sister, and the same writer's *Branwell Brontë* (1961) gives credit to his promise as a painter and disposes of claims made for him as an author; also by Winifred Gerin: *Charlotte Brontë: The Evolution of Genius* (1967) and *Emily Brontë* (1971). *The Four Brontës* by Lawrence and E. M. Hanson (1949) surveys the family history comprehensively with generous quotations from the novels. The various writings on the Brontës and the editions of their works by Clement K. *Shorter between 1896 and 1911 involved much pioneer study and still merit consultation.

Brook Kerith, The. Novel by George *Moore published in 1916. Impressed by his grandmother's stories of prophets and kings, the child Joseph of Arimathea dreams that he is visited by the prophet Samuel and resolves that he too must become a prophet. His father, a wealthy fish-salter, permits him to be taught Hebrew and Greek, but his interest turns later to his father's business until a visit to Jerusalem at the Feast of the Passover acquaints him with the doctrinal disputations of the Sadducees and Pharisees. From these he turns to the Essenes, an ascetic and celibate community, and goes to stay in their place of retreat above the river Jordan. There he teaches Hebrew and Greek to proselytes, finds philosophical discussion spiritually barren, and obtains leave to seek out John the Baptist, whom he finds is away on a journey with a new disciple named Jesus, subsequently recognized by Joseph as a young shepherd he had glimpsed among the Essenes. He becomes a follower of Jesus, and the narrative takes up the gospel story to the point of the crucifixion. Joseph gets permission to take the body of Jesus from the cross and with help carries it to the tomb. Alone there, he sees Jesus's eyes come open, and finding him alive he carries him by night to his own house, where he slowly recovers and at length returns to the Essenes as a shepherd on the hills above the brook Kerith. Years later Paul takes temporary refuge among them, learns the identity of Jesus and hears his story disclaiming messiahship. The two journey together on the road to Caesarea and part outside the city, Paul to embark for Italy to preach the resurrection story unchanged, Jesus to encounter a party of monks from India with beliefs resembling those of the Essenes.

Brooke, Jocelyn (Jocelyn Bernard Brooke, 1908-1966). Born at Sandgate, Kent; educated (briefly) at King's School, Canterbury, before going to Bedales and thence to Oxford. Worked as bookseller, wine-merchant, and in other trades, and as a medical orderly during World War II, after which he had a literary success with *The Military Orchid* (1948), a fascinating offshoot of his interest in botany, shown more exhaustively in *The Wild Orchids of Britain* (1950). His writings include *The Dog at Chambercrown* (1955), an auto-biographical 'excursion', novels, poetry, children's books, and a study of Ronald *Firbank (1951).

Brooke, Rupert (Rupert Chawner Brooke, 1887-1915). Born at Rugby, son of a master at the public school there, where he was educated and at Cambridge. He was one of the founders of the Marlowe Society, the University drama club, for which he acted in Marlowe's *Dr Faustus* and Milton's *Comus*. Graduating in 1909, he then travelled on the Continent and when in England lived at the Old Vicarage, Grantchester, which he made famous in the poem bearing that title. From May 1913 to June 1914 he travelled across America and among the South Pacific islands, as well as visiting New Zealand. On the outbreak of World War I he took a commission in the Royal Naval Division, and after sharing in the unsuccessful expedition to Antwerp went with the Division in February 1915 to the Dardanelles. He declined a staff post, but did not live to take any active part in the attack against the Turks at Gallipoli. On 23 April 1915 he died from blood poisoning and sunstroke and was buried on the Greek island of Skyros. His early death on war service made him a symbolic figure of patriotism and sacrifice, and his poetry (*Poems*, 1911, and *1914 and Other Poems*, 1915) achieved an exceptional and long-sustained popularity, largely on account of the role for which public opinion cast him posthumously as the young hero. He had uncommon physical beauty, was abounding with eager life, and even if as a poet he was acclaimed beyond the measure of his talent,

he wrote a handful of poems likely to survive the fluctuations of literary fashion, which a generation after his death under-rated him as extravagantly as he had formerly been overpraised. If in 1914-15 he took a romantic view of war, it was because he had not experienced the disillusion and horror that was to come in the later stages of the world conflict. He left his money and the proceeds from royalties on his poems to be divided between three fellow poets–Lascelles *Abercrombie, Walter *de la Mare, and W. W. *Gibson. His friend Edward *Marsh published in 1918 a collected edition of Brooke's poems, with a personal Memoir. The first full biography was by Christopher *Hassall (1964).

Brooke, Stopford (Rev. Stopford Augustus Brooke, 1832-1916). Born in Donegal; ordained and appointed a royal chaplain (1872) he later became a Unitarian minister. His *Primer of English Literature* (1876) was used by innumerable students well into the present century and was again produced in an enlarged edition in 1924, the supplementary chapter being provided by George *Sampson. Stopford Brooke also wrote *On Ten Plays of Shakespeare* (1905) and *Ten More Plays of Shakespeare* (1913), and (as editor and author) on many other literary subjects and on religion.

Brooke, Tucker (Charles Frederick Tucker Brooke, 1883-1946). Born in West Virginia; educated at the university there, at Chicago, and (as a *Rhodes Scholar) at Oxford. Taught at various American universities, mainly at Yale. As an authority on Elizabethan drama he was as well known among English students as in America, his widely used books including *The Tudor Drama* (1911) and several volumes on Marlowe, Shakespeare, and other contemporaries.

Brookfield, Charles (1857-1913). Educated at Westminster and Cambridge. Acted in the theatre companies of Ellen Terry, the Bancrofts, and Beerbohm Tree, but was chiefly known as a man-about-town. He wrote plays, including *Dear Old Charlie* (adapted from the French), which was frequently cited as an example of the Censor's leniency to frivolously salacious plays while banning serious works. Angry criticism consequently followed the announcement in 1911 of Brookfield's appointment as Examiner of Plays.

Brooks, Cleanth (1906-). Born in Kentucky; educated at American universities and (as a *Rhodes Scholar) at Oxford. Taught in the English department of Louisiana State University, and from 1947 as Professor of English at Yale. An advocate and leading propagator of the *New Criticism which concentrates on the structural and linguistic factors in poetry and other literary forms, Brooks's writings had a considerable academic influence both in and beyond America, though his approach and methods were viewed with disfavour by those who set a higher value upon the human values of literature than upon technical analysis. His works include *Modern Poetry and the Tradition* (1939), *The Well-Wrought Urn* (1947), and in collaboration with others *Understanding Poetry* (1938), *Understanding Fiction* (1943), *Understanding Drama* (1947), *Modern Rhetoric* (1949).

Brooks, Van Wyck (1886-1963). Born at Plainfield, New Jersey; educated there, and in Europe and at Harvard. Worked as a journalist in London and New York, as a lexicographer, teacher of English, and translator from the French. His most notable work was as a critic, literary historian and biographer: *The World of H. G. Wells* (1915), *America's Coming of Age* (1915), *The Ordeal of Mark Twain* (1912; new edn 1933), *Life of Emerson* (1932), *The Flowering of New England* (1936), *The World of Washington Irving* (1944), *The Times of Melville and Whitman* (1947); *On Literature To-day* (1941). His *Autobiography* appeared in 1965, collecting volumes published in his lifetime. *The Opinions of Oliver Allston* (1941) are mainly his own, and contain interesting matter on contemporaries.

Brophy, Brigid (Brigid Antonia Brophy, 1929-). Daughter of the following. Educated at St Paul's Girl's School and Oxford. Author of *The Crown Princess* (1953), *The King of a Rainy Country* (1956), *The Finishing Touch* (1953), *Don't Never Forget* (1966), etc. *Mozart the Dramatist* (1964), *Black and White: a Portrait of Aubrey Beardsley* (1968), *Prancing Novelist* (1973); *The Burglar, a play with preface* (1968).

Brophy, John (1899-1965). Born in Liverpool; educated at Holt and (after service in World War I, for which he enlisted while under age) at Liverpool and Durham Universities.

Worked as a journalist, as a teacher in Egypt, and as a copywriter, before he was established as an author. His many novels include *The Bitter End* (1928), *Flesh and Blood* (1931), *Waterfront* (1934), *Immortal Sergeant* (1942), *Portrait of an Unknown Lady* (1945), *Turn the Key Softly* (1951), *The Front Door Key* (1960). Also: *Fanfare* (1930; essays); with Eric *Partridge, *Songs and Slang of the British Soldier 1914-18* (1930).

Broughton, Rhoda (1840-1920). Author of numerous popular novels of sentiment, from *Cometh Up as a Flower* (1867) to *A Waif's Progress* (1905).

Brown. See *Gentleman Brown.

Brown. See *Susan Brown.

Brown, Father. Roman Catholic priest-detective in crime stories by G. K. *Chesterton.

Brown, George Douglas. See *Douglas, George.

Brown, Hilton (1890-1961). Born at Elgin, Scotland; educated at the Academy there and at St Andrew's University. In the Indian Civil Service, 1913-34; and on the B.B.C. staff, 1940-46. He wrote numerous novels, among them *Ostrich Eyes* (1928), 'a story of middle-class lives done with unsentimental force and candour', but they made no permanent mark. He also wrote a study of Rudyard *Kipling* (1945).

Brown, Ivor (Ivor John Carnegie Brown, 1891-1974). Born in Malaya of Scottish parentage; educated in England at Cheltenham and Oxford; entered the Civil Service but left it and concentrated on writing, spending many years in journalism—as dramatic critic of the *Manchester Guardian* (1919-35) and other papers, and acted as editor of *The Observer* (1942-48). Published books on politics and public affairs, on *H. G. Wells* (1922), volumes of theatre essays, some novels, *Shakespeare* (1949), a number of studies in the use of language, among them *A Word in Your Ear* (1942), *No Idle Words* (1949), *Having the Last Word* (1950), and topographical and travel books *The Heart of England* (1935), *Winter in London* (1951), *Summer in Scotland* (1952).

Brown, John Mason (1900-1969). Born in Kentucky; educated at Harvard. Dramatic critic on several leading American papers and author of books on the theatre: *The*

Modern Theatre in Revolt (1929), *The Art of Playgoing* (1936), *Seeing Things* (1946; 1948; 1950) and several other volumes of collected essays on plays in performance.

Brown, Ladbroke. *See* *'Savonarola' Brown.

Brown, Lionel (1888-1964). Born and educated in Ireland. As a playwright he achieved moderate success with *To Have and To Hold* (1937), *The Incalculable Factor* (1941), *For Dear Life* (1948), and other pieces, some written for broadcasting.

Brown, Maurice (1881-1955). Born at Reading; educated at Winchester, Eastbourne and Cambridge. Founded and directed theatre companies in England and America. First producer of **Journey's End* by R. C. Sherriff (at Savoy Theatre, London, 1929). Author of *We Sailed in Convoy* (1942).

Brown on Resolution. Novel by C. S. *Forester published in 1929. Albert Brown, illegitimate son of Agatha Brown and Lieut-Commander Saville-Samarez, joins the navy at fifteen after his mother's death, and by 1914, seven years later, has through steady promotion become a Leading Seaman on the third-class cruiser *Charybdis* in the Pacific. At the outbreak of war with Germany *Charybdis* encounters *Ziethen*, a more heavily-gunned commerce raider, and is sunk by her. Brown, the only unwounded survivor, is taken on board *Ziethen*, which has been holed by a shell from *Charybdis* and makes for Resolution, an uninhabited island of volcanic origin in the Galapagos group. There in a landlocked harbour *Ziethen* anchors and prepares to forge and fit a new armour-plate and so enable the raids against food ships and other merchant vessels to be resumed. Brown, determined to do something to delay her departure, escapes from observation and steals a rifle, ammunition and water-bottles. Reaching land, he climbs the razor-sharp volcanic and cactus-covered cliffs, and takes cover behind lava blocks which enable him to train the rifle on the men working to repair *Ziethen* and to kill and wound several. Landing parties fail to reach his hiding place, but a straying German seaman detects and wounds him, leaving him to die in delirium. He had delayed *Ziethen* forty-eight hours, long enough to prevent her

escaping destruction by H.M.S. *Leopard*, a battle cruiser commanded by Captain Saville-Samarez.

Brown, Valentine. Marries Phoebe Throssel in J. M. Barrie's **Quality Street* (1902).

Browne, E. Martin (Elliott Martin Browne (1900-   ). Educated at Eton and Oxford. Assistant Professor of Drama, Carnegie Institute, Pittsburgh, 1927-30; produced all T. S. *Eliot's plays; Director of the *British Drama League, 1948-57.

Browne, Thomas Alexander. *See* Rolf *Boldrewood.

Browne, Wynyard (Wynyard Barry Browne, 1911-1964). Born in London; educated at Marlborough and Cambridge. His lifelong devotion to literature was productive of success in two widely separated periods of his life, first with *Queenie Molson* (1934), *Sheldon's Way* (1935) and other novels, and second with plays, among which *The Holly and the Ivy* (1950) was outstanding both as a popular success and as a work combining dramatic skill, stylistic merit, and convincing characterization.

Browning, Oscar (1837-1923). Historian and educationist; taught at Eton and King's College, Cambridge, where he had considerable influence among large numbers of undergraduates in whose later memoirs his name frequently appears.

Bruce Lockhart. *See* Lockhart.

Bruller, Jean. *See* *Vercors.

Bryant, Sir Arthur (Arthur Wynne Morgan Bryant, 1899-   ; knighted 1954). Born in Norfolk; educated at Harrow and Oxford; called to the Bar, but settled to a distinguished career as historian and biographer. Though his view of history tends towards the heroic and is designed for a non-academic audience, his skill and sense of style represent popularization at its best. His writings include a three-volume life of Samuel Pepys (1933; 1935; 1938), biographical studies of Charles II (1934), George V (1936), Stanley Baldwin (1937), and an edition of the war diaries of Lord Alanbrooke, *The Turn of the Tide* (1957). A pageant of English history is given in *The Years of Endurance, 1793-1802* (1942), *Years of Victory, 1802-1812* (1942), and *The Age of Elegance, 1812-1832* (1950).

Bryce, James (1838-1922; 1st Viscount Bryce, 1914). Historian and statesman; Regius Professor of Civil Law in the University of Oxford (1870-93); British Ambassador in Washington (1907-13); wrote *The American Commonwealth* (1888), *Modern Democracies* (1921), and much else.

Bryher (pseudonym of Annie Winifred Ellerman, 1894-). Born in Margate, daughter of the shipping magnate; educated privately and in Eastbourne. Wrote book reviews for the *Saturday Review* and other papers before publishing her first novel *Development* (1920), followed by *The Fourteenth of October* (a story of the Norman Conquest, 1952), *The Player's Boy* (1953), *Roman Wall* (1954), *The Heart of Artemis* (1963), *Visa for Avalon* (1965), *The Days of Mars* (1972).

Buchan, John (1875-1940; 1st Baron Tweedsmuir, 1935). Born at Perth; educated at Glasgow and Oxford; called to the Bar, 1901; private secretary to Lord Milner in South Africa, 1901-03; Director of Information in World War I; M.P. for the Scottish Universities, 1927-35; Governor-General of Canada, 1935 until his death. Although he was an able statesman and administrator, his chief talent was as a writer of stories of adventure and international intrigue, in which field he was unsurpassed in his time. Since his level of achievement showed little fluctuation, the following books are typical rather than 'best': *The Thirty-Nine Steps* (1915), *Greenmantle* (1916), *Mr Standfast* (1919), *The Three Hostages* (1924). He also wrote several biographies: *Montrose* (1928), *Sir Walter Scott* (1932), *Cromwell* (1934).

Buchanan, Robert Williams (1841-1901), copious writer of verse and fiction popular in the 19th century, but remembered since only for his intemperate attack on Swinburne, Rossetti and others in a pseudonymous article headed 'The Fleshly School of Poetry' (*Contemporary Review*, October 1871) which Rossetti answered in 'The Stealthy School of Criticism' (*Athenaeum*, December 1871).

Buchman, Frank (Frank Nathan Daniel Buchman, 1878-1961). Born in Pennsylvania; ordained as a Lutheran minister (1902) and worked among the poor in Philadelphia. After experiencing while on a visit to England in 1908 'a vision of the Cross' which he fixed as the turning point of his life, he returned to America to become a Y.M.C.A. secretary and start the type of evangelism he was later to conduct on a worldwide scale and to develop into, first, the 'Oxford Group' and then 'Moral Re-Armament' (M.R.A.). Confident claims were made for the transforming effect of these movements in private lives, and for their potential value in redirecting international politics. On the other hand, strong criticism was made of methods deemed by the unsympathetic to be 'dangerous from medical and psychological viewpoints', while questions concerning the sources of abundant funds remained unanswered.

Buck, Pearl (*née* Pearl Sydenstricker, 1892-1973). Born in West Virginia of missionary parents with whom she settled in China while a child; educated in Shanghai and in Virginia. Returned to China, married Dr J. L. Buck, a missionary, and taught in the English departments of universities there. She had written (and won newspaper prizes) from early years, but not until 1931 did she achieve notable success. Then, her second novel, *The Good Earth*, made a deep impression with its knowledge and affectionately sympathetic understanding of China's labouring people. Later, she became involved in controversy with missionary organizations and left China. In America she entered publishing for a while and continued to write novels as well as turning biographer with lives of her parents (*The Exile* and *Fighting Angel*, both 1936). While her advocacy of the cause of the coloured races inclined her to venture upon inadequately informed criticisms, her personal devotion was generously displayed in the foundation of Welcome House in Pennsylvania where Asiatic-American children are nurtured in homes providing affection and stability. Confessing an incurable itch to write, Pearl Buck added abundantly to her output of novels and other works, but her reputation rests upon the early novels on Chinese themes, which include *East Wind, West Wind* (1929), *The Young Revolutionist* (1931), *Sons* (1932), *The Mother* (1934).

Buckle, G. E. (George Earle Buckle, 1854-1935). Born at Twerton-on-Avon, Somerset; educated at Winchester and at Oxford where he won the Newdigate Prize in 1875. Studied law but adopted journalism as his profession, and after a few months in a subordinate position on *The Times* he became its editor in 1884. During his editorship the Parnell case occurred, and developments in organization and a change of ownership created further difficulties for him and he resigned in 1912. He completed the official biography of Benjamin Disraeli after the original author (Monypenny) died, and was responsible for vols 3-6 (1914-20). Later he continued the work previously done by A. C. *Benson and Lord Esher as editors of Queen Victoria's Letters and assisted with the first volume of the *History of 'The Times'* published in the year of his death.

Bucktrout, Gervase. House-agent who befriends widowed Lady Slane in V. Sackville-West's *All Passion Spent* (1931).

Budge, Sir Wallis (Ernest Alfred Thompson Wallis Budge, 1857-1934; knighted 1920). Educated at an elementary school and then employed by a firm of wholesale stationers and booksellers. He studied Hebrew and Syriac in his spare time, and his natural ability led to funds being made available to send him to Cambridge. While still an undergraduate there he published works on Assyrian texts, and after graduating was eventually appointed to the Department of Oriental Antiquities at the British Museum, and from 1894 to 1924 was Keeper of the Department of Egyptian and Assyrian Antiquities there. He took part in various archaeological expeditions in Egypt and the Sudan and was one of the foremost authorities on Egyptology. His many scholarly works include an *Egyptian Hieroglyphic Dictionary* (1900) and an edition of *The Book of the Dead* (1898); he also wrote an autobiographical record, *By Nile and Tigris* (1920).

Buffalo Bill. *See* William Frederick *Cody.

Bulldog Drummond (Captain Hugh Drummond). Chief character in stories bearing his nickname (1920 onward) by *Sapper.

Bullen, Arthur Henry (1857-1920). Editor and publisher, devoted especially to 16th and 17th century poetry and drama; controller of the Shakespeare Head Press, Stratford-on-Avon (1904-20).

Bullen, Frank Thomas (1857-1915). Born in Paddington, London, of impecunious parents. The death of an aunt with whom he lived left him destitute, and he at length went to sea as a cabin boy. About 1875 he embarked from Bedford, Massachusetts, on a whaling vessel, an experience recorded in *The Cruise of the 'Cachalot'* which made him immediately famous when it was published in 1898 and remains a minor classic of seafaring life. Bullen afterwards worked for a while in the Meteorological Office, London, a confining occupation from which he escaped to regular journalism. He wrote many other books, but only the one has survived.

Bullett, Gerald (Gerald William Bullett, 1893-1958). Born at Forest Hill, London; educated at a private day-school before going to work in a bank. His first novel *The Progress of Kay* was published in 1916 while he was serving in the Royal Flying Corps. At the end of World War I he studied at Cambridge with a government grant and graduated in 1921. Thereafter he lived by writing—as a reviewer, essayist, short story writer, and novelist. Among his works of fiction are *The History of Egg Pandervil* (1928), *Nicky, Son of Egg* (1929), *The Jury* (1935), *The Elderbrook Brothers* (1945), *Cricket in Heaven* (1949), *The Daughters of Mrs Peacock* (1957). He also wrote poems, studies of G. K. Chesterton, Walt Whitman, and Modern English Fiction, and compiled several anthologies.

Bullock, Sir Alan (Alan Louis Charles Bullock, 1914-   ). Knighted 1972. Educated at Bradford and Oxford. Master of St Catherine's College, Oxford, from 1960. Author of *Hitler: A Study in Tyranny* (1952); *The Life and Times of Ernest Bevin* (2 vols, 1960, 1967).

Bunin, Ivan (1870-1953). Born in Voronezh; educated at home and at Moscow University. Left Russia in 1919 and lived for the rest of his life in France. One of the outstanding pre-Revolution writers, producing both verse and prose, his international repute rested mainly upon his novel *The Village* (1910).

Bunter, Billy. The fat schoolboy in stories and television plays by Frank *Richards.

Bunting, Daniel George. *See* Daniel *George.

Burgess, Anthony (1917-   ). Educated in Manchester. Lecturer, English master, education officer, Malaya and Brunei (1954-9). Author of many novels: *Time for* a *Tiger* (1956), *A Clockwork Orange* (1962), *Tremor of Intent* (1966), etc. *The Novel Today* (1963), *Here Comes Everybody: An Introduction to James Joyce* (1965). Also wrote as Joseph *Kell.

Burgess, Bessie. In Sean O'Casey's *The *Plough and The Stars* (1926) a street fruit-vendor, forty, hardened by toil and somewhat coarsened by drink.

Burgess, Gelett (Frank Gelett Burgess, 1866-1951). Born in Boston; educated at Massachusetts Institute of Technology. Author of many humorous books, including *Are You a Bromide?* (1907). Though his quatrain 'The Purple Cow' is known far and wide, his name is not equally often attached to it.

Burgess, Mr. Father of the heroine in Bernard Shaw's *Candida* (1894).

Burgin, G. B. (George Brown Burgin, 1856-1944). Born in Croydon; educated at Totteridge. Secretary to Sir Samuel White Baker (Baker Pasha); Secretary, Authors' Club, 1905-8. Author of nearly a hundred novels, including *Herb of Healing* (1915), *One Traveller Returns* (1931), *Slaves of the Ring* (1936).

Buried Alive. Novel by Arnold *Bennett published in 1908. Priam Farll, a fifty-year-old famous but incurably shy painter, is living in an undistinguished South Kensington house attended only by his valet, Henry Leek. When Leek dies from double pneumonia, the doctor mistakes the master for the man and the death certificate is made out in the name of Priam Farll, the painter's shyness preventing him from having the error corrected. Unrecognized after forty years, Farll is presumed by his solicitor cousin to be the valet Henry Leek, and is paid off with a month's wages in lieu of notice. A letter addressed to Leek which had been delivered to Farll leads to a meeting with a Mrs Alice Challice, to whom Leek had written through the medium of a matrimonial agency. After Leek's body has been buried as that of the famous painter in Westminster Abbey, Farll marries Alice and they settle in her house at Putney as Mr and Mrs Leek. When her income from brewery shares fails and he decides that his painting must be their means of support, he confesses to her that he is Priam Farll, but she supposes him to be suffering from delusions, and is not moved from that belief when he paints a masterpiece, which, however, she can make little of and, to humour him, says is 'beautiful—for an amateur'. But an art expert recognizes the hand of Priam Farll in the 'posthumous' paintings, and the artist's true identity having been tardily established by means of a lawsuit, Farll and Alice escape from notoriety by leaving the country, and the valet's body is removed from the Abbey. Though the plot is basically fantastic and farcical it is treated within the limits of genuine comedy, and Alice, imperturbable, motherly, and matter-of-fact, is admirably drawn. Retitled *The Great Adventure* and with changed names for the principals, the story was successful in a dramatized version which ran at the Kingsway Theatre for nearly 700 performances from 25 March 1913.

Burke, Mat. Ship's stoker in Eugene O'Neill's *Anna Christie* (1921); in love with Anna.

Burke, Thomas (1886-1945). Born in London, orphaned in infancy, and began work at the age of fifteen with little formal education. Office work, assisting a bookseller, and several years in a literary agency preceded success as a writer of fiction specializing in stories of London's Chinatown, the life of which he had seen at first-hand while living in the east-end district of Poplar during boyhood: *Limehouse Nights* (1916), *Whispering Windows* (1920), *The Pleasantries of Old Quong* (1931). He also wrote nonfiction studies of London's east end, and an autobiography, *The Wind and the Rain* (1924).

Burnand, F. C. (Sir Francis Cowley Burnand, 1836-1917; knighted 1902). Editor of *Punch*, 1880-1906, and author of much humorous writing, including stage burlesques and farces.

Burnett, Mrs Frances Hodgson (*née* Frances Eliza Hodgson, 1849-1924). Married Dr Swan M. Burnett, 1873; divorced 1898. Married Stephen Townesend; divorced 1901. Born in England (Manchester), daughter of a successful hardware dealer who died while Frances was still an infant. When the family export business was bankrupted by the American Civil War, the Burnetts emigrated to the U.S. and lived in poverty in Tennessee, until Frances succeeded as a writer from the age of seventeen. Her *Little*

Lord Fauntleroy (1886) had an enormous and long-sustained vogue, though later and more sophisticated generations derided it as mawkish and intolerably sentimental. She nevertheless maintained her popularity among less critical readers, and her understanding of children compensated certain absurdities in her outlook and personal bearing. Among her books for children, *The Secret Garden* (1909) was still in circulation half a century later. She led an expensive and unsettled life between Europe and America, living for a while in Kent.

Burnett, Ivy Compton. *See* Ivy *Compton-Burnett.

Burnett, W. R. (William Riley Burnett, 1899-   ). Born in Springfield, Ohio; educated there and at Miami Military Institute. After working for some time as a statistician, he turned to full-time writing, producing novels mainly of city life depicted in a 'tough' realistic style. His first book *Little Caesar* (1929) was immediately successful, and among its numerous successors *The Asphalt Jungle* (1949) is outstanding.

Burnt Norton. Poem by T. S. Eliot, the first of his *Four Quartets* (1943); first published separately in 1936.

Burroughs, Edgar Rice (1875-1950). Born in Chicago; educated privately and at Michigan Military Academy. More than a decade in varied occupations seemed likely to lead to a life of permanent failure, but from 1914 he became known throughout the world as author of *Tarzan of the Apes.*

Burroughs, William S. (1914-   ). Expatriate U.S. writer of novels and other works subjectively concerned with drug addiction, among which *The Naked Lunch* (1959) was charged as obscene.

Bury, J. B. (John Bagnell Bury, 1861-1927). Historian and classical scholar; wrote histories of Greece and the Roman Empire, a *History of Freedom of Thought* (1914), and edited a standard edition of Gibbon's *Decline and Fall of the Roman Empire.*

Bush, Douglas (John Nash Douglas Bush, 1896-   ). Born in Canada (Morrisburg, Ontario); educated at Ontario and Harvard. Professor of English at Harvard from 1957. Author of *Mythology and the Renaissance Tradition* (1932), *Mythology and the Romantic Tradition* (1937), *Science and English*

Poetry (1950), and the volume on the Earlier Seventeenth Century (1945) in the *Oxford History of English Literature.*

Buss, Frances Mary. *See* Dorothea *Beale.

Bussy, Dorothy (*née* Dorothy Strachey; died 1960). Educated at Fontainebleau; married the painter Simon Bussy and continued to live in France. Her novel *Olivia* (1949) was highly praised, and her other works included *Fifty Nursery Rhymes, with a Commentary on English Usage for French students* (1950), and translations of the writings of André *Gide, who was one of her circle of distinguished friends.

Butcher, S. H. (Samuel Henry Butcher, 1850-1910). Born in Dublin; educated at Marlborough and Cambridge; taught at Eton and Cambridge before becoming Professor of Greek in the University of Edinburgh from 1882 to 1903. He did valuable work in education, but his reputation rests on the translation of Homer's *Odyssey* (1879) he made in collaboration with Andrew *Lang.

Butler, Samuel (1835-1902). Born at Langar, Nottinghamshire, son of the rector of the parish, and grandson of Dr Samuel Butler, headmaster of Shrewsbury School and later Bishop of Lichfield. Samuel (the grandson) was first educated by his father, then at Allesley, near Coventry, before attending Shrewsbury from 1848 to 1854, when he went up to St John's College, Cambridge, graduating in classics in 1858. Intended for the Church, he prepared in London for ordination until he recognized his inability to accept the essential doctrinal principles. After other professions had been considered and rejected, he emigrated to New Zealand in 1859 and set up as a sheep farmer, doubled the capital provided by his father, and returned to England in 1864 and settled at 15 Clifford's Inn, London, which remained his bachelor home until he died. Two of the main influences in his life originated, first, in the passion for Italy dating from the earliest visit with his parents in 1843, and, next, the passion for Handel's music acquired during schooldays. While he was in New Zealand his family compiled from his letters and other writings *A First Year in Canterbury Settlement*, published in 1863 and disliked by Butler, since his father had edited it with that strict Victorian regard for propriety from which the son violently dissented. Having returned from New Zealand with enough money to maintain himself in modest circumstances (though occasional financial crises beset him), he became a lifelong dilettante—an amateur of painting, music, and literature. A painting by him in the Tate Gallery, London (*Mr Heatherley's Holiday*) is reminiscent of the art school (the well-known Heatherley's) at which he took lessons, and other of his pictures were exhibited at the Royal Academy. His interest in music did not show itself in practice until he was middle-aged. After forming a friendship with Henry Festing Jones (who became his biographer), he composed either singly or in collaboration with Jones, and always in a Handelian style, chamber music (*Gavottes, Minuets, Fugues*, etc., 1885), *Narcissus, A Dramatic Cantata* (1888), and *Ulysses, A Dramatic Oratorio* (published posthumously, 1904). His dealings with literature were more serious and consistent. A lifelong controversialist and prober into accepted beliefs, old and new, he ventured into theological polemics with a privately printed and anonymous critical examination of *The Evidence for the Resurrection of Jesus Christ* (1865), expanded in *The Fair Haven* (1873), a volume published pseudonymously as by 'the late John Pickard Owen'. In between came the Utopian satirical novel *Erewhon* (1872), again issued anonymously. Though this is his best-known and most influential book, it brought him next to no profit; and inasmuch as the ideas it promulgated were a paradoxical reversal of current beliefs and attitudes, it had to wait for a new and heretical generation to recognize its subtlety and originality of outlook. Apart from *Erewhon, Erewhon Revisited* (1901) and *The *Way of All Flesh* (1903), Butler's writings are on the fringes of literature. His originality of mind and his intellectual independence are startlingly evident, yet his combativeness in maintaining them against all comers was carried into eccentricity and even crankiness. He opposed Darwin in several books, put forward confidently the opinion that the *Odyssey* was written in Sicily and by a woman, and proffered unorthodox theories concerning Shakespeare's *Sonnets*. His anti-Darwinian views on Evolution filtered down to the present century largely through the Prefaces of Bernard *Shaw. As an epigrammatist and projector of paradoxes he is presented in *The Notebooks of Samuel

Butler (1951 edn). The major antagonism of his life was towards his father, for reasons displayed in *The Family Letters of Samuel Butler 1841-1866* (1962) as well as in *The Way of All Flesh*. Also in the latter is Butler's most attractive piece of character-drawing, of Aunt Alethea, based on his friend Miss Savage. A very full account of his life is given in *Samuel Butler, Author of 'Erewhon', 1835-1902. A Memoir* by H. Festing Jones (2 vols 1919), and there have been many studies of his personality and writings. See also the Preface to Shaw's *Major Barbara*.

Butterfield, Sir Herbert (1900-   ; knighted 1968). Born at Oxenhope, Yorks; educated at Keighley grammar school and Peterhouse, Cambridge. Appointed Professor of Modern History, Cambridge, 1944, Regius Professor 1963; Master of Peterhouse from 1955. Author (among other works) of *George III, Lord North and the People* (1949), *The Origins of Modern Science* (1949), *Christianity in European History* (1951) and *The University and Education Today* (1962).

Buttle, Myra. Pseudonym under which Victor *Purcell wrote verse satires: *The Sweeniad* (1958) and *Toynbee in Elysium* (1960) attacking, respectively, T. S. *Eliot and the historian A. J. *Toynbee; and *The Bitch's Brew, or The Plot Against Bertrand Russell* (1960), championing Russell against detractors.

B.V. Initials (standing for Bysshe Vanolis) added to his name on title pages by James *Thomson (1834-82) to distinguish himself from the 18th-century poet of the same name. He was an enthusiastic admirer of Percy *Bysshe* Shelley and of Novalis (pseudonym of Friedrich Leopold von Hardenburg, 1772-1801) whose nom-de-plume Thomson adopted in the form of an anagram.

Byrne, Donn (Brian Oswald Donn-Byrne, 1889-1928). Born in Brooklyn of Irish parents; educated in Dublin, Paris, and Leipzig. Tried various occupations in South America and New York, working in the latter as journalist and lexicographer, until his novel *Messer Marco Polo* (1920) started him on a successful but brief literary career ended by a fatal motor accident. In addition to other novels and short stories published in his lifetime, e.g. *Blind Raftery*, 1924; *Hangman's House*, 1926; *Brother Saul*, 1927, he left much in manuscript, and among posthumous publications were *Field of Honour* (1929), *The Island of Youth* (1933).

Byrne, James. Pseudonym used by Edward William *Garnett for *Lords and Masters* (1911), a play in three acts.

Byron, Cashel. See *Cashel Byron's Profession*.

Byron, Robert (1905-1941). Born at Wembley; educated at Eton and Oxford; travelled in Greece, India, Tibet, Afghanistan, Persia, Russia, China and Egypt, sometimes as a journalist. Several books were an outcome of these travels, *The Road to Oxiana* (1937) being a masterpiece. His other books include *An Essay on India* (1931), *The Byzantine Achievement* (1929), *First Russia, Then Tibet* (1933).

Bywater, Ingram (1840-1914). Professor of Greek in the University of Oxford, 1893-1908. Celebrated for his translation of the *Poetics* of Aristotle (1900) and for scholarly editions of this and other classical texts.

Cabell, James Branch (1879-1958). Born at Richmond, Virginia; educated at William and Mary College. Worked as a journalist and genealogist, but from 1904 published novels, poems, and other writings which gained him for some years a high reputation. He created his own peculiar world of myth and romance in *Jurgen* (1919), which, with others in a like genre, is set in an imaginary land of Poictesme. Their rabelaisian flavour and mannered style attracted initiates and repelled the orthodox, whose lack of enthusiasm for Cabell's work was endorsed by later critics. *The Eagle's Shadow* (1904), *The Rivet in Grandfather's Neck* (1915), *The Cream of the Jest* (1917), *The Silver Stallion* (1926), *Something About Eve* (1927), *The Way of Ecben* (1929), are representative.

Caesar. The Roman emperor in *Androcles and the Lion* by Bernard Shaw.

Caesar and Cleopatra. Historical play in five acts by Bernard *Shaw written in 1898, published in *Three Plays for Puritans* (1900); first professional performances—in New York 1906, in England (Leeds) 1907. A Prologue added in 1912 and spoken by the god Ra, sketches Egyptian-Roman history up to the time Julius Caesar returned home. The original (now an alternative) Prologue, set on the Syrian border of Egypt, begins the play with news brought to the Egyptian guardsmen that their army has been defeated by the Roman legions under Caesar. They discuss what is to be done with Cleopatra, but are told by her chief nurse, Ftatateeta, 'a huge grim woman', that the queen is missing. She has fled to the desert and is sleeping between the paws of the great Sphinx, where she is discovered by Caesar, of whom she is terrified until he leads her to the palace and enthrones her. Caesar is next at Alexandria, in the palace of the boy king Ptolemy, the rival of his sister Cleopatra as ruler of Egypt. After a confused quarrel among those present, Caesar orders the hall to be cleared, and remains with Cleopatra alone until a messenger reports that the citizens have risen against the Romans. Besieged, Caesar orders the burning of ships in the harbour, whence the flames spread to the famous library of Alexandria. Caesar hastens to capture the Pharos island and its lighthouse. With his general, Rufio, and his secretary, Britannus, he gets to the lighthouse, where Cleopatra

follows them, hidden in carpets vended by Apollodorus, a foppish Sicilian. Cut off by the Egyptians they escape by swimming, Cleopatra being thrown into the sea for Caesar to rescue. Back in her palace, Cleopatra gives audience to Pothinus, Ptolemy's guardian, who is held as a hostage. He plans to drive out Caesar, but she suspects him of plotting to oust her and put Ptolemy on the throne, and he does in fact accuse her to Caesar of treachery. Cleopatra orders Ftatateeta to kill Pothinus, though Caesar has given him a safe conduct. When Ftatateeta is disclosed as his slayer, Rufio kills her. Having defeated the supporters of Ptolemy, who is drowned in the battle, Caesar sails for Rome, promising to send Cleopatra Mark Antony in exchange for himself.

Caetani, Princess Marguerite (*née* Marguerite Chapin, 1880-1963). Born in New London, U.S., she studied singing until her marriage in 1911 to an Italian nobleman and amateur composer, Roffredo, Prince of Bassiano. They settled in Paris, where the Princess became the benefactor of writers of various nationalities as editor of her literary review, *Commerce*, which ran from 1924 to 1932. Later they moved to Rome, where she started another and more influential review, *Botteghe Oscure*.

Cain, J. M. (James Mallahan Cain, 1892-   ). Born at Annapolis, Maryland; educated at Washington College. Worked as a journalist until his novel *The Postman Always Rings Twice* (1934) brought him the means to become an independent full-time writer. His fiction—which includes *Serenade* (1937), *Mildred Pierce* (1941), *Three of a Kind* (1943), *Galatea* (1953)—attracted by a fast-moving and forceful narrative style and by avoidance of sexual reticence.

Caine, Hall (Sir Thomas Henry Hall Caine, 1853-1931; knighted 1918). Born at Runcorn, Cheshire, the son of a Manx blacksmith. He received only an elementary education (in Liverpool and the Isle of Man) before starting work at fourteen in the office of a Liverpool architect, whence he returned after an interlude as school-teacher in the Isle of Man, and before changing to become a builder's assistant. Spare-time journalism and lecturing led to acquaintanceship with authors, chiefly Dante Gabriel Rossetti. In 1881 he moved to London as Rossetti's secretary, publishing *Recollections of D. G. Rossetti* in 1882, the year in which the poet died. It was at Rossetti's suggestion that Hall Caine made the Isle of Man the scene of a number of his novels: *The Deemster* (1887), *The Bondman* (1890), *The Manxman* (1894), *The Christian* (1897), etc. Other novels: *The Eternal City* (1901), *The Prodigal Son* (1904), *The Woman Thou Gavest Me* (1913). He rivalled Marie *Corelli in popularity and fortune; and, like her, earned disfavour with the critics. Several of his novels became extremely successful in stage adaptations. *A Life of Christ*, edited from an enormously long manuscript left at his death, was published in 1938. An autobiography, *My Story*, appeared as early as 1908.

Cakes and Ale, or The Skeleton in the Cupboard. Novel by W. Somerset *Maugham published in 1930. The narrator, Ashenden, himself a novelist, is suddenly invited to lunch by Alroy Kear, a much younger novelist who buttresses his popularity by flattery and self advertisement. He revives a former slim acquaintance with Ashenden so as to get from him facts about the early life of Edward Driffield, an eminent writer, whose biography Kear has been commissioned by the widow to write. Driffield, after neglect by the critics and a shady early life, was nursed into respectability and fame by his second wife. In boyhood Ashenden has been friendly with Driffield and his first wife, Rosie, formerly a barmaid, and he is shaken when the Driffields disappear, leaving their debts unpaid. Later, in London, Rosie becomes Ashenden's mistress before decamping to America with another lover, where they become prosperous. Many years later, widowed there, she reveals to Ashenden the truth behind a crucial episode narrated in Driffield's masterpiece. Alroy Kear's purpose is to extract from Ashenden details of the underside of Driffield's early life, to be used, he indicates, only allusively and with discretion and charm. His particular problem is 'how the devil am I to get over the first Mrs Driffield?' 'The skeleton in the cupboard', murmurs Ashenden, convinced that Kear will cook the facts and distort the picture. The novel portrays Rosie as an enchantingly lovable woman, though in the main it is a satire on literary circles. Driffield and Kear were widely regarded as caricatures of Thomas Hardy and Hugh

Walpole, an identification denied by Maugham.

Calamity Jane. Name applied to anyone with an habitually gloomy outlook which prognosticates disaster. Originally the nickname of Martha Jane Burke (*c.* 1852-1903) an American mining-camp character.

Calder, Ritchie (Peter Ritchie Calder, 1906- ; life peer 1966 as Baron Ritchie-Calder of Balmashannar). Born in Scotland; educated there at Forfar. Worked as journalist for various Scottish and English newspapers and periodicals, specializing as a disseminator of scientific knowledge in terms comprehensible by the lay mind. Montague Burton Professor of International Relations, Edinburgh, 1961-67. His numerous books include *Men Against the Desert* (1951), *Men Against the Jungle* (1954), *Science Makes Sense* (1955), *Living With the Atom* (1962), *The Evolution of the Machine* (1968).

Calderon, George (George Leslie Calderon, 1868-1913). Author of plays including *The Fountain* (1909), *The Little Stone House* (1911), a number of one-act plays, pamphlets on woman's rights, and a volume of impressions, *Tahiti* (not published until 1921).

Caldwell, Erskine (Erskine Preston Caldwell, 1903-). Born in Georgia, son of a Presbyterian minister; educated at the University of Virginia. Among his numerous novels, *Tobacco Road* (1932) and *God's Little Acre* (1933) attracted most attention, and achieved a sale of millions of copies in their various editions. Both deal with intermingled lust and religion in the lives of degenerate poor whites in Georgia; both were fruitlessly proceeded against on charges of obscenity; and both were credited with 'exhibiting his rich sense of folk humour as well as his indignation at social inequalities'. In a dramatized version *Tobacco Road* had a run of 3,182 performances in New York (1932 onward). cf. Christie, Agatha.

Caldwell, Taylor (Janet Taylor Caldwell, 1900-). Born in England (Manchester) but lived in the United States from 1907. Author of popular novels, *Dynasty of Death* (1938), *The Eagles Gather* (1940), and others.

Callaghan, Slim. Private detective in crime stories by Peter *Cheney.

Call of the Wild, The. Novel by Jack *London

published in 1903. The son of a St Bernard and a Scotch shepherd dog, Buck is born and brought up as 'a sated aristocrat' at Judge Miller's place in the sunny Santa Clara Valley, California, whence he is kidnapped and beaten until he is 'metamorphosed into a raging fiend' before being clubbed into insensibility and subjection by a dog-breaker. He is shipped to Alaska at the time of the 1897 Klondike goldrush and put into a sledge team, of which he at length makes himself leader by overcoming his predecessor in a ruthless fight. He passes from one owner to another, from the skilful and considerate to the incompetent and brutal. Under ill-treatment Buck at last rebels and is rescued when nearly beaten to death, by John Thornton, a gold-prospecter, who becomes his ideal master. He saves Thornton from drowning and later wins a wager for him by pulling a sledge with a half-ton load. Buck begins to be made restless by the howling of timber wolves and makes occasional excursions to them in the forest. When Indians attack the camp he tears at their throats and drives them off, but Thornton is already dead. A wolf-pack then moves in. Buck withstands them, but soon he finds the call of the wild irresistible and runs with the pack.

Callaghan, Morley (1903-   ). Born and educated in Toronto. Acquainted with Ernest *Hemingway, Scott *Fitzgerald and James *Joyce in Paris. Author of novels, *Strange Fugitive* (1928), *It's Never Over* (1930), *They Shall Inherit the Earth* (1935), *More Joy in Heaven* (1937), *The Loved and the Lost* (1951), *A Passion in Rome* (1961). *Morley Callaghan's Stories* (1959). *That Summer in Paris* (1963) is an account of his early experiences in France and also of his literary technique.

Calypso. A West Indian spontaneously improvised song with topical and/or personal references sung by workers or at public gatherings, usually outdoors. The origin of the word in this sense is untraced, having no discoverable connection with Calypso, a nymph in Homer's *Odyssey*.

Cambridge, Elizabeth (pseudonym of Barbara K. Hodges, *née* Webber, 1893-1949). Born in Hertfordshire; educated in Plymouth and Paris. Her first short stories were published during adolescence and she went on to write novels—*Hostages to Fortune* (1933), *The*

Sycamore Tree (1934)—depicting English village life with sensitive understanding.

Cambridge Platonists. A group of Christian philosophers centred on Cambridge University around the middle of the seventeenth century. Among their chief aims was to attempt to reconcile religion and reason, and to establish the conviction that right and wrong have real existence independently of any theory of divine purpose. They were opposed to both extremist wings of contemporary theology, followed the teachings of Plato as against those of the schoolmen disciples of Aristotle, and included mystics and transcendentalists among their number. A prominent member of the group was Henry More (1614-1687), who appears in Rose Macaulay's *They Were Defeated* (1932).

Cameron, John. See A. G. *Macdonell.

Cammaerts, Emile Leon (1878-1953). Born in Belgium; educated at the University of Brussels; settled in England in 1908 and became Professor of Belgian Studies in the University of London. His *Belgian Poems* (1915; 1916) were welcomed in World War I for their inspiring words during the German occupation of his country; and later, among much miscellaneous writing, he produced further verse and biography and history on Belgian themes, as well as books on art, religion, etc., and an autobiography, *The Flower of Grass* (1944).

Campbell, Gabrielle Margaret Vere (Mrs Arthur L. Long). See Marjorie *Bowen.

Campbell, Mrs Patrick (*née* Beatrice Stella Tanner, 1865-1940; married, 1884, Patrick Campbell, who was killed, 1900, in the South African War; married, 1914, George Frederick Myddleton Cornwallis-West). Starting in an amateur company, she became at length the leading actress of her generation, excelling in *The Second Mrs Tanqueray* by A. W. *Pinero, in plays by *Ibsen, and later as Eliza Doolittle in *Pygmalion* by Bernard Shaw, who was one of her chief admirers and also one of her most candid critics. She published some of Shaw's letters to her in *My Life and Some Letters* (1922); and Alan Dent edited in 1952 *Bernard Shaw and Mrs Patrick Campbell: Their Correspondence*, upon which a stage version was based—*Dear Liar: A Comedy of Letters*—by Jerome Kilty, who acted in it with his wife in Chicago in 1957 and in London in 1960. It is supposed that the 'strangely innocent relationship' between Shaw and Mrs Campbell is reflected in the Interlude of Shaw's play The *Apple Cart.

Campbell, R. J. (Rev. Reginald John Campbell, 1867-1956). Born in London; educated at Nottingham and Oxford universities; entered the Congregational denomination and was Minister of the City Temple, Holborn Viaduct, London, from 1903 to 1915. His publication of The New Theology (1907) stirred much controversy. He was ordained in the Church of England in 1916 and became Chancellor of Chichester Cathedral (1930-46). A man of staunch individuality and liberal opinions, and an early member of the *Fabian Society, he attracted many eminent lecturers to speak at the City Temple Literary Society meetings, which drew large audiences and stimulated enlightened interest in literature and public affairs. His numerous writings, mainly on theological subjects, include a Life of Christ (1921) and biographies of Thomas Arnold (1927) and David Livingstone (1929).

Campbell, Roy (Ignatius Roy Dunnachie Campbell, 1901-1957). Born in Durban of Irish and Scottish ancestry; educated at the High School there, but much of his childhood was occupied with free life in the bush and veld; left South Africa when he was seventeen and during a brief stay at Oxford became acquainted with many of the young writers of the period. After a period in France he returned for a while to South Africa, where he developed a strongly critical and satirical attitude towards politicians and their conduct of affairs. Again he went to France, settling in Provence as a fisherman and bullfighter. He joined the Franco forces in the Spanish Civil War, after moving to Toledo and becoming a Roman Catholic. In World War II he served with the British army in East Africa, was injured and invalided out, and entered the Talks Department of the B.B.C. In 1952 he bought a farm in Portugal and was killed in a motor accident there in 1957. Campbell was a man of imposing stature and physical strength, and by temperament a rebel against all the influences of contemporary civilization which impose uniformity and diminish individuality. His poetry, traditional in form, is belligerent in tone and spirit—as in the satirical volumes The Flaming

Terrapin (1924), The Wayzgoose (1928), The Georgiad (1931)—and sometimes expressive of the primitive life of native peoples and creatures of the wild, as in such short poems as 'The Zulu Girl', 'Horses on the Camargue', 'The Zebras', 'The Sisters', and others in the volumes entitled Adamastor (1930) and Flowering Reeds (1933). He also published translations of the poems of St John of the Cross (1951), Frederico Garcia *Lorca (1952), and Baudelaire, and plays by the classic Spanish dramatists Lope de Vega and Tirso de Molina. His prose works include an account of bull fighting, Taurine Provence (1932), and two autobiographical volumes, Broken Record (1934) and Light on a Dark Horse (1951).

Campion, Albert. Amateur detective in the crime stories of Margery *Allingham.

Camus, Albert (1913-1960). Born, educated, and for some years worked as actor and producer of plays, in Algeria. He was in France during the German occupation in World War II and was active in the Resistance. The ideas expressed in his earlier writings seemed to align with those inherent in the *Existentialism of *Sartre, though he afterwards became involved in controversy with him. Nevertheless, Camus' 'philosophy of the absurd' retained existentialist features without accepting its more pessimistic outlook. His novels include L'Etranger (1942) and La Peste (1947); among his plays are L'Etat de siège (1948; adaptation of La Peste) and Caligula (1938; performed 1946). Le Mythe de Sisyphe (1942) and L'Homme révolté (1951) are philosophical essays. See *Theatre of the Absurd.

Canadian Writers. While contemporary American literature has been competing on level terms with those of European countries since the 1920s, no Canadian writer born later than the 1880s has yet found a large audience in Britain. The popularity of the earlier books from Canada is accounted for by English fascination with life in 'the wild', as depicted in the animal stories of C. G. D. *Roberts (1860-1945) and Ernest Thompson *Seton (1860-1946); a more rollicking kind of wild life, mostly human and frequently of the bar-room and rough-neck type, gave the ballads and songs of Robert W. *Service (1874-1958) an immense and long-sustained circulation. Roberts's cousin, Bliss *Carman (1861-1929), was philosopher as well as lyric poet, and though he collaborated in three volumes of songs from 'Vagabondia', his poems are more delicate than robust, and had lost their previous wide appeal a decade or more before he died. The poems of Duncan Campbell *Scott (1862-1947) are largely and sympathetically concerned with the ways of the North American Indians, as are the paintings and prose works of Emily *Carr (1871-1945). Frederick Philip *Grove (1871-1948) had firsthand experience of the prairie and farming life dealt with in his realistic novels, which display nothing of the kindly sentiment which living on a farm distilled in *Anne of Green Gables* by L. M. *Montgomery (1874-1942), whose series of books following the same characters and their offspring were received with international and seemingly inexhaustible affection. Stephen *Leacock (1869-1944), like Ernest Thompson Seton, Robert W. Service and Marjorie *Pickthall (1883-1922), was a migrant from England. His collections of humorous sketches and parodies, combining an artless sense of fun with a cunningly injected measure of literary sophistication, gave pleasure to both the learned and the simple. He was also a distinguished economist and an historian. Marjorie Pickthall was a college librarian in Toronto and author of romantic and religious verse and prose. Mazo *de la Roche (1885-1961) succeeded in maintaining her own and her worldwide readers' interest in the Whiteoaks family through more than a dozen novels, steering the matriarch past her hundredth birthday. George (or Archibald) Stansfield Belaney (1888-1938), known to the public as *Grey Owl and trading on his personal appearance on lecture platforms in Red Indian dress, was also an immigrant from England. But Indian half-caste or not, he possessed genuine knowledge of the Canadian out-of-doors and displayed it in his books. The numerous poems of E. J. *Pratt (1883-1964)—on, variously and symbolically, whale fishery, death and immortality, the loss of the *Titanic*, fascism and war, the building of the Canadian Pacific Railway, Jesuit missions to the Indians—have been given renewed attention by younger critics. With W. E. *Collin (1893-   ) Canadian writing moved into the contemporary academic phase. His *The White Savannahs* (1936) undertook the first critical analysis of Canadian authors.

Robert *Finch (1900-   ) is to some degree a poet in debt to Matthew Arnold. A. J. M. *Smith (1902-   ) is metaphysical poet, literary historian and critic, and anthologist. Some lingering air of Paris in the heyday of the American expatriates exhales from the novels and short stories of Morley *Callaghan (1903-   ). Among other notable writers born in Canada in this century are Bruce *Hutchison (1901-   ), Earle *Birney (1904-   ), Hugh *MacLennan (1907-   ), A. M. *Klein (1909-   ), Robertson *Davies (1913-   ). Malcolm· *Lowry (1909-1957), sometimes claimed as a Canadian writer on account of fifteen years in British Columbia, was born in England and died there, and found his chief inspiration in Mexico.

The abundance of Canadian writers in both British and French Canada is demonstrated in *The Oxford Companion to Canadian History and Literature* compiled by Norah Story (1967). *A Literary History of Canada* edited by Carl F. Klinck (Toronto, 1965) surveys Canadian works written in English.

Canby, H. S. (Henry Seidel Canby, 1878-1961). Born at Wilmington, Delaware, U.S.; educated at Yale, where he became for a time a Professor of English. His chief activities were in journalism, as co-founder and (from 1924 to 1936) editor of the *Saturday Review of Literature*. In that journal and in his books his declared aim was 'to pass on sound values to the reading public'. Author of *Definitions* (1921; 1924), *American Estimates* (1929), *Classic Americans from Irving to Whitman* (1931), *The Age of Confidence* (1934), and biographies of Thoreau, Whitman, etc.

Cancel page. A leaf inserted in a book to replace a page found to contain error, libel, etc. after printing.

Candida. Play in three acts by Bernard *Shaw written 1894-5, published in *Pleasant Plays* (1898); first performed in Aberdeen 1897, in London 1900. In St Dominic's Parsonage, overlooking Victoria Park in northeast London, the Rev. James Mavor Morell is discussing forthcoming speaking engagements with his typist, Proserpine Garnett, when his curate, Rev. Alexander Mill, comes to tell him that his father-in-law, Burgess, is about to call. Described as 'a vulgar ignorant guzzling man', Burgess has not visited the house since Morell lost him a contract for workhouse clothing three years before because his low tender was based on sweated labour. While he is trying to ingratiate himself with Morell his daughter Candida, Morell's wife, returns from the country accompanied by Eugene Marchbanks, a morbidly sensitive eighteen-year-old poet who is romantically devoted to thirty-three-year-old Candida, whom he idealizes, refusing to believe that she is happily married and shuddering from the thought of her fingers 'dabbling in paraffin oil' while filling lamps. Candida scolds her husband for overworking, and tells him that his success as a preacher is because all the women are in love with him. He has become troubled, meanwhile, about Candida and Eugene, who has berated Morell with the taunt that his oratory is only 'the gift of the gab' and that his wife despises him in her heart. Finally, when Candida is asked to choose between them, she says 'I give myself to the weaker of the two': namely, to her husband, to whom she is an indispensable prop and protection, whereas the poet has lived 'without comfort or welcome or refuge' and 'learnt to live without happiness'.

Canfield, Dorothy (Dorothea Frances Canfield, 1879-1957; Mrs J. R. Fisher). Born in Kansas; educated in France and at Ohio and Columbia universities. Author of *The Bent Twig* (1915), *The Brimming Cup* (1921), *Seasoned Timber* (1939) and other novels, besides short stories, books for young readers, and books on the Montessori educational method.

Cannan, Denis (*né* Denis Pullein-Thompson, 1919-   ; son of Joanna *Cannan and her husband). Educated at Eton. Acted at Citizen's Theatre, Glasgow, 1946-48. Author of *Captain Carvallo* (1950) and other plays including a translation (1951) of *Colombe* by *Anouilh and an adaptation (1956) for the stage of *The Power and the Glory* by Graham *Greene.

Cannan, Gilbert (1884-1955). Born in Manchester; educated there and at Cambridge. Studied law and was called to the Bar in 1908, but turned to writing and theatre organization, being one of the pioneers at the Manchester Repertory Theatre. Although his ambition was to become a playwright, none of his writings for the theatre (*Miles Dixon*, 1910; *Mary's Wedding*, 1912; *Everybody's Husband*, 1917, etc.) was

successful. Among his novels *Round the Corner* (1913) has considerable merit. He married Mary Ansell, the divorced wife of J. M. *Barrie, in 1910. He was the drama critic at different times of *The Star* and *The Nation*, and as Gilbert Gunn is introduced among the critics in the Induction and Epilogue of *Fanny's First Play* by Bernard Shaw.

Cannan, Joanna (Joanna Maxwell Cannan, 1898-1961; married H. J. Pullein-Thompson, 1918). Born in Oxford; she was the daughter of Charles Cannan, Secretary to the Delegates of the Oxford University Press. Educated at Wychwood School. Her early stories were published during adolescence, and her first novel, *Misty Valley*, in 1923. Her mature fiction began with *High Table* (1931), dealing somewhat satirically with characters in a university setting, and was followed by other novels of irony and social comment, e.g. *Pray Do Not Venture* (1937), *Idle Apprentice* (1940), *Blind Messenger* (1941). She turned to detective novels—*Death at the Dog* (1941) etc.—and also wrote *A Pony for Jean* (1937) and other children's books, and a volume on *Oxfordshire* (1952).

Canning, Victor (1911-   ). Author of mystery novels: *The Golden Salamander* (1948), *The Venetian Bird* (1951), *The House of the Seven Flies* (1952), *Monasco Road* (1957), *Black Flamingo* (1962), *The Scorpio Letters* (1964), *Doubled in Diamonds* (1966).

Cannon, George. Marries Hilda Lessways bigamously in Arnold Bennett's *Clayhanger* trilogy (1910-16). He 'had rather the style of a slightly doggish stockbroker' and was by turns unqualified solicitor and boarding-house keeper. After serving a sentence for bigamy he was again imprisoned on a forgery charge but was at length found innocent and released from Dartmoor. He borrowed money from Edwin Clayhanger to go to America and subsequently repaid the loan.

Cantos. A prolonged sequence of poems by Ezra *Pound published in separate instalments from 1917 onward. There is no connected theme, but a mass of allusions and quotations drawn from the literatures of various countries and disquisitions on politics, economics, etc. Praised by sympathetic critics as a major masterpiece, the work has been stigmatized by others as pretentious and unintelligible.

apek, Karel (1890-1938). Born in Bohemia; educated in Prague, Berlin, and Paris. He was the son of a physician and intended to become a biologist, but turned to philosophy and then became passionately involved in the political life of Czechoslovakia between its achievement of independence after World War I and its dissolution by Hitler as a prelude to World War II. As a writer he achieved international renown with two plays *R.U.R.* (1921) and The *Insect Play* (1921), the latter written in collaboration with his elder brother Joseph Čapek (1887-1927)—both of which had a sombre prophetic significance as well as dramatic excellence on the stage. He also wrote novels, short stories, books on President Masaryk, and *Letters from England* (1925) which show a humorously affectionate appreciation of national manners and conduct and a penetrating view of foibles. Similar books were forthcoming for Italy (1926), Spain (1931), and Holland (1933).

pes, Godwin. Biology demonstrator, and later pseudonymous playwright Thomas More, who marries Ann Veronica Stanley in H. G. Wells's *Ann Veronica* (1909).

oote, Truman (1924-   ). Born in New Orleans; educated in New York. Author of novels (*Other Voices, Other Rooms*, 1948; *The Grass Harp*, 1951), short stories (*Tree f Night*, 1949; *Breakfast at Tiffany's*, 958), essays and a fact-finding account of mass murder, *In Cold Blood* (1966).

tain Brassbound's Conversion. Play in three cts by Bernard *Shaw written in 1899, ublished in *Three Plays for Puritans* (1900), erformed in London, 1900. Born in a ondon slum and speaking in an extreme 'ockney dialect, Felix Drinkwater is the nly convert of Leslie Rankin of the Free 'hurch of Scotland, who has served in Mogador with the North African Mission or twenty-five years. Drinkwater tells ankin that Sir Howard Hallam ('the angingest judge in England') and his ster-in-law, Lady Cicely Waynflete, have ist landed, proposing to make an expedition ito territory accounted dangerous. Rankin ecalls that he once knew Hallam's brother ho went to the West Indies. Drinkwater iggests as escort for the expedition, aptain Brassbound and his crew from the schooner *Thanksgiving*, a suggestion hardly welcomed by Rankin, for Brassbound is a dubious character nicknamed Black Paquito. Against Rankin's advice, Hallam and Lady Cicely start, escorted by Brassbound and accompanied by Drinkwater. Attacked on their journey, one of the party is wounded and nursed by Lady Cicely, who commandeers Brassbound's bed for the patient and begins to exercise the imperturbable and irresistible charm which later converts Brassbound from his declared intention of being revenged on Sir Howard, whom he accuses of misappropriating the West Indian estate of Miles Hallam, brother of Howard and father of the pseudonymous Brassbound. Meanwhile, Brassbound has sent messages to a local sheik, to whom he intended to hand over his English prisoners. They are rescued, and when Brassbound's conduct is made the subject of a formal inquiry by the captain of an American gunboat summoned to release the travellers, Lady Cicely's magnanimous evidence exonerates everyone, while she herself is barely saved from marrying Brassbound.

Caption. The printed title or longer description of a book-illustration.

Carbon-14. See *Radiocarbon dating.

Carco, Francis (pseudonym of François Marie Alexandre Carcopino-Tussoli, 1886-1958). Born at Nouméa, in the South Sea island of New Caledonia, of Corsican parents. The family moved to France when he was nine, but he had little formal education and was dominated by the primitiveness and violence of life in his birthplace, where his father had been inspector of prisons. He became the laureate both in verse and in prose of the deeper layers of bohemian Paris, for which he retained into later life a profound affection without unawareness of its moral and spiritual degeneracy. Influenced by the poems and life of Villon and by Baudelaire, he wrote *La Bohème et mon coeur* (1912; enlarged complete edn 1939); and among his many other works is *L'Homme Traqué* (1922; *The Hounded Man*). And see Katherine *Mansfield.

Carcopino-Tussoli, François Marie Alexandre. See Francis *Carco.

Card, The. Humorous novel by Arnold *Bennett published in 1911. ('*Card*: an amusing person; one given to freakish, clownish, or uninhibited behaviour'— *Webster's Dictionary*). Edward Henry Machin, called Denry by his widowed mother to save time, progresses from Board School boy to Bursley's youngest Mayor, by audacious manoeuvres beginning with a scholarship won through undetected manipulation of the results list. Dismissed from his first job as solicitor's clerk for supplying himself with an unauthorized invitation to a municipal ball where he dances with the Countess who gave it, he sets up as rent collector and estate agent. While on holiday at Llandudno he buys an old lifeboat, and by running half-crown trips to an offshore wreck is able to take home to his mother a hatbox filled with 1926 sovereigns. He contrives that the Countess's carriage shall break down in the country while she is on her way to open the new Policeman's Institute she has donated, rescues her and drives her to the function in his mule-drawn vehicle. Meanwhile he has started the Five Towns Universal Thrift Club, makes £4,000 a year from his enterprises, inveigles his mother from her little cottage to a labour-saving house he builds without her knowledge; invests in a newspaper; snatches a girl friend from her parents' side on the liner when they are emigrating to Canada, marries her, and honeymoons hilariously in the Alps. He achieves his mayoral ambition after saving the Bursley Football Club from bankruptcy and extinction by buying them 'the greatest centre forward in England'.

Cardew, Cecily. John Worthing's ward in Oscar Wilde's *The Importance of Being Earnest* (1895); marries Algernon Moncrieff.

Carducci, Giosuè (1835-1907). Born in Tuscany; educated in Florence and Pisa. Professor of Italian Literature at Bologna University, 1860-1904. Senator, poet, satirist, literary historian and critic, he was the outstanding Italian scholar and writer of his period.

Cardus, Sir Neville (1889-   ; knighted 1967). Born in Manchester of poor parents; educated at a Board School there, and at thirteen began work as a newspaper seller and delivery boy for the washing done at home by his parents. He continued his education at the public library, satisfying his passion for reading, and indulging outdoors his love of cricket. After a period of odd jobs, he began in 1904 seven years in the office of an insurance agent, meanwhile attending free lectures at Manchester University and through concertgoing acquired an understanding of music. In 1912 he applied for and got the post of assistant cricket coach at Shrewsbury School, was rejected as an army recruit in 1914, and in 1916 became for a few weeks music critic on the *Daily Citizen* northern edition, until shortage of newsprint forced him to return to insurance as a door-to-door collector of premiums. Taken on to the reporting staff of the *Manchester Guardian* early in 1917, he wrote for most sections of the paper until he became its senior cricket correspondent and music critic. His cricket articles are vividly written, with a sense of style which makes them part of the creative literature of the period in the several volumes in which they are collected: *A Cricketer's Book* (1921), *Days in the Sun* (1924), *Close of Play* (1955), etc. His music articles are reprinted in *Ten Composers* (1945) and *Talking of Music* (1957). His *Autobiography* (1947) was followed by *More Autobiography* (1950). He wrote for the Sydney *Morning Herald* 1941-47, having become familiar with Australia while accompanying English cricket teams there.

Caretaker, The. Play in three acts by Harold *Pinter performed in London in 1960 Aston, living in a squalid junk-filled upper room of an otherwise unoccupied house in west London, brings in Davies, an old tramp found quarrelling with the keeper of a local café where he worked as a cleaner Davies accepts Aston's offer to sleep there and tells how he came to leave his wife years before after only a week of married life. Throughout, the dialogue is, of set purpose, inconsequent and frequently incoherent as the three characters (the third is Aston's brother Mick) talk without effecting lucid communication. Davies' account of a fruitless journey to a monastery at Luton to beg a pair of shoes, and his longing to go down to Sidcup to get his 'papers' from a man he left them with fifteen years ago, are representative of the vein of tragicomedy and ambiguity that run throughout the play. A long monologue by Aston makes it appear that he underwent the nightmare experience of a brain operation and a lack of normality is shown in his endless fiddling with an electric plug and his often mentioned but never fulfilled intentio to build a shed in the weed-choked garden. Davies stays a while as caretaker in a continuous state of bewilderment, taunted when Mick visits the room and attributes fantastically improbable accomplishments to him. The script calls for the frequent pauses and silences which give a sinisterly disturbing further dimension to the play in performance. It was received by the critics as a notable contribution to the *Theatre of the Absurd.

rey, Lydia. Rich landowner, employer of Bashville in The *Admirable Bashville* by Bernard Shaw.

rey, Philip. Central character in Somerset Maugham's *Of Human Bondage* (1915). After releasing himself from an attempt to train as a chartered accountant, he has two years in Paris as an art student, but finally qualifies as a doctor. Marries Sally Athelny.

rey, Rosa Nouchette (1840-1909). Prolific writer of popular novels with a religious bent; *Herb of Grace* (1901) is characteristic.

ibbean Writers. No single group of writers made as distinctive a mark on English literature in the decades following World War II as the varied company of authors from the English-speaking Caribbean. But here is nothing definable as a school of West Indian writers. They are, individually, authors from a geographical region diverse a race and culture, and no unifying pattern as emerged to link them together—unless is their startling use of the English language, which brings brilliant sharpness and clarity to dialogue in their novels. 'West Indian English' has become recognized by anthropologists and linguistic specialists as a language with its own grammar and syntax rather than as a mere dialect. It enables writers from the West Indies to get effects with force and poignancy impossible in orthodox English. Many of the words used go back to Elizabethan and Cromwellian times, but though they would sound archaic in modern English usage, in the context of West Indian Creole they say precisely what they are meant to say. Writers from the English-speaking West Indies developed along lines quite different from those followed by writers born in French, Spanish, or Dutch-speaking Caribbean territories. The few authors who attracted notice in the early years of the present century came, as did their later counterparts, from varying ethnic groups

and social backgrounds. H. G. de Lisser (1877-1944), a Jamaican newspaper editor, and Claude McKay (1890-1948), an island policeman, represent the two poles of background and race. The others, some six novelists and a handful of poets, had their roots and ties variously situated between these two. Following World War II, through a B.B.C. programme, 'Caribbean Voices', and the pages of Little Magazines produced locally—*Bim* started in Barbados, *Kyk-over-Al* in what was then British Guiana, and *Focus* in Jamaica—a few of the poets and prose writers began to find an outlet for their work. Then in 1950 came the publication in Britain of *A Morning at the Office* by Edgar *Mittelholzer (1909-1965), the first of twenty-four books immensely varied in theme and locale. They ranged from historical novels to ghost stories, sociopolitical works, a travel book, the first part of an autobiography, and Gothic horror novels. In the same year V. S. *Reid (1913-) published in America *New Day*, a novel written largely in the vernacular, telling of an historical event of 1865, which did much to make Jamaicans aware of a heritage which the history books had for the most part discreetly ignored. George *Lamming (1927-) followed with his poetic and compelling books, and Roger *Mais (1905-1955) with three Hogarthian novels of poverty, despair, and prison life under a tropical sun. Samuel *Selvon (1923-), from Trinidad, began publishing humorous novels of life in his homeland and later among West Indians in London—rich, often satirical books using dialect dialogue in a way never before seen in print. Other Trinidad writers include V. S. *Naipaul (1932-), whose books won him international acclaim, and Michael *Anthony (1932-), whose stories of life in Trinidad are gently and beautifully evocative. John *Hearne (1926-) created a mythical Caribbean island called Cayuna as the setting for five novels—it is in fact Jamaica—all displaying a shapely and stylish technique, and all dealing in some measure with political themes. Andrew *Salkey (1928-) ranged from turn-of-the-century Jamaica to West Indians in contemporary London. He also edited the anthologies cited below, and wrote a successful series of children's books. Wilson *Harris (1921-) wrote a number of highly acclaimed novels, mostly set in the hinterland of Guyana and propounding a sense of history and of time and space and living of all men, not only those in his chosen region.

There is no dearth of poets in the Caribbean. Derek *Walcott (1930-   ) had collections of his poems published in both the United States and Britain. Edward *Brathwaite (1930-   ), historian as well as poet, published the first part of an ambitious long verse-narrative in 1967, the second part in 1968, and the third in 1969. Its theme is the quest for an identity by the black West Indian, and embraces the poet's own experiences in America, Britain, Africa, and the Caribbean. Few writers from the West Indies have been able to return home after becoming established; fewer still became known without leaving their own shores. They are scattered abroad—in Europe, in North and South America, in West Africa— a considerable body of talent, recognized but without immediate prospect of reward in their own lands.

Anthologies of West Indian writings include the following: edited by G. R. Coulthard, *Caribbean Literature* (1966); edited by O. R. Dathorne, *Caribbean Narrative* (1966), *Caribbean Verse* (1967); edited by John Figueroa, *Caribbean Voices* (1966); edited by Kenneth Ramchand, *West Indian Narrative* (1966); edited by Andrew Salkey, *West Indian Stories* (1960), *Stories from the Caribbean* (1965), *Caribbean Prose* (1967); edited by Anne Walmsley, *The Sun's Eye* (1968).

Critical essays on Wilson Harris, John Hearne, George Lamming, Roger Mais, V. S. Naipaul, V. S. Reid, Andrew Salkey, Derek Walcott, and others appear in *The Islands in Between*, edited with an Introduction by Louis James (1968). *See also* E. A. *Braithwaite.

Carman, Bliss (William Bliss Carman, 1861-1929). Born at Fredericton, New Brunswick, of Canadian-American descent; educated at Fredericton, at the University of Edinburgh, and at Harvard. Although he studied law and civil engineering and did a little school teaching and journalism, his life was given to poetry. His contemporary popularity as Canada's leading poet has for later critics been obliterated by the derivative nature of his work, its conventional technique and lack of original thought. He edited *The Oxford Book of American Verse* (displaced in 1950 by a new *O.B.A.V.*). His own

Collected Poems appeared in 1905 and *Later Poems* in 1921.

Carmen Sylva (pseudonym of Elizabeth, Queen of Rumania, *née* Princess Elizabeth of Wied, 1843-1916). Her writings in verse and prose became popular both in her own country and abroad, though critics found them over-sentimental.

Carnegie, Andrew (1835-1918). Born in Dunfermline, Scotland; was taken to America (Pittsburg) when twelve and after working at various trades became at length a multimillionaire ironmaster. He retired to Scotland in 1901 and endowed public libraries in Britain and the U.S. His benefactions totalled many millions, devoted to universities, peace organizations and to the Carnegie Foundation (established 1905) and the Carnegie Corporation (1911) from which grants are made to educational institutions and to individuals engaged in research. He wrote *The Empire of Business* (1902) and *Autobiography* (published 1920).

Carnegie, Dale (1888-1955). Born at Maryville, Missouri; educated at the State Teachers College, and studied dramatic art and journalism at New York and Columbia universities. Lectured on 'effective speaking' and applied psychology' in America, Europe and Africa. Author of *Lincoln the Unknown* (1932), but gained a national (and even international) audience with *How to Win Friends and Influence People* (1936), and *How to Stop Worrying and Start Living* (1948) His wife (Dorothy Reeder Carnegie) produced, in a similar vein, *How to Help Your Husband Get Ahead in His Business and Social Life* (1954).

Carp, Augustus. See H. H. *Bashford.

Carpenter, Edward (1844-1929). Born Brighton; educated at Cambridge; ordained in the Church of England but became an unbeliever when he was thirty. Turning socialism he wrote *Towards Democracy* (1883), and later works established him as a unconventional and advanced thinker. *Civilization: Its Cause and Cure* (1889) *Love's Coming of Age* (1896), *The Intermediate Sex* (1908); *My Days and Dreams* (autobiography, 1916).

Carpetbaggers. Contemptuous nickname given by Southerners to those sent from the North to assist Reconstruction measures after the American Civil War (1861-65). The term still sometimes applied to political transients from outside who concern themselves unwelcomely in the affairs of another community, and are therefore open to the gibe that they carry their own property in a travelling bag.

Carr, E. H. (Edward Hallett Carr, 1892-). Educated at Merchant Taylors' School, London, and Cambridge. After many years in the diplomatic service at home and abroad, he was Professor of International Politics at Aberystwyth from 1936 to 1947, assistant editor of *The Times* 1941-46, and a tutor at Oxford 1953-55. *Dostoevsky* (1931), *Karl Marx* (1934), *Michael Bakunin* (1937), and several volumes on international politics, preceded the works which marked him out as the best-informed contemporary English historian of modern Russia: *The Soviet Impact on the Western World* (1946), *A History of Soviet Russia* (9 vols, 1950-71), *The New Society* (1951), etc.

Carr, Emily (1871-1945). Born in British Columbia; studied art in San Francisco and in England and France. Her paintings were largely of Indian life and woodland scenes. Illness having prevented her from further painting, she turned to writing on similar themes: *Klee Wyck*—'the laughing one', her name among the Indians (1941), a collection of stories and sketches, with reporoductions of paintings by herself; *The Book of Small* (1942), childhood reminiscences; *Growing Pains* (posthumously 1946; autobiography).

Carr, John Dickson (1905-). Born in Pennsylvania. Author of numerous detective novels under his own name (e.g. *It Walks by Night*, 1930; *The Mad Hatter Mystery*, 1933; *The Emperor's Snuff Box*, 1942; *The Devil in Velvet*, 1951). As Carr Dickson, *The Plague Court Murders*, 1934; *The Red Widow Murders*, 1935. As Carter Dickson, *The Judas Window*, 1938; *He Wouldn't Kill Patience*, 1944; *Graveyard to Let*, 1949; *The Cavalier's Cup*, 1953. Also under his own name, *The Life of Sir Arthur Conan Doyle* (1949).

Carrados, Max. Blind detective in crime stories by Ernest *Bramah.

Carritt, E. F. (Edgar Francis Carritt, 1876- 964). Born in London; educated at Bradfield and Oxford. Tutor (afterwards University Lecturer) in Philosophy, Oxford

University. His special interest was aesthetics and material originating in his lectures is preserved in *The Theory of Beauty* (1914; new edn 1923), *What is Beauty?* (1932) and *Introduction to Aesthetics* (1949). He also published *The Theory of Morals* (1928), *Morals and Politics* (1935), and *Ethical and Political Thinking* (1947).

Carroll, Paul Vincent (1900-1968). Born in Ireland, at Blackrock, near Dundalk; educated by his schoolmaster-father and in Dundalk and Dublin. Began his career as a teacher in Glasgow, but from 1937, when his play *Shadow and Substance* was a success both at the *Abbey Theatre, Dublin, and in New York, he devoted himself to writing for the stage and films and television. In 1943 he and James *Bridie helped to found the Citizens' Theatre in Glasgow, Carroll becoming a director and adviser on productions. His *Three Plays* (1944) contains *The White Steed; The Things that are Caesar's*; and *The Strings, My Lord, are False.*

Carson, Kit (Christopher Carson, 1809-1968). American frontier guide and soldier. He appears as hero in numerous popular stories and has become a legendary figure. In Willa Cather's *Death Comes for the Archbishop* (1927) two sides of his character are shown.

Carson, Rachel L. (Rachel Louise Carson, 1907-1964). Born at Springfield, Pennsylvania; educated there and at Pennsylvania College for Women, studying zoology there and at Johns Hopkins University, Baltimore. Taught for a short time at the University of Maryland before joing the U.S. government Fish and Wildlife Service where, after World War II, she became chief editor of its publications. Her interest in oceanography and marine biology had already been shown in an essay 'Undersea' published in the *Atlantic Monthly* in 1937 and developed into her first book, *Under the Sea-Wind* (1941). Ten years later *The Sea Around Us* (1951) brought her tremendous success not only in the U.S. and Britain but also in other countries. The book is a serious brief presentation of the state of scientific knowledge of the sea, a fascinating 'story of how the young planet Earth acquired an ocean', and, through its author's skill as a writer, a piece of literature. This was followed by *The Edge of the Sea* (1956) dealing with life on the seashore, but her most influential, and controversial, book was *Silent Spring* (1962), an indictment of the use of poisonous chemical fertilizers by farmers. She claimed that these were destructive of animals and birds and injurious to humans.

Carswell, Catherine (*née* Catherine Roxburgh Macfarlane, 1879-1946; married H. P. M. Jackson 1903; divorced 1908; married Donald Carswell 1915). Born in Glasgow; educated at school and University there, and later studied music in Germany. Became dramatic and literary critic on the *Glasgow Herald* from 1907 to 1915. She was one of D. H. *Lawrence's close friends and after his death wrote *The Savage Pilgrimage: A Narrative of D. H. Lawrence* (1932). Other books by her include novels, *Open the Door* (1920) and *The Camomile* (1922); biographies, *The Life of Robert Burns* (1930) and *The Tranquil Heart: A Portrait of Giovanni Boccaccio* (1937); and an autobiography, *Lying Awake* (1950), compiled from the papers she left.

Carte, Richard D'Oyly (1844-1901). Born in Soho, London; educated at University College School and the University of London. Beginning in his father's musical-instrument business, he became associated with W. S. Gilbert (1836-1911) and Arthur Sullivan (1842-1900) as manager and producer of their comic operas for which he built the Savoy Theatre, whence the title Savoy Operas, by which they became collectively known. The D'Oyly Carte Opera Company continued in full activity after his death and was endowed as a trust by Bridget D'Oyly Carte when the copyright in the operas finally expired in 1961.

Carter, Howard (1874-1939). Born in London; educated privately and trained as a draughtsman by his father, an animal painter. He went to Egypt as a draughtsman to the Archaeological Survey Department, and later became Inspector-in-Chief of the monuments of Upper Egypt and Nubia. In 1902 he began excavations in the Valley of the Tombs of the Kings, making important discoveries before, in November 1922, he made his greatest find at Thebes, the hoard of treasure described in detail in his own account *The Tomb of Tut-ankh-Amen* (3 vols, 1923-33). The buried boy king belonged to the Eighteenth Dynasty (14th century B.C.).

Carter, John (John Waynflete Carter, 1905-

). Born at Eton, educated there and at Cambridge. Outstanding as a bibliographer, his major achievement (in collaboration with Graham Pollard) was the exposure of the literary forgeries of T. J. *Wise, in *An Enquiry into the Nature of Certain Nineteenth Century Pamphlets* (1934). Also author of *Taste and Technique in Book-collecting* (1948), *ABC for Book Collectors* (1952), *Books and Book-Collectors* (1956).

Carthew, Maud. Governess and lifelong friend of Michael Fane in Compton Mackenzie's *Sinister Street* (1913-14); marries Captain Ross and after he is killed in the Boer War becomes a Roman Catholic.

Cartland, Barbara (Barbara Hamilton Cartland, 1904-   ). Author of numerous romantic novels and biographies, and some plays and books on personal and domestic subjects.

Carton, R. C. (pseudonym of Richard Claude Crichett, 1856-1928). After some years of experience as an actor he devoted himself to playwriting with success, in which his wife (*née* Katherine Mackenzie Compton) shared as leading lady. His most popular pieces were *Liberty Hall* (1892), *Lady Huntworth's Experiment* (1900), *Mr Preedy and the Countess* (1909). His *Dramatic Works* appeared in print 1900-14.

Cary, Joyce (Arthur Joyce Lunel Cary, 1888-1957). Born in Ireland (Londonderry); educated at Tunbridge Wells, Clifton and Oxford; studied art in Edinburgh and Paris. A considerable part of his childhood was spent in Ireland, as his *The House of Children* (1941) demonstrates. He served with a British Red Cross unit in Montenegro during the Balkan War, 1912-13, in the latter year entered the Nigeria Political Service as an adminstrative officer and district magistrate, and was wounded while with the Nigerian Regiment in the Cameroons in World War I. Resigning from the Colonial Service in 1920 on account of ill-health, he settled in Oxford and spent the next twelve years training himself to become a novelist, and disciplining an innately over fertile creative imagination. But though Cary's literary conscience forbade his dealing with topics and person until he was confident of full comprehension of the material, his chief power as a novelist was more instinctive than acquired. He was endowed with the rare ability to clothe himself with the diversified personalities of his created characters, whether they were African men and women (as in *Aissa Saved*, 1932, *The *African Witch*, 1936, and **Mister Johnson*, 1939), or wartime cockney evacuated children (**Charley is my Darling*, 1940), or a scurrilous painter-genius (Gully Jimson in *The *Horse's Mouth*, 1944), or a cabinet minister (Chester Nimmo in *Prisoner of Grace*, 1952, **Except the Lord*, 1953, and *Not Honour More*, 1955). The variety and range of subjects and characters and the force of his narrative drive did not breed verbal economy or elegance of style in Cary's novels, but in a generation of finicking talents he stood out as a genuine creator. His *Cock Jarvis* (which he started in 1924 but left unfinished) was published after his death (1973).

sey Jones. American train-driver killed in a crash in 1900 and hero of a popular ballad first printed in 1909.

spary, Vera (1904-   ). Born and educated n Chicago. After working in an advertising agency, and then conducting her own correspondence courses in ballet dancing and film script writing, she turned novelist, beginning with *The White Girl* (1929). Her chief success was with the crime story *Laura* (1943).

ssandra (pseudonym of Sir William Neil Connor, 1909-1967; knighted 1966). Born at Muswell Hill; educated variously. After working as a clerk and in advertising, he joined the *Daily Mirror*. For that paper he wrote from 1935 the outspoken and often gloomily prophetic articles which made him national figure approved by most of the paper's readers but rarely by those in authority. Published *The English at War* (1940), *Cassandra's Cats* (1960).

t-off. A printer's estimate of the number of words in a manuscript, or the number of book-pages it will occupy, upon which the publisher's preliminary costing is based.

tle, Agnes (*née* Agnes Sweetman, died 1922). Born in Ireland; married Egerton Castle and collaborated with him in many novels.

tle, Egerton (1858-1920). Born in London; educated at the universities of Paris, Glasgow and Cambridge, and at Sandhurst Military College. Worked as a journalist and was a director of Liverpool newspapers. In

collaboration with his wife he wrote many popular novels (*The Pride of Jennico*, 1898; *The Incomparable Bellairs*, 1904; *If Youth but Knew*, 1906; etc.), several of which were dramatized. He was also highly skilled in fencing, upon which he wrote and lectured, and captained the British team at the 1908 Olympic Games.

Casuarina Tree, The. Volume of six short stories by W. Somerset *Maugham published in 1926 and containing 'Before the Party', 'P & O', 'The Outstation', 'The Force of Circumstance', 'The Yellow Streak', 'The Letter' (rewritten later as a play).

Cat on a Hot Tin Roof. Play in three acts by Tennessee *Williams performed in New York in 1955. The Pollitts, wealthy Mississippi cotton planters, are gathered to celebrate the father's ('Big Daddy's') sixty-fifth birthday. The favourite son, Brick—drunkard, drug addict, and latent homosexual—is married to 'the cat', Maggie, who aims to overcome his reluctance to father a child which she desires to prevent Big Daddy's wealth from going to Gooper, the other son with numerous children, who has planned a trusteeship enabling him to control the property after the father's expected early death from cancer. Maggie frustrates the plan by announcing prematurely that she is pregnant, a condition she hopes to achieve forthwith. The title is the American equivalent of 'a cat on hot bricks' the English saying applied to a restless, resentful person in an uncomfortable situation.

Catalogue raisonné. A descriptive, annotated catalogue of books, works of art etc., divided by subject groups where appropriate.

Catcher in the Rye, The. Novel by J. D. *Salinger published in 1951. Seventeen-year-old Holden Caulfield, due to be expelled from school for neglecting his studies, decides not to stay until the school term ends, but to go to a New York hotel until he is expected home. The last of his days at the school and his subsequent aimless wanderings—drinking, 'dating', dancing, mainly with disgust—are detailed without gloss in the monotonously repetitive and impoverished vocabulary of a mentally and morally underdeveloped adolescent. He categorizes most men and women as 'phonies', considers himself from time to time a madman, and has occasional bouts of vertigo. An ambiguous figure, he can be diagnosed either as a psychotic or as 'a symbol of purity and sensitivity'—the aspect in which he was seen by those of contemporary age who made the book a conspicuous success as well as a social portent. Its uniqueness lies in its ironic exposure of the current debasement of the English language.

Catharsis. Term (Greek *katharsis*) used by Aristotle in the *Poetics* to denote the purgation (emotional and spiritual cleansing) by pity and terror which he believed to be effected in the audience present at performances of great poetic tragedies. The word has been adopted in relation to any literary or dramatic work calculated or presumed to have such an effect.

Cather, Willa (Willa Sibert Cather, 1873-1947). Born in Virginia and brought up from an early age on her father's ranch in Nebraska. After being taught at home and at a Nebraska high school, she went to the University of Nebraska, and became a journalist in Pittsburg. Following an interval as teacher of English, she went to New York as managing editor of a popular magazine, but, from 1913 when *O Pioneers!* started her successful literary career, she ranked as one of the most distinguished novelists of the period, esteemed abroad as well as in her own country. Though her most praised and most widely circulated novel was *Death Comes for the Archbishop* (1927), the standard of her work both in style and in substance was on a high level throughout. The emotional reticence and classical grace and sobriety of her novels was in sharp contrast to much American fiction of the period, a fact likely to ensure the survival of *My Antonia* (1918), *A Lost Lady* (1923), *Shadows on the Rock* (1931), as well as the two books named above.

Caucasian Chalk Circle, The. Play in Six Scenes by Bertolt *Brecht, written 1944-5: (1) The Struggle for the Valley; (2) The Noble Child; (3) The Flight into the Northern Mountains; (4) In the Northern Mountains; (5) The Story of the Judge; (6) The Chalk Circle. The opening scene is among the ruins of a Caucasian village after the defeat of the Nazis in World War II. The men and women of two villages are disputing the possession and future cultivation of the valley. Those to whom 'the valley has belonged for centuries' wish to retain it as grazing land; the contrary plan is to build a dam on the mountain lake and irrigate a large tract of infertile land, including the disputed valley, for fruit growing. A peasant woman announces that in honour of the visiting delegates a play has been arranged, called 'The Chalk Circle' and derived from the Chinese. The remaining five scenes consist of the performance of this play part folk tale and part revolutionary propaganda. Various strands are entwined in the complex plot, the main one dealing with the flight of Grusha, a kitchenmaid who escapes with the baby son of the Governor of a city in which the Palace Guard has mutinied. After the long and adventurous flight, the Governor's Wife catches up with Grusha, and in the ensuing dispute for possession of the child, judgment is given 'To establish the true mother/By the famous test of the Chalk Circle'. A chalk circle is drawn on the floor and the child placed in the centre: 'The true mother is she who has the strength to pull the child out of the circle towards herself'. But when the test is made and Grusha lets go of the child saying 'Am I to tear him to pieces? I can't do it!' the child is given to her. The moral is stated in the closing lines of the play '. . . what there is shall belong to those who are good for it, thus/The children to the maternal, that they thrive;/ . . . And the valley to the waterers, that it should bear fruit.' In its multitude of characters, its disregard of limitations of place and time and its introduction of passages of verse and song, the play is devised in terms of the 'epic theatre', by means of which Brecht aimed to free drama from the artificial confines of the modern stage.

Causley, Charles (Charles Stanley Causley 1917-). Born at Launceston, Cornwall educated there and at Peterborough Teacher; literary editor of B.B.C. (West Region) magazines. Author of several collections of poems, including *Hands Dance* (1951), *Farewell, Aggie Weston* (1951), *Survivor's Leave* (1953), *Union Street* (1957), *Johnny Alleluia* (1961 edited *Modern Folk Ballads* (1966).

Caudwell, Christopher (pseudonym Christopher St John Sprigg, 1907-193

Born in Putney; educated at the Benedictine School, Ealing; became a reporter on the *Yorkshire Observer*, and later editor and director in a firm of aeronautical publishers. He wrote text books on aeronautics and invented an infinitely variable gear. In 1935 he joined the Poplar (east London) Communist Party; in the following year spent some time in Paris, and on the outbreak of the Civil War in Spain joined the International Brigade and was killed in February 1937. Under his own name of Sprigg he produced seven detective novels between 1933 and 1939 (*Crime in Kensington*, etc.). As Christopher Caudwell he wrote studies of poetry and prose literature in its political and psychological setting, all issued posthumously: *Studies in a Dying Culture* (1938), on Bernard Shaw, T. E. Lawrence, D. H. Lawrence, H. G. Wells, Pacifism and Violence, Love, Freud, and Liberty; *Further Studies in a Dying Culture* (1949), on 'bourgeois' religion, aesthetics, history, psychology, and philosophy; *Illusion and Reality* (1937), on poetry, mythology, politics, and psychotherapy. A sympathetic critic viewed his writings as 'the first comprehensive attempt to work out a Marxist theory of art'; but although his exceptional intelligence was widely recognized, his later work was accommodated single-mindedly within a rigid framework of political preconceptions. Also as Christopher Caudwell he wrote a novel *This My Hand* (1935), *The Crisis in Physics* (1939), and *Poems* (1965).

Causerie. Informal writing or conversation on literary (or other) subjects, often as part of a series.

Cautionary Tales. Verses by Hilaire *Belloc published in 1907, with a further collection, *New Cautionary Tales*, in 1930. They include 'Henry King, who chewed bits of String, and was early cut off in Dreadful Agonies', 'Charles Augustus Fortescue, who always Did what was Right, and so accumulated an Immense Fortune', 'Sarah Bing, who could not read and was tossed into a thorny hedge by a Bull', 'About John, who lost a Fortune by Throwing Stones'.

Cavafy, C. P. (pseudonym of Konstantinos Kavaphes, 1863-1933). Born in Alexandria, of Greek parentage. After the death of his father in 1876, he spent three years in England and briefly visited Paris and Athens

before settling again in Alexandria for the rest of his life. His poems were first introduced to English readers in E. M. *Forster's *Pharos and Pharillon* and then more comprehensively in *The Poems of C. P. Cavafy* (translated by John Mavrogordato, 1952). His poetry influenced a number of the young contemporary English writers; and an appreciation of his work appears in *The Creative Experiment* (1949).

Cavell, Edith (1866-1915). English nurse who served in Belgium in World War I and made no distinction of nationality in tending the wounded. She succoured many Allied soldiers and aided a number to escape, a humanitarian course of action which led to one of the abhorred war crimes of the Germans who executed her by shooting. Her last words became famous ('I realize that patriotism is not enough. I must have no hatred or bitterness towards anyone'), and are carved on the statue of her erected in London near the National Portrait Gallery, St Martin-in-the-Fields church, and Trafalgar Square.

Cavendish Laboratory. Established in 1873 as a department of the University of Cambridge. It became the research centre for a succession of famous scientists conducting experiments which culminated in the 'splitting', or disintegration, of the atom in 1932 by Lord *Rutherford and his colleagues. Rutherford was a student of Sir J. J. Thomson (1856-1940), who had made the Cavendish Laboratory 'the greatest research institution in the world'.

Cavor. Inventor of 'Cavorite' in H. G. Wells's *The *First Men in the Moon* (1901).

Cazamian, Louis (1877-1965). Born at Saint-Denis, in the island of Réunion, between Madagascar and Mauritius; educated in Paris. Professor of English Language and Literature in the University of Paris 1925-45. Author of a number of works on English writers (Wordsworth, Shelley, Browning, Carlyle, etc.), *The Development of English Humour* (1930; 1952), *A History of French Literature* (1955), and in collaboration with Emile *Legouis *A History of English Literature* (1927 and later editions).

Cecil, David (Lord Edward Christian David Cecil, 1902-   ). Born at Hatfield House, being the younger son of the 4th Marquess of Salisbury; educated at Eton, and at

E

Oxford, where he became Professor of English Literature from 1948. Achieved a literary success with *The Stricken Deer* (1929)—(a study of the poet William Cowper), and published other literary and biographical studies, including *Early Victorian Novelists* (1934), *Jane Austen* (1935), *The Young Melbourne* (1939), *Hardy the Novelist* (1943), *Two Quiet Lives* (Dorothy Osborne and Thomas Gray, 1948), *Lord M.* (1954), *The Fine Art of Reading* (1957), *Max* (biography of Sir Max *Beerbohm, (1964), *The Cecils of Hatfield House* (1973).

Cecil, Henry (pseudonym of Henry Cecil Leon, 1902-). Born in Middlesex; educated at St Paul's School, London, and at Cambridge. Called to the Bar, 1923; County Court Judge from 1949. Began to write in childhood, but did not succeed in getting a book published until *Full Circle* appeared in 1948. He followed this with a series of humorous novels on the experiences of a young barrister, *Brothers in Law* (1955), *Friends at Court* (1956), and other aspects of legal life, such as *Much in Evidence* (1957): the first of these reached a wider audience in film and television versions.

Celestial Omnibus, The. Short stories by E. M. *Forster published in 1911. Besides the title story, the volume includes 'The Story of a Panic', 'The Other Side of the Hedge', 'Other Kingdom', 'The Curate's Friend'—all on supernatural themes associated with extra-sensory perception—and 'The Road from Colonus', in which an elderly Englishman, visiting Greece for the first time, almost miraculously escapes death.

Céline, Louis Ferdinand (pseudonym of Louis Ferdinand Destouches, 1894-1961). Born in Paris; received little education in early life, but after serving in World War I, during which he received severe wounds, he studied medicine, qualified, and held appointments in the U.S., Africa, and France. Meanwhile he was writing novels of despair, praised by many for their force and uncompromising realism but condemned by others as debasing and obscene. The most widely known in English translation is *Journey to the End of Night (Voyage au bout de la nuit, 1932)*.

Celtic Twilight. W. B. *Yeats's volume *The Celtic Twilight* (1893) established the term as descriptive of the atmosphere of Irish traditional lore with its suggestion of mysticism and mistiness, its supernormal creatures—

fairies, ghosts, and 'little folk'—and its vaguely heroic past. Something of the same sort is also dominant in the stories and plays of Fiona *Macleod (William Sharp) who was brought up on the myths and legends of the western highlands of Scotland. The term is sometimes used derisively of the Irish literary renaissance in its strongly Gaelic aspects.

Cendrars, Blaise (pseudonym of Frédéric Sauser-Hall, 1887-1961). Born in Paris of Swiss and Scottish parentage; travelled widely in early life, and from the age of fifteen spent several years in China and Russia. Thereafter he led a wandering existence, visiting many countries and trying many occupations, including authorship of various kinds, producing novels and poetry based upon his adventurous life: *Nineteen Elastic Poems* (1919), *Sutter's Gold* (1926), *African Saga* (1927), *Antarctic Fugue* (1948).

Censorship of books. Although no direct literary censorship exists in Great Britain, civil or criminal proceedings can be taken against any published work which, on information received, the police and the Director of Public Prosecutions examine and consider obscene. The offence that has to be proved to the satisfaction of magistrates in a court of first instance or of a jury in a higher court is that the publication tends to deprave and corrupt. Until the Obscene Publications Act 1959, main attention was concentrated upon the protection of the morals of young and immature potential readers, but the new legislation was designed to prevent literature from being judged wholly by adolescent standards, and to allow defendants to call qualified witnesses to testify to the literary, intellectual, or other relevant merit of the work. Under the pre-1959 law, successful actions had been brought for the suppression of James Joyce's *Ulysses,* Radclyffe Hall's *The *Well of Loneliness,* D. H. Lawrence's *The *Rainbow,* and other novels. An action by the Public Prosecutor in 1959 against the publishers of an English edition of an American novel, *The Philanderer* by Stanley *Kauffmann failed and was notable for the principles expressed by Mr Justice Stable in his summing-up (included in the 1954 *Penguin Books reprint of Kauffmann's book). The publicity given to this case drew attention also to the treatment of the defendant—a reputable and respected publisher—who was subjected to routine police measures designed for criminals. The first prosecution under the 1959 Act was brought against the publishers (Penguin Books Ltd) of an unexpurgated edition of *Lady Chatterley's Lover*. They had previously notified the Director of Public Prosecutions of their intention to issue the book. The trial at the Old Bailey, before Mr Justice Byrne and a jury of nine men and three women, was remarkable for the evidence given on behalf of the novel, the author (who died in 1930), and the publishers, by a succession of men and women of letters and by religious and educational witnesses, and remarkable also for the fact that no evidence was called by the prosecution. Though the judge's summing up conformed to the correct legal standard of impartiality, it appeared to be emotionally weighted against the book, but the jury gave a verdict of Not Guilty. A fairly widespread impression that they had given the right verdict for wrong reasons did not detract from the general view that the result was a vindication of common sense and of the right to freedom of expression in defensible causes. A weakness in the 1959 Act was disclosed by the refusal of the judge in the *Lady Chatterley* case to allow reference to be made to deliberately debasing fiction whose unrestricted sale to young and old alike stirred no evident concern in the department of the Director of Public Prosecutions. Those who oppose actual or attempted literary censorship on any pretext deprecate the inflated commercial profit which results from any prosecution under the obscenity laws. While the sales of the Penguin Books edition of *Lady Chatterley's Lover* would undoubtedly have been much above average, since no unexpurgated version had been published in England since its first appearance in 1928, the abortive trial created so great an additional demand that Penguin Books' accounts for 1960 showed an item of £62,000 as profit on the sales of the 2s 6d edition between 10 Nov. 1960 and 31 Dec. 1960. This sum was considerably diminished, however, by the costs of the legal action, which the judge declined to grant to Penguin Books, although the prosecution was a test case brought by the authorities. A publisher is compelled to incur the expense of printing and distributing a book before he can know whether action will or will not be taken against it. No official opinion can be obtained by submitting a manuscript or other copy to the police or the Director of Public Prosecutions. The crime, if any, lies in 'offering for sale'. Subsequent prosecutions have produced inconsistent results. *And see* Pornography.

Centre 42. An organization of writers, painters, composers, actors, stage designers, and others, cooperating with trade unions, originated by Arnold *Wesker and set up at the beginning of the 1960s to promote festivals of the arts, exhibitions of craft work, and other activities designed particularly for working people. By encouraging the creative arts and crafts in centres and among groups previously catered for mainly or exclusively by *'pop culture', it was hoped to stimulate among culturally undeveloped wage-earners a liking and desire for good music, intelligent plays, poetry, and other media for enlightened employment of the increasing leisure available in the Welfare State. The council of the Centre included Labour leaders in parliament and the T.U.C., and its exhibitions and festivals were available for location in factories, housing estates, universities, clubs, public houses, or any other premises where a suitable audience could be reached.

Chamber Music. A collection of lyrics by James *Joyce published in 1907.

Chamberlain, Houston Stewart (1855-1927). Born at Southsea; educated privately, and at Cheltenham and Versailles. Married the daughter of Wagner the composer; wrote on music, philosophy, and history in German; settled in Germany and became naturalized there. During World War I his anti-British fervour made him notorious in the country of his birth and obloquy consequently attached at the time to his survey of European culture, *Die Grundlagen des neunzehuten Jahrhunderts* (1899) translated as *The Foundations of the Nineteenth Century* (1911).

Chambers, Charles Haddon (1860-1921). Born in Sydney, N.S.W.; educated at schools there; entered the Australian Civil Service. Spent a period as a stockrider, then migrated to England, intending to occupy himself in journalism but actually becoming a successful playwright with *Captain Swift* (produced 1888, published 1902). His best play is *The Tyranny of Tears* (produced 1899; published 1902).

Chambers, E. K. (Sir Edmund Kerchever Chambers, 1866-1954; knighted 1925). Born in Berkshire; educated at Marlborough and Oxford. His professional career was spent in the Board of Education, where he rose to the position of Second Secretary; but he won fame as one of the leading authorities on Shakespeare and on the history of the stage: *The Medieval Stage* (1903), *The Elizabethan Stage* (1923), *Shakespeare: A Survey* (1925), *William Shakespeare* (1930).

Chambers, Jessie. The young woman friend of D. H. *Lawrence who served as his model for Miriam in *Sons and Lovers* and was in other ways important in relation to his early writings. Their personal relationship (begun in 1901) was frustrated by the Lawrences' mother–son attraction, and they ceased to meet or correspond in 1913, by which time D. H. Lawrence was living in Italy with Frieda Weekley (*née* von Richthofen) whom he married after her divorce in 1914. Jessie Chambers later became Mrs John Wood and lived until 1944. In 1935 she published *D. H. Lawrence: A Personal Record by E.T.*, a valuable source of information about Lawrence's upbringing and early education (new edition with further material, 1965). The initials E.T. are from *Eunice Temple,* the title of a novel Jessie Chambers began to write about 1913 but destroyed unfinished.

Chambers, R. W. (Raymond Wilson Chambers, 1874-1942). Born in Yorkshire; educated at the Grocers' School, and at the University of London, where he became Professor of English Language and Literature from 1922 to 1941. He wrote largely on Anglo-Saxon poetry, but did not neglect later writers, his *Thomas More* (1935) being the product of long study. His most original and valuable work is *The Continuity of English Prose from Alfred to More and his School* (1932).

Chambers, R. W. (Robert William Chambers, 1865-1933). Born in Brooklyn; studied art in New York and Paris, and had early success as a painter and illustrator; but from 1893 to the end of his life he wrote scores of popular novels, largely on European and American historical themes: *The Red Republic* (1894), *Lorraine* (1896), *Cardigan* (1901), *The Maid at Arms* (1902). He also wrote on social themes, as in *The Fighting Chance* (1906) and *The Firing Line* (1908). Though many other novels followed, it was in his early books that his gifts as a storyteller were most absorbingly shown.

Chambers, Whittaker (1901-61). Born on Long Island; educated at Columbia University, joined the Communist Party in 1925 and became a Soviet agent in Washington. Left the Party in 1938, joined the staff of the American magazine *Time* and rose to be a senior editor until 1948. In that year he became a world-renowned ambiguous figure as a witness against Alger Hiss in the espionage investigations which led to the famous trial and the imprisonment of Hiss. Fantastic features in Chambers's evidence, and the atmosphere of national hysteria in which the trial was conducted, left the case in a fog of mystery which Chambers's self-pitying autobiography, *Witness* (1952), did not disperse. He became a Quaker and retired to his farm in Maryland, where he died.

Chance. Novel by Joseph *Conrad published in 1914. Born in the east end of London and starting his career as junior clerk to a dock company, de Barral marries a sailor's daughter who encourages him to accept a post in a west end bank. He branches out on his own as founder of a Thrift Association, promising 10 per cent interest on all deposits. When money pours in he opens branches up and down the country under various titles and, becoming the prey of swindlers, is induced to put vast sums into fraudulent schemes which bankrupt him and lead to long imprisonment. Meanwhile, after his wife's death, he places their young daughter Flora in the care of a governess, who taunts her maliciously and deserts her when de Barral crashes. Flora, suicidally agonized by her father's misfortune and the governess's abuse, is befriended by a Mr and Mrs Fyne, and is deterred from killing herself by Mrs Fyne's brother, Captain Roderick Anthony, who persuades her to elope. They marry, and when de Barral leaves prison they provide for him on board Anthony's ship *Ferndale*. De Barral regards Flora's marriage as traitorous to himself, and in hatred puts poison into Captain Anthony's drink. Detected by the second mate of the *Ferndale,* Powell, de Barral swallows the poisoned liquor himself and dies. Some years later the *Ferndale* is sunk in a collision. Flora and Powell are among those rescued but the Captain goes down with his ship. The story is told mainly by Marlow, frequently present in Conrad's fiction as detached observer and indirect narrator. Here he presents the encounters and events as operations of chance. Despite its complex structure, this novel was the first of Conrad's works to attract the general public.

Chandler, Raymond (Raymond Thornton Chandler, 1888-1959). Born in Chicago; educated in England at Dulwich College. Did some freelance writing for London papers before returning to the U.S. where (after serving with the Canadian forces and the R.A.F. in World War I) he worked as an accountant and an oil company executive from 1919 to 1932. Beginning with *The Big Sleep* (1939) he quickly became recognized in America and elsewhere as the originator of a new type of crime novel, in which ingenuity of plot and detection combined with a distinctive and distinguished literary style within a framework of 'tough' speech and action, practised no less by his private detective Philip Marlowe than by the criminals he unmasks. He discussed his methods in *The Simple Art of Murder* (1950) where, also, he names Dashiel *Hammett with admiration. His other books are *Farewell My Lovely* (1940), *The High Window* (1942), *The Lady in the Lake* (1943), *The Little Sister* (1949), *Trouble is My Business* (1950), *The Long Goodbye* (1953), and *Playback* (1958).

Chanty. See Shanty.

Chapbooks. Thin paper-covered booklets, originally carried by chapmen (pedlars) and other itinerant salesmen, as part of the stock of small cheap articles they hawked around the country to cottage wives and at fairs, etc. The contents of chapbooks were similar to the unsophisticated material printed on *broadsheets. They were a common type of popular literature in the 16th-18th centuries, and have been imitated occasionally with more refined contents and improved production in the present century—e.g. by the *Poetry Bookshop, the Saltire Society in Scotland, etc.

Chapin, Harold (1886-1915). Born in Brooklyn, U.S., but was brought to England in 1888 and lived there until he joined the army and was killed in France. His mother was an actress and the boy appeared as Marcus in *Coriolanus* at Stratford-on-Avon at the age of seven. He was afterwards educated at schools in London and Norwich before taking up a stage career in 1902, playing many parts before joining the Glasgow Repertory Theatre in 1910 as producer. Meanwhile he had also taken to playwriting with *Augustus in Search of a Father* (1910), and among his later pieces were *The Autocrat*

of the Coffee Stall (1911), *The Dumb and the Blind* (1911), *Art and Opportunity* (1912). His plays were collected in *The Comedies of Harold Chapin* (1921), and his letters in *Soldier and Dramatist*, with a Memoir by Sidney *Dark (1916).

Chapman, R. W. (Robert William Chapman, 1881-1960). Born at Eskbank, Scotland; educated at Dundee High School and Oxford. Spent his working life with the Oxford University Press, becoming Secretary to the Delegates (1920-42). His interest in lexicography enabled him to take a useful part in the later stages of the great *Oxford English Dictionary* and other important work, and he was an expert on the text of Jane Austen's and Anthony Trollope's novels. His edition of Jane Austen's works (novels, letters, and juvenilia) is unlikely to be superseded. He also had an unrivalled knowledge of Samuel Johnson's writings, shown particularly in the edition of Johnson's letters (3 vols, 1952).

Charley Is My Darling. Novel by Joyce *Cary published in 1940. A semi-tragic story of children evacuated to the country from poor city homes in World War II.

Charley's Aunt. Farce by Brandon *Thomas, first produced in 1892 and frequently revived in the present century.

Charlton, H. B. (Henry Buckley Charlton, 1890-1961). Born at Bingley, Yorkshire; educated at Leeds University and in Berlin. Professor of English Literature, Manchester University, 1914-57. Author of *Shakespearian Comedy* (1938), *Shakespearian Tragedy* (1948), other literary studies, and *Portrait of a University* (1951).

Charlus. See *Remembrance of Things Past.

Charnwood, Lord (Godfrey Rathbone Benson, 1864-1945; 1st Baron Charnwood, 1911). Mainly a politician and worker in public causes, but also wrote on religious and philosophical subjects, and produced biographies of Abraham Lincoln (1916) and Theodore Roosevelt (1923), the former being particularly successful.

Charteris, Leslie (pseudonym of Leslie Charles Bowyer Yin, 1907-   ). Born in Singapore, son of a Chinese surgeon and an English mother; educated at unspecified schools and at Cambridge. Began to write at a very early age and had the first of his many crime novels

Meet the Tiger published when he was twenty-one. He then spent an adventurous period in Malaya, trying several occupations (including pearl fishing, gold seeking, and bar tending) before the publication of *Enter the Saint* (1930) started his prosperous career as the recorder of the adventures of the imaginary Simon Templar, 'gentleman burglar', who reappeared in a long succession of 'Saint' novels.

Chase, Mary (*née* Mary Coyle, 1907-   ; married Robert Lamont Chase, 1928). Born of Irish parents at Denver, Colorado; educated at the High School and University there. Became a journalist and then turned to playwriting in 1937 with moderate success until she achieved sudden fame and an immensely long run with *Harvey* (produced 1944, published 1950), a comedy-fantasy in which the name-character is a man-size invisible white rabbit.

Chase, Mary Ellen (1887-   ). Born in Maine; educated at Blue Hill Academy and at the University there, supporting herself by small sums earned from short stories. Became a school teacher and at length Professor of English Literature at Smith College. Spent many holiday periods in England, about which she wrote with sympathy and understanding in *England Now* (1936). Her books include essays, literary and biblical studies, children's stories, and novels, the best known in the last category being *Mary Peters* (1934), one of several dealing with working people on the seaboard of Maine.

Chase, Stuart (1888-   ). Born in New Hampshire; educated at a High School in Massachusetts, at the University there, and at Harvard. Studied economics, banking, and accountancy. Beginning with *The Tragedy of Waste* (1935) he wrote a number of books on the effects of the machine age on human welfare, including *Men and Machines* (1929), *The Economy of Abundance* (1934) and *The Proper Study of Mankind* (1948). One of his most important books, *The Tyranny of Words* (1938; rewritten as *The Power of Words* 1954), discourses on propagandist manipulation of language.

Chasuble, Canon. Marries Miss Prism in Oscar Wilde's *The Importance of Being Earnest* (1895).

Chatham House. Colloquial short title for the *Royal Institute of International Affairs*, which has its headquarters at Chatham House, St James's Square. The building was formerly the residence, in turn, of William Pitt, Earl of Chatham, of the Earl of Derby, and of Gladstone.

Chatterley, Lady Constance. Central character in D. H. Lawrence's *Lady Chatterley's Lover* (1928).

Chaucer, Daniel. Pseudonym under which Ford Madox *Hueffer (alias Ford Madox Ford) wrote *The Simple Life Limited* (1911) and *The New Humpty-Dumpty* (1912).

Chauvelin. French agent in Baroness Orczy's *The*Scarlet Pimpernel* (1905).

Chauvinism. Extreme and uncritical patriotism, such as is expressed in the phrase 'our country right or wrong' (spoken by the American naval commander Stephen Decatur in 1816). The word derives from the name of a fanatically devoted soldier in Napoleon's army, Nicolas Chauvin.

Chehov, Chekhov. *See* Tchekhov.

Chell, Countess of. Born of 'poor but picturesque parents', marries the wealthy Earl of Chell, and is 'determined to be identified with . . . social progress in the Five Towns', where she becomes known as 'Interfering Iris'; a leading character in Arnold Bennett's *The *Card* (1911).

Cheney, Peter (pseudonym of Reginald Evelyn Peter Southouse-Cheney, 1896-1951). Born in Ireland; educated at the Mercers' School and London University. Worked as law clerk, actor, and editor, and served and was badly wounded in World War I. *This Man is Dangerous* (1936) was followed by a long line of crime novels which, both in language and in action, emulate the 'tough' American style and achieved an enormous circulation. He formed The Cheney Organisation to coordinate his ceaseless activities as a writer. His chief characters were Slim Callaghan, private detective, and the ambiguous Lemmy Caution, who moved amid a large company of glamorous, luscious, and frequently dangerous 'dames'.

Cherry Orchard, The. Comedy in four acts by Anton *Tchekhov performed in Moscow in 1904. (English translation by Constance *Garnett 1923). Madame Ranevsky, owner of the cherry orchard, returns bankrupt from France, where she has resided with her lover since the death of her alcoholic husband and the accidental death of her young son. The cherry orchard is to be sold by auction to pay her debts unless the money can somehow be raised to save it. Madame Ranevsky and her brother Gaev think of only improbable sources from which they might borrow, and she rejects the one practical suggestion. This comes from a friend, the rich merchant Lopahin, who proposes that the cherry trees be cut down, the land divided into building lots and leased for the building of summer villas. This he estimates will ensure them a satisfactory income. Madame Ranevsky replies scornfully that their cherry orchard is the only interesting and remarkable thing in the whole province, and Gaev interposes that it is even mentioned in the Encyclopaedia. The household abounds in eccentric and feckless characters: Gaev continually makes strokes on an imaginary billiards table with an imaginary cue; the former governess, Charlotta, does card tricks and bits of ventriloquism; the clerk, Epihodov, is un-decided whether to live or shoot himself, but always carries a revolver; Trofimov, 'a perpetual student' (formerly tutor to the dead child), deplores the state of Russia in eloquent prophetic speeches declaring that to live in the present they must expiate their past. At the auction Lopahin buys the orchard, and the play ends with the departure of the family and the sound of axes felling the trees. Only old Firs, the valet aged eighty-seven, is left behind, forgotten and murmuring 'nothing left . . . all gone!'

Cheshire Cat. In *Alice in Wonderland,* the animal that is able to disappear, its grin being the last thing left visible.

Cheshire Cheese. An eating-house in Wine Office Court, Fleet Street, famous as a meeting-place of poets and men of letters, from Ben Jonson's time. It is frequently though mistakenly supposed that it was the rendezvous of Samuel Johnson and the Literary Club. The Rhymer's Club founded by W. B. *Yeats and others met there regularly for reading and criticism of one another's poems.

Chesterton, Mrs Cecil (*née* Ada Elizabeth Jones, 1870-1962). Born in London of a family of journalists whose profession she adopted; contributed to various periodicals pseudonymously as Sheridan Jones. In 1917 she married Cecil Chesterton (brother of G. K. *Chesterton) and, after his death in the following year, travelled widely. A period of living among destitute people provided her

with material for *In Darkest London* (1926) and led to the major work of her life in the foundation of the Cecil Houses where home-less women could find for a few pence comfortable temporary lodging and food.

Chesterton, G. K. (Gilbert Keith Chesterton 1874-1936). Born at Campden Hill, London; educated at St Paul's school and at the Slade School of Art in the University of London. But although his talent for drawing found at length an outlet in humorous illustrations for books by his devoted friend Hilaire *Belloc, it was in journalism that he first made a reputation, writing for *The Bookman,* the *Daily News* and other papers, but particu-larly for *The Illustrated London News,* to which he contributed essays weekly from 1905 to 1930. These and other essays were collected in numerous volumes, e.g. *Tremend-ous Trifles* (1909), *Alarms and Discursions* (1910), *The Uses of Diversity* (1920), *Generally Speaking* (1928), *All I Survey* (1933), *As I Was Saying* (1936). His versatil-ity makes it impossible to forecast in which department of literature he will in future be considered most important; or, indeed, whether he will in the long run be regarded as having at all the genius and importance credited by his contemporaries, especially by Belloc whose valuation is set out in *On the Place of Chesterton in English Letters* (1940). His facility in production, the range of his interests, his journalistic faculty of dis-coursing and arresting attention on almost any topic, and, above all, the gift of paradox indulged to the point where his wit seemed to circle in pursuit of its own tail—all these characterists may lead to a drastic winnow-ing of his fecund output. His verse embraces many moods, from the historico-legendary narrative poem, *The Ballad of the White Horse* (1911), and *Lepanto* (in *Collected Poems*, 1915), to the drinking songs first interspersed in the novel *The *Flying Inn* (1914) and reissued separately as *Wine, Water and Song* (1915) and to such brief satirical pieces as 'Elegy in a Country Churchyard' and 'Antichrist, or the Reunion of Christendom' (see *Collected Poems*, 1933). Among his novels, *The Flying Inn* is less esoteric than *The Napoleon of Notting Hill* (1904), *The Man Who Was Thursday* (1908), *The Ball and the Cross* (1909), and *Manalive* (1912), but his longest-lasting success in fiction was with *The Innocence of Father Brown* (1911), crime stories with a Roman Catholic priest-detective modelled on his friend the Rev. John O'Connor; these were continued in *The Wisdom of Father Brown* (1914), *The Incredulity of Father Brown* (1926), *The Secret of Father Brown* (1927), and collected in *The Father Brown Stories* (1929). Chesterton became a Roman Catholic in 1922, after a prolonged pilgrimage from agnosticism through socialism to Christianity. One of the first products of his newfound faith was *St Francis of Assisi* (1923). He had previously written several biographical and critical studies of writers and others: *G. F. Watts* (1902), *Robert Browning* (1903) *Charles Dickens* (1906), *Bernard Shaw* (1909; enlarged edition, 1935), *Thackeray* (1910), *William Black* (1910), and later on *William Cobbett* (1925), *Robert Louis Stevenson* (1927), *Chaucer* (1932), *St Thomas Aquinas* (1933). While personal idiosyncrasy robbed certain of these of importance, he was excellent on Browning and Dickens and appreciative of Shaw's intellectual honesty and moral courage, though dissenting from most of his opinions. Chesterton edited *The Eye Witness* from 1916 to 1923 (the title was changed to *The New Witness* from November 1921) and ran his own paper *G. K.'s Weekly* from 1925 to 1936. It was as a person as much as as a writer that he impressed himself on his own generation. A brilliant and ebullient conversationalist, in figure a modern Falstaff, in outlook a pre-Reformation Englishman, as an opponent of 'money, power and imperialism' he spoke and wrote against the Boer War, and as a champion of integrity in public life he supported the critical attitude adopted by his brother Cecil towards statesmen and others implicated in the financial transactions which became known as 'the Marconi Scandal' of 1912.

Chetham-Strode, W. (Warren Chetham-Strode, 1897-1974). Born in Middlesex; educated at Sherborne. Served in World War I; was in business from 1919 to 1932, and in government departments from 1939 to 1945. His career as a playwright began with *Sometimes Even Now* (1933), and later plays included *Young Mrs Barrington* (1945) and *The Guinea Pig* (1946), as well as numerous writings for the cinema and television.

Chiang Yee (1903–   ). Born in Kiyukiang; educated there and at Nanking University; Following experience as a science teacher and government official in China he migrated to England, where he taught at the School of Oriental Studies in the University of London.

The Silent Traveller in Lakeland (1937), written in English and illustrated in colour and black-and-white by himself, was the first of a succession of popular books with similar titles dealing with London, the Yorkshire Dales, Oxford, New York, Edinburgh, etc. The self-given nickname 'silent traveller' derives from his Chinese pseudonym meaning 'dumb walking man'.

Child, H. H. (Harold Hannyngton Child, 1869-1945). Born at Gloucester; educated at Winchester and Oxford. He turned from brief periods as solicitor's clerk and then as actor, to journalism, becoming from 1902 a valuable and adaptable member of *The Times* staff, helping to found *The Times Literary Supplement*, and contributing dramatic and literary criticism, and light leading articles. He also wrote the libretto for Vaughan Williams's opera *Hugh the Drover* (1911) and a small book on *Thomas Hardy* (1916). Collections of his articles are contained in *Love and Unlove* (1921), and in *Essays and Reflections* issued posthumously (1948).

Childers, Erskine (1870-1922). Born in London of Anglo-Irish parentage; educated at Haileybury and Cambridge; from 1895 to 1910 he held a clerkship in the House of Commons. He served with the British forces both in the Boer War of 1899 to 1901 and in World War I, though he had from at least as early as 1914 been a passionate advocate of Irish independence, and after the German defeat he settled in Dublin and was elected a member of the rebel parliament. After the Irish Free State was established in 1921 he took arms against the new government, and served with the Republicans until he was captured on 10 November 1922, court martialled, and shot on the 24th. In addition to a few political books and two on his experiences with the British army in the South African war, he wrote *The *Riddle of the Sands* (1903).

Chiltern Hundreds. A British member of Parliament is not permitted to resign his seat, but may apply for the post of Steward of the Chiltern Hundreds (districts of the Chiltern hills once infested by highway robbers, whom the Steward was appointed to stamp out). The stewardship now exists only in name, but by a legal fiction it continues to rank as 'an office of profit under the Crown', acceptance of which conventionally obliges an M.P. to seek re-election. If he does not stand again, he automatically ceases to be a member of Parliament and a by-election must follow.

Chinoiserie. Applied to buildings and examples of decorative art imitative of Chinese works. The style was popular in England in the 18th century: examples are the pagoda by Sir William Chambers (1726-96) in Kew Gardens and wallpapers and furniture in the Victoria and Albert Museum and other collections.

Chips with Everything. Play in two acts by Arnold *Wesker performed in London in 1962. One of a group of nine young recruits sharing the same Royal Air Force hut, Thompson (nicknamed Pip) alone is not from a working-class family. For training they are under the immediate control of Corporal Hill, whose one ambition and determination is to drill them into an obedient and efficient unit. By the day of the Passout Parade he has succeeded with all but two. Washington (nicknamed Smiler) has tried to run away but has returned with bleeding feet, which are washed by Wingate; he is put back to another unit. The second nonconformist, Pip, after refusing an order during bayonet practice, is threatened with a court martial. He obeys the order with desperate cynical violence at a second chance. He is characteristic of the theoretical equalitarian who rebels against his own class without uprooting ingrained contempt for the classes below. He describes a café in the east end of London where he went for a cup of tea and an old man sat beside him: 'I saw the menu, stained with tea . . . and on top it said—God I hated that old man—it said "Chips with everything". Chips with every damn thing. You breed babies and you eat chips with everything.'

Chirol, Sir Valentine (Ignatius Valentine Chirol, 1852-1929; knighted 1912). Born abroad of English parents; educated mainly in France and Germany. Worked in the Foreign Office, travelled in many countries 1876-92, became Berlin correspondent of *The Times* in 1892, and in 1896 became head of its foreign news section. Wrote books on political problems in the Middle and Far East and India, and *Fifty Years in a Changing World* (1927). He was a profound student of foreign affairs and his views were valued by governments and the press.

Chisholm, Hugh (1866-1924). Born in London; educated at Felsted School and Oxford. Editor and leader-writer on London evening

papers; Financial Editor, *The Times*, 1913-20. Editor of the famous 11th (Cambridge) edition of the *Encyclopaedia Britannica* (1911).

Chitterlow, Harry. Author of the money-making farce *The Pestered Butterfly* in H. G. Wells's *Kipps* (1905).

Chloe. Wife of Charles Hornblower in John Galsworthy's *The *Skin Game* (1920). When a secret in her past is made known she commits suicide.

Chocolate Soldier, The. Nickname of Captain Bluntschli in Bernard Shaw's *Arms and the Man,* and the title of the musical play (1910) based on it.

Cholmondeley, Alice. *See* Elizabeth, Countess von Arnim.

Cholmondeley, Mary (1859-1925). Born in Shropshire, daughter of the rector of Hodnet. A semi-invalid throughout her life, she lived in and through her novels, which began with a mystery story, *The Danvers Jewels* (1887; published under the pseudonym Pax). *Red Pottage* (1899), an attack on middle-class hypocrisy, made her famous and assured the success of her subsequent novels: *Moth and Rust* (1902), *Notwithstanding* (1913) and others, all somewhat dully moralizing. *Under One Roof* (1918) is her autobiography.

Chowdler, Rev. Henry. Housemaster at Chiltern School in G. F. Bradby's *The *Lanchester Tradition* (1913). He provokes a crisis by rebelling against the new headmaster.

Christian Science. *See* Mary Baker *Eddy.

Christiansen, Arthur (1904-63). Born at Wallasey, Cheshire; educated at the Grammar School there. When sixteen he started work on the local paper; four years later moved to Liverpool; in 1925 became London editor of the *Liverpool Evening Express*, but next year became news editor of the *Sunday Express* and in 1929 its assistant editor. From 1933 to 1957 he was editor of the *Daily Express*, seeing its circulation more than double, to over 4 million daily. His concentration on the visual presentation of news, requiring minimum expenditure of mental effort by readers, brought criticism from those who held that journalism has a higher public duty.

Christie, Dame Agatha (*née* Agatha Mary Clarissa Miller, 1891-   ; married (1) Archibald Christie, 1914; (2) Max Mallowan, 1930). Born in Torquay of an American father;

educated at home by her mother and from the age of sixteen in Paris; studied singing, but her ambition to make a career in opera was frustrated by an unsuitable voice. Encouraged by her mother, and later by Eden *Phillpotts, she had her first detective novel *The Mysterious Affair at Styles* published in 1920. By 1970 she had written and published seventy detective novels and was nicknamed the Queen of Crime. The sales of her books total a hundred million or so and her appeal is universal. She also wrote detective plays with equal success, usually adaptations of her novels. *The Mousetrap* was performed continuously in London for many years, the longest run in the history of the theatre. Her best-known fictional creation was Hercule Poirot, the Belgian detective in many of her novels, who relies upon a psychological approach and the employment of 'the little grey cells' (his catch phrase). In later books she introduced a woman detective, the elderly Miss Marple. Her enormous output was on a generally high level and her ingenuity inexhaustible. It is difficult to pick either her best novels or her worst, though *The Murder of Roger Ackroyd* (1926) springs the greatest surprise. Frequently the characterization is as engaging as the mystery, e.g. in *The Hollow* (1946) and *Crooked House* (1949). Journeys in the Middle East with her second husband, an archaeologist, led to detective novels set in that region: *Murder in Mesopotamia* (1936), *Death on the Nile* (1937). Under a pseudonym, Mary Westmacott, she wrote *Absent in the Spring* (1944) and *The Rose and the Yew Tree* (1948), and other non-crime novels. D.B.E. 1971.

Christie, Anna. Central character in Eugene O'Neill's *Anna Christie* (1922).

Christie, Campbell (Campbell Manning Christie, 1893-1963). Born in India; educated in England at Clifton and the Woolwich military academy; entered the army and rose to the rank of Major-General. After his marriage he and his wife collaborated as playwrights (see next entry).

Christie, Dorothy (*née* Dorothy Casson Walker,). Born in India; married Campbell Christie in 1914 and with him wrote a number of successful plays including *Family Group* (1935), *Grand National Night* (1946), *His Excellency* (1950), *Carrington V.C.* (1953), and others less well received.

Christie, John (1882-1962). Born at Glynde-

bourne, Sussex, his family's home for seven centuries; educated at Eton and Cambridge. Taught physics at Eton before succeeding his father as owner of the estate. After serving in World War I he developed an interest in music, and on marrying Audrey Mildmay, an opera singer, in 1931 began producing an annual summer season of opera which, beyond all expectations, was to make Glyndebourne a place of musical pilgrimage from 1934 when, in the theatre built next to the manor house, the first performances (of Mozart) were given. His wife sang in early productions and her death in 1953 was a severe deprivation; but Christie was a single-minded enthusiast and Glyndebourne became synonymous with perfection in operatic production. Singers, instrumentalists, conductors, and stage designers of international repute contributed to the fame of the theatre in its beautiful South Down country; and not the least of its founders' achievements was to attract a genuinely music-loving and aesthetically disciplined audience from various social levels to what might, under other direction, have degenerated into a snob ritual.

Christina Allaby. *See* Christina *Allaby.

Christmas Garland, A. Volume of parodies of contemporary writers by Max *Beerbohm. It consists of a series of discourses on Christmas themes, imitating in succession the style and mannerisms of *Kipling, A. C. *Benson, *Wells, *Chesterton, *Hardy, Frank *Harris, *Bennett, *Galsworthy, G. S. *Street, *Conrad, Edmund *Gosse, *Belloc, Bernard *Shaw, Maurice *Hewlett, George *Moore, and George *Meredith.

Christopher Christopherson. Swedish captain of a coal barge, and father of Anna in Eugene O'Neill's *Anna Christie* (1921).

Christopher Robin. The child (the author's son) named, and for whom the verses were written, in *When We Were Very Young* (1924) and *Now We Are Six* (1927) by A. A. *Milne. *Winnie the Pooh* (1926) and *The House at Pooh Corner* (1928) were also written for him.

Christy Mahon. *See* Christy *Mahon.

Church, Richard (Richard Thomas Church, 1893-1972). Born in London; educated at Dulwich College; worked as a civil servant from the age of sixteen until he was forty. By that time he had written much verse, fiction, biography and essays, but his outstanding success was the autobiographical *Over the Bridge* (1955), continued in *The Golden Sovereign* (1957). *The Porch* (1937) attracted most attention among his novels. *Collected Poems* (1948) was supplemented by later books of verse.

Churchill, Florence. Aunt of four of the Sanger children in Margaret Kennedy's *The *Constant Nymph* (1924). She marries Lewis Dodd, the young composer-friend of the Sangers, who finds her 'silver sty' too confining and they part.

Churchill, Randolph (Randolph Frederick Edward Spencer Churchill, 1911-68). Son of Sir Winston S. Churchill; educated at Eton and Oxford. After several unsuccessful attempts he became a member of Parliament, 1940-45, but was most prominent as a controversial journalist, frequently expressing disapproval of newspapers and their owners, evidence of the irascible moral courage which made him notorious. He wrote *Fifteen Famous English Homes* (1954), *What I said about the Press* (1957), *The Rise and Fall of Sir Anthony Eden* (1959), *Lord Derby* (biography, 1960), *Twenty-One Years* (1965). He was working on the official Life of his father, and had been warmly commended for so much as was published before his death.

Churchill, Winston (1871-1947). Born at St Louis; educated at Annapolis Naval Academy. From 1898 he devoted himself to writing novels on American historical and social themes: *Richard Carvel* (1899), *Coniston* (1906), *Mr Crewe's Career* (1908), *The Inside of the Cup* (1913), etc. Though his books received much contemporary acclaim and sold in vast numbers, his romantic presentation of history was in the fashion of his day and his popularity waned. He ceased to write for publication many years before he died, being throughout of independent means. There was no relationship between him and the following, who used the initials W.S. to distinguish his books from those of the American writer.

Churchill, Winston S. (Sir Winston Leonard Spencer Churchill, 1874-1965; knight of the Garter, 1953). Born at Blenheim Palace, son of Lord Randolph Churchill and his American wife; educated at Harrow and Sandhurst. He began a military career in 1895, served in the Spanish-American War in Cuba, with British forces in India and the Sudan, and while acting as a war correspondent in South Africa was captured by the Boers. The classic story of his escape is an exciting chapter in his partial autobiography *My Early Life* (1930). His first books all dealt with military campaigns he had seen at first hand, but his earliest substantial work was *Lord Randolph Churchill* (1906), the biography of his father. Meanwhile he had begun a political career as M.P. for Oldham in 1900, and for the next half-century and more he was to hold a succession of ministerial and cabinet offices, punctuated by periods on the Opposition side in Parliament, and culminating in his greatest period—as Prime Minister and inspirer of his nation in World War II. Since the deeds of statesmen tend to be remembered only as pictures in the continuous pattern of history, the memory of Churchill is likely to be more vividly preserved by his contributions to literature and oratory, in which he recaptured the grand manner and did not refrain from a florid and picturesque style when these were needed to stir the imagination and fire the courage of readers and hearers in times of national danger. His literary output was vast, even though it was a secondary product in a life mainly devoted to public affairs. Though when temporarily out of politics he wrote some ephemeral journalism, his major writings are classics of history and biography: *The World Crisis 1916-18* (6 vols, 1923-31); *Marlborough: his Life and Times* (4 vols, 1933-8), *The Second World War* (6 vols: *The Gathering Storm*, 1948; *Their Finest Hour*, 1949; *The Grand Alliance*, 1950; *The Hinge of Fate*, 1950; *Closing the Ring*, 1951; *Triumph and Tragedy*, 1954), *A History of the English-Speaking Peoples* (4 vols, 1956-58). Ten volumes of his wartime and post-war speeches were published. His early writings include a novel, *Savrola* (1900). Painting became a leisure-time occupation in later decades, his achievements in that being recognized by election in 1948 as a Royal Academician Extraordinary. His widow was made a life peeress in 1965 as Baroness Spencer-Churchill.

Churchill, Winston Spencer (1940-   ), grandson of the preceding; educated at Eton and Oxford; travelled extensively as correspondent for various newspapers; elected to parliament, 1970; author of *First Journey* (1964), *The Six Day War* (with his father, Randolph, 1967), a record of the Israeli-Arab war.

Circle, The. Comedy in three acts by W. Somerset *Maugham, performed in London in 1921. The setting is the drawing room of the Champion-Cheneys' house in Dorset. Arnold Champion-Cheney, M.P., thirty-five, married to Elizabeth, still in her twenties, continues to bear resentment because his mother, Kitty, ran away thirty years before with Lord Porteus, whose wife refused to divorce him. Clive Champion-Cheney, Arnold's father, arrives unexpectedly on the day Kitty and Porteus are also coming. They have been invited at Elizabeth's insistence, and she is left to explain the dilemma to her father-in-law. An embarrassing encounter seems unavoidable, but in fact the one-time rivals for Kitty converse amicably. Elizabeth and Clive (left with only Edward Luton, a visitor from Malaya in love with Elizabeth and she with him) discuss Porteus and Kitty who, once romantic lovers, have ruined one another. 'She's a silly worthless woman because she's led a silly worthless life', is Clive's summing-up; and of Porteus he says: 'Can you imagine that that was a brilliant young man, whom everyone expected to be Prime Minister? Look at him now. A grumpy sodden old fellow with false teeth.' Both Kitty and Porteus try to dissuade Elizabeth from going away with Luton, as she tells Arnold she intends. He declares he will not divorce her and orders Luton from the house. His father advises him that a self-sacrificing attitude will shake Elizabeth's resolve, and it seems that the scheme has worked. But the masterfulness of Luton wins her back to him, and just as Clive is gloating over his own cleverness the starting-up of the runaways' car is heard.

Cities of the Plain. English title of part four of Marcel Proust's novel. *A la recherche du temps perdu* (*Remembrance of Things Past*). *Sodome et Gomorrhe* is the part-title in the original.

Clandon, Mrs Lanfrey. Author of the *Twentieth Century Treatises* (on Cooking, Creeds, Clothing, Conduct, Children, Parents), and mother of Gloria, Dorothy, . and Philip Clandon in Bernard Shaw's *You Never Can Tell* (1895).

Clara Dawes. In D. H. Lawrence's *Sons and Lovers* (1913); leaves her husband, Baxter Dawes, who fights with Paul Morel, her lover; later returns to Baxter after the two men are reconciled.

Clarendon Press. The printing and publishing organization of the University of Oxford. The first book was printed at Oxford in 1478 by a printer from Cologne, but it was not until 1586 that the University was authorized to print by a Star Chamber decree. The present name dates from the early 18th century when the University was given perpetual copyright in the Earl of Clarendon's *History of the Great Rebellion* which it published in 1702-4. The Clarendon Press is responsible for learned works and for educational books of all grades. Its London business and overseas branches, using the title Oxford University Press, publish books of a general kind as well as marketing those with the Clarendon Press imprint. C.P. and O.U.P. are a single body functioning as a department of the University and under the control of a University-appointed committee, the Delegates of the Press.

Clark, Alfred Alexander Gordon. See Cyril *Hare.

Clark, G. N. (Sir George Norman Clark, 1890- ; knighted 1953). Educated at Manchester and Oxford. Editor of the *English Historical Review*, 1920-25. Professor of Economic History, Oxford, 1931-43; Professor of Modern History, Cambridge, 1943-47; Provost of Oriel College, Oxford, 1947-57. Author of *The Seventeenth Century* (1929), *The Later Stuarts* (1934), *Science and Social Welfare in the Age of Newton* (1937), *The Wealth of England* (1946), *Early Modern Europe* (1957), and other historical works.

Clark, John Pepper (1935-). See *African writers.

Clark, Kenneth (1903- ; Baron Clark of Saltwood, 1969). Educated at Winchester and Oxford. Worked with Bernard *Berenson in England and Florence. Keeper of the Department of Fine Art, Ashmolean Museum, Oxford (1931-33); Director of the National Gallery, London (1934-45); Slade Professor of Fine Art, Oxford (1946-50). Author of *The Gothic Revival* (1929), *Leonardo da Vinci* (1939), *Landscape into Art* (1949), *The Nude* (1955), *Civilization* (1969), *Another Part of the Wood* (autobiographical; 1974), etc.

Clarke, Arthur C. (Arthur Charles Clarke, 1917-). Educated in Taunton and London. Research on radar, interplanetary exploration, communications satellites, and underwater exploration. Author of *Interplanetary Flight* (1950), *The Exploration of Space* (1951), and other scientific and technical works, as well as many volumes of science fiction reaching a high standard.

Clarke, Austin (1896-   ). Born in Dublin; educated there at the Jesuit Belvedere College and at the University. After a period as University lecturer in English he migrated to England and engaged in journalism, returning to Ireland in 1937, founding the Dublin Verse Speaking Society and the Lyric Theatre Company for the performance of his own and other verse plays. Beginning in 1917 with *The Vengeance of Fionn*, the first of his poems on Gaelic legends, he wrote *The Fires of Baal* (1930), *The Cattledrive in Connaught* (1925), etc. *Collected Poems* (1936), *Later Pòems* (1961). Among his verse plays are *The Flame* (1941), and *Viscount of Blarney and Other Plays* (1944), while his novels include *Bright Temptation* (1932), *The Singing Men at Cashel* (1936), and *The Sun Dances at Easter* (1952). *Collected Plays* (1963), *Twice Around the Black Church* (autobiography, 1960), *A Penny in the Clouds* (memoirs, 1968).

Classics. Originally used of literary works of ancient Greece or Rome, the term has come to be used more and more loosely. In relation to English literary works it is legitimately attached to those whose reputation for excellence has been maintained through successive generations. Latterly, 'modern classics' has become a publishers' label for a heterogeneous range of books of recent date conforming to current fashions in subject and style, whether dictated by public favour or academic vogue. In the vocabulary of sport and trade, 'classic' has been adopted as descriptive small-change for a horse or dog race, clothing, or any commercial product, at the manufacturer's or retailer's whim.

Claudel, Paul (1868-1955). Born at a village in the province of Aisne; educated at provincial schools and in Paris, where he studied philosophy, law, and political science. From 1890 he was in the diplomatic service, and after holding consular appointments in many parts of the world became French Ambassador in Japan and then in the U.S. and (1933-35) in Belgium. In World War II he was Minister of Propaganda. The major event in early life was his conversion to Roman Catholicism in 1886, soon after he had fallen under the spell of Rimbaud's poetry. He was also influenced by Mallarmé and Verlaine. His own literary output was extensive and varied, comprising poetry, plays, and essays on metaphysics, sociology, poetics, and religion. In English-speaking countries he is best known for the plays *The Tidings Brought to Mary (L'Annonce faite à Marie,* 1912*)* and *The Hostage (L'Otage,* 1911*)*.

Claudius Clear. *See* Sir William Robertson *Nicoll.

Clayhanger. Novel by Arnold *Bennett published in 1910, the first of a trilogy continued with *Hilda Lessways* (1911) and completed with *These Twain* (1915). On the day he leaves school at the age of sixteen in 1872, Edwin Clayhanger resolves to tell his father, Darius Clayhanger, that he will not go to work in the family printing business in Bursley, one of the *Five Towns. Darius had been sent to work at the age of seven by his poverty-stricken parents, labouring up to eighteen hours a day and frequently thrashed. When the family, completely destitute, were rescued after one night in the workhouse by Darius's Sunday-school teacher, Mr Shushions, a job is found for the boy as a printer's devil. From that beginning Darius progresses until he owns the leading printers in Bursley, with a stationery and bookseller's shop attached. Edwin, in spite of his resolution, finds himself drawn into his father's business, his protest that he wants to become an architect being virtually ignored. He lives at home with his sisters, Maggie and Clara, occasionally visited by widowed Auntie Hamps, 'a damned fine woman' of independent means, their dead mother's younger sister. Edwin becomes friendly with the family of Mr Osmond Orgreave, the town's chief architect, and in their house meets Hilda Lessways, whom he thinks ugly and at first dislikes, though increasingly fascinated by her self-contained air of mystery. They fall in love, and Edwin, bent on marriage, asks his father for an increase on his weekly wage of 17s 6d and is offered a rise of half a crown. Hilda has meanwhile gone to Brighton to visit a friend. She sends Edwin ardent though brief love letters, which cause him to be doubly dismayed by the sudden news that Hilda has married. They do not meet again until years later when Janet Orgreave has nine-year-old George Cannon staying with her, and tells Edwin that the child's mother is Hilda, who is widowed and in difficulties. Edwin finds her in Brighton as the penniless proprietor of a bankrupt shabby boarding-house, with the brokers' man in charge. Edwin settles her debts but she soon repays the money. She confesses that she is not a widow and, later, that Cannon married her bigamously and is in prison. Edwin and Hilda are drawn together again when she returns to Bursley while her child is seriously ill at the Orgreaves. The novel has a panoramic historical background of the period from the 1870s to the early 1890s, with the 1880 Sunday-schools Centenary and the 1887 Jubilee of Queen Victoria as set pieces. The prolonged decline and death of Darius is a painful clinical study of the mental and physical disintegra- of an indomitable old man.

Clayhanger Family, The. Trilogy by Arnold *Bennett published under this title in one volume in 1925, comprising *Clayhanger (1910), *Hilda Lessways (1911), *These Twain (1916). The first of these is surpassed only by Bennett's masterpiece, The *Old Wives' Tale.

Clayton, Richard H. M. See William *Haggard.

Clemens, Samuel Langhorne. See Mark *Twain.

Clemo, Jack (John Reginald Clemo, 1913-　　). Born in Cornwall; educated at a council school, leaving when he was twelve. Impair- ment of sight and hearing from childhood resulted in complete blindness and deafness in middle age. He began to write at the end of his schooldays, but a Cornish newspaper provided almost the only outlet for his verse and stories before the publication of a novel Wilding Graft (1948), an autobiography, Confession of a Rebel (1949), and collections of verse including The Clay Verge (1951), The Invading Gospel (1958), A Map of Clay (1961), Cactus on Carmel (1967).

Cleveland, John. Fellow and tutor, St John's College, Cambridge, from 1634 to 1645; royalist and metaphysical poet. He is a lead- ing character as the lover of Julian Cony- beare in Rose Macaulay's *They Were Defeated (1932).

Clewes, Howard (Howard Charles Vivian Clewes, 1912-　　). Born in York, brother of the following; educated at Merchant

Taylors' School. Worked in advertising 1931-57. Wrote novels (Dead Ground, 1946; The Mask of Wisdom, 1948; An Epitaph for Love, 1952), a study of Stendhal (1940), Image in the Sun (a play, 1955), and film scripts.

Clewes, Winston (Winston David Armstrong Clewes, 1906-　　). Born in Leeds, brother of the preceding; educated in York, Derry (Northern Ireland), and London. While mainly occupied as a business executive, he was also active as a spare-time novelist: The Violent Friends (1944) is a fictional treatment of the relationship of Jonathan Swift with Stella and Vanessa. Among his other novels are Journey into Spring (1948) and Men at Work (1951).

Cliché. Overworked and therefore stale words and phrases used by indolent writers and speakers, especially by critics and politicians as a thought-saving device.

Clifford, Lady. See Mrs Henry *de la Pasture.

Clifford, Martin. See Frank *Richards.

Clifford, Mrs W. K. (née Lucy Lane, died 1929; married William Kingdon Clifford, eminent mathematician, in 1875). Born in Barbados. After the death of her husband in 1879 she undertook journalistic work and then turned to the writing of fiction, producing children's stories (Anyhow Stories 1882) and novels, Mrs Keith's Crime (1885), Aunt Anne (1893), Sir George's Objection (1910) and others. Love Letters of a Worldly Woman (1891) had a contemporary vogue. She also wrote several plays.

Clitheroe, Jack. Bricklayer and Commandant in the Irish Citizen Army in Sean O'Casey's The *Plough and the Stars (1926).

Clitheroe, Nora. Wife of Jack Clitheroe, above.

Cliveden Set. See *Astor Family.

Cloak and Dagger. Facetious phrase applied to spy stories and similar fiction.

Cloak and Sword. Originally applied descrip- tively in its Spanish form (capa y espada) to the 17th-century plays of Calderón and others; later extended to pseudo-historical and romantic novels and plays of love and intrigue such as The Prisoner of Zenda (Anthony Hope, 1894), Under the Red Robe (Stanley Weyman, 1894), If I were King (Justin Huntly McCarthy, 1901).

Clodd, Edward (1840-1930). Employed as

Secretary of the London Joint Stock Bank for the main part of his working life, though his interests were chiefly in literature, science, philosophy, and in a rationalistic approach to religion. His circle of friends included many outstanding literary men, some of whom he benefited much. Among his own writings were *Jesus of Nazareth* (1880), *The Story of Creation* (1888), and an autobiography, *Memories* (1916).

Cloete, Stuart (1897-   ). Born in Paris, of South African parentage; educated in Paris and England. After being severely wounded during World War I he spent some years in South Africa, where he bought a dairy farm, but returned to England in order to devote himself to writing. After several discouraging years he had a popular success with *Turning Wheels* (1937), designed to be the first of a series of novels dealing with South African life. He lived for a time in the U.S. but settled in South Africa after World War II. Other novels by him include *Watch for the Dawn* (1939), *Congo Song* (1943), *The Curve and the Tusk* (1952), *The Gambler* (1973). *Against These Three* (1945) is a biographical account of President Kruger, Cecil Rhodes, and the Matabele chief Lobengula.

Cloud Cuckoo Land. Historical novel by Naomi *Mitchinson published in 1925. The title comes from the city built in the sky in Aristophanes' *The Birds*.

Clowes, Evelyn Mary. *See* Elinor Mordaunt.

Clutton-Brock, Arthur (1868-1924). Art critic (mainly for *The Times*) and writer on literary subjects, e.g. *Shelley: the Man and the Poet* (1909).

Clyde Griffiths. Central character in Theodore Dreiser's *An *American Tragedy* (1925).

Cobb, Humphrey (1899-1944). Born in Florence of American parents; educated in the U.S. Served in France with the Canadian forces in World War I and was wounded and gassed. Experiences gathered there gave him basic material for *Paths of Glory* (1935), one of the outstanding realistic novels of the war.

Cobb, Irvin S. (Irvin Shrewsbury Cobb, 1876-1944). Born in Kentucky; had little education. He began working at odd jobs in early adolescence, and subsequently became a local newspaper reporter and for a while its editor. His wider reputation was made as a humorous writer, chiefly of short stories in

which the central character is Judge Priest, 'a kindly, hospitable old Confederate veteran', as in *Old Judge Priest* (1915), etc. Others among his many books are *Cobb's Anatomy* (1912), *Oh, Well, You Know How Women Are!* (1919), *A Laugh a Day* (1923). *Myself to Date* (1923) and *Exit Laughing* (1941) tell his own story.

Cobden-Sanderson, T. J. (Thomas James Cobden-Sanderson, 1840-1922). Born at Alnwick. Became the leading English bookbinder of the period and, as an associate of William Morris, one of the pioneers in the modern revival of fine printing. In 1900 he founded, and until it closed in 1916 controlled, the famous Doves Press. His *Journals, 1879-1922* were published in 1926.

Cockerell, Douglas Bennett (1870-1945). Brother of the following; a few varied and exciting years in Canada followed his education at St Paul's School in London; on returning home he took to bookbinding as craftsman and teacher, and became for the rest of his life the leading practitioner of that craft. He wrote *Bookbinding and the Care of Books* (1901).

Cockerell, Sir Sydney (Sydney Carlyle Cockerell, 1867-1962; knighted 1934). Born at Beckenham, Kent, brother of the preceding; educated at St Paul's School. After working (1889-92) in the family coal-merchant business he began to follow his own inclinations in the field of arts and crafts, becoming secretary of the Arts and Crafts Society when it was founded in 1888, and later assisted William Morris, who appointed him as literary executor. He wrote the history of Morris's Kelmscott Press, and from 1908 to 1937 was Director of the Fitzwilliam Museum at Cambridge, which he made into one of the foremost of such institutions. His correspondents included a great number of the outstanding men and women of the time, and two volumes of their letters to him were published under the editorship of Viola Meynell, *Friends of a Lifetime* (1940) and *The Best of Friends* (1956). His own writings included works on medieval illuminated manuscripts and early woodcut illustrations.

Cocktail Party, The. Three-act comedy in verse by T. S. *Eliot first performed at the Edinburgh Festival in 1949 (published, 1950). Though described by the author as a comedy, the play moves on several levels. The inconsequent cocktail badinage of act one, with Julia Shuttlethwaite as an amusing chatterer, is in the tone of drawing-room comedy. Domestic drama enters when the absence of the hostess, Lavinia Chamberlayne, attributed to a visit to a sick aunt, is admitted to be due to her having left her barrister husband, Edward Chamberlayne, whose mistress, Celia Coplestone, visits him after other guests have gone, and after a mysterious Unidentified Guest, in conversation with Edward, has steered the piece on to the morality play level. In a later scene this Unidentified Guest appears as Sir Henry Harcourt-Reilly, psychiatrist, in whose consulting room Lavinia and Edward, exposed as an unlovable woman and as a man incapable of loving, are reconciled on the basis that they must make the best of a bad job. Celia also seeks Reilly's advice and, confessing to a sense of sin, is offered alternative ways of redemption. She chooses the way on which she must 'journey blind . . . towards possession / Of what you have sought for in the wrong place.' To both Celia and the Chamberlaynes, Reilly's parting words are the same: 'Go in peace . . . work out your salvation with diligence.' In the last act the Chamberlaynes have settled down to a recognition 'that life is only keeping on', though a guest at their latest cocktail party had brought news that Celia joined an austere nursing order and during a native insurrection was crucified near an ant-hill in Kinkanja.

Cocteau, Jean (1891-1963). Born near Paris. Influenced in youth by the writings of André *Gide, he began to publish poetry when he was seventeen, and thereafter became a leading figure in all the arts, either as himself a practitioner or as an advocate and commentator. He did much to publicize and make fashionable avant garde painting, music, ballet, plays, and films. Among his own numerous writings the best known are the verse plays Orphée (1927), La Voix humaine (1930), La Machine infernale (1934), L'Aigle à deux têtes (The Eagle with Two Heads, 1946), the novel Les Enfants terribles (1929), and Opium, Journal d'une désintoxication (Opium: The Journal of an Addict, 1930).

Cody, Captain (William Frederick Cody, 1846-1917). Born in Iowa. Served as a frontier scout and earned the nickname 'Buffalo Bill' from his killing thousands of buffaloes under a contract to supply meat to railway workers. Later he became an actor in melodramas and

in 1883 started the Wild West Show which he toured in America and Europe. In 1904 he published an autobiography which is as often imaginative as factual.

Cody, S. F. (Samuel Franklin Cody, 1862-1913). Born in Texas. Became a naturalized Englishman and a pioneer aviator, inventing man-lifting kites, airships, and aeroplanes. Killed in an aeroplane crash.

Coffee-table book. Any lavishly produced and illustrated large volume designed less for reading than to be displayed to visitors as a cultural status symbol.

Coffin, Robert P. T. (Robert Peter Tristram Coffin, 1892-1955). Born at Brunswick, Maine; educated at Bowdoin, Princeton, and (as a Rhodes scholar) at Oxford. Professor of English at Wells College, Aurora, New York, 1921-34. Gave numerous public readings of his own poems throughout the U.S., drawing upon published volumes, Dew and Bronze (1927), Ballads of Square-Toed Americans (1933), Saltwater Farm (1937), Maine Ballads (1938); Collected Poems (1939). He also wrote biography, history, novels, essays, and literary criticism. The central concern of his work was his native Maine and the life of its people.

Cohan, George M. (George Michael Cohan, 1878-1942). American playwright, actor, and theatre manager. Author of vaudeville songs and sketches and full-length plays: Little Johnny Jones (1904), Forty-Five Minutes from Broadway (1906), The Song and Dance Man (1923). He wrote one of the most popular songs of World War I, 'Over There'.

Cokane, William de Burgh, a character in *Widowers' Houses by Bernard Shaw; friend of Dr Harry Trench, whose scruples about the source of his income are deprecated by Cokane.

Cokeson. Managing clerk to James & Walter How in John Galsworthy's *Justice (1910). He tries unsuccessfully to save Falder from prison and its mentally and morally destructive effects.

Cold Comfort Farm. Novel by Stella *Gibbons published in 1932. It parodies the earthy dialect novels of rural life which had been in vogue, such as some by Mary *Webb, Sheila *Kaye-Smith, T. F. *Powys. Having been left inadequately provided for when her parents died, and having no inclination to work, Flora Poste goes to stay with her Starkadder cousins at Cold Comfort Farm, Howling, Sussex. She finds it 'crouched, like a beast about to spring, under the bulk of Mockuncle hill', while the inhabitants display various shades of primitive subnormal mentality, with sexuality and religious fanaticism prominent. Flora's Aunt Ada Doom, who leaves her upstairs room only twice a year, exercises matriarchal remote control over the numerous sons and other relatives, and reiterates maddeningly that she 'saw something nasty in the woodshed' long ago. Flora determines to inject sweetness and light into the oppressive atmosphere and succeeds so far beyond expectation as to persuade Aunt Doom to make an air trip to Paris, 'dressed from head to foot in the smartest flying kit of black leather'.

Collage. A mode among painters of sticking scraps of paper and other materials to the picture surface as part of the design. In poetry and prose, the incorporation of passages, phrases, etc. in a language other than that of the main work: e.g. in T. S. Eliot's The *Waste Land (1922).

Cole, G. D. H. (George Douglas Howard Cole, 1889-1958). Born at Ealing, London; educated at St Paul's School and Oxford. After holding university appointments in the provinces and London, returned to Oxford and became Chichele Professor of Social and Political Theory there from 1944. He took a prominent part in socialist and Labour Party politics and became chairman of the *Fabian Society. He was also active in the Adult Education movement both as a tutor and as Vice-President of the Workers' Educational Association. He wrote extensively on economics, trade unionism, and Guild Socialism; published biographies—William Cobbett (1924), Robert Owen (1925)—and some poems; and in collaboration with his wife, Margaret *Cole, produced numerous detective novels.

Cole, Dame Margaret (née Margaret Isabel Postgate, 1893- ; D.B.E. 1970; married G. D. H. Cole, 1918). Born in Cambridge; educated at Roedean and Girton. Classics mistress at St Paul's Girls' School, 1914-16. Collaborated with her husband in many books, including detective novels. Wrote independently Local Government for Beginners (1927), Marriage (1938), Books and the People (1938), Beatrice Webb (1945),

The Story of Fabian Socialism (1961), Life of G. D. H. Cole 1971. Secretary, Fabian Society, 1939 to 1953.

Coleridge, Mary Elizabeth (1861-1907). Poet (Poems Old and New, 1907), novelist (The Seven Sleepers of Ephesus, 1893; The King with Two Faces, 1897), and essayist (Gathered Leaves, 1910). She was descended from the family of Samuel Taylor Coleridge through his nephew, her grandfather.

Coles, Cyril Henry. See Manning *Coles.

Coles, Manning (pseudonym of Adelaide Frances Oke Manning, died 1959, and Cyril Henry Coles, 1901-65). The former was born in London and educated at Tunbridge Wells; the latter, also born in London, was educated at Petersfield. Coles served as a British Intelligence agent in Germany during part of World War I. The two writers collaborated in numerous spy stories and detective novels, including Drink to Yesterday (1940), The Fifth Man (1946), Diamonds in Amsterdam (1949), Night Train to Paris (1952), Crime in Concrete (1960).

Colette (Sidonie Gabrielle Colette, 1873-1954). Born at Saint-Sauveur-en-Puisage, Burgundy; educated locally, but more particularly by her innate love of the countryside and by unrestricted reading at home with her mother for whom she had lifelong gratitude and devotion. When twenty she married Henry Gauthiers-Villars, a versatile writer whose wide-ranging productions were amplified by ghost-writers in his employ. He was, however, a genuine and perceptive music critic and intimate with the artistic and bohemian set in Paris, a startlingly new environment for his wife, nearly twenty years younger than himself and accustomed hitherto only to village life. Willy (Gauthiers-Villar's pseudonym) quickly tired of Sidonie, who became bored and hysterical from neglect. As a time-filling compensation he urged her to write of her girlhood, and her first book Claudine à l'école was published in 1900. But this and other Claudine books which followed in the next few years bore only Willy's name as author, and he alone had the public credit and enjoyment of their merit and popularity. It was at his insistence, however, that their true author sauced these books with titillating amorous passages which largely accounted for their immediate success, though the esteem in which they were subsequently held was due to their subtle and sensitive portrayal of character and feeling and to the excellence of their literary style. The first books on which her own name appeared (as Colette Willy) was *Dialogues de bêtes* (1904), a series of conversations between a dog and a cat. She was divorced from Gauthiers-Villars in 1906, but continued to write as Colette Willy until 1916, after which she used Colette only as her pen name. From 1906 to 1914 she acted on the vaudeville stage, a literary product of that experience being *L'Envers du music-hall* (1913). Early country life was recollected in *Le Retraite sentimentale* (1907) and *Les Vrilles de la vigne* (1908); other autobiographical elements appear in *La Maison de Claudine* (1923) and *Mes Apprentissages* (1936). Her mother is beautifully portrayed in *Sido* (1929). Long before she died Colette was acknowledged as one of France's finest writers and she received high public honours. Among outstanding books not mentioned above are *Chéri* (1920) and *La Fin de Chéri* (1926); *Le Blé en herbe* (1923); *La Naissance du jour* (1928), *Gigi* (1945).

Collie, Ruth. *See* Wilhelmina *Stitch.

Collier, John (1901-). Born in London; educated privately. Author of poems (*Gemini*, 1931, etc.); several volumes of short stories (*No Traveller Returns*, 1931; *The Devil and All*, 1934; *Fancies and Good Nights*, 1951; and others), and novels, of which the first, *His Monkey Wife, or Married to a Chimp* (1930), a satire, attracted most attention.

Collin, W. E. (William Edwin Collin, 1893-). Born in England; educated at Durham and in France and Canada. Professor of Romance Languages, University of Western Ontario, 1925-60. Author of *The White Savannahs* (1936), pioneer critical essays on Canadian authors.

Collingwood, R. G. (Robin George Collingwood, 1889-1943). Born at Cartmel, Lancashire, son of the following; educated at home and at Rugby and Oxford, becoming tutor and lecturer in the University on philosophy and Roman history, and from 1935 to 1941 Professor of Metaphysical Philosophy. He was a man of immense learning and widespread interests embracing art, music, and sailing. In addition to his eminence as a philosopher he was an unequalled expert on Roman Britain, writing a volume with that title in 1921 (revised 1932) and collaborating in the first volume of the Oxford History of England (*Roman Britain and the English Settlements*, 1936). His other works include *Speculum Mentis, or The Map of Knowledge* (1924), *An Essay on Philosophical Method* (1933), *The Principles of Art* (1938), *An Essay on Metaphysics* (1940), *The New Leviathan* (1942). *An Autobiography* (1939) is the best introduction to his remarkable personality.

Collingwood, W. G. (William Gershom Collingwood, 1854-1932). Father of the preceding; artist, antiquarian, and Professor of Fine Art at University College, Reading. Wrote several books on the Lake District, his home for many years; best known for his *Life of Ruskin* (1900), he having been both friend and secretary to Ruskin.

Collins, Norman (Norman Richard Collins, 1907-). Born and educated in London. After working on the staff of publishers and as assistant literary editor of the *News Chronicle* he concentrated on novel writing, following his first book *The Facts of Fiction* (1932). From the 1940s he was largely associated with radio and took an active part in the establishment of commercial television in England. Among his novels *Love in Our Time* (1939) and *London Belongs to Me* (1945) are representative.

Collins, W. E. (1893-). *See* Canadian writers.

Collis, John Stewart (1900-). Educated at Rugby and Oxford. Writer on (principally) nature subjects: e.g. *Forward to Nature* (1927), *While Following the Plough* (1946), *Down to Earth* (1947), *The Triumph of the Tree* (1950), *The Worm Forgives the Plough* (1973). Other books include: *Shaw* (1925), *Marriage and Genius* (1963), *Life of Tolstoy* (1969), *The Carlyles* (1972); *Bound Upon a Course* (autobiography, 1971).

Collis, Maurice (1889-). Born in Dublin; educated in England at Rugby and Oxford. Entered the Indian Civil Service and was a district magistrate in Burma from 1912 to 1934 (apart from a period with the army in Palestine during World War I). After leaving the I.C.S. he became a full-time writer, producing *Siamese White* (1936) and numerous other books on Eastern subjects, including *Trials in Burma* (1938), *The Land of the Great Image* (1943), *Marco Polo* (1950), as well as an autobiography *The Journey Outward* (1952) and *Somerville and Ross: A Biography* (1968).

Collyer, Hester. Wife of Sir William Collyer and mistress of Freddie Page in Terence Rattigan's *The *Deep Blue Sea* (1952), where she is the central character.

Colophon. Publisher's or printer's pictorial device or symbol traditionally appearing at the end of a book. Now the symbol is usually on the title-page.

Colston-Baynes, Dorothy Julia. See Dormer *Creston.

Colum, Mary Gunning (*née* Mary Gunning Maguire, died 1957; married Padraic *Colum in 1912). Educated in Ireland and Holland; went with her husband to the U.S. in 1914, and from the early 1930s contributed to leading journals articles which gained her the reputation of being one of the best literary critics in America. Her one published book in this kind is *From These Roots* (1937); *Life and the Dream* (1947; new edn. 1967) is a volume of personal memoirs.

Colum, Padraic (1881-1972). Born at Longford, Ireland; educated locally; worked as a railway clerk in Dublin. Became, with W. B. *Yeats and others, a pioneer in the Irish literary revival, and wrote plays, *The Land* (1905) and others for the *Abbey Theatre. Co-founder and for a while editor of the *Irish Review*. A close personal study of Hawaiian folklore (made at the request of the government of Hawaii) resulted in two volumes, *At the Gateways of the Day* (1924) and *The Bright Islands* (1925). His numerous works include (besides plays), *Collected Poems* (1953), short stories, essays, children's books, *An Anthology of Irish Verse* (1948), *A Treasury of Irish Folklore* (1955), and a novel *Castle Conquer* (1923). He settled in the U.S. in 1939.

Colvin, Sidney (Sir Sidney Colvin, 1845-1927; knighted 1911). Born near Woodbridge, Suffolk; educated privately and at Cambridge. Became art critic to the *Pall Mall Gazette* and moved among such painters as Burne-Jones, Rossetti, and G. F. Watts. Appointed Slade Professor of Fine Art at Cambridge in 1873, Director of the Fitzwilliam Museum there in 1876, and from 1884 to 1912 Keeper of Prints and Drawings at the British Museum. His genius for friendship attracted a number of the outstanding poets, novelists and public men of the 19th century and, later, Joseph *Conrad; but his outstanding service was to Robert Louis Stevenson, who was greatly helped by Colvin and his wife (formerly Mrs A. H. Sitwell), to both of whom many of Stevenson's best letters were written. In addition to essays on art and guides to museum collections, Colvin wrote biographies of Landor (1881) and Keats (1887; and a larger work in 1917). He also edited the standard edition (in four volumes) of *The Letters of Robert Louis Stevenson* (1911).

Comfort, Alex (Alexander Comfort, 1920-   ). Born in London; educated at Highgate School, at Cambridge, and at London Hospital Medical College, where he became Lecturer in Physiology in 1948. While continuing medical research he wrote novels (*The Power House*, 1944, etc.), short stories (*Letters from an Outpost*, 1947), poems (*A Wreath for the Living*, 1943; *All But He Departed*, 1951; etc.) as well as plays and volumes on social problems including *Art and Social Responsibility* (1946) and *Authority and Delinquency in the Modern State* (1950).

Commitment. Although it would be difficult to find in the history of literature any period in which writers, whether factual or imaginative, entirely divorced themselves or their works from some critical link with the political and social circumstances of their age, the demand that poets, novelists, and others should accept as morally and intellectually imperative the principle of *commitment* was a particular product of the 1930s and after. Such issues as the great industrial depression in the decade before World War II, the Spanish Civil War (1936-39), the Hitler régime in Germany, and, after the War, nuclear armaments, stirred chivalrous and humanitarian impulses in many writers. Some, such as George *Orwell, became physically engaged as well as using their literary talent in behalf of a chosen cause, but most were satisfied to give support by deploying their abilities in poetry and fiction. The goodwill and honesty of purpose which animate 'committed' writers are beyond question. The case advanced in opposition to them is that 'committed' poems and 'committed' novels and stories tend to degrade the imaginative forms of literature and bring them to the level of propaganda; and that imaginative creation is a function of timeless cosmic vision, not of temporal localized partisanship.

Common Reader, The. The title of volumes of essays by Virginia *Woolf: first series 1925; second series 1932. They contain much of her best writing, and in suitability to their medium are superior to her novels. They range over many periods and types of literature, past and contemporary, but in critical penetration and sensitive excellence of prose style they appeal rather to the uncommon than the common reader. Further collections of her essays were published posthumously: *The Death of the Moth* (1942), *The Moment and other essays* (1947), *The Captain's Death-Bed* (1950); *Collected Essays* embodying all the above (4 vols., 1966-7).

Companionate Marriage. A form of trial marriage advocated by the American Judge *Lindsey as a means of avoiding or minimizing unhappy permanent contracts.

Companionship of Literature. *See* *Royal Society of Literature.

Compton, Joseph (1891-1964). Director of Education, Manchester (1925) and Ealing (1937-1957). Chairman of the *National Book League and from 1958 head of its education department, with a special interest in drama, poetry, speech training and verse speaking. Author of *The Curtain Rises* (1927), *Spoken English* (1941), etc.

Compton-Burnett, I. (Ivy Compton Burnett, 1892-1969). Born at Pinner, Middlesex, daughter of a leading homeopathic physician by his second wife. Her morally cramping though intellectually fruitful education at Royal Holloway College, the death of her brothers and joint suicide of two sisters, the oppressiveness of home life under a demanding imperious stepmother, are detailed in Hilary Spurling's *Ivy When Young* (1974) which covers her first thirty-five years. Though the direct autobiographical element in her novels is small, their unique quality, uniting the sombre and the melodramatic, nevertheless had its roots in her early life. A gap of fourteen years separated her immature first novel (*Dolores,* 1911) from its successor, *Pastors and Masters* (1925), followed by *Brothers and Sisters* (1929), *Men and Wives* (1931), *Daughters and Sons* (1937), *Parents and Children* (1941), *Elders and Betters* (1944), *Darkness and Day* (1951), *Mother and Son* (1955), *A Father and his Fate* (1957),

A God and his Gifts (1963), and others. Her characters, particularly the numerous children, are for the most part stripped of the pretence, or humbug, or tender consideration which normally cushions the impact of one human being upon another, and the implied dictum 'truth is brutality' is set up in opposition to the comfortable doctrine that 'Truth is Beauty'. Virtue is not rewarded, evil goes unpunished; and unabashed yet unspeakable horror creeps below a skin of Edwardian primness. The author's reputation with critics and fellow authors was due chiefly to her ruthless acceptance of the truth about human nature as it appeared to her to be, though limitation of experience restricted her range and prevented her from giving as fair a showing to the infinite diversity of individuals as to covert (even, sometimes, overt) baseness in human types. The Compton-Burnett novels resemble those of her own best-liked author, Jane Austen, in relying on conversation, not on narrative or description; and also like Jane Austen's they abound in wit and mordant humour. Both writers adopt a mainly objective attitude towards their characters, an attitude more remarkable in the later novelist since she contemplates her human monsters with imperturbable acceptance.

Computers. The possible utility of computers in the literary field has become a subject of speculation by scholars and others who envisage their employment in a variety of ways, ranging from the composition of poems to the solution of problems of authorship, the compiling of indexes, translating, and the almost instantaneous performance of routine tasks of scholarship otherwise requiring prolonged human labour.

Comstock, Anthony (1844-1915). Crusader against obscene literature in the U.S., founder of the Society for the Suppression of Vice, and promoter of the Comstock Law (1873) for the exclusion of indecent matter from the American mails. A remarkable ultra-Puritan, he was the subject of a biographical study by Heywood Broun and Margaret Leech, *Anthony Comstock: Roundsman of the Lord* (1927).

Conan Doyle. *See* Sir Arthur Conan *Doyle.

Conditioned reflex. *See* *Pavlov.

Connage. *See* *Rosalind Connage.

Connection, The. Play in two Acts by Jack Gelber, first produced in New York in 1959 and in London in 1961. The characters are mainly drug addicts, and in keeping with their condition the play itself is uncoordinated and is presented as a formless improvisation with jazz music taking a prominent part. In New York it became a cult product of the *'beat generation', but had only a brief run on the London stage. The English printed text (1961) included a commendatory Preface by Kenneth *Tynan.

Connell, John (pseudonym of John Henry Robertson, 1909-65). Educated at Loretto School and Oxford. On the staff of the *Evening News* from 1932. Author of novels (*Lyndesay*, 1930; *The House by Herod's Gate*, 1947; *Midstream*, 1948; etc) and biographical and critical studies (*W. E. Henley*, 1949; *Winston Churchill, the Writer*, 1956).

Connell, F. Norreys (until 1920, the pseudonym of Conal O'Connell O'Riordan, 1874-1948). Born in Dublin and educated in Jesuit schools. Studied for the army, but suffered a spinal injury and turned to the stage, acting in England before becoming Director of the *Abbey Theatre in Dublin in 1909. Being unfit for military service, he went to France in World War I to run a rest centre for the troops. President of the Irish Literary Society from 1937. Author of plays—*The Piper* (1908), *His Majesty's Pleasure* (1925), *The King's Wooing* (1929), *Captain Falstaff and Other Plays* (1935); novels—*In the Green Park* (1894), *The Fool and His Heart* (1896), *Adam of Dublin* (1920), *Adam and Caroline* (1921), *In London* (1922), *Married Life* (1924), *Judith Quinn* (1939). Works later than 1920 were published under his birth name.

Connelly, Marc (Marcus Cook Connelly, 1890-   ). Born in Pennsylvania; educated at Washington, Pa. Worked as a journalist in Pittsburg and also in New York, where he also wrote lyrics and other material for musical comedies before achieving his great success with the Negro play *Green Pastures* (1929), adapted from a book by Roark *Bradford. In collaboration with George *Kaufman he wrote other successful plays, among them *Beggar on Horseback* (1923) and *Merton of the Movies* (1925).

Conner, Reardon (Patrick Reardon Conner, 1907-   ). Born in Dublin, educated there and in Cork. Settled in England; worked in London as a landscape gardener, and during and after World War II in government departments; also as book reviewer and publisher's reader. Author of *Shake Hands with the Devil* (1933), *Salute to Aphrodite* (1935), *The Sword of Love* (1938), *The Devil Among the Tailors* (1947), *Hunger of the Heart* (1950), *The House of Cain* (1952) and other novels and numerous short stories. Under the pseudonym Peter Malin: *River, Sing Me a Song* (1939), *Kobo the Brave* (1950) and other books for boys.

Connington, J. J. (pseudonym of Alfred Walter Stewart, 1880-1947). Born in Glasgow; educated at Glasgow, Marburg and London universities. From 1901 he held university appointments in chemistry, becoming Professor of Chemistry at Queen's University, Belfast, from 1919. In addition to a number of scientific works under his birth name, he wrote under his pseudonym a long series of detective novels beginning with *Nordenholt's Million* (1923) and including *Murder in the Maze* (1927), *The Case with Nine Solutions* (1928), *The Sweepstake Murders* (1931), *No Past is Dead* (1942), *The Dangerfield Talisman* (1945), etc., and *Alias J. J. Connington* (1947), an autobiography. His fictional detectives are Sir Clinton Driffield and Mark Brand.

Connolly, Cyril (Cyril Vernon Connolly, 1903-1974). Educated at Eton and Oxford. After contributing to various periodicals from 1927, he founded *Horizon in 1939 and edited it until it ceased in 1950. He was for a year literary editor of *The Observer* and afterwards a leading critic on the *Sunday Times*. Author of *The Rock Pool* (novel, 1935), *Enemies of Promise* (autobiography, 1938), *The *Unquiet Grave* (1944), *The Condemned Playground* (essays, 1944), *The Evening Colonnade* (1973).

Connor, Ralph (pseudonym of Charles William Gordon, 1860-1937). Born in Ontario; educated at Toronto University and Edinburgh; studied for the Presbyterian Church, and spent some time as a missionary among miners and lumbermen in the Rocky Mountains region, before becoming (from 1894 until he died) minister of a Winnipeg church, with an interval as chaplain to the Canadian forces in World War I. He wrote novels which draw extensively upon his active personal experiences and are designed to inculcate sound religious principles: *Black Rock* (1898), *The Sky Pilot* (1899), *The*

Man from Glengarry (1901), *The Girl from Glengarry* (1933), and many others.

Connor, Sir William Neil. *See* Cassandra.

Conquest, Owen. *See* Frank *Richards.

Conquest, Robert (George Robert Acworth Conquest, 1917-   ). Born at Great Malvern; educated at Winchester, Oxford and Grenoble. Editor of anthologies of contemporary verse *New Lines* Series 1 and 2 (1956, 1963). His own books of poetry include *Between Mars and Venus* (1962) and *Arias from a Love Opera and Other Poems* (1969). *The Great Terror* (1968) is an account of Stalinist purges.

Conrad, Joseph (pseudonym of Józef Teodor Konrad Korzeniowski, 1857-1924). Born near Berdichev in the Ukraine region of Poland, the only child of Apollo and Evelina Korzeniowski. His father had little practical sense, and though at St Petersburg University Apollo studied law and languages, and later acted as an estate manager, his interests were mainly literary and political. He wrote poems and plays and translated works by Victor Hugo and some small part of Shakespeare; but his revolutionary activities attracted the attention of Poland's Russian masters, and in 1862, with his wife and child, he was banished to Vologda in northern Russia, where the rigorous climate and hardships of exile directly contributed to the death of Józef's mother early in 1865, when he was little more than seven years old. During the next three or four years the boy, periodically ill, shared the time between his father and his maternal uncle (Thaddeus Bobrowski), until in 1869 Apollo was allowed to go with him to Cracow, where Józef went to his first school. His father died in May of that year, and although the guardianship of Józef was otherwise intended by his parents, Thaddeus voluntarily assumed responsibility for his nephew's welfare and up to the time of his own death twenty-five years later he served conscientiously as mentor, friend, and financial adviser and supplier to a frequently difficult charge. A tutor was engaged for the boy, who at the age of fifteen began to express a determination to become a sailor, though born in a country with no seacoast. The tutor's efforts to dissuade him having been fruitless, he was at length allowed (in 1874) to join the French merchant navy at Marseilles, whence he made his first sea voyage to Martinique,

returning to Marseilles in May 1875. He then voyaged to the West Indies as apprentice in the French sailing ship *Mont Blanc,* while during a further voyage to the West Indies as steward in 1876 he met, on the *Sainte-Antoine,* the Corsican Dominic Cervoni who became the model for leading characters in Conrad's novels. Of this part of Józef's life comparatively little is known, though apparently he took part in a disastrous smuggling and gun-running adventure for the supporters of Don Carlos VII, whose family had long been claimants to the Spanish throne. He also became involved with a Spanish girl, unidentified except in the character of Doña Rita in *The *Arrow of Gold,* written by Conrad long after (1917-18). A wound received in Marseilles in 1878, and long believed to have been received in a duel, appears to have been self-inflicted. In a letter to a friend, Thaddeus Bobrowski told that he had been summoned from Kiev to Marseilles, where Józef, having lost borrowed money in a first gambling venture at Monte Carlo, had shot himself near the heart. The letter was first published in *Joseph Conrad: A Critical Biography* by Jocelyn Baines (1960). Shortly after (April 1878) he joined the crew of the British ship *Mavis* sailing from Marseilles to Constantinople with cargo, and returned on her to England, landing in this country for the first time on 18 June 1878, at Lowestoft, knowing only a few words of English. In October of that year he went from London to Australia on a wool clipper, remaining with her until she reached London again a year later. In June 1880 he qualified by examination as a Second Mate in the British Merchant Service; in December 1884 as a First Mate; and in August 1886 became a naturalized British subject (anglicizing his name as Joseph Conrad thenceforward), three months before passing the Board of Trade examination for a Master's certificate. In the intervening years he had served as an officer on English sailing ships: on another clipper to Sydney; on the barque *Palestine* to Bangkok (a voyage on which he subsequently based *Youth*); on the *Rivesdale* to Madras; on the *Narcissus* from Bombay to Dunkirk (drawn upon for *The *Nigger of the 'Narcissus',* 1897). Early in 1887 he sailed as First Mate on the *Highland Forest* from Amsterdam to Java, but left her at Singapore to go into hospital for treatment for an injured leg. Between August 1887 and the following January he was Mate on the *Vidar* (his first steamship) trading to and from Singapore via the Malay Archipelago. Next engaged as Master of the *Otago,* he resigned the command in April 1889 after sailing from Bangkok to Singapore, Sydney, Mauritius, Melbourne, and Adelaide. In London lodgings, sometime in the later part of 1889, he began to write a novel. Before this progressed far, he fulfilled a long-felt desire to go to the Congo, first discussing the project with his uncle, whom he visited in Poland early in 1890. He arrived in Africa in May to take command of a Belgian company's river steamer, the captain of which had been killed. To reach the vessel he had to travel far up the river Congo and then proceed 200 miles by caravan track, a thirty-six days' journey. Though the months he spent in Africa gave him material for one of his most impressive stories, *Heart of Darkness,* it permanently undermined his health. Back in London at the beginning of 1891, he was unemployed until November, when he sailed from Plymouth as First Mate on the clipper *Torrens* for Adelaide. During the voyage he showed to a passenger as much as was written of his novel and was encouraged to continue. Among the passengers was another future novelist, John *Galsworthy, who became one of Conrad's close friends. His uncle died in February 1894 and in April Conrad finished the novel which had been in slow progress for five years. It was accepted by Fisher Unwin and published in April 1895 as *Almayer's Folly.* Attempts to get another sea appointment came to nothing, and by 1898 he had abandoned any expectation of returning to the merchant service. His career as sailor and ship's officer lasted almost a quarter of a century. The rest of his life, a further quarter of a century, though less arduous was in other respects more exhausting. As a writer he was physically handicapped by recurrent gout and other ills, and was often mentally drained by the difficulties of composition. He wrote slowly, and frequently despaired when his brain seemed barren and words failed to come. Moreover, as a novelist he had exacting aesthetic standards, treating story-telling not merely as the provision of entertaining fiction but as a medium for profound investigation of human character and motive in action, as the expression of a philosophy of life, and as literary art on the highest level. Though he had no marked inventive ability —most of his novels and shorter stories were

rooted in experience, either his own or that of others reported to him—he had unique imaginative power that transmuted, after long gestation, actual happenings of temporary significance into matter made permanent and vital in his books. His wife (*née* Jessie George), whom he married in London in March 1896, quickly recognized that she was not his mental equal and that she could do little to compensate the inner solitude that was at once a necessity and a torment to him. But she wisely encouraged his companionship with men of his own intellectual calibre, and in matters of health and domesticity was invaluable to him, despite her own illnesses and, for many years, their poverty and chronic indebtedness. From the date of his first published novel, eighteen years passed before *Chance brought a first glimpse of popularity and prosperity in 1913, although with fellow authors, qualified critics, and a limited public he had long been ranked as a writer of exceptional genius. The rapidity with which he mastered the English language was astonishing. Even if he never wrote quite as a born Englishman, he wrote the language incomparably better than most educated Englishmen do. His earlier works, frequently concerned with the tropics and distant East, are exotic in expression as well as in setting. A certain exuberance of style and vividly colourful scene-painting, fascinating to his first admirers and to many readers still, was found distasteful by critics in a new generation who gave fuller praise to his later works and preferred Conrad in monochrome. Yet the luminosity of the prose in his early, and in some less early, books distinguishes them from all else in English literature and redeems the intermittently lush passages. Much has been made of his supposed persistent sense of guilt and betrayal in having cut himself off from Poland, while the pessimistic mental and spiritual cast of a number of his fictional characters has been interpreted as the reflection of his own disturbed conscience. But his outlook was always sardonic and his writings are steeped in irony and dominated by fatalism. He detested revolutionaries little less intensely than he hated the Russian oppressors of his nation, and even if he had remained or returned to Poland his innate aristocratic temper would have disinclined him to support or sympathize with any democratic uprising. The convictions he held and subtly commended through characters in his books were so deeply rooted as to appear pre-natal rather than as the product of any sense of personal faithlessness, however easy it may be to apply to himself in relation to Poland the declaration of faith made in his *A Personal Record:* 'Those who read me, know my conviction that the world . . . rests on a few very simple ideas; so simple that they must be as old as the hills. It rests notably .'. . on the idea of Fidelity.' In his wrestling with words and with the material stresses of life he endured much agony of mind, which was not the less genuine even when it was not endured with stoical dignity but shrilled into complaining letters to his friends. The complexity of his mental processes is shown in his narrative method. He rarely told (or, indeed, wished to tell) a story in direct terms: he doubled back and forth with numerous involutions of time and place, revealing character by the gradual fitting together of aspects and phases of personality. His most notable device was the invention of a more or less detached narrator named Marlow, who—in *Lord Jim* (1900), *Youth* (1902), *Heart of Darkness* (1902), and *Chance* (1914)—acts as a receiver and sifter of evidence from various sources, thus enabling events and persons to be viewed from different angles, with consequent enlargement of the reader's understanding. As the epigraph on the title page of his last completed novel, *The Rover,* Conrad chose lines from Spenser: 'Sleep after toyle, port after stormie seas/Ease after warre, death after life, does greatly please.' Both the title and the epigraph are appropriate to Conrad himself. He died at his home—Oswalds, Bishopsbourne, near Canterbury—on 3 August 1924. Recognition had come to him tardily, both in the shape of the money he needed and in the offer of a knighthood (which he declined) a few weeks before his death. Since he died, Conrad has received more critical attention than most writers of the period. Formerly regarded as pre-eminently a writer about the sea, emphasis has come to be laid on the political element in his novels, and on his use of symbolism and imagery. Though these factors may bulk larger in the minds of critics conforming with current fashions than they did in Conrad's mind, it is true that he considered the art of the novel no less important than its content. *Nostromo* (1904) is generally regarded as his finest novel, though *Lord Jim* (1900) is preferred by many readers. His principal works, in addition to those already named, are: *Typhoon* (1903), *The *Secret Agent* (1907), *Under Western Eyes* (1911), *Twixt Land and Sea* (1912; including 'The *Secret Sharer' and *'Freya of the Seven Isles'), *The Mirror of the Sea* (reminiscences, 1912), *Victory* (1914), *The Shadow Line* (1917).

Constant Nymph, The. Novel by Margaret *Kennedy published in 1924. On the journey to stay with his friend Albert Sanger and family at their chalet in the Austrian Tyrol, Lewis Dodd, young composer of *Revolutionary Songs* and Symphony in Three Keys, encounters a stranger who introduces himself as Kiril Trigorin. He also is bound for the chalet, invited because he is arranging a ballet for Sanger's opera *Akbar.* At railhead they are met by Teresa (Tessa) aged fourteen and Paulina aged twelve, two of the numerous Sanger children, only some of whom are legitimate. They proceed in a cart already occupied by a dead pig, and from the foot of the mountain pass below the chalet they have to walk, to the great discomfort of fat Trigorin. Living at the chalet is the brood nicknamed Sanger's Circus: Kate (the capable one) and Caryl, children of the great composer's first wife, an Australian opera singer who died in time for him to marry his pregnant mistress, Evelyn Churchill, an English girl pupil of good family, twenty years younger than himself; Antonia, Tessa, Paulina, and Sebastian are borne by Evelyn, who dies when she is thirty; Susan, the other child now at the chalet, is the daughter of Sanger's present mistress, Linda, a dazzling blonde from an Ipswich tobacconist's. Trigorin immediately becomes slavishly attached to her. Lewis has written a short opera, *Breakfast with the Borgias,* to be performed by the family for Sanger's birthday. The girls have been brought up in a thoroughly amoral atmosphere, and Antonia (eighteen) already has a wealthy lover, Jacob Birnbaum, nicknamed Ikey Mo, whom she later marries. Lewis considers Tessa 'the pick of the bunch' and, rightly, believes her innocent: 'Innocence was the only name he could find for the wild, imaginative solitude of her spirit.' From childhood she has loved Lewis. When Sanger dies suddenly and the news reaches the Churchills, Tessa, Paulina, and Sebastian are brought to England by their mother's brother Charles and niece Florence, Paulina remaining behind with Birnbaum. Florence falls in love with Lewis Dodd and marries him. Having social as well as artistic aspirations, she aims to bring Lewis and the Sanger children into conformity with conventional English standards. The children are sent to boarding school, but are intractable and run away. Lewis rebels against being kept in a 'silver sty'. The marriage breaks down and Lewis starts for the Continent. At the last moment Tessa joins him at the station and they travel together to Brussels, where Tessa collapses and dies while struggling to open an unyielding window in the hotel bedroom.

Constant Wife, The. Comedy in three Acts by W. Somerset *Maugham first produced in Cleveland, U.S. in 1926, and in London in 1927. The setting throughout is the drawing-room in the Harley Street residence of John Middleton, F.R.C.S., and Constance, his wife. Martha Culver and Mrs Culver, Constance's sister and mother, visit the house after hearing from another source that her husband is having an affair with a married close friend of them all, Marie-Louise Durham. Martha has convinced herself that Constance is a very unhappy but unsuspecting person and that she must be told of her husband's infidelity. Her mother, however, is determined that Constance shall not be told, for she insists that the philanderings of men are of no great importance and that when women are faithful it is because they have no inclination to be otherwise. Before long it is found that Constance has been aware of the situation for some time. She tells the others that after five rapturously happy years following their marriage she and her husband fell out of love simultaneously, and that during the intervening ten years she has lived happily and contentedly with John and felt no ill will on account of his affairs with Marie-Louise and others. But now that his dallyings have become a matter of gossip she accepts an offer she previously refused to go into partnership with her friend Barbara Fawcett, a successful interior decorator. Meanwhile Mortimer Durham, Marie-Louise's husband, has found John's cigarette case under her pillow, but Constance covers up for her by declaring that she left the case there while she was visiting Marie-Louise. Mortimer apologizes abjectly to the two women and John, and later at Constance's suggestion he compensates his wife for his accusations by buying her a valuable pearl necklace and taking her for a long voyage.

By the time she returns, John has recovered from his infatuation and he asks Constance to break the news to Marie-Louise. But before Constance can do so, Marie-Louise tells her that during the voyage a younger man has displaced the former lover. John, now repentant and supposing that his original relationship with Constance can be restored, is shocked and astounded by her announcing that, having in the intervening twelve months earned a considerable sum in her partnership with Barbara, she is going for a six weeks' holiday in Italy with Bernard Kersal, who has loved her since she was a girl, and is now on vacation from his business in Japan. Even more than in most of Maugham's plays, the plot is of less moment than the dialogue, in which the wit is matched by the truth of the comments on human motives and relationships.

Conte. (French) short story.

Conundrum of the Workshops, The. Poem by Rudyard *Kipling written in 1890 on the theme of creation and criticism, the voice of the Devil as critic whispering 'It's pretty, but is it Art?'

Conybeare Family. Father (Dr **Michael**), sons (**Francis** and **Christopher**), and daughter (**Julian**)—leading characters in Rose Macaulay's *They Were Defeated* (1932). Julian falls in love with the Cambridge scholar and poet John Cleveland (1613-58), and is killed accidentally when he is attacked by her brother Francis. Christopher (Kit) adds to the father's distresses by becoming a Papist and going to France as assistant to Sir Kenelm Digby (1603-65; sailor, turncoat, dabbler in alchemy, etc.).

Cook, George Cram (1873-1924). Born in Iowa; educated at Iowa and Harvard. Became a university lecturer in English, then a farmer, journalist, novelist, founder of the Provincetown Players (Provincetown, Massachusetts) and the Playwrights' Theatre, New York, producing at both places plays by Eugene *O'Neill. As his third wife he married Susan *Glaspell, and they lived in Greece for the last three years of his life. He wrote several novels, some poems, plays (in collaboration with Susan Glaspell), and *Evolution and the Superman* (1906), and *Battle-Hymn of the Workers* (1912).

Cooke, Alistair (Alfred Alistair Cooke, 1908-). Born in Manchester; educated there and at Cambridge and Harvard. From 1934 he was on the staff of the British Broadcasting Corporation, first as film critic and from 1938 as commentator on American life and affairs. His ease and intimacy of manner, ideally suited to radio, made him one of the most successful of all broadcasters, without conscious exploitation of 'personality', the cult disease of the medium. His weekly 'Letter from America' consistently attracted a large body of listeners who appreciated his often light-hearted yet always serious and courteous treatment of well chosen and wide-ranging material. A selection of his broadcasts *Letters from America* was published in 1952, and a further selection in 1968. His account of the Alger Hiss case, *A Generation on Trial* (1950), penetrated the fog of official and popular prejudice. *Alistair Cooke's America* (1973).

Cookman, A. V. (Anthony Victor Cookman, 1894-1962). Born at Salisbury, where he became a local newspaper reporter before moving to the *Manchester Guardian*, for which after World War I he served as special correspondent in Ireland. From 1925 until his death he was on the staff of *The Times* first as a parliamentary reporter, and from 1939 as dramatic critic.

Cooper, Lady Diana (- , Viscountess Norwich). Born Diana Manners, daughter of the 8th Duke of Rutland. Played the part of the Madonna in *The Miracle* (produced by Max *Reinhardt) in England, America, and Continental countries. Married Duff *Cooper (afterwards Viscount Norwich) in 1919. Wrote her recollections in *The Rainbow Comes and Goes* (1958), *The Light of Common Day* (1959), *Trumpets from the Steep* (1960).

Cooper, Duff (Alfred Duff Cooper, 1890-1954; 1st Viscount Norwich, 1952). Born at Norwich; educated at Eton and Oxford. Entered the Foreign Office; Member of Parliament 1924-45 and held various ministerial offices; British Ambassador to France 1944. Wrote a biography of *Haig* (1935, 1936) and other books; his *Talleyrand* (1932) ranks as one of the best biographies produced in the second quarter of the 20th century.

Cooper, Edith Emma. See Michael *Field.

Cooper, Giles (Giles Stannus Cooper, 1918-66). Born in County Durham; educated at Lancing and Grenoble; served in Burma in World War II. He had studied at a drama school, and after the war wrote a succession of stage plays: *Never Get Out!* (1950), *Everything in the Garden* (1962), *Out of the Crocodile* (1963) and others. From 1957 he was prolific and much esteemed as a radio and television playwright.

Cooper, William (pseudonym of H. S. Hoff, 1910-). Educated at Cambridge. Civil Service Commissioner 1945-58. Consultant to the Atomic Energy Commission from 1958. Author of *Scenes from Provincial Life* (1950), *Scenes from Married Life* (1961), and other novels which were more successful than those previously published under his own name: *Trina* (1934), *Rhéa* (1935), *Lisa* (1937), *Three Marriages* (1946).

Coote, Chester. House agent and social and cultural snob in H. G. Wells's *Kipps* (1905). While Kipps has money he patronizes him, but cuts him afterwards.

Coppard, A. E. (Alfred Edgar Coppard, 1878-1957). Born at Folkestone; educated at an elementary school in Brighton; when nine years old became a tailor's shop boy in Whitechapel and afterwards an office boy in Brighton. Meanwhile he was educating himself, and in 1907 went as accountant to a firm of engineers in Oxford. There he began to write short stories and in 1919 decided to make writing his profession. After a period of consequent poverty he began to attract a select though always limited audience, and though he became one of the most applauded writers of his generation he had from time to time to support himself and his family by resuming commercial employment. His stories combine a prose of poetic quality with a style close to spoken narrative and owing much to folklore. More than a dozen volumes appeared, from *Adam and Eve and Pinch Me* (1921) to *The Dark-Eyed Lady* (1947). *Collected Tales* appeared in 1948, *Collected Poems* in 1928, and an autobiography *It's Me, Oh Lord* in 1957.

Copyright. Under the Copyright Act 1956 all literary, dramatic, and musical works are protected against unauthorized reproduction until fifty years after the last day of the year in which the author or composer dies. The symbol © with the date of first publication and the copyright owner's name, printed on the back of the title page of a book or (usually) at the end of an article, newspaper, or other publication, serves as a declaration that the work is legally protected. Outside Great Britain other requirements may operate, though most countries observe similar regulations under the Universal Copyright Convention. Infringement of an author's rights is likely to occur when plays are produced by amateurs unaware, or casually unobservant, of copyright protection. It is a legal offence to perform, or to read to a public audience, any copyright play without the copyright owner's permission applied for and obtained in writing before rehearsals begin. The same restrictions apply to performances of musical works. The Act requires publishers to deposit a copy of every book published with the British Museum, the Bodleian Library, Oxford, The University Library, Cambridge, the National Libraries of Scotland and Wales, and the Library of Trinity College, Dublin.

Corbett, Jim (James Edward Corbett, 1875-1955). Born at Nani Tal, Kumaon, in the Himalayan region of India; educated at the English school there. Became a railway official in charge of labour forces. In World War I he recruited a large Indian labour battalion for service in France, and in World War II trained British troops in jungle fighting. He spent much of his life in ridding the Kumaon area of man-eating tigers, and his account of these exploits is excitingly yet modestly told in the books which brought him great success after his retirement: *Man Eaters of Kumaon* (1946), *The Man-Eating Leopard of Rudraprayag* (1948) and *The Temple Tiger* (1954). Other aspects of Indian life are viewed in *My India* (1952) and *Jungle Lore* (1953). He moved to Kenya (after the partition of India) and died there.

Corbusier, Le (pseudonym of Charles Edouard Jeanneret, 1887-1965). Born at La Chaux-de-Fonds, Switzerland; studied architecture in Paris and Germany. A leader of the modern international style in building, he popularized the principle that *Une maison est une machine-à-habiter* ('a house is a machine for living in') and applied machine forms and engineering resources to his architectural designs, which had a worldwide influence. Author of *Vers une architecture* (1922; English translation *Towards a New Architecture*), *Urbanisme* (1924; *The City of Tomorrow*), *La Maison des Hommes* (1942), etc.

Corelli, Marie (pseudonym of Mary Mackay, 1855-1924). Born in London, the illegitimate child of Charles Mackay, song writer, and Ellen Mills, a widow whom he later married as his second wife. Mary, always mystifying the circumstances of her birth, claimed to have been his adopted daughter and deferred her birth date to 1864, alleging that her actual father was Italian. From that self-created myth derived the name she used from girlhood. Educated by governesses and (briefly) in a convent school, she trained as a pianist and showed considerable talent as a performer. From 1885, however, she devoted herself to writing and with *A Romance of Two Worlds* (1886), began the remarkable career as novelist which brought her almost unexampled popularity with the public (including some readers high in Church and State), though little but derision from professional critics. In the perfervid prose of her novels she conducted a crusade against the sins of Society, concerning which she was totally uninformed; yet her undisciplined imagination, moral hysteria, and lack of self-criticism or any sense of absurdity enabled her to produce during more than a quarter of a century an outpouring of fiction in which romance, sentimentality, religiosity, and a genuine craving to be 'in tune with the Infinite' combined to impress and delight millions. With the fortune made from her books she bought a house (Mason Croft) at Stratford-on-Avon, and lived there from 1901 until her death more than twenty years later. Her attitude of further dignifying Shakespeare's birthplace by her presence there, coupled with her desire to play Lady Bountiful to the town, acted as an irritant, and robbed her of the credit that would otherwise have been her due for good-heartedness and generosity. If as a writer she is in retrospect negligible, as a psychological study she is incomparable. The adoring friend of many years with whom she lived at Mason Croft, Bertha Vyver, wrote *Memoirs of Marie Corelli* (1930). Among her own books *Open Confession* (1925) is a semi-fictional unveiling of belated passion, in which a minor artist, Arthur Severn, was the other (misinterpreted) principal. Perhaps the most acclaimed of her novels (which latterly she withheld from reviewers) were *Thelma* (1887), *Barabbas* (1893), *The Sorrows of Satan* (1895), *The Master Christian* (1900), *Temporal Power* (1902), *The Treasure of Heaven* (1906), *The Life Everlasting* (1911).

Cornelius. Treacherous Malacca Portuguese in Joseph Conrad's *Lord Jim* (1900).

Cornford, Frances (*née* Frances Crofts Darwin, 1886-1960; married F. M. *Cornford, 1908). Born at Cambridge, daughter of Sir Francis Darwin and granddaughter of Charles Darwin; educated at home. She wrote many brief lyrical poems, carefully wrought in traditional metres and sensitive and graceful in content and expression. Though known to a wider public mainly by two verse epigrams ('To a Fat Lady Seen from a Train' and the lines on Rupert *Brooke beginning 'A young Apollo golden haired'), her output of verse was considerable: *Poems* (1910), *Spring Morning* (1915), *Autumn Midnight* (1923), *Mountains and Molehills* (1934), *Travelling Home* (1948), etc.; *Collected Poems* (1954).

Cornford, F. M. (Francis Macdonald Cornford, 1874-1943). Born at Eastbourne; educated at St Paul's School and Cambridge. A highly accomplished classical scholar, he became Professor of Ancient Philosophy at Cambridge from 1931-39, and wrote much on classical themes, culminating in a translation of Plato's *Republic* (1941). A little volume of satirical verse on local university themes, *Microcosmographia Academica* (1908), long delighted connoisseurs.

Corno di Bassetto. See Bernard *Shaw.

Corridors of Power, The. Novel by C. P. *Snow, published 1964.

Corvo, Baron (pseudonym of Frederick William Serafino Austin Lewis Mary Rolfe, 1860-1913). Born in Cheapside, London; educated at a north London school and as an unattached student at Oxford, before joining the Church of Rome and studying unsuccessfully for the priesthood at Catholic seminaries in England and Rome. He worked spasmodically as a school-teacher, private tutor, photographer's assistant, painter, and Labour politician's secretary, being frequently in abject poverty and as frequently in debt. A man of eccentric character and incorrigibly quarrelsome, he libelled and alienated most of the many who befriended and at times supported him. He claimed to have received the title Baron Corvo from the Duchess Sforza-Cesarini while he was living in Italy in the 1880s, a claim never either disproved or confirmed. Much of his life remains obscure, despite *The Quest for Corvo* (1934), a brilliant work of biographical detection by A. J. A. *Symons. Corvo finally settled in Venice, living in depravity and dying there in squalor. His published writ-

ings began with *Stories Toto Told Me*, a series of folklore legends of Catholic saints supposed to have been recounted to the author by an Italian peasant boy. Six of these were printed in The *Yellow Book* from 1895 onward, and republished with numerous additions in 1898. *Chronicles of the House of Borgia* (1901) and *In His Own Image* (1901) preceded his masterpiece, *Hadrian the Seventh* (1904, dramatised 1968), in which his remarkable prose style and unique personality are displayed, and his feud with the Roman Catholic Church ingeniously resolved. In addition to *Don Tarquinio* (1905), and *The Weird of the Wanderer* (1912), he left several unpublished books, which subsequently appeared: *The Desire and Pursuit of the Whole* (1934), *Hubert's Arthur* (1935), *Nicholas Crabbe, or, The One and the Many* (1958)—all in some degree symptomatic of his persecution mania.

Cory, Adela Florence. See Laurence *Hope.

Cosmopolitans. Volume of short stories by W. Somerset *Maugham published in 1926. The twenty-nine stories in it were written for an American magazine *Cosmopolitan*, the publisher specifying in the commission that each story should be limited to the space afforded by two facing pages of his periodical. Within the brief compass thus imposed the author contrived to produce brilliant compressed pieces which have humorous and/or satirical point, and occasionally tragic force. Though there is no room for developed characterization, there is effective thumbnail portraiture.

Costain, Thomas B. (Thomas Bertram Costain, 1885-1965). Born in Canada; settled in the U.S. Author of best-selling historical novels: *The Black Rose* (1945), *The Silver Chalice* (1952), *The Last Plantagenets* (1962), and others. He also wrote a history of Canada up to the late eighteenth century, *The White and the Gold* (1954).

Cosway. See *Antoinette Cosway.

Cosy. A cliché prevalent in the 1950s and after among book reviewers, who applied it to writings in which normality and optimism were more evident than a squalid and despairing presentation of human beings and their affairs.

Cotterill, Nellie. Marries Denry Machin in Arnold Bennett's The *Card* (1911).

Coulton, G. G. (George Gordon Coulton, 1858-

1947). Born at King's Lynn; educated at Felsted and Cambridge. He entered the Anglican Church but turned from parish work to schoolmastering and coaching until about 1908. An interval of study and writing on medieval subjects was followed by a renewed association with Cambridge lasting for the rest of his life. His stalwart Protestantism and support of conscription involved him in controversy on two fronts—with Roman Catholics and with pacifists; but the vigour of his convictions was matched by the depth of scholarship displayed in *Five Centuries of Religion* (4 vols, 1923, 1927, 1936, 1947), *The Medieval Village* (1925), *Medieval Panorama* (1938). *Fourscore Years* (1943) is his autobiography.

Country of the Blind, The. Short story by H. G. *Wells included in *The *Time Machine and other Stories* (1895). Cut off from the outside world by a vast landslip, a mountain valley in the Andes becomes in the course of many generations peopled by a community entirely blind. While with a mountaineering party in Ecuador, one of the guides, Nunez, is precipitated into the isolated valley by a snow avalanche. He reaches a village where the houses have no windows and the people live in total darkness within, believing their country to be roofed like a cavern. When Nunez tells them of 'the beauties of sight, of watching the mountains, of the sky and the sunrise' they conclude that he is mad. Pondering this proverb 'In the country of the blind the one-eyed man is king', Nunez decides that, being fully-sighted, he can establish himself as master of the sightless, but his attempts to attack are frustrated by his opponents' defensive mechanism of sense and smell. When he and a girl, Medinasaroté, fall in love, her relatives will not countenance her marrying an idiot; but a great doctor advises that Bogota (their name for Nunez) can be cured if the 'irritant bodies' affecting his brain—his eyes—are removed. His love for the girl causes him to agree to the operation, but on the last day the splendour of the visible world constrains him and he climbs the mountain wall blocking the gorge.

Couperus, Louis (Louis Marie Anne Couperus, 1863-1923). Born at The Hague, educated in Java (where his father was in the service of the Dutch government) and at the University of The Hague. A prolific novelist, he became well known beyond his own country during his lifetime. Of his books translated into English, *Old People and the Things that Pass* (1918) received most attention.

Courage, James. See *New Zealand Writers.

Courcelles, Master de, Canon of Paris; one of the framers of the 'indictment of The Maid on sixty-four counts' in Bernard Shaw's *Saint John* (1921).

Cournos, John (1881-). Born in Kiev; taken in the early 1890s to America where he first learned English and endured hardship until he succeeded in journalism. Returned to Europe shortly before World War I and was employed by the British government in Russia and elsewhere, but settled again in the United States in 1931. Author of novels (*The Mask*, 1919; *The New Candide*, 1924; etc.), verse, plays, and *Autobiography* (1935).

Court Theatre. See Royal Court Theatre.

Courthope, W. J. (William John Courthope, 1842-1917). Born in Sussex; educated at Harrow and Oxford. He became an examiner in the Education Office (now the Board of Education) and from 1887 to 1907 a Civil Service Commissioner. From 1895 to 1900 he was Professor of Poetry at Oxford. As an author his major work was *A History of English Poetry* (6 vols, 1895-1909). He also wrote a study of Addison (1882), *The Liberal Movement in English Literature* (1885), and *The Country Town and Other Poems* (published posthumously with a Memoir, 1920).

Courtly Love. The relationship between a married lady of the nobility and her knightly paramour, involving adultery and requiring the young man's unquestioning obedience to the lady's wishes and whims. It was wholly extra-marital. See *The *Allegory of Love* (1936) by C. S. Lewis.

Covey, The Young. A fitter in Sean O'Casey's *The *Plough and the Stars* (1926); twenty-five, 'with lines on his face that form a perpetual protest against life as he conceives it to be'.

Coward, Noel (Sir Noel Pierce Coward, 1899-1973; knighted 1969). Born at Teddington, Middlesex; educated at a day school, at the Chapel Royal School, Clapham, for singing, and for the stage at the Italia Conti Academy. He made a brief appearance as a page-boy in Charles Hawtrey's company, and after World War I settled to playwriting and had his first success with *The *Vortex* (1923). By 1925, when *Hay Fever* started a long run in

London, he was the most successful of the younger English playwrights, and set a mode of smart sophistication, amorality, and impudent humour, using the fashionable staccato clipped speech of his generation. Though several of his plays missed fire, he continued to produce at intervals comedies which were found equally beguiling by the smart set and by middle-class audiences, though austere dramatic and other critics deplored the lack of literary distinction in his writing. Yet, however apparent this short-coming may be in the printed texts of his plays, his stage sense of effective spoken dialogue was often faultless, for he was essentially a writer for the theatre, depending upon the nuances of skilled acting to fill-out and give dramatic effect to deliberately con-trived *lacunae* in the spoken and printed text. By such devices the censor could be circumvented, for a conversation about the Albert Hall could be used as the sole vocal accompaniment to an audaciously amorous passage in performance. Coward's profes-sional competence and versatility were displayed in acting, singing and composing as well as in playwriting. *Bitter Sweet* (1929), an operetta, was among his greatest successes; and two or three of his revues achieved a legendary repute. Since he was for many years regarded as hardly more than a brittle and cynical sophisticate, *Cavalcade* (1931), which was both a family chronicle and a pageant of patriotism, aroused critical astonishment and public applause; and sub-sequently in *This Happy Breed* (1943) and several one-act plays he showed knowledge and understanding of working-class people. In his own special *genre* of amorous comedy *Private Lives* (1930) and *Design for Living* (1933) were peak achievements; and *Blithe Spirit* (1941) was one of his most successful experiments in comedy-farce. Most of his plays have been published. Parts of his life-story are in *Present Indica-tive* (1937) and *Future Indefinite* (1954).

Cox, A. B. (Anthony Berkeley Cox, 1893-1971). Wrote several detective stories under this name: *The Professor on Paws* (1926); *Mr Priestley's Problem* (1927), etc. *See also* Anthony *Berkeley, and Francis *Iles.

Cozzens, James Gould (1903-   ). Born in Chicago; educated at Staten Island Academy, Kent College, and Harvard. After a period of schoolteaching in Cuba and twelve months in Europe, he became for a year in 1938 an associate editor on *Fortune*. Then lived a retired life in the country. His first novel (*Confusion*, 1924) was published while he was still at Harvard, but his first success came seven years later with *S.S. San Pedro* (1931), a striking tale of disaster at sea. *The Last Adam* (1933), *Castaway* (1934), and *The Just and the Unjust* (1942) were among the other novels which preceded his prize-winning *Guard of Honour* (1948) and the ambitious *By Love Possessed* (1956). *Morn-ing, Noon, and Night* (1969).

Craig, Gordon (Edward Gordon Terry, 1872-1966). Born at Harpenden, son of Ellen Terry and Edward Godwin; educated at Bradfield College and Heidelberg. While only six he made his first stage appearance, and continued to act, mainly in Henry Irving's company, until he was twenty-five. He then turned to wood-engraving and stage designing, displaying uncommon talent in the former art and unique genius in the latter. After some early productions in London theatres which were remarkable for his innovations in scenery, lighting, and stage management, he worked mainly on the Continent, where he was subjected to less restriction of his idiosyncratic and combative personality and less financial limitation than in England. His greatest practical triumph as a designer and producer was with *Hamlet* at the Moscow Art Theatre in 1911, while as founder and director of the School for the Art of the Theatre in Florence he had an incalculable influence on the international theatre. His publications include *On the Art of the Theatre* (1911), *The Theatre Advancing* (1921), *Woodcuts and Some Words* (1924), *Henry Irving* (1930), *Ellen Terry and Her Secret Self* (1931), and the autobio-graphical *Index to the Story of My Days* (1957). The assumed surname Craig was given to him and his sister Edith by their mother, from the Scottish islet Ailsa Craig. Edward Craig: *Gordon Craig* (1968).

Craig, Hardin (1875-   ). Born in Kentucky; educated locally and at Princeton, in Germany and at Oxford. Editor of *Two Coventry Corpus Christi Plays* (1902), *Machiavelli's 'The Prince'* (1944), *Richard II* (1911). Author of *The Enchanted Glass: The Eliza-bethan Mind in Literature* (1936).

Craigie, Mrs. *See* John Oliver *Hobbes.

Craigie, W. A. (Sir William Alexander Craigie, 1867-1957; knighted 1928). Born in Dundee;

educated there and at St Andrew's; studied Scandinavian languages in Copenhagen. Lecturer in Scandinavian Languages, Oxford, 1905-16; Professor of Anglo-Saxon there, 1916-25. Worked on the *Oxford English Dictionary* for many years, as joint-editor with Henry *Bradley, 1901-33. Wrote numerous books on the English language, on Scandinavian and Icelandic subjects, and *The Study of American English* (1927). Started and edited *A Historical Dictionary of American English*, 1936-43, and *A Dictionary of the Older Scottish Tongue* from 1931 onward.

Crampton, Fergus. Long separated from his wife, who adopted the name Clandon for herself and their children, in Bernard Shaw's *You Never Can Tell* (1895).

Cran, Marion (*née* Marion Dudley, 1875-1942). Born in South Africa; educated in England; trained at hospital in Dublin; on staff of *Connoisseur* and *Burlington Magazine;* held various official appointments in the Commonwealth. Founded the Mayfair Garden Club and wrote extensively on gardens.

Crane, Hart (Harold Hart Crane, 1899-1932). Born in Ohio. He resisted attempts to establish him in commercial employment but was for a while an advertisement copywriter in New York before a patron enabled him to travel and devote himself to poetry. He succeeded in producing two long symbolic and mystical poems, *White Buildings* (1926) and *The Bridge* (1930), which, though dismissed as unintelligible by some critics, were regarded by literary scholars as an outstandingly important addition to American poetry. In despair after years of constant dissipation, Crane drowned himself while returning home after living for some months in Mexico. A number of additional pieces were included in *Collected Poems* (1933). *The Complete Poems and Selected Letters and Prose of Hart Crane,* edited by Brom Weber, came out in 1968.

Crane, Stephen (1871-1900). Born in New Jersey; educated at Lafayette College and Syracuse University. He worked as a newspaper reporter in New York before publishing *Maggie: A Girl of the Streets* (1893), a novel in the realistic mode then prevalent on both sides of the Atlantic. This was followed by his masterpiece, *The Red Badge of Courage* (1895), the immediate success of which has been surpassed by the greater

esteem in which it has been held in the twentieth century. Subtitled 'An Episode of the American Civil War' and presenting a remarkably convincing study of a young soldier's fear and compensating courage on the battlefield, *The Red Badge* was the product not of personal experience (for Crane was an infant at the time of the Civil War) but of his reading. Crane afterwards spent several years as a war correspondent in Mexico, Cuba, and Greece; he lived for periods in England and died of consumption in Germany. 'The Open Boat' (included in a volume with that title in 1898) is a short story based on personal recollection of exposure on the sea after a shipwreck.

Crankshaw, Edward (1909-). Born in Essex; educated at Bishops Stortford; travelled in Europe; contributed articles on music, literature and other arts to various papers, and later specialized as a student of Soviet affairs. Author of *Joseph Conrad: Aspects of the Art of the Novel* (1936), *Britain and Russia* (1945), *Russia by Daylight* (1951), *Khrushchev's Russia* (1959), *The Fall of the House of Habsburg* (1963), *Maria Theresa* (1969), and novels; *Nina Lessing* (1938), *The Creedy Case* (1954).

Crawford, Francis Marion (1854-1909). Born in Italy; educated in U.S. and at Cambridge; became an accomplished linguist and editor of the *Indian Herald* in Allahabad. *Mr Isaacs* (1882) was the first of many novels, romantic and historical, among them *A Tale of a Lonely Parish* (1886), *A Cigarette Maker's Romance* (1890), *A Rose of Yesterday* (1897), *Cecilia: A Story of Modern Rome* (1902), *The Prima Donna* (1908). He also wrote a play produced in Paris by Sarah Bernhardt, *Francesca da Rimini* (1902), and a critical study *The Novel: What It Is* (1893).

Creasey, John (1908-1973). Born and educated in London. After twelve years as a clerk from the age of fifteen he turned to writing and estimated that between 1932 and 1973 he produced 560 books, mainly crime novels, using besides his own name 28 pseudonyms: Gordon Ashe, Norman Deane, Michael Halliday, Kyle Hunt, Peter Manton, J. J. Marric, Richard Martin, Anthony Morton, Jeremy York, etc.

Creative Evolution. The 'gospel' of Bernard *Shaw, expressing his conviction that human improvement depends upon 'the simple fact that the will to do anything can and does, at a certain pitch of intensity set up by conviction of its necessity, create and organize new tissue to do it with'. *See* his Preface to *Back to Methuselah* (1921).

Creatures of Circumstance. The final volume of short stories by W. Somerset *Maugham, published in 1947. Two of his best stories 'The Kite' and 'The Colonel's Lady' are included.

Creston, Dormer (pseudonym of Dorothy Julia Colston-Baynes (-   ). Author of *Enter a Child* (1939), reminiscences of the author's childhood; *Andromeda in Wimpole Street: The Romance of Elizabeth Barrett Browning* (1929); *Fountains of Youth* (1936), a biography of Marie Bashkirtseff; *In Search of Two Characters: Some Intimate Aspects of Napoleon and his Son* (1945); *The Youthful Queen Victoria* (1952).

Creswell, H. B. (Harry Bulkeley Creswell, 1869-1960). Educated at Bedford Grammar School and Trinity College, Dublin. Trained and practised as an architect, designing houses, churches and commercial and public buildings. He wrote several novels in which humour and technical knowledge of architecture and building were pleasantly combined into cautionary tales for those employing designers and constructors: *The Honeywood File* (1929), *The Honeywood Settlement* (1930), *Grig* (1942), *Grig in Retirement* (1943) and, on different themes but equally sagacious and amusing, *Thomas* (1918) and *Thomas Settles Down* (1919).

Crich, Gerald. In D. H. Lawrence's *Women in Love* (1920), mine manager and owner; becomes the lover of Gudrun Brangwen and dies accidentally while with her in the Swiss Alps.

Crichel Down Case. Farming land at Crichel Down in Dorset, compulsorily acquired by the Air Ministry in 1937 and no longer wanted in 1949, was passed to the Ministry of Agriculture to use or sell. The former owners were told that their claim to buy back or lease the land would be considered when it was put out to tender. Nevertheless the land was equipped at public expense and let without tender to a farmer who had had no previous connection with it. Following a public outcry and questions in Parliament, a Statutory Inquiry was held and uncovered 'incompetence, muddle, folly, and mis-

judgment' largely due to an official who was 'accustomed to having his own way' and resented anyone 'questioning anything that he had done or querying any decision that he had come to'. On the principle that the Minister concerned is responsible for the actions of his subordinates, the Minister of Agriculture resigned. The case has become a classic of official despotism such as an *Ombudsman is intended to check.

Crichton, the butler in *The *Admirable Crichton* by J. M. Barrie.

Criterion, The. Quarterly critical review founded in 1922, financed by Lady Rothermere, edited by T. S. *Eliot up to the last number in 1939. No 1 included Eliot's *The *Waste Land*, and among the contributors at various times were W. H. *Auden, G. K. *Chesterton, James *Joyce, D. H. *Lawrence, Louis *MacNiece, Ezra *Pound, George *Saintsbury, and many foreign writers. A complete reprint in eighteen volumes was published in 1967.

Criticism. *See* *Book Reviews; *Dramatic Criticism; *Literary Criticism.

Croce, Benedetto (1866-1952). Born in the Abruzzi, Italy; educated in a socially exclusive Catholic school and at the University of Rome, studying law. Being of a wealthy family he had no need to practice as a lawyer and devoted himself to history and philosophy. He became a senator in 1910 and Minister of Public Instruction for a year in 1920-21, but otherwise stood apart from active participation in public affairs, though his philosophical and other writings had an implicit (but by his countrymen mainly unregarded) political significance. His philosophy is complex and insusceptible to simple definition, for he was 'an accomplished specialist and, at the same time, a universal thinker' ranging over aesthetics, philosophy, ethics, religion, politics, economics. He was, in the terminology of philosophers, an 'idealist' and an anti-romantic. Of an extensive output of writings, the following are among those translated into English: *The Essence of Aesthetic* (1921), *The Conduct of Life* (1924), *A History of Italy, 1871-1915* (1929), *History of Europe in the Nineteenth Century* (1933), *Politics and Morals* (1944), *My Philosophy* (1949).

Crock of Gold, The. Prose fantasy by James *Stephens published in 1912. Two Philosophers and their wives—the Grey Woman of Dun Gortin and the Thin Woman of Inis Magrath—living in a dark pine wood, have two children: a boy called Seumas Beg and a girl called Brigid Beg, born on the same day. When the children are ten years old, the husband of the Grey Woman declares that he is old enough and wise enough to put an end to his life, which he does by gyrating rapidly until he drops dead. The Grey Woman then does likewise and the Thin Woman buries the two bodies under the hearthstone. A neighbouring farmer, Meehawl MacMurrachu, comes to consult the surviving Philosopher about his wife's stolen washboard. The Philosopher says leprecauns have taken it, and sends him to look under a certain tree. There, instead of the washboard, Meehawl finds a crock full of gold which has taken the leprecauns thousands of years to amass. In revenge, Seumas and Brigid are kidnapped. Meanwhile, Meehawl's daughter, the shepherd girl Caitilin, meets Pan, the Master of the Shepherds, and disappears. The leprecauns release Seumas and Brigid, whom the Philosopher then sends in search of Caitilin, but neither they, nor, later, the Philosopher himself can persuade Caitilin to leave Pan's cave. Failing to recover their crock of gold, the leprecauns denounce the Philosopher to the Police, accusing him of the murder of the two buried under the hearthstone. He is imprisoned and taken away for trial. Having watched the police exhume the bodies, Seumas and Brigid play imitatively by digging in the wood, where they unearth the crock of gold hidden by Meehawl and restore it to the leprecauns. The children and their mother journey to the abode of the god, Angus Óg, to seek his aid. Caitilin has become the bride of Angus Óg, and they descend to earth and release the Philosopher. Though the story is set in the realm of myth and fairy tale, there is a less fanciful interest in the conversations and monologues which form the main part of the book and embody much wisdom and, in the sad stories of the Philosopher's fellow prisoners, much sympathetic feeling.

Crockett, S. R. (Samuel Rutherford Crockett, 1860-1914). Born in Kirkudbrightshire; educated at Cowper's School, Castle Douglas, and at Edinburgh University. Following experience as a tutor abroad and as a journalist in London, he studied theology

and was ordained in 1886 as a Free Church minister. His principal activity, however, was as a prolific novelist, the best known of his popular writings being *The Stickit Minister* (1893), *The Lilac Sunbonnet* (1894), *Kit Kennedy* (1899), *The White Plumes of Navarre* (1909). See The *Kailyard School.

Croft-Cooke, Rupert (1904-   ). Born in London; educated at Tonbridge. Taught in Paris and Buenos Aires; lectured in Switzerland and Spain. Author of many novels including *Troubadour* (1930), *Cosmopolis* (1932), *The Man in Europe Street* (1939), *The Moon in My Pocket* (1948); *The Verdict of You All* (autobiography, 1955), plays, some poems, and books on *Rudyard Kipling* (1948), *English Cooking* (1961), etc.

Crofts, Freeman Wills (1879-1957). Born in Dublin; educated in Belfast. Started as a railway engineer, but having in 1920 published an extremely popular detective novel, *The Cask,* he resigned from the railway in 1929 and turned wholly to the writing of mystery novels, most of which were linked with some aspect of his technical knowledge of engineering. The solutions are mostly the achievement of Inspector French of Scotland Yard. A few of the many titles are *Inspector French's Greatest Case* (1925), *The Sea Mystery* (1928), *Mystery in the Channel* (1931), *The 12.30 from Croydon* (1934), *Death of a Train* (1946).

Crofts, Sir George. A character in *Mrs Warren's Profession* by Bernard Shaw. He finances the brothels managed by Mrs Warren.

Crompton, Richmal (pseudonym of Richmal Crompton Lamburn, 1890-1969). Born in Lancashire; educated there and in London; taught in schools as a senior classics mistress until 1924. She published the first collection of stories about 'the freckle-faced mud-encrusted perpetual eleven-year-old school-boy' as *Just William* in 1922, and more than thirty volumes of his further exploits and misdeeds followed up to the time of her death, with sales totalling several million. She wrote a larger number of other novels, some of superior merit, but William stayed with his creator to the end.

Cronin, A. J. (Archibald Joseph Cronin, 1896-   ). Born at Cardross, Scotland; educated at Dumbarton Academy and studied medicine at Glasgow University; qualified in 1919 after working in the naval medical ser-

F

vice during World War I. Held hospital appointments, became Medical Inspector of Mines in 1924, and practised in London 1928-30. The immediate success of his first novel, *Hatter's Castle* (1931) determined him to abandon medicine for literature and in succeeding years he produced a large number of popular novels, including *The Stars Look Down* (1935), *The Citadel* (1937), *The Keys of the Kingdom* (1942), *Crusader's Tomb* (1956), *The Judas Tree* (1961), *A Question of Modernity* (1966). *Jupiter Laughs,* a play, was produced in 1940.

Cronin, Vincent (Vincent Archibald Patrick Cronin, 1924-   ). Son of the preceding; educated at Ampleforth, Harvard, and Oxford. Author of *The Golden Honeycomb* (1954, a portrait of Sicily), *The Last Migration* (1957, Persia), *The Letter after Z* (1960), *Louis XIV* (1964), *Four Women in Pursuit of an Ideal* (1966), *Napoleon* (1971).

Crothers, Rachel (1878-1958). Born in Illinois and educated there. Studied acting in New York and became an instructor. Author of *A Man's World* (1909), *Nice People* (1920), *As Husbands Go* (1931), *Susan and God* (1938), and many other plays.

Crowley, Aleister (pseudonym of Edward Alexander Crowley, 1875-1947). Notorious as a practitioner of black magic and dealer in the occult. Author of numerous books on those subjects; also published several books of verse.

Croy. See *Kate Croy.

Crozier, Eric (Eric John Crozier, 1914-   ). Born in London; educated at University College School and Royal Academy of Dramatic Art. Author of libretti for operas by Benjamin Britten: *Albert Herring* (1947), *Let's Make an Opera* (1949), and (with E. M. Forster) *Billy Budd* (1951).

Cruelty, Theatre of. See *Theatre of Cruelty.

Cubism. A type of abstract painting which aims to penetrate beyond surface appearances and single vision and to depict persons and objects from varying angles simultaneously and three-dimensionally. The pioneers, and chief exponents, of Cubism were Pablo Picasso (1881-   ) and Georges Braque (1882-1963). The first Cubist exhibition was in Paris in 1907. The theory derived from Cezanne's principle that the painter's treatment of Nature should have the cylinder, the sphere, and the cone as basic forms. In the

work of Picasso's successors Cubism branched in various ways.

Cullen, Sir Patrick. Retired Irish physician in Bernard Shaw's *The *Doctor's Dilemma* (1906). He is sceptical of new methods of treatment and holds that 'most discoveries are made regularly every fifteen years'.

Cullum, Ridgwell (1867-1943). Born in London. In adolescence went to South Africa, where he took part in the gold rush and then worked in the diamond mines. He afterwards had an adventurous life in the Yukon and the United States, at various times being fur-trader, hunter, and cattle-rancher, as well as fighting against the Sioux. These experiences gave him rich material for the novels he wrote from 1903 until his last years, Canada being the main scene: *The Hound from the North* (1903), *The Night Riders* (1906), *The Watchers of the Plains* (1909), *The Law of the Gun* (1919), *Bull Moose* (1931).

Cultures. See *Pop Culture. The *Two Cultures.

Cummings, Bruce Frederick. See Barbellion.

cummings, e. e. (edward estlin cummings, 1894-1962). Born in Cambridge, Massachusetts; educated at Harvard. Service as an ambulance driver in France during World War I led to his imprisonment by the French on a mistaken charge of treason, and this experience provided him with material for *The Enormous Room* (1922), an autobiographical record written as a kind of modern *Pilgrim's Progress.* His other writings are mainly in verse forms distinguished by eccentricities of line division, capitalization, punctuation, and other typographical and verbal oddities, collected in *Poems 1923-1954* (1954). He preferred not to use capital initials in his name.

Cunninghame Graham, R. B. (Robert Bontine Cunninghame Graham, 1852-1936). Born in London of an ancient Scottish family on his father's side and of a mother of Spanish descent; educated at Harrow and in Brussels. When seventeen he made the first of his visits to South America, where he delighted in the robust life of the plains and rode much with the *gauchos.* The expert knowledge he acquired was put at the service of the British government in World War I, when he was commissioned to revisit Argentina to buy horses for the army. For a while he was Liberal M.P. for north-west Lanarkshire, but he turned socialist, became a disciple of William Morris, and in February 1887 received a six weeks' prison sentence for assaulting the police in Trafalgar Square during a demonstration by the unemployed. In spite of his democratic convictions he was by nature an aristocrat, in appearance and bearing combining the dignity and authority of a Spanish grandee and a Scottish laird. His friends called him 'Don Roberto', a city in Argentina was given that name in honour of him, and *Don Roberto* is the title of the biography written by his friend A. F. *Tschiffely in 1937. Further travels took him to Spain and North Africa, and his fearless quest of adventure led him to undertake the dangerous journey into Morocco which resulted in his splendid travel-book *Mogreb-el-Aksa* (1898). He also published several collections of stories and essays, vigorous in style and precisely phrased: *Thirteen Stories* (1900), *Success* (1902), *Charity* (1912), *Brought Forward* (1916). He died in Buenos Aires, but was buried in Scotland beside the grave of his wife, who died in 1906 (they married in 1879). An amusing brief characterization of Cunninghame Graham is in Bernard Shaw's Notes to *Captain Brassbound's Conversion*, where the playwright acknowledges a debt to *Mogreb-el-Aksa*.

Curle, Richard (Richard Henry Parnell Curle, (1883-1968). Born in Scotland; educated at Wellington. He became acquainted with numerous writers, particularized in *Caravansary and Conversation* (1937), and especially with Joseph Conrad: *The Last Twelve Years of Joseph Conrad* (1928), *Joseph Conrad and his Characters* (1959). He also wrote travel books, two novels, and on women, stamp collecting, first editions, etc.

Curnow, Allen (Thomas Allen Monro Curnow, 1911-   ). Born at Timaru, New Zealand; educated at Christchurch and Auckland. Worked on the literary staff of New Zealand and London newspapers. Lecturer in English at Auckland University from 1951. Author of *Island and Time* (1941), *Sailing or Drowning* (1943), *At Dead Low Water* (1949), *The Axe* (verse play; 1949), *Poems 1949-57* (1957), *A Small Room with Large Windows* (1962), and other books of verse. Editor of *A Book of New Zealand Verse* (1946), *The Penguin Book of New Zealand Verse* (1960). See *New Zealand Writers.

Currier and Ives (Nathaniel Currier, 1813-88 and J. Merritt Ives, 1824-95). Printers and publishers in the U.S. of a series of crudely coloured lithographic prints in the second half of the nineteenth century. They were produced cheaply for the popular market and have little artistic merit, but as representations of many aspects of American life of the period they have historical interest and for this and acquisitive reasons are collected and preserved in the present century.

Curtain-raisers. Generic title given to one-act plays which, in the pre-1914 period, were frequently staged at the beginning of a theatrical performance, before the curtain was raised on the principal play of the evening. Among the writers of one-act plays at that time were J. M. *Barrie, Lady *Gregory, Gertrude Jennings, Bernard *Shaw, and W. B. *Yeats. After increased costs had made it uneconomic to include them as curtain-raisers in the professional theatre, one-act plays found their main production outlet in the programmes of amateur societies.

Curtis, Peter. Pseudonym used by Norah *Lofts for several of her novels.

Curwood, James Oliver (1878-1927). Born in Michigan; while a boy worked on a farm in Ohio, afterwards going to the University of Michigan from 1898 to 1900. Although he began to write fiction in childhood, his first published novel was *The Courage of Captain Plum* (1908), published after he had spent several years as a newspaper reporter and editor. He wandered much, particularly in northern Canada and among Eskimos, and had experience in trapping wild animals. His many extremely popular novels have small literary value, but he was an effectively robust storyteller, and his concentration on adventures in the wild life of the north was a product of first-hand experience, however extravagantly heightened in terms of fiction. *Nomads of the North* (1919) and *The Valley of Silent Men* (1920) are typical.

Curzon of Kedleston, 1st Marquis (George Nathaniel Curzon, 1859-1925). Born at Kedleston Hall, Derbyshire; educated at Eton and Oxford. Travelled extensively in Europe, the East, and America. Had a distinguished parliamentary career before going to India as Viceroy (1899-1905), where he ruled in splendour before incurring Indian disfavour and quarrelling with Lord Kitchener the Commander-in-Chief. Chancellor of Oxford University from 1907. He held Cabinet appointments after his return from India, and hoped to succeed Lloyd George as Prime Minister, an ambition frustrated by his being in the Lords not in the House of Commons. He was an intimate friend of the popular novelist Elinor *Glyn after the death of his wife and until he re-married in 1917 the widowed Mrs Grace Duggan, mother of the future historical novelist Alfred *Duggan. As the product of his early travels, Curzon wrote on Asian affairs: *Russia in Central Asia* (1889), *Persia and the Persian Question* (1892), *Problems of the Far East* (1894). His other writings were: *Lord Curzon in India* (1906), *Modern Parliamentary Eloquence* (1913), *War Poems and Other Translations* (1915), *Tales of Travel* (1923).

Cushing, Harvey (Harvey Williams Cushing, 1869-1939). Born in Ohio. Became one of the world's most eminent surgeons and held professorships of neurology and surgery at Harvard and Yale. In addition to important professional works he wrote an outstanding biography, *The Life of Sir William Osler* (1925), the British physician and Professor of Medicine at Oxford, and *From a Surgeon's Journal* (1936).

Cusins, Adolphus. Professor of Greek in Bernard Shaw's *Major Barbara*. In love with Barbara Undershaft, he joins in some of her Salvation Army activities and is later nominated by her father to inherit the Undershaft munitions business. Certain of his scholarly characteristics were modelled on those of Shaw's friend Professor Gilbert *Murray.

Cutcliffe Hyne. *See* C. J. Cutcliffe *Hyne.

Dada (French, hobby horse). A movement publicized by Louis *Aragon, André *Breton, Tristan Tzara and others in the post-World-War I period after tentative beginnings in Zurich about 1916. An account by Tzara of its début in Paris in 1920 is given in translation by Edmund Wilson as an appendix to his *Axel's Castle. An outcome of war hysteria, Dada was irrational, nihilistic and destructive. At a 'performance' in Paris, Tzara records that on the stage he 'read aloud a newspaper article while an electric bell kept ringing so that no one could hear what I said . . . all I wanted to convey was simply that my presence on the stage, the sight of my face and my movements, ought to satisfy people's curiosity and that anything I might have said really had no importance'. He speaks also of idiocy, unexpectedness, and brutality as features of Dada, and of the 'anti-literary' aim of its publications. The movement had offshoots in other European countries and in America, and an early development in *Surrealism. After some years of waning interest, the impulse behind Dada revived in the anti-art and anti-hero cult of the 1940s and later, and notably in the products of the *Theatre of the Absurd.

Daddy Long Legs. Sentimental American novel by Jean *Webster published in 1912. It tells the story of an orphan girl and her subsequent romance with her guardian, and was extremely popular on both sides of the Atlantic.

Daffodil Fields, The. Narrative poem in seven-line stanzas rhyming a b a b b c c (rhyme royal) by John *Masefield published in 1913. On his deathbed Nicholas Gray of Rye-meadows Farm in Shropshire, now bankrupt, pledges his friends Keir and Occleve to continue the education of his son Michael until the lad finishes at a school in France. They consent, but when Michael is summoned home to his dying father he tells them that he has been expelled and is glad, for he has had his fill of 'farming by the book'. He goes to work on a cattle ranch in Argentina, asking Mary Keir, who loves him and he her, to wait for him until he returns after three years. She promises, though Lion Occleve hopes to displace him. Michael soon stops writing to Mary, and when Lion goes out to deliver to the South American buyer a famous bull-calf from the Shropshire farm, he seeks out Michael and finds him living with a 'dark Spanish beauty'. On returning home, Lion at length persuades Mary to marry him. When this news reaches Michael he comes back to England, reviving Mary's love, and they go away together to Wales. The two men meet and fight in the daffodil fields, both are mortally wounded, and Mary dies of a broken heart. The poem combines the tragic spirit of a traditional ballad with passages of natural description centring on the daffodil fields.

Daglish, Eric Fitch (1892-1966). Born in London; educated there and in Germany. Science correspondent of a London evening paper, 1923-5. Author and illustrator with wood engravings of many books on animals, birds, insects, wild flowers, etc.

Daiches, David (1912-). Lived in Scotland as a child; educated at Edinburgh and Oxford. Taught at Chicago University 1937-43; in English government service 1943-6; Professor of English at Cornell University 1946-61; University Lecturer in English at Cambridge, 1951-61; Professor of English, University of Sussex from 1961. Author of *The Place of Meaning in Poetry* (1935), *The King James Bible* (1941), studies of *Virginia Woolf* (1942), *Robert Louis Stevenson* (1947), *Robert Burns* (1950), *Willa Cather* (1951), *John Milton* (1957); *Critical Approaches to Literature* (1956); *A Critical History of English Literature* (1960), *Two Worlds: An Edinburgh Jewish Childhood* (1956).

Dain Waris. Son of Doramin, a Patusan chief, in Joseph Conrad's *Lord Jim* (1900); becomes Jim's 'war-comrade'; killed in an ambush. Dain's father shoots Jim, who accepts responsibility for his friend's death.

Dakers, Elaine. See Jane *Lane.

Dalcroze, Emile Jaques- (1865-1951). Swiss composer best known as the originator of *Eurhythmics.

Dale's Diary, Mrs. A serial dealing with the experiences of a country family of the professional classes which ran for over ten years as a B.B.C. programme. Though widely and lastingly popular, particularly among women, it received acute minority criticism on account of its alleged snobbishness. It was later renamed The Dales, and came to an end in 1969 after more than 5,000 episodes.

Dallas, Eneas Sweetland (1828-79). Born in Jamaica; educated at Edinburgh University. In addition to journalistic writings he published *Poetics* (1852) and a study of literary criticism *The Gay Science* (1866) which aroused new interest and received measured praise from other critics around the middle of the present century.

Dallas, Ruth (1919-   ). Born at Invercargill, New Zealand. She grew up on a farm, an experience that influenced her poetry of 'mountain, hill, and sea', of shell and bird and nature in its many changing moods. Author of *Country Road* (1953), *The Turning Wheel* (1961), *Day Book* (1966). See *New Zealand Writers.

Dalloway, Clarissa. Wife of Richard Dalloway, M.P., with one daughter, Elizabeth, in Virginia Woolf's *Mrs Dalloway* (1925).

Danby, Frank (pseudonym of Mrs Julia Frankau, 1864-1916). Author of many popular novels, from *Dr Phillips, a Maida Vale Idyll* (1887) to *The Story behind the Verdict* (1915), with *The Heart of a Child* (1908) as the best known. She also wrote *Eighteenth Century Colour Prints* (1900), biographies of engravers, and *The Story of Emma, Lady Hamilton* (1910). See Gilbert *Frankau and Pamela *Frankau, her son and granddaughter, both novelists.

Dane, Clemence (pseudonym of Winifred Ashton, died 1965). Born at Blackheath; educated in England and abroad. Spent a year in Geneva teaching French; studied art in London at the Slade School and in Dresden; worked as a portrait painter and later as an actress before settling to authorship. Her first novel, *Regiment of Women* (1917), made her well known and equal success attended *Legend* (1919). She won even wider renown with her first play *A *Bill of Divorcement* (1921), one of the outstanding stage successes of the interwar period. Her career as a playwright continued with *Will Shakespeare* (1921), *Granite* (1926), *Wild Decembers* (about the Brontës; 1933), etc., and she dramatized Max Beerbohm's story *The Happy Hypocrite* (1936). Her later novels include *Broome Stages* (1931), *The Moon is Feminine* (1938), and *He Brings Great News* (1944). Her *Tradition and Hugh Walpole* (1929) is a study of an admired contemporary.

Dangerous Corner. Play in three acts by J. B. *Priestley performed in London in 1932. After dinner at the country house of Robert and Freda Caplan, they and their guests— Gordon and Betty Whitehouse (brother and sister-in-law of the Caplans), Olwen Peel and Charles Stanton (an executive and a director, respectively, of the Caplan publishing firm), and Maud Mockridge (novelist), begin a discussion of the adage 'let sleeping dogs lie' which is controverted by Robert's insistence that truth must always be told however disturbing the consequences may be. Stanton remarks that 'telling the truth is about as healthy as skidding round a corner at sixty', to which Freda responds 'And life's got a lot of dangerous corners'. A remark made by Olwen when a musical cigarette box is opened leads to a prolonged course of truth-telling which opens up a disturbing chapter of recent family history and culminates in Robert's shooting himself. After a moment's stage blackout, the opening moments of the play are identically re-enacted up to Olwen's remark about the musical cigarette box. This time her words pass unnoticed, Gordon turns on the wireless, and 'they are all very gay as they dance to the music'. The dangerous corner has been harmlessly passed.

Daniels, Elder. Alias of 'Boozy Posnet', Blanco's hypocritical brother in Bernard Shaw's *The *Shewing-up of Blanco Posnet* (1909).

Dannay, Frederick. See Ellery *Queen.

D'Annunzio, Gabriele (1863-1938). Born in Pescara; educated at Prato and University of Rome. He became a prolific versifier from schooldays onward and was already a notorious amorist before adolescence ended. After a period on the staff of the Roman newspaper *La Tribuna,* he devoted himself to literary work, novels and plays, which made him the outstanding Italian author of the period and gave him a world reputation, to which his amours (particularly his years of association with the great actress Eleonora Duse) contributed. As propagandist and aviator for the Allies during World War I he showed himself a man of action, and won great applause from his countrymen when he defied the League of Nations towards the end of 1919 by leading a raid on Fiume in Dalmatia. Later he became a vociferous supporter of Mussolini, receiving from him the title Prince of Monte Nevoso in 1924. As a prince in Renaissance Italy, d'Annunzio might have vied with the Medici and the Borgias; in his own time, despite his brilliant literary talent, he was a contemptible yet dangerous anachronism. He fascinated women, and unscrupulously exposed his mistresses to the public in his writings, as with Duse in *The Flame of Life* (*Il Fuoco*, 1899). Though he has been described as a pioneer of realism in modern Italian literature, his writings are also gothically romantic, as though written in a state of high fever, while nevertheless preserving stylistic beauty and clinically precise observation of character. His novels include *The Triumph of Death* (*Il Trionfo della Morte*, 1896) and *The Virgins of the Rocks* (*La Vergine delle Rocco*, 1879); his plays, *La Gioconda* (1899), *The Dead City* (*La Citta Morta*, 1898), *Francesca da Rimini* (1901).

Daphnis and Chloe, The Pastoral Loves of. A retelling by George *Moore of a Greek romance of about the second century A.D., possibly by Longus. With erotic overtones it tells of a boy and girl abandoned in infancy, brought up by shepherds, and of their union and eventual discovery of their parents. Moore's version was published in 1924.

Dare, Simon. Pseudonym of Marjorie Huxtable, author of numerous romantic novels.

Dark Comedy. Alternative title for plays of the *Theatre of the Absurd and *Theatre of Cruelty schools. Also called Black Comedy.

Dark Lady of the Sonnets, The. Play in one act by Bernard *Shaw written in 1910 and performed in London in the same year in support of the project for a National Theatre. On the terrace of Whitehall Palace, at midsummer in the late 16th century, Shakespeare is challenged by a Beefeater, whom he bribes with money and tickets for the Globe Theatre. Shakespeare has a tryst with Mary Fitton, the Dark Lady, and when a cloaked woman appears, sleep-walking, he takes her to be Mary and wakes her, finding only when the right Mary arrives that the cloaked woman, whom he was about to kiss, is Queen Elizabeth. When Mary enters, she cuffs the other two apart. Discovering Elizabeth's identity, she shrieks 'Will: I am lost: I have struck the Queen!' He responds, in capitals and with many exclamation marks, 'Woman: you have struck William Shakespeare!' He picks up numerous quotations for his plays from the others' lips, and delivers a long plea to the Queen for a theatre 'endowed out of the public revenue'. She approves the proposal but with impressive foresight says that England will lag in the rear of other countries and follow them only to be in the fashion.

Dark, Sidney (1874-1947). Born in London. Wrote many kinds of journalism for the *Daily Mail* and *Daily Express;* edited the *Church Times,* 1924-41. Wrote on *Thackeray* (1912), *Dickens* (1919), *W. S. Gilbert* (1923), *R. L. Stevenson* (1931), and numerous other books on a variety of subjects, religious and secular.

Darkness at Noon. Novel by Arthur *Koestler written in German, published in English translation by Daphne Hardy in 1940. An imaginative but authentic picture presented through the experiences of one victim of the Stalin period in Russia during the 1930s. Rubashov, one of the Old Bolshevik founders of the Soviet Union, is arrested at night and imprisoned. His only means of communication is by a tapping code with a Tsarist prisoner in the next cell. He is subjected to a series of prolonged interrogations, first by an 'old college friend and former battalion commander', Ivanov; then, when Ivanov too has been discarded, by Gletkin, one of the 'generation of modern Neanderthalers' produced by the philosophy of State omniscience and infallibility. Rubashov recalls his own past, when allegiance to the Party made him a blind instrument of human destruction; now he is himself trapped by means of torture-extracted evidence from a young acquaintance, and by his own admission that utterances and statements made by himself can be represented as dangerous to the régime and as threatening the life of 'No. 1', i.e. Stalin. In the end he is marched from his cell and shot in the back of the head while walking along a cellar corridor.

Darling Dora. Dora Delaney, Bobby Gilbey's girlfriend in Bernard Shaw's *Fanny's First Play* (1905).

Darling, Justice (Charles John Darling, 1849-1936, 1st Baron Darling, 1924). His legal knowledge and eminence as a judge were impaired by a tendency to facetiousness on the bench, while his judicial reputation was damaged by his loss of control of the court proceedings during the notorious 'Black Book' libel action in 1918. See Noel Pemberton *Billing.

Darling family: Mr and Mrs, Wendy Moira Angela, John, and Michael, in J. M. Barrie's *Peter Pan* (1904).

Darling, Fraser (Frank Fraser Darling, 1903-

). Born and educated in Scotland; student of agriculture and animal genetics, and Director of the West Highland Survey (1944-1950); author of a large number of scholarly works and popular surveys of bird and animal life in Scotland, and of the fishing industry there. These include *A Herd of Red Deer* (1937), *Bird Flocks and the Breeding Cycle* (1938), *A Naturalist on Rona* (1939), *Island Farm* (1943), *Natural History in the Highlands and Islands* (1947). He also wrote *Wild Life in an African Territory* (1960).

Darlington, W. A. (William Aubrey Darlington, 1890-   ). Born at Taunton; educated at Shrewsbury and Cambridge. Beginning as a schoolmaster, he turned to journalism and (1920-68) was dramatic critic of the *Daily Telegraph*. Author of novels and plays, including *Alf's Button* (novel, 1919; film, 1920; play, 1924), volumes of theatre essays (*Through the Fourth Wall*, 1922, etc.), and an autobiography (*I Do What I Like*, 1947).

Darwin, Bernard (1876-1961). Born at Downe in Kent, the grandson of Charles Darwin; educated at Eton and Cambridge; studied law and was called to the Bar, but after practising for a few years he became for the next forty-six years golf correspondent of *The Times*. He also wrote a number of books on the game, compiled an anthology of sport (*The Game's Afoot*, 1926), wrote articles on Dickens (on whose books and life he was an authority) and short biographies of Dickens and W. G. Grace. He had a ready and graceful pen (see his Preface to the *Oxford Dictionary of Quotations*, written in two hours or so shut up in an office by his friend the publisher Sir Humphrey Milford); and his autobiographical volumes *Green Memory* (1929), *Life is Sweet, Brother* (1940), and *Pack Clouds Away* (1941) communicate his personal zest.

Dashwood, Mrs Edmée Elizabeth Monica. *See* E. M. *Delafield.

Dauber. Narrative poem in seven-line stanzas rhyming a b a b b c c (rhyme royal) by John *Masefield published in 1913. Signed on as lampman and painter on a speedy sailing vessel, the chief character is the twenty-one-year-old son of a Gloucestershire farmer. He refused to follow his father's occupation, and having found in the farmhouse attic a mouldering sketchbook that belonged to his dead mother, he determines to become an artist. Drawn to ships and the sea as subjects,

he purposes to familiarize himself with these by joining a clipper, a vessel of great beauty. Nicknamed Dauber by the crew, he is jeered at by all on board, and his pictures are obliterated and mutilated. The ship runs into foul weather round Cape Horn, but though he is terrified while working aloft, he comes through with enough credit to surmount the prejudice of his tormentors. The clipper sails on with the prospect of good weather to Valparaiso, but she is caught in a fierce gale and this time Dauber falls from a yardarm and is killed. The poem is notable both for its account of sea life before steam and for the vivid descriptions of men battling against tempests.

Davenport, Marcia (Mrs Russell Davenport; *née* Marcia Gluck; 1903-   ). Born in New York; educated in the U.S. and France. Worked on the *New Yorker* and as a music critic. Engaged in relief work for Czechoslovakia, 1945-48. Author of *Valley of Decision* (1942), *East Side, West Side* (1947), *My Brother's Keeper* (1954) and other novels, preceded by *Mozart* (1932), a biography.

Davidson, The Rev Alfred. Fanatical missionary in Somerset *Maugham's story, *Rain*. He commits suicide after being seduced by Sadie Thompson, the prostitute he set out to convert.

Davidson, John (1857-1909). Born in Scotland at Barrhead; educated in Greenock and Edinburgh. Worked variously as analyst's assistant, schoolteacher, and clerk before settling in London from 1889, contributing to periodicals and publishing in the last century several books of verse, among which *Fleet Street Eclogues* (1893) is best known. In the present century he published *The Testament of a Man Forbid* (1901), *Selected Poems* (1904), *The Theatrocrat* (1905) containing a description of his 'materialistic and rebellious philosophy', *The Triumph of Mammon* (1907) and other verse. He committed suicide.

Davidson, Lawrence H. Pseudonym under which D. H. *Lawrence wrote *Movements in European History*, a school textbook published in 1921. He took the pen-name from Davidson Road School, Croydon, where he taught for a brief period.

Davie, Donald (Donald Alfred Davie, 1922-   ). Educated in Barnsley and at Cambridge. Lecturer in Dublin University, 1950-

57, Cambridge University, 1958-64; Professor of Literature, University of Essex, 1964-68; Professor of English, Stanford University, California, from 1968. Author of *Brides of Reason* (1955), *A Winter Talent* (1957), *Events and Wisdoms* (1964), and other books of verse; *Purity of Diction in English Verse* (1952), *Articulate Energy* (1957), etc.

Davies, David. *See* Ivor *Novello.

Davies, Gwendoline Elizabeth (c. 1880-1951); **Davies, Margaret Sidney** (1885-1963). *See* *Gregynog Press.

Davies, Rhys (1903-). Born in the Rhondda Valley, South Wales; educated at Porth. Afterwards lived mainly in London and Paris. Author of short stories and novels: *The Withered Root* (1927), *A Pig in a Poke* (1931), *Honey and Bread* (1935), *Tomorrow to Fresh Fields* (1941), *The Black Venus* (1944), *The Dark Daughters* (1947), *Collected Stories* (1955), *Nobody Answered the Bell* (1971).

Davies, W. H. (William Henry Davies, 1871-1940). Born in Newport, Mon., the son of a publican. A minimum of elementary education during an undisciplined boyhood was followed by the deliberate choice of a tramp's life. He made his way to New York, all but penniless, and in the following years lived from hand to mouth as a casual labourer, beggar, and cattle-boat man, interspersed with brief prison sentences. While train-jumping in Canada en route for the Klondike he fell and injured a leg, which had to be amputated. He returned to England, sleeping in men's lodging houses, and occupying his days by writing poems, a collection of which he had printed at his own expense in 1905 as *The Soul's Destroyer*. He despatched copies to well-known people, inviting them to send him the money for the book. The chief of those who responded was Bernard Shaw, who also wrote an Introduction for *The *Autobiography of a Super-Tramp* (1908) which led to Davies's being taken up by literary London. Thereafter he wrote copiously, producing an almost non-stop flow of brief and simple nature lyrics, from *New Poems* (1907) to *Poems* (1940). The final and inclusive edition of his *Collected Poems*, totalling more than 600 pieces, was published in 1943. He also wrote a few novels (*A Weak Woman*, 1911; *Dancing Mad*, 1927; etc.) and some non-fictional prose (*The True Traveller*, 1912; *My Garden*, 1933), and *True Travellers: A Tramp's Opera in Three Acts* (1923).

Richard J. Stonesifer: *W. H. Davies* (1963).

Davies, Robertson (William Robertson Davies, 1913-). Born in Canada; educated there and at Oxford. Acted in England with the Old Vic company; later worked in Canada as editor of periodicals. Lecturer in English, University of Toronto, 1960. Articles on life and literature from his periodicals reprinted in *The Table Talk of Samuel Marchbanks* (1949), *A Voice from the Attic* (1961). Also wrote comedies and novels.

Davin, Dan (1913-). Born in New Zealand. In World War II he served with the New Zealand Division in Crete and North Africa and wrote an account of the island campaign, *Crete* (1953). After the war he settled in Oxford on the Secretariat of the Clarendon Press. Author of novels—*Cliffs of Fall* (1945), *For the Rest of Our Lives* (1947), *Roads from Home* (1949), *The Sullen Bell* (1956), *No Remittance* (1959); short stories—*The Gorse Blooms Pale* (1947). Editor of *New Zealand Short Stories* (anthology; 1953).

Daviot, Gordon (pseudonym of Elizabeth Mackintosh, 1897-1952, who also wrote under the name of Josephine *Tey). Born and educated at Inverness; worked as a physical training instructress before turning to write short stories and plays, her first success in the theatre being with the historical *Richard of Bordeaux* (1932). Other plays include *The Laughing Woman* (1934) and *The Stars Bow Down* (1949). Under this pen-name she also wrote *Kif* (1929) and other novels, as well as *Claverhouse* (1937), a biography of the seventeenth-century scourge of the Covenanters, the Jacobite leader, John Graham of Claverhouse, Viscount Dundee.

Davis, Richard Harding (1864-1916). Born in Philadelphia; worked as a journalist there and in New York and as a war correspondent in several campaigns, including World War I. Though a prosperously successful novelist, short-story writer and playwright, as well as a social luminary, his vast earnings were dissipated by the time he died. His fiction included *The Exiles* (1894), *The Bar Sinister* (1903), *The Lost Road* (1913). Among his plays are *The Dictator* (1904) and *Peace Manoeuvres* (1914). He also wrote travel books arising from his experiences as war correspondent.

Dawes, Clara. *See* *Clara Dawes.

Dawson, Geoffrey (George Geoffrey Robinson, 1874-1944; assumed the name Dawson in 1917). Born in Yorkshire; educated at Eton and Oxford; entered the Civil Service and in 1901-05 was seconded as secretary to Lord *Milner in South Africa. He resigned from the Civil Service to become Editor of the *Johannesburg Star* (1905-10). In 1911 he joined the staff of *The Times* in London, and in August of the next year became its Editor. He resigned when *Northcliffe took over the paper, but again became editor (1923-41) when John Jacob Astor assumed control after Northcliffe's death. Being a power behind the scenes as a confidant of leading statesmen, Dawson was suspected of having a prime role in the appeasement policy towards Hitler during the years preceding World War II.

Day, Clarence, Jr (Clarence Shepard Day, 1874-1935). Born in New York; educated there and at Yale. After working for a while with his stockbroker father, he joined the navy and afterwards turned to journalism before becoming a victim of crippling arthritis. He turned his parents into delightful copy for the books which brought him a devoted public, *Life with Father* (1935) and *Life with Mother* (1936), collections of sketches which combine the qualities of the familiar essay and the short story. Among his other writings *This Simian World* (1920) is more sardonic in mood.

Day-Lewis, Cecil (1904-1972). Poet Laureate, 1968. Born in Ireland; educated at Sherborne and Oxford. Taught at schools in Oxford and Helensburgh and at Cheltenham College, but from 1935 concentrated on writing—as a poet under his own name but using the pseudonym Nicholas *Blake for detective novels. He had begun to write verse in early boyhood, and while at the University edited *Oxford Poetry 1927*. During the 1930s his name was commonly linked with those of W. H. *Auden and Stephen *Spender as a 'left wing' poet, but when after World War II their political affiliations loosened, Day-Lewis became a more individual figure with a traditional and classical bent, as his translation of *The Aeneid of Virgil* (1952) indicates. His early poems were published as *Country Comets* (1928), *Transitional Poem* (1929), *From Feathers to Iron* (1931), *The Magnetic Mountain* (1933). Subsequent volumes include *Collected Poems* (1935), *Poems 1943-1947* (1948), *An Italian Visit*

(1954), *The Room and other Poems* (1965). Prose writings: *A Hope for Poetry* (1934), *Revolution in Writing* (1935), *Poetry for You: A Book for Boys and Girls on the Enjoyment of Poetry* (1944), *The Poetic Image* (1947); *The Friendly Tree* (a novel, 1936), *The Otterburn Incident* (a story for young readers, 1948).

Dead Sea Scrolls. Fragments of Old Testament and other writings found in caves in the Qumran Valley at the northern end of the Dead Sea in 1947 and later. They were apparently of the library of a Jewish monastic brotherhood, hidden on the approach of some anticipated calamity. Their examination by biblical scholars has thrown additional light on scriptural history.

Dean, Susie. Concert party comedienne in J. B. Priestley's *The *Good Companions* (1929).

Deane, Norman. See John *Creasey.

Dear Brutus. Comedy in three acts by J. M. *Barrie performed in London in 1917. A group of married men and women—Mr and Mrs Dearth, Mr and Mrs Coade, Mr and Mrs Purdie—with unmarried Lady Caroline Laney and Joanna Trout, are invited by a quaint Mr Lob to stay at his house in the country in the week of midsummer eve. Finding that his butler, Matey, has stolen their rings, the women agree not to report to the police if Matey tells them what it is they have in common that has caused Lob to bring them together. The butler speaks of Lob's great age—'He says he is all that is left of Merry England'—and warns the women not to 'go into the wood'. When the men return from the dining room, all except Mrs Coade and Lob nevertheless go to look for this wood, which they are told appears on midsummer eve but never twice in the same place. When the curtains are opened 'an endless wood of great size . . . has come close to the window', replacing the garden. It is 'the wood of the second chance'. Those who enter it experience dream lives. The middle-aged dissolute and childless artist, Dearth, becomes a respectable painter with a much-loved daughter. His wife marries a former suitor and is deserted and left penniless. When they return from the wood to reality, Purdie moralizes that something 'makes us go on doing the same sort of fool things, however many chances we get', and he quotes from Shakespeare: 'The fault, dear Brutus, is not in our stars,/But in ourselves, that we are underlings.'

Dearden, Harold (1883-1962). Born at Bolton; educated at Bromsgrove and Cambridge; trained and practised as a physician and medical psychologist, but became best known as the author of novels (*Such Women are Dangerous*, 1933; *Death in the Lens*, 1934; etc.), memoirs and personal reflections (*The Doctor Looks at Life*, 1924; *The Science of Happiness*, 1925; *The Wind of Circumstance*, autobiography, 1938). In the theatre he was successful with *Interference* (1927) written in collaboration with Roland *Pertwee, *Two White Arms* (1928), and other plays. His directly professional writings included *A New Way with the Insane* (1923).

Death Comes for the Archbishop. Novel by Willa *Cather published in 1927. An account of missionary journeys in New Mexico in the latter half of the 19th century by Father Vaillant and his newly appointed Bishop (afterwards Archbishop) Father Latour. In their journeys through desert country where mission settlements were often hundreds of miles apart, they rely for transport mainly on two mules, Contento and Angelica. The two priests' understanding of Mexicans and Indians gives them a strong hold on the people, and their ministrations revive the Catholic fervour of scattered communities long cut off from the rites of the Church. Their story embraces legends and miracles, historical episodes such as the American government's ejection of the Navajos from their own lands and their ultimate return, the setting-up of a new mission by Father Vaillant in Colorado at the time of the gold rush, and the achievement of Bishop Latour's ambition to build a fine cathedral in Santa Fé. Throughout, descriptions of the Mexican landscape are prominent, and in spite of sandstorms and drought the country has beauties where 'sheep were grazing under the magnificent cottonwoods and drinking at the streams of sweet water; it was like an Indian Garden of Eden'. Among the characters is Kit Carson the legendary frontiersman, shown in his heroic stature but also as the scourge of the Navajos.

Death of a Hero. Novel by Richard *Aldington published in 1929. In a Prologue the death of Acting Captain E. F. George Winterbourne in France on 4 November 1918 is received by his erotic mother with extravagantly assumed grief and by his father with sentimental religiosity. It is considered possible that George intentionally exposed himself to German machine-gun fire intending to be killed. His friend the narrator, regarding George's death as a symbol of 'the damnable stupid waste and torture' of the War, makes 'a desperate effort to wipe off the blood-guiltiness' by writing the life of George Winterbourne, showing how the mismanaged lives of his parents and grandparents, and his mismanaged schooling, shaped his character. He becomes a not very good painter, and the lover of Elizabeth Paston and her friend Fanny, marrying the former notwithstanding their amoral views on free love when she panics on imagining that she is pregnant. The sections anatomizing the prewar London intelligentsia are bitterly ironical and subject the artistic and literary circles of the period to angry satire. The latter part of the book deals with George's army experiences at home and in France, showing that the cumulative effects of prolonged heavy bombardment, machine-gun fire, gas attacks, rat-and-lice-infested trenches and dugouts, and mutilated and decaying bodies, 'rent his mind to pieces . . . a wrecked man, swept along in the swirling cataracts of the War'. Finally, 'Something seemed to break in Winterbourne's head. He felt he was going mad, and sprang to his feet. A line of bullets smashed across his chest like a savage steel whip. The universe exploded darkly into oblivion.'

Death of a Salesman. Play by Arthur *Miller, described by the author as 'Certain private conversations in two acts and a Requiem'; performed in New York and in London in 1949. A traveller in small goods, Willy Loman, is failing as a salesman in his middle sixties and prepares for suicide in order that Linda, his devoted and compassionate wife, shall be provided for from insurance if his employers decline to give him an office post that will take him off the road. His two sons, Happy and Biff, have failed to fulfil his ambitions for them, Happy working in a store and Biff on a farm after drifting through a number of jobs, with intermittent thieving. Willy Sloman's addiction to illusion and make-believe centres on his determination to build up Biff's ego, casting him as a young hero on the sports field and a great man in business. With his faculties in decline, past and present merge for Willy and he holds imaginary conversations, particularly with his dead brother Ben, who made a fortune in Alaska, where Willy declined to accompany him. Biff at length tears down the veil of illusion by telling his father, 'I never got anywhere because you blew me so full of hot air . . . . I am not a leader of men, Willy, and neither are you. You were never anything but a hard-working drummer who landed in the ash-can like all the rest of them!'

Death of the Heart, The. Novel by Elizabeth *Bowen published in 1938. 'Born docile' and by nature naively innocent and emotionally defenceless, Portia Quayne is committed when sixteen to the care of her married half-brother Thomas, when their father and later his second wife, Portia's mother, are dead. After a happy first marriage enduring for more than thirty years, the father in his late fifties fell in love with a young widow, Irene. Explaining the situation remorsefully to his wife when Irene became pregnant, Mr Quayne is idealistically but masterfully divorced by Mrs Quayne, who makes Thomas agree that they 'must do everything possible to help Irene, and the poor little coming child', whose lives thereafter are mainly spent flitting between cheap hotels and dark flats on the Riviera. After Mr Quayne's death, Portia and her mother continue this rootless existence, compensated by their affectionate companionship. When Irene dies, Portia, sent to London to stay with Thomas and his wife Anna in their Regent's Park house, finds no human warmth or understanding with her relatives, but is befriended and watched over by Matchett, an old family servant. Portia is enrolled for lessons at a private academy in Cavendish Square and finds there her only personal friend, Lilian, until she becomes romantically attached to Eddie, a protégé of Anna's. Portia's diary, blandly recording her unsophisticated impressions and opinions, is found and read with indignation by Anna, causing her indifference to turn to active dislike. Eddie encourages Portia to believe they are in love, but her childlike faith in him is shaken when he flirts with Daphne, the daughter of Mrs Heccomb, Anna's former governess, with whom Portia goes to stay while her brother and sister-in-law are on holiday abroad. When questioned about her flirtatiousness with Eddie, Daphne brutally taunts Portia, driving her further in upon herself. Bewildered and distraught by the self-enclosed Eddie's rejection, she is finally

desolated when she learns that Anna (as well as Eddie to whom she had lent it) has read her diary and both, she believes, consider her a laughingstock. She attempts to take refuge with Major Brutt, an elderly acquaintance of Anna's who has treated her kindly, and refuses to return home unless they 'do the right thing'. Though this 'right thing' is unspecified, Thomas and Anna interpret it as meaning that only Matchett could persuade her, and she is sent to bring Portia back.

De Banke, Cécile (1889-1965). Born in the east end of London and educated there. In her mid-twenties she went to South Africa and remained for fifteen years, until 1930, working as an actress and instructor in speech training. She then migrated to the U.S., and from 1932 until her retirement was Associate Professor of Speech at Wellesley College, Mass. Author of *Hand over Hand* (1957), an account of her early life in London; *Bright Weft* (1958) and *American Plaid* (1961), dealing with her years in South Africa and America. She also wrote *The Art of Choral Speaking* (1937), *Tabby Magic* (1959).

Decadents. A term commonly applied to certain English writers flourishing in the last decades of the 19th century—Oscar *Wilde, Ernest Dowson, Arthur *Symons, and others. Their precursors in France in the 1880s founded a review, *Le Décadent*, and congregated in literary coteries, contemptuous of religion and morality, obsessed by a sense of futility, and avid of sensation in any form.

De Chair, Somerset (1911-   ). Educated in New South Wales and at Oxford. M.P. for S.W. Norfolk, 1935-45; for S. Paddington, 1950-51. Author of *Red Tie in the Morning* (1937), *The Dome of the Rock* (1948), *Bring Back the Gods* (1962), and other novels; *Collected Verse* (1970); and several books on political and military history.

Decline and Fall. Novel by Evelyn *Waugh published in 1928. Set upon and 'debagged' by undergraduate drunks, Paul Pennyfeather, a theological student, runs through the quadrangle of his Oxford college without his trousers and is sent down for indecent behaviour. He becomes a teacher at a small boarding school in Wales, grandiloquently named Llanabba Castle, where no serious attempt at education is made by either himself or his colleagues—Mr Prendergast, formerly a clergyman until he had *Doubts*, and Captain Grimes, a heavy drinker who has lost a leg, is repeatedly 'in the soup', but is engaged to the Principal's daughter, Flossie Fagan, whom he bigamously marries. On an hilariously misorganized Sports Day, Paul attracts the attention of wealthy Mrs Beste-Chetwynde, mother of one of the boys, whose tutor he is invited to become. Before Paul leaves the school Grimes has disappeared, believed drowned, while Philbrick the butler, having told each teacher a different highly coloured life story, is arrested on charges of impersonation and false pretences. As tutor to Peter Beste-Chetwynde, Paul becomes familiar with social life in Mayfair and at King's Thursday, a Tudor country mansion before being rebuilt 'clean and square' when bought by Mrs Margot Beste-Chetwynde. Paul and Margot become engaged, but on the wedding morning he is arrested, having become innocently involved in the white slave traffic, which he then learns is the source of Margot's wealth. He gets a seven-year sentence and while in jail meets Grimes again, now a fellow convict, and Prendergast, now a prison chaplain. After serving a few months of his sentence Paul is suddenly conducted to a nursing home at Worthing, where he is reported to have died on the operating table. Smuggled aboard Margot's yacht, he stays at her villa at Corfu, before returning unrecognized to Oxford to take up theology again.

Decline of the West, The. A study in the philosophy of history by Oswald *Spengler. Published in the German original (*Der Untergang des Abendlandes*) in 1918-23 and in its English translation in 1926-29 (one volume edition 1933).

Decoud, Martin. Costaguanan journalist in Joseph Conrad's *Nostromo* (1904); in love with Antonia Avellanos; accompanies Nostromo on the silver-laden lighter; left alone with the treasure on the islet, he becomes demented by solitude and sleeplessness and drowns himself.

Deep Blue Sea, The. Play by Terence *Rattigan performed in London in 1952. In a dingy furnished flat in north-west London, Hester Collyer—a woman in her middle thirties 'with a thoughtful remote face'—tries to commit suicide. She is found unconscious before the unlit gasfire by occupants of other flats in the house, to whom she is known as Mrs Page. Information reluctantly given by the landlady discloses that Hester is the wife

of Mr Justice (Sir William) Collyer and that she is living with Freddie Page, a now unemployed test pilot. She is revived by another tenant, Mr Miller, a middle-aged German ex-doctor recently jailed for some unspecified malpractice, now employed as a bookmaker's clerk but giving voluntary night service at a hospital. Page's immediate whereabouts being unknown to them, her rescuers telephone for Collyer. In the ensuing conversation between him and Hester, she attributes her suicide attempt to anger at Page, who she thinks has never loved her, hatred of herself for uncontrollably desiring him, and consequent shame at being alive. When Page returns from a weekend's golf, he suddenly remembers he has forgotten Hester's birthday, and when he learns of her suicide attempt he supposes it was due to this trivial cause, until he reads the note she wrote to him and meant to destroy. Since he had a plane crash some time before, he has lost his nerve and been drinking heavily, but he now tells Hester he is going to South America, alone, to be a test pilot again. She again prepares for suicide, but Miller talks her into 'facing life', as he himself has learned to do, finding that 'to live without hope is to live without despair'.

Deeping, Warwick (George Warwick Deeping, 1877-1950). Born at Southend, Essex; educated at Merchant Taylors' School and Cambridge; qualified as a doctor at Middlesex Hospital but after a year in medical practice turned novelist, producing some sixty popular books up to 1947, of which *Sorrell and Son* (1925) was best known.

Defence of Cosmetics, A. Essay by Max *Beerbohm first published in The *Yellow Book*, April 1894; reprinted in revised form as 'The Pervasion of Rouge' in The *Works of Max Beerbohm* (1896); republished separately under its original title in a limited edition (New York, 1922).

Degeneration. English title of a work by Max *Nordau (1849-1923), a Jewish writer and physician born in Hungary, attacking the new movements in art then current. Originally published in German as *Entartung* in 1893, it is chiefly notable for provoking a lengthy reply from Bernard *Shaw in the form of an open letter to Benjamin Tucker (editor of an American periodical *Liberty*), who had urged Shaw to read and answer Nordau's attack. The 'open letter' was first printed in *Liberty*, republished as a pamphlet in England twelve years later (1908) as *The Sanity of Art*, and included in Shaw's *Major Critical Essays* (1932).

Dehan, Richard (pseudonym of Clotilda Inez Mary Graves, 1863-1932). Born at Buttevant, County Cork. Author of several plays and a Drury Lane Theatre pantomime *Puss in Boots* (1888), and of many novels under her own name. Her most popular success as Richard Dehan was *The Dop Doctor* (1910), a novel set in South Africa.

Dehn, Paul (Paul Edward Dehn, 1912-   ). Educated at Shrewsbury and Oxford. Worked as film critic to London newspapers. Author of screen plays and several volumes of poems including *The Day's Alarm* (1949), *Romantic Landscape* (1952), *Collected Poems* (1965).

Dekobra, Maurice (pseudonym of Ernest Maurice Tessier, 1885-1973). Born in Paris and educated at the University there; foreign correspondent for French newspapers; author of a large number of sophisticated cosmopolitan novels with a worldwide circulation in many languages, the best known being *La Madone des Sleepings* (1927; English translation *The Madonna of the Sleeping Cars*).

De Kruif, Paul (1890-   ). Born in Michigan of Dutch descent, and educated at the University there. Worked as a bacteriologist and pathologist, then turned to writing popular books on medical and allied subjects: *Microbe Hunters* (1926), *Men Against Death* (1932), *The Male Hormone* (1945), and others; *The Sweeping Wind* (autobiography, (1962). Helped Sinclair Lewis with expert knowledge for *Arrowsmith.

Delafield, E. M. (pseudonym of Edmée Elizabeth Monica de la Pasture, 1890-1943). Born in Monmouthshire, daughter of Mrs Henry *de la Pasture. Nursing service during World War I and work for the Ministry of National Service preceded her main career as a novelist. Her output of fiction was prolific and her readers were moderate in number until the popular success of *The Diary of a Provincial Lady* (1930) encouraged her to follow it with *The Provincial Lady Goes Further* (1932), *The Provincial Lady in America* (1934), and *The Provincial Lady in Wartime* (1940). A successful film was based upon these books,

which may be considered precursors of the B.B.C.'s Mrs *Dale's Diary. Her *Messalina of the Suburbs* (1923) was suggested by the Thompson-Bywaters murder case. Other novels include *Thank Heaven Fasting* (1932), *Faster! Faster!* (1936), *Nothing is Safe* (1937); she also wrote three plays, *To See Ourselves* (1930), *The Glass Wall* (1933), *The Mulberry Bush* (1935); and a book on *The Brontës* (1938).

De la Mare, Walter (1873-1956). Born in Kent; educated at St Paul's Choir School, where he founded and edited the *Chorister's Journal*. When seventeen he became a clerk in the office of an international oil company and by the time he left in 1898 had begun to contribute stories to periodicals under the pseudonym Walter Ramal, which he also used for his first book of poems *Songs of Childhood* (1902). Recognition of the exceptional talent he showed in that volume, in the prose fantasy *Henry Brocken* (1904), and in *Poems* (1906), led to the grant of a small Civil List pension in 1908, a help towards his becoming a full-time writer. He also benefited (with Lascelles *Abercrombie and W. W. *Gibson) under the will of Rupert *Brooke. The foundations of wider fame were securely laid by *The Listeners and Other Poems* (1912) and *Peacock Pie* (1913), and the novel *Memoirs of a Midget* (1921). The entirely individual character of his writings eludes definition. Though 'child poems' are important in his work, with their childlike but never childish simplicity is interwoven adult subtlety and profundity. The tendency to compare him to Blake is inapposite, since while he is consistently elusive he is seldom obscure; he wrote no Blakean 'prophetic books'. In the nearly nine hundred pages of his complete poems, only *Winged Chariot* (1951) is of substantial length. (Its penultimate section avers that Poetry is 'the endeavour, faithfully and well . . . To enshrine (in language) the inexpressible'—a key to De La Mare's poetry.) He was essentially a lyric poet whose finest and most memorable effects could be achieved in fewest lines, and often in 'silence' poems where 'the inexpressible' is enshrined in the interspaces of language, demanding the utmost imaginative response of the reader. De la Mare continued to publish new poems up to the age of eighty, the collections including *Motley* (1918), *The Veil* (1921), *The Fleeting* (1933), *Memory* (1938), *The

DE LA MARE167DE MORGAN

Burning Glass (1945), *Inward Companion* (1950). *O Lovely England* (1953), all with 'other poems'. Short stories are collected in *The Riddle* (1923), *Broomsticks* (1925), *The Connoisseur* (1926), *The Lord Fish* (1933), *The Wind Blows Over* (1936), and other volumes. He also compiled inimitable anthologies of prose and verse, most notably *Come Hither* (1923 and later editions). In the Introduction to *A Choice of de la Mare's Verse* (1963), W. H. Auden, its compiler, wrote of him as 'a poet who continued to mature, both in technique and wisdom, till the day of his death'. *The Complete Poems of Walter de la Mare* (1969) provides a definitive text and includes many previously uncollected poems and a number not published before.

Deland, Margaret (Mrs Lorin Deland, *née* Margaret Wade Campbell, 1857-1945). Born in Pennsylvania; educated privately; studied art in New York. Author of *John Ward, Preacher* (1888), *The Wisdom of Fools* (1894), *The Awakening of Helena Richie* (1906), *The Hands of Esau* (1914), and numerous other novels, besides *Old Chester Tales* (1899), *Old Chester Days* (1935) and other collections of short stories, and an autobiography *If This Be I* (1935).

Delaney, Dora. See *Darling Dora.

Delaney, Shelagh (1939-   ). Born in Salford, the daughter of a bus inspector; educated at a nearby secondary school until she left at seventeen to be a shop assistant, followed by work of other kinds before Joan *Littlewood's production of *A Taste of Honey* (1958) brought her success as a playwright. Her next play, *The Lion in Love* (1960) and other writings attracted less attention.

De la Pasture, Mrs Henry (*née* Elizabeth Lydia Rosabelle Bonham, 1866-1945; married (1) Henry de la Pasture (died 1908); (2) Sir Hugh Clifford). Born in Naples, daughter of a British Consul. Her novels include *Deborah of Tod's* (1897), *Peter's Mother* (1905), *The Man From America* (1906), *The Lonely Lady of Grosvenor Square* (1907). She also wrote plays, some dramatized from her novels. *See also* E. M. *Delafield, her daughter.

De la Roche, Mazo (1885-1961). Canadian novelist whose many books about the Whiteoaks, a family her stories followed in detail through several generations, brought her an international body of readers of the English and numerous translated editions. *Jalna* (1927) the first of the series, was followed by *Whiteoaks* (1929) and more than a dozen others including *Centenary at Jalna* (1958) and *Morning at Jalna* (1960). A dramatized version of *Whiteoaks* was successful in the U.S. and also in London, where it had more than 800 performances.

Dell, Floyd (1887-   ). Born in Illinois. Editor in Chicago of the *Evening Post* and in New York of *Masses* from 1914-17. Author of *Moon-Calf* (1920), *An Old Man's Folly* (1926), *The Golden Spike* (1934); some plays; *Love in Greenwich Village* (poems and stories, 1926), *Love in the Machine Age* (1930), a study of *Upton Sinclair* (1927); an autobiography *Homecoming* (1933).

De Madariaga. See Don Salvador de *Madariaga.

De Morgan, William (William Frend De Morgan, 1839-1917). Born in London, son of Augustus De Morgan, Professor of Mathematics at University College, which he helped to found. The son was educated there, then studied at the Royal Academy Schools, became associated with members of the Pre-Raphaelite movement, and designed stained glass and tiles for the firm started by William Morris to render 'the commonplace things of life more beautiful'. For nearly fifty years De Morgan was occupied as a master potter, producing not only decorated tiles, but also vases, dishes and bowls which made him known as 'perhaps the greatest of all English ceramic artists', particularly in respect of his rediscovery of the lost art of lustreware. Specimens of his ware were collected by connoisseurs and for the Victoria and Albert and other museums. De Morgan's perfectionism and lack of commercial acumen, however, brought the factory to bankruptcy in 1905 and ended his career as a ceramic artist. During an illness shortly before, his wife encouraged him to resume a novel he had begun but discarded after two chapters, and in 1906 when he was sixty-seven published *Joseph Vance* started him on a second successful career. In the remaining decade of his life he completed seven more novels—*Alice for Short* (1907), *Somehow Good* (1908), *It Never Can Happen Again* (1909), *An Affair of Dishonour* (1910). *A Likely Story* (1911),

When Ghost Meets Ghost (1914), *The Old Madhouse* (published posthumously in 1919) —and an unfinished one, completed by his wife and published as *The Old Man's Youth* (1921). De Morgan's books, though entirely original, were in the amplitude of their structure, their depth of characterization, and their humour, a throwback to the mid-Victorian novel, for his reading of fiction, considerable until then, had virtually ceased when he took to pottery around 1860.

Dempsey, Father. Parish priest in Bernard Shaw's *John Bull's Other Island* (1904).

Dennis, C. J. *See* *Australian Writers.

Dennis, Geoffrey (Geoffrey Pomeroy Dennis, 1892-1963). Born at Barnstaple; educated at North Country schools and then at Oxford after three years in an estate agent's office. Army service was followed by years of service with the League of Nations and a period with the B.B.C.; from 1949-57 he was English editor for *Unesco in Paris. The great promise of his first novel *Mary Lee* (1922), dealing with a Plymouth Brethren group in the last century, was scarcely fulfilled by his later fiction, in which abundant and almost grotesque fancy and attraction to supranormal experience tended to lessen his control of a potentially impressive prose style. This aspect of his writing is displayed in *Harvest in Poland* (1925), *Declaration of Love* (1927), *Sale by Auction* (1932); and in *The End of the World* (1930). *Coronation Commentary* (1937) was withdrawn owing to a charge of libel by the Duke of Windsor (the abdicated Edward VIII), but republished in America. *Till Seven* (1957) is a record of early boyhood.

Denry Machin. Central character in Arnold Bennett's *The Card* (1911). Christened Edward Henry, his mother adopted the time-saving abbreviation.

Densher, Merton. Journalist in Henry James's *The *Wings of the Dove* (1902); secretly engaged to Kate Croy; loved by Milly Theale.

Dent, Alan. *See* *Dramatic criticism.

Dent, J. M. (Joseph Mallaby Dent, 1849-1926). Publisher, and founder of the firm of J. M. Dent & Sons Ltd and of *Everyman's Library. Born in Darlington, the son of a house painter; educated at a Wesleyan elementary school; apprenticed to a printer and later to a bookbinder. Started for London in 1867 with a box of clothes, his fare, and half-a-crown; began to work there for a bookbinder, from 8 a.m. to 8 p.m. for 12*s* 6*d* a week. On completing his apprenticeship he set up on his own account as a binder. Engaged in social work and local government, and became Secretary of the Shakespeare Society. Started as a publisher in 1888, establishing the Temple Library as the first of the many series issued in succession by his firm, which within a few years had taken an assured place among the leading London publishing houses.

De Polnay, Peter (1906-). Educated privately in England, Switzerland and Hungary. Lived in Kenya as a farmer. Author of *Angry Man's Tale* (1938). *Water on the Steps* (1943), *The Umbrella Thorn* (1946), *An Unfinished Journey* (1952), *The Crack of Dawn* (1960), *Garibaldi* (1960) and numerous other books.

De Profundis. The title given to the abridged version of the last prose work of Oscar *Wilde as edited by Robert *Ross and published in 1905. The same title was used in 1949 for 'the first complete and accurate version of "Epistola: in Carcere et Vinculis"'; with an Introduction by Vyvyan *Holland, Wilde's younger son. The document which gave rise to both editions was written in Reading Gaol as an eighty-page letter to 'Bosie' (Lord Alfred *Douglas), whose friendship led to Wilde's two-year prison sentence. It was not allowed to leave the gaol until Wilde was released, when he gave the original to his loyal friend Ross, who presented it to the British Museum in 1909, with instructions that it should be kept sealed for sixty years. Ross provided Douglas with a typed copy. The main theme of the letter is that Douglas's constant importunity nullified Wilde's repeated efforts to end the friendship; that his extravagant exploitation of Wilde's hospitality ruined the latter financially and bankrupted him; and that he used Wilde as a tool in his campaign of hatred against his father, the 8th Marquess of Queensberry, whose denunciations caused Wilde's downfall. The letter also records the writer's passage from bitter hatred to humility while in prison, acknowledges his own measure of responsibility, and digresses into comments on the character of Hamlet and, lengthily, on the nature of Christ.

De Selincourt, Aubrey (1894-1962). Educated at Rugby and Oxford. Became a schoolmaster from 1921 to 1929 and in 1931 headmaster of Clayesmore School, Dorset. Author of books on the sea (*Family Afloat*, 1940; *The Channel Shore*, 1953; *The Book of the Sea*, 1961, etc.), topographical volumes (*Dorset*, 1947; *The Isle of Wight*, 1948), some fiction; translator of Herodotus.

De Selincourt, Ernest (1870-1943). Born in Streatham, London; educated at Dulwich and Oxford. Professor of English Language and Literature in the University of Birmingham, 1908-35. Professor of Poetry, Oxford, 1928-33. Author of *English Poets and the National Ideal* (1915), *The Study of Poetry* (1918); a biography, *Dorothy Wordsworth* (1933). Edited *The Letters of William and Dorothy Wordsworth* (1935-39), *The Journals of Dorothy Wordsworth* (1942). The definitive edition of *The Poetical Works of William Wordsworth* on which he was engaged from 1940 was completed by Helen Darbishire.

Desert Rats. British armoured divisions with long service in the Western Desert (North Africa) during World War II. Derisively so named by Mussolini, from their insignia of a rat on a coloured ground, they adopted it as their own nickname.

Design for Living. Comedy in three acts by Noel *Coward performed in New York in 1933; in London 1939; published 1933. Otto Mercuré a painter and Leo Sylvus a playwright, devoted friends, are both in love with Gilda, an interior decorator. She is in love with both and alternates between them, causing outbursts of jealousy that only temporarily breach the friendship of the two men. A time comes when she feels she has overcome her passion, and she runs away to New York and marries Ernest Friedman, a wealthy art dealer and old friend of all three. Two years later Otto and Leo seek her out there and she finds herself still emotionally bound. The author has described the play's title as 'ironic rather than dogmatic' and the three principal characters as 'glib, over-articulate, and amoral creatures' who 'force their lives into fantastic shapes and problems because they cannot help themselves'.

Destouches, Louis Ferdinand. See Louis Ferdinand *Céline.

Detective fiction. Edgar Allan Poe is usually regarded as the originator of this type of imaginative literature with his story 'The Purloined Letter' published in 1845. Emile Gaboriau wrote detective novels in French from 1866 to 1873. But it was the Sherlock Holmes stories by Conan *Doyle, spanning the years from 1879 to 1905, that established a genre which has since attracted a multitude of writers, among them G. K. *Chesterton, E. C. *Bentley, Dorothy L. *Sayers, Nicholas *Blake (C. Day-Lewis), Michael *Innes (J. I. M. Stewart), Agatha *Christie and others beyond numbering. In America Dashiell *Hammett and Raymond *Chandler wrote the best of the 'tough thrillers' in which amoral characters on both sides of the legal fence and of both sexes practised violence, in prose of distinguished quality, while Erle Stanley *Gardner provided readers and television viewers with a long series of ingenious law court triumphs by Perry Mason over district attorneys and shady witnesses.

Deus ex machina (Latin, the god from the machine). A term derived from ancient classical drama, where apparently insuperable problems were solved by the sudden intervention of one of the gods from Olympus, brought on to the stage by some mechanical apparatus. The term has since been used of any person or influence intervening unexpectedly to settle a seemingly insurmountable difficulty.

Deutsch, Babette (1895-   ). Born in New York; educated at the Ethical Culture School and Columbia University. Author of *Banners* (1919). *Honey Out of the Rock* (1925), *Epistle to Prometheus* (1931), *Take Them, Stranger* (1944), *Animal, Vegetable, Mineral* (1954), and other volumes of poems. *A Brittle Heaven* (1926), *Rogue's Legacy* (on Francois Villon, 1942), and other novels; *Poetry in 'Our Time'* (1952); *Walt Whitman* (1941).

De Voto, Bernard (Bernard Augustine De Voto, 1897-   ). Born in Utah; educated at the University there and at Harvard. Editor of the *Saturday 'Review of Literature*, 1936-8; contributor to *Harper's Magazine* from 1935. Author of *The Crooked Mile* (1924), *Mountain Time* (1947), and other novels, but best known for his writings on Mark Twain and for other literary studies, including *The Literary Fallacy* (1944), and for a history of early exploration in America, *The Course of Empire* (1952).

Devil's advocate. A person who aims to destroy the reputation of another by scandalous means. The term comes from the Roman Catholic practice, prior to canonization of a saint, of having all his/her sins enumerated before the ecclesiastical court by an advocate presumed to be appearing on behalf of the devil.

Devil's Disciple, The. 'A Melodrama' in three acts by Bernard *Shaw, written 1896-7, performed in New York 1897, in London 1899; published in *Three Plays for Puritans,* 1900. In a New Hampshire farmhouse at the time of the American War of Independence, Mrs Dudgeon, a bitterly puritanical widow, is visited by the Presbyterian Rev. Anthony Anderson with news of the will made by her recently dead husband leaving nearly everything to his son Richard, a smuggler who lives with gypsies and is known as the Devil's Disciple. After the reading of the will, Mrs Dudgeon, outraged by its terms, curses Richard. Anderson, hearing that the British intend to capture and hang Richard as a rebel, invites him to call, so that he can be warned. After Richard's arrival Anderson is called away to Mrs Dudgeon who is taken ill, and while he is absent British soldiers come to arrest the minister himself. Since they know Anderson only by name, Richard puts on the minister's coat (left behind for mending) and is marched off as Anderson, after impressing upon Judith Anderson that she must get her husband out of harm's way. But in spite of Judith's pleading when he returns, the minister rides off to save Richard, though Judith thinks he is running away. She goes to see Richard, intending to tell the court-martial who he really is, but he convinces her that it is useless and also denies that he is sacrificing himself out of love for her. Judith nevertheless declares to the court that he is not her husband, but Richard is told that unless Anderson surrenders by noon he will be hanged in his place. While he is on the gallows awaiting execution, he is saved by Anderson's arrival bearing a safe-conduct.

Dewey Decimal System. A method of library cataloguing devised by Melvil Dewey (1851-1931), librarian of Amherst College, Massachusetts. The system has been widely adopted in America and elsewhere.

Dewey, John (1859-1952). Born in Vermont; educated at the University there and at Johns Hopkins University, Baltimore. Held professorships in philosophy at the Universities of Michigan, Minnesota, and Chicago and at Columbia University, and was for the main part of his career considered America's outstanding philosopher and educationist. His works include: *Psychology* (1886), *Studies in Logical Theory* (1903), *How We Think* (1909), *Democracy and Education* (1916), *Human Nature and Conduct* (1922), *Art as Experience* (1934), *Freedom and Culture* (1939), *Problems of Men* (1946).

Dial, The. American magazine published from 1880 to 1929, monthly except for a period of fortnightly publication. Among its eminent contributors in the present century were Thomas *Mann, T. S. *Eliot, Harold *Laski, Van Wyck *Brooks, Conrad *Aiken.

Dickinson, G. Lowes (Goldsworthy Lowes Dickinson, 1862-1932). Born in London; educated at Charterhouse and Cambridge; studied, but did not practise, medicine. Lecturer in Political Science at Cambridge, 1896-1920. Among his writings on historical, political and philosophical subjects, *The Greek View of Life* (1896) has been most enduring; his inflexible pacifism inspired *War: Its Nature, Cause, and Cure* (1923) and other writings. The rest of his books included *The Meaning of Good* (1901), *Letters from John Chinaman* (1901), and *After Two Thousand Years: A Dialogue between Plato and a Modern Young Man* (1930). His friend E. M. *Forster wrote his biography, *Goldsworthy Lowes Dickinson* (1934).

Dickson Carr. *See* John Dickson *Carr.

Dickson, Carter. *See* John Dickson *Carr.

Dies irae (Latin, day of wrath). Used to signify the Day of Judgment in a medieval hymn opening thus. Extended loosely to any modern occasion of dire consequence.

Dickens, Monica (Monica Enid Dickens, 1915- ; Mrs R. O. Stratton). Great-granddaughter of Charles Dickens. Educated at St Paul's Girls' School, London. Settled in Massachusetts with her American husband. Author of *One Pair of Hands* (1939), *Thursday Afternoons* (1945), *Flowers on the Grass* (1949), *My Turn to Make the Tea* (1951), *The Angel in the Corner* (1956), *Kate and Emma* (1964), and other novels.

Digest. A magazine confined to abridged versions of articles and books published elsewhere. Some have earned vast popularity, but also some critical disfavour on the ground that they tend to discourage sustained reading and mental effort. In a different category, scientific and technical digests (often called 'abstracts') are required to disseminate indispensable information about relevant expert publications which workers in those fields must study.

Dine, S. S. Van. *See* S. S. *Van Dine.

Dinesen, Isak. *See* Karen *Blixen.

Disappointed Man. *See* *Journal of a . . .

Disenchantment. A view of World War I by C. E. *Montague published in 1922, one of the first of the antiwar books of that period. Concealing his age, the author enlisted at the beginning of the war, quickly finding his and others' patriotic idealism eroded by the cynicism and incompetence of the N.C.O.s and officers appointed to instruct recruits. Disillusion at home turned to disgust and hatred among the rank and file in France, slaughtered by the carrying out of impossible orders given by distant commanders ignorant of the realities of modern warfare. The book also discusses the attitude of army chaplains, the influence of politicians, the make-believe of war correspondents and other journalists, the functions of propaganda and military intelligence, the patronizing insolence of civilians who kept safe and grew fat at home, 'ready to give up less of what was pleasant and to do less of what was hard'. 'There was a bad smell about; the air stank of bad work in high places.' The final chapters—'Any Cure?' and 'Fair Warning'—survey the prospects for England in the aftermath of war and have now to be read in the circumstances of another post-war age. As a distinguished prose work as well as a moving document of human endurance under mental, moral and physical stress, *Disenchantment* survives.

Disher, Willson (Maurice Willson Disher, 1893-1969). Born in London; illness in early years restricted his education, but by his late teens he was already theatre and music hall critic for leading London papers. In subsequent years he became the historian of most forms of light public entertainment: *Clowns and Pantomimes* (1925), *Fairs, Circuses and Music Halls* (1942), *Melodrama: Plots that Thrilled* (1954), *Victorian Song* (1955), etc. He settled in Spain and died there.

Dismal Science, The. Name applied by Thomas Carlyle to Political Economy. Cf. *The *Gay Science.

Disney, Walt (Walter Elias Disney, 1901-66). Born and educated in Chicago. Was a commercial artist until 1923, when he went to Hollywood and, after some unsuccessful efforts in cartoon films, started his forty years of fame and wealth with the Mickey Mouse and Silly Symphony animated cartoons. Other film characters invented by him —the hound Pluto and Donald Duck, etc.— made, like Mickey Mouse, a worldwide appeal and established themselves as part of the Disney modern mythology. From these short films he branched out into a series of full-length cartoons in colour with accompanying music, starting in 1937 with *Snow White and the Seven Dwarfs*. In later years he turned to non-cartoon film versions of *Treasure Island, Peter Pan*, and other literary classics for young people. All his work was 'wholesome, warm-hearted, and entertaining—in his own specialized field of gentle fantasy he produced work of incomparable artistry and of touching beauty' (*The Times*, 12 Dec. 1966).

Dissociation of sensibility. Phrase used by T. S. *Eliot in his essay 'The Metaphysical Poets' (1921) to signify the departure (most influentially by Milton and Dryden) from the characteristic manner of the 16th-17th century poets, who 'possessed a mechanism of sensibility which could devour any kind of experience'. When the 'dissociation of sensibility' set in, thought and feeling split apart, and 'while the language became more refined, the feeling became more crude'. Eliot's phrase became an item of critical small change as repeated, almost cabbalistically, by teachers and their pupils in the following decades.

Ditzen, Rudolf. *See* Hans *Fallada.

Diver, Maud (*née* Katherine Helen Maud Marshall, died 1945; married Lieut.-Col. T. Diver). Born in India; settled in England 1896 onward. Achieved wide and long sustained popularity with novels in mainly Indian settings: *Captain Desmond, V.C.* (1907), *Candles in the Wind* (1909), *Siege Perilous* (1924), and others.

Divine Fire, The. Novel by May *Sinclair published in 1904. Its hero. Savage Keith Rickman, a Keats-like person, is described as having 'the soul of a young Sophocles battling with that of a junior journalist'.

Dixon, James. Central character in Kingsley Amis's *Lucky Jim* (1954).

Dobell, Bertram (1842-1914). Born at Battle, Sussex. His parents' lack of means cut short his schooldays and compelled him to spend some time in menial occupation until he started in Charing Cross Road what became known as one of London's most notable bookshops. His own poems (*Rosemary and Pansies,* 1903; *A Century of Sonnets,* 1910; etc.) and prose writings (on Charles Lamb and James Thomson, B.V.) brought him some repute, but his name is more lastingly associated with the seventeenth-century metaphysical writer, Thomas Traherne, whose unpublished manuscripts Dobell discovered and issued: the *Poems* in 1903 and the prose *Centuries of Meditations* in 1908.

Dobson, Austin (Henry Austin Dobson, 1840-1921). During his professional career in the Civil Service he wrote a considerable number of poems, many in the fixed-verse forms fashionable in the 1870s-1880s and often conceived in a playful manner of 18th-century pastiche (*Vignettes in Rhyme,* 1873; *Proverbs in Porcelain,* 1877; *At the Sign of the Lyre,* 1885). He was also in demand as a provider of introductions to English classics (Jane Austen's novels among them) and as author of biographical studies of *Henry Fielding* (1883), *Oliver Goldsmith* (1888), *Horace Walpole* (1890), and *Fanny Burney* (1903), among others.

Dobson, Zuleika. Central character in Max Beerbohm's *Zuleika Dobson* (1911).

Doctor's Dilemma, The. Tragedy in four acts and an Epilogue by Bernard *Shaw written in 1906 and performed in London in the same year. Dr Ridgeon, just knighted as Sir Colenso Ridgeon, receives congratulations from a succession of medical and surgical colleagues at his West-end consulting room. He has discovered a cure for consumption, but is at present able to provide the necessary vaccine for ten patients only. He is therefore prevented from agreeing to treat the artist-husband of Jennifer Dubedat who comes to plead for him, though Ridgeon invites her to bring him to a dinner to celebrate the knighthood. At the dinner it becomes evident that though Dubedat is a genius as a painter he is unscrupulous as a man. Ridgeon's dilemma is whether to save him or a poverty-stricken east-end doctor, Blenkinsop, 'an honest decent man; but is he any use? Dubedat's a rotten blackguard; but he's a geniune source of pretty and pleasant and good things.' A way out is found when Sir Ralph Bloomfield Bonnington, 'a very eminent physician', agrees to treat Dubedat, but he bungles it and the patient dies, while Ridgeon succeeds in curing Blenkinsop. At a retrospective exhibition of Dubedat's pictures, Ridgeon tells Jennifer that he is in love with her and had no wish to save Louis. He is astounded to hear that she has already remarried. Though described by the author as a tragedy, a main interest of the play is in the long and frequently comic discussion-passages between the doctors.

Dodd, Lewis. Young composer in Margaret Kennedy's The *Constant Nymph* (1924). He marries Florence Churchill, aunt of his friend Albert Sanger's children—Antonia, Tessa, Paulina, and Sebastian. Tessa accompanies him to Brussels when he parts from his wife, and she dies in a hotel there.

Dominic. Corsican sailor and friend of Monsieur George in Joseph Conrad's The *Arrow of Gold* (1919).

Don Fernando; or, Variations on some Spanish Themes. By W. Somerset *Maugham, published in 1935 (revised edition 1950). Don Fernando, a tavern keeper and curio dealer in Seville, forces upon the unwilling author (Maugham himself) an old book which proves to be an early life of Ignatius Loyola, founder of the Society of Jesus (the Jesuits). From that beginning, Maugham's narrative develops into an account of his search for a topic on which to base a book about Spain, which was not to be a mere travel book. In the course of rejecting one topic after another, he deals with many aspects of Spain in her Golden Age and leads the reader on by a sequence of disquisitions on the Jesuit founder's *Spiritual Exercises,* and on Cervantes, Lope de Vega and Calderòn (the leading Spanish playwrights), the original Don Juan story, the Spanish language, the paintings of El Greco and Zurbarán, and the Spanish national character.

Don Juan in Hell. Title given to Act III sc. ii of Bernard Shaw's *Man and Superman* (1903) when detached and performed separately as a one-act play. Conceived as a dream experienced by John Tanner, in which he appears as Don Juan, Ann Whitefield as Doña Ana, Roebuck Ramsden as the Statue, while the Devil is not unlike the brigand, Mendoza, whose romantic verses have sent Tanner to sleep. In the void Don Juan encounters an old crone who has died at the age of seventy-seven, a faithful daughter of the Church and therefore indignant at finding herself not in heaven. Told that those in hell can will to be any age they choose, she is whisked to a handsome twenty-seven, and as Doña Ana immediately recognises the man as Don Juan Tenorio, her earthly pursuer who killed her father in a duel. Juan tells Ana that her father will come from heaven to meet her if she so wishes. He does appear of his own accord as the Statue and, calling up the Devil, says he has left heaven for ever because it is 'the most angelically dull place in all creation. . . . Nobody could stand an eternity of heaven.' When Ana nevertheless declares that she will go to heaven at once 'for happiness', Juan warns her that if happiness is what she wants she must stay where she is, 'for hell is the home of the unreal and of the seekers for happiness. It is the only refuge from heaven, which is . . . the home of the masters of reality.' He intends to transfer to heaven where 'there is the work of helping Life in its struggle upward'. In reply to a prolonged speech by the Devil, enumerating the follies and crimes of mankind, Juan attributes it all to Man's cowardice and adds that 'you can make any of these cowards brave by putting an idea into their heads . . . men will never really overcome fear until they imagine they are fighting to further a universal purpose . . . universal liberty and equality' and, later on, 'men will die for human perfection'. He exalts the philosopher as one possessed with a purpose beyond his own, 'because the philosopher is in the grip of the Life Force'. Juan departs to heaven, The Statue goes down with the Devil to his palace, and Doña Ana vanishes into the void crying 'I believe in the Life to come. A father! a father for the Superman!'

Donisthorpe, Ida M. Loder. See Pansy.

Donkin. Contemptible member of the crew in Conrad's The *Nigger of the 'Narcissus'* (1897). Mutinous, 'with shifty eyes and a yellow hatchet face', he displays 'his talents for shirking work, for cheating, for cadging'.

Doolittle, Alfred. *Eliza's dustman father, one of the 'undeserving poor', in Bernard Shaw's *Pygmalion* (1914).

Doolittle, Hilda. See *H. D.

Dop Doctor, The. Novel with a South Africa setting by Richard *Dehan published in 1910.

Dora. Colloquial name (from the initials) of the Defence of the Realm Act passed in Britain during World War I. A number of its provisions were retained after the war and in so far as they gave the government powers of interference with individual freedom, 'Dora' became an epithet for old-maidish bureaucratic meddling.

Doramin. A Patusan chief in Joseph Conrad's *Lord Jim* (1900); father of *Dain Waris.

Doran, Barney. Owner of a flour mill at Rosscullen in Bernard Shaw's *John Bull's Other Island* (1904). He is 'recklessly untidy', blasphemous and intolerant; he declares that 'There's too much blatherumskite in Irish politics'.

Dorling, Henry Taprell. See Taffrail.

Dorset, Duke of. The 'splendid youth' in Max Beerbohm's *Zuleika Dobson* (1911) who drowns himself for love of Zuleika, an example of devotion followed by all the other Oxford undergraduates.

Dos Passos, John (John Roderigo Dos Passos, 1896-1970). Born in Chicago of Portuguese-American descent. A somewhat broken schooling while travelling with his parents in Europe preceded education at Harvard. He served in World War I and then did journalistic work in America and elsewhere before settling as a novelist. Two or three works of fiction inspired by his war experiences, a book of verse (*A Pushcart at the Curb*, 1922) and a collection of essays (*Rosinante to the Road Again*, 1922) preceded *Manhattan Transfer* (1925), the first of the novels in which he employed original literary devices to portray the swarming life of New York. Through a discontinuous technique which sketches and at length draws together a variety of separate characters typical of their place and period, a realistic impression of the great city is contrived. The method was developed in the novels forming the trilogy *U.S.A.* (1938): *The 42nd Parallel* (1930), *1919* (1932), and *The Big Money* (1936). Here the author presents his view of the contemporary United States as a nation degenerating under the impact of commercialization. He uses a kind of prose montage with elements drawn from newspapers, posters, and popular songs, interspersed with biographical sketches of actual persons and the author's own observations under a recurrent heading, 'The Camera Eye'. These political and sociological novels had a strong leftward bias, later offset in *Adventures of a Young Man* (1939), dealing fictionally with Communist treatment of a deviationist. Dos Passos's works include other novels, travel books, plays including *The Garbage Man* (1926), and *The Best Times: An Informal Memoir* (1968). *See also* Huey *Long.

Doublethink. In George Orwell's **Nineteen Eighty-four* (1949), the use of words in their narrowed 'Newspeak' sense, which supersedes their original meaning.

Doughty, C. M. (Charles Montagu Doughty, 1843-1926). Born in Suffolk; educated at Portsmouth Naval School and Cambridge; his journeyings in 1875-77 provided him with material for *Travels in Arabia Deserta* (1888), the greatest prose work written of that region, though it was not recognized as a masterpiece of knowledge of the desert tribes as well as of literature until renewed attention was drawn to it in World War I by T. E. *Lawrence (Lawrence of Arabia), who wrote the Introduction to a new and definitive edition in 1936. Doughty's literary style was idiosyncratic, making no concessions to ease of reading, and this factor limited his audience, particularly for the epical poems: *The Dawn in Britain* (6 vols, 1906), *Adam Cast Forth* (1908), *The Cliffs* (1909), *The Clouds* (1912), *Mansoul, or The Riddle of the World* (1920).

Douglas, Lord Alfred (Lord Alfred Bruce Douglas, 1870-1945). Born near Worcester, son of the 8th Marquess of Queensberry; educated at Winchester and Oxford; from 1891 he associated with Oscar *Wilde, and was sent abroad in the hope of breaking the friendship, to which his parents objected. In 1895 his father was involved in a libel action brought against him by Wilde, who was arrested at the end of the case, which Queensberry won. When Wilde's imprisonment ended, the friendship was intermittently resumed till Wilde died in 1900. Douglas was incurably spendthrift and pathologically quarrelsome. A wealthy friend bought and made him editor of *The *Academy*, 1907-10, but he had no staying power. He was repeatedly entangled in litigation and in 1923 was sent to prison for libelling Winston Churchill. He wrote two books (largely

contradictory) about Wilde and himself, and *Autobiography* (1929). He also published a good deal of verse, among which his *Sonnets —In Excelsis* (1924) and *Sonnets and Lyrics* (1935)—have been highly praised.

Douglas, Clifford Hugh. *See* *Social Credit.

Douglas, George (pseudonym of George Douglas Brown, 1869-1902). Born in Ayrshire; educated there and at Glasgow and Oxford universities. Lived by teaching and miscellaneous writing before achieving his one notable success, *The *House with the Green Shutters,* in the year before he died.

Douglas, Keith (1920-44). Born at Tunbridge Wells; educated at Christ's Hospital and Oxford. As an officer in the Tank Corps in World War II he served in North Africa and in Normandy, where he was killed. His poems are a cold ironic commentary with a powerful undercurrent of controlled fury against the calamities and miseries and human wastage of war: *From Alamein to Zem-Zem* (1946); *Collected Poems* (1951; new edition with an Introduction by Lawrence *Durrell, 1966).

Douglas, Lloyd (Lloyd Cassel Douglas, 1877-1951). Born in Indiana; educated in Ohio and at a Divinity School. Ordained in the Lutheran ministry and spent years as pastor in several churches of that body. After a number of books on specifically religious themes, his novels *Magnificent Obsession* (1929) and *Forgive Us Our Trespasses* (1932) launched him into the company of best sellers. His popularity was increased by *The Robe* (1942) and *The Big Fisherman* (1948). All his writings had an ethical and religious motive which made devoted readers inattentive to the stylistic and other shortcomings which were observed by literary critics.

Douglas, Norman (George Norman Douglas, 1868-1952). Born in Scotland; educated at Uppingham and Karlsruhe. Served in the British Foreign Office from 1893 to 1901, his facility with languages enabling him to go as a diplomat to St Petersburg. He studied science and wrote books on zoology before taking to fiction, at first unsuccessfully, with *Unprofessional Tales* (1901), published under the pseudonym Normy. For a while he was assistant editor of the *English Review* in London, but for most of the rest of his life lived on the island of Capri which, with the neighbouring islands in the Gulf of Salerno, provided material for *Siren Land* (1911). His first (and almost only) real success came with *South Wind (1917), which remains unique in English literature. Later works include *They Went* (1921), *Fountains in the Sand* (1923), *Old Calabria* (1928), *London Street Games* (1931), *Looking Back* (memoirs; 1932).

Douglass, Frederic. 'Quiet, grave white-haired negro', who visits the President and is told of the decision to abolish slavery in Drinkwater's *Abraham Lincoln (1918). He is based on a historical character (*c.* 1817-1895), a slave who bought his freedom with money earned during a lengthy stay in Britain.

Dover Wilson. *See* J. Dover *Wilson.

Dowell, John and **Florence.** American millionaire and his adulterous wife in Ford Madox Hueffer's *The *Good Soldier* (1915).

Doyle, Sir Arthur Conan (1859-1930; knighted 1902). Born in Edinburgh of an Irish family which included his uncle Richard Doyle, the *Punch* artist; educated at Roman Catholic schools (Stonyhurst and in Austria) and as a medical student in Edinburgh. He practised as a physician in Southsea, as an oculist in London, and spent best part of a year as a ship's doctor on vessels voyaging to the arctic and the tropics. The inability of the medical profession to provide him with an adequate income turned his attention to writing, where, indeed, his true interests lay. His reading had made him well acquainted with the detective fiction of Edgar Allan Poe, Wilkie Collins and Emile Gaboriau, and he invented and introduced Sherlock Holmes as the leading character of *A Study in Scarlet* printed in *Beeton's Christmas Annual for 1887*. In that year he had also published the first of his historical novels, *Micah Clarke* (1889), a story of the Monmouth Rebellion in 1685 and its aftermath in the Bloody Assize. The credit due to Conan Doyle as a stirring historical novelist has been limited by the lasting popularity of his detective stories and the cult which successive generations of Sherlock Holmes enthusiasts have grafted upon them. *The White Company* (1890), set in 14th century England and France, was followed by *The Refugees* (1893), *The Exploits of Brigadier Gerard* (1895), *Rodney Stone* (1896), and *Sir Nigel* (1906). He served in the Army Medical Corps in South Africa

and wrote *The Great Boer War* (1900). He also wrote a history of World War I. In his later years he became an ardent spiritualist and wrote a *History of Spiritualism* (1926). His deep sense of justice led him to stir public conscience and official action in the case of Oscar Slater, a German condemned in 1909 for a Glasgow murder but pardoned and released years later as the outcome of Conan Doyle's campaign.

Doyle, Laurence. Of the firm of Doyle and Broadbent, civil engineers, Westminster, in Bernard Shaw's **John Bull's Other Island.* Broadbent accompanies him to Ireland.

Doyle, Lynn (pseudonym of Leslie Alexander Montgomery, 1873-1961). Born in Downpatrick; educated in Dundalk. Until he reached retiring age he worked as bank clerk and bank manager, meanwhile writing brilliant comic stories: *Ballygullion* (1908), *Lobster Salad* (1922), *Me and Mr Murphy* (1930), *The Shake of the Bag* (1939), *Green Oranges* (1947), *Back to Ballygullion* (1953) and other volumes. He also wrote novels which are less characteristic.

Drabble, Margaret (1939-   ; Mrs Clive Swift). Born in Sheffield; educated in York and at Cambridge. Author of *The Garrick Year* (1964), *The Millstone* (1965), *Jerusalem the Golden* (1967), *The Waterfall* (1969) and other novels. Criticism: *Wordsworth* (1966), *Arnold Bennett* (1974).

Drake. 'An English Epic' by Alfred *Noyes, published in 1908.

Drake's Drum. Poem by Sir Henry *Newbolt published in 1896.

Drama. A cold breath from Scandinavia was still blowing through the English theatre when the new century began. The production of Ibsen's *Ghosts* in London in 1891 had been met with transports of abuse from the *Daily Telegraph* critic, but in the same year Bernard Shaw's *Quintessence of Ibsenism* was published, and in the next year, when J. T. Grein's *Independent Theatre (which had produced *Ghosts*) was twelve months old, the new age of English drama—designedly realistic, intellectual, and critical of the state of society—opened with the production of Shaw's first play, **Widowers' Houses.* Ibsen's disturbing works continued to be performed in English translations, and there was a sufficient reading public for his plays by 1906-8 to justify a six-volume collected edition in English edited by William *Archer. From the 1880s the commanding writers for the London stage had been Henry Arthur *Jones and A. W. *Pinero, both of whom made some attempt at realism and social criticism as the Ibsenite influence took hold, but neither was in accord with the new spirit and their popularity waned after Jones's *The Liars* (1897) and Pinero's *His House in Order* (1906). By that time the Court Theatre repertory season (1904-7) had established Shaw with 701 performances of eleven of his plays, and had introduced John Galsworthy with *The *Silver Box* (1906), Granville Barker (who, with J. E. Vedrenne, controlled the season) with *The *Voysey Inheritance* (1905), and other British dramatists, besides Maurice *Maeterlinck, Gerhart *Hauptmann, Ibsen (*Hedda Gabler* and *The Wild Duck*) in translations; and Gilbert *Murray's versions of Euripides' *Trojan Women, Electra,* and *Hippolytus,* which were soon to achieve considerable popularity in print until a later generation viewed them coldly. Though he was faced with long-continued disapproval from dramatic critics and others accustomed to conventional *well-made stage pieces, Shaw continued to write notable plays until within a few years of his death at the age of ninety-four; and after his death he survived the denigration which undermined the contemporary reputation of Galsworthy and J. M. Barrie who, with Shaw, headed English drama until a new order appeared after World War I. In the post-war period the London theatres fell into the maw of financiers with resources enough to bear inflated rents and crippling costs of production. Before the war, the *Abbey Theatre, Dublin, the *Gaiety Theatre, Manchester (both subsidised at first by Miss A. E. F. *Horniman) and the *Birmingham Repertory Theatre under Barry *Jackson had challenged the long monopoly of London. In Dublin, W. B. *Yeats, J. M. *Synge, Lady *Gregory and others provided the Irish Players with distinguished literary and acting material; Manchester produced a group of local dramatists, among whom Stanley *Houghton (with *Hindle Wakes,* 1912) and Harold *Brighouse (with *Hobson's Choice,* 1916) reached a wider public also; Birmingham's most acclaimed success was *Abraham Lincoln* (1918) by John *Drinkwater, followed by Eden *Phillpotts's unpretentious rural comedy, *The Farmer's Wife* (1916), and

Rudolf *Besier's *The *Barretts of Wimpole Street* (1930). In London Noel *Coward, trained as an actor, first attracted attention with *The *Vortex* (1923), a grim little play, and quickly went on to become the most prosperous playwright of his generation, with a skilled stage sense which disguised and triumphed over the frequent triviality of the dialogue. 'Thrillers' (i.e. crime and detection plays) came to occupy much time and space in the theatres, among the most accomplished providers being Edgar *Wallace and Agatha *Christie (whose *The Mousetrap* had run continuously in London for nearly 20 years by 1970). Beginning with *French Without Tears* in 1936, Terence *Rattigan had a series of successes (*The *Winslow Boy,* 1946, *The *Deep Blue Sea,* 1952, and others). His defence in the preface to the second volume of his *Collected Plays,* of that ageless playgoer dubbed Aunt Edna, serves to uphold Dr Johnson's assertion that 'the drama's laws the drama's patrons give', a view contested by the young 'new wave' playwrights of the 1950s and after, who, as reformers 'committed' to some philosophical or propagandist purpose, felt bound to register aggressive contempt of those who expected only to be entertained in the theatre. History repeated itself in so far as the Court Theatre in London became again (as in 1904-7) the centre of a new drama. There John *Osborne's *Look Back in Anger,* performed in 1956, established the English Stage Company, and, in the years that followed, plays in the new manner were welcomed. A strong external influence on the drama of the period came from the stage works of Bertolt *Brecht (1898-1956), while Samuel *Beckett's *Waiting for Godot* (1956), at first received with bewilderment, took its place in the *Theatre of the Absurd which, with the *Theatre of Cruelty, developed numerous offshoots. Whether English drama of the reign of Elizabeth II is destined to as long life as that of Elizabeth I cannot be prophesied. Of those whose talent has given promise of staying power, the names of John *Arden, Harold *Pinter, and Arnold *Wesker may be added to that of John Osborne. After World War II much was said and done on English stages which would not have escaped censorship or police action before. Despite this liberalizing attitude of the licensing authority (the Lord Chamberlain, advised by his Examiner of Plays), agitation for the abolition of the censorship revived and was more successful than in 1909 (*see* the Preface to Bernard Shaw's *The *Shewing-up of Blanco Posnet*). Censorship was abolished by the Theatres Act 1968. *See also* *American Writers.

Dramatic art. *See* *Royal Academy of Dramatic Art.

Dramatic Criticism. The conditions under which dramatic critics on daily papers work do not make for high literary quality nor for more than snap judgements. To rush from a theatre at curtain-fall to a telephone to dictate, or to the office to scribble, a critical notice to go forthwith on to the machine printing the approaching day's paper, is an exacting task, though less so now than when, earlier in this century and before, the dramatic critic had a whole column or more to fill. Those who write for weekly periodicals have an easier task, and it is from one such source, the *Saturday Review*, that the most brilliant and lastingly enjoyable modern dramatic criticism, Bernard *Shaw's, came in 1895-98 (*see below*). It is not intended here to include under this heading any writings other than those dealing with performances witnessed in the theatre. Reviews and studies of printed texts fall outside the present category, which is, more precisely, theatre criticism. Dramatic criticism as named here looks only in part at drama as literature, as a medium of vocal communication; it is no less the dramatic critic's function to weigh and consider the degree of merit in the actors' interpretation of the author's words, and to assess the value of the contributions made by producer and stage designer. Since (until the coming of the cinema and television) only the text of a play had a permanent existence as a source of interest or reference, a rare skill was needed by a dramatic critic to recreate in memorable words the evanescent features of a vanished performance. This rare skill is displayed abundantly by Shaw in the three volumes of *Our Theatres in the Nineties* (1931), reprinting his *Saturday Review* articles, where trivial plays of long ago as well as masterpieces; bad, mediocre, and great performances by players, many of whom are no longer otherwise remembered even as names; all are fascinatingly resuscitated in Shaw's pages. The articles of his successor on the *Saturday Review*, Max *Beerbohm, are collected in *Around Theatres* (2 vols, 1924; 1 vol edn, 1953); those of

A. B. *Walkley, for many years dramatic critic of *The Times*, in *Dramatic Criticism* (1903) and other volumes. His friend Bernard Shaw dedicated *Man and Superman* to him, and also poked good-humoured fun at him as Mr Trotter, one of the dramatic critics in *Fanny's First Play*. Desmond MacCarthy's *The Court Theatre 1904-1907* (1907) is a valuable record of an epoch-making venture in theatre history. Other collections: C. E. *Montague: *Dramatic Values* (1911); James Agate: *Buzz, Buzz* (1918), etc., Alan Dent: *Preludes and Studies* (1942); Harold Hobson: *Verdict at Midnight* (1952).

Dramatic Irony. An effect achieved in a play when a character's words are intended by the dramatist to have a meaning for the audience different from (or additional to) the meaning they have for the speaker; or by an event in the action of the play which throws back an ironical light on something spoken earlier.

Dreadful Dragon of Hay Hill, The. Allegory by Max *Beerbohm published in 1928. Set in the year 39,000 B.C., it imagines a community of cavemen drawn into a coherent society while a dragon is ravaging. As soon as the creature has been slain they disintegrate once more.

Dreiser, Theodore (Theodore Herman Albert Dreiser, 1871-1945). Born in Indiana; educated at schools there and at Indiana University. From the early 1890s he did journalistic and editorial work in Chicago and New York. *Sister Carrie* (1900), his first novel, was censored and withdrawn on the allegation of obscenity. This and a similar experience with *The Genius* (1915) involved him and others in a prolonged struggle in support of free expression, and their degree of success can be measured by comparing the uninhibited writings of the next generation with Dreiser's own. He published around a dozen novels and a larger number of non-fictional prose volumes, as well as some verse and plays. Whatever of his may drop from notice, it is probable that *An *American Tragedy* (1925) will endure among its nation's literature of that period. It has the inevitability of true tragedy with less of the drab realism of the author's earlier novels (among them *Jennie Gerhardt*, 1911), and the directness and pace of its narrative style contrast strikingly with the turgidity of much of Dreiser's prose. His autobiography is *A Book About Myself* (1922).

Dreyfus Case, The. Notorious miscarriage of justice involving Captain Alfred Dreyfus, an officer in the French artillery, who was accused of passing secret defence documents to the Germans. He was condemned in 1894 to transportation to the penal settlement on Devil's Island, French Guiana. Repeated demands from eminent persons for a retrial were obstructed by the military authorities and anti-Jewish influences until 1899, when he was again adjudged guilty, notwithstanding that a Major Esterhazy had been proved to be the traitor and a Colonel Henry a perjured witness. Dreyfus's supporters continued to assert his innocence and demand his release, the most influential being the statesman and subsequent Premier, Georges Clemenceau, and Emile Zola the novelist whose 'open letter' 'J'accuse' published in a newspaper (*Aurore*) in 1898 charged the military with conspiracy and led him to take refuge in England to escape imprisonment for libel. Although Dreyfus was pardoned by President Loubet in 1899, it was not until 1906 that his condemnation was legally reversed and his military rank restored. His innocence was proved finally by the publication of relevant German documents. The Dreyfus affair marked the climax of antisemitism on the Continent, until it revived under Hitler.

Driffield, Edward. Distinguished elderly novelist, husband of Rosie, in Somerset Maugham's *Cakes and Ale* (1930). He was thought to be modelled on Thomas Hardy, though the author denied it.

Drinkwater, Felix. Undernourished slum-bred Cockney, a murderer of the English language, in Bernard Shaws *Captain Brassbound's Conversion* (1900).

Drinkwater, John (1882-1937). Born in Leytonstone, London, the son of a schoolmaster turned actor; educated at Oxford High School. Employed as an insurance clerk in Midland towns, particularly in Birmingham and Manchester, until 1909. By that time his interests had turned towards literature, and the enthusiasm he developed for the theatre led him to become in 1907 co-founder of The Pilgrim Players, which became the *Birmingham Repertory Theatre in 1913, with Drinkwater as manager. His first pub-

lished work appeared at his own expense as *Poems* (1903), and was followed by several other books of verse which gave him prominence among the contemporary *Georgian poets (*Collected Poems*, 1923); he also wrote one-act plays. The production of his *Abraham Lincoln* (1918) at Birmingham and afterwards in London, brought him critical esteem and popular success, but subsequent plays on *Mary Stuart* (1921), *Oliver Cromwell* (1921), *Robert E. Lee* (1923), and *Robert Burns* (1925) were inferior. Such claim as his plays may have to a permanent place in the English stage repertory will depend on *Abraham Lincoln* and *Bird-in-Hand* (1928), a comedy. He also wrote much miscellaneous prose, mainly literary and biographical studies, and a two-volume autobiography: *Inheritance* (1931); *Discovery* (1932).

Drummond, Captain Hugh. See *Bulldog Drummond.

Dry Salvages, The. Poem by T. S. Eliot, the third of his *Four Quartets* (1943); first published separately in 1941. Named from 'a small group of rocks, with a beacon, off the N.E. coast of Cape Ann, Massachusetts.'.

Dubedat, Louis. The unscrupulous and tubercular young artist in The *Doctor's Dilemma* by Bernard Shaw. The dilemma facing the doctor, Sir Colenso Ridgeon, is whether he shall save the life of this scoundrelly genius or that of a worthy, useful, but undistinguished physician.

Du Bois, W. E. B. (William Edward Burghardt Du Bois, 1868-1963). Born in Massachusetts of French Huguenot and African descent. Educated in State schools, Fisk University (Tennessee), Harvard, and Germany. Became Professor of History and Economics at Atlanta University and later head of its department of Sociology. A foundermember of the National Association for the Advancement of Coloured People, he edited its periodical The Crisis for many years, and in 1960 settled in Ghana, where he adopted African citizenship and undertook preparatory work for the projected *Encyclopaedia Africana*. He was a prolific writer, occasionally of novels (*The Quest of the Silver Fleece* 1911; *The Dark Princess*, 1928), but mainly on the history and treatment of coloured peoples: *The Suppression of the African Slave Trade* (1896), *The Souls of Black Folk* (1903), *John Brown* (1909), *The Negro* (1915)

Black Folk: Then and Now (1939), *Colour and Democracy* (1945), *The World and Africa* (1947). *Dusk of Dawn* (1940) is his autobiography.

Dubliners. Short stories by James *Joyce published in 1914. Centred on diverse characters in the Irish capital, the stories are written in traditional prose prefiguring none of the experimental features of Joyce's later style. Contents: 'The Sisters'; 'An Encounter'; 'Araby'; 'Eveline'; 'After the Race'; 'Two Gallants'; 'The Boarding House'; 'A Little Cloud'; 'Counterparts'; 'Clay'; 'A Painful Case'; 'Ivy Day in the Committee Room'; 'A Mother'; 'Grace'; 'The Dead'.

Dubois, Blanche. Central character in Tennessee Williams's *A *Streetcar named Desire* (1947).

Dudgeon, Mrs Annie. Bitter tyrannical puritan widowed mother of Dick Dudgeon in Bernard Shaw's *The *Devil's Disciple* (1897).

Dudgeon, Dick. Central character in Bernard Shaw's *The *Devil's Disciple* (1897).

Duff Cooper, Alfred (Viscount Norwich). *See* Duff *Cooper.

Duggan, Alfred (Alfred Leo Duggan, 1903-64). Born in Buenos Aires; educated at Eton and Oxford, travelled in the Levant and Galapagos Islands collecting specimens for the British Museum. In 1950 (*Knight with Armour*) he started a new and successful career as author of historical novels distinguished by scrupulous scholarship and avoidance of romantic heroics: *The Conscience of the King* and *The Little Emperors* (both 1951), *Leopards and Lilies* (1954), *Devil's Brood* (1957), *Lord Geoffrey's Fancy* (1962). His subjects embraced Roman and Celtic Britain, the Crusades, and medieval and later England. His widowed mother became the second wife of the 1st Marquis Curzon in 1917.

Duhamel, Georges (1884-1966). Born in Paris. Qualified as a physician and surgeon, but devoted his time almost entirely to writing, becoming one of the founders of L'Abbaye, a community of authors and artists established at Créteil, near Paris, which disbanded after little more than a year, having failed to be self-supporting. Duhamel's outstanding work is the sequence of novels named collectively *Chronique des Pasquier*

(1933-45), translated into English as *The Pasquier Chronicles* in several volumes.

Dujardin, Edouard (1861-1949). French symbolist poet, playwright and novelist, and writer on religious subjects. His place in the history of literary development depends mainly upon his introduction of the *'interior monologue' into fiction in his novel *Les Lauriers sont coupés* (1888), the source to which James *Joyce ascribed his own extended use of this device.

Du Maurier, Daphne (1907-   ; Lady Browning; married Lieut. Gen. Sir Frederick Browning). Born in London, granddaughter of George Du Maurier, novelist and illustrator (1834-96) and daughter of Sir Gerald Du Maurier, actor-manager (1873-1934); educated at home and in Paris. Began to write in girlhood and published her first novel in her mid-twenties, *The Loving Spirit* (1931). One of the most popular women novelists of her generation, she achieved prolonged success with *Rebecca* (1938). Her uncommon story-telling ability and dramatic sense are disciplined by a prose style above the common level of romantic fiction. *Gerald: A Portrait* (1934) is a biography of her father; and her interest in the Brontës is shown directly in *The Infernal World of Branwell Brontë* (1960).

Dunn, Ellie. A leading character in Bernard Shaw's *Heartbreak House* (1917); daughter of Mazzini Dunn, who gets confused with Billy Dunn, burglar in the same play.

Dunne, Finley Peter. *See* *Mr Dooley.

Dunne, J. W. (John William Dunne, 1875-1949). Educated privately. Served in the Boer War 1900-01; afterwards attached to the government Balloon Factory. Pioneer of British military aircraft. Later he wrote on philosophical subjects, his personal experience of dreams as prefigurations of future happenings leading to the widely influential *An *Experiment with Time* (1927), followed by *The Serial Universe* (1934), *The New Immortality* (1938), *Nothing Dies* (1940). The first of these inspired J. B. *Priestley's *Time and the Conways* and other of his plays. *See also* 'An *Adventure'.

Dunne, Mary Chavelita. *See* George *Egerton.

Dunois. Bastard of Orleans. French commander in Bernard Shaw's *Saint Joan* (1924).

Dunsany, Lord (Edward John Moreton Drax

Plunkett, 18th Baron Dunsany, 1878-1957). Born in London; educated at Eton and Sandhurst. After serving in World War I became Professor of English Literature in Athens. He was a prolific writer of fiction (*The Gods of Pegana*, 1904; *The King of Elfland's Daughter*, 1924; *The Man Who Ate the Phoenix*, 1949), drama (*Plays of Gods and Men*, 1917; *Plays for Earth and Air*, 1937), essays (*Unhappy Far-Off Things*, 1919), poems (*Fifty Poems*, 1929; *To Awaken Pegasus*, 1949); autobiography (*Patches of Sunlight*, 1938).

Dunsterville, Lionel Charles (1866-1946). Educated at the United Services College, Westward Ho!, Devonshire, where he was a schoolfellow of Rudyard *Kipling, in whose novel *Stalky & Co* (1899) he appears as Stalky.

Durant, Will (William James Durant, 1885-). Born in Massachusetts; educated in Jersey City. Author of popularizing volumes in philosophy and history: *The Story of Philosophy* (1926), *The Story of Civilization* in several volumes (1935-53).

Durrell, Gerald (Gerald Malcolm Durrell, 1925- ; brother of the following). Born in India; educated privately in France, Italy, Switzerland and Greece. Studied Zoology in England at the Whipsnade branch of the Royal Zoological Society, and undertook animal collecting expeditions in Africa and Central and South America which provided ample material for his entertaining and well received books: *The Overloaded Ark* (1953), *The Drunken Forest* (1956), *Encounters with Animals* (1958), *The Whispering Land* (1961), *Two in the Bush* (1966), *Beasts in My Belfry* (1973). *My Family and other Animals* (1956) is an account of his childhood on Corfu.

Durrell, Lawrence (Lawrence George Durrell, 1912-). Born in India; educated there at Darjeeling and in England at Canterbury. Worked in the Foreign Service in Greece, Egypt and Yugoslavia, and for the British Council in Greece and Argentina. Author of novels which at first received little attention except from a limited number of critics, but at the completion of The Alexandria Quartet (*Justine*, 1957; *Balthazar*, 1958; *Mountolive*, 1958; *Clea*, 1960) he

received wider acclaim. *Tunc* (1968). His *Collected Poems* (1960); *The Black Book* (1938; 1973). *Reflections on a Marine Venus* (1953) and *Bitter Lemons* (1958) are fruit of his travels. An early novel *Panic Spring* (1937) was published under the pseudonym Charles Norden.

Durrenmatt, Friedrich (1921-). Born and educated in Switzerland. Dramatist and novelist. His plays, frequently in the contemporary 'black comedy' and *'Theatre of Cruelty' mode, became well known abroad, produced in stage adaptations from the German originals: in English, *The Visit* (from *Der Besuch der alten Dame*) 1955; *The Physicists* (from *Die Physiker*) 1962.

Duvallet, Lieutenant. French naval officer, involved with Margaret Knox in a Boat-Race-night difficulty with the police in Bernard Shaw's *Fanny's First Play* (1905).

Dynamo. Play by Eugene *O'Neill, the unsuccessful production of which in 1929 dissuaded the author from his original intention of following it with two further plays to form a trilogy. The dynamo is represented symbolically as a god which destroys its worshippers.

Dynasts, The. 'An epic-drama [mainly in verse] of the war with Napoleon: in three parts, nineteen acts, and one hundred and thirty scenes' by Thomas *Hardy, originally published in three volumes (1904, 1906, 1908). The period covered by the action is ten years, 1805 to 1815, and it moves forwards and backwards from England to various places on the European mainland involved in Napoleon's campaigns up to his final defeat at Waterloo. It was designed to represent and account for the Human Tragedy, to which end Hardy introduces not only the main human antagonists in this struggle for the domination and liberation of Europe, but also groups of 'phantom intelligences' created 'as spectators of the terrestrial action'—a variant of the chorus in Greek tragedy. As well as monarchs, statesmen, military and naval commanders, representatives of the common people appear; in particular, rustics of Hardy's own region of Wessex who provide humour.

Eagle, Solomon. See *Solomon Eagle.

Earlforward, Henry. Inherits his uncle T. T. Riceyman's secondhand bookshop in Arnold Bennett's *Riceyman Steps* (1923); lives in miserly fashion before and after marrying widowed Violet Arb.

Earlham. By Percy *Lubbock published in 1922. The author recovers in memory the happy summers spent in boyhood at Earlham Hall near Norwich, tenanted by members and relatives of the extensive Gurney family, Quaker bankers, social reformers, and philanthropists. By the boy, Earlham was memorized as 'a beautiful old house, red and mellow, spacious, sun-bathed', rambling and on changing levels indoors as the earliest (1642) building had been added to in successive generations. Mystifying features were external windows apparently without rooms inside; an eleven-sided bedroom, fear-inspiring to a small boy wakeful in the darkness; a locked 'Bluebeard's chamber', which was only a storeroom. With the freedom of the house, young Lubbock had friends among the domestics no less than among his relatives: Mrs Chapman, mistress of her 'beautiful art' as cook and dispenser of luscious teatime cakes to the children in her private apartment, 'The Room'; the red-bearded butler, pounding the gong; 'our well-beloved Rose, the housemaid' who 'somehow made a drama' of her work; above all the old superannuated nurse of the family, holding court in her upper room. A plethora of aunts and uncles included the seven sisters Kitty, Betsy, Rachel, Richenda, Hannah, Louisa, and Priscilla Gurney, of whom Betsy later became world-renowned as Mrs Elizabeth Fry, the prison reformer, while Richenda had talent as a pupil of Old Crome, founder of the famous Norwich School of watercolour painters. But the most enduring and best-loved memory at Earlham was of the boy's grandmother, widow of a Gurney but remarried to the Rev W. N. Ripley, thirty years rector of St Giles's, Norwich, before becoming incumbent of the living of Earlham. 'Grandmother' shed light and joy all around her in life, and her many-faceted character illuminates the book throughout.

Early English Text Society. 'Founded in 1864 by F. J. Furnival, with the help of Richard Morris, Walter Skeat, and others, to bring the mass of hitherto unprinted Early English literature within the reach of students and provide sound texts'. By 1970 it had published over 250 volumes, including a large number of 'texts already printed but not in satisfactory or readily obtainable editions'.

Earp, Ruth. Dancing teacher temporarily engaged to Denry Machin in Arnold Bennett's *The *Card (1911); becomes well-to-do Mrs Capron-Smith.

Earwicker. See *Finnegans Wake.

Easmon, Sarif. See *African Writers.

East Coker. Poem by T. S. Eliot, the second of his *Four Quartets (1943); first published separately in 1940. Named from the village of East Coker in Somerset, from which his ancestors came and where his ashes were buried, Easter 1965, in St Michael's Church.

Eastaway, Edward. Pseudonym of Edward *Thomas.

Eastman, Max (Max Forrester Eastman, 1883-). Born in New York State; educated in Pennsylvania and at Columbia University. Co-founder and editor of socialist periodicals, *Masses* in 1911 and *The Liberator* in 1919. He joined but later left the Communist Party, and wrote several political books on Soviet Russia which he visited in the 1920s. Author of volumes of poems; *The Enjoyment of Poetry* ('a study of the psychology of literature', 1913; enlarged edn 1951), *The Sense of Humour* (1921), *The Literary Mind* (1931), *Art and the Life of Action* (1934), *The Enjoyment of Laughter* (1936), and a candid autobiography *Enjoyment of Living* (1948).

Eberhart, Mrs Mignon (*née* Mignon Good, 1899- ; married A. C. Eberhart, civil engineer). Born in Nebraska, and educated there. Author of many detective novels: *The Patient in Room 18* (1929), *The White Cockatoo* (1932), *The Glass Slipper* (1938), *The Man Next Door* (1940), *The Unknown Quantity* (1953), etc.

Eberhart, Richard (Richard Ghormley Eberhart, 1904-). Born in Minnesota; educated at Dartmouth College (New Hampshire) and Harvard, and in England at Cambridge. *Collected Poems, 1930-1960* (1960); *Fields of Grace* (1972).

Eclectic. A style in art, etc., drawing upon many sources or models, especially of diverse kinds: *eclectic taste*, the capacity for enjoying many kinds of things.

G

Eddington, Sir Arthur Stanley (1882-1944; knighted 1930). Born at Kendal, Westmorland; educated at Owen's School, Manchester, and at Cambridge. Chief assistant to the Astronomer Royal, Greenwich, 1906-13; Professor of Astronomy at Cambridge, 1913. His particular study of the General Theory of Relativity from the time *Einstein enunciated it in 1915, resulted in his own *Mathematical Theory of Relativity* (1923). His important astronomical researches made him one of the outstanding astrophysicists of his period, and for other scholars Eddington's *Fundamental Theory* (published posthumously in 1946) is an important work. He was also a lucid popularizer, conveying in admirable prose mathematical and philosophical concepts in *The Nature of the Physical World* (1928) which might otherwise remain ungraspable by the average intelligent mind. This book, widely read, was a masterpiece for its purpose, and a disproof of the theory that science and literature are incompatible.

Edelman, Maurice (1911-   ). Born in Cardiff; educated there and at Cambridge. M.P. from 1950. Author of *A Trial of Love* (1951), *Who Goes Home* (1953), *The Happy Ones* (1957), *A Call on Kuprin* (1959), *The Prime Minister's Daughter* (1964), *Shark Island* (1967), *Disraeli in Love* (1972), and other novels.

Eddy, Mary Baker Glover (*née* Mary Baker, 1821-1910). Born in New Hampshire; educated at local schools and privately; married three times, adopting the names Glover and Eddy from her first and last husbands. From Congregationalism she turned to and founded Christian Science, organizing the First Church of Christ, Scientist, at Boston in 1879. Wrote the official textbook of the movement, *Science and Health with Key to the Scriptures*, in 1875. Started *The Christian Science Monitor* as a daily paper in 1908. She attributed her 'discovery' of Christian Science to reading in St Matthew 9:2-7 of Christ's curing the man sick of a palsy, while she was herself prostrated by a supposedly fatal accident.

Edison, Thomas Alva (1846-1931). Born in Ohio; began when twelve to sell newspapers on the railways and was soon publishing the first paper printed as well as sold on a train. He turned to telegraphy, patented improvements in communication and a vast number of inventions, among them the phonograph which, leading to the gramophone, has a literary bearing in making possible the recorded oral transmission of poetry, plays, etc.

Editio princeps (Latin, first edition). Such an edition of a famous work is sought after by scholars as showing the original intention of the author, free from subsequent textual interpolations, emendations, or corruptions.

Edna. See *Aunt Edna.

Egoist, The, An *avant-garde* magazine which developed from a feminist paper, *The New Freewoman*, of which Harriet *Weaver was co-founder. In making its changed appeal it published James Joyce's *Portrait of the Artist as a Young Man* as a serial, and while Richard *Aldington was assistant editor (Harriet Weaver remained nominal editor) it became a medium for the *Imagist poets. T. S. Eliot became assistant editor in 1917. The magazine ran from 1914 to 1919, first fortnightly, then monthly.

Education of Henry Adams, The. Autobiography of Henry *Adams (1838-1918), first printed privately and not published for general circulation until 1918, after his death. Adams, a younger member of the distinguished American family of statesmen, travelled extensively in Europe and acted as secretary to his father, Charles Francis Adams, who served as Minister to England during the American Civil War. The autobiography, which has the sub-title 'A Study of Twentieth Century Multiplicity', is wideranging, embracing acute criticism of his education at Harvard and in Germany, disquisitions on diplomacy and Darwinism, history, and physics, metaphysics and mysticism. Its place in literature is determined by the excellence of its prose style.

Egerton, George (pseudonym of Mary Chavelita Dunne, 1860-1945). Born in Melbourne, Australia. Educated privately and travelled widely in adventurous circumstances, including a voyage to South America in a sailing ship. Her first husband, H. H. W. Melville, died in 1889 a year after their marriage, and it was from the Christian name of her second husband Egerton Clairmonte that she took her pseudonym. On his death in 1901 she married Reginald Golding Bright, a well-known literary agent. Her first novel *Keynotes* (1893) brought her acclaim, and was followed by *Discords*

(1894), *Fantasies* (1898) and others. In these she portrayed with more intimacy than was familiar at that time the stresses of marriage and other problems of a woman's life.

Eggheads. A slang term (imported from America) for scholars and serious-minded persons generally, and an example of the sneer vocabulary of the 1950s and after. It superseded 'highbrows'.

Eglinton, John (pseudonym of William Kirkpatrick Magee, 1868-1961). Born in Dublin; became Assistant Librarian in the National Library there; appears in George Moore's *Hail and Farewell* and James Joyce's *Ulysses*. Author of *Pebbles from a Brook* (1901), *Anglo-Irish Essays* (1917), *Irish Literary Portraits* (1935), *A Memoir of A.E.* (George William Russell) (1937), *Confidential; or, Take It or Leave It* (1951). Editor of *Letters of George Moore: to Eduard Dujardin* (1929); to John Eglinton (1942).

Ehrenburg, Ilya (Ilya Grigoriyevich Ehrenbourg, 1891-1967). Born and educated in Russia. Took part in revolutionary action during the Tsarist régime and went into exile mainly in France until he returned to his own country at the time of the Bolshevik Revolution. In World War II he was engaged as a war correspondent on the eastern front, and was made famous by his vivid despatches (collected and translated in *The Tempering of Russia*, 1944). Before and after, his novels attracted considerable attention: *The Loves of Jeanne Ney* (1923), *A Street in Moscow* (1930), *The Fall of Paris* (1942), *The Storm* (1949), *The Ninth Wave* (1952), etc.

Einstein, Albert (1879-1955). Formulated the special theory of Relativity in 1905 and the general theory in 1916, overturning traditional Newtonian physics.

Einstein, Alfred (1880-1952). Author of numerous works on musical themes and composers, including *Mozart: His Character and His Work* (1945), *The Italian Madrigal* (3 vols, 1949), *Schubert: A Musical Portrait* (1951).

Ekwall, Eilert (Bror Oscar Eilert Ekwall, 1877-1964). Born and educated in Sweden. Professor of the English Language, University of Lund, Sweden. Author of *Shakespere's Vocabulary* (1903), *Old English Dialects* (1917), *English River Names* (1928), *Concise Oxford Dictionary of English Place*

Names (1936; 4th edn 1960), *Street-Names of the City of London* (1954), *The Population of Medieval London* (1956).

Ekwensi, Cyprian (1921-). See *African Writers.

Élan vital. Term used by Henri *Bergson in '*Evolution créatrice* (1907; English edition, *Creative Evolution*, 1911) to express his belief that evolution is not a mechanistic process as postulated by Darwinism but is the outcome of intuitive desire. The idea was given wider currency by Bernard *Shaw, whose term 'the Life Force' embodies the same belief, developed by him in *Man and Superman* and in the Preface to *Back to Methuselah* on Creative Evolution.

Elegy. A poetical lament for (usually) a dead friend. Originally a classical Greek form, English elegies in less restricted metres include Milton's *Lycidas* (1638: for Edward King), Shelley's *Adonais* (1821; for John Keats), Tennyson's *In Memoriam* (1850; for A. H. Hallam), Arnold's *Thyrsis* (1866; for A. H. Clough); in the present century W. B. Yeats's *In Memory of Major Robert Gregory* (included in *The Wild Swans at Coole*, 1919, and in *Collected Poems*, 1950) and W. H. Auden's *In Memory of W. B. Yeats* (included in *Another Time*, 1940).

Elfine Starkadder. Youngest of the family in Stella Gibbons's *Cold Comfort Farm* (1932). From being a fey rural romantic she is transformed by Flora Poste into a marriageable young lady.

Eliot, Lewis. Narrator in C. P. Snow's *Strangers and Brothers* sequence of novels.

Eliot, T. S. (Thomas Stearns Eliot, 1888-1965). Born at St Louis, Missouri, U.S.; educated at Smith Academy and Harvard, and, after graduating, studied in Germany and at Oxford and the Sorbonne in Paris. Having settled in England he became, first, a teacher at Highgate School, London, and then from 1919 to 1922 a bank clerk. Meanwhile he had been assistant editor of *The *Egoist, and in 1917 appeared his first separately published poems *Prufrock and other Observations,* followed two years later by *Poems.* He became editor of *The *Criterion when it was started in 1922 and until it ceased to appear in 1939. In the first number *The *Waste Land, the foundation poem of his subsequent great reputation, was printed. Though it was at first as much attacked as praised, it created an enthusiastic and increasing audience for the poetry which followed: *Poems 1909-1925* (1925), *Ash *Wednesday* (1930), *Collected Poems 1909-1935* (1936), *Burnt Norton* (1936), *East Coker* (1940), *The Dry Salvages* (1941), *Little Gidding* (1942)—collected and republished as *Four *Quartets* (1944). A more genial aspect of his versifying was shown in *Old *Possum's Book of Practical Cats* (1939), written for children, but possibly destined to be his enduring work, as *Alice in Wonderland* is of the sometime eminent mathematician C. L. Dodgson. As an experimental dramatist Eliot began with *Sweeney Agonistes* (1932), a fragment of 'an Aristophanic melodrama'. *The Rock* (1934) of which he retained only the choruses in his collected poems, was written as a pageant play in aid of a London churches fund. In his other five plays—*Murder *in the Cathedral* (1935; written for the annual festival of Canterbury Cathedral), *The* *Family *Reunion* (1939), *The* *Cocktail *Party* (1950), *The Confidential Clerk* (1954), *The Elder Statesman* (1959)—Eliot put into operation his theory that verse drama should conform to natural speech-rhythms and not be consciously poetic. His commanding position in contemporary English literature was due as much to the authority of his critical and other prose writings as to the originality of his verse technique. Many had assumed from *The Waste Land* that his attitude was that of an agnostic in matters of belief, and of a revolutionary in regard to literary form; while it seemed natural that as an American he would favour a non-monarchical régime. But he declared in the Introduction to *For *Lancelot Andrewes* (1928, the year in which he became a naturalized British subject) that he was 'classicist in literature, royalist in politics, and anglo-catholic in religion'. Eliot's first volume of essays *The Sacred Wood* (1920) preceded *Homage to John Dryden* (1924), to whom as a classicist Eliot's admiration and allegiance remained inflexible. He was critical of Shakespeare and Milton, but was prominent among those who brought back into favour the metaphysical poets, especially Donne. His extensive prose output included *Andrew Marvell* (1922), *Dante* (1929), *The Use of Poetry and the Use of Criticism* (1933), *Elizabethan Essays* (1934), *Essays Ancient and Modern* (1936), *What is a Classic?* (1945), *Milton* (1947), *Notes Toward the Definition of Culture* (1948), *Poetry and Drama* (1951), *On Poetry*

and Poets (1957); and on religious themes: *After Strange Gods* (1934) and *The Idea of a Christian Society* (1939). The widespread acceptance of Eliot as a superlatively great poet and great critic was unparalleled; as a literary arbiter he had been equalled in modern times only by Samuel Johnson in the 18th century. Much of the adulation he received was probably born of fashion rather than of comprehension, for his writings were the product and expression of erudite scholarship beyond the grasp of more than a minority of those who applauded. Though personally modest and no contriver of his own reputation, as a critic he was not without intellectual arrogance; and though as a poet he profoundly influenced a whole generation of writers, only posterity will be competent to judge whether Eliot led English poetry into productive new territory or into a cul-de-sac. *Complete Poems and Plays* (1 vol edn, 1969).

Eliza Doolittle. Covent Garden flower girl, heartlessly transformed by Henry Higgins in Bernard Shaw's *Pygmalion (1914).

Elizabeth, Queen of Rumania. See *Carmen Sylva.

Elizabeth (pseudonym of Mary Annette Beauchamp, afterwards Countess von Arnim, and later Countess Russell, 1866-1941). Born in Sydney, Australia, cousin of Katherine *Mansfield; educated at home. While touring in Italy she met Count Henning August von Arnim, whom she married in 1891, and until his death in 1910 they lived on his extensive estate near the Baltic coast of Pomerania. There she bore and brought up the children who appear as the April, May, and June babies in her first novel *Elizabeth and her German Garden* (1898), which gave a foretaste of the humour, wit and irony which were to develop in the many works that followed. In the first books her husband as well as the children appear, and her characterization of him as 'the Man of Wrath' is marked by the union of sentiment and bland irony which gave her writing its distinctive tone and, during the period of her first marriage, kept her wit within the bounds of optimism. After six years of widowhood she married the 2nd Earl Russell (elder brother of Bertrand *Russell) in 1916, but their marriage was a failure and ended in 1919. Her earlier group of books included *The Solitary Summer* (1899), *The Benefactress* (1902), *The Adven-*

tures of Elizabeth in Rugen (1904), *The Princess Priscilla's Fortnight* (1906), *Fraulein Schmidt and Mr Anstruther* (1907), and *The Caravanners* (1909). They were followed by novels of a darker tone; her wit became more incisive and at times displayed the sharp teeth of malice which had before been guarded. *The Pastor's Wife* (1914), *Vera* (1921), *Expiation* (1929) and *Father* (1931) belong to this group, but in *The Enchanted April* (1923), perhaps her best book, there was a return to the happier manner. Among other novels are *The Jasmine Farm* (1934) and *Mr Skeffington* (1940). *In the Mountains* (1920) was published anonymously; for *Christine* (1913) she used the pseudonym Alice Cholmondeley. *All the Dogs of my Life* (1936) is autobiographical. In London her circle of literary friends included many of the outstanding writers of the period, even though her personal charm and wit did not guarantee invariably smooth relationships, as Hugh *Walpole had found in 1907 when acting as tutor to the eldest daughters in Germany. She went to America in 1939 and died at Charleston, South Carolina.

Leslie de Charmes: *Elizabeth of the German Garden* (1958).

Ellerman, Annie Winifred. *See* Bryher.

Elliot, Frederick. Central character in E. M. Forster's *The *Longest Journey* (1907). Rickety as a child, he is nicknamed Rickie by his father and is so called all his life. Not succeeding as a writer, he becomes a schoolmaster married to a dominating and avaricious woman, Agnes (*née* Pembroke). While rescuing a drunken half-brother he is run down and fatally injured at a level crossing.

Ellis, Havelock (Henry Havelock Ellis, 1859-1939). Born in Surrey; educated privately but spent a good deal of his childhood voyaging with his father, a sea captain. Went to Australia and taught in New South Wales, 1875-79, experiences recollected in his novel *Kanga Creek* (1922). Back in England he studied at St Thomas's Hospital and qualified as a physician, but devoted himself to literature and science, editing the Mermaid Series of 16-18th century dramatists (1887-9) and the Contemporary Science Series (1889-1914). Though his interest in literature continued to the end, his most famous work was *The Psychology of Sex* (in seven volumes, 1897-1928), a study which led in England to the prosecution of the pub-

lisher of the early volumes and the banning of the work, subsequently printed only in the American edition, though the futility of censorship was demonstrated by surreptitious importation which made it as familiar in Britain as in countries where it circulated normally. Ellis's pioneering investigations opened up a field of inquiry which others explored with minute particularity and often with abandon in the following generation. He was also a graceful literary essayist— *Little Essays of Love and Virtue* (1922), *Impressions and Comments* (3 vols, 1914, 1921, 1924). Autobiography: *My Life* (1940). A vital experience was his long and devoted friendship with Olive *Schreiner.

Eloi. The people living in the upper world and preyed on by the underworld Morlocks in H. G. Wells's *The *Time Machine* (1895).

Elsie Sprickett. Widowed after two nights of marriage in 1915, she becomes charwoman to Mrs Arb and Henry Earlforward in Arnold Bennett's *Riceyman Steps* (1923). After her employers' marriage she is resident general servant until their deaths; rescues, nurses, and marries Joe, a shell-shocked and malarial ex-soldier, and jointly with him is engaged as 'staff' by the local physician.

Elton, G. R. (Geoffrey Rudolph Elton, *né* Ehrenberg, 1921-   ). Born at Tuebingen, Germany; educated in Prague and at London University. Professor of Constitutional History, Cambridge, from 1967. Author of *England Under the Tudors* (1955), *The Tudor Constitution* (1960), *Renaissance and Reformation* (1963), *The Future of the Past* (1968).

Elton, Godfrey (1892-1973; 1st Baron Elton of Headington, 1943). Born in Buckinghamshire; educated at Rugby and Oxford. Lecturer in Modern History, Oxford, 1919-39; General Secretary, Rhodes Trust, 1939-59 (*see under* Cecil John *Rhodes). Among his books are *The Revolutionary Idea in France 1789-1878* (1923), *General Gordon* (1954), whose *Khartoum Journal* he edited (1961), *The Unarmed Invasion* (1965) on the immigration problem.

Elton, Oliver (1861-1945). Born in Norfolk; educated at Marlborough and Oxford. Lecturer in English Literature at Owen's College, Manchester, 1890-1901; Professor of English Literature, Liverpool University, 1901-25. He wrote on various periods and aspects of literature, a six volume *Survey of English Literature* covering the period 1730-1880 (1912, 1920, 1928), *The English Muse* (1933, on poetry from the Anglo-Saxon period to 1918), and a memoir of his friend C. E. *Montague (1929).

Elwin, Malcolm (1903-   ). Born in Nottinghamshire; educated at local schools and Oxford. Author of biographical studies of *Charles Reade* (1931), *Thackeray: A Personality* (1932), *Savage Landor* (1941); editor of *The Essential Richard Jefferies* (1948) and of various writings of Benjamin Robert Haydon, R. L. Stevenson, and Charles Lamb.

Elwin, Verrier (1902-64). Son of a Bishop of Sierra Leone; educated at Oxford, where he became Vice-Principal of Wycliffe Hall and Chaplain of Merton College, before going to India as a missionary in 1927. A few years later he began to live among native tribes, and thereafter devoted himself mainly to the study of their religion, customs, songs, and literature, on all of which he wrote: *Leaves from the Jungle* (1936), *Folk Tales of Mahakoshal* (1944), *Folk-Songs of Chhattisgarh* (1946), *Myths of Middle India* (1949), *The Tribal Art of Middle India* (1952), *The Religion of an Indian Tribe* (1955). He was appointed to official posts bearing on tribal affairs both before and after independence.

Ely, G. H. *See* Herbert *Strang.

Elyot Chase, Divorced husband of Amanda in Noel Coward's *Private Lives* (1930).

Emerson, George. Marries Lucy Honeychurch in E. M. Forster's *A *Room with a View* (1908).

Eminent Victorians. Biographical essays by Lytton *Strachey published in 1918: 'The End of General Gordon'; 'Florence Nightingale'; 'Cardinal Manning'; 'Dr Arnold'. The Introduction, in effect a manifesto, denigrates the customary form and style of English 'Standard Biographies' with 'their ill-digested masses of material, their slipshod style, their tone of tedious panegyric, their lamentable lack of selection, of detachment, of design'. The author's own declared aim was to 'attack his subject in unexpected places . . . shoot a sudden, revealing searchlight into obscure recesses', to lower a bucket into the great ocean of material and 'bring up to the light of day some characteristic specimen . . . to be examined with a careful

curiosity'. He insisted that biography is an art and, therefore, that the biographer, considered as an artist, must select and arrange, not simply accumulate. The book had a startling success, a host of imitators in the following decade or more, and as many detractors. Strachey's outstanding gift of irony was beyond the capacity of his imitators, who failed to effect the revolution in English biographical writing which *Eminent Victorians* appeared to promise or threaten. The detractors accused Strachey of anti-Victorian prejudice leading to suppression and distortion, but the book survives as a masterpiece of literary art and humanization.

Emotive language. In speech or writing, the use of words and phrases intended to do more than convey their literal and rational meaning and to play upon the feelings or passions of the hearer or reader. Emotive language is common and legitimate in poetry and much fiction, often delusive in preaching, potentially a danger in political oratory.

Empathy. The ability to enter into the feelings and sensations of another; to achieve imaginative identity with that other, not simply contemplate from without. In literature empathy is invaluable, even if rare; it is notable in Browning's poetry and in the novels of Joyce *Cary.

Emperor Jones, The. Play in eight scenes by Eugene *O'Neill performed in New York in 1920. Brutus Jones, a Negro former Pullman car attendant in the U.S., escapes from jail there and, as a stowaway, reaches a West Indian island, where he gains power over the natives and sets himself up as Emperor, with Henry Smithers, a low-class white cockney trader, as a kind of major-domo. Jones, finding his 'palace' deserted, learns from Smithers that his generals and cabinet ministers have rebelled, stolen the horses, and taken to the hills, preparatory to hunting him down. Jones, having foreseen that his reign would be short, has stored up money and hidden food in various spots ready to escape when revolution comes. He has also created the legend that ordinary weapons cannot harm him and that nothing but a silver bullet could kill him. In his own revolver are five lead bullets and a silver one. He boasts to Smithers that he can safely escape from pursuit along forest paths, and at nightfall reaches its edge, already tired.

He fails to locate the first of his caches of food, and in continuous monologue expresses his growing fears and horrible imaginings. He gradually empties his revolver, firing at apparitions, and has his clothes torn to rags until he has lapsed back to naked savagery, frenzied by the never-ending beat of tom-toms. He fires his last bullet, the silver one, at a visionary crocodile and, emerging weaponless at dawn from the forest at the same place as he went in, is killed by silver bullets which his enemies have moulded in the night.

Empirical. Based on experience, not theory.

Empson, William (1906-   ). Born in Yorkshire; educated at Winchester and Cambridge. Held university professorships in English Literature in Tokyo and Peking; Professor of English Literature in the University of Sheffield from 1953. His *Seven Types of Ambiguity* (1930), *Some Versions of Pastoral* (1935), and *The Structure of Complex Words* (1951) had a marked influence on contemporary students of English literature. His *Collected Poems* were published in 1955.

Encounter. A monthly publication founded in 1953 by the Congress for Cultural Freedom, with Stephen *Spender as joint editor in its early years. The first number included contributions by Virginia Woolf, Christopher Isherwood, Edith Sitwell, Cecil Day-Lewis, and Albert Camus. It has continued to attract leading writers of various nationalities.

En-dor, The Road to. An escape story of World War I by E. H. Jones published in 1919.

Enemies of Promise. Autobiography by Cyril *Connolly published in 1938. It surveys critically his education at Eton and the social and other influences of his time which are considered as acting as 'enemies of promise', handicapping the development of writers with an intellectual rather than a popular aim. The book includes much comment on contemporary authors of repute.

Engagement. *See* Commitment.

English Association, The. Founded in London in 1906 to bring together those interested in English Language and Literature and to spread as widely as possible the knowledge and enjoyment of the literature. Organizes lectures and conferences; publishes a magazine, *English,* three times a year, and annually *The Year's Work in English Studies, Essays and Studies,* and the Presidential Addresses. Admits subscription-paying Members, Branch Members, and Life Members.

Eng. Lit. (English Literature). An abbreviation in vogue in the 1950s and later among book reviewers and others who adopted a contemptuous attitude to the teaching of English literature in universities and schools, and sometimes to English literature as such, though Eng. Hist. and Eng. Geog. were not thus designated.

English Review, The. Founded in 1908 with Ford Maddox *Hueffer as editor, this monthly became famous with its publication of novels by Joseph *Conrad and H. G. *Wells in instalments of unusually generous length and of John Masefield's extended narrative poems *The *Everlasting Mercy* and its successors. Having changed its editor and its price (from half-a-crown to a shilling), after a few years, *The English Review* became less distinguished and suffered, in common with other periodicals, from the restrictions and crippling financial effects of World War I and ceased publication.

Enright, D.. J. (Dennis Joseph Enright, 1920-   ). Educated at Leamington and Cambridge; tutor, lecturer, or professor in universities in England and abroad. Poet (*The Laughing Hyena,* 1953; *Some Men are Brothers,* 1960; *The Old Adam,* 1965), novelist (*Academic Year,* 1955; *Insufficient Poppy,* 1960), critic—*Conspirators and Poets* (1966). His reminiscences in *Memoirs of a Mendicant Professor* (1969) include accounts of his brushes with authority in Thailand and Singapore.

Ensor, R. C. K. (Sir Robert Charles Kirkwood Ensor, 1877-1950; knighted 1955). Educated at Winchester and Oxford. Held academic appointments at the London School of Economics and at Oxford colleges. Sometime leader-writer for London dailies, and from 1940 to 1953 (as 'Scrutator') contributor of weekly articles on foreign affairs to the *Sunday Times.* Author of several volumes of verse; *Modern Socialism* (1903), *Courts and Judges in France, Germany, and England* (1933) and (volume 14 in the Oxford History of England) *England 1870-1914* (1936).

Épater le bourgeois. To shock or flabbergast the middle classes, a traditional sport of the *avant garde.*

Ephesian (pseudonym of Carl Eric Bechhofer Roberts, 1894-1949). Born in London and educated there at St Paul's School and later at Berlin University; practised as a barrister; served with British military mission in Russia and as foreign correspondent of *The Times* and other English, Continental and American newspapers; private secretary (1924-30) to the 1st Earl of *Birkenhead, a study of whom he wrote in 1926. Author of many other books, including considerations of Winston *Churchill (1927), Stanley Baldwin (1936), Verlaine (1937); *The Truth about Spiritualism* (1932); a novel concerning Charles Dickens, *This Side Idolatry* (1928); and plays and other novels, alone or in collaboration with C. S. *Forester and George Goodchild.

Epstein, Sir Jacob (1880-1959; knighted 1954). Born in New York, studied in Paris, and settled in England from 1905. Almost certainly the greatest sculptor and modeller to have worked in the country of his adoption, he also became the most controversial, since he worked in an Eastern and symbolic tradition at variance with the familiar naturalistic convention. His many commissions included the Oscar Wilde memorial in the Père Lachaise cemetery, Paris; the W. H. Hudson memorial (Rima) in Hyde Park, London, and portrait bronzes of Bernard Shaw, Joseph Conrad, Cunninghame Graham, and others eminent in the arts and affairs. Among his latest and most impressive works were 'Christ in Majesty' for Llandaff Cathedral and 'St Michael overcoming Satan' for Coventry Cathedral. He wrote *The Sculptor Speaks* (1931) and an autobiography *Let there be Sculpture* (1940; enlarged edn 1955).

Erskine, John (1879-1951). Born in New York; educated at Columbia. Professor of English, Columbia University, 1916-37. A many-sided man with inexhaustible energy, he not only won academic distinction both as student and as teacher, but also performed as a concert pianist with famous orchestras. With W. P. *Trent he edited the *Cambridge History of American Literature,* and among his own writings were *The Elizabethan Lyric* (1903), *The Kinds of Poetry* (1920), *The Literary Discipline* (1923), and other works on literary subjects, and his *Collected Poems* came out in 1922. He made a first appearance as novelist with *The Private Life of Helen of Troy* (1925), following it with *Galahad* (1926), *Adam and Eve* (1927), and

Tristan and Isolde (1932), impish satirically humorous redressings of the originals.

Ertz, Susan (1894-   ). Born in England of American parents, but from the time she was twelve she lived for six years in California, receiving private education there. Settled in England from 1914; married Major J. R. McGrindle, 1932. Her first novel, *Madame Claire* (1922), remained her best and best known; others are *Now East, Now West* (1927), *The Proselyte* (1933) and *The Prodigal Heart* (1950).

Ervine, St John (St John Greer Ervine, 1883-1971). Born in Belfast. Wounded in World War I. Manager of *Abbey Theatre, Dublin, 1915. Professor of Dramatic Literature, Royal Society of Literature. 1933-36. As dramatic critic for *The Observer* after World War I his notices were given authority by his practical experience as playwright and theatre manager. *Mixed Marriage* (1910) and *Jane Clegg* (1911), and *John Ferguson* (1914), which had established him prominently among the naturalistic dramatists of the pre-war period, were followed by plays with a wider appeal: *Anthony and Anna* (1926), *The First Mrs Fraser* (1928), and *Robert's Wife* (1937) had literary merit as well as long runs on the London stage. His later plays were less successful. He also wrote several novels— *Mrs Martin's Man* (1914), *The Wayward Man* (1927)—biographies of *Parnell* (1925), General Booth (*God's Soldier,* 1934), and *Bernard Shaw: His Life, Work and Friends* (the definitive biography; 1956).

Escaped Cock, The. Original title of D. H. Lawrence's *The *Man Who Died.*

Escapist literature. Description applied mainly to romantic fiction which takes its readers into a dream world; also applied austerely to all reading matter which is not committed to social realism.

Essay. In its lighter form, for entertainment more than for information, the essay in the present century flourished mainly in the earlier decades. Under the influence of Charles Lamb, E. V. *Lucas wrote copiously, and Robert *Lynd several volumes (collected from *The New Statesman*) in a not dissimilar style, using Y.Y. as his signature in the periodical. A. G. *Gardiner wrote in *The Star* newspaper as 'Alpha of the Plough' and Oswald *Barron in the *Evening News* as 'The Londoner'. Max *Beerbohm's essays continued to be unique; Maurice *Hewlett produced four collections which merit revived attention; G. K. *Chesterton and Hilaire *Belloc were notable essayists as well as poets and novelists. Alice *Meynell published mostly in the previous century, but her Collected Essays (1914) brought her agreeably to the notice of a new generation. The popularity of the essay waned in the later decades, though it continued to be practised with distinction by Harold *Nicolson and J. B. *Priestley, while newcomers to the genre included Richard *Church, William *Golding, Margaret *Lane, Alison *Uttley. Virginia *Woolf's Common Reader and other volumes, on a level hardly equalled by her contemporaries, come into the category of criticism rather than into that of the essay as considered here.

Essenes. An ascetic and communistic religious sect in Palestine which flourished for some four centuries up to about A.D. 200. They figure in George Moore's novel The *Brook Kerith (1916) and in his play The Passing of the Essenes (1930).

Esson, Louis. See *Australian Writers.

Establishment, The. A term, usually of disgruntlement, current among journalists and others in the 1950s and 1960s. It signified not so much the established order of Government and Church as a supposedly more or less conspiratorial hidden hand operated collectively by organizations wielding authority without bearing responsibility, in order to maintain the status quo. The suspect bodies included the Army, the B.B.C., the Public Schools, High Society, All Souls College (Oxford), and The Times. Those who viewed 'The Establishment', so called, as a mere political and social myth, retaliated by charging the Anti-Establishment with the suppressed desire to become itself the alternative Establishment. A volume entitled The Establishment, edited by Hugh Thomas (1959), delivered the main attack. The claim to first use of the term in this sense became a matter of controversy. That it was not its recent users' invention appeared to be settled by a letter to The Times Literary Supplement (1 April 1965) quoting Coleridge's complaint that as a political journalist he was 'Unthanked and left worse than defenceless by the Friends of the Government and the Establishment' (12 September 1814).

Estragon. One of the two tramps in Samuel

Beckett's *Waiting for Godot (1954). Nicknamed Gogo.

Ethan Frome. Short tragic novel by Edith *Wharton published in 1911. On a poor farm in Massachusetts, Ethan Frome falls in love with his nagging and hypochondriac wife's young cousin, Mattie Silver. Zeena, the wife, drives out Mattie, and while on their way to the station Ethan and Mattie decide to die rather than part, but their endeavour to kill themselves by crashing their snow-sledge into a tree results in their being permanently crippled and at the mercy of Zeena.

Euphemism. Avoidance of plain words by the substitution of terms or phrases considered more polite or genteel or less emotionally disturbing.

Euphuism. The elaborately mannered prose style used by John Lyly in Euphues (1579); any later literary style employing similar artificial devices.

Eurhythmics. A system of musical training by association with rhythmical physical movement, invented by Emile Jaques *Dalcroze (1865-1951). It aims at complete coordination of all the human faculties, thus assisting every aspect of individual development.

Evans, Sir Arthur (Arthur John Evans, 1851-1941; knighted 1911). Born in Hertfordshire; educated at Harrow and Oxford. Keeper of the Ashmolean Museum, Oxford, 1884-1908. Engaged in archaeological investigations in Crete, where (1900-08) he excavated the Minoan palace of Knossos, one of the greatest achievements in the history of archaeology. Author of The Mycenaean Tree and Pillar Cult, 1901; The Palace of Minos at Knossos (4 vols, 1922-35); and other works.

Evans, Caradoc (David Evans, 1878-1945). Born in Wales; at board school in Cardiganshire he learned hardly any English; worked as a draper's apprentice and assistant for years and studied at the Working Men's College in London. Having left the drapery business, he found employment in publishing houses and became an editorial assistant. He returned to live in Wales, where he was bitterly disliked for the unfavourable view of the Welsh people he gave in My People (1915), Capel Sion (1916), My Neighbours (1920). He also wrote novels—Nothing to Pay (1930), Wasps (1934)—and a play, Taffy (1924). He married, as her second husband, the novelist then writing as Oliver *Sandys.

Evans, Joan (-   ). Half-sister of Sir Arthur Evans (above). Medieval scholar and archaeologist; educated at Berkhamsted and Oxford. Author of *Life in Mediaeval France* (1925; 1957), *St Joan of Orleans* (1926), *Monastic Life at Cluny* (1931), *Romanesque Architecture of the Order of Cluny* (1938), *Art in Mediaeval France* (1948), *History of Jewellery 1100-1870* (1953), *The Diaries of John Ruskin* (1956, 1958, 1959), *Prelude and Fugue* (autobiography, 1965).

Everlasting Mercy, The. Narrative poem in rhyming couplets by John *Masefield published in 1911. Its first appearance, in *The *English Review*, created a literary and extra-literary sensation by its uninhibited colloquialism, mixing of religion and near-blasphemy, 'unpoetic' characters, and frequently strained rhymes. Saul Kane tells the story of his unregenerate early life—'I drunk, I fought, I poached, I whored'—his brutal prize fight with Bill Myers, his debauches in pubs and with women. He becomes seemingly devil-possessed—'Out into the street I ran uproarious, / The devil dancing in me glorious'—and is hell-bent for damnation until Miss Bourne, a Quaker, who 'went round at ten / To all the pubs in all the place / To bring the drunkard's soul to grace', rebukes his indecencies, saying 'every drop of drink accursed / Makes Christ within you die of thirst, / . . . every dirty word you say / Is one more flint upon His way.' After closing-time he walks until dawn, conscious that 'the bolted door' of his soul 'had broken in': 'I knew that I had done with sin / I knew that Christ had given me birth.' He is newly aware of the beauties of Nature, being cleansed in spirit and vision by Christ's 'everlasting mercy'.

Everyman's Library. A series of reprints projected in 1904-05 by J. M. *Dent to include the classics of English and foreign literature in English translations. The original aim was to reach one thousand volumes at a shilling each, and a beginning was made in February 1906 with fifty volumes and a further 100 appeared in the same year. World War I slowed down production and increased the price and it was not until 1956 that volume 1000 was reached with a new translation of the *Metaphysics* of Aristotle. The first work in 1906 was Boswell's *Life of Johnson* in two volumes. The editor of the series for many years was Ernest *Rhys, and it was he who chose the name and the epigraph—'Every-

man, I will go with thee, and be thy guide'—from the medieval morality play, *Everyman.*

Evoe. *See* E. V. *Knox.

Ewer, Monica (*née* Monica Thompson, died 1964). Educated in Belgium and at Bedford College, University of London. Author of many novels, including *Insecurity* (1930), *Fifty Bob a Week* (1934), *Marriage Isn't Easy* (1945), *End of the Road* (1951); also *Play Production for Everyone* (1924).

Except the Lord. Novel by Joyce *Cary published in 1953. An old man, Chester Nimmo, relives in memory the several periods of his life, from boyhood in a Devonshire moorland hamlet, through the years of his growth and early earnings from hard ill-paid labour, his emancipation from a rigid religious environment, and his experiences of socialism, trade unionism, and Liberal Party politics. His father, a lay preacher to village congregations believing passionately in the imminence of the Second Advent of Christ, unwittingly contributes to the boy's growing scepticism when gatherings he arranges on the moors to greet the expected descent of the Lord Jesus are fruitless. Chester's development is crucially affected by the fascinated horror he experiences while watching a fairground melodrama in which the murderer becomes for him at once 'the villain, the devil—and the hero'. In a later phase Nimmo returns to religion and preaches to his father's congregation, but his life becomes mainly political, involving him in labour troubles and violence and treachery by colleagues. At the end, after giving forty years of his life to 'the party of freedom', he finds himself 'an old and broken man . . . thrown into the gutter'. Though Nimmo's public life is central to the narrative, its human interest is mainly embodied in the characters of his father, his sister Georgina, and his brother Richard. *Except the Lord,* the first of a trilogy, was followed by *Prisoner of Grace* (1952) depicting Nimmo as his wife Nina sees him, while in *Not Honour More* (1955) he is seen from the viewpoint of Nina's second husband, Jim Latter. The title *Except the Lord* is from the opening words of Psalm 127 in the Prayer Book version.

Existentialism. A term used for a loosely defined philosophy which has had conflicting religious and atheistic manifestations. In its religious aspect it goes back to *Kierkegaard, but popular interest in existentialism was excited, mainly after World War II, by the writings of Jean-Paul *Sartre. As far as their convictions can be defined briefly and intelligibly, existentialists of the Sartre school hold that we can know nothing but that we exist and are solely responsible for ourselves as existing creatures, that there is no God to share or exact responsibility. This view led some to a conviction of the utter futility and absurdity of life, expressed in such writings as those of Samuel *Beckett and the plays of *Ionesco. But in Thornton *Wilder's novel, The Ides of March, Caesar writes to a friend: 'How terrifying and glorious the role of man if, indeed, without guidance and without consolation he must create from his own vitals the meaning for his existence and write the rules whereby he lives'.

Experiment with Time, An. An account by J. W. *Dunne of his arrival at the concept of serial time by analysis of the content of his dreams recorded in writing immediately on waking and found to be composed of images of past experience and future experience blended together. The book, first published in 1927, attracted widespread attention, reflected in, e.g. the 'time plays' of J. B. Priestly—Time and the Conways (1937), I Have Been Here Before (1937). To the 1947 paperback edition of Three Time Plays Priestley contributed an Author's Note giving a simplified account of Dunne's theory. See also An *Adventure.

Expressionism. Originally a term denoting visual works of art expressing some inner vision or intellectual bias or spiritual turmoil of the individual artist rather than actual features of the external world. Extended to literature, aspects of Expressionism enter into the poetry of T. S. *Eliot (The Waste Land etc.), the prose of James *Joyce, the plays and other writings of Samuel *Beckett.

Eyles, Leonora (1889-1960). Born in Staffordshire; married D. L. *Murray. Author of Margaret Protests (1919), The Woman in the Little House (1922), Shepherd of Israel (1929), They Wanted Him Dead (1936), The Ram Escapes (1953). Commonsense About Sex (1956). Also books on women's careers and home economics.

Eynsford-Hill, Freddie. In Bernard Shaw's postscript to *Pygmalion (1914) the author reports that Eliza married Freddie and was set up in a South Kensington flower shop (later a prosperous greengrocery) by Colonel Pickering.

Fabian Society, The. Founded in 1884 to establish Socialism by 'the emancipation of Land and Industrial Capital from individual and class ownership, and the vesting of them in the community for the general benefit'. The 'Basis' of the Society, from which the foregoing phrase is taken, was formulated in 1887, and it added: 'For the attainment of these ends the Fabian Society looks to the spread of Socialist opinions, and the social and political changes consequent thereon. It seeks to achieve these ends by the general dissemination of knowledge as to the relation between the individual and Society in its economic, ethical, and political aspects.' Although the Society's aim was to bring into being a Socialist state, it did not formally ally itself with any political party nor require its members to do so. Although Bernard *Shaw, a member of the Executive Committee from 1885 to 1911, declared that 'the Fabians were at first as bellicose as the others' (i.e. the Social Democratic Federation and similar militant bodies), the Society as such worked through lectures and tracts, trusting in political education, not political agitation. The success of its methods was demonstrated at length by the number of Fabians who became members of Parliament and subsequently ministers in the first British Labour Government in 1924. Its most influential publication was *Fabian Essays* published in 1889, first in an edition of 1,000 copies, but eventually reaching a sale of nearly 50,000. The essayists were Bernard *Shaw, Sidney *Webb, William Clarke, Sydney *Olivier, Graham *Wallas, Mrs *Besant, and Hubert *Bland. Although great success attended the Society's public lectures during many years, its membership was composed more largely of an intellectual élite than of the proletarian rank and file. Extensions of its work were ensured through its organization of the London School of Economics in 1895 and the foundation in 1913 by Bernard Shaw, Mr and Mrs Sidney Webb and others, of *The *New Statesman* which, though not formally linked with the Society, expressed its policy for many years. Among the eminent members of the Fabian Society (besides those already named) were Granville *Barker, Rev. R. J. *Campbell, G. D. H. *Cole, St John *Ervine, Rev. Stewart Headlam, J. Ramsay MacDonald (Britain's first Socialist Prime Minister), Rebecca *West, and H. G. *Wells (who left the Society in 1908 after five years' member-

ship in which he attempted unsuccessfully to gain personal control in leading it into more aggressively propagandist ways). The name adopted by the Society relates to the 3rd century B.C. Roman consul Fabius who in the campaign against Hannibal avoided direct battle and chose instead to pursue and worry the enemy. The title page of Fabian Tract No. 1, issued in 1884, bore this epigraph: 'For the right moment you must wait, as Fabius did most patiently when warring against Hannibal, though many censured his delays; but when the time comes you must strike hard, as Fabius did, or your waiting will be in vain, and fruitless.' Critics have challenged this as a historical statement on the ground that Fabius never did strike hard; but the delaying tactics of the Fabians at length bore fruit when the Labour Government of 1945-51 'struck hard' in its nationalization programme. Bernard Shaw's collected volume of *Essays in Fabian Socialism* (1932) contains much of the material he wrote for the Society in the 1890s and 1900s.

Edward R. Pease: *The History of the Fabian Society* (1916) covers its achievements up to 1915; Margaret Cole: *The Story of Fabian Socialism* (1961) continues the history and gives impressions of some of its outstanding members.

Fabre, Jean Henri Casimir (1823-1915). Spent the main years of his life in retirement, engaged on entomological study leading to his great ten-volume work *Souvenirs entomologiques* (1879-1907); sections translated into English include: *Insect Life* (1901), *The Life and Love of the Insect* (1911), *Social Life in the Insect World* (1912), *The Wonders of Instinct* (1918), *Animal Life in Field and Garden* (1921), *Curiosities of Science* (1927).

Façade. Poems by Edith *Sitwell published in 1922. A public recital of twenty-one of the thirty-three pieces was given later by the author, speaking through a megaphone projecting from a backcloth designed by John Piper, and with accompanying music by William Walton. The composer afterwards adapted the music as an orchestral suite and for an amusing popular ballet. The *Façade* poems include 'Country Dance', 'Fox Trot', 'Polka', 'Mazurka', 'Waltz', and 'Hornpipe' in metres appropriate to the several dance-measures; and other verses in various modes—baroque, rococo, comic—

including 'Trio for Two Cats and a Trombone'.

Fair, A. A. *See* Erle Stanley *Gardner.

Fairburn, A. R. D. (Arthur Rex Dugard Fairburn, 1904-57). Born and educated in Auckland, New Zealand; worked as clerk, journalist, script writer, university lecturer in the theory and history of art. Author of *He Shall Not Rise* (1930), *Dominion* (1938), *Three Poems* (1952), *Strange Rendezvous* (1952). *See* *New Zealand Writers.

Fairfax, Hon Gwendolen. Daughter of Lady Bracknell in Oscar Wilde's *The Importance of Being Earnest* (1895); marries John Worthing.

Fairfield, Cicily Isabel. *See* Rebecca *West.

Fairless, Michael (pseudonym of Margaret Fairless Barber (1869-1901). Born at Rastrick, Yorkshire. Becoming an invalid, she turned from nursing to writing and her book of essays *The Roadmender*, finished shortly before she died, had long-sustained success from the year of its publication soon after her death. Other volumes followed, *The Gathering of Brother Hilarius* (1901) and *The Grey Brethren* (1905).

Falder. Young solicitors' clerk in John Galsworthy's *Justice* (1910). Convicted of forgery, he serves a prison sentence and kills himself when rearrested.

Falk: A Reminiscence. Story by Joseph *Conrad published in 1903 in *Typhoon and Other Stories*. The narrator, commanding a barque trading to an Eastern up-river port, frequently visits his friend Hermann, captain of the *Diana*, when their ships are at neighbouring berths. Mrs Hermann and their children live on board and also a niece, barely nineteen, physically splendid but, in the story, always silent. Another assiduous visitor to the *Diana*, Falk, is the owner and commander of the only tugboat on the river, and occasion comes when he refuses ever again to tow the narrator's ship. Hearing that the cause of this refusal is jealousy, the narrator convinces Falk that he is not a rival for Hermann's niece, and even undertakes to 'speak for' him, since he says, mysteriously, 'I have been unfortunate once' —in some other, unspecified, connection. After the narrator has cleared the way with Hermann, Falk makes his declaration of love but insists that 'he could not marry a woman unless she knew of something in his life that

happened ten years ago'. Later, he tells the narrator the full story of disaster which befell a ship he was on, and of how he was finally driven to cannibalism. When Falk reveals the bare fact on the *Diana*, Hermann raves in horror, but the niece weeps from pity and the uncle becomes reconciled to the marriage.

Falkner, J. Meade (John Meade Falkner, 1858-1932). Born in Wiltshire; educated at Marlborough and Oxford. Became tutor in the household of the head of the armaments firm of Armstrong Whitworth; was appointed Secretary to the firm and (1915-20) its Chairman. Though his business career was remarkably successful, his personal interests were scholarly and literary, and after his retirement he served as Honorary Librarian at Durham Cathedral Chapter Library and Honorary Reader in Palaeography to the University of Durham. He was also an authority on Church music. The most important of his three novels, *The *Nebuly Coat* (1903), displays the variety of his cultural interests—music, architecture, heraldry, genealogy—all woven into a romantic story. *Moonfleet* (1898) is a tale of smugglers on the Dorset coast, and *The Lost Stradivarius* (1895) is one of the best of all lengthy ghost stories. In addition, Falkner wrote handbooks for travellers, on Oxfordshire and Berkshire, a *History of Oxfordshire*, and poems.

Fallada, Hans (pseudonym of Rudolf Ditzen, 1893-1947). His novel of postwar Germany, *Little Man, What Now?* (in German 1932; English translation 1933), on an average man confronting the social problems of his time, won him international acclaim.

Family Reunion, The. Verse play in two parts and six scenes by T. S. *Eliot performed in London in 1939. The scene is laid at Wishwood, a country house in the north of England, on the afternoon and evening of the Dowager Lady Monchensey's birthday. Her younger sisters, Ivy, Violet, and Agatha, her brothers-in-law, the Hon Gerald and the Hon Charles Piper, and Mary, daughter of a deceased cousin of Lady Monchensey, are awaiting the return from abroad of Harry, Lord Monchensey, who has been away eight years. In discussion it appears that his wife had disappeared from a liner in mid-ocean. When he arrives he declares that he pushed her overboard; and he believes himself pursued by 'the sleepless hunters / That will not let me sleep'—the Eumenides or Furies of Greek tragedy, with which Eliot's play is remotely linked. The dialogue is for the most part highly metaphysical and such 'plot' as is intermittently apparent involves Agatha: 'Thirty-five years ago', says Lady Monchensey to her, 'You took my husband from me. Now you take my son', for Agatha has impressed upon Harry that he has a long journey to undertake and must leave Wishwood. To his mother he says: 'all my life has been a flight / And phantoms fed upon me while I fled. . . . Now they will lead me. I shall be safe with them.'

Fane, Michael. Chief character in Compton Mackenzie's *Sinister Street* (1913-14), the theme of which is 'the youth of a man who presumably will be a priest'. His sister Stella becomes a concert pianist before marrying Alan Merivale.

Fanfrolico Press. See Jack *Lindsay.

Fanny's First Play. 'An easy play for a Little Theatre' in an Induction, three acts, and an Epilogue by Bernard *Shaw, first staged anonymously in London in 1911, the year in which it was written. In a country house owned by Count O'Dowda, a stage has been prepared for a private performance to which the leading dramatic critics have been invited. O'Dowda, a Count of the Holy Roman Empire, has hitherto made his home in Venice so as to escape from England 'befouled with industrialism'. His daughter Fanny, educated at Cambridge, has written a play of which he has been told nothing except that the hero is a Frenchman. He is giving her the performance as a birthday present and is confident that the play will be like 'a Louis Quatorze ballet painted by Watteau'. When Fanny's play begins (after the Induction devoted to the gathering of the critics) the scene is a middle-class home in a London suburb, whence Mr and Mrs Gilbey's son Bobby has been missing for a fortnight. A 'young lady of hilarious disposition', Dora Delaney ('Darling Dora'), calls to tell them that Bobby is in gaol waiting to be bailed out after a half-drunken frolic. In another part of London, Mr Gilbey's partner, Knox, and Mrs Knox are distressed because their daughter Margaret, engaged to Bobby Gilbey, has not been heard of for a fortnight. She then arrives in company with a Frenchman, Lieutenant Duvallet, who, she says, has been

extremely kind. On boat-race night she got so excited by the hymn-singing at a Salvation Festival in the Albert Hall that she went on to a music hall where she met Duvallet. Afterwards the two got caught up in a brawl between students and police and were arrested. Margaret's tussle with the police and her time in Holloway prison have given her a view of reality, and enlightened her in a way that makes nonsense of her parents' 'silly little hole of a house and all its pretences'. Margaret and Darling Dora have met in prison, and they meet again with Bobby and Duvallet at the Gilbeys' house, where, after much discussion of parent–child relationships, Bobby pairs off with Dora Delaney and Margaret with Juggins the Knoxes' footman, who is really the brother of a duke. In the Epilogue, Fanny's father expresses himself as shocked by her play. The critics, from whom the authorship has been kept secret, dispute as to who wrote it, naming several leading playwrights. Fanny at length enlightens them, declares that she is a suffragette, and confesses that, like her characters, she too has been in gaol.

Far Away and Long Ago. Autobiography of childhood and youth by W. H. *Hudson published in 1918. It records life on the South American pampas from 1841, where he developed from infancy the lifelong affinity with Nature which made birds and animals, trees and flowers and grass, indispensable to him. His personal story gives primacy to inanimate things and the lesser living creatures, though he and his family were also brought in contact with a variety of native people and scattered settlers. Educated at home by schoolmasters whose eccentricity was more evident than their scholarship, he and his brothers were little hampered in their preference for outdoor pursuits. He became familiar not only with the many birds that flocked in and about the plantation, but also with opossums, armadillos, snakes, rats, and rarer creatures. Among the many anecdotes and experiences is the account of a tramp nicknamed The Hermit, who called for food periodically at every house in a fifty-mile radius, wearing huge boots of undressed cowhide and an ankle-length garment of scraps of the same material 'stuffed with sticks, stones, hard lumps of clay, rams' horns, bleached bones' and fastened round him with straps of hide. He spoke no recognizable language, and died alone, his wasted body in its grotesque coverings being found on the prairie. Daily insight into the often primitive and brutal lives of the gauchos was varied by a more civilizing intimacy with neighbours descended from the old Spanish families who colonized the wide pampas in the seventeenth and early eighteenth centuries, though it was an old gaucho landowner who had a vital influence on Hudson during the period of spiritual turmoil and preoccupation with the mystery of death and immortality which darkened the end of his boyhood.

Farewell to Arms, A. Novel by Ernest *Hemingway published in 1929. Lieutenant Frederic Henry, an American serving with an Italian ambulance unit in World War I, is introduced to an English V.A.D. nurse, Catherine Barkley, at the British hospital in Gorizia. Her fiancé, to whom she had been engaged for years, has been killed in France some months before. Henry is much attracted to her, but though at first she holds aloof they become lovers. During an Austrian bombardment he is severely wounded and evacuated to the American hospital in Milan where he is operated on. Catherine, now pregnant, succeeds in being transferred and helps to nurse him. He returns to the front shortly before the Austro-German offensive breaks through the Italian defences at Caporetto and the great retreat begins. The three vehicles in Henry's charge have to be abandoned in the mud, and with two companions he continues on foot. After evading advancing Germans, he is pulled from the retreating column by Italians searching for deserters, and only escapes summary execution by diving into the river and swimming across. He jumps a freight train and reaches Milan. Finding that Catherine has gone to Stresa he follows her there, and they stay at a hotel until he is warned that his arrest for desertion is imminent. A friendly barman at the hotel provides them with a boat in which they row at night across the lake to Switzerland, where they are temporarily held in custody but at length reach Lausanne. Catherine goes into hospital to have the baby, but dies after being delivered of a stillborn child.

Farigoule, Louis. See Jules *Romains.

Farjeon, Eleanor (1881-1965). Born in London; educated privately. She was one of the rare writers whose books find a devoted audience among both children and grown-ups:

Nursery Rhymes of London Town (1916), *Martin Pippin in the Apple Orchard* (1921), *Martin Pippin in the Daisy Field* (1937), *The Little Bookroom* (1955). Plays: *The Silver Curlew* (1948), and with her brother, Herbert Farjeon (1887-1945), *The Two Bouquets* (1936), *An Elephant in Arcady* (1938), *The Silver Slipper* (1944). She also wrote a memoir of *Edward Thomas: The Last Four Years* (1958), and the autobiographical *A Nursery in the Nineties* (1935; reissued 1960).

Farleigh, John (1900-65). Born and educated in London. Worked as a commercial artist and art teacher. Came into prominence when commissioned to illustrate with wood engravings Bernard Shaw's *The *Adventures of the Black Girl in Her Search for God* (1932). Later he also made illustrations for Shaw's *Back to Methuselah* and engravings for D. H. Lawrence's *The *Man Who Died. Author of *It Never Dies: Lectures and Essays* (1946), *The Creative Craftsman* (1950). Autobiography: *Graven Image* (1940).

Farmer's Glory. 'A pen picture of farming life in Southern England and Western Canada' by A. G. *Street published in 1932. Though using fictional names (the author appearing as Jim Blanchard), it is a straight autobiographical record of a young Wiltshire farmer's life on the land and his personal relationships with other agricultural workers. From an agricultural school, young Street went to work on his father's farm, starting at the bottom at a wage of seven shillings a week, and learning during the following years the whole craft of arable and dairy farming in the period before mechanization. Desiring fuller responsibility than his father allowed, he spent three hard but satisfying years ploughing, threshing and cooking for bachelor co-workers under primitive conditions 150 miles from Winnipeg. He returned to England in the first year of World War I, was rejected for military service, and resumed work on the farm, becoming its owner when his father died in 1917. While he deplored 'the waning of the glory' as farming ceased to be prosperous in the postwar decades, he adapted to the changing methods, installing machines and concentrating on milk production. With enthusiasm for his profession and outspokenness about State officials, 'gentlemen farmers', and changing standards of work, he combined human understanding of the men around him. The book has many anecdotes and much humour as well as lucidly communicated knowledge of farming techniques.

Farnol, Jeffrey (John Jeffrey Farnol, 1878-1952). Born in Warwickshire; educated privately. Attempts to set him to a business career failed, and little more came of a period of art study. In 1902 he went to New York, painted stage scenery, and wrote the novel published in England as *The Broad Highway* (1910), the first of a long series of romantic novels which continued until 1951, by which time the large public with whom they had been extremely popular had been superseded by a disillusioned and sophisticated generation.

Farrell, James T. (James Thomas Farrell, 1904-   ). Born in Chicago and educated at schools and the University there. Worked as a clerk, garage attendant, book salesman, and undertaker. Author of a series of realistic novels, *Studs Lonigan* (1932-35), etc.

Farson, Negley (James Negley Farson, 1890-1960). Born in New Jersey; educated in Massachusetts and at the University of Pennsylvania. After experience as an aviator and in business, he became foreign correspondent for a Chicago newspaper and travelled and voyaged in Europe and the East. Author of *Sailing Across Europe* (1926), *The Way of a Transgressor* (1935), *Last Chance in Africa* (1949), *Caucasian Journey* (1951).

Father and Son. A Study of Two Temperaments by Edmund Gosse published in 1907. This 'scrupulously true . . . record of educational and religious conditions which, having passed away, will never return', traces a boy's recollections of his upbringing from infancy to the end of his teens. The only child of rigidly puritanical parents belonging to the Plymouth Brethren, an exclusive sect of self-styled 'saints', he was from birth 'dedicated to the Lord'. His father, Philip Henry Gosse, an eminent marine zoologist, and his mother, Emily Gosse, author of religious verse and widely circulated Evangelical tracts, conducted their lives in conformity with an unshakable conviction that the Bible is true in an absolute sense and is the sole guide for Christian living. Mrs Gosse died early in the life of her child, whose memories of living alone in her company during the time she was receiving useless treatment for her fatal malady are related

with tragic pathos. She laid on her husband the dying injunction that he should bring up the boy 'in the nurture and admonition of the Lord', a task the father's own spiritual devotion welcomed and faithfully laboured to fulfil. They moved from London to Devonshire, where Philip Gosse conducted his marine studies and wrote his books, with his son as sole companion and, at times, his innocent parodist, writing and drawing in imitation of his father. As leader of a local congregation of the Brethren, Mr Gosse imposed inflexible discipline based on his assurance that he was God's confidant as interpreter of the Divine Will. No secular reading nor pleasure of any kind was allowed to his son on the Lord's Day; fiction was at all times prohibited until a less fanatical stepmother brought Sir Walter Scott's works into the house. The admission of the boy to 'breaking of bread' (Communion)—an adult privilege—was secured by the father through ingeniously contrived favouritism. In serio-comic circumstances the boy received 'adult baptism' by total immersion. The determination from his birth to 'keep him unspotted from the world' insulated him from other children, and not until he went to boarding school did he make contact with other minds and develop his own to the point where he demanded the right to think for himself, and finally broke from the bondage of misconceived parental love.

Father Brown. Catholic priest and detective in G. K. *Chesterton's *Innocence of Father Brown* (1911), *The Wisdom of Father Brown* (1914), etc.

Father Figure. Term from the vocabulary of psychiatry, applied in common use to a political leader or other person who serves as an emotional or ideological substitute for a father.

Faulkner, William (William Harrison Falkner (*sic*), 1897-1962). Born in New Albany, Mississippi; educated at the University of Mississippi, to which he returned after serving with the Canadian and British flying corps. Settling to writing, he began with a volume of poems *The Marble Faun* (1924), his first novel, *Soldier's Pay*, following two years later. His later novels constitute a saga of the degeneration of a family and community in the Deep South, named by the author as the county of Yoknapatawpha, with the town called Jefferson as its centre. Faulkner's first three novels made little impression, but with *The Sound and the Fury* (1929) he gathered an audience which continued to regard him as a novelist of genius, in spite of dissenters by whom he was variously described as a 'chronicler of decay, of viciousness, of perversion, of cruelty', a creator of characters who are 'twisted shapes in the chaotic wreckage of a mad world', a writer of 'slippery and heavily mannered prose'. Offsetting such American voices, the anonymous writer of *The Times* obituary notice said: 'He brought to life a fictional world, the highest mark of a novelist's achievement, he developed a distinctive unmistakable style, and, under cover of his own myth of the South, he created stories with universal implications. One has only to savour the complex, rich and subtle texture of Faulkner's writing to know that for all the critical diatribes about his violence, his primitivism, and his obsession with lust and incest, here is a great literary imagination.' His novels, in addition to the above, include *As I Lay Dying* (1930), *Light in August* (1932), *Absalom, Absalom!* (1936), *The Hamlet* (1940).

Fausset, Hugh l'Anson (1895-1965). Born in Westmorland; educated at home, and at Sedburgh and Cambridge. Two books of verse preceded the succession of critical writings which constituted his main work: *Keats* (1922), *Tennyson* (1923), *John Donne* (1924), *Coleridge* (1926), *Tolstoy* (1927), *The Lost Leader: A Study of Wordsworth* (1933), *Whitman* (1942). Also wrote novels— *Between the Tides* (1943) and *The Last Days* (1945), an autobiography, *A Modern Prelude* (1933), and studies in Buddhism and other Eastern religions, and was a prolific reviewer for literary periodicals.

Faust, Frederick Schiller. *See* Max *Brand.

Fauves, Les. Literally, 'the wild beasts': the name given by a critic in 1905 to Matisse, Derain, Vlaminck, Rouault, and others exhibiting in that year at the Paris Salon, on account of the violence of colour, distortion, and other features then unfamiliar in paintings. The term has since been adopted descriptively without malice.

Feemy Evans. The local prostitute in Bernard Shaw's *The *Shewing-up of Blanco Posnet* (1909). She breaks down when about to testify against Blanco.

Fell, Dr. Detective in crime novels by John Dickson *Carr.

Fellow travellers. Applied to those who are sympathetic to Communists without belonging to the Party.

Female of the Species, The. Poem written in 1911 by Rudyard *Kipling, with the much-quoted refrain 'The female of the species is more deadly than the male'.

Ferber, Edna (1887-1968). Born in Michigan; educated at schools in Wisconsin. In her teens she became a reporter and continued in journalism until she had major successes as short-story writer with *Emma McChesney & Co* (1915) and later as novelist with *So Big* (1924), *Show Boat* (1926), *Cimarron* (1929), *American Beauty* (1931), etc. *Show Boat* was adapted as a popular musical play and *Cimarron* as an exciting film. In collaboration with George S. *Kaufman she wrote *Dinner at Eight* (1932), *Stage Door* (1938) and other plays. *A Peculiar Treasure* (1939) tells her life story.

Ferguson, Helen. Nurse in Ernest Hemingway's *A *Farewell to Arms* (1929).

Fermor, Patrick Leigh (Patrick Michael Leigh Fermor, 1915-   ). Born in London; educated at Canterbury. Served in Greece, Albania, and Crete in World War II. Author of *The Traveller's Tree* (1950), an account of the Caribbean islands; *Mani* (1958), on southern Greece; and other travel books. *The Violins of St Jacques* (1953), a short novel, concerns an island in the Antilles submerged in a volcanic eruption.

Ferrovius. A Christian prisoner in *Androcles and the Lion* by Bernard Shaw; he is a powerful man and, as he feared beforehand, in the arena his combative instinct overcomes his faith and he slays six gladiators instead of submitting to martyrdom, and is enrolled in the Pretorian Guard.

Festschrift (German: celebration in writing). A collection of essays or other literary pieces written by colleagues or sometime pupils etc. in honour of an eminent scholar or author and presented on a birthday or at retirement. One such was given to Bernard *Shaw, entitled *G.B.S. 90* (1946), offering tributes by twenty-seven contemporaries.

Fettercairn House. The home near Aberdeen of a descendant of one of James Boswell's executors, where a mass of Boswell Papers came to light in 1930-31. Bought by an American collector, they were acquired by Yale University in 1949 and volumes containing them began to appear in the 1950s. *See also* Malahide Castle.

Feuchtwanger, Lion (1884-1958). Born in Munich; educated there and in Berlin. Playwright and novelist, he achieved international success in the 1920s with two historical novels translated into English as *Jew Süss* (1926) and *The Ugly Duchess* (1927). Persecuted in Germany during the Hitler period, he escaped and settled in America.

Fiction. At the beginning of the century only George Meredith (1828-1909) and Thomas Hardy (1840-1928) survived of the great Victorian novelists; both had abandoned prose and returned to poetry. Rudyard *Kipling, the most praised and politically the most condemned of the then living writers, published his prose masterpiece, *Kim*, in 1901, and continued for many years to add to his short stories, the medium in which he won fame long before. In the same year H. G. *Wells's *The *First Men in the Moon* appeared, appropriately ushering in the concept of Space Travel which was to become a commonplace before the century ended. While Wells's fiction was to be ambiguously poised between science and sociology, between imaginative creation and contemporary commentary, Joseph *Conrad's (his *Lord Jim* came out in 1900) was poised between sea adventure and cosmopolitan politics, between stored observation and matured recollection. By the time Wells died in 1946 his reputation was ebbing, his prose had deteriorated, and his hopes for the unification of mankind in a peace-committed One World State were shattered. Conrad died in 1924, scarcely suspecting that half a century later he would become the subject of academic study with critical assessments mounting high. This was perhaps inevitable since his concern with the technique of composition was only less than that of Henry *James, of whom he was in some degree a disciple. James's own novels in the present century—The *Wings of the Dove* (1902), *The *Ambassadors* (1903), *The *Golden Bowl* (1904) are in his third and most involuted style: his three periods were named ironically by Philip *Guedalla as 'James I, James II, and the Old Pretender'. In line with the growth of interest in ob-

scurity in the second half of the century, James's three novels named became critics' favourites. Arnold *Bennett, the first regional novelist of the century, began his Staffordshire Potteries series with *Anna of the Five Towns* (1901), reaching his peak with *The *Old Wives' Tale* (1908) and *Clayhanger* (1910). John *Galsworthy (who as a passenger on one of Conrad's ships encouraged him to become a novelist) had originally no intention of pursuing Soames *The Man of Property* (1906) beyond that one book, but he did reappear in later novels to make *The *Forsyte Saga* (1922), a family chronicle which continued in several more books. Wells, Bennett, and Galsworthy were superseded by a generation of writers who turned the English novel into new paths: D. H. *Lawrence, James *Joyce, Virginia *Woolf, though these three had nothing in common except preoccupation with mental and emotional states and subconcious promptings. In a lecture (1924) called 'Mr Bennett and Mrs Brown', Virginia Woolf devalued Arnold Bennett's method of depicting character by the accumulation of detail, suggesting that a Mrs Brown or any other did not come alive by such means. Her own method, an impressionistic not a descriptive one, has been dispraised on the ground that all her characters are aspects of Virginia Woolf, never a Mrs Brown among them. The *stream-of-consciousness school of novelists, making much use of the *interior monologue technique, has Joyce's *Ulysses* as its monumental achievement. For those of average intellect it is largely unreadable. Even less readable is Dorothy *Richardson's multivolumed *Pilgrimage*, devoted to long-sustained interior monologues of Miriam Henderson, who is so enduringly dull that the merits of the author's experimental technique are obscured. George *Moore, Aldous *Huxley, Robert *Graves, Walter *de la Mare, Rose *Macaulay, Elizabeth *Bowen, Rosamund *Lehmann, are among scores of praised novelists. Hugh *Walpole, whose *Mr Perrin and Mr Traill* (1911) promised greatly, was ultimately handicapped by his own competence and facility, which faded into mediocrity. J. B. *Priestley's later novels did not excel *The *Good Companions*; Somerset *Maugham was undervalued by the critics until the approval of the common reader brought them to heel; E. M. *Forster, confining himself to five novels, won unique critical distinction. Perhaps the last of the English traditional novelists, Joyce *Cary is also among the best. Crime fiction became peculiarly a favourite medium for women writers. Agatha *Christie, with more than fifty such novels behind her, became in her seventies the Grand Old Lady of detective fiction; Margery *Allingham and Ngaio *Marsh also combined literary merit with ingenuity and suspense. For more than a decade Dorothy *Sayers ranked as the most 'literary' of the writers in the crime-and-detection category, but the mannerisms of her amateur investigator, Lord Peter Wimsey, grew tedious. Outside this genre, later women writers much praised include Ivy *Compton-Burnett and Iris *Murdoch. A school of social-protest fiction, disguised in the early examples as irreverent comedy, began with John Wain's *Hurry on Down (1953) and Kingsley Amis's Lucky Jim (1954). John Braine's novel of a young man on the make, *Room at the Top (1957) gave a popular impetus to the novel of provincial life, a type to which, in a raw industrial setting, Alan *Sillitoe's Saturday Night and Sunday Morning (1958) was a turbulent addition. See also American Writers. It is impossible to touch here on the multitude of short-story writers. They are dealt with fully in The Modest Art by T. O. Beachcroft (1968).

Field, Michael. Joint pseudonym of Katharine Harris Bradley (1848-1914) and her niece Edith Emma Cooper (1862-1913). The former was born in Birmingham and educated at Cambridge and in Paris; the latter was born in Kenilworth, Warwickshire. They collaborated indistinguishably from 1889 in the production of over a score of volumes of verse (Wild Honey, 1908, etc) and poetic tragedy (Borgia, 1905, etc) which were well received in literary circles. They were acquainted with prominent mid- and late-Victorian writers, and extracts from their journals were published posthumously as Works and Days (1933).

Field, Rachel (Rachel Lyman Field, 1894-1942). American author of All This and Heaven Too (1938) and other novels, children's books (Hitty: Her First Hundred Years; The Life and Adventures of a Wooden Doll, 1932) and one-act plays (The Cross-Stitch Heart, etc, 1927).

Fielding, A. (pseudonym of Dorothy Fielding, of whom no personal details have been published). Author of many detective novels

from The Eames-Erskine Case (1924) and including The Footsteps that Stopped (1926), The Net Around Joan Ingilby (1928), Tragedy at Beechcroft (1935), Murder in Suffolk (1938), Pointer to Crime (1944).

Fielding, Cyril. Principal of the Government College, Chandrapore, in E. M. Forster's A *Passage to India (1924); friend of both Dr Aziz and Adela Quested, Fielding believes him innocent and her mistaken in the charge she brings against Aziz.

Fin de Siècle. End of century: applied to writers of the 1890s whose 'decadence' was taken to be a characteristic of the dying century.

Finch, Robert (1900-   ). Born in Long Island, N. Y.; educated in Toronto and Paris. Author of Poems (1946), The Strength of the Hills (1948), A Century has Roots (1953), Dover Beach Revisited (1961), Acis in Oxford (1961), Silverthorn Bush (1966), and other collections of verse.

Finchley, Sondra. See *Sondra Finchley.

Findlater, Jane Helen (1866-1946). Born in Edinburgh; educated at home. Author of The Green Graves of Balgowrie (1896), Rachel (1899). The Story of a Mother (1902), Seven Scots Stories (1912); in collaboration with Kate Douglas *Wiggin, The Ladder to the Stars (1906); in collaboration with her sister Mary *Findlater, Crossriggs (1908), Penny Monypenny (1911), Beneath the Visiting Moon (1923), and (reminiscences) Seen and Heard Before and After 1914 (1916). Eileen Mackenzie: The Findlater Sisters (1965).

Findlater, Mary (1865-1964). Born in Perthshire; educated at home. Author of Over the Hills (1897), Betty Musgrave (1899), The Rose of Joy (1903), A Blind Bird's Nest (1907), and of other novels in collaboration with her sister (see Jane Helen *Findlater above).

Finger Prints. The system of criminal detection by the impression and classification of finger prints, so often referred to in detective fiction, derives largely from the researches of Sir Francis Galton (1822-1911) who published Finger Prints (1893) and Fingerprint Directory (1895). The Bertillon system, based upon physical measurements, was superseded by the fingerprint system, the utility of which is now frequently countered by glove-wearing criminals.

Finland Station, To the. *See* Edmund *Wilson.

Finlayson, Roderick (Roderick David Finlayson, 1904-   ). Born and educated in New Zealand. Author of collections of short stories—*Brown Man's Burden* (1938), *Sweet Beulah Land* (1942); novels—*Tidal Creek* (1948), *The Schooner Came to Atia* (1952), *The Springing Fern* (1965); non-fiction—*Our Life in this Land* (1940). *See* *New Zealand Writers.

Finnegans Wake. Novel by James *Joyce published as a whole in 1939, following the appearance of sections at intervals during the seventeen years it was known only as Work in Progress. It represented the ultimate stage of Joyce's experiments with language and, as his own recordings of parts make clear, is more an oral creation than a written one, a fact attributable to the author's near-blindness through the years of composition. The central character is H. C. Earwicker and the period overtly covered is one night of his dreams and nightmares. It compacts an immense amount of learning and a vast body of allusions; and though its verbal bulk is enormous, more of its multiple significances are underneath the words than in them. It defies summarization and will almost certainly continue to defy comprehension by all but such devotees of Joyce as are prepared to trace its learning and allusions to their manifold sources in Irish history and topography, in works by Giordano Bruno (Italian philosopher, 1548-1600), Giovanni Battista Vico (Italian philosopher and historian, 1668-1744), Freud, Jung, and others, and, perhaps above all, in the linguistic inventions and fragmentations and combinations by Joyce himself.

Firbank, Ronald (Arthur Annesley Ronald Firbank, 1886-1926). Born in London, the son of a wealthy company director; educated at Uppingham and Cambridge. He left the University in 1909 without graduating and spent the next years in travelling in Spain, Italy, the Middle East and North Africa. Sunstroke while he was a child made him delicate, and although he was to acquire numerous friends after the publication of his first novel in 1915, he was always shy and timid in company, and was mostly unaccompanied in his frequent concert- and theatre-going. He had a variety of eccentricities, such as having in his apartment a palm tree, to water which he engaged a gardener to visit him twice daily; and he wrote his books on piles of blue postcards. These peculiarities were recorded by his friend Sir Osbert Sitwell, who also perceived in Firbank's novels 'a new revelation of style, and of a wit that rippled the surface of every page without ever breaking it', adding that the chief claim to be made for him is 'his startling technical achievement' in the mastery of the dialogue which makes Firbank's books almost wholly conversation pieces, often inconsequent and baffling to readers accustomed to novels sustained by logical narrative. His books were few and brief—*Vainglory* (1915), *Inclinations* (1916), *Caprice* (1917), *Valmouth* (1918), *Santal* (1921), *The Flower Beneath the Foot* (1923), *Prancing Nigger* (1924), *Concerning the Eccentricities of Cardinal Pirelli* (1926). They are at once extravagantly artificial, fragile, and bizarre, a throwback to the 1890s and a realization in prose of the delicacy and degeneracy of Beardsley's art at its most ambiguous.

First Edition Club. *See* A. J. A. *Symons.

First Men in the Moon, The. Novel by H. G. *Wells published in 1901. Risky business transactions having made him bankrupt, Mr Bedford goes into retirement at Lympne in Kent, intending to write a play. His literary plans are sidetracked by the forming of a friendship with a neighbour, Mr Cavor, engaged on scientific research directed towards the invention of a substance 'opaque to gravitation'—i.e. one that will cut off the gravitational pull of both the earth and the sun. By accident, a sheet of metal alloy he is experimenting with suddenly displays this opacity, and, by releasing everything above it from the force of gravity, it produces the effects of a vast explosion, causing widespread damage. Naming the substance Cavorite, the inventor overcomes its disastrous potentialities by constructing a glass-lined steel sphere large enough to accommodate two men, the outside being cased with adjustable shutters of Cavorite which can be drawn aside from within to control the direction of the sphere's movement as it flies through space. Having taken aboard food and other necessaries, Cavor and Bedford close the airtight manhole cover and start the sphere on its journey to the moon. As the flight progresses, they experience the phenomenon of weightlessness, and in due course touch down on the moon, seeming to be surrounded by hummocks of snow which prove to be solidified air, frozen in the intense cold of the lunar night. At sunrise the hummocks thaw, liquefying and vaporizing to form the surrounding atmosphere. In the increasing warmth, vegetation develops with visible rapidity from seed pods to full-grown plants, their complete life cycle embraced within a single day before the arctic cold destroys them. Leaving the sphere, the travellers wander in the landscape and lose their way back. They witness animals and men (naming them mooncalves and Selenites) rising from underground habitations. Unable to locate the sphere, Cavor and Bedford satisfy their hunger with an edible growth which has an intoxicating effect, and enables the Selenites to capture and imprison them, fettered, underground. Unpleasant treatment and a fierce conflict ensue before they escape to the surface. They separate to search by different routes for the sphere, which is reached by Bedford when he is delirious with exhaustion. Having reason to believe that Cavor is dead, he gropes into the sphere and, fumbling with the switches, plunges the machine on course back to the earth. After he has ended his written account of the adventure, messages picked up on a Dutch electrician's apparatus are identified as originating from the moon. The sender is Cavor. He narrates his life among the Selenites in their underground cities, tells how he slowly manages verbal communication with them, and describes their physical structure and social organization. The series of sixteen messages, lucid up to the seventh, becomes increasingly broken and repetitive, ending finally with an incomplete sentence giving no clue to Cavor's fate.

Fisher, Dorothy Canfield. *See* Dorothy *Canfield.

Fisher, H. A. L. (Herbert Albert Laurens Fisher, 1865-1940). Born in London; educated at Winchester and Oxford and in France and Germany; Member of Parliament 1916-26; as President of the Board of Education he introduced the 1918 Education Act. Warden of New College, Oxford, from 1925. Author of biographies of *F. W. Maitland* (1910), *James Bryce* (1927), and a *History of Europe* (1935) which had a wide circulation.

Fisher, Vardis (Alvero Vardis Fisher, 1895-

). Born in Idaho; educated at the Universities of Utah and Chicago; taught English at Utah and New York universities. Author of many novels, the most ambitious being a series of twelve, collectively titled *The Testament of Man*, beginning from prehistoric times with *The Darkness and the Deep* (1943) and coming down to modern times.

Fitt, Mary (pseudonym of Kathleen Freeman, 1897-1959). Educated at the University College of South Wales, and became lecturer in Greek there, 1919-46, after which she wrote books on Greek subjects under her own name (*The Work and Life of Solon*, 1926; *Greek City-States*, 1950; etc) and, as Mary Fitt, detective novels including *Death and Mary Dazill* (1941) and *Sweet Poison* (1956).

Fitzgeorge, Mr. Octogenarian millionaire and collector in V. Sackville-West's *All Passion Spent* (1931).

Fitzgerald, F. Scott (Francis Scott Key Fitzgerald, 1896-1940). Born at St Paul, Minnesota; educated there and in New Jersey and at Princeton; served in the American army in World War I. Publishing his first novel *This Side of Paradise* in 1920, he was regarded for the remaining twenty years of his life as the embodiment and mouthpiece of the intelligent young in the 1920s— the period bearing the label he used in his *Tales of the Jazz Age* (1922). This followed his second novel *The Beautiful and Damned* (1922). His later work included three further novels—*The *Great Gatsby* (1925), *Tender is the Night* (1934), *The Last Tycoon* (unfinished; published posthumously, 1941); and two collections of short stories, *All the Sad Young Men* (1926), *Taps at Reveille* (1935). He himself became infected by the febrile spirit of the age and died burnt out.

Five Towns, The. English Staffordshire pottery towns—Tunstall, Burslem, Hanley, Stoke-upon-Trent, and Longton: they are now incorporated in the federated Borough of Stoke-on-Trent. Most of the more important novels of Arnold *Bennett are set in the Five Towns region.

Flaggon, Rev Septimus. Newly appointed headmaster of Chiltern School in G. F. Bradby's *The *Lanchester Tradition* (1913). He has a critical encounter with the Rev Henry Chowdler, a senior housemaster.

Flaherty, Margaret. Known as Pegeen Mike in J. M. Synge's The *Playboy of the Western World* (1907).

Flanders, Jacob. Central character in Virginia Woolf's *Jacob's Room* (1922).

Flashback. A cinematic device whereby episodes or other material from the past are interpolated in a current narrative. Used as a literary device it enables the salient features of a lifetime to be drawn into a novel with a time scale limited to, say, a few hours.

Flecker, James Elroy (*né* Herman Elroy Flecker, 1884-1915). Born in London; educated in Cheltenham and at Uppingham and Oxford; later studied languages at Cambridge. Entered the Consular Service, and was stationed at Constantinople and Beirut before recurrent tuberculosis compelled him to retire for treatment in Switzerland, where he died. His half-dozen books of verse published between 1908 and 1915 (*Collected Poems,* 1916) were distinguished by their evocation of the music and colour of 'the Gorgeous East', qualities that caused his play *Hassan* (staged in 1922) to be greeted by critics and public alike as a masterpiece, though it is tainted by a sadistic strain. The expectation that *Hassan* and his non-dramatic verse would place Flecker lastingly among the English poets and poet-dramatists has not been fulfilled, for the verbal magnificence came to appear more as tinsel than as gold, and he is remembered by hardly more than the few pieces that deservedly persist in anthologies, notably 'The Golden Road to Samarkand' and 'The Old Ships'.

Fleet Street. Generic term for the London newspapers, the offices of which have long been mainly concentrated in that street. Even those papers situated outside the zone —e.g. *The Times* and the *Daily Mirror*— come under the general colloquial heading.

Fleming, Sir Alexander (1881-1955). Born in Ayrshire; educated at Kilmarnock; worked as a shipping clerk in London for several years before becoming a student at the medical school of St Mary's Hospital. After qualifying, he worked under Sir Almroth Wright in the bacteriological laboratory there. Besides valuable pioneering work with vaccines, he discovered by chance in 1928 penicillin, a natural mould found to possess unique antibiotic properties against many harmful bacteria. He was knighted in 1944 and became internationally renowned.

Fleming, Ian (Ian Lancaster Fleming, 1908-64). Educated at Eton and Sandhurst and in Munich and Geneva. Began his career with Reuters, continued it in banking and stockbroking; joined the navy at the beginning of World War II and became attached to Naval Intelligence; afterwards (1945-59) Foreign Manager of a major newspaper combine. Starting to write in 1952 he quickly found himself with a following voracious for his spy and secret-service novels. The sadistic and amorous episodes in which the central character James Bond, Secret Agent, is frequently involved roused protests which enhanced rather than diminished the popularity of the books and of the films derived from them. The books appeared in quick succession and include *Casino Royale* (1953), *Moonraker* (1955), *Diamonds are Forever* (1956), *Doctor No* (1958), *Goldfinger* (1959), *On Her Majesty's Secret Service* (1963). *See also* The *Book Collector.*

Fleming, Oliver. Occasional pseudonym of Philip *MacDonald.

Fleming, Peter (Robert Peter Fleming, 1907-1971). Born in London, brother of Ian; educated at Eton and Oxford. Travelled extensively, in Mexico and Brazil, Russia, China and Japan, and in Eastern and Central Asia as special correspondent of *The Times*. The travel books originating in the journeys —*Brazilian Adventure* (1933), *One's Company* (1934), and *News from Tartary* (1936)— are among the best written in the period, excellent in style, though with some excessive cultivation of understatement. His later work includes *The Flying Visit* (a novel, 1940), *A Forgotten Journey: A Diary of a Journey through Russia, Manchuria and Northern China in 1934* (1952). *The Siege at Peking* (1959) is an account of the Boxer rising.

Fleshly School of Poetry, The. See R. W. *Buchanan.

Fletcher, C. R. L. (Charles Robert Leslie Fletcher, 1857-1934). Born in London; educated at Eton and Oxford, where he became a history tutor at Magdalen College from 1889 to 1906, later returning to Eton to teach history. Author of biographies, *An Introductory History of England* (5 vols, 1904-23), and in collaboration with Rudyard

*Kipling *A School History of England* (1911).

Fletcher, John Gould (1886-1950). Born in Arkansas; educated privately and at Harvard; lived in London, 1909-14. Published his first poems in 1913 (*The Dominant City; Fire and Wine; Fool's Gold; The Book of Nature; Visions of the Evening*) as one of the *Imagist group, and continued to write verse throughout his life. *Selected Poems* (1938) is a representative sampling. He also wrote on the painter *Paul Gauguin* (1921), *Some American Poets* (1921), *The Two Frontiers: A Study in National Psychology* (1930), and an autobiography, *Life is My Song* (1937).

Fletcher, J. S. (Joseph Smith Fletcher, 1863-1935). Born in Halifax, Yorkshire; started his career as a journalist in London, but later produced scores of novels, beginning with *When Charles the First Was King* (1894). Early in the twentieth century he turned to detective fiction and thereafter confined himself mainly to that genre with considerable popularity but limited critical acclaim: *The Amaranth Club* (1918), *The Middle Temple Murder* (1918), *The Charing Cross Mystery* (1923), *The Kang-Le Vase* (1926) are typical. His other writings include books on Yorkshire, and *Collected Verse, 1881-1931* (1931).

Flibbertigibbet. A word appearing in English literature at various times and with varying meanings from the 16th century. In earliest use it meant a gossiper or chatterer; Shakespeare uses it as a title for 'the foul fiend' (*King Lear* III iv 118). In modern colloquial usage it is applied to a flighty chattering girl.

Flint, F. S. (Frank Stewart Flint, 1885-1960). From poverty, elementary school, and work as a barber's lather-boy, he mastered Latin and French at evening schools and at nineteen gained entry to the Civil Service where he rose to be Chief of the Overseas Section (Statistics Division) of the Ministry of Labour. For some years he was prominent as a poet in the *Imagist movement with *In the Net of Stars* (1909), *Cadences* (1915), and *Otherworld* (1920), but after a domestic bereavement he published no more verse, though he undertook numerous translations from French and German, and plays and poems of Emile *Verhaeren.

Flower, Sir Newman (Walter Newman Flower, 1879-1964; knighted 1938). Born at Fontmell Magna, Dorset; educated at Whitgift School.

He started work at the Harmsworth Press, then joined the publishing house of Cassell & Co in 1906 and, having made a success of its magazines, reorganized the book department, and in 1927 became proprietor and managing director of the firm. Among the famous works he was instrumental in getting for Cassell's were Sir Winston *Churchill's history of *The Second World War* and his *History of the English-Speaking Peoples*. Newman wrote studies of *Handel* (1923; rev. edn 1959), *Schubert* (1928; rev. edn 1949), and an autobiography, *Just as it Happened* (1950).

Flower, Robin (Robin Ernest William Flower, 1881-1946). Born at Leeds of Irish ancestry; educated there and at Oxford; on the staff of the British Museum (Department of Manuscripts), 1906-44. He learnt Irish during his frequent visits, translated the autobiography of Tomás O Crohan, *The Islandman* (1934), and wrote *The Irish Tradition* (published posthumously, 1947) and a fragment of the history of Irish literature he had planned. *Eire* (1910), *The Pilgrim's Way* (1927) and *The Western Island* (1944) are among his other books.

Flower Children. *See* Hippies.

Fluther Good. Carpenter in Sean O'Casey's *The *Plough and the Stars* (1926). 'In an argument he usually fills with sound and fury generally signifying a row.'

Flying Inn, The. Novel by G. K. *Chesterton published in 1914. To evade a Prohibition Act sponsored by Lord Ivywood, stipulating that alcoholic drinks are to be sold only in selected premises designated by a pictorial sign, Humphrey Pump, landlord of the Old Ship Inn at Pebbleswick-on-Sea, and his friend, Captain Patrick Dalroy, a gigantic Irish adventurer late of the Royal Navy and sometime self-styled King of Ithaca, uproot the Old Ship sign and decamp with it and a big keg of rum and 'a great solid drum of a cheese'. They wander afield, setting up the inn sign temporarily outside whatever places they visit, thus making them appear premises entitled under the Act to serve alcohol. This compels amending legislation to be rushed through Parliament. Ivywood's teetotal enthusiasm is linked with a scheme for the unification of Christendom and Islam, a cause in which he gives patronage to Misysra Ammon, an itinerant advocate of temperance and vegetarianism who crazily traces back everything European to Moslem sources. Among those caught up in the fantastic narrative are Ivywood's relatives Lady Joan Brett, Lady Enid Wimpole and the Hon Dorian Wimpole ('Poet of the Birds'); Hibbs However, of the *Pebbleswick Globe*; the dog Quoodle and a donkey. The novel embodies several of Chesterton's best poems, including 'The Saracen's Head', 'Old Noah he had an Ostrich Farm', 'A Song Against Grocers', 'A Song about Vegetarianism', 'Nebuchadnezzar the King of the Jews', 'Mr Mandragon the Millionaire', 'The Song of Quoodle', 'St George for England', 'Feast on wine or fast on water', 'The town of Roundabout', 'The rolling English road', 'Who goes home?'.

Flying Officer X. Pseudonym used by H. E. *Bates for stories written during World War II.

Flyte, Lord Sebastian. Younger son of the Marquis of Marchmain in Evelyn Waugh's *Brideshead Revisited* (1945); brother of Lady Julia Flyte and younger sister Lady Cordelia.

Fogazzaro, Antonio (1842-1911). Born at Vicenza. Wrote many novels, from *Miranda* (1874) to *Leila* (1911) in which his chief aim was to bring the Catholic Church to face honestly the problems of the modern world. Though he reached an extensive international public with *Il Santo* (*The Saint*, 1906), considered his greatest novel, it was banned to Catholics by the Vatican authorities, who put it on the Index.

Fogerty, Elsie (1865-1945). Born at Sydenham, where she was educated privately until she went to Paris to study under the actor Coquelin *âiné*. She taught English and speech training in various schools during many years, and founded the Central School of Speech Training and Dramatic Art, which has continued the valuable work she pioneered. Her methods of verse and prose speaking ousted the artificialities of old-style elocution, and many actors and actresses as well as innumerable teachers were indebted to her, though on the stage the virtue of clear articulation was later abandoned.

For Lancelot Andrewes. Essays by T. S. *Eliot published in 1928. Lancelot Andrewes (1555-1626), a learned theologian and one of the translators engaged on the Authorized Version of the Bible, had been one of Queen Elizabeth's chaplains and successively Bishop of Chichester, Ely, and Winchester.

For Whom the Bell Tolls. Novel by Ernest *Hemingway published in 1940. An American university lecturer in Spanish from Montana, Robert Jordan, serving with the Republicans in Spain during the Civil War, is instructed to blow up a bridge across a gorge. The explosion is to be timed with absolute precision to prevent Falangist reinforcements using the bridge to oppose a Republican attack aiming to capture Segovia. The American joins a party of guerrillas camping at a cave in the mountains and led by Pablo, renowned as a military organizer. Those in the camp include Pablo's woman, Pilar; Maria, a young girl who has seen her parents executed by the enemy and has herself been subjected to multiple rape; Anselmo, an old peasant and faithful guide; Rafael, a gipsy, and others; while in a post higher up the mountain are eight men under El Sordo. Despite his past record as a ruthlessly committed Republican, Pablo is now regarded with suspicion by his companions, even by Pilar, who assumes the leadership of the party. Pablo is consequently in immediate danger of being killed by one or other of his associates as a potential traitor. With the encouragement of Pilar, Robert Jordan and Maria become lovers, and through her passionate devotion the girl's state of shock due to her dreadful experiences is relieved. A troop of Falangist cavalry supported by aircraft annihilate El Sordo's group before Jordan is ready to call on their aid in his mission; and when the time is approaching, it is found that Pablo has stolen the exploder and detonators from the dynamite packs and decamped. Anselmo, sent to watch the road, reports the passing of guns and vehicles, indicating that the Falangists are well prepared for the Republican attack. Jordan dispatches a warning to headquarters, but a crazed commissar holds up the message until it is too late to countermand the attack. Pablo, having relented, returns and confesses that he has thrown the stolen articles into the river. Jordan proceeds with his mission, employing bombs to explode the dynamite. The bridge is destroyed, but Anselmo and others are killed in the operation, and Jordan, while retreating, is thrown from his horse with a fractured thigh and, unable to escape, lies with a submachine gun ready to kill before he is himself killed by the enemy. The title is from John Donne's Devotions (XVII): 'Any man's death diminishes me, because I am involved in Mankind; And therefore never send to know for whom the bell tolls; it tolls for thee.'

Forbes, Rosita (*née* Joan Rosita Torr, 1893-1967; married Colonel Ronald Forbes). Spent years in expeditions to many countries, producing unconventional travel books based on her experiences: e.g. *From Red Sea to Blue Nile* (1925), *Sirocco* (1927), *Conflict: Angora to Afghanistan* (1931), *A Unicorn in the Bahamas* (1939). Also wrote several novels and three autobiographical volumes: *Gypsy in the Sun* (1944), *Appointment with Destiny* (1946), *Appointment in the Sun* (1950).

Forbes-Robertson, Sir Johnston. *See* Forbes *Robertson.

Ford, Ford Madox. Under this name Ford Madox *Hueffer published some of his best work, notably the sequence of war novels centred on the character named Christopher Tietgens: *Some Do Not* (1924), *No More Parades* (1925), *A Man Could Stand Up* (1926), *Last Post* (1928): republished with the collective title *Parade's End* (1950-51). He also used this name for travel books, reminiscences, other novels, and a vast collection of literature from Confucius to modern times *The March of Literature* (1939). He founded the *transatlantic review* in Paris 1924, having earlier (1908 and after) been the benefactor of Conrad, Masefield, and others as founder-editor of *The *English Review*.

Forester, C. S. (Cecil Scott Forester, 1899-1966). Born in Cairo; educated in London at Dulwich College; studied medicine at Guy's Hospital but turned to writing. An ironically conceived crime novel, *Payment Deferred* (1926); a powerful story of individual courage and endurance in World War I, *Brown on Resolution* (1929); other fiction and two biographies were followed by *Death to the French* (1932) and *The Gun* (1933), historical novels of the Peninsular War. In 1937 came the first of the series of Hornblower novels on which Forester's reputation and success were chiefly founded: *The Happy Return* (1937), *Flying Colours* (1938), *A Ship of the Line* (1938)—later gathered into a single-volume trilogy as *Captain Horatio Hornblower*. In spirit Hornblower

appears somewhat as a fictional recreation of Nelson, and various stages of his career are covered in *Lord Hornblower* (1946), *Mr Midshipman Hornblower* (1950), *Hornblower in the West Indies* (1958), etc. Among his other notable novels are *The *African Queen* (1935) and *The Ship* (1943). Though Forester's name seldom appears in formal literary histories, he combined the ability to give pleasure to a multitude of readers with the skill to write good and unpretentious prose. In *Long Before Forty* (published posthumously, 1967) he told of his life up to the age of thirty-one; and in 'Some Personal Notes' in the same volume is his account of the origin and progress of the Hornblower Cycle. *See also* *Ephesian.

Forman, Harry Buxton (1842-1917). Born in London; educated at Teignmouth; a senior official in the Post Office until 1907. He edited the works of Keats and his letters to Fanny Brawne, the works of Shelley, and wrote of Elizabeth Barrett Browning and others. After the literary forgeries of his friend T. J. *Wise were exposed, Forman was suspected by some investigators of having been involved, but no conclusive evidence appeared.

Format. The physical style in which a printed book is chosen (by publisher or designer) to appear: i.e. height and width of page, name and size of type, type-area on page etc, and general appearance.

Forster, E. M. (Edward Morgan Forster, 1879-1970). Educated at Tonbridge and Cambridge. He lived for a while in Italy and in 1921 became secretary to the Maharaja of Dewas Senior, an experience he described years later in *The Hill of Devi* (1953). His high place among the English novelists of this century is based on an unusually small output—*Where Angels Fear to Tread* (1905), *The *Longest Journey* (1907), *A *Room with a View* (1908), *Howards End* (1910), *A *Passage to India* (1924), *Maurice* (1972)—and two collections of short stories—*The *Celestial Omnibus* (1923) and *The Eternal Moment* (1928). He also wrote 'a domestic biography' of *Marianne Thornton* (1956). His contributions to periodicals, extended over many years, provided material for two collections of essays—*Abinger Harvest* (1926) and *Two Cheers for Democracy* (1951)—while *Aspects of the Novel* (1927) contains his Clark Lectures delivered at Cambridge in that year. An outcome of his official work in Egypt in World War I was *Alexandria: A History and a Guide* (1922), and in the following year *Pharos and Pharillon* appeared. One of his early visits to India had been with his friend of Cambridge student days, G. Lowes *Dickinson, whose biography he wrote in 1924. Although Forster was mostly thought of as an austere and withdrawn figure, his insistent theme was the human need to unify in personal relationships, expressed with characteristic verbal economy in 'only connect', words so bandied about by admirers as to become less a proverb than a cliché. The fame of *A Passage to India* was as much political as literary, for while it is absorbing in characterization and incident, its impact was made as a presentation of the deep-lying racial resentments between Indians and their overlords and overladies under British rule. The book probably did much to further the conviction that India must be made independent, since Forster's novel had a considerable vogue among British intellectuals. Forster was not by temperament inclined to sink his individuality in any corporate body, though he was often regarded as one of the *Bloomsbury Group in the post-1918 period. Among its members his reputation reached its peak, and his literary influence was strong on Virginia *Woolf. A spinsterish tone marks a good deal of his writing, and as a liberal in a period of decaying liberalism he was acutely and sadly conscious of clinging to a seemingly lost cause. The opinion that he was preeminently a novelists' novelist is doubtless correct, for his ironical subhumour, his muted prose style, and the largely unfictional nature of his fiction, reflective rather than inventive—these are qualities perceived and appreciated more by other writers than by unprofessional readers.

Forsyte Saga, The. Composite novel by John *Galsworthy published in 1922, assembling the following:
The Man of Property (1906). From their yeoman origins the Forsytes have, by hard work, hard saving, and shrewd investing, established themselves in the 1880s in houses around Hyde Park, and are taking a vigorous part in the life of the upper middle-classes in Victorian London. Timothy Forsyte retired from publishing when he was forty, and in his Bayswater Road house the family gather every Sunday afternoon to exchange news. Soames, a hard-headed solicitor who is the typical Forsyte of the next generation, buys land at Robin Hill, on the outskirts of London, on which to build a house for himself, his beautiful but antagonistic wife Irene, his collection of pictures—and in time, he hopes, his sons. Everything he possesses is, to him, *property*. He selects as architect for the new house Philip Bosinney, who is engaged to June, granddaughter of Jolyon, the eldest of the 'old' Forsytes. Soames's choice is disastrous. Irene and Bosinney fall in love; Soames sues the young architect for exceeding his estimates; Irene leaves Soames, but Bosinney is run over and killed in a fog. When June, still in love with Bosinney, begs her grandfather to buy Robin Hill and pay the costs of the lawsuit, he agrees and effects the purchase after Bosinney's death.
Interlude: Indian Summer of a Forsyte. By 1892 old Jolyon has been living at Robin Hill for three years with young Jolyon and his second wife and their children, Jolly and Holly. While the young Jolyons are on holiday in Spain with June, Old Jolyon meets Irene again and, like most men who know her, falls under the spell of her beauty. He takes her out in London, entertains her at Robin Hill, and arranges for her to give music lessons to Holly. He dies while he is waiting for her one afternoon, but has left her £15,000 in his Will.
In Chancery (1920). By 1899, when Roger Forsyte dies, the 'old' Forsytes are much depleted and the next generation in command. Soames is preoccupied by his problems as an undivorced man. He is now forty-five and longs for a son. He wishes to marry Annette, whose mother keeps a small French restaurant in Soho. He visits Irene, falls under her spell again, but is repulsed. Irene and Jolyon meet in Paris and Soames foists a divorce suit on them. They are now in love and do not defend the suit. The affairs of Soames's sister, Winifred Dartie, are troubling the family. Her husband, Monty, goes to South America with a dancer, taking Winifred's pearls. She brings an action for restitution of conjugal rights as a preliminary to divorce. This is felt as a disgrace by her son Val, particularly when he falls in love with his cousin Holly Forsyte. Monty returns and Winifred takes him back. Val and Jolly Forsyte go to fight in the Boer War, and Holly goes out as a nurse. Jolly is killed, Val

wounded, and news of Val and Holly's marriage reaches the family in England. Irene and Jolyon marry, and Soames marries Annette. On the day that her daughter is born, Soames's father, old James Forsyte, dies.

Interlude: Awakening. This is a brief account of Jon Forsyte's happy childhood with his parents, Jolyon and Irene, at Robin Hill.

To Let (1921). By 1920 Fleur Forsyte, Soames's daughter, and Jon, Jolyon and Irene's son, are both nineteen. They know nothing of Forsyte history or of the feud between their families. They meet for the first time at June Forsyte's picture gallery off Cork Street and fall in love. Their feelings are strengthened when they meet again, and Fleur determines to find out about the family feud and to marry Jon whatever the opposition. She learns of Soames and Irene's former marriage from her mother's too-close friend, Prosper Profond. Keeping Jon in ignorance of this, she begs him to elope to Scotland with her. Jon tells his parents that he and Fleur are determined to marry, so Jolyon gives him the account of the family feud which he has written, and while Jon is still stunned by this, Jolyon dies suddenly from heart failure. Fleur does not regard this as a reason for their not marrying but after witnessing a meeting between Irene and Soames, the boy aligns himself with his mother. Fleur then rushes into a fashionable marriage with Michael Mont, a baronet's son who has been pursuing her. Jon goes off to see the world. Other Forsytes appear from time to time. June tries to help the young lovers. Monty Dartie is dead, so Soames and his family see more of Winifred and her young married daughter Imogen. Timothy, last of the old Forsytes, reaches the age of 100, and his death means the break-up of the family gathering-place in Bayswater Road.

The Forsyte chronicles continue in *A Modern Comedy* (1929) and conclude in *The End of the Chapter* (1934).

Fortune, Reginald. Amateur detective in stories by H. C. *Bailey.

Fortunes of Richard Mahony, The. Novel in three volumes by Henry Handel *Richardson: *Australia Felix* (1917), *The Way Home* (1925), *Ultima Thule* (1929); in one volume under the collective title, 1930. Young Dublin-born Richard Townshend Mahony, F.R.C.S., M.D., Edin., lured by 'the rose-

water romance of the English press', leaves his 'tidy little country practice' in England and emigrates to Australia at the time of the gold rush in the early 1850s. He tramps from Melbourne to Ballarat, where six months' digging for gold reduces him to skin and bone. Bartering his 'last pinch of gold-dust for a barrow-load of odds and ends', he opens the 'Diggers' Emporium'. A young friend, Purdy Smith, who has followed him as an emigrant, introduces him to Tilly and Jinny, daughters at Beamish's Family Hotel in Melbourne, where Mahony also meets Mary Turnbull, a girl from England on a visit to her brothers. She and Mahony marry, and the store at Ballarat prospers until he declines to support the diggers in militant action against the state authorities. Boycotted, he sells up, and is persuaded by his wife, more level-headed than himself, to set up in medical practice instead of retreating at once to England. Though an able practitioner, he alienates patients by his reserve and brusqueness. Morbidly sensitive to any suspicion of patronage or snobbery by upper-class acquaintances, he becomes virtually a recluse, and over the years grows more and more dominated by books, studying in solitude the contemporary conflict between science and religion and turning later to spiritualism. When the Mahonys' fortunes are at a low ebb, his shares in a seemingly dubious gold mine unexpectedly soar and make them rich. They return to Europe, where he lavishes gifts on Mary and spends improvidently. A telegram informing him that his financial agent has absconded calls him back alone to Australia, where he learns that he is ruined. He hides the full truth from Mary, who joins him with the son and twin daughters born late in their marriage. For the rest of his life he makes ill-directed attempts to get their affairs on to a firm basis again, but only Mary's commonsense and devotion hold off disaster until his complete mental and physical collapse forces her to take an ill-paid job as postmistress at a remote settlement, where she also tends her stricken husband in his last days. The Mahonys' tragic story is set amid a family and social chronicle introducing a large gallery of lesser characters.

47 Workshop. Name given to the experimental stage for playwriting and other drama students set up at Harvard by Professor G. P. *Baker. It operated for twenty years

(1905-25), Eugene *O'Neill being one of the future notable playwrights who began there.

Fougasse (pseudonym of Cyril Kenneth Bird, 1887-1965). Born in London; educated at Cheltenham and King's College, London; studied art and design, and took to drawing for periodicals when disabled in World War I. He joined the staff of *Punch,* became art editor in 1937, and editor in 1949 until 1953. His drawings were comic in themselves without aid from captions, and were much employed on commercial posters and in official publicity as well as in *Punch.* He collected his drawings in a succession of volumes from 1921 to 1947.

Four Freedoms, The. Speaking to Congress on 6 January 1941 President F. D. Roosevelt proclaimed that the four essential human freedoms are: freedom of speech and expression; freedom of worship; freedom from want; freedom from fear.

Four-letter words. Euphemistic term for nouns and verbs (not all confined to four letters) in the erotic vocabulary, long tabu in print and polite conversation, though in constant daily oral misuse as meaningless expletives. Regarded as obscene, but after the failure of the case against *Lady Chatterley's Lover* in 1960 they appeared increasingly in print, including the *Oxford English Dictionary (Supplement,* vol. I 1972).

Four Million, The. Volume of short stories by O. *Henry published in 1906. The title is a satirical counterblast to the New York social register's assumption that of the inhabitants of the American capital only the chosen Four Hundred were important. O. Henry drew his characters from the whole population. What is generally ranked as his best story, 'The *Gift of the Magi', is among the twenty-five in this collection.

Four Quartets. Poem in four parts by T.S. *Eliot: *Burnt Norton* (1936), *East Coker* (1940), *The Dry Salvages* (1941), *Little Gidding* (1942), intended by the author 'to be judged as a single work' and published together under the collective title in 1944. Accepted as Eliot's masterpiece, it treats 'a subject of extreme complexity, which is constantly eluding formulation in words', and the poem has consequently been regarded as impenetrably obscure by readers without time or patience or knowledge to explore and penetrate the depths of its

erudition. Inapt as it is for summarization or easy exposition, its beauties and profundities are only intermittently revealed in unmethodical reading, and require some such detailed and learned examination as is undertaken in *The Art of T. S. Eliot* (1949) by Helen Gardner, who analyses its diction, metrical structure, imagery, musical affinities, variations of locale, conceptions of time, philosophic and religious principles.

Fournier. *See* *Alain-Fournier.

Fourteen Points, The. In a statement to Congress on 8 January 1918 President Wilson set out the fourteen conditions on which the U.S. was prepared to make peace to end World War I. They included: Open covenants openly arrived at; Freedom of navigation; Removal of economic barriers; Establishment of a general association of nations.

Fourth Dimension. Time: 'a dimension in addition to the three dimensions length, breadth, and thickness that is assumed to exist in order to satisfy certain mathematical analogies and that in the theory of relativity constitutes the time coordinate used along with the rectangular coordinates x, y, z to locate a point' (*Webster's Third New International Dictionary,* 1961). Extended from the sphere of physics and mathematics to that of philosophy, and to supranormal experience and imaginative speculation, the Time theme absorbs attention in a number of modern literary works, among them H. G. Wells's *The *Time Machine,* Moberly and Jourdain's *An *Adventure,* J. W. Dunne's *An *Experiment with Time,* Balderston and Squire's *Berkeley Square,* J. B. *Priestley's 'time plays', and more intensively in Marcel Proust's *A la recherche du temps perdue (*Remembrance of Things Past).* And compare Kipling's story 'An error in the Fourth Dimension' included in *The Day's Work* volume.

Fowler, Francis George (1870-1918). Brother of H. W. *Fowler.

Fowler, H. W. (Henry Watson Fowler, 1858-1933). Educated at Rugby and Oxford. Taught for some years at Sedburgh School until 1899; thereafter, in collaboration with his brother Francis George Fowler, produced *The King's English* (1906) which, represented as *A Dictionary of Modern English Usage* in 1926, became world-famous as a standard of reference for writers of English everywhere, though by the 1950s those who favoured a more flexible or even a looser style dissented from certain features of 'correctness' in Fowler which they regarded as academic quirks and prejudices.

Fowler, Sydney (pseudonym of Sydney Fowler Wright, 1874-   ). Educated at High School in Birmingham and practised in that city as an accountant for some twenty-five years before turning to authorship as poet, novelist, biographer and anthologist. His many novels include *The Island of Captain Sparrow* (1928), *The Siege of Malta* (1942), while *The Bell Street Murders* (1931) and *Who Killed Reynard?* (1947) are among his large output of crime fiction.

Foyle, W. A. (William Alfred Foyle, 1885-1963). Born in London; educated at Owen's School, Islington. After failing for the Civil Service, he and his brother Gilbert started as booksellers, and after a modest start elsewhere opened premises in Charing Cross Road which expanded progressively until the firm of W. & G. Foyle claimed to be 'The World's Greatest Bookshop'. Later activities included the monthly Literary Luncheons organized by W. A. Foyle's daughter Christina, with celebrated authors as guests; book clubs and a lecture agency. In 1949 the William Foyle Annual Poetry Prize of £250 was founded.

Frame, Janet (1924-   ). Born in Dunedin, New Zealand; educated in Otago. Lived for a while in England. Wrote some poetry, but chiefly novels: *Owls Do Cry* (1957), *Faces in the Water* (1961), *The Edge of the Alphabet* (1962), *Scented Gardens for the Blind* (1963), *The Adaptable Man* (1965), *See* *New Zealand Writers.

France, Anatole (pseudonym of Jacques Anatole François Thibault, 1844-1924). Born in Paris; received a classical education at a Jesuit college, but became a sceptic later. He achieved distinction as one of the leading French novelists, and most of his books became popular in England in translations, the best known being: *The Crime of Sylvestre Bonnard* (1906), *Thaïs* (1909), *Penguin Island* (1909), *The Gods are Athirst* (1912), *The Revolt of the Angels* (1914), *The Man who Married a Dumb Wife* (1915). He spent many years on *The Life of Joan of Arc* (1909) and published several volumes of essays *On Life and Letters* (1911, 1914, 1922, 1924).

In the Preface to *La Vie litteraire* he wrote: 'Le bon critique est celui qui raconte les aventures de son âme au milieu des chefs-d'oeuvre.' (The good critic is he who relates the adventures of his soul among masterpieces.)

France, Ruth (1913-68). Born in North Canterbury, New Zealand; educated there and in Australia. Worked as a librarian and yacht-hand. Author of novels—*The Race* (1958), *Ice Cold River* (1961); books of verse (under the pseudonym Paul Henderson)—*Unwilling Pilgrim* (1955), *The Halting Place* (1961). See *New Zealand Writers.

Francis, M. E. (pseudonym of Mrs Francis Blundell, née M. E. Sweetman, c. 1855-1930). Born near Dublin; educated at home and in Brussels; settled in Lancashire. Author of many novels including *The Duenna of a Genius* (1898), *Galatea of the Wheatfield* (1909), *Many Waters* (1922), *The Evolution of Oenone* (1928).

Frankau, Gilbert (1884-1952). Educated at Eton. His mother was the novelist who wrote as Frank *Danby. Having been invalided after serving in Belgium and France in World War I, he settled to writing, first with novels in verse and other poems (*Poetical Works*, 1923), then with prose fiction: *The Love Story of Aliette Brunton* (1922) and other novels, but becoming best known with *Peter Jackson, Cigar Merchant* (1919), in which he was on familiar ground, since he had spent some time before the war in the family cigar business. In World War II he served in the R.A.F. Later titles include *Oliver Trenton K.C.* (1951). Autobiography: *Self-Portrait* (1939).

Frankau, Joan. Sister of Gilbert Frankau. See Joan *Bennett.

Frankau, Pamela (1908-67). Daughter of Gilbert Frankau above. Author of novels and short stories, including *The Marriage of Harlequin* (1927), *The Willow Cabin* (1949), *The Winged Horse* (1953), *The Bridge* (1957), *The Road Through the Woods* (1960), *Slaves of the Lamp* (1965); also *I Find Four People* (autobiography, 1935). In *Pen to Paper: A Novelist's Notebook* (1961) she describes her writing methods and some of its incidental embarrassments.

Frapp, Nicodemus. Baker cousin, called 'Uncle', of George Ponderevo in H. G. Wells's *Tono-Bungay* (1909). The atmosphere of pious hypocrisy and squalor disgusts George when he is compelled to live with the Frapp family.

Fraser, Lady Antonia (*née* Pakenham, 1932-). Daughter of the Earl of *Longford; educated at Ascot and Oxford. Author of biographies—*Mary Queen of Scots* (1969), *Cromwell* (1973)—and various books for children.

Fraser, Ronald (Sir Arthur Ronald Fraser, 1888-1974; knighted 1949). Educated at St Paul's School. Disabled in World War I. He rose to senior rank in the Civil Service and held diplomatic appointments in Buenos Aires and Paris, 1933-49. Wrote more than twenty novels, including *The Flying Draper* (1924), *Landscape with Figures* (1925; 1952), *Rose Anstey* (1930), *A House in the Park* (1937), *Sun in Scorpio* (1949), *Bell from a Distant Temple* (1954), *City of the Sun* (1961); also *Latin America: A Personal Survey* (1953).

Frazer, J. G. (Sir James George Frazer, 1854-1941; knighted 1914). Born in Glasgow; educated at Helensburgh, and at the Universities of Glasgow and Cambridge; studied law in London and was called to the Bar, but did not practise. He wrote essays (*Sir Roger de Coverley and other Literary Pieces*, 1920; etc) and edited and translated Ovid and other classical writers, but his main life-work was as an anthropologist, becoming world-renowned as the author of numerous books on that subject. His major work *The *Golden Bough* is a masterpiece as a unique contribution to anthropological study and as literature, since Frazer was an eminent prose writer. First issued in sixteen volumes between 1890 and 1915, *The Golden Bough* was abridged for a one-volume edition in 1922.

free association. A method of proceeding mentally from one word or idea to another randomly suggested by it though apparently unrelated, and so in sequence until some psychologically productive result is achieved, a method used in psychoanalysis. Its analogues in literature are *stream of consciousness and *interior monologue.

free verse. Poetry governed only by rhythm, and avoiding metre, rhyme, and stanzaic structure. It aims to overthrow the barriers between natural speech rhythms and poetic diction. The supreme master of free verse is Walt Whitman (*Leaves of Grass*, 1855).

Freeman, Austin (Richard Austin Freeman, 1862-1943). Born in London; studied at the Middlesex Hospital Medical School, qualified as surgeon and physician. Held surgical appointments in West Africa and joined an expedition upon which his first book, *Travels and Life in Ashanti and Jaman* (1898), was based. Returning to England he held other surgical and medical posts until bad health forced his retirement. From 1905 he was a full-time writer of crime novels, with Dr John Thorndyke as amateur detective of a type then new in fiction. Thorndyke uses methods of detection depending upon accurate scientific data, and Freeman's books are as much studies in forensic medicine as mysteries of crime: often their attraction comes not from discovering the identity of the criminal, but from following Thorndyke's step-by-step scientific investigation.

Freeman, H. W. (Harold Webber Freeman, 1899-). Born in Essex; educated at the City of London School and Oxford. Utilized experience as a farm-worker in his novels: *Joseph and His Brethren* (1928), *Down in the Valley* (1930), *Chaffinch's* (1941), *The Poor Scholar's Tale* (1954).

Freeman, John (1880-1929). Born in Dalston, London; educated in Hackney; started work as boy clerk in a large insurance organization of which he eventually became secretary. Before he was thirty he published his first volume of poems, followed by several others included in *Collected Poems* (1928). He did not reach as wide an audience as some of his friends among the poets of the period, but contemporary critics regarded him as one of the best of the Georgians. He wrote studies of *George *Moore* (1922) and *Herman Melville* (1926), and other prose works.

Freeman, Kathleen. See Mary *Fitt.

Freeman, M. E. (*née* Mary Eleanor Wilkins; Mrs Charles Manning Freeman; 1852-1930). Born in Massachusetts; educated privately and at boarding school in Vermont. Author of about twenty volumes of short stories, a dozen novels, and a few books of verse—all popular in their time.

Fremantle, Anne (*née* Anne Jackson; married the Hon Christopher Fremantle 1910). Born in France; educated at Cheltenham and Oxford; became an American citizen in 1947. Contributor to leading English periodicals; special correspondent of *The Times* in Moscow 1936. Author of biographies of *George Eliot* (1931) and others; novels, poems, etc. and editor of *The Wynne Diaries* (1935-37).

French, Alice. *See* Octave *Thanet.

French, Inspector. Scotland Yard detective in crime novels by Freeman Wills *Crofts.

French Academy (L'Académie française). Founded in Paris in 1634 under the aegis of Cardinal Richelieu, with forty members, the number to which it is still limited. Its original purpose was to perfect the French language. Its members have included many of France's greatest men of letters, but men prominent in other professions may now be elected by the remaining members when a vacancy occurs. The official green uniform dates from 1801.

French, Paul. Pseudonym of Isaac *Asimov for *David Starr, Space Ranger* (1953), *Lucky Starr and the Pirates of the Asteroids* (1954).

Freud, Sigmund (1856-1939). Born in Freiburg, Moravia; studied medicine in Vienna, graduated in 1881, then specialized in neurology, and later studied psychopathology in Paris. He used hypnosis in the treatment of hysteria, but turned from this to a method of 'free association' in which the patient in a relaxed condition was encouraged to utter whatever came spontaneously into consciousness without rational control. This treatment and the interpretation of dreams Freud named 'psychoanalysis'. He laid strong emphasis on the part played by the unconscious in individual development, and originated the theory of infantile sexuality and the *Oedipus complex. His published works include *The Interpretation of Dreams* (1900), *The Psychopathology of Everyday Life* (1904), *Three Contributions to the Sexual Theory* (1905), *Beyond the Pleasure Principle* (1920), *The Ego and the Id* (1923). Freud's theories and later developments of and diversions from them have had a revolutionary influence on belief and morals and consequently in literature. The writings of, among many others, James *Joyce, T. S. *Eliot, and their followers must have been profoundly different but for the almost universal percolation of Freudianism.

Freya of the Seven Isles: A Story of Shallow Waters. By Joseph *Conrad, included with two other stories in '*Twixt Land and Sea* (1912). Neilson, a Dane, called by all his English acquaintances 'old Nelson', worked out East for English firms for many years before retiring with his daughter Freya to an island in the Dutch East Indies, part of a group named the Seven Isles. Timid of the power of the Dutch authorities to dispossess him, and aware of their suspicion and detestation of Englishmen, Neilson 'did not look with a favourable eye' on young Jasper Allen, captain and owner of a sailing vessel, the brig *Bonito,* which he bought in dirty and neglected condition and transformed into a thing of beauty. Jasper and Freya fall in love and both are also deeply in love with the *Bonito,* which is to be their home together when they marry. Neilson persuades himself that Jasper is 'just company' for Freya, that he amuses the girl, nothing more. Knowing that her father would never allow her peaceably to marry an Englishman, Freya makes Jasper agree to a runaway match when she is twenty-one, a wait of two years. Meanwhile she is pursued by a gross middle-aged Dutch naval lieutenant, Heemskirk, in command of the gunboat *Neptun.* Maliciously jealous when he sees Freya kissing Jasper, he attempts to make love to her, and has his face soundly slapped. In revenge he waylays the *Bonito* and, alleging that there is 'something fishy' about Jasper's business, insists on towing the brig to Makassar for investigation. On the way he deliberately runs the *Bonito* immovably on to a reef, where it slowly breaks up. Heemskirk reports the loss as an accident, and also accuses Jasper of gun-running. The guns have in fact been stolen and sold up-river by Schultz, the drunken mate of the *Bonito* who, remorseful, hangs himself. Robbed of the ship they loved and of the prospect of marriage, Jasper wastes into 'a skeleton in dirty clothes', spending his days on 'a lonely spit of sand' watching the brig become a grey ghost of a wreck. Freya, lonely and without hope, her vitality sapped by anaemia, contracts pneumonia and dies in Hong Kong.

Froebel, Friedrich Wilhelm August (1782-1852). German originator of a system of education which aims to ensure the natural and spontaneous growth of children's minds. He opened an orphanage, trained teachers there, and spent the last fifteen years or so of his life organizing kindergarten schools.

Frome, Ethan. Central character in Edith Wharton's *Ethan Frome* (1911); married to

Zeena (Zenobia) Frome.

Frost, Robert (Robert Lee Frost, 1874-1963). Born in San Francisco; taken to Lawrence, Mass., after the death of his father in 1884, and attended school there before spending a year at Dartmouth College, which he left voluntarily to work in a cotton mill. In 1897, three years after he married, he took a two-year course at Harvard. Having failed as a farmer in New Hampshire, he migrated with his wife and young daughters to England in 1912 and farmed there for three years, returning to the U.S. in 1915, again to farm, though for the remainder of his life he was much sought by American colleges and universities as a visiting lecturer and poet-in-residence. While still a schoolboy, he had felt that his true vocation was as a poet, and while in England he met most of the young poets. Friendship there with Edward *Thomas was a natural consequence of affinity between their poetic outlook and manner of expression. It was in London that his first books of verse were published— *A Boy's Will* (1913), *North of Boston* (1914). Through his New England father and Scottish-born mother he inherited tendencies and affections that gave his poetry a spare clarity and deepseated mystical quality, often below a deceptive but beautiful simplicity, rooted in ideals and traditions independent of current literary fashions. Though he was admired and affectionately regarded by most contemporaries—writers and readers—in the English-speaking lands, as a poet he stood apart through the timeless quality of his verse. *Complete Poems* (1949); *In the Clearing* (1962).

Fry, Christopher (pseudonym of Christopher Harris, 1907-   ). Born in Bristol; educated at Bedford. Some experience as a school teacher and much more as member and director of repertory companies in Bath, Tunbridge Wells, and Oxford culminated in success as a verse playwright, after initial failures. He had ambitions as an author from boyhood, and among his early ventures for the stage was the provision of material for a London revue. The first of his plays to be published was *The Boy with a Cart* (1939) written for a Sussex village church festival. *The Firstborn* (1946) received little attention, but *A Phoenix Too Frequent* (1946) made it evident that his verbal gifts and cultured humour offered something new and welcome in the English theatre. The promise was fulfilled in *The *Lady's Not for Burning* (1949), which had not only a prolonged stage success but also astonishingly large sales in book form. Its coruscating fountain of words caused him to be acclaimed by some as a new Christopher Marlowe, though he was rebuked by other critics to whom his Elizabethan eloquence and verve seemed betrayals of the literary puritanism which had been imposed on contemporary English verse by the innovations of T. S. *Eliot, by whom Fry had been influenced in his apprentice writings and whose ideals he appeared again to follow after *Venus Observed* (1950). Although *A Sleep of Prisoners* (1951) was praised as his best play by critics who had hitherto underrated him, he did not again display the imaginative force and verbal abundance which had made him unique. *The Dark is Light Enough* (1954) and *Curtmantle* (1961) attracted diminishing attention. In the intervals of original work he translated plays by *Anouilh (*The Lark, Ring Round the Moon*) and *Giraudoux (*Tiger at the Gates, Duel of Angels, Judith*) and worked on biblical and other film scripts. *The Lady's Not for Burning, Venus Observed, The Dark is Light Enough,* and *A Yard of Sun* (1970) represent the four seasons (spring, autumn, winter, summer).

Fry, Roger (Roger Eliot Fry, 1866-1934). Born in London; educated at Cambridge, where he took a science degree; then studied art in London and Paris. Director of the Metropolitan Museum of Art in New York, 1905-10. His interest in the works of Cézanne, Van Gogh, Gauguin and other modernist painters led him to organise in London in 1910 an exhibition of their pictures, applying to them the term he originated—*Post Impressionists. In 1913 he started the *Omega Workshops which had a strong influence on contemporary British art and design, and his writings were received by artists and by a proportion of the interested public as the gospel of new movements tending away from representational art and towards the abstract. Among close friends who helped to propagate his ideals were some of the *Bloomsbury Group, including Vanessa *Bell and her sister Virginia *Woolf who wrote Roger Fry's biography in 1940. In the last year of his life he was appointed Slade Professor of Fine Art in the University of Cambridge. His most widely read book is *Vision and Design* (1920); other writings

H

include *Giovanni Bellini* (1899), *Transformations* (1926), *Cézanne* (1927), *Henri Matisse* (1930), *Reflections on British Painting* (1934).

Fry, Ruth (Anne Ruth Fry, 1878-1962; sister of Roger Fry). Born at Highgate; educated principally at home. A lifelong member of the Society of Friends, her energies were devoted for some half-century to the international services of Quaker relief organizations and pacifist movements. She wrote *A Quaker Adventure* (1926), *Quaker Ways* (1937), *Everyman's Affair: A Plea for a Sane Peace* (1941), *Three Visits to Russia* (1942), and various other books and pamphlets.

Ftatateeta. Chief of the queen's women in Bernard Shaw's **Caesar and Cleopatra* (1900). She murders Pothinus by order of Cleopatra and is herself killed by Rufio.

Fulbright scholarships. Available to U.S. citizens with a college degree or its equivalent for an academic year's study in educational institutions in other countries, the language of which the applicant must know. The scholarships cover necessary transport, teaching fees, books, and maintenance. Named after Senator J. William Fulbright, who instigated the scheme put into action by the Fulbright Act of 1946.

Fulford, Roger (Roger Thomas Baldwin Fulford, 1902-   ). Educated at Lancing and Oxford. Member of *The Times* staff, 1933; lecturer in English, University of London, 1937-48. Author of historical and biographical works: *George IV* (1935), *The Prince Consort* (1949), *Queen Victoria* (1951), *Votes for Women* (1957; a history of the suffrage campaign), *Hanover to Windsor* (1960). Editor (with Lytton *Strachey) of *The Greville Memoirs* (1937).

Fuller, Roy (Roy Broadbent Fuller, 1912-   ). Born in Lancashire; educated at Blackpool. All his professional life was spent as a solicitor; wrote on the law and practice of Building Societies. From 1939 published much poetry written in his leisure: *Collected Poems*, 1962. Elected Professor of Poetry at Oxford, 1968-1973.

Furnivall, F. J. (Frederick James Furnivall, 1825-1910). Born in Surrey; educated privately and at the Universities of London and Cambridge. Helped to found (in 1854), and taught at, the Working Men's College. Secretary of the Philological Society from 1862, having in the previous year become Editor of the Society's *New English Dictionary* which developed into the *Oxford English Dictionary*. Founded the *Early English Text Society in 1864, and later the Chaucer, Ballad, New Shakespeare, Wiclif, Browning, and Shelley Societies.

Futurism. *See* Filippo Tommaso *Marinetti.

Fyleman, Rose (1877-1957). Born in Nottingham; educated at the University College there; studied singing in London and abroad; made some professional appearances and was for a while a teacher. From 1918, when her *Fairies and Chimneys* was published, she concentrated on the production of verse, short plays and stories, mainly for children. Her many books include *The Rainbow Cat* (1922), *The Easter Hare* (1932), *Over the Tree Tops* (1949), and about fifty others.

G.B.S. Familiar designation of George Bernard *Shaw. The initials were used as his signature for much of his early journalism, on his many postcards, and in the title of the book presented by his friends on his ninetieth birthday: *G.B.S. 90*. He came to dislike his first name, saying 'I hate being George-d'.

G.K.C. The initials by which G. K. *Chesterton was customarily known.

Gaiety Theatre, Manchester. An old theatre bought and renovated by Miss A. E. F. *Horniman in 1908 as the home of the company she established there until 1917. The work done by her players and writers in those years constituted one of the most fruitful chapters in the history of modern English drama. Some two hundred plays were performed, the majority of them by living authors, and some specially written for 'Miss Horniman's Company' by local playwrights—Stanley *Houghton, Harold *Brighouse, Allan *Monkhouse and others of the group which became known as the Manchester School. Though it made an invaluable contribution to both entertainment and culture, it was financially unprofitable and the building ended as a cinema.

Galbraith, John Kenneth (1908-   ). Born in Ontario; educated at Toronto and California Universities. Professor of Economics, Harvard, from 1949; U.S. ambassador to India, 1961-63. *The *Affluent Society* (1958) made him internationally celebrated.

Gale, Zona (1874-1938). Born in Wisconsin; educated at the University there. Author of *Friendship Village* (1908), *Bridal Pond* (1930), and other volumes of short stories; several novels—*Mr Pitt* (1924), *Borgia* (1929), etc; a book of verse (*The Secret Way*, 1921); an autobiography, *When I Was a Little Girl* (1913) and *Portage, Wisconsin* (1928). Her chief success was *Miss Lulu Bett* (1920) a novel she dramatized in the same year.

Galley. Technical name for a printer's proof on which any corrections are to be made before the work proceeds to its next stage (page proof), prior to going on the printing machine. *See* *Proof corrections.

Gallup, George Horace (1901-   ). Born in Iowa. For many years Professor of Journalism in American universities. Founded the American Institute of Public Opinion in 1935 and established the Gallup Polls organization which spread to other countries and,

together with rival companies, made public opinion polls, by 'random sampling', a method of statistical forecasting of election results, testing customers' sales potential, preferences in radio and television programmes, etc.

Galsworthy, John (1867-1933). Born at Kingston, Surrey; educated at Bournemouth, Harrow, and Oxford. Studied law and was called to the Bar in 1890, but practised only for a short time. He travelled widely as a young man, and became acquainted with Joseph *Conrad, ship's officer on one of the voyages, encouraging him to continue with his first novel. In 1905 Galsworthy married the divorced wife of his cousin, their association having begun some years earlier when her first marriage proved unhappy. These experiences are reflected in *The Man of Property* (1906) and the later novels which were to constitute *The *Forsyte Saga* (1922). Adopting the pseudonym John Sinjohn, Galsworthy began his writing career with *From the Four Winds* (1897), followed by *Jocelyn* (1898), *The Villa Rubein* (1900), and *A Man of Devon* (1901). *The Island Pharisees* (1904) and all its successors were published under his own name. He was moved throughout life by an acute sense of social justice, and though he aimed to hold the balance fairly between rich and poor, between the powerful and the helpless, his emotions were always engaged on the side of the underdog. He saw human existence in terms of the hunters and the hunted: with varying emphasis and in a variety of guises this is the theme of the majority of his novels and plays. In addition to *The Forsyte Chronicles*, which embrace the *Saga* and some dozen or so other novels and shorter stories, Galsworthy's prose fiction includes *The Country House* (1907), *The Patrician* (1911), *The Dark Flower* (1913), *The Freelands* (1915), and the collection of his short stories *Caravan* (1925). He was equally prolific as a dramatist who for many years rivalled Bernard *Shaw and J. M. *Barrie in popularity and shared with them the attentive notice of dramatic and literary critics. *The *Silver Box* (1906), *Strife* (1909), *Justice* (1910), and *The *Skin Game* (1920) are in lasting interest of subject matter and in technical skill the best of his many plays. Fickleness of literary fashion led to the rapid decline of Galsworthy's reputation in the decades following his death, though it seems improbable that the plays named above will remain permanently neglected; and in spite of critical and academic disfavour *The Forsyte Saga* continued to be widely read, even before it became in the late 1960s the most popular and lengthiest of all television serials, causing some clergy to change their service times so that the congregation should not miss any of the twenty-six Sunday evening instalments. Independently of its literary merits or demerits, this sequence of novels preserves a view of the Edwardian upper middle class which social historians will not undervalue.

Galton, Sir Francis. *See* *Finger prints.

Gamesmanship. *See* Stephen *Potter.

Garden family, The. In Rose Macaulay's *Told by an Idiot* (1923): The Rev. **Aubrey** Garden who in a succession of changes of belief moves from Anglicanism to Romanism, Dissent, Agnosticism, Ethicism, Theosophy, Christian Science, Spiritualism, Higher Thought; **Victoria**, his eldest daughter, marries, has a large family, thinks life 'certainly a comedy', and becomes in middle age 'a merry, skimming matron'; **Maurice** marries (and after many years happily divorces) a 'silly, common, nagging wife', and becomes editor of the *Gadfly*, a left-wing periodical; **Rome**, temporarily shaken out of her cultivated attitude of detachment by a tragically-ended love, brightens her later years by observing 'the cheerful spectacle of a world of fools': **Stanley**, before and after her marriage and divorce, supports 'movements' and fights for 'causes'; **Irving** marries a titled girl and makes a fortune; **Una** achieves happiness and serenity as a prosperous farmer's wife.

Gardiner, A. G. (Alfred George Gardiner, 1865-1946). Born at Chelmsford. After experience in provincial journalism he joined the *Daily News* and was its editor, 1902-19. One of the last of the great editors, he was also one of the last periodical essayists with the gift of combining lucidity, readability, and a naturally graceful prose style. The essays he contributed to *The Star* (the evening paper allied to the *Daily News*) were written under the pseudonym Alpha of the Plough and collected in *Pebbles on the Shore* (1916), *Leaves in the Wind* (1918), *Windfalls* (1920), *Many Furrows* (1924). Under his own name he wrote *Prophets, Priests, and Kings* (1908; essays on eminent contemporaries.)

Gardner, Dame Helen (1908-   ). Educated in London and Oxford; became University Lecturer, London and Oxford, and in 1966 Merton Professor of English Literature, University of Oxford. D.B.E. 1967. Author of *The Art of T. S. Eliot* (1949), *The Divine Poems of John Donne* (1952), *The Business of Criticism* (1960); edited the *New Oxford Book of English Verse 1250-1950* (1972).

Gardner, Erle Stanley (1889-1970). Born in Massachusetts; practised as a lawyer in California for over twenty years. In 1932 he began the series of crime novels with as their almost invariable climax, a court scene in which Perry Mason, advocate for the defence, outwits the prosecuting attorney and exposes the real criminal. The three stock characters —Perry Mason himself, his secretary Della Street, and the private detective he employs, Paul Drake—though hardly more than puppets, are likeable puppets, and the cases in which they become involved always provide a gripping narrative. Already popular with a multitude of readers, the Perry Mason cases captured audiences millions strong on television. Of Gardner's hundred or so novels, varying little in quality, only the first and one of the more recent can be named here: *The Case of the Velvet Claws* (1932), *The Case of the Glamorous Ghost* (1955).

Gardner, Frank. Son of the Rev. Samuel Gardner who, when young and before ordination, had been one of Mrs Warren's lovers in Bernard Shaw's *Mrs Warren's Profession* (1893-94). Since the paternity of Vivie Warren is not known, it is maliciously alleged that she is Frank's half-sister.

Garland, Hamlin (Hannibal Hamlin Garland, 1860-1940). Born in Wisconsin; educated in Iowa. Author of *Main-Travelled Roads* (1891) and other collections of short stories; *A Member of the Third House* (1892) and other novels, and, outstandingly, *A Son of the Middle Border* (1917).

Garnett, Constance (*née* Constance Black, 1861-1946, married Edward *Garnett). Educated at Brighton and Cambridge. Renowned for her many translations of Russian masterpieces by Turgenev, Dostoevsky, Chekhov, Gogol, and Tolstoy.

Garnett, David (1892-   ). Born in Brighton;

educated privately and at the Royal College of Science. Started a London bookselling business in 1919. In 1920 he had great success with his short fantasy novel *Lady Into Fox, its originality being not quite matched by *A Man in the Zoo* (1924) and *The Grasshoppers Come* (1931). His subsequent novels were closer to traditional intellectual fiction. *A Rabbit in the Air* (1932) deals with his first efforts as an aviator. His grandfather was Richard *Garnett and his parents Edward *Garnett and Constance *Garnett.

Garnett, Edward (Edward William Garnett, 1868-1937). Born in London; educated privately. Becoming a publishers' reader and literary adviser, he was the discoverer and encourager of numerous authors, among them Joseph *Conrad. Garnett's own writings were secondary to those he helped others to produce: they include *Hogarth* (1911), *Turgenev* (1917), a volume of essays *Friday Nights* (1922), and *The Trial of Jeanne d'Arc and other Plays* (1931). *And see* James *Byrne.

Garnett, Prosperine. *See* *Prosperine Garnett.

Garnett, Richard (1835-1906). Educated privately. At the age of twenty-two he joined the library staff of the British Museum and from 1875 to 1890 was Superintendent of the Reading Room. He wrote short lives of Milton, Carlyle, and Emerson, a *History of Italian Literature*, and a volume of poems, but his only surviving book is *The Twilight of the Gods* (1888), a collection of short stories.

Garvin, J. L. (James Louis Garvin, 1868-1947). Born in Birmingham. After some twenty years of varied journalistic experience in the provinces and London, he became Editor of the virtually moribund Sunday *Observer* and almost overnight turned it into one of the most influential newspapers of the period, remaining Editor until 1942. A notable feature was his forceful leading article each week in rhetorical prose and of exceptional length. But while his political opinions were strong, they did not exclude the enlightened interest in literature and the other arts which made his paper required reading for a large non-political following. He wrote a *Life of Joseph Chamberlain* (3 vols, 1932-34) and was Editor-in-Chief of the 13th-14th editions of the *Encyclopaedia Britannica*.

Gascoyne, David (1916-). Born in Salisbury;

educated at the Cathedral Choir School there, and in London. Influenced by French *surrealist poets. Author of *The Vagrant* (1950), *Night Thought* (1956), and other verse.

Gate Theatre, Dublin. Founded in 1928 to present a wider range of plays than those at the *Abbey Theatre, which were almost wholly concerned with Irish themes. The Gate produced masterpieces of all countries and periods.

Gate Theatre, London. Founded in 1925 as an experimental theatre for the production of plays appealing to a limited audience and impracticable for the commercial theatres. Run on a membership basis and ranking as a private theatre, it was able to present plays (such as the *Lysistrata* of Aristophanes) to which the Lord Chamberlain's licence for public performance would not be granted. Revues noted for their satirical wit were also staged. The premises (in one of the railway arches in Villiers Street, leading from Charing Cross main-line station to the Thames Embankment) were much damaged during World War II.

Gatsby, Jay, born James Gatz, in Scott Fitzgerald's *The *Great Gatsby* (1926).

Gauguin, Paul (Eugène Henri Paul Gauguin, 1848-1903). Born in Paris, son of a French journalist and a Peruvian Creole mother. He married and became a prosperous stockbroker, painting in his spare time. In the late 1880s he left his wife and family and spent the rest of his life as a painter in various places, settling finally in Tahiti from 1895 and living as a native. In Somerset Maugham's novel *The *Moon and Sixpence* (1919) Charles Strickland is a fictional projection of Gauguin.

Gaunt, William (1900-). Born in Hull; educated there and at Oxford; travelled widely in Europe. Author of *Bandits in a Landscape*, a study of romantic painting (1937), *The Pre-Raphaelite Tragedy* (1942), *The Aesthetic Adventure* (1945), *The Study of Sculpture* (1957); topographical books: *Chelsea* (1954), *Kensington* (1958), *London* (1961); *The Lady in the Castle* (novel, 1956).

Gawsworth, John (pseudonym of Terence Ian Fytton Armstrong, 1912-1970). Poet, critic, and editor. *Collected Poems* (1948); *Ten Contemporaries* (two series: 1932; 1933); editor of the *English Digest* (1939-41) and other periodicals including *The Poetry Review*, 1948-52; compiled numerous anthologies.

Gay Science, The. A discussion of criticism by Eneas Sweetland *Dallas published in 1866. It declared that 'the immediate end of art is to give pleasure'. Though still not widely known, the book has been frequently praised and commended in the present century.

Geddes, Sir Patrick (1854-1932; knighted 1932). Born in Perth; educated at the Universities of London, Edinburgh, and Paris. Professor of Botany at University College, Dundee, 1889-1914. A many-sided man, his works included *The Evolution of Sex* (1889) and influential writings on town-planning: *A Study in City Development* (1904), and *Cities in Evolution* (1913).

Genet, Jean (1910-). First attracting notice by a disorderly life, he later became renowned as one of the *black-comedy playwrights with *The Maids* (*Les Bonnes*, 1945), *The Balcony* (*Le Balcon*, 1956), and *The Blacks* (*Les Nègres*, 1958). His novel *Our Lady of the Flowers* (*Notre-Dame des fleurs*, 1943) and autobiography, *The Thief's Journal* (*Journal du voleur*, 1949) also received considerable attention.

Genoux. Lady Slane's devoted French maid in V. Sackville-West's *All Passion Spent* (1931). She becomes housekeeper and companion when widowed Lady Slane retires to Hampstead.

Gentleman Brown. Nickname of a rapacious scoundrel in Joseph Conrad's *Lord Jim* (1900). He is responsible for the death of *Dain Waris and indirectly for that of Jim.

Gentleman in the Parlour, The. 'A Record of a Journey from Rangoon to Haiphong' by W. Somerset *Maugham, published in 1930. The title comes from the author's first reading of Hazlitt's essays, where he found the phrase in 'On Going a Journey'. In a 1935 Preface, Maugham remarks that a book of travel gives its author an opportunity to write 'prose . . . cultivated for its own sake', and *The Gentleman in the Parlour* is one of his most conscientious endeavours in a cultivated prose style. Though there is much about the places visited during this journey through Burma, Siam, Cambodia, and Annam, the narrative is enlivened by conversations with persons encountered *en*

route and by observations and reflections on a variety of matters.

Gentleman with a Duster, A. *See* Harold *Begbie.

Gentlemen Prefer Blondes: The Illuminating Diary of a Professional Lady. Novel by Anita *Loos published in 1925, farcically satirizing the 'gold-digging' young women of the period. Lorelei, a semi-illiterate film extra with a gentleman friend 'who is known practically all over Chicago as Gus Eisman the Button King', collects diamonds from him and a complete set of Joseph Conrad's works from another gentleman friend who is an English novelist and says she reminds him quite a lot of Helen of Troy. She takes to reading good books to improve her mind, and is given a trip to Europe with Dorothy, her girl friend, so that she can become more educated. She finds Dorothy unrefined, and is upset because Dorothy goes around 'with gentlemen who do not have anything' instead of with one who is 'really quite wealthy and can make a girl delightful presents'. On the boat Lorelei extracts secret information about new aeroplanes from an American and passes it on to an English agent. The two girls spend some time in London, where they are introduced to titled ladies who all try to sell them something—bead headbands, a dog, a portrait said to be by Whistler—but Lorelei's interest is aroused by nothing but a diamond tiara for 7,500 dollars which she cajoles Piggie (her name for Sir Francis Beekman) into buying for her, before she and Dorothy take off for Paris, which 'must be much more educational than London'; but she finds French gentlemen's politeness unproductive, 'because kissing your hand may make you feel very very good but a diamond and safire bracelet lasts forever'. Most of their time in Paris is occupied in outings with Lady Beekman's solicitors, who are engaged to recover the diamond tiara Piggie has given Lorelei. The two go on to the 'central of Europe', where Lorelei has a session with 'Dr Froyd' in Vienna. She takes up with wealthy Henry H. Spoffard, who always gets his photo in all the papers 'because he is always senshuring all of the plays that are not good for peoples morals', and in the end she marries him so that she and H. Gilbertson Montrose can spend their time working on a film scenario while Henry runs a Welfare League and gives his spiritual aid to the small-part film girls who tell him all their problems. For 'a girl like I', she decides, 'everything always turns out for the best'.

George, Daniel (pseudonym of Daniel George Bunting, 1890-1967). Essayist, critic, and anthologist: *Tomorrow Will Be Different* (1933), *All in a Maze* (1938), *A Book of Anecdotes* (1957), *A Book of Characters* (1959), *The Anatomy of Love* (1962), etc.

George, Monsieur. Central character in Joseph Conrad's *The *Arrow of Gold* (1919).

George, Stefan Anton (1868-1933). Educated in Berlin, Munich, and Paris. Up to 1914 he travelled over almost the whole of Europe, then settled in Germany until he went into exile in Switzerland, having refused the patronage of the Nazi rulers. A volume of his poems appeared in English translation in 1943.

George, W. L. (Walter Lionel George, 1882-1926). Born in Paris; educated there and in Germany. Acted as special correspondent for various English newspapers. His writings included *The Making of an Englishman* (1914) and other novels; *Anatole France* (1915), *The Intelligence of Woman* (1917), *A Novelist on Novels* (1918), *A London Mosaic* (1921).

Georgian Poetry. Title of five anthologies of contemporary verse issued from the *Poetry Bookshop between 1912 and 1922. The early volumes were edited by (Sir) Edward *Marsh under the initials E.M. When literary fashions changed the previously acclaimed Georgian Poets were derided as 'the weekend school', though a number of the still-approved poets were among them.

Gerhardie, William (William Alexander Gerhardie, 1895-   ). Born in St Petersburg; educated there and at Oxford. British Military Attaché in Petrograd (formerly St Petersburg; now Leningrad) 1917-18; served with the British Military Mission in Siberia, 1918-20. He wrote *Anton Chehov: A Critical Study* in 1923, following a novel in which he had skilfully infused into English prose the tone and manner of Chehov: *Futility: A Novel on Russian Themes* (1922). Later novels included *The Polyglots* (1925), *Pending Heaven* (1930), *My Wife's the Least of It* (1938); *Pretty Creatures* (1927) is a collection of short stories. He also wrote *The Romanoffs: An Historical Biography* (1940), *Highlights of Russian History* (1949), *The Life and Times of Lord Beaverbrook*

(1964), and for a collected revised edition of his works in 1947 he provided an Introduction, 'My Literary Credo'.

Gethryn, Colonel Anthony. Detective in crime novels by Philip *MacDonald.

Ghosting. Writing books, articles, etc for another person whose name will appear as author. Sometimes a profitable form of hack-writing.

Gibbings, Robert (Robert John Gibbings, 1889-1958). Born in Cork; educated at University College, Cork; studied art in London. From 1924 to 1933 controlled the *Golden Cockerell Press; Lecturer in Book Production, University of Reading, 1936-42. He was one of the leaders in the contemporary revival of wood-engraving and illustrated many books, including his own, some of the latter being issued by the Press he directed, usually in limited editions. In 1940 he had his first popular success with *Sweet Thames Run Softly*, in which the robust charm of his literary style equalled the firm beauty of his engravings. These qualities were maintained in succeeding volumes: *Coming Down the Wye* (1942), *Lovely is the Lee* (1944), *Coming Down the Seine* (1953). Attractive though these records of European river voyages are, Gibbings was probably at his best when discoursing on and depicting more exotic scenes, the fruit of his travels in the South Seas: *Iorana!: A Tahitian Journal* (1932), *Blue Angels and Whales* (1938). *Over the Reefs and Far Away* (1948).

Gibbon, Lewis Grassic (pseudonym of James Leslie Mitchell, 1901-35). Born in Kincardineshire, educated at a local school and at Mackie Academy, Stonehaven. Work as a reporter and as airforce clerk was followed by an archaeological journey to the Maya region of Central America, and in 1928 he published *Hanno, or The Future of Exploration*. Encouraged by H. G. Wells he turned to short-story writing, which resulted in the collection called *Calends of Cairo* (1931). Two novels, *Stained Radiance* (1930) and *The Thirteenth Disciple* (1931) preceded his masterpiece, the trilogy (later collected in one volume as *A *Scots Quair*, 1946), *Sunset Song* (1932), *Cloud Howe* (1933), and *Grey Granite* (1934). For these and *Niger: The Life of Mungo Park* (1934) he used his pseudonym; his other writings, which included *The Conquest of the Maya* (1934), were issued under his own name.

Gibbons, Stella (Stella Dorothea Gibbons, 1902-   ). Born in London; educated at the North London Collegiate School and University College. Worked for ten years as a journalist. The resounding success she had with her first published novel, *Cold Comfort Farm* (1932), overshadowed the rest of her books, which included *Enbury Heath* (1935), *Nightingale Wood* (1938), *The Matchmaker* (1949), *Conference at Cold Comfort Farm* (1949), *The Swiss Summer* (1951), *Here Be Dragons* (1956), *The Weather at Tregulla* (1962), *Starlight* (1967), and other novels; several books of short stories, *Beside the Pearly Water* (1954) etc. Her *Collected Poems* appeared in 1950.

Gibbs, Cosmo. Brother of Sir Philip *Gibbs. *See* Cosmo *Hamilton.

Gibbs, Sir Philip (Philip Hamilton Gibbs, 1877-1962; knighted 1920). Educated privately. Spent some years as publisher's editor and as a journalist on the *Daily Mail* and other papers, coming into public prominence as a war correspondent with the armies in France and Belgium, 1914-18. His published works —fiction and non-fiction—are numerous, and include one of the best novels on journalistic life, *The Street of Adventure* (1909).

Gibson, W. W. (Wilfrid Wilson Gibson, 1878-1962). Born at Hexham, Northumberland; educated privately. His whole life was given to poetry, the chief characteristic of his massive output being the endeavour to provide a voice for the 'inarticulate poor'. He came into prominence with the 'Georgian' poets in the years preceding World War I, and with Lascelles *Abercrombie and Walter *de la Mare was one of the writers to whom Rupert *Brooke willed his property and the proceeds from his poems. Gibson's verse would be more effective if there were less of it: though genuinely compassionate for unfortunate, deprived, and suffering people, the 'voice' he provided became monotonous and reiterative. His *Collected Poems* (1926) drew upon a large number of preceding volumes, including *Stonefolds* (1907), *Daily Bread* (1910), *Fires* (1912), *Livelihood* (1917), *Neighbours* (1920), etc. Among later volumes were *The Golden Room and Other Poems* (1928), *Highland Dawn* (1932), *The Alert* (1942), and *Within Four Walls* (1950).

Gide, André (André Paul Guillaume Gide, 1869-1951). Born in Paris; educated privately and at the École Alsacienne. His early religious upbringing exercised a lifelong influence in conflict with a powerful innate strain of revolt from orthodox beliefs and morals, so that his life and writings reveal 'many of the antinomies upon which his dynamic equilibrium rests: the soul and the flesh, life and art, expression and restraint, the individual and society, classicism and romanticism, Christ and Christianity, God and the Devil' (*Columbia Dictionary of Modern European Literature*, 1947, p. 323). For a brief period he figured among the symbolist writers in Paris (*see* *Symbolism), before visiting North Africa and living at Biskra, where he acknowledged the homosexual impulses which had been a source of inner torment. He went to Central Africa in 1925 as an envoy of the French Colonial Ministry, the outcome being two books (translated into English and combined as *Travels in the Congo*, 1929) which led to important reforms. A visit to Russia in 1935 as a convinced Communist resulted in the disillusioned *Return from the U.S.S.R.* (1937). Gide's fictional and personal writings —the two kinds are rarely distinguishable— were frequently attacked as shamelessly immoral, though his stature as a European literary genius ceased to be disputed before his death. *Les Faux-Monnayeurs* (1926; in English as *The Counterfeiters,* 1927) is generally considered his outstanding novel. His *Essay on Montaigne* (1929) was his tribute to one in whom he recognized a sceptical spirit akin to his own. He also wrote on *Oscar Wilde* (1905) and *Dostoievsky* (1925). Among the other works by Gide translated into English are the autobiographical *If it Die* (1935) and *Journals* (4 vols, 1947-49).

Gideon, Superintendent (later **Commander**). Scotland Yard detective in crime novels by J. J. *Marric.

Gifford Lectures. Courses of lectures on natural theology and ethics delivered by invitation in Scottish universities, the lecturers nominated being eminent in theology and philosophy. The first course was delivered in 1888, funds for their foundation and continuance having been provided under the will of Adam Gifford (1820-87), Lord of Session. In their published form the Gifford Lectures have made substantial contributions to knowledge.

Gift of the Magi, The. Short story by O. *Henry included in *The *Four Million* (1906).

Having only one dollar and eighty-seven cents, Della, Mrs James Dillingham Young, is desolated because she hasn't money to buy a Christmas present for her young husband. They have two much-cherished possessions, his gold watch and her beautiful hair, which reaches below her knees when let down. She cuts off her hair, sells it for twenty dollars, and buys a platinum chain for Jim's watch. When he gets home on Christmas Eve he stares at her with a curious expression, then produces a package from his pocket. Della finds inside a set of combs, pure tortoise-shell with jewelled rims, which she had longed for—'just the shade to wear in the beautiful vanished hair'. She then holds out the platinum chain for his watch, only to find that he has sold it to get the money to buy the combs.

Gilbert, Anthony. Pseudonym used by Lucy Malleson for her detective novels: *Death at Four Corners* (1929), *The Man in Button Boots* (1934), *He Came by Night* (1944), *Snake in the Grass* (1954), and many others. *See also* Anne *Meredith.

Gilberte. *See* *Remembrance of Things Past.

Gilbey, Mr and **Mrs,** and their son **Bobby,** in Shaw's *Fanny's First Play* (1911).

Gilda. Central character in Noel Coward's *Design for Living* (1939).

Gill, Eric (Arthur Eric Rowton Gill, 1882-1940). Born in Brighton; educated there and at Chichester School of Art; apprenticed to a London architect, but turned to sculpture and lettering, becoming renowned as a stone-carver and as a designer of type-faces, particularly the Gill Sans Serif fount much used by publishers and commercial artists for books and display work. Gill was also an accomplished writer, mainly on topics embracing craftsmanship, social welfare and Christianity: *Clothes* (1931), *Beauty Looks After Herself* (1933), *Money and Morals* (1924), *Work and Leisure* (1935), *The Necessity of Belief* (1936), *Work and Property* (1937), *Autobiography* (listed by himself as *Autopsychography,* 1940). *See also* *Golden Cockerell Press.

Gilmore, Dame Mary (*née* Mary Cameron, 1865-1962; D.B.E. 1937). Born at Goulburn, N.S.W.; educated in N.S.W. She joined the New Australia movement which founded a community settlement in Paraguay in 1893, and after the failure of the experiment she

taught and did journalistic work in various parts of South America, and also married there, returning to Australia in 1902. For many years she contributed to Labour publications in Sydney, and wrote a great deal of verse which established her as one of Australia's leading poets of her generation: *Fourteen Men* (1954), *Selected Verse* (1969), etc. She was also the author of essays and stories, in which she wrote sympathetically of the aborigines, her personal contact with whom had begun in childhood. Autobiographical: *Old Days: Old Ways* (1934), *More Recollections* (1935).

Gino Carella. Italian second husband of Lilia Herriton in E. M. Forster's *Where Angels Fear to Tread* (1905).

Ginsberg, Allen (1926-). Born in New Jersey. A leading figure in the *Beat movement, the advocates of which, both in the U.S. and abroad, accepted him as their major poet with the publication of *Howl and Other Poems* (1956), which was arraigned for obscenity but cleared. He voiced the spirit of protest prevalent among the young men and women of his period, and his work has been likened to that of Walt Whitman. Later volumes: *Kaddish and Other Poems* (1961), *Reality Sandwiches* (1963).

Giraudoux, Jean (Hippolyte Jean Giraudoux, 1882-1944). Born at Bellac; educated there and in Paris. He entered the French diplomatic service and at various times was employed on official duties in Russia, America, and elsewhere. He wrote novels from 1920 onward, but had his chief successes in the theatre, both in his own country and in England, with *Amphitryon 38* (1929), and the plays translated as *The Madwoman of Chaillot* (1947) and (by Christopher *Fry) *The Tiger at the Gates* (1955), *Duel of Angels* (1958) and *Judith* (1962).

Gissing, George (1857-1903). Born at Wakefield in Yorkshire; educated at a Quaker boarding school in Worcestershire and at Owens College, Manchester, where he had a brilliant record; but, convicted of petty theft in 1876, he served a brief sentence, and then was sent by friends to America. He taught languages for a few months, became destitute in Chicago, contributed short stories to the *Tribune* there, and returned to England in 1877. For a while he studied philosophy in Germany. Two unfortunate marriages (his alcoholic first wife died miserably) committed him to a lifetime of drudgery as an ill-paid novelist, though he was a scholarly writer of high distinction and integrity. His outstanding novels are *New Grub Street* (1891); *Born in Exile* (1892)—in which Godwin Peake is partly the author himself; *The Odd Women* (1893). His *Charles Dickens: A Critical Study* (1898), remains one of the best books on the novelist who influenced him deeply, though he lacked humour. The solid and grim qualities of most of his novels denied him popularity, but his near-genius has earned him limited and lasting respect. He is now remembered chiefly by *The *Private Papers of Henry Ryecroft* (1903), a scarcely disguised autobiographical record in which the pleasures of life and thought outvie darker memories.

Glasgow, Ellen (Ellen Anderson Gholson Glasgow, 1874-1945). Born in Richmond, Virginia; educated privately. Her novels, dealing unsentimentally and unromantically with the people of the Southern States and their ideas, prejudices and illusions, include *The Voice of the People* (1900), *The Wheel of Life* (1906), *Virginia* (1913), *Life and Gabriella* (1916), *Barren Ground* (1925), *The Romantic Comedians* (1926), *The Sheltered Life* (1932), *In This Our Life* (1941); short stories: *The Shadowy Third* (1923).

Glaspell, Susan (1882-1948; Mrs George Cram Cook). Born in Iowa; educated at Drake University there and at the University of Chicago. Helped to found the Provincetown Players in Provincetown, Cape Cod, who produced her one-act plays *Suppressed Desires* (written 1914), which ridicules psychiatry, and *Trifles* (1916). The best known of her full-length plays is *Alison's House* (1930) supposedly suggested by some aspects of the life and posthumous influence of Emily Dickinson (1830-86). Susan Glaspell also wrote *The Inheritors* (1921) and *The Verge* (1921), and novels including *The Glory of the Conquered* (1909), *Judd Rankin's Daughter* (1945).

Gloomy Dean, The. *See* W. R. *Inge.

Glover, Denis (Denis James Matthews Glover, 1912-   ). Born at Dunedin, New Zealand; educated at Auckland and Christchurch. Started printing-presses at school and university, and later had his own printing works. Author of *The Wind and the Sand* (1945), *Sings Harry* (1951), *Arawata Bill*

(1953), *Enter Without Knocking* (1964), and other collections of verse; *Hot Water Sailor* (autobiography; 1962).

Glyn, Elinor (*née* Elinor Sutherland, 1864-1943; married Clayton Glyn). Born in Jersey, Channel Islands; educated mainly through extensive reading in early years. Her husband died in 1915 and she had a passionate friendship with Lord *Curzon which ended at his second marriage in 1917 (to the widowed mother of Alfred *Duggan). Elinor Glyn began her remarkable career as a novelist with *The Visits of Elizabeth* (1900), and had published several others before *Three Weeks* (1907) made her at once immensely popular with the public and a target for the critics. *Three Weeks* became inseparably associated with the image of love-on-a-tiger-skin, and the absurdity of its overheated romanticism did not avert accusations of immorality. It may perhaps be regarded as an early forerunner of *Lady Chatterley's Lover* without the apocalyptic solemnity of D. H. *Lawrence. The many later novels of Elinor Glyn did nothing either to diminish or to increase her reputation as an efficient saleswoman of the sex-appeal which constituted her gospel of romance.

Glyndebourne. *See* John *Christie.

Gobbledegook. Derisive term for language not intelligible by normal standards: e.g. in bureaucratic documents and correspondence, in the jargon of literary and art critics, in nonsense songs, and in such linguistically experimental works as those of Gertrude *Stein and James *Joyce's *Finnegans Wake*. The word derives onomatopoeically from farmyard poultry utterances.

Godden, Rumer (Margaret Rumer Godden, 1907-   ; Mrs Haynes Dixon). Born in Sussex; spent part of her childhood in India; educated there and at Eastbourne. In later years she alternated between England and India where she ran a small girl's school. Her intimate knowledge of India gives a unique quality of sensitive understanding to such of her novels as *Black Narcissus* (1938), *Breakfast with the Nikolides* (1941), and *The River* (1946). Other novels include *A Fugue in Time* (1945), *A Candle for St Jude* (1948), *Kingfishers Catch Fire* (1953), *An Episode of Sparrows* (1955), *The Greengage Summer* (1958), *The Tale of the Tales* (1971).

Godot. The mysterious being named but never

appearing in Samuel Beckett's *Waiting for Godot* (1954).

Gogan, Mrs. Charwoman in Sean O'Casey's *The *Plough and the Stars* (1926); forty, doleful-looking, fidgety and nervous, aflame with curiosity.

Gogarty, Oliver St John (1878-1957). Born in Dublin; educated at Stonyhurst, Trinity College (Dublin), and Oxford. He had a distinguished career as a surgeon, and acquired a large circle of eminent literary friends in both Ireland and England. He was appointed a Senator of the Irish Free State in 1922, but after his country was renamed Eire in 1936 he was in opposition to its political leaders, ceased to be a Senator, and from 1939 lived in the U.S. His ebullience and incisive wit are displayed in *As I Was Going Down Sackville Street* (1937), *Tumbling in the Hay* (1939), and other prose writings. He was also an accomplished versifier whose *Collected Poems* (1952) merit more attention than they have received.

Golden Bough, The. A Study in Magic and Comparative Religion by Sir James George *Frazer in twelve volumes published 1890-1915, to which were added in 1936 *Aftermath: A Supplement.* Among the innumerable topics of this vast work are: Priestly Kings; Sympathetic Magic; Magical Control of the Weather; The Worship of Trees; Tabooed Acts, Persons, Things, and Words; Myths of Diana, Adonis, Attis, Osiris, Isis, Dionysus, Demeter, Persephone, Balder, and others; Gods and Goddesses of Fertility and Vegetation; The Corn Mother; The Transference of Evil; Scapegoats; Fire Festivals. The 'golden bough' (identified with mistletoe) is the branch 'which, at the Sibyl's bidding, Aeneas plucked before he essayed the perilous journey to the world of the dead'. Virgil 'tells how two doves, guiding Aeneas to the gloomy vale in whose depth grew the Golden Bough, alighted upon a tree "whence shone a flickering gleam of gold. As in the woods in winter cold the mistletoe . . . is green with fresh leaves and twines its yellow berries about the boles; such seemed upon the shady holm-oak the leafy gold, so rustled in the gentle breeze the golden leaf." The inference is almost inevitable that the Golden Bough was nothing but the mistletoe seen through the haze of popular poetry or of popular superstition.' Why the mistletoe, to ordinary

eyes a mere tree-parasite, became, for the initiated, charged with mystical properties, is the problem ramifying in Frazer's thousands of pages.

Golden Bowl, The. Novel by Henry *James published in 1904. On the eve of the wedding in London of the daughter of an American millionaire, Maggie Verver, and Prince Amerigo, an impecunious Italian, his superseded love, Charlotte Stant, arrives unannounced from New York, ostensibly to attend the wedding. She stays with Mrs Assingham, a friend of them all, who is troubled by Charlotte's reappearance, for it was she who introduced Maggie to the Prince after he broke with Charlotte when they agreed they were too poor to marry. Throughout the narrative Fanny Assingham continues to feel, and to express to her husband, concern as her friends' affairs develop, but Colonel Robert Assingham customarily treats his wife's misgivings with irony and amused tolerance. On arrival, Charlotte, a 'magnificently handsome and supremely distinguished' young woman, induces the Prince to accompany her on excursions around London, professedly in search of a wedding present for Maggie, who is unaware of their meetings or of their past relations. No suitable present is found, but at a small antique shop in Bloomsbury they inspect a gold-covered crystal bowl which is blemished by a crack undetected by Charlotte but apparent to Amerigo. Their conversation in Italian is understood by the old antique dealer, who, detecting that Charlotte is attracted by the golden bowl, says he will keep it for her. Maggie is utterly devoted to her father, Adam Verver, a widower who since his wife's death has filled the gap in his life by acquiring an expert knowledge of antiques and works of art, for his priceless collection of which he has genuine love. When Maggie bears a son, the child and its mother become central in Mr Verver's life, and Maggie spends much of her time with her father and the infant, guilelessly leaving Amerigo to companionship with Charlotte. Maggie, says Fanny Assingham, 'wasn't born to know evil'. Charlotte's interest is also engaged on behalf of Mr Verver when Maggie and Amerigo go to the Continent for a lengthy visit. During the young people's absence, Mr Verver finds Charlotte an agreeable and intelligent companion. She accepts his proposal of marriage after receiving an enthusiastic congratulatory message from Maggie and an ambiguous one from Amerigo. Charlotte and the Prince continue their meetings after her marriage, but such suspicions as Maggie may have remain latent until, by accident and co-incidence, she, too, is attracted by the golden bowl in the Bloomsbury shop. Having sold it to her at a high price without declaring its flawed condition, the antique dealer's troubled conscience leads him to call on Maggie and offer reparation. While with her, he recognizes in the room photographs of the two who had previously inspected the bowl, and remembers the exact date. This reveals to Maggie that Amerigo and Charlotte had been meeting surreptitiously between the dates of her engagement and her marriage. She displays the golden bowl on her mantelshelf and tells the whole story to Fanny Assingham, who handles and smashes the bowl just as Amerigo comes into the room. Left alone with him, Maggie faces him with her knowledge of his infidelity. She afterwards denies to Charlotte that she has anything against her, and they all become enmeshed in a web of lies, spoken and unspoken. The situation is resolved by Mr Verver's return to America with Char-lotte, and a complete reconciliation between the Prince and Maggie, whose love of him has not weakened. Fundamently good people, their hidden flaws are symbolized by the imperfect golden bowl.

Golden Cockerel Press. Founded in 1920 by Harold Taylor to print and publish 'litera-ture worthy of typographic devotion and care'. It played a leading part in the move-ment for good printing which inspired book production in the decades following World War I, and by the end of 1934 it had issued a hundred titles. The founder died in 1924 and the Press was taken over by Robert *Gibbings until in 1933 it passed to Christopher Sandford, Francis Newbery and Owen Rutter. Its first book was twelve tales by A. E. *Coppard, *Adam and Eve and Pinch Me*, and thereafter the titles were fairly evenly divided between other works by living writers and past classics. The most famous production is *The Four Gospels* with sixty-five wood-engravings by Eric *Gill, a magnificent quarto bound in white pigskin. Gill also embellished other Golden Cockerel books, and most of the other notable wood-engravers of the period

illustrated one or more volumes, with Gibbings's own work outstanding. In 1931 a specially cut type designed by Gill, called Golden Cockerel Face, was first used.

Golding, Louis (1895-1958). Born in Man-chester; educated there and at Oxford. Among his many novels, those dealing with Jewish life are outstanding: e.g. *Magnolia Street* (1931), *Five Silver Daughters* (1934), *Mr Emmanuel* (1939), etc. Others include *The Camberwell Beauty* (1935). He also published poems, *Shepherd Singing Ragtime* (1921) and other collections, a book on *James Joyce* (1933) and *The World I Knew* (1940).

Golding, William (William Gerald Golding, 1911-). Educated at Marlborough and Oxford. Author of novels—*The *Lord of the Flies* (1954), *The Inheritors* (1955), *Pincher Martin* (1956), *Free Fall* (1959), *The Spire* (1964), *The Pyramid* (1967), *The Scorpion God* (1971); essays—*The Hot Gates* (1965); play—*Brass Butterfly* (1958).

Goldring, Douglas (1887-1960). Born in Greenwich; educated at Felsted School and Oxford. From 1917 for some ten years he was engaged editorially on several periodi-cals, including *The *English Review* in 1909 under Ford Madox *Hueffer, an experience which provided him with material for *South Lodge: Reminiscences of Violet Hunt, Ford Madox Ford and the English Review Circle* (1943).

Goldsmith, Peter. Pseudonym used by J. B. *Priestley as collaborator with George *Billam in *Spring Tide* (1936), a comedy.

Gollancz, Sir Victor (1893-1967; knighted 1965). Born in London; educated at St Paul's School and Oxford. After four years as a teacher he went into publishing and in 1928 started his own firm with immediate success. The Left Book Club which he ran for some years before, through, and after World War II as propaganda against the dictatorships, combined political idealism and business acumen. He wrote two auto-biographical volumes addressed to his grand-son *My Dear Timothy* (1950), *More for Timothy* (1953). He also compiled two anthologies, *From Darkness to Light* (1956) and *A Year of Grace* (1959).

Golliwog. See Florence *Upton.

Gooch, G. P. (George Peabody Gooch, 1873-1968). Born in London; educated at Eton, King's College (London), and Cambridge; later studied in Berlin and Paris. Liberal M.P. for Bath, 1906-10. Editor of the *Contemporary Review*, 1911-60. Historical works: *English Democratic Ideas in the Seventeenth Century* (1898), *English Political Thought from Bacon to Halifax* (1915), *Nationalism* (1920), *The Second Empire* (1960) etc. *Under Six Reigns* (1958; autobiography).

Good Companions, The. Novel by J. B. *Priestley published in 1929. Jesiah (Jess) Oakroyd, unjustly dismissed by his firm in Bruddersford, Yorkshire, and tired of his nagging wife, packs his tools and takes to the road to find adventure 'down South'. At about the same time Inigo Jollifant loses his teaching job for defying and mocking his headmaster's wife; and Elizabeth Trant, freed by her father's death, buys her nephew's car and sets off to tour England's cathedral cities. After preliminary adventures the three meet and also fall in with the Dinky Doos, a stranded concert party. Elizabeth's money, Inigo's skill as composer of popular tunes, and Jess's craftsmanship are placed at the party's disposal, and a new company, The Good Companions, is started. Then for a while the adventures of them all are the adventures of the company: failure and heartbreak, success and romance, catching-up on the past—these in touching individuals touch them all. Eventually the company breaks up and the Companions part: Elizabeth has met and married the Scottish doctor she loved years before; Inigo's music takes him to the top in the wake of Susie Dean, the Companions' comedienne, who becomes a musical comedy star; and Jess, after returning to Bruddersford to be with his wife who is dying, goes to Canada to live with his beloved daughter Lily and her family, and to brood happily on his memories of life on 't' road'.

Good, Fluther. *See* *Fluther Good.

Good Soldier, The: *A Tale of Passion*. Novel by Ford Madox *Hueffer published in 1915. An American couple, John and Florence Dowell, form a friendship with Captain Edward Ashburnham and his wife Leonora while in Nauheim, which they all visit for part of the summer to benefit Florence and the Captain as sufferers from heart trouble. Ashburnham, the owner of an estate in Hampshire, is 'an excellent magistrate, a first-rate soldier, one of the best landlords' in the county. Dowell relates the story of the progress of the friendship on the Continent and in England, and of its disastrous sequel after more than nine years, in a narrative which departs from chronological order as he learns out of sequence the events concerning the four. Briefly, and keeping closer to the time-order of the happenings, Leonora resents the generosity with which her husband treats the tenants and workers on his estate, and her lack of sympathy and increasing coldness drive him into a succession of amorous affairs. The drain on his means which the first of these causes, leads Leonora to take control of his finances. She restores prosperity, but her heartless treatment of their dependents makes a deeper rift in the marriage. Meanwhile, Dowell discovers that Florence's supposed weak heart is only a cover for her adultery with a young American. She also becomes Ashburnham's secret mistress. When her infidelity is revealed she commits suicide. A young girl, Nancy Rufford, the daughter of a friend stationed in India, is taken into their home by the Ashburnhams and falls in love with Edward. He, too, loves her, but is determined that no sexual relationship shall develop. Leonora tells Nancy of his past infidelities, but says she must 'give herself' to save him, for he is dying of love for her. Both women are Roman Catholics, and know that Leonora's advice would commit Nancy to mortal sin. Edward sends Nancy back to her father in India. After receiving a desolating telegram from her, sent on the voyage, he kills himself. Nancy loses her reason and returns to England to live on the Ashburnham estate, which Dowell buys, Leonora having remarried and moved.

Goodman, Arnold Abraham, Baron 1965 (1913-). Educated in London and Cambridge. Solicitor; official adviser in numerous capacities, and appointed to serve on many public bodies (Arts Council, British Council, Commissions, Tribunals of Enquiry, etc.); Director/Chairman/Governor/ of Royal Opera House, Royal Shakespeare Theatre, Sadler's Wells Trust; President, National Book League (1972).

Goodwin, Archie. Nero Woolf's resident assistant in detective stories by Rex *Stout. He takes an ironic and humorously disrespectful though loyal view of his employer.

Gopaleen, Myles na. *See* Brian *O'Nolan.

Gordon, Charles William. *See* Ralph *Connor.

Gordon, Janet. *See* Cecil *Woodham-Smith.

Gordon, Neil. Pseudonym used by A. G. *Macdonell for detective novels.

Gordon Clark, A. A. *See* Cyril *Hare.

Gore, Charles (1853-1932). Born at Wimbledon; educated at Harrow and Oxford. Ordained in the Anglican Church, 1878. Librarian of Pusey House, Oxford, 1884-93. Chaplain in the Royal household, 1898-1901. Successively Bishop of Worcester (1902-04), Birmingham (1905-11), and Oxford (1911-19). A man of commanding personality and powerful intellect, he was an ardent controversialist holding unorthodox theological views which estranged him from some Church leaders and others. He established the Community of the Resurrection, a brotherhood of celibate priests, and devoted his money to the furtherance of Anglican purposes. His numerous writings included *The Creed of the Christian* (1895), *Spiritual Efficiency* (1904), *The New Theology and the Old Religion* (1908), *The Question of Divorce* (1911), *Christian Moral Principles* (1921), *Christ and Society* (1928).

Gore-Booth, Constance. *See* Countess *Markievicz.

Gore-Booth, Eva (Eva Selina Gore-Booth, 1870-1926). Born in Sligo; educated privately. Became an advocate of women's suffrage during the militant movement in the years preceding World War I. Author of some dozen books of verse, mostly on Irish themes, including *Poems* (1898), *Unseen Kings* (1904), *The Agate Lamp* (1912), *The Death of Finovar* (1916), *The Shepherd of Eternity* (1925). Her sister Constance became Countess *Markievicz.

Goryan, Sirak. Pseudonym used by William *Saroyan for some early writings, including 'The Daring Young Man on a Flying Trapeze' when first published as a single story.

Gosheron. Lady Slane's sympathetic builder in V. Sackville-West's *All Passion Spent (1931).

Gosse, Sir Edmund (Edmund William Gosse, 1849-1928; knighted 1925). Born in London; educated privately. His parents were members of a rigid evangelical body, the Plymouth Brethren, the father being Philip Henry Gosse, whose life the son wrote in 1890. Assistant Librarian at the British Museum, 1867-75; Lecturer in English Literature, Trinity College, Cambridge, 1884-90; Librarian, House of Lords, 1904-14. Between 1873 and 1900 he published poems, books on Gray, Raleigh, Donne, Fielding, Browning and other classic authors, and did much to gain acceptance in England for the works of Scandinavian writers (*Northern Studies*, 1879; *Henrik Ibsen*, 1908). In the new century he produced a dozen or so collections of essays on varied subjects and published *Collected Poems* (1911). Also wrote *The Life of Algernon Charles Swinburne* (1917), and biographical studies of *Jeremy Taylor* (1904), *Coventry Patmore* (1905), and *Sir Thomas Browne* (1905). After World War I he contributed a weekly article on current books to the *Sunday Times* which made him something of an arbiter of literary taste, though many thought him overbearingly opinionated. Amid his extensive output of mostly routine work that has passed from notice, Gosse produced one book that stands with the masterpieces of English literature, *Father and Son* (1907), though it was at first attacked as unfilial.

Gottlieb, Max. Professor of Bacteriology and Martin's sponsor and inspirer in Sinclair Lewis's *Martin Arrowsmith* (1925).

Goudge, Elizabeth (Elizabeth de Beauchamp Goudge, 1900-1970). Born at Wells, Somerset (daughter of the Rev. Henry Leighton Goudge, Regius Professor of Divinity in the University of Oxford, 1923-39); educated at Southbourne and the University of Reading. Author of novels and short stories of romance and sentiment: *Island Magic* (1932), *A City of Bells* (1934), *Green Dolphin Country* (1944), *Gentian Hill* (1950), *The Scent of Water* (1963), etc.; of children's books including *The Little White Horse*; and of biographies of Christ (*God So Loved the World*, 1951) and *St Francis of Assisi*.

Gould, Bernard. *See* Sir Bernard *Partridge.

Gould, Charles. Administrator of the San Tomé silver mine in Joseph Conrad's *Nostromo* (1904). He says 'I pin my faith to material interests', believing that they will, ensure 'law, good faith, order, security'. Mrs Gould, his wife, 'the first lady of Sulaco', takes a more idealistic stand.

Gourlay, John. Prosperous merchant and arrogant citizen in George Douglas's The *House with the Green Shutters* (1901). Brought low by a turn of Fortune's wheel, he is killed by his son John, who poisons himself.

Gourmont, Remy de (1858-1915). Born in Normandy; educated at Coutances and the University of Caen. Worked at the National Library in Paris, 1884-91; one of the founders of the famous *Mercure de France* which in the 1890s was a medium for the Symbolists, among whom de Gourmont was an outstanding and learned critic. *Une Nuit au Luxembourg* (1906; English translation *A Night in the Luxembourg*, 1912) is described as a philosophical fantasy, and in common with his other novels is highly analytical and deficient in human feeling. He also wrote short stories, poems, and several volumes of criticism. His work as a whole had a strong influence on other writers in France and beyond.

Gowers, Sir Ernest (Ernest Arthur Gowers, 1880-1966; knighted 1928). Educated at Rugby; entered the Civil Service and retired in 1930, having reached high rank. He continued his public service afterwards for many years on Commissions, etc., and at the request of the Treasury wrote *Plain Words* (1948) as a guide to the proper use of English by officials in government offices. This was also bought in very large numbers by the general public, and was followed by *An ABC of Plain Words* (1951); a combined edition, *The Complete Plain Words*, appeared in 1954. The excellent guidance given does not appear to have produced more than a temporary effort towards brevity and clarity in official correspondence, good English being the plain Englishman's bane.

Graham, Ennis. *See* Mrs *Molesworth.

Graham, Harry (Harry Jocelyn Clive Graham, 1874-1936). Born in London; educated at Eton and Sandhurst. Joined the Coldstream Guards and became a captain, serving in South Africa and in France in World War I. He was a voluminous writer of verse and prose, particularly noted for *Ruthless Rhymes for Heartless Homes* (1899) and *More Ruthless Rhymes* (1930)

which may be regarded as pioneer examples of the 'sick humour' which had a cult vogue in the 1950s-1960s, though Graham's rhymes were genuinely comic and without sadistic intention. Other verse: *Fiscal Ballads* (1905), *Verse and Worse* (1905), *Deportmental Ditties* (1909), *The Motley Muse* (1913), *Rhymes for Riper Years* (1916). He also published several volumes of humorous essays—*The World We Laugh In* (1924), etc.—and was part author of a number of plays.

Graham, R. B. Cunninghame. *See* *Cunninghame Graham.

Graham, Stephen (1884-   ). Born in England but spent many years travelling (mainly on foot) in Russia and writing about that country, its people and its leaders: *A Vagabond in the Caucasus* (1910), *Undiscovered Russia* (1911), *With the Russian Pilgrims to Jerusalem* (1913), *Through Russian Central Asia* (1916), *Life of Peter the Great* (1939), *Stalin: An Impartial Study* (1931; 1939). Service in World War I led to a ruthless study of army conditions *A Private in the Guards* (1919); a visit to America and friendship with Vachel *Lindsay produced *Tramping with a Poet in the Rockies* (1922); and among his many other books are *Under-London* (1923), *London Nights* (1925), *The Gentle Art of Tramping* (1927), *Twice Round the London Clock* (1933), *Thinking of Living* (1949), *Part of the Wonderful Scene* (autobiography, 1964).

Grahame, Kenneth (1859-1932). Born in Edinburgh; educated at St Edward's School, Oxford; joined the staff of the Bank of England and became its Secretary from 1898 until his retirement. Reserved in human relationships, he had a great love of outdoor life and wild creatures, as his masterpiece *The *Wind in the Willows* (1908) demonstrates. His earlier books—*Pagan Papers* (1893), *The Golden Age* (1895), *Dream Days* (1898) though largely about children continue to delight adult readers, and at least *The Golden Age* seems bound to find a permanent niche in English literature.

Grand Guignol. Adopting the name of an eighteenth century French character in provincial puppet plays, a theatre with this title was established in Paris in the next century and a Grand Guignol season was given in London by English actors in 1920-22. The essential element of the Guignol plays (usually in one act) was horror in numerous bloodcurdling manifestations. In a solemnly pretentious form the genre reappears in the *Theatre of Cruelty and *Black Comedy types of play around the 1960s.

Grand, Sarah (pseudonym of Mrs Frances Elizabeth McFall, *née* Clarke, 1862-1943). Born in Ireland; married an army surgeon at sixteen and spent several years in the Far East. Associated herself with the women's freedom movement, an interest reflected in her novels, among which *The Heavenly Twins* (1893) is inseparably linked with her name. She was Mayoress of Bath six times between 1923 and 1929. Though her books are extravagant in style and frequently absurd, they not only entertained a large public but also mirror certain matters of contemporary social interest, e.g. *Adnam's Orchard* (1912), *The Winged Victory* (1916).

Granville-Barker, Harley. *See* Granville *Barker.

Graves, A. P. (Alfred Percival Graves, 1846-1931). Born in Dublin, son of the Bishop of Limerick; educated at Windermere College and University of Dublin. In Civil Service, 1869-75; H. M. Inspector of Schools, 1875-1910. Took a leading part in the Irish literary and musical revival. Published many books of Irish and Welsh songs and ballads; author of the famous popular song, 'Father O'Flynn'. Father of Robert *Graves.

Graves, Clotilda Inez Mary. *See* Richard *Dehan.

Graves, Robert (Robert V. Ranke Graves, 1895-   ). Born in London, son of A. P. *Graves; educated at Charterhouse and Oxford. Service with the British army in France in World War I accounted for a good many of the poems in his earliest collections—*Over the Brazier* (1916), *Goliath and David* (1916), *Fairies and Fusiliers* (1917)—and also for *Goodbye to All That: An Autobiography* (1929; rev. edn 1957) which brought him into general notice. Though he was at first linked with the *Georgian Poetry group, he followed a personal line free from any coterie. The poems of his middle period are 'dry' in so far as they are dedicated to verbal precision

and the avoidance of adulterating emotionalism. The later poetry is less denuded of natural feeling. He was elected Professor of Poetry in the University of Oxford 1961-66. As well as being outstanding among the poets of his generation, he was an excellent historical novelist with a range extending from Roman times (*I Claudius*, 1934; *Claudius the God*, 1934) and the Byzantine period (*Count Belisarius*, 1938), to Puritan England (*Wife to Mr Milton*, 1943) and on to the American War of Independence (*Sergeant Lamb of the Ninth*, 1940, *Proceed, Sergeant Lamb* 1941). A variety of miscellaneous works includes a collection of essays on poetry *The Common Asphodel* (1949); *The Greek Myths* (1955); (as editor) *English and Scottish Ballads* (1957). *More Poems* (1961), *Collected Short Stories* (1965), *Love Respelt* (1965), *Collected Poems* (1965), and later poems (1966-72).

Grayson, David (pseudonym of Ray Stannard *Baker, 1870-1946). Writing under this pen-name the author had wide popular success with essays in successive volumes, the tone of which is indicated by the titles: *Adventures in Contentment* (1907), *Adventures in Friendship* (1910), *Adventures in Understanding* (1925) etc.

Great Adventure, The. *See* *Buried Alive.

Great Betrayal, The. *See* Julien *Benda.

Great Gatsby, The. Novel by F. Scott *Fitzgerald published in 1926. James Gatz, son of 'shiftless and unsuccessful farm people', drifts aimlessly until, when seventeen, he becomes the protégé of a copper magnate and changes his name to Jay Gatsby. Left 25,000 dollars at the early death of his benefactor, Gatsby eventually becomes a millionaire with a bachelor mansion on Long Island where he gives lavish parties eagerly attended by vast numbers of guests, mainly uninvited. One of those actually invited, Nick Carraway, narrator of the story, is cousin of the girl Daisy, with whom Gatsby had a love affair while an army officer during World War I. While he is in Europe with the American forces, his romantic dream of life with Daisy is dispersed by news of her marriage to Tom Buchanan; but after the War he renews relations with her, and in a stormy scene tells Buchanan that Daisy is going to leave him and live with Gatsby. Buchanan retaliates by declaring that Gatsby has become wealthy by discreditable means. Daisy and Gatsby leave by car with Daisy driving. She hits and kills a woman who has rushed into the road, but drives on. The dead woman, Mrs Wilson, is the mistress of Buchanan, who tells her distraught husband that Gatsby was the driver. Wilson shoots Gatsby and commits suicide. Nick takes charge of Gatsby's funeral arrangements and invites the dead man's intimate friends. None attend. The novel has symbolic undertones, typified by the great ashtips neighbouring Gatsby's mansion, and an oculist's vast poster with gigantic eyes brooding over the refuse heaps.

Green, Anna Katherine (1846-1935). Born in Brooklyn. She was one of the pioneers of the detective novel in America with *The Leavenworth Case* (1878), many others following, up to *The Step on the Stair* (1923).

Green, Anne (1899-   ). Born in Savannah, Georgia; elder sister of Julian Green (see below); educated in Paris. Author of *The Selbys* (1930), *Reader, I Married Him* (1931), *The Lady in the Mask* (1942), *The Old Lady* (1957) and other novels; *With Much Love* (1948; autobiography).

Green, Henry (pseudonym of Henry Vincent Yorke, 1905-1973). Educated at Oxford, became an engineer and, later, Managing Director of an Engineering Company in Birmingham. Author of *Living* (1929), *Party Going* (1939), *Loving* (1945), *Concluding* (1948), *Nothing* (1950), and other novels. He relies chiefly on dialogue and his novels have been described as 'elegant and witty but ambiguous comedies of manners'. *Pack My Bag* (1930) is autobiographical.

Green, Julian (Julian Hartridge Green, 1900-   ). Born in Paris of American parents; sister of Anne Green (see above); educated in Paris and in America at the University of Virginia. Later studied art and music but turned to literature with novels which he chose to write in French. Though grim, if not morbid, his books caused him to be regarded as one of the most distinguished French novelists of the period: *Mont-Cinere* (1926; English translation, *Avarice House*, 1927); *Le Voyageur sur la Terre* (1926; *The Pilgrim on the Earth*, 1929); *Le Visionnaire* (1934; *The Dreamer*, 1934), and numerous later novels. The autobiographical *Memories of Happy Days* (1942) was written in English.

Green, F. L. (Frederick Lawrence Green, 1902-1953). Born in Portsmouth; educated at the Salesian College, Farnborough. Settled in Northern Ireland. Of his dozen or more novels the best known are *On the Night of the Fire* (1939) and *Odd Man Out* (1945). For the latter he also wrote a film script which made a successful and exciting picture presenting visually the characteristic theme of Green's novels—a man pursued, whether physically or symbolically.

Green Mansions. Novel by W. H. *Hudson published in 1904. Electing to be known as Mr Able, only, Abel Guevez de Argensola relates to his friend the story of his experiences among savage tribes in the region of the upper Orinoco after he had fled from Venezuela as a political refugee. While living in an Indian village he explores a forest which the natives of the village will not enter. He hears from an unseen source a voice of great beauty which appears to follow him closely. The Indians declare that it comes from 'the daughter of the Didi', a malevolent spirit, but Abel discovers at length that it is the voice of a shy lovely girl who reproaches him angrily when he is about to crush a poisonous snake, for she protects all living creatures. While following her he falls from a high bank and on recovering consciousness finds that he has been found and tended by a ragged old man, who states that the girl is his seventeen-year-old grandchild, called Rima. To Abel she appears more a sprite than a human, a familiar of birds and animals and insects, weaving her garments from spider filaments. The old man, Nuflo, is reluctantly persuaded to tell Abel the story of how the child was left on his hands at the death of her mother, who had suddenly appeared to a gang he was with, standing near a mountain cave: 'her head was surrounded by an aureole like that of a saint in a picture'. Nuflo helps her from the mountain, called Riolama, to the nearest Christian village, where the priest names her child Riolama, shortened to Rima. The mother speaks an unknown language, accountable only on the theory that she was the sole survivor of a small remote community massacred by enemies. Rima induces Nuflo and Abel to go with her on the long and fruitless journey from the forest to Riolama, since she has long believed that she would find there her mother's people. Though Rima and Abel have fallen in love, she insists on journeying back to the forest alone, leaving Abel to follow with Nuflo. When the men reach the forest they see that Nuflo's house has been destroyed, and Abel is told that Rima is dead, the Indians having burned down the tree in which she had taken refuge. Mad for revenge, Abel leads a rival tribe in an attack on the Indians' village which wipes out the inhabitants. He returns to civilization and sets apart in his house a darkened chamber for a cinerary urn containing the ashes of Rima.

Green, Paul (Paul Eliot Green, 1894-   ) Born in North Carolina; educated at the University there and at Cornell University. Author of many plays, particularly about American Negroes: *In Abraham's Bosom* (1927), *Roll, Sweet Chariot* (1934); and poor whites *The Field God* (1927), *The House of Connelly* (1932).

Greene, Graham (1904-   ). Born at Berkhampstead; educated at the school there (when his father was headmaster) and at Oxford. He joined the staff of *The Times* in 1926 and remained until 1940; worked in the Foreign Office during World War II. Began his career as a novelist with *Babbling April* (1925) and quickly became one of the most discussed contemporary writers. He divided his fictional works into two categories—entertainments and novels—though there is no clear line of demarcation. After joining the Roman Catholic Church his novels were much concerned with shabby souls in process of disintegration, veering towards damnation but not beyond reach of salvation. The combination of religion with crime or degeneracy is found nauseating by a minority of readers but inspiring by others. As a storyteller Greene is in the tradition of John *Buchan, whose influence he acknowledged, as also that of the French novelist, Mauriac, whose religious outlook he shared. As well as novels (*The Man Within*, 1929; *Brighton Rock*, 1938; *The Power and the Glory*, 1940; *The Heart of the Matter*, 1948; *The End of the Affair*, 1951; *The Quiet American*, 1955; *Our Man in Havana*, 1958; *A Burnt out Case*, 1961; *The Honorary Consul* (1973), and others) Greene has written successful plays (*The Living Room*, 1953; *The Potting Shed*, 1957; *The Complaisant Lover*, 1959, etc.) and films based on the plays. *Collected Stories* (1972).

Greenwich Village. The Bohemian quarter of New York. Many writers of good repute and high achievement lived there in the 1920s, but it was also a haunt of undesirables. *The Improper Bohemians* by Allen Churchill (1961) is subtitled 'A Re-creation of Greenwich Village in its Heyday'.

Greenwood, Walter (1903-1974). Born in Salford, Lancashire; educated at a local Council school. Through many years after leaving school he had a succession of ill-paid jobs and experience of unemployment before writing a novel exposing the kind of life endured by those on a bare subsistence level, *Love on the Dole* (1933). It had great success both as a book and on the stage in the dramatized version (in collaboration with Ronald Gow). Greenwood continued to write both plays and novels, but without equalling this success. *Love on the Dole* is one of the few books of the 1930s which give an authentic impression of how the economic collapse of that decade affected the unmoneyed classes.

Greet, Ben (Sir Philip Barling Ben Greet, 1857-1936; knighted 1929). Born on a recruiting ship in the Thames, commanded by his father; educated at the Royal Naval School in London. After a brief period of teaching he went on the stage in 1879 and seven years later began to organize open-air performances of Shakespeare. He toured extensively at home and abroad with his own repertory company, and in 1914 established himself for some years at the *Old Vic and gave many performances for schools at the request of the educational authorities. Later he presented English plays in Paris and also took a leading part in running the Open Air Theatre in Regent's Park, London. At the beginning of the century he was associated with the revival of *Everyman* by William *Poel and was responsible for many subsequent performances of it.

Gregory, Lady (*née* Isabella Augusta Persse, 1852-1932; married Sir William Gregory, a former colonial governor). Born in County Galway, Ireland; educated privately. After her husband's death in 1892 she developed her literary interests and, meeting W. B. *Yeats, became a collaborator in making the *Irish Players at the *Abbey Theatre, Dublin, one of the most famous companies in the world. She became not only its practical man-of-all-work, but also wrote for it a series of one-act plays, mainly of peasant life, which stand high in the dramatic output of the Irish literary revival: they include *Spreading the News* (1904), *Hyacinth Halvey* (1906), *The Gaol Gate* (1906), *The Rising of the Moon* (1907), *The Workhouse Ward* (1908). Her full-length plays (*The Travelling Man*, 1910, and others) are less remarkable, but she performed a notable feat in translating several of Molière's plays into the dialect of Western Ireland (*The Kiltartan Molière*, 1910).

Gregynog Press. Founded at Gregynog Hall, Montgomeryshire, in 1923 by Gwendoline Davies and her sister Margaret, whose grandfather, David Davies (born 1818), started work in a sawmill when he was eleven, became a civil engineering contractor, Liberal M.P., and millionaire. His granddaughter Gwendoline was a pioneer collector of Post-Impressionist paintings, and both sisters were benefactors of literature, education, and the arts and crafts. They planned to make Gregynog a centre for fine pottery, weaving, furniture-making, and printing, but only the book production side (type setting, wood-engraving, printing, and binding) developed. As with other such enterprises, the work of the Gregynog Press was ended by World War II, but the forty-two works it printed and published were among the finest examples produced by the private presses. Seven of the books were in Welsh; those in English included Charles Lamb's Elia essays in two volumes, Caxton's translation of Aesop, books of selected poems of George Herbert, Henry Vaughan, Christina Rossetti, Lascelles Abercrombie, W. H. Davies; selected poems and selected essays by Edward Thomas; Gilbert Murray's translation of the plays of Euripides in two folio volumes; *Shaw Gives Himself Away*, an autobiographical miscellany by Bernard Shaw (1939). *See also* *Golden Cockerel Press; *Nonesuch Press.

Greig, Maysie (died 1971). Born and educated in Australia; worked as a journalist there and in London, where she settled. Author of '200 romantic novels in England and America'. Also wrote as Jennifer Ames.

Grein, J. T. (Jacob Thomas Grein, 1862-1935). Born in Amsterdam; educated in Holland, Germany, and Belgium; settled in London and became a naturalized British subject

in 1895. An enthusiastic lover of the theatre and a fecund dramatic critic, he wrote for papers in England and abroad and published (1899-1905) five volumes of *Dramatic Criticism*. His sure place in the history of the theatre rests on his founding the *Independent Theatre, London, in 1891. Starting with Ibsen's *Ghosts,* it presented Bernard Shaw's first play *Widowers' Houses* in 1892 and thus paved the way for the new 'intellectual drama' that was to dominate the English stage in the early decades of the present century.

Grenfell, Sir Wilfred (Wilfred Thomason Grenfell, 1865-1940; knighted 1927). Born in Cheshire; educated at Marlborough and Oxford. Studied medicine and became famous as a medical missionary working in Labrador, founding the International Grenfell Association with land-based hospitals and hospital ships. He wrote many books, including *Harvest of the Sea* (1906), *Labrador* (1909), *The Adventure of Life* (1912), *Northern Neighbours* (1923), and two autobiographical narratives, *A Labrador Doctor* (1923) and *Forty Years for Labrador* (1932).

Grensted, L. W. (Rev. Canon Laurence William Grensted, 1884-1964). Born in Lancashire; educated at Liverpool and Oxford. Professor of the Philosophy of the Christian Religion, Oxford, 1930-50; Canon Theologian of Liverpool Cathedral, 1930-41. Author of *The Making of Character* (1928), *The Study of Theology* (1939), *The Psychology of Religion* (1952), etc.

Grey, Zane (1872-1939). Born in Zanesville, Ohio; educated at the University of Pennsylvania. Abandoned his first practice as a dentist and then struggled as a writer for several years before the publication of *Riders of the Purple Sage* (1912) started him as a pioneer of 'Westerns' and inducted him into the class of million-sale novelists. He continued to write on similar lines for the rest of his life.

Grey of Fallodon, 1st Viscount (Edward Grey, 1862-1933; inherited his grandfather's baronetcy in 1882; created viscount in 1916). Born in London; educated at Winchester and Oxford. Liberal M.P. for Berwick-on-Tweed, 1885-1916. As Foreign Secretary (1905-16) it fell to him to announce in the House of Commons on 3 August 1914 the Government's intention to resist Germany, thus bringing Great Britain into World War I.

Historians have taken a critical view of him as a statesman, and his reputation now rests upon his quality as an amateur naturalist. His *Fly Fishing* (1899), *Fallodon Papers* (1926) and *The Charm of Birds* (1927) compare well with the writings of Izaak Walton, Gilbert White of Selborne and W. H. *Hudson. He also wrote his memoirs as *Twenty-Five Years, 1892-1916* (1925).

Grey Owl (pseudonym of Archibald Stansfeld Belaney, 1888-1938). Born in Hastings and educated there. His father had married in America a woman alleged by her son to be of Indian descent. He emigrated to Canada in 1903, worked as a guide and trapper, lived and married among the Indians. Served in World War I, and married an English woman in 1917, his Indian wife having left him. He returned alone to Canada to live again among Indians. Became a ranger in national parks and a popular lecturer on wild life. His assumption of native costume and the belief or illusion that he was part Indian contributed materially to his success as speaker and as author of *The Men of the Last Frontier* (1931), *Pilgrims of the Wild* (1934), *Tales of an Empty Cabin* (1936). His Indian mistress from 1925 to 1937, Anahareo published *My Life with Grey Owl* (1940). A biography, *Wilderness Man* (1974), is by his English publisher and friend Lovat Dickson.

Gribble, Leonard (Leonard Reginald Gribble, 1908-   ). Born in London. His own biographical summary states: 'In 1928 wrote first detective story, in 1950 completed hundredth book'. Among them are: *The Stolen Home Secretary* (1932), *Who Killed Oliver Cromwell?* (1937), *The Arsenal Stadium Mystery* (1939), *Atomic Murder* (1947), *Death Pays the Piper* (1956).

Grierson, Sir Herbert (Herbert John Clifford Grierson, 1866-1960; knighted 1936). Born in the Shetland Isles at Lerwick; educated at Aberdeen and Oxford. Professor of Rhetoric and English Literature in the University of Edinburgh, 1915-35; Rector of that University, 1936-39. Editor of *The Poems of John Donne* (1912), *Metaphysical Poets: Donne to Butler* (1921), *The Poems of John Milton* (1925), *Lyrical Poetry from Blake to Hardy* (1928). Author of *The Background of English Literature* (1925), *Cross Currents in the Literature of the Seventeenth Century* (1929), *The English Bible* (1944), *Rhetoric and English Composition* (1945).

Grieve, Christopher Murray. *See* Hugh *MacDiarmid.

Griff, Alan. Pseudonym under which Donald *Suddaby wrote *Lost Men in the Grass* (1940).

Griffith, Hubert (Hubert Freeling Griffith, 1896-1953). Educated at St Paul's School and in Berlin; studied art at the Slade School, London. Worked on metropolitan and provincial papers, mainly as dramatic critic, and also London editor during World War II of publications on Russia sponsored by the British Ministry of Information. Wrote *Iconoclastes, or the Future of Shakespeare* (1927), *Seeing Soviet Russia* (1932), *This is Russia* (1944); and several plays including *Tunnel Trench* (1924); *Red Sunday* (1929), *Youth at the Helm* (1934), as well as others translated from German and Russian.

Griffiths, Clyde. *See* *Clyde Griffiths.

Grigson, Geoffrey (1905-   ). Born in Cornwall; educated at Leatherhead and Oxford. He came into prominence as the founder in 1933 of *New Verse* a periodical devoted to modernist poetry; it ran until 1939. A period on the staff of London newspapers preceded his main work as author or editor of a large number of books on literature and art, anthologies etc. Collections of his own verse include *Under the Cliff and Other Poems* (1943) and *The Isles of Scilly and Other Poems* (1946), *Collected Poems* (1963), *Discoveries of Bones and Stones* (1971). Autobiographical, *The Crest on the Silver* (1950).

Grile, Dod. *See* Ambrose *Bierce.

Grimble, Sir Arthur (Arthur Francis Grimble, 1888-1956; knighted 1938). Born in Hong Kong; educated at Chigwell School and Cambridge, and in France and Germany. Joined the British Colonial Service, in which he rose to be Governor of the Seychelles (1936-42) and then of the Windward Islands (1942-48). His two books of reminiscences, adventurous in spirit and rich in entertaining stories, were immediate best-sellers: *A Pattern of Islands* (1952) and *Return to the Islands* (published posthumously, 1957).

Grimshaw, Beatrice (Beatrice Ethel Grimshaw, 1871-1953). Born in Ireland; educated in Belfast, France, and London. Travelled widely and often alone among the South Sea islands, producing many books arising from her often hazardous experiences: e.g. *From Fiji to the Cannibal Islands* (1907), *The Sorcerer's Stone* (1914), *The Terrible Island* (1920), *The Victorian Family Robinson* (1934). She settled in Australia in 1940.

Grove, Frederick Philip (1871-1948). Born in Russia of English parents; educated in Berlin; studied archaeology. Worked in Canada as a farm labourer, village schoolmaster, and farmer. Wrote a number of books on prairie life; realistic novels, *Settlers of the Marsh* (1925), etc; an autobiography, *In Search of Myself* (1927), and numerous other books.

Grub Street. The former name of Milton Street in the City of London: 'inhabited by writers of small histories, dictionaries, and temporary poems, whence any mean production is called *grubstreet*' (Johnson's Dictionary, 1755). The title of George *Gissing's *New Grub Street* (1891) alludes to the plight of similarly needy authors.

Guedalla, Philip (1889-1944). Educated at Rugby and Oxford. Practised as a barrister, 1913-23, and in following years was an unsuccessful parliamentary candidate in several constituences. While engaged in legal and public life he wrote *Ignes Fatui: A Book of Parodies* (1911), *The Partition of Europe, 1715-1815* (1914), *Supers and Supermen* (1920), *The Industrial Future* (1921), *The Second Empire* (1922), *A Council of Industry* (1925). His later years were devoted almost entirely to writing and he became established as a biographer with *Palmerston* (1926), *Gladstone and Palmerston* (1928), *The Duke* (of Wellington) (1931), *The Queen and Mr Gladstone* (1933), *Mr Churchill: A Portrait* (1941). While his literary style owed something to the witty Lytton *Strachey mode and employed certain mannerisms from that source, Guedalla relied upon historical research rather than psychological intuition.

Guermantes family. See *Remembrance of Things Past*.

Guignol. See *Grand Guignol.

Guiney, Louise Imogen (1851-1920). Born in Massachusetts; educated at a convent school in Rhode Island. After working in turn as journalist, postmistress, and assistant at Boston Public Library, she migrated to England in 1895 and settled in a Gloucestershire village. Much of her verse and prose

was written in the last century from 1884, but her collected poems, *Happy Ending*, appeared in 1910 (enlarged edn 1927), and among her prose works belonging to the present century are *Robert Emmet: His Rebellion and His Romance* (1904), *Blessed Edmund Campion* (1908) and other Catholic writings. Her *Letters* were published in 1926.

Guinness, Nurse. The old nannie, now housekeeper, in Shaw's *Heartbreak House* (1919).

Gulley Jimson. See Jimson.

Gumbril, Theodore. Inventor of Gumbril's Patent Small-Clothes in Aldous Huxley's *Antic Hay* (1923).

Gunn, Mr. Dramatic critic in the Induction and Epilogue to Shaw's *Fanny's First Play* (1911). The name glances at that of a contemporary dramatic critic, Gilbert *Cannan.

Gunga Din. One of the *Barrack Room Ballads* by Rudyard *Kipling, the last line of which is frequently quoted facetiously: 'You're a better man than I am Gunga Din!' Gunga Din was a regimental *bhisti* (water-carrier) in the British army in India.

Gunn, Gilbert. See Gilbert *Cannan.

Gunn, Neil, M. (Neil Miller Gunn, 1891-1973). Born in Scotland at Caithness; after attending the village school he was educated privately in Galloway. Passed into the Civil Service about 1906 and remained in the service until he resigned in 1937, having in his last post as a Customs and Excise officer become intimate with most of the Western Highlands and islands of Scotland. His first novel *The Grey Coast* (1926) and its numerous successors—*Morning Tide* (1931), *Highland River* (1937), *Young Art and Old Hector* (1942), *The Well at the World's End* (1951) and others—depict the hard lives and varied characters of the fishing and scattered farming people of the Highlands. *Whisky and Scotland* (1935) deals with that world-famous national product; *Off in a Boat* (1938) and *Highland Pack* (1950) are the product of his voyaging and travelling among the islands and mountains; *The Atom of Delight* (1956) is his autobiography.

Gunn, Thom (Thomson William Gunn, 1929-). Born in London; educated at University College School there and at Cambridge. Lived abroad for lengthy periods

(Paris, Rome, Berlin) and settled in California from 1954 teaching English in the University at Berkeley. He and Ted *Hughes were ranked as the representative poets of their period. Author of *Fighting Terms* (1954), *My Sad Captains* (1961), *Poems 1950-1966* (1969), etc. Described as writing with 'formal precision and elegance' but also with 'energy and violence', his poems are equally at ease with classical references, with youths on motor cycles, and with the 'slow passion' of a snail's 'deliberate progress'.

Gunther, John (1901-1970). Born in Chicago; educated at schools and the University there. Correspondent of the *Chicago Daily News* in London 1924-26, and in most of the European capitals, 1926-35. From 1936 travelled independently in India, China, Japan, and Latin America. *Inside Europe* (1936 and later revisions) created a vogue for similar books surveying current conditions and events with an acute journalistic eye: *Inside Asia* (1939; 1942), *Inside Latin America* (1941), *Inside U.S.A.* (1947), *Inside Africa* (1955), *Inside Russia Today* (1958), *Inside Europe Today* (1961).

Gurdjieff, George Ivanovitch (1868-1949). Born at Alexandropol in the Caucasus of Greek parents from Asia Minor. Nothing is recorded of his early life up to the time he studied medicine and for the priesthood. From about 1890 he travelled mysteriously in the East, apparently in Persia, Turkestan, Chitral, India, and in Tibet, where he is said to have been tutor to the Dalai Lama, and for ten years the chief Russian secret agent there. He was in Moscow in 1914, presenting *The Battle of the Magi,* a ballet of ancient sacred dances revealing 'oriental magical techniques'. While in the East he acquired from esoteric teachers occult knowledge which he summed up in the phrase 'I deal in Solar energy'. A group gathered round him in Russia until the Revolution scattered them, when he moved to Tiflis and started in a small way the Institute for the Harmonious Development of Man, which was to bring him both fame and notoriety when, from 1922, it was established palatially in the Chateau of Avon, near Fontainebleau, with about sixty disciples, mainly Russians, but with English and Americans also. Gurdjieff was to some a messiah, an inspired master of secret knowledge and supernatural powers; to others he was a charlatan and mountebank exercising evil hypnotic influence. The basic

tenet of his teaching was the need to harmonize and unite man's physical, intellectual, and emotional faculties and so effectuate a 'whole man' in place of one in whom, as is invariably the case, a single faculty is in command. Since most of the disciples were intellectuals they were set to arduous, even exhausting physical labour, with a bare minimum of sleep. The regimen was not uniformly successful and there were numerous defections. The best-known English resident, Katherine *Mansfield, was in search of a miracle to restore her husband's love, which had been destroyed by the horror of her tubercular affliction. She hoped for a physical cure which, with her already existing intellectual and emotional faculties, would make her again a happily balanced and desirable wife. Her disease continued its deadly course, and she died after rather more than three months in the Institute.

Guthrie, John. Scottish crofter in Lewis Grassic Gibbon's *A *Scots Quair* (1932-34); his daughter **Christine,** who marries a neighbouring farmworker and runs the croft with him after her father's death. When she is left a widow with one child, Ewan, after her husband's death in France in World War I, she marries the Rev. Robert Colquohoun. When he dies and a third marriage is a failure, she returns alone to farm the croft where she was born.

Guthrie, Thomas Anstey. *See* F. *Anstey.

Gwynn, Stephen (Stephen Lucius Gwynn, 1864-1950). Born in County Dublin; educated at St Columba's College in Ireland and at Oxford. After teaching for several years, lived in London from 1896 to 1904, when he made his home in Ireland and became M.P. for Galway City, 1906-18. Served with the British army in World War I. He produced many books on a variety of subjects—politics, gardens, fishing, exploration, poetry, drama, painting, topography. His *Collected Poems* appeared in 1924, and among other books were several volumes of essays, biographical and critical studies of *Thomas Moore* (1904), *Captain R. F. Scott* (of the Antarctic) (1929), *Sir Walter Scott* (1930), *Horace Walpole* (1932), *Mary Kingsley* (1932), *Swift* (1933), *Mungo Park* (1934), *Goldsmith* (1935), *R. L. Stevenson* (1939), and several volumes on Ireland and its political history. *Experiences of a Literary Man* (1926) is autobiographical.

H.D. (Initials used as pen name by Hilda Doolittle, 1886-1961). Born at Bethlehem, Pennsylvania; educated at Philadelphia and Bryn Mawr; settled in Europe from 1911 and died at Zurich. She married Richard *Aldington in 1913 and with him and others became well known as one of the *Imagist poets, a group which flourished in the 1910s. Her verse is strongly classical in character, austere and spare, and relying for its cool beauty on images derived from ancient Greek mythology tempered by descriptions drawn from modern Greek landscape. She collaborated with Aldington (from whom she was after some years divorced) in translations from Greek and Latin and in a volume of verse *Images, Old and New* (1915). Her independent works include *Sea Garden* (1916), *Hymen* (1921), *Heliodora and other poems* (1924); a play in classical form, *Hippolytus Temporizes* (1927); *The Walls do not Fall* (1944), *Tribute to Angels* (1945), and *Flowering of the Rod* (1946), a verse trilogy; and several novels, among them *Bid Me to Live* (1961), semi-autobiographical and containing a striking word-portrait of D. H. *Lawrence. She also translated the *Ion* of Euripides.

H.M. See Sir Henry *Merivale.

Hack writer. An author who does drudging routine jobs rather than original work, either in a publisher's employ or as a freelance. *See* Grub Street.

Hackett, Francis (1883-1962). Born in Ireland at Kilkenny; educated at Kildare. Went to the United States in 1901. Worked on the *Chicago Evening Post* and the *New Republic* from 1906 to 1922. Later divided his time between America, Ireland and Denmark, his wife's native land. His chief popular success as a writer was with *Henry the Eighth* (1929) an entertaining biography in somewhat hectic prose. Other works: *Ireland: A Study in Nationalism* (1918), *The Story of the Irish Nation* (1922); *Francis the First* (1924); *Queen Anne Boleyn* (biographical novel, 1939); other novels—*That Nice Young Couple* (1924), *The Green Lion* (1935), *The Senator's Last Night* (1943); literary criticism—*Horizons* (1918), *On Judging Books* (1947); *I Chose Denmark* (1940).

Haddock. The plaintiff in most of the *Misleading Cases* by A. P. *Herbert.

Haddon, Christopher. Pseudonym used by John Leslie *Palmer.

Haden. *See* *Lily Haden.

Hadrian the Seventh. Novel by 'Baron *Corvo' (pseudonym of Frederick Rolfe), published in 1904. It was in some degree an exercise in literary revenge for the slights Rolfe received from official Roman Catholicism. In the novel George Arthur Rose, a fictional extension of the author himself, is elected Pope, taking as his pontifical title Hadrian VII. In language combining English colloquialism with hieratic pomp the book is mainly an account of Hadrian's remarkable conduct as Pontiff up to the day of his death, when the College of Cardinals declared epigrammatically that 'He would have been an ideal ruler if He had not ruled'.

Haggard, Sir Rider (Henry Rider Haggard, 1856-1925; knighted 1912). Born at Bradenham, Norfolk; educated at Ipswich. Went to South Africa as Secretary to the Governor of Natal in 1875 and held other official appointments before running an ostrich farm until 1881, when he returned to England to study law, was called to the Bar (1884) but did not undertake regular practice. Thereafter for the rest of his life he travelled in many countries and served on a large number of Royal Commissions and government committees. His special interest in agriculture and rural affairs is expressed in *A Farmer's Year* (1899), *Rural England* (1902), *The Poor and the Land* (1905), but his fame and prosperity came from the series of strikingly original novels of African adventure, among which *King Solomon's Mines* (1885), *Allan Quartermain* (1887), *She* (1887), and *Ayesha, or the Return of She* (1905) have been long remembered as classics in their kind.

Haggard, William (*pseud.* of Richard Henry Michael Clayton, 1907-   ). Educated at Lancing and Oxford. Served in Indian Civil Service and Army (1931-46). Author of numerous novels of mystery and international intrigue, *The Telemann Touch* (1958), *The Powder Barrel* (1965), *The Protectors* (1972), etc.

Hahn, Emily (1905-   ). Born in St Louis; studied geology and engineering at the University of Wisconsin; lived for a period in China which provided material for biographies of *The Soong Sisters* (1941) and *Chiang Kai-Shek* (1955). Other books: *Raffles of Singapore* (1946), *Congo Solo* (1935), *England to Me* (1949); novels—*With Naked Foot* (1934), *Mr Pan* (1942).

Haig, Fenil. Pseudonym under which Ford Madox *Hueffer wrote *The Questions at the Well, With Sundry Other Verses for Notes of Music* (1893).

Hail and Farewell. Autobiographical reminiscences by George *Moore in three volumes: *Ave* (1911), *Salve* (1912), *Vale* (1914). They give a firsthand account of the beginnings of the *Irish Literary Theatre, in which, with W. B. *Yeats, Edward *Martyn, and Lady *Gregory, he was actively concerned. As a voluntary propagandist on behalf of the Gaelic League which aimed to revive the Irish language as a medium for literature, he was soon convinced that the endeavour would fail since (as he came to believe and argue) Catholics had produced no real literature since the Renaissance. Though born into a Catholic family and educated (in profound misery) at Oscott College, he developed aggressively Protestant convictions which at times threatened to estrange him from his brother, Colonel Moore, whose younger son he offered (as he here relates) to have educated as a Protestant. He gives memorable character sketches of Yeats, Lady Gregory, J. M. *Synge, *AE (G. W. Russell) and others, never underestimating genius nor failing to disclose such individual foibles as mingle with it. His friendship with Edward Martyn was imperilled by Martyn's objection to the figure he cuts in Moore's pages, though to detached readers at a distance in time he appears a lovable person, not least because he is presented often in a humorous light. The charge made by Irish contemporaries that Moore wrote in malice is hard to understand, except on the supposition that they saw themselves and one another as 'faultily faultless... splendidly null'. It is probable that the account of the doings of the Department of Agriculture and Art in Ireland in which Moore poses Sir Horace Plunkett and Thomas Gill satirically as Flaubert's Bouvard and Pécuchet, was more than somewhat irritating to the principals, but it is a grand piece of sustained comic writing. In recurring to his ten years in Paris, the author draws masterly pen-portraits of Manet, Monet, Degas, Renoir and other Impressionist painters in whose circle he moved, and of the cocottes who swirled around the studios.

Haldane, J. B. S. (John Burdon Sanderson Haldane, 1892-1964). Born at Oxford. Educated at Eton and Oxford. Held appointments in biochemistry, physiology, and genetics in Cambridge and London before appointment as Professor of Biometry in the University of London, 1937-57. He emigrated to India in 1957 and became naturalized as an Indian citizen three years later. Outstanding among contemporary scientists, he was a lucid popularizer in many articles for the Communist *Daily Worker*, and a vigorous controversialist. Author of *Possible Worlds* (1927), *Science and Ethics* (1928), *The Inequality of Man* (1932), *The Marxist Philosophy and the Sciences* (1938), *Science and Everyday Life* (1939), *Everything has a History* (1951) and many other writings including a children's story *My Friend Mr Leakey* (1937).

Haldin, Victor Victorovitch. Revolutionary and assassin in Joseph Conrad's *Under Western Eyes* (1911); betrayed by Razumov, he is hanged. His sister **Nathalie** living in Geneva is visited by Razumov there and, unaware of his treachery, falls in love with him; shamed, he confesses.

Halevy, Élie (1870-1937). Born at Étretat; educated at the Lycée Condorcet and the École Normale Supérieure. Professor of Political Science in Paris from 1898. He became well known as an historian in England with his monumental *History of the English People in the 19th Century* written in French in five volumes published in his lifetime, with three further volumes projected but unfinished. The period covered is from the year of Waterloo (1815), and traverses the Reform Bill crisis, the Imperialism of 1895-1903, and the transition to social democracy, 1905-14.

Halfway House. Novel by Maurice *Hewlett published in 1908, the first of a trilogy continued with *Open Country* (1909) and completed with *Rest Harrow* (1910). See John *Senhouse.

Hall, Radclyffe (Marguerite Radclyffe Hall, 1886-1943). Born in Bournemouth; educated at the University of London and in Germany. Her first books—in verse: *'Twixt Earth and Stars* (1906), *Poems of the Past and Present* (1910), *Songs of Three Countries* (1913), *The Forgotten Island* (1915)—attracted little attention. She then turned to novel-writing with more success: *The Forge* (1924), *The Unlit Lamp* (1924), *Adam's Breed* (1926); but although the last-named was awarded literary prizes in Britain and France, it was *The Well of Loneliness* (1928) that made her name a household word. A London court declared the book obscene and ordered its destruction, though it was cleared of a similar charge in the United States. Its theme—lesbianism—was treated in the vein of tragedy and with no tendency to deprave; it is, indeed, more dull than alluring, and when, years later, the fact of sexual inversion became frankly recognized in Britain, the novel was reprinted and circulated without hindrance or comment. Radclyffe Hall's subsequent novels were quietly received: *The Master of the House* (1932), *The Sixth Beatitude* (1936).

Hall, Willis (1929-   ). Educated in Leeds. Author of *The Long and the Short and the Tall* (1959), *A Glimpse of the Sea*, and (in collaboration with Keith *Waterhouse) other plays.

Hallam, Sir Howard. The 'hangingest judge in England', in Shaw's *Captain Brassbound's Conversion.*

Halliday, Michael. *See* John *Creasey.

Hamilton, Charles. *See* Frank *Richards.

Hamilton, Cicely (*née* Cicely Mary Hammill, 1872-1952). Born in London; worked as a journalist and actress. Among her many plays, *Diana of Dobson's* (1908) and *Just to Get Married* (1910) made most impression. Also wrote *Lament for Democracy* (1940); and (in collaboration with Lilian *Bayliss) *The Old Vic* (1926).

Hamilton, Clive. Pseudonym of C. S. *Lewis.

Hamilton, Cosmo (1872-1942). Assumed name (by deed poll) of Cosmo Gibbs, brother of Sir Philip *Gibbs. Worked on two or three London newspapers and periodicals before achieving success as a playwright, chiefly with the libretti of popular musical plays: *The Belle of Mayfair* (1906), *The Catch of the Season* (1904), *The Beauty of Bath* (1906). He also wrote non-musical plays, novels, and an autobiography, *Unwritten History* (1924).

Hamilton, Sir George Rostrevor (1888-1967; knighted 1951). Born in London; educated at Bradfield and Oxford; in Civil Service, 1912-53. Author of many books of verse (*Collected Poems and Epigrams*, 1958), compiled several classical and other anthologies, and published volumes of literary essays, notably *The Tell-Tale Article* (1949); autobiography: *Rapids of Time. Sketches from the Past* (1965).

Hamilton, Mary Agnes (*née* Mary Agnes Adamson, 1884-1966; Mrs C. J. Hamilton). Born in Manchester; educated at Glasgow and Cambridge. Labour M.P. for Blackburn,

1929-31; a Governor of the B.B.C. 1933-7. Author of *The Labour Party* (1939); *Newnham* (her college at Cambridge; 1936); novels —*Less Than the Dust* (1912), *Dead Yesterdays* (1916), *Murder in the House of Commons* (1931). *Outlines of Greek and Roman History* (1913), *Ancient Rome* (1922); *Remembering My Good Friends* (1944), *Up-hill All the Way* (1953; autobiography). She also wrote biographies: *Sidney and Beatrice Webb* (1933), *J. Ramsay MacDonald* (1929); the first version of the latter (1925) was published under the pseudonym Iconoclast.

Hamilton, Patrick (Anthony Walter Patrick Hamilton, 1904-62). Born at Hassocks, Sussex; educated at Westminster School. Began an acting career in 1921 but turned to writing. His novels were mainly concerned with modern city life, particularly its grim and sinister aspects: *Craven House* (1926), *The Plains of Cement* (1934), *Twenty Thousand Streets Under the Sky* (1935), *Hangover Square* (1941). His principal success was with *Rope* (1929) and *Gas Light* (1938), plays in which fear and horror were melodramatically treated with an underlying moral intention. Among his radio plays were *Money with Menaces* and *To the Public Danger* (both 1939).

Hammett, Dashiell (Samuel Dashiell Hammett, 1894-1961). Born in Maryland; educated at the Polytechnic Institute in Baltimore and took a number of unexciting jobs before becoming a private detective with the Pinkerton agency. After service in World War I he started writing detective stories in a style that pioneered the 'tough' school of American crime fiction in which he and Raymond *Chandler became the masters. Hammett's success was great but his output small. Best are *The Maltese Falcon* (1930) and *The Glass Key* (1931); the others are *Red Harvest* (1929), *The Dain Curse* (1929), and *The Thin Man* (1932)—the last named making his name most widely known in a film series.

Hammond, Barbara (*née* Lucy Barbara Bradby, 1873-1961; married J. L. *Hammond, 1901). Educated at St Andrew's and Oxford. She and her husband wrote jointly *The Village Labourer, 1760-1832* (1911), *The Town Labourer, 1760-1832* (1917), *The Skilled Labourer, 1760-1832* (1919), *Lord Shaftesbury* (1923), *The Rise of Modern Industry* (1925), *The Age of the Chartists* (1930), *The Bleak Age* (1934). These works are the product of deep and wide scholarship and thorough documentation, but their success with a large reading public was due to the Hammonds' excellent literary style and humane outlook.

Hammond Innes. See Ralph Hammond *Innes.

Hammond, J. L. (John Lawrence Le Breton Hammond, 1872-1949). Educated at Bradford and Oxford. Editor of the weekly political and literary review *The Speaker*, 1899-1906; leader writer and special correspondent to London and Manchester newspapers. Wrote jointly with his wife Barbara *Hammond the celebrated works listed in the entry on her, above. Author (by himself) of *Charles James Fox* (1903), *Life of C. P. *Scott* (1934), *Gladstone and the Irish Nation* (1938).

Hamps, Mrs Clara. 'Auntie Hamps' in Arnold Bennett's *Clayhanger* (1910) and *These Twain* (1916). Called by some 'a damned fine woman', she had 'terrific vitality', 'a glorious digestion', and much-paraded piety which seemed to her nephew and nieces 'the baffling garment of effusive insincerity in which she hid her soul'. A great comic character, she was a 'pillar of society, a champion of the conventions, and a keeper-up of appearances'; 'she placed religion above morality; hence her chicane, her inveterate deceit and self-deceit'.

Hamsun, Knut (pseudonym of Knut Pedersen, 1859-1952). Born in Norway. He described himself as a farmer and claimed to have 'no education'. Apprenticed to a shoemaker, he became by turns a clerk, a county school teacher, and, during periods in North American States, a street-car conductor, lecturer, and deep-sea fisherman. From 1889 he divided his time between writing and farming in Norway. *Growth of the Soil* (1920) and *Hunger* (1921) laid the foundations of his international reputation as a novelist. Other novels: *Shallow Soil* (1914), *Pan* (1920), *Mysteries* (1927), *The Women at the Pump* (1928), *August* (1932). In both World Wars he incurred odium for his pro-German utterances.

Hanaud. The solver of mysteries in the crime novels of A. E. W. *Mason. Described as 'a great detective of the Sûreté in Paris', he appears in *At the Villa Rose* (1910), *The House of the Arrow* (1924), and others.

Hankey, Donald (1884-1916). Educated at Rugby, Woolwich Military Academy, and Oxford. After a period as a commissioned officer of the regular army, stationed in Mauritius, he resigned in 1907 and studied at Oxford. A visit to East Africa in 1910 was followed by theological training, but he decided against ordination. Disguising himself as a workman, he tramped in Surrey and Sussex, sleeping in common lodging-houses, in order to familiarize himself with the life of the poor and the 'feel' of destitution. In 1912 he went steerage to Australia in order to ascertain why boys emigrating from Britain did not fit in, and on return to England lived in the Oxford Mission Settlement in Bermondsey, helping with the Boys Club there. He enlisted when World War I started in August 1914 and was killed in France in October 1916. A series of essays published earlier in 1916, *A Student in Arms*, mainly on army life at home and in the trenches, made his name widely known, and a second series was issued posthumously in the next year. *Letters of Donald Hankey*, introduced by Edward Miller (1919), covers the phases of his life from 1903, when he left Rugby, to a few days before his death. His specifically Christian publications were *The Lord of All Good Life* (1914), *A Passing in June* (1915) and *Religion and Common Sense* (1917), but all his writings were religious in purpose.

Hanley, Gerald (Gerald Anthony Hanley, 1916-). Born in Ireland. Started farming in Kenya about 1932; served with the British forces in Africa and Burma in World War II, the latter phase of his service yielding *Monsoon Victory* (1946). At the end of the war he worked on films in India, with the B.B.C. in England, but in 1950 settled in the Punjab as a novelist: *The Consul at Sunset* (1951), *The Year of the Lion* (1954), *Drinkers of Darkness* (1955), *Without Love* (1957), *The Journey Homeward* (1961), *Gilligan's Last Elephant* (1962), *Warriors and Strangers* (1971).

Hanley, James (1901-). Born in Dublin. Had only elementary education before going to sea as a stoker in 1914. Returning to shore work after ten years, he did mainly unskilled work until the publication of *Drift* in 1930 started him as a novelist. *Boy* (1931) and *The Furys* (1934) are representative of his perfervid sympathy with the wretched on land and sea. Other novels: *Captain Bottell* (1933), *Hollow Sea* (1938), *Our Time is Gone* (1940). *Sailor's Song* (1948), *The Closed Harbour* (1952), *The Welsh Sonata* (1954), *Say Nothing* (1962); short stories: *Men in Darkness* (1931), *Half-an-Eye* (1937), *People are*

Curious (1938), *A Walk in the Wilderness* (1950); essays: *Soldiers Wind* (1938), *Between the Tides* (1939), *Don Quixote Drowned* (1953); autobiography: *Broken Water* (1937).

Hannay, James Owen. *See* George *Birmingham.

Happy Hypocrite, The: A Fairy Tale for Tired Men. Story by Max *Beerbohm, first published in *The *Yellow Book*, Oct. 1896; reissued as a booklet, 1897; reprinted in *A *Variety of Things*, 1928; dramatized by the author and produced at the Royalty Theatre, London, in December 1900.

Hardcastle family. In Walter Greenwood's *Love on the Dole*, **Mr Hardcastle**, miner; **Sally** Hardcastle, his daughter, mill worker; **Harry** Hardcastle, son, apprenticed as engineer. During the depression of the 1930s, father and son become unemployed, and the family is only saved from destitution by the influence of the local bookmaker when Sally becomes his mistress.

Hardinge, George, 3rd Baron Hardinge of Penshurst. *See* George *Milner.

Hardwicke, Sir Cedric (Cedric Webster Hardwicke, 1893-1964; knighted 1934). Born at Lye, Worcestershire. Failing to qualify as a physician he became an actor and for some years from 1922 displayed exceptional talent in plays by Bernard *Shaw: *Heartbreak House, Back to Methuselah, Too True to Be Good*, and *The Apple Cart* in which his performance as King Magnus is unlikely to be equalled. In New York on the night of Shaw's death (2 November 1950) he delivered a tribute to the playwright to whom he owed so much. He was also an outstanding success as Churdles Ash in Eden *Phillpotts's *The Farmer's Wife* and as Mr Barrett in *The *Barretts of Wimpole Street* by Rudolf Besier. He wrote two autobiographical volumes, *Let's Pretend* (1932) and *A Victorian in Orbit* (1961).

Hardy, Thomas (1840-1928). Born at Bockhampton, Dorsetshire; educated at Dorchester and in London at King's College. Articled to an ecclesiastical architect (1856-61) and sketched and measured many country churches; worked in a London architect's office (1862-67) and became a prizeman of the Royal Institute of British Architects. From 1865-68 he wrote numerous poems which remained unpublished until the next century, his energies as an author being given from the beginning of the 1870s to the series of prose works which enrolled him among the great English novelists. After the publication of *Jude the Obscure* (1895), he abandoned fiction, his last two novels having been attacked by critics on religious and moral grounds. It is wholly as a poet that Hardy belongs to 20th century literature. Though it has been commonly assumed that he forsook the novel as a literary form on account of hostile criticism, his first love as well as his last love was poetry. It may be assumed that his great series of novels constitute a completed body of work which released him to revive and develop his dormant poetic genius. The publication of *Wessex Poems* (1898), which include verses written from 1865 onward, did not mark the acceptance of Hardy for a place among the major English poets. The charge of pessimism often brought against him as a novelist was revived, as it continued to be for the remaining thirty years of his life. His verse forms, too, were held to be crabbed and his vocabulary harsh. No ready-made audience was awaiting him; he had in part to create it, and it was in other part created by the impact of war and the aftermath of war from 1914 onward. *Poems of the Past and of the Present* (1901), *Time's Laughing stocks and other Verses* (1909), *Satires of Circumstance* (1914), *Lyrics and Reveries* (1914), *Moments of Vision* (1917), *Late Lyrics* (1922), *Human Shows and Far Fantasies* (1925), and *Winter Words* (1928) contributed hundreds of lyrics and brief narrative poems to his total output, while amid much that is metaphysically profound are poems that became almost universally known and loved: e.g. 'In Time of 'the Breaking of Nations', 'Weathers' ('This is the weather the cuckoo loves'), 'When I set out for Lyonesse', 'The Oxen' ('Christmas Eve, and twelve of the clock'). Meanwhile, in three parts (1904, 1906, 1908), the greatest of Hardy's works appeared: *The *Dynasts*. Notwithstanding attempts to belittle it in the decades following Hardy's death, this vast epic-drama is a supreme achievement of imagination and intellect.

Hare, Cyril (pseudonym of Alfred Alexander Gordon Clark, 1900-1958). Born at Mickleham, Surrey; educated at Rugby and Oxford. Called to the Bar 1924; County Court Judge from 1950. Author of crime novels: *Tenant for Death* (1937), *Tragedy at Law* (1942), *When the Wind Blows* (1949), *An English*

Murder (1951), *He Should Have Died Here-after* (1958), etc.

Harland, Henry (1861-1905). Born in Russia (St Petersburg) of American parents; educated in Rome and Paris and at Harvard. Worked as a journalist in New York and wrote novels as Sidney Luska, a pseudonym he abandoned on settling in London in 1900, where he became the first editor of *The *Yellow Book*. The best-known of his writings is *The Cardinal's Snuff-box* (1900). Other novels and short stories: *Grey Roses* (1895), *Comedies and Errors* (1898), *My Friend Prospero* (1904).

Harmsworth, Alfred Charles William. *See* Lord Northcliffe.

Harmsworth, Harold Sydney. *See* Lord Rothermere.

Harraden, Beatrice (1864-1936). Born in London; educated in Dresden and in England at Cheltenham and the University of London. Her first novel, *Ships That Pass in the Night* (1893), was an immediate, vast and long-lasting success not equalled by her later books: *Hilda Strafford* (1897), *Katharine Frensham* (1903), *Out of the Wreck I Rise* (1912), *Where Your Treasure Is* (1918), *Search Will Find It Out* (1928).

Harris, Christopher. *See* Christopher *Fry.

Harris, Frank (James Thomas Harris, 1856-1931). The facts of his life are obscured by the accepted opinion that he was a seemingly pathological liar whose erotic autobiography, *My Life and Loves* (1923-27), is not to be trusted except where its assertions are verifiable from independent sources. He named both Galway in Ireland and Tenby in Wales as his birthplace; claimed to have won a scholarship to Cambridge which he was too young to take up at fifteen and was, instead, given a solatium of £10 which he spent on a steerage passage to New York, working there as a shoeblack, labourer on the building of Brooklyn bridge, and hotel worker. Returned to England and became in turn editor of the *Evening News*, *Fortnightly Review*, and other journals, excelling as editor of the *Saturday Review* (1894-98), which became under his control the outstanding weekly of the period, among the writers he engaged being Bernard Shaw, who contributed his famous theatre essays week by week from 1895 to 1898. Harris's later career as an editor was mainly discreditable, for it was alleged that the scandal sheets he ran briefly from time to

time were used as instruments of attempted blackmail. He was a writer of legitimate fiction of some merit, though the early repute of his short-story volumes, *Elder Conklin* (1894) and *Montes the Matador* (1900), has not been sustained; nor did his novels—*The Bomb* (1908), *Great Days* (1914)—make much impression. More attention was given to his literary studies, *The Man Shakespeare* (1911), *The Women of Shakespeare* (1911), and a play, *Shakespeare and His Love* (1910), though they receive no praise from scholars. The biography of *Oscar Wilde* (1920) is generally considered his best work; the *Life of Bernard Shaw* (1931) owes most to Shaw himself, who completed it to benefit the author's legatees after his death. Four series of *Contemporary Portraits* (1915-23) contain work of varying merit.

Harris, John Benyon. *See* John *Wyndham.

Harris, Wilson (Henry Wilson Harris, 1883-1955). Born in Plymouth; educated there and at Cambridge. From 1908 successively news editor, leader writer and diplomatic correspondent of the *Daily News*. Editor of the *Spectator* 1932-53. Author of *The League of Nations* (1929), *The Future of Europe* (1932), a biography of *J. A. Spender* (1945), *Life So Far* (autobiography, 1954).

Harris, Wilson (1921-   ). Born and educated in Guyana, where he became a land surveyor travelling in the interior, the setting of most of his novels. Settled in England. Author of *Palace of the Peacock* (1960), *The Far Journey of Oudin* (1961), *The Whole Armour* (1962), *The Secret Ladder* (1963), *The Waiting Room* (1967), and other novels; *Eternity to Season* (poems, 1954); *Tradition and the West Indian Novel* (1965).

Harrison, Frederic (1831-1923). Born in London; educated there and at Oxford; called to the Bar (1858) and practised; Professor of Jurisprudence and International Law at Lincoln's Inn (1877-89); he was a Radical in politics and a Positivist in philosophy, undertaking propaganda in both fields. His writings include *The Meaning of History* (1862), *Oliver Cromwell* (1888), *The Philosophy of Common Sense* (1908), *On Society* (1918). His friendship was an important source of support in early years to George *Gissing, who was for a time engaged as tutor to Harrison's son, Austin Harrison, afterwards editor of *The *English Review.*

Harrison, G. B. (George Bagshawe Harrison, 1894-). Born in Sussex; educated at Brighton and Cambridge. Teacher at Felsted; lecturer at Cheltenham and King's College, London. Professor of English, Queen's University, Kingston, Ontario, 1943-49; Professor of English, University of Michigan from 1949. Many writings on Shakespeare, other Elizabethans and Jacobeans, and *John Bunyan: A Study in Personality* (1928).

Harrison, Henry Sydnor (1880-1930). Born in Tennessee; educated at Columbia University. A brief experience of journalism preceded his beginnings as a novelist. The immense popular success of *Queed* (1911) and *V.V.'s Eyes* (1913) was unaccompanied by critical approval, and these and later novels were not long celebrated.

Harrison, Mrs Mary St Léger. See Lucas *Malet.

Hart, B. H. Liddell. See B. H. *Liddell Hart.

Hart, Frances Noyes (*née* Frances Newbold Noyes, 1890-1943; Mrs Edward Henry Hart). Born in Maryland; educated privately and in Italy and France and at Columbia University. Her detective novel *The Bellamy Trial* (1927) was one of the first crime stories to concentrate interest on a prolonged account of court proceedings. Other novels: *Hide in the Dark* (1929), *Pigs in Clover* (1931), *The Crooked Lane* (1934).

Hart, Moss (1904-61). Born in New York and educated there. Author of numerous plays, frequently in collaboration with George S. *Kaufman: Once in a Lifetime* (1930), *Merrily We Roll Along* (1934), *You Can't Take It With You* (1936), *The Man Who Came to Dinner* (1939).

Hartley, L. P. (Leslie Poles Hartley, 1895-1972). Born at Whittlesea; educated at Harrow and Oxford. Collections of short stories: *Night Fears* (1924), *The Killing Bottle* (1932), *The Travelling Grave* (1951), *The White Wand* (1954), *Two for the River* (1961). Novels: *Simonetta Perkins* (1925), *The Boat* (1950), *My Fellow Devils* (1951), *The Go-Between* (1953), *A Perfect Woman* (1955), *The Hireling* (1957), *Facial Justice* (1960), *The Brickfield* (1964), *The Betrayal* (1966); and, outstandingly, the trilogy embracing *The Shrimp and the Anemone* (1944), *The Sixth Heaven* (1946) and *Eustace and Hilda* (1947), of which the first is a memorable study of the brother and sister in childhood.

Hašek, Jaroslav (1883-1923). Born in Prague.

Became a bank clerk before World War I, in which he served with an Austrian security corps and spent a long time in a Russian prisoner-of-war camp. His satirical novel *The Good Soldier Schweik* (abridged English edition, 1930), intended as pacifist propaganda, had a worldwide circulation translated into various languages. Though its propagandist purpose was not overlooked, the book established itself as a classic on account of the brilliant characterization of Schweik himself, an indomitable simpleton with wisdom beyond the wisest.

Hassall, Christopher (Christopher Vernon Hassall 1912-63). Born in London; educated at Brighton College and Oxford; son of John Hassall (famous as poster artist) and brother of Joan Hassall, wood engraver. Friendship with Ivor Novello led to Hassall's becoming the successful librettist in several of Novello's light operas, a form of composition he pursued also for more serious works, including Sir William Walton's *Troilus and Cressida*. Lyrical and narrative poems appeared in *Poems of Two Years* (1935), *Penthesperon* (1938), *S.O.S. Ludlow* (1941), *The Red Leaf* (1957). *Devil's Dyke* (1936), *Christ's Comet* (Canterbury Cathedral Festival, 1937), *Out of the Whirlwind* (performed in Westminster Abbey, 1953), are verse dramas. He also wrote biographies of Stephen Haggard, an actor who died young (*The Timeless Quest*, 1948), *Edward Marsh, Patron of the Arts* (1959), and *Rupert Brooke* (1964). *Ambrosia and Small Beer* (1964) contains correspondence between himself and Sir Edward Marsh.

Hassall, John (1868-1948). Born at Walmer; educated in Devon and at Heidelberg; studied art in Antwerp and Paris, after trying farming with his brother in Canada. Became one of the most celebrated poster-artists of his generation. Father of Christopher *Hassall and Joan Hassall (wood-engraver).

Hassan: The Story of Hassan of Bagdad and how he came to make the Golden Journey to Samarkand. Play in five acts by James Elroy *Flecker published in 1922; performed in London in 1923. Hassan, a poor confectioner, lovesick for a beautiful young woman who recently came into his shop, is persuaded by his friend and confidant, Selim, to send her a gift of sweets compounded with a magic love potion. He learns that her name is Yasmin, and on going to her house finds that Selim has treacherously forestalled him. Taunted by the lovers, he collapses in a swoon and is found when Haroun al Raschid, the Caliph of Bagdad, and his followers, disguised as merchants, come to a house with no door and have to be drawn up in a basket. Ishak, the Caliph's poet, tired of his job, sends up the unconscious Hassan instead of himself. Inside the house, the host has Hassan washed, scented and handsomely clad; but the Caliph, Jafar his vizier, and Masrur his negro executioner, find they have been trapped. The host is Rafi, King of the Beggars of Bagdad, in rebellion against the tyrannous Caliph. Rafi seeks revenge because Pervaneh, his betrothed, has been abducted and taken to Haroun's seraglio. Rafi and his company of beggars leave their guests imprisoned within iron shuttered walls, from which they are rescued when Hassan suggests a means of getting a message out. For this he is raised to be the Caliph's personal friend. Rafi and his followers are captured, and he and Pervaneh are given the choice of a day and night of love, 'unfettered and alone', followed by torture and death, or freedom on condition that she agrees to become the Caliph's wife. They choose love and death. Hassan, who has angered the Caliph by interceding for them, is forced to watch their end and falls in a faint. He is roused by Ishak and they join the pilgrim caravan to Samarkand. The play is mainly in poetic prose with occasional lyrics, notably 'The War Song of the Saracens' and 'The Golden Road to Samarkand'.

Hauptmann, Gerhart (Gerhart Johann Robert Hauptmann, 1862-1946). Born in Silesia; educated in Breslau and later studied sculpture there and in Rome. After acting for a short time in Berlin, his first play *Before Sunrise*, produced there in 1889, drew him into the current of the new drama of Ibsen, Strindberg and others who revolutionized playwriting by making it a medium more of earnest social comment than of entertainment. Later plays (as translated into English): *The Weavers* (1892), *Lonely Lives* (1898), *The Sunken Bell* (1900), *Hannele* (1908).

Haw Haw, Lord. Derisive title given by British listeners to William Joyce, who broadcast Nazi propaganda from Germany during World War II. He was captured at the end of the war, convicted in London of high treason, and hanged. His drawling intonation was responsible for his being named Haw Haw. The nickname had been briefly borne previously for similar reasons by Norman

Baillie-Stewart, a renegade British Officer.

Hawk, Affable. *See* *Affable Hawk.

Hawkes, Jacquetta (*née* Jacquetta Hopkins, 1910-   ; married (1) Christopher Hawkes; (2) J. B. *Priestley). Born in Cambridge and educated there; daughter of the eminent biochemist Sir Frederick Gowland Hopkins, pioneer in vitamin research. She read archaeology and anthropology at the University and published *Archaeology of Jersey* in 1939; *Early Britain* (1945), *Man on Earth* (1954). Her outstanding success was *A Land* (1951). Other writings: *Symbols and Speculations* (poems; 1948), *Fables* (tales; 1953), and books in collaboration with J. B. Priestley.

Hawkins, Anthony Hope. *See* Anthony *Hope.

Hay, Ian (pseudonym of Major-Gen. John Hay Beith; 1876-1952). Educated at Fettes and Cambridge. Served in France in World War I and as a member of the British War Mission to the U.S. His account of the men who enlisted in the early stages of the war (*The First Hundred Thousand*, 1915) had a great success, as also had his novels (*A Man's Man*, 1909; *A Safety Match*, 1911; *The Middle Watch*, 1930; *The Housemaster*, 1936), and plays adapted from his novels.

Hay Fever. Light comedy in three acts by Noel *Coward performed and published in 1925. The author describes it as 'far and away one of the most difficult plays to perform' since 'it has no plot at all, and remarkably little action'. A retired actress, Judith Bliss, living with her novelist husband David, their daughter Sorel, and cartoonist son Simon, in an untidy house at Cookham, has invited for the weekend a callow young admirer, Sandy Tyrell, not knowing that each of the others has also invited a guest without notice: David an ingenuous awkward girl, Jackie Coryton; Sorel a diplomat, Richard Greatham; Simon Myra Arundel, who, Judith declares, 'goes about using Sex as a sort of shrimping net'. The Blisses 'never attempt to look after people when they come' and the weekend becomes a pandemonium of bickering and a tangle of spurious declarations of love. After breakfast on the second day the guests slip away unnoticed while the Bliss family are noisily disputing about David's knowledge or ignorance of the topography of Paris.

Hayek, F. A. (Friedrich August von Hayek,

1899-). Born in Vienna; educated at the University there. Professor of Economic Science and Statistics in the University of London, 1931-50; Professor of Social and Moral Science in the University of Chicago from 1950. His writings on economics and monetary theory exercised considerable influence on competent readers, while *The Road to Serfdom* (1944), more widely concerned with the condition of the contemporary world, circulated and aroused interest far beyond the academic field.

Hayes, Carlton (Carlton Joseph Huntley Hayes, 1882-1964). Born at Afton, New York; educated at Columbia University, where he afterwards became Professor of History 1919-50. Author of *British Social Politics* (1913), *Political and Social History of Modern Europe* (1916), *Historical Evolution of Modern Nationalism* (1931), and later historical works.

Hayward, John (John Davy Hayward, 1905-65). Born in London; educated at Gresham's School and Cambridge. Though disabled by paralysis in his twenties he became well known as a compiler of anthologies and editor of the works of Rochester, Donne, and Swift, and the *Letters* of St Evremonde. He was also an authority on antiquarian books, co-founder and Editorial Director of *The* **Book Collector*, and a vice-president of the Bibliographical Society. *And see* Bibliography.

Hazlewood, Guy. Central character in Compton Mackenzie's *Guy and Pauline* (1915) and friend of Michael Fane in **Sinister Street* (1913-14).

Heard, G. F. Name used by Gerald *Heard for his novels and short stories.

Heard, Gerald (Henry Fitzgerald Heard, 1889-). Born in London; educated at Sherborne and Cambridge. Books on history, science, ethics, and religion—*The Ascent of Humanity* (1929), *The Social Substance of Religion* (1931), *The Emergence of Man* (1932), *Science in the Making* (1935), *Exploring the Stratosphere* (1936), *The Creed of Christ* (1940), etc. As G. F. Heard: *A Taste for Honey* (1941), *Murder by Reflection* (1945), *The Notched Hairpin* (1952); *The Great Fog and other Weird Tales* (1947), *The Lost Cavern and other Tales of the Fantastic* (1948). Settled in California.

Hearne, John (1926-). Born in Canada of Jamaican parents; educated in Jamaica and (after serving in the R.A.F. in World War II) at Edinburgh and London Universities; taught in English schools and became a staff tutor for the University of the West Indies. Author of *Voices Under the Window* (1955), *Stranger at the Gate* (1956), *The Faces of Love* (1957), *Autumn Equinox* (1959), *Land of the Living* (1961), and other novels, as well as short stories, poems, etc.

Hearst, William Randolph (1863-1951). Born in San Francisco; educated at Harvard. Beginning with the San Francisco *Examiner*, which was owned by his father, he bought the New York *Morning Journal* and a large number of other papers, becoming the most clamorous newspaper magnate in the United States. He aimed to become a power in politics and ran campaigns in opposition to national leaders. Sensationalism in the presentation of news, often slanted in conformity with his own irresponsible passions, was almost the sole aim of the journalistic empire he controlled. He was the American counterpart of *Northcliffe in Britain, though with none of Northcliffe's original scruples.

Heart of Darkness. Story by Joseph *Conrad published in 1902 in **Youth and Two Other Stories*. One of four friends on a cruising yawl waiting in the sea-reach of the Thames for the turn of the tide, *Marlow tells of his appointment by a Continental trading company to succeed one of their river-steamer captains who has been killed by natives in central Africa. He goes out on a French ship to the mouth of the big river he is to traverse. On reaching the Company's station thirty miles up-river he finds 'objectless blasting' work going on, and is horrified by what he describes as 'a grove of death', in which diseased and starving outcast native workers of the Company are slowly dying. He begins to hear of a Mr Kurtz, described as 'a first-class agent . . . a very remarkable person' in charge of the farthest trading-post, 'a very important one, in the true ivory-country. . . . Sends in as much ivory as all the others put together.' The next stage of Marlow's journey is a two-hundred-mile tramp with native carriers to the Central Station on a backwater of the big river, where he finds that the steamer he was appointed to command is sunk. Raising and repairing the vessel takes months, during which Marlow gathers more information about Kurtz, particularly from an aristocratic young agent (engaged as brickmaker but without material essential for brickmaking) who refers to Kurtz as a 'uni-

versal genius'. When at length Marlow succeeds in getting the repaired steamer close to
its destination, a rain of arrows greets them
from the dense jungle, killing the native
helmsman. The white passengers fire futilely,
but the attackers retreat in panic at the sound
of blasts from the steam whistle. Before Kurtz
appears, a mortally sick man borne on a
stretcher, Marlow has been given cause to
believe him demented by years of solitude,
evil, and 'hollow at the core'. He dies on the
steamer's return down the river, after prolonged raving discourse—hiding 'in the magnificent folds of eloquence the barren darkness of his heart'. The words in which a native
boy announces his end, 'Mistah Kurtz—he
dead', were taken by T. S. *Eliot as epigraph
for his poem 'The Hollow Men' (1925).

Heartbreak House: A Fantasia in the Russian
manner on English themes. Play in three acts
by Bernard *Shaw performed in New York
in 1920 and in London in 1921; begun before
the outbreak of World War I, finished during
the war, published in 1919. An eccentric 88-
year-old retired master mariner, Captain
Shotover, lives with his daughter Hesione,
her husband Hector Hushabye, and Nurse
Guinness (former nannie, now housekeeper)
in a Sussex villa, where he has had the main
room built and fitted 'to resemble the after
part of an old-fashioned high-pooped ship
with a stern gallery'. Hesione has invited a
young friend, Ellie Dunn, to stay, but finding
no one about when she arrives she falls asleep
in a chair until Nurse Guinness is called by
the Captain when he sees the girl through the
window. He upbraids his household for their
lack of hospitable manners, but himself upsets
Ellie by asking if her father is the Dunn, ex-
pirate, he once had as a boatswain. He tells
her of his daughters: Hesione, who runs the
house, and of Ariadne (Addie) and 'her num-
skull of a husband'. Ariadne then arrives
from abroad, furious that no one is at home
to receive her, and says to Ellie: 'My husband
is Sir Hastings Utterword, who has been
governor of all the crown colonies in succession'. When she kisses her father, who refuses
to recognize her, he tells her she should grow
out of kissing strange men who may be trying
to attain 'the seventh degree of concentration', which he states at intervals during the
play is his own aim. Hesione rushes in to Ellie,
affectionately apologetic, and it is revealed
that Ellie is engaged to Boss Mangan, 'a
perfect hog of a millionaire for the sake of

her father', Mazzini Dunn, who arrives and is
mistaken by the Captain for his former boatswain. Mazzini, a clever idealist with no commercial skill, is bested by financiers, the latest
being Mangan, who to his own profit has provided Mazzini with capital. Ellie supposes
this is a generous act she must repay by
marrying him. When Mangan is in the house
as a guest, Ellie hypnotizes him while sooth-
ing his headache, and in the trance he hears
an unflattering conversation between Hesione
and Ellie about himself. Ellie has also told
Hesione that she is in love with a Marcus
Darnley she met at a concert, who told her
excitingly heroic stories about himself, but
who now proves to be Hector Hushabye,
Hesione's romancing and ladykilling husband. Lady Utterword's diamonds are stolen
by a burglar who is caught and discovered to
be Billy Dunn, the Captain's pirate-boatswain
and Nurse Guinness's vanished husband. In
the final scene in the garden a prolonged discussion is ended when bombs dropped in an
air raid explode the Captain's dynamite in a
nearby gravel pit and kill Mangan and the
burglar, who have sought shelter there. The
heart of the play is in the Captain's oracular
and prophetic utterances. Shaw's 'heartbreak
house' was contemporary England, in danger
of destruction because her leaders were like a
drunken skipper lying in his bunk while the
crew gamble in the forecastle. Ellie feels herself to be Captain Shotover's spiritual wife.
When she talks of marrying Mangan for his
money and the fine things it will provide, the
Captain replies: '. . . if you sell yourself, you
deal your soul a blow that all the books and
pictures and concerts and scenery in the
world won't heal.'

Heaslop, Ronny. City Magistrate at Chandrapore, in E. M. Forster's *A *Passage to India*
(1925); breaks off his engagement to Adela
Quested after she withdraws her charge
against Dr Aziz.

Heath-Stubbs, John (John Francis Heath
Stubbs, 1918-   ). Born in London; educa-
ted in Sussex and the Isle of Wight and at
Oxford. Collections of poems: *Wounded
Thammuz* (1942), *Beauty and the Beast* (1943),
The Charity of the Stars (1949), *The Swarm-
ing of the Bees* (1950). Criticism: *The Darkling
Plain* (1950).

Hecate County, Memoirs of. *See* Edmund
*Wilson.

Hecht, Ben (1894-1964). Born in New York.

Worked as a circus acrobat and then as a journalist before turning novelist and playwright, succeeeding mainly in the theatre and cinema, notably (in both media) with *The Front Page*, in collaboration with Charles MacArthur (staged 1928, filmed later). He incurred odium in Britain with his unmeasured condemnation of her as mandatory power in Palestine before Israel became an independent nation.

Heidegger, Martin (1889-   ). Born at Messkirch, Baden; educated at the University of Freiburg where he subsequently became Professor of Philosophy from 1929 to 1945. One of the leading German philosophers of his time, he was much influenced by *Kierkegaard and, against his own declaration, was regarded as one of the propounders of *Existentialism. His writings, too abstruse for general comprehension, mostly remain in their original German, but *Existence and Being* (1949) and *An Introduction to Metaphysics* (1960) are available in English translations.

Heinemann, William (1863-1920). Born at Surbiton, soon after his parents had migrated from Hanover to England; educated in Dresden and privately in England. Studied music in Germany, but his love of books led him to train in publishing. He started his own business in 1890. He was successful from the start and within a few years many of the leading contemporary authors, especially novelists and playwrights, were in his list and most remained with him: A. W. *Pinero, Somerset *Maugham, Max *Beerbohm, H. G. *Wells, John *Galsworthy, John *Masefield, as well as numerous less remembered but often more popular and profitable writers. The sound foundations he laid kept William Heinemann Ltd in the forefront of English publishing for long after his death, and its interests extended to other countries. His own few plays—*The First Step* (1895), *War* (1901), etc.—published by another firm were of no great merit.

Hellman, Lillian (1907-   ). Born in New Orleans; educated at New York and Columbia Universities. Internationally renowned as a playwright, principally with *The Children's Hour* (1934), *The Little Foxes* (1939), *Watch on the Rhine* (1941), *Another Part of the Forest* (1946), *Toys in the Attic* (1960). Her experiences in Spain and Russia and her contacts with leading writers in the U.S. are described in *An Unfinished Woman* (1969) and *Pentiments: A Book of Portraits* (1974).

Hemingway, Ernest (Ernest Miller Hemingway, 1899-1961). Born at Oak Park, Illinois, and educated there. A short term as reporter on a Kansas City newspaper preceded service in the Italian army in World War I, during which he was wounded. These experiences gave rise to the novel *A *Farewell to Arms* (1929), which was the first important landmark in the growth of his literary reputation. In the early 1920s he settled in Paris, one among the many American expatriates then congregated there. *Men Without Women* (1927), a collection of short stories, highlights the characteristic Hemingway prose style, with its clipped staccato dialogue and affectation of tough masculinity. He was probably the inspirer of the contemporary cult of enthusiasm for bullfighting as a spectacle, which was taken up by other English-speaking authors, following on Hemingway's *Death in the Afternoon* (1932), one of the products of his sojourns in Spain where, during the Civil War, he acted as correspondent for an American news agency and also gestated his novel, *For Whom the Bell Tolls* (1940). As is suggested by the title of his bull-fighting book, mentioned above, death was one of Hemingway's main preoccupations—a consummation towards which he felt or assumed a distinctive urge. This death-wish, generated by the first World War and facilitated by the second—Hemingway served in both—also became a widespread cult, and may have served to inflate his reputation. The legend of the man will need to diminish before the ultimate value of his writings can appear. His last short novel *The Old Man and the Sea* (1952) was thought by some to be his masterpiece after the relative failure of *Across the River and Into the Trees* (1950). Mention should also be made of his early novel *The Sun Also Rises* (1926).

Hémon, Louis (1880-1913). Born in Brest. He spent some years in London and lived his last year in Canada, where he was accidentally killed by a train. A completed novel published after his death, *Maria Chapdelaine* (English translation 1921), gave him posthumous fame.

Henderson, Archibald (1877-1963). Born in North Carolina; educated at University of North Carolina, Cambridge, Berlin, and Paris. At his own university he progressed from the post of Instructor in Mathematics in

1898 to Professor and Head of the Department till his retirement in 1948. Though eminent as a mathematician and leading early interpreter in America of the theory of relativity (he had worked with Einstein in Berlin), it was as a literary biographer that he became more widely known. He was first in the field with a full-length book on Shaw—*George Bernard Shaw, His Life and Work* (1921), which was followed by *Table Talk of G.B.S.* (1925) and other writings on the playwright, culminating in *George Bernard Shaw: Man of the Century* (1956). In the course of preparing these works he visited Shaw on a number of occasions, and they frequently corresponded. He also wrote *Mark Twain* (1911), *O. Henry: A Memorial Essay* (1914), and on other modern authors.

Henderson, Mary. First pseudonym of O. H. Mavor; *see* James *Bridie.

Henderson, Miriam. Central character in Dorothy *Richardson's *Pilgrimage* sequence (1915-38).

Henderson, Paul. *See* Ruth *France.

Henderson, Sylvia. *See* Ashton-Warner, Sylvia.

Henley, W. E. (William Ernest Henley, 1849-1903). Best known as a close friend of Robert Louis Stevenson, with whom he collaborated in a volume of plays (1892) containing *Deacon Brodie*, *Macaire*, etc., and as editor from 1888 to 1893 of the *National Observer* (originally the *Scots Observer*) and other periodicals in which he encouraged a number of young men (including Rudyard *Kipling and Joseph *Conrad) who afterwards became leading writers in the new century. Henley was himself a poet of some originality, often using unrhymed metres more in the mode of the next generation than of his own. His imperialism made him, like Kipling, unpopular with the anti-imperialists, whose opinion of his writings was dictated by political prejudice. *Collected Poems* appeared in 1908, and from 1894 to the year of his death he collaborated in the compilation of a *Dictionary of Slang*.

Henriques, R. D. (Robert David Quixano Henriques, 1905-67). Born in London; educated at Rugby and Oxford. Joined the British army as a professional soldier and had much experience of foreign service from 1926 onward as a commissioned officer, with an interval in the Territorial Army from 1933 to 1939 during which he farmed in the Cots-

wolds, was unsuccessful in publishing, and engaged in a hunting trip in Africa. In World War II he was recalled to the army, took part in Commando raids, and was active as a staff officer in the invasions of Italy and France. At the end of the war he toured the U.S. on a War Bonds mission, before taking up farming again in England. His many and varied experiences provided background material for novels: *Death by Moonlight* (1938), *No Arms, No Armour* (1939), *The Journey Home* (1944), *A Stranger Here* (1953), *Red over Green* (1955). Other books: *The Cotswolds* (1950), *Marcus Samuel, First Viscount Bearstead* (1960), *From a Biography of Myself* (1969).

Henry, Frederic. Central character in Ernest Hemingway's *A *Farewell to Arms* (1929); lieutenant in an Italian ambulance unit in World War I; lover of Catherine Barkley.

Henry, O. (pseudonym of William Sydney Porter 1862-1910). Born in North Carolina. He had little schooling and from 1875 drifted through various occupations—in shops and offices, on a ranch, in a bank, and as a journalist. In 1898 he was given a five-year prison sentence in Ohio on a charge of embezzling funds of the bank in which he had worked, though there has remained some doubt of the justice of the accusation. Good conduct abbreviated the prison term considerably, and from 1901 he lived mainly in New York, where his contacts with an almost unlimited range of city types below the exclusive social levels gave him basic material for the hundreds of short stories he wrote in his last five years. These were immensely popular for a decade or more after he died and will continue to attract by their humanity, humour, compassion and gentle irony. The author's outstanding technical device—the surprise ending—decreases in surprisingness by frequent repetition, though it is effective in many of the stories, among which 'The *Gift of the Magi' is perhaps the best. Henry's *milieu* is aptly indicated by the title of his second collection, *The *Four Million* (1906)—the swarming multitudes of the highways and byways, in contradistinction to 'the four hundred' of the American aristocracy's Social Register. Other volumes: *Waifs and Strays* (1906), *The Voice of the City* (1908), *Sixes and Sevens* (1911).

Henson, Hensley (Herbert Hensley Henson, 1863-1947). Born in London; educated privately and at Oxford. Ordained 1887. Vicar of Barking, 1888-95; Canon of Westminster, 1900-12; Dean of Durham, 1912-18. Successively Bishop of Hereford, 1918-20, and Durham, 1920-39. His unorthodox views on the Virgin Birth and the New Testament miracles aroused considerable opposition which he faced with great integrity of mind. Author of *Sincerity and Subscription* (1903), *The Liberty of Prophesying* (1909), *The Oxford Groups* (1933), *Bishoprick Papers* (1946), and a three-volume autobiography, *Retrospect of an Unimportant Life* (1942-50).

Henty, G. A. (George Alfred Henty, 1832-1902). Born near Cambridge; educated at Westminster and Cambridge. Employed as correspondent for London papers in the Crimean and Franco-Prussian wars. He then became for several decades the most successful living writer of historical novels for boys, the majority centred on some campaign in which British forces served with success or distinction. The scores of titles included: *With Moore at Corunna* (1898), *With Buller in Natal* (1901), *With Roberts to Pretoria* (1902), *With the Allies to Pekin* (1904). They ceased to appeal to the more sophisticated young people of later generations, and Henty's novels for adults (*A Woman of the Commune*, 1895; etc) are almost entirely forgotten.

Heppenstall, Rayner (John Rayner Heppenstall, 1911-   ). Born in Yorkshire; educated at the University of Leeds and in Calais and Strasbourg. Author of *Poems 1933-1945* (1946) and later collections. As a novelist (*The Lesser Infortune,* 1953; *The Greater Infortune,* 1960; *The Connecting Door,* 1962; *The Woodshed,* 1962) he employs 'a modified stream-of-consciousness' technique.

Herbert, A. P. (Sir Alan Patrick Herbert, 1890-1971; knighted 1945). Born in London; educated at Winchester and Oxford. He studied law and was called to the Bar in 1918 after war service with the Royal Navy. For many years a contributor to *Punch,* he was witty, adroit and technically accomplished as a writer of light verse and humorous prose. His *Misleading Cases in the Common Law* (1929 and later collections) made effective use of his legal knowledge in poking fun at some of the anomalies and absurdities of court procedure, usually involving a client he named Haddock, acceptable as a fictional

persona of the author. As a novelist his outstanding book, *The Water Gypsies* (1930), is a product of his love of boats and the river. From 1935, until the Labour Government abolished parliamentary representation for the universities in 1950, he was independent member for Oxford University, and interested himself especially in divorce-law reform, introducing the Matrimonial Causes Bill which became law in 1938. The same subject was the theme of his novel, *Holy Deadlock* (1934). He also campaigned for better English in *What a Word* (1935), while among other products of his manifold interests and versatility were lyrics for *Riverside Nights* (1926) and several operas— *Tantivy Towers* (1930), *Bless the Bride* (1947) and others. *A Book of Ballads* (1949) contains the best of his light verse.

Herford, Oliver (1863-1935). Born in Sheffield; educated at Lancaster College and (after his family settled in America) in Ohio. Later studied art in London and Paris, but became reputed as a writer of humorous verse; often with animals as the main theme: *Rubaiyat of a Persian Kitten* (1904), *A Little Book of Bores* (1906), *Cupid's Encyclopedia* (1910), and many other volumes, besides plays.

Hergesheimer, Joseph (1880-1954). Born in Philadelphia; educated at Germantown; studied art at the Pennsylvania Academy. His first novel (*The Lay Anthony*) was published in 1914, his last (*The Foolscap Rose*) in 1934, after which he deliberately ceased to write. He had a spell of limited popularity in England with *The Three Black Pennys* (1917), *Gold and Iron* (1918), and *Java Head* (1919). Autobiography: *The Presbyterian Child* (1923).

Heron, Irene. Marries Soames Forsyte in *A Man of Property* (1906), the first-published part of *The *Forsyte Saga* (1922). Later, after divorce, she marries Young Jolyon Forsyte.

Herrick, Robert (1591-1674). Vicar of Dean Prior in Devonshire and prolific lyrical poet. He is a leading character in Rose Macaulay's **They Were Defeated* (1932).

Herrick, Robert (1868-1938). Born in Cambridge, Mass; educated there and at Harvard, where he became a Professor of English, 1893-1923. Government Secretary of the Virgin Islands from 1935. Author of realistic novels: *The Real World* (1901), *The Common Lot* (1904), *One Woman's Life*

(1913), *Waste* (1924), *The End of Desire* (1932) and several volumes of short stories.

Herries family. In the several parts of Hugh *Walpole's Herries Chronicle: Rogue Herries* (1930), *Judith Paris* (1931), *The Fortress* (1932), *Vanessa* (1933).

Herriton family. In E. M. Forster's *Where Angels Fear to Tread* (1905): **Mrs Herriton,** mother of **Harriet** and **Philip**; mother-in-law of **Lilia,** widow of **Charles Herriton** and mother of **Irma.** Lilia remarries in Italy and dies in childbirth.

Herself Surprised. Novel by Joyce *Cary published in 1941, the first of a trilogy continued with *To be a Pilgrim* (1942) and completed with *The *Horse's Mouth* (1944), each book a first-person narrative by one of the three chief characters.

In this first of the novels, Sara, brought up on a farm, her father a freeholder and working foreman, her mother a teacher, goes into domestic service and by the year of Queen Victoria's Diamond Jubilee (1897) is cook to the Monday family in a southern cathedral town. The son Matthew, partner in a foundry business, escapes from domination by his mother and sister by marrying Sara, who at first finds herself fitting uneasily into the changed social environment, choosing clothes that are too bright and 'loud', after the manner of her exuberant friend from childhood, Rosina Balmforth, called Rozzie, wife of a publican. Sara is nevertheless happy with her husband and four daughters, until Matt becomes violently jealous of a rich friend, Hickson, whose mild advances to Sara have not, however, been encouraged by her. Further discord arises from the presence and importunities of Gulley Jimson, a painter of genius but an unprincipled scrounger, who has been provided with a studio in the Mondays' house. Though Sara is without illusions about Jimson, he has a compelling influence on her, and after her husband's death she lives with him as his mistress, only leaving him when he knocks her about. Now middle-aged, she takes a post as cook at a rat-infested country house owned by Mr Wilcher, an elderly solicitor with sexual urges towards young girls. Sara admits him to her bed, and after a fire at his town house he takes a small suburban house, proposing to marry her, but his elder daughter has Sara arrested for theft. Over the years she has been purloining small

articles and had already been in prison for giving bad cheques when she was heavily in debt on account of Gulley Jimson, who continued to batten on her. Sara's self-portrait is of a naively innocent, amoral, yet Christian woman who accepts herself and others according to their nature, without shame or self-pity, having malice towards none and charity towards all.

Hersey, John (John Richard Hersey, 1914-). Born in China; educated in the U.S. at Yale and in England at Cambridge. War correspondent in Europe and the Pacific for American periodicals during World War II. *Men on Bataan* (1942), *A Bell for Adano* (1944), *Hiroshima* (1946), *The Wall* (1950) reflect in their several ways his wartime memories.

Herzog, Émile. *See* André *Maurois.

Hesione. *See* Hushabye.

Hewitt, Martin. Detective in crime novels by Arthur *Morrison.

Hewlett, Maurice (Maurice Henry Hewlett, 1861-1923). Born in Kent; educated in London; studied law and was called to the Bar but did not practise. Keeper of Land Revenue Records, 1896-1900. He became immediately successful with his romantic historical novel, *The Forest Lovers* (1898), and followed it with other romances of the medieval period *Richard Yea-and-Nay* (1900), *The Queen's Quair* (1904), *The Fool Errant* (1905). In the modern trilogy *Halfway House* (1908), *Open Country* (1909) and *Rest Harrow* (1910), the central character, John *Senhouse, is an advocate of voluntary poverty, a theme near to the heart of the author, who aspired towards the simple life and had deep fellow-feeling for the poor, particularly for farm labourers, whose age-long part in the history of the English nation he memorialized in his long narrative poem, *The Song of the Plow* (1916), which deserves to be remembered for its presentation of a neglected phase of English history. Hewlett's later novels—which included in *Frey and His Wife* (1916), *Thorgils* (1917), and *Gudrid the Fair* (1918) excursions into northern mythology—are of less account than the essays written in his last period and collected as *In a Green Shade* (1920), *Wiltshire Essays* (1921), *Extempory Essays* (1922) and *Last Essays* (posthumously, 1924). His love of Italy was shown in such earlier books as *Little Novels of*

Italy (1899) and the non-fictional *Earthwork out of Tuscany* (1895) and *The Road in Tuscany* (1904). He published several volumes of lyrical poems and miscellaneous prose.

Hext, Harrington. Pseudonym used by Eden *Phillpotts for *Number 87* (1922), *The Thing of Their Heels* (1923), *Who Killed Diana?* (1924).

Heyer, Georgette (1902-1974). Author of popular historical romances set largely in the Regency period: *The Regency Buck* (1935), *The Corinthian* (1940), *Penhallow* (1942), *Arabella* (1949), *The Quiet Gentleman* (1951), *Bath Tangle* (1955); also many detective novels, including *Footsteps in the Dark* (1932), *Death in the Stocks* (1935), *Detection Unlimited* (1953).

Heyerdahl, Thor (1914-   ). Born in Larvik, Norway; educated at the University of Oslo. Engaged in archaeological and anthropological research in the Pacific and British Columbia, 1937-40. On active service with a Free Norwegian parachute unit, 1940-45. To test his theory that Polynesia could have been settled by Indians from the western seaboard of South America, he constructed a raft of balsa-wood logs held together by rope, and with a few companions traversed in 101 days the 4,300 miles of ocean from Callao in Peru to Tuamotu Island in the South Pacific, thus demonstrating the possibility of a trans-Pacific migration in prehistoric times. The account of his voyage was published in Norway in 1948 and in England as *The Kon-Tiki Expedition*. A later book, *Aku-Aku* (1958), endeavoured to account for the origin and explain the method of erection of the great hewn statues on Easter Island, representative specimens of which are in the British Museum.

Heyst, Axel. Central character in Joseph Conrad's *Victory* (1915). His inherited philosophy of detachment as an 'unconcerned spectator' of human affairs is overborne by his spontaneous practical sympathy in rescuing Captain Morrison from financial ruin and Lena from sexual persecution.

Heyward, Du Bose (1885-1940). Born in Charleston. Family misfortune deprived him of educational advantages and forced him into clerical work at an early age. He

began to write verse, published in *Carolina Chansons* (1922) and *Skylines and Horizons* (1924), without notable success, but his novel of negro life, *Porgy* (1925), became increasingly famous on reaching the stage first as a straight play and then as an opera, *Porgy and Bess*, with George Gershwin's music.

Hibbert, Christopher (1924-   ). Educated at Radley and Oxford. Author of historical and biographical works, including *The Road to Tyburn* (1957), *King Mob* (1958), *Corunna* (1961), *The Battle of Arnhem* (1962), *The Court at Windsor* (1964), *Garibaldi and His Enemies* (1965), *The Making of Charles Dickens* (1967), *London* (1969).

Hichens, Robert (Robert Smythe Hichens, 1864-1950). Born in Kent; educated at Tunbridge Wells and Clifton, and in London at the Royal College of Music. After a course at a school of journalism he began to contribute to magazines, and in 1894 published with immediate success *The Green Carnation*, a satire on the contemporary aesthetic movement which, on account of its period associations, seems the only book by Hichens that is likely to survive. In his lifetime, however, it was obscured by the popular appeal of such novels as *The Garden of Allah* (1904) and *Bella Donna* (1909), both of which had long runs when adapted for the stage and further acclaim as films. The list of Hichens's later novels and short stories is lengthy but, apart from *The Paradine Case* (1933), holds little interest.

Higgins, Henry. Central male character in Shaw's *Pygmalion* (1914); professor of phonetics; teaches Eliza Doolittle to speak pure English. Modelled on Henry Sweet, 'greatest British philologist and chief founder of modern phonetics' (*D.N.B.*). A character with the same name appeared in a farce by Charles Selby, *The Boots at the Swan* (1842), in a revival of which Ellen Terry at the age of eight took the part of Jacob Earwig (the 'Boots') in 1855.

High Wind in Jamaica, A. Novel by Richard *Hughes published in 1929. Following an earthquake and a hurricane which demolishes their house and devastates the landscape, Mr and Mrs Bas-Thornton, English settlers in Jamaica, send their five children to be schooled in England. John, the eldest, Emily, aged ten, Edward, Rachel and the three-year-old Laura, are accompanied on the ship by a distant neighbour's children, Margaret Fernandez (thirteen) and her little brother Harry. Leaving Montego Bay on the barque *Clorinda*, the children find life on board as entertaining as a circus, until the barque is boarded by pirates disguised as women passengers from an apparently harmless schooner, to which the children are removed while the *Clorinda* is ransacked of stores and specie. Captain Jonsen intended to return his young captives to their rightful vessel after transhipping the plunder, but Captain Marple and his crew escape with the *Clorinda* and he reports that the children have been murdered by the pirates. The Thorntons and Harry Fernandez, after their initial discomfort and bewilderment, 'settled down quietly to grow', scarcely noticing the absence of John, who, unknown to them, fell and broke his neck while ashore in Santa Lucia, where Jonsen failed to persuade the Chief Magistrate's wife to relieve him of the children. When the pirates take another vessel and tie up the Dutch captain, he is left bound in the cabin where Emily is lying with an injured leg. He tries to reach a knife to cut his bonds; but Emily, in terror of him and screaming unheard by the crew, seizes the knife and kills him. Margaret, who has spent most of the voyage in Jonsen's cabin, is suspected of the crime and thrown overboard, but is rescued by other members of the crew. By a plausible tale Jonsen induces the captain of a Dutch steamer to take the children. There, and when they reach England, they are, to their amazement, idolized as young heroes and heroines escaped from deadly peril. When Jonsen and his crew are captured and brought to trial, no charges against them can be got from the children. But when Emily breaks down in court, her hysterical recollection of the Dutch captain's death is interpreted as evidence of murder against the pirates.

Highet, Gilbert (Gilbert Arthur Highet, 1906-   ). Born in Glasgow; educated there and at Oxford. Professor of Greek and Latin, Columbia University, New York, 1938-50, and Professor of Latin Language and Literature there from 1950. In his writings he combines genuine scholarship with skill as a popularizer, and he exercised this conjoint faculty as a book reviewer for *Harper's Magazine* and broadcaster in New York, some of this material being published in *People, Races and Books* (1953). Other works: *The Classical Tradition: Greek and Roman Influences on Western Literature* (1949), *The Art of Teaching* (1951), *Man's Unconquerable Mind* (1954), *The Migration of Ideas* (1954), *A Clerk of Oxenford* (1954), *Juvenal the Satirist* (1954), *The Anatomy of Satire* (1962).

Hilda Lessways. Novel by Arnold *Bennett published in 1911, the second volume of the trilogy begun with *Clayhanger* (1910) and completed with *These Twain* (1916).
Hilda Lessways, born at Turnhill in the *Five Towns pottery district of Staffordshire and living there in 1878 with her widowed mother, is drawn into acquaintanceship when twenty-one with George Cannon, 'indefinitely older than herself', a local solicitor who becomes her mother's rent collector. At his suggestion Hilda takes a phonography course and, as 'the only girl in the Five Towns who knew shorthand', is installed as 'editorial secretary' when Cannon starts a shortlived newspaper. From a former school friend, Janet Orgreave, Hilda learns that Cannon's quarrelsome half-sister, Sarah Gailey, is in need, unknown to him, and she is deputed to inform him. Cannon sets Sarah up in a boarding-house in London where her friend, Hilda's mother, goes to stay with her. Hilda receives a telegram from Sarah with the news that her mother is ill; but, absorbed in her work on the paper, she delays going to London. Her mother has died before Hilda arrives, and she is overwhelmed by a conviction of sin. Janet Orgreave finds her in London and they go up to Bursley together. There Hilda is introduced to Edwin Clayhanger and is excited by his non-religious views. She is persuaded by Cannon to return to London to dissuade Sarah Gailey from giving up the boarding-house. He also reveals that he is not a qualified solicitor and, threatened with prosecution for acting as one, is leaving the Five Towns and going into the hotel business. He transfers Sarah from London to another boarding-house in Brighton. There, Hilda becomes engaged to him and they marry at the registrar's office in Lewes. Later, a malicious servant girl spreads the news that Cannon already has a wife in Devonshire. He admits that he has married Hilda bigamously, and at once goes 'out of the house and out of her life'. She visits Janet Orgreave, who is unaware of the marriage, and while in Bursley she and

Edwin Clayhanger fall in love. Hilda is called back to Brighton by an urgent telegram from Sarah, who is now bedridden. Finding that she is pregnant, Hilda writes to Janet that she is married to George Cannon and asks her to tell Edwin. (Her future, until she marries Edwin, is outlined in *Clayhanger* and their married life is detailed in *These Twain*.)

Hill, Jenny. Salvation Army lassie in Shaw's **Major Barbara* (1905).

Hillary, Sir Edmund (1919-   ; knighted 1953). Born in New Zealand; educated there at Auckland. Joined expeditions to the Himalayas and as a member of that of 1953 (led by Col. John Hunt) was the first to reach the summit of Everest, accompanied by the Indian Sherpa, Norgay Tenzing. The story was told by Sir John Hunt (knighted 1953) in *The Ascent of Everest* (1953) and *Our Everest Adventure* (1954). Hillary, as leader of the New Zealand Transantarctic Expedition, completed the overland journey to the South Pole early in 1958, and with a fellow member, Sir Vivian Fuchs, wrote *The Crossing of Antarctica* (1958).

Hillary, Richard (Richard Hope Hillary, 1919-1943). Born in Sydney, Australia; educated in England at Oxford where he was an excellent oarsman and went to Germany with a University crew which defeated the Germans in a contest for the Hermann Goering Cup. As a pilot in the Royal Air Force he was shot down and badly disfigured in 1940 two days after World War II really began. A series of plastic surgery operations on his face and other treatment kept him in hospital for some two years, but he insisted on returning to active service with the R.A.F. and was killed when his plane crashed shortly after. His personal record, *The Last Enemy* (published in 1942), written in moving prose, is a masterpiece of the war.

Hillcrist. Country gentleman in Galsworthy's *The *Skin Game* (1920); 'about fifty-five . . . refined, rather kindly, . . . rather cranky countenance'; resents encroachments by Hornblower, newly rich manufacturer. **Jill,** his daughter and ally, 'upstanding . . . nineteen . . . pretty, manly face', outspoken and slangy.

Hilton, James (1900-1954). Born at Leigh, Lancashire; educated at school and uni-

versity in Cambridge. He contributed to various English and Irish papers and made his name with *Goodbye, Mr Chips* a sentimental story with a school background first published in the *British Weekly* at the end of 1933 and as a book in the following year. For some years, however, Hilton's main contribution to literature seemed to be *Lost Horizon* (1933), its *dolce far niente* land of **Shangri-La* creating restful longings in its many thousands of readers and providing them with a simple philosophy distilled in persuasive prose. Other novels: *Contango* (1932), *Knight Without Armour* (1933), *We are Not Alone* (1937). For *Murder at School* (1931) he used the pseudonym Glen Trevor.

Hindle Wakes. A play in three acts by Stanley **Houghton 'about Lancashire people', performed first in London in 1912. Alan Jeffcote, son of a prosperous cottonmill owner, and Fanny Hawthorne, a weaver at the mill, spend a weekend together at Llandudno 'for a bit of fun'. Her father, a lifelong friend of Nathaniel Jeffcote but now one of his employees, is outraged by the discovery of the young couple's escapade and, in conformity with local standards of morality with the fervent support of his wife and Nathaniel Jeffcote, determines that they shall marry, although Alan is engaged to Beatrice, daughter of the Mayor, Sir Timothy Farrar. She, too, insists that it is his duty to marry Fanny. When all four parents assemble 'to settle when the wedding's to be', Fanny disrupts the whole plan by stoutly refusing to marry Alan 'to turn him into an honest man'. She declares that she will leave home and live her own life on what she earns as a weaver; Alan goes off to cajole Beatrice. Written at the height of the campaign for the emancipation of women, the play had great success as a startling declaration of independence and manifesto of 'the new morality' by Fanny Hawthorne.

Hindsight. Wisdom after the event. Declaring what should have been done when it is too late to do it.

Hindus, Maurice (Maurice Gerschon Hindus, 1891-1969). Born in Russia; taken to the United States in 1905 knowing no English; educated there in piecemeal fashion and eventually at Harvard. Visits to Russia in the 1920s and during World War II resulted in a number of books, among them *Humanity*

Uprooted (1929), *Moscow Skies* (1936), *Mother Russia* (1943), *The Cossacks* (1946).

Hinkson, Mrs Katherine. *See* Katherine *Tynan.

Hippies. Successors to the *Beatniks, and like them originating in California. They affected to renounce the ways and means of contemporary materialistic society, from which they became known as 'drop-outs'. Their principles were opposed to 'taking a job', except as an occasional means of keeping alive; they 'slept rough' and in London in the late 1960s resorted to 'squatting' in (taking unauthorized possession of) vacant buildings. They adopted shabbiness in clothes and personal appearance, and some were in fashion as drug addicts. While a proportion of the cult were genuine ascetics and high principled, they were infiltrated by others of hooligan breed. As disciples of peace their slogan was 'Make love not war', and among them were those who took the name 'flower children' and wore ornaments designed to identify them. Their title derives from the jazz age slang 'hip'—'with it' (i.e. in conformity with the *mores* of the cult).

Hiroshima. An account of the effects of the first atom bomb on the Japanese city, by John *Hersey (1946).

History of Mr Polly, The. Novel by H. G. *Wells published in 1910. Alfred Polly, aged 37½, is introduced sitting on a stile and suffering from indigestion due to the unsuitable meals provided by his wife. He has been educated partly at a National School by mainly untrained teachers, and then 'finished off' incompetently at a private school. At fourteen he starts work in a 'rather low-class' department store, and afterwards drifts from job to job until a small legacy from his father enables him to take a little shop of his own at Fishbourne after marrying his cousin Miriam. Fifteen years as a shopkeeper, stocking clothes for men and boys, having led only to bankruptcy, he plans to commit suicide and arson simultaneously in a way to make it appear that he has fallen downstairs with a paraffin lamp and been burnt to death. His widow would then benefit by both fire and life insurance. In the event, he causes 'the great Fishbourne fire' but, rescuing an old lady, is applauded as a hero. He next decides to 'clear out', and takes to the

country roads of Kent and Sussex in spring time, coming ultimately to the Potwell Inn, where the plump landlady employs him as odd-job man. Her drunken nephew Jim makes violent attempts to drive Polly away, but is routed and disappears after a destructive night raid in which he steals Polly's clothes and, being eventually found drowned, is taken to be Polly, at the inquest. Miriam collects the life insurance, and when Polly revisits Fishbourne some years later he finds that she has opened a teashop. He returns to the Potwell Inn and settles there with the plump woman.

Hobbes, John Oliver (pseudonym of Pearl Mary Teresa Richards, 1867-1906; Mrs R. W. Craigie). Born in Boston, U.S.; educated there and in London and Paris. Her family settled in England while she was young and she continued to live there. Her first novel *Some Emotions and a Moral* (1891) created rather more interest than the rest of her fiction, which included *The Serious Wooing* (1901), *Love and the Soul-Hunters* (1902), *The Flute of Pan* (1905). She also wrote plays—*The Wisdom of the Wise* (1900) and others—and many articles in English newspapers and periodicals.

Hobson, Harold. *See* Dramatic Criticism.

Hobson's Choice. A Lancashire comedy by Harold *Brighouse performed and published in 1916. Henry Horatio Hobson, bootmaker in Salford, a widower with three unmarried daughters, tyrannizes over the younger two—Victoria (21) and Alice (23)—but is unable to dominate Maggie (30), who both keeps house and manages the shop with imperturbable efficiency. Albert Prosser, son of the local solicitor, frequently visits the shop to court Alice, but Maggie puts a stop to it by making him buy a pair of boots when he asks only for bootlaces. Mrs Hepworth, an aristocratic customer, demands to know who made her latest pair of boots, and Hobson hesitates to give the workman's name, thinking that she is dissatisfied. When the maker, Willie Mossop, mentally stunted from childhood but a skilful craftsman, is called from the underground workshop, Mrs Hepworth tells him the boots are the best she's ever had and that wherever he goes he will have her custom. Though Maggie is considered a permanent old maid by her family, she browbeats the shy Willie into marrying her, and the business they set up in their new home, a two-room cellar, takes away almost all Hobson's trade. While intoxicated, he falls through a corn-merchant's trap door in the pavement on to a soft pile of bags and lies there sleeping. Threatened with an action for trespass, Hobson agrees to settle out of court for £500, only to find that Maggie, in concert with legally-trained Albert Prosser, has plotted the threatened lawsuit and is dividing the 'damages' between her sisters as marriage portions. She and Willie prosper while Hobson's business dwindles, and they return to the shop, with Maggie's father as a sleeping partner in the new firm of Mossop and Hobson.

Hockaby, Stephen. See Gladys *Mitchell.

Hocking, Joseph (1860-1937). Born in Cornwall, brother of the following; educated at Manchester. He became a nonconformist minister in 1884 after several years as a surveyor. Between 1891 and 1936 he wrote about fifty novels, a number of them with Cornish settings, others on religious or historical themes. Among the latest were *Prodigal Daughters* (1922), *Prodigal Parents* (1923), *Felicity Treverbyn* (1927), *Deep Calleth Deep* (1936).

Hocking, Silas K. (Silas Kitto Hocking, 1850-1935). Born at St Stephen's, Cornwall, and educated there. Became a Methodist minister in Lancashire and elsewhere from 1870 until his resignation in 1896, after which he devoted himself to authorship, adding to the numerous popular novels of religion and sentiment he had been producing since 1878. Among those published in the present century, *A Modern Pharisee* (1907), *The Shadow Between* (1908), and *Watchers in the Dawn* (1920) are characteristic in content and style.

Hodges, Barbara K. (*née* Webber). See Elizabeth *Cambridge.

Hodgson, Ralph (1871-1962). Born at Darlington, Durham. A withdrawn man whose reticence was lifelong, little is known of his personal life, beyond that he ran away from school, was in America from 1889 to 1921, worked as a newspaper and magazine artist in London before World War I, and founded a private press which printed broadsheets and chapbooks illustrated by Claud Lovat Fraser and issued from the *Poetry Book-

shop in London, whence also came the volumes of *Georgian Poetry which included several of Hodgson's best-known pieces, 'The Song of Honour', 'Eve', 'The Gipsy Girl', 'The Bull'. These aroused expectations that he would develop and become not only the best of the Georgians but possibly the major poet of the age. But *The Last Blackbird and other Lines* (1907) and *Poems* (1917), both slim in extent, had no followers until forty years later, when *The Skylark and Other Poems* (1958) appeared in an England where only few remembered him. He had been for some time Lecturer in English at the University of Sendai, Japan, and had afterwards settled in America. The early poems named above are distinguished by metrical skill, forceful utterance, and intense compassion, especially for birds and animals.

Hoff, H. S. (Harry Summerfield Hoff). See William *Cooper.

Hoffe, Monckton (pseudonym of Reaney Monckton Hoffe-Miles, 1881-1951). Born in Connemara. Acted in his own and other plays. Author of *The Little Damozel* (1909), *The Faithful Heart* (1921), *Many Waters* (1928), *Four Days* (1944), etc.

Hogben, Lancelot (Lancelot Thomas Hogben, 1895-   ). Born in Hampshire; educated at Tottenham and Cambridge. Held various university appointments before that of Professor of Medical Statistics in the University of Birmingham, 1947-61. Vice-Chancellor and Principal, University of Guyana, 1963. In addition to learned scientific and mathematical works, he produced valuable popularizations, *Mathematics for the Million* (1936), and *Science for the Citizen* (1938).

Hoggart, Richard (Herbert Richard Hoggart, 1918-   ). Educated at schools in Leeds and at the University there; served in the Royal Artillery 1940-46. Professor of English, Birmingham, from 1962; Director of the Centre for Contemporary Cultural Studies there from 1964; deputy Director-General of Unesco from 1970. With *The Uses of Literacy* (1957) he made an immediate impact. *Higher Education: Demand and Response* (1969) records changes of attitude among young people.

Holcroft, M. H. (Montague Harry Holcroft, 1902-   ). Born at Rangiora, New Zealand; educated at Christchurch. Worked as journalist and editor. Author of numerous prose works, notably *Discovered Isles* (1951), which aimed to examine 'the nature of creative problems in New Zealand', but has been described as, in effect, 'a study of New Zealand civilization'. *See* *New Zealand Writers.

Holland, Vyvyan (Vyvyan Beresford Holland, 1886-1967). Born in London, son of Oscar *Wilde; educated abroad and at Stony-hurst and Cambridge. Practised as a barrister before World War I, in which he served. Author of *The Mediaeval Courts of Love* (1927), *On Bores* (1935), *Son of Oscar Wilde* (autobiography, 1954), *Hand-Coloured Fashion Plates, 1770-1899* (1955), and many translations.

Holme, Constance (1880-1955; Mrs F. B. Punchard). Born in Westmorland where she passed all her life and celebrated in her novels. These made no marked impact when first published, but they had a vogue when reissued later in The World's Classics in consequence of admiration of them by Sir Humphrey Milford of the Oxford University Press. Principal titles, with dates of original publication: *The Lonely Plough* (1914), *The Splendid Fairing* (1919), *The Trumpet in the Dust* (1921).

Holmes, Sherlock. Detective in crime stories by A. Conan *Doyle.

Holtby, Winifred (1898-1935). Born in York-shire; educated at Scarborough and Oxford. Joined the staff of *Time and Tide* as assistant to Lady *Rhondda and was a director of the paper from 1926. She wrote novels of high merit and originality, the most praised, *South Riding* (1936), being a large-scale representation of life and public service in her own much-loved county. *Mandoa! Mandoa!* (1933), with an African setting, satirizes the impact of European civilization on an unsophisticated people. Her under-estimated *Poor Caroline* (1931) is both a moving character-study and an unobtrusively skilful exposure of a charitable organization with a vested interest in indefinite survival after its function is exhausted. Other books: *The Land of Green Ginger* (1927); collections of short stories—*Truth is Not Sober* (1934), *Pavements at Anderby* (1937); *Virginia Woolf: A Critical Study* (1932). She is commemorated in *Testament of Friendship* (1940) by Vera *Brittain.

Honeychurch, Lucy. Marries George Emerson in E. M. Forster's *A* *Room with a View* (1908).

Honeywill, Ruth. In Galsworthy's *Justice* (1910); married to a brutal drunkard; plans to go away with Falder.

Hook, Captain. Pirate in Barrie's *Peter Pan* (1904).

Hoosier. A colloquial name for people living in Indiana. Among the writers to whom the word has been applied, or who have used it, are James Whitcombe *Riley, 'the Hoosier poet'; Meredith *Nicholson (*The Hoosiers* and *A Hoosier Chronicle*); Theodore *Dreiser (*A Hoosier Holiday*). The origin of the nickname is uncertain, but it may originally have been applied to suggest raw rusticity. *See also* Booth *Tarkington.

Hopalong Cassidy. *See* Clarence E. *Mulford.

Hope, Anthony (pseudonym of Sir Anthony Hope Hawkins, 1863-1933; knighted 1918). Born in London; educated at Marlborough and Oxford. Studied law and practised at the Bar until the publication in 1894 of *The Dolly Dialogues* and *The* *Prisoner of Zenda* started his successful career as novelist. Though *The Dolly Dialogues* had an im-mediate vogue, it is now no more than a period museum piece of contemporary society frivolity and outmoded wit. *The Prisoner of Zenda* and its sequel *Rupert of Hentzau* (1898), on the other hand, are established romantic classics and their setting in the imaginary domain of Ruritania has given a word to the English language. The author's numerous other novels have sunk into oblivion. His *Memories and Notes* came out in 1927.

Hope, Laurence (pseudonym of Adela Florence Cory, 1865-1904; Mrs M. H. Nicolson). Born in Gloucestershire; educated in Richmond. Went to India in 1889, where her father was an army officer, and married there (her husband was promoted as Lieutenant-General Nicolson in 1899). She wrote a large number of impassioned lyrics in a pseudo-oriental style, published as *The Garden of Kama* (1901), *Stars of the Desert* (1903), *Indian Love* (1905). Set to music, some of these enjoyed a prolonged vogue among drawing-room, concert and radio vocalists. Mrs Nicolson committed suicide a few weeks after the death of her husband.

Hopkins, Gerard Manley (1844-1889). Born at Stratford, Essex; educated at Highgate and Oxford. In 1866 he joined the Roman Catholic Church, having come under the influence of the Oxford Movement while at the University. He became a member of the Jesuit Order (Society of Jesus) in 1868 and was ordained in 1877, serving variously in the next years as parish priest, missioner, preacher, and in Jesuit schools as teacher of Classics (which he had read at Oxford). In the last five years of his life he was Professor of Classics at University College, Dublin. He had won the poetry prize at Highgate School when he was sixteen, and continued to write poems until, for some seven years, his literary energy lay dormant under the stress of religious preoccupation, reviving in 1876 with the writing of his longest poem (in thirty-five stanzas) 'The Wreck of the Deutschland', dedicated to five Franciscan nuns drowned when the ship sank in December 1875. This poem is, in effect, a compendium of the varied technical devices which give Hopkins's poetry its uniqueness: 'a total complex of style, in which the natural strong beat of the freer kinds of English verse is reinforced by alliteration, assonance, internal rhyme, and half-rhyme'. This analysis is given in the Introduction to the third edition (1948) of Hopkins's poems by W. H. Gardner, who also speaks of the poet's 'constitutional lack of imaginative "staying power"', his 'nervous debility', 'deep spiritual unrest', and 'melancholia'. The true stature of Hopkins among the English poets will not be determined with certainty until his work is cleared of the fog of partiality spread around it by critics who have viewed him more as a 'Catholic poet' than as a poet unadjectived; and until the attraction of his technical innovations has waned, along with the desire to imitate his use of what he called *'Sprung Rhythm'. He steadfastly declined to let his poems appear in print. Many of them were sent in letters to his friend Robert *Bridges, who from time to time after Hopkins's death allowed a few pieces to be included in anthologies, and at length edited, with notes, a first collected edition in 1918. The second edition in 1930, with additional poems and a critical introduction by Charles *Williams, marked the beginning of what 'can only be called a "Hopkins cult"' (Gardner's words in the third edition). The paradox of Hopkins's life was that while religion inspired him with an intense sense of duty, it failed to serve as a source of Christian consolation and inward peace. His was a troubled soul in which faith and the creative instinct were at constant war, a tortuous experience to which certain features of his poetry may be traced—its intricacy, its verbal involutions, and its not infrequent obscurity. A great deal of light is thrown on his personality and his poetry by *The Letters of Gerard Manley Hopkins* (edited by Claude Colleer Abbott, 3 vols, 1955-6) and *The Journals and Papers of Gerard Manley Hopkins* (edited by Humphry House and Graham Storey, 1959).

Horizon. A monthly founded in 1939 and edited throughout by Cyril *Connolly 'to give to writers a place to express themselves, and to readers the best writing we can obtain'. The first number came out in January 1940 and the last (No. 121) in 1950. *The Best of Horizon*, a selection (1950).

Horler, Sydney (1888-1954). Born in Essex; educated in Bristol, where he became a journalist until 1911, when he went to Manchester and later to Fleet Street. Became a publishers' editor before starting to write the first of more than 150 mystery novels, beginning with *The Mystery of No. 1* (1925).

Horn, Alfred Aloysius (born Alfred Aloysius Smith, 1861(?)-1931). Born in Lancashire; educated in Liverpool; went to West Africa as a trader in ivory and rubber, and had gravitated to the level of a down-and-out in Johannesburg when he was persuaded by Ethelreda *Lewis, who heard extraordinary stories from him, to write down all he could remember of his experiences. She edited his rough manuscripts and, after repeated rejections, induced a publisher to issue a selection under the title *Trader Horn* in 1927. Although John *Galsworthy was convinced of the genuineness of the tales of jungle life and wrote an Introduction to the book, it was sceptically received by critics. Doubts of its authenticity, however, did not prevent it from becoming an immediate success, though the popularity was short-lived and not extended to two books that followed.

Hornblower. Manufacturer in John Galsworthy's *The *Skin Game* (1920); father of Charles Hornblower, husband of Chloe.

Hornblower, Chloe. *See* Chloe.

Hornblower, Horatio. Character who appears at various stages of his naval career in novels by C. S. *Forester.

Horniman, A. E. F. (Annie Elizabeth Fredericka Horniman, 1860-1937). Born at Forest Hill, London; educated privately and studied art at the Slade School; secretary to W. B. *Yeats for several years. During the rest of her life she devoted her wealth to the support of theatres, defying the opposition of her family. In turn she subsidized the Avenue Theatre in London (*c.* 1894) during a season when the plays produced included Yeats's *The Land of Heart's Desire* and **Arms and the Man* by Bernard Shaw. She next (1904-7) financed the *Abbey Theatre, Dublin, and from 1907-1921 the *Gaiety Theatre, Manchester, Repertory Company, building up a fine company of players and encouraging a local school of playwrights (among them Stanley *Houghton, Harold *Brighouse and Allan *Monkhouse), as well as producing English and foreign classics, old and new. She accumulated a large library of plays which the *British Drama League received as a gift from her.

Hornung, E. W. (Ernest William Hornung, 1866-1921). Born at Middlesbrough; educated at Uppingham. Lived in Australia for two years from 1884 and thereafter devoted himself to writing. He married the sister of Arthur Conan *Doyle, and as a counterblast to the infallibility of Sherlock Holmes invented the character A. J. Raffles, a gentleman burglar, who made his first entrance in *The Amateur Cracksman* (1899), with the author's brother-in-law as dedicatee: 'To A.C.D. This Form of Flattery'. Raffles became lastingly popular and made reappearances in *A Thief in the Night* (1905) and *Mr Justice Raffles* (1909). The early Australian period is reflected in *A Bride from the Bush* (1890) and *Stingaree* (1905).

Horse's Mouth, The. Novel by Joyce *Cary published in 1944, the final volume of the trilogy begun with **Herself Surprised* (1941) and continued with **To Be a Pilgrim* (1942). In 1957 an illustrated edition of *The Horse's Mouth* was published with a self-portrait and eight other drawings by the author, and an originally rejected chapter 'The Old Strife at Plant's'; this edition also has a preface by Andrew Wright and indentification of the numerous William Blake

quotations in the novel. Cary described *The Horse's Mouth* as 'the story of an artist, and his adventures both in art and life, told by himself'.

Gulley Jimson, the son of a once popular painter of pretty girls in pretty gardens, explains that he never meant to be an artist, until, while a contented clerk in London and happily married, he one day pushed about a blot on an envelope to make it look like a face: 'from that moment I was done for'. He goes to art classes, loses his office job, sells his belongings, nearly starves, and is left by his wife. As a painter he works through many styles, coming to Blake and Persian carpets and Raphael's cartoons, and at last takes to painting on walls. He grows more and more eccentric, and less and less squeamish about money and women. As Sara Monday's lover he is prominent in *Herself Surprised*, has just served a prison sentence when he appears at the beginning of *The Horse's Mouth,* and in becoming scurrilous and entirely amoral has developed into one of literature's great comic characters, facing society's animosity without rancour and fighting it without scruple. He leaves prison with two-and-sixpence; takes up again with a former female crony, Coker, barmaid and chucker-out; and returns to his old studio, a derelict boathouse, where he left unfinished a vast canvas of The Fall, from which someone has in the meantime cut away part of Adam's anatomy. A would-be pupil—a stammering schoolboy Gulley calls Nosy—brings a patch of canvas to repair Adam, but in spite of the boy's persistent pleading the old artist (he is now in his late sixties) refuses to teach him to paint. Gulley resumes contact with Sara Monday, who has in the past unlawfully acquired a number of his sketches and drawings, which he is anxious to get back when a critic, A. W. Alabaster, plans an illustrated 'Life and Works of Gulley Jimson'. Alabaster also brings him in touch with a wealthy collector, Sir William Beeder, whose wife Gulley proposes to paint in the nude, reminiscent of Goya's Duchess of Alva. While the Beeders are on a three-month visit to America, Gulley takes illegitimate possession of their mansion flat and starts to paint a mural of The Raising of Lazarus in one of the rooms. A sculptor acquaintance also invades the flat, introducing through a window a large block of stone for a war memorial which he proceeds to carve. By the time the Beeders return, most of their belongings, even the bathroom taps, have gone to raise money for food and drink. Gulley's career ends when he falls from a high staging erected in a disused chapel where he has started work on a twenty-five feet by forty feet painting of The Creation.

Horst Wessel Song. *Die Fahne Hoch* ('Raise the flag! . . .') written by Horst Wessel (1907-30) and adopted as the party anthem by the German National Socialists (Hitler's Nazis).

Hotson, Leslie (John Leslie Hotson, 1897-   ). Born in Ontario; educated at Harvard. Held various university appointments preliminary to the Professorship of English at Haverford College, Pennsylvania, 1931-41. Devoting himself to Elizabethan scholarship, with remarkable acumen he discovered documentary evidence shedding new light on *The Death of Christopher Marlowe* (1925), and made other discoveries and some not unanimously approved conjectures embodied in *Shakespeare Versus Shallow* (1931), *I, William Shakespeare* (1937), *The First Night of Twelfth Night* (1954), *Shakespeare's Wooden O* (1959).

Houghton, Claude (pseudonym of Claude Houghton Oldfield, 1889-1961). Born at Sevenoaks, Kent; educated at Dulwich College; accountant and civil servant. Notable among his large number of distinctly original novels are *Chaos is Come Again* (1932), *I am Jonathan Scrivener* (1934), *Hudson Rejoins the Herd* (1939).

Houghton, Stanley (William Stanley Houghton, 1881-1913). Born in Cheshire; educated at Manchester Grammar School. Went into his father's cotton-merchant business before becoming a dramatic critic and book reviewer on the *Manchester Guardian* from 1906 to 1912. Miss *Horniman's Repertory Company, then flourishing at the Gaiety Theatre in Manchester, performed his first play, *The Dear Departed*, in 1908; and the same company chose for production on a London visit in 1912 *Hindle Wakes*, a play which made Houghton immediately famous, though it had the less fortunate result of bringing him to live in London, where a bout of being extravagantly lionized interfered with his writing and at length repelled him. He then went to Paris in the few remaining months of his life. *The Younger Generation* (1910), successful in both Manchester

and London, has claims to a lasting place in the English repertory alongside *Hindle Wakes*, both being among the best products of what came to be known as the Lancashire school of dramatists. It is not improbable that *The Younger Generation* would have been vociferously greeted if it had first appeared forty years later, when revolting adolescents had become folk heroes, though Houghton's play differed from the angry-young-men dramas of the 1950s in not casting off civilized manners.

Hoult, Norah (1898-   ). Born in Dublin; educated in England; worked as a journalist for London and provincial papers. Her first book, *Poor Women* (short stories; 1928), was warmly and deservedly praised, and was followed by a regular succession of novels less noticed, among them *Time! Gentlemen, Time!* (1930), *Holy Ireland* (1935), *Coming From the Fair* (1937), *Augusta Steps Out* (1942), *There Were No Windows* (1944), *Journey into Print* (1954), *Father and Daughter* (1957), *Husband and Wife* (1959), *Last Days of Miss Jenkinson* (1962), etc.

House With the Green Shutters, The. Novel by George *Douglas published in 1901. John Gourlay, quarrier, grain-merchant, and carrier, having made himself the most prosperous citizen of the small Scottish town of Barbie, adopts an attitude of social superiority and holds himself aloof from the rest of the townsfolk, who hate and fear his domineering 'brute force of character'. Though a skinflint in other ways, he spends lavishly on building and making improvements to the House with the Green Shutters, of which he is morbidly proud as a symbol of his wealth and importance. His wife, attractive when they married, has degenerated under his bullying into a downtrodden dull-witted slut. She is passionately and over-indulgently fond of her son John, whom Gourlay consequently detests, while the daughter Janet, an unlovely child, is his favourite because her mother seems to neglect her. James Wilson comes back to Barbie after an absence of fifteen years and opens a grocery, provision, and iron-mongery store. He hopes to be well received by Gourlay, but 'the big man' taunts him insultingly because Wilson's father was only a molecatcher. Gourlay's prosperity is slowly eroded by the storekeeper's growing success, which enables Wilson to break into branches of business which Gourlay previously monopolized. Determined not to be out-done, Gourlay sends his son to the same High School as Wilson's boy and on to Edinburgh University. There, John becomes a toper but nevertheless in his first year gains distinction by winning the coveted Raeburn Prize with an essay on 'An Arctic Night' which, though poor in grammar and spelling, and running to only half-a-dozen small pages, is placed above longer and more literate entries by showing 'a wonderful imagination.' That is the limit of young Gourlay's academic success, for his active imagination brings fears that aggravate his innate moral weakness. He continues to drink heavily and, a negligent, disorderly, and insolent student, is finally expelled. This ruins his father's hope that a brilliant son would compensate the accumulating disasters which have brought his own fortunes crashing down. On returning in disgrace to Barbie, John gets hurt in a drunken brawl in the Red Lion and reaches home in a murderous rage. His father has already heard of the trouble at the inn and, regarding it as 'a new offence of his offspring', sneers at him when he enters the house. Maddened further by this, he leaps at his father and with a heavy poker strikes a blow which kills him, in the presence of Janet and their mother. They satisfy the doctor that the fatal wound is due to falling from a step-ladder and hitting his head on the iron fender. Though no suspicion falls on John, except in whispered gossip, his disturbed imagination torments him with bad dreams and the conviction that his father's eyes are always watching him. They learn that Gourlay's account at the bank is overdrawn and that they will lose the house because the mortgage-interest is unpaid. With Elizabethan completeness the Gourlay family comes to a doomful end in the house with the green shutters.

Household, Geoffrey (Geoffrey Edward West Household, 1900-   ). Born in Bristol; educated at Clifton and Oxford. Travelled and worked in 'foreign capitals' and the United States. Author of *The Spanish Cave* (1936), *Rogue Male* (1939), *Watcher in the Shadows* (1960), *Things to Love* (1963), *Olura* (1965), and other novels of ordeal and adventure; *The Salvation of Pisco Gabor and Other Stories* (1939); *Against the Wind* (autobiography; 1958).

Housman, A. E. (Alfred Edward Housman, 1859-1936). Born at Fockbury, Worcester-

shire; brother of the following; educated at Bromsgrove and Oxford; civil servant (in the Patent Office), 1882-92. Professor of Latin, University College, London, 1892-1911; Professor of Latin in the University of Cambridge from 1911. Although as a student at Oxford he had an undistinguished academic record, he later became renowned as a meticulous classical scholar with a scathing pen for other scholars' shortcomings. His scrupulous regard for accuracy and attention to minute textual problems were shown in his editions of Manilius (author of *Astronomica*, a Latin poem in five books; Housman's edition was issued in five volumes, 1903, 1912, 1916, 1920, 1930), Juvenal (1905) and Lucan (1926). In 1896 *A Shropshire Lad* made him famous overnight as a poet, and although subsequent fluctuations of taste among critics led to its reputation being subject to ups-and-downs, the book continues to hold a distinctive and perhaps unique place in English literature. Not until a quarter of a century later did its successor appear with a title *Last Poems* (1922) suggesting finality, but *More Poems* was published posthumously in the year he died. The total of his poetic output is small in bulk (*Collected Poems,* 1939), and the individual poems are brief, always compressed, and frequently laconic. But if they leave much unsaid, they say all that is needful through the interspaces of what is said. Housman's personality was enigmatic, and burdened by a private grief which remains unfathomed beyond what may be deduced from his poems. His own intermittent poetic processes are fascinatingly indicated in *The Name and Nature of Poetry* (1933), a lecture delivered in Cambridge.

Housman, Laurence (1865-1959). Born at Bromsgrove, Worcestershire; brother of the preceding; educated at Bromsgrove; studied art in London and was first occupied as a book illustrator. *An Englishwoman's Love Letters* (1900) which he published anonymously created a stir, for though fictitious it was taken to be an actual correspondence. His large and varied output is beyond enumeration. He was attracted to the theatre by collaborating with Granville *Barker in *Prunella,* a fantasy produced at the Court Theatre in 1906. He struck a successful vein with two series of one-act plays, collected as *Little Plays of St Francis* (First series, 1922;

Second series, 1931) and *Victoria Regina* (1934) dealing in numerous episodes with Queen Victoria and her reign.

Howard, Sidney (Sidney Coe Howard, 1891-1939). Born at Oakland, California; educated at the University of California, and at Harvard where he studied under G. P. *Baker. After service with the American army in World War I he worked on various periodicals, but is chiefly known as a dramatist: *They Knew What They Wanted* (1924) and *The Silver Cord* (1927) were his most successful plays.

Howards End. Novel by E. M. *Forster published in 1910. While a guest at Howards End, the Hertfordshire home of the Wilcoxes whom she and her elder sister Margaret met on a Continental holiday, Helen Schlegel sends Margaret a brief romantically impulsive note saying that she and young Paul Wilcox are in love. Their Aunt Juley (Mrs Munt) rushes to Howards End, bent on rescuing Helen from what she is convinced is an undesirable entanglement; but on arrival she finds that Helen has already wired: 'All over. Wish I had never written. Tell no one.' Paul kissed her at evening in the garden, a flirtation already faded next morning. The Schlegels, orphaned of their naturalized German father and English mother, live with their aunt in West London, cultivating artistic and intellectual interests. At a Queen's Hall concert (the author's account of which includes a celebrated passage on Beethoven's Fifth Symphony) Helen, leaving early, mistakes for her own an umbrella belonging to a neighbouring young man in the audience. Margaret, conducting him to their house to retrieve the umbrella, gathers that the young man, Leonard Bast, is poor and aspires after culture. He is an insurance clerk 'at the extreme verge of gentility', living in a basement flat with his blowsy wife, Jacky, years older than himself. The Wilcoxes take a furnished flat opposite the Schlegels' house, and Margaret establishes a friendship with Mrs Wilcox, who returns to Howards End without mention of the desperate illness from which she soon dies. After the funeral her family receive a note she wrote in hospital saying: 'I should like Miss Schlegel (Margaret) to have Howards End', a property she had inherited in her own right. The Wilcoxes destroy the note, of which Margaret knows nothing. Later, the sisters, having come to regard Leonard Bast as

something of a protégé, tell Mr Wilcox of his circumstances. Leonard leaves the insurance company, which Wilcox says is on the verge of bankruptcy, and takes a job·in a bank, soon becoming unemployed when staff is reduced. The Schlegels are outraged when Wilcox is indifferent to the plight of Leonard and Jacky. Helen turns up unexpectedly at the Wilcoxes' other house at Oniton in Shropshire, bringing the Basts, during the wedding celebrations of Wilcox's daughter Evie. Helen declares extravagantly that the Basts are starving. When Wilcox and Jacky, now half-drunk, encounter in the garden, they recognize one another, having long ago secretly been lovers during the first Mrs Wilcox's lifetime. Margaret, who in the meantime has become engaged to Wilcox, condones his offence and they marry quietly. Helen disappears for a while on the Continent and endeavours to elude contact when back in England. She is with child by Leonard Bast, to whom she was momentarily drawn by a mutual sense of loneliness and by her conviction of injustice. Wilcox's elder son Charles, supposing that Leonard has 'played about with' and seduced Helen, thrashes him with the flat of a sword. Leonard falls dead from heart failure. Charles receives a three-year sentence for manslaughter. Helen's child is born and the sisters are united at Howards End, which is to be left to Margaret absolutely by Wilcox, who tells her barely a half-truth about his first wife's dying request. The epigraph and basic philosophy of the novel, 'Only connect . . .' express Forster's rooted belief that the pains and penalties of civilized man arise from inability or failure to 'connect without bitterness until all men are brothers'.

Hoyle, Sir Fred (1915-   ; knighted 1972). Born in Yorkshire; educated there and at Cambridge; Professor of Astronomy, Cambridge, 1958-73. Author of *The Nature of the Universe* (1950), *Galaxies, Nuclei and Quasars* (1965), *From Stonehenge to Modern Cosmology* (1972) and other scientific works; also novels, *The Black Cloud* (1957), and with G. Hoyle *Fifth Planet* (1963), *Seven Steps to the Sun* (1970), *The Inferno* (1973), etc.

Hubris. A term from the Greek, warning against overweening pride or boastful self-confidence incurring the wrath of the gods, from whom punishment and ruin come. The Elizabethan conception of Fortune's Wheel, on which the hero reaches the topmost point and then plunges to destruction as the wheel comes full circle, expresses a corresponding idea.

Hudson, Stephen (pseudonym of Sydney Schiff, 1869?-1944). Novelist and translator; author of *War-Time Silhouettes* (1916), *Richard Kurt* (1919), *Elinor Colhouse* (1921), *Prince Hempseed* (1923), *Tony* (1924), *Myrtle* (1925), *A True Story* (1930; revised and enlarged edition 1965), *The Other Side* (1937). He translated *In Sight of Chaos* by H. Hesse (1923) and *Time Regained*, vol. 12 of *Remembrance of Things Past* by Marcel *Proust (1941). Hudson was strongly averse to personal publicity and declined to provide autobiographical information.

Hudson, W. H. (William Henry Hudson, 1841-1922). Born in Argentina of American parentage; brought up on his father's farm and worked on it until his health was permanently impaired at the age of fifteen. He migrated to England in 1869. From boyhood he had been intensely devoted to bird-watching and nature study, and from 1885, when his first book *The Purple Land* was published, he wrote almost exclusively as a naturalist, though his command of clear English and an exceptionally attractive and unpretentious literary style gave his books an unrestricted appeal. Both *The Purple Land* and *Green Mansions* (1904) have South American settings, and when after his death Jacob Epstein was commissioned to sculpt a Hudson Memorial to be set up in Hyde Park, he chose Rima, the bird-girl heroine of *Green Mansions*, as subject. The subsequent besmearing of the memorial was a customary ignorant attack on Epstein as an artist and in no way concerned with Hudson the writer. To *Birds in a Village* (1893), *British Birds* (1895) and *Birds in London* (1898), he added in the new century *Birds and Man* (1901), *Adventures Among Birds* (1903), and *Birds in Town and Village* (1919). A *Shepherd's Life* (1910) is a delightful classic of English country work and lore, while *Far Away and Long Ago* (1918) has few equals in autobiographical literature. Other books: *Idle Days in Patagonia* (1893), *A Crystal Age* (1906), *Afoot in England* (1909), *A Traveller in Little Things* (1921).

Hudson, W. H. (William Henry Hudson, 1862-1918). Born in London; educated privately; began journalism in London, then became Private Secretary to Herbert *Spencer

before going to New York as assistant librarian at Cornell University until he was appointed Professor of English Literature at Stanford University, California, 1892-1901, and then Professorial Lecturer, University of Chicago, 1902-03. He returned to England and served as a staff lecturer to the London University Extension Board. His *Outline History of English Literature* (1913) had a long life in schools and was frequently reprinted (with additional chapters by another hand after his death). The remainder of his work was chiefly in editing volumes of selections of English and American poets and writing on miscellaneous literary and historical subjects.

Hueffer, Ford Madox (1873-1939). His birth name was Ford Hermann Hueffer, to which he added, as further Christian names, Joseph Leopold Madox; changed his surname to Ford in 1919 (he was the grandson on his mother's side of the Victorian painter Ford Madox Brown), and alternated between Ford Madox *Ford and Ford Madox Hueffer on the title pages of his books. Born at Merton in Surrey; educated in Folkestone and at University College School, London. Founded *The *English Review* in 1908 as a half-crown monthly, and during his editorship printed in lengthy instalments some of the best work of Joseph *Conrad, H. G. *Wells and other leading authors. An uneasy friend to Joseph Conrad, he collaborated with him in *The Inheritors* (1901) and *Romance* (1903), while (as Ford Madox Ford) he wrote *Joseph Conrad: A Personal Remembrance* (1924). As Hueffer his principal works were *Ford Madox Brown* (1896), *Rossetti* (1902), *The Pre-Raphaelite Brotherhood* (1907), *Ancient Rights and Certain New Reflections* (memories; 1911), *The Critical Attitude* (1911), and numerous novels, best of which include the historical trilogy—*The Fifth Queen* (1906), *Privy Seal* (1907), and *The Fifth Queen Crowned* (1908); *The *Good Soldier* (1915). The novels inspired by his service in France during World War I, *Parade's End*, and other works were first published under his Ford pseudonym.

Hughes, Langston (James Langston Hughes, 1902-67). Born in Missouri; educated in Cleveland and at Columbia University; worked as a sailor, cook, and hotel attendant before resuming education at Lincoln University, Pennsylvania, after his first volume of poems, *The Weary Blues* (1926), had attracted attention. Other writings on Negro life: verse—*Dear Lovely Death* (1931), *Shakespeare in Harlem* (1942); plays— *Mulatto* (1936), *The Sun Do Move* (1942); novel—*Not Without Laughter* (1934); short stories—*The Ways of White Folks* (1934), *Simple Speaks His Mind* (1950); *The Big Sea* (1940) and *I Wonder as I Wander* (1956), autobiographical. Edited *Poems from Black Africa* (1963).

Hughes, Richard (Richard Arthur Warren Hughes, 1900-   ). Born at Weybridge; educated at Charterhouse and Oxford. Adventurous and unorthodox, he wandered about Europe, and later travelled in North America and the West Indies. His first (one-act) play *The Sister's Tragedy* was published with others in 1924; he also wrote poems—*Gipsy Night* (1922) and *Confessio Juvenis* (1926)—and short stories—*A Moment of Time* (1926)—before his scarifying novel about a group of children, *A *High Wind in Jamaica*, appeared in 1929. Later works: *In Hazard* (allegorical novel, 1938); children's stories—*The Spider's Palace* (1931), *Don't Blame Me* (1940). In 1961 he began a multi-volume novel *The Human Predicament* with the first part *The Fox in the Attic*.

Hughes, Ted (1930-   ). Educated at Cambridge; married Sylvia *Plath. He and Thom *Gunn were ranked as the representative poets of their period. Author of *The Hawk in the Rain* (1957), *Lupercal* (1960), *Wodwo* (1967), *Crow* (1970), and poems and stories for children. Though there is often a forceful roughness of language in his poetry, his imaginative perception is acute, as in lines from 'The Thought-Fox': 'Cold, delicately as the dark snow,/A fox's nose touches twig, leaf'.

Hull, E. M. (Edith Maude Hull). No dates or other biographical information are available about the author of *The Sheik* (1925), which was scorned by literary critics but eagerly read by multitudes. It was published at the time when titillating sex-appeal stories and films were in vogue, before their 'torrid suggestiveness' was superseded by naked sexuality in novels and other writings after World War II. *The Sheik* (impersonated by Rudolph Valentino) had worldwide currency in its cinema version. 'Desert love' was further exploited in E. M. Hull's

later but less popular books. That she was personally familiar with at least the scenic setting of the novels is made apparent by her *Camping in the Sahara* (1927).

Hull, Richard (pseudonym of Richard Henry Sampson, 1896-   ). Born in London; educated at Rugby. After service with the British army in World War I he became a chartered accountant and continued in that profession up to and after World War II, in which he also served. His first detective novel *The Murder of My Aunt* (1935) was followed by *Murder Isn't Easy* (1936), *And Death Came Too* (1942), *Invitation to an Inquest* (1950), and others.

Hulme, T. E. (Thomas Ernest Hulme, 1883-1917). Born in Staffordshire; educated at Newcastle-under-Lyme and Cambridge. Lived in Canada, Belgium, Italy and Germany at various times, usually studying philosophy. In London he had a remarkable influence on other thinkers and writers, and after he was killed in Belgium while serving with the British army in World War I he became almost legendary in *avant garde* circles as an unfulfilled and war-destroyed genius. His translations of Bergson's *Introduction to Metaphysics* and Georges Sorel's *Reflections on Violence* appeared in 1912, otherwise only a few poems and articles were published in his lifetime. Posthumously: *Speculations* (1924) edited by Sir Herbert Read, *Further Speculations* (1955), edited by Sam Hynes, and *Notes on Language and Style* (1929) were gathered from his manuscripts and uncollected essays.

Humanism. The philosophical attitude of Renaissance scholars who, turning away from medieval preoccupation with the hereafter, concerned themselves more with humanity in the present life. Obscurantist scholasticism gave way to the study of classical writers and to the conception of Man as central in the universe.

Hume, Fergus (Ferguson Wright Hume, 1859-1932). Born in England of New Zealand parentage; educated in Dunedin and at the University of Otago. He became a barrister in New Zealand, but went to Australia and lived there for three years before settling in England from 1888, a year or so after his first detective story *The Mystery of a Hansom Cab* was published in Melbourne. This was said to have had the largest sale in the history of detective fiction, a dubious claim though undoubtedly its circulation was huge. Fergus Hume wrote well over a hundred other novels, but never equalled the success of *The Mystery of a Hansom Cab*, which preceded by several years the first of Conan Doyle's Sherlock Holmes stories.

Humphreys, Eliza Margaret J. *See* Rita.

Huneker, James (James Gibbons Huneker, 1860-1921). Born in Philadelphia; studied law but spent more time as a music student in Paris and elsewhere. Among the numerous papers and periodicals to which he later contributed musical and dramatic criticism in America and Europe, was the (London) *Saturday Review*, from which he compiled the first collection of Bernard Shaw's theatre articles, *Dramatic Opinions and Essays* (2 vols, New York, 1906; London, 1907). Huneker's own works included *Chopin: The Man and His Music* (1900), *Melomaniacs* (1902), *Iconoclasts* (1905), *Egoists* (1909), *Ivory, Apes and Peacocks* (1915); *Variations* (1921) was the first of three autobiographical volumes; *Painted Veils* (1920) is a novel of Bohemian life in New York and Paris, introducing real musicians and writers among its fictional characters.

Hunt, Kyle. *See* John *Creasey.

Hunt, Violet (1866-1942). Born in Durham, daughter of the Victorian painter Alfred William Hunt, who had her instructed in his own profession, which he intended her to follow. She turned to writing, however, contributed to the *Pall Mall Gazette*, and published her first book, *The Maiden's Progress: A Novel in Dialogue* in 1894; but her novels are of less importance and interest than her recollections and reminiscences of the Pre-Raphaelite circle and of later authors and artists of whom she had personal knowledge: *The Wife of Rossetti* (1932), *Those Flurried Years* (1926). *The Cat* (1905), which she described as 'animal autobiographies', was a product of her passion for cats. She lived for years from 1911 with Ford Madox *Hueffer, and her idiosyncrasies as a hostess can be observed in the account by Douglas *Goldring of their home on Campden Hill, London, *South Lodge* (1943).

Huntly, Frances E. *See* Ethel Colburn *Mayne.

Hurry on Down. Novel by John *Wain pub-

lished in 1953. University-educated, 'with a mediocre degree in History', Charles Lumley determines to break with his middle-class upbringing and to detach himself from its approved occupations and social observances. He becomes, first, a window-cleaner, then an export delivery driver taking cars from the factories to the docks, a job he is introduced to by a casual acquaintance, Teddy Bunder, who turns out to be a drug distributor. Although drawn into the racket unawares and loathing it, Lumley continues in it because he needs the money in order to establish himself with Veronica Roderick, known to him as the niece of a rich company director. A former school friend, Harry Dogson, now a journalist, tries to persuade Lumley to smuggle him into the export docks, where he hopes to get material for articles exposing the drug traffic, not suspecting that Lumley is implicated. Refused help, Dogson nevertheless inspires a police raid on the docks and is murdered by the racketeers. Bunder, believing that Lumley has blabbed, pushes him out of the stolen fast car in which they are escaping and leaves him shattered on a country road. During his long treatment in hospital, Lumley's romantic affair with Veronica is ended when he learns that she is Roderick's mistress, not his niece. After a period as a hospital orderly he becomes chauffeur to a onetime patient, Samuel Braceweight, a wealthy chocolate manufacturer, until young Walter Braceweight, a born mechanic frustrated by parents but benevolently regarded by Lumley, crashes his experimental engine into his father's Daimler. A brief job as chucker-out at a sleazy night club precedes a profitable three-year contract with a team of radio comics and a resumption with Veronica.

Hurst, Fannie (1889-1968; Mrs J. S. Danielson). Born in Ohio; educated at Washington University and at Columbia. She gathered background and foreground knowledge for her novels and short stories by living and working among the underprivileged, whom she portrays in fiction both realistically and emotionally but with genuine sympathy and understanding as in, e.g., *Lummox* (1923), 'a study of a Scandinavian servant girl'. Other novels: *Mannequin* (1926), *Back Street* (1931), *Hallelujah* (1944), *Anywoman* (1950), *God Must Be Sad* (1961);

short stories: *Gaslight Sonatas* (1918), *Humoresque* (1919), *Song of Life* (1927), *We Are Ten* (1937); autobiography: *Anatomy of Me* (1958).

Hushabye, Hesione. Daughter of Captain Shotover in Shaw's **Heartbreak House* (1919); married to Hector Hushabye.

Hutchinson, A. S. M. (Arthur Stuart-Menteth Hutchinson, 1879-1971). Born in India; studied medicine at St Thomas's Hospital in London, but turned to journalism, becoming editor of *The Daily Graphic* (1912-16). Published his first novel *Once Aboard the Lugger* in 1908 but made no great mark until 1920, when *If Winter Comes* had extraordinary popular success, its hero, Mark Sabre, embodying the sentimental idealism of the immediate post-war mood. The novel was cold-shouldered by the upper literary critics, and its popularity with unprofessional readers was not extended to *This Freedom* (1922), *One Increasing Purpose* (1925), *It Happened Like This* (1942), *A Year that the Locust . . .* (autobiography, 1935).

Hutchinson, R. C. (Ray Coryton Hutchinson, 1907-   ). Born in London; educated in Somerset (Monkton Combe) and Oxford. Worked in advertising for Colmans of Norwich until 1935, when he decided to live by writing. Several novels—*Thou Hast a Devil* (1930) and others—preceded *Testament* (1938) which had considerable success. Other novels: *Shining Scabbard* (1936), *The Fire and the Wood* (1940), *Elephant and Castle* (1949), *Journey with Strangers* (1952), *A Child Possessed* (1964), etc.

Hutchison, Bruce (1901-   ). Born in Ontario; educated in British Columbia; journalist and newspaper editor. Author of *The Hollow Men* (a political novel, 1944), and of non-fictional works including *Mr Prime Minister, 1867-1964* (1964), on the men who have held that office in Canada during the period indicated.

Hutton, Edward (1875-1969). Educated at Highgate School and Blundells. An expert in Italian history and culture. His biographies of cities include *Rome* (1909), *Venice and Venetia* (1911, 4th edn 1954), *Naples and Campania Revisited* (1958). He also contributed volumes on *Gloucestershire*, *Somerset* and *Wiltshire* to the Highways and Byways series. The Cosmati mosaics

in Westminster Cathedral and Buckfast Abbey are to his designs.

Huxley, Aldous (Aldous Leonard Huxley, 1894-1963). Born at Godalming, Surrey; educated at Eton and Oxford. The distinguished family to which he belonged included Thomas Henry Huxley, his grandfather; Arnold of Rugby, his great-grandfather on his mother's side; Mrs Humphry *Ward, the novelist, his aunt; Sir Julian *Huxley his elder brother. His father Leonard Huxley was editor of the *Cornhill Magazine*. From early years he suffered from a severe eye affection which prevented his entering the medical profession, and after leaving Oxford he began work as a literary journalist and dramatic critic before achieving early repute as a writer of fiction which held up a mirror to that circumscribed section of the contemporary world in which he moved. From *Crome Yellow* (1921) onward for rather more than a decade he wrote a sequence of novels which passed by stages from being brilliant, witty and ironical to being sombre, satirical and bitter. He was closely in touch with the leading writers and other intellectuals of his generation, more especially with D. H. *Lawrence, an edition of whose *Letters* he published in 1932 with an introduction which remains one of the best things written on Lawrence, who also appears thinly veiled among the characters in **Point Counter Point* (1928). The gusto and audacity of Huxley's earlier novels—among which **Antic Hay* (1923) and *Those Barren Leaves* (1925), are outstanding—are offset by weakness of character-drawing which causes them to slide effortlessly over the contours of the reader's mind without an adequate measure of mental penetration. With **Brave New World* (1932), however, his writing took a prophetic rather than a merely diagnostic turn, and the theme of a conditioned world in which the individual and his individuality are obliterated was a horrifying vision that was to be made more horrible by the actualities of the world of the later 1930s and turned into nightmare by George *Orwell in **Nineteen Eighty-Four* (1949). Huxley's later novels, e.g. *Eyeless in Gaza* (1936), **After Many a Summer* (1939), *Ape and Essence* (1948) are oppressively darkened by his Swiftian fixation of despair and disgust, without Swift's sustained narrative power. Some of

Huxley's best work is in his *Collected Short Stories* (1957) and *Collected Essays* (1960). He lived for several years in Italy and settled in America from 1938; his developing interest in mysticism and supranormal states was displayed in *The Perennial Philosophy* (1946), *The Doors of Perception* (1956) and other writings, while *The Art of Seeing* (1943) tells of the system of eye-training advised by a New York doctor, which held off the threat of blindness.

Huxley, Elspeth (*née* Elspeth Josceline Grant, 1907- ; married Gervas Huxley 1931). Born in London; educated in Nairobi and at Reading and Cornell Universities. Her authoritative writings on African affairs include *Lord Delamare and the Making of Kenya* (1935) and (in collaboration) *Race and Politics in Kenya* (1944). *The Flame Trees of Thika* (1959) is a record of her childhood with her family in Kenya, followed by *The Mottled Lizard* (1962); *Four Guineas* (1954) is among her travel books, and she has also written novels, including *Red Strangers* (1939), *The Walled City* (1948); and detective stories: *The Merry Hippo* (1963) and others.

Huxley, Sir Julian (Julian Sorell Huxley, 1887- ; knighted 1958). Born in London; brother of Aldous Huxley; educated at Eton and Oxford. Held university and other appointments in zoology, physiology and biology in England and the U.S.; Secretary of the Zoological Society at the London Zoo, 1935-42; visited West and East Africa as adviser on native education and the conservation of wild life. A prolific writer, his books include *Essays of a Biologist* (1923), *Religion without Revelation* (1927), *Ants* (1929), *Bird-watching and Bird Behaviour* (1930), *Africa View* (1931), *What Dare I Think?* (1931), *At the Zoo* (1936), *Democracy Marches* (1941), *Man in the Modern World* (1947), *Evolution in Action* (1953), *From an Antique Land* (1954), *New Bottles for New Wine* (1957). In collaboration with H. G. Wells and his son G. P. Wells, Huxley wrote *The Science of Life* (1929), a companion book to Wells's famous *Outline of History*. He was Director General of *UNESCO 1946-48.

Huxtable family. Henry Huxtable, surviving partner in the Peckham drapery store of Roberts & Huxtable; his wife Katherine,

and their spinster daughters, Laura, Minnie, Clara, Julia, Emma and Jane, in Granville Barker's *The *Madras House* (1910).

Huxtable, Marjorie. See Simon *Dare.

Hyams, Edward (Edward Solomon Hyams, 1910-). Born in London; spent some years on the Continent after leaving school and was then 'first introduced to French satire, the influence of which he has never shaken off'. Worked in a tobacco factory before travelling again, in southern Europe and North America. His wide range of interests, besides writing, includes gardening and fruit-growing and the restoring of grape-culture and vineyards to England. Author of numerous novels including *The Wings of the Morning* (1939), *William Medium* (1947), *The Astrologer* (1950), *Gentian Violet* (1953), *All We Possess* (1961), *A Perfect Stranger* (1964). Edited *Vineyards in England* (1953) and (with a joint editor) *The Orchard and Fruit Garden: A New Pomona* (1961). *The *New Statesman: The History of the First Fifty Years 1913-1963* (1963). *From the Waste Land* (autobiography; 1950). Also made a very large number of translations.

Hybris. See Hubris.

Hyde, Douglas (1860-1949). Born in County Roscommon; educated at Trinity College, Dublin. Went to Canada for a short time as Professor of Modern Languages in the University of New Brunswick. Returning to Ireland he became President of the Gaelic League from its foundation in 1893 until 1915, and took a leading part in the establishment of the *Irish Players, writing plays in Gaelic and furthering in every way the literary renaissance, in connection with which he was elected President of the Irish National Literature Society in 1894-5. He was a Senator in the Free State Parliament in 1925 and 1935, and when his country assumed the status of an independent republic he became the first President of Eire from 1938 to 1945. Writings by him available in English include: *Beside the Fire* (1890), *Love Songs of Connaught* (1894), *A Literary History of Ireland* (1899), *Mediaeval Tales from the Irish* (1899), *The Bursting of the Bubble and Other Irish Plays* (1905), *Legends of Saints and Sinners* (1915).

Hyde, Montgomery (Harford Montgomery

Hyde, 1907-   ). Born in Belfast; educated at Sedbergh and Queen's University, Belfast; called to the Bar 1934; Conservative M.P. for Belfast 1950-59. His publications include *The Rise of Castlereagh* (1933), *The Trials of Oscar Wilde* (1948; 1962), *The Trial of Roger Casement* (1960); and among his many biographies *Judge Jeffreys* (1940), *Mr and Mrs Beeton* (1951), *Carson* (1953), *Lord Reading* (1967).

Hyde, Robin (pseudonym of Iris Guiver Wilkinson, 1906-1939). Born in Cape Town; educated and settled in New Zealand. Worked as a journalist. Author of *The Desolate Star* (1929), *The Conquerors* (1935), and other verse including *Persephone in Winter* (1937); and of novels including *Passport to Hell* (1936), *Nor the Years Condemn* (1938), *Check to Your King* (1936), *Wednesday's Children* (1937), *The Godwits Fly* (1938). See *New Zealand Writers.

Hyne, C. J. Cutcliffe (Charles John Cutcliffe Wright Hyne, 1865-1944). Born at Bibury, Gloucestershire; educated at Bradford and Cambridge. Travelled and voyaged over most of the world and wrote a vast amount of fiction from which the character of Captain Kettle survived to give the author fame. Kettle's first appearance was in the book originally titled *Honour of Thieves* (1895) but renamed *The Little Red Captain* (1902), *The Adventures of Captain Kettle* (1898) having meanwhile established the character visually through Stanley L. Wood's illustrations, as a strutting little man with a jutting triangular beard. Many other Kettle volumes followed, down to *Ivory Valley* (1938), the central character passing through several transmogrifications, appearing in the mid-1920s as the Reverend Sir Owen Kettle, K.C.B. Other Cutcliffe Hyne books: *Through Arctic Lapland* (1898), *Mr Horrocks, Purser* (1902), *McTodd* (1903), *Kate Meredith* (1907), *My Joyful Life* (1935).

Ibáñez, Vicente Blasco (1867-1928). Born at Valencia; studied law in Madrid, but devoted himself to republican political journalism which resulted in imprisonment and exile, and from 1909 to 1914 he lived in Argentina. Meanwhile he was also writing novels dealing realistically with Spanish provincial life, but it was with the war novel *The Four Horsemen of the Apocalypse* (1918) that he became internationally successful. Among his other novels, *Blood and Sand* (1908) and *Our Sea* (1918) have also been popular in English translations.

ibid. Contraction of Latin *ibidem*, in the same place. Used in footnotes to indicate that the reference or quotation comes from the identical source of the one immediately preceding it. If a reference to some different source has intervened, the title or name of the relevant book, author, or other source should be repeated in place of *ibid.* (with chapter and page number where appropriate).

Ibsen, Henrik (1828-1906). Norwegian poet and playwright. Though his last play, *When We Dead Awaken*, was issued in 1899 and his works belong chronologically to the 19th century, his influence continued strongly in the 20th century as a pervasive force rather than as an isolatable factor, as it had been in the early work of *Shaw. The *Archer translations of Ibsen's work, valued for many years, fell out of favour with succeeding generations, and comprehensive series of new translations were made by R. Farquharson Sharp (for *Everyman's Library), Michael Meyer, and J. W. McFarlane. Numerous English stage productions of Ibsen's plays have been seen in the present century, the most ambitious being the complete performance of *Peer Gynt* at the Old Vic in 1921, though Laurence Irving's production of *The Pretenders* (1913) in which he played Skule was no less memorable.

iconoclast. See Mary Agnes *Hamilton.

Ida Arnold. Middle-aged woman with 'a rich Guinness voice' and 'big blown charms' in Graham *Greene's *Brighton Rock* (1938). She suspects that Fred Hale's sudden death was not from natural causes and determines to expose his killers.

Ides of March, The. Novel by Thornton *Wilder published in 1948. A series of documents originating in the author's imagination constitute this 'fantasia on certain events and persons of the last days of the Roman republic' culminating in the assassination of Caesar on 15 March 44 B.C. . . . . In journal-letters to his friend Lucius Mamilius Turrinus (sometime a general in the Roman army, captured and mutilated by the Belgians, and now living in Capri), Caesar expresses his disbelief in the superstitious rites of the soothsayers by which his actions are intended to be governed, questions the existence of the gods, and reveals those aspects of his character which incline him to clemency and stoicism towards conspiracies. His love of poetry makes him the friend of Catullus, whose heartless treatment by Clodia (the Lesbia of the poems) angers Caesar. Her notorious profligacy is capped when she profanes the sacred mysteries of the Bona Dea (a ceremony secret to women) by smuggling in her brother in female clothes. Letters between Caesar and Cleopatra on her prolonged visit to Rome, details of which are given also in letters by others, are among the striking features of this fictional projection of a critical phase of world history.

Iles, Francis. A pseudonym of Anthony Berkeley *Cox under which he wrote the famous detective story *Malice Aforethought* (1931), and the less notable *Before the Fact* (1932) and *As for the Woman* (1939). Cox also wrote as Anthony *Berkeley.

Image. A word used by public relations professionals and others to denote a mental picture, genuine or spurious, created and fostered by propaganda to gain public approval and support for a product, a person or company, or a political or bureaucratic organization.

Image, Imagery. Terms common in literary criticism to denote the similes and metaphors used in poetry and creative prose, often of recurrent types serving as an index to a writer's mental (or subconscious) processes. An impetus was given to this type of literary study by Professor Caroline *Spurgeon's *Shakespeare's Imagery and What it Tells Us* (1935).

Imagism. An Anglo-American movement in poetry, usually dated as beginning with the invention of the word *Imagiste* by Ezra *Pound in an appendix to his *Ripostes*

(1912). Elsewhere he wrote: 'An "Image" is that which presents an intellectual and emotional complex in an instant of time.' Richard *Aldington in the Preface to *Some Imagist Poets* (1915) defined the principles of the movement as: 'To use the language of common speech . . . to employ always the exact word. . . . To create new rhythms. . . . To present an image . . . poetry should render particulars exactly and not deal in vague generalities. . . . To produce poetry that is hard and clear. . . . concentration is of the very essence of poetry.' Leading Imagist poets, besides Pound and Aldington, were *H.D. (whose early verses best show the clean sculptured form, clarity, and compression implicit in Imagist theory), F. S. *Flint, Ford Madox *Ford, Amy *Lowell. For a summary discussion of the movement, with quotations, see 'Imagism and the New Poetry' (ch. 5 of *A Map of Modern English Verse* by John Press, 1969).

Impasto. In painting, laying on pigment thickly with palette knife or thumb instead of brushes. It gives a low-relief appearance to the picture surface, with a vibrant effect as the light or the viewpoint changes.

Impressionism. As applied to paintings (e.g. those of Monet, Renoir, and their followers) the term relates to the presentation on the picture surface of the fleeting impressions made on the painter's retina by the constantly changing effects of light on the observed scene or object; in music, Debussy and Delius are among the impressionists, representing transitory scenes in elusive sound; in poetry, impressionism and symbolism are allied; in fiction Virginia Woolf's novels are more impressionistic than descriptive; in criticism Walter Pater's passage in *The Renaissance* on the Mona Lisa is frequently cited as a classic example.

Inchfawn, Fay (pseudonym of Mrs Elizabeth Rebecca Ward, 1881-). Author of popular books of verse (including *The Verse Book of a Homely Woman*, 1920), novels, essays, religious and children's books, reminiscences, etc.

Incunabula. Books printed before A.D. 1501, with or without illumination.

Independent Theatre Society. Founded in 1891 by J. T. *Grein for the stage production of plays of literary and artistic merit which commercial managers cold shouldered. It hired existing theatres for its occasional performances and was instrumental in putting Ibsen's *Ghosts* on the London stage. It also staged Bernard Shaw's first play *Widowers' Houses* in 1892.

Index, On the. The common expression indicating that the book named is not to be read by Roman Catholics, since it is listed in the *Index Librorum Prohibitorum*. The *Index Expurgatorius* gives references to passages to be excised from other books, which are then allowed to Roman Catholics in the mutilated form.

Inflated language. 'When you marry', sings Tessa in *The Gondoliers*, 'Every goose becomes a swan.' The transformation has been found more easily achievable in the common practice since World War II of naming 'clerks' 'clerical officers'; 'shorthand-typists' 'secretaries'; 'secretaries' 'personal assistants'; 'cooks' 'catering officers'; 'commercial travellers' 'sales representatives'; 'advertising agents' 'practitioners in advertising'; 'evening institutes' 'colleges of further education'; 'technical institutes' 'universities'; the list seems inexhaustible. The effect of such 'escalating of nomenclature' is to rob words of their descriptive function and downgrade them as terms of vanity and flattery, or of bureaucratic officialese.

Inge, W. R. (William Ralph Inge, 1860-1954). Born at Crayke, Yorkshire, son of the Rev. William Inge, Provost of Worcester College, Oxford; educated at Eton and Cambridge. Became an assistant master at Eton and tutor at Oxford; then a vicar in London, Professor of Divinity at Cambridge (1907-11), and Dean of St Paul's Cathedral, London, from 1911 to 1934. His learning, classical scholarship, and forthright and incisively expressed views on public affairs and modern tendencies received more attention than his less-publicized services to the Church. Over a period of many years he contributed to the *Evening Standard* and other papers articles that were widely read and discussed. His indifference to current trends and his forcefully expressed doubts concerning political and social reforms commonly assumed to be beneficial, led to his being nicknamed 'the Gloomy Dean'. Many of these articles were collected in *Outspoken Essays* (1919; Second Series, 1922), *Lay Thoughts of a Dean* (1926) and *More Lay Thoughts of a Dean* (1931). His scholarly works include *Christian Mysticism*

(1899), *Studies of English Mystics* (1906), *The Philosophy of Plotinus* (1918), *The Platonic Tradition* (1926), and various writings on more directly religious topics. An autobiography, *Vale* (1934) and *The Diary of a Dean* (1949) are among his personal writings, and he was also the author of a volume on *England* (1953). As Dean of St Paul's he was a worthy successor in a line of eminent theologians from John Donne onward, and he refuted the charge of gloominess by declaring: 'I have tried only to face reality, to be honest, and to refuse to be foolishly optimistic.' The worthiness of his literary work is determined as much by the excellent gravity of his prose as by his rejection of humbug.

Ingpen, Tertius. District Factory Inspector in Arnold Bennett's *These Twain* (1916). He is an amateur musician, plays the piano, violin, and clarinet, takes part in the Clayhangers' musical evenings, and becomes their good and honest friend, even to the point of telling Hilda that 'the proper place for women is the harem. . . . If you don't like the mere word, let's call it . . . the drawing-room and the kitchen.' He is a bachelor, but has a visiting woman friend whose husband is in an asylum. He confides this information to Edwin Clayhanger when he has recovered from a nearly fatal accident while inspecting the hardware factory of Albert Benbow, Edwin's brother-in-law.

Ingram, Sir Bruce (Bruce Stirling Ingram, 1877-1963; knighted 1950). Born in London; educated at Winchester and Oxford. Editor from 1900 of the *Illustrated London News*, founded in 1842 by his grandfather.

Innes, Hammond (Ralph Hammond Innes, 1913-   ). Author of many best-seller adventure-and-mystery novels: *Wreckers Must Breathe* (1940), *The White South* (1949), *Campbell's Kingdom* (1952), *The 'Mary Deare'* (1956), *Atlantic Fury* (1962) etc. Also a history of the Spanish conquests in Mexico and Peru, *The Conquistadors* (1969).

Innes, Michael. Pseudonym used by John Innes Mackintosh *Stewart for crime novels with Inspector Appleby as the detective. The originality of these books consists largely in the extent to which intellectual ingenuity overrides the routine

mystification of the average thriller. Their appeal is, consequently, more academic than popular in the widest sense. They include *Death at the President's Lodging* (1936), *Hamlet, Revenge!* (1937), *Lament for a Maker* (1938), *Appleby on Ararat* (1941), *The Daffodil Affair* (1942), *The Hawk and the Handsaw* (1948), *Appleby Talking* (1954). See the entry under his own name for biographical information and titles of other books.

Inscape. A term devised by Gerard Manley *Hopkins to denote the 'one-ness' uniting a complex of qualities or characteristics in a natural object or scene; to the 'energy of being' which upholds all things he applied the word *instress*. Hopkins's own explication of the term is in the Author's preface to the MS. of his poems, printed in current editions. *And see* *Sprung Rhythm.

Insect Play, The. By Karel and Joseph *Čapek. Produced in Czech in 1921; translated into English by Paul Selver (1923) as *And So Ad Infinitum*. With characters drawn from the insect world it satirizes political tyranny but does not overlay legitimate theatrical effect with propaganda.

Insulin. *See* Frederick *Banting.

Interfering Iris. *See* Countess of *Chell.

Interior monologue. A literary device emanating from William James's 'stream of consciousness' concept, whereby a novelist records, without imposed logical order or arrangement, the whole flux of impressions, thoughts and impulses prompted by external stimuli or welling up from the subconscious. The extreme example is the long-sustained unspoken soliloquy of Molly Bloom set down entirely unpunctuated at the end of James Joyce's *Ulysses. See also* Edward *Dujardin.

International Affairs. *See* *Royal Institute of International Affairs.

Ionesco, Eugène (1912-   ). Of Rumanian descent; educated in Bucharest and Paris; became a French citizen. Regarded as one of the leading figures in the *Theatre of the Absurd movement, his plays (written in French) had a vogue in other countries also. Among those performed in London are *The Chairs* and *Rhinoceros*. His works have been translated into English (by Donald Watson and Derek Prouse).

Irish Literary Theatre. Founded in Dublin in 1899 by W. B. *Yeats, Edward *Martyn, George *Moore, and others as the first practical outcome of the movement towards an Irish literary renaissance which had been stirring through the preceding twenty years. The first public performance in the Antient Concert Rooms introduced Yeats's *The Countess Cathleen* and Martyn's *The Heather Field*. Its beginnings are surveyed from a personal angle by George Moore in *Ave* (1911: vol. I of *Hail and Farewell*). At first an amateur venture, it developed into the *Abbey Theatre with its ultimately wide-travelling and world-renowned company, the Irish Players, performing works by native playwrights, among the later of whom J. M. *Synge and Sean *O'Casey were pre-eminent, though, as modern prose realists, their works drew the movement away from the original intention of reviving the ancient poetic legends and folklore of Ireland. Lady *Gregory's important part in the movement is acknowledged by Moore in the work cited above, where her misconceptions are also touched on.

Irish Players. The company of actors and actresses based on the *Abbey Theatre in Dublin, as a professional development of the amateur *Irish Literary Theatre. The brothers Frank and William Fay, originally amateur actors, played a leading part in training and directing the Players, as well as performing in most of the plays. The company travelled in England and elsewhere, becoming internationally famous with the plays of J. M. *Synge, Lady *Gregory, and others.

Iron, Ralph. *See* Olive *Schreiner.

Irony. In speech and writing, presenting actual intended meaning under cover of a statement which expresses the opposite, i.e. saying one thing but meaning another. *See also* *Dramatic irony.

Irwin, Margaret (died 1967). Born at Highgate, London; educated at Clifton and Oxford. Author of mainly historical novels: *Still She Wished for Company* (1924), *None So Pretty* (1930), *Royal Flush* (1932), *The Gay*

Galliard (1941). *Young Bess* (1945), *Elizabeth, Captive Princess* (1948), and *Elizabeth and the Prince of Spain* (1953) form a trilogy.

Isabel Rivers. Daughter of General Sir Graham Rivers, V.C. Political and literary assistant and subsequently mistress of Richard Remington in H. G. Wells's *The *New Machiavelli* (1911). With their child they settle in Italy.

ISBN. *See* *Standard Book Numbering.

Isherwood, Christopher (Christopher William Bradshaw Isherwood, 1904-). Born in Cheshire; educated at Repton and Cambridge; studied medicine in London (1928-29), but went to Berlin as a teacher of English (1930-33). As a writer he came into prominence in the 1930s as collaborator with W. H. *Auden in three plays—*The Dog Beneath the Skin* (1935), *The *Ascent of F.6* (1937), and *On the Frontier* (1938)—and a travel book which was the product of a visit to China with Auden, *Journey to a War* (1939). His other writings include fiction—*All the Conspirators* (1928), *The Memorial* (1932), *Mr Norris Changes Trains* (1935), *Goodbye to Berlin* (1939), *Prater Violet* (1945), *The World in the Evening* (1954); travel (in South America), *The Condor and the Cows* (1949); *Exhumations* (essays, 1966); autobiography, *Lions and Shadows* (1938). He settled in America in 1939, writing film scripts; later developed a particular interest in Eastern religion and philosophy, translating (with an Indian collaborator) *The Bhagavad-Gita* (1944) and cognate works. He became an American citizen in 1946.

Ivory tower. An imaginary place to which a person is said to withdraw from contact with actuality in the world outside. It is particularly applied, usually as a term of reproach, to those of a romantic or meditative temperament who do not engage in practical affairs. The case for the recluse is stated by E. M. *Forster in his essay 'The Ivory Tower' (*London Mercury*, Dec 1938, pp 119-30: 'The conviction . . . sometimes comes to the solitary individual that his solitude gives him something finer and greater than he gets when he merges in the multitude.').

Jacks, L. P. (Lawrence Pearsall Jacks, 1860-1955). Born in Nottingham; educated there and at the University of London, Manchester (Unitarian) College in Oxford, Göttingen, and Harvard. He became a Unitarian minister in 1887, serving churches in London, Liverpool, and Birmingham. A wider public knew him as the author of *Mad Shepherds and other Human Studies* (1910) and a large number of similar collections of essays combining a religious, ethical, sociological and humanistic outlook with an admirable prose style. His practical knowledge of life in industrial centres was sympathetically displayed in *The Legends of Smokeover* (1922) and *The Heroes of Smokeover* (1926). He edited the *Hibbert Journal* from its beginnings in 1902 until 1947 and wrote two autobiographical volumes: *Confessions of an Octogenarian* (1942) and *Observations of a Nonagenarian* (1952).

Jacks, M. L. (Maurice Leonard Jacks, 1894-1964). Son of L. P. *Jacks. Educated at Bradfield and Oxford. Headmaster of Mill Hill School, 1922-1937; thereafter Director of Oxford University Institute of Education. Author of *Education as a Social Factor* (1937), *The Education of Good Men* (1955), etc.

Jackson, Sir Barry (Barry Vincent Jackson, 1879-1961; knighted 1925). Born in Birmingham; trained as an architect. Developing a passion for acting, he formed the Pilgrim Players, an amateur company whose success led Jackson to build in 1913 the Birmingham Repertory Theatre, which he ran with unique distinction for more than twenty years, producing a great number of plays, new and old, British and foreign. One of his outstanding successes was with John Drinkwater's *Abraham Lincoln*, and he was the first to stage Bernard Shaw's *Back to Methuselah* in its entirety. In 1929 he started the Malvern Festival, a summer season devoted mainly to Shaw's plays. He wrote *The Theatre and Civil Life* (1922) and translated and adapted several French and Russian plays.

Jackson, Charles (Charles Reginald Jackson, 1903-68). Born in New Jersey. Wrote much for broadcasting. Best known for *The Lost Weekend* (1944) a powerful novel of five days in the life of a drunkard. Other novels on *outré* subjects: *The Fall of Valor* (1946),

The Outer Edges (1948). Short stories: *The Summer Side* (1950), *Earthly Creatures* (1953).

Jackson, Holbrook (1874-1948). Born in Liverpool; educated at 'various schools' but was mainly self-taught through his love of books. After some youthful experience in business he turned to journalism first as co-editor with A. R. *Orage of the *New Age* in 1907, then worked editorially on *T.P.'s Weekly* from 1911 to 1916; founded and edited one of the first of the 'little magazines', *To-day* (1917-23), with leading contemporary poets and essayists among the contributors. He wrote the first English book on *Bernard Shaw* (1907; H. L. *Mencken's *George Bernard Shaw: His Plays* preceded it in 1905), and his *The Eighteen-Nineties* (1913) is an indispensable study of the writers of that period. His well-informed interest in typography produced *A Brief Survey of Printing* (in collaboration with Stanley *Morison, 1923) and *The Printing of Books* (1938), as well as a study of *William Caxton* (1933). Holbrook Jackson was among the last of the old-style booklovers whose lives were absorbed by everything internal and external relating to books: see his *The Anatomy of Bibliomania* (vol. i, 1930; ii, 1931), *A Bookman's Holiday* (1945), *The Reading of Books* (1946).

Jackson, Shirley (1919-65, Mrs S. E. Hyman). Born in San Francisco; educated at Syracuse (N.Y.). Author of novels and short stories, frequently dealing with tragic and psychopathic subjects: *The Lottery* (1949), *Hangsaman* (1951), *The Bird's Nest* (1954), *The Haunting of Hill House* (1959), *We Have Always Lived in the Castle* (1962). More light-hearted are the books about her children: *Life Among the Savages* (1953), *Raising Demons* (1957).

Jacob, Naomi (Naomi Ellington Jacob, 1889-1964). Born at Ripon; educated at Middlesbrough. Worked successively as a teacher, a secretary, and an actress. From 1926 when her first novel *Jacob Ussher* was published, she became a voluminous writer of fiction and claimed that her output was two novels a year, having her first notable success with *Four Generations* in 1934. She also wrote a biography of Marie Lloyd—*Our Marie* (1936), and several autobiographical volumes beginning with *Me: a Chronicle about Other People* (1933).

Jacob's Room. Novel by Virginia *Woolf published in 1922. From his first appearance as a wilful small boy on a Cornwall beach wandering from his recently widowed mother, Jacob Flanders is presented in a series of episodes from his Oxford years, residence and social contacts in London, and times in Paris, Greece, and elsewhere, up to World War I, when a few of his friends gather in his Bloomsbury room, dealing with his possessions and asking 'Did he think he would come back?' He is seen impressionistically at social gatherings, in company with mistresses, at the opera house, in the British Museum Reading Room, as well as abroad at Versailles and on the Acropolis. He is characterized in discontinuous glimpses projected through observations of acquaintances on differing social levels. Much of the book's interest lies in its poetic presentation of city and country scenes.

Jacobs, W. W. (William Wymark Jacobs, 1863-1943). Born in London; educated privately; in Civil Service (G.P.O. Savings Bank), 1883-89. Beginning with *Many Cargoes* (1896) he wrote nearly a score of volumes, mainly of short stories but including some novels, treating with distinctive humour of longshoremen, barge crews, night watchmen and others who live by the sea and boats but are not ocean-going sailors. Notwithstanding the limitations of character and environment in these books, Jacobs played many ingenious comic variations on his themes and his rendering of the cockney (London) dialect was more convincing than the attempts made by most other writers. Though his place in literature may be small, he worked a vein of humour that was entirely his own and inimitable. He was also occasionally a master of horror, as with *The Monkey's Paw* both as a story and as a play. The humorous books include *The Skipper's Wooing* (1897), *Light Freights* (1901), *The Lady of the Barge* (1902), *Sailor's Knots* (1909), *Night Watches* (1914), *Sea Whispers* (1926).

James, Henry (1843-1916). Born in Boston, U.S., son of Henry James (1811-82; best known as a disciple of Swedenborg) and brother of William *James; educated privately, mostly abroad, and at Harvard Law School. His early cosmopolitan schooling had been directed in accordance with his father's conviction that 'children should not be allowed to take root in any religion,

political system, ethical code, or set of personal habits', and to this can be traced Henry James's adopted attitude as an analytical observer of the conduct of men and women in cultured society. He lived mainly in Europe, from 1876 in England where he became a naturalized English citizen in 1915. Though most of his novels and short stories were published in the 19th century, his fame in Great Britain was much enhanced after World War II, when his subtlety in character analysis and his complex prose style were in harmony with the increasing intellectualization of literary study. Popular attention was also drawn to him by the success of dramatizations of certain of his stories (*Washington Square*, as *The Heiress*; *The Turn of the Screw* as an opera with music by Benjamin Britten; *The Aspern Papers*). This posthumous acceptance of James in the theatre had its ironical aspect for he had desperately tried and dismally failed to become a playwright on his own account. The novels he published in the present century—*The *Wings of the Dove* (1902), *The *Ambassadors* (1903), *The *Golden Bowl* (1904)—have been variously estimated: by some as masterpieces displaying his literary art at its highest; by others as exhibitions of his prose at its most involved. He progressed—or regressed—from a relatively simple style in his early novels to tortuous attempts at refinement and exactitude of meaning through infinite qualification. Since praise often amounting to adulation of James became a cult in the 1940s and later, critical assessments grew unreliable. His mind and manner were unique and his influence was strong on other authors who sought to raise novel writing to the level of a fine art and to underplay its function as fictional narrative and storytelling. He discussed his own aims in the prefaces written for the heavily revised New York edition of his works (1907-09). These, together with three autobiographical volumes —*A Small Boy and Others* (1913), *Notes of a Son and Brother* (1914), *The Middle Years* (1917)—are valuable though never easy aids.

James Joyce Collection. Harriett *Weaver's collection of Joyce first editions and association copies was presented by her to the *National Book League in 1957.

James, Montague (Montague Rhodes James, 1862-1936). Born in Kent; educated at Eton and Cambridge, where he became Director of the Fitzwilliam Museum (1894-1908), Provost of King's College (1905-18), and Vice-Chancellor of the University (1912-15). From 1918 he was Provost of Eton. Though his accomplishments as a biblical scholar are on record in his almost innumerable publications on relevant themes, his literary reputation rests on *Ghost Stories of an Antiquary* (1905) and several similar volumes brought together in *Collected Ghost Stories* (1931).

James, Norah C. (Norah Cordner James, 1900-). Born in London; educated at various schools there; studied art at the Slade School; worked as a wartime civil servant and later as a trade union organizer and in other posts. Author of *Sleeveless Errand* (1929), *The Lion Beat the Unicorn* (1935), *Women are Born to Listen* (1937), *The Long Journey* (1941), *Over the Windmill* (1954), *The Green Vista* (1963), and other novels; *I Lived in a Democracy* (autobiography 1939).

James, William (1842-1910). Born in New York, brother of Henry *James. In early years travelled much in Europe with the family, and in 1868 graduated at Harvard Medical School, but did not practise. Turning to philosophy and psychology, he at length became Professor of Philosophy at Harvard. Outstanding among his writings are *Varieties of Religious Experience* (1902), established as a classic; *Pragmatism* (1907), *The Meaning of Truth* (1909).

Jameson, Storm (Margaret Storm Jameson, 1897-   ; Mrs Guy Chapman). Born at Whitby, Yorkshire; educated at Scarborough, and at Leeds University and University College, London. Author of *Modern Drama in Europe* (1920), *Morley Roberts: The Last Eminent Victorian* (1961), and many novels, notably *The Lovely Ship* (1927), *The Voyage Home* (1930) and *A Richer Dust* (1931). Autobiography: *Journey from the North* (I, 1969; II, 1970).

Janeites, The. Name given by Rudyard *Kipling to enthusiastic admirers of Jane Austen and her novels, in his story with that title included in *Debits and Credits* (1926).

Jarry, Alfred (1873-1907). Author of *Ubi Roi* (1896; Eng. trs. 1951; Eng. stage adaptation London 1966), a play prefiguring the irrational characteristics of the *Theatre of the Absurd. Antonin *Artaud and Roger *Vitrac founded the theatre named after him in Paris.

Jazz Age, The. Specifically the 1920s, when young men and women indulged in a whirl of frenetic social excitement or dissipation fostered by the collapse of moral standards during and following World War I. The term was established by Scott *Fitzgerald in his *Tales of the Jazz Age* (1922).

Jean Ogilvie. Niece of the Rev. Mr McCrimmon in James Bridie's *Mr Bolfry* (1943), in which she is a leading character.

Jeans, Sir James (James Hopwood Jeans, 1877-1946; knighted 1928). Born in London; educated at Merchant Taylors' School and Cambridge. Professor of Applied Mathematics at Princeton University, U.S., 1905-09; Lecturer in Applied Mathematics in the University of Cambridge, 1910-12; Secretary of the Royal Society, 1919-29; Professor of Astronomy in the Royal Institution, 1935-46. Wrote works for experts on Mechanics, Mathematics, Electricity and Magnetism, Radiation and the Quantum Theory, Astronomy and Cosmogony, etc. Having command of a lucid and attractive prose style, he had an enormous popular success with *The Universe Around Us* (1929) which was maintained by *The Mysterious Universe* (1939), *The Stars in their Courses* (1931), and *Through Space and Time* (1934). His other publications included *Science and Music* (1937).

Jeeves. Manservant and general consultant to Bertie Wooster in numerous comic stories by P. G. *Wodehouse.

Jeffers, Robinson (John Robinson Jeffers, 1887-1962). Born in Pittsburgh; educated at the University there and in Switzerland and Germany; studied medicine at the University of South Carolina and forestry at the University of Washington. Built himself a house in a part of California where he was able to indulge his passion for solitude and his love of wild life. He became one of the outstanding American poets of his generation with *Roan Stallion* (1925), *Dear Judas* (1929), *Give Your Heart to the Hawks* (1933), *Be Angry at the Sun* (1941), *The Double Axe* (1948), and other volumes in which he expresses a frequently unmeasured distress in contemplation of the devil's dance of humanity.

Jekyll, Gertrude (1843-1932). Born in London; studied art but bad eyesight prevented her practising as a painter and she turned to flower cultivation and writing on gardens.

Her striking personality made her something of a legend in her lifetime and seemed to invest even her old gardening-boots, which became the subject of one of Sir William Nicholson's most effective still-life paintings. Author of *Home and Garden* (1900), *Roses for English Gardens* (1902), *Flower Decoration in the House* (1907), *Children and Gardens* (1908), *Old English Household Life* (1925), *A Gardener's Testament* (1937).

Jennet Jourdemayne. Leading character in Christopher Fry's *The *Lady's Not for Burning* (1948). Supposed a witch, she is accused of turning a man into a dog.

Jennings, Elizabeth (Elizabeth Joan Jennings, 1926-   ). Born in Lincolnshire; educated in Oxford; library assistant there, 1950-58; later publishers' reader. Her volumes of poems include *Poems* (1953), *A Way of Looking* (1955), *A Sense of the World* (1958), *Song for a Birth or a Death* (1961), *The Mind Has Mountains* (1966), *Collected Poems* (1967), *Lucidities* (1970).

Jerome, Jerome K. (Jerome Klapka Jerome, 1859-1927). Born at Walsall, Staffordshire; educated in London. Worked as railway clerk, actor, reporter, teacher and editor of periodicals. His ample literary output included the lastingly popular *Three Men in a Boat* (1889), and *The Passing of the Third Floor Back* (1908), a modern morality play set in a Bloomsbury boarding-house and on the theme of spiritual transformation effected in other lodgers during the transit of the Christlike Stranger. Autobiography, *My Life and Times* (1926).

Jerrold, Douglas (1893-1964). Born in Scarborough; educated at Westminster and Oxford. Left the Civil Service in 1923 and became a publisher for the rest of his life. Editor of the *English Review* (1930-36); of the *New English Review* (1945-50). Author of political and historical works and novels (*The Truth About Quex*, 1927; *Storm over Europe*, 1930). He was a descendant of Douglas Jerrold (1802-57), playwright, novelist, and author of the comic *Mrs Caudle's Curtain Lectures* (1845).

Jesse, F. Tennyson (Friniwyd Tennyson Jesse (died 1958; Mrs H. M. Harwood). Started as a journalist; in World War I worked for the Ministry of Information and afterwards for the Hoover National Relief Commission. Her novels impress by narrative power and force uncommon in women writers: *The*

Milky Way (1913), *Tom Fool* (1926), *Moonraker* (1927), *The Lacquer Lady* (1929). *A Pin to See the Peep Show* (1934) attracted more than literary attention by being based on the actual murder case of Thompson and Bywaters, which created much doubt as to the justice of Mrs Thompson's execution.

Jim, Tuan. Chief character in Conrad's *Lord Jim* (1900).

Jimson, Gulley. Painter and narrator in Joyce Cary's *The *Horse's Mouth* (1944). He also appears in *Herself Surprised* (1941) and is mentioned in *To Be a Pilgrim* (1942).

Joad, C. E. M. (Cyril Edwin Mitchinson Joad, 1891-1953). Born in London; educated at Blundell's School and Oxford. Civil Servant, 1914-30. Head of the Department of Philosophy, Birkbeck College, University of London, from 1930. Author of many popular but mostly ephemeral books on philosophical subjects. As a member of the B.B.C. Brains Trust he was one of the first 'radio personalities', his frequent 'It depends what you mean by . . .' in response to questions becoming a facetious catch-phrase among listeners. *The Testament of Joad* (1937) is autobiographical.

Joan, St. *See* *Saint Joan.

Joe Lampton. Principal character in John Braine's *Room at the Top* (1957). He reaches the top by seducing and marrying Susan Brown, a wealthy man's daughter, but feels himself responsible for the death of Alice Aisgill, a married woman whose lover he had long been.

John Bull's Other Island. Play in four acts by Bernard *Shaw written and performed in 1904; published in 1907. In the London offices of Doyle & Broadbent, civil engineers, Tom Broadbent prepares for a journey to Ireland, where he is to develop an estate at Roscullen for the Land Development Syndicate in which he has a major financial interest. He proposes to take with him Tim Haffigan as his self-styled 'Irish Secretary' to smooth the way for his project, but his partner Larry Doyle is contemptuous of Haffigan as a Glasgow-born drunken 'seedy swindler' talking like a stage Irishman. Larry agrees to go with Broadbent, though warning him against sentimentality about Ireland, a country where the climate debauches the inhabitants with dreaming and imagining which disables them from dealing with reality. Larry has not been back to Ireland since he left it for America eighteen years before. He tells Broadbent of Nora Reilly, about whom he was romantic when they were seventeen and who is still waiting for him, though he is now indifferent. At Roscullen, before they arrive, Nora is encouraged to hope that she will not be thought 'coarse and dowdy'. She talks with Peter Keegan, a much-travelled ex-priest who converses with insects and animals, and, being thought mad, has been dismissed from the priesthood. Larry having declined an invitation to become parliamentary candidate for Roscullen, Broadbent is adopted and also becomes engaged to Nora Reilly. He rhapsodizes about Roscullen's golden future when the Syndicate has made it a prosperous tourist centre, but Keegan foresees a time when 'this poor desolate countryside becomes a busy mint in which we shall all slave to make money for you'.

John O'London's Weekly. A periodical with literary articles and book reviews for a popular audience not attracted by weightier publications. It aimed to follow in the path of *T. P.'s Weekly* but was less substantial. John O'London was the pseudonym of Wilfred *Whitten, editor of the paper. Founded 1919; ceased publication 1936.

Johns, W. E. (Captain William Earl Johns, 1893-1968). Born and educated at Hertford; qualified as a surveyor. Served in the Royal Flying Corps in World War I; was shot down and sentenced to death, but escaped, was recaptured, and kept in a punishment camp till the war ended. Founded in 1932 and edited *Popular Flying*. Turning to fiction for young people, he created Biggles, an airman hero, whose exploits he recorded in many extremely popular short stories and novels. In World War II Worrals of the W.A.A.F., Biggles's girl counterpart, was invented, and also Gimlet of the Commandos.

Johnson. Young Nigerian clerk, mission-educated and in temporary government employment, in Joyce Cary's *Mister Johnson* (1939).

Johnson, Hewlett (1874-1966). Born at Macclesfield; educated there and at Manchester and Oxford. Ordained in 1905 and, after holding a variety of other Anglican appointments, became Dean of Canterbury from 1931 until he retired in 1963. His propagandist enthusiasm for Soviet Russia and

Communist China earned him the title of 'the Red Dean' and much angry criticism. Following a visit to Russia he wrote *The Socialist Sixth of the World* (1940), followed in succeeding years by other books in support of Communism, including *China's New Creative Age* (1953).

Johnson, Lionel (Lionel Pigot Johnson, 1867-1902). Born at Broadstairs, Kent; educated at Winchester and Oxford. Worked as a critic and book-reviewer in London; where he became prominent in the Rhymer's Club, which included W. B. *Yeats among its members. Johnson became a Roman Catholic and developed the passion for Ireland shown in *Ireland and Other Poems* (1897). Though that and *Poems* (1895), and in prose *The Art of Thomas Hardy* (1894), were the only books he published, he is regarded as one of the key figures of the 1890s, possibly because his alcoholism is regarded as symptomatic of the somewhat mythical decadence of the writers of that period. A collection of his journalistic writings was published posthumously—*Post Liminum: Essays and Critical Papers* (1911).

Johnson, Louis (1924-). Born in Wellington, New Zealand. Worked as a teacher and in journalism and advertising. Author of *The Sun Among the Ruins* (1951), *Roughshod Among the Lilies* (1951), *New Worlds for Old* (1957), and other verse. Founded in 1952 and edited *New Zealand Poetry Yearbook*. See *New Zealand Writers.

Johnson, Pamela Hansford (1912- ; Lady Snow, wife of C. P. *Snow). Born and educated in London; worked in a bank until she turned novelist with *This Bed Thy Centre* (1935). Later novels include *The Trojan Brothers* (1944), *An Avenue of Stone* (1947), *Catherine Carter* (1952), *The Unspeakable Skipton* (1959), *An Error of Judgement* (1962), *Cork Street, Next to the Hatter's* (1965). She has also written critical studies of Ivy Compton Burnett, Proust, and Thomas Wolfe, and a play, *Corinth House* (1948). Her reflections after attending as a reporter the Moors Murder trial were published as *On Iniquity* (1967), an inquiry into certain aspects of the contemporary 'permissive society'.

Johnston, Denis (William Denis Johnston, 1901-). Born in Dublin; educated at Dublin, Edinburgh and Cambridge, and studied at Harvard Law School. Director of the Dublin

Gate Theatre, 1931-36, then worked in various capacities for the B.B.C. Head of Department of Theatre, Smith College, Massachusetts, from 1961. Author of numerous plays including *The Old Lady Says 'No!'* (1929), *The Moon in the Yellow River* (1931), *A Bride for the Unicorn* (1933), *The Golden Cuckoo* (1939), *The Scythe and the Sunset* (1958). Autobiography: *Nine Rivers from Jordan* (1953). *Collected Plays* (2 vols, 1960).

Johnston, H. H. (Sir Harry Hamilton Johnston, 1858-1927; knighted 1896). Born in London; educated at grammar school and King's College there; studied art at the Royal Academy. Joined expeditions into various regions of Africa, held consular and other Government offices, and wrote voluminously on African topics. After his retirement he turned his attention to fiction, producing 'continuations' of Dickens's *Dombey and Son* (*The Gay Dombeys*, 1919) and *Our Mutual Friend* (*The Veneerings*, 1922), and of Bernard Shaw's *Mrs Warren's Profession* (*Mrs Warren's Daughter*, 1920). He published an autobiography, *The Story of My Life* (1923).

Johnston, Mary (1870-1936). Born in Virginia, daughter of a Confederate army officer; educated at home. She wrote novels dealing mainly with life in the Old South or with the Civil War period. Though she took care to ensure the accuracy of the historical references and facts, her characters were excessively romantic, and her style lush, but her books abound in stirring incidents. Her first success was with *To Have and to Hold* (1895); best known among the others are *Lewis Rand* (1908), *The Long Roll* (1911), *The Great Valley* (1926).

Joliffe, Euphemia. Gentle and kindly landlady of Bellevue Lodge in J. Meade Falkner's *The *Nebuly Coat* (1903). Her half-brother Martin and his daughter Anastasia also bear the name, but are in fact descended from the titled Blandamers.

Jollifant, Inigo. Schoolmaster turned concert-party entertainer in Priestley's *The *Good Companions* (1929).

Jones. 'Plain Mr Jones', card-sharper of gentlemanly appearance and 'evil intelligence' in Joseph Conrad's **Victory* (1915).

Jones, David (1895-1974). Born in Kent. Studied at Camberwell and Westminster Schools of Art. His drawings and paintings are in various national galleries of art, including the Tate Gallery, London. Author of *In Parenthesis* (1937) an experimental work in prose and free verse; *The Anathemata* (1952), *The Wall* (1955), *The Sleeping Lord* (1974).

Jones, E. B. C. (Emily Beatrix Coursolles Jones; Mrs F. L. *Lucas; died 1966). Novelist: *Quiet Interior* (1920), *The Singing Captives* (1921), *The Wedgwood Medallion* (1922), *Inigo Sandys* (1924), *Helen and Felicia* (1927), *Morning and Cloud* (1931). She reviewed fiction for leading literary periodicals, and the opinions she expressed there 'were a sure guide for the highbrows'. She was an intimate of the *Bloomsbury Group and Lytton *Strachey frequently corresponded with her.

Jones, E. H. *See The Road to *En-dor.*

Jones, Gwyn (1907-). Educated at Tredegar and University of Wales; became a schoolmaster and university lecturer, and from 1940 Professor of English Language and Literature at Aberystwyth. Founded (1939) and edited until 1948 the *Welsh Review*. Author of *Richard Savage* (1935), *The Green Island* (1946), *The Flowers Beneath the Scythe* (1952), *The Walk Home* (1962), and other novels; *The Buttercup Field* (1945), *The Still Waters* (1948), and other collections of short stories. Also books on Welsh and Scandinavian legends.

Jones, Henry Arthur (1851-1929). Born in Buckinghamshire; educated at the local village school. For fifteen years he worked as a draper's assistant and commercial traveller, taking to playwriting in his spare time. The first of his plays to be performed was *It's Only Round the Corner* (1878), followed by *A Clerical Error* (1879). Success came with *The Silver King* (1882), written in collaboration with Henry Herman, a melodrama remembered mainly for one sentence: 'Oh God, put back thy universe and give me yesterday!'. Jones thereafter became identified with 'the new drama' which aimed at the naturalistic treatment of serious social themes and led from A. W. *Pinero and Jones to Bernard *Shaw. To appreciate the significance of Jones's contributions it is essential to view them in the setting of their own time and in conjunction with the work of immediately contemporary playwrights. He never altogether shed his addiction to melodrama and emotional extravagance, but it was his choice of themes not his treatment of them that made him a genuine pioneer, even if a timid one, in the redirection of English drama along lines that converged towards Ibsenite realism. Jones's weakness lay in his reluctance to carry the social and individual problems he posed to their legitimate conclusion, if that conclusion would be unacceptable in the moral atmosphere of the day. Thus the last act of *Michael and His Lost Angel* (1896), for example, falls into a bog of sentimentality unredeemed by its theatrical 'daring'. Other notable plays: *The Dancing Girl* (1891), *The Case of Rebellious Susan* (1894), *The Triumph of the Philistines* (1895), *The Liars* (1897), *Mrs Dane's Defence* (1900). If any of Jones's plays survives on the stage, it is likely to be the last-named; its third act offers an impressive display of mounting dramatic tension.

Jones, Jack (1884-1970). Born in Merthyr Tydfil; educated at elementary school there. From the age of twelve until he was forty he worked as a miner; served in World War I; became a trades union official, 1923-28. Author of novels—*Rhondda Roundabout* (1934), *Bidden to the Feast* (1938), *Off to Philadelphia in the Morning* (1947), *River Out of Eden* (1951), *Choral Symphony* (1955), etc; plays—*Land of My Fathers* (1937), *Transatlantic Episode* (1947), and others; autobiography—*Unfinished Journey* (1937), *Me and Mine* (1946), *Give Me Back My Heart* (1950).

Jones, Rufus (Rufus Matthew Jones, 1863-1948). Born in Maine of Quaker parentage; educated at the Friends' School, Providence, Rhode Island, and at Haverford College, where he later taught philosophy for many years. He became the leading Quaker publicist of his generation, writing on the history and principles of that religious body and on mysticism: *Spiritual Reformers in the 16th and 17th Centuries* (1914), *Later Periods of Quakerism* (1921), *The Flowering of Mysticism* (1939).

Jones, Sheridan. Pseudonym of Ada Elizabeth Jones (Mrs Cecil *Chesterton).

Joneses. *See* *Keeping up with the . . .

Jordan, Robert. Chief character in Ernest Hemingway's *For Whom the Bell Tolls* (1941); American university lecturer serving with the Republicans in the Spanish Civil War.

Joseph, M. K. (Michael Kennedy Joseph, 1914-). Born in London; lived in New Zealand from 1924; educated in Auckland and at Oxford. Served in Normandy in World War II. Professor of English, University of Auckland. Author of verse collections—*Imaginary Islands* (1951), *The Living Countries* (1957); *I'll Soldier No More* (war novel; 1958), etc. *See* *New Zealand Writers.

Joseph Vance. Novel by William *De Morgan published in 1906. In this subtitled 'Ill-written Autobiography' the narrator (Joseph Vance himself) sits in his Bloomsbury lodgings writing of his life from when he was the poor seven-year-old son of uneducated London parents, up to his sixties when, a successful civil engineer, he returns temporarily from engagements in South America to gather material at the British Museum for his labour of love, a History of Musical Instruments. His progress from poverty to affluence dates from a fight between his drunken father, Christopher Vance, and a sweep, which puts old Vance into hospital for several weeks with an injured back, after he has lost his job as a warehouseman. Mrs Vance is 'taken notice of' by philanthropic Dr Randall Thorpe while drawing from her depleted account at the Savings Bank. In the meantime Vance has bought for fifteen-pence a secondhand signboard reading 'C. Dance, Builder. Repairs. Drains promptly attended to'. He gets a neighbouring sign-painter to alter 'Dance' to 'Vance', and puts up the board outside. Dr Thorpe, having noticed the sign, engages Vance to attend to the drains at the Thorpe family's Poplar Villa. This commission starts Vance on an ever-enlarging career as a master builder, based on the principle of always getting others to do the work. His boy Joseph, accompanying Vance to Poplar Villa on the first visit, immediately conceives a child's love for Lossie (born Lucilla) Thorpe, aged about fifteen. He becomes a protégé of Dr Thorpe who, discovering latent intellectual ability in the boy, assumes responsibility for his education at boarding school and Oxford, and also welcomes him into the family circle at Poplar Villa, where Lossie binds him to her with the same affection as she gives to her baby brother, also christened Joseph but pet-named Beppino. Old Vance prospers despite outbreaks of drunkenness, until in one of these bouts he causes a gas explosion leading to the complete destruction of his works by fire, a calamity aggravated by his having failed to post the now overdue insurance premiums. Before Joseph Vance leaves Oxford he is desolated by Lossie's marriage and departure to India with her husband General (afterwards Sir Hugh) Desprez. Some years later Joseph finds partial consolation in marrying Janey Spencer, younger sister of Lossie's best friend, but Janey is eventually drowned when a ship she and Joseph are on is wrecked off the coast of Portugal. Lossie's husband is killed while on military service. He and Joseph had established a friendly relationship and conspired together to keep from Lossie the knowledge that, shortly before marrying an English heiress, Beppino has, in Florence and under the assumed name of Giuseppe Vance, married an Italian girl who dies in childbirth. These facts become known to Joseph after the death of Beppino from typhoid while honeymooning with his English wife. Joseph makes himself responsible for the child's upbringing in Italy, and subsequently takes him to South America as assistant on civil engineering projects. Correspondence between Lossie and Joseph ceases when he does not deny rumours that he is the father of the child born in Italy, and it is not until many years have passed that Lossie learns of Beppino's duplicity. She searches out Joseph in London and, in old age, their enduring love is refreshed. De Morgan's narrative embraces a complex of family relationships interwoven with those of Lossie and Joseph, and running through a wide range of moods and emotions, from comic to tragic.

Jourdain, Eleanor (died 1924). *See* An **Adventure.

Jourdemayne. *See* *Jennet Jourdemayne.

Journal of a Disappointed Man, The. Selected entries from the diary of W. N. P. *Barbellion (pseudonym of Bruce Frederick Cummings) published in 1919. Except the laconic final note, 'Barbellion died on December 31 [1917]', the *Journal* gives a factual account of the author's experiences and opinions from January 1903, when he was thirteen, to October 1917. Cummings lived until

October 1919. He set down in the diary upon which the *Journal* draws, an autobiographical record of the vocational interest in natural history which led him from detested work as a local newspaper reporter to a desired appointment on the staff of the British Museum (Natural History). Glimpses of his work as a zoologist run through the recital of his manifold interests, in which a love of music is prominent. His subjective exposition of Beethoven's Fifth Symphony and the description of Sir Henry Wood conducting, are illustrative of the enthusiasm aroused in him by many aspects of life. From boyhood his health was poor, and bouts of illness culminated in the onset of disseminated sclerosis, not revealed to him until after his marriage, though known before and accepted as a burden by his wife. While the slow approach of death inevitably occasioned increasing anguish and protest, the *Journal* is devoted more to the art of living than to the craft of dying. It records friendships and loves and hates, the beauty of earth and its creatures, and the depths and shallows of the author's inner life.

Journey's End. Play in three acts by R. C. *Sherriff performed in 1928, published in 1929. Set in a British dug-out in the front line near St Quentin in March 1918, at the time the great German attack is expected to begin, it concerns a group of officers headed by Captain Stanhope, the company commander, with his second-in-command, Osborne, and Lieutenants Trotter (a former ranker) and Hibbert. Stanhope, still only twenty-one, has been in and out of the front line in France for three years with little respite, drinking hard to overcome his shattered nerves. Middle-aged Osborne says, 'There isn't a man to touch him as a commander of men.' Hibbert, complaining of neuralgia, wants to go sick, but Stanhope threatens to shoot him, recognizing that his nerve has given way. Afterwards Stanhope confesses that his own fears are equal to Hibbert's. A new young subaltern, Raleigh, joins the company straight from the school where Stanhope had been hero-worshipped by the other boys. He is in love with Raleigh's sister and dreads that the boy's letters home will reveal him as a drunkard, though before the war he neither drank nor smoked. When Osborne and Raleigh are sent on a raid to take prisoners for identification,

Osborne is killed, but Raleigh captures a German and is promised recommendation for a M.C. Next day he is mortally wounded at the beginning of the German attack and dies in the dug-out a moment before it is destroyed by a shell.

'Joxer' Daly. In Sean O'Casey's *Juno and the Paycock* (1925) the boon companion of 'Captain' Jack Boyle; he is around sixty but looks much older, with a face 'like a bundle of crinkled paper', eyes with 'a cunning twinkle', and an invariable grin.

Joyce, James (James Augustine Aloysius Joyce, 1882-1941). Son of John Stanislaus Joyce, a Collector of Rates in Dublin, who in 1887 moved with the family to Bray, where the children were first taught, briefly, by a governess and then at a kindergarten. In 1888 James was sent to Clongowes Wood College, a Jesuit institution in Co. Kildare. To maintain a standing there among other boastful pupils, he conferred imaginary grandeur on his family, meanwhile winning distinction in religious knowledge, music, and games. When John Joyce retired on a small pension in 1891, James left Clongowes, and after an interlude of home study and attendance at the Christian Brothers' School in Dublin he was admitted to Belvedere College, a Jesuit dayschool there. He won several annual exhibitions carrying monetary awards, with which he tried unrewardingly to bolster the declining family fortunes. While still at school he began to write both verse and prose, passed through a phase of religious enthusiasm, had his first sexual encounters, and read widely in contemporary authors. In his last year at Belvedere his previous exemplary conduct gave way to rebellious neglect of study, though he continued to excel in English. He went in 1898 to University College, Dublin, his outstanding achievement while there being the acceptance by the *Fortnightly Review* (April 1900) of an article by him on 'Ibsen's New Drama', a review of the recently published *When We Dead Awaken*. By this time he had extended his reading to the works of other continental authors, studying and mastering languages for this purpose. In May 1900 he and his father visited London, where James attempted without success to pave the way to a journalistic appointment, though he managed to enlist the interest of William *Archer, Ibsen's English translator. Having graduated

in the autumn of 1902, Joyce then cultivated the acquaintanceship of W. B. *Yeats, Lady *Gregory, George *Moore, J. M. *Synge, George *Russell and others who were fostering the cultural renaissance centred on the *Irish Literary Theatre. In his contacts with Russell and Yeats he created an impression in which their sense of his intelligence and imagination was tempered by dislike of his arrogance and crude manners. He was later to become one of the strongest opponents of the Irish literary movement. In October 1902 he entered the Medical School in Dublin, but almost immediately his father's financial imprudence made it impossible to meet the requisite fees and expenses. Joyce thereupon sought work as a tutor, but finding none available he left Ireland and continued his medical studies in Paris while supporting himself there as a teacher of English. He represented this voluntary exile as enforced by antagonism towards him on the part of the university authorities in Dublin, a first bout of his lifelong inclination to self-pity. Though he earned a little by teaching and book-reviewing, he was compelled to beg from his family and friends, and borrowed from a pupil when he was called back to Dublin to his mother's sick-bed. In the interval of a few months until she died, Joyce perambulated Dublin and had much talk with Irish friends, particularly with Oliver St John *Gogarty, who succeeded in breaking down Joyce's determination to overcome his drinking habits. In the months following his mother's death he began an autobiographical novel at first called *Stephen Hero*, and was also writing the poems afterwards collected in *Chamber Music* and the first of the stories subsequently published as *Dubliners*. Apart from £1 each for such of these stories as were accepted for publication in the *Irish Homestead*, and correspondingly small fees for occasional reviews, Joyce earned nothing by his writings at that time. Having a good tenor voice, he had thoughts of becoming a professional singer and once appeared in the same concert programme as John McCormack. He was also for a short period a schoolteacher. Meanwhile he had fallen in love with the girl, Nora Joseph Barnacle, whom he married years later (in 1931). With her he again departed for the Continent on borrowings from his friends. They reached Paris in October 1904, and moved on to Zurich, where Joyce failed to get an expected post as a teacher of English to Swiss students. After a similar disappointment in Trieste, they settled at Pola (then under Austrian control but now the Yugoslavian town renamed Pulj). There they stayed from November 1904 to March 1905, Joyce teaching at the Berlitz School and continuing with that organization when they returned to Trieste which, except for brief visits elsewhere, became their home until the summer of 1915. At Joyce's instigation his younger brother, Stanislaus, joined them in Trieste in October 1905, and took a similar teaching post. The combined household was far from happy or peaceful. By now, Joyce had a son as well as Nora to support, and he grew increasingly intolerant of her mental limitations and indifference to his literary preoccupations. He was frequently drunk, Stanislaus's attempts to sober him being ineffective. Joyce continued to write, completing the *Dubliners* stories, adding chapters to *Stephen Hero*, and alternately railing against the Irish and using them as copy. The Berlitz School was not flourishing, and Joyce migrated to Rome, working there from July 1906 to the following March as correspondence clerk in a bank. He then resumed his English teaching in Trieste on a part-time basis, helping out the family income by newspaper articles in Italian and by lectures at the University. *Chamber Music*, published by Elkin Matthews in London in May 1907, brought a few moderately favourable reviews but no money. Again he and Nora and (now) two children were supported by Stanislaus, to whose burdens James's illness from rheumatic fever was shortly added. One of its after-effects was the beginning of the eye trouble which was to be an increasing affliction. In July 1909 he took his elder child, Georgie, on a visit to Dublin, paying the travelling expenses from a year's fees in advance from a private pupil. While there he mixed with old friends and newer acquaintances among the journalists, absorbing more of the Dublin atmosphere and spirit that were to form the main current in his writings from first to last—a love-hate relationship curiously rooted in Joyce's conviction that by writing about Dublin he was at the same time penetrating to the heart of all cities and all mankind. He left Dublin for Trieste in September, but was again in Ireland a

month later as agent for a partnership he had initiated in Trieste to start cinemas in Dublin and other Irish cities where none existed. Their first picture theatre opened in the capital in December, but Joyce did not stay to see it through its infancy and the scheme had collapsed by July 1910, some six months after his further return to Trieste and renewed penury. Meanwhile he was in angry dispute with the Irish publishers who had accepted *Dubliners* but later demanded that he should delete references to Queen Victoria and Edward VII which were held to be offensive. Joyce refused and in a personal letter to George V, enclosing a proof of the questioned story, he invited the king's opinion, but was of course informed that no opinion could be given. In July 1912 Nora visited their families in Dublin and was immediately followed there by Joyce. They stayed until September and that was the last he saw of Ireland. *Dubliners* was published in June 1914, not by the Dublin firm (who had destroyed all but the one copy in the author's possession) but by Grant Richards in London. Though it was received with respectful reviews, the sales were negligible. Yet Joyce had by this time 'arrived' in terms of *avant-garde* acclaim led by Ezra *Pound, through whom *A *Portrait of the Artist as a Young Man* (the title of the rewritten *Stephen Hero*) was serialized in *The Egoist* from February 1914 to September 1915. Thus encouraged, he began **Ulysses*, the progress and reception of which were to be at least as much a part of 20th-century literary history as of Joyce's personal life. Ejected from Trieste by the war, the family moved back to Zurich, and apart from occasional visits abroad (including the one to London in 1931, when he and Nora married), that was his home for the rest of his life. Soon after this migration to Switzerland, the active interest of friends and other admirers obtained for him a grant from the *Royal Literary Fund and in August 1916 a Civil List grant. *A Portrait of the Artist as a Young Man* was published in book form in New York in December 1916 and in an English (imported) edition in February 1917. An operation for glaucoma in August still further impaired his eyesight, and it has been suggested that the failure of his bodily vision was an important factor in the increasing approximation of his prose to the aural character of music and away from rationality. *Ulysses* began publication as a serial in the New York *Little Review* in March 1918, and its successive instalments brought the editors of the magazine into disfavour with the authorities. Ultimately they were charged with publishing obscene matter and fined. Joyce's financial situation had been eased by donations from rich American patronesses, though the fickleness of these enthusiasts made this source liable to sudden stoppage. His books, however, were at last bringing in money, especially after the issue in 1921 of the complete and unexpurgated *Ulysses* in Paris. The next seventeen years were given to the writing of *Work in Progress*, published in 1939 as *Finnegans Wake*, his last book. He died on 13 January after an operation for duodenal ulcer. No assured forecast can yet be made of Joyce's future rank among the novelists, if indeed 'novels' is an appropriate label for books of the unique character of *A Portrait of the Artist*, *Ulysses*, and *Finnegans Wake*. The first of these presents no difficulty as prose, but its combination of spiritual torment, realism, and aesthetic theory assembled within a framework intensely personal yet also objective, gave it no affinity with the English Novel as practised up to that time. In its character as autobiography it provides the essential explanation of Joyce's bitter hatred of the Roman Catholic Church from his adolescence onward, though the very intensity of his antagonism acted throughout as a bond. Whatever may be the imaginative stature and esoteric significance of *Ulysses* and *Finnegans Wake*, they are likely to join the company of such classics as Rabelais's *Gargantua and Pantagruel* and Burton's *Anatomy of Melancholy*, masterpieces much praised but little read. It was Joyce's fate to imagine himself a modern Prometheus pierced and torn by the dark gods, and in that aspect his two biggest works may be regarded by the non-sympathetic as protracted gestures of moral and linguistic defiance. Edmund *Wilson's essay, 'The Dream of H. C. Earwicker' on *Finnegans Wake* (in *The Wound and the Bow*) records that 'Joyce once said to a friend: "The demand that I make of my reader is that he should devote his whole life to reading my books." '

The James Joyce Collection of his first editions and association copies made by

Harriet *Weaver was presented by her to the *National Book League in 1957.

Joyce, William. *See* Haw Haw.

Juggins. Footman to the Gilbeys in Shaw's *Fanny's First Play* (1911). He turns out to be the brother of a duke and becomes engaged to Margaret Knox.

Jung, Carl (Carl Gustav Jung, 1875-1961). Born in Switzerland. Studied medicine in Basle and psychiatry in Paris. Professor of Psychology at the University of Zurich, 1933-41, and at Basle from 1943. Dissenting from the prominence given to sexual phenomena in the system of psychoanalysis established by *Freud, Jung's long professional association with him was severed in 1913. Jung's beliefs were highly transcendental and comprehensible to few but initiates, though terms he used, such as 'complexes', 'introversion', 'extroversion' 'the collective unconscious', became familiar in current speech. His writings include *The Theory of Psychoanalysis* (1912), *The Psychology of the Unconscious* (1916), *Psychological Types* (1923), *Psychology and Religion* (1938), *Psychology and Alchemy* (1952).

Jungle, The. Novel by Upton *Sinclair published in 1906. Lured to America by the promise of good wages in a free country, a group of twelve leave their farming community in Lithuania and settle in Chicago, where Jurgis Rudkus's magnificent physique immediately gets him picked for employment from among the daily crowd begging for work in the stockyards, where thousands of hogs and cattle are slaughtered every day and nothing is wasted; whether diseased or not, every scrap of flesh goes for food as hams and bacon, dressed or canned beef, sausages, lard, and in various faked guises, such as 'devilled chicken'. What remains—bones, blood, guts, sweepings and filth—becomes 'peerless fertilizer'. Jurgis begins as a sweeper of entrails, earning 'more than a dollar and a half in a single day' of twelve hours. The Lithuanians find themselves cheated on every hand by agents and others, particularly in the buying of a house on which there are charges undisclosed to them, and from which they are ultimately ejected. Jurgis marries Ona Lukoszaite, a young girl from his own country, and in conformity with Lithuanian tradition and custom an open-house wedding feast has to be given, even though it leaves them all penniless. Ona gets work in the ham packing department, and some time after the birth of her first child she is forced to submit sexually to the departmental boss. Jurgis attacks him and is imprisoned; Ona dies at the birth of a second child. Rebelling against accumulating injustices, Jurgis turns into an enemy of society, becoming tramp, thug, strike-breaker, and political grafter, before embracing socialism with its expectation of 'the rallying of the outraged working men of Chicago to our standard'.

The novel's exposure of conditions in the slaughterhouses and meatpacking factories led to investigations ordered by the Theodore Roosevelt government and to consequent legislation.

Juno and the Paycock: A Tragedy in Three Acts by Sean *O'Casey performed in 1924; published in 1925. The setting throughout is a combined living-room and bedroom in a Dublin tenement house in 1922, when the 'Diehards' (extreme Republicans) are fighting the supporters of the lately founded Irish Free State. Mary Boyle is reading from the newspaper to her brother Johnny the account of the finding of the shot-ridden body of a neighbour's diehard son, Commandant Tancred, on a country road. Johnny, wounded in the Easter 1916 uprising and with a bomb-shattered arm, protests hysterically that there is too much reading about butchery. Mrs Boyle (Juno) returns from shopping and argues against trade unions with Mary, who is on strike. With Johnny unemployed and the father, work-shy 'Captain' Jack Boyle, strutting 'like a paycock' in and out of the Dublin snugs (pubs) with his boozing companion Joxer Daly, Juno alone works to feed them all. Jerry Devine, a Labour leader in love with Mary, brings news of a job for the Captain (a title, mocks Juno, based on his single venture on the water, on a collier from Dublin to Liverpool). In a comic scene the Captain and Joxer discuss the unhappy prospect of going after the job, and Boyle complains of pains in his legs. Charles Bentham, a self-satisfied schoolteacher whom Mary is attached to, comes with information that a relative has left a fortune to Boyle. In anticipation of the money, they borrow prodigally to buy furniture and other goods. Trouble returns when Mary is found to be pregnant by Bentham, who has gone abroad; accumulates when no fortune appears, owing to a wrongly-drawn will; and culminates in Johnny's summary execution for having betrayed Tancred.

Juno Boyle. In Sean O'Casey's **Juno and the Paycock* (1925), the wife of 'Captain' Jack Boyle. She is forty-five, with 'a look of listless monotony and harassed anxiety' and 'an expression of mechanical resistance'. In other circumstances 'she would probably be a handsome, active and clever woman'.

Jupp, Mrs. Landlady of Ernest Pontifex's lodging in Samuel Butler's *The *Way of All Flesh* (1903). She was modelled on Mrs Boss, a modern Mrs Quickly, employed by Butler's cousin. A selection of her memorable sayings is given as 'Bossiana' in *Butleriana* (Nonesuch Press, 1932), extracted from Butler's Notebooks.

Jurgis Rudkus. Lithuanian immigrant working in the Chicago stockyards and in other capacities in Upton Sinclair's *The *Jungle* (1906).

Jusserand, Jules (Jean Adrien Antoine Jules Jusserand, 1885-1932). Born in Lyons; educated there and in Paris. Became in succession Councillor at the French Embassy in London, Minister in Denmark, and from 1903 to 1924 French Ambassador in Washington. He was a distinguished scholar with a profound knowledge of English life and literature, manifest in *English Wayfaring Life in the Middle Ages* (1889), *The English Novel in the Time of Shakespeare* (1890), *A Literary History of the English People* (1906-13). His other books included *A French Ambassador at the Court of Charles II* (1892) and *With Americans of Past and Present Days* (1916).

Justice. A Tragedy by John *Galsworthy performed and published in 1910. Inquiry into the cause of an unaccountable reduction in the bank balance of James & Walter How, solicitors, reveals that a cheque for £9 has been altered to £90 by twenty-three-year-old Falder, one of their clerks, who was sent to cash it and has kept the balance. Suspicion would have fallen on a fellow clerk, Davis (who sailed for Australia three days after the date of the cheque), but for the proved fact that the counterfoil could not have been altered until two days after Davis had left.

Falder is in love with Ruth Honeywill, married to a continuously brutal husband, from whom she cannot get free, cruelty alone being at that date insufficient ground for divorce. Consequently Falder has made plans to go to South America with Ruth and her two young children, a project for which he needed the money fraudulently obtained. The elder How, head of the firm, insists on prosecuting, against the wish of his son Walter, who drew the cheque, and against the plea for leniency by Cokeson, their humane managing clerk. Falder's relationship with a married woman is regarded as evidence of depravity aggravating the crime of forgery, for which, after a moral homily by the judge, he is sentenced to three years penal servitude. Cokeson not only visits him in prison but also calls on the Governor in the hope of impressing on him that solitary confinement will be mentally disastrous to the young man. In a wholly wordless scene showing Falder in his cell, silence and solitude drive him and other prisoners to frenzied beating with their fists on the cell doors. After serving the sentence, news of his record gets round to wherever he finds work and prevents him from getting references when he changes jobs. Cokeson's intercession is on the point of getting him taken back into the firm, when he is arrested anew for 'obtaining employment with a forged reference'. He breaks from the detective-sergeant's grasp and throws himself down the stairs, breaking his neck. It was believed that prison reforms were made after Winston Churchill (then Home Secretary) had seen the play.

Kafka, Franz (1883-1924). Born in Prague. Studied law and worked as a government insurance official for some years from 1907. He suffered much from ill-health aggravated by wartime privation and died from tuberculosis. His abnormally sensitive nature, mystical tendencies, and bouts of despair, coupled with his encroaching lung disease, created a tormented and abnormal personality. Nevertheless he was hailed in unmeasured terms by English, American, German and French writers as a genius of the first order, and a wide and deep though possibly unenduring influence was exercised by the novels he left in incomplete form and which were, in spite of his expressed wishes, published posthumously: translated into English as *The Castle* (1930), *The Metamorphosis* (1937), *The Trial* (1937), *Amerika* (1938).

Kai Lung. See Ernest *Bramah.

Kailyard School. Kailyard=kitchen garden, cabbage patch. The term was applied to a group of late nineteenth-century authors of stories about Scottish cottagers, among them Ian *Maclaren, S. R. *Crockett, J. M. *Barrie.

Kaiser, Georg (1878-1945). Born and educated in Magdeburg. Worked in Argentina and spent some time in Spain and Italy before returning to Germany, from which he went into exile in Switzerland after the Nazis usurped power. During the vogue in the 1920s for *Expressionism in drama his plays—*From Morn to Midnight* (in German, 1916; Eng. trans., 1920), *The Coral* (1917; 1929), *Gas I* (1918; 1924), *Gas II* (1920)—were internationally applauded as were those of his younger contemporary Ernst *Toller. In their period these two were accorded similar high rank to that occupied by Bertolt *Brecht after World War II. Though Kaiser's aim was to contribute to the drama of ideas, he was less a productive thinker than a stage craftsman more successful in dramatic action than in rational presentation.

Kane, Saul. Central character in *The *Everlasting Mercy* by John Masefield.

Kapek, Karel. See Čapek.

Kate Croy. A leading character in Henry James's *The *Wings of the Dove* (1902); secretly engaged to Merton Densher.

Katharsis. See Catharsis.

Katzin, Olga. See Sagittarius.

Kauffmann, Stanley (1916-   ). Born and educated in New York; worked as publishers' editor and contributor to various periodicals. His novels include *The Hidden Hero* (1949), *A Change of Climate* (1955), *The Very Man* (1956), *If It Be Love* (1960). *The Philanderer* (*The Tightrope* in U.S.) (1953) was the subject of an unsuccessful obscenity trial in London in 1954. See *Censorship of Books.

Kaufman, George S. (George Simon Kaufman, 1889-1961). Born and educated in Pittsburg. After varying commercial employment he contributed regularly to Washington and New York papers before collaborating with Marc *Connelly, Moss *Hart and others in a large number of popular stage successes: with Connelly, *Merton of the Movies* (1922), *Beggar on Horseback* (1924); with Moss *Hart, *You Can't Take It With You* (1936), *The Man Who Came to Dinner* (1939); with Edna *Ferber, *The Royal Family* (1927), *Dinner at Eight* (1932), *Stage Door* (1936); with J. P. *Marquand, *The Late George Apley* (1946); with Howard Teichmann, *The Solid Gold Cadillac* (1954).

Kavaphes, Konstantinos. See C. P. *Cavafy.

Kavanagh, Patrick (1905-1967). Born in Inniskeen, County Monaghan, son of a small farmer; worked as a journalist on Irish papers in Dublin, where he cultivated the reputation of being 'a character eloquent and irascible', to meet whom was 'a tourist attraction'. Though long regarded as a major Irish poet, his writings were of varying merit: *The Great Hunger* (1942) was considered his best poem, an opinion he ceased to share; other verse: *A Soul for Sale* (1947), *Come Dance with Kitty Stobling* (1960), *Collected Poems* (1964). He also wrote two novels, *The Green Fool* (1938) and *Tarry Flynn* (1948) which is largely autobiographical. *Self Portrait* came out in 1964 and *Collected Prose* in 1967.

Kaye-Smith, Sheila (1887-1956), Born at St Leonards, Sussex; educated privately. She married an Anglican clergyman (the Rev. T. P. Fry) in 1924, but both became Roman Catholics five years later. Between 1908 and 1923 she wrote regional novels set in the county of Sussex and concerned largely with a local family, the Alards: the best are *Sussex Gorse* (1916), *Tamarisk Town* (1919),

Green Apple Harvest (1920), *Joanna Godden* (1921), *The End of the House of Alard* (1923). Her later and more numerous novels are less noteworthy, with the possible exception of *The History of Susan Spray* (1931). Autobiography: *Three Ways Home* (1937).

Keable, Robert (1887-1927). Born at Ravenham, Bedfordshire; educated at Whitgift Grammar School and Cambridge. Ordained as an Anglican clergyman in 1911 and, after serving as curate in a Bradford (Yorkshire) parish, went as a missionary to central Africa, 1912-20. Following the end of World War I, during which he was a chaplain in France, he withdrew from the Church and became for a year or two a schoolmaster. His health broke down and he went to live in the South Seas, where he died at Tahiti. None of his writings attracted particular attention until the publication of *Simon Called Peter* (1921), a novel based on his own loss of faith, a theme then regarded as sensational, fascinating, and shocking. The book had only small literary merit and was soon forgotten, its sequel *Recompense* (1925) failing to revive interest. Keable's later works include *Tahiti: Isle of Dreams* (1926).

Kear, Alroy. A character in *Cakes and Ale* by Somerset Maugham, generally supposed to have been a satirical thrust at Hugh *Walpole.

Keegan, Peter. Former priest in Shaw's *John Bull's Other Island* (1904). Regarded by the Church as 'a poor madman' he was dismissed from the priesthood. He regards animals and insects as his friends and brothers, and eloquently defends his dream of a holy Ireland against the Land Development Syndicate plans for hotels and golf links.

Keeping up with the Joneses. Colloquial phrase for the form of snobbery which leads to emulation of the social standing of neighbours or others, or to the acquiring and display of possessions as a status symbol in rivalry with someone else.

Kell, Joseph. Pseudonym used by Anthony *Burgess for *One Hand Clapping* (1961) and *Inside Mr Enderby* (1963; reissued under his own name, 1967).

Keller, Helen (Helen Adams Keller, 1880-1968). Born in Alabama. An illness deprived her of sight and hearing before she was two years old, and her education was conducted by a friend who communicated lessons by the manual alphabet tapped out on her hand; the same method enabled her to become a graduate of Harvard. She learned to type, was proficient in French and German, and made a special study of philosophy. Her life was devoted to international service for the blind, deaf, and dumb. She published *The Story of My Life* (1902), *Optimism* (1903), *The World I Live In* (1908), *Out of the Dark* (1913), *Midstream: My Later Life* (1930), *Helen Keller's Journal* (1938). *Teacher* (1956) was an account of Anne Sullivan, to whom she owed her education, and who was her constant companion.

Kelly, George (George Edward Kelly, 1887-). Born in Philadelphia; educated privately. Was for some years an actor in theatres and music-halls, writing sketches for the latter. Of his full-length plays *Craig's Wife* (1925) made the chief mark, though *The Torchbearers* (1922) is most widely known, by its remarkable popularity among amateur actors.

Kennedy, Charles Rann (1871-1950). Born in Derby; educated in Birmingham. Worked as a clerk, then went on the stage, appearing in London and New York in Shakespeare, Shaw, Greek drama, and his own plays, of which the best is *The Servant in the House* on a similar theme to *The Passing of the Third Floor Back* by Jerome J. *Jerome. Kennedy became an American citizen in 1917 and was for some years head of the Drama Department at a college in Millbrook, New York.

Kennedy, Margaret (1896-1967; Lady Davies; married Sir David Davies, 1925). Born in London; educated at Cheltenham and Oxford. Began to write while still a young girl but published nothing before a historical manual, *A Century of Revolution* (1922). With her second novel *The *Constant Nymph* (1924), a tale of an unconventional musical family, she scored a rarely precedented success which extended from the book to the play with the same title written in collaboration with Basil Dean. A sequel, *The Fool of the Family*, came out in 1930. She had a further stage success with *Escape Me Never!* (1934). Her later books include the novels *The Midas Touch* (1938), *Lucy Carmichael* (1951), *Troy Chimneys* (1952), *Act of God* (1955), and a critical study, *Jane Austen* (1950).

Kenny, Charles J. A pseudonym used by Erle Stanley *Gardner for *This is Murder* (1936).

Kenyon Review. *See* John Crowe *Ransom.

Keown, Eric (Eric Oliver Dilworth Keown, 1904-1963). Educated at Highgate and Cambridge. Joined the staff of *Punch* in 1928 and was its dramatic critic from 1945. Author of *The Complete Dog's Dudgeon* (1938), *Peggy Ashcroft* (1955), *Margaret Rutherford* (1956).

Ker, W. P. (William Paton Ker, 1855-1923). Born in Glasgow; educated there and at Oxford. After six years as Professor of English Literature and History in the University of South Wales he was appointed to the Chair of English Literature at University College, London, holding also the Professorship of Poetry at Oxford from 1920. He was a genial and inspiring teacher with a love as well as deep knowledge of medieval literature and history, subjects he made attractive both in lectures and in books: *Epic and Romance* (1897), *The Dark Ages* (1904), *Essays on Medieval Literature* (1905), *English Literature: Medieval* (in the Home University Library, 1924). He also edited the Berners translation of Froissart (1901-3).

Kerouac, Jack (1922-1969). Born in Massachusetts; educated at Columbia University. His association with the *Beat movement is reflected in *On the Road* (1957) and its sequel *Big Sur* (1962). *The Dharma Bums* (1958) adds Zen Buddhism to the Beat theme.

Kersh, Gerald (1911-1968). Born in Middlesex; educated in London. Worked in a variety of occupations; served in World War II, an experience leading to *They Die With Their Boots Clean* (1941) and *The Nine Lives of Bill Nelson* (1941). He wrote many other novels, often on horrific themes in forceful prose. He became an American citizen in 1959, regarding himself as 'a refugee from the Welfare State'.

Kesselring, Joseph (1902-1967). Born in U.S. Among his varied literary works (verse, plays, fiction) *Arsenic and Old Lace* (1941) was an outstanding success on the stage in New York and London and brought him a fortune. A bizarre comedy, it concerns two adorable old ladies who, with kindly intention, dispose of solitary old gentlemen and bury them on the premises.

Keyes, Frances Parkinson (*née* Frances Parkinson Wheeler, 1885-1970; married Senator H. W. Keyes). Born at Charlottesville, Virginia; educated in Boston, Geneva and Berlin. Travelled in many countries, east and west. Her writings fall into several categories, but are mainly novels, including *Queen Anne's Lace* (1930), *Dinner at Antoine's* (1949), *Blue Camellia* (1957), *Roses in December* (1960).

Keyes, Sidney (1922-1943). Born at Dartford, Kent. Killed while on service in North Africa. With Alun *Lewis he was one of the only two young soldier poets who attracted particular attention during World War II. *Collected Poems* (1945) included the earlier books *The Iron Laurel* (1942) and *The Cruel Solstice* (1944).

Keynes, J. M. (John Maynard Keynes, 1883-1946; 1st Baron Keynes 1942). Born in Cambridge; educated at Eton and Cambridge, where he was one of the circle influenced by the teaching of G. E. *Moore, the philosopher whose theories were propagated not only by Keynes but also by the friends who, with him, were later to be designated 'the *Bloomsbury Group'. He entered government service, first at the India Office (1906-8); his interests were mainly in economics and finance; he was editor of the *Economic Journal* from 1911 to 1944 and was a Treasury official 1915-19. The turning point in his life came when he went as principal representative of the Treasury at the Paris Peace Conference during the first half of 1919. Convinced that the punitive reparations imposed on the Central Powers would prove disastrous to Europe, he resigned from the Treasury and published his views in *The Economic Consequences of the Peace* (1919) a brilliant analysis which not only attacked the Versailles Treaty but also characterized the British and French Prime Ministers and the American President with merciless but masterly satire. The book was astoundingly influential though its conclusions were often bitterly challenged, and deplored by some politicians and others who came to regard it as an incentive to the revival of German aggression. It can be held that Keynes's power lay as much in his mastery of words as in the depth of his knowledge and his strength of argument, for he was one of the few men in British history who could endow 'the dismal science' of political economy with the graces of literary art. In the years between the two World Wars, Keynes published *A Treatise on Probability* (1921), *A Tract on Monetary Reform* (1923), *The End of Laissez-Faire* (1926), *A Treatise on Money* (2 vols, 1930), and *The General Theory of Employment, Interest and Money* (1936). His views on national finance won a degree of government acceptance which laid the monetary foundations of the Welfare State. He was made a Director of the Bank of England in 1941. His more general contributions to literature are *Essays in Persuasion* (1931), *Essays in Biography* (1933), and *Two Memoirs* (posthumously 1949). He was an active supporter of the arts and married the Russian ballerina Lydia Lopokova in 1925.

Keyserling, Hermann von (1880-1946). Born in Livonia; educated privately and at the Universities of Geneva, Dorpat and Heidelberg. He described the School of Wisdom he founded at Darmstadt in 1920 as 'a centre of inspiration as opposed to information and education' and its inspirational rather than rational basis has prevented his philosophy from making any widespread impact, though his *Travel Diary of a Philosopher* (1919; Eng. trans. 1925) was widely read.

Kierkegaard, Sören Aaby (1813-55). Danish philosopher and theologian, who became antagonistic to orthodox organized Christianity. His writings began to impress many readers in other countries nearly a century after his death. His books are regarded as prefiguring *Existentialism* in its religious, not atheistic, aspect.

Kieschner, Sidney. See Sidney *Kingsley.

Kilmer, Joyce (1886-1918). Born in New Brunswick; educated at Rutgers College and Columbia University. He displayed considerable facility as a journalist and published essays and two books of verse from which only the single poem 'Trees' is remembered, through its favour with anthologists.

Kim. Novel by Rudyard *Kipling published in 1901. Kim, born Kimbell O'Hara of poor white parents, grows up in Lahore as a native after his parents' early deaths. A meeting with a Tibetan lama wandering through India seeking the Four Holy Places fires Kim's imagination, and he attaches himself to the old man as his *chela* (disciple). He begs money for the journey from his friend Mahbub, a horse-trader; but Mahbub, who works for the British Secret Service, uses him to carry a vital message to Colonel Creighton in Umballa. Soon after this mission is accomplished, Kim's identity is discovered, and he has to submit to the normal education of a white boy, with the promise of a job with the Secret Service if he completes his course at school. Apart from lapses in the school holidays, when he goes native again and rejoins the lama, Kim conforms and is rewarded by being tested and trained for his future work by Lurgan Sahib. In due course he is allowed to leave school and, under cover of a journey into the hills with his lama, undertakes his first commission, relieving spies of their papers and passing them to Hurree Babu, another secret agent, to deliver to the right quarter. Kim is physically and emotionally ill after this excursion; but, helped by the devoted care of the lama, he recovers in time to be with the old man when he decides that his quest is completed and he has won salvation both for himself and his disciple. The interest and attraction of the book are not confined to the story, but consist as much in the teeming pageant of Indian life, particularly on the Grand Trunk Road which runs straight for fifteen hundred miles, bearing India's traffic —all castes and kinds, bankers and tinkers, pilgrims and potters, 'all the world going and coming . . . such a river of life as nowhere else exists in the world'.

Kimmins, Anthony (1901-64). Educated at the Royal Naval College and served in the Navy and Fleet Air Arm. Author of *While Parents Sleep* (1932), *The Amorous Prawn* (1960) and other plays, and worked in the film industry as a director and script writer.

King-Hall, Stephen (1893-1966; knighted 1954; life peer 1966). Educated in Lausanne and at Osborne and Dartmouth; retired from the navy in 1929 with the rank of Commander; member of Parliament, 1939-44. Started in 1936 the *King-Hall News Letter* to give 'the news behind the news', continuing it until 1959. Founded the Hansard Society in 1944. Author of numerous political and historical books; *My Naval Life* (1952); in collaboration with Ian *Hay wrote successful comedies —*The Middle Watch* (1930), *The Midshipmaid* (1932), and others.

Kingsley, Mary St Leger. *See* Lucas *Malet.

Kingsley, Sidney (pseudonym of Sidney Kieschner, 1906-   ). Educated in New York and at Cornell University. Became an actor in New York and then worked for a film company. *Men in White* (1933), a play with a hospital setting, was a success in New York, London, and elsewhere, and *Dead End* (1936) portrays convincingly contrasting types in the slum region of New York's East Side. His other plays include *Detective Story* (1949) and *Darkness at Noon* (1951) a dramatized version of the novel by Arthur Koestler.

Kingsmill, Hugh (pseudonym of Hugh Kingsmill Lunn, 1889-1949). Born in London; educated at Harrow and Oxford and Trinity College, Dublin. Worked for some years in the travel agency organized by his father, Sir Henry Lunn. Author of novels, including *The Fall* (1919); short stories, *The Dawn's Delay* (1924); books on *Matthew Arnold* (1928), *Frank Harris* (1932), *Samuel Johnson* (1933), *Dickens* (*The Sentimental Journey*, 1934), and *D. H. Lawrence* (1938); various books in collaboration; a volume of parodies, *The Table of Truth* (1933), and *An Anthology of Invective* (1929).

Kipling, Rudyard (Joseph Rudyard Kipling, 1865-1936). Born in Bombay, son of J. Lockwood Kipling, principal of the School of Art there and later Director of the Lahore Museum. Sent to England while still a child and spent with an unsympathetic relative several unhappy years, relieved by visits to the Burne-Jones household, his mother being the sister of Lady Burne-Jones and of Mrs Baldwin, wife of the future Prime Minister, Stanley Baldwin. In 1878 he began his schooling at the United Services College, Westward Ho!, Devonshire, his experiences and friendships there being semi-fictionally commemorated some years later in *Stalky and Co.* (1899), where Kipling portrayed himself in the character called Beetle. He went back to India in 1882 and started work as a journalist on the *Civil and Military Gazette* in Lahore, moving to Allahabad in 1887 where he became assistant editor of the *Pioneer,* and in 1889 its overseas correspondent, travelling in China and Japan, America, Africa, and Australia. He had already begun his literary career with the immediate success of *Departmental Ditties* (Lahore, 1886), followed in rapid succession by *Plain Tales from the Hills* (1887), *Soldiers Three, The Story of the Gadsbys, In Black and White, Under the Deodars, The Phantom Rickshaw,* and *Wee Willie Winkie* (all 1888)—the last named having particular interest as the first of his stories for children. Most of this early work was written for the journals that employed him, and much was reprinted in slim paper-bound collections which became much-sought collectors' pieces in later years. Before his first stay in England he had been brought up by an Indian nurse and was as proficient in Hindustani as in English. He acquired considerable insight into the ways of the native people and also of the rank and file of the British army. *Barrack Room Ballads* (1892), like some of the earlier prose tales, demonstrated in language and theme his admiring even if subconsciously patronizing affection for the private soldiers he typified humorously in his representative three—Ortheris, Learoyd and Mulvaney. His rendering of cockney and other 'common' speech, while skilfully contrived to safeguard his characters from being unrealistically endowed with literary English, is not free from the suspicion of 'talking down'. His attitude to the Indians as 'subject peoples' was uncompromisingly imperialistic, though also idealistic, for *service* as a sacrificial exercise was always high in Kipling's catalogue of virtues. But whatever self-abnegating ideal might underlie his conception of overlordship, of the principle of ruling for the good of the ruled, he could not escape political odium at a time when the wave of anti-imperialism was beginning to rise towards the crest it was to reach a few years after Kipling's death. With the publication of *Life's Handicap* (1891) his unique ability as a writer of short stories became unquestionable. His narrative gift was grippingly displayed as much in comic as in grimly dramatic stories and, in all, his mastery of detail was evident. Indeed, his care to know to the last bolt and nut the construction and working of whatever object had a place in his stories has been charged against him as a fault, a source of mechanical constriction in his prose. But he wrote in a period when craftsmanship still received credit, and as a literary craftsman Kipling is unique. Of his three novels, only *Kim* (1901) is important: *The Light that Failed* (1891) is itself a failure, and *Captains Courageous* (1897) mediocre. He settled in England in 1889, living first in London and in Sussex from 1902 when he published *Just So Stories for Little Children* which, with the earlier *Jungle Book* (1894) and *Second Jungle Book* (1895) and the later *Puck of Pook's Hill* (1906) established him as a nursery classic. Whatever may be thought of the general body of his verse, at least a handful of his ballads seems sure to survive, and also such quiet English poems as 'The Way Through the Woods'. Of his prose not yet mentioned, there are notable stories in *Many Inventions* (1893), *The Day's Work* (1898), *Traffics and Discoveries* (1904), *Rewards and Fairies* (1910), *A Diversity of Creatures* (1917); *Debits and Credits* (1926) includes his remarkable tribute to Jane Austen in the story 'The Janeites' and the poem beginning 'Jane lies in Winchester' and ending 'Glory, love, and honour unto England's Jane'. Extremely reticent about his personal life, he told little in the unfinished autobiography *Something of Myself* (posthumously, 1937). His poem 'Recessional' written at the time of Queen Victoria's Diamond Jubilee, 1897, when the British Empire was at its apogee is at once a solemn hymn and a prophetic dirge. He also collaborated with C. R. L. *Fletcher in *A School History of England* (1911).

Kipps. Novel by H. G. *Wells published in 1905. Arthur Kipps, 'Art' or 'Artie' to familiars, brought up by an aunt and uncle at New Romney and schooled at a 'middle-class academy' in Hastings, is apprenticed to a draper in Folkestone. Before leaving for the shop he gives half a divided sixpence to his girl friend Ann Pornick as a love-token, keeping the other half himself. Towards the end of his apprenticeship he takes up 'technical education' by joining a wood-carving class conducted by a Miss Helen Walsingham, to whom he later becomes engaged after learning through an advertisement shown to him by his friend Chitterlow that he has been left a fortune by his grandfather. Through the Walsinghams he enters local Society, being groomed by Helen, a process uncongenial to him and made intolerable by renewed affectionate contact with Ann Pornick who, after several years' separation, still cherishes the half-sixpence. Kipps shelves these social and personal complications by a trip to London, where he meets by accident Ann's brother Sid, now a thriving bicycle maker. Back in Folkestone he calls on Ann at the house where she is a servant and he has been a

dinner guest. Hesitantly agreeing to run away to London and marry him, she goes with him to her brother's, and after their honeymoon they search for a house at Hythe and elsewhere in Kent, deciding at length to build. Kipps then learns that all but a small fraction of his fortune has been embezzled by Helen's brother. For a living he opens a bookshop in Hythe, where he and Ann and their child settle, fortified by a cheque for £2000, Kipp's share of the profits from a successful farce by Chitterlow in which he had invested.

Kirkup, James (1923-   ). Educated in South Shields and at Durham University. From 1950 lecturer and Professor of English Literature in England, Sweden, Spain, Malaya, and Japan; Poet in Residence, and Visiting Professor, Amherst College, Mass. from 1968. Author of several volumes of poems, among which *A Correct Compassion* (1952) is best known; verse plays, fiction, travel books; autobiography, *The Only Child* (1957); also *England, Now* (1965), *Japan, Now* (1966), *Frankly Speaking* (1966).

Kitchen-sink Drama. Derisive term applied to a type of stage play in vogue after World War II in which sombre aspects of household life are quasi-realistically presented, e.g. by John *Osborne, Arnold *Wesker, and Harold *Pinter, among others.

Kitchin, C. H. B. (Clifford Henry Benn Kitchin, 1895-1967). Born at Harrogate; educated at Clifton and Oxford. Called to the Bar; member of the Stock Exchange; journalist and novelist. His most successful book was a detective novel, *Death of My Aunt* (1929), which is ranked as a classic in its kind. Other novels: *Streamers Waving* (1925), *Mr Balcony* (1927), *The Sensitive One* (1931), *Birthday Party* (1938), *Death of His Uncle* (1939), *The Auction Sale* (1949), *The Secret River* (1956), *The Book of Life* (1960).

Kittredge, G. L. (George Lyman Kittredge, 1860-1941). Born in Boston; educated at Harvard, where he became Professor of English Literature, 1894-1936, and was an eminent Shakespearean, an exacting scholar and a daunting yet greatly admired and respected personality. He edited an edition of separate plays by Shakespeare and wrote *Chaucer and His Poetry* (1915), *A Study of Sir Gawain and the Green Knight* (1916), *Sir Thomas Malory* (1925) and studies of witchcraft.

Klein, A. M. (Abraham Moses Klein, 1909-
). Born and educated in Montreal.
Barrister from 1933 to 1954. Author of
Hath Not a Jew (1940), *The Rocking Chair*
(1948) and other collections of verse.

Knight, Wilson (George Wilson Knight, 1897-
). Born in Surrey; educated at Dulwich
and Oxford. Professor of English Literature,
University of Leeds 1956-62, after being
Reader there, 1946-56, and Professor of
English in the University of Toronto, 1931-
40. While in Toronto he staged Shakespeare
productions at the Hart House Theatre and
in England later at Leeds. His writings on
Shakespeare showed original insight and
occupied a distinctive place in contemporary
scholarship: *The Wheel of Fire* (1930), *The
Imperial Theme* (1931), *The Burning Oracle*
(1939), *The Starlit Dome* (1941), *The
Sovereign Flower* (1958), *The Golden Labyrinth* (1962) and other books on Byron,
Nietzsche, Myth and Miracle, and Christian
topics.

Knole. A mainly fifteenth-century house near
Sevenoaks, Kent. One of the largest private
residences in England, it was in the possession of the Sackville family from the sixteenth century until they passed it to the
National Trust in 1946. Its literary associations (beginning with Thomas Sackville,
1st Earl of Dorset, as part author of *The
Mirror for Magistrates* and of the first
English tragedy, *Gorboduc*, in the 1560s)
include, in the twentieth century, its being
the birthplace of Edward and Victoria
*Sackville-West, to the latter of whom is
dedicated Virginia Woolf's *Orlando* (1928),
some part of which is set in a country
mansion recognizable as Knole.

Knox, E. V. (Edmund George Valpy Knox,
1881-1971). Son of the Rt Rev. E. A. Knox,
Bishop of Manchester, a stalwart Evangelical
Protestant; educated at Rugby and Oxford.
Joined the staff of *Punch* in 1921 and was
editor 1932-49. Most of his humorous
articles, poems, and parodies appeared
in that periodical under the pseudonym
Evoe before republication in book form:
Parodies Regained (1921), *These Liberties*
(1923), *Fiction as She is Wrote* (1923), *Folly
Calling* (1932).

Knox, Ronald (Ronald Arbuthnott Knox, 1888-
1957). Brother of the preceding; educated at
Eton and Oxford. Ordained as an Anglican
clergyman in 1912 and was chaplain of

Trinity College, Oxford, until he resigned in
1917, having been converted to Roman
Catholicism. Entered the Roman priesthood
1919; became Catholic chaplain to the
University of Oxford, 1926-39, Domestic
Prelate to the Pope in 1936, and a member of
the Papal Academy of Theology from 1957.
In 1939 he undertook a new English translation of the Bible from the Latin Vulgate,
completing the Old Testament in 1944 and
the New Testament in 1950. His miscellaneous secular writings included detective
novels—*The Viaduct Murder* (1925), *The
Three Taps* (1927), *The Footsteps at the Lock*
(1928), *The Body in the Silo* (1933); and
Essays in Satire (1928), *Caliban in Grub
Street* (1930), *Barchester Pilgrimage* (1935),
Let Dons Delight (1939).

Knox, Mr and **Mrs.** Puritanical parents of
Margaret Knox, who takes an independent
line, in Shaw's *Fanny's First Play* (1911).

Koestler, Arthur (1905-   ). Born in Budapest;
educated in Vienna. He emigrated to Palestine
in 1926, later became foreign correspondent
for German newspapers, and in 1930 Science
Editor and Foreign Editor in Berlin. He
joined the Communist Party and in 1933
spent a year in the Soviet Union, moving
from there to Paris, and in 1936 went to
Spain as a reporter in the Civil War, being
captured by Franco's supporters and condemned to death but released under an
International Red Cross prisoner exchange
agreement. His experiences in Spain led to
his renouncing Communism and the Communist Party, and to his best known book
Darkness at Noon (1940), which had been
preceded by *Spanish Testament* (1938) and
The Gladiators (1939). Numerous later
works include *Dialogue with Death* (1942),
The Yogi and the Commissar (1945), *The Act
of Creation* (1964), and two autobiographical
volumes, *Arrow in the Blue* (1952), *The
Invisible Writing* (1954). Until about 1922 he
wrote in Hungarian, then in German until
1940; afterwards in English.

Korzeniowski, Józef Teodor Konrad. *See*
Joseph *Conrad.

Kouyoumdjian, Dikran. *See* Michael *Arlen.

Kreymborg, Alfred (1883-   ). Born in New
York. Author of several volumes of poems,
Mushrooms (1916), *Blood of Things* (1920),
The Lost Sail (1928), *Manhattan Man* (1929),
Prologue to Hell (1930); collections of verse

plays; *I'm No Hero* (1933) and other novels; *Troubadour* (1925), an autobiography.

Kurtz, Mr. Company agent and ivory trader in Joseph Conrad's *'Heart of Darkness'. Almost a legendary figure he is regarded variously: by some as a 'universal genius', but finally—by Marlow—as a 'soul satiated with primitive emotions, avid of lying fame, of sham distinction, of all the appearances of success and power'.

Ladvenu, Brother Martin. In Shaw's *Saint Joan* (1923). Holds up a cross for Joan to see at her burning.

Lady Chatterley's Lover. Novel by D. H. *Lawrence privately printed abroad in 1928; not published in full in England until 1960 after an obscenity prosecution failed. Sir Clifford Chatterley, Bt, is paralysed from the waist down and rendered sexually impotent by wounds received in World War I. He inherits coalpits in Derbyshire, and the family seat, Wragby Hall, where he and his wife live. Cut off from active life, he becomes self-enclosed and takes refuge in writing magazine stories. The mutual devotion between him and his wife weakens into estrangement. She has a brief and unsatisfying affair with Michaelis, a young Irish playwright, and is then drawn into association with her husband's gamekeeper, Oliver Mellors, a man of working-class origin, commissioned in the war after serving in the ranks in India. Their intercourse is described in colloquial terms employing words tabu in print until the result of the Chatterley case ushered them into the literary vocabulary on a par with their age-old daily verbal usage. Though Clifford Chatterley had told his wife previously that he would condone her bearing a child by another man, he refuses to divorce her so that she can marry again before she gives birth to Mellors's child. His refusal is due to his opinion that the gamekeeper is socially inferior. Lawrence wrote three versions of *Lady Chatterley's Lover*, the one outlined here being the third and until 1944 the only published version. The first was issued in the U.S. as *The First Lady Chatterley* in 1944 (in England not until 1972, together with the second version as *John Thomas and Lady Jane*). The sexual passages in the first are less boldly explicit than in the final version. Partly for that reason but also because, as his wife wrote, it came 'out of his own immediate self', the first draft has been considered the best.

Lady into Fox. Prose fantasy or fable by David *Garnett, published in 1922. Silvia, wife of Richard Tebrick, living in Oxfordshire in 1880, is suddenly changed into a small bright red vixen while the pair are out walking one afternoon. For some time she retains the delicate and affectionate manners which had made her an ideal young wife before her metamorphosis, eating the same food, and wearing human garments. But gradually she develops animal habits, hunting and killing, and burrowing in the earth. At length she disappears and is given up for lost by her husband, until she reappears with five cubs, whom he names Sorel, Kasper, Selwyn, Esther, and Angelica. 'Thus Mr Tebrick had a whole family now to occupy him, and, indeed, came to love them with very much of a father's love and partiality.' The cubs grow up and disappear, leaving the mother vixen as his sole companion. One morning huntsmen and hounds break into his garden, killing the vixen and mauling Tebrick terribly: 'in the end he recovered his reason and lived to be a great age; for that matter he is still alive'.

Lady of Quality. Pseudonym under which Enid *Bagnold wrote *Serena Blandish, or The Difficulty of Getting Married* (1925).

Lady's Not For Burning, The. Verse comedy in three acts by Christopher Fry performed in 1948; published in 1949. Thomas Mendip, a discharged soldier from the Flanders wars, comes to the house of Hebble Tyson, Mayor of the small market town of Cool Clary in about the year 1400, declaring that he has committed murder and insists on being hanged. The fretful and dilatory Mayor expresses disbelief, reluctant to be bothered with him or with a new arrival, Jennet Jourdemayne, who has been chased through the town as a witch accused of turning into a dog the local rag-and-bone man, Matthew Skipps, though he is the one that Thomas Mendip claims to have killed. The Mayor, having put Jennet and Thomas under arrest, conspires with the Chaplain and Justice Tappercoom to eavesdrop on a conversation between the two prisoners, hoping that 'one or other by their exchange of words/Will prove to be innocent. or we shall have proof/Positive of guilt'. As the result, Jennet is sentenced to be burnt next day; but Thomas, 'found guilty/Of jaundice, misanthropy, suicidal tendencies/And spreading gloom and despondency' is condemned to attend a convivial party that night. As Skipps appears, proving that he is neither dead nor a dog, Jennet is allowed to leave the town unobserved and Thomas goes with her.

La Farge, Oliver (Oliver Hazard Perry La Farge, 1901-63). Born in New York; educated at Groton and Harvard. While still a child he developed a close interest in the lives of the American Indians, later became an anthropologist and ethnologist, and was a research assistant in anthropology at Columbia University 1931-33. His first novel *Laughing Boy* (1929) and others that followed show his deep understanding of the Navajos and other indigenous tribes of North America.

Lagerlof, Selma (Selma Ottiliana Lovisa Lagerlof, 1858-1940). Born in Sweden; educated at home and later at a teachers' seminary. Became a schoolmistress until the success of *Gosta Berling's Saga* (1898; Eng. trans. 1918), a novel based on folk tales, made it possible for her to travel abroad. Few of her later books enjoyed such international repute as *Gosta Berling,* though *The Wonderful Adventures of Nils* (1907) has appealed to children.

Lallans. Lowland Scots dialect used by some contemporary poets, Hugh *MacDiarmid and others.

Lambert, Leslie Harrison. *See* A. J. *Alan.

Lambsbreath, Adam. Cowman in Stella Gibbons's *Cold Comfort Farm* (1932).

Lamburn, Richmal Crompton. *See* Richmal *Crompton.

Lamming, George (1927-   ). Born and educated in Barbados; teacher in Trinidad and Venezuela before going to England in 1950, where he worked in factories; travelled extensively in West Africa, North America, and the Caribbean. Author of semi-autobiographical novels—*In the Castle of My Skin* (1953), *The Emigrants* (1954), *Season of Adventure* (1960); also essays and poems, and autobiographical observations, *The Pleasures of Exile* (1960).

Lamotte, Annette. Soames Forsyte's second wife in Galsworthy's *The *Forsyte Saga* (1922).

Lampoon. A satirical attack on a person in verse or prose, usually malicious in intention and often virulent in tone, though not necessarily lacking truth and wit.

Lampton, Joe. *See* *Joe Lampton.

Lancaster, Florence and her son **Nicky.** Chief characters in Noel Coward's *The *Vortex* (1923).

Lancaster, Osbert (1908-   ). Born in London; educated at Charterhouse and Oxford. Studied law unsuccessfully and turned to art at the Slade School. He developed a gift for satirical caricature mainly aimed at monstrosities of architecture and interior decoration: *Progress at Pelvis Bay* (1936), *Homes, Sweet Homes* (1939), *Drayneflete Revealed* (1949). *Pocket Cartoons* (1940) and its successors reproduce small drawings of individual types contributed morning by morning to the *Daily Express* from 1939. *All Done from Memory* (1953) preserves recollections of his childhood. *Classical Landscape With Figures* (1947) is the product of a period in Athens during World War II. Other books: *The Year of the Comet* (1957), *Here, of All Places* (1959), *Signs of the Times* (1961), *The Littlehampton Bequest* (1973).

Lancelot Andrewes, For. *See* *For Lancelot Andrewes.

Lanchester Tradition, The. School novel by G. F. *Bradby published in 1913. Founded by a bequest in the seventeenth century from a local farrier, Chiltern School ranked as hardly more than a county grammar school when the Rev. Dr Abraham Lanchester became headmaster at the end of the eighteenth century. He left it 'one of *the* public schools of England . . . an institution of National, almost Imperial, importance'. With irony and humour the author details the ways of the school and its masters and boys under the spell of the Lanchester tradition which, in brief, represents 'a certain immutability and fixity of things, an as-it-was-in-the-beginning-is-now-and-ever-shall-be attitude towards life' that appeals to those with the 'best conservative instincts' and has been strictly maintained by the Rev. Dr Gussy during his twenty-four years as headmaster. He has now notified his coming retirement on appointment to a vacant Deanery, and the Governing Body, or Council, meets to select a new head. Of more than a score of candidates, only two are ultimately in the running, but when each receives the same number of votes at the Council meeting and the Chairman declines to give a casting vote, compromise is reached by appointing a hitherto unsupported younger candidate, the Rev. Septimus Flaggon. Most of the school staff are hostile to the new headmaster, and antagonism grows between Mr Flaggon and the Rev. Henry Chowdler, a senior housemaster who for many years past has 'run' Dr Gussy and been 'the master mind that shaped the destinies of the school'. The friction culminates in open rebellion by Chowdler and a request for his resignation which he treats as notice of dismissal entitling him under the school Statutes to appeal. At the Council meeting to consider the appeal, the voting is again equal, but this time the Chairman does give a decisive vote, with consequences of great moment to both the antagonists and to the Lanchester tradition.

Land, The. Poem of ninety-six pages by V. *Sackville-West published in 1926. In varied metres—blank verse, irregular rhymed verse, and interspersed lyrics—it progresses through the English seasons from Winter to Autumn, detailing the labour imposed upon Man by Nature in growing and gathering the produce of the land. It is localized in the Weald of Kent, the author's home territory. Avoiding the romantic and merely picturesque interpretation of country life, this 'mild continuous epic of the soil' recognizes such imperatives as 'marl and dung' in the 'loutish life' of the tillers and reapers: 'Strange lovers, man and earth! their love and hate/Braided in mutual need; and of their strife/A tired contentment born'. The vagrant frozen to death in the winter night; the shepherd robbed of his Christmas by the weakly new-born lamb; the yeoman planning 'his year for pasture or for seed'; the farm worker fighting the Wealden clay, 'that yellow enemy' that sucks at his horses' hooves and sinks his waggon wheels in the mud in winter, and hardens as brick and opens in root-withering cracks in summer— these are among the aspects comprehended in the author's declaration, 'The country habit has me by the heart'. Her survey of the year's work includes the sowing and rotation of crops, the pruning and training of hops (and their gathering by Cockney hop-pickers), the control of pests in the orchards, the rearing of young stock, bee culture, sheep shearing and dipping, harvesting, thatching, country crafts, ploughing, threshing, hedging and ditching, foresting, cider making, hop drying in the oast houses which are distinctive in the landscape of Kent. The author's love of gardening is well represented (at Sissinghurst she made one of the great gardens of England), and there are sections on wild flowers of the countryside. Though rejecting 'the easier uses of made poetry', *The Land* is a poem no less than a chronicle, and (as the epigraph and final

lines indicate) it has classical roots in the *Georgics* of Virgil.

Landfall. See Charles *Brasch.

Lane, Allen (Sir Allen Lane Williams Lane, 1902-1970; knighted 1952). Founder of *Penguin Books after earlier experience in the publishing firm of John Lane (The Bodley Head) from 1919 to 1936. His success as a popularizer and educator with Penguin Books and Pelican Books was recognized in the knighthood he received in 1952. When shares in the company were offered for sale to investors in 1961 it was said that he 'became a millionaire overnight', the 750,000 shares bringing applications for 150 times that number.

Lane, Jane (pseudonym of Elaine Kidner, Mrs Andrew Dakers). Author of many historical novels, including books for children; also biographies of *Titus Oates* (1949) and others.

Lane, John (1854-1925). Born in Devon; educated at local schools. From 1869 to 1887 he was a clerk in the Railway Clearing House. In the latter year, with Elkin Mathews as partner, he set up as an antiquarian bookseller in London, taking as shop sign 'The *Bodley Head'. He next turned to publishing, issuing his first book (by Richard *Le Gallienne) in 1889 and gathering among his authors in following years William Watson, Francis Thompson, and other outstanding men of the 'nineties', with *The *Yellow Book* (1894-97) as his most celebrated publication. He continued to flourish in the new century as a general publisher with numerous popular authors on his list. He was more morally adventurous than publishers of longer standing, and took on H. G. Wells's *The *New Machiavelli* (1911) after others refused it. *And see* Allen *Lane.

Lane, Margaret (1907-   ). Educated at Folkestone and Oxford; married (1944) the Earl of Huntingdon. Newspaper reporter and special correspondent in London and New York (1928-38). Author of *Edgar *Wallace: The Biography of a Phenomenon* (1938), the father of her first husband; *The Tale of Beatrix *Potter* (1946), *The Brontë Story* (1953). *Purely for Pleasure* (1966), a book of essays, opens with a sympathetic study of Flora *Thompson, valuable as the only biographical record of the author of

*Lark Rise. Novels: *Faith, Hope, No Charity* (1935), *Where Helen Lies* (1944), *A Smell of Burning* (1965), etc.

Lane, Ralph Norman Angell. *See* Norman *Angell.

Lang, Andrew (1844-1912). Born at Selkirk; educated at Edinburgh, St Andrews, and Oxford. Among his friends was Robert Louis Stevenson, one of whose poems addresses him as 'Andrew with the brindled hair'. He was the author of a large and varied range of books, among them collections of poems in the fixed-verse style which had a popular revival with Edmund *Gosse, Austin *Dobson, and others in the late decades of the nineteenth century: those by Lang are in his *Ballads and Lyrics of Old France* (1872), *Ballades in Blue China* (1880), *Rhymes à la Mode* (1884). His *Letters to Dead Authors* (1886) is still praised by connoisseurs of the essay. He wrote several books on Homer, and collaborated with Walter *Leaf and E. J. *Myers in a prose translation of the *Iliad* (1882) and with S. H. *Butcher similarly for the *Odyssey* (1879). Other interests are shown by *Myth, Ritual, and Religion* (1887), *Prince Charles Edward* (1900), and *A Book of Romance* (1902), but he is now actively remembered only by *The Blue Fairy Book* and others, each designated by a different colour.

Lanyon, Joyce. Widow; Martin's second wife in Sinclair Lewis's *Martin Arrowsmith* (1925).

Lardner, Ring (Ringold Wilmer Lardner, 1885-1933). Born in Michigan; educated in Chicago. Worked on papers in Boston, St Louis, and Chicago, mainly as a sports reporter. Achieved popular and critical success with books that were enjoyed by the majority for their colloquial humour but were read by others as bitter satire: *You Know Me, Al* (1916), *Gullible's Travels* (1917), *Treat 'Em Rough* (1918), *The Big Town* (1921), *The Story of a Wonder Man* (1927).

Lark Rise. Autobiography by Flora *Thompson published in 1939. Apart from the use of fictional names for places and persons, the book is a first-hand record of life in the 1880s in an Oxfordshire hamlet near the borders of Northamptonshire and Buckinghamshire: Lark Rise is Juniper Hill; the 'mother village' (named Fordlow in the book) is Cottisford; the author herself (the daughter of a stonemason and a former children's nurse) appears as Laura. Her story presents the cottagers' hard but not invariably unhappy lives at the time when farm workers' standard wages were ten shillings a week and a family pig was commonly fattened in a sty beside the cottage to be killed for winter bacon. Men working in the fields and talking, drinking and singing old country songs in the village inn; children at play and in schools; wives and mothers at their many tasks and simple social alleviations—all have a place in this humanized account of a phase of English rural history not otherwise recorded with literary skill from the grass-roots angle. The record is continued through later stages of Laura's development in *Over to Candleford* (1941) and *Candleford Green* (1943). *Lark Rise to Candleford* (1945) assembles the trilogy in a single volume.

Larkin, Philip (Philip Arthur Larkin, 1922-   ). Born at Coventry; educated there and at Oxford. After work in different libraries, became Librarian of the University of Hull. Author of novels (*Jill*, 1946; *A Girl in Winter*, 1947), but more highly regarded for his poems (*The Less Deceived*, 1955; *The Whitsun Weddings*, 1964; *High Windows*, 1974). *All What Jazz* (essays, 1970); editor *The Oxford Book of Twentieth Century English Verse* (1973).

Larkins, Miriam. *See* *Miriam Larkins.

Lasenby, Lady Mary—Lady Catherine—Lady Agatha. Daughters of The Earl of Loam in *The *Admirable Crichton* by J. M. *Barrie.

Laski, Harold (Harold Joseph Laski, 1893-1950). Born in Manchester; educated there and at Oxford. Became Lecturer in History at McGill University, Toronto, 1914-16; at Harvard, 1916-20; Yale, 1919-20; in Political Science at Cambridge, 1922-25. Professor of Political Science in the University of London from 1926. On the Executive Committee of the Labour Party, 1936-49, and Chairman of the Party, 1945-6. A speech he made in the provinces during the general election campaign in 1945 was reported in a local newspaper as advocating revolution by violence. Laski brought an action for libel but lost the case, opposing counsel (Sir Patrick Hastings) having quoted damagingly from books in which he expressed extreme Marxist views. He was a brilliant teacher with a large student following, and a fluent and lucid writer: *The Problem of Authority* (1917), *A Grammar of Politics* (1925), *Communism* (1927), *Liberty in the Modern State* (1930), *The Dangers of Obedience* (1930), *The Crisis and the Constitution* (1932), *Democracy in Crisis* (1933), *Parliamentary Government in England* (1938), *Reflections on the Revolution of Our Time* (1943), *The American Democracy* (1948).

Laski, Marghanita (1915-   ; Mrs J. E. Howard). Born in London, granddaughter of the Chief Rabbi and daughter of Judge Laski; educated in Manchester, at St Paul's School in London, and at Oxford. Author of *Love on the Super-Tax* (1944), *Tory Heaven* (1948), *Little Boy Lost* (1949), *The Village* (1952), *The Victorian Chaise-Longue* (1953); also *Ecstasy: A Study of Some Secular and Religious Experiences* (1961), *Domestic Life in Edwardian England* (1964), etc. Her second novel, *To Bed with Grand Music* (1946), was published under the pseudonym Sarah Russell.

Latour, Jean Maria. Bishop, later Archbishop, in Willa Cather's **Death Comes for the Archbishop* (1927).

Laura Trevelyan. In Patrick White's **Voss* (1957) the niece of Mrs Bonner, wife of the chief sponsor in Sydney of Voss's expedition. Laura and Voss experience a mystical relationship during his distant journey and in his dying moments.

Laureate. See *Poets Laureate.

Laver, James (1899-   ). Born in Liverpool; educated there and at Oxford. Keeper in the Departments of Engraving and of Paintings, Victoria and Albert Museum, London, 1938-59. Writer on art: *History of British and American Etching* (1929), *Whistler* (1930), *French Painting and the Nineteenth Century* (1937), *Titian* (1950), *Fragonard* (1956); on costume: *Nineteenth Century Costume* (1929), *English Costume in the Eighteenth Century* (1931), *Fashions and Fashion-Plates* (1943), *Tudor Costume* (1951); and on a variety of other subjects. His witty novel *Nymph Errant* (1932) was extremely successful in print, and on the stage as a play with music; and as a poet he produced in *Love's Progress* (1929) a brilliantly clever pastiche of Pope in his lighter moods. Children's books included *Tommy Apple* (1935), *Tommy Apple and*

Peggy Pear (1936), and some plays for children. Autobiography: *Museum Piece* (1963).

Lavin, Mary (1912-   ; Mrs MacD Scott). Born in Massachusetts; began her schooling there but later studied in Dublin and remained in Ireland. Her first collection of stories *Tales from Bective Bridge* (1942) was launched with an enthusiastic preface by Lord *Dunsany. Later books: *The House in Clewe Street* (1945), *Mary O'Grady* (1950), both novels; several volumes of short stories including *The Becker Wives* (1946), *At Sally Gap* (1947), *A Single Lady* (1951), *The Great Wave* (1961), *In the Middle of the Fields* (1966), *Collected Stories* (I 1971, II 1973).

Lavinia. The young woman Christian prisoner in **Androcles and the Lion* by Bernard Shaw; she makes a resolute defence of her faith in discussion with the Captain of the Roman guard.

Lavish, Miss. Uses the pseudonym J. E. Prank in E. M. Forster's *A *Room with a View* (1908).

Lawler, Ray. See *Australian Writers.

Lawless, Anthony. Occasional pseudonym of Philip *Macdonald.

Lawrence, D. H. (David Herbert Lawrence, 1885-1930). Born at Eastwood, Nottinghamshire, son of a coalminer married to a schoolteacher who came to despise her uncultured and frequently drunken husband, and forged an emotionally restrictive link with her son which was largely accountable for his later inadequacy in intimate relationships with women, and for the sexual torments to which in imagination he was to subject many of his fictional characters. It was also in boyhood that the first symptoms appeared of the lung affection which at length killed him at the age of forty-four. His education began at the local Council school, but when thirteen he won a scholarship to Nottingham High School. He started work at the age of sixteen as a clerk in a surgical appliance firm at 13s a week, but soon left to become a pupil teacher in Eastwood. At eighteen he went to the University College at Nottingham, matriculated two years later, and as a certificated teacher was on the staff of Davidson Road School, Croydon, until 1911. While at the University he began his first novel which, with other writings, was sent by an Eastwood friend, Jessie *Chambers, to Ford Madox *Ford, then editing the *English Review, for an opinion. Ford, much impressed, passed the novel to William Heinemann, who published it as The White Peacock in 1911. Lawrence then abandoned teaching and set himself to live by writing. In 1912 he made the first of the many journeys abroad on which much time and energy were to be expended during the rest of his life. Early in the same year he first met the wife of Professor Ernest *Weekley of Nottingham University, she having been born as Frieda von Richthofen, daughter of a German baron. She and Lawrence eloped to the Continent and were married after she had been divorced in 1914. Thereafter the tie between them, though often badly strained by temperamental antagonisms and jealousy, never snapped, and in the legend of Lawrence Frieda never loses importance. Meanwhile the second and third of his novels had been published—The Trespasser (1912) and in the next year *Sons and Lovers, which reflects much of his early life at home, while the character of Miriam represents, from his angle, Jessie Chambers. Though critics at a later date were prone to name The *Rainbow (1915) as his most important novel, Sons and Lovers has strong claims, since the apocalyptic Laurentian manner had not then over-whelmed his style. The Rainbow had, however, a crucial place in Lawrence's life since it was condemned and confiscated as obscene. This and the suspicion of being German spies which caused him and his wife to be prohibited from remaining in Cornwall where they were then living, promoted that tendency to persecution mania which occasional residence in his own country was thereafter to incite. When World War I ended, they went to Italy and in the following years to Australia, New Zealand, the South Seas, California, New Mexico, and thence back to Italy in 1926, after which he moved from place to place in Europe in unavailing endeavour to check his progressively deteriorating health. He died in a sanatorium at Vence in the south of France. With few authors is it harder than with Lawrence to consider the work apart from the man. His magnetic personality drew into his circle a multitude of conflicting personalities, including lion-hunting women who preyed and were preyed upon. Within a few decades the literature about Lawrence had become immense, among it a good deal of adulatory biography, some creating unconsciously the impression that he was often ridiculous and a scrounger. The fact that not only The Rainbow but also his paintings, some of his poems and *Lady Chatterley's Lover (1928) brought him what could be represented as persecution by the authorities, made him in the eyes of non-conforming critics and scholars a symbol of defiance who must be accorded unmeasured praise in an age when defiance appeared in itself a good. Law-rence's 'obscenity' was often the product of his bloodless purity—his incapacity for the average sensual man's sexual experience. With the possible exception of The *Man Who Died (1931) he wrote no unblemished masterpiece. As a writer of descriptive nature prose he had few equals; it was when dealing with human relationships that his style became clotted and turgid in the throes of his preoccupation with the love–hate theme. His hatred of industrialism was at once justified and extreme—foaming-at-the-mouth in a good cause: futile emotional ism substituting for the hard labour of practical reform. The direct products of Lawrence's wanderings were the travel books Twilight in Italy (1916), Sea and Sardinia (1921), Mornings in Mexico (1927), Etruscan Places (1932) and, among the novels, Kangaroo (1923) and The Plumed Serpent (1926). Other novels: *Women in Love (1920), *Aaron's Rod (1922). His many short stories are among his best work: England My England (1922) and other volumes. Light is thrown upon aspects of his fiction by Psychoanalysis and the Un-conscious (1921) and Fantasia of the Un-conscious (1922). His quarrel with authority provoked Pornography and Obscenity (1930). His poems, and also his short stories, are available in collected editions. Studies in Classic American Literature (1923) was a pioneer work in England; Movements in European History (1921) was published under the pseudonym Lawrence H. Davidson. His letters to a fellow-student at Notting-ham University College, written between 1906 and 1912, were published in 1968 as Lawrence in Love.

Lawrence, Frieda. See Frieda von *Richthofen.

Lawrence, Hilda (née Hilda Kronmiller; married Reginald Lawrence, 1924). Born and educated in Baltimore; worked for publishers in New York. Author of *Blood upon the Snow* (1944), *A Time to Die* (1945), and other mystery novels with a psychological interest, the most impressive being *Death of a Doll* (1947).

Lawrence, T. E. (Thomas Edward Lawrence, 1888-1935). Born at Tremadoc in Wales of unmarried parents; educated at Oxford High School and at the University. From 1910 to 1914 he engaged in archaeological surveys in Syria, Mesopotamia, Egypt, and Sinai under D. G. Hogarth, Flinders *Petrie, and Leonard *Woolley. In the early months of World War I he joined the British Intelligence Service in Egypt and continued until the autumn of 1916, when he went to the desert to organize the Arabs, who had begun their revolt against their Turkish rulers. As a leader in this guerrilla campaign he won the esteem of the Arab chieftains and aided their eventual victory. He went with the Arab delegation to the Versailles Peace Conference in 1919, and served the British Government in the following years as adviser on the Middle East. At the end of 1922 he embarked on that quest for personal obscurity which in practice brought him more into public notice than if he had remained in Oxford with the Fellowship of All Souls College to which he had been elected in October 1919. His reasons for this withdrawal have been variously stated by himself and others. He enlisted in the lowest rank of the Royal Air Force under the assumed name of Ross. His identity having been discovered he was discharged, and then rejoined as T. E. Shaw, remaining until the spring of 1935, when he went to live by himself in a Dorset village. Fascinated by speed, he accepted a fast motor cycle and died a few days after it crashed. In 1919 he began to write his account of the Arab campaign and had most of the first draft, several hundred thousand words, stolen on Reading station. Having previously destroyed his notes, he was compelled to write the second version from memory, but it was a third version that he published as *Seven Pillars of Wisdom* in a strictly limited edition in 1926. A shortened version appeared as *Revolt in the Desert* (1927). After his death *Seven Pillars of Wisdom* was reprinted in an edition for general sale. Many accepted the book as a literary masterpiece of the

first order, for the popular title 'Lawrence of Arabia' created an uncritical mystique. Viewed objectively, it fails on two counts: its style is not the man, but an eclectic creation; and the self-conscious determination against self-revelation enshrouds the narrative. The story he had to tell was heroic and terrible, and much of its heroism and terror come through, but a soul is excluded. What *Seven Pillars* might have been if Lawrence had allowed his self free play can be deduced from his natural style as displayed in his letters (*The Letters of T. E. Lawrence* edited by David Garnett, 1938). Lawrence made a prose translation of. Homer's *Odyssey* (1932), and an account of his Air Force experiences under the assumed names is given, again disappointingly, in *The Mint*, which circulated privately in his lifetime but was not published for sale until 1955.

The legend of Lawrence as hero persisted and was little examined before Richard *Aldington's *Lawrence of Arabia: A Biographical Enquiry* was published twenty years after his death. Violently attacked by Lawrence advocates and marred by some irrelevant spleen, the book nevertheless offered evidence in support of Aldington's conviction that the legend had been self-created by a pathological egoist.

Lawson, Henry (1867-1922). *See* *Australian Writers.

Laye, Camara (1928-   ). *See* *African Writers.

Leacock, Stephen (Stephen Butler Leacock, 1869-1944). Born in Hampshire. His family emigrated to Canada when he was seven to farm in Ontario, where he was educated at Upper Canada College, and taught there, 1891-99, after graduating at the University of Toronto. Then studied at the University of Chicago and in 1901 joined the staff of McGill University where he remained (as Head of the Department of Economics from 1908) until his retirement in 1936. He published *Elements of Political Science* (1906) and some later serious works, but was best known as the author of a long series of humorous books beginning with *Literary Lapses* (1910), followed by *Nonsense Novels* (1911), *Sunshine Sketches of a Little Town* (1912), *Moonbeams from the Larger Lunacy* (1915) and many others. *The Boy I Left Behind Me* (1946) is autobiographical.

Leaf, Munro (1905-   ). Born in Maryland; educated at the State University there and at Harvard. Author of (mostly) children's books, among which *Ferdinand* (1936), 'the story of a little bull who would not fight', has been much enjoyed outside (as well as in) America.

Leaf, Walter (1852-1927). Born in London; educated at Harrow and Cambridge. Became a banker and financial expert, but also an Homeric scholar collaborating with Andrew *Lang and E. J. *Myers in a well-received prose translation of the *Iliad* (1882). Author of *Troy: A Study in Homeric Geography* (1912), *Homer and History* (1915), *Banking* (1926).

Leavis, F. R. (Frank Raymond Leavis, 1895-   ). Born in Cambridge; educated there at the Perse School and at the University. Held the post of University Reader in English at Cambridge from 1959, having been a Fellow of Downing College since 1936. In 1932 he took the main part in founding *Scrutiny, a literary quarterly he also edited until it ceased publication in 1953. Devoted to the principle that the study of literature should be based on close textual analysis, and holding that all worthwhile criticism is related to 'particular arrangements of words on the page', Leavis enforced these views in his lectures and through the articles in *Scrutiny*, communicating a conviction of his rightness to a generation of students, many of whom, as future teachers and lecturers at home and abroad, propagated the intellectual puritanism which scholars of a more liberal mind believed sterile. *Mass Civilization and Minority Culture* (1930), his first book, established the position he continued to maintain, that 'culture has always been in minority keeping', with the corollary that an intellectual élite must be bred to sustain it. That this might lead to arrogance of mind was suggested by Leavis's manner as a controversialist, which reached its climax in the Richmond Lecture (delivered at Cambridge in February 1962) embodying an attack on Sir Charles (later Lord) *Snow whose *The Two Cultures* had recently attracted much attention. Leavis's critical judgments of individual authors and contemporary movements are expressed in *D. H. Lawrence* (1930), *New Bearings in English Poetry* (1932), *For Continuity* (1933), *Revaluation: Tradition and Development in*

English Poetry (1936), *The Great Tradition: George Eliot, Henry James, and Joseph Conrad* (1948), *The Common Pursuit* (1952), *D. H. Lawrence: Novelist* (1955). In 1963 he published *Scrutiny: A Retrospect* in connection with its twenty-volume reissue in that year. *Letters in Criticism* (1974).

Leavis, Queenie (*née* Queenie Dorothy Roth,   - ; Mrs F. R. Leavis). Author of *Fiction and the Reading Public* (1932).

Leblanc, Maurice (1864-1941). Born in Rouen; educated in France, England, and Germany. Creator of the fictional character Arsène Lupin who began in Leblanc's early stories as a criminal but developed into a master detective: *The Exploits of Arsène Lupin* (1907), *The Hollow Needle* (1910), *The Crystal Stopper* (1913), *The Eight Strokes of the Clock* (1922), *Arsène Lupin Intervenes* (1929).

Ledwidge, Francis (1891-1917). Born in Ireland. Began work on the land and did other manual labour before becoming a trade-union secretary. Served with the British forces in World War I and was killed in Belgium. Encouraged by Lord *Dunsany he had made headway as a poet with *Songs of the Field* (1915) and *Songs of Peace* (1916). Dunsany wrote a preface for the *Complete Poems* (1919).

Lee, John A. (John Alexander Lee, 1891-   ). Born in Dunedin, New Zealand; educated at Albany. Farm worker and civil servant. Member of N.Z. Parliament, 1922-28, 1931-43. Author of *Children of the Poor* (1934), *The Hunted* (1936), *Shining with Shiner* (1944), *Shiner Slattery* (1964), and other novels. See *New Zealand Writers.

Lee, Laurie (1914-   ). Born in Gloucestershire; educated at a village school and in Stroud; worked with various film units and as Publications Editor at the Ministry of Information in World War II. Author of several volumes of poems—*The Sun My Monument* (1944), *The Bloom of Candles* (1947), *My Many-Coated Man* (1955), etc.—and of a widely praised autobiography, *Cider With Rosie* (1959), followed by *As I Walked Out One Midsummer Morning* (1969). *And see under* *Poetry (p.423).

Lee, Manfred B. See Ellery *Queen.

Lee, Sir Sidney (Solomon Lazarus Lee, 1859-1926; knighted 1911). Born in London; educated at the City of London School and at Oxford. As a protégé of F. J. *Furnival he became assistant editor of the *Dictionary of National Biography* when it was projected in 1882 under the editorship of Sir Leslie *Stephen. Lee wrote hundreds of the entries and became editor from 1891. Amplifying articles which first appeared in the *D.N.B.*, he published *Shakespeare* (1898) and *Queen Victoria* (1902). *The Life of Shakespeare* (1915; revised edn. 1925) was a further enlarged biography. His *Life of King Edward VII* (vol I 1925) was completed after Lee's death by A. S. Markham (vol II 1927). Other works: *Great Englishmen of the Sixteenth Century* (1904; 1925), *Shakespeare and the Modern Stage* (1906), *The French Renaissance in England* (1910), *Principles of Biography* (1911). He was Professor of English Language and Literature at East London College (University of London) 1913-24.

Lee, Vernon (pseudonym of Violet Paget, 1856-1935). Born at Boulogne-sur-Mer of British parents. Her education was patchy, since her mother and father moved from place to place on the Continent before settling in Florence, but she had a natural aptitude for scholarship and languages. Her *Studies of the Eighteenth Century in Italy* (1880) was immediately praised for its intellectual brilliance and her learning was matched by her conversation, witty and critically incisive though often cocksure and sometimes insolent. She began many friendships with eminent artists and writers, but her arrogant tongue and pen led to estrangements, even from England through her antagonistic attitude in World War I. Her books were numerous and varied in subject-matter. Her style was mannered and, though carefully cultivated in early works, became inferior as she grew older. Her reputation at its best was confined to a limited circle and she was little remembered after her death. A fair view of her work can be had from *Belcaro* (essays; 1883), *The Beautiful* (1913); *The Spirit of Rome* (1905), *The Sentimental Traveller* (1907); *Gospels of Anarchy* (1908), *Proteus, or The Future of Intelligence* (1925); and, from among her novels, *Miss Brown* (1884), a satire on the friends she made in England in artistic and literary circles.

Left Book Club. Started by Victor *Gollancz in 1936 for the monthly distribution, to members, of books with socialist interest published by his own firm and mostly specially commissioned. It continued until 1947.

Left Hand, Right Hand! Collective and first volume title of autobiography in four volumes by Osbert *Sitwell: *Left Hand, Right Hand!* (1945); *The Scarlet Tree* (1946); *Great Morning* (1948); *Laughter in the Next Room* (1949). A fifth (supplementary) volume, *Noble Essences; or, Courteous Revelations* (1950), described by the author as 'a book of characters', has chapters on Edmund *Gosse, Ronald *Firbank, Wilfred *Owen, Ada *Leverson, W. H. *Davies, Arnold *Bennett, among others. The whole work, Osbert Sitwell's major achievement, is an impressive sustained display of contemporary English prose style, and a unique portrait of an age, in which the author's parents, sister, brother and servants in their family home, Renishaw, are lovingly and divertingly characterized, while the account of the larger world in which he moved in adult years comprehends much of what was best in the artistic and intellectual life of his time.

Le Gallienne, Richard (Richard Thomas Le Gallienne, 1866-1947). Born and educated in Liverpool. After years as an accountant he settled in London. From 1887 to 1943 he wrote copiously in verse and prose, achieving considerable acclaim and popularity, which proved impermanent. He migrated first to the U.S. and later to France. His books in the present century include *The Life Romantic* (1900), *An Old Country House* (1902), *The Romantic '90s* (1926), *From a Paris Garret* (1943).

Legouis, Emile Hyacinthe (1861-1937). Born at Honfleur; educated there and at the Universities of Caen and Paris. Specialized in English studies as Lecturer and Professor in the University of Lyon, 1885-1904, and as Professor of English Language and Literature in Paris at the Sorbonne, 1904-32. He wrote much on English poets and poetry: *Wordsworth and Annette Vallon* (1922) told their early love story, which Wordsworth had deleted from the first published edition of *The Prelude* (1850; restored in 1926 edition). In collaboration with Louis Cazamian, Legouis wrote *A History of English Literature* (1924; Eng. trans. 1926) much used by students.

Lehmann, John (John Frederick Lehmann, 1907-). Born in Buckinghamshire; educated at Eton and Cambridge. Contributor to the *New Statesman* and other periodicals; partner and general manager of the Hogarth Press (1938-46); founded his own publishing house in 1946 and was its managing director until it came under other control in 1952. Did much to encourage young writers as founder and editor of the 'little magazine' *New Writing* (1936-50). He also founded *The London Magazine* (1954). Author of *A Garden Revisited* (1931), *Forty Poems* (1942) and other books of verse; a study of *Edith Sitwell* (1952); and an autobiography, I. *The Whispering Gallery* (1955), II. *I Am My Brother* (1960), III. *The Ample Proposition* (1966).

Lehmann, Rosamond (Rosamond Nina Lehmann, Mrs Wogan Phillipps, 1903-). Born in London, sister of the preceding; educated privately and at Cambridge. Author of *Dusty Answer* (1927), *A Note in Music* (1930), *The Weather in the Streets* (1936), *The Ballad and the Source* (1944), *The Echoing Grove* (1953), and other novels.

Lehmann, R. C. (Rudolf Chambers Lehmann, 1856-1929). Born near Sheffield; educated at Highgate and Cambridge. A barrister, he was better known as an oarsman and from 1890 to 1919 as a regular contributor to *Punch*. Liberal M.P. for a Leicester constituency, 1906-11. He was a skilful writer of light verse and humorous prose sketches: *Mr Punch's Prize Novels* (1893), *Anni Fugaces* (1901), *Crumbs of Pity* (1903), *Light and Shade* (1909), *Sportsmen and Others* (1912); also *Rowing* (1897), *The Complete Oarsman* (1908), *Charles Dickens as Editor* (1912). Father of Rosamond and John Lehmann.

Leighton, Clare (Clare Veronica Hope Leighton, 1899-). Studied art in Brighton and at the Slade School, London, and became a leading wood-engraver, illustrating classic and modern novels, and also her own writings, *The Farmer's Year* (1933), *Four Hedges* (1935), *Southern Harvest* (1942). *Tempestuous Petticoat* (1948) is an entertaining record of her parents, Marie Connor *Leighton and Robert *Leighton, both writers.

Leighton, Marie Connor (*née* Marie Connor; died 1941). Born at Clifton; educated mainly in France. A prolific writer of stories of mystery and sensation, she made a great hit with *Convict 99* and continued with devoted industry for many years to retain the public who welcomed her novels.

Leighton, Robert (died 1934). Born in Scotland; educated in Liverpool. Editor of *Young Folks* (1884-5): Literary Editor of the *Daily Mail* (1896-9). His numerous books were mainly for boys or on dogs: *The Pilots of Pomona* (1892), *The Golden Galleon* (1897), *With Nelson in Command* (1905), *Softfoot of Silver Creek* (1926); *Dogs and All About Them* (1910), *The Complete Book of the Dog* (1922). Husband of Marie Connor *Leighton and father of Clare *Leighton.

Leishman, J. B. (James Blair Leishman, 1902-1963). Born in Cumberland; educated at northern schools and Oxford. Became senior lecturer in English Literature at Oxford from 1947. His chief successes were with verse translations from the German of Rilke and the Latin of Horace. His writings on English literature included *The Metaphysical Poets* (1934), *The Monarch of Wit* (John Donne) (1951), *Themes and Variations in Shakespeare's Sonnets* (1961).

Lemaitre, Brother John. Of the Order of St Dominic; deputy for the Chief Inquisitor at the trial of the Maid in Shaw's *Saint Joan* (1923).

Lena. English girl violinist in Zangiacomo's Ladies' Orchestra in Joseph Conrad's *Victory* (1915). Befriended by Axel Heyst, she elopes with him.

Lena Lingard. Daughter of a Norwegian farmer settled in Nebraska in Willa Cather's *My Ántonia* (1918). From tending her father's cattle she goes to work for a local dressmaker and later has a successful dressmaking business of her own in San Francisco, though as a girl she was thought flighty and irresponsible.

Lenormand, Henri-René (1882-1951). Author of *Time Is a Dream* (1923), *Man and His Phantoms* (1928), *In Theatre Street* (1937).

Lensky, Lydia. In D. H. Lawrence's *The *Rainbow* (1915), the daughter of a Polish landowner and widow of a doctor and revolutionary exiled in England; she marries Tom Brangwen as her second husband.

Anna, her daughter by the first marriage, becomes the wife of Will Brangwen, Tom's nephew.

Lentulus. A young Roman courtier in *Androcles and the Lion* (1912) by Bernard Shaw.

Leon, Henry Cecil. *See* Henry *Cecil.

Leonard, Frederick. *See* Frederick *Lonsdale.

Le Queux, William (William Tufnell Le Queux, 1864-1927). Born in London; educated there and in Italy; travelled extensively in the Balkans and northern Africa; claimed to have intimate knowledge of secret service of other countries and to have been consulted on such matters by the British government. Also claimed to have forecast the 1914-18 war in *The Invasion* (1908). His numerous and widely read novels were of the sensational cloak-and-dagger and undercover-information genre. The best known was *Secrets of Monte Carlo* (1899); others include *The Crystal Claw* (1924), *Hidden Hands* (1925), *The Fatal Face* (1926), *Blackmailed* (1927); also books on *German Spies in England* (1915), *Rasputin, the Rascal Monk* (1920), etc.

Leroux, Gaston (1868-1927). Author of *The Mystery of the Yellow Room* (1908), *The Perfume of the Lady in Black* (1909), *The Phantom of the Opera* (1911), and other mystery and detective novels.

Leslie, Doris (*née* Doris Oppenheim; Lady Fergusson Hannay). Educated in London and Brussels; studied acting in London and art in Florence. Author of *The Starling* (1927), *The Echoing Green* (1929), *Full Flavour* (1924) and other novels; *Royal William* (William IV, 1941), *Polonaise* (Chopin, 1943), *A Wreath for Arabella* (Arabella Stuart, 1948), *That Enchantress* (Abigail Hill, 1950), *The Great Corinthian* (the Prince Regent, 1952) and other biographical portraits.

Leslie, Sir Shane (John Randolph Shane Leslie, 1885-1971; succeeded to his father's baronetcy in 1944). Born in London; educated at Eton and Cambridge. Author of novels: *The Oppidan* (1922), *The Cantab* (1926) and others; biography: *Cardinal Manning* (1921), *George IV* (1926), *The Skull of Swift* (1928), *Studies in Sublime Failure* (1932); *Poems* (1928); current

history: *The End of a Chapter* (1916). Also *The Film of Memory* (1938), *Salutation to Five* (1951), *Long Shadows* (1966), etc.

Lessing, Doris (Mrs Lessing, *née* Doris May Tayler, 1919-). Born in Persia; lived on a farm in Rhodesia, 1924-49; settled in England. Her novels, mostly written in the natural conversational style of oral narration, include *The Grass is Singing* (1950), *Five* (short novels, 1953), and an ambitious sequence entitled collectively *Children of Violence* (*Martha Quest*, 1952; *A Proper Marriage*, 1954; *A Ripple from the Storm*, 1958; *Landlocked*, 1965; completed with *The Four Gated City*, 1969). Her short stories are collected in *The Habit of Loving* (1957), *A Man and Two Women* (1963), *African Stories* (1964). Non-fiction: *Going Home* (1957), on a visit to Southern Rhodesia; *In Pursuit of the English* (1960).

Lessways, Hilda. In Arnold Bennett's *Clayhanger* novels (1910-16) marries Edwin Clayhanger after having been deceived into bigamy by George Cannon.

L'Estrange, C. J. *See* Herbert *Strang.

Leverson, Ada (Mrs Ernest Leverson, *née* Ada Beddington, 1865-1936). Born in London; educated privately; married when nineteen the son of a diamond merchant, and a hardened gambler. Neglected by her husband she developed literary interests and friendships with prominent authors—George Moore, Oscar Wilde (who nicknamed her The Sphinx and inscribed to her under that title a copy of 'The Ballad of Reading Gaol'), Max Beerbohm, Somerset Maugham, the Sitwells. She wrote for *The Yellow Book* in 1895, for *The Criterion* in 1926, and in between contributed parodies to *Punch* and a weekly column for women (signed Elaine) in *The Referee*, a Sunday paper. She also published six witty novels— *The Twelfth Hour* (1907), *Love's Shadow* (1908), *The Limit* (1911), *Tenterhooks* (1912), *Bird of Paradise* (1914), *Love at Second Sight* (1916). They were reissued in 1951.

Lewis, Alun (1915-44). Born in South Wales. From teaching in Wales he went in 1942 to India as a lieutenant in the British army and was killed while fighting against the Japanese in Burma. In 1942 his first books were published: *Raiders' Dawn and other Poems* and a volume of short stories, *The Last Inspection*. His remaining poems, *Ha! Ha!*

Among the Trumpets (1942), came out a few months after his death with an Introduction by Robert Graves. A miscellany of his letters and hitherto uncollected short stories, *In the Green Tree*, was published in 1949. Alun Lewis was one of the two young soldier poets (the other was Sidney *Keyes) whose verses received particular praise in World War II.

Lewis, Cecil (Cecil Arthur Lewis, 1898-   ). Born at Birkenhead; educated at Dulwich, University College School, and Oundle. Served in the Royal Flying Corps from 1915; became one of the founders of the B.B.C. and during its first adventurous years was known affectionately through the Children's Hour as Uncle Caractacus; chairman of the Programme Board, 1922-26. His *Sagittarius Rising* (1937) is an account of flying in World War I, and *Farewell to Wings* came in 1964, after service with the R.A.F. through World War II. Other writings: *The Trumpet is Mine* (travel; 1938), *Pathfinders* (novel; 1943); *Never Look Back* (autobiography, 1974). Sheep farming in South Africa, 1947-50.

Lewis, Cecil Day. See C. *Day-Lewis.

Lewis, C. S. (Clive Staples Lewis, 1898-1963). Born in Belfast; educated at Malvern and Oxford; Fellow and Tutor, Magdalen College, Oxford, 1925-54; Professor of Medieval and Renaissance English at Cambridge from 1954. His writings on literary subjects include *The Allegory of Love: A Study in Medieval Tradition* (1936), *A Preface to Paradise Lost* (1942), *English Literature in the Sixteenth Century* (1954); *Studies in Words* (1960), and *An Experiment in Criticism* (1961). He also wrote several novels of a kind in which religion and science fiction combined: *Out of the Silent Planet* (1938), *Perelandra* (1943); a number of children's books: *The Lion, the Witch and the Wardrobe* (1950), *The Voyage of the 'Dawn Treader'* (1952), *The Magician's Nephew* (1955); and a vastly popular series of books on religious themes beginning with *The *Screwtape Letters* (1942). He used the pseudonym 'Clive Hamilton' (from his mother's surname) for his first book, *Dymer* (1926).

Lewis, D. B. Wyndham (Dominic Bevan Wyndham Lewis, 1894-1969). Wrote the humorous Beachcomber column in the *Daily Express* from 1919 to 1924 (when the

pseudonym was taken over by J. B. *Morton). In the *Daily Mail* from 1925-30 he contributed under the heading *At the Sign of the Blue Moon* and wrote as Timothy Shy in the *News Chronicle* from 1934. His books include *At the Green Goose* (1923), *At the Sign of the Blue Moon* (1924), *The Nonsensibus* (1936). Also biographies of *François Villon* (1928), *King Spider* (Louis XI of France, 1930), *Emperor of the West* (Charles V, 1932), *The Hooded Hawk* (1946; as *James Boswell*, 1952), *Dr Rabelais* (1957), *Molière: The Comic Mask* (1959).

Lewis, Eiluned (Mrs G. Hendrey). Born in Wales; educated in London; worked on the *News Chronicle* and *Sunday Times*. Author of *Dew on the Grass* (1934), *The Captain's Wife* (1943), *The Leaves of the Tree* (1953).

Lewis, Ethelreda (died 1946). Born in London; lived in South Africa and wrote of that country in such novels as *The Harp* (1925) and *Flying Emerald* (1926), but her greatest success was as the transcriber of the adventures of Trader *Horn.

Lewis, Sinclair (Harry Sinclair Lewis, 1885-1951). Born in Minnesota; educated at the local High School and at Yale. Between 1908 and 1916 he had no settled occupation and drifted through a variety of journalistic and other jobs. His first five novels, from *Our Mr Wrenn* (1914) to *Free Air* (1919) had no special distinction, but with *Main Street* (1920) and *Babbitt* (1922) he became a force in American literature and was among the first to make English readers aware of the development of indigenous American fiction with a socially critical and satirical purpose. These two novels laid a specimen Middle West community and type of business man under the microscope and scalpel, and though humour bubbled in them there was an undercurrent of destructive satire that was to turn bitter and intermittently sour in such later novels as *Arrowsmith* (1925) and *Elmer Gantry* (1927), which exposed the possibility of prosperous charlatanry in medicine and research and the disguising of hypocrisy in a religious cloak. Though Sinclair Lewis swam in the tide of debunking that swept America and Britain after World War I, the merit of his iconoclastic novels lay more in the verve of his literary style and his skill as a narrator than in any permanent effect of his message. Though it was said that babbitry perished under the exposure of Babbitt, the patient made a sure recovery. *Dodsworth* (1929), *Ann Vickers* (1933), and *It Can't Happen Here* (1935) are the best of Sinclair's later novels, which included much indifferent work.

Lewis, Wyndham (Percy Wyndham Lewis, 1884-1957). Born in the United States (in Maine) of English parents; brought to England in childhood and educated at Rugby; studied art at the Slade School and became equally notable as writer and as painter, his portraits of Edith Sitwell, T. S. Eliot and others (Tate Gallery, London) being regarded as among the finest products of contemporary art. Explosive in all forms of expression, he was most praised by the *avant garde,* who asserted the importance and value of his writings, though little in them was intelligible to the average reader. In association with Ezra *Pound he started in 1914 a characteristic literary irritant in unorthodox typography, *Blast: Review of the Great English Vortex.* Though intended as a periodical, its second number in 1915 was also the last. The Vorticism it propounded had something in common with the Futurism of *Marinetti, and a similarity of outlook led to Lewis's being suspected later of Fascist sympathies. His writings cannot be neatly classified, since those which are ostensibly novels partake also of the nature of non-fictional prose with excursions into a heightened style veering towards the poetic. But, in all, there is the tone of an author at odds with his environment. *Tarr* (1918), nearest to a straight novel, is his most intelligible and possibly his best book, though his admirers placed *The Childermass* (1928) and *The Apes of God* (1930) higher. Other works: *The Art of Being Ruled* (1925), *Time and Western Man* (1927), *The Diabolical Principle* (1930), *Hitler* (1931), *The Doom of Youth* (1932), *The Revenge for Love* (1937); verse: *One-Way Song* (1933); autobiographies: *Blasting and Bombardiering* (1937), *Wyndham Lewis: The Artist from 'Blast' to Burlington House* (1939).

Lewisham, George E. Chief character in Wells's *Love and Mr Lewisham* (1900); schoolmaster; marries Ethel Henderson.

Lickcheese. A character in *Widowers' Houses* (1892) by Bernard Shaw. He acts as rent collector for Sartorius, the slum property owner, and later becomes wealthy himself by ignoble means.

Liddell Hart, B. H. (Sir Basil Henry Liddell Hart, 1895-1970; knighted 1966). Born in Paris; educated at St Paul's School (London) and Cambridge. After active service in World War I he became, in turn, military correspondent of the *Daily Telegraph* and *The Times,* exercising marked influence on British military thought through his articles and other writings, including an officially-commissioned manual, *Infantry Training* (1920). He lectured to military academies in numerous countries, was described by Germans as 'the theoretical originator of mechanized warfare', and as adviser to the British Minister of State for War in 1937-38 endeavoured to hasten army reorganization. His command of a lucid literary style made military history and biography attractive and intelligible to an enlarged company of readers: *Paris: or The Future of War* (1925), *Great Captains Unveiled* (1927), *The Decisive Wars of History* (1929), *Sherman: Soldier, Realist, American* (1929), *Foch: The Man of Orleans* (1931), *The Ghost of Napoleon* (1933), *Colonel Lawrence: The Man Behind the Legend* (1934), *T. E. Lawrence: In Arabia and After* (1934), *The Other Side of the Hill* (1948; new edn 1951), *Defence of the West* (1950), *A History of the Second World War* (1962).

Liebling, A. J. (Abbott Joseph Liebling, 1904-63). Born in New York; educated at Dartmouth College and Columbia University. Worked as a sports reporter on the *New York Times* and later on the *New Yorker*, serving as its Paris correspondent in World War II and then as commentator on New York life, and particularly on the vagaries of the newspaper press.

Life and Letters. A monthly periodical first published in 1923, edited by Desmond *MacCarthy. Later it was subtitled 'An International Monthly of Living Literature', edited by Robert Herring. In 1939 it absorbed the *London Mercury.*

Life Force. A recurrent term in the writings of Bernard *Shaw which he equated at times with the Will of God, the Holy Ghost, and other terms in the vocabulary of orthodoxy. In the Preface to *Androcles and the Lion* he wrote: 'the Life Force (or whatever you choose to call it) cannot be finally beaten by any failure, and will even supersede humanity by evolving a higher species if we cannot master the problems raised by the multiplication of our own numbers'. When Tanner in *Man and Superman* is inveigled into proposing marriage by Ann Whitefield, he declares 'I am in the grip of the Life Force'; while Ann (as Doña Ana de Ulloa) in the Hell scene of that play, exits crying to the universe: 'I believe in the Life to Come. A father! a father for the Superman!'

Lilia. See *Herriton family.

Lilith. Originating in ancient Eastern mythology as an evil spirit and thence obtaining mention in ancient Hebrew literature in various guises (in one version as a pre-Eve wife of Adam), Lilith also appeared in Goethe's *Faust,* in Rossetti's poem, *Eden Bower,* and in *Back to Methuselah* by Bernard Shaw. In the first part of the last-named work she is spoken of by the Serpent in the Garden of Eden as having produced Adam and Eve by parthenogenesis; in the final part she delivers the long closing speech on birth and the endless continuity of life, which is one of the finest passages in Shaw's works.

Lily Haden. The girl of easy morals by whom Michael Fane is infatuated in Compton Mackenzie's *Sinister Street* (1913-14).

Lily Sabina. See Sabina.

Limerick. A comic verse in fixed five-line form rhyming *a a b b a,* lines 1, 2, and 5 having three metrical feet, lines 3 and 4 two only. The origin of the name is uncertain, though it has been suggested that such verses began as improvised party pieces after each of which the company sang as a refrain, 'Won't you come up, come up, won't you come up to Limerick?', though the relevance is not evident. The principal writer of Limericks is Edward Lear (*Book of Nonsense,* 1846, and later collections) though his are less witty than the numerous later anonymous ones, many of which are accounted improper and unprintable.

Lin Yutang (1895-   ). Born in Amoy, China; educated there at Christian schools, and in America and Germany. Professor of English, University of Peking, 1923-26; Chancellor of Nanyang University, Singapore, 1954-55. Author of *My Country and My People* (1935), *The Importance of Living* (1937), *A Leaf in the Storm* (1941), *Peace is in the Heart* (1950), *The Importance of Understanding* (1961).

Lindbergh, Anne (*née* Anne Spencer Morrow, 1906-   ; Mrs Charles Lindbergh). Born in New Jersey, daughter of Dwight Whitney Morrow, sometime U.S. Ambassador to Mexico; educated in New York and at Smith College, Massachusetts. Married in 1929 Colonel Charles Lindbergh, the first man to fly alone across the Atlantic from New York to Paris in 1927 (see his *The Spirit of St Louis,* 1953). She took much active interest in aeronautics. Author of *North to the Orient* (1935), *Listen, the Wind* (1938), *Gift from the Sea* (1955), *The Unicorn* (1958).

Lindsay, Jack (1900-   ). Born in Melbourne, Australia, son of the following; educated in Brisbane; settled in England from 1926. Ran the Fanfrolico Press, devoted to fine printing. His extensive literary output is miscellaneous in range and character, including translations of Greek and Latin classics as well as original verse and verse drama, biographies, history, political surveys, novels, art criticism, autobiography (*Life Rarely Tells,* 1921; *The Roaring Twenties,* 1960).

Lindsay, Norman (Alfred William Norman Lindsay, 1879-1969). Born in Creswick, Victoria; father of the preceding and of the following. Studied art and from 1901 was chief cartoonist on the *Sydney Bulletin.* Author of novels: *A Curate in Bohemia* (1913), *Red Heap* (1931), *The Cautious Amorist* (1934), *The Age of Consent* (1938). *Creative Effort: Essays on Life and Art* (1920). *Dust or Polish* (1950). He was also an outstanding book illustrator and artist in several other media.

Lindsay, Philip (1906-58). Born in Sydney, Australia, son of the preceding; educated in Brisbane; worked as a journalist in Sydney; settled in England from 1929. Wrote many historical novels, including *London Bridge is Falling* (1934), *Pudding Lane* (1940), *My Lord Admiral* (1949), *The Counterfeit Lady* (1954); historical studies of English kings; a biography of *Don Bradman* (1951); an autobiography, *I'd Live the Same Life Over* (1941).

Lindsay, Vachel (Nicholas Vachel Lindsay, 1879-1931). Born in Springfield, Illinois; educated there and at Hiram College, Ohio; studied art in Chicago and New York. He was unsuccessful as a black-and-white illustrator, and failing to find other employment he set out on prolonged tramping excursions as a poet-beggar, selling leaflets of his verses, such as *Rhymes to be Traded* *for Bread* (1912). He undertook lecture engagements for the Y.M.C.A. and the Anti-Saloon League, resulting in one of his prose books *Adventures While Preaching the Gospel of Beauty* (1914), that 'gospel' being among his chief preoccupations. The main source of his celebrity, however, was in the original poems he declaimed in public wherever he found an audience: 'The Congo', 'General William Booth Enters Into Heaven' (the title-poems of two volumes, 1913, 1914), 'Abraham Lincoln Walks At Midnight', 'The Santa-Fé Trail'. He thus did much to pave the way to the later revival of oral poetry, though there was little immediate sign of achievement beyond the excitement he could create by his own dramatic manner of delivery. His poetic ability declined in later years, his best work being in the pieces named above (included in *Collected Poems*, 1923).

Lindsey, Benjamin Barr (1869-1943). U. S. judge and social reformer. He was among the first to set up juvenile courts for dealing humanely with young offenders, but this service was for a time obscured by his advocacy of Companionate Marriage, which provoked much unfavourable comment and some uproar. Lindsey's plan was to permit young couples to live together for a trial period before committing themselves to a permanent alliance, thus reducing the frequency of hasty marriages, prolonged marital disharmony, and the consequent high divorce rate. His proposals were made before pre-marital sexual relationships became commonplace.

Lingard, Lena. See *Lena Lingard.

Linguistics. Comprehensive term for the several branches of language study: etymology (origin, formation, and development of words), semantics (meanings), phonetics (speech sounds), morphology (forms and inflexions), syntax (structure of sentences).

Linklater, Eric (1899-1974). Born in Penarth; educated at Aberdeen and began to study medicine in the University there, but abandoned it for an English course. Wounded in World War I. Assistant Editor in Bombay of *The Times of India*, 1925-27; awarded a Commonwealth Fellowship for 1928-30 tenable in the U.S. Commanded the fortress of the Orkney Islands, 1939-41; then worked in the Public Relations Directorate of the War Office, 1941-45. Rector of

Aberdeen University, 1945-48. His time in the U.S. led to the most amusing of his novels, *Juan in America* (1931) which was hardly equalled by *Juan in China* (1937) after a visit to that country. His first novels— *White Maa's Saga* (1929) and *Poet's Pub* (1929)—were set in his native region; after the Juan books the most enjoyable of his novels, and in characterization the best, was *Private Angelo* (1946), an hilarious story of postwar Italy. During World War II he wrote several effective 'conversations' for radio: *The Raft* and *Socrates Asks Why* (1942), *The Great Ship* and *Rabelais Replies* (1944), and a play, *Crisis in Heaven* (1944). His other books include *The Corpse on Clapham Common* (1971), *The Voyage of the Challenger* (1972).

Lippmann, Walter (1889-1974). Born in New York; educated at Harvard. Held editorial posts on the *New Republic*, the *New York World,* and *Herald Tribune.* One of the most scholarly of American journalists and political commentators, his *A Preface to Politics* (1913), *A Preface to Morals* (1929), *The Good Society* (1937), and *Essays in the Public Philosophy* (1955) are among the books by which he influenced current thinking in the U.S. and elsewhere.

Literary criticism. The change of emphasis from appreciation (i.e. enjoyment) of literature to its study in depth as an academic discipline, has done much towards diverting literary criticism from its standing as a branch of the Humanities to becoming ancillary to processes of technical investigation. The appointment of Sir Arthur *Quiller-Couch as the first King Edward VII Professor of English Literature at Cambridge in 1912 brought into the field of English Studies a successful writer of original imaginative prose and verse who also had the reputation of being a brilliant critic and an inspiring lecturer. He reached an enthusiastic audience in and far beyond Cambridge with *On the Art of Writing* (1916), *On the Art of Reading* (1920), and three series of *Studies in Literature* (1918, 1922, 1929). But meanwhile a mood of intellectual puritanism had set in, largely under the influence of T. S. *Eliot, whose first collection of essays on poetry and criticism, *The Sacred Wood*, came out in 1920, followed by Percy *Lubbock's *The Craft of Fiction* (1921), by original works in a new austere or difficult mode by Eliot, James *Joyce and others, and by I. A. *Richards's

Principles of Literary Criticism (1924). Richards was a lecturer in English at Cambridge University from 1922 to 1929. The English School there became throughout following decades the stronghold of literary study devoted mainly to textual analysis, with emphasis on such elements as imagery and symbolism. At Oxford, Lord David *Cecil, as the first Goldsmith's Professor of English Literature, kept closer to traditional lines of study, producing a sensitive study of William Cowper, *The Stricken Deer* (1929), which was widely popular. With the multiplication of universities after World War II, most with departments of English Studies, the academic tide crept up the beach of literature, engulfing the earlier centuries and reaching to a few approved writers of the present age—Joseph Conrad, D. H. Lawrence, W. B. Yeats, James Joyce, T. S. Eliot —who came to be referred to satirically as 'O.K. authors'. Theses abounded and seeped into publishers' lists, taking in this century the place occupied by theological works and collections of sermons in the past. In 1968 the author of a reassessment of Conrad remarked: 'Conrad has become established as a modern classic, a writer who is widely studied, examined, written about and researched into'; but, he added, ' I have the impression that his apparently unchallengeable status among the critics has not been accompanied by a comparable popularity with the common reader'. The prevalent type of literary criticism diverted literature from the ordinary reader, so that a teacher with a strong interest in literature is moved to express his wish 'to get as far away as possible from the kind of detailed textual study that delights scholars but has done much to stifle the enjoyment of books by the young. . . . Many boys and girls leave school without having read a single work of literature apart from their set books'. Most of contemporary English Studies has nothing to do with the human values of literature. Unless reading by students and others teaches them how to live, it teaches them nothing.

Little Gidding. Poem by T. S. Eliot, the last of his *Four Quartets* (1943); first published separately in 1942. Named from the village of Little Gidding in Huntingdonshire where the Anglican scholar-divine Nicholas Ferrar (1592-1637) founded an austere religious community in 1625. It was dispersed when Cromwell's troops raided it in 1646.

Little magazines. Periodicals produced on a non-commercial basis for a limited circulation. Appealing to a literary and artistic coterie of restricted interests, the financial means available are frequently too small to keep a little magazine long in being. The importance and the quality of contents of such publications vary widely: some serve as nurseries of genius; others are mainly channels of selfconscious eccentricity or mirrors for mutual admiration.

Littlewood, Joan. As Director of' Theatre Workshop at the Theatre Royal, Stratford, in the eastern part of London, from 1945, she encouraged young playwrights. Her productions, mostly with a critical contemporary relevance and in a realistic mode, included *A Taste of Honey* by Shelagh *Delaney and *The Hostage* by Brendan *Behan.

Littlewood, S. R. (Samuel Robinson Littlewood, 1875-1963). Born at Bath; educated at Merchant Taylors', and at Dover College and St Paul's. Went into journalism and became dramatic critic on various papers, including the *Daily Chronicle, Pall Mall Gazette, Morning Post,* and *Daily Telegraph*; editor of *The Stage* 1943-52. Author of children's books, a manual on *Dramatic Criticism* (1939), and *Elizabeth Inchbold and Her Circle 1753-1821* (1921).

Live Like Pigs. Play in seventeen scenes by John *Arden performed in 1958; published in 1961. The Sawney family (Sailor Sawney, Big Rachel and her son Col, Rosie and her daughter Sally) called by the author 'nomads' and 'direct descendants of the "sturdy beggars" of the sixteenth century' but regarded as gipsies by their neighbours, are moved from the derelict tramcar in which they have been living on a caravan site, to a house on a Council estate in a northern industrial town. Their next door neighbours —the Jacksons—are respectable lower middle-class: Mrs Jackson, Doreen their daughter, and Jackson a Co-operative Society official. Mrs Jackson's attempt to be sociable is abusively rejected by the Sawneys, who find it beyond their ability to adapt themselves to the new way of living. Col complains to next-door Doreen: 'You got a house. . . . Then you got a bit of garden. . . . Then you got the concrete bloody road and two blue coppers thumping up and down it. I'll tell you, I'm going off me nut already.' Blackmouth, a former lover of Rosie and father of Sally, descends as a lodger on the Sawneys after a term in prison, bringing with him Daffodil, his present doxy, and her crazy mother, the Old Croaker. Col attempts to seduce the not unwilling Doreen; Blackmouth rages in the street after a knife fight with Col over Daffodil; Old Croaker goes up and down the gardens pulling down the washing and tearing it up. The exasperated neighbours attack the Sawneys, who are rescued by the police but have to give up the house for infringing the Council regulation banning lodgers.

Llewellyn, Richard (pseudonym of Richard Dafydd Vivian Llewellyn Lloyd, 1907-   ). Born at St David's, Wales; educated there and in Cardiff and London; worked in film studios before writing *Poison Pen* (1938), a stage success in London, and *How Green Was My Valley* (1939), a novel about a Welsh mining family, which was an immediate best-seller. Later novels: *None But the Lonely Heart* (1943), *A Few Flowers for Shiner* (1950), both concerned with Cockney characters. Also several plays.

Lloyd, Richard Daffyd Vivian Llewellyn. *See* Richard *Llewellyn.

Loam, The Earl of. Elderly Radical peer who urges equality upon his reluctant family and servants in *The *Admirable Crichton* (1902) by J. M. Barrie.

Lob. The Puck-like host in J. M. Barrie's *Dear Brutus* (1917).

Locke, W. J. (William John Locke, 1863-1930). Born in British Guiana; spent part of his childhood in England; educated, afterwards, in Trinidad and then again in England, at Cambridge. Became a schoolmaster until his health broke down, then was Secretary of the Royal Institute of British Architects, 1897-1907, by which time he had published several novels, including *The Morals of Marcus Ordeyne* (1905) and *The Beloved Vagabond* (1906). These, with *Simon the Jester* (1910), *The Joyous Adventures of Aristide Pujol* (1912), and *Stella Maris* (1913), represent his romantic, compassionate, and humorous narrative style at its most attractive. He continued to write novels for most of his remaining years and added some plays, but changing tastes diminished his popularity.

ockhart, Bruce (Sir Robert Hamilton Bruce Lockhart, 1887-1970; knighted 1943). Born in Scotland; educated in Edinburgh, Paris, and Berlin. Spent a few years in Malaya on a rubber plantation, then entered the diplomatic service and went to the British Consulate in Moscow. In 1918 he was arrested by the Bolsheviks and imprisoned until he was exchanged for a Russian held in England. Leaving the Consular service, he took up banking in Central Europe, followed by journalism in London, 1929-37; then joined the Political Intelligence Department and was Director-General of Political Warfare, 1941-45. His first book *Memoirs of a British Agent* (1932) was a popular success; later he wrote *Return to Malaya* (1936), *My Scottish Youth* (1937), and others.

Lodge, Sir Oliver (Oliver Joseph Lodge, 1851-1940; knighted 1902). Born in Staffordshire; educated at Newport (Shropshire) and University College, London. Professor of Physics, University College, Liverpool, 1881-1900; Principal of the University of Birmingham, 1900-19. His researches in electromagnetism, radiation, inventions indispensable to wireless broadcasting, made him a world-famous physicist. His writings included both scholarly scientific works and popular books such as *Pioneers of Science* (1892), *Man and the Universe* (1908), *Modern Problems* (1912). He had become President of the Society for Psychical Research in 1901, but when the death of his son Raymond in World War I led to the writing of *Raymond, or Life and Death* (1916) surprise was expressed that so eminent a scientist placed confidence in spiritualism. He wrote *My Philosophy* in 1933, following his autobiography *Past Years* (1931).

Lofting, Hugh (Hugh John Lofting, 1886-1947). Born in Maidenhead; educated at Chesterfield. Worked as a civil engineer in Canada, Africa, and Cuba, but having been wounded in World War I he turned to the production of children's books telling the adventures of the imaginary Dr Dolittle, described as 'an eccentric country physician with a bent for natural history and a great love of pets' who gives up his practice in order to devote his skill to animals. They became immediately popular and rank among the classics for children: *The Story of Dr Dolittle* (1920), *The Voyages of Dr Dolittle* (1922), *Dr Dolittle's Post Office* (1923) and others, doing his rounds at Circus, Zoo, Caravan, Garden, in the Moon, etc—all with the author's own illustrations. Lofting settled and died in

America. Doctor Dolittle was reincarnated
in the film on him made in the beautiful
Somerset village of Castle Combe in 1967.

Lofts, Norah (*née* Norah Robinson, 1904-   ;
married Geoffrey Lofts and, after his death,
Dr Robert Jorisch). Author of, mainly,
novels: *Out of this Nettle* (1939), *The Silver
Nutmeg* (1947), *Heaven in Your Hand* (1959),
The Lost Ones (1969). Pseudonymously as
Peter Curtis: *Dead March in Three Keys*
(1940), *Lady Living Alone* (1944), *The
Devil's Own* (1959).

Logical Positivism. A philosophical system,
of Austrian origin, emanating mainly from
Ludwig *Wittgenstein's *Tractatus Logico-
Philosophicus* (1921; Eng. trans. 1922). It
aimed to create a comprehensive philosophy
of science, emphasising the basically linguistic
nature of philosophical problems, in opposition to traditional metaphysics. Its leading
English advocate was A. J. *Ayer.

Log-rolling. Praise by authors of each other's
books in the expectation of material benefit
or to curry favour. Of two nineteenth-century
historians an anonymous lampoonist wrote:
'Stubbs butters Freeman, Freeman butters
Stubbs'.

Lolita. Novel by Vladimir *Nabokov. The
impending publication of an English edition
in 1959 caused much controversy on account
of the alleged immoral tendency of the book,
which had already appeared in America. No
official action was taken against it, however,
and the agitation ceased after the English
edition appeared. The sexual precocity of the
young girl Lolita attracted most attention,
and her proclivities gave temporary currency
to the word 'nymphet' applied to her.

Lolly Willowes; or, The Loving Huntsman.
Novel by Sylvia Townsend *Warner published in 1926. After living in London for many
years with her elder brother Henry and his
wife Caroline and their children (who call her
Auntie Lolly), Laura Willowes becomes restless and astonishes the family by suddenly
announcing that she is going off to live by
herself at Great Mop, a secluded Buckinghamshire hamlet in the heart of the Chilterns.
She takes rooms in a cottage with a Mrs
Leak, a satisfactory and non-interfering
landlady. Laura goes on long solitary walks,
buys odd Christmas presents at the village
shop for her relatives, and learns from Mrs
Leak all about the idiosyncrasies of the

villagers. She makes friends with Mr Saunter,
formerly a Birmingham bank clerk, now
living in a wooden hut and keeping poultry.
Laura helps him with the hens and takes to
thinking of herself as the henwife in the
fairy tale, 'close cousin to the witch'. She
is 'growing every day . . . more rooted in
peace' until she is disturbed by a visitor from
the outside world, her nephew Titus, who,
though a favourite, becomes a nuisance
when he settles in the neighbourhood and
interposes himself between her and the spirit
of the place, with which she had hitherto
communed in a kind of mystical love. She
now feels that she is being drawn back into
the family entanglements she had with
difficulty freed herself from, but ' "No!" the
woods seemed to say, "No! We will not let
you go." ' One night when she returns late
to her lodgings while Mrs Leak is out, she
finds a small kitten in her room. As she bends
to stroke it, it writhes round her hand and a
drop of blood oozes from the scratches it
gives her. She is convinced that the 'round
red seal of her blood' is a sign that 'She,
Laura Willowes, in England, in the year
1922, had entered into a compact with the
Devil': 'he had done little for nine months
but watch her. Near at hand but out of sight
the loving huntsman couched in the woods,
following her with his eyes.' Mrs Leak invites her for a late night stroll and leads her
to a nearby hilltop where a crowd of people
are dancing. At the end of this Witches'
Sabbath, Laura sits out on the cool turf of
the common until morning, when a man
dressed as a gamekeeper comes out of the
wood. It is Satan disguised. Then and later
she has amicable conversations with him. On
an occasion when he appears as a jobbing
gardener, she learns that she is irrevocably
a witch. She says it all seems perfectly
natural, to which he replies 'That is because
you are in my power: you will never escape
from me, for you can never wish to.'

Lomax, Charles. 'A young man about town . . .
afflicted with a frivolous sense of humour';
engaged to Sarah Undershaft in Bernard
Shaw's *Major Barbara* (1905); will be a
millionaire in ten years' time (when thirty-
five).

Lombroso, Cesare (1836-1909). Born in Verona;
educated at the University of Turin, where
he became Professor of Forensic Medicine
and Psychiatry. He was a pioneer in the
scientific study of criminal mentality and put

forward the theory (long accepted but now discredited) that there is a 'criminal type' recognizable by physical characteristics.

London, Jack (John Griffith London, 1876-1916). Born in San Francisco, illegitimate son of W. H. Chaney, an itinerant astrologer, and Flora Wellman. The father was of Irish descent, and though leading a vagabond life had some learning in languages and apparently a literary style with characteristics that his son inherited. The mother married a John London a few months after the birth of her child, who thereafter bore the name by which he became famous. Jack London was brought up in hardship and poverty, with insatiable reading of books from the public library as his refuge from the misery of home and the succession of laborious odd jobs he had to undertake for a pittance, until he lit out as a tramp in his early teens and served a brief term in prison for vagrancy. He took to the sea as an oyster pirate and seal fisher, embraced Socialism, attended for a few months a course at the University of California, and in 1896 set off for the Klondyke during the gold rush but returned penniless. His varied reading, resumed omnivorously at this time, led to often conflicting enthusiasms, but political and philosophical confusion did not weaken the power he was developing as a writer from 1899, when his first story 'An Odyssey of the North' was accepted by the *Atlantic Monthly*. Though from that time his writings brought him large sums, his spendthrift habits, ostentatious hospitality, and alcoholism kept him in financial difficulties and led to the dwindling of his creative abilities. Some doubt was expressed as to the cause of his death, but the evidence points to the probability that he intentionally took an overdose of drugs. Jack London's reputation has passed through three phases: from being ranked as a writer of rattling good stories, he next fell into neglect and, when remembered at all by critics, was dismissed with hardly a second thought; he has now returned as literature. While the majority of his novels and short stories are unlikely to attain academic repute, classic rank is accorded to, at least, *The *Call of the Wild* (1903), and **White Fang* (1905). It might be nonsense to claim that the dogs in these books are dogs-as-they-really-are, 'thinking' as dogs think, and behaving with rational dog-logic, yet this is the conviction Jack London creates, for his

animals observe as by nature the internal laws of the imaginative animal universe he creates. The visit he made to the east-end of London in 1902 gave him grim material for *The People of the Abyss* (1903); *John Barleycorn* (1913) and *Martin Eden* (1909) owe much to autobiographical experience; *The Iron Heel* (1907), with its seemingly prophetic interest as a foreshadowing of totalitarian despotism, may claim a place on the short roll of important political novels.

London Library. Largely through the active influence of Thomas Carlyle, this institution was founded in 1840 as a lending and reference library for subscribers. It still renders valuable service to the thousands of scholars and serious readers of all kinds who depend upon its resources. At first situated in Pall Mall, it moved to its present building in St James's Square in 1866.

London Mercury, The. Founded and edited by J. C. *Squire. From its beginning in 1919 it was for a decade or more the leading English literary and art monthly but lost its hold as new, experimental types of writing became common. It ceased separate publication in 1939 and was merged with *Life and Letters* (which ran from 1928 to 1950). Selections from the magazine's contents were published in *The Mercury Book* (1926) and *The Mercury Book of Verse* (1931).

Londoner, The. See Arthur Oswald *Barron.

Long, Mrs Gabrielle (*née* Gabrielle Margaret Vere Campbell, 1886-1952; Mrs Arthur Long). See Marjorie *Bowen.

Long, Huey (Huey Pierce Long, 1893-1935). U.S. politician; Governor of Louisiana, 1928-32; Senator from 1930. Though his State administration was efficient and he improved some public services, he adopted totalitarian methods resembling those of the European dictators and was assassinated on the steps of his State capitol after he had announced that he would stand as a candidate at the next election for U.S. President. He was described as ruthless, violent, unprincipled, and flagrantly corrupt (*Dict. Amer. Biog.*). His character and career are assumed to have inspired several contemporary novels: *Sun in Capricorn* (1942) by Hamilton *Basso, *Number One* (1943) by John *Dos Passos, *All the King's Men* (1946) by Robert Penn *Warren.

Longest Journey, The. Novel by E. M. *Forster

published in 1907. Invited to Cambridge for a weekend by their friend Frederick Elliot, called Rickie because he was a rickety child and is lame, Agnes Pembroke and her much older brother Herbert discuss her recent engagement to Gerald Dawes, known to Rickie as a prefect and 'athletic marvel' at school. Not long after, Gerald dies from an injury at football, and Rickie, having seen the lovers together, finds his enthusiasms deflected from Greek gods and heroes to the imaginative transfiguration of 'a man who was dead and a woman who was still alive'. Rickie grew up in great loneliness hating his father but loving his mother despite her reticence and lack of intimacy with him. Both parents died when he was fifteen. He intends, after graduating, to live as a writer, but, discouraged by a publisher's comments, he accepts a teaching post at the small public school where Herbert Pembroke is a housemaster, Agnes, now married to Rickie, acting as housematron. The new master becomes disillusioned when he realizes that Pembroke has only 'one test for things— success: success for the body in this life or for the soul in the life to come', and has no educational ideals. While staying with an aunt and her somewhat uncouth nephew, Rickie is shocked to learn that the nephew, Stephen Wonham, is his half-brother. He knows that his father and mother had lived apart for a period, and concludes that Stephen is his father's illegitimate son. Unknown to Rickie, Agnes has been intriguing to persuade the aunt to dispatch Stephen to Canada as a remittance man. When Rickie discovers this, the estrangement that has been growing between himself and Agnes breaks into an open quarrel. Stephen declines to go abroad, and, in conversation with one of Rickie's Cambridge friends, Stewart Ansell, produces documents establishing his parentage. Agnes tries to bribe Stephen to 'agree to perpetual silence', but Ansell, hating her ways, shames her by revealing the secret in the school dining-hall in the presence of the boys: Stephen is Rickie's mother's illegitimate son, not his father's. Although Stephen has become a drunkard, with hooligan tendencies, Rickie will not tolerate his being made an outcast, as Agnes wishes. In the train while the brothers are on the way to visit their aunt, Stephen promises to reform, but that same night he gets helplessly drunk again. Rickie finds him lying on the rails at a level crossing and, pushing

Stephen to safety, is himself fatally injured. His ruling principle in life was drawn from Shelley's *Epipsychidion* (lines 143-156), inveighing against those who 'commend to cold oblivion' all but one, and 'travel to their home among the dead . . ./With one chained friend' . . . and, so, 'The dreariest and the longest journey go'.

Longford, 7th Earl of (Francis Aungier Pakenham, 1905-   ), politician and publicist. Author of *Causes of Crime* (1958), *The Idea of Punishment* (1961), *Five Lives* (1964), **Pornography* (1972), *A Grain of Wheat* (1974). *And see* Lady Antonia *Fraser, and the following.

Longford, Countess of (1906-   ); wife of the preceding. Author (as Elizabeth Pakenham) of *Jameson's Raid* (1960); (as Elizabeth Longford) of *Victoria R.I.* (1964), *Wellington: Years of the Sword* (1969), *Wellington: Pillar of State* (1972).

Lonsdale, Frederick (pseudonym of Frederick Leonard, 1881-1954). Born in Jersey, Channel Islands; worked as a page-boy on a transatlantic liner and as a sailor before enlisting for five years in the army. By 1928 he was a successful London dramatist with three plays running simultaneously. It was with comedies set to music by others that he flourished in his first phase—*The King of Cadonia* (1908), *The Balkan Princess* (1910), *The Maid of the Mountains* (1916). He moved on to a series of well-constructed non-musical pieces characterized by high spirits, sparkling wit, and genial satire: *Aren't We All* (1923), *Spring Cleaning* (1923), *The Last of Mrs Cheney* (1925), *Canaries Sometimes Sing* (1929).

Look Back in Anger. Play in three acts by John *Osborne performed in 1956, published in 1957. In a one-room furnished flat in a Midland town on a Sunday evening, Alison Porter is ironing clothes, while Jimmy, her husband, and their friend, Cliff Lewis, sprawl in armchairs reading the day's newspapers. A graduate from one of the younger universities, Porter, having tried journalism, advertising, and selling vacuum cleaners, is now keeping a sweet-stall in partnership with Lewis. They are all in their middle twenties and the Porters have been married four years, living in an atmosphere of sensual passion and raucous hatred. Except when in the grip of physical desire, he persistently taunts Alison with sneers at her upbringing and abuse of her upper middle-class family, her father Colonel Redfern having commanded a Maharaja's army in India, while Porter comes from working people. When Alison's actress friend, Helena Charles, after one of his raging outbursts of hatred, says 'You think the world's treated you pretty badly, don't you?' he describes how he learnt at the age of ten what it was to be angry and helpless, when he watched his father slowly dying after returning wounded from the Spanish Civil War: 'I was the only one that cared.' Finding she is pregnant, and keeping that news from her husband, Alison goes to stay with her parents. Helena and Jimmy fall in love and live together in the flat while Alison is away; but Helena, discovering that she believes what she is doing is wrong and evil, leaves and returns to the stage. Alison returns, the baby having died, and she and Jimmy resolve to co-exist as 'rather mad, slightly satanic, and very timid little animals' wary of the 'cruel steel traps lying about everywhere'.

Loos, Anita (1893-   ). Born in California. While still a child she appeared on the stage in her father's company before having regular schooling. In her teens she was writing successful film scenarios and contributing to newspapers, but this precocious literary adolescence was outstripped by the immediate fame of her first novel *Gentlemen Prefer Blondes: The Illuminating Diary of a Professional Lady* (1925), which made her hardly less than a dollar millionairess, established a questionable phrase in the popular vocabulary, and encouraged an almost universal profusion of bleached hairstyles. Its sequel *But Gentlemen Marry Brunettes* (1928) received less credence. Other writings: *Happy Birthday* (play: 1947); *A Mouse is Born* (novel; 1951); *A Girl Like I* (autobiography, 1967).

opahin. The rich merchant in Tchekhov's The *Cherry Orchard* (1904) who buys the orchard to cut down the trees and lease it in building lots.

orac, E. C. R. (pseudonym of Edith Caroline Rivett). Author of about forty detective novels.

orca, Federigo Garcia (1899-1936). Born in Grenada; educated at the University of Grenada and started the university theatre there. His poems, inspired largely by peasant and gipsy life, made him internationally famous; those translated into English include *Lament for the Death of a Bullfighter* (trans. 1937), *Poems* (trans. 1939), and *Gipsy Ballads* (trans. 1953). The best known of his plays, translated as *Blood Wedding* (1933), is the first of a dramatic trilogy (*Three Tragedies of Lorca,* trans. 1947). His visit to America is described in *The Poet in New York* (trans. 1940). He was killed soon after the Civil War began, reputedly by political enemies.

Lord Jim. Novel by Joseph *Conrad published in 1900. Born in an English country parsonage, Jim (he has no surname in the book) trains as a merchant seaman and in due time holds the post of mate on the steamship *Patna*. While carrying some 800 pilgrims from an Eastern port towards Mecca, the *Patna* strikes, with only a slightly perceptible shock, a submerged object—perhaps a capsized timber-laden vessel. Jim finds that the *Patna* has been holed below the water-line and that the only bulwark is dropping flakes of rust and appears to be giving way under pressure of the sea-water flooding the forepeak. He reports to the skipper, 'a sort of renegade New South Wales German', and the engines are stopped. Only seven life-boats are carried, one of which the captain, aided by the two engineers and the donkey-man, prepares to lower. Jim looks on, astounded by the other white men's evident intention to abandon the ship and the pilgrims, who are unaware of the accident. In the struggle to release the lifeboat, George the donkey-engineer collapses and dies from heart-failure, noticed only by Jim. The life-boat is lowered and the captain and engineers shout repeatedly to George to jump. At last, impelled by some unwilled force, it is Jim who jumps into the boat. As they look back at the *Patna,* seeing its masthead light is no longer visible, they believe the ship has sunk, and the captain so reports when a steamer picks them up. But when they are landed, news is given to them that the *Patna,* still afloat, has been towed to Aden by a French gunboat. Only Jim has the moral courage to face questioning at the Court of Inquiry: the captain absconds; the engineers retire to hospital. Finding the captain and Jim guilty of disregarding their plain duty by 'abandoning in the moment of danger the lives and property confided to their charge', the Court cancels their certificates. The narrator throughout is Captain *Marlow, who looks beyond Jim's tragic lapse and perceives his true quality. Through friends, Marlow gets him successive shore jobs, which Jim flees from as talk of his disgrace follows him. Finally, again through Marlow, he is appointed agent and manager of a remote trading-post at Patusan far up a tropical river. There he quickly leaps 'into the trust, the love, the confidence of the people' of Doramin, an elderly chief, whose young warrior son, Dain Waris, becomes the comrade of the white man, whom they name Tuan Jim, i.e. Lord Jim. His worthless predecessor as manager of the trading-post, Cornelius, a Malacca Portuguese, ill-uses his stepdaughter; her life is transformed when Jim takes her as his nominal wife, calling her Jewel. She cherishes him and saves his life from assassins, but is in constant fear that he will, like all other white men, return to his own country. A notorious piratical ruffian known as Gentleman Brown comes to Patusan in a stolen schooner, demanding food for his men and intent on making trouble. His plan to burn and kill being frustrated, he gets from Jim the promise of 'a clear road to go back whence we came'. Cornelius, however, betrays the Patusans by showing Brown and his men a narrow channel at the back of the island, whence they kill Dain Waris and annihilate the force guarding the river. Cornelius is stabbed to death by Jim's Malay servant. Dain Waris's body is brought into Doramin's camp and laid at his father's feet. Jim approaches, saying 'I am come in sorrow . . . I am come ready and unarmed.' Doramin, staring with 'an expression of mad pain', shoots his son's friend: 'the white man sent right and left . . . a proud and unflinching glance. Then with his hand over his lips he fell forward, dead.'

Lord of the Flies. Novel by William *Golding published in 1954. A wrecked aeroplane-load of evacuee boys is marooned on an uninhabited island, the remnants of the plane with the pilot and other adults being washed out to sea. Ralph and a bespectacled fat boy, Piggy, separated from the rest, find a conch shell which is used as a trumpet to summon the others. Among these is Jack Merridew, leader of a choir-school group in uniform. A meeting of all the boys to choose a leader elects Ralph, who deputes some to build shelters, others to make and maintain a fire, the smoke from which is their only possible

signal to attract a ship to rescue them. Jack and his party are to act as hunters of the wild pigs in the jungle, to provide meat. The fat boy's spectacles, used as a burning glass, are the sole means of igniting a fire. Soon, slackness delays work on the shelters, the fire is not maintained, and a nightmare of one of the younger boys starts a panic fear of a beast from the sea. A general breakdown of morale develops when the rule of law and order under Ralph's leadership is undermined by Jack, representing power and destruction, and lapsing into savagery when he and the other hunters paint their bodies with coloured earths and indulge in primitive ritual dances around slain pigs and later around one of the boys whom they slaughter in their frenzy after he has crawled, terrified, from the Lord of the Flies, which is only a fly-infested pig's head stuck on a pole. The beast superstition is supported when a billowing parachute from an exploding aircraft lodges ghostlike on the summit of the island. Jack degenerates wholly into blood lust; Piggy is robbed of his spectacles and killed; and Ralph is hunted almost to death before a naval vessel reaches the island.

Lorelei. Chief character in Anita Loos's *Gentlemen Prefer Blondes* (1925).

Loss leaders. A term of American origin applied to articles offered for sale below normal prices, usually in large department stores and supermarkets, in the expectation that customers attracted into the premises by the advertised 'bargain line(s)'—usually varied from day to day or week to week—will also be drawn to make other purchases at unreduced prices and thus compensate any loss to the proprietors on whatever led them in. See *Net Book Agreement.

Lossie Thorpe. In William De Morgan's *Joseph Vance* (1906), the younger daughter of Dr Randall Thorpe. Joseph aged seven first sees her when she is about fifteen and thinks her for the rest of his life 'the most beautiful thing in heaven or earth'.

Lost Generation, The. A term in frequent use after World War I in reference (a) to the host of young men killed; (b) to the young men who survived physically but were afterwards spiritually and morally adrift. The term is said to have been originated by Gertrude *Stein, and it was in the writings of certain American novelists (e.g. those of Scott

*Fitzgerald) that the mood of the surviving lost generation' was presented.

Lost Lady, The. Novel by Willa *Cather published in 1923. While climbing on a cliff face, nineteen-year-old Marian Ormsby falls and breaks both legs. After lying helpless all night she is rescued by a search-party led by Captain Daniel Forrester, a widower twenty years older, whom she marries. Forrester, a railroad contractor, has pioneered lines through the middle-west, and has built his house at a lovely spot called Sweet Water, which he had first seen when, a young man, he worked as a waggon-driver across the great grass plains from Nebraska City to Denver. The Captain and his second wife are at Sweet Water only in summer, until a fall from his horse incapacitates Forrester and they live there all the year. Marian Forrester is beautiful and gracious, and much liked and admired by the scattered neighbours, particularly by young Niel Herbert, the nephew of their friend Judge Pommeroy. Mrs Forrester befriends the boy, who grows up idealizing her until he stumbles on the truth that she is drinking overmuch and is also sexually involved with Frank Ellinger, a coarse middle-aged bachelor. Thereafter, to Niel, she is increasingly a 'lost lady', as her beauty and fine nature become contaminated by baser qualities formerly unsuspected. She is 'betrayed by what is false within'. Niel loses sight of her for many years after her husband's death, and last hears of her having died in California as the third wife of 'a rich cranky old Englishman'.

Lost Weekend, The. See Charles *Jackson.

Loti, Pierre (pseudonym of Louis Marie Julien Viaud, 1850-1923). Born at Rochefort, of devotional Huguenot parents who intended him for the Church. He went instead into the French navy and voyaged to many parts of the world, including the South Seas, where the Tahiti women's nickname for him provided the pseudonym he adopted as author, as well as background experiences for the novel *Rarahu, or The Marriage of Loti* (1890). Though this and other exotic books with a sensuous atmosphere became regarded as characteristic of Loti, his posthumous reputation is maintained by the very different *Pêcheur d'Islande* (1886; Eng. trans. *An Island Fisherman*, 1887), a tale of the Breton coast. His books in the present century include *Disenchanted* (1906), *On*

Life's Byways (1914), *Notes of My Youth* (1924).

Louka. The Petkoffs' disdainful servant girl in Shaw's *Arms and the Man* (1894). Major Sergius Saranoff flirts with her and engages to marry her when Raina jilts him for Bluntschli.

Louys, Pierre (pseudonym of Pierre Louis, 1870-1925). Born in Ghent; educated in Paris; associated with the *Symbolists, and with André *Gide and others in literary journalism. He practised a temporarily successful deception with *Songs of Bilitis* (1894) which was accepted as a translation from the ancient Greek. This, like *Aphrodite* (1896), *The Adventures of King Pausole* (1900) and others, attracted by their sensuality, but *The Woman and the Puppet* (1898) has psychological interest as a study of moral disintegration.

Love on the Dole. Documentary novel by Walter *Greenwood published in 1933. Within a fictional framework it gives a faithful impression of the lives of industrial workers and their families during the early 1930s, when some three million men in Britain suffered prolonged unemployment, receiving only 'the dole' (the vernacular name for out-of-work pay) of less than £1 a week from the State, supplemented in extreme cases by minute sums from the 'workhouses' (Poor Law institutions). The Hardcastle family in the novel consists of husband and wife, daughter (Sally) and son (Harry). In his last weeks at school Harry does part-time work for a pawnbroker for half-a-crown a week. Sally is a millworker. On leaving school Harry is apprenticed to an engineering firm, but is given no training and at the end of his seven years indentures is left to join the vast body of the permanently unemployed. The father being also workless, Sally becomes the mainstay of the family. She wards off the lewd attentions of Sam Grundy, bookmaker, and of Ned Narkey, 'a huge fellow with the physique of a Mongolian wrestler'—both notorious woman-hunters. She falls in love with Larry Meath, a maintenance engineer of studious habits and socialist convictions who is an effective orator at street meetings. Their imminent marriage is prevented when Larry, while with a demonstration of unemployed against the Means Test, is injured in a clash with the police. He contracts pneumonia and dies, and Sally is compelled to borrow from Grundy to make up the cost of Larry's cremation. Harry, meanwhile, learns that his girl friend, Helen Hawkins, is pregnant by him. They are compelled to marry, though virtually penniless, and have to accept charity and parish relief. Broken in spirit by grief and poverty, Sally becomes Sam Grundy's mistress and, through his influence, both Harry Hardcastle and his father find employment with the local bus company. Throughout, a group of old women degraded by penury and excessive childbearing serves as a kind of witches' chorus: Mrs Nattle, who 'obliges her neighbours' by pawning on commission, advances small sums to them as agent for Alderman Grumpole the moneylender, and runs an illicit whisky-selling business at '3d a nip'; Mrs Jike, fortune-teller and fake medium; Mrs Dorbell, 'a beshawled, ancient, lugubrious woman', who pawns the food-tickets and goods she gets from charities; Mrs Bull, untrained midwife and layer-out of the dead.

Low, Sir David (David Alexander Cecil Low, 1891-1963; knighted 1962). Born in Dunedin, New Zealand; became cartoonist on papers in Christchurch (N.Z.) and Sydney before settling in England. For many years from 1919 onward he ranked as the most brilliant and accomplished cartoonist and caricaturist of the period, working for *The Star,* the *Evening Standard,* the *Manchester Guardian,* and the *New Statesman.* Many collections of his drawings were published in book form, including *A Cartoon History of Our Times* (1939), *Years of Wrath* (1949), and *The Fearful Fifties* (1960). In *Lions and Lambs* (1928) by Low and Lynx his literary collaborator was Rebecca *West, and in *Low and Terry* (1934) Horace Thoroughgood. Low's *Autobiography* appeared in 1956.

Lowell, Amy (Amy Lawrence Lowell, 1874-1925). Born at Brookline, Massachusetts, of the family which had included Lowell the nineteenth-century poet and other distin-. guished New Englanders; educated privately. Possessed of ample means, she was able to indulge studied eccentricities of dress and habits as a protective shield against constitutional physical handicaps. In her middle twenties she determined to become a poet and spent the next ten years on an apprenticeship of preparatory silence which closed with the publication of *A Dome of Many Coloured*

Glass (1912). At that date the *Imagists were in the forefront of the 'new poetry' and Amy Lowell aligned herself with Ezra *Pound, *H.D. and others in that movement, though her attachment was neither close nor long-lasting, for, with whatever measure of overdone self-assurance, she had genuine independence of mind and creative ability. She was a pioneer in declaring that poetry had to be released from restrictions of metre and be governed by a fundamental rhythm and the cadences of good speech, principles which governed her poems in *Sword Blades and Poppy Seed* (1914), *Men, Women and Ghosts* (1916) and *What's O'Clock?* (1916). In prose she produced a study of *Six French Poets* (1915), *Tendencies in Modern American Poetry* (1917), and in 1925 an overburdened biography, *John Keats,* in two volumes.

Lowell, Robert (Robert Traill Spence Lowell, Jnr, 1917-   ). Born in Boston, U.S.; educated at Kenyon College and Harvard. Author of numerous books of verse including *Lord Weary's Castle* (1946), *Life Studies* (1959), *For the Union Dead* (1964), *Notebook* (1970), *The Dolphin* (1973).

Lowes, John Livingstone (1867-1945). Born in Indiana; educated in Pennsylvania and at Leipzig, Berlin and Harvard. Professor of English at Harvard, 1918-30, and of English Literature there, 1920-39. His *Convention and Revolt in Poetry* (1919) attracted attention which was eclipsed by his next book *The Road to Xanadu* (1927) a study of Coleridge's sources which gave a new impetus to painstaking academic re-erection of the preliminary scaffolding of imaginative creations. Later works: *Of Reading Books* (1930), *The Art of Geoffrey Chaucer* (1931), *Essays in Appreciation* (1936).

Lowndes, Mrs Belloc (née Marie Adelaide Belloc, 1868-1947; married F. S. Lowndes). Sister of Hilaire *Belloc. She wrote novels of various types and in large numbers, making her chief mark with murder mysteries, especially *The Lodger* (1913), suggested by the unsolved, so-called Jack-the-Ripper crimes which terrified London's east-end in 1888-89. She also wrote three autobiographical volumes *I, Too, Have Lived in Arcadia* (1941), *Where Love and Friendship Dwelt* (1943) and *Merry Wives of Westminster* (1946).

Lowry, Malcolm (Clarence Malcolm Lowry,

1909-57). Born at Wallasey, Cheshire; educated at Cambridge. Reacting against his wealthy family (his father was a Liverpool stockbroker), he went to sea, and then became a wanderer in several countries, a dipsomaniac, a voluntary down-and-out; but he had found in Mexico the inspiration for *Under the Volcano* (1947), an autobiographical novel acclaimed as a masterpiece. An earlier novel, *Ultramarine*, was published in 1933; *The Selected Letters of Malcolm Lowry* in 1967. He died by misadventure near Lewes in Sussex.

Lubbock, Percy (1879-1965). Born in London; educated at Eton and Cambridge. Curator of the Pepys Library in Magdalen College, Cambridge, 1906-08, and author of an entertaining study of the diarist, *Samuel Pepys* (1909). His prose masterpiece is *Earlham* (1922), a beautifully written account of his childhood at the family mansion in Norfolk. *The Craft of Fiction* (1921) is an illuminating even though intermittently laborious analysis of the technique of novel-writing centred mainly on Tolstoy, Flaubert and Henry James. Other books: *Roman Pictures* (1923), *The Region Cloud* (1925), *Shades of Eton* (1929), *Portrait of Edith *Wharton* (1947).

Lucas, E. V. (Edward Verrall Lucas, 1868-1938). Born at Eltham, Kent; educated in Brighton, and apprenticed to a bookseller there before becoming a reporter on a Sussex local paper. He then attended University College, London, and worked for the evening *Globe* newspaper for a time from the spring of 1893. In that year he was commissioned to write a memoir of Bernard Barton, a friend of Charles Lamb (*Bernard Barton and His Friends*, 1893), and from that time it was as biographer of Lamb and editor of his collected letters, essays, and other writings that Lucas expressed his deepest enthusiasm. Even more fruitfully, he was Lamb's disciple in a long succession of essay volumes, though he had an original strain which made him other than an imitator of Lamb. He was probably the prime mover in that revival of the familiar, light-hearted essay blending humour and sentiment which was a feature in English literature in the early decades of the present century. Representative volumes of such essays by Lucas: *Fireside and Sunshine* (1906), *Character and Comedy* (1907), *Loiterer's Harvest* (1913), *Adventures and Enthusiasms* (1920),

Events and Embroideries (1926), *Adventures and Misgivings* (1938). He also wrote novels, called 'Entertainments', in a kind of extended essay style relying largely upon discursive conversation and little upon plot: the best of these, *Over Bemerton's* (1908), is set above a bookshop. Two of his anthologies are among the best of their kind, *The Open Road* (1899) and *The Gentlest Art* (letters; 1907). Topography, travel, and paintings were among the other subjects on which he wrote with enthusiasm; he was also a frequent contributor to *Punch* and head of a leading firm of publishers. Autobiography: *Reading, Writing, and Remembering* (1932).

Lucas, F. L. (Frank Laurence Lucas, 1894-1967; married E. B. C. *Jones). Born in Yorkshire; educated at Rugby, and at Cambridge where he became University Reader in English. Scholar, literary historian, and critic, he was antagonistic to the new fashions in poetry and criticism. He wrote much on Greek classical, English, and French literatures, and published novels— *The River Flows* (1926), *The Wild Tulip* (1932), *Doctor Dido* (1938); *Poems* (1935). His entertaining literary studies include *Authors Dead and Living* (1926), *The Decline and Fall of the Romantic Ideal* (1948), *The Search for Good Sense* (1958), *The Art of Living* (1959).

Lucas, Victoria. See Sylvia *Plath.

Lucius Septimus. Military tribune in Shaw's *Caesar and Cleopatra* (1898); murderer of Pompey; a turncoat, he offers to serve Caesar when he knows victory is imminent.

Lucky. Driven as a slave by Pozzo in Samuel Beckett's *Waiting for Godot* (1954).

Lucky Jim. Novel by Kingsley *Amis published in 1954. James Dixon, a young lecturer on probation in the history department of a provincial university, feels it necessary to keep on good terms with Professor Welch, though he detests and despises him. Dixon is disliked by certain senior members of the Faculty, and the continuation of his appointment depends upon the goodwill of Welch, who impresses upon Dixon the importance of getting his article on Medieval Shipbuilding Techniques published. It is accepted by a new journal, but the author is unable to extract any forecast of the date of publication, which is necessary to put him in better standing with the university authorities. Dixon is drawn into a sympathetic relationship with Margaret Peel, a physically unattractive colleague, who has taken an overdose of sleeping tablets due, it is thought, to her having been jilted by a Mr Catchpole. She and Dixon are among the company invited to a weekend party at the Welches' country house, where they meet the Professor's son Bertrand, an uncouth minor painter, and his girlfriend, Christine Callaghan, by whom Dixon is much attracted. Bored by the amateur musicians at the party, Dixon gets drunk at the local pub and after returning to the house falls asleep in a stupor on the bed. Next morning he finds that his cigarette has burned great holes in the sheet and blankets. He cuts away the charred portions, then calls in Christine, who helps him to remake the bed with the damaged clothes at the bottom, out of sight. He leaves without informing or apologizing to his hostess. Catchpole gets in touch and convinces him that Margaret Peel's story of jilting, and her suicide attempt, were only neurotic. Bertrand warns Dixon to leave Christine alone, but gets the worst of a fight. Dixon's college career has a farcical ending when he is drunk and finally collapses on the platform while giving a public lecture on Merrie England before a crowded audience including the Principal and most of the College Council. His dismissal is fully compensated by his engagement as a well-paid private secretary to Christine's wealthy uncle, Julius Gore-Urquhart.

Ludwig, Emil (1881-1948). Born in Breslau; educated there and at Heidelberg. He attracted most attention as a prolific biographer, particularly with his books on *Napoleon* (1927), *Bismarck* (1927), *Goethe* (1928), *Christ The Son of Man* (1928). His style was highflown and inflated and his vogue rapidly dwindled.

Lugg, Magersfontein. Albert Campion's manservant in detective stories by Margery *Allingham. Formerly an old lag, he has many comic turns of speech.

Luhan, Mabel Dodge (*née* Mabel Ganson, 1879-1962; married Edwin Dodge after the death of her first husband, and Antonio Luhan, a Mexican Indian, as her fourth husband). Born in Buffalo; educated there and in Maryland. A wealthy woman, she

aspired to be a patron of the arts, presided over salons at which she gathered numerous celebrities; among the geniuses she collected the chief was D. H. *Lawrence, of whom in Mexico she wrote *Lorenzo in Taos* (1932). Other books: *Winter in Taos* (1932) and *Intimate Memories* (4 vols, 1933-37).

Lunn, Hugh Kingsmill. See Hugh *Kingsmill.

Lupin, Arsène. Central character in crime novels by Maurice *Leblanc.

Luska, Sidney. Pseudonym under which Henry *Harland published novels of Jewish immigrant life in the United States in the 1880s (*Mr Sonnenschein's Inheritance*, etc.). He afterwards wrote under his own name.

Lyall, David. See Annie S. *Swan.

Lyall, Edna (pseudonym of Ada Ellen Bayly 1857-1903), writer of popular novels with strong religious (and some political) sentiment: *Donovan* (1882), *We Two* (1884), *The Hinderers* (1902), and others.

Lynd, Robert (1879-1949). Born in Belfast; educated there at Queen's College. Migrated to London, where he was Literary Editor of the *News Chronicle* and for many years the regular weekly contributor of an essay to the *New Statesman* over the pseudonym 'Y.Y.' He and E. V. *Lucas were in the van of the revival of essays in the Charles Lamb tradition. *The Pleasures of Ignorance* (1921), *The Blue Lion* (1923), *I Tremble to Think* (1936), *Life's Little Oddities* (1941) are typical collections of Lynd's essays.

Lynd, Robert S. (Robert Staughton Lynd, 1892-). Born in Indiana; educated at Princeton and Columbia. Author in collaboration with his wife H. M. Lynd (*née* Helen Merrell), of *Middletown* (1929), which applied the scientific methods of anthropology to 'A Study of Contemporary American Culture' and set a pattern since followed by many social researchers. They also wrote *Middletown in Transition* (1937).

Lysistrata. The Powermistress-General in *The *Apple Cart* (1929) by Bernard Shaw who took her name from the satirical comedy with that title by the ancient Greek Aristophanes.

Maartens, Maarten (pseudonym of Jozua Marius Willem Van Der Poorten-Schwartz, 1858-1915). Born in Amsterdam; educated in England and at Bonn and Utrecht. His first three books (poems and verse plays) were written under his birth name but with *The Black Box Murder* (1889) he adopted the pseudonym, writing always in English. *The Sin of Joost Aveling* (1889) is the first of a sequence of novels, set among Dutch farm workers and fishermen, which were widely read and praised in England and America, where he was admired both for his writings and for his personal integrity. Other novels: *An Old Maid's Love* (1891), *The Price of Lis Doris* (1909), *Eve* (1912). Short stories: *My Poor Relations* (1903), *The Healers* (1906), *The New Religion* (1907).

Macaulay, Dame Rose (1889?-1958; D.B.E. 1958). Born in Cambridge, daughter of G. C. Macaulay, a classical scholar and lecturer in the University there; educated at Oxford. From the time *Potterism* (1920) was published, she was popular, and earned critical respect, as a satirical novelist. While not greatly gifted in detaching her fictional characters from her own convictions, she had a rare ability to couple the acerbities of satire with compassion and a rich sense of fun, even though she could, when her uncompromising mood took over, chasten humanity as a 'mass of stupid, muddled, huddled minds', greedy, ignorant, sentimental, and truthless. After *Dangerous Ages* (1921) she produced the best of her satirical novels, *Told by an Idiot* (1923), followed it with *Orphan Island* (1924), *Crewe Train* (1926), *Keeping up Appearances* (1928), and *Staying with Relations* (1930), before turning to a strikingly different subject and period in *They Were Defeated* (1932), her finest though not most popular novel and the one by which she deserves to be longest remembered. *The World My Wilderness* (1950) shows with uncanny skill and acute understanding the unsettling and bewildering effects of a war-conditioned mentality on an intelligent and cultured English girl and a French youth amid the bombed ruins of London around St Paul's. Her last novel, *The Towers of Trebizond* (1956), part travel book, part spiritual quest, has autobiographical undertones made apparent posthumously when her *Letters to a Friend: 1950-2* were published (1961). Among her miscellaneous writings are: *A Casual Commentary* (essays; 1925), *Some Religious Elements in English Literature* (1931), *The Writings of E. M. Forster* (1938), travel books, books of verse including *Poems* (1927); and some prose anthologies.

McCabe, Joseph (1867-1955). Educated at Roman Catholic Schools in Manchester and London, and at Louvain University. Became a Franciscan monk and priest as 'Father Anthony'. After several years as a Professor of Scholastic Philosophy and Rector of Buckingham College, he left the Church and was thereafter a violent dissenter from Roman Catholicism, writing *Twelve Years in a Monastery* (1897), *The Decay of the Church of Rome* (1909) and a great number of books on miscellaneous subjects, including biographical studies of Talleyrand, Bernard Shaw and others, and volumes on evolution, rationalism, physics, and religion.

MacCarthy, Sir Desmond (1878-1952; knighted 1951). Born at Plymouth; educated at Eton and Cambridge. He edited the *Eye Witness* and other periodicals, including *Life and Letters*, and was among the foremost dramatic and literary critics of his generation, being for some years the principal book reviewer for the *Sunday Times*. His detailed account of the famous season at the Court Theatre under Granville *Barker which established Bernard Shaw and other playwrights is an invaluable record: *The Court Theatre 1904-1907: A Commentary and a Criticism* (1907). His articles and essays are collected in *Portraits* (1931), *Criticism* (1932), *Experience* (1935), *Drama* (1940), *Shaw* (1951), *Memories* (1953), *Humanities* (1954). For his articles in the *New Statesman* (1913 onward) he used the pseudonym Affable Hawk in succession to J. C. *Squire as Solomon Eagle. MacCarthy's daughter married Lord David *Cecil.

McCarthy, Justin (1830-1912). Born in Cork. Journalist in Liverpool and London, 1853-68; visited U.S., 1868-71. M.P. for Irish constituences, 1879-1900. Author of *A History of Our Own Times* (7 vols, 1879-1905) and other historical works, as well as popular novels including *Dear Lady Disdain* (1875).

McCarthy, Justin Huntly (1861-1936). Son of the preceding; educated at University College, London. Irish Nationalist M.P., 1884-92. Married Cissie Loftus, a leading actress; became a popular playwright with *If I Were King* from his novel with the same title on François Villon (1901). Other novels: *The King Over the Water* (1911), *In Spacious Times* (1916), *Henry Elizabeth* (1920). He also wrote other plays, and several historical works: *England Under Gladstone* (1884), *Ireland Since the Union* (1887), *The French Revolution* (4 vols, 1890-97).

McCarthy, Mary (1912-   ). Born in Seattle; educated at a Convent School there and later at Vassar College; wrote book reviews and dramatic criticism for periodicals; her marriage to Edmund *Wilson ended in divorce. Author of much-praised incisively satirical novels and short stories: *The Company She Keeps* (1942), *The Oasis* (1949), *The Groves of Academe* (1952), *A Charmed Life* (1954), *The Group* (1963); autobiography, *Memories of a Catholic Girlhood* (1957).

McCarthyism. After World War II Senator Joseph McCarthy (1908-1957) incited, and as chairman presided over, a series of meetings of the U.S. Senate Permanent Investigating Subcommittee, in which reckless charges of communist activity or sympathy were brought against innumerable people, some of whom held high administrative office and were loyal and honoured citizens. His methods were entirely unscrupulous, using the 'smear' as a weapon intended to destroy the reputation of anyone opposed to his malicious campaign, which was a source of discredit to his country. The term has survived him as a label for any political heresy hunt.

McComas, Finch. Solicitor and friend of the Clandon family in Shaw's *You Never Can Tell* (1895).

McCrae, John (1872-1918). Born in Ontario; educated there and at the University of Toronto, where he studied medicine. Army medical officer in South Africa in Boer War, and in Flanders in World War I, during which he died of an infection. Author of *A Text Book of Pathology* (1914), but became widely known by his poem 'In Flanders Fields' (first published in *Punch* in 1915), included in the volume with the same title in 1919.

McCrimmon, Rev. Mr. Free Church minister in James Bridie's *Mr Bolfry* (1943).

McCullers, Carson (*née* Carson Smith, 1917-1967; Mrs R. McCullers). Born in Georgia; educated there and in New York. Novels: *The Heart is a Lonely Hunter* (1940), *Reflections in a Golden Eye* (1941), *The Member of the Wedding* (1946; dramatized 1951). The description of the last named as a story of 'tormented adolescence' strikes the keynote of the author's preoccupation with psychological disturbance. Later novels: *The Ballad of the Sad Café* (1951), *Sweet as a Pickle and Clean as a Pig* (1964).

McCutcheon, George Barr (1866-1928). Born in Indiana; educated at Purdue University. Tried acting and journalism without success and was in his mid-thirties before his first novel *Graustark*, about an imaginary romantic kingdom, was published in 1901 with great profit to the publisher who had bought it outright for a small sum. Graustark was the setting for other popular novels, but it was with the 'comic fantasy' *Brewster's Millions* (1902; dramatized 1906) that he became most widely celebrated.

MacDiarmid, Hugh (pseudonym of Christopher Murray Grieve, 1892-   ). Born in Langholm, Dumfriesshire: educated there and in Edinburgh. He gained acceptance as the most notable Scottish dialect poet of his time, and was politically prominent as a founder of the Scottish Nationalist Party and as an ardent admirer of Lenin: *First Hymn to Lenin* (1931), *Second Hymn to Lenin* (1935). Other poems: *Sangschaw* (1925), *Penny Wheep* (1926), *A Drunk Man Looks at the Thistle* (1926), *To Circumjack Cencrastus* (1930), *Kist of Whistles* (1947), *Collected Poems* (1962), *A Lap of Honour* (1967). *Lucky Poet. A Self Study in Literature and Political Ideas* (1943), *In Memoriam James Joyce. From a Vision of World Language* (1955).

MacDonagh, Donagh (1912-1968). Son of Thomas *MacDonagh; born and educated in Dublin. Became a barrister, and in 1941 a District Justice in Wexford (later in Dublin). Author of *Happy as Larry* (1946), a verse play successful in London and the U.S. and in translations. Other plays include *Step-in-the-Hollow* (1957). Co-editor with Lennox *Robinson of the *Oxford Book of Irish Verse* (1958).

MacDonagh, Thomas (1878-1916). Born in County Tipperary; educated in religious schools and at Dublin University. Became a teacher before appointment as a Professor of English Literature in Dublin. Joined the Irish Volunteers and was executed following the Easter Rising 1916, in which he was a commander. He was a fine poet: *Through the Ivory Gate* (1902), *Songs of Myself* (1910), *Lyrical Poems* (1913); *Collected Poems* (posthumously, 1917) with an Introduction by James *Stephens.

MacDonald, Betty (*née* Anne Elizabeth Campbell Bard, 1908-1958; Mrs D. C. MacDonald). Born in Colorado; educated in Seattle and at the University of Washington. With her first husband, Robert Heskett, she embarked upon the chicken-rearing enterprise which resulted in the more profitable literary product *The Egg and I* (1945), a highly enjoyable and successful work of humour. *The Plague and I* (1948) resulted from her months as a sanatorium patient. Other books: *Anybody Can Do Anything* (1950), *Onions in the Stew* (1955) and several stories for children, including *Mrs Piggle-Wiggle* (1947).

MacDonald, George (1824-1905). Born at Huntly; educated in Aberdeen and in London at the theological college of the Congregational Church, of which he became a minister, but was forced into retirement by ill health. From 1856 to the end of the century he wrote poems and novels, among them *At the Back of the North Wind* (1871) and *The Princess and the Goblin* (1872) which have become children's classics. His principal adult novels are *David Elginbrod* (1863) and *Robert Falconer* (1868). Convinced that he was undeservedly neglected, C. S. *Lewis published *George MacDonald: an Anthology* in 1945.

MacDonald, Philip (-   ). Grandson of George *MacDonald. Service in Mesopotamia in World War I led to his novel *Patrol* (1928). He became well known as a writer of detective novels: *The Rasp* (1924), *The Noose* (1930), *R.I.P.* (1933) and others. For other books he used the pseudonyms Oliver Fleming, Anthony Lawless, Martin Porlock.

Macdonell, A. G. (Archibald Gordon Macdonell, 1895-1941). Born in Aberdeen; educated at Winchester. Served in World War I and afterwards joined the staff of the League of Nations Union, 1922-27. Unsuccessful Liberal parliamentary candidate for Lincoln 1923, 1924. Among his books, *England, Their England* (1933), a comic

fictional commentary upon some English names and customs, was much praised and continues to be read. Other books: *Napoleon and His Marshals* (1934), *A Visit to America* (1935), *My Scotland* (1937), *Autobiography of a Cad* (1939), *The Crew of the Anaconda* (1940). Under the pseudonym Neil Gordon he wrote *The Silent Murders* (1929), *Murder in Earls Court* (1933), *The Shakespeare Murders* (1933) and other detective novels; and as John Cameron: *The Seven Stabs* (1929) and *Body Found Stabbed* (1932).

McDougall, William (1871-1938). Born in Lancashire; educated at Manchester, Cambridge, and St Thomas's Hospital, London. After holding other university appointments, was Professor of Psychology, Duke University, North Carolina, from 1927. He was one of the most influential psychologists of his generation, both as a teacher and as author of *Introduction to Social Psychology* (1908), *The Group Mind* (1920), *Outline of Psychology* (1923), *Outline of Abnormal Psychology* (1926), *Character and the Conduct of Life* (1927), *Psycho-Analysis and Social Psychology* (1936).

Macfall, Haldane (Chambers Haldane Cooke Macfall, 1860-1928). Educated at Norwich and Sandhurst. Author of *The Wooings of Jezebel Pettyfer* (1897), a novel with a West Indian setting, other novels, and books on *Whistler* (1905), *Ibsen* (1906), *Beardsley* (1927); *Old English Furniture* (1908); *A History of Painting* (1910).

McFee, William (1881-1966). Born in London; educated in Suffolk; apprenticed as a mechanical engineer. Went to sea on a tramp steamer in 1906 and became a chief engineer. He had decided in 1912 to live in the U.S., and settled there after finally retiring from the sea ten years later. After his first (non-fictional) *Letters From an Ocean Tramp* (1908) he wrote a series of novels with Chief Engineer Spenlove as leading character. These made McFee one of the foremost sea-writers. In addition to novels—*Casuals of the Sea* (1916), *Captain Macedoine's Daughter* (1920), *Command* (1922), *Sailors of Fortune* (1929), *The Beachcomber* (1935), *Spenlove in Arcady* (1941)—he wrote essays collected in *Harbours of Memory* (1921) and *More Harbours of Memory* (1934), and a biography of *Sir Martin Frobisher* (1928).

McGinley, Phyllis (1905-   ). Born in

Ontario; educated in Colorado and at the Universities of Utah and California. Worked as a teacher and in advertising and journalism. Author of, mainly, light verse—*On the Contrary* (1934), *A Pocketful of Wry* (1940), *Stones from a Glass House* (1946), *The Love Letters of Phyllis McGinley* (1954), *Times Three: Selected Verse from Three Decades* (1960)—and children's books: *The Horse Who Lived Upstairs* (1944), *The Most Wonderful Doll in the World* (1950).

Machen, Arthur (1863-1947). Born in Caerleon, Monmouthshire, a region with legendary associations which either exercised a permanent influence on Machen's mind and imagination or were in tune with his inborn tendencies. After some ineffective private schooling he started work with a London publishing firm, then tried teaching and free-lance journalism with little encouragement. The book by which he was to be long known, *The Hill of Dreams*, came out in 1907, but he had previously published *The Great God Pan* (1894), *Hieroglyphics* (1902) and other stories. In 1915 *The Bowmen and Other Legends of the War* gave him his first and almost only glimpse of popularity, for it included the myth of 'The Angels of Mons' which he had invented, though credulous people had believed that in the 1914 retreat from Mons the British army had been led by a visionary company of angels. Machen's books in general appealed strongly to a limited company of connoisseurs of the supernatural and tales of horror, in which he was a master.

Machin. *See* *Denry Machin.

MacInnes, Colin (1914-   ). Son of Angela *Thirkell (who wrote under the surname of her second husband) and grandson of J. W. *Mackail. Born in England; educated in Australia. Published his first novel (*To the Victors the Spoils*) in 1950; became more widely known with *Absolute Beginners* (1959). He has been described as a 'documentary moralist' treating scenes of 'criminal or semi-criminal life in which conventional morality is shaken'; but 'the reformer's dice are loaded' for the wrong-uns get the best lines. Other novels: *City of Spades* (1957), *Mr Love and Justice* (1960), *All Day Saturday* (1966). Non-fiction: *England, Half English* (1961).

McInnes, Helen (Helen Clark McInnes, 1907-   ). Born in Glasgow; educated at Helensburgh and Glasgow University. Married Gilbert *Highet in 1932 and settled in New York when he was appointed Professor of Latin and Greek at Columbia University. They became American citizens in 1951. Author of *Above Suspicion* (1941), *Assignment in Brittany* (1942), *Neither Five Nor Three* (1951), *Pray For a Brave Heart* (1955), *North From Rome* (1958), *Decision at Delphi* (1961), *The Venetian Affair* (1963), *The Salzburg Collection* (1968), and other novels. *Home is the Hunter* (play, 1964).

Mackail, Denis (Denis George Mackail, 1892-1971). Born in London, son of the following; educated at St Paul's School and at Oxford. Worked for a while as a designer in the theatre, and in government departments and the British Museum Print Room. Author of many novels of humour and sentiment: *Tales from Greenery Street* (1928), *Another Part of the Wood* (1929), *Summer Leaves* (1934), *London Lovers* (1938), *Huddleston House* (1945), *It Makes the World Go Round* (1950). He also wrote a biography of J. M. *Barrie, *The Story of J.M.B.* (1941).

Mackail, J. W. (John William Mackail, 1859-1945). Born in Bute, Scotland; educated at the Universities of Edinburgh and Oxford. Married in 1888 Margaret Burne-Jones, daughter of the painter; their son was Denis *Mackail and one of their daughters became Mrs Angela *Thirkell. Though he was a brilliant classical scholar, Mackail turned from academic life and accepted appointment as Examiner and Assistant Secretary to the Board (afterwards Ministry) of Education, 1885-1919. He was also for a time Professor of Ancient Literature at the Royal Academy, and Professor of Poetry at Oxford, 1906-11. The most important of his writings is *The Life of William Morris* (1899), a biography of classic quality based on long personal acquaintance. Other works: *Select Epigrams from the Greek Anthology* (1890), *The Springs of Helicon* (1909)—on the progress of English poetry from Chaucer to Milton—*Lectures on Greek Poetry* (1910), *The Approach to Shakespeare* (1930), *Studies in Humanism* (1938). He also made an English verse translation of Homer's *Odyssey* (1905-10; new edition 1932).

Mackay, Mary. *See* Marie *Corelli.

McKenna, Stephen (1888-1967). Born in

London, nephew of Reginald McKenna (1863-1943), the Liberal statesman and banker; educated at Westminister and Oxford. Held government appointments at home and abroad. Author of many socio-political novels, among which *Sonia* (1917) attracted most attention; others include *The Reluctant Lover* (1912), *Ninety-Six Hours' Leave* (1917), *Saviours of Society* (1926), *Portrait of His Excellency* (1934), *Pearl Wedding* (1951), *A Place in the Sun* (1962). Autobiographical: *While I Remember* (1921). *Reginald McKenna 1863-1943: A Memoir* (1948).

McKenney, Ruth (1911-   ). Born in Indiana; educated in Cleveland and at Ohio State University. Worked as a journalist until 1936. Though she disclaimed a capacity for humorous writing it was the rich comedy of *My Sister Eileen* (1939; dramatized 1941) that gave her outstanding success both in its literary and its stage versions. Her novels include *Jake Horne* (1943); and her non-fictional works a regional study, *Industrial Valley* (1939), personal records in *Love Story* (1950), and others.

Mackenzie, Sir Compton (Edward Montague Compton Mackenzie, 1883-1972; knighted 1952). Born in West Hartlepool of a famous stage line, his father being Edward Compton and his mother belonging to the Bateman family. Educated at St Paul's School, London, and at Oxford. Studied law but turned to writing, publishing *Poems* (1907) and having immediate success with his first novel *The Passionate Elopement* (1911) and the following *Carnival* (1912). But among the almost innumerable books he wrote later, *Sinister Street* (2 vols, 1913, 1914) remains as the classic Oxford novel of its period, while *Guy and Pauline* (1915) best reflects the mood and atmosphere of what might be called the Rupert *Brooke generation. The critical acclaim which placed the young Compton Mackenzie among those who were thought to be effecting a renaissance of the English novel became muted as his books acquired popularity among a wider public. In World War I he served at the Dardanelles and in Greece, and recorded his experiences in *Gallipoli Memories* (1929), *Athenian Memories* (1931), and *Greek Memories* (1932). The last-named was suppressed as contravening the Official Secrets Act, but was reissued as *Aegean Memories* in 1940. *Sylvia Scarlett* (1918) and *Sylvia and*

Michael (1919) align with his early books; in later years he enjoyed considerable popularity with such humorous Scottish novels as *The Monarch of the Glen* (1941) and *Whisky Galore* (1947), the latter suggested by the sinking of a whisky-laden cargo-boat near the isle of Eriskay. A six-volume novel, *The Four Winds of Love*, began in 1937 with *The East Wind*, continued with *The South Wind* (1937), *The West Wind* (1940), *West to North* (1940), and was completed with *The North Wind* (2 vols, 1944, 1945). His range of personal enthusiasms embraced recorded music and cats. As founder in 1923 and editor until 1961 of *The Gramophone*, he did much to develop the widespread interest and informed taste which created a large audience for classical records. He was President of the Siamese Cat Club and author of *Cat's Company* (1960). He planned a multi-volume autobiography, *My Life and Times*, of which *Octave One* and *Octave Two* were published in 1963, with further Octaves annually to 1970.

Mackenzie, Faith Compton (*née* Faith Stone; died 1960). Married Compton *Mackenzie in 1905. Author of *The Sibyl of the North* (1931), on Queen Christina of Sweden; *The Cardinal's Niece* (1935), *Napoleon at the Briars* (1943), and other books including the autobiographical *As Much as I Dare* (1938) and *More Than I Should* (1940).

McKerrow, R. B. (Ronald Brunlees McKerrow, 1872-1940). Educated at Harrow, London and Cambridge. Professor of English in Tokyo, 1897-1900; Lecturer in English Literature, King's College, London, 1914-19. Founded and edited (1925-40) *The Review of English Studies*; Secretary of the Bibliographical Society from 1912. Author of editions of Elizabethan writers, *An Introduction to Bibliography for Literary Students* (1927), *Prolegomena for the Oxford Shakespeare* (1939), a valuable prelude for an enterprise it had been hoped he would live to complete.

Mackintosh, Elizabeth. See Gordon *Daviot, and Josephine *Tey—pseudonyms used by Elizabeth Mackintosh.

Maclagan, Bridget. Pseudonym under which Mary *Borden published her first two novels: *Mistress of Kingdoms* (1912), *Collision* (1913).

Maclaren, Ian (pseudonym of John Watson,

1850-1907). Born in England (Manningtree, Essex) of Scottish parentage; educated at Stirling and Edinburgh. Entered the ministry and held pastorates in Perthshire, Glasgow, and Liverpool. His *Beside the Bonnie Brier Bush* (1894), a collection of stories of simple Scottish rural life, was a pioneer product of the *Kailyard School and had enormous success. His later works included *Kate Carnegie and Those Ministers* (1897) a volume of sketches of Glasgow life called *St Jude's* (1907), and some theological writings. He was for a brief period towards the end of his life Principal of Westminster College, Cambridge, which he had helped to found, and he also had a part in the foundation of Liverpool University.

Maclaren-Ross, Julian (1913-1964). Author of *Of Love and Hunger* (novel; 1947), *The Stuff to Give the Troops* (short stories; 1944), *The Weeping and the Laughter* (autobiography of childhood; 1953) and numerous articles in periodicals. *Memoirs of the Forties* (1965) includes his recollections of working alongside Dylan *Thomas in a London office.

McLaverty, Michael (1907-   ). Born in County Monaghan; educated in Belfast. Author of novels: *Call My Brother Back* (1939), *Lost Fields* (1941), *In This Thy Day* (1945), *The Three Brothers* (1948), *Truth in the Night* (1951), *School for Hope* (1954); and collections of short stories: *White Mare* (1943), *The Game Cock* (1949).

MacLeish, Archibald (1892-   ). Born in Illinois; educated in Connecticut and at Yale and Harvard; studied law, and after serving in World War I practised in Boston 1920-23. Then turned to literature, having published his first poems, *Tower of Ivory* in 1917. From 1923 he lived in France for five years, during that time writing *The Happy Marriage* (1924), *The Pot of Earth* (1925), *Nobodaddy* (a verse play, 1925), *Streets in the Moon* (1926) and *The Hamlet of A. MacLeish* (1928). Having returned to America, he was editor of *Fortune* (1929-38), Librarian of Congress (1939-44), and an Assistant Secretary of State (1944-45). Professor of Rhetoric and Oratory at Harvard 1949-62. His output of poetry and verse-drama has included, in addition to the above, *Conquistador* (1932), *Actfive and Other Poems* (1948); *Songs for Eve* (1954) was preceded by *Collected Poems* (1952); *J.B.* (verse play, 1958).

Macleod, Fiona (pseudonym of William Sharp, 1855-1905). Born in Paisley; educated at Glasgow University. His early life was spent mainly in the western highlands of Scotland, but after leaving the University he spent some time in Australia and the South Seas before settling in London from 1879, becoming familiar with D. G. Rossetti and his circle. He travelled widely in Europe, America and North Africa and published much verse and prose under his own name— e.g. *Earth's Voices* (1884), *Sospiri d'Italia* (1906); biographies of Rossetti, Shelley, Browning, and others; *Children of Tomorrow* (1890) and other novels; also anthologies of sonnets, etc. None of these has survived, and he is now remembered only by the pseudonym he steadfastly declined to acknowledge. The Fiona Macleod stories and plays are in the *Celtic twilight mode, in which Sharp was a leading practitioner: *Pharais: a Romance of the Isles* (1894), *The Mountain Lovers* (1895), *The Sin Eater* (1895), *The Immortal Hour* (1900).

McLuhan, Marshall (Herbert Marshall Mc-Luhan, 1911-   ). Born in Alberta, educated in Manitoba and at Cambridge; Director, Centre for Culture and Technology, Toronto, from 1963. Author of *Understanding Media* (1964), *The Medium is the Masssage* (sic) (1967), and other writings extolling electronic devices, especially television, as a cultural medium dismissive of books and reading. In *McLuhan and the Future of Literature* (English Association, 1969) Rebecca *West cogently questioned both the validity of his theories and his ability to communicate them intelligibly.

McManus, Seumas (1869-1960). Born in County Donegal; self-taught by reading and working on the mountain farms of his home district, becoming a schoolmaster there until he visited New York and sold there all the stories he had written. He repeated the expedition in subsequent years with equal encouragement. Among his books are: *The Leadin' Road to Donegal* 1896), *Well of the World's End* (1959).

MacMullan, Charles Walden Kirkpatrick. *See* C. K. *Munro.

Macnamara, Brinsley (pseudonym of John Weldon, 1875-1963). Born in Westmeath, Eire. Joined the *Irish Players at the *Abbey Theatre in Dublin, became one of its directors, and afterwards Registrar of the National Gallery of Ireland. He wrote novels (including *The Valley of the Squinting Windows*, 1918) and various plays for the Abbey Theatre, starting with *The Rebellion in Ballycullion* (1919).

MacNeice, Louis (1907-1963). Born in Belfast; educated in England at Marlborough and Oxford. Held academic posts at Birmingham and Bedford College, London, in the 1930s, and in that decade was regarded as one of the outstanding younger poets alongside W. H. *Auden and Stephen *Spender, whose leftish political views he shared at the time. During World War II and after he became an outstanding writer of broadcast plays for the B.B.C., making a deep impression with *The Dark Tower*, published with other radio scripts in 1940. He translated *The Agamemnon of Aeschylus* (1936) and Goethe's *Faust* in an abridged form (1951). Though his poetry probably has enduring qualities absent from the work of the more publicized poets of his generation it found a smaller and less vocal public, though his *Collected Poems* (1949) constitute, *The Times* said, 'a body of verse in which lyricism, wryness, sharp observation, sometimes even slapstick humour' are intermingled and presented with the 'delicate and fastidious craft . . . of a robust but equally fastidious mind'. In collaboration with Auden he wrote *Letters from Iceland* (1937), and independently a travel book of the Western Isles of Scotland, *I Crossed the Minch* (1938), a study of *The Poetry of W. B. Yeats* (1941), and a children's story *The Penny that Rolled Away* (1954). *The Strings Are False* (unfinished autobiography; published posthumously, 1965).

McNeile, Herman Cyril. *See* Sapper.

McCrae, Hugh. *See* *Australian Writers.

M'Taggart, J. M. (John M'Taggart Ellis M'Taggart, 1866-1925). Born in London; educated at Clifton and Cambridge. He developed the peculiar distinction of combining atheism with membership of the Church of England, and his belief in the immortality of the soul is set out in *Some Dogmas of Religion* (1906). A Lecturer in Philosophy at Cambridge from 1897 to 1923, he wrote *Studies in the Hegelian Dialectic* (1896), *Studies in Hegelian Cosmology* (1901), *A Commentary on Hegel's Logic* (1910), and *The Nature of Existence* (vol i, 1921, vols ii

and iii posthumously, 1927). As a philosopher he was unorthodox and as influential with those who dissented from his views as with those who agreed. It is said that 'his arguments for the unreality of time bewitched [Bertrand] *Russell and drove [G. E.] *Moore to philosophizing in protest'.

MacWhirr, Captain. In command of the *Nan-Shan* in Joseph Conrad's *Typhoon* (1903). His literal mind and dauntless temperament make him imperturbable in any crisis and his ship a 'floating abode of harmony and peace'.

Madariaga, Don Salvador De (1886-   ). Born in Corunna, Spain; educated in Madrid and Paris. First worked as a mining engineer, then spent several years as a journalist in London, and took a leading part in the League of Nations, later becoming Spanish ambassador in the United States and (1932-34) in France. Appointed Professor of Spanish Studies in the University of Oxford in 1928. His writings in English include: *The Genius of Spain* (1923), *Englishmen, Frenchmen, Spaniards* (1928), *I, Americans* (i.e. 'First Epistle to the Americans', 1930), *Don Quixote* (1934), *Christopher Columbus* (1939), *The Rise of the Spanish American Empire* (1947), *The Fall of the Spanish American Empire* (1947), *On Hamlet* (1948), *Essays with a Purpose* (1953), and a novel, *Heart of Jade* (1944).

Madge, Charles (Charles Henry Madge, 1912-   ). Born in South Africa; educated in England at Winchester and Cambridge. Reporter on the *Daily Mirror*, 1935-36; founded Mass-Observation 1937; undertook various sociological and industrial surveys. Professor of Sociology, University of Birmingham, from 1950. Author of *The Disappearing Castle* (1937), *The Father Found* (1941) and other collections of poems, as well as prose studies arising from his professional interests.

Madras House, The. Comedy in four acts by Granville *Barker performed in 1910; published in 1911. The weekly Sunday-morning after-church gathering of the Huxtable family in their house at Denmark Hill, consists of Henry Huxtable (surviving partner in the Peckham drapery firm of Roberts & Huxtable), his wife, and their six spinster daughters, differing from one another only as lead pencils do 'after some weeks' use; a matter of length, of sharpening, of wear': their ages range from thirty-nine to twenty-six. Visiting them on the present occasion are Philip Madras (son of Mr Huxtable's married but deserted sister Amelia) and his friend Major Hippisly Thomas, who inform Huxtable of a conference arranged to discuss a plan by an American to take over the Peckham firm and also the Madras House in Bond Street, of which Philip is the present head, his father Constantine Madras having long since retired to Arabia and become a Mohammedan. Miss Yates, first assistant in the costume department at Roberts & Huxtable, has been 'got hold of' by 'some West End Club feller' while on temporary transfer to the Madras House, and is pregnant. The housekeeper at Peckham, Miss Chancellor, who regards herself as guardian of the girl assistants' morals, reports that she has caught Miss Yates and Brigstock of the hosiery department kissing. Regarding this as an insinuation that Brigstock is responsible for the young woman's pregnancy, his wife threatens an action for slander. Miss Yates, interviewed by Philip, declines to name the father of her coming child and accepts all responsibility. At the Madras House conference, the manager puts on a mannequin parade to impress the American purchaser, Eustace Perrin State. Constantine Madras, who is present, expresses his horror at scantily dressed girls being thus exhibited, and says he found himself obliged to leave England, 'where women are . . . encouraged to flaunt their charms on the very streets'. As a Mohammedan he advocates the seclusion of women and polygamy, and he turns out to have been Miss Yates's lover. Philip has been asked by Hippisly Thomas to warn Jessica his wife against flirting. He does so and also reproves her privileged way of life: 'I want an art and a culture that shan't be just a veneer on savagery . . . but it must spring in good time from the happiness of a whole people.'

Maeterlinck, Maurice (Maurice Polydore Marie Bernard Maeterlinck, 1862-1949). Born at Ghent; educated at a Jesuit school and at the University of Ghent where he studied law and practised for a while, before he was drawn into the circle of the *Symbolists during a short stay in Paris. From 1889 he published poems and verse plays, his first enduring success being *Pelleas and Melisande* (1892), upon which Debussy's opera was based in 1902. For two or three decades thereafter Maeterlinck became a world figure with plays and such prose works as *The Treasure of the Humble* (essays, 1897) and *The Life of the Bee* (1901). His theatre reputation reached its height with *The Blue Bird* (1909) which enchanted children by the fairylike story of Tytyl and Mytyl and impressed adults by its mystical element. *Monna Vanna* (1902) stirred some excitement and moral disfavour by a scene in which the heroine was to be imagined as naked under her cloak, and some short plays including *The Death of Tintageles* (1899) were in vogue in England and elsewhere in the early years of this century. The laudation of Maeterlinck as 'the Belgian Shakespeare' did not survive World War I, though it is questionable whether the subsequent neglect of his writings has been more perceptive than the former extravagant praise.

Magee, William Kirkpatrick. *See* John *Eglinton.

Maggie Verver. *See* Verver.

Maggie Wylie. Marries John Shand, M.P. in J. M. Barrie's *What Every Woman Knows* (1908).

Magnus, King. Chief character in *The *Apple Cart* (1929) by Bernard Shaw. Faced by his Cabinet with an ultimatum which, if accepted, would make him 'a dumb king' forbidden to express publicly or to inspire any public expression of his views on political affairs, he threatens to abdicate and then to stand as a parliamentary candidate for Windsor. Knowing that he would be certain of election and thus become the dominant member in Parliament, the Cabinet withdraws the ultimatum.

Mahon, Christy. Treated as a hero in J. M. Synge's *The *Playboy of the Western World* (1907) until his story of having killed his father is disproved by Old Mahon's arrival.

Mahony, Richard. Dr Richard Townshend Mahony, and his wife **Mary** (*née* Turnbull), central characters in Henry Handel Richardson's trilogy *The *Fortunes of Richard Mahony* (1930).

Mailer, Norman (1923-   ). Born in New Jersey; educated in Brooklyn and at Harvard. Served with the American forces in the Pacific during World War II, his first novel *The Naked and the Dead* (1948) being an outcome of that experience.

Mainly on the Air. Broadcasts and other pieces by Max *Beerbohm, published in 1946 and containing six radio talks ('London Revisited', 'Speed', 'A Small Boy Seeing Giants', 'Music Halls of My Youth', 'Advertisements', 'Playgoing'). The other previously uncollected material is 'From Bloomsbury to Bayswater', 'Old Carthusian Memories', 'The Top Hat', 'Fenestralia'.

Mair, G. H. (George Henry Mair, 1887-1926). Educated at Aberdeen and Oxford. On the *Manchester Guardian* editorial staff, 1909-14; worked in various government departments during World War I; Assistant Director, League of Nations Secretariat, from 1919. Author of an edition of Wilson's *Arte of Rhetorique* (1908), *English Literature: Modern* (1911 and many later editions).

Mais, Roger (1905-55). Born in Jamaica. Author of *The Hills Were Joyful Together* (1953), *Brother Man* (1954), *Black Lightning* (1955); reissued as *The Three Novels of Roger Mais* (1966).

Mais, S. P. B. (Stuart Peter Brodie Mais, 1885-). Born in Matlock; educated at Halifax and Oxford. Taught in public schools, 1909-20, and again in World War II; literary critic for London morning and evening newspapers, 1918-26; leader writer on *Daily Telegraph*, 1926-31. His scores of books are mainly on the teaching and use of the English language, on literature, and on travel.

Major Barbara. Play in three acts (four scenes) by Bernard *Shaw written and performed in 1905; published in 1907. Lady Britomart Undershaft surprises her twenty-four-year old son Stephen and her daughters Barbara and Sarah by announcing that she has asked their father Andrew Undershaft to come that evening. She separated from him when the children were very young, because he refused to make Stephen heir to the fabulously wealthy armaments business of Undershaft and Lazarus, of which Andrew is the head. He will not break the centuries-old tradition that the firm must always pass to a foundling. Under a settlement made at the time of the separation the family have ample means, but Lady Britomart wants more as marriage portions for the girls. When Andrew comes he mistakes for his son, in turn, Charles Lomax, engaged to Sarah, and Adolphus Cusins, engaged to the other daughter, introduced to her father as 'Major Barbara Undershaft, of the Salva-

tion Army'. Andrew says he is interested in the Salvation Army, and that its motto 'Blood and Fire' might be his own. He and Barbara make the bargain that he will visit her 'Salvation Shelter' and that she will go the day after to his cannon works. In the yard of the shelter at West Ham, Snobby Price and Rummy Mitchens, pretending converts, are finishing a meal of bread and margarine and syrup and diluted milk and are joined by a hungry elderly-looking man, Peter Shirley, a fitter, thrown out of work as too old, though only forty-six. Bill Walker, a cockney bully, comes in looking for his 'girl', Mog Habbijam, who has been converted. He assaults Jenny Hill, a young Salvationist, and old Rummy Mitchens, but is subdued by Barbara, who troubles his conscience. Having been sent to Canning Town to find Mog, he returns indignant but cowed after being thrashed and prayed over by her new chap. Meanwhile Undershaft and Cusins have arrived while Barbara has been at an open-air meeting. She returns, excited at having collected 4s 10d. Mrs Baines, a Commissioner, comes in and announces that Lord Saxmundham (formerly Bodger), whisky distiller, has offered a donation of £5000 if £5000 more can be raised. Undershaft gives this. Though Mrs Baines justifies acceptance of the money, Barbara is heartbroken by the thought that they have sold themselves to 'Drunkenness and Murder'. Bill Walker gloats because £1 from him was refused but not the rich men's money. Barbara takes off her S.A. badge. Next day Lady Britomart fails again to induce Andrew to make Stephen his successor, but when the family and the suitors visit the armaments works it is discovered that Adolphus Cusins is technically a foundling, for his parents' marriage in Australia was not legal in England. He agrees to change his name and become the next Andrew Undershaft. Barbara approves his decision, convinced that among those employed by Undershaft and Lazarus 'is where salvation is really wanted'.

Major, Charles (1856-1913). Born in Indiana and educated there; studied and practised law. Author of historical novels, of which *When Knighthood Was in Flower* (1898) and *Dorothy Vernon of Haddon Hall* (1903) were the most celebrated.

Malahide Castle. James Boswell, Samuel Johnson's biographer, left his unpublished manuscripts and other papers to his executors. They were long thought to have been destroyed, but in 1925 a cache was discovered at Malahide Castle, near Dublin, where the papers had been taken by a Boswell descendant. More of his manuscripts were unearthed there in 1930, 1937, and 1940. See *Fettercairn House for a note on their disposal.

Malapropism. A confusion of words comically characteristic of Mrs Malaprop in Richard Brinsley Sheridan's The Rivals (1775): e.g. 'progeny of learning' (prodigy), 'contagious countries' (contiguous), 'mistress of orthodoxy' (orthography). Any similar locutions by others.

Malet, Lucas (pseudonym of Mary St Léger Kingsley, Mrs W. Harrison, 1852-1931). Born at Eversley, Hampshire, daughter of Charles Kingsley the Victorian novelist and Protestant clergyman. Before she became a Roman Catholic in 1897 she had published novels which won considerable popularity but were subsequently trimmed to accord with her changed faith: Colonel Enderby's Wife (1885), The Wages of Sin (3 vols, 1890, 1892, 1894). Later novels included The Gateless Barrier (1900), Sir Richard Calmady (1901), The Far Horizon (1906), The Survivors (1923).

Malin, Peter. See Reardon *Conner.

Malinowski, Bronislaw (Bronislaw Kasper Malinowski, 1884-1942). Born in Poland; educated at Cracow University. Joined anthropological expeditions to New Guinea, Melanesia, Australia and elsewhere. Professor of Anthropology, University of London, from 1927. Author of important pioneer works in the study of primitive communities: The Family Among the Australian Aborigines (1913), Argonauts of the Western Pacific (1922), Crime and Custom in Savage Society (1926), The Father in Primitive Psychology (1927), The Sexual Life of Savages in North West Melanesia (1929).

Malleson, Lucy. See Anthony *Gilbert and Anne *Meredith.

Mallock, W. H. (William Hurrell Mallock, 1849-1923). Born in Devon; educated privately and at Oxford. Having no need to adopt a profession, he travelled widely, wrote on religion, philosophy, sociology, 'classes and masses', politics, economics—his stated aim being 'to expose the fallacies of Radicalism and Socialism'. His only surviving work is

The New Republic (1877), a Utopian satire in which certain of his contemporaries appear under fictional names, e.g. Ruskin as Mr Herbert.

Malone, Louis. Pseudonym used for certain early writings by Louis *MacNeice; derived from Malone Road, Belfast, where he was born.

Malraux, André (1901-   ). Born in Paris; educated there; studied archaeology and oriental languages. Visited Indo-China, but abandoned his archaeological work there for political activities in south-east Asia, in China, and later in Europe. While serving with the French army in World War II he was wounded and taken prisoner but escaped to America and then joined the Resistance. Held various government appointments in France after the war and became Minister of State for Cultural Affairs in 1960. Author of Les Conquérants (1926-27; Eng. trans. The Conquerors 1929), La Condition Humaine (1933; Eng. trans. Man's Fate, 1934), Psychologie de l'art (1950; Eng. trans. The Psychology of Art, 1949-51), La Métamorphose des Dieux (1957; Eng. trans. The Metamorphosis of the Gods, 1960).

Maltby, H. F. (Henry Francis Maltby, 1880-1963). Born in South Africa; educated in England at Bedford School. He started as an actor in 1899, appearing in many stage plays and subsequently in films for which he also wrote scenarios. A prolific playwright, his chief successes were with The Rotters (1915), and A Temporary Gentleman (1919). His memoirs appeared as Ring Up the Curtain (1950) and Curtain Up (1952).

Man and Superman: A Comedy and a Philosophy. Play in four acts by Bernard *Shaw performed (without the removable third act) in 1905; first complete performance (in Edinburgh) 1915; published in 1903 with an 'Epistle Dedicatory' to A. B. *Walkley and, at the end, 'The Revolutionist's Handbook' and 'Maxims for Revolutionists' credited to John Tanner, the leading character in the play.

Roebuck Ramsden, a model of respectability in his early sixties, opens the play in his study in Portland Place, where he is visited by Octavius Robinson and by John Tanner who bursts in to announce that he and Ramsden have been appointed joint Guardians of Ann Whitefield under the will of her recently dead father. Ramsden declares that he will not act with Tanner, whose opinions he abhors; while Tanner says he will not act at all as guardian to Ann, whom he considers an unscrupulously self-willed young woman, getting her own way by pleading that she is 'only an orphan'. Octavius, on the other hand, sees her with love-bemused eyes as a paragon. When Ann enters she turns on the whole battery of feminine wiles and wheedles Ramsden and Tanner into acceptance of the joint guardianship. Dismay is felt by the conventionally respectable persons present when it is learned that Octavius's sister Violet is pregnant, but their immediate assumption that the child is illegitimate is baseless, for Violet is secretly married to Hector Malone, son of a wealthy American who had other plans for Hector. When Octavius proposes to Ann, she refers him to Tanner as her guardian, but he, warned by his chauffeur, 'Enry Straker, that Ann has marked down Tanner himself as the husband she is after, goes off at once on a continental tour, leaving behind the party (Ann, Violet, Hector, Octavius and Ramsden) he was to have accompanied. In the Sierra Nevada, while listening to poetry recited by a love-lorn brigand, Tanner falls asleep and has the dream which becomes the usually omitted but important scene known as *Don Juan in Hell,* constituting a one-act play effective for separate performance (first so performed in 1907). After Tanner wakes he is rejoined by the rest of the original party and they go on to Granada, where Hector's father at length condones Violet's marriage to his son. Ann refuses Octavius's proposal, alleging that her mother is determined that she shall marry Tanner. Mrs Whitefield dismisses this allegation as being only Ann's way of intimating her own wish to marry Tanner. Finally, left alone with Ann, Tanner feels drawn irresistibly to her against his will: 'We do the world's will not our own. . . . The Life Force. I am in the grip of the Life Force' he cries and, as the others return, Ann exclaims 'I have promised to marry Jack' and faints in his arms.

Man Who Died, The. Story (issued separately as a short novel) by D. H. *Lawrence published in 1931. Originally called *The Escaped Cock,* the changed title was approved by the author before his death in 1930, after part of the story had appeared in an American magazine. H. T. Moore (in *The Intelligent Heart,* 1955) traces the first title

to 'a little white rooster coming out of the egg' seen by Lawrence in a toyshop window. In the finished story 'The Man' rises from his tomb and lives for a while with peasants near Jerusalem who own the cock, before making his way to Lebanon. There, in the temple of Isis, the priestess designates him as Osiris and heals the wounds in his hands and feet and sides, taking death out of him. Her body becomes to him 'the soft white rock of life . . . "On this rock I built my life. . . . I am risen!" ' The priestess conceives by him and wishes to keep him with her in a house she will build by the temple, but he departs, saying 'I shall come again, sure as Spring', and to himself: 'I have sowed the seed of my life and my resurrection.'

Manchester School. Collective title of the group of playwrights who wrote for Miss *Horniman's Company at the Gaiety Theatre, Manchester, between 1907 and 1921, chiefly Stanley *Houghton and Harold *Brighouse.

Mancroft, Lord (Arthur Michael Samuel, 1872-1942; 1st Viscount Mancroft, 1937). Born at Norwich; educated at the Grammar School there. Conservative M.P. for Farnham, Surrey (1918-37) and held various ministerial offices. Author of *A Life of Giovanni Battista Piranesi* (1910), *The Herring: Its Effect on the History of Britain* (1915), *The Mancroft Essays* (1923; enlarged edn 1937).

Mandalay. One of the *Barrack Room Ballads* by Rudyard *Kipling, made additionally familiar by musical settings to which it was frequently sung by baritones at concerts.

Mander, Jane (Mary Jane Mander, 1877-1949). Born in Auckland, New Zealand. Worked as a teacher and journalist. Wrote novels including *The Story of a New Zealand River* (1920), *The Passionate Puritan* (1922), *The Strange Attraction* (1923), *Allan Adair* (1925), *The Besieging City* (1926), *Pins and Pinnacles* (1928). See New Zealand Writers.

Manichaeism. A doctrine derived from ancient pagan nature-worship and codified by Mani, a third-century A.D. Persian prophet. He taught that daylight and darkness symbolize the spiritual conflict between good and evil which dominates the whole universe. As a religion Manichaeism spread widely in the Roman Empire and the East, imposing asceticism on its adherents. It was regarded as heretical by the Christian Church, and as an organized faith came to an end about A.D. 500, though certain Manichaean tenets have continued to attract individual non-Christians down to the present time.

Manifold, John (1915-). Born in Australia; educated at Geelong and in England at Cambridge. Author of music criticism in English and Australian periodicals and of *Death of Ned Kelly and Other Ballads* (1941); *Selected Verse* (1946); and in prose, *The Amorous Flute: An Unprofessional Handbook for Recorder Players* (1948).

Mankowitz, Wolf (1924-). Educated in East Ham and at Cambridge. Author of *A Kid for Two Farthings* (1953), *The Biggest Pig in Barbados* (1965), and other novels; *The Mendelman Fire* (short stories; 1957); *The Bespoke Overcoat* (plays; 1955) and several musical plays; works on ceramics, *Wedgwood* (1953), *The Portland Vase* (1953), *An Encyclopedia of English Pottery and Porcelain* (1957); numerous films, 1954 onward.

Mann, Erika (1905-). Born in Munich, daughter of Thomas Mann; studied for the stage in Berlin and elsewhere. Married W. H. *Auden, 1935. Author of *School for Barbarians* (1938), *The Lights Go Down* (1940), *Gang of Ten* (1942).

Mann, Heinrich (1871-1950). Born in Lübeck, brother of Thomas Mann; educated in Berlin. Author of novels including *Professor Unrat* (1904) from which *The Blue Angel* (1932), the film made famous by Marlene Dietrich's performance, was adapted.

Mann, Klaus (1906-1949). Born in Munich, son of Thomas Mann; educated there. Settled in America in 1936 and became a naturalized citizen in 1943. Author of novels including *Pathetic Symphony* (1938), based on the life of Tchaikovsky; plays, and an autobiography *The Turning Point* (1942).

Mann, Mary E. (*née* Mary E. Rackham, died 1929; Mrs Fairman Mann). Born at Norwich. Author of *A Lost Estate* (1889), *The Pattern Experiment* (1899), *The Mating of a Dove* (1901), *Olivia's Summer* (1902), *The Eglamore Portraits* (1906), *Astray in Arcady* (1910), and other novels.

Mann, Thomas (1875-1955). Born in Lübeck; had only irregular periods of formal education. Spent some time with his brother in Rome, and before returning to Germany in 1898 he had written most of *Buddenbrooks* (published in 1901; Eng. trans. 1924), a novel tracing a family resembling his own. Though its success was not immediate, it has become accepted as one of the several masterpieces written by the author, who is ranked as the greatest German novelist of the century. *The Magic Mountain* (1924; trans. 1927) and *Dr Faustus* (1947; trans. 1948) are his other novels, with *Death in Venice* (1913; trans. 1916) as a masterly shorter story.

Manners, Lady Diana. *See* Lady Diana *Cooper.

Manners, John Hartley (1870-1928). Born in London; educated privately. Became an actor; settled in America; married Laurette Taylor, a celebrated film actress; wrote numerous plays, among which *Peg O' My Heart* (1912) was outstanding with a first run of over 600 performances in New York and over 700 in London in 1914-16.

Mannin, Ethel (Ethel Edith Mannin, 1900-). Born in London of Irish ancestry; educated at Council school which she left in her early teens to work in advertising, an experience which led to *Sounding Brass* (1925), her satirical third novel. Other novels: *Green Willow* (1928), *Rose and Sylvie* (1938), *The Dark Forest* (1946), *Late Have I Loved Thee* (1948), *Pity the Innocent* (1957); also short stories, travel books, children's books, works on education; autobiography: *Confessions and Impressions* (1930), *Privileged Spectator* (1939), *Stories from My Life* (1973).

Manning, Adelaide Frances Oke. *See* Manning *Coles.

Manning, Frederic (1887-1935). Born in Sydney, son of Sir William Manning, mayor of that city; educated there until he migrated to England in 1902. Wrote book reviews for *The Spectator*; published books of verse, *The Vigil of Brunhild* (1907), *Poems* (1910), and a volume of essays *Scenes and Portraits* (1909). In spite of indifferent health he joined the army and served in France in World War I. His novel *Her Privates We* (1930), published under the pseudonym Private 19022, is one of the classics of the war, which it aimed to present from the point of view of the lower ranks. Though T. E. *Lawrence is said to have recognized Manning's style, it was not until after his death that the author's identity was openly revealed. In addition to the edition for general sale an unexpurgated version was printed for private circulation, *The Middle Parts of Fortune*, the titles for both editions being taken from *Hamlet*, and with the Shakespearean ambiguity.

Mannon family. In Eugene O'Neill's **Mourning Becomes Electra* (1931): **Ezra Mannon**, murdered by his wife **Christine** with poison obtained from her lover, Adam Brant; **Lavinia**, daughter of Ezra and Christine; **Orin**, Lavinia's brother, who shoots Brant, an act leading to his mother's suicide and subsequently to his own.

Mansfield, Katherine (pseudonym of Kathleen Mansfield Beauchamp, 1888-1923). Born in Wellington, New Zealand, daughter of (Sir) Harold Beauchamp, wealthy merchant and banker; cousin of **Elizabeth (Countess von Arnim); educated at schools in Wellington and (1903-06) in London at Queen's College, Harley Street; married (1) G. C. Bowden, (2) J. M. *Murry. After leaving London for home she read widely, fell under the influence of the introspective *Journal* of Marie Bashkirtseff (1860-84), and wrote in prose and verse, having several 'Vignettes' published (1907) in the *Native Companion*, an Australian monthly. She returned to London in 1908 on a small yearly allowance from her father, supplemented by contributions from Ida Baker (who appears in Katherine's *Letters* and *Journal* as L.M., 'Lesley Moore', and sometimes as 'Jones', fictional names conferred by Katherine). Though frequently much stormed against, Ida remained a generous and wholly devoted friend from Queen's College days onward to the time of Katherine's death. 'To see what it felt like, for a book she was writing' (she explained), Katherine married George Charles Bowden in March 1909 and left him next morning. She moved to Liverpool and was briefly in the chorus of a light opera company there. Next in Bavaria, she was desolated by losing, through miscarriage, a baby whose father was not her husband, whom she rejoined temporarily in London. At his suggestion she submitted stories to A. R. *Orage, editor of the *New Age*, who accepted them and asked for more. Her connection with that paper began what was to be an illustrious career as a short story writer of international repute who became also, with later stories, the virtual founder of a distinctive New Zealand literature. Though the impressionistic style of her stories led to her being

customarily regarded as a follower of **Tchekhov, signs are not wanting in her apprentice work that she might have developed independently on similar lines. In 1911 an abortion terminated her pregnancy by an undisclosed man, just before her parents arrived for the coronation of George V. Her first book of stories, *In a German Pension*, published that year brought critical praise. Having been shabbily treated by the *New Age*, she turned to **Rhythm*, a new quarterly of literature and art founded and edited by John Middleton *Murry and Michael *Sadleir. A first meeting with Murry at the end of 1911 was crucial both for her work and in personal relations. *Rhythm* printed a story and two poems by her in the spring of 1912 and from April she and Murry were sharing a flat, frugally and at first platonically. While she was becoming a celebrated writer her health was declining and a long series of moves from place to place began. In December 1913 she and Murry went to live in Paris, where Francis *Carco, already well known to Murry, befriended them and undertook to give French language lessons to Katherine. She continued to write, contributing stories again to the *New Age*, to the **English Review*, and reviewing for the *Athenaeum* when Murry became its editor. Their circle of literary friends included D. H. *Lawrence and his wife, from whom they were intermittently estranged, however, by Lawrence's rages. The death of Katherine's much loved young and only brother in France in World War I was a grievous blow, though also the source of inspiration for the best of her stories. The memory of their times together in their native country and the places they explored there, convinced her that she had a debt of love to pay 'to make our undiscovered country leap into the eyes of the Old World'. The first fruit of this resolve was **Prelude*, the story published singly in book form in 1918 and usually considered her finest achievement. In that year, after her divorce, she and Murry married. Also published separately, in 1920, *Je ne parle pas français* took as its title the phrase she had used on being introduced to Francis Carco in Paris in 1913. The publication of *Bliss and Other Stories* (1921) and *The Garden Party and Other Stories* (1922) made her fame secure. Her increasing illness, from pulmonary tuberculosis, was for a while relieved by a stay in Menton, 1920-21, but she at length

M

abandoned hope of a cure there and after further wanderings entered the *Gurdjieff Institute at Fontainebleau in October 1922 and died there in January 1923. Published posthumously: *The Dove's Nest and Other Stories* (1923), *Something Childish and Other Stories* (1924); *Collected Stories* (1945). *Novels and Novelists* (1930; reviews); *Journal* (1927, 1954), *Letters* (1928, 1951), *Scrapbook* (1939).

Manton, Peter. See John *Creasey.

Manuscripts, Preparation of. See Advice for *Authors.

March, William (pseudonym of William Edward March Campbell, 1893-1954). Born in Alabama; studied law at the University there. After serving in World War I he became for the rest of his life one of the heads of a leading steamship company. Author of *Company K* (1933), *The Looking Glass* (1943), and other novels, including *The Bad Seed* (1954), a story of a young girl murderess which is characteristic of his mastery of horror.

Margaret Seddon. Marries Richard Remington in H. G. Wells's *The *New Machiavelli* (1911).

Marinetti, Filippo Tommaso (1876-1944). Born in Egypt; educated in France and Italy; settled in Milan, where he became the leader of the Futurist movement, which was antagonistic to traditional values and ideas and derided it as 'past-ism'. He also exercised a strong influence upon the young intellectuals of Paris, where he published his manifesto of *Futurism in *Figaro* in 1909. He and his followers were advocates of violence, both physical and in ideas and imagination; they affected to despise virtue, beauty, and compassion, idolized machinery and all the paraphernalia of modern industry, and preached a debased philosophy degrading women and gnawing at the foundations of Christianity. In politics their trend was towards Fascism and in literature and art they had as offspring such 'anti-art' groups as the Dadaists and Surrealists. In England the Vorticists and P. Wyndham *Lewis's shortlived periodical *Blast* owed something to Marinetti.

Maritain, Jacques (1882-1973). Born and educated in Paris. He joined the Roman Catholic Church in 1906 and became subsequently the leading contemporary advocate of the theological philosophy of Thomas Aquinas, opposing Luther, Descartes, Pascal, Rousseau, and all political -isms which do not conform to Roman Catholic principles. Among his works translated into English are: *Three Reformers* (1928), on Luther, Descartes, and Rousseau; *Art and Scholasticism* (1930), *The Angelic Doctor* (i.e. Aquinas; 1931), *Freedom in the Modern World* (1935), *Scholasticism and Politics* (1940), *Science and Wisdom* (1940), *Religion in the Modern World* (1941), *Art and Poetry* (1943), *Man and the State* (1949).

Marjoram, J. See R. H. *Mottram.

Markham, Edwin (Edwin Charles Markham, 1852-1940). Born in Oregon; became a school teacher in California. 'The Man with the Hoe' (published with other verses in a volume with that title, 1899), which became one of America's most popular poems, was suggested by Jean François Millet's painting of a work-bowed field labourer. *Lincoln and Other Poems* (1901) was the only one of his later books to achieve popularity.

Markievicz, Countess (*née* Constance Georgine Gore-Booth, 1868-1927; married Count Casimir de Markievicz of Poland, 1900). She became an impassioned supporter of the Irish Nationalist movement, and as an active member of the Irish Volunteers in the Easter Rising of 1916 was sentenced to death. The sentence was commuted to imprisonment for life, but after hunger-striking almost to death she was released in 1917 and was afterwards elected to Parliament as a Sinn Fein member, thus becoming the first woman M.P. qualified to sit at Westminster, though, in conformity with Sinn Fein policy, she did not take her seat. *See also* Eva *Gore-Booth.

Marlow, Charles. Character who acts as narrator and interlocutor in stories and novels by Joseph *Conrad. He first appeared in *Youth* (1902). In the Author's Note of 1917 to that story in the collected edition of his works (vol. 5), Conrad wrote of Marlow's origin, disclaiming that he was the product of a meditated plan. 'He haunts my hours of solitude, when, in silence, we lay our heads together . . . but as we part at the end of a tale I am never sure that it may not be for the last time. . . . Of all my people he's the one that has never been a vexation to my spirit. A most discreet, understanding man. . . .'

Marlow, Louis. See Louis *Wilkinson.

Marlowe, Philip. Detective in crime novels by Raymond *Chandler.

Marquand, J. P. (John Phillips Marquand, 1893-1960). Born in Delaware; educated in Massachusetts and at Harvard. Worked as a journalist in Boston and New York, contributed many stories to large-circulation magazines, and became widely known as the creator of the Japanese detective in *Thank You, Mr Moto* (1936), *Think Fast, Mr Moto* (1937), *Mr Moto is So Sorry* (1938). With *The Late George Apley* (1937) he established a high reputation in sophisticated literary circles, this satire on Boston society being followed by other novels in a similar setting: *H. M. Pulham, Esquire* (1941), *Point of No Return* (1949) and others.

Marquis, Don (Donald Robert Perry Marquis, 1878-1937). Born in Illinois; educated at Knox College and studied art with little success. Became an actor, then a popular journalist in New York. He wrote some serious poems and plays, but became famous only as a comic writer with such specifically American humour as *The Old Soak's History of the World* (1924). Two of his books have, however, survived the Atlantic passage with no loss of hilarious appeal: *archy and mehitabel* (1927) and *archys life of mehitabel* (1933), without capital letters because Archy the cockroach, who taps out the narratives concerning himself and Mehitabel the alley cat by jumping on the keys, cannot work the shift key.

Marric, J. J. Pseudonym under which John *Creasey wrote several novels dealing with Scotland Yard's operations against criminals: *Gideon's Day* (1955) and others, introducing Superintendent (afterwards Commander) Gideon's name in the titles.

Marriott, Charles (1869-1957). Born in Bristol; educated privately and at South Kensington. Trained and worked as a photographer and dispenser, before turning novelist and becoming art critic on *The Times*, 1924-40, and Lecturer in Art at the University of Liverpool, 1938-39. Author of *The Column* (1901), *The House on the Sands* (1903), *The Intruding Angel* (1909), *The Unpetitioned Heavens* (1914), *An Order to View* (1922), and other novels; *Modern Art* (1917), *Augustus John* (1918), *Modern English Architecture* (1924).

Marriott Watson. See H. B. Marriott *Watson.

Marsh, Sir Edward (Edward Howard Marsh, 1872-1953; knighted 1937). Born in Cambridge, the son of the Master of Downing College; educated at Westminster and Cambridge. Entered the Civil Service and was for many years Private Secretary to Winston Churchill. He had many friends among writers and artists and edited the famous anthologies of *Georgian Poetry published from 1912 to 1922. Among the young poets he encouraged was Rupert *Brooke, writing a *Memoir* of him as a preface to the *Collected Poems* (1918). He translated into English verse the *Fables of La Fontaine* (1931), the *Odes of Horace* (1941), and made prose translations of other works. He was valued by Winston Churchill, Somerset Maugham and others as a vigilant watchdog over their proofs and prose; while as a Trustee of the Tate Gallery and Chairman of the Contemporary Art Society for many years, and as a collector of pictures, he did much to encourage living painters. *A Number of People* (1939), his autobiography, serves as an informative and entertaining footnote to the history of his time.

Marsh, Dame Ngaio (Ngaio Edith Marsh, 1899-   ; D.B.E. 1966). Born at Christchurch, New Zealand; educated in that country at St Margaret's College and at the School of Art in Christchurch, and was an actress for two years before coming to England in 1928 as partner in an interior decorating business. From 1934 she was one of the outstanding writers of detective novels, enjoying no less praise from the critics than popularity with the general public. Her Roderick Alleyn is an upper-crust Scotland Yard detective; Sergeant Fox his assistant and butt is a shrewd stooge; and Agatha Troy, an artist who becomes Alleyn's wife, is knowledgeably drawn. Ngaio Marsh, sometime a play-producer and drama lecturer in New Zealand, has placed some of her most effective crime novels in theatre settings: *Enter a Murderer* (1935), *Final Curtain* (1947), *Opening Night* (1951). Other titles: *Vintage Murder* (1937), *Colour Scheme* (1943), *Died in the Wool* (1945), *Scales of Justice* (1954), *Death at the Dolphin* (1967), *Black as He's Painted* (1974).

Marshall, Archibald (1866-1934). Born in London; educated at Highgate and Cambridge. Visited Australia and U.S., abandoned an intention to become a Church of England clergyman, and settled to journalism.

A comic first novel *Peter Burney: Undergraduate* (1899), was followed by *Exton Manor* (1907), and in 1909 by *The Squire's Daughter*, the first of a series dealing with a landed family, the Clintons. He wrote many other novels, also collections of short stories, and in his last years was best known as the author of humorous pages in *Punch: Simple Stories* (1927), *Simple Stories from Punch* (1930). Autobiography: *Out and About* (1933).

Marshall, Bruce (Claude Cunningham Bruce Marshall, 1899-   ). Born in Edinburgh; educated there, and at Glenalmond and St Andrew's. Wounded and taken prisoner in World War I. An accountant by profession. Author of *Father Malachy's Miracle* (1931), *Yellow Tapers for Paris* (1943), *All Glorious Within* (1944), *The Bank Audit* (1958), *Father Hilary's Holiday* (1965), and other novels.

Marshall, Christabel. See Christopher Marie *St John.

Martens, Paul. See Neil *Bell.

Martin, Kingsley (Basil Kingsley Martin, 1897-1969). Educated at Mill Hill and Cambridge. Lecturer at the London School of Economics, 1923-27; on the *Manchester Guardian*, 1927-31. Editor of the *New Statesman*, 1931-60. Author of *The Triumph of Palmerston* (1924), *The British Public and the General Strike* (1927), *The Press the Public Wants* (1947), *Harold Laski: A Memoir* (1953). Autobiographies: *Father Figures* (1966), *Editor* (1968).

Martin, Richard. See John *Creasey.

Martin, Stella. Pseudonym used by Georgette *Heyer for *The Transformation of Philip Jettan* (1923).

Martin, Violet Florence. See Martin *Ross.

Martínez Sierra, Gregorio (1881-1947). Born in Madrid. Worked as an actor, journalist, and novelist, but best known as a dramatist. Through translations, mainly by Granville Barker and his wife Helen, several of his plays became very popular in England: *The Cradle Song* (1911; Eng. trans. 1917), *The Kingdom of God* (1915; 1923), *The Romantic Young Lady* (1918; 1923), *A Hundred Years Old. Collected Plays* (in Eng., 2 vols, 1923).

Martindale, Rev. C. C. (Cyril Charlie Martindale, 1879-1963). Born in India; educated at Harrow; joined the Roman Catholic Church and the Society of Jesus and continued his education at Oxford where he had an exceptionally distinguished career as a classical scholar. He wrote prolifically and with extraordinary variety in the service of his religion, producing, notably, biographies of R. H. *Benson and Bernard Vaughan (brother of the Cardinal).

Martyn, Edward (1859-1924). Born in Galway; educated at Catholic schools in Dublin and Windsor, and at Oxford University, but claimed to be 'chiefly self-educated'. Started the Palestrina Choir of male singers in Dublin, and attempted to reorganize liturgical music, church architecture and stained glass. He was one of the founders, with W. B. *Yeats and others, of the Irish Dramatic Movement in 1899 and of the Irish Theatre in Dublin. His plays *The Heather Field* (1899) and *Maeve* (1899) were among the first produced by the *Irish Players. He is a prominent character in his friend George Moore's *Hail and Farewell* (1911-14), where he is portrayed with affectionate humour which failed to amuse him.

Martyr, Weston (Joseph Weston Martyr, 1885-1966). Born in Southampton; when fifteen went to sea. After turning to goldmining in South Africa, engaging in merchant, steamship, trading and banking business, acting as a consul, pioneering ocean yacht racing, etc., he devoted himself to writing. *The Southseaman* (1923), his most notable book was followed by *The £200 Millionaire* (1931), *A General Cargo* (1935), *Paradise Enow* (1936), and his autobiography *The Wandering Years* (1939).

Marvin, F. S. (Francis Sydney Marvin, 1863-1943). Born in London; educated at Merchant Taylors' School and Oxford. Became an Inspector of Schools, 1890-1924. Author of *The Living Past* (1913), *The Century of Hope* (1919), *The Modern World* (1929), *The Nation at School* (1933).

Marx, Karl (1818-1883). Born at Trier; educated in Bonn and Berlin. Lived in Paris from 1843 until he was expelled two years later; then settled in Brussels where, with Friedrich Engels, he wrote and published the *Communist Manifesto* (1848) which led to Marx's expulsion from Belgium. He lived in London from 1849 with his family, and spent a great deal of his time in the British Museum Reading Room, studying economics and the capitalist system, which he set about to destroy by means of his monumental work *Das Kapital* (vol. i, 1867). This was unfinished when he died, the last two volumes being edited by Engels and published in 1885 and 1895. The world-changing influence of Marx's theories in the present century is common knowledge, though history has still to justify his assertion that under Communism the State would wither away.

Mary Poppins. See P. L. *Travers.

Maschwitz, Eric (1901-69). Born in Birmingham; educated at Repton and Cambridge. After a short period as a publishers' magazine editor he joined the B.B.C. and was editor of *Radio Times* for six years from 1927. Thereafter, except for war service 1940-45, he was mainly engaged in writing musical plays—*Balalaika* (1936), *Carissima* (1948), *Belinda Fair* (1949), and others—and in various senior capacities with the B.B.C. Also author of novels, and of *No Chip on my Shoulder* (autobiography; 1957).

Masefield, John (1878-1967). Born at Ledbury, Herefordshire; educated at King's School, Warwickshire, and (in compliance with his wish for a career at sea) on the training-ship *Conway*, whence he was apprenticed on a sailing vessel bound *via* Cape Horn for Chile. After a bout of ill-health he reached New York as a junior officer on an Atlantic liner, left the sea, and passed the next few years in various unskilled jobs, including one as bar attendant in a hotel saloon. Such leisure as he had was given to intensive reading, and when he returned to England in 1897 he was determined to be a writer. Contributions in prose and verse were accepted by London periodicals, and he was engaged by the *Manchester Guardian,* in which he originated the daily 'Miscellany' column where many later writers found hospitality for light essays and articles with a literary and humane tone. Masefield settled in London with J. M. *Synge among his friends, and in a later poem 'Biography' he recalls the night walks they took around the streets of Bloomsbury, a district not then affected by the to-be-renowned *Bloomsbury Group. The publication of his first collection of poems, *Salt-Water Ballads* (1902), and the prose stories and

sketches in *A Mainsail Haul* (1905), gave him a firm footing in contemporary literature, while his position was consolidated by more verse—*Ballads* (1903), *Ballads and Poems* (1910); more short stories—*A Tarpaulin Muster* (1907); two novels—*Captain Margaret* (1908) and *Multitude and Solitude* (1909); and *The Tragedy of Nan* (1909) and *The Tragedy of Pompey the Great* (1910), his first plays. In a period when literary sensations were rarer than journalists made them later, Masefield's long narrative poem *The *Everlasting Mercy* made an immediate sensation when it came out in *The *English Review* late in 1911. As an account of the conversion of a drunken blasphemer it was acceptable to Christian readers, but as a repository of blasphemer's language it repelled them, and from the literary angle it appeared an incongruous display of pedestrian jog-trot and often ludicrous rhymes mixed on uneasy terms with passages of fine poetry. A generation later such incongruities startled less. Masefield explored this vein further in *The *Widow in the Bye Street* (1912), *Dauber* (1913) and *The *Daffodil Fields* (1913). He was also writing novels of adventure—*Lost Endeavour* (1910), *Martin Hyde* (1910), *Jim Davis* (1911). Journeys to the battle fronts during World War I produced one of his most moving books, *Gallipoli* (1916), and also *The Old Front Line* (1917) and *The Battle of the Somme* (1919). The best of his narrative poems *Reynard the Fox* (1919) was followed by volumes of miscellaneous verse, with further plays—*The Trial of Jesus* (1923), *Tristan and Iseult* (1927), among others—and further novels—*Sard Harker* (1924), *Odtaa* (1926), *The Bird of Dawning* (1933), etc. In the first poem in his first book he had declared his intention of concerning himself with the underprivileged, and compassion had been a keynote in most of his writings since. The Labour government recommended him as successor when Robert *Bridges the Poet Laureate died in 1930. His output of verse and prose continued during the following decades, though his most memorable work belongs to the earlier period.

Masochism. A form of (usually sexual) perversion which causes a person to take pleasure in having pain inflicted on him/her or suffering humiliation. The word is from the name of Leopold von Sacher-Masoch (1836-95), Austrian lawyer and novelist, whose writings are concerned with this abnormality. See Sadism.

Mason, A. E. W. (Alfred Edward Woodley Mason, 1865-1948). Born at Dulwich; educated there and at Oxford. Took to the stage as a member of F. R. Benson's Shakespeare Company and the Compton Comedy Company, both touring mainly in the provinces. He turned to writing as a profession, with *A Romance of Wastdale* (1895) as his first novel and *The Four Feathers* (1902) and *The Broken Road* (1907) as the most notable books of his first period. Beginning with *At the Villa Rose* (1910) he started a new phase as one of the most distinguished writers of crime novels, with Hanaud the French detective in the front rank of fictional mystery-solvers. The standard set by Mason in that novel was maintained in *The Witness for the Defence* (1913), *The House of the Arrow* (1924), *No Other Tiger* (1927), *The Prisoner in the Opal* (1929). As a biographer he wrote *Sir George Alexander and the St James's Theatre* (1935) and *The Life of Francis Drake* (1942).

Mason, Arthur Telford. See *Artemas.

Mason, Perry. Central character, as counsel for the defence, in the long series of crime novels by Erle Stanley *Gardner. His ingenious performances on behalf of his clients brought him into frequent conflict with District Attorneys, but he was invariably vindicated by whatever trial judge he appeared before in open court.

Mason, R. A. K. (Ronald Alison Kells Mason, 1905-   ). Born and educated in Auckland, New Zealand. Worked as a teacher, company secretary, public works foreman, and landscape gardener. Author of *In the Manner of Men* (1923), *The Beggar* (1924), *No New Thing* (1934), *End of Day* (1936), *This Dark Will Lighten* (1941), *Collected Poems* (1962), and other collections of verse. See *New Zealand Writers.

Mason, Stuart (pseudonym of Christopher Sclater Millard). Author of *A Bibliography of Oscar Wilde: With a Note by Robert Ross* (1914), *Oscar Wilde: Art and Morality* (1915), *Oscar Wilde and the Aesthetic Movement* (1920). Under his birth name he published *The Printed Work of Claud Lovat Fraser* (a bibliography, 1923).

Mason, Walt (1862-1939). Born in Ontario; self-educated; settled in the U.S. He wrote sentimental prose-poems which he claimed were 'published daily in more than 200 papers in the United States and Canada'. Collections of his writings appeared as *Rhymes of the Range* (1910), *Walt Mason's Business Prose Poems* (1911), *Rippling Rhymes* (1913), *Terse Verse* (1917), *Walt Mason, His Book* (1918).

Mason-Dixon Line. The boundary line between Maryland and Pennsylvania as fixed in the 1760s by Charles Mason and Jeremiah Dixon, English astronomers and surveyors. At the time of the Civil War it was popularly used of the dividing line between the Northern and Southern States.

Massingham, Harold John (1888-1952). Born in London, son of the following; educated at Westminster and Oxford. Worked as a journalist, contributing to the *Athenaeum*, the *Nation*, and the *Spectator*; retired to the country for the sake of his health and to pursue the nature studies which were his dominant interest. Author of *St Francis of Assisi* (1913), *Dogs, Birds and Others* (1919), *Some Birds of the Countryside* (1921), *In Praise of England* (1924), *Downland Man* (1926), *Birds of the Sea Shore* (1931), *English Downland* (1936), *Shepherd's Country* (1938), *Wisdom of the Fields* (1945), *Faith of a Fieldsman* (1951).

Massingham, H. W. (Henry William Massingham, 1860-1924). Born at Norwich; educated there and worked on local newspapers. Moved to London, where he became, in turn, Editor of the *Star* and the *Daily Chronicle*; and from 1907 to 1923 of the *Nation*, being during those years one of the most influential political journalists until the Liberal Party he supported fell into decline.

Masson, David (1822-1907). Born in Aberdeen; educated there and in Edinburgh. Worked as a journalist in Aberdeen and later in London as a contributor to text-books, etc. Professor of English Literature, University College, London, 1853-65; editor of *Macmillan's Magazine*, 1858-65; Professor of Rhetoric and English Literature, University of Edinburgh, 1865-95. Author of the *Life of Milton* (6 vols, 1859-80) which treats the poet in relation to the history of his time and was for long the standard biography. Masson also produced editions of the works of Milton, and De Quincey, and wrote lives of Thomas Chatterton and De Quincey.

Masterman, C. F. G. (Charles Frederick Gurney Masterman, 1874-1927). Born in Sussex; educated at Weymouth and Cambridge; contributed to the *Nation* and *Athenaeum* and, as Literary Editor, to the *Daily News*. One of the most brilliant of the younger Liberal statesmen, he held ministerial office from 1908 to 1915. Author of *Tennyson as a Religious Teacher* (1899), *F. D. Maurice* (1907), *The Condition of England* (1909).

Masters, Edgar Lee (1868-1950). Born in Kansas; studied law and practised in Chicago, 1891-1920. He had published collections of poems and a verse-drama of no outstanding quality before, in the *Spoon River Anthology* (1915), he wrote with a degree of originality and astringency uncommon in American poetry at that time. The *Anthology* comprises more than two hundred free-verse epitaphs on the men and women buried in the churchyard at Spoon River, an imaginative projection of, probably, Master's boyhood home. In total the book creates the impression that there was an uncommon concentration of misery in Spoon River, though this impression is in a measure compensated by the ingenuity of the author's method. His only other work of note is *Lincoln: the Man* (1931), an exercise in belittlement.

Masters, John (1914-). Born in Calcutta; educated in England at Wellington and Sandhurst military college. Returned to India in 1934 and served in the Middle East and Burma in World War II. Settled in the U.S. after India became self-governing. Author of novels with an Indian setting, mainly centred on episodes in the history of British rule: *Night Runners of Bengal* (1951), *Bhowani Junction* (1954), *The Venus of Konpara* (1960), *To the Coral Strand* (1962), *Fourteen Eighteen* (1965).

Masters, The. Novel by C. P. *Snow published in 1951. Vernon Royce, Master of a Cambridge college, is dying, and the Fellows have to consider the choosing of his successor. Two candidates from among themselves are Paul Jago, Senior Tutor, whose sensitivity and love for the college appear vital to his supporters, and Redvers Crawford, a brilliant scientist with competent, polished manners. The Master's illness is prolonged, and strong feelings develop among the supporters of both candidates. Ronald Nightingale switches to Crawford, hoping that this will ease his own path to academic honours; this disgusts Walter Luke, a miner's son, who then pledges firm support for Jago. Mrs Jago is made aware by an anonymous circular that she is not fitted for Master's wife. Jago him-

self criticizes his supporters, Chrystal and Brown, for their negotiations with Sir Horace Timberlake, which have produced a promise of £120,000 for the development of the college on the science side; the resentful Chrystal finally decides to support Crawford. The Master dies. The Fellows reverently attend his funeral, then resume their bickering. The outside world now plays a part, for it is 1937, and the septuagenarian Eustace Pilbrow returns from the Continent having switched from Jago, whom he considers the better man, to the forward-thinking radical Crawford, whom he regards as indispensable for the troubled days ahead. Crawford is elected at a ceremony conducted with dignity by the aged Senior Fellow, Maurice Gay. The novel is one of the *Strangers and Brothers* sequence with Lewis Eliot as narrator.

Mata Hari (Margarete Gertrude Zelle, 1876-1917). Born at Leeuwarden in the Netherlands; became a dancer on the French stage, adopting the name by which she was to become notorious. Accused of spying for the Germans in World War I, she was condemned and shot in Paris. 'Mata Hari' has since become a more or less facetious generic name for any beautiful woman wrongly or rightly suspected as an enemy agent.

Matson, Norman (Norman Häghejm Matson, 1893-). Author of *Flecker's Magic* (1926), a fantasy commended by E. M. *Forster in *Aspects of the Novel; Day of Fortune* (1928), *Bats in the Belfry* (1942) and other fiction; and *The Log of the Coriolanus* (1930), an account of his voyage across the south Atlantic and back.

Matthiessen, F. O. (Frances Otto Matthiessen, 1902-50). Born in California; educated at Yale, Oxford, and Harvard, later becoming a teacher at Yale and then at Harvard. He advocated the unification of literary study with social and political activity. Depressed by the state of the world in the cold war period, he committed suicide. Author of *The Achievement of T. S. Eliot* (1935 and later editions), *American Renaissance* (1941), *Henry James: The Major Phase* (1944), *The Responsibilities of the Critic* (1952); editor of the *Oxford Book of American Verse* (1950).

Mattingly, Garrett (1900-62). Professor of European History, Columbia University, New York. Author of *Catherine of Aragon* (1942), *Renaissance Diplomacy* (1955), and *The Defeat of the Spanish Armada* (1959). which was praised by other historians as a work of scrupulous scholarship and widely read by the public as an entrancing narrative.

Maude, Aylmer (1858-1938). Born at Ipswich; educated in London at Christ's Hospital and in Moscow, later becoming a teacher of English there and a business executive. Established a friendship with Leo Tolstoy and from the later 1890s devoted most of the rest of his life to translating Tolstoy's works and writing *Tolstoy and his Problems* (1901), *Life of Tolstoy* (The First Fifty Years, 1908; Later Years, 1910), *Tolstoy on Art and Its Critics* (1924), *Family Views of Tolstoy* (1926), *Leo Tolstoy and His Works* (1930). He also wrote *Marie *Stopes: Her Work and Play* (1924).

Maugham, Robin (Robert Cecil Romer Maugham, 2nd Viscount Maugham, 1916-   ). Son of the 1st Viscount, Lord Chancellor and brother of Somerset *Maugham. Educated at Eton and Cambridge. Served in World War II; called to the Bar, 1945. Author of *Come to Dust* (1945), *Line on Ginger* (1949), *The Rough and the Smooth* (1951), *The Man With Two Shadows* (1958), and other novels. *Somerset and All the Maughams* (1966).

Maugham, W. Somerset (William Somerset Maugham, 1874-1965). Born in Paris, the youngest of six brothers, their father being solicitor to the British Embassy and their mother reputedly 'the most beautiful woman in Paris'. After the mother's death in 1882 and the father's two years later, William's schooling in France ended and he was sent to England where, at Whitstable in Kent, he lived in the austere household of his uncle the Rev. H. M. Maugham, vicar of All Saints'. His life there and at the King's School, Canterbury, are reflected in part in two of his novels *Of Human Bondage* (1915) and *Cakes and Ale* (1930). In the former, the physical affliction (clubfoot) of the hero, Philip Carey, represents Maugham's own early handicap of a pronounced stammer, which made his schooldays a period of torment through mockery by boys and masters alike. He also showed a tendency to tuberculosis, from which his mother had died, and he was sent from school for a period to the south of France, where he began to develop the liking for French literature— especially the short stories of Maupassant— that was to have a marked influence both upon the form of his own mature writings and

upon the unillusioned attitude towards the human material displayed in them. Early in the 1890s he spent a year at Heidelberg, attending a philosophy course at the University, and incidentally acquiring a love of the theatre and of painting, thus laying the foundations of his future success as a playwright and also of his connoisseurship as an art collector. On returning to England he resisted his uncle's wish that he should enter the Church (he was already a non-Christian) and chose a medical career, studying at St Thomas's Hospital in London and qualifying as a physician and surgeon in 1897. During that period he had intensive experience of the miseries of childbirth among slum patients, and learned the hardship of their lives, distilling the experience in semi-fictional terms in *Liza of Lambeth* (1897), which holds a place among the realistic novels of the turn of the century. Maugham made no further practical use of his medical qualification, but used a small private income for travels on the Continent, particularly in Italy and Spain, acquiring a love of Spanish life and art such as informs at least two of his subsequent books *Don Fernando* (1935; revised edition 1950) and *Catalina* (1948). Settling in Paris, he moved among painters and writers, lived in Montparnasse, and for several years made little impression with his own writings. Besides novels he was composing plays from 1892 onward, but none was published until *A Man of Honour* in 1903. In the same year it was put on by the Stage Society for the two performances to which the Society's productions were normally limited, and there was nothing in its reception to foreshadow the unexampled success that had befallen Maugham by 1908, when four of his plays *(Lady Frederick, Jack Straw, Mrs Dot* and *The Explorer)* were simultaneously West End successes in London, and were soon equally well received in the United States. From that time he was an established playwright until 1933, when he abandoned the theatre. During those years his outstanding plays were *Smith* (1909), *Caesar's Wife* and *Home and Beauty* (1919), *The *Circle* (1921), *East of Suez* (1922), *Our Betters* (1923), *The *Constant Wife* (1927), *The Sacred Flame* (1929), *The Breadwinner* (1930), *For Services Rendered* (1932), and *Sheppey* (1933), the last two being the most serious of his plays and the least acceptable by audiences accustomed to the preceding witty comedies and satires. Meanwhile, Maugham has achieved a further popularity with his numerous mordant short stories, ranging from the collection entitled *Orientations (1899) to Creatures of Circumstance (1947). Many of these were a product of his travels among the islands of the South Seas. During World War I he acted as a secret agent in the British Intelligence Service. A direct outcome of that assignment was the volume of stories called Ashenden, or The British Agent (1928), set in Switzerland, France, Italy and Russia, and detailing a variety of the author's experiences. After the war he travelled widely, leaving little of the world unvisited. Two entertaining travel books are among the products of these wanderings: *On a Chinese Screen (1922) and The *Gentleman in the Parlour (1930). Towards the end of his career as a writer he published several volumes with a strong personal note: The Summing Up (1938), Strictly Personal (1942), A Writer's Notebook (1949), The Vagrant Mood (1952), Points of View (1958). The position of Somerset Maugham among British authors has been ambiguous. His quality as an entertainer in his plays and short stories led to his being for many years cold-shouldered by critics. His sardonic view of human behaviour, in which amorality was a common factor, caused the squeamish to view him with disfavour even if they could not resist his talent for presenting unorthodoxy with brilliant readability. Indifferent to critical or moral opinion, he followed his own path and was at length able to contemplate with wry indulgence the spectacle of professional critics belatedly overtaking popular opinion, though some still refused to acknowledge Maugham as a prose stylist. As an irresistible storyteller he has hardly been surpassed, either as a novelist in *Cakes and Ale, or in the majority of his shorter tales, one of which, *Rain, fascinated film and stage adapters for many years and brought its author not inconsiderable fortune. He made collected editions of what he wished to preserve: Complete Short Stories (3 vols, 1951), Collected Plays (3 vols, 1931), Far and Wide (2 vols, containing nine novels, 1955), each with a new Preface by himself. Though much has been written about him, he preserved an objective attitude towards biographers and directed that there should be no official 'life' of him and that none of his letters should be published. See also *Cosmopolitans, The *Mixture as Before, The *Trembling of a Leaf.

aundy Money. Silver coins specially minted (pennies, fourpenny pieces, etc.) for distribution by the Sovereign to thirteen poor persons on Maundy Thursday (the day preceding Good Friday). In England the custom was begun by Edward III in 1368, and is a relic of the abandoned custom of a ceremonial royal washing of the feet of poor people on that day (see St John 13: 4-17).

Mauriac, François (1885-1970). Born in Bordeaux; educated at Roman Catholic schools there. He came to be considered the greatest French novelist of his time and much of his fiction is dominated by problems of religion. From a large output the following are among those translated into English: The Kiss of the Leper (1922; trans. 1930), Thérèse (1927; 1928), The Desert of Love (1925; 1929), The Viper's Tangle (1932; 1933), The Frontenac Mystery (1933; 1952). He also wrote plays: Asmodée (1938; 1939) and others; and much miscellaneous prose, including Proust's Way (1950), Letters on Art and Literature (1953).

Maurier, Daphne du. See Daphne *Du Maurier.

Maurois, André (pseudonym of Émile Herzog, 1885-1967). Born at Elbeuf; educated there and at Rouen and Caen. Served as a liaison officer with the British army in World War I, an experience that led to The Silence of Colonel Bramble (1918), his first book, which became even more popular in England than in France. Among the several biographies of Englishmen that he wrote Ariel: The Life of Shelley (1924) made most impression.

Maurya. The old mother in J. M. Synge's *Riders to the Sea. She loses her husband and her six sons by drowning.

Mavor, Osborne Henry. See James *Bridie.

Max. See Max *Beerbohm.

Maxwell, Gavin (1914-69). Born in Wigtownshire; educated at Stowe and Oxford. Served with the Scots Guards in World War II. In 1945 he bought the island of Soay and in Harpoon at a Venture (1952) gives an account of his attempt to establish a shark fishery there. God Protect Me from My Friends (1956) is a biography of the Sicilian outlaw Guiliano; A Reed Shaken by the Wind (1957) describes a journey among the Marsh Arabs of southern Iraq; Ring of Bright Water (1960) deals with his two pet otters, and has a sequel in Raven Seek Thy Brother (1968). The House of Elrig (1965) is an autobiography of his early years.

Maxwell, Mrs M. E. See Miss *Braddon.

Maxwell, W. B. (William Babington Maxwell, 1866-1938). Born in Surrey, his mother being the novelist who wrote under her maiden name, M. E. *Braddon, to whom he acted as secretary for a time. From 1901 with *The Countess of Maybury* he wrote scores of novels, of which the earlier received more attention than those published in the changed conditions after World War I, in which he served in France. Among his novels are *The Ragged Messenger* (1904), *The Guarded Flame* (1906), *The Rest Cure* (1910), *Spinster of This Parish* (1922), *The Case of Bevan Yorke* (1927). He also published collections of short stories, *Odd Lengths* (1907), *Children of the Night* (1925). Autobiography: *Time Gathered* (1937).

Mayakovsky, Vladimir Vladimirovich (1893-1930). Born in a village in the Caucasus. While still a schoolboy in Moscow he was imprisoned for revolutionary activities, and was equally nonconforming when he turned to literature, writing poetry in a modified Futurist mode (*see* Marinetti). An English introduction to his work is *Mayakovsky and his Poetry*, compiled by Herbert Marshall (London, 1942; rev. edn 1945). His *Mystery-Bouffe: An heroic, epic and satiric representation of our epoch*, translated by G. R. Noyes and A. Kaun, is in *Masterpieces of Russian Drama* (New York, 1933).

Mayerling. The shooting of Crown Prince Rudolf of Austria and his young mistress, Baroness Marie Vetsera, in the royal hunting lodge in the Austrian village of Mayerling on 30 January 1889, continues to attract writers both as a romantic and tragic love story and as an unsolved mystery. The couple were found dead after the Austrian Emperor had ordered his son to end the liaison. Alternative theories are that Rudolf and Marie made a suicide pact (as was officially given out); or that he shot the girl and then himself; or that they were murdered in a cloak-and-dagger plot. The smuggling out, in a carriage, of Marie's body, fully dressed and as if alive, provided a gruesome climax to the affair.

Maynard, Theodore (1890-1956). Born in India; educated in England. After intending to become a Unitarian minister, he became converted to Roman Catholicism. Settled in the United States and became an American citizen. *Collected Poems* (1946). Many prose works on Roman Catholic subjects.

Mayne, Ethel Colburn (died 1941). Born, and educated privately, in Ireland. Adopted temporarily the pseudonym Frances E. Huntly for stories she contributed to *The *Yellow Book*, but published her first book *The Clearer Vision* (1898) under her own name. She continued to write fiction but became better known for her biographies and literary studies: *Byron* (1912), *Browning's Heroines* (1913), *The Life and Letters of Anne Isabella, Lady Noel Byron* (1929), *A Regency Chapter* (1939).

Mayne, Rutherford (pseudonym of Samuel J. Waddell, 1879-1967; brother of Helen *Waddell). Born in Japan; educated in Belfast; worked as a civil servant in Ireland, but in earlier years was on the stage with the Ulster Literary Theatre and also acted at the *Abbey Theatre in Dublin, for which two of his plays were written. His published plays include: *The Turn of the Road* (1907), *The Drone* (1912), *Bridge Head* (1939).

Mayo, Katherine (1868-1940). Born in Pennsylvania; educated privately in Boston and Cambridge (Massachusetts). Travelled widely; worked as a research assistant for other authors before publishing her first book *Justice to All* (1917), a study of the Pennsylvania police. *Isles of Fear* (1925) criticized American administration in the Philippines. Her most controversial work, *Mother India* (1927), an exposure of the Indian child-marriage system, was indicative of her well-intentioned but sometimes intemperate methods as a social reformer.

Mead, Margaret (1901-   ). Born in Philadelphia; educated there and in Indiana and at Columbia University, graduating in Psychology and Anthropology. Her first-hand studies in the culture of primitive societies are among the most important works of anthropological research: *Coming of Age in Samoa* (1928), *Growing Up in New Guinea* (1930), *Male and Female* (1949), *Growth and Culture* (1951).

Meats, Henry. Alias Brother Aloysius, alias Henry Barnes, in Compton Mackenzie's *Sinister Street* (1913-14). Michael Fane first encounters him as a visitor at Clere Abbey, and later engages him as guide through the London underworld in search of Lily Haden. He ends as the murderer of a prostitute.

Mee, Arthur (1875-1943). Born and educated at Stapleford, Nottinghamshire. Started as a journalist on the local evening paper before moving to London on the staff of the *St James's Gazette* in 1900. Joined the Harmsworth organization as literary editor of the *Daily Mail*, 1903-5, and for some thirty years following he edited various Harmsworth publications issued in serial parts: their *Self-Educator* (1906), *History of the World* (1907), *Natural History* (1911), *Popular Science* (1912). His name was mainly associated with the *Children's Encyclopedia* (1908 and later editions), a pioneer work which stimulated the interest and imagination of unnumbered young people for a generation or more. He supplemented this during a quarter of a century with a monthly publication on similar lines *My Magazine* and with a large number of books for children. Although Mee was lacking in academic scholarship, he was a devoted and skilled popularizer and no mean educator. Among his enterprises was the *Children's Newspaper*, a weekly he started and edited in 1919. It ran for forty-six years, reaching a very large circulation before it ceased publication in 1965.

Megaera. The scolding wife of Androcles in *Androcles and the Lion* (1912) by Bernard Shaw.

Meiklejohn, J. M. D. (John Miller Dow Meiklejohn, 1836-1902). Born and educated in Edinburgh. Became the first Professor of the Theory, History, and Practice of Education, University of St Andrews from 1876. A translation of Kant's *Critique of Pure Reason* was among his works, but his claim to renown rests upon the schoolbooks he wrote or sponsored. Though now superseded, they were of a higher educational standard than was general in textbooks at that time, and their solid merit is still apparent: *English Language* (1886), *The Art of Writing English* (1899), *English Literature* (1904).

Melba, Dame Nellie (*née* Helen Porter Mitchell, 1861-1931). Born and educated in Australia at Melbourne, from which she derived her stage name; studied operatic singing in Paris, and in 1887 made a triumphant début in Brussels as Gilda in Verdi's *Rigoletto*. Thereafter she was accepted as one of the world's principal prima donnas for the next forty years.

Mellors, Oliver. Sir Clifford Chatterley's gamekeeper in D. H. Lawrence's *Lady Chatterley's Lover* (1928); Constance Chatterley becomes his mistress.

Melmoth, Sebastian. Name used by Oscar *Wilde

after his release from Reading Gaol, when he went into exile in France. He adopted it from *Melmoth the Wanderer* by Charles Maturin (1782-1824), a remote ancestor on his mother's side. *See* Speranza.

Melville, Frederick (1876-1938) and **Walter** (1875-1937). Brothers, proprietors of the Lyceum Theatre in London for many years, and authors of preposterous but enormously popular melodramas: *The Worst Woman in London* (1899), *The Girl Who Took the Wrong Turning* (1906), *The Ugliest Woman on Earth* (1904), *The Bad Girl of the Family* (1909) and others. These brought fortunes to the authors, Frederick leaving £314,228 and Walter £205,861.

Memoirs of Hecate County. *See* Edmund *Wilson.

Menander. *See* Charles *Morgan.

Mencken, H. L. (Henry Louis Mencken, 1880-1956). Born and educated in Baltimore; worked on newspapers there. Became editor of the *Smart Set* and from 1924 to 1933 of the *American Mercury*. His *George Bernard Shaw: his Plays* (1905) was the first book on Shaw, and Mencken was also a force in directing attention to the young contemporary writers in his own country. He was one of the key figures in the American literary scene with his sceptical and often sardonic and irreverent attitude towards conventions, dogmas, and institutions, whether literary, religious or political. Among his miscellaneous writings were *The Philosophy of Friedrich Nietzsche* (1908), *A Book of Burlesques* (1916), *In Defense of Woman* (1917), *A Book of Prefaces* (1917), *Damn: A Book of Calumny* (1917), *Treatise on the Gods* (1930), *Treatise on Right and Wrong* (1934). His anarchic disposition made him as distrustful of democracy as he was bitter towards totalitarianism: his view of the former is expressed in *Notes on Democracy* (1926). The quintessence of Mencken is in his essays entitled *Prejudices* (six series, 1919-27), but his outstanding work is *The American Language* (1919 and later editions; with Supplement I, 1945, and Supplement II, 1948). Autobiography: *Happy Days: 1880-1892* (1940), *Newspaper Days* (1941), *Heathen Days* (1943).

Mendes, Catulle (1841-1900). Born in Bordeaux. He was one of the pioneers of the *Parnassian movement in French poetry. He also wrote plays, novels, and criticism and served a term of imprisonment for the alleged obscenity of his *Le Roman d'une Nuit* (1883). His *Rue des Filles-Dieu, 56* (1895), a one-act comedy in verse, was translated as *Number 56* (1928).

Mendip, Thomas. *See* *Thomas Mendip.

Menen, Aubrey (1912-   ). Born in London; educated at the University of London. His father was Indian and during World War II Aubrey Menen became a leading English-language radio broadcaster in India. With the publication of *The Prevalence of Witches* (1948) he made his mark as a sprightly and witty novelist with an acute eye for current absurdities, which he surveyed from a closer angle in the non-fictional *Dead Man in the Silver Market* (1953). Other novels: *The Stumbling Stone* (1949), *The Backward Bride* (1950), *The Duke of Gallodoro* (1952), the last two set mainly in Italy.

Mercer, Cecil William. *See* Dornford *Yates.

Mercury, The London. *See* *London Mercury.

Meredith, Anne. Pseudonym used by Lucy Malleson for *The Stranger* (1939), *The Sisters* (1948), *The Innocent Bride* (1954), and other novels. *Three a Penny* (autobiographical reminiscences, 1940). *See* Anthony *Gilbert for her detective novels.

Meredith, George (1828-1909). Born at Portsmouth; educated privately and in Germany. He and Thomas *Hardy were the most celebrated novelists of the late 19th century and both were distinguished poets, though, unlike Hardy, Meredith published his poems also in the last century except the minor collection *A Reading of Life* (1901). The little-known essay *Comedy and the Uses of the Comic Spirit* (1897) still has relevance.

Merezhkovsky, Dmitry Sergeyevich (1865-1941). Born and educated in St Petersburg (Leningrad) and at the University of Moscow. Implicated in the abortive anti-Tsarist revolution of 1905 he left Russia, but was no less antagonistic to the Soviet régime after 1917 and settled in Paris, attacking the Bolsheviks in *The Kingdom of Antichrist* (1922). He wrote poetry and criticism as well as historical novels with a religious and philosophical purpose. Of these, the trilogy *Christ and the Antichrist* had some success in a four-volume translation: *Julian the Apostate* (1899), *The Death of the Gods* (1901), *The Romance of Leonardo da Vinci* (1902), *Peter and Alexis* (1905).

Merivale, Sir Henry. Detective in crime novels by John Dickson *Carr.

Mermaid Theatre. Originating in 1951 as a private (prefabricated) theatre of Elizabethan type adjoining Bernard Miles's house in northwest London, it was re-erected at the Royal Exchange in the City of London in the Coronation year of Elizabeth II (1953), performances of Shakespeare and Ben Jonson and Purcell's *Dido and Aeneas* being given there. The permanent theatre, at Puddle Dock, Upper Thames Street, built inside a bombed warehouse, opened in May 1959 with Bernard Miles, the founder of the whole Mermaid enterprise, as director. Plays by Ibsen, Shaw, Brecht, and others, both modern and earlier, were included in a catholic repertory.

Merrick, Leonard (name taken by deed poll by Leonard Miller, 1864-1939). Born in London; educated privately and at Brighton College. Began to study law but was compelled for financial reasons to seek other employment, and went to South Africa and worked in Kimberley for a few years. After returning to England he went on the stage and later was unsuccessful as an actor in New York. Between 1892 and 1930 he published almost a score of novels. Believing that his books were unfairly neglected, a group of eminent fellow-writers cooperated in 1918 to reissue his novels in a collected edition, each of the sponsors providing an introduction to a particular novel. *Conrad in Quest of his Youth* (first edition 1903) was commended in the 1918 edition by J. M. *Barrie who spoke of it as 'the best sentimental journey' since Laurence Sterne's. Other introducers were H. G. *Wells (*The Quaint Companions*, 1903), A. W. *Pinero (*The Position of Peggy Harper*, 1911), Granville *Barker (*One Man's View*, 1897), G. K. *Chesterton (*The House of Lynch*, 1907). For reasons difficult to determine, this multiple tribute failed to attract an adequate reading public to Merrick's books, though they are enjoyable minor classics with gaiety and colour and unmawkish sentiment to compensate their glimpses of tragedy.

Merriman, Henry Seton (pseudonym of Hugh Stowell Scott, 1862-1903). Born at Newcastle upon Tyne; educated at Loretto and Wiesbaden. After beginning as an insurance underwriter's clerk, he took to novel-writing with *Young Mistley* (1888). Travelling extensively abroad, he put his knowledge of foreign countries and their history into *The Slave of the Lamp* (1892), *From One Genera-

tion to Another (1892), *With Edged Tools* (1894), *The Sowers* (1896), *In Kedar's Tents* (1897), *The Velvet Glove* (1901), *Barlasch of the Guard* (1902), *The Last Hope* (1904).

Merton, Thomas (Father M. Louis, 1915-   ). Born in France of Anglo-American parentage; educated in England at Cambridge and in the U.S. at Columbia. He passed from Communism to Roman Catholicism and wrote his first book (*Thirty Poems,* 1944) and its successors in verse and prose under a profound religious conviction. He became a priest after entering a Trappist monastery in 1941. Poems: *Figures for an Apocalypse* (1947), *Tears of the Blind Lions* (1949). Autobiography: *The Seven Storey Mountain* (1948), *The Waters of Siloe* (1949). Other works: *Seeds of Contemplation* (1949), *No Man Is an Island* (1955).

Merton Densher. *See* Densher.

Merwin, Samuel (1874-1936). Born in Illinois and educated there. He spent some time in China and among his novels *Silk: A Legend* (1923) is a story (*c.* A.D. 100) of the great highway along which silk, both raw and in finished materials, was borne by camels, asses and mules and in ox-carts, from China westward to Asia Minor and thence to the markets of the Roman Empire.

Metalious, Grace (1924-64). Born and educated in New Hampshire. Her novels of American small-town communities were heavily charged with erotic episodes, with associated incidents of rape, abortion, and violent death. The first *Peyton Place* (1957), was reported as having world sales of more than eight million copies by 1963, and corresponding popularity extended to the film based on it, and to her other novels *Return to Peyton Place* (1960), *The Tight White Collar* (1960) and *No Adam in Eden* (1963).

Metaphysical poetry. Term applied by Samuel Johnson to the writings of a group of seventeenth century poets, among whom John Donne had already been criticized by Dryden: 'he affects the Metaphysics . . . where Nature only should reign'. Andrew Marvell, Abraham Cowley, Richard Crashaw, George Herbert, and Henry Vaughan are among the metaphysicals, employing complexity of thought and spiritual apprehension, far-fetched imagery, a craggy and sometimes violent colloquial manner of expression (e.g. Donne's 'Busy old fool, unruly Sun': 'For God sake hold your

tongue, and let me love'; 'Go, and catch a falling star, / Get with child a mandrake root'). Neither the urbane eighteenth century nor the romantic nineteenth was in harmony with the metaphysical poets, but they returned to favour in the present century, scholars and critics giving much labour to study of Donne's writings and to editing definitive editions; while T. S. Eliot and the host of his disciples returned to metaphysical modes in their verse.

Metaphysics. A word now interpreted as 'beyond or transcending physics' and designating the philosophy of mind as distinct from *physics,* the science of matter and energy; originally it related only to the placing of certain sections in the works of Aristotle after his *Physics.*

Metchnikoff, Elie (1845-1916). Born in Russia. Became a Professor at the Pasteur Institute in Paris. Conducted fruitful research on immunology. Author of *The Nature of Man* (1903), *Immunity in Infective Diseases* (1906), *The Prolongation of Human Life: Optimistic Essays* (1907).

Metellus. A young Roman courtier in **Androcles and the Lion* (1912) by Bernard Shaw.

Method, The. A style of acting and stage-direction in vogue in the U.S. and Britain after World War II. Said to derive from the teachings of **Stanislavsky in An Actor Prepares* (1926), its leading principle was that the actor must lose himself completely in the part he is playing and completely identify himself with the character. (This would seem to have been the aim of all good acting from time immemorial.) It led to a generation of actors practising extreme naturalism in action and in speech, and was possibly responsible for much slovenly and inaudible stage dialogue which suggested that players were no longer taught the actor's first lesson: how to speak. 'The Method' was considered by some critics to be based on a misconception of Stanislavsky's purpose.

Methuselah. *See* *Back to Methuselah.

Mew, Charlotte (Charlotte Mary Mew, 1870-1928). Born in London, daughter of an architect; educated privately. Lived for a while in Paris but mainly in London at Bloomsbury. A desperately unhappy woman, overwhelmed by ill-health, family deaths, hopeless love, and poverty, she committed suicide, though through the efforts of Thomas *Hardy and others she had been granted a small Civil List pension. Her poems, unique in form, match in content the acute sensibility of her own nature. She contributed to The *Yellow Book, but except for the few published in The Farmer's Bride (1916), and The Rambling Sailor (posthumuously, 1929) she destroyed all her poems.

Meyer, Kuno (1858-1919). Professor of Celtic in the University of Liverpool (1895-1911). Translated Selections from Ancient Irish Poetry (1911); made valuable contributions to Irish lexicography. Mentioned in George Moore's *Hail and Farewell.

Meynell, Alice (née Alice Christiana Gertrude Thompson, 1847-1922; married Wilfrid *Meynell, 1877). Born at Barnes in Surrey; educated by her father, who was a friend of Dickens. She lived in Italy as a child and in 1872 joined the Roman Catholic Church. After marriage, she and her husband, though never drawn into Society, were on terms of friendship with most of the contemporary men and women of literary genius—Tennyson and Browning, Rossetti and Meredith, Ruskin and George Eliot—but most of all with Coventry *Patmore and with Francis *Thompson whom their hospitality rescued from destitution. While still a girl her poems had been warmly praised by the older writers, especially her sonnet 'Renouncement'. Her output of verse and prose was small but always scrupulously fine in style and content; her poems, it was said by J. L. *Garvin, were composed less of sounds than of silences. Her verse was published in Preludes (1875), Poems (1893), Other Poems (1896), Later Poems (1901), Collected Poems (1912), A Father of Women (1917), Last Poems (posthumuously, 1923). Essays: The Rhythm of Life (1893), The Colour of Life (1896), The Spirit of Place (1898), Ceres' Runaway (1909), Selected Essays (1914), Hearts of Controversy (1917), The Second Person Singular (1921). She was the mother of Everard, (Sir) Francis, and Viola Meynell (her biographer).

Meynell, Everard (1882-1926). Son of Alice and Wilfrid Meynell. Author of The Life of Francis Thompson (1913), Corot and his Friends (1908). See also Serendipity.

Meynell, Sir Francis (1891-   ; knighted 1946). Born in London; son of Wilfrid and Alice Meynell; educated at Downside and at Trinity College, Dublin. Contributed to London newspapers; founded and directed the *Nonesuch Press; took a leading part in the revival of fine printing and book-design.

Author of The Typography of Newspaper Advertisements (1929), Seventeen Poems (1945), English Printed Books (1946); editor of The Week-End Book (1923), The Nonesuch Century (1936).

Meynell, Viola (1886-1956). Born in London, daughter of Wilfrid and Alice Meynell. Author of poems: The Frozen Ocean (1931); novels: Modern Lovers (1914), Narcissus (1916), Antonia (1921), Follow Thy Fair Sun (1935); biography: Alice Meynell: A Memoir (1929).

Meynell, Wilfrid (1852-1948). Born at Newcastle upon Tyne; educated in Croydon and York. Though born into a Quaker family and taught in Quaker schools, he was converted to Roman Catholicism in 1871; married Alice Thompson in 1877; became editor of the Catholic Weekly Register, 1881, and contributed to various London weeklies and quarterlies. Author of Journals and Journalism (under the pseudonym John Oldcastle, 1880); The New Disraeli (1903), Verses and Reverses (1912), Aunt Sarah and the War (1914), Rhymes with Reasons (1918), Come and See (1919).

Michael Fane. See Michael *Fane.

Michaëlis, Karen (née Karin Marie Bech Brondum, 1872-1950; married Sophus Michaëlis). Born in Denmark; educated privately. Author of many novels, The Dangerous Age: Letters and Fragments from a Women's Diary (1911) having a large international circulation. Other novels in English translations: Elsie Lindtner (1912), The Governor (1913); children's books: Bibi (1927), Bibi Goes Travelling (1935).

Michener, James Albert (1907-   ). Born in Pennsylvania; educated there at Swarthmore College, at the University of St Andrews, and at Harvard. Professor at Colorado State College of Education, 1936-41. Served in the South Pacific in World War II. Author of Tales of the South Pacific (1947), The Fires of Spring (1949), The Bridges at Toko-ri (1953), Sayonara (1954).

Mickey Mouse. See Walt *Disney.

Middleton, Richard (Richard Barham Middleton, 1882-1911). Born at Staines, Middlesex; educated at St Paul's and Merchant Taylors' Schools and University of London. After six years as a clerk, he resigned without means, and little is known of his doings in the remaining few years before he committed suicide in Brussels. Born out of his time, he would have fared better among the aesthetes and decadents of the 1890s. He made a few contributions to periodicals but issued nothing in book form. The following were published after his death: *Poems and Songs* (1912), *The Ghost Ship and other Stories* (1912), the title story being considered his masterpiece; essays: *The Day Before Yesterday* (1923).

Mildred Rogers. Teashop waitress in Somerset Maugham's *Of Human Bondage* (1915). She has a malign influence on Philip Carey and ends as a prostitute.

Miles. See Neil *Bell.

Miles, Reaney Hoffe. See Monckton *Hoffe.

Milestones. Play in three acts by Arnold *Bennett and Edward Knoblock, performed in London in 1912.

The scene throughout is the drawing-room of the Rheads' house in Kensington Gore, London. Act I takes place in the late evening of 29 December 1860, the day on which the first iron vessel in the British navy has been launched. John Rhead, partner in the Thames-side iron foundry of Sibley, Rhead & Sibley is convinced that the future success of the firm lies in amalgamation with Macleans, an old-established shipbuilding firm who are about to change over from wooden to iron vessels. The Sibleys, however, agree with the 'five-sixths of the experts in England [who] have no belief whatever in the future of iron ships'. John Rhead therefore withdraws from the partnership in order to join Macleans. Rose Sibley, engaged to Rhead, defies her father's and brother's objection to her marrying him; but her brother Sam Sibley's engagement to Gertrude Rhead, John's sister, is broken off. Act II, dated 1885, shows the same drawing-room, partially refurnished in contemporary taste. John Rhead, now a successful shipbuilder aged fifty, is as sceptical of the future of steel ships as his former partners were of iron ones. Gertrude Rhead has dwindled into 'a faded, acidy spinster with protective impulses for her niece Emily', the only child of John and Rose. John Rhead has found in the drawing office of his works a brilliant young inventor, Arthur Preece, who has fallen in love with Emily, but her parents forbid the engagement since they intend her to marry the middle-aged Lord Monkhurst (formerly Ned Pym) who is pulling political strings to get a baronetcy for

John Rhead. In Act III the drawing-room has 'undergone an entire change' of furnishing and decoration in the style of 1912. The occasion is the golden wedding of Sir John Rhead, Bart, and Lady Rhead. Their daughter Emily bowed to their determination that she should marry Monkhurst, and she is now a widow with a daughter of twenty-four, the Hon. Muriel Pym, and a son of twenty-two, Gerald, the present Lord Monkhurst. He is 'a young man-about-town . . . tall, hollow-chested, careless in his manners, very self-assured, and properly bored'. Muriel, by contrast, 'is a handsome girl . . . rather thin and eager, with a high forehead and much distinction'. 'She has herself under absolute control' and is unshaken by her family's objection to her marrying her cousin Richard Sibley, an engineer specializing in reaping-machines, with whom she intends to emigrate to Canada. Arthur Preece, now a Labour M.P., has meanwhile forced Sir John Rhead to 'take up steel on a big scale' and made a great deal of money. He also deals with Rhead's labour troubles, and is at length instrumental in overcoming the stubborn old man's objection to Richard Sibley as a husband for his granddaughter Muriel. Emily and Arthur Preece resume their former relationship, after twenty-six years, and the play ends with Muriel bringing a flower to her grandparents as they sit on either side of the fire while Gertrude at their request sings in an adjoining room one of the songs of their young days 'in a cracked and ancient voice, very gently and faintly'.

Milford, Sir Humphrey (Humphrey Sumner Milford, 1877-1952; knighted 1936). Educated at Winchester and Oxford. Joined the Clarendon Press, Oxford, in 1900 and was Publisher to the University from 1913-45, operating from the Oxford University Press in London, which expanded greatly under his direction and established important branches overseas. Himself an indefatigable reader with liberal tastes, and a man of wide vision, he was served with devotion by his staff, who found him the ideal publisher, humorous though exacting. His reprints of Trollope's novels in the World's Classics series initiated the Trollope revival.

Millar, George (1910-　　). Born near Glasgow; educated at Loretto and Cambridge; trained as an architect and practised, 1930-32, before turning to journalism in London. Served in World War II; taken prisoner but escaped to

England and then went into occupied France as an agent with the Resistance. Author of *Maquis* (1945), *Horned Pigeon* (1946), *Through the Unicorn Gates* (1950), *A White Boat from England* (1951). Settled as a farmer in Dorset.

Millard, Christopher. See Stuart *Mason.

Millay, Edna St Vincent (1892-1950). Born in Maine; educated at Barnard College and Vassar. Her poem, 'Renascence', first published in an annual of verse when she was twenty, brought her considerable attention, and though she did not greatly please the critics she continued to satisfy a larger body of readers than poetry normally attracts. Her earlier books of lyrics—*Renascence and other Poems* (1917), *A Few Figs From Thistles* (1921), *Second April* (1921), *The Buck in the Snow* (1928)—were strongly personal and subjective, but she enlarged her vision in *Conversation at Midnight* (1937) and subsequent volumes. *The Harp Weaver and other Poems* (1923) showed her mastery of the sonnet form and the *Collected Sonnets* (1941) may prove her enduring contribution to American poetry.

Miller, Alice Duer (*née* Alice Duer, 1874-1942; Mrs H. W. Miller). Born in New York; educated at Columbia University. She became a successful writer of fiction, among her well-known novels being *Come Out of the Kitchen* (1916), *The Charm School* (1919); and (short stories) *Come Out of the Pantry* (1933); but she was most widely (if only temporarily) celebrated for her verses *The White Cliffs of Dover* (1940), a tribute to England's resolute and solitary stand against Hitler's onslaught in the early stages of World War II.

Miller, Arthur (1915-   ). Born and educated in the Harlem district of New York. While employed as a warehouse hand he felt the urge to become a writer and saved money to enable him to study at the University of Michigan. Some early disappointments with plays were followed by the success of *All My Sons* (1947), **Death of a Salesman* (1949), *A View from the Bridge* (1955), *After the Fall* (1963), *The Creation of the World and Other Business* (1972). Also short stories and films.

Miller, Henry (1891-   ). Born in New York. His education was sketchy owing to his nonconforming nature, and for many years he knocked about the world, moving in and out of many jobs, including a period as hawker of his own writings. While living in Paris, his novel *Tropic of Cancer* (1934) was published there, and *Tropic of Capricorn* followed in 1939. Though long banned in England and America as obscene, they were openly published and sold in English editions in the 1960s with little protest, their erotic content being conformable with the new moral freedom. As a writer he has been extravagantly praised and uncompromisingly dispraised by critics of equal authority. Other books: *The Cosmological Eye* (1939), *The Wisdom of the Heart* (1941), *The Colossus of Maroussi* (1941), *The *Air-Conditioned Nightmare* (1945), *The Books in My Life* (1952), *The Rosy Crucifixion* (trilogy: *Sexus; Plexus; Nexus:* 1949-59); *My Life and Times* (1972).

Miller, Joaquin (pseudonym of Cincinnatus Hiner Miller, 1841-1913). Supposed to have been born in a covered waggon while passing through the borderlands between Indiana and Ohio, and to have become, 'at various times, horse thief, Portland lawyer, pony-express messenger, newspaper editor, and Indian fighter'. It was his ambition to be accepted as 'the American Byron', and his poems had a long vogue, not only in America but also in England, where he published *Pacific Poems* (1870) and *Songs of the Sierras* (1871).

Miller, Leonard. See Leonard *Merrick.

Miller, Mary Britton. See Isabel *Bolton.

Millin, Sarah Gertrude (*née* Sarah Gertrude Liebson, 1889-1968; Mrs P. Millin). Born and educated in South Africa, at Kimberley. Her husband was a Judge of the Supreme Court in South Africa. Author of biographies of *Cecil Rhodes* (1933; new edn 1952), *General Smuts* (1936); novels: *The Dark River* (1920), *God's Stepchildren* (1924), *Mary Glenn* (1925), *The Burning Man* (1952), *The Wizard Bird* (1962); autobiography: *The Night is Long* (1941), *The Measure of My Days* (1955).

Milly Theale. American girl in Henry James's *The *Wings of the Dove* (1902); comes to England with her companion, Mrs Stringham; loves Merton Densher; dies in Venice.

Milne, A. A. (Alan Alexander Milne, 1882-1956). Born in London: educated at Westminster and Cambridge; did journalistic work in London and was Assistant Editor of *Punch*, 1906-14. His humorous essays from that periodical were collected in *The Day's Play* (1910), *The Holiday Round* (1912), *The Sunny Side* (1922), and other volumes. It was also to *Punch* that he contributed the verses that became a children's classic when brought together in *When We Were Very Young* (1924). Equal success was achieved by *Now We Are Six* (1927), and by their prose companions, *Winnie the Pooh* (1926) and *The House at Pooh Corner* (1928). The verses are skilfully and appealingly contrived, and the Pooh books stand with Kenneth Grahame's *The *Wind in the Willows*, which Milne adapted as a play in *Toad of Toad Hall* (1929). He was also a popular writer of light comedies, *Mr Pim Passes By* (1919), *The Dover Road* (1923), *The Truth About Blayds* (1923). Other books: *The Red House Mystery* (detective novel, 1921); *It's Too Late Now* (autobiography, 1939).

Milner, Alfred, 1st (and only) Viscount (1854-1925). Born in Germany, where his father was a university lecturer; educated there and in England at King's College, London, and at Oxford. Was on the staff of the *Pall Mall Gazette* (1882-85); helped to found the Toynbee Hall educational settlement in east London, and, after holding official appointments in Egypt, was High Commissioner in South Africa, 1897-1905, a period which spanned the Boer War and the subsequent period of reconciliation and brought much dissent from his policies. His later political career was a distinguished one, leading him into the War Cabinet, 1916-18, but he was to be most frequently remembered by references to 'Milner's kindergarten', the young statesmen-to-be who served under him in South Africa. Author of *England in Egypt* (1892), *The Nation and the Empire* (1913), *Questions of the Hour* (1923).

Milner, George (pseudonym of George Edward Charles Hardinge, later 3rd Baron Hardinge of Penshurst, 1921-   ). Educated at Eton and Royal Naval College, Dartmouth. Served in the Navy, 1940-47. Worked in publishing firms. Author of crime novels: *Stately Homicide* (1953), *Shark among Herrings* (1954), *The Scarlet Fountains* (1956), *Your Money and your Life* (1957).

Mint, The. Experiences and reflections of T. E. *Lawrence while serving in the R.A.F. under an assumed name as T. E. Shaw; published in New York 1936, in London 1955.

Miriam Larkins. Marries Alfred Polly in Wells's *The *History of Mr Polly* (1910).

Miriam Leivers. In D. H. Lawrence's *Sons and Lovers* (1913), farmer's daughter in love with Paul Morel.

Mirsky, Dmitry Svyatopolk (born 1890). Born Prince Mirsky; educated at the University of St Petersburg (Leningrad) and served in the Tsarist army. Settled in England after the Bolshevik Revolution, and held an appointment as lecturer in Russian literature at King's College, London, 1922 to 1932. He returned to Moscow, having changed his attitude to the Soviet régime and developed anti-British views. Although he was welcomed home by the Russians and appeared to be highly regarded, it seems that he incurred disfavour after a year or two, and nothing more was heard of him. He contributed to Soviet journals, and while in England wrote *Contemporary Russian Literature, 1881-1925* (1925), *Pushkin* (1926), *A History of Russian Literature, from the Earliest Times to the Death of Dostoyevsky* (1927), *Lenin* (1931), and later *The Intelligentsia of Great Britain* (1935).

'Miss Buss and Miss Beale'. *See* Dorothea *Beale.

Miss Lonelyhearts. *See* Nathanael *West.

Mr Bolfry. Play in four scenes by James *Bridie performed in 1943, published in 1944.
Cully, a young intellectual, and Cohen, a Jewish cockney shopkeeper, are billeted in a Free Kirk minister's manse in the Scottish Highlands while serving as gunners in the Royal Artillery in World War II. Jean Ogilvie, niece of the Rev. Mr McCrimmon, the minister, is convalescing in the manse after the bombing in London of the government building where she works. She and the two soldiers are drawn into theological argument with the minister, Jean categorically denying the Calvinistic beliefs of her uncle. Cully is less intolerant, and when she asserts that he is on the minister's side, he replies: 'I'm on nobody's side. I'm a sort of Devil's Advocate.' Among McCrimmon's books is the 16th-century Reginald Scot's *Discoverie of Witchcraft*, which the three consult late that night, in response to Jean's 'I wish we could raise the Devil and get him to speak for himself.' They follow instructions given by Scot to conjure a 'great and terrible divell' who bears several names, one being Bolfry. In a crash of thunder the outer door swings open and a mackintoshed figure with a dripping umbrella comes in, announcing himself as Dr Bolfry, but dressed in exactly the same way as Mr McCrimmon. With great eloquence Bolfry discourses on Good and Evil, Heaven and Hell, Body and Soul, Creation and Destruc-

tion, Life and Death. When Cohen says he is 'bored bloody stiff', Bolfry retorts: 'If you are alive, Mr Cohen, you should be interested in everything—even in the phenomenon of a Devil incarnate explaining to you the grand Purpose in virtue of which you live, move and have your breakfast.' At the end of a lengthy sermon by Bolfry on a text from William Blake, McCrimmon snatches up a knife and chases him out of the house and over a cliff into a calm sea: 'where he dived, the water boiled like a pot'. Next morning McCrimmon thinks he was drunk or delirious, Jean says she had 'an eerie dream', Cully suggests they were victims of mass hypnotism. Their attempts to rationalize are nullified when Jean suddenly notices the umbrella left behind. As she screams out 'It's Bolfry's', the umbrella 'gets up and walks by itself out of the room'.

Mr Dooley (pseudonym of Finley Peter Dunne, 1867-1936). Born in Chicago and had many years of experience as reporter and editor in Chicago and New York during which he invented the character he named Mr Dooley, making him the medium for astute satirical running comments on public affairs, delivered in Irish dialect. Collected in about a dozen volumes, from *Mr Dooley in Peace and in War* (1898) to *The 'Mr Dooley' Papers* (1938), they led to the author's being regarded as the greatest American humorist since Mark Twain.

Mister Johnson. Novel by Joyce *Cary published in 1939.
In a prefatory essay to the 1952 edition the author calls Johnson 'a young clerk who turns his life into a romance, he is a poet who creates for himself a glorious destiny'. He is a Nigerian mission-school youth on probation as a government clerk to the white District Officer at Fada station, which consists of no more than half-a-dozen old thatched houses, a fort, and a police barracks. Johnson is absurdly incompetent, apart from an aptitude for copperplate handwriting, but he has delusions of importance and grandeur, even to the point of claiming that the king of England is his personal friend. He is benevolently treated by Rudbeck, Assistant District Officer, who has an obsessive passion for cutting new roads through the bush, though his Treasury grant for this purpose is entirely inadequate. Johnson curries favour with Rudbeck by encouraging the road mania and devising a scheme for meeting the cost by

switching funds granted for other purposes. He is also given charge of the construction gang and has the road completed in quick time. He is continuously insolvent himself, borrowing more each time he can no longer avoid repaying an existing debt; and he buys his native girl-wife on a complicated instalment plan. He has an almost innocent disregard of truth and honesty—even a capacity for believing his lies are true and his thieving honest—and when Rudbeck is at length compelled to discharge him for peculation and extortion, Johnson goes to work at the Fada Company store owned by Gollup, a dipsomaniac white man who beats his loving native wife senseless as a regular weekly exercise. Johnson steals goods and money from Gollup, and after he is kicked out he returns at night to the store to rob the cash drawer, using a key he has purloined. With the money thus obtained he plays the part of a rich and generously hospitable friend among the natives, but on a further night foray to replenish his funds he is discovered by Gollup, whom he stabs and kills. Johnson decamps, but is caught, tried, and condemned to be hanged. He professes no fear of death, but on the execution morning he makes the request, which is refused verbally but at the last moment granted in fact, that Rudbeck shall shoot him.

Mr Priestley. Detective in crime novels by Anthony *Berkeley.

Mr Weston's Good Wine. Novel by T. F. *Powys published in 1927.
In a Ford delivery van two strangers reach the country town of Maidenbridge on their way to the village of Folly Down, where the elderly driver announces himself as Mr Weston, wine merchant, offering a brand called Mr Weston's Good Wine. In a ledger in the van are the names of potential customers. Michael, his junior partner, operates an electrical apparatus which advertises the wine by writing its name on the sky in 'bright and shining letters'. Among the leading villagers is the Rev. Nicholas Grubb, who has not believed in God since his sportive young wife was killed while saving their child, Tamar, who had jumped on the railway line to recover the picture of an angel she had dropped. Other villagers are Thomas Bunce, landlord of the Angel Inn, and his daughter Jenny; Luke Bird, who preaches to the birds and animals, has converted a bull, and is in love with Jenny; Mrs Vosper, procuress for

Squire Mumby's sons, who ravish the village girls she entices to 'lie down in the oak-tree bed'; Mr Grunter, the sexton, who is believed locally to be the seducer of the girls. Tamar longs to be loved by an angel and is at length joined in mystical marriage to Michael. Within its realistic and sensual framework the narrative is an allegory of love and death, with the visitors as God and the archangel. The title occurs in Jane Austen's *Emma* (ch. 15): 'She believed he had been drinking too much of Mr Weston's good wine, and felt sure that he would want to be talking nonsense.'

Mrs Dalloway. Novel by Virginia *Woolf published in 1925.

In preparation for her evening party, Clarissa, wife of Richard Dalloway, M.P., goes to Bond Street to buy flowers. While she is in the florist's shop, a tyre bursts with a loud report outside, and the traffic is held up until the affected car, with some eminent passenger, is able to move on. As well as by Mrs Dalloway from the shop, the incident is watched from the pavement by Septimus Warren Smith and his Italian wife, Lucrezia, who are thus linked tenuously with the narrative. Smith is suffering mentally from delayed effects of shell shock in the war, and on the way to a nerve specialist he and Lucrezia rest in Regent's Park, where his strange behaviour is noticed by Peter Walsh on his way from a morning call on Mrs Dalloway. Long before, Peter had been in love with Clarissa, and after she refused to marry him he spent many years in India, where he becomes involved with a married woman and returns to London on divorce business. His renewal of friendship with Clarissa stirs a varied range of memories of the past in both. Clarissa recalls especially a deep friendship between herself and daring, reckless Sally Seton. At the Dalloways' party that evening the eminent guests include the Prime Minister and Sir William and Lady Bradshaw, from whom Clarissa hears of a young patient of Bradshaw's, Septimus Warren Smith, who, a few hours before, killed himself by jumping from a window. Clarissa is puzzled when a Lady Rosseter is announced, until she sees that it is her old friend Sally Seton, who is married to a rich manufacturer in Manchester and has five sons. The book concentrates on the interior life of the characters, giving a minor place to external happenings.

Mrs Warren's Profession. Play in four acts by Bernard *Shaw written 1893-4, published in *Plays Unpleasant* in 1898. Refused a licence by the Lord Chamberlain for public performance, it was presented privately by the Stage Society in January 1902. A licence having at length been granted, the first public performance in England was given at Birmingham in 1925. In America it was publicly performed in 1905 but the theatre was closed by the police; the performers were charged with disorderly conduct but acquitted.

Vivie Warren, a self-confident young woman of twenty-two, has tied with the third wrangler in the mathematical tripos at Cambridge and has been devilling in the Chancery Lane office of her friend Honoria Fraser, practising as an actuary. While relaxing at her cottage in Surrey, Vivie is visited by her mother, who is usually abroad, and by Sir George Crofts and Mr Praed, friends of Mrs Warren. They are joined by the local clergyman, the Rev. Samuel Gardner, and his twenty-year-old son Frank, who is on affectionate terms with Vivie. Crofts tries to bribe Mrs Warren into supporting his plan to marry her daughter, and later that night the mother tells Vivie that she will have to make up her mind to see a good deal of Crofts, supposing that she and Vivie will henceforward be much together. When Vivie presses in vain for the name of her father, Mrs Warren tells how she and her sister Liz escaped from poverty by becoming prostitutes and later started a chain of brothels in European capitals. Next day Crofts proposes marriage to Vivie and, infuriated by her refusal, declares that her education had been paid for out of the profits on the £40,000 he invested in her mother's business. She calls him a 'capitalist bully' and he retaliates by alleging that she is Frank's half-sister, Samuel Gardner having been one of Mrs Warren's lovers before he entered the Church. Though at first horrified by the thought that they might unknowingly have made an incestuous marriage, they reach the conviction that Crofts' allegation is a malicious lie. Vivie nevertheless tells Frank that brother and sister is the only suitable relation for them. She refuses the money her mother offers to enable her to live in luxury, and goes into working partnership with Honoria Fraser.

Mitchell, Gladys (Gladys Maude Winifred Mitchell, 1901-   ). Educated at Isleworth and University of London. After writing historical novels under the pseudonym Stephen

Hockaby, she turned to crime fiction in which Mrs Bradley (later Dame Beatrice Bradley) is featured as the detective: *Dead Men's Morris* (1936), *Tom Brown's Body* (1949), *Spotted Hemlock* (1958), *Say It With Flowers* (1960), and many others. Also wrote children's books: *Holiday River* (1948), *Seven Stones Mystery* (1949), *The Malony Secret* (1950), *Caravan Creek* (1954).

Mitchell, James Leslie. *See* Lewis Grassic *Gibbon.

Mitchell, Margaret (1900-49; Mrs John R. Marsh). Born in Atlanta; educated there and at Smith College, Massachusetts. Prevented by family responsibilities from qualifying as a doctor, she wrote for an Atlanta newspaper and married in 1925. From her family, all of whom were deeply interested in the history of the Southern States, she had throughout her childhood and adolescence heard stories of the Confederacy and the Civil War, and from the knowledge thus acquired she created *Gone With the Wind* (1936), a thousand-page novel which was to become the most widely circulated of all best-sellers, its sales in nearly twenty languages totalling many millions, while the film based on it was also record-breaking. Though subsequently meeting the denigration which is the common aftermath of phenomenal success, *Gone With the Wind* has genuine merit as a sustained narrative achievement, and among its characters the memorable, tempestuous, Southern beauty Scarlett O'Hara. Margaret Mitchell wrote no other book.

Mitchens, Mrs Romola. *See* *Rummy Mitchens.

Mitchison, Naomi (*née* Naomi Margaret Haldane, 1897- ; Mrs G. R. (later Lady) Mitchison, her husband being made a life peer in 1964). Born in Edinburgh; educated at Oxford. For some years from 1923 she was the outstanding historical novelist of her generation, combining wide scholarship with a narrative method which humanized history and avoided the archaism of language which robbed much English historical fiction of the sense of actuality. Later, the author became preoccupied with public affairs and community life in Scotland. Her novels include *The Conquered* (1923), *When the Bough Breaks* (1924), *Cloud Cuckoo Land* (1925), *Black Sparta* (1928), *The Hostages* (1930), *The Corn King and the Spring Queen* (1931), *The Delicate Fire* (1933), *The Swan's Road* (1954), *The Far Harbour* (1957), *Small Talk*

(autobiography, 1973), *A Life for Africa* (1973).

Mitford, Nancy (Nancy Freeman Mitford, 1904-1973; Hon. Mrs Peter Rodd). Born in London; her father became Lord Redesdale when his brother was killed in World War I; educated at home. *Pursuit of Love* (1945), a novel set in the kind of environment in which she was reared, substitutes wit and humour for social snobbery. In addition to other novels— *Love In a Cold Climate* (1949), *The Blessing* (1951)—her books include *Madame de Pompadour* (1953, 1968), *Voltaire in Love* (1957), *The Sun King* (1966).

Mittelholzer, Edgar (Edgar Austin Mittelholzer, 1910-65). Born and educated in British Guiana, where he worked as a Customs officer and in other capacities before settling in England in 1948 on the staff of the British Council. With the publication of *Corentyne Thunder* in 1941 he began his career as a novelist and with *A Morning at the Office* (1950) became recognized as outstandingly important among the group of writers who were creating a *Caribbean imaginative literature. His later writings included *Shadows Move Among Them* (1951), *Children of Kaywana* (1952), *Kaywana Blood* (1958), *The Wounded and the Worried* (1962), and the non-fictional *With a Carib Eye* (1958) and *A Swarthy Boy* (autobiographical, 1963).

Mixture as Before, The. Volume of ten short stories by W. Somerset *Maugham published in 1940, with the title adopted from a review in *The Times* of his *Cosmopolitans*.

Moberley, Anne, died 1937. *See An Adventure.*

Molesworth, Mrs (*née* Mary Louisa Stewart, 1839-1921; married Major R. Molesworth). Born in Rotterdam; educated in Switzerland. Having written *Lover and Husband* (1869) and other novels under the pseudonym Ennis Graham, she found her true bent as author of fairy tales and other children's books which have become classics: *Carrots* (1876), *The Cuckoo Clock* (1877).

Molnar, Ferenc (1878-1952). Born in Budapest; educated and studied law there and in Geneva, but turned to journalism. Settled in America in 1940. Wrote novels, but was chiefly a playwright, though only his early light comedies are outstanding: *Liliom* (1921), *The Swan* (1922), *The Guardsman* (1924).

Mommsen, Theodor (1817-1903). Born in Schleswig; educated at Kiel. Professor of Law in Leipzig, Zurich, and Breslau, and of Ancient History in Berlin. His great *History of Rome* (3 vols, 1854-55) is still a standard work.

Moncrieff, C. K. Scott. *See* C. K. *Scott-Moncrieff.*

Monday. *See* *Sara Monday.

Monkhouse, Allan (Allan Noble Monkhouse, 1858-1936). Born at Barnard Castle, Durham; educated privately. Joined the staff of the *Manchester Guardian* in 1902 and remained on the paper until 1932, principally as dramatic critic. He wrote novels–*Love in a Life* (1903), *Men and Ghosts* (1918), *My Daughter Helen* (1922)—but was best known as one of the Manchester School of playwrights associated with Miss A. E. F. *Horniman's Company at the *Gaiety Theatre there: *Mary Broome* (1912), *The Education of Mr Surrage* (1913), *The Conquering Hero* (1923).

Monro, Harold (Harold Edward Monro, 1879-1932). Born in Brussels; educated in England at Radley and Cambridge. Founded the Samurai Press and in 1912 started the *Poetry Review* and opened the *Poetry Bookshop in Bloomsbury which became a rendezvous for many of the young writers and the publishing house of the famous volumes of *Georgian Poetry. In 1919 he founded *The Monthly Chapbook* which he edited till 1925. He was himself a poet whose work had qualities that have been too little recognized: *Poems* (1906), *Strange Meetings* (1917), *The Earth for Sale* (1928), *The Winter Solstice* (1928), and other volumes; *Collected Poems* (1933).

Monroe, Harriet (1860-1936). Born in Chicago; educated in Georgetown, District of Columbia. In 1912 she started *Poetry: A Magazine of Verse,* which ran for many years and fostered the talent of numerous young poets and paid for their contributions. Her own poems are of little merit: *Valeria and Other Poems* (1892), *Columbian Ode* (1893), *The Passing Show* (verse plays, 1903).

Monsarrat, Nicholas (Nicholas John Turney Monsarrat, 1910-   ). Born in Liverpool; educated at Winchester and Cambridge. Studied law and worked in a solicitor's office but turned to writing. His chief early success was with *H.M. Corvette* (1942), a product of his service with the navy in World War II. *East Coast Corvette* (1943) and *Corvette Command* (1944) followed. Later books *Leave Cancelled* (1945), *The Cruel Sea* (1951), *The Story of Esther Costello* (1953), *The Nylon Pirates* (1960). *Life is a Four-Letter Word* (autobiography, I, 1966, II, 1970).

Montague, C. E. (Charles Edward Montague, 1867-1928). Born in London; educated there and at Oxford. He joined the *Manchester Guardian* in 1890, married the daughter of the editor-proprietor, C. P. *Scott, and became his principal assistant, also acting for some time as the paper's dramatic critic and collecting some of the articles in *Dramatic Values* (1911). Although over-age for military service he dyed his hair and enlisted in the army when war started in 1914, was in France until his health failed, and afterwards did less-exacting war duties. His *Disenchantment* (1922) was among the earliest of the books which gave an unromantic and unheroic view of war, though he had himself shown exceptional courage on the battlefront. Other of his writings arising from the war were some of the short stories in *Fiery Particles* (1923) and the novels *Rough Justice* (1926) and *Right off the Map* (1927). His first novel *A Hind Let Loose* (1910) is a humorous account of newspaper life in which a journalist writes leading articles in two local papers of opposing political views. *A Writer's Notes on his Trade* (1930) gives insights into Montague's literary methods.

Montessori, Maria (1870-1952). Born in Rome. She became the first woman to be granted the degree of Doctor of Medicine by the University of Rome. Having made a close study of subnormal children, she instituted a system of education which enabled them to compete with those having no mental handicap, and later she evolved the Montessori System, applicable to all children, which spread to many countries. The chief aims in the Montessori curriculum are: the training of the senses and of speech; control of the limbs and movements of the body; teaching of writing and reading, and of arithmetic—the overriding principle being free spontaneous development. She published *The Montessori Method* (Eng. trans. 1913) and *The Secret of Childhood* (1936). *See* Friedrich *Froebel.

Montgomery, Leslie Alexander. *See* Lynn *Doyle.

Montgomery, L. M. (Lucy Maude Montgomery, 1874-1942). Born in Prince Edward Island and educated there. Became a teacher and contributed to periodicals; married the Rev. Ewan

Macdonald, a Presbyterian minister and settled in Toronto. Her first book *Anne of Green Gables* (1908) and later 'Anne' books made her world-renowned.

Montherlant, Henri de (Count Henri Millon de Montherlant, 1896-1972). Born in Paris; educated partly in England. Served and was severely injured in World War I and was also wounded in World War II, afterwards incurring bitter criticism based on the allegation that he was 'the one prominent French author who . . . welcomed and adulated the enemy', though his literary skill was never questioned. Author of *The Bullfighters* (trans. 1927), *Pity for Women* (trans. 1938), and other novels.

Monthly Chapbook, The. *See* Harold *Monro.

Moody, D. L. (Dwight Lyman Moody, 1837-99). *See* Ira D. *Sankey.

Moody, William Vaughn (1869-1910). Born in Indiana; educated there and in New York and at Harvard. Became an instructor and afterwards assistant professor of English in the University of Chicago. His writings include verse plays—*The Masque of Judgment* (1900), *The Fire Bringer* (1904); *Selected Poems* (1931); *The Great Divide* (1906) and other prose plays.

Moon and Sixpence, The. Novel by W. Somerset *Maugham suggested by the life of Paul Gauguin; published in 1919.

Charles Strickland, a 'good, dull, honest, plain' middle-aged stockbroker, suddenly deserts his charming wife and family after seventeen years of marriage and goes alone to Paris. In boyhood he wished to become a painter but was compelled into business by his father. For a year before his flight he took lessons in painting, unknown to his family; and in Paris declared with insistence 'I've got to paint', being manifestly possessed by a daemon which made him indifferent to social obligations, public opinion, and the fate of his wife. Though he paints in a manner that is derided by the majority, he is recognized as a genius of rare originality by Dirk Stroeve, a Dutch painter of commonplace genre pictures, with an English wife, Blanche, whom he adores sentimentally. Blanche hates Strickland, and for a long time refuses absolutely Dirk's urgent plea that they should have him brought to their apartment from the filthy attic in which Strickland is lying seriously ill with no one to look after him. Blanche gives

way when Dirk reminds her that she was once glad of a helping hand when in distress. She proves a devoted nurse during Strickland's illness, and when he has recovered she desolates her husband by leaving him and going away with Strickland. Apart from intermittent bouts of physical need, Strickland regards domestic intimacy with a woman as an intolerable intrusion on his overmastering passion for painting. Excluded from all but a fragment of his life, Blanche poisons herself. Later Strickland lives as a down-and-out in Marseilles until he becomes involved in a tavern fight and, to escape reprisals, works his passage to Tahiti, where he settles and marries a native girl and paints the pictures which make him famous after he is dead.

Moore, Frankfort (Frank Frankfort Moore, 1855-1931). Born in Limerick; educated in Belfast; travelled in Africa, India, the West Indies, South America and elsewhere; worked as a journalist. Among his many works of fiction and non-fiction, *The Jessamy Bride* (1897) was best known. The title of *Fanny's First Novel* (1913) was no doubt suggested by Bernard Shaw's *Fanny's First Play* (1911).

Moore, George (George Augustus Moore, 1852-1933). Born at Moore Hall, Ballyglass, County Mayo, son of an Irish M.P. who ran a racing stable. Educated in England at the Roman Catholic Oscott College, but became an agnostic in later life. Though intended for a military career, his inclinations were towards art, and after his father's death in 1870 he went to Paris and mixed with the poets and artists there for some ten years and made half-hearted attempts to study painting. By 1880, when he returned to London (with occasional visits to his Irish property), he had decided to become a writer. Under the influence of Zola he produced seven works of fiction before *Esther Waters* (1894) put him in the forefront of contemporary novelists. That book has continued to be ranked as the masterpiece of the realistic movement which was in full swing at the time. Meanwhile—in addition to the novels, *A Modern Lover* (1883), *A Mummer's Wife* (1885), *A Drama in Muslin* (1886) and others—he had written *Confessions of a Young Man* (1888), *Impressions and Opinions* (1891) and *Modern Painting* (1893), and had become art critic to a London periodical, *The Speaker*. He retired to Ireland in 1899 on account of his opposition to the Boer War and lived in Dublin from

1901 to 1911, then settled again in London at 121 Ebury Street, near Victoria Station, an address made famous by his residence there for the rest of his life. His first phase as a novelist and short-story writer ended with the series of books comprising *Celibates* (1895), *Evelyn Innes* (1898), *Sister Teresa* (1901), *The Untilled Field* (1903), and *The Lake* (1905). In succeeding years he published *Reminiscences of the Impressionist Painters* (1906), *Memoirs of My Dead Life* (1906), and **Hail and Farewell* in three volumes—*Ave* (1911), *Salve* (1912), *Vale* (1914). This autobiographical trilogy portrayed, sometimes through Moore's distorting lens, those with whom he associated in Dublin; but despite the fury aroused, it is a work of surpassing literary skill and enduring interest, whether it is to be viewed as a true record or as an amalgam compounded in the crucible of the author's creative imagination. His second and final phase as a novelist began with *The *Brook Kerith* (1916). That and *Héloise and Abélard* (1921) and **Aphrodite in Aulis* (1930) are written in austere prose contrasting with the lush style of much of Moore's earlier fiction. Other late works: fiction—*A Storyteller's Holiday* (1918), *Peronnik the Fool* (1924), *Ulick and Soracha* (1926); essays, etc., *Avowals* (1919), *Conversations in Ebury Street* (1924), *A Communication to My Friends* (1933); translation (from the Greek), *The Pastoral Loves of Daphnis and Chloe* (1924). At intervals he wrote plays, including *The Strike at Arlingford* (1893), *The Bending of the Bough* (1900), *The Apostle* (1911), *Esther Waters* (1913), *The Passing of the Essenes* (1930).

Moore, G. E. (George Edward Moore, 1873-1958). Born in London; educated at Dulwich and at Cambridge where he became University Lecturer in Moral Science, 1911-25, and Professor of Philosophy, 1925-39. Editor of the quarterly philosophical journal *Mind*, 1920-47. As a teacher at Cambridge his philosophical and ethical principles deeply influenced J. M. *Keynes, E. M. *Forster and others who were later to constitute what became known as the *Bloomsbury Group. The major statement of his principles is *Principia Ethica* (1903), his only other works being *Ethics* (in the Home University Library, 1912), *Philosophical Studies* (1922), and *Some Main Problems of Philosophy* (1953). T. Sturge *Moore was his brother and the poet Nicholas Moore his son.

Moore, John (John Cecil Moore, 1907-67).

Educated at Malvern. Author of, mainly, books both fictional and factual on English country life: *Country Men* (1934), *The Cotswolds* (1937), *The Countryman's England* (1939), *Portrait of Elmbury* (1945), *Brensham Village* (1946), *Come Rain, Come Shine* (1956), *The Waters Under the Earth* (1965). He also published *The Life and Letters of Edward *Thomas* (1939).

Moore, Marianne (Marianne Craig Moore, 1887-1972). Born in St Louis; educated at Bryn Mawr College; studied at a commercial college and was for several years a shorthand teacher before becoming an assistant at the New York Public Library, 1921-25, and then editor of *The Dial* in its last three years, 1926-29. She said of her own poems that they were written in a 'patterned arrangement' to produce an effect of 'flowing continuity', and her view of the world has been described as 'witty, cerebral, ironic' and comparable with that of Emily Dickinson. Her several volumes of verse include *Poems* (1921), *The Pangolin* (1936), *What Are Years?* (1941), *Nevertheless* (1944); *Collected Poems* (1951).

Moore, Mrs. Mother of Ronny Heaslop (son by her first marriage) in E. M. Forster's *A *Passage to India* (1924); accompanies Adela Quested to Chandrapore; dies on the return voyage.

Moore, T. Sturge (Thomas Sturge Moore, 1870-1944). Born at Hastings, brother of G. E. *Moore. Bad health brought his schooling to an early close, but he made some study of art and became an accomplished woodengraver. He published more than a dozen volumes of verse which received much critical praise but little general attention: a collected edition in four volumes appeared in 1932-33. He also wrote prose studies of several painters: *Altdorfer* (1900), *Dürer* (1904), *Correggio* (1906); and *Art and Life* (1910).

Moorehead, Alan (Alan McCrae Moorehead, 1910-   ). Born in Australia (at Croydon in Victoria); educated in Melbourne at the Scotch College and the University. Wrote for newspapers in Australia and England. His experiences as a war correspondent led to success as a writer with *Mediterranean Front* (1941), *A Year of Battle* (1943), *The End in Africa* (1943): collected as *African Trilogy* (1944). Later books: *Montgomery* (1946), *The Rage of the Vulture* (1948), *The Traitors* (1952), *Gallipoli* (1956), *The Russian Revolution* (1958), *No Room in the Ark* (1959), *The*

White Nile (1960), *The Blue Nile* (1962), *Cooper's Creek* (1963), *The Fatal Impact* (1966) (the last two deal with, respectively, central Australia and the South Sea islands), and *Darwin and the Beagle* (1969).

Moraes, Dom (1938-   ). Born in Bombay, son of an English-educated barrister who became Editor of *The Times of Ceylon* and later of *The Times of India*. His early years were spent between Bombay and Colombo and touring with his father to Australia, New Zealand, and South-East Asia. After schooling in Bombay he came to England when sixteen, spent some time on the Continent, and finished his formal education at Oxford. From boyhood he read voraciously in books by recent English and French authors, made the acquaintance of Stephen Spender, W. H. Auden, and other writers, and had his first book *Poems* published with acclaim in 1957. He settled in England after briefly revisiting India. Later books: poetry—*Poems* (1960), *John Nobody* (1965), *Poems 1955-65* (1966); travel—*Gone Away* (1960); autobiography—*My Son's Father* (1968).

Moral rearmament. Religious movement started in 1921 as the 'Oxford Group' by an American evangelist, Frank *Buchman. Renamed (1938) in response to protests from Oxford and elsewhere that the original title was misleading.

Morand, Paul (1889-   ). Born and educated in Paris; entered the French diplomatic service and became Ambassador at Berne in 1944 after having held embassy appointments in London, Rome, Madrid, Siam and Bucharest. Among his numerous books the two volumes of short stories *Open All Night* (1923) and *Closed All Night* (1924) made him most widely known beyond France.

Moravia, Alberto (pseudonym of Alberto Pincherle, 1907-   ). His novels achieved international popularity, notwithstanding what has been described as 'grim, hopeless realism', 'a constantly sombre and haggard atmosphere', 'melancholic cruelty', and 'morbid love of the sadistic and the grotesque'. Translations into English: *The Time of Indifference* (1953), *The Fancy Dress Party* (1948), *The Woman of Rome* (1949), *Conjugal Love* (1951), *Two Women* (1958).

Mordaunt, Elinor (*née* Evelyn May Clowes, 1877-1942; sometime Mrs Mordaunt). Born in Nottinghamshire; educated at home. Her first marriage to a planter in Mauritius was a prelude to later travels which took her to

many countries. She wrote travel books and many novels, among which *Full Circle* (1931; published in America as *Gin and Bitters* by A. Riposte) was intended as a counterblast to *Cakes and Ale* by Somerset *Maugham, but she was competing out of her class.

More. A second volume of essays by Max *Beerbohm, published in 1899, and containing twenty pieces, including 'Some Words on Royalty', 'Madam Tussauds', 'Groups of Myrmidons', 'The Sea-Side in Winter', 'Ouida' [to whom the book is dedicated], 'The Blight on Music Halls', 'A Cloud of Pinafores', 'At Covent Garden'.

More, Paul Elmer (1864-1937). Born in St Louis; educated at Washington and Harvard Universities. His life was divided between formal scholarship and literary journalism: he taught Sanskrit at Harvard, philosophy at Princeton, and in New York was editor of *The Nation* from 1909 to 1914. Author of *Shelburne Essays* (14 vols, 1904-34), in which he advocated 'a return to classic values in a period of romantic stress and groping for standards' and aligned himself with Irving *Babbitt as a leading proponent of the *New Humanism. Other works: *Life of Benjamin Franklin* (1900), *Platonism* (1917), *Hellenistic Philosophies* (1923), *The Demon of the Absolute* (1928), *Pages from an Oxford Diary* (autobiographical, 1937).

Morel family. In D. H. Lawrence's *Sons and Lovers* (1913): Walter Morel, miner; Gertrude, his wife; their children, William, Annie, Paul, Arthur.

Moresby, Louis. *See* Lily Moresby Adams *Beck.

Morgan, Charles (Charles Langbridge Morgan, 1894-1958). Born in Kent, educated at naval colleges and Oxford. Served in the navy both before and during World War I. He joined the staff of *The Times* in 1921 and was its dramatic critic from 1926 to 1939. He became a popular and for some time a critically approved novelist with *The Fountain* (1932), but the philosophical content of that and other novels was superficial and his prose style grew increasingly suave and ponderous, as in the essays he contributed to *The Times Literary Supplement* under the pseudonym Menander and collected in *Reflections in a Mirror* (1944) and *Second Reflections in a Mirror* (1945). Other novels: *My Name is Legion* (1925), *Portrait in a Mirror* (1929), *Sparkenbroke* (1936), *The Voyage* (1940), *The*

Judge's Story (1946). Plays: *The Flashing Stream* (1938), *The River Line* (1952; dramatized from his 1949 novel with the same title), *The Burning Glass* (1953). He also wrote a publishing history of *The House of Macmillan* (1943); *Epitaph on George Moore* (1935, a sketch for an unwritten biography); and *Ode to France* (1942), a country for which he had an impassioned devotion. *Selected Letters of Charles Morgan*, edited and with a Memoir by Eiluned Lewis (1967).

Morgan, William De. See William *De Morgan.

Morison, Samuel Eliot (1887-   ). Born in Boston; educated at Harvard, where he became Professor of History (1925-55). Author of the *Oxford History of the United States* (1927), *Admiral of the Ocean Sea: A Life of Christopher Columbus* (1942), *History of U.S. Naval Operations in World War II* (15 vols, 1947-62), *Paul Jones: A Sailor's Biography* (1960).

Morison, Stanley (1889-1967). A member of *The Times* staff and typographical adviser to the Cambridge University Press and the Monotype Corporation, he designed the New Roman type for *The Times*, adopted in 1932 for that paper as well as by other printing houses. He edited *The History of the Times* (4 vols, 1935-52), and was editor of *The Times Literary Supplement* from 1945 to 1947. Author of books on typography and typographers and the art of printing.

Morley, Christopher (Christopher Darlington Morley, 1890-1957). Born at Haverford, Pennsylvania; educated there and (as a Rhodes Scholar) at Oxford. Worked for publishers and as a contributor to newspapers, and to the New York *Saturday Review of Literature* from 1924 to 1939. His writings are hard to classify, often spanning in one and the same book more than a single category — *belles lettres*, fiction, autobiography, gossip, criticism, conversation. He belonged to the dwindling company of those formerly called bookmen, and much of his work is in a whimsical yet archly sophisticated mode. The somewhat mystifying *Thunder on the Left* (1925) attracted a good deal of puzzled attention, while his nearest to a conventional novel in style, *Kitty Foyle* (1939), was found morally unconventional by conventional readers.

Morley, Edith (Edith Julia Morley, 1875-1964). Born in London; educated in Kensington,

Hanover, and King's College and University College, London. Professor of English Language, Reading University, 1908-40. As a scholar she concentrated on editing the valuable literary remains of the diarist Henry Crabb Robinson (1775-1867), publishing a selection entitled *Blake, Coleridge and Wordsworth* (1922); *Correspondence of Crabb Robinson with the Wordsworth Circle* (1927), *Henry Crabb Robinson on Books and their Writers* (1938); *The Life and Times of Henry Crabb Robinson* (1935).

Morley, John (1838-1923; 1st Viscount Morley of Blackburn, 1908). Born at Blackburn; educated at Cheltenham and Oxford. Liberal M.P. from 1888; held various Cabinet offices until he resigned in 1914 in protest against war. His *Life of Gladstone* (1903) was long regarded as the standard biography. He edited the *Fortnightly Review*, 1867-82, and the *Pall Mall Gazette*, 1880-83. Valuable service for students was rendered by his editorship of the English Men of Letters series, in which he wrote the volume on *Edmund Burke* (1879), and the English Statesmen series, to which he contributed *Robert Walpole* (1889). Other works: *Voltaire* (1872), *On Compromise* (1874), *Rousseau* (1876), *Diderot and the Encyclopaedists* (1878), *Richard Cobden* (1881; new edn. 1896), *Studies in Literature* (1891), *Oliver Cromwell* (1900).

Morlocks. The race living in perpetual darkness underground and capturing the above-ground people (the Eloi) as food in H. G. Wells's *The *Time Machine* (1895).

Morrison, Arthur (1863-1945). Born in Kent. He wrote detective stories—*Martin Hewitt, Investigator* (1894), *Adventures of Martin Hewitt* (1896) and others; a volume on oriental art—*The Painters of Japan* (1911)—having himself acquired pictures by Chinese and Japanese artists (his fine collection passed to the British Museum); and realistic stories of London slum life: *Tales of Mean Streets* (1894), *A Child of the Jago* (1896), *The Hole in the Wall* (1902).

Mortimer, John (1923-   ). Educated at Harrow and Oxford; studied law and practised as a barrister. Author of several novels but better known as a radio and stage dramatist: *The Dock Brief and Other Plays* (1959), *The Wrong Side of the Park* (1960), *A Voyage Round My Father* (1970), *Five Plays* (1971).

Mortimer, Penelope (née Penelope Ruth Fletcher, 1918-). Author of *The Pumpkin Eater* (1962), *The Home* (1971), and other novels.

Mortimer, Raymond (1895-). Educated at Malvern and Oxford. Sometime Literary Editor of the *New Statesman*. He wrote on the paintings of Manet and Duncan Grant; and in *Channel Packet* (1942) published a collection of his literary articles.

Morton, Anthony. See John *Creasey.

Morton, Guy Mainwaring. See Peter *Traill.

Morton, H. V. (Henry Vollam Morton, 1892-). Born and educated in Birmingham; worked on the staffs of London newspapers but left journalism when the success of his books permitted. Author of *The Heart of London* (1925) and other books on London; *In Search of England* (1927), and similar volumes on Scotland (1929), Ireland (1930), Wales (1932); and other travel books relating to the Middle East (1941), South Africa (1948), Spain (1954), Rome (1957), the Holy Land (1961).

Morton, J. B. (John Cameron Andrieu Bingham Michael Morton, 1893-). Educated at Harrow and Oxford. Wrote in the *Daily Express* as Beachcomber from 1924. Author of humorous books—*The Cow Jumped Over the Moon* (1924), *Mr Thake* (1929) and later 'Thake' volumes; *The Dancing Cabman* (verse, 1938); *Hilaire Belloc: A Memoir* (1955) and other biographies; studies of the French Revolution, etc.

Morton, Sir Robert. Counsel for the defence in Terence Rattigan's *The *Winslow Boy* (1946).

Mosher, T. B. (Thomas Bird Mosher, 1852- 1923). Publisher of the 'Mosher Books' and *The Bibelot* (1895-1915), which were most attractively produced and cherished by collectors but not by English authors, since Mosher was disposed to take advantage of discrepancies in the copyright laws of Britain and the United States.

Mossop, Willie. Married by capture by Maggie Hobson in Harold Brighouse's *Hobson's Choice* (1916).

Mottram, R. H. (Ralph Hale Mottram, 1883- 1971). Born at Norwich; educated there and in Lausanne. Encouraged by John *Galsworthy he turned from a business life to that of a writer. Service in Flanders during World War I provided a setting for his first and very successful novel *The Spanish Farm* (1924),

followed by *Sixty-Four, Ninety-Four* (1925) and *The Crime at Vanderlynden's* (1926), the three books being collected in *The Spanish Farm Trilogy* (1927). Mottram wrote many other novels, *A History of Financial Speculation* (1929) and *A History of the East India Company* (1940). Under the pseudonym J. Marjoram he published *Repose and Other Verses* (1906) and *New Poems* (1909).

Moult, Thomas (1885-1974). Born in Derbyshire; educated in Manchester. Undertook welfare work in Borstal institutions and prisons. Literary, dramatic, and music critic for *Manchester Guardian* and other newspapers and periodicals. Author of *Snow Over Eldon* (1920), *The Comely Lass* (1923) and other novels; *Down Here the Hawthorn* (1921) and other poems; biographical and critical studies of *J. M. Barrie* (1928), *Mary Webb* (1932), *W. H. Davies* (1934); editor of numerous anthologies of poems and of books on cricket by Jack Hobbs (*Playing for England*, 1931) and Len Hutton (*Cricket is My Life*, 1949).

Mourning Becomes Electra. Trilogy of plays by Eugene *O'Neill (performed and published in 1931) based on the Greek tragedy of Agamemnon, betrayed by his wife Clytemnestra while away at the Trojan War, and murdered by her and her lover Aegisthus, who are in turn killed by Orestes and Electra, children of Agamemnon and Clytemnestra.

In O'Neill's drama, centred on the Mannon residence in a New England seaport, built in the style of a Greek temple, Christine Mannon begins an adulterous affair with Captain Adam *Brant while her husband General Ezra Mannon is with the Federal army in the Civil War. Her daughter Lavinia, obsessed by jealous hatred of her mother and adoration of her father, threatens to make the illicit relationship known unless they end it. Christine obtains poison from Brant and gives it to her husband in place of medicine for an attack of angina on the night he returns from the war. Lavinia finds the remainder of the poison when her mother faints in the bedroom as Ezra dies. Her brother Orin, home from the war, is at first incredulous when Lavinia denounces Christine as adulteress and murderess, for mother and son are passionately attached. He is convinced, however, by Lavinia's production of the remaining poison and by finding his mother together with Brant in the latter's ship. He kills Brant, and when told of this Christine shoots herself. Orin, demented by horror, is taken by his sister on a voyage to China and Pacific islands, from which she returns almost transfigured into a beautiful likeness of her mother, but Orin remains haggard and lifeless. The two feel bound together by the consciousness of inherited guilt, while Orin displays incestuous feelings for Lavinia. Continuing to be tormented by remorse he commits suicide, making it appear as an accident while cleaning a revolver. Lavinia, the last of the doom-ridden family, determines to punish herself by passing the remainder of her life shut away in the deserted and decaying Mannon mansion.

Mphahlele, Ezekiel (1919-   ). *See* *African Writers.

Muckraking. Term applied to a series of investigations by journalists and others in the U.S. into charges of corruption in politics and commerce. Though Theodore Roosevelt used the word in an attack on this reform movement in 1906, 'muckraking' ceased to be a derogatory label when widespread corruption was proved and exposed. The movement ran throughout a decade or more from 1902, and its history is given in the *Autobiography* of Lincoln *Steffens, while light is thrown on specific instances in such novels as *The *Jungle* by Upton *Sinclair and *Susan Lenox* and others by David Graham *Phillips.

Mudie, Charles Edward (1818-90). Born in Chelsea, son of Thomas Mudie, a secondhand bookseller who lent books at 1*d* a volume and in 1840 started a bookselling and stationer's business in Bloomsbury. Charles Mudie published in 1844 the first English edition of James Russell Lowell's poems and an oration by Emerson, but his claim to remembrance is his starting in 1842 the book-circulating enterprise which developed into the famous Mudie's Library situated at the corner of New Oxford Street and Museum Street from 1852 until it closed in 1937. 'Mudie's' became a power in the publishing world through its ability to exercise a form of censorship by declining to stock or circulate any book to which exception was taken on moral or other grounds. Among those who objected to Mudie's methods was George *Moore who published in 1885 a pamphlet *Literature at Nurse; or, Circulating Morals,* 'strictures upon the selection of books in circulation at Mudie's Library'. Since Mudie's order might run to thousands of copies, their support was important to publishers and authors.

Muir, Edwin (1887-1959). Born in the northern Scottish isle of Orkney. The family having moved to Glasgow he worked as a clerk and in other jobs there from the age of fourteen until 1919, when he married and migrated to London, where he worked as assistant to the editor of the *New Age,* A. R. *Orage. From 1921 they lived on the Continent, first in Prague and in the south of France before returning to Scotland in 1927. Muir and his wife (*née* Willa Anderson) translated *Kafka's *The Castle* and *The Trial* and various works by German writers. After World War II he worked for the British Council in Pragué and Rome until he was appointed Warden of Newbattle Abbey College (for adult education), Midlothian, in 1950. Between 1955 and 1958 he was a Visiting Professor at Universities in the United States and England. He wrote three novels—*The Marionette* (1927), *The Three Brothers* (1931), *Poor Tom* (1932); several volumes of criticism—*Transition* (1926), *The Structure of the Novel* (1928), *Essays on Literature and Society* (1949), *The Estate of Poetry* (posthumously, 1962, with a Foreword by Archibald *MacLeish). Poems—*First Poems* (1925), *Chorus of the Newly Dead* (1926), *Variations on a Time Theme* (1934), *Journeys and Places* (1937), *The Narrow Place* (1943), *The Labyrinth* (1949); *Collected Poems 1921-1958* (posthumously, 1960). Autobiography—*The Story and the Fable* (1940) reissued as *Autobiography* (1954).

Muir, Ramsay (John Ramsay Bryce Muir, 1872-1941). Educated at Liverpool and Oxford. Professor of Modern History, Liverpool University, 1906-13; at Manchester University, 1913-21. Liberal M.P. for Rochdale, 1923-4. Author of *Peers and Bureaucrats* (1910), *History of the British Commonwealth* (Vol. I, 1920; II, 1922), *How Britain is Governed* (1930), *Civilization and Liberty* (1940).

Mukerji, Dhan Ghopal (1890-1936). Born in Calcutta; educated at a missionary school and studied at the Universities of Calcutta, Tokyo, and California. His *A Son of Mother India Answers* (1928) was provoked by Katherine *Mayo's *Mother India.* Among his other writings are *Gay-Neck* (1927; a book on birds for children), and the autobiographical *Caste and Outcast* (1923).

Mulford, Clarence Edward (1883-1956). Born in Illinois; educated there and in New York, where he began work on the staff of a technical journal. He made an intensive study of the history of the American West and wrote a long series of short stories and novels of cowboy adventure ('Westerns') with a lame hero, Hopalong Cassidy, whose popularity in the books was further extended by dramatic adaptations for television. His books include *Bar 20* (1907), *Hopalong Cassidy* (1910), *Rustler's Valley* (1924), *The Bar 20 Rides Again* (1926), *The Round-Up* (1933).

Mulgan, John (John Alan Edward Mulgan, 1911-45). Born in Christchurch, New Zealand; educated there and at Auckland University and Oxford. Journalist. Author of *Poems of Freedom* (1938), *Man Alone* (novel, 1939), *Report on Experience* (autobiography; posthumously 1947). See *New Zealand Writers.

Mumford, Lewis (1895-   ). Born on Long Island; educated at high school and New York and Columbia Universities. Worked as a journalist in London and New York. His writings in periodicals and books show deep concern for the restoration of moral values and civilized standards in philosophy, literature and the arts, and his interest in the planning of cities is a product of his conviction that architectural environment has a metaphysical influence. Author of *The Story of Utopias* (1922), *Sticks and Stones* (1924), *The Golden Day* (1926), ' *The Brown Decades* (1931), *Technics and Civilization* (1934), *The Culture of Cities* (1938), *Faith for Living* (1940), *The Condition of Man* (1944), *City Development* (1945), *Art and Technics* (1952), *The City in History* (1961).

Munro, C. K. (pseudonym of Charles Walden Kirkpatrick MacMullan, 1889-   ). Born in Ireland; educated at Harrow and Cambridge. Entered the Civil Service and became Under-Secretary at the Ministry of Labour. Wrote about a dozen stage plays, his greatest success being the boarding-house comedy *At Mrs Beam's* (1922). Other plays: *Wanderers* (1915), *The Rumour* (1923), *Storm* (1924), *The Mountain* (1926), *Mr Eno* (1928), *Ding and Co.* (1934); also plays for broadcasting, and essays (*The True Woman*, 1931; *Watching a Play:* lectures, 1933; *The Fountains in Trafalgar Square*, 1952).

Munro, Hector Hugo. See Saki.

Munro, Neil (1864-1930). Born in Inverary, Argyllshire; educated at the local school. Worked as a lawyer's clerk before turning to journalism, at length becoming Editor of the *Glasgow Evening News* (1918-27). He wrote some verse, collected in *The Poetry of Neil Munro* (1931) and some miscellaneous prose including *The Clyde: River and Firth* (1907), but was most celebrated for his historical novels of the Scottish highlands—*John Splendid* (1898), *Gilian the Dreamer* (1899), *Doom Castle* (1901), *Children of Tempest* (1903)—and for his humorous dialect tales—*The 'Vital Spark'* (1906), *The Daft Days* (1907), *Fancy Farm* (1910), *Ayrshire Idylls* (1912), *Jaunty Jock* (1918).

Munthe, Axel (Axel Martin Fredrik Munthe, 1857-1949). Born in Sweden; educated at the University of Uppsala; studied medicine and qualified in Paris, and practised there, becoming increasingly renowned as a psychiatrist. On returning to his own country he became physician to the Queen of Sweden, then lived for some years in the isle of Capri, and finally spent his last decade as a guest in the Royal Palace, Stockholm. He published *Memories and Vagaries* (1897); *Letters from a Mourning City* (1899), an account of Naples afflicted by cholera; *Red Cross and Iron Cross* (1916), about France in World War I; and leapt into international popular fame with *The Story of San Michele* (1929), a unique volume of reminiscences touched with imagination. *And see* Mrs Bernard *Shaw.

Murder in the Cathedral. Religious play in verse by T. S. *Eliot, first performed (in an abbreviated form) in the Chapter House of the Cathedral at the Canterbury Festival, June 1935. It was the first of Eliot's poetic dramas (apart from the 'verse libretto' for *The *Rock*) and initiated the principles expounded in his *Poetry and Drama* lecture (1950) and exemplified in his later secular verse plays.

The 'murder in the cathedral' is that of Thomas Becket at Canterbury in 1170, the characters in the play, besides the Archbishop himself, being a Chorus of Women, Three Priests, Four Knights, Four Tempters, a Herald, and Attendants. The drama opens with a chorus of the poor women of Canterbury lamenting Becket's seven years' absence in exile, but a Herald arrives to announce to them and the Priests that the Archbishop is returning. But despite this welcome news, they all (except the Second Priest) are fearful that King Henry II's reconciliation with him is treacherous. Becket enters and foresees 'Little rest in Canterbury/With eager enemies restless about us.' A long scene follows with the Tempters.

who bring, in their speeches, temporal temptations and then the temptation to 'Seek the way of martyrdom, make yourself the lowest/ On earth, to be high in heaven.' But Becket sums up as the scene closes: 'Now is my way clear, now is the meaning plain: . . ./The last temptation is the greatest treason :/To do the right deed for the wrong reason.' The Interlude gives Becket's sermon preached in the cathedral on Christmas morning 1170. Part II of the play is concerned first with a dialogue of the Priests and then with the coming of the four Knights, who charge Becket with 'rebellion to the King and the law of the land', and convey the King's command 'That you and your servants depart from this land'. When he declines they abuse him and say they will come again for 'the King's justice'. The Priests, failing to induce Becket to barricade himself in the Cathedral, drag him away and bar the door, but he commands them to open it and the Knights, now half-drunk, return and kill him. The four murderers then address the audience in turn, making a prose apologia, protesting that their action was 'perfectly disinterested' and, in the closing words of the last speaker, urging that since Becket ordered the door to be opened to them, a verdict of Suicide while of Unsound Mind should be rendered.

Murdoch, Iris (Jean Iris Murdoch, 1919-   ; Mrs J. O. Bayley). Born in Dublin; educated in London, Bristol, and Oxford; lecturer in philosophy at Cambridge, and at the Royal College of Art. Author of *Sartre: Romantic Rationalist* (1953) and of numerous novels, including *Under the Net* (1954), *The Flight from the Enchanter* (1955), *The Bell* (1958), *A Severed Head* (1961), *The Time of the Angels* (1966), *Bruno's Dream* (1969). At her best she has a gift of uproarious humour, as in the progress and outcome of the prolonged London pub-crawl in *Under the Net*, and in the shareholders' meeting in *The Flight from the Enchanter*. In the latter, too, her sense of pathos and tragedy is shown in the account of the life and death of Mina the refugee dressmaker. Her rapid succession of later novels displayed some loss of coherence, and overpreoccupation with symbolism and sexual vagaries.

Murray, D. L. (David Leslie Murray, 1888-1962). Born in London; educated at Harrow and Oxford. Dramatic critic of the *Nation*, 1920-23; editor of *The Times Literary Supplement*, 1938-44. Author of *The Bride Adorned*

(1929), *The English Family Robinson* (1933), *Regency* (1936), *Tale of Three Cities* (1940), *Folly Bridge* (1945), *Outrageous Fortune* (1952), and other novels; and of *Pragmatism* (1912), *Scenes and Silhouettes* (1926), *Disraeli* (1927).

Murray, Gilbert (1) (George Gilbert Aimé Murray, 1866-1957). Born in Sydney, Australia, son of Sir Terence Murray, President of the New South Wales Legislative Council; educated in London at Merchant Taylors' School and at Oxford. From 1889-99 he was Professor of Greek in the University of Glasgow, and from 1908 until his retirement in 1936 Regius Professor of Greek in the University of Oxford. He produced critical editions of Greek classics in the original language, but became more widely celebrated with his many English verse translations of the tragedies of Euripides, Sophocles, Aeschylus, and some of the comedies of Aristophanes. Although in academic circles these were increasingly devalued as misrenderings into an inappropriate metrical form (mainly rhyming couplets), they did inestimable service for Greekless English readers and theatregoers to whom the great Athenian tragedies would otherwise have remained unknown. Murray was an ardent supporter of the League of Nations (as Chairman of the League of Nations Union, 1923-38), and was Professor of Poetry at Harvard in 1926. He was affectionately caricatured by his great friend Bernard *Shaw as Adolphus Cusins in *Major Barbara*. In addition to his critical editions and translations of Greek plays, he wrote: *The Rise of the Greek Epic* (1907), [*Four*] *Five Stages of Greek Religion* (1913, 1925, 1951), *Euripides and his Age* (Home University Library, 1913), *The Classical Tradition in Poetry* (1927), *Aristophanes: A Study* (1933), *Aeschylus, Creator of Tragedy* (1940), *Stoic, Christian, and Humanist* (1940), *Hellenism and the Modern World* (1953), several books on political and pacifist themes, and two original plays—*Carlyon Sahib* (1899) and *Andromache* (1900).

Murray, Gilbert (2). Pseudonym of Richard Newman Wycherley, writer on Methodism.

Murray, T. C. (Thomas C. Murray, 1873-1959). Born in County Cork; educated at St Patrick's Training College; became a teacher and headmaster. Author of plays for the Irish Theatre, including *Birthright* (1910), *Maurice Harte* (1912), *Autumn Fire* (1924), *Illumination* (1939).

Murry, John Middleton (1889-1957). Born in London; educated at Christ's Hospital and Oxford. Joined the staff of the *Westminster Gazette,* contributed to *The Nation* and from 1913 to *The Times Literary Supplement.* After service in the War Office from 1916 to 1919 he became editor in turn of the *Athenaeum,* 1919-21, and the *Adelphi,* 1923-48. He married Katherine *Mansfield in 1913 and after her death in 1923 published much about her, including *Letters of Katherine Mansfield* (1928; 1951), *The Life of Katherine Mansfield* (1933), *Katherine Mansfield and other Literary Portraits* (1949; 1959), *The Journal of Katherine Mansfield* (1954). He was an influential if self-conscious critic, being most successful with *Keats and Shakespeare* (1925), *Studies in Keats* (1930; 1939), *William Blake* (1933), *Jonathan Swift* (1954). His friendship with D. H. *Lawrence, an uneasy one, produced *Son of Woman* (1931). Autobiography: *Between Two Worlds* (1935).

Muses. In classical Greek mythology, the nine lesser goddesses presiding over and inspiring the arts and some other activities: Clio, the muse of history, Calliope, of epic poetry, Erato, of love poetry; Euterpe, of lyric poetry; Melpomene, of tragedy; Polyhymnia, of sacred song; Terpsichore, of choric dance; Thalia, of comedy; Urania, of astronomy. The father of the nine was Zeus, the chief of the gods, their mother Mnemosyne (Memory).

Music of Time, The. See Anthony *Powell.

My Ántonia. Novel by Willa *Cather published in 1918.

When he was ten, Jim Burden was sent to live with his grandparents in Nebraska, both his parents having recently died. On the journey 'across the great midland plain of North America' he first met the Shimerdas, a family of poor immigrants from Bohemia, of whom only the young daughter Ántonia (pronounced Áñ-ton-ee-ah) can speak a few words of English. They are bound for the same destination as Jim, Black Hawk, where they had bought unseen a neglected homestead with only a hovel to live in. The family consists of father and mother, son Ambrosch (nineteen), a younger subnormal boy Marek, a small girl Yulka, and fourteen-year-old Ántonia, who learns more English from Jim as they become fast friends and ramble together. The hard life the Shimerdas have to endure overwhelms Mr Shimerda, and in misery and loneliness he kills himself. With neighbours' help and hard work on the land

by Ambrosch and Antonia, their condition improves, and later Ántonia becomes cook to the prosperous Harling family, until in a rebellious mood she takes a supposed easier job with the Cutters, an ill-conditioned couple, he being notorious as a moneylender and rake. Subsequently he makes a frustrated attempt to rape Ántonia, and in the end murders his wife and commits suicide. Jim's friendship with Ántonia continues in the intervals between his absence at college, but he loses contact with her for longer periods when she goes away to Denver to marry a train conductor, who deserts her, however, before the wedding and she returns home pregnant. After a further interval of twenty years, Jim visits her where she is living happily married to a farmer of her own nationality and with numerous children. Though Ántonia is central to the book it abounds with other interests; nature scenes; characterizations of Ántonia's friends of several nationalities, among whom Lena Lingard is outstanding as Jim's occasional companion at the theatre and elsewhere during his university sessions; and interpolated episodes such as the retrospective account by the dying Russian farmhand, Pavel, of the tragic pursuit of a wedding sledge-party by a famished wolf pack.

Myers, F. W. H. (Frederic William Henry Myers, 1843-1901). Born at Keswick; educated at Cheltenham and Cambridge. One of Her Majesty's Inspector of Schools, 1872-1900. As a poet his chief work was *St Paul* (1867). Prose books: *Wordsworth* (1881), *Essays Modern and Classical* (1885), *Science and a Future Life* (1893). He was a founder (and President) of the Society for Psychical Research and wrote *Human Personality and Its Survival of Bodily Death* (published posthumously, 1903). Father of the following.

Myers, L. H. (Leopold Hamilton Myers, 1881-1944). Born in Cambridge, son of the preceding; educated at Eton and Cambridge. He travelled widely and lived for a short time in Colorado. Although he long desired to be a writer, he did not publish anything until his novel *The Orissers* appeared in 1921. *The Clio* followed in 1925, and in 1929 *The Near and the Far,* the first of a sequence of four novels continued with *Prince Jali* (1931), *The Root and the Flower* (1935), *The Pool of Vishnu* (1940)—and republished as one volume (1943) under the title of the first book. These constitute a finely written meditative story in an

Indian setting in the time of the Mogul emperor Akbar (sixteenth century), but in spirit it is outside time and place and ranks as one of the most distinguished contemporary fictional works.

My Fair Lady. Play with music by Frederick Loewe and libretto by Alan Jay Lerner based on Bernard Shaw's *Pygmalion*. Produced in New York in 1956 and in London in 1958, it ran for several years in both places and outstripped previous records for a musical play.

Myles na Gopaleen. *See* Brian *O'Nolan.

Mysticism. A term susceptible of varied definitions and interpretations, evolving from a multitude of individual spiritual attitudes. If there is a common feature, it is a sense of one-ness with God, attained through meditation, contemplation, and self-surrender. Inasmuch as the mystic aspires to direct spiritual communion with the Deity, he is likely to be at variance with the dogmas of organized religion.

Nabokov, Vladimir (1899-   ). Born in Russia; educated at St Petersburg and in England at Cambridge; settled in the United States in 1940, where he became a university professor, dividing his academic interests between zoology and Russian literature, and his literary activities between fiction and biography. His novels include *The Real Life of Sebastian Knight* (English edition, 1960), and the controversial **Lolita* (English edition, 1959).

Naidu, Sarojini (*née* Sarojini Chattopadhyay, 1879-1949; married M. G. Naidu). Born in Hyderabad; educated there and in London and Cambridge. Took a leading part in social, educational, and political work on behalf of India, engaging especially in welfare activities for women and students, and travelling widely as lecturer. First Indian woman President of the Indian National Congress; Chancellor of the University of Allahabad. Author of three volumes of poems written in English, a number of which have been translated into various Indian and other languages: *The Golden Threshold* (1905), *The Bird of Time* (1914), *The Broken Wing* (1917). Known as 'the nightingale of India' and also noted for her witty and outspoken comments on fellow members of the National Congress.

Naipaul, V. S. (Vidiadhar Surajprasad Naipaul, 1932-   ). Born in Trinidad; educated there and at Oxford; settled in England. Author of novels—*The Mystic Masseur* (1957), *The Suffrage of Elvira* (1958), *Miguel Street* (1959), *A House for Mr Biswas* (1961), *Mr Stone and the Knight's Companion* (1963), *The Mimic Men* (1967); short stories—*A Flag on the Island* (1967); travel books—*The Middle Passage: The Caribbean Revisited* (1962), *An Area of Darkness: An Experience of India* (1964).

Name and Nature of Poetry, The. Lecture by A. E. *Housman delivered in Cambridge and published in 1933. It includes an engaging personal account of the preliminary symptoms of poetic production.

Namier, Sir Lewis (Lewis Bernstein Namier, 1888-1960; knighted 1952). Born in Russia; educated in England at Oxford. Served in British army and Intelligence Department in World War I. Professor of Modern History in the University of Manchester 1931-53. His books on eighteenth century history threw new light on English politics in that period and had a marked influence on other historians' approach to the politics and parties of the age: *The Structure of Politics at the Accession of George III* (1929), *England in the Age of the American Revolution* (1930). Other works: *Germany and Eastern Europe* (1915), *Skyscrapers* (1931), *In the Margin of History* (1939), *Conflicts* (1942), *1848: The Revolution of the Intellectuals* (1946), *Diplomatic Prelude 1938-1939* (1949), *Europe in Decay 1936-40* (1950), *Avenues of History* (1952), *In the Nazi Era* (1952), *Vanished Supremacies* (1958).

Nansen, Fridtjof (1861-1930). Born in Norway; educated at Oslo and Naples. Undertook famous expeditions in Arctic regions, particularly in the *Fram*; reached what was until then (1895) the nearest point to the North Pole. Norwegian Ambassador in London, 1906-08. After World War I did valuable service in connection with relief work in Russia and elsewhere, becoming League of Nations High Commissioner for Refugees. Received Nobel Peace Prize in 1922. Professor of Oceanography, University of Oslo, from 1908. Author of *Farthest South* (2 vols, 1897), *In Northern Mists* (1911), *Through Siberia* (1914), *Hunting and Adventures in the Arctic* (1925), *Through the Caucasus to the Volga* (1931).

Narayan, R. K. (1906-   ). Born in Madras; educated there and in Mysore. Contributed many of his short stories to the Madras newspaper *Hindu*. Author of *Swami and Friends* (1935), *The English Teacher* (1945), *Mr Sampatch* (1949), *The Financial Expert* (1952), *The Guide* (1958), *The Man-Eater of Malgudi* (1961), *Gods, Demons and Others* (1964).

Naturism. Synonym for nudism as practised in the regimen of a nudist colony; also applied to the prescribed dietetic and other routine of any health organization opposed to a sedentary life, slaughtered animal food, medicinal drugs, etc.

Nash, Ogden (Frederic Ogden Nash, 1902-1971). Born in New York State; educated in Rhode Island and at Harvard. Worked in publishing firms for some years. Became celebrated as author of humorous verses with uniquely ingenious rhymes and metrical forms: *Hard Lines* (1931), *The Primrose Path* (1935), *The Bad Parents' Garden of Verse* (1936), *I'm a Stranger Here Myself* (1938), *The Face is Familiar* (1940), *Family Reunion* (1951), *Collected Verses* (1961).

Nathan, Daniel (pseudonym of Frederic Dannay). See Ellery *Queen.

Nathan, G. J. (George Jean Nathan, 1882-1958). Born in Indiana; educated at Cornell and Indiana Universities and in Italy at the University of Bologna. With other American authors he was co-founder of *The American Mercury* and *The American Spectator* and contributor of theatre articles and dramatic criticism to numerous periodicals and reference books. With H. L. *Mencken he led the iconoclastic school of American criticism in the 1920s and following decades. Author of *The Popular Theatre* (1918), *The American Credo* (1920), *The Critic and the Drama* (1922), *Materia Critica* (1924), *The House of Satan* (1926), *Since Ibsen* (1933), *The Theatre of the Moment* (1936), *Encyclopaedia of the Theatre* (1940), *The Theatre Book of the Year* (annually from 1943-4).

Nathan, Robert (Robert Gruntal Nathan, 1894-). Born in New York; educated in Switzerland and at Harvard. Worked as a solicitor and teacher of journalism. Author of many novels including *Autumn* (1921), *The Son of Amittai* (1925; American title *Jonah*), *The Fiddler in Barly* (1926), *The Bishop's Wife* (1928), *Journey of Tapiola* (1938), *Winter in April* (1938), *Mr Whittle and the Morning Star* (1947). Poems: *Youth Grows Old* (1922), *A Cedar Box* (1929), *Morning in Iowa* (1944), *Darkening Meadows* (1945).

Nation, Carry (1846-1911). Militant American temperance reformer who spent most of her life from 1890 raiding saloons with a hatchet which she carried for damaging the premises and property. She was both a dedicated nuisance and an object of popular derision, and was frequently arrested. She lectured on both sides of the Atlantic, and wrote her autobiography as *The Use and Need of the Life of Carry A. Nation* (1904).

National Book Council. Founded in 1925 to promote interest in books and reading, with John Masefield as its first President. In 1944 it was reconstituted as the *National Book League.

National Book League. Founded in 1944, as successor to the *National Book Council, to promote the habit of reading and a wider recognition of the contribution made by books to the enjoyment of leisure and the enrichment of cultural life, and to educational and technological progress. Presidents: John Masefield, 1944-49; Lord Justice Birkett, 1949-54; Sir William Haley, 1954-63; H.R.H. The Duke of Edinburgh, from 1963.

While the policy and direction of the League are entirely independent, it has the support of publishers and booksellers, national, educational, commercial and industrial institutions, as well as of authors and the public; and it works in collaboration with the book trade and with government and local authorities. At its headquarters in a fine eighteenth-century house at 7 Albemarle Street, London, it has a bibliographical library, exhibition and reading rooms, a Book Information Bureau and Education Department. Harriet *Weaver presented to the League in 1957 her James Joyce Collection of first editions and association copies, and there are other special collections. Annotated booklists giving up-to-date information about books on particular subjects are published, besides the quarterly journal *Books.* Membership on a subscription basis is available to all. The League also has a branch office in Glasgow.

Naturalism. As a literary term, naturalism is usually accepted as a synonym for realism, though attempts are sometimes made to distinguish between the two, regarding naturalism as an extreme form of realism. Though nature and reality are not prerogatives of any single social class, naturalistic or realistic prose and verse are usually concerned with the lives of the poor and depressed. While such writings almost always claim to be rooted in social facts, they are frequently coloured by overstatement and sentimentality when written by external observers, and by self-pity when the authors are of the class depicted. The master of modern naturalism was Emile Zola in novels written in the late 1860s onward. His disciple in English literature was George *Moore, and others in England were George *Gissing, Richard *Whiteing, Arthur *Morrison, Somerset *Maugham in *Liza of Lambeth*. Later books in the mode by authors writing at firsthand include *Love on the Dole* by Walter Greenwood and *The Ragged Trousered Philanthropists* by Robert Tressell. Naturalism in form rather than in subject matter was attempted by the stream-of-consciousness novelists, Dorothy *Richardson, James *Joyce and others. In verse, John Masefield's *The *Everlasting Mercy, The *Widow in the Bye Street,* and similar narrative poems, are in the naturalistic manner.

Naylor, Eliot. Pseudonym under which Pamela *Frankau wrote *The Offshore Light* (1952).

Neale, J. E. (Sir John Ernest Neale, 1890-   ; knighted 1955). Born in Liverpool; educated at the Universities of Liverpool and London. Professor of Modern History in the University of Manchester, 1925-7; Professor of English History in the University of London, 1927-56. Author of *Queen Elizabeth* (1934), *The Age of Catherine de Medici* (1943), *The Elizabethan House of Commons* (1949), *Elizabeth I and Her Parliaments 1559-1581* (1953), *Elizabeth I and Her Parliaments 1584-1601* (1957).

Nebuly Coat, The. Novel by J. Meade *Falkner published in 1903.

A young architect, Edward Westray, is sent by his principal, Sir George Farquhar, Bart., to superintend the restoration work at Culerne Minster, formerly, until the Dissolution, the Abbey Church of St Sepulchre. Started in the twelfth century, the Norman work of the nave received later additions in the choir and elsewhere, and finally the great central tower was built, resting on the arches of the crossing. While being shown round the Minster at his first visit, Westray notices particularly, at the head of the middle division of the great window in the south transept, 'a shield of silver-white crossed by waving sea-green bars'. This, he is told in heraldic terms, is the coat of arms of the local nobility—the Blandamers—'barry nebuly of six, argent and vert', commonly known as the nebuly coat. Old Lord Blandamer died a few years previously at a great age, crabbedly contributing nothing to the restoration fund. His grandson and heir has for years been travelling abroad. Westray takes lodgings at Bellevue Lodge, hitherto a coaching inn named The Hand of God. Miss Euphemia Joliffe, the gentle elderly landlady of Bellevue, has her young niece Anastasia as companion and occasional helper. From his fellow lodger, Mr Sharnall, the Minster organist, Westray learns that Miss Joliffe's half-brother and Anastasia's father Martin Joliffe, recently died, believing himself the true heir of the late Lord Blandamer. In Westray's room is a large still-life of flowers painted by Sophia, mother of Martin and Euphemia. Sophia 'put about she was a widow' and had a three-year-old boy, Martin, when she married Farmer Joliffe. Westray considers the flower painting hideous and crude, but Miss Joliffe cherishes it and believes it valuable. Though in need of money she refuses an offer of £50 from a London art dealer. Certain papers which Martin hoped might yield evidence supporting his claim were passed for inspec-

tion to Sharnall the organist, who tells Westray that 'that's where the light's coming from, out of Martin's papers'. The present Lord Blandamer returns from abroad unannounced, and undertakes to bear the cost of all necessary restoration work at the Minster, where Westray has been rebuffed by Sir George and by the Rector for expressing concern about the safety of the tower. Lord Blandamer calls at Bellevue Lodge several times to confer with Westray and has also been alone in Sharnall's room. The organist, a heavy drinker, is found dead in the organ loft one night with a wound at the back of his head, presumed to have been caused by striking the pedal-board which was supporting his head. Westray questions this conclusion, believing Sharnall has been murdered. Anastasia declines a proposal of marriage from Westray, because she has conceived a romantic devotion to Blandamer. She accepts a proposal from him, and after their marriage they spend a prolonged honeymoon on the Continent. During their absence Miss Joliffe prevails on Westray to have the flower painting in the lodgings to which he moved after Anastasia refused him. The frame is damaged in transit and some old documents are revealed. Among them is a marriage certificate proving that Sophia was the former Lord Blandamer's wife before she became Mrs Joliffe, and that Martin was in fact the rightful heir. It is also found that Sophia's flower piece has been painted on top of a Blandamer portrait in which the nebuly coat also appeared. Westray concludes that the present claimant murdered Sharnall to prevent him from extracting conclusive evidence from Martin's papers. Since Anastasia has borne a son and heir, Westray decides not to proceed against Blandamer. To welcome the couple on their return home, a full peal has been rung on the Minster bells. This adds to Westray's fears for the tower, and while it is obviously in danger he goes up to the belfry to make a further inspection. Caught behind a jammed door, he is released by Blandamer, who is unable to escape from the tower before it collapses and crushes him.

Negative Capability. In a letter dated 21 Dec. 1817, Keats remarked that Coleridge was 'incapable of remaining content with half-knowledge'. Earlier in the letter he wrote: 'Negative Capability, that is, when a man is capable of being in uncertainties, mysteries, doubts, without any irritable reaching after fact and reason'.

Nehru, Shri Jawaharlal (1889-1964). Born in Allahabad; educated in England at Harrow and Cambridge; studied law and practised as a barrister in the High Court of Allahabad. Joined the non-violent non-cooperation campaign for Indian independence in conjunction with Gandhi, and was several times imprisoned by the British for his political activities. President of the Indian National Congress, 1929, 1936, 1937, 1946, 1951-54. Prime Minister of India from 1947 until his death. Author of *Soviet Russia* (1929), *India and the World* (1936), *Autobiography* (1936), *Glimpses of World History* (1939), *Independence and After* (1953; his speeches 1949-53).

Neill, A. S. (Alexander Sutherland Neill, 1883-1973). Born at Kingsmuir, Angus; educated there and at Edinburgh. Worked in various trades and professions before becoming joint-founder of the International School in Dresden in 1921, afterwards transferring it to England. His educational system and the free discipline which was among its principles won him both enthusiastic support and strong opposition. He wrote books on matters related to his educational methods and convictions: *A Dominie's Log* (1915), *A Dominie Dismissed* (1916), *A Dominie's Five, or Free School* (1924), *The Problem Child* (1926), *The Problem Parent* (1932), *The Problem Teacher* (1939), *The Problem Family* (1948), *The Free Child* (1953).

Nesbit, E. (Edith Nesbit, 1858-1924). Born in London; educated in France and Germany and in London. In 1880 she married Hubert *Bland. She wrote unremarkable novels, short stories, and books of verse before producing in 1899 the first of the children's books which were to make her financially independent of her profligate first husband (who died in 1914) and to give her enduring repute. *The Story of the Treasure Seekers* (1899) was followed by *The Would-Be-Goods* (1901), *Five Children and It* (1902), *The Phoenix and the Carpet* (1904), *The Story of the Amulet* (1906), *Wet Magic* (1912), and others. Her successful formula was to involve her ordinary children (mostly members of the Bastable family) in extraordinary events of an Arabian Nights character. She was an ardent member of the *Fabian Society and, as one of her numerous literary and political friends among its members, Bernard *Shaw unwittingly inspired in her warm feelings which met with no response. *See also* Fabian *Bland.

Net Book Agreement. Until 1899, booksellers at their individual discretion and without regard to publication prices, sold books at discounts which often varied sharply from shop to shop. This resulted in much competitive underselling and reduction of profits below the margin necessary to maintain booksellers in business unless they treated books as a mere sideline to other more profitable wares. At the instigation of Frederick Macmillan, the Publishers' Association and the Associated Booksellers signed in February 1899 the Net Book Agreement whereby, as a condition of supply to retailers, no book was to be sold at other than the net price fixed by the publisher. This assured booksellers of a fair margin of profit and protected them against undercutting, especially by financially powerful rivals who might otherwise treat books as *'loss leaders'. In 1905 The Times Book Club, founded as an advertising inducement to increase the newspaper's circulation, began a determined campaign against the Agreement and provoked what came to be known as The Book War and led to a libel action by John Murray in which he was awarded £7,500 against *The Times*, which at length capitulated.

Nevins, Alan (1890-1971). Born in Illinois; educated at the University there and at Columbia. Worked on the *Evening Post, Nation, Sun,* and *World,* all in New York. Professor of American History, Columbia University, 1931-58. Author of *The American States During and After the Revolution* (1925), *The Emergence of Modern America* (1927), *The Gateway to History* (1938), *The Making of Modern Britain* (1943), *The Emergence of Lincoln* (1950) and numerous other historical works, and biographies of Rockefeller (1940), Ford (1953; 1957) and others.

Nevinson, H. W. (Henry Woodd Nevinson, 1856-1941). Born in Leicester; educated at Shrewsbury and Oxford, and later studied in Germany. Worked on London and Manchester newspapers as leader writer, war correspondent, and special investigator of the slave trade in Portuguese dependencies. Author of *Ladysmith* (1900), *Books and Personalities* (1905), *A Modern Slavery* (1906), *Essays in Freedom* (1909), *Essays in Rebellion* (1913), *The English* (1929), *Rough Islanders, or The Natives of England* (1930), *Thomas Hardy* (1941), *Visions and Memories* (posthumously,

1944). *Changes and Chances* (1923), *More Changes, More Chances* (1925) and *Last Changes, Last Chances* (1928) are autobiographical. After his first wife's death he married Evelyn *Sharp in 1933.

New Age, The. *See* A. R. *Orage.

New Criticism, The. A title given to the theories of a number of literary critics, mainly American, opposed to Romanticism and concentrating on a philosophical and linguistic approach to poetry and imaginative prose. The New Criticism was by no means the product of an associated group, and diverse aspects appear in the writings of I. A. *Richards (*Principles of Literary Criticism,* 1924), English born but for many years a teacher at Harvard, R. P. *Blackmur, Cleanth *Brooks, J. C. *Ransom, Yvor *Winters. The critical writings of T. S. *Eliot had a notable influence. The title was applied by Ransom in *The New Criticism* (1941). *And see* *Textual analysis.

New Deal. Name given to the economic and other measures introduced in the United States by President F. D. Roosevelt in 1933 to counteract the disastrous effects of the current financial collapse and consequent widespread unemployment and destitution. Though its social legislation and public works projects were effective in relieving distress, the New Deal antagonized a large section of American industrialists and others who were opposed to Federal intervention and the introduction of State benefits.

New Machiavelli, The. Novel by H. G. *Wells published in 1911 and marking in Wells's career as a writer the division between his earlier novels of humour, character and invention and those of political and social inquiry and analysis.
In this book Richard Remington surveys his own life from childhood up to the time he withdrew from political affairs in early middle age, as Niccolo Machiavelli the Florentine statesman did in the sixteenth century, before turning to the writing of the classic of political science and statecraft *The Prince* (1517), which earned him lasting fame and also execration. But Remington recognizes that his book must be altogether different from Machiavelli's, inasmuch as its aim is not to instruct a prince or king or lord how to rule, but to appeal to the multitude for 'the unification of human effort, the ending of confusions': 'There is, moreover, a second

great difference in kind between my world and Machiavelli's. We are discovering women.' Remington, the son of an inefficient science teacher and an unquestioningly pious mother, passes from the City Merchants' School to Cambridge. After graduating, he obtains a Fellowship, but abandons it when he has some success with two books and sundry articles in periodicals. He makes contact with social and political circles in London and is taken up by Altiora and Oscar Bailey, single-minded indefatigable researchers fashioned after the pattern of Beatrice and Sidney Webb, seeing human beings as 'types' to be drilled by experts in an efficient, passionless, emasculated world. While staying with relatives in Staffordshire, Remington meets Margaret Seddon, the well-to-do stepdaughter of a provincial solicitor, and five years later, when he is twenty-seven, encounters her again at the Baileys'. Altiora contrives to throw them together, and they fall in love and marry. At the 1906 General Election Remington becomes one of the overwhelming majority of Liberal M.P.s, but he gradually becomes dissatisfied with the Government and joins the Opposition as one of the Young Tories. At the next election he is returned as a Conservative and founds and edits a successful political and literary periodical, the *Blue Weekly*. He becomes prominent as a leading advocate of the Endowment of Motherhood. His career is wrecked when his liaison with a brilliant young woman, Isabel Rivers, becomes known. Their determination to part breaks down and they go to live in Italy, where Remington sets down his life story, 'to show a contemporary man in relation to the state and social usage', to give 'the broad lines of my political development, and how I passed from my initial liberal-socialism to the conception of a constructive aristocracy'.

New Statesman, The. Founded as 'A Weekly Review of Politics and Literature' in 1913 by Beatrice and Sidney *Webb with support from Bernard Shaw and others associated with the *Fabian Society. Though the paper is dedicated to Socialist principles and gives general support to the Labour Party, it preserves an independent critical attitude to all political parties. Many of its readers, while dissenting strongly from its political views, are attracted by the high standard and integrity of its literary pages. Its past editors are Clifford Sharp (from the beginning to 1930), Kingsley *Martin (1930 to 1960), John Freeman (1961 to 1965, when he was appointed British High Commissioner in India until he went in 1969 to Washington as British Ambassador). The Literary Editors of the *New Statesman* have included J. C. *Squire (using the pseudonym Solomon Eagle), Desmond *MacCarthy (Affable Hawk), Raymond *Mortimer, V. S. *Pritchett, Walter *Allen. Most of the celebrated contemporary authors have contributed to the paper from time to time, the most remarkable feat of sustained writing being the weekly essays (signed Y.Y.) by Robert *Lynd which appeared regularly for many years. Perhaps the most famous and controversial issue of the *New Statesman* was No. 84 (14 November 1914) which carried as a 32-page separate supplement Bernard Shaw's *Common Sense About the War,* expressing opinions far from common when the war had gone on for only three months.

New Yorker, The. Weekly periodical started by Harold *Ross in 1925. Though celebrated for its sophisticated and sometimes recondite humour, it has been hospitable to a great deal of writing on matters of serious public interest and concern. Literary articles, stories, and verse have been contributed by most notable American (and some British) writers. Its style and ideas have influenced journals in other countries, e.g. in the use of its caption 'Profiles' for biographical sketches of prominent living men and women. Cartoons and comic drawings in the *New Yorker* manner have also had a widespread influence on artists and editors elsewhere. See *Ross and the New Yorker* (1952) by Dale Kramer; *My Years with Ross* (1959) by James *Thurber.

New Zealand Writers. As in other lands settled by immigrants from Britain, early New Zealand writings in English dealt with aspects of the land and its indigenous people and with the occupations and trials of the newcomers from Europe. And when at length creative and imaginative literature developed alongside the literature of fact, English traditions, modes of thought, and literary forms prevailed until the land was occupied by generations born in New Zealand, not arriving from outside. The Victorian historian James Anthony Froude prophesied after his visit in the 1880s that it would be 'in the unexhausted soil and spiritual capabilities of New Zealand that the great English poets, artists, philosophers, statesmen and soldiers of the future will be born and nurtured'. Some twenty years before, Samuel *Butler (1835-1902), in

A First Year in Canterbury Settlement (1863) said that New Zealand was fitted to preserve physical rather than intellectual health and catered best for those who concentrated on money-making. Butler's later repute in England as the author of *Erewhon* (begun in New Zealand) and of *The Way of All Flesh* may still draw readers to the account of his sheep-farming venture in the Canterbury region, but a more attractive work on colonial life is *Station Life in New Zealand* (1870) by Lady (Mary Anne) Butler (1831-1911). These, however, are pioneer works, almost primitives from the present-century angle, and English readers remained virtually unconscious of New Zealand as a cradle of literary genius for nearly another half-century, when Katherine *Mansfield made her indelible impression as a short-story writer comparable with Tchekov. She left Wellington in the first years of this century to complete her education in London, and except for three years back in New Zealand from 1906 to 1909 she spent the rest of her uneasy life in Europe. As a writer she was caught imaginatively between the two worlds. Such stories as 'Prelude' and 'At the Bay', steeped in the atmosphere of her own country, identify her as distinctively a New Zealand writer, while in the bulk of her stories the vision is cosmopolitan. Her emotional range was wide and her sympathies and understanding deep. Few writers have equalled her portrayals of children, a feature far removed from the tragically sensitive and moving creation of the old charwoman in 'Life of Ma Parker', the bleak spinsterhood of 'Daughters of the Late Colonel', and the desolation of the fading film actress in 'Pictures'. Her several volumes, from *Bliss* (1920) to *Something Childish* (1924), are brought together in *The Collected Stories of Katherine Mansfield* (1945). While she was establishing an international reputation through her contacts with the larger literary world, a more restricted though not in a creative sense necessarily narrower school of fiction was appearing in New Zealand. William *Satchell (1860-1942) produced novels which, while owing more than enough to English models, were nevertheless invigorated by the life around him in the Auckland area: *The Toll of the Bush* (1905); *The Greenstone Door,* an historical novel (1914). Jane *Mander (1877-1949) dealt in *The Story of a New Zealand River* (1920) with the timber industry and in *Allen Adair* (1925) with a young man reluctantly and unprofitably forced to Oxford who returns to settle to the useful but unacademic life of a storekeeper. The umbilical attachment to the literature of the 'mother country' still remained, however, and not until the 1930s was the separation to seem complete. In that decade John A. *Lee (1891-   ) and Robin *Hyde (1906-39) published documentary novels 'exploring tracts of New Zealand experience not touched before'—e.g. Lee's Children of the Poor (1934); Robin Hyde's Passport to Hell (1936), The Godwits Fly (1938). Two pronouncements from this period are significant. Robin Hyde wrote in a magazine article in 1938: 'in our generation . . . we loved England still, but we ceased to be "for ever England". We became, for as long as we have a country, New Zealand.' John *Mulgan (1911-45), in Report on Experience (1947), said: 'If you try to . . . forget the country of your youth, as I did for a long time, you will lose the fight and wither internally of homesickness.' The realization had come that New Zealand literature must have its roots in the soil of New Zealand and interpret the life of its people; that it must use its own idiomatic tongue, not as something quaint and rather comic, in the Australian A. B. ('Banjo') *Paterson style, but as the living language of common intercourse and everyday communication. Among the first and most important of those who founded what can be called the new New Zealand literature was Frank *Sargeson (1903-   ), whose novels are less striking than his short stories (Collected Stories, 1964; English edition with an introductory salute by E. M. *Forster, 1965). These range in length from less than a single page ('Park Seat') to the eighty pages of 'That Summer'. All are true story telling as differentiated from story writing: men talking colloquially, idiomatically, and with clarity in English which is like a language refreshed by release from literary mannerisms. Mulgan's novel Man Alone (1939) explores what E. H. McCormick describes (in the book cited below) as 'a world of the underdog and the fugitive' and represents in the character of Johnson 'the patient indestructible mass of humanity, borne along on the stream of history'. Janet *Frame (1924-   ) reached a public in the U.S. and Britain as well as in her own country with Owls Do Cry (1957), a complex novel which treats of a family within a community. No more than passing mention can be made here of a few other outstanding fiction writers and representative books:

Roderick *Finlayson (1904-   ; Brown Man's Burden, 1938, stories of Maoris), Dan *Davin (1913-   ; The Gorse Blooms Pale, 1947, short stories; Roads from Home, 1949, novel), James Courage (1905-   ; The Young Have Secrets, 1954, novel), Ruth *France (1913-   ; The Race, 1960, novel). See also Sylvia Ashton *Warner.

New Zealand began a golden age of poetry in the 1930s. The poets were political, satirical, practical, explosive. They were young men caught in the economic depression who could no longer make the expensive migration to Europe and looked long and hard at New Zealand instead. They caught also the wave of independence, of emotional separation from Britain, and wrote with more than a widespread competence. Their exuberant reworking of a European tradition produced imagery and tone in which New Zealanders recognized their own environment and their own attitudes as something not alien to but certainly different from British patterns of thought.

Mary Ursula *Bethell (1874-1945), of an older generation than these, did not publish the verses she had written in letters until she was in her middle fifties, but her Collected Poems issued five years after her death included many pieces expressive of the New Zealand landscape and of 'its implications in geological and temporal history, in time and in eternity'. Charles *Brasch (1909-   ), the youngest of the 'thirties poets', produced his first collection in 1939, The Land and the People and other Poems, followed by further volumes including Ambulando (1964). Mainly a landscape poet, incorporating nature elements—'a leisurely gull', 'mermaid grass', 'silvered lichens', 'huddling trees/Pressed flat by the wind'—into 'Rest on the Flight into Egypt' and numerous others, he had in view also (in 'Ephebe in 1954') the 'mechanic Hamlet', the 'metal centaur', the 'Rider of a quivering machine' in 'Crash helmet, goggles, leather jacket'. This leap from the timelessness of natural things to the temporalities of urban life, indicates the immensity of the material which the contemporary poet has to face and wrestle with, for few are disposed to turn their backs even to its most intractable elements. Of these, politics is the chief; and since politics can no longer be localized and insulated it has dominated the poetic imagination. R. A. K. *Mason (1905-   ), described by McCormick as, through political involvement, New Zealand's 'supreme poetic casualty' of the thirties, is by no means the last such casualty. A recital of influences and a discussion of subject matter and technique cannot be attempted here. The accomplishment of the poets already named and of those mentioned below has, from a distance, to be gauged from anthologies where the following will be represented: A. R. D. *Fairburn (1904-57), Denis *Glover (1912-   ), M. K. *Joseph (1914-   ), Gloria *Rawlinson (1918-   ), Ruth *Dallas (1919-   ), J. K. *Baxter (1926-   ), C. K. *Stead (1932-   ). Allen *Curnow (1911-   ), himself a major poet, edited *A Book of Verse* (1945) and *The Penguin Book of New Zealand Verse* (1960). *Verse for You* (Book three, 2nd edn 1966) edited by J. G. Brown, and *Modern Verse for You* (1968) edited by P. W. Day and J. G. Brown, are school anthologies with a generous selection of New Zealand verse included.

Landfall, a literary quarterly founded in 1947 by Charles Brasch and edited by him for twenty years, did much to stimulate the writing of poetry and creative prose. *New Zealand Short Stories* (vol. I edited by Dan Davin, 1953; vol. II edited by C. K. Stead, 1966) are in the World's Classics series (Oxford). Outstanding as an introductory survey is E. H. McCormick's *New Zealand Literature* (1959), on which the present entry is mainly based. *See also* Hone *Tuwhare, Maori poet.

Newbolt, Sir Henry (Henry John Newbolt, 1862-1938; knighted 1915). Born at Bilston, Staffordshire; educated at Clifton and Oxford; later studied law and practised as a barrister from 1887 until 1899. In the next year he became editor of Murray's *Monthly Magazine*. The first of his long list of books came out in 1892, and he became lastingly celebrated with the poem 'Drake's Drum', first printed in the *St James's Gazette* in 1896 and included with other verses in *Admirals All* (1897). He continued to write sea songs—*The Sailing of the Long-ships* (1902), *Songs of the Sea* (1904), *Songs of the Fleet* (1910), the last two collections being given wider popularity when set to music by Sir Charles Stanford. Like 'Drake's Drum', Newbolt's 'Clifton Chapel' (*Clifton Chapel and Other Poems*, 1908) was long remembered. He also wrote some fiction, criticism, military and naval history, and an autobiography *My World as In My Time* (1932).

Newby, P. H. (Percy Howard Newby, 1918-

). Born at Crowborough, Sussex; educated at Hanley and Cheltenham. Served in France and Egypt in World War II. Lecturer in English Literature at Cairo University, 1942-6. Joined B.B.C. 1949 and became Controller of the Third Programme. Author of *A Journey to the Interior* (1945), *Agents and Witnesses* (1947), *The Young May Moon* (1950), *The Picnic at Sakkara* (1955), and other novels.

Newdigate Prize. Founded in 1805 by Sir Roger Newdigate (1719-1806), M.P. for Oxford University, as an annual prize for an original poem on a set subject by an Oxford undergraduate. The prize-winning poems have contributed little of note to English literature.

Newman, Bernard (1897-1968). Born in Leicestershire; educated at Bosworth. His novel *The Cavalry Went Through* (1930), and the later *Spy* (1935) were highly praised in retrospect (*The Times*, 27 February 1968) by Sir Basil *Liddell Hart—the first for its military acumen, the other as a subtle psychological study. From the middle thirties he devoted much of his time and energy to cycling abroad. He was said to have toured in sixty countries, and produced over a hundred travel books and novels. Autobiography: *Speaking from Memory* (1960). For more than a dozen of his spy stories he used the pseudonym Don Betteridge.

Newman, Ernest (pseudonym of William Roberts, 1868-1959). Born and educated in Liverpool. After working as a teacher of music he was music critic of the *Manchester Guardian* (1905), of the *Birmingham Post* (1906-19), of the *Sunday Times* (1920-58). He became the recognized English authority on the life and works of Richard Wagner, writing numerous books on him, and others on Bach, Gluck, Beethoven, Liszt, Richard Strauss, and Elgar.

Newnes, Sir George (1851-1910; baronet 1895). Born in Matlock; educated in Yorkshire and at the City of London School. Began work when sixteen and was employed commercially until he started the weekly *Tit-Bits* at Manchester in 1881 (transferred to London three years later) thus becoming the pioneer in journalism for the masses, preceding by seven years Alfred *Harmsworth's *Answers*. Among Newnes's other publications were the *Strand Magazine* (1891) and the *Westminster Gazette* (1893). He was Liberal M.P. for Newmarket (1885-95), for Swansea (1900-

10). The publishing firm he started is still active under his name.

Newspeak. The 'only language in the world whose vocabulary gets smaller every year', in George Orwell's *Nineteen Eighty-four* (1949).

Newton, A. E. (Alfred Edward Newton, 1863-1940). Born in Philadelphia; educated privately. Started to work at an early age for Philadelphia booksellers, then went into an electrical firm, but became celebrated as a book collector and author of attractive essays on his hobby. He built up a remarkable library of rare books which was, at his own request, dispersed after his death. Author of *The Amenities of Book-Collecting* (1918), *This Book-Collecting Game* (1928), *End Papers* (1933); *Dr Johnson: A Play* (1923).

Newton, Eric (1893-1965). Born and educated in Manchester, where he was also employed as a designer of mosaics from 1918 to 1933, examples of his work in that medium being executed for churches in other parts of the country. He made a wider reputation as art critic on the *Manchester Guardian* and the *Sunday Times*; he rejoined the *Guardian* in 1956 and remained with it until his death. He lectured extensively, was Slade Professor of Fine Art at Oxford, 1959-60, and wrote *The Artist and His Public* (1935), *European Painting and Sculpture* (1941), *The Meaning of Beauty* (1950), *The Arts of Man* (1960), *The Romantic Rebellion* (1962).

Nichols, Anne (1891-1966). American actress and playwright whose *Abie's Irish Rose*, produced in New York in 1922, ran for 2327 performances until 1927, a record up to that time. She also wrote *Down Limerick Way* (1919), *The Happy Cavalier* (1921), *The Land of Romance* (1922), and other plays.

Nichols, Beverley (John Beverley Nichols, 1899-   ). Born in Bristol; educated at Marlborough and Oxford. The precocious talent he displayed while at the University continued to be evident in following years, for he published the first of his autobiographies, *Twenty-Five*, in 1926, having already written three novels — *Prelude* (1920), *Patchwork* (1921), *Self* (1922). He became a popular contributor to newspapers and periodicals, and though continuing to produce novels found his vocation in writing with humour and sentiment on gardens and country matters: *Down the Garden Path* (1932), *A Thatched Roof* (1933), *A Village in a`Valley* (1934), *Merry Hall* (1951), etc. His views on

politics, religion and pacifism were subject to fluctuation; in World War II he was for a time a press correspondent in India, resulting in *Verdict on India* (1944); and he continued his autobiography in *All I Could Never Be* (1949). His later works include: *Laughter on the Stairs* (1953), *Murder by Request* (1960), *Forty Favourite Flowers* (1964), plays, and books on cats. *Father Figure* (autobiography, 1972).

Nichols, Robert (Robert Malise Bowyer Nichols, 1893-1944). Born in the Isle of Wight; educated at Winchester and Oxford. Served for a while on the Western Front in World War I and then in government service till the war ended. Professor of English Literature at Tokyo University, 1921-4. Author of *Invocation* (1915), *Ardours and Endurances* (1917) which linked him with the war poets of the period, *Aurelia* (1920), *Such Was My Singing* (1942), and other poems; *Guilty Souls* (1922) and other plays; and some miscellaneous prose volumes.

Nicholson, Meredith (1866-1947). Born in Indiana. Worked from the age of fifteen in miscellaneous jobs; from 1933 to 1940 held office as U.S. Minister in, successively, Paraguay, Venezuela, and Nicaragua. He wrote poems —*Short Nights* (1891), *Poems* (1906); essays —*The Provincial American* (1913), *The Valley of Democracy* (1918), *Old Familiar Faces* (1929); and novels, the most successful being *The House Of a Thousand Candles* (1905), followed by *The Port of Missing Men* (1907), *The Siege of the Seven Suitors* (1910) and others. In *The Hoosiers* (1900) he wrote a study of Indiana authors—'Hoosier' being a title of uncertain origin applied to them— and also *A Hoosier Chronicle* (1912) a partly autobiographical novel.

Nicholson, Norman (Norman Cornthwaite Nicholson, 1914-   ). Born at Millom, Cumberland; educated locally. Author of *The Old Man of the Mountains* (1945), *A Match for the Devil* (1955), both verse plays on biblical themes; collections of poems— *Five Rivers* (1944), *Rock Face* (1948), *The Pot Geranium* (1954); literary studies—*H. G. Wells* (1950), *William Cowper* (1951).

Nicoll, Allardyce (John Ramsay Allardyce Nicoll, 1894-   ). Educated in Stirling and at Glasgow University. Lecturer in English, Loughborough College; then Lecturer, later Professor, of English Language and Literature in the University of London, before going to the United States as Professor of the

History of Drama and Dramatic Criticism at Yale. Professor of English, University of Birmingham, 1945-61. As an author he concentrated on the history of drama and the theatre, producing works invaluable to students and teachers: *A History of English Drama 1660-1900* (6 vols., 1952-9, combining his earlier books on the several periods from the Restoration to the late 19th century), *The Development of the Theatre* (1927), *Masks, Mimes, and Miracles* (1931), *The Theory of Drama* (1931), *Shakespeare* (1953), *The Elizabethans* (1956), *The World of Harlequin: A Study of the Commedia dell'Arte* (1963), studies of *William Blake* (1922), *John Dryden* (1923), and editions of the works of Cyril Tourneur and others. He was also Editor of the annual *Shakespeare Survey* from its start in 1948 until 1965.

Nicoll, Sir William Robertson (1851-1923; knighted 1909). Born in Aberdeenshire; educated in Aberdeen at the Grammar School and University. Ordained into the Free Church, he served as minister in Dufftown (1874-7) and Kelso (1877-85). In London as editor of the Nonconformist *British Weekly* from 1886 he had considerable political and literary influence, his weekly articles under the heading 'The Letters of Claudius Clear' being an attractive feature, mainly on books. He also edited The *Bookman*, a literary monthly, from 1891, and a religious monthly, *The Expositor*, from 1885. His many books included biographies of *Ian *Maclaren* (1908) and *Emily Brontë* (1910); *The Day Book of Claudius Clear* (1905), *The Problem of Edwin Drood* (1912), *A Bookman's Letters* (1913), and a large number of religious works.

Nicolson, Sir Harold (The Hon. Harold George Nicolson, 1886-1968; knighted 1953. Born in Teheran, Persia; son of Sir Arthur Nicolson (later Lord Carnock) who was then *chargé d'affaires;* educated at Wellington and Oxford. Joining the Foreign Office, he served in embassies or legations in Madrid, Constantinople, Teheran, and Berlin, until he resigned in 1929, having meanwhile served on the British Delegation to the Paris Peace Conference in 1919. National Labour M.P. for West Leicester 1935-45. Author of literary studies—*Paul Verlaine* (1921), *Tennyson* (1923), *Byron: The Last Journey* (1924), *Swinburne* (1926); biographies —*Lord Carnock* (1930), *Curzon: The Last Phase* (1934), *King George V: His Life and Reign* (1952); *The Development of English*

Biography (1928), *The English Sense of Humour* (1947); and several books of essays including *Public Faces* (1932), *Small Talk* (1937), *Marginal Comment* (1939), *Some People* (1944; new edn 1959), *Comments* (1948). *Diaries and Letters, 1930-62* edited by Nigel Nicolson (3 vols, 1966-67-68). *And see* Sackville-West, V.

Niebuhr, Reinhold (1892-1971). Born in Missouri; educated at Elmhurst College and Yale; studied for the ministry and became pastor of an Evangelical Church in Detroit from 1915 to 1928; Professor of Ethics and Theology, Union Theological Seminary, New York, from 1928. One of the leading theologians of his time, he sought to link the teaching of the Christian Church with social and political ethics. The Gifford Lectures he was invited to deliver at Edinburgh in 1939 were printed in *The Nature and Destiny of Man* (2 vols, 1941-43), his outstanding book. Other works: *Moral Men and Immoral Society* (1932), *Beyond Tragedy* (1937), *Christianity and Power Politics* (1940), *The Children of Light and the Children of Darkness* (1944), *Christian Realism* (1953), *The Structure of Nations and Empires* (1959).

Niemöller, Martin (Friedrich Gustav Emil Martin Niemöller, 1892-   ). Born in Westphalia; educated at Elberfeld; served in the German navy, 1910-19. Then studied theology, became a Protestant pastor, and drew international interest and admiration as an active religious opponent of the Nazi régime, which led to his imprisonment in a concentration camp from 1937 to 1945. After the war he was elected President of the Office of Foreign Affairs of the Evangelical Church in Germany.

Nigger of the 'Narcissus', The: *A Tale of the Sea*. Novel by Joseph *Conrad published in 1897. Last aboard while Mr Baker, the chief mate of the sailing ship *Narcissus,* is mustering the crew for the return voyage from Bombay to London, a gigantic Negro from St Kitts announces himself suddenly as James Wait when the roll-call is ending. The other members of the crew include old Singleton, an able seaman with nearly half a century's experience; Craik, a little Irishman nicknamed Belfast; the cook, fanatically religious; Donkin, a new hand, a ragged Cockney scrounger and seditious work-dodger who has absconded without his kit from an American ship. The master, a Scot, Captain Allistoun, had commanded the *Narcissus* since she was built. Wait goes sick with a racking cough from the beginning of the voyage, takes permanently to his bunk, and, understood to be a dying man, dominates the ship. The *Narcissus* runs into a gale and almost capsizes. Wait has to be hacked out of the sickbay while the vessel is heeled over, but only abuses his rescuers. After the gale the *Narcissus* is becalmed, and the misadventures of the voyage are attributed to the malign influence of the death-haunted Negro. The cook so terrifies him by preaching hell-fire, that he declares he is now well and will go back to duty. The captain, convinced that he has been shamming all along, orders Wait to remain off deck to the end of the voyage. Incited by Donkin, the crew become mutinous at this, but the captain calms them and quells Donkin who has thrown an iron belaying pin. Singleton's prophecy that the sick man will die when they sight land and that favourable winds will then follow is fulfilled. Wait is buried at sea.

Nightingale, Florence (1820-1910). Born in Florence; trained as a nurse in Germany and France. Leading a party of nearly forty other nurses she went to the Crimea in 1854 and against considerable military and political opposition organized and controlled an efficient and sanitary nursing service for the wounded and sick in the war between Britain and Russia. When the war ended she continued her campaign for the improvement of army medical services and nurses' training, raising funds in England to establish a teaching institution for nurses. Her *Notes on Nursing* (1859) remained for many years the standard manual. She was inflexible in pursuing her aims, and spared neither her opponents nor her friends in the causes for which she fought with almost demoniac energy. The official biography of her was written by Sir Edward Cook (*The Life of Florence Nightingale*, 1913), but more interest was aroused by Lytton *Strachey's brilliant controversial essay in *Eminent Victorians* (1918) and by Cecil *Woodham-Smith's *Florence Nightingale* (1950).

Nijinsky, Vaslav (1890-1950). Born in Kiev; trained at the Imperial School of Ballet, St Petersburg. As the leading male dancer in Diaghilev's company he became a legendary figure from the time he first performed in Western Europe (Paris 1909) until his career ended in 1917, when he became incurably insane. His most famous roles were in *Le Spectre de la Rose* (to Weber's 'Invitation to the Dance'), *L'Après-midi d'un Faune* (to Debussy's music and Nijinsky's own choreography), and *Petrouchka* (Stravinsky).

Nikola, Dr. *See* Boothby.

Nimmo, Chester. Central character in novels by Joyce *Cary. *See *Except the Lord*.

Nine Muses, The. *See* Muses.

Nineteen Eighty-four. Novel by George *Orwell published in 1949.

By the year of the title, the world is divided between Oceania, Eurasia, and Eastasia. London is the chief city of Airstrip One (formerly Britain), the control centre of Oceania. At the apex of Oceanic society is Big Brother, infallible and all-powerful; next below him comes the Inner Party (less than 2 per cent of the population), followed by the Outer Party, and then by the dumb masses (the 'Low', or 'proles'), numbering some 85 per cent. Plastered everywhere are posters of the enormous face of the leader, with the caption BIG BROTHER IS WATCHING YOU. No one has ever seen him or knows when he was born, though it is 'reasonably sure that he will never die'. The approved language is Newspeak, which in its final version will have a minimum vocabulary, so narrowing the range of thought that there will be no words to express anything unapproved by the régime. The three slogans of the Party are 'War is Peace', 'Freedom is Slavery', 'Ignorance is Strength'. The functions of government are divided between the Ministry of Peace (concerning itself with war), the Ministry of Love (law and order), the Ministry of Plenty (economics and rationing), and the Ministry of Truth. In the last-named the central character of the book, Winston Smith, is engaged in expunging from past newspapers and published books everything contrary to current policy, falsifying events, and fabricating past utterances of Big Brother and his henchmen to bring them into line with the changed requirements of the moment. Though ubiquitous television screens and microphones record whatever is said and done, Smith goes into secret opposition and links up with Julia, a girl in the same Ministry; under the aegis of O'Brien, a senior official, they agree to work with an underground organization known as the Brotherhood, not suspecting that O'Brien is entrapping them. They are eventually arrested and subjected to prolonged torture and degradation. O'Brien tells Smith that confession and submission are not enough; the aim is to capture the mind, to bring the heretic 'over to our side ... genuinely, heart and soul. We make him one of ourselves before we kill him.' In the end Smith's shattered mind tells him 'He had won the victory over himself. He loved Big Brother', but there is no escape from the bullet from behind.

Niven, Frederick (Frederick John Niven, 1878-1944). Born in Valparaiso, Chile; educated in Glasgow. Worked in Scotland as a librarian, and after spending some time in Canada worked for Glasgow and Dundee papers before finally settling in British Columbia. Author of many novels, including *A Wilderness of Monkeys* (1911), *The Porcelain Lady* (1913), *Cinderella of Skookum Creek* (1916), *Penny Scot's Treasure* (1918), *Treasure Trail* (1923), *The Paisley Shawl* (1931), *Under Which King?* (1943).

Nobel Prize for Literature. One of the five prizes offered annually since 1901 under the will of Alfred Bernhard Nobel (1833-96), Swedish inventor and maker of explosives. Most of his fortune of £2 million was left for the annual prizes in (as well as literature) physics, chemistry, physiology (or medicine), and service for peace. Among the best-known recipients of the literature prize (for work of an idealist tendency) are: Rudyard Kipling (1907), Selma Lagerlöf (1909), Maurice Maeterlinck (1911), Gerhart Hauptmann (1912), Rabindranath Tagore (1913), Romain Rolland (1915), Knut Hamsun (1920), Anatole France (1921), W. B. Yeats (1923), Bernard Shaw (1925), Henri Bergson (1927), Sigrid Undset (1928), Thomas Mann (1929), Sinclair Lewis (1930), John Galsworthy (1932), Luigi Pirandello (1934), Eugene O'Neill (1936), Pearl Buck (1938), André Gide (1947), T. S. Eliot (1948), Bertrand Russell (1950), François Mauriac (1952), Sir Winston Churchill (1953), Ernest Hemingway (1954), Albert Camus (1957), Boris Pasternak (1958), John Steinbeck (1962), J. P. Sartre (1964), Samuel Beckett (1969), Alexander Solzhenitsyn (1973).

Nonesuch Press. Of the private presses (so called to distinguish them from commercial firms) started after World War I, the Nonesuch Press had the advantage that its founder, Francis *Meynell, had from birth a literary background, and from the beginning of his working life a thorough training in typography and printing processes. Moreover, whereas other private presses were devoted to hand operations regardless of cost, the Nonesuch Press was begun by Meynell in 1923 with the firm intention of using the existing machine-equipped printing houses, reserving to himself and his colleagues every detail of book design and selection of paper, binding materials, etc. By demonstrating that machine-produced books could be as good as those hand-produced and could be sold at a fraction of the price, the Nonesuch Press effected a revolution which raised the general standard of printing and book-making. Of the first hundred Nonesuch books published up to 1932, thirty-six were new (i.e. not previously published), while among the older works most had newly edited texts by reputable scholars. Nearly fifty of the hundred were illustrated in monochrome or colour by leading artists, using various techniques—copperplate engraving, wood engraving, line drawing, colour stencils, lithography, collotype. The seven-volume edition of Shakespeare is described as 'the finest of all editions of our greatest poet'. *See also* *Golden Cockerel Press; *Gregynog Press.

Nordau, Max (Max Simon Nordau, 1849-1923). Born in Budapest, and educated there; studied medicine and practised as a physician in Budapest and Paris. Wrote copiously on various subjects but is now remembered mainly as the author of *Entartung* (1893), translated into English as *Degeneration* and attacked in one of Bernard *Shaw's major critical essays *The Sanity of Art*.

Norden, Charles. *See* Lawrence *Durrell.

Nordhoff, Charles Bernard (1887-1947). Born in London of American parentage. Taken to the U.S. while an infant; educated at Stanford and Harvard. Served in France in World War I and afterwards settled in Tahiti. In collaboration with James Norman Hall he wrote, mainly novels, about the South Seas.

Normyx. Pseudonym used only for his first book by Norman *Douglas.

Norris, Charles G. (Charles Gilman Norris, 1881-1945). Born in Chicago, brother of Frank *Norris; educated at the University of California; married Kathleen Thompson (*see* Kathleen *Norris). Author of realistic novels with a social purpose: *Salt* (1917), *Brass* (1921), *Bread* (1923), *Pig Iron* (1925), *Seed* (1930), *Flint* (1944).

Norris, Frank (Benjamin Franklin Norris, 1870-

1902). Born in Chicago, brother of the preceding; educated in California; studied art in London and Paris. Went to South Africa in 1895 and wrote for American papers on the war there until he was captured by the Boers and sent out of the country. He also acted as war correspondent in the Spanish-American conflict. While still a student he had been influenced by the realism of Zola, and his own novels are in that mode: *McTeague* (1899); *The Octopus* (1901) and *The Pit* (posthumously, 1903) were to be completed as a trilogy called 'The Epic of the Wheat', but he died with the third part (*The Wolf*) unwritten.

Norris, Kathleen (*née* Kathleen Thompson, 1880-1966; Mrs Charles G. Norris). Born in San Francisco; educated privately and at the University of California. Author of many popular novels including *Mother* (1911), *Certain People of Importance* (1922), *Margaret Yorke* (1930), *The Maiden Voyage* (1942). Autobiography: *Noon* (1925); *Family Gathering* (1959).

Northcliffe, Viscount (Alfred Charles William Harmsworth, 1865-1922; baronet 1903; baron 1905; Viscount Northcliffe of St Peter-in-Thanet 1917). Born near Dublin of an English father and Ulster-Scottish mother. Educated in Hampstead. After a beginning as freelance journalist he started *Answers* (to correspondents) in 1888 and *Comic Cuts* in 1890 before acquiring the *Evening News* (1894) and founding the *Daily Mail* in 1896, followed by the *Daily Mirror* (1903) which failed as a women's paper but became an immense success when quickly changed to an illustrated *'tabloid'. Meanwhile the *Daily Mail* had consolidated the newspaper revolution with which the name of Harmsworth will always be associated. Sold at a halfpenny, it presented news in compressed and mentally unexacting style, departing radically from the heaviness and longwindedness to which the British newspapers were accustomed. The *Mail* also boosted its circulation by a succession of stunts, one at least of which had a lasting influence on the development of aviation. In 1908 Northcliffe became the proprietor of *The Times* with fluctuating success. In his time he was the most powerful of the new race of British press magnates, but his desire for political power (mainly evident in World War I) was frustrated, and in his final years his mind was shattered by megalomania. *See also* Rothermere.

Norton, Charles Eliot (1827-1908). Born in Cambridge, Massachusetts; educated privately and at Harvard. Professor of the History of Art, Harvard University, 1873-97; Editor of the *North American Review*, 1861-68. Author of *Church Building in the Middle Ages* (1876), *The Poet Gray as a Naturalist* (1903); editor of editions of the letters of Carlyle, Ruskin, and others. The Charles Eliot Professorship at Harvard for visiting lecturers commemorates him.

Norway, Nevil Shute. *See* Nevil *Shute.

Norwich, Viscount. *See* Alfred Duff *Cooper.

Norwich, Viscountess. *See* Lady Diana *Cooper.

Nostromo. 'A Tale of the Seaboard' by Joseph *Conrad published in 1904. The San Tomé silver mine, fabulously rich and the most important thing in the South American Republic of Costaguana, has experienced numerous vicissitudes as revolutions and counter-revolutions have brought the country under the temporary rule of one or other of the warring political parties who have formed 'governments' that are usually little better than robber bands. One such government, 'the fourth in six years' forces a perpetual concession of the now derelict silver mine upon Señor Gould in full settlement of large compulsory loans. For the unwanted concession he is forced to pay, at once, five years' royalties on the estimated output of the mine —though the concessionaire has no means of working it. He voices his indignation and despair to his son Charles in England, where the Goulds, an English family, settled for generations in Costaguana, customarily receive their education. After his father's death, Charles Gould returns to South America with his young wife, to live in the Casa Gould, the family mansion in Sulaco, the chief port of Costaguana, where Captain Joseph Mitchell is superintendent of the Ocean Steam Navigation Company's business, with Nostromo, formerly a Genoese sailor, as foreman of the lightermen. Nostromo lives with fellow Genoese, Giorgio Viola and his wife Teresa and daughters Linda and Giselle. At once feared, respected, admired, and incorruptible, Nostromo is relied on for numerous services by the aristocrats, and for justice by the workers, with whom he stands as a Man of the People. Charles Gould, with the backing of North American financiers, imports machinery and recruits labour to reopen the mine, which he runs with success, and in cynical conformity with the customary expectations of rapacious Costaguanan officials. His workers are treated humanely, and , his wife is regarded with general affection as 'the first lady of Sulaco'. In the latest revolutionary outbreak, the reigning President-Dictator, Don Vincente Ribiera, barely escapes on board a steamer of Captain Mitchell's Company. A young Spanish creole journalist, Martin Decoud, who has spent years as a dilettante in Paris, returns to Costaguana and is persuaded by Don José Avellanos, a leading supporter of the Ribiera government, to start and edit in Sulaco a paper supporting Ribiera. Decoud and Don José's daughter Antonia fall in love. A valuable consignment of silver from the mine, which must be got out of the country before the rebels can capture it, is loaded from Sulaco jetty into a lighter manned by Nostromo, who is reluctant to have Decoud with him. The plan is to transfer the silver to a steamer at sea, but on a pitch-dark night the two men find great difficulty in reaching the Isabels, islets offshore, where Nostromo intends to take cover until the steamer is sighted next day. In the darkness the lighter is hit and slightly damaged by a rebel troopship and has to be run aground on the Great Isabel, the largest of the islets. Nostromo and his companion bury the oxhide boxes containing the silver ingots in a cavity. Nostromo leaves Decoud with the treasure and gets back to Sulaco. No rescuer appearing, Decoud is driven by solitude and sleeplessness to load his pockets with ingots and drown himself. The rebels in Costaguana are overcome, mainly as a consequence of a desperate and heroic ride by Nostromo to summon loyal forces. Prolonged peace ensues and prosperity from the mine. But the once incorruptible Nostromo is corrupted by the silver, which he alone knows has not been sunk. He buys a trading schooner and secretly by night collects a few ingots at a time. A lighthouse is built on the Great Isabel. Linda is given charge of the light and, with her father and sister, goes to live there. Nostromo, supposedly affianced to Linda, is in love with Giselle, and Linda sees them meeting. Mistaken by old Viola for an intruder for whom he is watching, Nostromo is shot. In his dying moments in Sulaco hospital he sends for Mrs Gould and offers to tell her where the treasure is. But she wishes to hear no more of the silver: 'No one misses it now', she says. 'Let it be lost for ever.'

Not Honour More. Novel by Joyce *Cary published in 1955. See *Except the Lord.

Notes and Queries. A periodical founded in 1849 (by W. J. Thoms, 1803-85, author of antiquarian works and deputy-librarian of the House of Lords from 1863) as 'a medium of inter-communication for literary men, artists, antiquaries, genealogists, etc.' From the beginning to the present it has been a widely used source of information on literature and learning, and its back volumes are a valuable repository of varied lore communicated by experts and frequently no less valuably by scholarly eccentrics. It was taken over by the Oxford University Press during World War II and edited by Frederick *Page from 1943 to 1959. It continued under other editors 'For Readers and Writers, Collectors and Librarians'.

Novello, Ivor (pseudonym of David Davies, 1893-1951). Born in Cardiff, son of the celebrated vocalist, Clara Novello (Mrs Davies); educated at Magdalen College School, Oxford. He sprang into fame in 1915 with the patriotic wartime song 'Keep the Home Fires Burning'. For the rest of his life he had almost continuous success as composer, playwright, producer, and actor on stage and screen, rivalling Noel *Coward as a versatile man of the theatre. His non-musical plays include The Truth Game (1928), A Symphony in Two Flats (1929), Party (1932), Proscenium (1933), but his greatest successes were as composer of Glamorous Night (1935), Careless Rapture (1936), The Dancing Years (1939), Perchance to Dream (1945), King's Rhapsody (1949), all with lyrics by Christopher *Hassall.

Noyes, Alfred (1880-1958). Born at Wolverhampton; educated at Oxford. He became the most popular and prolific poet of his generation and the only one since Tennyson to live by his poetry. Though much of it was facile, and in an age of increasing intellectualization in poetry considered shallow by critics, he had a genuine gift for ballad and narrative verse of a romantic kind. Among his numerous books of verse the most successful were The Flower of Old Japan (1903), Forty Singing Seamen (1907), Drake: An English Epic (1906-8), Tales of the Mermaid Tavern (1913), The Elfin Artist (1920), Shadow-of-a-Leaf (1924), Songs of the Torch Bearers (3 vols, 1922, 1925, 1930). His miscellaneous prose included Some Aspects of Modern Poetry (1924) and a life of Voltaire

(1936) which he successfully defended against censorship by the Roman Catholic Church, which he had joined in 1930. *Two Worlds of Memory* (1953) is autobiographical.

Nymphet. Sexually provocative adolescent girl; diminutive from nymphomaniac. The word was popularized by its application to Lolita in the novel by V. *Nabokov.

Nzekwu, Onuora (1928-   ). *See* *African Writers.

Obey, André (1892-   ). Born and educated at Douai, where he also studied music. After World War I, in which he was twice severely wounded, he worked as music and theatre critic and sports writer on Paris newspapers, published novels and essays, but had his chief successes as a playwright: *Noë*, which in translation as *Noah* (1935) also made him celebrated in England; *Le Viol de Lucrèce* (1931), written on the model of Greek tragedy, was used in an English adaptation by Ronald Duncan as the basis of Benjamin Britten's opera *The Rape of Lucretia*. Later works, less acclaimed, include *Maria* (1946), *Lazare* (1951).

Objective. As applied to literature, that which deals judicially with the matter presented or discussed, unaffected by the author's personal enthusiasms or prejudices.

Objective correlative. Term coined by T. S. *Eliot in his essay on *Hamlet* (1919) and debased into a cliché by a host of borrowers in the following decades. The original passage read: 'The only way of expressing emotion in the form of art is by finding an "objective correlative"; in other words, a set of objects, a situation, a chain of events which shall be the formula of that *particular* emotion; such that when the external facts, which must terminate in sensory experience, are given, the emotion is immediately evoked.'

O'Brien, Edward J. (Edward Joseph Harrington O'Brien, 1890-1941). Born in Boston; educated there and at Harvard; lived mainly in England from 1922, the year he married Romer *Wilson. Though he wrote some plays (*The Flowing of the Tide*, 1910; *The Bloody Fool*, 1917) and verse (*White Fountains*, 1917; *Distant Music*, 1921), he was better known as editor of numerous collections of short stories—*The Best American Short Stories* (annually, 1915-40), *The Best British Short Stories* (annually, 1921-40), and others.

O'Brien, Flann. *See* Brian *O'Nolan.

O'Brien, Kate (1897-1974). Born in Limerick; educated there and in Dublin. Lived some years in London and in Spain. Her first work made public, the play *Distinguished Villa* (1926), was succeeded by successful novels dealing with Irish middle-class life and religious conflict, e.g. *Without My Cloak* (1931), or with Spanish themes, *Mary Lavelle* (1936), *That Lady* (1946). Also *The Flower of May* (1953), *Presentation Parlour* (1963), etc.

O'Byrne, Dermot. *See* Arnold *Bax.

O'Casey, Sean (anglicization of Shaun O'Cathasaigh, 1880-1964). Born in poverty in Dublin, the youngest of a large family; his father's early death and his own chronically bad eyesight seriously limited and shortened his elementary education and it was not until he was thirteen that he began to read. Thenceforward he read omnivorously. He began work in an ironmonger's shop, and from the age of eighteen laboured for some twelve years as a road-worker. He learned Gaelic, became an active trade unionist, and began to write plays, the first three being rejected by the *Abbey Theatre, which accepted the next *The Shadow of a Gunman* (1923). In the meantime he had taken a leading part in organizing the Irish Citizen Army in 1914 and took part in the 1916 Easter Rebellion. These events served as a background to his first produced play and to *The *Plough and the Stars* (1926) which caused rioting in the Dublin theatre, the audience considering that the Protestant author was insufficiently pro-Irish. His greatest and most successful play *Juno and the Paycock* (1924, published 1925) placed him at once among the world's dramatists of genius, and demonstrated that the superficial realism of his plays and their pervasive and often bitter irony was transcended by power of character-drawing—at once moving and monumental. Like other great playwrights he was master of both tragedy and humour, interweaving the comic, the absurd, and the profoundly tragic, and penetrating to 'the deep heart's core' of the men and women he created. The tumult in Dublin over *The Plough and the Stars* led O'Casey to leave Ireland and settle in England for the rest of his life, though he was at times an intemperate political critic of Britain. He wrote many more plays—among them *The Silver Tassie* (1929), *Within the Gates* (1933), *The Star Turns Red* (1940), and *Red Roses for Me* (1943)—but none was welcomed by theatre managers and producers, though a minority of critics and others, impressed by their symbolism, praised them highly. In his later years O'Casey devoted himself to an immense autobiography in six volumes—*I Knock at Any Door* (1939), *Pictures in the Hallway* (1942), *Drums Under the Windows* (1945), *Inishfallen Fare Thee Well* (1949), *Rose and Crown* (1952), *Sunset and Evening Star* (1954)—all reissued as a single-volume paperback in 1964.

O'Cathasaigh, Shaun. *See* Sean *O'Casey.

O'Connor, Frank (pseudonym of Michael O'Donovan, 1903-66). Born in Cork and educated there at the Christian Brothers' School. Worked as a librarian in Dublin and elsewhere. Highly regarded as a short-story writer comparable in form with Tchekov: *Guests of the Nation* (1931), *The Saint and Mary Kate* (1932), *Bones of Contention* (1936), *Crab Apple Jelly* (1944), *The Stories of Frank O'Connor* (1953). Non-fiction: *The Book of Ireland* (1958); *Art of the Theatre* (1947) reflects his period of association with the *Abbey Theatre in Dublin. Poems: *Kings, Lords, and Commons* (1960). Autobiography: *An Only Child* (1961), *My Father's Son* (unfinished; published posthumously, 1968).

O'Connor, T. P. (Thomas Power O'Connor, 1848-1929). Born in Athlone; educated there and at Queen's College, Galway. Spent three years from 1867 as a reporter in Dublin, and then worked as a journalist in London. Nationalist M.P. for Galway, 1880-85; for the Scotland Division of Liverpool from 1885. He founded and was the first editor of the London evening *Star* and other newspapers, and of *T.P.'s Weekly* which for many years from 1902 did commendable service in fostering a love of reading and providing first steps to literary appreciation. O'Connor's own articles combined a popular approach with sound knowledge and enthusiasm. His books included *Lord Beaconsfield: A Biography* (1879), *Gladstone's House of Commons* (1885), *The Parnell Movement* (1886), *Napoleon* (1896); *Memoirs of an Old Parliamentarian* (autobiography, 1929).

Odets, Clifford (1906-63). Born in Philadelphia; educated at New York schools. Following long experience as an actor (partly with the Theatre Guild and the Group Theatre in New York) he turned to playwriting successfully with *Waiting for Lefty* (1935) which, like *Awake and Sing* (written 1933; produced 1935) and most of his serious work, is concerned with the economic and political struggles of the working classes: all literature, he held, should have a propagandist aim. *Till the Day I Die* (1935) was an attack on Nazi tyranny; *Golden Boy* (1937), young violinist turned prosperous prize-fighter, was a popular success, though the author declared it to be an allegory against materialism; the last of his successful plays, *Winter Journey* (1950; entitled *The Country Girl* in America)

was more concerned with human character than with theme. In the 1940s and after he did much work in Hollywood as film writer and director.

O'Donovan, Michael. *See* Frank *O'Connor.

Odtaa (One damn thing after another). Novel by John *Masefield published in 1926.

Of Human Bondage. Autobiographical novel by W. Somerset *Maugham published in 1915. Written in a first version about 1897 as *The Artistic Temperament of Stephen Carey,* unpublished; rewritten *c.* 1911-13. In it, Maugham recorded, 'fact and fiction are inextricably mingled; the emotions are my own, but not all the incidents are related as they happened, and some of them are transferred to my hero not from my own life but from that of persons with whom I was intimate'.

Orphaned in early childhood, Philip Carey, the son of a surgeon, is placed in charge of his clergyman uncle, at Blackstable (Whitstable) in Kent, where he is much loved by his aunt but repressed by the rigid and narrow piety of her husband. The boy is handicapped by a club foot, which causes him to be taunted as a cripple at King's School, Tercanbury (Canterbury) and is a frequent source of misery in later life. He resists pressure from his uncle and the headmaster to train for Holy Orders, and on leaving school spends a year as a student in Germany, living with a family in Heidelberg recommended by an acquaintance of his uncle, a Miss Wilkinson, who is staying at the vicarage when he returns home. She is a sentimental amorous spinster, twice his own age, and a grotesque affair with her introduces Philip to sexual experience. He begins a professional career as articled clerk to a London chartered accountant, but is a failure. Fired by reading Murger's *Vie de Bohème,* and having some talent for drawing, he enrols as an art student in Paris, where he spends two happy years, learning to paint and also developing a philosophy of life through discussion and argument with fellow students and other habitues of the art schools and cafés and music halls. At the end of the two years he is compelled to recognize that as an artist he has little but manual dexterity, and, not satisfied to become a merely mediocre painter, turns to the profession in which his father was successful, and enters the Medical School of St Luke's (St Thomas's) Hospital,

London. His progress becomes seriously impeded by a humiliating obsessive passion for a teashop waitress, Mildred Rogers. Though he sees her clearly as an ignorant heartless slut with ludicrous mock pretensions to gentility, he fails to cure himself of this besetting emotional affliction, though it is dulled for a time when she goes away to marry a German who has been a customer at the teashop. Through the years ahead she reappears disruptively at intervals in Philip's life, until she finally sinks into prostitution. His medical studies are interrupted when he loses in speculations what money he had, and for a time he becomes a down-and-out, hungry and homeless. A patient, Thorpe Athelny, who forms a friendship with him, is instrumental in getting him work as a shopwalker. Philip resumes his studies when he inherits from his uncle enough to pay the fees. When at length he qualifies, he goes as a *locum* to a crochety old Dr South at a Devon fishing port. The patients come to prefer the young man and South offers him a partnership in the practice. Philip has become an intimate of the large Athelny family and when Sally agrees to marry him he decides to accept Dr South's offer. The title is that of one of the books in Spinoza's *Ethics*.

O'Faolain, Sean (1900-). Born in Dublin; educated at the National University there and in the U.S. at Harvard. Lecturer in English at St Mary's College, Middlesex, 1929-33. Director of the Arts Council of Ireland from 1957. His first book, *Midsummer Night Madness* (1932), is an outstanding collection of short stories, and his first novel, *A Nest of Simple Folk* (1933) is his best. Other writings: biographies—*Constance Markievicz* (1934), *King of the Beggars: A Life of Daniel O'Connell* (1938), *De Valera* (1939), *The Great O'Neill* (1942); travel books—*Summer in Italy* (1949), *South to Sicily* (1953); literary history—*The Short Story* (1948), *The Vanishing Hero* (1956). A collected edition of *The Stories of Sean O'Faolain* came out in 1958. His other books include *I Remember! I Remember!* (1962), *The Heat of the Sun* (1966).

O'Flaherty, Liam (1897-). Born in the Aran Islands, off the coast of Galway; trained for the priesthood but abandoned the idea of entering the Church and studied for a while at University College, Dublin. Served with the British in France in World War I until he was invalided out in 1917. He travelled extensively,

working in various manual capacities at sea and on land. He took an active part in militant unemployed demonstrations in Dublin in 1922 and was compelled to leave Ireland. The attention he received for his novel *The Informer* (1926) was not maintained by *The Martyr* (1927), *The Assassin* (1928), *The Puritan* (1931), *Famine* (1937), *Insurrection* (1950), the impact of brutalized realism diminishing with repetition. He also wrote short stories in a gentler tone: *Spring Sowing* (1926), *The Fairy Goose* (1929), *The Wild Swan* (1932); collected, *The Short Stories of Liam O'Flaherty* (1956). Other writings: *Life of Tim Healy* (1927), *A Tourist's Guide to Ireland* (1929); autobiographies—*Two Years* (1930), *Shame the Devil* (1934).

Ogden, C. K. (Charles Kay Ogden, 1889-1957). Educated at Rossall and Cambridge. Originated Basic English to function on a vocabulary of only 850 words. Though it aimed to simplify the language, mainly for non-English learners, it was criticized on the ground that it necessitated circumlocution to express meanings not provided for by the limited vocabulary. Basic English received commendation from Winston Churchill during World War II, but Ogden declared that he was 'bedevilled by officials, 1944-46'.

Ogilvie, Jean. See *Jean Ogilvie.

Ogpu. Initials of the Russian words naming the secret political police of the U.S.S.R.

O'Hara, John (John Henry O'Hara, 1905-1970). Born in Pennsylvania; educated at several schools, and worked in a considerable number of different jobs before turning to journalism in various capacities on papers in Pennsylvania and New York. His novels and short stories portray with caustic observation and sometimes brutal realism the fast-living, often aimless and worthless members of the middle and lower social classes, the vigour of his narrative redeeming the unattractiveness of the characters. Novels: *Appointment in Samarra* (1934), *Butterfield 8* (1935), *Hope of Heaven* (1938), *A Rage to Live* (1949), *From the Terrace* (1958); short stories: *Files on Parade* (1939), *Pal Joey* (1940; used also as the basis of a popular musical play), *Pipe Night* (1954); essays: *Sweet and Sour* (1954).

O.K. A slang expression (of uncertain origin) expressing agreement with something said, or willingness to accede to some request. Originating in America, it seems likely to be admitted into standard English, though still objected to by purists.

O.K. authors. A term used ironically in the 1950s and 1960s by critics of the current mode of literary study in universities and schools which limited attention and approval to a few writers who were subjected to microscopic textual analysis. The critics claimed that literature was thus put into intellectualist blinkers and liberal and humanistic values ignored.

Oklahoma! The first of the new style American musical plays which became popular in and after World War II. Though less painstakingly realistic than some of its successors, such as *West Side Story*, it eschewed the frivolity of pre-war musical comedies. Based on a play *Green Grow the Lilacs* by Lynn Riggs, the libretto was by Oscar Hammerstein and the music by Richard Rodgers. Produced in New York in March 1943 it ran for well over 2,000 performances—a record for a musical play up to that time, but outstripped later by *My Fair Lady*. Both were correspondingly successful in their London productions at Drury Lane Theatre.

Old Possum's Book of Practical Cats. Volume of humorous cat-poems by T. S. *Eliot, first published in 1939 though they had been in private circulation during several years previously among the children (and others) for whom they were originally written. Immortalizing Macavity the Mystery Cat, Growltiger, Skimbleshanks, and others, they show a gift of comic verse that ranks Eliot with Edward Lear and Lewis Carroll.

Old Vic. Theatre in Waterloo Road, London, originally founded as the Coburg in 1818 and renamed the Victoria Theatre in 1833. It went through vicissitudes as a home of melodrama and as a music-hall, and had little repute until Emma Cons, social worker and temperance reformer, bought it and restarted it as a temperance music-hall in 1880 and' renamed it the Royal Victoria Hall and Coffee Tavern. It continued under Emma Cons's niece, Lilian *Bayliss, and from 1914 built a fine reputation with Shakespeare productions, completing the cycle of his thirty-seven plays by 1923. Damaged by bombing in World War II it was afterwards reconstructed, and having long been regarded as an unofficial National Theatre it was given that name and status in 1962, pending the building of a new theatre to be so designated on the South Bank area of the Thames.

Old Wives' Tale, The. Novel by Arnold *Bennett published in 1908. It is the intention of the parents that their daughters Constance and Sophia Baines shall work in the family shop when they leave school. Baines's is the leading drapers in Bursley, one of the Five Towns in the Staffordshire Potteries. Constance, docile and conformable, is content to go into the business, but Sophia, self-willed and turbulent, insists on becoming a teacher. Their father, John Baines, has been bedridden for many years and requires constant attention; their mother relies on Samuel Povey, formerly their apprentice, for the efficient management of the shop. Sophia has caught occasional glimpses of an attractive commercial traveller, Gerald Scales, who calls at Baines's, and on an occasion when she is left to watch over her father she runs down to the shop to talk to Scales. On returning to the bedroom she finds her father dead. Feeling herself responsible, and remorseful for her previous disobedience, she joins her sister to work in the shop. She furthers her acquaintance with Scales and takes surreptitious walks with him. When these become known to her mother, Sophia is forbidden to continue the meetings. She goes to visit an aunt in another part of the county but, instead, elopes to London with Scales. He fails to persuade Sophia to postpone marriage until they reach Paris, to which they go after a hasty wedding in London. The family in Bursley lose contact with Sophia. Constance marries Samuel Povey, but several years pass before their only child, Cyril, is born. Samuel dies, mortally distressed by the execution of his brother for the murder of a dipsomaniac wife. The Baines's shop is bought by a neighbouring chemist, Critchlow, who then marries Maria Insull, twenty-five years a Baines assistant, and carries on the drapery shop with her, while Constance continues to live in the bricked-off house. Her son, Cyril, departs for London, having won a national art scholarship. Meanwhile, in Paris, Sophia has been deserted by Scales, after being taken to various 'sights', including a public execution by guillotine. Sophia becomes seriously ill and is taken in care by two nurses turned prostitutes. After her recovery she goes into partnership with one of them in a low-class boarding house, which she runs with profit throughout the siege of Paris in the Franco-Prussian war.

Afterwards she buys the Pension Frensham 'in the cold and correct Rue Lord Byron', catering for English visitors. News of her reaches Constance, and letters pass between the sisters. Sophia sells the Pension at a price which makes her a rich woman. She returns to England and lives with Constance. An urgent message reaches her that Gerald Scales is dangerously ill in Manchester. She sets off immediately but he dies in poverty before she arrives. The shock and exertion cause her own death soon after. Towards the end of the next year Constance receives six months' notice to quit her house but she dies before the period expires.

Oldcastle, John. *See* Wilfrid *Meynell.

Oldfield, Claude Houghton. *See* Claude *Houghton.

Oldmeadow, E. J. (Ernest James Oldmeadow, 1867-1949). Born at Chester; educated at the King's School there. Wrote much journalism, novels, books on food, on Schumann and Chopin, and religious works. Editor of *The Tablet*, 1923-36, and author of the standard biography of *Francis, Cardinal Bourne* (vol. 1, 1940; vol. 2, 1944). Under the pseudonym Louis Barsac he published a book of verse, *Shadows and Fireflies, in* 1898.

Ole-Luk-Oie. *See* E. D. *Swinton.

Olivia. Short novel by Dorothy *Bussy, published in 1949 as 'Olivia, by Olivia'. Autobiographical in form, it is an account of a year the narrator spent as a girl in a French school, preceded by an outline of her parentage and early education at an English boarding school. Soon after reaching the French school, Olivia develops a deep and enduring affection for one of the teachers. Another of the staff is bitterly jealous of any affection her colleague shows to others, and she at length commits suicide. The book is notable for the lucid, restrained and delicate prose in which this story of tragic love and passion is told.

Olivier, Edith (1879-1948). Born at Wilton, Wiltshire; educated at home and St Hugh's College, Oxford. Mayor of Wilton, 1938-41. Author of *The Love Child* (1927), *As Far as Jane's Grandmother's* (1929), *The Triumphant Footman* (1930), *Dwarf's Blood* (1931) and other novels; *Moonrakings* (short stories, 1930); *The Eccentric Life of Alexander Cruden* (a biographical study of the compiler of *Cruden's Concordance;* 1934). Her auto-

biography, *Without Knowing Mr Walkley* (1938) was so titled on account of her early interest in the stage and her wish (unfulfilled) to meet A. B. *Walkley, dramatic critic of *The Times.*

Olivier, Sydney, 1st Baron (1859-1943; knighted 1907; 1st Baron Olivier, 1924). Educated at Lausanne, Tonbridge, and Oxford. Held office in the Colonial Service in the West Indies, and in other government departments; Secretary for India, 1924. Secretary of the *Fabian Society, 1886-90, and a fellow contributor with Bernard *Shaw and Sidney *Webb to the Fabian Essays and Tracts. Author of *Jamaica: The Blessed Island* (1936) and various writings on socialism and economics.

Ollivant, Alfred (1874-1927). Educated at Rugby and the Royal Military Academy, Woolwich. His career as an artillery officer having been ended by a spinal injury, he turned to writing and with *Owd Bob* (1898) became the author of what is still regarded by many as the best of all dog stories. None of his later books repeated this success.

O'Malley, Mary Dolling, *née* Sanders. *See* Ann *Bridge.

Oman, Carola (Carola Mary Anima Oman, 1897-   ; Lady Lenanton). Born at Oxford, daughter of the following; educated at Wychwood School, Oxford. Served with the British Red Cross in France in World War I. A versatile writer, she produced biographies— notably of *Nelson* (1947) and *Sir John Moore* (1953), *David Garrick* (1958); historical novels—*The Road Royal* (1924), *Crouchback* (1929), *Over the Water* (1935); novels of modern life—*Fair Stood the Wind* (1930), *Somewhere in England* (1943); children's books—*Alfred, King of the English* (1939), *Robin Hood* (1949); poems—*Menin Road* (1919).

Oman, Sir Charles (Charles William Chadwick Oman, 1860-1946; knighted 1920). Born in India; educated in England at Winchester and Oxford. Chichele Professor of Modern History, University of Oxford, from 1905; Conservative M.P. for the University, 1919-35. A leading historian, his works included *A History of Greece* (1888), *Warwick, the King Maker* (1891), *A History of Europe, 476-918* (1893), *A History of the Art of War in the Middle Ages* (1898; new edn. 1924), *A History of the Peninsular War, 1807-14*

(7 vols., 1902-30), *The Great Revolt of 1381* (1906), *Wellington's Army* (1912), *The Coinage of England* (1931), *On the Writing of History* (1939). Autobiographical—*Things I Have Seen* (1933), *Memories of Victorian Oxford* (1941).

Ombudsman. The title, derived from the compound Swedish word (*justitieombudsman*), now widely adopted for the official named 'Parliamentary Commissioner' in the Act appointing him in Britain and elsewhere in the Commonwealth. His functions vary in detail from country to country, but his overriding duty can be briefly stated as 'to protect the citizen against maladministration or oppression by civil service departments or illegal extension of powers by Ministers'. Except under pressure, governments in office are disinclined to initiate or support parliamentary bills directed towards the appointment of an Ombudsman, and the British 'Parliamentary Commissioner for Administration', as he is named in the Act of 1967, is hedged about by restrictions not generally approved, notably that he can only investigate complaints made to him by a member of Parliament. The aggrieved citizen has therefore to submit to the member's judgment, possibly inexpert or even biased against him, and has no right of direct approach to the Commissioner who, moreover, under the 1967 Act, could only investigate complaints of 'injustice in consequence of maladministration' by the administrative authority. Local government matters, the health service, and employment conditions in the public service, were at first excluded from the Commissioner's scope. His only ultimate sanction is a report to Parliament, for he has no direct power to order remedial action when he finds in a complainant's favour. *And see* *Crichel Down Case.

Omega Workshops, The. Started in Fitzroy Square, west-central London, in 1913 by Roger *Fry as an outcome of his enthusiasm for the *Post Impressionist movement in art. He and his associates—Vanessa *Bell, Duncan Grant, and others—convinced that the decorative art of early twentieth-century England was 'mean and pretentious when compared with the decorative art of savages', carried the Post-Impressionist and *Fauves formula into the design and decoration of furniture, carpets, curtains, lampshades, pottery, and other household articles and materials. Though the Omega productions aroused antagonism at the time because of their departure from conventional standards of design and symmetrical form, they anticipated much that was to be in vogue in the generations following the closure of the Workshops in 1920. An exhibition of Omega work at the Victoria and Albert Museum in 1964 occasioned an article by Quentin Bell (Vanessa and Clive Bell's son) in *The Listener* (30 January 1964) on which the present entry is based.

Ommanney, F. D. (Francis Downes Ommanney, 1903-   ). Educated at Aldenham School: studied zoology at the Royal College of Science, and became lecturer in that subject at Queen Mary College, London (1926-9). Later appointments included membership of the Scientific Staff of the *Discovery* Committee (1929-39), work on fishery surveys in African and Far Eastern oceans; Reader in Marine Biology, University of Hong Kong, 1957-60. In addition to scientific publications he wrote outstanding popular books based on his experiences in various regions: *South Latitude* (1938), dealing with whale-fishery operations and including an impressive account of adventure and physical endurance in Antarctica, *North Cape* (1939), *The Shoals of Capricorn* (1952), *Isle of Cloves* (1955), *Eastern Windows* (1960). *The House in the Park* (1944) is an account of his early years, and *The River Bank* (1966) of his later life.

On a Chinese Screen. Volume of brief sketches of Chinese people and places, and of Europeans living and working in China, by W. Somerset *Maugham. A product of the author's travels in the Far East, it was published in 1922 and is marked by sympathetic understanding of various types and classes of the population and by often penetrating critical observation of the attitude and conduct of foreign residents.

O'Neill, Eugene (Eugene Gladstone O'Neill, 1888-1953). Born in New York, son of a prominent American actor; educated in Roman Catholic schools and at Princeton and Harvard. He drifted through several occupations before spending a year at sea, 1910-11, followed by a brief period as actor in the same company as his father, then as a reporter, until tuberculosis immobilized him temporarily. After leaving the sanatorium he took to playwriting, and in 1914 became a student in Professor G. P. *Baker's drama department at Harvard—the celebrated *47

Workshop, of which he was to become the most famous member, though he formed a more productive association with the Provincetown Players (first in Provincetown, Massachusetts, and then in New York), who undertook in 1916 the staging of *Bound East for Cardiff*, the first of his plays to be performed; they also produced several other one-act plays by him in the following years. It was already evident that O'Neill was a uniquely gifted playwright likely to raise American drama to a level comparable with the best in Europe, and his first full-length play, *Beyond the Horizon* (1920), established him. In the years ahead his works alternated between the traditional-realistic and the experimental-mystical, with the theatregoing public acclaiming the former and the younger generation of critics excited by the latter. But though *Anna Christie* (1921) is grimly realistic, yet not without a dilution of melodrama and sentimentality, The *Emperor Jones* (1920) and *The Hairy Ape* (1922), though mystical by implication, are not devoid of realism. Even in his later period when symbolism with Freudian overtones predominated in such plays as *The Great God Brown* (1926), *Desire Under the Elms* (1924), *Strange Interlude* (1928), *Dynamo* (1929), *Mourning Becomes Electra* (1931) and *The Iceman Cometh* (1946), he was still able to write *Ah, Wilderness* (1933), 'a pleasant New England folk comedy'. If O'Neill had been born half-a-century earlier it is possible that his career would have been that of a dramatist upon whom managers could rely for a succession of theatrically effective plays; as it was, he grew up into a period of revolutionary ideas beyond the capacity of his mental equipment to bring under technical control, if not beyond the capacity of stage-drama itself. He was never commonplace, and while his failures may in a final assessment be counted as more numerous than his successes, they must be seen as the ambitious failures of a man whose reach exceeded his grasp.

Onions, C. T. (Charles Talbut Onions, 1873-1965). Born in Birmingham; educated there at King Edward VI School and Mason College. After teaching for three years he worked from 1895 on the staff of the Oxford English Dictionary, becoming one of its chief editors from 1914 to 1933, when the *Shorter Oxford English Dictionary* which he compiled was published. He also produced a valuable *Shakespeare Glossary* (1911; enlarged edn. 1953), new editions of the *Anglo-Saxon Reader in Prose and Verse* originally edited by Henry *Sweet, and *Advanced English Syntax* (1904).

Onions, Oliver (George Oliver Onions, 1873-1961). Born at Bradford; studied art in London and worked in a commercial studio. His intention to become a painter was diverted into a different channel from 1901 when his first book *The Compleat Bachelor* was published. A career in contemporary popular journalism, *Little Devil Doubt* (1909), was followed by *Good Boy Seldom* (1911), *In Accordance with the Evidence* (1912, the first volume of a trilogy reissued as a single work in 1925 with a new title, *Whom God Hath Sundered*). In later years his output was sporadic, and it was a new public that welcomed *The Story of Ragged Robyn* (1945) and *Poor Man's Tapestry* (1946), historical novels in a distinctive personal manner, the former set in the 17th century, the latter in the earlier period of the Wars of the Roses. He also wrote short stories of the supernatural, notably *Widdershins* (1911). *See also* Berta *Ruck.

O'Nolan, Brian (in Irish, Briain O Nuallain, 1912-66). Born in Tyrone; educated in Dublin; entered the civil service. Under the pseudonym Flann O'Brien wrote his first novel *At Swim-Two-Birds* (1939; reprinted 1960), which was 'recognized by a small circle . . . as a masterpiece in the tradition of *Ulysses,* and has been regarded as the only true successor to that book. In a dazzling cascade of wit, scholarship and prose-poetry it follows the picaresque adventures of a number of human and fairy characters through an enchanted Ireland' (Brian Cleeve: *Dictionary of Irish Writers,* 1967)—an interpretation helpful to readers perplexed by the interfolding narrative. Other novels: *The Hard Life* (1961), *The Dalkey Archive* (1965), *The Third Policeman* (posthumously 1968). As Myles na Gopaleen he wrote for many years in the *Irish Times*.

Open Country. Novel by Maurice *Hewlett published in 1909, the second in a trilogy begun with *Halfway House* (1908) and completed with *Rest Harrow* (1910). *See* John *Senhouse.

Open diplomacy. A term in frequent use by students of politics convinced that World War I was the outcome of secret treaties negotiated by national leaders and not revealed to their peoples. Though it was hoped that 'open diplomacy' through public debate in the League of Nations (afterwards in the United Nations) would prevent secret commitments likely to result in war, later experience that open diplomacy could degenerate into obstructive propaganda designed to exploit public ignorance, led to a counteracting belief that delicate and perplexing affairs of state may be dangerously prejudiced by ill-informed popular judgment.

Opium of the People. 'Religion is the opium of the people': translation from the German in Karl Marx's Introduction to *Criticism of Hegel's Philosophy of Right. See *Poison of the People.

Oppenheim, E. Phillips (Edward Phillips Oppenheim, 1866-1946). Born in London; educated in Leicester. Author of more than a hundred novels chiefly concerned with 'secret international documents, shifty diplomats, and seductive adventuresses': *The Mysterious Mr Sabin* (1901), *Mr Grex of Monte Carlo* (1915), *The Great Impersonation* (1920), *The Million Pound Deposit* (1930), *The Last Train Out* (1941). Autobiography: *The Pool of Memory* (1941).

Orage, A. R. (Alfred Richard Orage, 1873-1934). Born in Yorkshire; educated privately before training as a teacher, afterwards teaching for some twelve years in Leeds. He moved to London in 1906 and became, from the next year until 1922, editor of the *New Age,* a weekly periodical of unorthodox Socialism with a large number of distinguished contributors—Bernard *Shaw, H. G. *Wells, G. K. *Chesterton, *Hilaire Belloc, Arnold *Bennett, Ezra *Pound, and Katherine *Mansfield among them. From 1922 to 1931 he lectured in America on psychological topics and proselytized the theories of *Ouspensky and of *Gurdjieff, for whose institute at Fontainebleau he collected funds and for a period joined. On his return to London he founded the *New English Weekly* in 1932, mainly to advocate the *Social Credit system. He wrote *Friedrich Nietzsche* (1911), *The Art of Reading* (1930), and his *Social Credit* and *Political and Economic Writings* appeared posthumously (1935).

Orators, The. An English Study in verse and prose by W. H. *Auden published in 1932. It combines parody with prophecy of a revolutionary overthrow of the British social establishment, the middle classes being castigated as 'the enemy'.

Orczy, Baroness (Emmuska Orczy, 1865-1947, married Montagu Barstow). Born in Hungary; educated in Brussels and Paris; studied painting in London and exhibited in the Royal Academy. As a writer she produced a volume of detective stories, *The Old Man in the Corner* (1909), with similar collections in *Unravelled Knots* (1925) and *Lady Molly of Scotland Yard* (1910). These remain little known, being overshadowed by *The Scarlet Pimpernel* (1905) which, both as a novel and as a play produced in the same year, became one of the greatest popular successes of the century. Ingenious and sentimental, its story of the intrepid Englishman, Sir Percy Blakeney, who smuggles endangered aristocrats out of France during the Revolution has an irresistible appeal except to those who demand distinguished prose as the corollary of excitement. The author's several other Pimpernel books failed to repeat the success of the first. Among her other novels were *The Emperor's Candlesticks* (1899), *Beau Brocade* (1908), *The Laughing Cavalier* (1914), *The Turbulent Duchess* (1935).

Order of Merit. Founded in 1902 as a high distinction for eminent men and women, without conferring a title. It is limited to twenty-four members, and has two divisions, civil and military. Members are entitled to use O.M. after their names. The strict limitation of numbers has made it the most valued distinction. It has been conferred on the following authors: John Morley (1902), W. E. H. Lecky (1902), George Meredith (1905), James Bryce (1907), Alfred Russel Wallace (1908), Thomas Hardy (1910), George Otto Trevelyan (1911), Henry James (1916), A. J. Balfour (1916), J. M. Barrie (1922), F. H. Bradley (1924), J. G. Frazer (1925), George A. Grierson (1928), Robert Bridges (1929), Samuel Alexander (1929), John Galsworthy (1929), Montague James (1930), G. M. Trevelyan (1930), J. W. Mackail (1935), John Masefield (1935), H. A. L. Fisher (1937), A. S. Eddington (1938), J. H. Jeans (1939), Gilbert Murray (1941), Sidney Webb (1944), A. N. Whitehead (1945), Winston S. Churchill (1946), T. S. Eliot (1948), Bertrand Russell (1949), G. E. Moore (1951), Walter de la Mare (1953), G. P. Gooch (1963), E. M. Forster (1969), Veronica Wedgwood (1969), Sir Isaiah Berlin (1971).

O'Rell, Max (pseudonym of Léon Paul Blouet, 1848-1903). Born in France, educated in Paris; taken prisoner in the Franco-Prussian

War; afterwards settled in England as journalist and master at St Paul's School. Turned to authorship after 1887 and produced many widely circulated comic books on English ways and English women, from *John Bull's Womankind* (1884) to *Rambles in Womanland* (1903).

Orgreave family. Friends of Edwin in Arnold Bennett's *Clayhanger* trilogy (1910-16). **Charlie** was his school friend, later a doctor; **Janet,** in Auntie Hamps's opinion, waited in vain for years hoping that Edwin would propose. In the Orgreaves' house he met Hilda Lessways.

Orientations. W. Somerset *Maugham's first volume of short stories, published in 1899. Regarding them as immature, the author did not admit them to the three-volume *Complete Short Stories* (1951). One story, however, 'A Bad Example' provided the subject for Maugham's last play, *Sheppey* (1933).

O'Riordan, Conal (Conal O'Connell O'Riordan, 1874-1948). *See* F. Norreys *Connell.

Orlando: *A Biography.* Prose fantasy by Virginia *Woolf published in 1928.
Late in the 16th century, Orlando, a handsome boy of sixteen, is slicing with his sword at the shrivelled head of a Moor hanging from the rafters of an attic in the immense country house of the English lord who had slain him in Africa. From this substitute for the warlike ventures in which he is too young to join, Orlando turns to his more immediate passion — poetry — and resumes writing 'AEthelbert: A Tragedy in Five Acts' with 'horrid plots', 'noble sentiments', and such abstract characters as Vice, Crime, and Misery. While enjoying solitude on a hill above the house, he sees the Queen's cavalcade arriving and hurries down to put on Court attire and attend the Queen. She sees him as 'the very image of a noble gentleman', confers on him the Order of the Garter, but is in a torment of jealous rage when she catches him kissing a girl. During the Great Frost (described at length in a celebrated passage) he encounters a Muscovite princess while skating at the royal carnival on the frozen Thames. A love affair between them ends abruptly with her unannounced departure on the Muscovite Embassy ship as a great thaw breaks up the ice. Orlando retires to his country house, takes to reading particularly the works of Sir Thomas Browne, and returns to his own writings—'forty-seven plays, histories, rom-

ances, poems . . . all romantic and all long'. Desiring literary company, he summons from London Nicholas Greene, 'a very famous writer at the time', but is taken aback by the poet's decrepit appearance, receding chin and slobbering lips. Greene assures Orlando that the art of poetry is dead in England; that Shakespeare wrote some scenes that were well enough but got them from Marlowe; that Donne is a mountebank; and that the great age of literature is past. He talks incessantly about himself and his many diseases, but is good company, witty and irreverent. He departs with a promise from Orlando of a pension of £300 a year paid quarterly. To escape from an uninvited and unwelcome visitor, a Romanian Archduchess, Orlando prevails upon Charles II to send him as Ambassador Extraordinary to Constantinople. His success there leads Charles to honour him with the Order of the Bath and a Dukedom. After a night with Rosina Pepita, a dancer, he falls into a seven-day trance. On waking he finds his sex has changed and that he is now a woman. As the Lady Orlando she lives on through the centuries: is launched into London society in the reign of Queen Anne; entertains Swift and Addison and Alexander Pope (his tongue flickering like a lizard's) in her house at Blackfriars; hobnobs with the trollops of Leicester Square; submissively adopts the Victorian crinoline; marries Marmaduke Bonthrop Shelmerdine, a sailor; moves to Mayfair. Old Nicholas Greene reappears newly incarnated as a knight, a Litt.D., and a Professor, 'the most influential critic of the Victorian age', still declaring that 'the great days of literature are over'. He undertakes to find a publisher for her poem, 'The Oak Tree' (begun when she was an Elizabethan boy and worked on intermittently since); it wins the Burdett Coutts Memorial Prize of 200 guineas. Orlando has a baby; and reaching the year 1928, has her own car in which, after shopping at Marshall & Snelgrove's, she drives back to the great house in Kent (which, in actuality, is Knole, near Sevenoaks, the ancestral home of the Sackvilles and the birthplace of Victoria *Sackville-West, Virginia Woolf's poet friend, to whom *Orlando* is dedicated).

Orr, Christine (Christine Grant Millar Orr, 1899-1963; Mrs Robin Stark). Born in Edinburgh; educated there and at Oxford. Author of *The Player King* (1931) and other historical novels; of *Miss Scott of Castle*

Street (1952) and other plays. She also did much radio work for the B.B.C. in Edinburgh.

Ortega y Gasset, José (1883-1955). Born in Madrid; educated at Jesuit schools and at the Universities of Madrid, Leipzig, and Berlin. Professor of Metaphysics, Madrid, 1908; Professor of Philosophy, Lima, Peru, 1941. Took an active part in Spanish politics, but dissented from policies of both sides in the Civil War and went into exile. One of the most influential thinkers of his time, his writings achieved an international reputation. Those translated into English include *The Revolt of the Masses* (1932), *Toward a Philosophy of History* (1941), *The Mission of the University* (1944), *The Dehumanization of Art* (1948), *Notes on the Novel* (1948).

Orton, Joe (John Kingsley Orton, 1933-67). Born in Leicester; studied at *R.A.D.A. and was an actor before he became a playwright acceptable to some, repulsive to others. Finding people 'profoundly bad, but irresistibly funny', his bizarre sense of humour was prone to urge him to shock by indecency posing as 'protest'—as when he defaced public library books with obscene intent. He was murdered by a companion, who then killed himself. Orton's plays were *Entertaining Mr Sloane* (1964), *Loot* (1966), *Crimes of Passion* (1967).

Orwell, George (pseudonym of Eric Blair, 1903-50). Born in Bengal; educated in England at Eton. Service with the Indian Civil Police in Burma, 1922-7, having bred a hatred of colonialism, he resigned and returned to Europe to live in Paris, where he wrote without success and took refuge in menial occupations and private teaching. He then settled unwillingly in London as a bookseller's assistant until 1935, by which time he had published *Down and Out in Paris and London* (1933) and *Burmese Days* (1934) and was able to move into the country, where he ran a general shop until he went to Spain in 1936 to fight with the Republicans in the Civil War. He was both severely wounded and thoroughly disillusioned while there, and though when he resettled in England he maintained a theoretical attachment to left-wing principles he was out of sympathy with all political parties. Until 1945 he had only limited success with his books, which by then included *Keep the Aspidistra Flying* (1936), *The Road to Wigan Pier* (1937), *Homage to Catalonia* (1938), *Coming Up for Air* (1939),

though he was extending his public by his contributions to the *Observer* and other papers. Volumes of essays include *Inside the Whale* (1940), *Shooting an Elephant* (1950). The publication of *Animal Farm: A Fairy Story* (1945) rocketed him to success, and in the year before his death his novel of a horrifying totalitarian future *Nineteen Eighty-four* (1949) brought renewed attention.

Osborne, John (John James Osborne, 1929-). Educated at Belmont College, Devon. Acted in the provinces and at the Royal Court Theatre in London, where the production of his play *Look Back in Anger* in 1956 opened a new period in modern drama—the drama of the depressed and self-pitying young—though Osborne did not confine himself to the mode. Later plays (with their publication dates): *The Entertainer* (1957), *The World of Paul Slickey* (1959), *Luther* (1960), *Inadmissible Evidence* (1965), *A Bond Honoured* (1966), *A Sense of Detachment* (1972).

O'Shea, Katherine. *See* Charles Stewart *Parnell.

O'Sullivan, Seumas (pseudonym of James Sullivan Starkey, 1879-). Born and educated in Dublin. Acted in the Irish National Theatre company in Dublin and London. Founded the *Dublin Magazine* in 1923 and continued to edit it. A prolific poet, his published volumes include *The Twilight People* (1905), *Verses Sacred and Profane* (1908), *Requiem and Other Poems* (1917), *Collected Poems* (1940). Essays: *Impressions* (1912), *Mud and Purple* (1917), *Essays and Recollections* (1944).

Otherly, Mrs. In Drinkwater's *Abraham Lincoln* (1918) the mother of a killed son who pleads with the President to stop the war.

Ouida (pseudonym of Louise de la Ramée, 1839-1908). Born at Bury St Edmunds, of Anglo-French parentage. Of her at-one-time immensely popular but gushingly romantic novels *Under Two Flags* (1867) has been longest remembered as a remarkable period piece. Other novels: *Strathmore* (1865), *Tricotrin* (1869), *Moths* (1880).

Our Betters. Comedy in three acts by W. Somerset *Maugham performed in Atlantic City, U.S. in 1917; in London, 1923; published in 1923. A modern morality play, it scarifies rich American women who barter their wealth for European titles, and European titled and other men who are parasites on these women.

Pearl Saunders has become Lady George Grayson, Minnie Hodgson the Duchess de Surennes, and Flora van Hoog the Princess della Cercola. Sir George Grayson is for the most part an absentee husband: 'he generally dines out when Pearl is giving a party because he doesn't like people he doesn't know, and he seldom dines at home when they're alone, because it bores him'. Pearl's constant heavy debts are paid by an elderly American lover, Arthur Fenwick. During a weekend party at her country house she is caught in the arms of Antony Paxton, a youth who is the kept man of the Duchesse de Surennes. The Princess della Cercola married her Italian when she was twenty, seeing him 'as the successor of a long line of statesmen and warriors'. His family having been ruined by speculation, he sold himself for five million dollars to Flora van Hoog, to whom he was first indifferent, then bored by her, and finally hated her. Their child died, she returned to America, but finding herself a stranger there she settled in England; and of herself and other expatriated American women she says 'here we're strangers too'. It is Pearl's intention to bring about a match between her sister Bessie and Lord Bleane. After long hesitation Bessie accepts Bleane, until, distressed by the conduct of her sister and others and revolting against the atmosphere around them, she confesses to him that she only wanted a title, withdraws from the engagement, and closes the play with the words: 'I'm sailing for America next Saturday.'

Our Man in Havana. Novel by Graham *Greene, published in 1958.

Our Town. Play in three acts by Thornton *Wilder performed and published in the U.S. in 1938. Played in a bare setting except for essential tables and chairs which can be variously arranged to represent a drug-store counter and church pews in Act II with a projected colour transparency for the stained-glass window; and graves in Act III. All hand properties are imaginary, as also are the milkman's cart and Bessie, his horse.

The action centres on the Gibbs and Webb families in the small town of Grover's Corners, New Hampshire. In Act I, 'Daily Life' (1901), Mrs Gibbs and Mrs Webb go about their domestic occupations and get their children— George and Rebecca Gibbs and Wally and Emily Webb—off to school. The Stage Mana-

ger participates throughout, providing descriptive and explanatory matter and in Act II, 'Love and Marriage' (1904), taking part as the Minister at the wedding of George Gibbs and Emily Webb. Act III, 'Death' (1913), is located in the Grover's Corners cemetery at the funeral of Emily. Several townsmen and townswomen who have died previously are joined by Emily who, when the mourners have left, chooses to revisit her home on her twelfth birthday in 1899. Before returning to her grave she exclaims: 'Oh, earth, you're too wonderful for anybody to realize you'; and asking 'Do any human beings ever realize life while they live it?—every, every minute?', is answered: 'The saints and poets, maybe.'

Ouspensky, P. D. See Uspensky.

Outward Bound. See Sutton *Vane.

Overton, Mr. Godfather of Ernest Pontifex, and trustee of the fortune left for him by his aunt, Alethea Pontifex, in Samuel Butler's *The *Way of All Flesh* (1903).

Owen, John Pickard. Pseudonym under which Samuel *Butler wrote *The Fair Haven*.

Owen, Wilfred (1893-1918). Born at Oswestry, Shropshire; educated at Birkenhead and Shrewsbury. He worked in France at the Berlitz School, Bordeaux, and later as a private tutor, until he became a British infantry officer in World War I. In letters home he gave a realistic account of the tribulations of trench warfare. A period in hospital in England preceded further service with his regiment in France and the winning of the Military Cross before he was killed in November 1918, a week before the war ended. He had been drawn to poetry since childhood. The verses written in his last years—published after his death, *Poems* (1920)—were quickly recognized as the most remarkable of the war poems, both for technical originality and intense humanity and compassion. In two pieces particularly—'Strange Meeting' and 'Anthem for Doomed Youth'—he spoke for the generations wasted in war. A new edition —*The Collected Poems of Wilfred Owen* with Introduction and Notes by C. Day *Lewis and a Memoir by Edmund *Blunden—was published in 1963. Benjamin Britten's *War Requiem,* composed for the dedication ceremony of the new cathedral at Coventry (1962), incorporated poems by Owen. Almost the only notable dissenting opinion about his poems was voiced by W. B. *Yeats, who, as editor, excluded Owen with other war poets from the *Oxford Book of Modern Verse,* and also wrote (in *Letters on Poetry from W. B. Yeats to Dorothy Wellesley,* 1940) that he considered him 'unworthy of the poet's corner of a country newspaper', adding: 'I did not know I was excluding a revered sandwichboard Man of the Revolution, and that somebody has put his worst and most famous poem in a glass case in the British Museum—however, if I had known it, I would have excluded him just the same. He is all blood, dirt and sucked sugar stick . . . he calls poets "bards", a girl a "maid", and talks about "Titanic wars". There is every excuse for him, but none for those who like him.'

Oxenham, John (pseudonym of William Arthur Dunkerley, 1852-1941). Born and educated in Manchester; travelled widely in connection with his father's wholesale provision business for several years up to 1881, then started periodicals, *The Idler,* and, later, *Today* in conjunction with Jerome K. *Jerome. From 1898, with *God's Prisoner,* he wrote many novels, but had his greatest success with a small book of verses, *Bees in Amber* (1913). Refused by publishers, it was issued at his own expense and sold several hundred thousand copies.

Oxford Group, The. *See* Frank *Buchman, *and* Moral Rearmament.

Oxford University Press. *See* *Clarendon Press.

Oz, The Wizard of. Popular children's film based on the story, *The Land of Oz* by L. F. *Baum.

P.E.P. An association for investigating and preparing expert reports on Political and Economic Planning.

Packard, Vance (Vance Oakley Packard, 1914-). Educated at Pennsylvania and Columbia Universities. His books of social criticism include *The Hidden Persuaders* (1957), *The Status Seekers* (1959), *The Sexual Wilderness* (1968), *A Nation of Strangers* (1972).

Page, Frederick (1879-1962). Born in modest circumstances and largely self-educated, he worked for the Oxford University Press from 1899 until his retirement in 1952, continuing for a further seven years the editorship of **Notes and Queries* which he undertook in 1943. Although only one original book was published under his own name—*Patmore: A Study of Poetry* (1933)—he served as literary midwife to many authors.

Paget, Violet. *See* Vernon **Lee.

Pain, Barry (Barry Eric Odell Pain, 1864-1928). Born at Cambridge; educated at Sedbergh and Cambridge. From 1886 to 1890 he worked as an army coach, and then as a London journalist. He had graduated from the University as a classical scholar, but his reputation as author was made with humorous stories of London cockney and suburban characters, as in *Eliza* (1900), *Eliza's Husband* (1903), *Exit Eliza* (1912), *Mrs Murphy* (1913), *Edwards: The Confessions of a Jobbing Gardener* (1915), and many other volumes.

Pakenham. *See* Longford, Earl of; Fraser, Lady Antonia.

Pakington, Humphrey (The Hon. Humphrey Arthur Pakington, 5th baron Hampton, 1888-). Served in the navy, 1903-20, and 1939-45; trained as an architect from 1928 and practised as a partner in the family firm of architects. Author of novels— *Four in Family* (1931), *Family Album* (1939), *Aston Kings* (1946), *The Washbournes of Otterley* (1948); also *How the World Builds: An Introduction to Architecture* (1932), *English Villages and Hamlets* (1935); and an autobiography, *Bid Time Return* (1958).

Palinurus. Pseudonym under which Cyril Connolly wrote *The *Unquiet Grave*. In Virgil's *Aeneid* Palinurus falls into the sea from Aeneas's ship, of which he was the pilot.

Palladian. Architecture in the style of Andrea Palladio (1518-1580), based on that of Vitruvius (Rome, 1st century A.D.) whose treatise *De Architectura* was seminal for Palladio's *Quattro Libri dell' Architettura* (1570), a work that greatly influenced Renaissance buildings and, in England, especially those of Inigo Jones (1573-1652) and Sir Christopher Wren (1632-1723). The Palladian style persisted in many countries down to the present century.

Palmer, Henrietta Eliza Vaughan (Mrs Arthur Stannard). *See* John Strange **Winter.

Palmer, Herbert (Herbert Edward Palmer, 1880-1961). Born in Lincolnshire; educated at Woodhouse Grove School and at the Universities of Cambridge and Bonn. From 1899 to 1921 worked as a teacher in English and French schools, as a tutor in Germany, and as a lecturer in English Literature for the Workers' Educational Association. He wrote much verse, *Collected Poems* (1933) and later volumes. *The Teaching of English* (1930), *Post-Victorian Poetry* (1938); *The Mistletoe Child* (autobiography, 1935).

Palmer, John Leslie (1885-1944). Born in London; educated at Birmingham and Oxford; dramatic critic on the *Saturday Review*, 1910-15; author of *The Comedy of Manners* (1913), books on the contemporary theatre and on Bernard **Shaw (1915), **Kipling (1915) and others. In collaboration with Hilary St George **Saunders he wrote numerous thrillers (e.g. *The Seven Sleepers*, *The Six Proud Walkers*, etc.) under the pseudonym Francis Beeding, and with the same collaborator others under the pseudonym David Pilgrim. Novels published under his own name include *The King's Men* (1916); and under the pseudonym Christopher Haddon, *Under the Long Barrow* (1939).

Palmer, Vance. *See* **Australian Writers.

Panem et circenses. *See* **Bread and circuses.

Pankhurst, Dame Christabel (1880-1958; D.B.E. 1936). Born and educated in Manchester. With her mother and sister (see the following) she took an active part in the militant women's suffrage campaign of the 1910s but desisted from violence when war started in 1914. In later years she described herself as a 'religious propagandist' and directed her natural ardour wholeheartedly into preaching the Protestant

Evangelical doctrine of the Second Coming of Christ. In that cause she wrote *The Lord Cometh: The World Crisis Explained* (1923; revised edn 1934), *Pressing Problems of the Closing Age* (1924), *The World's Unrest: Visions of the Dawn* (1926), *The Uncurtained Future* (1940).

Pankhurst, Emmeline (*née* Emmeline Goulden, 1857-1928; Mrs R. M. Pankhurst). Born in Manchester; educated there and in Paris. Her parents and her husband (Dr R. M. Pankhurst), a barrister, whom she married in 1879) were social reformers and advocates of votes for women, a cause taken up from 1868 by Mrs Pankhurst. When her husband died in 1898, she supported her family by acting as a Registrar of Births and Deaths, resigning in 1907, four years after she had founded (with her daughter Christabel) the Women's Social and Political Union. The members of the W.S.P.U. conducted an increasingly violent campaign from 1905, and in the following years Mrs Pankhurst was among those who served terms of imprisonment, during which her constitution was undermined by repeated hunger-striking. Shortly before she died, the suffrage was given to women on the same terms as men. Her statue stands close to the Houses of Parliament, in Victoria Tower Gardens. Her autobiography, *My Own Story*, was published in 1914.

Pankhurst, Sylvia (Estelle Sylvia Pankhurst, 1882-1960). Born and educated in Manchester; studied art there and in London and Venice. Abandoned art to assist her mother and sister in the women's suffrage campaign and was imprisoned several times. She broke away from the W.S.P.U. to found the *Workers' Dreadnought* which claimed to pursue a more democratic policy. From 1914 she worked on behalf of various social and political causes, British and foreign, supporting in particular the struggle of Ethiopia against Fascist Italy. Among her numerous writings are *The Suffragette Movement* (1931) and *The Life of Emmeline Pankhurst* (1935).

Pansy. Pseudonym of (1) Isabella Macdonald Alden (1841-1930), American writer of Sunday School books, *Four Girls at Chautauqua* (1887), *Following Heavenward* (1889) and scores of others. (2) Ida M. Loder Donisthorpe, author of *Fireside Poems* (1929).

Panter-Downes, Mollie (Mollie Patricia Panter-Downes, 1906- ; Mrs Clare Robinson). Born in London; educated privately and in Brighton. Her first novel *The Shoreless Sea* (1924) was written when she was sixteen. Other books: *The Chase* (1925), *Storm Bird* (1929), *My Husband Simon* (1931), *Nothing in Common But Sex* (1932), *One Fine Day* (1947). During World War II she contributed to the *New Yorker* weekly articles collected in *Letter from England* (1940), *At the Pines* (on Swinburne; 1971).

Pantheism. The belief that everything in the universe is a revelation of God. 'Earth's crammed with heaven,/And every common bush afire with God' (E. B. Browning: *Aurora Leigh*, book vii).

Paperbacks. Trade term for books in paper covers, usually reprints of popular works, and usually published at prices below those charged for books in more durable binding. Their success began in 1935 with *Penguin Books, first published at sixpence each, a project for which failure and bankruptcy was widely prophesied. By the 1950s, however, paperbacks had become a staple product of the book trade, with many competing series, both British and American, and whole departments given over to their display and sale in bookshops, stores, and newsagents. A few of their competitors imitated an early development by the Penguin Books organization, whose non-fiction Pelican Books, started in 1937 as an educational series of reprints, soon became a library of new books specially commissioned from specialist authors. The reprint side of the paperback trade became a valuable additional source of income not only to authors but also to the non-paperback publishers in whose discretion lay at first the power to grant or refuse a licence for the reprinting of any copyright book first published by themselves. Although the percentage royalty paid on low-priced paperbacks is necessarily small per copy, the large editions (frequently 30,000 copies as an initial printing, but sometimes a multiple of that number if the book is a 'best-selling' novel that has been filmed or televised in some form) and the pressure of competition from other paperback sources, enables or compels publishers to offer large advance payments on account of royalties. A substantial advance payment and the possibility of a sale reaching a million or more copies in a few weeks or months is a golden prospect for authors and for their original publishers. Though fiction accounts for the great bulk of paperback sales, there have been unpredictable successes among non-fiction books, perhaps the most remarkable being the three-quarters of a million copies of the Penguin translation of Homer's *Odyssey* between 1946 and 1956. In the later 1950s several publishers of 'serious' books, including the University Presses, began to publish their own paperback series. Most of the books included (e.g. G. E. *Moore's *Principia Ethica*) could have no prospect of achieving a mass sale and their prices were accordingly high when compared with those of the popular series, even though these had been forced up by wartime and postwar economics from 6*d* to, variously, 2*s* 6*d*, 3*s* 6*d*, 5*s*, 7*s* 6*d*, and higher. By the early 1960s there had arisen the so far unanswered question of whether the revolution in book production and bookselling brought about by paperbacks might not, like nearly all revolutions, become destroyed by its own offspring through the flooding of the market by many thousands of novels indiscriminately chosen. *See* Appendix.

Papini, Giovanni (1881-1956). Born and educated in Florence. Edited several Italian periodicals; under the Fascist régime became Professor of Italian Literature in the University of Bologna, after having made an international reputation with his *Life of Christ* (1921). His other writings included *Twilight of the Philosophies* (1906), *A Finished Man* (novel; 1913), *St Augustine* (1929), *Life and Myself* (1930).

Parade's End. A series of linked novels by Ford Madox *Ford: *Some Do Not . . .* (1924), *No More Parades* (1925), *A Man Could Stand Up* (1926); a final volume *The Last Post* (1928), bringing the sequence to a somewhat sentimentalized conclusion, afterwards regretted by the author, was later detached from its predecessors. The trilogy pivots on the experiences of Christopher Tietjens, the younger son of a wealthy Yorkshire country gentleman. An exceptionally skilled statistician holding a post in the Department of Statistics until World War I, he suffers in France a brain injury which impairs his memory, and on returning to duty is appointed to a relatively quiet base camp as officer in charge of a draft, until he is sent up to the front line to avoid a

court martial when his malicious, lascivious and sadistic wife embroils him with a senior officer. In the trenches he endures the full horrors of war, but survives to return to Valentine Wannop, his young woman friend in England, whose earlier agreement to become his mistress was frustrated by the war.

Pares, Sir Bernard (1867-1949; knighted 1919). Born in Surrey; educated at Harrow and Cambridge. Specialized in Russian studies and became Professor of Russian History, Language and Literature in the Universities of Liverpool, 1908-17, and London, 1919-36, and Director of the School of Slavonic Studies, 1922-39. Author of *Russia and Reform* (1907), *Day by Day with the Russian Army* (1915), *A History of Russia* (1926), *My Russian Memoirs* (1931), *Moscow Admits a Critic* (1936), *The Fall of the Russian Monarchy* (1939).

Pares, Richard (1902-1958). Son of the preceding. Educated at Winchester and Oxford. Professor of History in the University of Edinburgh, 1945-54. Author of *War and Trade in the West Indies* (1936), *Colonial Blockade and Neutral Rights* (1938), *King George III and the Politicians* (1953), *Yankees and Creoles* (1956).

Pargeter, Edith (1913-   ). Educated at a local Church school and at the County High School, Coalbrookdale. Worked as a chemist's assistant before succeeding as a novelist. Author of *The City Lies Foursquare* (1939), *Reluctant Odyssey* (1946), *The Coast of Bohemia* (1949), *This Rough Magic* (1953), *The Soldier at the Door* (1954), *The Scarlet Seed* (1963), etc.

Parker, Dorothy (*née* Dorothy Rothschild; Mrs E. P. Parker; later Mrs Alan Campbell, 1893-1967). Educated in New Jersey and New York; began as a journalist on *Vogue* and *Vanity Fair* and was later on *The New Yorker*; her reputation rests on her witty, satirical, humorous and technically accomplished verse collected in *Not So Deep as a Well* (1936); she also wrote short stories collected in *Here Lies* (1939), film scenarios, and served as a press correspondent during the Spanish Civil War.

Parker, Sir Gilbert (Horatio Gilbert George Parker, 1862-1932; knighted 1902; baronet 1915). Born in Ontario; educated at the University of Toronto, where he became

o

Lecturer in English, 1883-85, then travelled extensively and was for several years in Australia as an editor of the Sydney *Morning Herald.* Settled in England from 1898 and was in 1900 elected Conservative M.P. for Gravesend which he continued to represent until 1918. Meanwhile he established himself as a novelist with *Pierre and His People* (1892), *The Translation of a Savage* (1894), *When Valmond Came to Pontiac* (1895), *The Seats of the Mighty* (1896), *The Right of Way* (1901), *A Ladder of Swords* (1904), *The Judgment House* (1913), *Carnac's Folly* (1922). He also wrote a *History of Old Quebec* (1903).

Parker, Louis N. (Louis Napoleon Parker, 1852-1944). Born in France of American parentage; educated in European countries and studied at the Royal Academy of Music in London. Director of Music at Sherborne School, 1873-92, afterwards making a wider reputation as a deviser of historical pageants for several English cities. He also wrote numerous plays, among which *Rosemary* (1896), *Pomander Walk* (1910), *Disraeli* (1911), *Drake* (1912), and *Joseph and His Brethren* (1913) had contemporary success.

Parkinson, Cyril Northcote (1909-). Born in County Durham; educated in York and at the Universities of Cambridge and London. Taught history as a schoolmaster; Raffles Professor of History, University of Malaya, 1950-58. Author of historical works—*Trade in the Eastern Seas* (1937), *War in the Eastern Seas* (1954), *The Evolution of Political Thought* (1958). The publication of **Parkinson's Law* at once made his name a household word. Later books developing similar themes: *The Law and the Profits* (1960), *In-Laws and Outlaws* (1962), *A Law unto Themselves* (1966), *Mrs Parkinson's Law* (1968).

Parkinson's Law. Formulated by C. Northcote *Parkinson in *Parkinson's Law, or The Pursuit of Progress,* published in 1957 (U.S.; in England 1958). On the hypothetical axioms that '(1) "An official wants to multiply subordinates, not rivals" and (2) "Officials make work for each other" ', the author based his 'law': 'Work expands so as to fill the time available for its completion.' The idea is pursued with a combination of seriousness, humour, and wit through chapters treating of various aspects of management and administration. The

words 'Parkinson's law' have passed into common speech in satirical reference to any organization, official or commercial, which appears to be extravagantly over-staffed.

Parnassians. The late nineteenth-century poets so called owed the title to the publication of their poems serially in *Le Parnasse contemporain* from 1866. They were in reaction from Romanticism, and cultivated an objective approach, their interests embracing philosophy, science, politics, antiquity, natural description. Leading members of the group included Leconte de Lisle, Sully Prudhomme, José-Maria de Heredia, Baudelaire, Mallarmé, Verlaine.

Parnell, Charles Stewart (1846-1891). Irish M.P. for County Meath and later for the City of Cork; leader of the Home Rule party in the House of Commons and a heroic figure to his countrymen. In 1887 *The Times* printed letters alleged to be by Parnell, approving the murder in Dublin in 1882 of the Chief Secretary and Under-Secretary. A commission appointed by the government revealed that the letters had been forged by an Irish journalist, Richard Pigott, who confessed and shot himself in Madrid in 1889. An action against *The Times* was settled by the payment of £5000 to Parnell who, although thus vindicated, was later discredited in Ireland as well as in England by the exposure of his liaison with the wife of a Captain O'Shea, who obtained a divorce. Parnell married Katherine O'Shea a few months before his death at Brighton. Though Victorian and Roman Catholic morality virtually outlawed Parnell as a consequence of the divorce, he has been restored in memory as one of the greatest fighters in the long and finally successful struggle for Irish independence. In the present century his story has been resurveyed in *Parnell* by Katherine O'Shea (1914), *Parnell* by St John *Ervine (1925), and *Parnell Vindicated* by Henry Harrison (1931). A play by Lennox *Robinson, *The Lost Leader* (1918), is based on a Parnell legend.

Parody. Imitation with satirical intent of writings by others, though Swinburne guyed his own mannerisms in 'Nephelidia'. The outstanding parodies of the present century are in *A *Christmas Garland* (1912) by Max *Beerbohm; other examples are *Parodies Regained* (1921) by E. V. *Knox,

Collected Parodies (1921) by J. C. *Squire, *Brief Diversions* (1922) by J. B. *Priestley.

Parrington, Vernon (Vernon Louis Parrington, 1871-1929). Born in Illinois; educated at Harvard. Professor of English in the University of Washington from 1912. He contributed to various encyclopaedias and was engaged at the time of his death on an important historical survey of American literature concentrating on the ideas expressed in it: *Main Currents in American Thought* (3 vols, 1927-30, the third volume having remained uncompleted). He also wrote *The Connecticut Wits* (1926) and *Sinclair Lewis: Our Own Diogenes* (1927).

Parrish, Anne (1888-1957). Born in Colorado; educated there and in Delaware; studied painting in Philadelphia. Author of *The Perennial Bachelor* (1925), *Semi-Attached* (1924), *All Kneeling* (1928), *The Methodist Faun* (1929) and other novels.

Parry, Sir Hubert (Charles Hubert Hastings Parry, 1848-1918; knighted 1895; baronet 1902). Born at Bournemouth; educated at Eton and Oxford. In addition to his many distinguished musical compositions, including an oratorio based on Milton's *Blest Pair of Sirens*, he wrote *The Art of Music* (1893), *Johann Sebastian Bach* (1909), *Style in Musical Art* (1911), and was Professor of Music in the University of Oxford, 1899-1908.

Partington, Dame. In popular phraseology, to behave like Dame (or Mrs) Partington is to indulge in some foolish vain endeavour. The name comes from a speech by Sydney Smith (1771-1845) in 1831, in which he likened the House of Lords' obstruction of the Reform Bill to the attempts of a Dame Partington to stem an Atlantic flood with her mop.

Partridge, Sir Bernard (1861-1945; knighted 1925). Born in London; educated at Stonyhurst Roman Catholic College. Trained as a designer in stained glass, but went on the stage for a few years under the name Bernard Gould, acting with Henry Irving and Forbes Robertson. From 1891 until his death he was on the staff of *Punch* and was its chief cartoonist from 1909.

Partridge, Eric (Eric Honeywood Partridge, 1894-   ). Born in New Zealand; educated at the Universities of Queensland and Oxford. Lecturer in English Literature at Manchester and London Universities, 1925-27. Founded and managed the *Scholartis Press*, 1927-31. Wrote two or three literary studies before concentrating on words, their etymology and current usage, and becoming the most original, forceful and entertaining lexicographer of his time: *Words, Words, Words* (1933), *Name This Child* (1936), *A Dictionary of Slang and Unconventional English* (1937), *A World of Words* (1939), *A Dictionary of Clichés* (1940), *Usage and Abusage: A Guide to Good English* (1942), *Shakespeare's Bawdy* (1947), *English: A Course for Human Beings* (1949), *British and American English since 1900* (1951).

Passage to India, A. Novel by E. M. *Forster published in 1924. Before she will agree to become engaged to Ronny Heaslop, Adela Quested travels to India with Mrs Moore (his mother by her previous marriage) and visits him at Chandrapore, where he is stationed as City Magistrate. Explaining Adela's purpose to her son, Mrs Moore says: 'She knows you in play, as she put it, but not in work, and she felt she must come and look round, before she decided— and before you decided.' The friendly attitude of the two newcomers to the Indians is resented by the established British officials and their wives, and both Mrs Moore and Adela are disturbed by the discovery that Ronny is also opposed to equality of social intercourse between the two races. While Mrs Moore is visiting a nearby mosque by moonlight, alone, she converses with and likes a young Indian whom she afterwards learns is Dr Aziz, assistant to the British Civil Surgeon at the Chadrapore hospital. Mutual liking develops between Aziz and Mrs Moore and Adela, who accept his invitation to join a party, including Cyril Fielding, Principal of the Government College, to visit the caves in the Marabar Hills. Adela, meanwhile, has at first decided against Ronny, but changes her mind, and plans for their marriage at Simla are put in hand. Aziz's excursion to the Marabar caves involves a train journey followed by an elephant ride, with a number of servants to deal with food and impedimenta. Fielding arrives too late to join the train, and the two Englishwomen and the Indians go on without him. In the first cave they enter, Mrs Moore is overcome by the stuffiness and the echoing noise and goes into the open air again, leaving Adela and Aziz with a guide to continue 'the slightly tedious expedition'. There are a number of caves at the top of the track, and Aziz steps into one to light a cigarette. When he comes out a minute later he finds only the guide, who tells him that the lady 'had gone into a cave', but he cannot specify which one. At that moment Aziz sees a car coming toward the hills on the road from Chandrapore. He supposes that Miss Quested has recognized friends and gone to join them. He returns to where Mrs Moore is resting, finds Fielding with her, and learns from the chauffeur that Miss Quested has departed in the car with Miss Derek, a nurse friend, driving. Fielding goes back with the main party, and when the train reaches Chandrapore Aziz is arrested. Miss Derek has reported to the Superintendent of Police that Adela rushed down to her from the caves in a distraught condition and is now ill and in the care of the Superintendent's wife. The charge made by Adela is that Aziz followed her into the cave and made insulting advances. The only British who believe Aziz innocent are Fielding, who has long been his friend, and Mrs Moore, who leaves for England before the trial and dies at sea. As Adela recovers, she has doubts about her charge and considers the possibility of hallucination. At the stormy trial, while giving evidence, she endeavours to reconstruct the critical day's happenings as in a vision, with the result that she declares in court: 'I have made a mistake . . . Dr Aziz never followed me into the cave.' The novel is essentially a tragedy of racial tensions and antagonism, in which the case of Dr Aziz is a symbolic episode.

Passfield, Lord. See Sidney *Webb.

Passion, Poison, and Petrifaction, or The Fatal Gazogene. One-act 'Brief Tragedy for Barns and Booths' performed at the Theatrical Garden Party in Regent's Park in 1905. Although written by Bernard *Shaw as a piece of knockabout nonsense and included by him among his *Tomfooleries, attempts have been made since his death to give it solemn importance as a forerunner of the *Theatre of the Absurd.

Pasternak, Boris (Boris Leonidovich Pasternak, 1890-1960). Born in Moscow; educated there and in Germany. From 1914 he published several collections of verse which

established him as one of Russia's foremost poets, but his novel *Dr Zhivago* (English trans. 1958), which gave him a great international reputation, also earned him the disfavour of, and mean persecution by, the Soviet authorities, who forbade his acceptance of the Nobel Prize for Literature awarded him in 1958.

Pastiche. See Parody.

Paston, George (pseudonym of Emily Morse Symonds; died 1936). Born in Norwich. Her novels and plays were mostly feminist in tone (novels: *A Bread and Butter Miss,* 1894; *A Modern Amazon,* 1894; plays: *The Pharisee's Wife,* 1904; *Nobody's Daughter,* 1910), though *Clothes and the Woman* (performed in London, 1920) was of lighter substance. She was more celebrated for her *Little Memoirs of the 18th century* (1901), *Little Memoirs of the 19th century* (1902), *Mrs Delany* (1900), *Side-Lights on the Georgian Period* (1902), *The Life of George Romney* (1903), *At John Murray's* (1932) is a history of that long-established publishing house.

Pastoral. A type of poetry or of prose romance treating either actual or ideal country life. The earliest extant examples are by ancient Greek poets, pre-eminently Theocritus (3rd century B.C.), and the greatest in Latin by Virgil (70-19 B.C.). Many pastorals in verse, drama, and prose were written in Elizabethan England (e.g. Shakespeare's *As You Like It,* scenes in *The Winter's Tale,* etc.). Pope's *Pastorals* (in Tonson's *Poetical Miscellany* 1709) are youthful work. In the present century there are *The Song of the Plow* (1916) by Maurice *Hewlett, *The *Land* (1927) by V. *Sackville-West, and poems by Edmund *Blunden (*The Shepherd,* 1922) and others. A personal view is taken in William Empson's critical work *Some Versions of Pastoral* (1935).

Patch, Blanche (Blanche Eliza Patch, 1879-1966). Daughter of a clergyman; became a dispenser; met Bernard *Shaw at the Webbs' house in Wales and became his secretary from 1920 until he died, typing all his plays from *Saint Joan* onward. She wrote *Thirty Years with G.B.S.* (1951).

Paterson, A. B. (Andrew Barton Paterson, 1864-1941). Born in Australia; educated in Sydney; studied law and practised as a solicitor, but from the time of the Boer War became a war correspondent for

Australian papers in several campaigns. He wrote novels, but was best known by his popular verses which earned him the nickname Banjo Paterson; among these was 'Waltzing Matilda' (adapted from a traditional source) which has become the popular national song of Australia.

Path to Rome, The. An account by Hilaire *Belloc, published in 1902, of his journey on foot from Toul in the valley of the Moselle which 'runs straight towards Rome', 250 leagues away, as the poem at the end of the book assesses the distance. The plan, to proceed in a straight line, had to be modified when the endeavour to cross the Alps in a blizzard failed; the intention to walk by night and rest during the hot June days did not always prevent exhaustion; and the vow to travel only on foot had to be relaxed when cash ran short, and a short train ride and, again, a lift by bullock cart was necessary to reach the next bank. Though there is no lack of description of the route followed or of the places passed through, 'the peculiar virtue of this book', as the author purposed, is in recording more than most travel-book writers observe: 'I am astonished at a thousand accidents, and always find things twenty-fold as great as I supposed they would be, and far more curious; the whole covered by a strange light of adventure.' So, the magnificence of scenery, the sensations experienced at night in the forest, and other rigours of the pilgrimage, are kept in due proportion by the attention given to people: nuns haymaking; a peasant driving 'the largest Tun or Barrel that ever went on wheels', filled with wine made by himself; innkeepers surly or hospitable, reluctant to provide a bed or generous with food. If the journey threatens at times to become tedious, the narrative is relieved by digressions—on windows, on wine, on 'shifty-eyed people', on Sussex place-names, on the corrupting effects of wealth, on 'the Faith'—and by stories and anecdotes. It is also interrupted from time to time by dialogues between the author and an imagined reader (Auctor and Lector), a humorous device which permits the discussion of such matters as literary style, a topic on which Auctor inveighs against pedantry. The author's farewell to his readers is preceded by a parable relating a conversation between St Michael and the Padre Eterno disposing of mankind's illusion of being the supreme achievement of the Creator.

Pathetic fallacy. The emotional attribution of human qualities and abilities to external things. Ruskin wrote in *Modern Painters* (Part IV, chapter xii), quoting lines from Charles Kingsley's *Alton Locke*: '"They rowed her in across the rolling foam—/The cruel, crawling foam". The foam is not cruel, neither does it crawl. The state of mind which attributes to it these characters of a living creature is one in which the reason is unhinged by grief. All violent feelings have the same effect. They produce in us a falseness in all our impressions of external things, which I would generally characterize as the "Pathetic Fallacy".'

Paton, Alan (Alan Stewart Paton, 1903-). Born and educated in Pietermaritzburg; worked as a school teacher until 1935, when he became principal of the largest reformatory for African boys, and some years later visited similar institutions in Europe and America. His sympathy with the coloured peoples of South Africa found written expression in his novels, *Cry, the Beloved Country* (1948) and *Too Late the Phalarope* (1953), which made him famous abroad but antagonized the advocates of racial segregation (*apartheid*) in his own country. He also wrote *The Land and People of South Africa* (1955), *Hope for South Africa* (1959), and *Debbie Go Home* (short stories, 1961), *The Long View* (1969).

Paul, Cedar (*née* Gertrude Mary Davenport). Born in Hampstead; studied in Paris, Genoa, and London, and as an opera singer in Dresden and Stuttgart. Her career as a singer was interspersed with work as a writer and translator in collaboration with Eden Paul (see below), their joint translations including medical, scientific, political, and other works by French, Russian, Italian, and German authors. Died 1972.

Paul, Eden (Maurice Eden Paul, 1865-1944). Born in Dorset, son of Kegan Paul (see below); educated at University College, London; studied medicine at London Hospital and from 1895 to 1912 practised in the Far East and in the Channel Islands and London. Founder and editor of the Nagasaki Press, Japan, 1897-99; Paris correspondent of the London *Daily Citizen*, 1912-14. Author of *Socialism and Science* (1909), *Karl Marx and Modern Socialism*

(1910), *Psychical Research and Thought Transference* (1911), *The Sexual Life of the Child* (1921), *Chronos, or the Future of the Family* (1930). In collaboration with Cedar Paul (see above): *The Appreciation of Poetry* (1920), *Creative Revolution* (1920), *Proletcult* (1921), *Communism* (1921), and many translations.

Paul, Elliot (Elliot Harold Paul, 1891-1958). Born at Malden, Massachusetts; educated there and at Maine University. Literary editor of Paris editions of *Chicago Tribune* (1925-26). *New York Herald* (1930); co-editor of *transition* (1927-28). Author of *Life and Death of a Spanish Town* (1937), *A Narrow Street* (1942), *Springtime in Paris* (1950).

Paul, Kegan (Charles Kegan Paul, 1828-1902). Born in Somerset; educated at Ilminster, Eton, and Oxford. Ordained in the Church of England, he held various livings and a chaplaincy at Eton, but retired from the Church, with whose teaching he ceased to agree. In 1877 he took over the publishing business of H. S. King in Cornhill and transferred it to Paternoster Square as C. Kegan Paul & Co until Alfred Trench joined as partner in 1881, when his name was added to the firm's title. Amalgamation followed later and the publishing business became, and has continued as, Routledge and Kegan Paul Ltd. Kegan Paul wrote books on Shelley and William Godwin, but joined the Roman Catholic Church in 1890.

Paul, Leslie (Leslie Allen Paul, 1905-   ). Born in Dublin; educated in London. From the age of twenty engaged in welfare work. Among his books, the autobiographical *Angry Young Man* (1951) made probably the first use of a phrase which later became a cliché. Other writings: *Annihilation of Man* (1944), *The Meaning of Human Existence* (1949), *The English Philosophers* (1953), *Sir Thomas More* (1953), *The Boy Down Kitchener Street* (1957), *Nature into History* (1957), *Persons and Perception* (1961), *Son of Man* (1961), *Eros Rediscovered* (1970).

Pavlov, Ivan Petrovich (1849-1936). Born near Ryazan, son of a village priest; studied medicine in St Petersburg (Leningrad), where he later became Director of the Institute of Experimental Medicine. He was made world-renowned by his work on conditioned reflexes, by which he demonstrated that the saliva normally produced by a dog when seeing or smelling food, will also be produced by the sound of a bell independently of food after the dog has been conditioned by repetition to link the sound with the expectation of food. The employment of advertising techniques and political and other means of conditioning human reflexes for particular ends is a development from Pavlov's experiments.

Paye, Robert. *See* Marjorie *Bowen.

Payne-Townshend, Charlotte Frances. *See* Mrs Bernard *Shaw.

Peabody, Josephine Preston (1874-1922). Born in New York; educated in Boston and at Radcliffe College (Cambridge, Mass). Wrote poems from early years; published her first collection of verse, *The Wayfarers,* in 1898. Lecturer in English Literature at Wellesley College, Mass, 1901-03. In 1910 she won the Stratford-on-Avon Shakespeare Memorial Theatre prize competition for a verse play with *The Piper* (suggested by Browning's poem 'The Pied Piper of Hamelin'). Her *Collected Poems* and *Collected Plays* were published posthumously (1927).

Peach, L. du Garde (Lawrence du Garde Peach, 1890-1975). Educated in Manchester, Göttingen, and Sheffield. Lecturer in English Language and Literature, University of Göttingen, 1912-14; Lecturer in English, University College of the South West, 1922-26. Author of many humorous articles in *Punch* and several hundred broadcast plays and plays for youth groups. *Collected Plays* (4 vols, 1955).

Peacock Pie. Book of poems by Walter *de la Mare published in 1913. Though ostensibly a collection of light verse for children it contains some of the author's most memorable poetry: e.g. 'Nicholas Nye', 'Hide and Seek', 'Tillie', 'Miss T'.

Peake, Mervyn (1911-68). Born in China, son of a medical missionary; educated at Tientsin and later in Kent when his parents came to England; studied at the Royal Academy Schools and in drawing and writing displayed a unique mastery of the grotesque, as shown in his novels, *Titus Groan* (1946), *Gormenghast* (1950), *Titus Alone* (1959), re-issued as a trilogy in 1967. He also published verse—*Rhymes Without Reason* (1944), *The Glassblowers* (1950), *The Rime of the Flying Bomb* (1962), a play—*The Wit to Woo* (1957), and illustrated numerous books.

Pearse, Padraic (Padraic Henry Pearse, 1879-1916). Born in Dublin; educated at the Christian Brothers' School. Made a special study of Irish Gaelic, took a leading part in the work of the Gaelic League, and founded a boys' school conducted in both Irish and English. In the 1916 Easter Rising he commanded the Irish Republican Army and was proclaimed President of the Provisional Government. Having been captured, when the headquarters of the Rising were abandoned, he was tried and executed. His *Collected Works* were published in 1917 and a volume of *Poems* a year later.

Pearson, Sir Arthur (Cyril Arthur Pearson, 1866-1921; baronet 1916). Born in Somerset; educated at Winchester. Joined the journalistic staff of George *Newnes and became manager of the firm. In 1890 he formed his own company, founding *Pearson's Weekly* and going on to establish a large number of other periodicals. He started the *Daily Express* in 1900, acquired the *Standard* and control of the *St James's Gazette* in 1905, and with these and his other publications competed with *Harmsworth and Newnes as one of the pioneers of the 'new journalism' catering for a mass public. Owing to failing sight he sold all his journals and became totally blind about 1912. Thereafter he devoted himself to the welfare of the blind, establishing in 1915 St Dunstan's, the now famous home for blinded soldiers and sailors. Author of *Victory over Blindness* (1919).

Pearson, Edmund (Edmund Lester Pearson, 1880-1937). Born in Massachusetts; educated at Harvard. Qualified in librarianship and was on the staff of the New York Public Library from 1914 to 1927. As a writer he specialized in the study of murder and murderers, becoming a recognized authority in the literature of the subject: *Studies in Murder* (1924), *Five Murders* (1928), *Instigation of the Devil* (1930), *More Studies in Murder* (1936), *The Trial of Lizzie Borden* (1937). Other books: *The Librarian at Play* (1911), *Theodore Roosevelt* (1920), *Queer Books* (1928), *Dime Novels* (1929). See William *Roughead, his British counterpart as a student of criminology.

Pearson, Hesketh (1887-1964). Born in Worcestershire; educated at Bedford Grammar School. Started work in a City office, left to go on the stage and continued as an actor

until 1931. Thereafter he wrote a long sequence of lively biographies: of Erasmus Darwin, Sydney Smith, Gilbert and Sullivan, Dr Johnson, Shakespeare, Conan Doyle, Dickens, and others—most notably of Bernard Shaw whose personal acquaintance and cooperative benevolence enabled Pearson to produce in *Bernard Shaw* (1942) one of the most readable and reliable studies of Shaw as playwright and person. A year after Shaw's death, *G.B.S.: A Postcript* (1951) appeared, and ten years later a new edition amalgamated the two books. *The Whispering Gallery* (1926), published anonymously and purporting to set down actual conversations of eminent living persons, was a spoof which brought him into passing disrepute, since it claimed to be by a diplomat of long experience. His reminiscences appeared in *Thinking it Over* (1938), and he collaborated with Hugh *Kingsmill in travel books and other volumes.

Pearson, Karl (1857-1936). Born in London; educated there and at Cambridge; studied law and was called to the Bar, but turned to other branches of learning. In the University of London he was Professor of Applied Mathematics and Mechanics, 1884-1911, Professor of Eugenics, 1911-33, and Professor of Geometry, 1891. He applied statistical methods to the study of evolution and eugenics, and by examples was responsible for the widespread inception of statistical laboratories. He founded in 1902 and edited until 1930 the learned journal *Biometrika*, and in addition to professional publications his books include *The Life, Letters and Labours of Francis Galton* (1914-30), and *The Grammar of Science* (1892 and later editions), his most widely circulated work.

Peary, Robert (Robert Edwin Peary, 1856-1920). Born in Pennsylvania; educated at Bowdoin College, Maine. Served in the U.S. Navy, joined many expeditions to the arctic regions, and on 6 April 1909 became the first to reach the North Pole. Author of *Northward Over the Great Ice* (1898), *Nearest the Pole* (1907), *The North Pole* (1910).

Peck, Winifred (Lady Peck, wife of Sir James Peck; *née* Winifred Frances Knox, 1882-1962). Born in Oxford; educated at Wycombe Abbey and Oxford. As the daughter of a bishop and sister of Ronald *Knox and E. V. *Knox she was brought up in an atmosphere of devotion and culture favourable to the impulse of imaginative creation which turned her to literature, mainly as a novelist in *The Skies are Falling* (1936), *A Garden Enclosed* (1941), *Winding Ways* (1952), and many others. *A Little Learning* (1952) and *Home for the Holidays* (1955), two of her most attractive books, recall her childhood days.

Pedro. Semi-human Caliban-like servant of Jones and Ricardo in Joseph Conrad's *Victory* (1915).

Pegeen Mike. Nickname of Margaret Flaherty in J. M. Synge's *The *Playboy of the Western World* (1907). Christy Mahon, the playboy, falls in love with her.

Péguy, Charles (Charles Pierre Péguy, 1873-1914). Born at Orleans of a peasant family; scholarships took him to a teachers' training college and to the Sorbonne in Paris. He then started a socialist bookshop and in 1900 a periodical, *Les Cahiers de la Quinzaine,* to which afterwards-celebrated writers contributed verse, essays, criticism and fiction. It continued until the beginning of World War I, in which Péguy was killed. He became an ardent Roman Catholic. Author of three dramatic poems on Joan of Arc, books on the *Dreyfus affair, and various other prose works.

Peirce, Charles Sanders. *See* Pragmatism.

Pelican Books. *See* *Penguin Books.

Pelléas and Mélisande. Play by Maurice *Maeterlinck; it appeared in 1892 and was made more celebrated ten years later by Claude Debussy, who based on it his opera with the same title. Mélisande, 'a frail mysterious forest maiden' is wedded by a prince, Golaud, whose brother Pélleas falls in love with her and is killed by Golaud. Mélisande dies heartbroken.

Pemberton Billing. *See* Noel Pemberton *Billing.

Pemberton, Sir Max (1863-1950; knighted 1928). Born at Birmingham; educated at Merchant Taylors' School and Cambridge. Editor of *Chums,* a boys' weekly paper (1892-93) and of *Cassell's Magazine* (1896-1906). Author of many novels including *The Diary of a Scoundrel* (1891), *The Iron Pirate* (1893), *The House Under the Sea* (1902), *Wheels of Anarchy* (1908), *Captain Black* (1911). He was a director of Northcliffe Newspapers

from 1920, and wrote *Lord Northcliffe: A Memoir* (1922). Autobiography: *Sixty Years Ago and After* (1936).

Pembroke, Herbert. Schoolmaster and brother-in-law of Rickie Elliot in E. M. Forster's *The *Longest Journey* (1907). His sister *Agnes marries Rickie.

Pen Portraits and Reviews. A volume of miscellaneous articles by Bernard *Shaw of varying dates from 1892 to 1927, collected in 1931. The chief pieces are on William *Archer, Samuel *Butler, William Morris, G. K. *Chesterton and Hilaire *Belloc, Dean W. R. *Inge, Henry Arthur *Jones, Henry Irving and Ellen *Terry.

Penguin Books. A series of paper-covered pocket-size reprints started in 1935 by Allen *Lane with a first batch of ten titles (eight novels, one biography, and one autobiography) costing sixpence each. Although failure had been almost unanimously prophesied, the first ten were immediately successful and there was no abatement of success as more and more volumes were added. In 1937 original books on current topics began to be included as Penguin Specials, while earlier in the same year an educational series (Pelican Books) unlimited in range of subject had been launched. Although World War II forced up prices and shortage of paper temporarily depressed the high production standard previously maintained by the series, it also increased the demand for books, since time was given to reading by many whose leisure had been spent otherwise before the war. In addition to adding extensively to Penguins and Pelicans, four subsidiary series were started by the firm during the war: King Penguins (small finely colour-illustrated books on such subjects as Roses, Birds, The Bayeux Tapestry, Elizabethan Miniatures, Russian Icons, etc.); Puffin Picture Books and Puffin Story Books (for children); and Penguin Modern Painters. After the war the range was still further extended: Penguin Classics (translations from various languages, new versions 'in contemporary English without any transgressions of scholarship or textual accuracy'); Penguin Scores (pocket-size editions of musical masterpieces); Penguin Poets; the Penguin Shakespeare (single plays); Penguin Reference Books; etc. By 1956, when it celebrated its coming of age, more than 1,100 Penguin titles had been published, more than 350 Pelicans, 165 Penguin Classics, and over 200 Puffins, besides smaller though impressive numbers in each of the remaining sub-series. At the time Penguin Books Ltd became a public company in 1961, a total of 250 million books had been sold, with an annual sale reaching 17 million. More far reaching than Penguin's own success was the general effect of the enterprise on the book trade (*see* *Paperbacks). The unsuccessful charge against the company in 1960 under the Obscene Publications Act led to the sale of 2 million copies of *Lady Chatterley's Lover* in less than two months (*see* *Censorship of Books).

Penicillin. A chemical substance derived from the green mould *penicillium notatum*, and used medically as an antibiotic in the treatment of various diseases. Its effect was first noticed by Sir Alexander *Fleming in 1928 when some of the mould which had developed in his laboratory worked destructively on bacterial cultures. It has since been produced synthetically and in World War II proved invaluable. It is only for use under medical supervision since it may create allergy or promote resistance in bacteria hitherto destroyed by it.

Pennell, Joseph (1857-1926). Born in Philadelphia; trained as an artist, specializing in book illustrations, etchings and lithographs. Married Elizabeth Robins (1855-1936), who must be distinguished from Elizabeth *Robins (1862-1952), both American and both authors. The Pennells settled in England and produced books jointly, including *The Life of James McNeill Whistler* (1908). She wrote a biography of *Mary Wollstonecraft* (1884) and published *The Life and Letters of Joseph Pennell* (1929).

Pennyfeather, Paul. Chief character in Evelyn Waugh's *Decline and Fall* (1928).

Pepys, Samuel. *See* Arthur *Bryant; J. B. *Fagan; H. B. *Wheatley.

Percy, Edward (pseudonym of Edward Percy Smith, 1891-1968). Educated at Haileybury and in France. In milling and corn business, 1909-30; member of Parliament, 1943-50. Author of *If Four Walls Told* (1922), *The Shop at Sly Corner* (1941), and other plays; he also wrote several novels.

Perelman, S. J. (Sidney Joseph Perelman, 1904-). Born in New York; educated at Brown University, Mass. One of America's

leading contemporary humorists, he wrote for the *New Yorker* and other periodicals, became a Hollywood film-script author, and wrote, among other books, *Strictly from Hunger* (1937), *Look Who's Talking* (1940), *Dream Department* (1943), *The Swiss Family Perelman* (1950), *Baby, It's Cold Inside* (1970).

Perry, Bliss (1860-1954). Born at Williamstown, Mass; educated there and in Berlin and Strasburg. Professor of English at Williams College, Mass, 1886-93; at Princeton, 1893-1900; and at Harvard, 1907-30. Editor of the *Atlantic Monthly*, 1899-1909. Author of several novels and numerous biographical and literary studies: *Walt Whitman* (1906), *Whittier* (1907), *Carlyle* (1915), *A Study of Prose Fiction* (1902), *The American Mind* (1912), *The American Spirit in Literature* (1918), *The Praise of Folly* (1923). Autobiography: *And Gladly Teach* (1935).

Personality. 'A personality is what you thought you were ... it lowers the people it acts on.' (Scott Fitzgerald: *This Side of Paradise*, 1920: Bk I, ch 3). The word had its greatest vogue in the 1950s and 1960s, as applied to television and radio performers and extended to politicians and others with a fabricated 'public image'.

Pertinax. Pseudonym used in succession by two French journalists: Charles Gérault (born 1878) and André Géraud (1882-1974).

Pertwee, Roland (1885-1963). Born at Brighton; studied art in London and Paris, then became an actor before turning to authorship as short story writer and dramatist. He worked with collaborators in several plays, e.g. *Interference* (1927) with Harold *Dearden. His chief stage success was *Pink String and Sealing Wax* (1943). Autobiography: *Master of None* (1938).

Pervaneh. Beloved by Rafi, King of the Beggars of Baghdad, in J. E. Flecker's *Hassan* (1922).

Pétain, Marshal (Henri Phillipe Omer Pétain, 1856-1951). His defence of Verdun and measures for dealing with the French mutinies in World War I made him appear a resolute figure, but this reputation was belied by his defeatism in World War II, when he surrendered France to the Germans and headed the collaborating Vichy government. He died in prison while serving the life sentence imposed on him at the treason trial after the war.

Peter Abelard. Novel by Helen *Waddell based on the disastrous love story of Abelard, the twelfth century theologian, and Héloise, the niece of Canon Fulbert. Published in 1933 the novel is in a more popular style than *Héloise and Abelard* (1921) by George *Moore.

Peter Pan: or, The Boy Who Would Not Grow Up. Play for children in five acts by J. M. *Barrie performed in 1904; published in 1928. Wendy, John, and Michael Darling, living with their parents in a top flat in Bloomsbury, have Nana, a Newfoundland dog, as their nurse. Mrs Darling tells her husband that a boy she had seen in the room flew out of the window when Nana sprang at him, and left behind his shadow, which she has rolled up and put away in a drawer. Jealous of Nana, Mr Darling chains her up in the yard before he and Mrs Darling go out to dinner, leaving the children in bed. When they are asleep the window is blown open and the boy flies in, attended by a fairy who appears only as a flitting star. Wendy is awakened by the sound of crying, and sees the boy, who is weeping because although he has found his shadow he cannot stick it on. Wendy says she will sew it on, and as she makes to do so he tells her his name is Peter Pan and that he ran away on the day he was born, and lived among fairies in Kensington Gardens because he heard his parents talking of what he was to be when he became a man: 'I want always to be a little boy and have fun.' He teaches Wendy and her brothers to fly, and with his attendant fairy, Tinker Bell, they go off to 'the Never Land' where Peter lives with 'the lost boys . . . the children who fall out of their prams'. There they are threatened by a pirate gang led by Captain Hook, and take refuge in 'the Home under the Ground' where Wendy acts as mother. In a fight above ground the pirates defeat a band of Red Indians who are guarding the children. Hook is always in deadly fear of a crocodile who has swallowed a clock which ticks inside him and acts as a warning to the pirate. Wendy and the boys are captured, and on the pirate ship Hook prepares to make them walk the plank, but when Peter beats him in a sword duel and frustrates his attempt to blow up the ship, he jumps overboard and is swallowed by the crocodile. Wendy and her brothers return home and find Mr Darling doing penance in the dog kennel. Peter

declines Mrs Darling's offer to adopt him, and she promises to let Wendy go to him for a week each year to do his Spring cleaning.

Peterkin, Julia (Julia Mood Peterkin, *née* Julia Mood, 1880-1961). Born in South Carolina. Wrote for leading magazines, reprinting her contributions in *Green Thursday* (1924). As the wife of a plantation manager in the Deep South she acquired a sympathetic understanding of the Negro workers, such as she displayed in her novels, *Black April* (1934), *Scarlet Sister Mary* (1928), *Bright Skin* (1932). In *Roll, Jordan, Roll* (1933) she dealt with their religion, superstitions, and customs.

Peters, Curtis Arnoux, jnr. *See* Peter *Arno.

Peters, Lenrie. *See* *African Writers.

Petrie, Sir Flinders (William Matthew Flinders Petrie, 1853-1942; knighted 1923). Born at Charlton, Kent; educated privately. Worked as an archaeologist from 1875, first on British sites, later in Greece and Palestine, but principally in Egypt, writing very many books on his researches and on the history and religion of Egypt. Autobiography: *Seventy Years in Archaeology* (1931).

Pevsner, Sir Nikolaus (1902-   ; knighted 1969). Educated at universities in Germany. On the staff of the Dresden Gallery, 1924-28; Lecturer on the History of Art in the University of Göttingen, 1929-33. Settled in England; Slade Professor of Fine Art in the University of Cambridge, 1949-55. Author of many books on architecture, painting and design, and of the Penguin series on *The Buildings of England,* county by county.

Phelps, William Lyon (1865-1943). Born in Connecticut; educated at Yale and Harvard. Professor of English Literature at Yale, 1901-33. Author of *Essays on Modern Novelists* ·(1910), *Browning* (1915), *The Twentieth Century Theatre* (1918), *American Literature* (1923-26), *The Courage of Ignorance* (1933); *Autobiography with Letters* (1939). His enthusiasms were many and were criticized as facile, but he communicated to a generation of students his genuine interest in the literature of his country.

Philip Carey. *See* Carey.

Philistines. Originally a tribe in south-west Palestine at enmity with the Israelites and hated by them as outsiders. The word was frequently applied by Matthew Arnold to people he considered uncultured, and in that sense it has continued in use, chiefly among the *avant garde*.

Phillipps Library. The world's greatest collection of manuscripts and rare books, made by Sir Thomas Phillipps (1792-1872), the eccentric son of a wealthy Birmingham manufacturer. Setting out with the impossible wish to have 'one copy of every book in the world', Phillipps acquired from many countries so great a mass of priceless manuscript and printed material, that the dispersal of the Library at auction sales and by private treaty to national libraries and private collectors was still uncompleted by 1970. When his grandson died in 1938 the sales negotiated to that date had brought in some £300,000, and it is some indication of possibly unplumbed riches that not until 1964 was one of the greatest treasures found 'scattered haphazardly through the remains of the vast collection of manuscripts'. This was books 1 to 9 of William Caxton's translation of Ovid's *Metamorphoses*, made in 1480. In 1688 Samuel Pepys bought (and bequeathed with the rest of his library to Magdalene College, Cambridge) books 10 to 15 of the Caxton manuscript. The earlier portion (long supposed destroyed), when recognized in the Phillipps collection, was bought at auction for £90,000 for America, but was returned to England and reunited with the Pepys section at Magdalene, the price being recouped by the publication of a facsimile of the whole manuscript in a limited edition. The five volumes of *Phillipps Studies* (1951-60) by A. N. L. Munby are for specialists, but *Portrait of an Obsession* (1967), adapted by Nicolas Barker from Munby's volumes, tells the fascinating story of Phillipps and his collection in a handier form.

Phillips, David Graham (1867-1911). Born in Indiana; educated there and at Princeton. Worked as reporter and special correspondent on papers in Cincinnati and New York. From 1902 became one of the leading *muckrakers, in articles and novels exposing abuses—journalistic, social, political, and financial—in the campaign then being conducted by writers and others. He was shot by a mentally deranged assassin. Phillips's novels include *The Great God Success* (1901), *The Master-Rogue* (1903), *Light-Fingered Gentry* (1907), *Old Wives for New* (1908), *The Fashionable Adventures of Joshua Craig*

(1909), and *Susan Lenox: Her Fall and Rise* (1917) which is usually considered his best book. Non-fiction: *The Reign of Gilt* (1905), *The Treason of the Senate* (1906).

Phillips, Hubert (1891-1964). Educated in Somerset and at Oxford. Held various educational and Liberal Party appointments. From 1930 to 1954 was on the staff of the *Daily Chronicle,* as chief leader writer, 1941-45, and at other periods as editor of the Bridge feature and Crossword Puzzles. His publications in prose and verse are almost innumerable; many of them deal with Bridge problems, puzzles, quiz questions, etc, but he also wrote on political subjects, and was a knowledgeable broadcaster.

Phillips, J. B. (Rev John Bertram Phillips, 1906-   ). Educated in London and Cambridge. Teacher at Sherborne Preparatory School, 1927-28; Curate, 1936-40, and Vicar, 1940-44 in London parishes, Vicar in Redhill, 1945-55, and Canon of Salisbury Cathedral from 1964. His widely circulated religious books include *Letters to Young Churches* (1947), *Plain Christianity* (1954), *New Testament Christianity* (1956), *The New Testament in Modern English* (1958), *A Man Called Jesus* (1959), *Ring of Truth* (1967).

Phillips, Stephen (1868-1915). Born near Oxford; educated at Stratford, Peterborough, and Oundle. Joined the F. R. Benson Shakespeare Company, acting with them from 1885 to 1892; then taught history for several years, meanwhile publishing several books of verse. A further volume *Poems* (1898) won him a prize of a thousand guineas offered by a literary weekly, *The Academy*; and the verse play, *Paolo and Francesca* (1900), produced with great success at the St James's Theatre by Sir George Alexander in 1902, led reputable literary critics to compare him favourably with the greatest tragic dramatists of the past. Sir Herbert Tree produced Phillips's *Herod* at His Majesty's Theatre in 1900 and continued the association with *Ulysses* (1902) and *Nero* (1906), by which time the author's reputation was plunging into a decline as rapid as its rise, and the publication of his *Collected Plays* in 1921 did nothing towards restoring it. Phillips was the last dramatist to win attention with verse plays in the Shakespearean blank verse mode. The disastrous failure in which his career ended was due in no small measure to the ineptitude of the critics who had so extravagantly overpraised him. The publisher's quotations from reviews at the end of *Paolo and Francesca* provide a wry comment on the vagaries of critical judgment, and are in line with Sir Sidney *Colvin's reply at a party to Maurice *Hewlett's question, 'Who is that ass at the other end of the room?'—'That is Stephen Phillips. We are all agreed that the genius of Shakespeare, the power of Michelangelo and the tenderness of Raphael are united in that one noble brow.' (*See* Van Wyck *Brooks: *The Opinions of Oliver Allston*, 1941, p 52).

Phillpotts, Adelaide Eden (*née* Mary Adelaide Phillpotts). Born at Ealing. Collaborated with her father (see below) in the successful plays, *The Farmer's Wife* (1924) and *Yellow Sands* (1926), the latter being published in a novelized version by her in 1930. Other writings: verse—*Illyrion* (1916); plays–*Arachne* (1920), *Savitri the Faithful* (1923), *Laugh with Me* (1938); novels—*Lodgers in London* (1926), *A Marriage* (1928), *What's Happened to Rankin?* (1938), *Our Little Town* (1942), *Stubborn Earth* (1951), *A Song of Man* (1959).

Phillpotts, Eden (1862-1960). Born in India; educated in England at Plymouth and trained in London for the stage, but recognizing his lack of acting skill he worked as an insurance clerk for ten years up to 1890. Thereafter, steadily avoiding social contacts outside his own family, he devoted himself entirely to writing and by the end of a lifetime of ninety-eight years he had written some 250 books, mainly novels, but also including volumes of poems and essays and more than a dozen plays. Many of his novels are set in Devonshire, the county he lived in and loved best, but *The Green Alleys* (1916) is set in the hopfields of Kent. In 1917 he published *The Farmer's Wife*, a novel which was later dramatized in collaboration with his daughter (see the preceding entry) and ran in London for over 1300 performances from March 1924, apart from later revivals. As well as being Phillpotts's greatest success it provided Cedric *Hardwicke with his most popular role. *Yellow Sands* by the same authors had a first run of more than 600 performances from November 1926. The best of his novels are those dealing with the Dartmoor region: *Children in the Mist* (1898), *The Secret Woman* (1905), *The Thief of Virtue* (1910), *Widecombe Fair* (1913), and others. He also wrote several crime

novels, including *A Voice from the Dark* (1925) and those published under the pseudonym Harrington *Hext.

Phoebe Throssel. 'Phoebe of the ringlets' to Valentine Brown, whom she marries. **Susan** her elder sister. In J. M. Barrie's *Quality Street* (1902).

Picaresque. (From the Spanish *picaro*=rogue, knave). Used descriptively of novels dealing with the adventures and wanderings of a rogue-hero.

Pickering, Colonel. Friend of Henry Higgins in *Pygmalion* (1913) by Bernard Shaw.

Pickthall, Marjorie (1883-1922). Born in Middlesex; taken to Canada while a child and educated in Toronto; settled in western Canada. Author of *The Drift of Pinions* (1913), *The Woodcarver's Wife* (1922), and other books of verse collected in the *Complete Poems of Marjorie Pickthall* (1927); she also wrote children's books, novels, and short stories.

Pickthall, Marmaduke (Marmaduke William Pickthall, 1875-1936). Born in Suffolk; educated at Harrow and abroad. Spent many years in the Middle East and in India, where he edited the *Bombay Chronicle*, 1920-24, and periodicals in Hyderabad and entered the Nizam's Educational Service there. He became a Muslim, and his writings include *The House of Islam* (1906) and *The Meaning of the Glorious Koran* (1930). His most successful book was *Saïd the Fisherman* (1903), a novel. Other writings: *The Valley of the Kings* (1909), *Oriental Encounters* (1918).

Pigott, Richard. *See* Charles Stewart *Parnell.

Piggott, William. *See* Hubert *Wales.

Pilgrim, David. Joint pseudonym of John L. *Palmer and Hilary St George *Saunders.

Pilgrimage. *See* Dorothy *Richardson.

Pincherle, Alberto. *See* Albert *Moravia.

Pinero, A. W. (Sir Arthur Wing Pinero, 1855-1934; knighted 1909). Born in Islington. Left school when he was only ten and was intended for a legal career, but turned to the theatre, first appearing in Edinburgh in 1874. He was an indifferent actor, and his real purpose was to acquire stage experience to qualify himself for playwriting. His first piece, *£200 a Year*, was produced in London in 1877. *The Money Spinner* (1881) was prophetic, for *The Magistrate* (1885), *The Schoolmistress* (1886), and *Dandy Dick* (1887)—known in theatre history as 'the Court Theatre farces'—made him famous and wealthy. By the end of the 1880s Ibsen and plays-with-a-purpose were becoming potent in the theatrical air of Europe, and Pinero's *The Second Mrs Tanqueray* (1893) was at least a shadow of things to come: a more sensationally noticed though in the long run a paler shadow than Bernard *Shaw's *Widowers' Houses* which was produced obscurely at a 'private' performance, the year before. Pinero's play, designed as a tragedy, now seems close to melodrama; and its 'daringness' in staging seriously a 'woman with a past' soon became no more than a stage cliché. But from the angle of 1893, *The Second Mrs Tanqueray* broke through a wall of conventions—theatrical, social, and moral. Viewed from any angle it is an effective piece of dramatic craftsmanship which survives the reproaches later brought against 'the well-made play' as 'mere stage carpentry'. Pinero's later plays tended to be variations on the Tanqueray formula, with *His House in Order* (1906) as its last resounding note. But while *The Second Mrs Tanqueray* survives as a historical landmark in the history of modern English drama, *Trelawny of the 'Wells'* (1898) will almost certainly survive as his best play.

Pinkie. The young gang leader and killer in Graham Greene's *Brighton Rock* (1938).

Pinter, Harold (1930-   ). Educated at a London grammar school; worked as an actor, 1949-57, then turned to playwriting, making a mark with short pieces in revues and on radio and television. A full-length play, *The *Caretaker* (1960), which had a long run in the theatre, put him among the leading dramatists of the day. He is a master of pregnant silences on the stage, signalling human failure to connect and communicate. He employs such silences also as a technical device to suggest the ominous and verbally-incommunicable, a feature that has caused his work to be named 'comedy of menace' and allied with the *Theatre of the Absurd. Later stage plays: *The Dwarfs* (1963), *The Homecoming* (1964), *Old Times* (1971).

Piper, John (1903-   ). Born at Epsom; educated there and in London at the Royal College of Art. In addition to his many paintings and the designs for stained glass in Eton College Chapel and Coventry Cathedral, he has written *Wind in the Trees* (poems, 1921), *British Romantic Painters* (1942), *Buildings and Prospects* (1949), and a number of guides to English counties.

Pirandello, Luigi (1867-1936). Born in Sicily; educated at the University of Rome and in Germany at Bonn. Worked as a teacher in Rome until his writings ceased to be neglected, then devoted himself to the theatre both as a playwright and as director of a company of actors touring on the Continent and in the U.S., performing his own plays. He used the drama as a complex medium in which philosophy, humour, religion, illusion, and a sense of ultimate human nothingness are ·fused in an elusive profundity which is always theatrically effective. Several of his plays have been translated and acted in English: *Six Characters in Search of an Author* (1921; in English 1922), *Henry IV* (1922), *Right You Are If You Think So* (1917; English 1922), *As You Desire Me* (1930; English 1931). He has been claimed as a precursor of the *Theatre of the Absurd.

Pitman, Sir Isaac (1813-1897; knighted 1894). Born at Trowbridge. Worked as a schoolmaster in Lincolnshire and Gloucestershire until he was dismissed in 1837 on joining the Swedenborg Church. He then started his own school in Bath and conducted it until 1843. He had learned the shorthand system of Samuel Taylor (*fl.* 1786-1816) and adapted it for his own *Stenographic Sound-Hand* (1837) which substituted a phonetic system for the methods based on spelling which had mostly been used before. The almost universal utilization of Pitman's shorthand became one of the romances of modern commerce, though manual shorthand is now threatened by mechanical and electronic devices.

Pitt, Frances (1888-1964). Author of many books on animal psychology and behaviour and other aspects of natural history: *Wild Creatures of Garden and Hedgerow* (1920), *Woodland Creatures* (1922), *Waterside Creatures* (1925), *The Intelligence of Animals* (1931), *Meet Me in the Garden* (1946), *Birds in Britain* (1948), *Nature Through the Year* (1950). She was a pioneer in widening public interest in wild life, largely through the articles she contributed to the *Evening News* for nearly forty years. She was also an able illustrator of her own books with photographs taken by herself.

Pitter, Ruth (1897-   ). Born in Essex; educated at London schools. Worked for a while in the War Office, then with an art and crafts firm until 1930, when she and a friend started on their own in a similar business in Chelsea, later moving to live in the country. She had written verse from childhood, and her *First Poems* (1920), like all that followed, were the product of refreshingly independent vision: *First and Second Poems* (1927), *Persephone in Hades* (1931), *A Mad Lady's Garland* (1934), *A Trophy of Arms* (1936), *The Spirit Watches* (1939), *The Rude Potato* (1941), *Pitter on Cats* (1946), *The Ermine* (1953). *Poems 1926-1966* (1968).

Place names. See Eilert *Ekwall.

Plain Words. See Sir Ernest *Gowers.

Plath, Sylvia (1932-1963). Born in America; married Ted *Hughes 1956. Her first collection of poems *The Colossus* was published in 1960, followed by *Ariel* (posthumously 1966). Pseudonymously as Victoria Lucas she wrote *The Bell Jar*, a novel (1963; reissued under her own name in 1966). *The Art of Sylvia Plath* (a symposium edited by Charles Newman, 1970) includes previously unpublished verse and prose.

Playboy of the Western World, The. Comedy in three acts by J. M. *Synge performed and published in 1907. Margaret Flaherty (called Pegeen Mike) daughter of Michael James Flaherty (called Michael James) is making out an order for supplies in their public house in a village on the coast of Mayo. Her father is leaving her alone for the night while he goes with others to a funeral wake. Shawn Keogh, a cousin she intends to marry if a papal dispensation is granted, is too afraid of the local priest to agree to stay alone with Pegeen till the morning. A weary and frightened and dirty young man comes in, giving his name as Christopher Mahon and explaining that he has been walking the roads for eleven days to escape the police after killing his father, who wanted to marry him to a widow more than twice his age. As this makes Christy a refugee

from what Michael James later calls 'the treachery of law', he is regarded as a hero by Pegeen Mike and all the village girls, and courted by the widow Quin. He displaces Shawn in Pegeen's affections, until the bubble of his fame is pricked when his father, Old Mahon, with a bandaged head but fully alive, arrives in pursuit of his son, whom he describes as lazy, poor-spirited, and far from heroic. Meanwhile Christy has been winning prize after prize at the village sports. When they meet, Christy is knocked down by his father. The ensuing fight ends with Old Mahon being chased outside and again hit over the head and apparently killed. Shawn and others pinion Christy, intending to hand him over as a murderer, but again Old Mahon revives and this time takes his son's part against 'the villainy of Mayo and the fools is here'. When Shawn rejoices that he and Pegeen will now be able to wed, she boxes his ears and breaks into 'wild lamentations': 'Oh my grief, I've lost him surely. I've lost the only playboy of the western world.'

Playfair, Sir Nigel (Nigel Ross Playfair, 1874-1934; knighted 1928). Born in London; educated at Harrow and Oxford. Joined F. R. Benson's Shakespeare Company; later acted in Bernard *Shaw's plays at the *Court Theatre, in Shakespeare under Sir Herbert Tree at His Majesty's, and under Granville *Barker at the Savoy. He came into greater prominence with his fruitful season at the Lyric Theatre, Hammersmith, which he managed from 1918 to 1932 and made during those years the most interesting playhouse in the London area. His outstanding production was the revival of the eighteenth-century John Gay's *Beggar's Opera* which reached nearly 1500 performances. His other well-staged productions included Congreve's *The Way of the World*, Farquhar's *The Beaux' Stratagem*, Wilde's *The Importance of Being Earnest*, Čapek's *The Insect Play*, Drinkwater's *Abraham Lincoln*, A. P. Herbert's *Riverside Nights*.

Plein-air. Painting which has an 'open-air' quality—an effect sought by, especially, the late 19th-century French Impressionists.

Plomer, William (William Charles Franklyn Plomer, 1903-1973). Born in South Africa; educated in England at Rugby; returned to Africa first as a farmer, then as a trader, before going to Japan, where he stayed for two years, returning to England via Manchuria, Siberia, Russia, Poland, etc. Worked in the Admiralty through World War II. Author of novels—*Turbott Wolfe* (1926), *Sado* (1931), *The Case is Altered* (1932), *Ali the Lion* (1936), *A Shot in the Park* (1955); short stories—*I Speak of Africa* (1927), *Paper Houses* (1929); biography—*Cecil Rhodes* (1933). *Collected Poems* (1960). Libretti for operas (by Benjamin Britten), *Gloriana* (1953), *Curlew River* (1964), *The Burning Fiery Furnace* (1966). Autobiography: *Double Lives* (1943).

Plough and the Stars, The. A Tragedy in Four Acts by Sean *O'Casey performed and published in 1926. Acts I and II take place in 1915, the first in Jack and Nora Clitheroe's living room, part of their flat in a Dublin Georgian house, now a tenement; the second in the bar of a pub, within sight and hearing of a speaker addressing a meeting outside in memory of Irish patriots. Acts III and IV take place in Easter week 1916 during the rebellion: first in the street outside the Clitheroe tenement; finally inside, in the room of Bessie Burgess, a street fruitseller. Fluther Good, a carpenter repairing a lock in the Clitheroe's room, and Mrs Gogan, a charwoman, discuss Jack and Nora, commenting particularly on Nora's 'swanky' ways. Peter Flynn, a labourer, Nora's elderly uncle, and the Young Covey, a fitter, Clitheroe's cousin, have a highly vocal part in the play, Peter indignantly reacting to the Covey's impudent taunts. Clitheroe, in ordinary life a bricklayer and ambitious to be made an officer in the Irish Citizen Army, rejects Nora's embraces when he learns that she has burned a letter appointing him a commandant. Peter, the Covey, Mrs Gogan, Bessie Burgess and others overhear the inflammatory speeches by Irish patriots outside; the two women quarrel and are turned out by the barman when they prepare to fight. When the rebellion begins, Nora exhausts herself in the streets searching vainly for her husband. The other men and women in the tenement join in the looting of the shops. When news of Clitheroe's death is brought to Nora she has a stillborn child and becomes demented. Bessie Burgess takes care of her, but is shot and killed while trying to get Nora away from a window she has rushed to and opened,

having got from her bed while Bessie was asleep.

Plumb, J. H. (John Harold Plumb, 1911-   ) Born in Leicester; educated there and at Cambridge where he became Professor of Modern English History from 1966. Author of *England in the Eighteenth Century* (1950), *Chatham* (1953), *Sir Robert Walpole* (I. 1956; II. 1960), *The First Four Georges* (1956), *Crisis in the Humanities* (1964), *The Growth of Political Stability in England, 1675-1725* (1967) and other historical writings.

Plunkett, Edward John Morton Drax. See Lord *Dunsany.

Plunkett, J. M. (Joseph Mary Plunkett, 1887-1916). Born in Dublin; educated there at Roman Catholic schools and in England at Stonyhurst. Editor of the *Irish Review* from 1913. Took part in the 1916 Easter Rising and was executed. Author of two collections of verse: *The Circle and the Sword* (1913) and *Poems* (1916).

Poel, William (*né* William Pole; 1852-1934). Born in London. Became an actor and changed the spelling of his name. Produced the First Quarto *Hamlet* in London in 1881. Became stage manager to F. R. Benson in 1883. Founded the Elizabethan Stage Society in 1895, and through his productions without scenery of seventeen Shakespeare plays and others by Marlowe, Ben Jonson, etc., had a deep influence on the staging of Elizabethan drama, both in regard to textual accuracy and to the speaking of blank verse. He also cooperated in the first modern production of the early morality play, *Everyman*, appearing himself as Death. Author of *Shakespeare in the Theatre* (1913). *See also* Ben *Greet.

Poetry. Little attention was given to poetry by readers in general between the death of Tennyson (1809-1892) and the outburst of poetry during the 1914-18 war by young men who, before the war, had no more thought of becoming poets than most of them had of becoming soldiers. The only poet widely read at the turn of the century was Rudyard *Kipling, and in the first decade of the new century Alfred *Noyes was said to be the only writer able to support himself by poetry alone. Robert *Bridges began to publish in the 1870s, but even his name was little known outside Oxford until he was appointed Poet Laureate in 1913 after the death of Alfred *Austin, who merited the title of 'dumb Laureate' more than Bridges, who was so called by the notorious rabble-rouser Horatio *Bottomley. Bridges had notable success with his anthology *The Spirit of Man* (1916) and leapt into astounding, if only temporary, fame with *The *Testament of Beauty* (1929). Of those who published verse between 1901 and 1914 Thomas *Hardy, retired novelist, was the most important, since to his outflow of lyrics the great epic drama *The *Dynasts* (1904-08) was added. Henry *Newbolt's *Songs of the Sea* (1904) had considerable repute, his 'Drake's Drum' becoming widely renowned as a song. The *Salt Water Ballads* (1902) of John *Masefield (Poet Laureate 1930-68) reached a limited public unprepared for the very different note struck in the succession of long quasi-realistic narrative poems he began with *The *Everlasting Mercy* (1911). In the same year, books of verse by Rupert *Brooke (*Poems*) and W. H. *Davies (*Songs of Joy*) appeared, and Brooke was also a prime mover in planning the first of the sequence of *Georgian Poetry* anthologies edited by Edward *Marsh which, beginning in 1912, were hoisted into contemporary fame by the new enthusiasm for poetry fostered from 1914 by the war. Passing mention must be made of Hilaire *Belloc's *Verses* (1910), G. K. *Chesterton's *Ballad of the White Horse* (1911) and *Poems* (1915), and Lascelles *Abercrombie's *Interludes and Poems* (1908). A greater poet than these, Walter *de la Mare, published *Poems* (1906), *The Listeners* (1912), *Peacock Pie* (1913) and numerous other collections until his death in 1956. D. H. *Lawrence's *Love Poems* (1913) were followed at intervals by verse collections of varying merit. Critics at a later date, ignorant of the genuinely idealistic spirit of young soldiers in the early months of the war, failed to understand the high praise given to Rupert Brooke's *1914 and other Poems* (1915) and to Julian Grenfell's isolated 'Into Battle', written shortly before he was killed in 1915. The human tragedies and disasters of war produced Siegfried *Sassoon's *Counter Attack* (1918) and Wilfred *Owen's *Poems*, published in 1920, two years after he was killed one week before the war ended. Owen was at length placed first among the war poets, and

verses by him served as a verbal accompaniment to the music of Benjamin Britten's *A War Requiem* (Coventry Cathedral, 1962).

Edith Sitwell, long regarded as an eccentric both in poetry and in person, had published several books before *Façade* (1922) made her widely known when the verses were declaimed through a megaphone in public to William Walton's music (1923), which was afterwards orchestrated as a popular ballet. Her later religious verse led to her being numbered with the few great English women poets. She was not immune from the revolutionary influence of T. S. *Eliot, whose *Prufrock* (1917) and, much more, *The Waste Land* (1922), together with his critical works in prose, made him for good or ill the literary arbiter of the English-speaking world for a generation or more. He and Gerard Manley *Hopkins, rediscovered from the previous century, brought about an unprecedented technical, mental, and spiritual upheaval in English poetry. It is probable, however, that the change of temper in the poetry of W. B. *Yeats was due to other causes, chiefly the troubles in Ireland from 1916 onward. He renounced the romanticism of his early period, becoming consistently metaphysical and intermittently political. In harmony with the spirit of the new age, the later Yeats was considered the greater. From the late 1920s until 1939 a desire to write 'poetry for the people' produced a good deal of verse with Marxist overtones, but without the lucidity needed to attract proletarian readers. World War II and succeeding events bred disenchantment with political panaceas, and there was some recourse to Christianity and other Eastern religions. The leading younger poets of the 1930s were Cecil *Day-Lewis, W. H. *Auden, and Louis *MacNeice. Auden lived in the U.S. from 1939 and became a naturalized American. MacNeice died in 1963. Day-Lewis succeeded Masefield as Poet Laureate in 1968. Of this group, Auden was the most productive and varied, possibly the most profound and esoteric.

The mood of dour necessity which governed the beginning and progress of World War II was unfavourable for poetry, and apart from some occasional verse of passing merit by established writers, the output of war poetry hardly extended beyond the publications, small in bulk, of Keith *Douglas, Sidney

*Keyes, and Alun *Lewis, all killed by 1944. Much effort was made after the war to encourage poets by subventions from public and private funds, and increases in publishers' sales of poetry were noted. Dylan *Thomas, though much of his verse escaped general comprehension, became in the late 1940s and early 1950s the most popular poet then living. This came about through the broadcast readings of his own poems, which he delivered in a mannered incantatory style exercising a partially hypnotic effect on listeners. (And see *Under Milk Wood.) Public reading and declamation of verse by authors making a 'personal appearance' attracted monster gatherings in London. Much curious contortion of language tended to bring work thus exhibited within the ambit of *Pop Culture, an end not always undesired by the organizers. In so far as this avalanche of verse was exhibitionist, it is unlikely to have made any permanent contribution to English literature. Indeed, few of those engaged aimed to write for posterity; their own age was their only desired audience. A smaller but still not inconsiderable number were producing poetry less intentionally ephemeral. A census of English poets compiled from the many contemporary anthologies (mostly for educational use) would be numerically impressive, and virtually beyond computation if the census sought to include American and Commonwealth writers also. Any selection of individual names is bound to be arbitrary, though D. J. *Enright, Thom *Gunn, Ted *Hughes, Elizabeth *Jennings, and Philip *Larkin were prominent among English poets born after 1920. In the 1970s Laurie *Lee and a neighbouring rural poet had encouraging success in a poetry-popularizing mission of their own devising, selling their locally produced Cotswold Ballads in the bars of country inns. And see *Barrow Poets. See also *American Writers, *Australian Writers, *Caribbean Writers, *New Zealand Writers.

Poetry Bookshop. A rendezvous for poets, poetry readers, and poetry buyers, started a few years before World War I. It was in romantically shabby premises in Devonshire Street, Bloomsbury, an area that has since passed through the grasp of developers. Controlled by Harold *Monro, it published broadsheets and booklets of poems by Ralph Hodgson with illustrations by Claude Lovat Fraser, and more substantial works, including the famous anthologies of verse by contemporary writers, edited by Edward *Marsh and entitled *Georgian Poetry (1912 onward). Lectures and poetry readings were given by Rupert *Brooke, Robert *Frost, and others, and among those to be seen there was Ezra *Pound.

Poetry Review. See Harold *Monro.

Poetry Society, The. Founded in London in 1909, by the mid-sixties it had approximately 4000 members. Weekly meetings for poetry reading are held, and it publishes The Poetry Review quarterly. Membership is by annual subscription.

Poets Laureate. See Alfred *Austin; Robert *Bridges; John *Masefield; C. *Day-Lewis; Sir John *Betjeman.

Poincaré, Raymond (Raymond Nicholas Landry Poincaré, 1860-1934). Born at Bar-le-Duc, north-east France; studied law. From 1887 was in politics and after holding lesser government offices was Premier for three terms between 1911 and 1929, the last two after he had been President of the French Republic from 1913 to 1920, a period including World War I.

Point Counter Point. Novel by Aldous *Huxley published in 1928. With a maximum of conversation and soliloquy and a minimum of description, aspects of London intellectual, artistic, political, and sexual life in the 1920s are displayed through representative characters, some with more or less satirical intent recognizably drawn from persons prominent at the time: e.g. Mark Rampion from D. H. Lawrence, Everard Webley from Oswald Mosley; while certain features or circumstances of Middleton Murry may be detected in Denis Burlap; of Augustus John in John Bidlake, and of others—such as the communist scientist Illidge—in originals whose reputation has faded.

When the fictitious novelist Philip Quarles reflects that in his writings 'he could manage the complications as well as anyone. But when it came to the simplicities . . . of the heart' he had 'no heart, no understanding', the confession can be interpreted as his creator's own, for the cerebral complications of this novel are broken only, brutally, by the debauchee Spandrell's sudden murder of Webley; and, pathetically, by the death of the Quarles's child from meningitis. On Spandrell's indulgence in complexities of vice, direct comment is made: 'The emotional results of all the possible refinements of vice seemed to him dully uniform. . . . The corruption of youth was the only form of debauchery that now gave him any active emotion.' Having, later, committed murder in circumstances which created 'the Webley mystery', he sacrifices himself by contriving to be shot by Webley's subordinates and dies while a Beethoven quartet is playing on the gramophone.

Poirot, Hercule. Belgian detective in crime novels by Agatha *Christie.

Poison of the people. 'Politics is the poison of the people', a retort of unstated origin to Karl Marx's 'Religion is the opium of the people'.

Pollard, A. F. (Albert Frederick Pollard, 1869-1948). Born at Ryde, Isle of Wight; educated at Portsmouth, Felsted, and Oxford. Assistant editor of the *Dictionary of National Biography*, 1893-1901; Professor of Constitutional History, University of London, 1903-31; Editor of *History* 1916-22; first Director of the Institute of Historical Research, 1920-31. Author of *The Jesuits in Poland* (1892), *England under Protector Somerset* (1900), *Henry VIII* (1902), *A Life of Thomas Cranmer* (1904), *Factors in Modern History* (1907), *The Reign of Henry VII from Contemporary Sources* (3 vols, 1913-14), *The Evolution of Parliament* (1920), *Factors in American History* (1925), *Wolsey* (1929).

Pollard, A. W. (Alfred William Pollard, 1859-1944). Born in London; educated there at King's College School and at Oxford. Joined the staff of the British Museum in 1883; Keeper in the Department of Printed Books, 1919-24. Professor of English Bibliography, University of London, 1919-32. Editor of *The Library*, 1903-34. Director of the *Early English Text Society, 1930-37. Author, or editor, of *English Miracle Plays* (1890), *Books About Books* (1893), *Early Illustrated Books* (1893), *Old Picture Books* (1902), *Life, Love, and Light; Practical Morality for Men and Women* (1911), *Shakespeare's Fight with the Pirates* (1917), *St Catherine of Siena* (1919), *Shakespeare's Hand in the Play of 'Sir Thomas More'* (1923).

Pollard, Graham (Henry Graham Pollard, 1903-). Born in London, son of A. F. Pollard (*see above*); educated at Shrewsbury and at the Universities of London and Oxford. Co-founder of Birrell & Garnett, antiquarian booksellers, which continued from 1924 to 1938. Reader in the History of Newspapers, University of London, 1939-42. President of the Bibliographical Society, 1960-61. In 1934 *An Inquiry into the Nature of Certain XIXth Century Pamphlets*, which he wrote jointly with John *Carter, exposed by typographical examination and scientific analysis of paper the spurious character of a number of rare 'first editions' put into circulation by T. J. *Wise. Also author of *T. J. Wise Centenary Studies* (1960), and numerous articles on book-collecting and related topics.

Pollock, Sir John (1878-1963). Educated at Eton, Cambridge, and Harvard Law School. Foreign correspondent of *The Times*. Author of historical and political works, and of plays including *Rosamond* (1910), *In the Forests of the Night* (1920), *The King's Arms* (1939), etc. Translator of plays by Tolstoy, Brieux, Henry Becque, and others.

Pollyanna. The 'glad child' in a series of children's stories by Eleanor *Porter.

Polnay, Peter de. *See* Peter *de Polnay.

Poltergeist. German for 'noisy spirit'; adopted into English as the term denoting the type of psychical phenomenon in which articles are violently displaced or thrown, or other mischievous tricks played, without a visible agent, assumed to be a ghost or disembodied spirit.

Ponderevo, Edward. In H. G. Wells's *Tono-Bungay* (1909) the inventor of the patent medicine bearing that name. His nephew George Ponderevo, F.R.S., aeronautical and marine engineer, is the narrator in the novel. Susan Ponderevo, Edward's wife, befriends George and takes a gently hilarious view of the financial and social rocketings in which her husband's activities involve her.

Ponsonby, Arthur (Arthur Augustus William Harry Ponsonby, 1871-1946; created Baron Ponsonby 1930). Son of Sir Henry Ponsonby (1825-95), Private Secretary to Queen Victoria. Educated at Eton and Oxford. Page of Honour to Queen Victoria, 1882-87. Entered the Diplomatic Service: stationed at Constantinople, 1894-97; at Copenhagen,

1898-99; in the Foreign Office, London, 1900-02. Liberal M.P. for Stirling, 1908-18; Labour M.P. for a Sheffield division, 1922-30, and a Minister in Labour governments during that period. Author of *The Camel and the Needle's Eye* (1909), *The Decline of Aristocracy* (1912), *Democracy and Diplomacy* (1915), *Religion in Politics* (1921), *Samuel Pepys* (1928), *Queen Victoria* (1933), *John Evelyn* (1934), *Life Here and Now* (1936), *Henry Ponsonby: His Life from his Letters* (1942). Selections with commentaries: *English Diaries* (1923), *More English Diaries* (1927), *Scottish and Irish Diaries* (1927).

Pontifex family. In Samuel Butler's *The *Way of All Flesh* (1903): **John Pontifex** (1727-1812), carpenter, organ-builder, and farmer, father of **George Pontifex**, who becomes wealthy as publisher of religious books; the **Rev. Theobald Pontifex**, son of the preceding and father of **Ernest Pontifex**, chief character in the novel; **Alethea Pontifex**, sister of Theobald, befriends her nephew, Ernest, and leaves her money to him. *See also* Allaby.

Poorten-Schwartz. *See* Maarten *Maartens.

Pop culture. From being simply a contraction of 'popular', 'pop' became in the 1950s and after a vogue word to which a special mystique attached. 'Pop culture' related to the whole range of (mainly adolescent) interests centred on jazz music for dancing and its derivatives. Small groups of young men (pop groups) playing guitars and singing such music into microphones were made internationally renowned through broadcasting and pop gramophone records, while their appearances in public often generated mass hysteria among undeveloped girls. The jazz idiom spread to art, design, poetry and other creative activities, being commonly expressed through rejection of form and the cultivation of incongruity in juxtaposing colours and associations of words. *And see* Beatniks.

Pope-Hennessy, James (1916-1974). Educated at Downside School and Oxford. Literary editor of the *Spectator* 1947-49. Author of *Monckton-Milnes*, I. *The Years of Promise* (1950) and II. *The Flight of Youth* (1952), *Lord Crewe, the Likeness of a Liberal* (1955), *Queen Mary* (1959), etc.

Pope-Hennessy, J. W. (John Wyndham Pope-

Hennessy, 1913-). Brother of the preceding. Director of the Victoria and Albert Museum, London, from 1967. Author of books on Italian painters and sculptors.

Poppins, Mary. *See* P. L. *Travers.

Porgy; Porgy and Bess. *See* Du Bose *Heyward.

Porlock, Martin. Occasional pseudonym of Philip *MacDonald.

Pornick, Ann. *See* *Ann Pornick.

Pornography. The widespread rejection of 19th century moral standards after World War II was profitably commercialized by the production of books, magazines, films, and (after the abolition of stage censorship in Britain in 1968) plays exploiting sex. The open display of publications trading in sexual material, verbal and pictorial, led Lord *Longford with selected associates to undertake an unofficial inquiry 'To see what means of tackling the problem of pornography would command general support'. The evidence collected from British and foreign sources is presented in *Pornography: The Longford Report* (1972), where relevant aspects of broadcasting, cinema, theatre, publications, advertising, and sex education are surveyed, and the proposal made that for the then legal phrase of tending 'to deprave and corrupt' there should be substituted that an article or performance 'is obscene if its effect, taken as a whole, is to outrage contemporary standards of decency or humanity accepted by the public at large'.

Porter, Eleanor H. (*née* Eleanor Hodgman, 1868-1920; Mrs J. L. Porter). Born in New Hampshire. Her early novels *Cross Currents* (1907), *The Turn of the Tide* (1908) were eclipsed by the children's books, *Pollyanna* (1913) and *Pollyanna Grows Up* (1915).

Porter, Gene Stratton (*née* Geneva Grace Stratton, 1868-1924; Mrs C. D. Porter). Born in Indiana, on her father's farm, where she spent her early years. After marriage she lived with her husband and daughter close to a primeval swamp called the Limberlost, 'a natural preserve of wild plants, moths, and birds' which gave a name and material for perhaps the most popular of her novels *A Girl of the Limberlost* (1909). Though she did not have the approval of literary critics, who found her slushily sentimental, she gained and held a vast body of less sophisticated readers with *The Song of the Cardinal* (1903), *Freckles* (1904), *The Harvester* (1911), *Laddie* (1913) and other novels. Non-fiction: *What I Have Done With Birds* (1907), *Birds of the Bible* (1909), *Homing With The Birds* (1919).

Porter, Jimmy. Central character in John Osborne's **Look Back in Anger* (1956). Coming from working people, he lives in a tormented love-hate relationship with his upper middle-class wife, Alison. Her friend Helena Charles says of him: 'He was born out of his time . . . he thinks he's still in the middle of the French Revolution. . . . He'll never do anything, and he'll never amount to anything.' He himself complains: 'No one can raise themselves out of their delicious sloth . . . how I long for a little ordinary human enthusiasm. . . . There aren't any good, brave causes left' just 'the Brave New nothing-very-much-thank-you'.

Porter, Katherine Anne (1890-   ). Born in Texas; educated at convent schools. Lectured on literature and the art of writing in several American universities. Author of *Flowering Judas* (1930), *Pale Horse, Pale Rider* (1939), *The Leaning Tower* (1944). *Collected Stories* (1965); *Collected Essays* (1969).

Porter, William Sydney. *See* O. *Henry.

Portrait of the Artist as a Young Man, A. Autobiographical novel by James *Joyce published in 1916. From babyhood the religious, moral, and intellectual development of Stephen Dedalus is traced through home and school influences and up to the late stages of his education at Trinity College, Dublin. As a small boy he is present at a serio-comic Christmas family dinner which is distempered by a bitter quarrel between Parnellites and anti-Parnellites; the former abusing the Catholic priests as murderers of Charles Stewart Parnell, the beloved Irish leader (1846-91) recently dead, while the opposition supports the Church passionately as God's instrument against Parnell's adultery. At Jesuit schools Stephen is variously treated by boys and masters, an occasion of unjust punishment by an unintelligent and brutal Father Dolan being a remembered and resented incident. In adolescence Stephen's sexual urges are accompanied by a sense of mortal sin, which is much aggravated when, during a 'retreat' at school, he hears sermons minutely detailing the topography of hell

and the processes of eternal punishment. Tormented by fear and remorse, he goes to an obscure Dublin church to seek absolution for sins he thinks too shocking to confess at the school chapel. After a prolonged period of spiritual tension, his religious fervour abates and the normal impulses of youth reassert themselves. He declines a suggestion that he should prepare for ordination and devote his life to the priesthood. At Trinity College his interests tend towards philosophy and literature, leading to much discussion of Aquinas, Aristotle, and aesthetics. He drifts farther from the Church, resisting his mother's religious pleading as well as his college friend Cranly's ambiguous arguing. He decides to leave Ireland, writing in his diary: 'Welcome, O life! I go to encounter . . . the reality of experience and to forge in the smithy of my soul the uncreated conscience of my race.'

Positivism. Any system of philosophy based on the evidence of the human senses and on scientific knowledge, not on metaphysics. It is particularly, though not exclusively, associated with the teaching of Auguste Comte (1798-1857), French philosopher. In England it had support from Herbert Spencer and Frederic Harrison, among others.

Postgate, Raymond (Raymond William Postgate, 1896-1971). Born at Cambridge; educated there at the Perse School, and at Liverpool and Oxford. Worked on the *Daily Herald* and other Labour papers. Author of *The Bolshevik Theory* (1920), *Revolution from 1789-1906* (1920), *Out of the Past* (1925), *Murder, Piracy and Treason* (1925), *History of the British Workers* (1926), *That Devil Wilkes* (1930), *Robert Emmet* (1931), *Karl Marx* (1933), *Life of George Lansbury* (1951), and books on food and wine.

Post-Impressionist Movement. A reaction against both Impressionism and representational art, and associated mainly with the paintings of Cézanne, Gauguin, and Van Gogh. An exhibition, Manet and the Post-Impressionists, organized in London (1910-11) by Roger *Fry, drew English attention to the movement. *See also* *Omega Workshops.

Potter, Beatrix (Helen Beatrix Potter, 1866-1943; Mrs William Heelis). Born in London;

lived many years in the Lake District. Famous for her little square children's books with illustrations from her own delicate water colours: *The Tale of Peter Rabbit* (1902), *The Tailor of Gloucester* (1903), *The Tale of Squirrel Nutkin* (1903), *The Tale of Jemima Puddle-Duck* (1908), *The Tale of Tom Kitten* (1911), and others.

Potter, Stephen (1900-1969). Educated at Westminster and Oxford. Secretary to Henry Arthur *Jones; contributor to various periodicals; on staff of the B.B.C. Author of *D. H. Lawrence: A First Study* (1930), *The Muse in Chains* (1937), *Potter on America* (1956), *Steps to Immaturity* (1959). His *Gamesmanship* (1947) gave a suffix '-manship' much used by others in following years to denote any activity otherwise described as 'skating on thin ice'. In Potter's book it was intended to refer to conduct in games which kept no more than a hair's breadth within the rules.

Pottle, F. A. (Frederick Albert Pottle, 1897-). Born in Maine; educated at Colby College and Yale. Professor of English and Public Orator at Yale. Most of his writings were concerned with James Boswell, whose newly discovered papers he worked on as editor.

Pound, Ezra (Ezra Loomis Pound, 1885-1972). Born in Idaho; educated at Hamilton College, New York, and at the University of Pennsylvania. Lived in London from 1908 to 1920, becoming closely acquainted with T. S. *Eliot and other intellectualist writers by whom he was highly esteemed as a poet. He settled in Italy in 1924 and during World War II made broadcasts which led in 1946 to his being charged in the U.S. with treason. Experts having certified that he was mentally unsound he was committed to a mental hospital. His combative nature, the aggressiveness of his critical prose, and the extremity of his anti-conventional verse technique caused him and his writings to be subjects of acrid debate, even among literary scholars, especially the long series of *Cantos I-LXXI* (1925-40). Other poetry: *Personae* (1909), *Exultations* (1909), *Ripostes* (1912), *Lustra* (1917), *Quia Pauper Amavi* (1919), *Selected Poems* (1949). Prose: *The Spirit of Romance* (1910), *How to Read* (1931), *Polite Essays* (1936).

Povey, Samuel. In Arnold Bennett's *The *Old Wives' Tale* (1908); apprenticed to John Baines, draper, in Bursley; becomes manager of the business after Baines's death; marries Constance Baines; dies following · his brother Daniel's execution for murder.

Powell, Anthony (Anthony Dymoke Powell, 1905-). Born in London; educated there and in Kent, and at Eton and Oxford. Worked in a publishing firm, and as a book reviewer and film scenario writer before serving throughout World War II. Author of *Afternoon Men* (1931), *Venusberg* (1932), *From a View to a Death* (1933), *What's Become of Waring?* (1939). His most ambitious venture began with *A Question of Upbringing* (1951), the first of a linked series of novels with individual titles, under the group title *The Music of Time*.

Powell, Dilys (Elizabeth Dilys Powell). Educated in Bournemouth and at Oxford. Joined the editorial staff of the *Sunday Times* 1928 and was its film critic from 1939. Lived for some years in Greece. Author of *Descent from Parnassus* (1934), *Remember Greece* (1941), *The Traveller's Journey is Done* (1943), *Coco* (1952), *An Affair of the Heart* (1957). *The Villa Ariadne* (1973), centred on the house built by Sir Arthur *Evans at Knossos, ranges over the guerrilla war against the Germans in Crete.

Power, Eileen (1889-1940; Mrs M. M. Postan). Educated at Bournemouth and Oxford schools and at Cambridge. Professor of Economic History, London School of Economics, 1931-40. Best known for her books on medieval subjects: *Medieval English Nunneries* (1922), *Medieval People* (1924) and others.

Powicke, Sir Maurice (Frederick Maurice Powicke, 1879-1963; knighted 1946). Born at Alnwick; educated at Stockport Grammar School, Owen's College (Manchester), and Oxford. Professor of Modern History, Queen's University, Belfast, 1909-19; of Medieval History, University of Manchester, 1919-28; Regius Professor of Modern History, Oxford, 1928-47. He was one of the leading medieval scholars of his time, among his published works in this field being *The Loss of Normandy, 1189-1204* (1913; 2nd edn 1961), *Stephen Langton* (1928), *Medieval England* (1931), *The Christian Life in the Middle Ages* (1935), *The Reformation in*

England (1941), *The Thirteenth Century* (1953; 2nd edn 1962).

Powys, J. C. (John Cowper Powys, 1872-1963). Born in Derbyshire, brother of the two following; educated at Sherborne and Cambridge. From 1904 to 1934 he was mainly occupied with lecture tours in the United States, and his output of immensely long novels was for the most part a product of later life, his sixties to eighties, though his remarkable literary and imaginative gifts as a novelist had already been displayed in *Wolf Solent* (1929) and, even more, in *A Glastonbury Romance* (1933). These were followed by *Maiden Castle* (1936), *Owen Glendower* (1941), *Porius* (1951), and *The Brazen Head* (1956). He also wrote on *Dostoievsky* (1946) and *Rabelais* (1947); Homeric studies—*Atlantis* (1954) and *Homer and the Aether* (1959); some philosophical and critical essays, poems—*Lucifer* (1956), etc.—and *Autobiography* (1934). His last home, a cottage at Blaenau-Festiniog, in the mountainous north of Wales, became a place of pilgrimage for admirers from many quarters who rated his novels as among the world's greatest, though their appeal is more esoteric than general.

Powys, Llewellyn (1884-1939). Born at Dorchester, brother of J. C. and T. F. Powys; educated at Sherborne and Cambridge. Farmed in Kenya, 1914-19; journalist in New York, 1920-25; then travelled in Palestine, the West Indies, and settled in Switzerland, where he died. His novels and other writings express his innate buoyant paganism and love of living: *Black Laughter* (1924), *Skin for Skin* (1925), *The Verdict of Bridlegoose* (1926), *Apples Be Ripe* (1930), *Love and Death* (1939) and other novels. Non-fiction: *The Pathetic Fallacy* (1930), *A Pagan's Pilgrimage* (1931), *Glory of Life* (1934), *Earth Memories* (1934), *Damnable Opinions* (1935), *Dorset Essays* (1935); with J. C. Powys, *Confessions of Two Brothers* (1916).

Powys, T. F. (Theodore Francis Powys, 1875-1953). Born in Dorset, brother of the two preceding; educated in Dorchester and neighbouring schools and lived throughout life in the rural quietness of his native county. Deeply religious, his novels have often the grim pessimism of a major prophet; but though the country people and life he depicted are often darkened by evil and tragedy they have also an element of grotesque humour, as well as literary distinction. The best of his fictional works, **Mr Weston's Good Wine* (1927), was almost the only one of his numerous books to be widely noticed, though there was ground for his brother J. C.'s opinion that T. F. was the most gifted member of a remarkable family. Other fiction: *The Left Leg* (1923), *Black Bryony* (1923), *Mr Tasker's Gods* (1925), *The House with the Echo* (1928), *Kindness in a Corner* (1930), *Goat Green* (1937).

Pozzo. The slave-master of Lucky in Samuel Beckett's **Waiting for Godot* (1954).

Pragmatism. Philisophical doctrine that beliefs and principles must be judged by their practical consequences, not according to abstract theorizing or blind faith. The word was introduced in this sense by Charles Sanders Peirce (1839-1914), American writer on logic, philosophy, and physics, in an article 'How to make our ideas clear' printed by *Popular Science Monthly* in 1878. The chief exponent, however, was William *James, brother of Henry *James, whose *Pragmatism* (1907) enlarged upon the doctrine as foreshadowed in the final chapter of his *Principles of Psychology* (1890).

Prank, J. E. Pseudonym of Miss Lavish in E. M. Forster's *A *Room with a View* (1908).

Pratt, E. J. (Edwin John Pratt, 1883-1964). Born in Newfoundland; educated at St John's and at Victoria College, University of Toronto, where he became Professor of English, 1920-53. Author of *Newfoundland Verse* (1923) and several other volumes of poems, including *Brebeuf and his Brethren* (1939). His *Collected Poems* (1944) was successively enlarged to include later works.

Praz, Mario (1896-   ). Born in Rome; educated there and in Florence. Professor of English Language and Literature, University of Rome, from 1934. Author of many books, of which the best known (in English translations) are *The Romantic Agony* (1933), *The Hero in Eclipse in Victorian Fiction* (1956), *Mnemosyne* (Literature and the Visual Arts, 1970).

Preece, Arthur. Inventor and, later, Labour M.P. in **Milestones* (1812) by Arnold Bennett and Edward Knoblock.

Preedy, George. One of several pseudonyms used by Mrs A. L. Long (*née* Gabrielle

Margaret Vere Campbell) who wrote mainly as Marjorie *Bowen.

Prelude. Story by Katherine *Mansfield first published, in separate form, in 1918 and included with other stories in *Bliss* (1920).

Stanley Burnell, a prospering New Zealand businessman and uxorious husband, buys 'dirt cheap' a house in the country, 'long and low built, with a pillared verandah and balcony all the way round'. While he is at the office, his family are left to move from the town: Linda, his indolent wife, her mother Mrs Fairfield and unmarried sister Beryl, and the three small Burnell children— Isabel, Kezia, and Lottie. The story, having no contrived plot, is composed of glimpses of the ambiguous relationship between husband and wife, of the affection of grand-mother and children, of Beryl's romantic communings with her mirror; of the little girls at 'make-believe' play with their boy cousins Pip and Rags Trout and Snooker the mongrel dog; of Pat the handy man and of Alice the servant girl working in the kitchen with her greasy little tattered *Dream Book* propped before her while working. Wandering alone in the garden, Kezia is entranced by the 'tangle of tall dark trees and strange bushes' and the variety of plants—camellias, roses of many kinds, verbena and lavender, pelargoniums, mignonette, pansies and daisies, Japanese sunflowers, red-hot pokers. The characters reappear in 'At the Bay' (in *The Garden Party*, 1922). Some are probably based on the author's relatives and acquaintances: *see* Antony Alpers: *Katherine Mansfield.*

Pre-Raphaelites. A group of artists and writers who formed (*c.* 1849) the Pre-Raphaelite Brotherhood in dissent from the standards prevailing in art since Raphael (1483-1520). They aimed at truth to Nature, in opposition to conventional idealization, but did not eschew symbolism. The leading members were Holman Hunt, John Everett Millais, and Dante Gabriel Rossetti. The *Germ*, the literary organ of the P.R.B., started in January 1850, expired after the fourth number. Their paintings made use of bright colours, were meticulous in detail, and were frequently done in the open air. The P.R.B. masterpiece, Millais's 'Christ in the House of His Parents' (now in the Tate Gallery), was savagely attacked, even by Dickens, but Ruskin defended the Brotherhood in his *Pre-Raphaelitism* (1851). In pictorial imagery

D. G. Rossetti's poems (e.g. 'The Blessed Damozel') and his sister Christina's ('The Goblin Market' etc) are Pre-Raphaelitish.

Prescott, H. F. M. (Hilda Frances Margaret Prescott, 1896-1972). Born in Cheshire; educated there and at the Universities of Oxford and Manchester. Worked for some time as a teacher, and was Vice-Principal of St Mary's College, University of Durham, 1943-48. *The Unhurrying Chase* (1925) and *The Man on a Donkey* (1952) are among the best historical novels of the period. She also wrote *The Lost Fight* (1928), *Flamenca* (1930), *Son of Dust* (1932); a detective novel, *Dead and Not Buried* (1938); *Jerusalem Journey* (1954), *Once to Sinai* (1957); and a biography of Mary Tudor, *Spanish Tudor* (1940).

Press Council. Set up in 1953 after a Royal Commission on the Press had recommended that such a Council should be established voluntarily. Under its revised constitution (1963) it has an independent Chairman and twenty per cent of lay members, the rest being nominated newspaper proprietors and editors and representatives of the journalists' Union and Institute. Its main functions are: To preserve the freedom of the Press; To uphold the highest professional and commercial standards; To consider and report upon complaints by the public (either individual persons or organizations) against the Press, or by the Press against any attempt to infringe its rights. Its remaining functions relate to the technical and commercial development of the Press. The Council has no penal authority, and can only rely upon the moral effect of its published conclusions, which have appeared to be ignored by censured papers.

Prester John. Legendary Christian king and priest (Prester=presbyter) supposed in the Middle Ages to be reigning somewhere in Africa or Asia. Mentioned humorously by Benedick in *Much Ado About Nothing* II, i, 278. Also the title of a novel by John *Buchan, published in 1910.

Price, Bronterre O'Brien. *See* *Snobby Price.

Priestly, Dr. Amateur detective in crime novels by John *Rhode.

Priestley, J. B. (John Boynton Priestley, 1894-). Born at Bradford, Yorkshire; educated there and at Cambridge. Served in World

War I and was thrice wounded. Contributed prolifically to papers and periodicals in London and the provinces and was recognized as exceptionally talented from the time of his earliest publications, *Brief Diversions* (1922) and *Papers from Lilliput* (1922). A dozen other books—mainly on literary subjects but also including two novels—intervened before the prodigious success of *The *Good Companions* (1929). Numerous other novels followed without equal acclaim, and it was as a playwright that Priestley scored his next great success with **Dangerous Corner* (1932), *Laburnum Grove* (1933), *Eden End* (1934). His second notable phase as a dramatist centred on the 'time plays', *Time and the Conways* (1937) and *I Have Been Here Before* (1937). *Cornelius* (1935) had been less well received and the author was provoked to reproach the critics and theatre audiences for their failure to share his own valuation of *Johnson Over Jordan* (1939), a modern morality. Among his later plays, *The Linden Tree* (1947) is outstanding. Priestley was a highly successful broadcaster and during World War II had a vast body of listeners to his homely and comforting Sunday night Postscripts (a selection was published in book form with that title in 1940). *Self-Selected Essays* (1932) gives a fair sampling of his writings in that class. *English Journey* (1934) is a sympathetic and compassionate plain-man's view of sections of the community during the Great Depression of the early 1930s. Other works: **Angel Pavement* (1930, probably the second best of his novels); autobiographical —*Midnight on the Desert* (1937), *Rain Upon Godshill* (1939). And many other works.

Prisoner of Grace. Novel by Joyce *Cary published in 1952. *See *Except the Lord.*

Pritchard, Katharine Susannah. *See* *Australian Writers.

Pritchett, V. S. (Victor Sawdon Pritchett, 1900-). Born in Ipswich; educated in London at Alleyn's School. In business until 1920, when he turned to journalism, writing in France and America as well as in England, where for two years he wrote the Books in General page for the *New Statesman* (of which he also became a Director) and did series of travel talks for the B.B.C. Author of novels—*Claire Drummer* (1929), *Elopement in Exile* (1932), *Dead Man Leading* (1932), *Nothing Like Leather* (1935), *Mr Beluncle*

(1951); short stories—*The Spanish Virgin* (1932), *You Make Your Own Life* (1938), *It May Never Happen* (1947); criticism—*In My Good Books* (1942), *The Living Novel* (1947), *Books in General* (1953). *A Cab at the Door: An Autobiography—Early Years* (1968).

Private Lives. Comedy in three acts by Noel *Coward performed and published in 1930. Amanda and Victor Prynne on their honeymoon at Deauville find that their estranged spouses Elyot and Sibyl Chase, also honeymooning, are at the same hotel in rooms with adjoining balconies. Amanda and Elyot find they still love one another and escape to Amanda's flat in Paris where, after an amorous evening, they quarrel as before their divorce and are struggling violently among overturned furniture when Sibyl and Victor arrive. Next morning, having spent the night in a separate room, Amanda keeps haughtily and silently aloof from Elyot until they go off together with their suitcases, leaving Sibyl and Victor angrily squabbling.

Private Papers of Henry Ryecroft, The. By George *Gissing published in 1903. Though purporting to be based on the diary of a recently dead Henry Ryecroft, this is Gissing's own work, in which he 'set down, as humour bade him, a thought, a reminiscence, a bit of reverie, a description of his state of mind, and so on'. While not wholly autobiographical, it draws largely on the author's personal experiences of poverty and deprivation in earlier years, and the opinions, enthusiasms, delights and dislikes attributed to Ryecroft are Gissing's own. He recalls the years when, as an unsuccessful author, he lived in London, sometimes in a garret, sometimes in a stone-floored front cellar rented at 4s 6d a week, short of food, and finding in the British Museum Reading Room the warmth he needed as well as material to satisfy his intellectual craving. Happier years had come, and speaking as Ryecroft in the Devon cottage to which he had retired on a modest legacy, he rejoices in the natural beauty of the countryside around him, and finds in his contacts with local folk such instances of the intelligence of the heart (which he has come to place above that of the brain) as his poor servantwoman displays. His meditations and observations embrace the manifold interests of an active and liberal mind: peace and war, civilization and democracy, poetry and music and painting, agriculture and climate, the seasons, flowers and birds; English inns and food; religion and philosophy. 'Now', he reflects, 'my life is rounded; it began with the natural irreflective happiness of childhood, it will close in the reasoned tranquility of the mature mind.'

Prokosch, Frederic (1908-   ). Born in Wisconsin; educated in Texas, in European countries and at Yale and Cambridge. Author of poetry—*The Assassin* (1936), *The Carnival* (1938), *Death at Sea* (1940); novels—*The Asiastics* (1935), *The Seven Who Fled* (1937), *Night of the Poor* (1939), *The Skies of Europe* (1942), *The Idols of the Cave* (1946), *A Tale for Midnight* (1955), *A Ballad of Love* (1960).

Proof corrections. Unless an author prepares his manuscript with scrupulous care he may cause alarming expense to the publisher (and himself for 'excess corrections' charges), and will probably delay the publication of his book. The ideal author who makes no proof corrections (other than of compositor's errors which have eluded the eye of the printer's reader) is rare; the author who has second, third, or tenth thoughts and starts to rewrite his book on the proofs is all too frequent. If a visit to a printing works can be arranged, the cost in time (and therefore in labour) of inserting or deleting even a comma can be demonstrated, to enlighten authors before proofs reach them. *See also* Advice for *Authors.

Proserpine Garnett. In Shaw's *Candida* (1894), secretary to the Rev. James Mavor Morell. She has what his wife, Candida, calls 'Prossy's complaint', i.e. like all Morell's enthusiastic women helpers and followers she is in love with him.

Proteus. The Prime Minister in The *Apple Cart* (1929) by Bernard Shaw.

Proust, Marcel (1871-1922). Born in Paris; educated there at the Lycée Condorcet. After a year's military service he studied law and political science, but constitutional weakness kept him from any other occupation than writing, first as a contributor to periodicals. A small collection of miscellaneous pieces of his verse and prose, *Les Plaisirs et les Jours*, was published in 1896 with a preface by Anatole *France, and during the next ten years Proust was accepted in the fashionable society and

literary salons of Paris. At length he tired of this way of life, and after the death of his parents (his father in 1903, his mother in 1905) he retired from active contact with the world, and lived mostly in isolation, in an airless room cork-lined to exclude noise. Tormented by neuroses and the homosexual problems which are a prominent theme in his greatest work, he feverishly confined himself year after year to the composition of that work. He first intended it to be a single volume called *A la recherche du temps perdu*, but while that title was retained for the whole it finally consisted of seven parts, published between 1917 and 1927, little more than half appearing in Proust's lifetime. Between 1922 and 1931 a translation was published in England as *Remembrance of Things Past*, the individual parts being *Swann's Way; Within a Budding Grove; The Guermantes Way; The Cities of the Plain; The Captive; The Sweet Cheat Gone; Time Regained*. Though it attracted no widespread attention at first, the stature of *A la recherche du temps perdu* was increasingly recognized and it has taken a place as one of the world's great novels, both for its quality as a creative literary masterpiece and as an analysis of a society in process of disintegration. Signs of any indebtedness to English prose may be hard to trace, but it is a fact that Proust was sufficiently impressed by Ruskin to translate painstakingly *The Bible of Amiens* and *Sesame and Lilies*. His own masterpiece was fortunate in its translators for the English version—C. K. *Scott-Moncrieff and (last section only) Stephen *Hudson, whose translation. of that section was superseded by Andreas Mayor's in 1970.

Prowse, R. O. (Richard Orton Prowse, 1862-1949). Born at Woodbridge, Suffolk; educated at Cheltenham and Oxford. Novels: *The Poison of Asps* (1892), *A Fatal Reservation* (1895), *Voysey* (1901), *James Hurd* (1913), *A Gift of the Dusk* (1920), *The Prophet's Wife* (1929), *Proud Ashes* (1934).

Pryce, Richard (1864-1942). Born in France of English parents; educated at Leamington. Author of many novels from *An Evil Spirit* (1887) to *Morgan's Yard* (1932) and plays mainly adapted from novels by Arnold Bennett, Christopher Morley, and others.

Psychological novel. One in which plot and events are subordinate to the interest aroused by the mental and psychic states of the characters.

Public image. *See* Image.

Public Lending Right. Under this title authors and their organizations claim that a charge of, say, 1p each time a book is borrowed should be made by public libraries and credited to the author through a central collecting and disbursing agency. It is argued that the privilege of borrowing gratis reduces the sale of an author's books and by thus lessening his income compels him to subsidize borrowers better off than himself. The scheme was opposed on such grounds as that municipal libraries were established as a *free* public service, that public-library purchases already benefit authors, and that the intricate accounting involved would be costly to ratepayers. A government enactment was long promised.

Pudney, John (John Sleigh Pudney, 1909-). Educated at Gresham's School, Holt. Journalist, Literary Editor, Director of publishing firm, producer and writer for B.B.C. Author of *Collected Poems* (1957) and later books of verse; novels, short stories, non-fictional prose, film scripts, etc.

Puff. Insincere or mercenary praise of a book, work of art, or commercial product. Mr Puff in R. B. Sheridan's *The Critic* (1781) enumerates the various sorts of puffing.

Pulp magazines. Cheaply produced publications on inferior (wood pulp) paper, native to America but spreading abroad. The contents are almost exclusively by hack writers, working to a predetermined editorial formula tailored to appeal to readers of undeveloped intellect. Though at first the formula demanded 'pure' youthful heroines and handsome, 'tough' but ultimately chivalrous heroes quelling black-hearted bad men, the trend has been towards brutality and eroticism, in conformity with the regress of popular taste and morals. Some of the kinds developed from pulp magazines are Westerns, science fiction, and crime novels.

Purcell, Victor (Victor William Williams Saunders Purcell, 1896-1965). Served in the Malayan Civil Service, dealing particularly with Chinese affairs, and some years later became University Lecturer in Far Eastern History at Cambridge. Wrote much on the Chinese language and poetry, Chinese

education, and the Chinese in southern Asia; also travel books, including *Chinese Evergreen* (1938). Author of satirical verse under the pseudonym Myra *Buttle.

Purdom, C. B. (Charles Benjamin Purdom, 1883-1965). Born in London. A pioneer in the Garden City Movement, he was among the founders of Letchworth and Welwyn Garden Cities and wrote *The Garden City* (1913) and other books on the subject. From 1928 he was the editor of various periodicals, and in 1939-40 General Secretary of the actors' trade union, British Equity. His lifelong interest in drama was shown in fruitful work as producer with amateur companies, as author of *Producing Plays* (1929; new edn 1951), *The Pleasures of the Theatre* (1932), *Harley Granville Barker* (biography, 1955), and as editor of *Letters of Bernard Shaw to Granville Barker* (1956).

Purple patch. A passage of inflated or overornate writing. In favour during the *fin de siècle* period it has since fallen into disrepute and is shunned by careful writers.

Pygmalion. A Romance in Five Acts by Bernard *Shaw performed in German translation in Vienna 1913, in the original in London 1914; published in 1916.
In the portico of St Paul's Church, Covent Garden, Henry Higgins, a Professor of Phonetics, is taking notes of the speechsounds of a cockney flower-girl, Eliza Doolittle. She protests, supposing that he will make trouble for her, but he explains that his interest is in 'her kerbstone English: the English that will keep her in the gutter for the rest of her days'. He tells a gentleman standing by that he could 'pass the girl off as a duchess' in a few months if she learned to speak properly, and the gentleman introduces himself as Colonel Pickering, a student of Indian dialects. He and Higgins know one another by repute, and next day Pickering calls on Higgins at his residence and laboratory in Wimpole Street and listens to speech records of 130 distinct vowel sounds. Eliza comes to ask Higgins to give her lessons so that she can be 'a lady in a flower shop' instead of selling in the streets, and offers to pay a shilling a lesson. Higgins puts her in charge of his housekeeper, Mrs Pearce, to live with them for six months, though Pickering and Mrs Pearce advise against the experiment. Eliza's father, Alfred Doolittle, a dustman, follows Eliza,

pretending to want to take his daughter away; but, describing himself as 'one of the undeserving poor', he barters her for £5. A few months later, on Higgins's mother's at-home day in Chelsea, Eliza converses in phonetically impeccable English, but her subject matter and vocabulary are startling. She is by now addicted to taxis, and when asked, on leaving, if she is going to walk, causes a sensation by replying 'Not bloody likely!' At the end of the period Higgins had specified, Eliza has passed as a duchess at a garden party, a dinner party, and the opera. She has also become a beautiful woman with sensitive feelings, though to Higgins she is only a successful experiment with no human claims. She takes refuge with Mrs Higgins, where her father comes and asks them to his wedding. Higgins had mentioned him to an American philanthropist who has left Doolittle £3000 a year. Eliza reproaches Higgins for his indifference to her as a human being, refuses to return to Wimpole Street or to let him adopt her, and threatens to set up as a rival teacher of phonetics. (In an epilogue which is not part of the stage play, Eliza is said to have married Freddie Eynsford-Hill, whom she met at Mrs Higgins's at-home, and the pair are set up in a flower-selling business by Colonel Pickering.) See also *My Fair Lady.*

Q. Pseudonym of Sir Arthur Thomas *Quiller-Couch.

Quality Street. Play in four acts by J. M. *Barrie performed in 1902. In a *Cranford*-like atmosphere about the year 1805 a group of refined ladies are gathered in the blue-and-white room of Miss Susan and Miss Phoebe Throssel's house in Quality Street. One of the visitors, Miss Fanny Willoughby, is reading aloud from a library book which shocks her elder sister Mary with its tale of hot, burning kisses. Susan informs the disapproving old maids that she is hourly expecting the young doctor Valentine Brown to propose to her sister, whom he calls 'Miss Pheobe of the ringlets'. Phoebe comes in excitedly from the street where she has just met Valentine, who is to call that afternoon to tell her something. The sisters assume that he is coming to tell Phoebe that he wants to marry her, but the news he brings is that he has enlisted and is going away the next day. Meanwhile, unknown to him, they have lost the money he advised them to invest and they have to start a school—'for genteel children only'. Ten years later Valentine Brown returns with only one hand, and is shocked to find Phoebe worn and aged by schoolmistressing. But by changing from her drab teaching clothes into a wedding dress made in vain by Susan long ago, and by letting the ringlets loose again from her cap, she is able to pass as a young and pretty imaginary niece, Livvy, and captivate Valentine, among others, at the ball he invited her to. But at length, judging Livvy to be a shocking flirt, he finds Phoebe 'the school-mistress in her old-maid's cap' is the one he loves.

Quaritch, Bernard (1819-99). Born in Saxony; apprenticed to a bookseller there and from 1839 to 1842 worked with a Berlin publishing house; then settled in London. In 1847 he started a small bookshop off Leicester Square, and in the 1850s was publishing Turkish and Arabic dictionaries and grammars. He built up a large stock of rare books and in 1860 moved to premises in Piccadilly. Continuing to buy valuable rarities at sales of famous libraries, he issued important annotated bibliographical catalogues. Among his publications of general books was the first edition of Fitzgerald's *Omar Khayyam*. By the time of his death Quaritch's was London's leading antiquarian book-sellers and it has continued in high esteem

down to the present time.

Quarterly Review, The. Founded in 1809 in the Tory interest, in opposition to the *Edinburgh Review* (1802-1929). Its early literary articles included such famous or notorious reviews as Sir Walter Scott's in praise of Jane Austen's *Emma* and John Wilson Croker's attack on Keats's *Endymion*, which provoked Byron's verse beginning 'Who killed John Keats?' and starting the legend that Keats was snuffed-out by a review. (Croker's article was printed in 1818; Keats died in 1821.) The *Quarterly* ceased publication in 1968; though (as *The Times* said) its quality remained high, its circulation had fallen. It was the last of the great quarterlies.

Quasimodo, Salvatore (1901-68). Italian poet, born in Sicily, which remained throughout the chief source of inspiration for his poems. Various of his writings in prose and verse have appeared in English translations.

Queen, Ellery (pseudonym used jointly by Frederic Dannay (1905-) and Manfred B. Lee (1905-1971) for crime novels in which the private detective is also named Ellery Queen. The first of their books, *The Roman Hat Mystery* (1929), was followed by a long sequence of others, including *The Dutch Shoe Mystery* (1931), *The Greek Coffin Mystery* (1932), *The Chinese Orange Mystery* (1934), *Halfway House* (1936), *The Dragon's Teeth* (1939), *There Was An Old Woman* (1943), *The Scarlet Letters* (1953). They also used the pseudonym Barnaby Ross for *The Tragedy of X* (1932), *The Tragedy of Y* (1932), *The Tragedy of Z* (1933), in which the detective is named Drury Lane; these and *Drury Lane's Last Case* (1933) have since been republished as by Ellery Queen. As Daniel Nathan, Frederic Dannay wrote *Golden Summer* (1953).

Quennell, C. H. (Charles Henry Bourne Quennell, 1872-1935). Architect and author of *Norwich Cathedral* (1900), *Modern Sub-urban Houses* (1906); joint author with his wife, Marjorie Quennell, of the books named in the following entry.

Quennell, Marjorie (*née* Marjorie Courtney, 1884-1972, Mrs C. H. B. Quennell). Born at Bromley, Kent; studied at several art schools. Author (with her husband, see preceding entry) of an educationally valuable illus-trated series of popular surveys: *A History of Everyday Things in England 1066-1799* in four parts (1918, 1919, 1933, 1934; later combined in one vol.), *Everyday Life in the Old Stone Age* (1921) and corresponding volumes for the *New Stone, Bronze,* and *Early Iron Ages* (1922), *Roman Britain* (1924), *Anglo-Saxon, Viking and Norman Times* (1926), *Homeric Greece* (1929), *Archaic Greece* (1931), *Classical Greece* (1932). Also wrote *The Good New Days* (1936).

Quennell, Peter (Peter Courtney Quennell, 1905-   ). Born in London, son of the two preceding; educated at Berkhamsted and Oxford. Contributed to leading periodicals; editor of the *Cornhill Magazine* (1944-51), then of *History To-day*. Author of verse—*Poems* (1926), *Inscription on a Fountain Head* (1929); novels—*The Phoenix-Kind* (1931); *Sympathy and other Stories*; biography, criticism, etc—*Baudelaire and the Symbolists* (1929), *Letters to Mrs Virginia Woolf* (1932), *Victorian Panorama* (1937), *Caroline of England: An Augustan Portrait* (1940), *Four Portraits* (1945), *John Ruskin: Portrait of a Prophet* (1949), *The Sign of the Fish* (1960), and several books concerning Byron.

Quested, Adela. Visitor to Chandrapore in E. M. Forster's *A *Passage to India* (1924). After she withdraws her charge against Dr Aziz she is ostracized by the British residents and Ronny Heaslop breaks off his engagement to her.

Quiller-Couch, Sir Arthur (Arthur Thomas Quiller-Couch, 1863-1944; knighted 1910). Born at Fowey, Cornwall; educated at Newton Abbot, Clifton and Oxford. Lecturer in Classics, University of Oxford, 1886-87; editor of *The Speaker*, 1887-99; King Edward VII Professor of English Literature, University of Cambridge, from 1912. He had a lifelong devotion to his native town and county, was Mayor of Fowey in 1937, and under the pseudonym 'Q', wrote what are probably the best novels and short stories about Cornwall, using the fictional name Troy Town for Fowey: *Dead Man's Rock* (1887), *Troy Town* (1888), *The Delectable Duchy* (1893), and many others; those written in the present century include *The Adventures of Harry Revel* (1903), *Hetty Wesley* (1903), *Poison Island* (1907). He published *Green Bays: Verses and Parodies*

(1893), *Poems and Ballads* (1896) and *Adventures in Criticism* (1896). He had what was in effect a new lease of life from the time he edited *The Oxford Book of English Verse* (1900), covering a much longer period than Palgrave's *Golden Treasury* (1861) and only second to it in popularity. Neither as anthologist nor as professorial lecturer has Q commanded the approval of later critics and scholars, for his interests were not primarily academic; his view of literature was far more humane than textual and analytical. To the generation of students he taught at Cambridge from 1912, literature became a living thing, and far beyond the University his lectures in their published form were both enlightening and delighting: *On the Art of Writing* (1916), *Studies in Literature* (3 series, 1918, 1922, 1929), *On the Art of Reading* (1920). He also edited the *Oxford Books of Ballads* (1910), *Victorian Verse* (1912), and *English Prose* (1925). *Memories and Opinions* (1944). *Q's Mystery Stories* (1937) gives a representative sampling of his shorter fiction.

Quintero, Joaquin Alvárez (1873-1944). Born at Utrera, Spain, brother of the following; both educated at Seville, and both worked for several years in government service at Madrid. They began to write plays while schoolboys and continued to do so for the rest of their lives; their total output is said to number over a hundred plays; among the few that became popular in England (in translations by Granville *Barker and his second wife Helen) are: *A Hundred Years Old, Fortunato, The Lady from Alfaqueque, The Women Have Their Way.*

Quintero, Serafin Alvárez (1871-1938). Brother of the preceding, and his collaborator.

Quisling, Vidkun (1887-1945). Born at Fyrisdal, Norway. Up to the outbreak of World War II he held diplomatic and political appointments, and in 1933 started a National Party on the lines of Hitler's Nazis. He urged nonresistance against the German invaders in 1940 and served as Prime Minister during the occupation. His surname became a synonym for traitor throughout the war but soon dropped from general use in English after his execution for treason when Norway was freed.

Quo Vadis? *See* Henryk *Sienkiewicz.

Rabinowitz, Solomon J. *See* Shalom *Aleichem.

Rackham, Arthur (1867-1939). Born and educated in London; studied at Lambeth School of Art; became celebrated as an illustrator with a distinctive personal style in which persons and natural objects—trees, etc.—often have a fairy-tale grotesquerie of form and a sinister atmosphere, with a wealth of detail. He illustrated, mainly in ominous colour, *de luxe* editions of *Rip Van Winkle* (1905), *Peter Pan* (1906), *Ingoldsby Legends* (1907), Wagner's *Ring of the Nibelung* (1910-11), Grimm's and Andersen's *Fairy Tales* (1909; 1932), *Midsummer Night's Dream* and *The Tempest* (1908; 1926), Dickens's *Christmas Carol* (1915), Ibsen's *Peer Gynt* (1936), and numerous others.

RADA. *See* *Royal Academy of Dramatic Art.

Radiocarbon dating. A method of determining the age of archaeological remains, introduced by Professor Willard Frank Libby, of Chicago (*Radiocarbon Dating*, 1952). The amount of radiocarbon (carbon-14) in living organisms remains invariable during life, and disintegrates at a known rate after death. If the amount remaining in any ancient specimen is compared with the amount in a corresponding living specimen, the age of the former can be stated within, it is calculated, plus or minus forty years. In *Dating the Past* (1946) Frederick E. Zeuner, speaking (in ch. x, sect. B) of 'the manifold interrelations of the various branches of science', deals with the time-rate of disintegration of radioactive material. More recent research in U.S. suggests that computer analysis of prehistoric fossil-tree rings throws doubt on the reliability of radiocarbon dating.

Raffles. The 'gentleman cracksman' in novels by E. W. *Hornung.

Rafi. King of the Beggars of Bagdad and lover of Pervaneh in J. E. Flecker's *Hassan.

Ragged Trousered Philanthropists, The. Novel by Robert *Tressell published (abbreviated) in 1914; full text 1955.
The misfortunes of a group of house-painters and decorators are set out in convincingly realistic detail which makes the book in this respect a reliable account of working-class conditions in Britain before World War I. The tyranny of employers, and more particularly of managers and foremen who are themselves of the working class; the perpetual threat and dread of unemployment; the inability of wives to manage and keep out of debt on their husbands' inhumanly low wages which hold families on or below the subsistence level: these aspects of labouring life in the pre-Welfare State era are rendered with distressing truth. As in other writings of its class, however, the impact is dulled by over-emphasis and repetition, and by inability or refusal to recognize that the perfecting of a social system depends upon an achieved perfectibility of mankind. The author's humorous passages misfire, while the episode in which a corpse is switched between coffins of rival claimants to the burial job is ludicrous rather than macabre or shocking. The central character, Owen, a dedicated socialist designer and house-painter with talent as a political orator, provides the title of the book in his reiterated assertion that employees are philanthropists accepting a pittance for work which produces wealth for employers. Since this is the classic proletarian novel and by an unprofessional writer, a recital of its literary shortcomings has little point.

Raglan, Lord (FitzRoy Raglan Somerset, 4th baron Raglan, 1885-1964). Born in London; educated at Eton and Sandhurst. Served with the army in the Far East and Middle East, but after retirement from military duties pursued his interest in folklore and anthropology. Author of *Jocasta's Crime* (1933), 'a study of the incest tabu'; *The Hero: A Study in Tradition, Myth and Drama* (1936); *Death and Rebirth* (1945), *The Origins of Religion* (1949), *The Temple and the House* (1964), and controversial writings on political topics.

Raimond, C. E. *See* Elizabeth *Robins (1862-1952).

Rain. The best known of the many short stories by W. Somerset *Maugham. First published in *The Smart Set*, a New York magazine, it was reprinted in *The *Trembling of a Leaf* in 1921. First entitled 'Miss Thompson', it is a tragico-satirical narrative of the moral collapse and suicide of a fanatical Christian missionary, the Rev. Alfred Davidson, who, after subjecting the prostitute Sadie Thompson to spiritual torment in his determination to convert her, is himself overcome by the eruption of suppressed sexual desire. The impact of the story is intensified by the described effects of the tropical rain and the 'seething, humid, sultry, breathless' atmosphere which combine to stretch the Europeans' nerves near to breaking point. Moreover, the crucial episode comes more shatteringly to the reader since it is not described but subtly implanted in the imagination. The characters of Davidson and Sadie are ruthlessly probed, as is that of Davidson's wife, who shares her husband's obtuse fanaticism. Film and stage versions made the story known throughout the world.

Rainbow, The. Novel by D. H. *Lawrence published in 1915; banned as obscene; reissued with modifications, but the original text was later restored.

The youngest of a prosperous but thrifty family at Marsh Farm in the Erewash valley on the Notts-Derby border, Tom Brangwen takes over the farm when his father dies. An older brother, Alfred, becomes a lace-designer in Nottingham. Tom marries Lydia Lensky, widow of a Polish doctor and revolutionary exiled in England, who has a young child, Anna. Though they are deeply in love, conflict develops for a while between Lydia and Tom, while he becomes lovingly devoted to Anna. After the birth of Lydia and Tom's sons, Tom and Fred, their parents turn again to each other. When Anna is approaching womanhood she falls in love with her stepfather's nephew, Will Brangwen, who, like his father, Alfred, is a lace-designer, but also an accomplished amateur wood-carver. Although the stepfather is distressed by the transference of Anna's love to the younger man, he reconciles himself to the marriage and leases a cottage for them in the nearby village of Cossethay, where Anna and Will spend an overwhelmingly rapturous honeymoon. Sated by passion, Anna begins to find Will's uxoriousness tedious; and when she girds against his religion and his interest in the village church (where he becomes choirmaster and restores carvings), a vein of hatred threads through their love. As each of their six children—Ursula, Gudrun, Theresa, Catherine, William, Cassandra—is born, Anna becomes wholly absorbed in the latest baby, while Ursula and her father grow strongly attached. The girl is also a solace to her grandmother,

Lydia, when the elder Tom Brangwen is drowned in a flood when the canal bank collapses. From the village school, Ursula and Gudrun go on to the Grammar School in Nottingham; Ursula 'a free, unabateable animal' owning no law nor any rule; Gudrun 'a shy, quiet, wild creature . . . pursuing half-formed fancies that had no relation to anyone else', and living by proxy in her sister, whom she considers 'clever enough for two'. As she passes through adolescence, Ursula adopts a confusing selective attitude towards Christianity, dissenting from injunctions concerning self-sacrifice and humility, and coming at length to feel she 'hated religion because it lent itself to her confusion'. About this time Anton, the son of Baron Skrebensky, a Polish exile friend of the Lenskys, comes to visit the Brangwens. A personable young army engineer, bringing intimations of a larger world, he fascinates Ursula and draws her to him. Their intermittent but physically intense courtship is ended by his departure to the Boer War, leaving Ursula in an overwrought and sensitive state in which 'her sexual life flamed into a kind of disease within her'. In her last terms at school she is shaken by a transitory lesbian experience with her class-mistress, Winifred Inger. Together they visit Ursula's uncle, Tom Brangwen, a Yorkshire colliery manager, whose mistress and then wife Winifred becomes. Having matriculated and left school, Ursula spends two miserable years as an elementary school teacher in Ilkeston, unable to control the class and humiliated by the headmaster. She then goes to college to study for a degree. In her last year there, when she is twenty-two, she hears again from Anton Skrebensky. They meet in Nottingham and soon plunge into uninhibited love-making which distracts Ursula from study. She fails to get her degree. Before Anton, now an officer, is due to leave for service in India, he begs her to marry him. After wavering, she decides against it until, believing herself pregnant, she writes, changing her decision. He cables from India: 'I am married'. Before this news arrives, Ursula is deliriously ill, having been caught in a stampede of horses while walking on a common in heavy rain. She finds there will be no child. Convalescent, she sits by her window, watching a rainbow forming: 'She saw in the rainbow the earth's new architecture, the old, brittle corruption of houses and factories swept away, the world built up in a living fabric of Truth, fitting to the over-arching heaven.' See also *Women in Love.

Raine, Kathleen (Kathleen Jessie Raine, 1908- ; Mrs Charles *Madge). Born in London; spent her early childhood in a northern English village; won scholarships to Cambridge, where she first developed as a poet. With later verse writings she achieved distinction among the metaphysically directed poets of the period: *Stone and Flower* (1943), *Living in Time* (1946), *The Pythoness* (1949), *The Year One* (1952); *Collected Poems* (1956); *On a Deserted Shore* (1973).

Rake's Progress. Hogarth's eighteenth-century series of paintings and engravings on this theme inspired the ballet (1935) by Gavin Gordon and the opera by Stravinsky (1951) with libretto by W. H. *Auden and Chester Kallman.

Raleigh, Sir Walter (Walter Alexander Raleigh, 1861-1922; knighted 1911). Born in London; educated there and at Edinburgh and Cambridge. Following a term as Professor of English at Aligarh, India, 1885-87, he was Professor of English at Liverpool, 1890-1900, then at Glasgow, 1900-04, before appointment as the first Professor of English Literature in the University of Oxford from 1904. There, his approach to the subject was liberal and humanistic, as *Quiller-Couch's was contemporaneously at Cambridge. His writings include *The English Novel* (1894), *Robert Louis Stevenson* (1895), *Style* (1897), *Milton* (1900), *Wordsworth* (1903), *The English Voyagers of the Sixteenth Century* (1906), *Shakespeare* (1907). He was commissioned at the end of World War I to write the official history of the Royal Air Force, but died with only one volume completed (published 1922). After his death a collection of prose pieces *Laughter from a Cloud* (1923) was edited by his son; and his wife issued *The Letters of Sir Walter Raleigh* (1926).

Ramal, Walter. See Walter *de la Mare.

Ramée, Marie Louise de la. See Ouida.

Rampion, Mark. Writer and painter in Aldous Huxley's *Point Counter Point* (1928). His views are akin to those of D. H. Lawrence.

Ramsden, Roebuck. A monument of Victorian respectability, appointed joint guardian of Ann Whitefield in Bernard Shaw's *Man and Superman* (1903). He strongly disapproves of his fellow guardian John Tanner.

Ranevsky, Madame. Owner of the bankrupt estate in Tchekhov's *The *Cherry Orchard* (1904).

Ransom, John Crowe (1888-1974). Born in Tennessee; educated at Vanderbilt University and in England at Oxford. Professor of Poetry at Vanderbilt University, 1924-37, then at Kenyon College, Ohio, where he edited the *Kenyon Review*, a quarterly specializing in 'the new criticism', propagating minute textual analysis, and publishing contemporary verse conforming to the approved mode. Ransom's own volumes of poems include *Poems About God* (1919), *Chills and Fever* (1924), *Two Gentlemen in Bonds* (1927), *Selected Poems* (1945). Criticism: *God Without Thunder* (1930), *The World's Body* (1938), *The New Criticism* (1941), *A College Primer of Writing* (1943).

Ransome, Arthur (Arthur Michell Ransome, 1884-1967). Born in Leeds; educated at Rugby. Worked in publishing until his late teens. Visited Russia before World War I and learned the language; returned there as a war correspondent. In the early 1920s he yachted in the Baltic; then, after visits to China and other countries, he wrote the first of the adventure novels which set a new literary standard in fiction for young readers without sacrificing narrative attraction: *Swallows and Amazons* (1931), *Pigeon Post* (1936), *We Didn't Mean to Go to Sea* (1938), *Secret Water* (1939), *The Big Six* (1940), *Great Northern?* (1947). Other books: *A History of Storytelling* (1909), *Old Peter's Russian Tales* (1916), *Six Weeks in Russia* (1919), *Racundra's First Cruise* (1923), *Mainly About Fishing* (1959).

Rasputin, Gregory Efimovich (1871-1916). Russian monk of peasant birth who exercised a baleful and disastrous influence at the Court of the last Romanoff rulers of Russia. His hold on the Tsarina was attributed to his pretence of supernatural powers beneficial to her ailing son. Through her he effected political backstairs operations and resisted efforts to remove him. He was with gruesome difficulty assassinated by

Grand Duke Dimitry and Prince Yusupov in an underground room of the Yusupov Palace.

Ratcliffe, Dorothy Una (*née* Dorothy Una Clough; died 1967). Born in Surrey of gipsy ancestry; educated in Weimar and Paris; married (1) Charles Ratcliffe, (2) Noel McGrigor Phillips, (3) Alfred Phillips. She was the author of many books of verse and prose, and also wrote peasant plays, devoting herself to the dialects of the Yorkshire dales, an area in which she lived following her first marriage. This phase of her career produced *Dale Dramas* (1923), *Dale Lyrics* (1926), *Dale Folk* (1927), *Lapwings and Laverocks* (1934); *Yorkshire Lyrics* (1960) contains her collected poems. Her later adventurous and wide-ranging travels are recorded in *South African Summer* (1933), *Equatorial Dawn* (1936), *News of Persephone* (1939), *Grecian Glory* (1941), *Icelandic Spring* (1950). Recollections: *Lady of a Million Daffodils* (1958). A relative by marriage of the first Lord Brotherton, she gave his library to Leeds University and added liberal endowments from her large fortune.

Rattigan, Sir Terence (Terence Mervyn Rattigan, 1911-   ). Knighted 1971. Educated at Harrow and Oxford. One of his earliest plays, *French Without Tears* (1936) ran for more than a thousand consecutive performances in London and was outstripped by *While the Sun Shines* (1943). Other plays: *Flare Path* (1942), *Love in Idleness* (1944), *The *Winslow Boy* (1946), **Adventure Story* (1949), *The *Deep Blue Sea* (1952), *Separate Tables* (1954), *In Praise of Love* (1973). Though in some measure cold-shouldered by critics, his plays achieved popularity without sacrifice of literary quality. *See* *Aunt Edna.

Raven, Charles (Charles Earle Raven, 1885-1964). Educated at Uppingham and Cambridge. Canon of Liverpool, 1924-32; Regius Professor of Divinity in the University of Cambridge, 1932-50; Master of Christ's College, Cambridge, 1939-50. His published works reflected his twin interests, theology and natural science: *Christian Socialism* (1920), *Christ and Modern Education* (1928), *War and the Christian* (1938); *John Ray, Naturalist: His Life and Works* (1942), *English Naturalists from Neckham to Ray* (1947).

Raverat, Gwen (*née* Gwendolen Mary Darwin, 1885-1957; Mrs Jacques Raverat). Born at Cambridge, granddaughter of Charles Darwin; studied at the Slade School and became an accomplished wood-engraver and illustrator. Her entertaining autobiographical *Period Piece* (1952) throws interesting light on her upbringing in a distinguished family. Her father, Sir George Darwin (1845-1912) was Professor of Astronomy in the University of Cambridge from 1883.

Rawlings, Marjorie Kinnan (*née* Marjorie Kinnan, 1896-1953; Mrs C. Rawlings). Born in Washington, D.C.; educated at the University of Wisconsin. She worked as a journalist until 1928, then bought an orange grove in Florida and in 1938 had great success with her story of a boy and his pet fawn, *The Yearling*. Other novels of Florida: *South Moon Under* (1933), *Golden Apples* (1935), *When the Whippoorwill* (1940), *The Sojourner* (1953). *Cross Creek* (1942), the address of her orange grove, treats of her experiences there.

Rawlinson, Gloria (Gloria Jasmine Rawlinson, 1918-   ). Born in Tonga, South Pacific; educated privately. Author of *Gloria's Book* (1932), *The Perfume Vendor* (1935), *Music in the Listening Place* (1939), *The Islands where I was Born* (1955), *Of Clouds and Pebbles* (1963), and other collections of verse.

Raymond, Ernest (1888-1974). Educated at St Paul's and at Chichester Theological College; ordained in the Anglican Church, 1914; resigned Holy Orders in 1923 after serving on six fronts in World War I. Had an immense success with his first novel *Tell England* (1922), and thereafter wrote many books including (among novels) *Damascus Gate* (1923), *Mary Leith* (1931), *We, the Accused* (1935), *The Last to Rest* (1941), *A Chorus Ending* (1951), *Mr Olim* (1961), *The Bethany Road* (1967); also *Through Literature to Life* (1928); *The Multabello Road* (play; 1932). *In the Steps of St Francis* (1938), *In the Steps of the Brontës* (1948), *Two Gentlemen of Rome: The Story of Keats and Shelley* (1952), *Paris, City of Enchantment* (1961). *The Story of My Days* (autobiography; 1968).

Razumov, Kirylo Sidorovitch. Student at St Petersburg University in Joseph Conrad's **Under Western Eyes* (1911). He betrays

Victor Haldin and goes as a police agent to Geneva, where he confesses his treachery and is permanently crippled and rendered stone deaf.

Rea, Lorna (*née* Lorna Smith, 1897-   ; Lady Rea). Born in Glasgow; educated at Malvern and Cambridge. She married in 1922 the Hon. Philip Russell Rea who succeeded as the second Baron Rea in 1935. Her first novel *Six Mrs Greenes* (1929), a striking success, was followed by *Rachel Moon* (1930), *The Happy Prisoner* (1931), *First Night* (1932), *Six and Seven* (1935).

Read, Conyers (1881-1959). Born in U.S.; educated at Harvard and Oxford. Professor in English History, University of Pennsylvania, 1934-51. As author of *Mr Secretary Walsingham and the Policy of Queen Elizabeth* (1925), *The Tudors* (1936), *Mr Secretary Cecil and Queen Elizabeth* (1955), *Lord Burghley and Queen Elizabeth* (1960) he was recognized by other historians as a leading authority on the Tudor period, while the ease and clarity of his style made his books acceptable to the ordinary reader.

Read, Sir Herbert (Herbert Edward Read, 1893-1968; knighted 1953). Born in Yorkshire; educated at Halifax and the University of Leeds. Served in France and Belgium in World War I. Was an Assistant Keeper at the Victoria and Albert Museum, London, 1922-31, and then held university appointments as Lecturer and Professor of Fine Art in Britain and the U.S., and as Professor of Poetry at Harvard. In addition to other works in verse and prose noted below, he wrote much on both fine and applied art, particularly on contemporary work which he consistently defended against critical attacks on innovating styles. *The Meaning of Art* (1931) is a lucid and persuasive introduction, liberal in outlook and drawing on a wide range of forms and periods. Other aspects are treated in *Art Now* (1933), *Art and Industry* (1934), *Art and Society* (1936), *Education Through Art* (1943), *The Grass Roots of Art* (1947), *The Philosophy of Modern Art* (1952), *The Art of Sculpture* (1956), *A Concise History of Modern Painting* (1959). Writings on literature: *English Prose Style* (1928), *Phases of English Poetry* (1928), *Wordsworth* (1930), *Form in Modern Poetry* (1932), *In Defence of Shelley* (1935), *Poetry and Anarchism* (1938). Other works: *Collected Poems* (1946); *Collected Essays* (1938); *Annals of Innocence and Experience* (autobiography; 1940).

Realism. See Naturalism.

Recessional. Poem by Rudyard *Kipling written in 1897 at the time of Queen Victoria's Diamond Jubilee. In retrospect it appears strikingly prophetic, for though written at the moment when the might and pride of the British Empire were at their peak it contains sobering lines, such as 'Lo, all our pomp of yesterday/Is one with Nineveh and Tyre!'.

Red Dean, The. See Hewlett *Johnson.

Redway, Ralph. See Frank *Richards.

Reed, Henry (1914-   ). Educated in Birmingham. Worked as teacher and journalist, and in the Foreign Office. Poet and critic, but best-known as a writer for broadcasting. *A Map of Verona* (poems, 1946). Adaptation of Herman Melville's *Moby Dick* (1947) for radio.

Reed, John (1887-1920). Born in Oregon; educated there and at Harvard. Travelled in Spain and Mexico and was in Russia at the time of the Bolshevik revolution which he described in his most widely known book, *Ten Days That Shook the World* (1919). He returned to Russia, died there of typhus, and was buried in the Kremlin.

Reed, Langford (Herbert Langford Reed, 1889-1954). Born in Clapham, London; educated there and at Hove. Contributed verse and prose to a large number of newspapers and periodicals. His collections of limericks became better known than his original writings, which included *The Life of Lewis Carroll* (1932). *The Complete Limerick Book* (1924) had several later editions.

Reed, Talbot Baines (1852-1893). Born in Hackney, London, son of Sir Charles Reed (Chairman of the School Board for London and head of a flourishing firm of typefounders); educated at the City of London School. He was one of the founders of the Bibliographical Society in 1892, after having spent many years on research for his *History of the Old English Letter-foundries, with Notes Historical and Bibliographical on the Rise and Progress of English Typo-*

graphy (1887; reissued, revised and enlarged 1952). Meanwhile he had been contributing to the *Boys' Own Paper* serial school stories which long remained popular in book form: *The Fifth Form at St Dominic's* (1881), *A Dog With a Bad Name* (1886), *The Master of the Shell* (1887), *The Cock House at Fellsgarth* (1891) and others.

Reese, Lizette Woodworth (1856-1935). Born in Maryland. She spent most of her life as a teacher, including four years in a school for coloured students. She published several collections of poems, from *A Branch of May* (1877) to *The Old House in the Country* (1936), with a volume of *Selected Poems* (1926). Though in language and diction she rarely departed from the conventional line of poetry to which early reading had accustomed her, in outlook and thought she bridged two periods. The prose books *A Victorian Village* (1929) and *The York Road* (1931) are autobiographical.

Reference books. Biographical, bibliographical, and other relevant factual information about writers, books, etc. is available in the reference works named below. *Annals of English Literature* (to 1950). *Cambridge Bibliography of English Literature* (1940. Supplementary volume 1957. Concise edn 1965). *Chambers's Biographical Dictionary. Chambers's Encyclopaedia. The Columbia Dictionary of Modern European Literature* (New York, 1947). *Encyclopaedia Britannica. Everyman's Dictionaries*: (1) *of Literary Biography, English and American*; (2) *of European Writers* (both Dent). *Oxford Companions to* (1) *English Literature*; (2) *American Literature*; (3) *Canadian History and Literature*; (4) *French Literature*; (5) *The Theatre*. *The Reader's Encyclopedia* (New York, Crowell; London, Black). *Twentieth Century Authors* (1942) and (1955) *First Supplement to the same* (New York, The H. W. Wilson Co.). *Whitaker's Almanack* (London, annually). *Who Was Who* (London, 1897-1915; 1916-1928; 1929-1940; 1941-1950; 1951-1960; 1961-1970; and at ten-year intervals). *Who's Who* (annually). Also the *International Who's Who* and the *Who's Who* volumes of various countries. Where no date is given above, the work is kept under revision and the latest edition should be consulted. Also *DNB*.

Regional novel. One in which the action or situation is confined to a circumscribed region, such as a county, district, city or town, whether actual (as in Arnold Bennett's *Five Towns) or imaginary (as in Anthony Trollope's Barsetshire). Thomas Hardy's Wessex novels pass in an area, embracing Dorset and parts of neighbouring counties, to which he restored the name of the old West Saxon kingdom, though the extent is not identical.

Régnier, Henri de (Henri François Joseph de Régnier, 1864-1936). Born at Honfleur; studied law but devoted himself to writing, first as a poet of the Symbolist school (as in *Poèmes anciennes et romanesques,* 1890), later as a classicist. He was also a fertile writer of fiction; *La Double Maîtresse* (1900) has been described as 'the first Freudian' novel, well in advance of the cult.

Reid, Forrest (1875-1947). Born in Belfast; educated there and at Cambridge. Contributed to literary periodicals. Author of novels—*The Gentle Lover* (1913), *Uncle Stephen* (1931), *Peter Waring* (1937), *Young Tom* (1944); critical studies—*W. B. Yeats* (1915), *Walter de la Mare* (1929).

Reid, V. S. (Victor Stafford Reid, 1913-   ). Born and educated in Jamaica, where he also worked as a journalist and editor, and in advertising. Author of novels—*New Day* (1950), *The Leopard* (1958)—and children's books: *Sixty-Five* (1960), *The Young Warriors* (1967).

Reinhardt, Max (*born* Max Goldmann, 1873-1943). Born near Venice. After starting as a bank clerk, he turned to acting in 1893, but from 1903 became a renowned producer and stage director, making use of modern improvements in lighting and other stage mechanism and achieving a unified art of the theatre which embraced designers, composers, choreographers, costumiers, etc. He was a master of spectacular productions employing large crowds of performers. He staged the *Oedipus Rex* of Sophocles in Vienna in 1910 and in London at Covent Garden in 1912, but his most impressive work was *The Miracle* in the vast arena of Olympia in London in 1911. At Salzburg he produced *Faust*, and plays by Shakespeare in New York. He settled in America as a refugee from the Nazi régime and died there.

Reith, Lord (John Charles Walsham Reith, 1889-1971; knighted 1927; baron 1940).

Educated at Gresham's School (Holt, Norfolk), at Glasgow Academy and at the Royal Technical School there. Apprenticed and worked as an engineer until World War I, in which he was wounded; then held government appointments until he became first General Manager of the British Broadcasting Company in 1922. When it was reconstituted as the British Broadcasting Corporation he was Director-General from 1927 to 1938. Thereafter he held important ministerial and other public appointments in war and peace, but his name is indelibly associated with his direction of the B.B.C. in its first phase. His idealism and vision as well as his organizing genius gave British broadcasting a world lead in efficiency and cultural value, for he was insistent that programmes should aim at the elevation of public taste and intelligence, an ideal to which his successors were not uniformly committed.

Réjane. Stage name of Gabrielle Charlotte Réju (1857-1920). Born in Paris; first appeared there in 1875 and excelled in comedy parts, though accomplished also in tragedy. She rivalled Sarah *Bernhardt in popularity and was equally acclaimed in her visits to London and New York.

Religious drama. An annual festival at Canterbury in the 1930s stimulated interest in religious plays, and produced T. S. Eliot's *Murder in the Cathedral* (1935), Charles *Williams's *Thomas Cranmer of Canterbury* (1936), Dorothy L. *Sayers's *The Zeal of Thy House* (1937), Christopher *Hassall's *Christ's Comet* (1938; published 1937). John *Masefield had written *Good Friday* (1916) and *The Coming of Christ* (1928). Christopher *Fry's *A Sleep of Prisoners* was performed in a church off Regent Street during the Festival of Britain in 1951. A great many religious plays continue to be performed by amateurs locally in churches and schools, with children or/and adult players, and frequently written by local authors. The Religious Drama Society was formed to encourage this movement.

Remarque, Erich Maria (1898-1970). Born and educated in Osnabrück. After World War I, in which he was severely wounded, he worked in a variety of jobs, from teaching to tombstone carving, before his war novel *All Quiet on the Western Front* (1929) became an international best-seller. It was outstanding among the books which were at that time depicting the horrors of war as experienced by the men in the trenches. Remarque continued as a novelist, with *The Road Back* (1931), *Three Comrades* (1937), *The Arch of Triumph* (1946), *A Time to Love and a Time to Die* (1954), *The Black Obelisk* (1957), and others. He lived for several years in Switzerland but later settled in America and became naturalized there.

Remembrance of Things Past. English translation in twelve volumes of Marcel *Proust's seven-part novel *A la recherche du temps perdu* (1913-27). C. K. *Scott-Moncrieff translated all but the final part of the French original; the rest was done by Stephen *Hudson after Scott-Moncrieff's death. The English edition (published 1922-31) has the following renderings of the original section titles: *Swann's Way* ('Du Côté de chez Swann'); *Within a Budding Grove* ('A l'ombre des jeunes filles en fleurs'); *The Guermantes Way* ('Le Côté de Guermantes'); *Cities of the Plain* ('Sodome et Gomorrhe'); *The Captive* ('La Prisonnière'); *The Sweet Cheat Gone* ('Albertine Disparue'); *Time Regained* ('Le Temps retrouvé'). The greatest novel of the century, entirely original in conception and execution, Proust's work is an intricate web of past and present, memory and immediate experience, appearance and reality, conscious and subconscious thought and emotion, with intertwining strands of love and jealousy, social snobbery and political passion, malice and personal intrigue. Among the two hundred or so characters the following are outstanding. Charles Swann, a wealthy middle-class country gentleman, admitted to the high society which for long excludes Odette de Crécy, his mistress and later his wife, the mother of his daughter Gilberte, with whom the young narrator (in part Marcel himself) is for a while in love. Gilberte afterwards marries Robert, Marquis de Saint-Loup, who has introduced Marcel into the exclusive Guermantes circle. Their kinsman, Charlus, who is dominant in later sections of the work, is shown in his irreconcilable complexity as a man of refined intellect, a ludicrously arrogant patron, an irresistible charmer, and a compulsive homosexual slowly degenerating through his relationships with the young violinist Morel and others of low breeding into a repellent and pitiable physical and mental wreck. Mme Verdurin, an incorrigible snob of bourgeoise origin, climbs into the aristocracy and gathers 'a little clan' into her weekly *salon* and acquires as her second husband the Prince de Guermantes. Albertine Simonet becomes Marcel's mistress. Though he discovers that she is a lesbian and is agonized by prolonged jealousy, he lives with her in Paris, keeping her in seclusion. She runs away and is killed in a riding accident. Of all the characters the narrator's beloved grandmother is the most beautifully drawn, and Françoise, the devoted though dictatorial family servant, the most solidly created and amusing. Though the major interest is in the surgically minute psychological dissection of the multitude of characters, there is also much incidental attraction: through the nature passages descriptive of Combray (probably Illiers, near Chartres) and Balbec (Cabourg on the Normandy coast), which with Paris are the novel's chief settings; and through the displayed interest in art (centred on the paintings of Elstir, who introduces Albertine to Marcel), literature (Bergotte's novels), music (compositions by Vinteuil). Though these names are fictional, Elstir has been taken as a composite of Monet and other Impressionists, Vinteuil as suggestive of Saint-Saëns, Bergotte unrelated. Echoes of the *Dreyfus case are recurrent throughout, splitting French society into two bitterly antagonistic groups. The basic structure is circular, the end linking on to the beginning through a moment of illumination (recorded in the final part) experienced by the narrator when, stumbling one day on uneven paving stones, he suffers a 'spiritual renewal' which reveals to him the way to the recovery of Lost Time and the resurrection (rather than the mere remembrance) of the Past, giving life to 'the being within me . . . which only appeared . . . through the medium of the identity of present and past'.

Stephen Hudson's translation of the final section was superseded (1970) by that of Andreas Mayor based on a revised edition of the French text.

Remington, Richard. Narrator and chief character in H. G. Wells's The *New Machiavelli* (1911). He is returned to Parliament as a Liberal in 1906, but becomes a Conservative M.P. at the next election. His political career ends when he leaves his wife (*née* Margaret Seddon) and settles in Italy with Isabel Rivers and their child.

Renaissance. The great Revival of Learning and Art in Western Europe conventionally dated from 1453, when Constantinople fell to the Turks and scholars fled, spreading Greek and Latin culture westward. The movement had earlier roots in Italy in the fourteenth century through Dante, Petrarch, and Boccaccio. In England the influence of Erasmus (1466-1536), the great Dutch humanist, was paramount. He lectured at Cambridge and was the friend of Sir Thomas More, John Colet, and others who laid the foundations of *Humanism and brought England into the full current of the Renaissance which, in literature, led to Shakespeare.

Renault, Mary (pseudonym of Mary Challans, 1905-   ). Educated at Bristol and Oxford; trained and practised as a nurse, but from 1939 (with a return to nursing throughout World War II) concentrated on the writing of novels. Her most notable successes were with a sequence on the Theseus legend: *The Last of the Wine* (1956), *The King Must Die* (1958), *The Bull from the Sea* (1962); later novels include *Fire from Heaven* (1970).

Renier, G. J. (Gustaaf Johannes Renier, 1892-1962). Born at Flushing, Holland; educated there and in Louvain, Ghent, and London. Acted as London correspondent of Dutch newspapers, 1914-27. Professor of Dutch History and Institutions in the University of London, 1945-57, having held lesser appointments there in the preceding years. His written works include biographies of *William of Orange* (1932), *Oscar Wilde* (1933), and *Robespierre* (1936), as well as books on Dutch history; but he struck a more original note with The *English: Are They Human?* (1931), a perceptive, sympathetic, and humorous view of his foster nation. *He Came to England* (1933) is subtitled '*A Self-Portrait*'.

Rennell of Rodd. See James Rennell *Rodd.

Repington, Charles À Court (1858-1925). Educated at Eton and Sandhurst. In military service from 1878 to 1902, reaching the rank of Lieutenant Colonel. Then became military correspondent for London newspapers, notably of The *Times* from 1904-18, his articles during World War I causing violent controversy by their forthright and sometimes intemperate criticism of the conduct of operations. Author of *The First World War* (1920), *After the War* (1922).

Repplier, Agnes (1858-1950). Born in Philadelphia; educated at a convent school there. From 1888 to 1937 she published collections of essays, traditional and distinguished in style and familiar in tone. *The Fireside Sphinx* (1901) is among the classics of cat lore, and *To Think of Tea* (1932) is *the* classic for tea-drinkers.

Rest Harrow. Novel by Maurice *Hewlett published in 1910, completing the trilogy begun with *Halfway House* (1908) and continued with *Open Country* (1909). See John *Senhouse.

Review of English Studies, The. See R. B. *McKerrow.

Review of Reviews. See Grant *Richards, W. T. *Stead, and Wickham *Steed.

Reviewing. See *Book Reviews.

Revolt in the Desert. Abridged edition by the author of T. E. Lawrence's *The *Seven Pillars of Wisdom* (1926); published in 1926.

Resurrection men. Critics and others who exhume dead reputations to provide cadavers for literary dissection.

Reynard the Fox; or, The Ghost Heath Run. Narrative poem in rhyming couplets by John *Masefield published in 1919. The grooming of the horses in the stables of The Cock and Pye begins the account of the meet and is followed by brief visual and character sketches of those assembling for the hunt: the parson, the doctor, the squire, the Manor set, farmers, the huntsman, the Master, and many others, young and old, male and female, portrayed with shrewd and deft Chaucer-like touches. Part II describes the run from the fox's angle as well as from that of the riders, the beat of the verse varying to suggest the speed of the horses and the fear and gradual tiring of the fox, who finds the earth he makes for stopped and barred with stakes, compelling him to further prolonged effort to reach a second earth, which is also stopped. Finally, almost dead with exhaustion, he finds refuge in a rabbit hide and the hounds lose him. The poem ends with a quiet coda of moonlight and midnight bells.

Reynolds, Quentin (Quentin James Reynolds, 1902-65). Born in New York; educated at Brown University, Rhode Island; studied law in New York. Became a reporter and foreign correspondent for American papers, and Berlin correspondent for the International News Service. In World War II he gave many heartening talks in England, but also saw the war at first hand in France, Africa, and the Pacific. He was particularly remembered by one B.B.C. broadcast in which he castigated Hitler under the Nazi leader's birth name, Schicklegrüber. His books include *The Wounded Don't Cry* (1940), *London Diary* (1940), *Don't Think It Hasn't Been Fun* (1941), *Only the Stars are Neutral* (1942), *They Fought for the Sky* (1958); also children's books and an autobiography *By Quentin Reynolds* (1964).

Rhead, John. Ironfounder and head of the family in *Milestones* (1912) by Arnold Bennett and Edward Knoblock. Becomes a baronet. **Gertrude,** spinster, is his sister.

Rhode, John (pseudonym of Cecil John Charles Street, 1884-   ). Author of many crime novels with Dr Priestley as the amateur detective: *Dr Priestley's Quest* (1926), *The Murders in Praed Street* (1928), *Poison for One* (1934), *Death on the Boat Train* (1940), *Nothing But the Truth* (1947), *Secret Meeting* (1951), *Grave Matters* (1955). Other books: *The Administration of Ireland* (1921), *Rhineland and Ruhr* (1923), *Hungary and Democracy* (1923), *Lord Reading* (1928).

Rhodes, Cecil John (1853-1902). Born in Hertfordshire, son of the vicar of Bishop's Stortford; educated there and intermittently at Oxford, having to interrupt his education with health visits to South Africa. With his brother and others he acquired a holding in the newly discovered diamond fields and at length had a leading part in establishing the De Beers Company. He sat in the South African Parliament from 1880 and took a major part in political affairs, leading to the expansion of British territory including that region named after him, Rhodesia. He was Prime Minister of the Cape, 1890-96, but resigned after he had been charged with implication in the Jameson Raid. He died in South Africa and was buried in the Matopo Hills. Though his political and financial activities have been severely criticized and often unreservedly condemned, his name is worthily commemorated by his endowment of the Rhodes Scholarships at Oxford which provide a three-year course for well over a hundred students from the U.S. and the British Commonwealth.

Rhodes Scholarships. See Cecil John *Rhodes.

Rhondda, Lady (*née* Margaret Haig Thomas, died 1958; succeeded as 2nd Viscountess Rhondda on the death of her father, the 1st Viscount, in 1918). She founded as a feminist weekly in 1920 *Time and Tide*, which developed into one of the leading English literary and political periodicals under her actual or, later, nominal editorship. It attracted a large number of distinguished women and men as contributors, and an able and enthusiastic staff and board of directors with Lady Rhondda as chairman. She had borne a considerable personal and financial burden in maintaining it, and the paper changed character when it passed into other hands after her death.

Rhymers' Club, The. Founded by W. B. *Yeats and Ernest *Rhys in 1891 with Lionel Johnson, Ernest Dawson, John Davidson, and Richard Le Gallienne among its members. They met at the *Cheshire Cheese to read and criticize one another's poems and to drink wine.

Rhys, Ernest (Ernest Percival Rhys, 1859-1946). Born in London; after experience as a mining engineer in the north of England, settled in London and became acquainted with prominent literary men. After experience as editor of the Camelot Series for a Tyneside publisher he undertook in 1906 the editorship of *Everyman's Library and is chiefly remembered for his fruitful connection with that enterprise.

Rhys, Jean (1894-   ). Born in Dominica, West Indies, daughter of a Welsh doctor and a Creole mother. Until in her middle teens she lived in the Windward Islands, then went to London, studied drama, and did some stage work. While in Paris, encouraged by Ford Madox *Ford, she began to write, and published a book of short stories *The Left Bank* (1927). Her novels—*Voyage in the Dark* (1934), *After Leaving Mr Mackenzie* (1937), *Good Morning, Midnight* (1939)— had no successor until *Wide Sargasso Sea* (1966) brought her back into esteem. *Tigers are Better-Looking* (1968) contains both reprinted and new short stories.

Rhys, Keidrych (1915-   ). Born and educated in Wales. Worked at various times as journalist, farmer, and public relations consultant; served in World War II. Founded and edited the magazine *Wales*. Author of *The Van Pool and Other Poems* (1941), *Angry Prayers* (1952), *The Expatriates*

(1964). Editor of *Poems from the Forces* (1942), *Modern Welsh Poetry* (1945).

Rhythm (1). Often confused with *metre*. While metre is governed by the regular recurrence of accented or stressed syllables, the nature of rhythm is basic in the universe and in human experience: the rhythm of the seasons, the rhythm of the waves, the rhythm of life—in all of which there is constant rhythmical motion and flow but not invariable formally timed recurrence. In literature, free verse is rhythmical; rhetorical or elevated prose may achieve rhythm, but is bad prose if it assumes a metrical beat.

Rhythm (2). An illustrated *avant-garde* quarterly of literature and art founded by J. Middleton *Murry and Michael *Sadleir in 1911, edited by Murry. It opposed aestheticism and proclaimed in words taken from J. M. *Synge that 'before art can be human again it must learn to be brutal', a creed in line with that of *Marinetti and the Futurists. *Rhythm* was the first English periodical to reproduce work by Picasso, and other art contributors included Derain and Augustus John. Katherine *Mansfield began to write in it in the spring number 1912 and became assistant to Murry (in place of Sadleir) when they began to live together. It lost money, was taken over by a small publisher, Stephen Swift, and turned into a monthly. Swift soon decamped, leaving Murry heavily in debt to the printers. *Rhythm* ceased publication with the March 1913 issue, but as the *Blue Review* was resuscitated after a few weeks but survived for only three issues, being finally closed down in July 1913.

Ribbentrop, Joachim Von (1893-1946). From being a wine merchant he became the Nazi Ambassador in Britain in 1936 and Foreign Minister in Germany from 1938, negotiating the pact with Soviet Russia which preluded World War II. Found guilty of war crimes at the Nuremberg trials, he was executed.

Ricardo. Jones's instinctively savage 'secretary' in Joseph Conrad's *Victory* (1915).

Rice, Alice Hegan (*née* Alice Caldwell Hegan, 1870-1942; Mrs Cale Young Rice). Born in Kentucky; educated privately; married Cale Young Rice (see below). She had great popular success with *Mrs Wiggs of the Cabbage Patch* (1901), an optimistically sentimental novel of a run-down widow and her family living in a city tenement; Mrs Wiggs views the world through rose-coloured spectacles and is justified by aid from rich benefactors. Other novels: *Lovey Mary* (1903), *A Romance of Billy Goat Hill* (1912); tales in collaboration with her husband. Autobiographical: *The Inky Way* (1940), *Happiness Road* (1942).

Rice, Cale Young (1872-1943). Born in Kentucky; educated in Indiana and at Harvard, married in 1902 Alice Caldwell Hegan (see preceding entry) and collaborated with her in *Turn About Tales* (1920), *Winners and Losers* (1925), *Passionate Follies* (1936). He wrote much verse and verse-drama: *Collected Plays and Poems* (1915) was added to by later volumes.

Rice, D. Talbot (David Talbot Rice, 1903-1972). Educated at Eton and Oxford. Concentrated on the study of Byzantine and Islamic art by repeated visits to their countries of origin and joined archaeological expeditions in Constantinopole and elsewhere in the Middle East. Author of *Byzantine Art* (1935), *The Icons of Cyprus* (1937), *The Background of Art* (1939), *The Beginnings of Christian Art* (1957), *Byzantine Icons* (1960).

Rice, Elmer (*born* Elmer Lion Reizenstein, 1892-1967). Born in New York; educated at high school there and later studied law, but did not practise. His first play, *Murder Trial* (1914), was immediately accepted and he went on to become one of the leading American playwrights with *The *Adding Machine* (1923) and **Street Scene* (1929). Other serious plays include *We, The People* (1933), *Judgment Day* (1934), *American Landscape* (1938), *A New Life* (1943). In addition he wrote lighter plays: *See Naples and Die* (1929), *The Left Bank* (1931), *Counsellor-at-Law* (1931), *Dream Girl* (1946); and several novels: *A Voyage to Purilia* (a satire on Hollywood; 1930), *Imperial City* (life in New York; 1937), *The Show Must Go On* (1949).

Riceyman Steps. Novel by Arnold *Bennett published in 1923. Formerly an insurance clerk, Henry Earlforward inherits his uncle T. T. Riceyman's secondhand bookshop, which has attached its name to the short stone-stepped passage in Clerkenwell where the shop stands. Opposite is widowed Mrs Violet Arb's 'general shop', recently acquired. She and the unmarried bookseller, both middle-aged, come into personal contact when she sends Elsie, their charwoman, across for a cookery book. Mrs Arb having declined to pay more than sixpence for the book he prices at a shilling, Earlforward makes it a gift and thus establishes a friendship which leads to their marriage. Earlforward, a relentless miser known locally as 'old skinflint', confines their honeymoon to a visit to Madame Tussauds, and as wedding present gives Violet a secondhand safe. As her present to Henry she engages a vacuum-cleaning firm to rid his house (now their home) of years of dirt and dust harboured by books piled on furniture and stairs, scattered on floors, and filling the bath. Elsie is engaged as general servant at £20 a year and is a loyal and tireless 'treasure', though, being stinted of food, hunger forces her to steal cheese and scraps of uncooked bacon. Undernourished, both Violet and Henry fall ill; she dies in hospital after an operation. Henry, confined to bed at home, is tended by Elsie, who also nurses Joe, her homeless young man, whom she has smuggled into the house while he is suffering from malaria. After Earlforward's death, Elsie and Joe marry: he becomes man-servant and she cook-general in the household of the local doctor.

Richards, Frank (pseudonym of Charles Hamilton, 1875-1961). Author of many hundreds of school stories published in periodicals from the 1890s, chiefly in the *Gem* (1907-39) and the *Magnet* (1908-40), with Billy Bunter, Tom Merry and others among characters perenially popular with boys and afterwards with radio and television audiences. From 1947 the stories had a renewed vogue in volume form as a series beginning with *Billy Bunter of Greyfriars School. The Autobiography of Frank Richards* (1952) lists other pseudonyms under which he wrote: Martin Clifford, Owen Conquest, Ralph Redway, Hilda Richards. His earliest stories were written under his birth name.

Richards, Grant (Franklin Thomas Grant Richards, 1872-1948). Educated at the City of London School; when fifteen went to work in a publishing firm and then with W. T. *Stead on the *Review of Reviews*. He started his own firm at the beginning of 1897 and in the following years published books by since-famous authors, including the earliest plays of Bernard *Shaw and the first edition of *The *Way of All Flesh* by Samuel Butler. Richards's own books include novels

—*Caviare* (1912), *Bittersweet* (1915), *Every Wife* (1824), *Vain Pursuit* (1931); a guide to the Riviera—*The Coast of Pleasure* (1928); reminiscences—*Memories of a Misspent Youth* (1932), *Author Hunting* (1934), *A. E. Housman, 1897-1936* (1941).

Richards, Hilda. See Frank *Richards.

Richards, I. A. (Ivor Armstrong Richards, 1893-   ). Born in Cheshire; educated at Clifton and Cambridge. Held university appointments at Cambridge, in China at Peking, and from 1914 in America at Harvard. His teaching, mainly concerned with the relationship of psychology and literature and the science of meaning, encouraged the growth of textual analysis as a leading academic discipline in literary study, at the cost of some diminishing of the more humane enjoyment of literature. With C. K. *Ogden he devised *Basic English, and in collaboration they wrote *The Meaning of Meaning* (1923). Richards's own writings are, chiefly, *Principles of Literary Criticism* (1924), *Science and Poetry* (1925), *Practical Criticism* (1929), *How to Read a Page* (1942); *Goodbye Earth and Other Poems* (1958), *The Screens and Other Poems* (1960).

Richardson, Dorothy M. (Dorothy Miller Richardson, 1873-1957; Mrs Alan Odle). Born in Abingdon, Berkshire; educated at day schools; worked as a teacher and as a clerk. She has repeatedly been referred to by other writers as an important innovator in the history of the modern English novel; yet her work has received only limited attention from critics and scarcely any from the general reader. Though she was scornful of the term 'stream of consciousness' as applied to her method, and little less so of 'interior monologue', the terms have continued to be used of her twelve-volume novel, *Pilgrimage,* devoted to what may best be called the life-in-the-mind of Miriam Henderson. The narrative throughout resembles a wide plain in which events are no more than slight undulations. This almost featureless literary landscape is a remarkable feat of cerebral rather than of imaginative creation, though it is in its way compelling and more deserving of tolerant and patient contemplation than of impulsive and impatient rejection. The separately published volumes appeared as *Pointed Roofs* (1915), *Backwater* (1916), *Honeycomb* (1917), *The Tunnel* (1919), *Interim* (1919), *Deadlock*

(1921), *Revolving Lights* (1923), *The Trap* (1925), *Oberland* (1927), *Dawn's Left Hand* (1931), *Clear Horizon* (1935), *Dimple Hill* (1938, as part of the whole in a single volume). Other writings include *The Quakers, Past and Present* (1914).

Richardson, Henry Handel (pseudonym of Ethel Florence Lindesay Richardson, 1870-1946). Born in Australia at Melbourne and educated there until she went to Germany to study music in Leipzig, where she met John G. *Robertson who became her husband. She read much in the literature of European countries and regarded Flaubert as chief mentor in the formation of the impersonal prose style of her novels: *Maurice Guest* (1908), *The Getting of Wisdom* (1910), *The Young Cosima* (1939). After her marriage she lived in Strasbourg until 1904 and then settled in England, only once visiting Australia to authenticate material for the first volume of the trilogy upon which her reputation as a novelist is mainly based: *Australia Felix* (1917), *The Way Home* (1925), *Ultima Thule* (1929). Republished in one volume as *The *Fortunes of Richard Mahony* (1930), it led to her being regarded at that time as the most accomplished of Australian-born novelists.

Richmond, Sir Bruce (Bruce Lyttleton Richmond, 1871-1964; knighted 1935). Born in Kensington; educated at Winchester and Oxford. Qualified as a barrister before becoming an assistant editor on *The Times* 1899 until he was appointed Editor of *The Times Literary Supplement* soon after its first appearance in 1902. Although he did not write for it himself, the high standards he set and the eminence and authority of those he engaged as willing contributors of reviews and articles quickly established the *Supplement* among the foremost critical journals. He retired from *The Times* in 1937.

Richthofen, Frieda Von (1879-1956). Sister of Manfred, Baron von Richthofen (1882-1918), famous German airman in World War I. She married Professor Ernest *Weekley, who divorced her when an association developed between her and D. H. *Lawrence. She and Lawrence married in 1914 and as Frieda Lawrence her name became virtually inseparable from his in the many books written about him. Though frequently tempestuous, their mutual devotion lasted until his death in 1930. His poems, *Look! We Have Come Through* (1917), and (in part) the novels *Women in Love* (1920) and *Kangaroo* (1923) suggest the trials and triumphs of their relationship. In *Not I, But the Wind* (1934) she detailed her reminiscences of Lawrence.

Ricketts, Charles (Charles de Sousy Ricketts, 1866-1931). Born in Geneva; educated in France. Founded the famous Vale Press (1896-1904) which published finely printed books which he designed and illustrated. With Charles *Shannon he edited *The Dial* (1889-97). He was painter, printer, book-illustrator, wood-engraver and stage-designer. Among the plays for which he designed scenery and costumes were Bernard Shaw's *The *Dark Lady of the Sonnets* (1910) and *Saint Joan* (1923), Oscar Wilde's *Salome* (1906), Shakespeare's *Henry VIII* (1925), and a new D'Oyly Carte production of *The Mikado*. His writings included *The Prado and its Masterpieces* (1903), *Titian* (1910), *Pages on Art* (1913); published posthumously: *Recollections of Oscar Wilde* (1932), *Unrecorded Histories* (1933), *Self-Portrait* (selected from his letters and journals; 1939).

Rickie. *See* Frederick *Elliot.

Riddle of the Sands, The: A Record of Secret Service. Novel by Erskine Childers published in 1903. Carruthers, a young man with 'a safe, possibly a brilliant, future in the Foreign Office', unexpectedly kept on duty in London in September while all his friends are away, receives a letter from a former Oxford acquaintance, Arthur H. Davies, written from the yacht *Dulcibella* at Flensburg, Schleswig-Holstein. It invites him for a spell of cruising and duck shooting in the Baltic. Carruthers wires his acceptance, and at the end of the month meets Davies at Flensburg and they go aboard the *Dulcibella*. Carruthers has to accustom himself to cramped quarters, for the yacht is a converted lifeboat, unlovely but businesslike and solid, flat-bottomed and drawing little water, but with a keel-plate which can be lowered in deep water, enabling the *Dulcibella* to go practically anywhere. Davies slowly admits that duck shooting is only a pretence. He has been cruising among the sandbanks behind the string of German Frisian Islands covering the mouths of the rivers Ems, Jade, and Weser, and has struck up an acquaintance with Dallmann, the owner of a smart

German sailing-yacht, the *Medusa*, on which he also meets and is attracted by Fraulein Dollmann, the owner's daughter. Dollmann undertakes to lead the *Dulcibella* on a short cut through the sands, but outsails the English boat, which runs aground and is nearly wrecked. Davies is sure that Dollmann intended to drown him as an intruder among the sands; and he and Carruthers, having discovered that Dollmann is English and a former officer in the Royal Navy, determine to expose him as a spy and frustrate whatever he may be plotting. The story follows their exciting and dangerous adventures, leading to a climax which (at that date) offered a warning for those responsible for the defence of England.

Riders to the Sea. Play in one act by J. M. *Synge performed in 1904; published in 1905. In a fisherman's cottage kitchen on 'An island off the West Coast of Ireland', Cathleen, a girl of about twenty, and her younger sister Nora are about to examine a bundle containing a shirt and a stocking taken from the body of a drowned man washed ashore far away in Donegal. Their old mother, Maurya, constantly lamenting the loss at sea of her son, Michael, as well as the earlier drowning of her husband and four other sons, watches by the shore for Michael's body. The sisters have no time to open the bundle for identification before they hear their mother returning. They hide it in the turf-loft. The last remaining son, Bartley, sets out to go by boat to Connemara, taking a red mare and a grey pony to the horse fair. He passes his mother while she is at the spring well, and she returns to the cottage keening and declaring that when she looked at the grey pony as it went by 'there was Michael upon it—with fine clothes on him and new shoes on his feet'. Her daughters convince her that Michael is dead by showing her the bundle of clothes which they have meanwhile identified. A group of mourning women comes with the news that Bartley has been knocked over into the sea by the grey pony and 'washed out where there is a great surf on the white rocks'. Maurya's years of lamentation are complete: 'They're all gone now, and there isn't anything more the sea can do to me.... No man at all can be living for ever, and we must be satisfied.'

Ridge, Pett (William Pett Ridge, 1857-1930). Born near Canterbury; educated in Kent and

London. Entered the Civil Service, then turned to writing as journalist and novelist. He took chief pleasure in wandering about the East-End of London, equipping himself to produce the mainly humorous stories of cockney life for which he was celebrated: *Mord Em'ly* (1898), *'Erb* (1903), *Mrs Galer's Business* (1905), *Name of Garland* (1907), *Nine to Six-Thirty* (1910), *Love at Paddington* (1912), *Rare Luck* (1924), *Affectionate Regards* (1929). Autobiographical: *A Story-Teller's Forty Years in London* (1923), *I Like to Remember* (1924).

Riding, Laura (*née* Laura Reichenthal, 1901-). Born in New York of American-Austrian descent; educated in Brooklyn and at Cornell University. Lived in England and on the Continent from 1925 to 1939, during which she wrote *A Survey of Modernistic Poetry* (1927), *A Pamphlet Against Anthologies* (1928), both in collaboration with Robert *Graves. Her *Collected Poems* were published in 1938, *Lives of Wives* (1939). She returned to America in 1939 and from 1941, when she married Schuyler Jackson, worked with him to produce a dictionary on original lines.

Ridler, Anne (*née* Anne Barbara Bradby, 1912-). Born at Rugby; educated at Downe House School and in London at King's College; married in 1938 Vivian Ridler, Printer to the University of Oxford from 1958. Author of several collections of verse: *Poems* (1939), *The Nine Bright Shiners* (1943), *A Matter of Life and Death* (1959); plays: *Cain* (1943), *The Shadow Factory* (1946), *The Trial of Thomas Cranmer* (1956).

Ridley, M. R. (Maurice Roy Ridley, 1890-1969). Born in Wiltshire; educated at Clifton and Oxford. Master at Clifton 1914-20; tutor in English Literature, Balliol College, Oxford, 1920-45; lecturer, Bedford College, London, from 1948. Author of *Poetry and the Ordinary Reader* (1930), *Keats's Craftsmanship* (1933), *Gertrude Bell* (1941), *Abraham Lincoln* (1944), *Studies in Three Literatures* (1961). Editor of the New Temple Shakespeare (1934-36), of *Antony and Cleopatra* and *Othello* (1953; 1957) in the New Arden edition, and of other classics.

R.I.I.A. See *Royal Institute of International Affairs.

Riley, James Whitcomb (1849-1916). Born in Indiana. After working as a sign-writer, and as play-cobbler with a company of itinerant actors, he joined the *Indianapolis Journal* from 1877 to 1885, contributing verses in the *Hoosier dialect which, with later poems, gained him wide popularity. He gave public readings of his poetry, which was invariably homely in sentiment and style. A 'biographical edition' of *The Complete Works of James Whitcomb Riley* was published in 1913.

Rilke, Rainer Maria (1875-1926). Born in Prague of Austrian parentage; educated in Prague, Munich and Berlin, after withdrawing from a military academy owing to illness. In 1905 he was for a while resident secretary to the French sculptor Auguste Rodin, one of whose pupils he married. He became internationally famous towards the end of his life and after, for poems recording his spiritual struggles and meditations on death and Man's relation to God. The mystical nature of his poetry and its pervading *angst* were found compatible with the prevailing spirit of the 1930s onward, when his writings were translated into English: *The Notebook of Malte Laurids Brigge* (1930), *Duino Elegies* (1948), *Sonnets to Orpheus* (1949), etc.

Rima. Name, shortened from Riolama, of the ethereal forest girl in W. H. Hudson's *Green Mansions* (1904). Epstein's representation of her on the Hudson memorial in Hyde Park, London, aroused controversy, being regarded by objectors as foreign to Hudson's description.

Rimbaud, Arthur (Jean Nicholas Arthur Rimbaud, 1854-1891). Born at Charleville. His education at the College de Charleville was ended when he ran away to Paris and was briefly jailed for travelling without a ticket. Sent home he twice ran away again, and became a prototype 'defiant, unruly adolescent', though he read voraciously, wrote poetry, and was invited to Paris by Verlaine with whom he formed a homosexual relationship. In 1872 they were in London for a short time. Rimbaud made attempts to break away from their dissolute life, and during a quarrel in Brussels in 1873 he was shot and wounded by Verlaine, who was imprisoned for two years. For the rest of his life Rimbaud was a vagabond, wandering in England, Germany, Italy, the Dutch East Indies, and the interior of Africa. A few months before his death, a diseased knee led to the amputation of a leg, and he died in hospital at Marseilles. In 1873 he published at his own expense *Une Saison en enfer*, a miscellany of snatches of verse and prose in which Rimbaud probes agonizingly his states of mind and soul. It attracted little attention then; but as author of that and *Les Illuminations* (1886), Rimbaud has since become one of the high-priests of the *Symbolist movement in poetry, with a powerful hold on writers, English as well as others, in the present century.

Rinehart, Mary Roberts (*née* Mary Roberts, 1876-1958; Mrs S. M. Rinehart). Born in Pittsburg; trained there as a nurse. A financial crisis several years after her marriage led her to write and her first stories were immediately accepted. From 1908, with *The Circular Staircase*, she became one of America's leading mystery novel writers; other books in that kind include *The Man in Lower Ten* (1909), *The Window at the White Cat* (1910), *The Breaking Point* (1922), *The State Versus Elinor Morton* (1934), *Haunted Lady* (1942). She also wrote humorous novels, *Tish* (1916), *More Tish* (1922), and others.

Riposte, A. See Elinor *Mordaunt.

Rita (pseudonym of Eliza Margaret Gollan, died 1938; Mrs W. D. Humphreys). Born in Scotland; taken to Australia while a child and educated in Sydney; returned to England in her early teens. Author of many romantic novels, some of which were regarded as excessively outspoken, though now considered insipid. In the present century she published *A Jilt's Journal* (1901), *Souls* (1903; her chief success), *Diana of the Ephesians* (1919), *The Great 'Perhaps'* (1926), among others. *Recollections of a Literary Life* (1936).

Rita, Doña. Inherits Henry Allègre's fortune in Joseph Conrad's *The *Arrow of Gold* (1919) and becomes a supporter of the Carlists and friend and lover of Monsieur George.

Ritchie, Lady (*née* Anne Isabella Thackeray, 1837-1919). Born in London, daughter of the Victorian novelist, William Makepeace Thackeray; married her cousin, an India Office Secretary who was knighted in 1907 as Sir Richmond Thackeray Ritchie. She wrote several novels which have continuing interest as period pieces: *The Story of Elizabeth* (1863), *The Village on the Cliff*

(1867) and, particularly, *Old Kensington* (1873). She also wrote reminiscences of the many eminent men she knew in her father's circle.

Ritchie, Sir Lewis (1886-1967). See Bartimeus.

Rivers. See *Isabel Rivers.

Rives, Amélie (1863-1945). Born in Virginia; educated privately; married, as her second husband, Prince Troubetzkoy. Author of *The Quick or the Dead* (1888), *The Golden Rose* (1908), *World's End* (1914), *Firedamp* (1930) and other novels; *Augustine the Man* (1906) and other verse plays; and poems, including *As the Wind Blew* (1922).

Rivett, Edith Caroline. See E. C. R. *Lorac.

Roberta Alden. Clyde Griffiths's victim in Theodore Dreiser's *An *American Tragedy* (1925).

Roberts, Carl Eric Bechhofer. See *Ephesian.

Roberts, Cecil (Cecil Edric Mornington Roberts, 1892-   ). Educated at Mundella Grammar School. Literary Editor, *Liverpool Post*, 1915-18; Editor, *Nottingham Journal*, 1920-25. Various official wartime posts. Author of many publications—poems, novels, plays, country books, etc.—among them *Poems* (1918); *Scissors* (1922), *Little Mrs Manington* (1926), *Victoria Four-Thirty* (1937); *Spears Against Us* (1939); *Pilgrim Cottage* (1933), *Gone Rustic* (1934); *And So to Bath* (1940), *And So to America* (1946), *And So to Rome* (1950).

Roberts, C. D. G. (Sir Charles George Douglas Roberts, 1860-1943; knighted 1935). Born at Douglas, New Brunswick; educated at the University there. Professor of English and French Literature, and of English and Economics, King's College, Nova Scotia, 1885-95. Though he wrote poetry—*Songs of the Common Day* (1893), *The Sweet o' the Year* (1925); and novels—*The Forge in the Forest* (1896), *The Backwoodsmen* (1909), *Lovers in Arcadie* (1924), he was best-known by his books on animal life—*The Heart of the Ancient Wood* (1900), *The Watchers of the Trails* (1904), *Red Fox* (1905), *Haunters of the Silences* (1907), *Eyes of the Wilderness* (1933).

Roberts, David. Strike-leader in John Galsworthy's *Strife* (1909). He refuses to compromise, but the strike is settled against his fanatical urging, after his wife's death due to privation.

Roberts, Elizabeth Madox (1886-1941). Born in Kentucky; educated at the University of Chicago. Author of poems—*Under the Tree* (1922), *Song in the Meadow* (1940); short stories—*The Haunted Mirror* (1932), *Not by Strange Gods* (1941); but her considerable reputation was built on novels in Kentucky settings—*The Time of Man* (1926), *My Heart and My Flesh* (1927), *The Great Meadow* (1930).

Roberts, Kenneth (Kenneth Lewis Roberts, 1885-1957). Born in Maine; educated at Cornell University. Worked on *Boston Post*, *Saturday Evening Post*, and other papers from 1909 to 1928. Author of *Arundel* (1930), *Rabble in Arms* (1933), *North-West Passage* (1937), *Lydia Bailey* (1947) and other novels; non-fiction—*I Wanted to Write* (1949), etc.

Roberts, Michael (1902-1948). Educated at Bournemouth, London, and Cambridge. Worked as a science teacher in Newcastle and then became Principal of the College of St Mark and St John, Chelsea, from 1945. Married Janet *Adam Smith. Author of *A Critique of Poetry* (1934). *Newton and the Origin of Colours* (1934), *The Modern Mind* (1937), *T. E. Hulme* (1938), *The Recovery of the West* (1941); books of verse—*Poems* (1936), *Orion Marches* (1939).

Roberts, Morley (1857-1942). Born in London; educated at Bedford School and Owen's School, Manchester. He worked in Australia on railway construction and on sheep and cattle ranches, at sea as a foremast hand, and on various projects in north America, Africa and the South Seas. Author of *The Western Avernus* (1887)—a record of solitary travel in North America, often in conditions of great hardship; *The Private Life of Henry Maitland* (1912)—a thinly veiled biography of his friend George *Gissing; *W. H. *Hudson, a Portrait* (1924). Among his many novels and short stories, which made no permanent mark, the best are *Rachel Marr* (1903), *The Man Who Stroked Cats* (1912), *Time and Thomas Waring* (1914).

Roberts, S. C. (Sir Sydney Castle Roberts, 1887-1966; knighted 1958). Born at Birkenhead; educated at Brighton College and Cambridge. Secretary, Cambridge University Press, 1922-48. Master of Pembroke College, Cambridge, 1948-58. His principal literary interests were in Dr Samuel Johnson and Sherlock Holmes. Author of *The Story of Doctor Johnson* (1919), *Samuel Johnson, Writer* (1927), *Doctor Watson* (1931), *Holmes and Watson* (1953).

Robertson, E. Arnot (Eileen Arnot Robertson; Mrs, later Lady, H. E. Turner, 1903-1961). Educated in Paris and Switzerland. Her first novel *Cullum* (1928) achieved success continued by, principally, *Three Came Unarmed* (1929), *Four Frightened People* (1931), and *Ordinary Families* (1933). She provided the text for *Thames Portrait* (1937), illustrated with photographs by her husband. In later years she wrote much film criticism, the vigour and independence of her judgments leading her into controversy and a lawsuit with a prominent film company. Though the final House of Lords verdict went against her in a libel action she brought against the company, public sympathy supported her in a fund raised to reimburse the heavy costs she had to bear.

Robertson, Forbes (Sir Johnston Forbes-Robertson, 1853-1937; knighted 1913). Born in London; educated at Charterhouse, at Rouen, and in London at the Royal Academy of Arts; went on the stage when twenty-one and in 1882 joined Henry Irving's Company. Three years later he made his first venture as actor-manager at the Lyceum, where he produced and played the leading part in *Hamlet*, being rated as the finest Hamlet of his time. He created the parts of Dick Dudgeon in Bernard Shaw's *The *Devil's Disciple* and of Caesar in Shaw's *Caesar and Cleopatra*, both in 1907; among his other notable parts were The Stranger in Jerome K. *Jerome's *The Passing of the Third Floor Back* (1908). He was an actor of great refinement and intellect, with a gracious presence and noble bearing. Autobiography: *A Player Under Three Reigns* (1925).

Robertson, J. G. (John George Robertson, 1867-1933). Educated at Glasgow and Leipzig Universities. Lecturer in English, Strasbourg University, 1896-1903; Professor of German Language and Literature, University of London, from 1903. Married Ethel Florence Lindesay Richardson, novelist, who wrote as Henry Handel *Richardson. Robertson was the author of *A History of German Literature* (1902), *Goethe and the Twentieth Century* (1912),

The Genesis of Romantic Literary Theory (1923), *Goethe and Byron* (1925), *Goethe* (1927; enlarged edn 1932).

Robertson, J. M. (John Mackinnon Robertson, 1856-1933). Born in Scotland on the Isle of Arran; educated at Stirling. Leader writer on the *Edinburgh Evening News*, 1878-84; then worked in London journalism. Liberal M.P. for Tyneside; a Minister in the Liberal government, 1911-15. Wrote several books on Shakespeare and others on Free Trade and Free Thought.

Robertson, W. Graham (Walford Graham Robertson, 1866-1948). Trained as an artist and illustrated many books. Author of the popular children's play, *Pinkie and the Fairies* (1908), and other stage pieces. His 'book of memories' *Time Was* (1931) is evocative of a vanished age.

Robertson Scott, J. W. *See* J. W. Robertson *Scott.

Robertson-Glasgow, R. C. (Raymond Charles Robertson-Glasgow, 1901-1965). Educated at Hindhead, Charterhouse, and Oxford. Played cricket for Oxford and Somerset, and after a period of teaching at his old school (St Edmund's, Hindhead) became cricket correspondent on London daily and weekly papers. Author of *The Brighter Side of Cricket* (1933), *Rain Stopped Play* (1948), *All in the Game* (1952). Autobiography: *46 Not Out* (1948).

Robins, Elizabeth (1855-1936). Married Joseph *Pennell and was his collaborator in various publications. Her own books included *The Feasts of Autolycus* (1896). *The Lovers* (1917), *The Life and Letters of Joseph Pennell* (2 vols, 1929), *Whistler the Friend* (1930).

Robins, Elizabeth (1862-1952). Born in Kentucky; educated in Ohio, She went on the stage at sixteen, and after touring extensively in the U.S. went with a company to Norway, where her interest was aroused in *Ibsen and his works. In 1889 she moved to London and through the next decade achieved fame as an intelligent and skilful actress in several English versions of Ibsen's plays before finally retiring from the stage in 1902. She had already written *George Mandeville's Husband* (1894), *The Open Question: A Tale of Two Temperaments* (1898), and other novels, adopting for those the pseudonym C. E. Raimond, derived

from the name of her brother Raymond. Journeying in search of him while he was in the Klondike, she acquired knowledge and experience employed with imaginative insight and masculine vigour in *The Magnetic North* (1904) and *Come and Find Me* (1908), novels which were for some time supposed to be written by a man. She settled in England, supported the women's suffrage movement, and in its aid wrote her play *Votes for Women* (1905). Her later novels included *The Florentine Frame* (1909), *My Little Sister* (1913), *Camilla* (1918), *Time is Whispering* (1923), *The Secret That Was Kept* (1926). Her early years in London led to the letters from Henry *James she published in *Theatre and Friendship* (1932). This, together with *Ibsen and the Actress* (1928), *Both Sides of the Curtain* (1940), and *Raymond and I* (posthumously, 1956), show the several aspects of a remarkable personality.

Robinson, Edwin Arlington (1869-1935). Born in Maine; educated there and at Harvard. From 1896 to 1909 he was variously employed in New York, for the last few years in the Custom House, to which he had been appointed after President Theodore Roosevelt had been impressed by the poems of Robinson, who was regarded as the outstanding modern American poet during the last twenty-five years of his life. He was at his best when he departed most from the English models who had influenced him strongly, though his character studies in the manner of Browning's dramatic monologues are among the poems which created the main contemporary interest in his work. In one of the most ambitious of these, *Captain Craig* (1902), he widens the scope of the monologue by incorporating verse-letters, ballads, and sonnets. Robinson's outlook on the world of his time was sombre and frequently satirical, and such humour as seeps in is for the most part sardonic. The charge of obscurity brought against him would not of itself have lost him favour with the new generation of critics if the approved symbolism were not encased in the impermeable solidity and bulk of his total output. Whatever 'modern' quality his mind possessed, it was nevertheless rooted in the old New England traditions of puritan metaphysics and transcendental hope: dominated by a 'sense of the tragedy of human life in a chaotic world', yet with an 'unfaltering mystic faith in a "glimmer" of 'light beyond'. Interest in earlier times was displayed in *Ben Jonson Entertains a Man from Stratford* (1916) and in the Arthurian trilogy: *Merlin* (1917), *Lancelot* (1920), *Tristram* (1927). His most popular piece was 'Miniver Cheevy' (in *Town Down the River*, 1910) whose mind dwelt overmuch on past times; he was 'born too late . . . called it fate, and kept on drinking'. Robinson's *Collected Poems* appeared in successive editions from 1921 to 1937.

Robinson, Lennox (Esmé Stuart Lennox Robinson, 1886-1958). Born in County Cork; educated at Bandon Grammar School. Manager of the *Abbey Theatre, Dublin (1910-14; 1919-23), where his first play (in one act) *The Clancy Name* was produced in 1908. Among his full-length plays *The Lost Leader* (1918) and *The Whiteheaded Boy* (1920) are outstanding. Other plays: *Crabbed Youth and Age* (1922), *The Round Table* (1922), *The White Blackbird* (1925), *The Far-Off Hills* (1931). Non-dramatic writings: *Towards an Appreciation of the Theatre* (1945), *Ireland's Abbey Theatre* (1951); *A Young Man from the South* (novel; 1917); *Eight Short Stories* (1919). Autobiography: *Three Homes* (1938), *Curtain Up* (1941). Edited *The Golden Treasury of Irish Verse* (1925), *Lady Gregory's Journals* (1946), and with D. *MacDonagh *The Oxford Book of Irish Verse* (1958).

Robinson, Rev. T. H. (Theodore Henry Robinson, 1881-1964). Born in Kent; educated at Mill Hill and Cambridge; biblical studies at Regent's Park College and the University of Gottingen. Professor of Hebrew and Syriac, Serampore College, Bengal, 1908-15; Lecturer in Semitic Languages, University College, Cardiff, 1915-27, and Professor there, 1927-44. He had an international reputation as an Old Testament scholar, publishing important textbooks for students, founding the Society for Old Testament Study in 1917, and taking a leading part from 1946 in connection with the New English Bible. In addition to linguistic and biblical studies for scholars, he wrote *The Decline and Fall of the Hebrew Kingdoms* (1926), *An Outline Introduction to the History of Religions* (1926), *The Poetry of the Old Testament* (1947).

Rococo. *See* Baroque, of which it is a later, extreme and sometimes fantasticated form, swirling and grotesque. In decorative art the rococo style prevailed in France in the mid-eighteenth century; in recent literature the term might be applied to Edith Sitwell's *Façade* (1922), Elinor *Wylie's novels, *Jennifer Lorn* (1923) and *The Venetian Glass Nephew* (1925), and Christopher *Fry's *Ring Round the Moon* (1950; from the French of Jean Anouilh).

Rodd, James Rennell (1858-1941; 1st Baron Rennell of Rodd, 1933). Born in London; educated at Haileybury and Oxford; entered the Diplomatic Service and became British Ambassador in Rome, 1908-19. Conservative M.P. for St Marylebone, 1928-32. Author of *Poems in Many Lands* (1883), *The Unknown Madonna* (1888), *The Violet Crown* (1891), *Ballads of the Fleet* (1897), *Love, Worship, and Death; Some Renderings from the Greek Anthology* (1916). Prose works: *The Customs and Lore of Modern Greece* (1892), *Sir Walter Raleigh* (1889), *Homer's Ithaca* (1927), *Rome of the Renaissance and Today* (1932). *Social and Diplomatic Memoirs* (3 series, 1922, 1923, 1926).

Rodgers, W. R. (William Robert Rodgers, 1909-1969). Born in Belfast; educated at Queen's University there. Entered the presbyterian ministry and served Loughall Church, Armagh, of that denomination from 1934-46; then was producer and script-writer for the B.B.C. until 1952. His poetry received considerable attention even from critics who judged it without enthusiasm: *Awake, and Other Poems* (1941), *Europa and the Bull* (1952).

Roethke, Theodore (1908-1963). Born in Saginaw, Michigan; educated at Michigan and Harvard. Professor of English at the University of Washington from 1948. Author of *Open House* (1941), *Words for the Winds* (1957), and other volumes of poems.

Rogers, Will (William Penn Adair Rogers, 1879-1935). Born in Oklahoma of part American-Indian descent; educated at school and military academy in Missouri; travelled around the world and joined a Wild West show in Australia and later in the U.S. His act in this developed into a popular vaudeville turn in which he combined the reciting of humorous monologues with the manipulation of a lasso. Then, by way of revues, the Ziegfeld Follies, films, and syndicated columns in newspapers, he developed into a national hero and living legend—a pioneer of the mass idols who were to proliferate in the *'pop culture' age after World War II. His humour was of the kind which does not survive vigorously in print: *What We Laugh At* (1920), *The Illiterate Digest* (1924), *Letters of a Self-Made Diplomat to His President* (1927), *Rogers's Political Follies* (1929). His death in an air crash led to sentimental excesses of grief but also to hospital and library foundations from popular subscriptions in memory of him.

Rohmer, Sax (pseudonym of Arthur Sarsfield Ward, 1883-1959). Born in Birmingham of Irish parentage. In early years he became fascinated by Egyptian history and later by the Far East and occult beliefs. Unproductive forays into office work and routine journalism preceded success as a writer of oriental mystery stories centring on Fu Manchu, a resourcefully sinister villain: *Dr Fu Manchu* (1913), *The Yellow Claw* (1915), *The Quest of the Sacred Slipper* (1919), *Yellow Shadows* (1925), *Fu Manchu's Bride* (1932), *The Drums of Fu Manchu* (1939).

Rolfe, Frederick William. *See* Baron *Corvo.

Rolland, Romain (1866-1944). Born in Burgundy; educated in Paris and Rome. Became Professor of the History of Art at the École Normale Supérieure and then of the History of Music at the Sorbonne. The best-known of his voluminous writings is the novel *Jean-Christophe* (10 vols, 1906-12), covering the life of a musical genius from birth to death. Among his other works are *Michelangelo* (1915), *Handel* (1916), *Gandhi* (1924), *Beethoven the Creator* (1929), *Goethe and Beethoven* (1931).

Rølvaag, Ole Edvart (1876-1931). Born in Norway of a seafaring family. Migrated to America; was educated there and later in Norway at the University of Oslo. He became an American citizen in 1908 and was Professor of Norwegian at St Olaf College, Minnesota, from 1907. He wrote all his published works in Norwegian, but his novels were well received in English translations, the most successful being *Giants in the Earth* (1924-25; trans. 1927), a grim story of the hardships endured in the 1870s by Norwegian settlers in the U.S.

This first part of a trilogy was continued and completed in *Peder Victorious* (1923; 1929) and *Their Fathers' God* (1931).

Romains, Jules (pseudonym of Louis Farigoule, 1885-1972). Born in a Cevennes village; brought up in Paris and educated there. He had a leading part in founding *Unanimisme*, a movement started around 1908-10 by a group of young writers committed to the principle of universal brotherhood and the development of a communal identity in which the individual willingly merges. From his large output of fiction and drama, the immense *Men of Goodwill* (27 volumes in the French original, 1932-47) became best known in England through translations by Gerard W. S. Hopkins.

Röntgen, Wilhelm Konrad von (1845-1923). Born in Prussia; educated in Switzerland. He held professional appointments in physics at German universities, his researches on electricity and magnetism while at Würzburg leading to the discovery of X Rays (or Röntgen-rays) in 1895, indispensable in modern medicine and surgery and for many industrial purposes.

Room at the Top. Novel by John *Braine published in 1957. Born in Yorkshire in 1921 and educated at the grammar school at Dufton, Joe Lampton becomes a junior clerk in the local Council offices. Finding 'Dead Dufton' 'a bit too sordid', he moves to Warley as an audit clerk at the Town Hall, lodging with a schoolmaster and his wife, the Thompsons, who treat him as a son, in place of their own boy, killed in an air accident. While in a Market Square café, he sees outside in an expensive car a young man and a girl of a social class much above his own, is filled with envious hatred, and determines that he will somehow gain money enough 'to enjoy all the luxuries which that young man enjoyed'. Through the Thompsons he joins the Warley dramatic society, and at a performance falls in love at first sight with Susan Brown, the young daughter of the wealthy owner of an engineering works. On the advice of Alice Aisgill, a married member of the dramatic society and a former repertory actress, who is impatient of Lampton's over-obvious sense of social inferiority, he telephones Susan and invites her to the ballet. He meets her again at a friend's birthday party and finds that she is in love with him. Meanwhile a rapturous affair has developed between Lampton and Alice Aisgill. Susan's parents let it be made known to him in a roundabout way that they object to her meeting him, but he continues to take her out until she learns of his continuing affair with Alice, whom he then decides to marry when she is divorced, though his friend Charles tries to convince him of the folly of taking a woman ten years older than himself. Charles persuades him to write to Susan, whom he promises to tell Alice that their association must end, but not until Alice comes out of hospital after an operation. This delay causes Susan to rage at him hysterically, but he subdues her masterfully and they make love. Some two months later he receives a call from Susan's father asking him to lunch. At their meeting Brown tries him by offering a bribe if he undertakes to give up Susan for good. When Lampton vehemently refuses, Brown admits that it was only a test offer: 'I wanted to be sure you were right for her.' Having learned that Susan is to have a baby, he had decided that she shall marry Lampton, whom he will buy a partnership in a firm of accountants in another town. Alice takes this news calmly, but that night she crashes her car. Conscience-striken, Lampton drinks himself helpless and is picked up in the street and taken to their home by friends.

Room with a View, A. Novel by E. M. *Forster published in 1908. Having been promised rooms with a view over the Arno, Lucy Honeychurch and her chaperoning cousin Charlotte Bartlett are indignant to find on arriving at the Pension Bertolini in Florence that their rooms look only into a courtyard. Their complaining at dinner is overheard by other visitors, and an elderly Mr Emerson offers to exchange with them the rooms he and his son George occupy. Miss Bartlett, hedged about by conventional gentility, considers this approach ill-bred, and the offer is declined until the Rev. Mr Beebe, whom the two ladies had known at Tunbridge Wells, assures them that no harm would come of acceptance. Lucy is conducted around Florence by Miss Lavish, a woman novelist at the pension, but is stranded by her at the door of Santa Croce. In the church she meets the Emersons and goes with them to see the Giotto frescoes. On a later occasion when Lucy goes out

alone, she sees two Italians quarrelling; one is stabbed and falls dead at her feet. She faints, and on recovering finds herself in the arms of George Emerson, who had seen the incident. A few days after, several of those at the pension go on a carriage excursion to the hills overlooking the Val d'Arno. Lucy becomes separated from the others; she falls at the edge of a slope covered with violets, where George Emerson appears and kisses her. Taking this as an insult, she and her cousin leave Florence hurriedly for Rome. After they return to England Lucy becomes engaged to Cecil Vyse. He despises the social obligations of their circle, and adopts a protective policy towards her which her independent spirit at length rebels against. The Emersons come to live in the vicinity, and Lucy, breaking off her engagement, marries George after vainly endeavouring to overcome their mutual attraction.

Roosevelt, Eleanor (née Anna Eleanor Roosevelt, 1884-1962; Mrs F. D. Roosevelt). Wife of President Franklin Delano Roosevelt (see the following entry), her distant cousin, whom she married in 1905. Though attention was directed to her mainly as 'the lady of the White House' during her husband's presidency, she was eminent in her own right as a social worker and author, and also acquired a practical knowledge of political and international affairs which qualified her to act as U.S. representative at the United Nations Assembly, 1945-52. She wrote for newspapers and magazines, and her books included *It's Up to the Women* (1933), *The Moral Basis of Democracy* (1940), *India and the Awakening East* (1954), *On My Own* (1958), *You Learn by Living* (1960), *Tomorrow is Now* (posthumously, 1964) and the autobiographical *This is My Story* (1937; as *The Lady of the White House* 1938) and *This I Remember* (1949).

Roosevelt, Franklin Delano (1882-1945). Thirty-second President of the United States; fifth cousin of Theodore Roosevelt. First elected in 1933, he was re-elected in 1936, and again in 1940 (the first President to serve a third term), and yet again in 1944. He introduced the 'New Deal' to overcome the great depression raging when he was first elected, and he had a leading part in the Grand Alliance in World War II. Author of *Whither Bound?* (1926); *The Happy Warrior* (1928)—on Alfred E. Smith,

Governor of New York; *Government—Not Politics* (1932), *Looking Forward* (1933). He married in 1905 a distant cousin, Anna Eleanor *Roosevelt, who survived him.

Roosevelt, Theodore (1858-1919). Twenty-sixth President of the United States, 1901-09. In domestic affairs he introduced reform measures designed to limit the power of the great commercial trusts, and supported legislation for meat inspection and pure food, which Upton Sinclair's revelations in *The *Jungle* (1906) had shown the need of. Roosevelt was also a prolific author; among his books are: *The Winning of the West* (4 vols, 1889-96), *The Strenuous Life* (1900), *African Game Trails* (1910; on his big-game hunting expeditions), *History as Literature* (1913), *Fear God and Take Your Own Part* (1916). His political philosophy is summed up in his much-quoted phrase, 'Speak softly and carry a big stick'. His life story is in *Theodore Roosevelt: An Autobiography* (1913).

Ros, Amanda McKittrick (*née* Anna Margaret McKittrick, 1860-1939). Born in Ireland at Ballynahinch, Co. Down; trained as a teacher at Marlborough Training College, Dublin, and taught at a school in Larne. In 1887 she married Andrew Ross, the Larne station master, changing her name to Ros when her first novel, *Irene Iddesleigh*, was published in Belfast in 1897. A second novel, *Delina Delaney* (1898), was followed by two books of verse, *Poems of Puncture* (1912) and *Fumes of Formation* (1933). She has been called 'the world's worst novelist', but the eccentricities of her language led to her books being cherished by connoisseurs of the absurd, and the richness of their unintentionally comic nonsense inspired several reprints of the two novels. The facts of her life, and her fancies concerning it and her writings, are recorded in *O Rare Amanda!* by Jack Loudan (1954).

Rosalind Connage. A leading character in Scott Fitzgerald's *This Side of Paradise* (1920). She loves Amory Blaine but marries a richer man.

Rose. The young waitress victimized by Pinkie, the gang-leader in Graham Greene's *Brighton Rock* (1938).

Rose, J. H. (John Holland Rose, 1855-1942). Born at Bedford; educated there, in Manchester at Owens College, and at Cambridge.

Professor of Naval History in the University of Cambridge, 1919-33. Author of *The Rise of Democracy* (1897), *Life of Napoleon* (1902), *Napoleonic Studies* (1904), *The Development of the European Nations, 1870-1921* (1923), *William Pitt and National Revival* (1911), *The Mediterranean in the Ancient World* (1933), *Man and the Sea* (1935).

Rosebery, Lord (Archibald Philip Primrose, 5th Earl of Rosebery, 1847-1929). Born in London; educated at Eton and Oxford; succeeded to the title 1868. Held ministerial appointments from 1881 in Liberal governments. Became Prime Minister in March 1894 when Gladstone retired, but was defeated at the General Election in the next year, and held no Government office thereafter. He was temperamentally alien to partisan politics, but distinguished as orator and writer. His books include *William Pitt* (1891), *Appreciations and Addresses* (1899), *Sir Robert Peel* (1899), *Oliver Cromwell* (1899), *Napoleon: the Last Phase* (1900), *Lord Randolph Churchill* (1906), *Chatham: his Early Life and Connections* (1910), *Miscellanies, Literary and Historical* (1921).

Rosenbach, A. S. (Abraham Simon Wolf Rosenbach, 1876-1952). Born in Philadelphia; educated at the University of Pennsylvania. As head of the Rosenbach Company, dealers in rare book and manuscripts, he was a prominent figure at important sales of private libraries and collections in America, England and elsewhere, and acquired many valuable items at record prices. In addition to important catalogues and bibliographies he wrote *The Unpublishable Memoirs* (1917), *Books and Bidders* (1928), *Early American Children's Books* (1933), *A Book Hunter's Holiday* (1936).

Rosenberg, Alfred (1893-1946). Born in Estonia. Became one of the most fanatical of Hitler's inner ring and was the fabricator of Nazi foreign policy and then controlled the party's cultural programme and political education system. In *The Myth of the Twentieth Century* (1930) he framed the odious racial doctrines which led to the extermination of millions in World War II. He was condemned at the Nuremberg war crimes trials and executed.

Rosenberg, Isaac (1890-1918). Born in Bristol;

educated at Council schools in the east-end of London; apprenticed as an engraver; then studied art at the Slade School. He went to South Africa for his health in 1914 but returned to England in the following year to join the army and was killed in France. His books of verse *Night and Day* (1912), *Youth* (1918), *Poems* (1922) were esteemed by other poets, and interest was revived by *Collected Works* (poetry, prose, letters and drawings) published in 1937, and a new edition of *Collected Poems* (1949).

Rosie Gann. The heroine of *Cakes and Ale* by W. Somerset *Maugham. While a barmaid at Blackstable she marries Edward Driffield, then an obscure writer. Before he has become famous she elopes with a prosperous local builder and goes with him to live in America. Though entirely amoral, she is fundamentally guileless, warm hearted and generous spirited, and one of the most attractive characters in modern fiction.

Ross, Alan (1922-   ). Educated at Hailey-bury and Oxford. Served in the Navy during World War II, afterwards becoming cricket correspondent to the *Observer*, accompanying English teams on tours of Australia, South Africa, and New Zealand. Editor of *The London Magazine*. Author of *Poems 1942-67* (1968) and books on cricket, travel, etc.

Ross, Barnaby. Pseudonym under which the Ellery *Queen partnership (Frederick Dannay and Manfred B. Lee) published several crime novels featuring a detective named Drury Lane. These included *The Tragedy of X* (1932), *The Tragedy of Y* (1932), and *The Tragedy of Z* (1933).

Ross, Harold Wallace (1892-1951). Born in Aspen, Colorado; educated in Salt Lake City, where he began work on the *Tribune* and then wandered as a roving newspaper reporter for several years until he reached San Francisco in 1916. There, as a water-front reporter and a member of the Press Club, he was known as Roughhouse Ross. When the U.S. entered the war against Germany in 1917 he joined the Engineers Regiment and went to France with the first contingent. Early in 1918 he became a member of the editorial board and eventually managing editor of *Stars and Stripes*, 'the official newspaper of the A.E.F.' with offices in Paris. After the war, a short period as editor of *The Home*

Sector, a civilian successor to *Stars and Stripes*, preceded his appointment to the *American Legion Weekly*, which he ran from 1920 to 1924, leaving it to become co-editor of *Judge*, an old-style humorous weekly. Ross had for some years contemplated starting a weekly magazine 'of reporting and humour . . . that would cover a big city' and on 21 February 1925 the first number of the *New Yorker* appeared. In the remaining quarter of a century of his life Ross was in control of the paper, which developed from near-failure to success, prosperity and international fame. See *Ross and the New Yorker*, by Dale Kramer (1952); *The Years With Ross*, by James *Thurber (1959).

Ross, Leonard Q. (pseudonym of Leo Calvin Rosten, 1908-   ). Born in Poland; taken to America in infancy and educated at schools and University in Chicago; later visited England to study at the London School of Economics. Held various university and other appointments in political science and statistical research in America, but known chiefly as a humorous writer with *The Education of H*y*m*a*n K*a*p*l*a*n* (1937). As Leonard Ross ('without the Q') he wrote screen plays.

Ross, Martin (pseudonym of Violet Florence Martin, 1865-1915). Collaborator with her cousin Edith Somerville in the *Somerville and Ross stories and novels of Irish life. She was born at Ross House in Galway; educated privately and at Alexandra College, Dublin.

Ross, Robert (Robert Baldwin Ross, 1869-1918). Born in Canada, son of the Attorney General there; educated in England. He wrote for the *Scots Observer* under the editorship of W. E. *Henley, and contributed dramatic criticism and book reviews to other journals. From 1900, when he bought the Carfax Gallery in St James's, he was largely instrumental in gaining attention for the paintings of young artists, many of whom became famous, and in later years he was appointed London Adviser to national and city Art Galleries in Australia and South Africa, and became a Trustee of the Tate Gallery, London. His chief claim to remembrance is his unwaveringly loyal friendship for Oscar Wilde, whose literary and dramatic executor he was appointed. The book published as *De Profundis* (1905) was an abbreviated version of the manuscript Wilde lodged with Ross (complete edition 1950), and Wilde's posthumous rehabilitation was largely due to the collected edition of his works which Ross caused to be published in 1908. *Friend of Friends* (1952), edited by Margery Ross, contains letters written to Ross by numerous notable correspondents and also extracts from his own published articles.

Ross, Sir Ronald (1857-1932; knighted 1911). Born in India, educated at boarding school in England; studied medicine at St Bartholomew's Hospital. After a few voyages as a ship's surgeon he entered the Indian Medical Service, was attached to regiments in Madras and Burma, and devoted his leisure to intensive literary study in several languages and to writing imaginative prose and verse. On leave in England he met Sir Patrick Manson (1844-1922), Medical Adviser to the Colonial Office and a founder of the London School of Tropical Medicine, and the combined researches of these two led to the identification of the anopheles mosquito as the infective agent of malaria in human beings and to the adoption of curative treatment and preventive measures. He wrote the valuable *Prevention of Malaria* (1910) and other medical works; his *Collected Poems* (1928) and the novels—*The Child of Ocean* (1889; revised edn 1932), *The Spirit of Storm* (1896), *The Revels of Orsera: A Medieval Romance* (1920),—are remarkable by-products; and his *Memoirs* (1923) record, without excessive modesty, the scope of his invaluable achievements.

Ross, T. E. *See* T. E. *Lawrence.

Ross Williamson, Hugh. *See* Hugh Ross *Williamson.

Rostand, Edmond (1868-1918). Born and educated in Marseilles. He had published poems (*Les Musardises*, 1890) and had several plays produced with considerable success—*Les Romanesques* (1894), *La Princesse lointaine* (1895), *L'Aiglon* (1900) but the enormous popularity and international fame of *Cyrano de Bergerac* (1897) aroused expectations which were disappointed by his later play, *Chantecler* (1910), which, however, lacked sentiment rather than literary merit. He was the most widely-acclaimed French verse dramatist at the turn of the century, and he found in the seventeenth century author-duellist

Cyrano de Bergerac a character he was able to endow with the fire of a great lover endeavouring by romantic eloquence to compensate the physical handicap of a grossly oversize nose. A skilful English translation of *Cyrano de Bergerac* by Gladys Thomas and M. F. Guillemard was published in 1898; a new verse translation by Brian Hooker in New York in 1924 (London, 1953), and another by Humbert *Wolfe in 1937.

Rostovtzeff, Michael I. (1870-1952). Born in Kiev; educated there and at St Petersburg (Leningrad). Professor of Latin, University of St Petersburg, 1898-1918; Professor of Ancient History, University of Wisconsin, 1920-25, and at Yale University, 1925-44. Outstanding among his writings are *A Social and Economic History of the Roman Empire* (1926), *A History of the Ancient World* (2 vols, 1926-27), *The Caravan Cities* (1932), *A Social and Economic History of the Hellenic World* (3 vols, 1941).

Roth, Cecil (1899-1970). Born in London; educated at the City of London School and Oxford. President of the Jewish Historical Society of England (1936-45 and later). Reader in Jewish Studies, University of Oxford, from 1939. Author of *The Last Florentine Republic* (1925), *A Short History of the Jewish People* (1936), *The Magnificent Rothschilds* (1939), *The Sassoon Dynasty* (1941), *History of the Jews in England* (1941), *The Jews of Medieval Oxford* (1951), *Life of Benjamin Disraeli* (1952), *The Historical Background of the Dead Sea Scrolls* (1958).

Rothenstein, Sir John (John Knewstub Maurice Rothenstein, 1901- ; knighted 1952. Son of the following). Born in London; educated at Bedales and Oxford. Director of the City Art Gallery, Leeds, 1932-34 and Sheffield, 1934-38; Director of the Tate Gallery, London, 1938-64. Author of *Eric Gill* (1927), *The Artists of the 1890s* (1928), *Nineteenth Century Painting* (1932), *The Life and Death of Conder* (1938), *Manet* (1945), *Turner* (1949), *Modern English Painters* (I. Sickert to Smith, 1952; II. Lewis to Moore, 1956), *The Tate Gallery* (1958), *Turner* (1960), *Augustus John* (1962). Autobiography: I. *Summer's Lease* (1965); II. *Brave Day, Hideous Night* (1966); III. *Time's Thievish Progress* (1970).

Rothenstein, Sir William (1872-1945; knighted

1931. Father of the preceding). Born and educated in Bradford, Yorkshire. Studied painting at the Slade School in London and at the Academie Julian in Paris. Professor of Civic Art, Sheffield University, 1917-26; Principal, Royal College of Art, London, 1920-35. He published collections of his portrait drawings and a *Life of Goya* (1900). Having moved in the circle of artists and writers who were active in the decades linking the old century and the new, his lively volumes *Men and Memories*: I, *1872-1900* (1931); II, *1900-22* (1932) give an entertaining and historically invaluable account of the artistic and literary scene. Less striking is *Since Fifty: Men and Memories, 1922-38* (1939).

Rothermere, Viscount (Harold Sydney Harmsworth, 1868-1940; baronet 1910; baron 1914; Viscount Rothermere of Hemsted 1919). Born in London. Closely associated with his brother, Viscount *Northcliffe, his exceptional financial acumen contributed vitally to the newspaper empire .they built. On his own account Rothermere founded the *Glasgow Daily Record* and the *Sunday Pictorial*, and he took over the *Daily Mail* and other publications after Northcliffe's death. He incurred disfavour in the 1930s by giving temporary support to the British fascist organization. He endowed the King Edward VII Chair of English Literature at Cambridge and other professorships.

Roughead, William (1870-1952). Born and educated in Edinburgh. Admitted as a Writer to the Signet (i.e. one of a chief-ranking order of solicitors in Scotland), 1893. Specialized as an author in the study of criminology: from 1906 he edited volumes in the Notable British Trials series, and later wrote *Malice Domestic* (1928), *The Evil That Men Do* (1929), *What is Your Verdict?* (1931), *Rogues Walk Here* (1934), *Knaves' Looking-Glass* (1935), *Rascals Revived* (1940), *Reprobates Reviewed* (1941). *See also* Edmund Lester *Pearson.

Routledge, George (1822-1888). Born in Cumberland; apprenticed to a bookseller in Carlisle; moved to London, and in 1836 opened his own bookshop near Leicester Square. Seven years later he began as a publisher in Soho Square, and in 1848 started the famous shilling Railway Library, in which half a million copies of *Uncle Tom's Cabin* were sold, while of another

volume in the series 20,000 copies were printed and bound within one week of the receipt of copy. He published many original works outside the Railway Library, and continued in personal control until the year before his death. The firm he founded continues as Routledge & Kegan Paul, Ltd. *See* Kegan *Paul.

Rowlands, Effie Adelaide. *See* Madame *Albanesi.

Rowse, A. L. (Alfred Leslie Rowse, 1903-   ). .Born at St Austell, Cornwall; educated there and at Oxford. Fellow of All Souls College, Oxford. Renowned as an Elizabethan scholar, his historical writings on the period include *Sir Richard Grenville of the 'Revenge'* (1937), *Tudor Cornwall* (1941), *The England of Elizabeth* (1950), *The Expansion of 'Elizabethan England* (1955), *Ralegh and the Throckmortons* (1962). In 1964, the year of the quatercentenary of Shakespeare's birth, he published studies of the life and work of the poet-dramatist, expressing opinions which provoked dissent from literary scholars and exasperated rejoinders from the historian. The crux of the controversy was the dating of the sonnets *(William Shakespeare: A Biography; Shakespeare's Sonnets)*. Other works: *A Cornish Childhood* (autobiography, 1942), *The Early Churchills* (1956), *The Later Churchills* (1958); *Poems, Chiefly Cornish* (1944), *Simon Forman: Sex and Society in Shakespeare's Age* (1974), *Peter the White Cat of Trenarren* (1974).

Royal Academy. The Royal Academy of Arts (at Burlington House, Piccadilly, London), founded in 1768 with George III as Patron and Sir Joshua Reynolds as President. Its main function is the holding of an annual Summer Exhibition of new paintings, drawings and sculpture. But it has also organized in the present century famous winter exhibitions of Old Masters of Italy and other European schools. In the Diploma Gallery on an upper floor is a permanent exhibition of paintings by members of the Royal Academy, consisting of the 'diploma pieces', i.e. the single paintings which newly elected members are required to present to the Academy. Small special exhibitions are also held in the Diploma Gallery from time to time. The Royal Academy Schools have continued from its foundation to train young artists. The exhibits for the Summer Exhibition are chosen by the Council of the Academy from the much larger number of works submitted from all quarters. Each Summer Exhibition customarily receives harsh criticism on the ground that the more advanced styles in contemporary art are inadequately represented, though it could fairly be pleaded that a national Academy is by its constitution the headquarters of academic art and that experimental art has its advocates and outlets elsewhere until, in turn, it becomes itself 'academic'. In later years the Academy has in fact been more hospitable to contemporary styles. Membership of the Academy is limited to forty full Members (designated R.A.) and thirty (originally twenty) Associates (A.R.A.).

Royal Academy of Dramatic Art. Founded in London by Sir Herbert Tree in 1904. it has become an established training centre for those intending a stage career as actors or actresses, or in any other capacity in the theatre, or as drama teachers. The Academy has its own fully equipped theatre for student productions.

Royal Court Theatre. On the east side of Sloane Square, London, replacing in 1870 an older theatre on the south side. A. W. *Pinero's early farces were produced there and in 1898 his famous *Trelawny of the 'Wells'*. The season of modern plays given under the *Vedrenne-Barker management from 1904 to 1907 was illustrious, establishing the reputation of Bernard *Shaw, whose *John Bull's Other Island* was seen there by Edward VII (whence the addition of 'Royal' to its name). Under other managements Shaw's *Heartbreak House* was done there in 1921 and his *Back to Methuselah* in 1924. The theatre was bomb-damaged in World War II, and after renovation was occupied by the newly formed English Stage Company, whose production of John Osborne's *Look Back in Anger* (1956) started a new trend.

Royal Institute of International Affairs. Founded in London in 1920 for the promotion of amity and understanding between the nations by objective historical study and presentation of current and recent world affairs. It publishes many relevant books by scholars of international repute and arranges lectures at Chatham House, its headquarters in St James's Square.

Royal Institution of Great Britain, The. Founded in London in 1799 by Benjamin Thompson (Count Rumford) for 'the promotion of science and the diffusion and extension of useful knowledge'. Sir Humphry Davy, Michael Faraday, John Tyndall, and Sir William Bragg are among those who have worked in its laboratories and lectured there. It continues special research under a resident Professor, and arranges lectures for senior pupils of schools in London and neighbouring counties. The famous Christmas Juvenile Lectures (started in 1826) retain their popularity. Its scientific library has well over 50,000 volumes, in addition to most current periodicals relevant to its work. The *Proceedings of the Royal Institution* appear at stated intervals during each year. The Institute's premises are in their original place at 21 Albemarle Street, London, W.1. 'It is not required of an intending member that he or she shall have made any contribution to science.'

Royal Literary Fund, The. Founded as the Literary Fund Society in 1790 by the efforts of David Williams, a Welsh dissenting ex-minister and pioneer educationist. He had mooted the idea for such a benevolent fund seventeen years earlier but received no encouragement. His purpose was to relieve needy geniuses and ensure that their studies, efforts and privations should not leave them in misery. There was to be no distinction of race, religion, politics, or sex. From 1790 funds accumulated, peers accepted office as President, and the Prince of Wales (later Prince Regent and then George IV) made generous contributions amounting to more than £5000 and also granted a charter which authorized the title Royal Literary Fund. Among the hundreds of authors or their dependants who have benefited from the Fund are Coleridge, Robert Burns's widow, Peacock, Leigh Hunt, John Clare, Tom Hood, Mary Russell Mitford, Richard Jeffries, Frederick Rolfe (Baron Corvo), Conrad, Ouida, Edith Nesbit, D. H. Lawrence, James Joyce. Some fifty persons are assisted each year, for the Fund has not become unnecessary in the Welfate State. It receives no income from public funds and its function is to help those undeservedly beset by misfortune, not to subsidize writing projects.

Royal Society, The. Founded in 1660 (granted the Royal Charter in 1662) as the Royal

Society of London for Promoting Natural Knowledge. Its original purpose was to promote the 'new experimental philosophy', though its early members included literary men upon whom was imposed the duty of 'a close, naked, natural way of speaking; positive expressions, clear senses, a native easiness'. It is now concerned exclusively with the natural sciences, and election to its limited Fellowship (F.R.S.) is the highest distinction receivable by a scientist. Its premises are at Burlington House, Piccadilly, London, W.1.

Royal Society of Arts. Founded in 1754 as the Royal Society for the Encouragement of Arts, Manufactures and Commerce. Its present activities are of various kinds: in 1936 it created the Faculty of Royal Designers for Industry (the R.D.I. is the highest distinction receivable by British commercial designers); and it conducts the largest number of examinations in commercial subjects.

Royal Society of Edinburgh, The. Founded in 1783, absorbing the Philosophical Society of Edinburgh, the Medical Society and the Society for Improving Arts and Sciences. It originally comprised a Physical side and a Literary one, but became predominantly scientific, Sir Walter Scott being its only literary President (from 1820 to 1832). Lord Kelvin was President for twenty-one years. Among other Presidents was Thomas Stevenson, father of Robert Louis Stevenson who read to the Society a paper 'On the Thermal Influence of Forests' in 1873. The library of the Society has some 150,000 volumes and a number of manuscripts.

Royal Society of Literature of the United Kingdom, founded in London in 1823. Holds lectures, poetry readings, and discussion meetings; publishes annually *Essays by Divers Hands*. Admits subscription-paying members, and (usually by election) Fellows of literary distinction. In 1961 the Society created a Companionship of Literature to be limited at any one time to not more than ten writers, men or women, of exceptional distinction in English letters, to be elected by unanimous vote of the R.S.L. Council. The five Companions first elected were Sir Winston Churchill, E. M. Forster, John Masefield, Somerset Maugham, and G. M. Trevelyan.

Royde-Smith, Naomi (Naomi Gwladys Royde-Smith, died 1964). Born in Wales; educated in London and Geneva. Literary Editor of the *Westminster Gazette*, 1912-22. Author of *The Tortoiseshell Cat* (1925), *Children in the Wood* (1928), *The Delicate Situation* (1931), and many other novels; *Mrs Siddons* (1931), *All Night Sitting* (1954), and other plays; biographies: *The Double Heart* (1931; a study of Julie de Lespinasse, whose literary salon was a feature of eighteenth-century French social life), and *Portrait of Mrs Siddons* (1933); and *A Private Anthology* (1924).

Ruark, Robert (Robert Chester Ruark, 1915-65). Born in North Carolina; educated at the university there; worked in various capacities as a journalist in the U.S.; spent some time in Kenya; then settled in London, where he died. In Africa he gathered material for *Horn of the Hunter* (1953) and for two novels *Something of Value* (1955) and *Uhuru* (1962) which led to his being banned from re-entry to the newly independent states in East Africa. His other writings included *Grenadine Etching* (1947), a parody of contemporary historical novels; two autobiographical volumes—*The Old Man and the Boy* (1957) and *The Old Man's Boy Grows Older* (1961); a collection of essays, *I Didn't Know It Was Loaded* (1948); and a novel satirizing American women, *The Honey Badger* (1965).

Ruck, Berta (1878-   ). Born in Wales; educated at Bangor; studied art in London and Paris; married Oliver *Onions. Author of many romantic novels; among them *His Official Fiancée* (1914), *Dancing Star* (1923), *The Lap of Luxury* (1931), *Bread and Grease Paint* (1943), *The Men in Her Life* (1954); autobiography: *A Story-teller Tells the Truth* (1935).

Rudbeck, J. H. Assistant District Officer in Nigeria, with a mania for road-making, in Joyce Cary's *Mister Johnson* (1939).

Rufford, Nancy. The girl in love with, and loved by, Edward Ashburnham in Ford Madox Hueffer's *The *Good Soldier* (1915). Their separation leads to tragedy for both.

Rummy Mitchens. Nickname of Mrs Romola Mitchens in Bernard Shaw's *Major Barbara* (1905); an 'old bundle of poverty and hard-worn humanity'; confesses to imaginary sins so as to be 'rescued' by the Salvation Army and fed at their West Ham shelter; named after the heroine of George Eliot's *Romola*, 'somebody me mother wanted me to grow up like'.

Runciman, Sir Steven (The Hon James Cochran Stevenson Runciman; 2nd son of 1st Viscount Runciman; 1903-   ; knighted 1958). Educated at Eton and Cambridge. Professor of Byzantine Art and History, University of Istanbul, 1942-45. Author of *Byzantine Civilization* (1933), *A History of the Crusades* (3 vols, 1951, 1952, 1954). *The Sicilian Vespers* (1958), *The White Rajahs* (1960), *The Fall of Constantinople, 1453* (1965), *The Last Byzantine Renaissance* (1970).

Running heads. Headlines (usually to right-hand pages) in a printed book which summarize or refer to the matter on the particular page as it differs from what precedes and follows. (The left-hand headlines usually give only the title of the book or of the chapter.)

Runyon, Damon (Alfred Damon Runyon, 1880-1946). Born in Kansas; educated in Colorado. Worked as a journalist in San Francisco, New York, and elsewhere, and in Mexico and Europe as war correspondent. He wrote numerous stories of gangsters in a unique farcical vein dependent on their portrayal as illiterate toughs whose hearts are simple because their minds are weak to the point of being virtually non-existent. The comedy of the stories depends largely on the originality and resourcefulness of the slang put into the characters' mouths. The several volumes are fairly sampled in *The Best of Runyon* (1940). *Guys and Dolls* (1932) was later drawn upon for a musical play with the same title.

R.U.R. *Rossum's Universal Robots*, a play by the Czech dramatist Karel *Čapek produced in 1923, dealing with the ultimate enslavement of human beings by the mechanical creatures (Robots) they have created and manufactured.

Ruritania. An imaginary country in *The Prisoner of Zenda* (1894) by Anthony *Hope. Adopted in common usage for any improbably romantic land of make-believe.

Russell, Bertrand (Bertrand Arthur William, 3rd Earl Russell, 1872-1970). Born in Wales; educated privately, and at Cambridge, where he had a distinguished career in mathematics and philosophy, and was also in the circle of young scholars who became eminent as thinkers and writers in later years. Russell's genius as a mathematician became evident in *Principia Mathematica* (1910), written in collaboration with A. N. *Whitehead. He had already published *The Philosophy of Leibniz* (1900), *Principles of Mathematics* (1903), *Philosophical Essays* (1910), and his subsequent works were numerous and varied. He combined scholarship with literary skill and a rare talent for popularization both in writing and as a broadcaster. On politics and education he held and expressed unorthodox opinions, and in World War I his pacifist intransigence led to imprisonment. He advocated free discipline in education and ran a school on that principle. His devotion to unpopular causes did not diminish with age: in his nineties he was active in nuclear disarmament demonstrations as a pavement-sitter in Whitehall. He succeeded as 3rd Earl Russell on the death of his brother in 1931, but rarely used the title. A brief selection of his books: *Mysticism and Logic* (1918), *Roads to Freedom* (1918), *The Analysis of Mind* (1921), *What I Believe* (1925), *On Education* (1926), *An Outline of Philosophy* (1927), *Sceptical Essays* (1928), *Marriage and Morals* (1929), *The Conquest of Happiness* (1930), *History of Western Philosophy* (1946), *Authority and the Individual* (1949), *Unpopular Essays* (1950), *Why I am Not a Christian* (1957), *My Philosophical Development* (1959), and three volumes of *Autobiography:* I *1872-1914* (1967), II *1914-1944* (1968), III *1944-1967* (1969).

Russell, Countess. Wife of the 2nd Earl Russell, whom she married after the death of her first husband Count von Arnim. *See* Elizabeth.

Russell, George William. *See* AE.

Russell, G. W. E. (George William Erskine Russell, 1853-1919). Born in London; educated at Harrow and Oxford. Liberal M.P. for Aylesbury, 1880-85, North Bedfordshire, 1892-95. Held ministerial offices between 1883 and 1895. Author of several volumes of light essays and memories: *Collections and Recollections* (2 vols, 1898, 1909), *A Londoner's Log-Book* (1902), *A Pocketful of Sixpences* (1907), *Portraits of the Seventies* (1916), *Politics and Personalities* (1917).

Russell, Sarah. *See* Marghanita *Laski.

Rutherford, Lord (Ernest Rutherford, 1871-1937; 1st Baron Rutherford of Nelson, New Zealand). Born in New Zealand; educated at schools and university there, and in England at Cambridge. Professor of Physics, McGill University, Montreal, 1898-1907; Professor and Director of the Physics Laboratories, University of Manchester, 1907-19; Professor of Experimental Physics and Director of the *Cavendish Laboratory, University of Cambridge, from 1919. Years of continuous research with colleagues led to the world-changing series of discoveries summarized in popular language as 'the splitting of the atom'—and to the dawn of the Nuclear Age.

Rutherford, Mark (pseudonym of William Hale White, 1831-1913). Born and educated at Bedford. He then studied theology and qualified for the Congregational ministry but was expelled from that body when he developed views incompatible with some tenets of its doctrine. Becoming a civil servant, he rose to the rank of Assistant Director of Contracts at the Admiralty. He has a lonely place in literature as author of impressive short novels constituting a personal spiritual pilgrimage: *The Auto-biography of Mark Rutherford* (1881) and *Mark Rutherford's Deliverance* (1885). His other novels are *The Revolution in Tanner's Lane* (1887), *Miriam's Schooling* (1890),

Catherine Furze (1894), *Clara Hopgood* (1896). Though they have claims to be ranked as lesser classics, their greyness of tone has kept them from being widely read. Other books: *Pages from a Journal* (1900), *John Bunyan* (1905), *More Pages from a Journal* (1910).

Rutter, Frank (Frank Vane Phipson Rutter, 1876-1937). Born at Putney; educated at Merchant Taylors' School and Cambridge. Art critic on the *Sunday Times* from 1903. Author of *Varsity Types* (1902), *The Path to Paris* (1908), *Rossetti, Painter and Man of Letters* (1909), *Whistler, a Biography and an Estimate* (1910), *Revolution in Art* (1910), *The Poetry of Architecture* (1923), *Since I Was Twenty-five* (1928).

Ryall, William Bolitho. *See* William *Bolitho.

Ryecroft, Henry. See *The *Private Papers of Henry Ryecroft* (1903) by George Gissing.

Ryder, Charles. Central character in Evelyn Waugh's *Brideshead Revisited* (1945).

Ryle, Gilbert (1900-   ). Educated at Brighton College and Oxford. Served as a commissioned officer in World War II. Professor of Metaphysical Philosophy in the University of Oxford from 1945. Editor of *Mind* from 1947. Author of *Philosophical Arguments* (Inaugural Lecture, 1945), *The Concept of Mind* (1949), *Dilemmas* (1954).

Sabatini, Rafael (1875-1950). Born in Italy; educated in Switzerland and Portugal; settled in England. Attained wide popularity with romantically coloured historical novels: *The Tavern Knight* (1904), *Bardelys the Magnificent* (1906), *The Sea Hawk* (1915), *Scaramouche* (1921), *Captain Blood* (1922), *Master-at-Arms* (1940), etc.

Sabin, A. K. (Arthur Knowles Sabin, 1879-1959). Born in Yorkshire. Officer in charge of the Bethnal Green Museum, 1922-40. One of the founders of the Samurai Press, hand-printing books for that and other private presses. Author of *Typhon and Other Poems* (1902), *The Death of Icarus* (1906), *New Poems* (1915), *East London Poems* (1931).

Sabina. Lily Sabina, a leading character in Thornton Wilder's *The *Skin of Our Teeth* (1942): maid to the Antrobus family, winner of an Atlantic City beauty contest, and camp auxiliary in the war.

Sackville, Lady Margaret (died 1963). Daughter of the 7th Earl de la Warr. Passed much of her life in Edinburgh. Wrote verse, from *Poems* (1901) to *Quatrains* (1960). *Collected Dramas* (1926); *Collected Poems* (1939).

Sackville-West, Edward (Edward Charles Sackville-West, 1901-65; succeeded his father as 5th Baron Sackville in 1962). Born at Knole, Kent, cousin of the following; educated at Eton and Oxford. Studied music, intending to become a concert pianist, but joined the *New Statesman* as music and book critic before spending a year in Germany. Author of *Piano Quintet* (1925), *The Ruin* (1926), *Simpson* (1921), *The Sun in Capricorn* (1934), and other novels; *The Rescue* (radio verse-drama, 1945); *A Flame in Sunlight* (on the life and writings of Thomas De Quincey; 1936); *Inclinations* (essays, 1949).

Sackville-West, V. (Victoria Mary Sackville-West, 1892-1962; married Harold *Nicolson, 1913). Born at Knole, Sevenoaks, Kent, daughter of Lord Sackville; educated at home, and was strongly influenced throughout her life by the history and natural beauty of Knole, which had been in the possession of her family since the sixteenth century. After marrying Harold (later Sir Harold) Nicolson she travelled with him in Persia and other countries to which he was posted as a diplomat, and among the literary products of these experiences were her travel

books *Passenger to Teheran* (1926) and *Twelve Days* (1928). She had begun to write much earlier, both in verse and prose, publishing *Poems of West and East* (1917) and *Heritage* (1918), her first novel. Her output thereafter was prolific and her best works rank among the classics of the period: *Knole and the Sackvilles* (1922), *The *Land* (pastoral poem, 1926), *All Passion Spent* (novel; 1931), *Pepita* (1937). She also wrote biographies of *Saint Joan of Arc* (1936) and, in *The Eagle and the Dove* (1943), of the two Saints Teresa; her *Collected Poems* appeared in 1933; and, among many other novels, *Seducers in Ecuador* (1924) and *The Edwardians* (1930) are notable. After her husband's diplomatic career closed, they settled in Kent, where her love of that county and especially of gardening led to the writing of several volumes of *Country Notes* (1939, etc) and garden books, *The Garden* (poems, 1946) and *In Your Garden* (1951, etc). Among her close friends was Virginia *Woolf, in whose *Orlando* she was the central figure, projected imaginatively as an historical phantasm. Her intimate diary, published in *Portrait of a Marriage* (1973) by her son Nigel Nicolson, is concerned largely with a tumultuous relationship with Violet *Trefusis, but also with the ultimate tranquil development of her marriage.

Sadism. Addiction to the deliberate imposing of physical pain or mental suffering on others, as a psychotic sexual perversion; from the name of its notorious practitioner, the Marquis de Sade (1740-1814), who died insane. See Masochism.

Sadleir, Michael (Michael Thomas Harvey Sadleir, 1888-1957). Born in Oxford, son of the following; educated at Rugby and Oxford. Altered the spelling of his surname to avoid confusion with his father. Joined the publishing firm of Constable and Co, of which he became Director. He developed a special interest in the life, literature and bibliography of the nineteenth century, and his best novel, *Fanny by Gaslight* (1940), presents vividly some raffish aspects of that period. His *Trollope: A Commentary* (1927; new edn 1945) is a standard work written at the height of the revival of interest in Trollope's writings; *Trollope: A Bibliography* (1928) supplements it. Other non-fiction: *Daumier* (1924), *Bulmer and his Wife, 1803-1836* (1931), *Blessington-Dorsay* (1933; new edn 1947), *Things Past* (essays; 1944).

Bibliographies: *Excursions in Victorian Bibliography* (1922), *The Evolution of Publishers' Binding Styles, 1770-1900* (1930), *Nineteenth Century Fiction: A Bibliographical Record* (2 vols, 1951). Biography—*Michael Ernest Sadler: A Memoir by his Son* (1949). Other novels: *Desolate Splendour* (1923), *The Noblest Frailty* (1925), *These Foolish. Things* (1937), *Forlorn Sunset* (1947).

Sadler, Sir Michael (Michael Ernest Sadler, 1861-1943; knighted 1919). Born at Barnsley, Yorkshire; educated at Rugby and Oxford. In the Department (now Ministry) of Education, 1895-1903; Professor of the History and Administration of Education, Manchester, 1903-11; Vice-Chancellor, Leeds University, 1911-23; Master of University College, Oxford, 1923-34. One of the leading and most enlightened educationalists of the time, he produced many reports on education in Britain and elsewhere. In addition to official papers, he wrote *Our Public Elementary Schools* (1926) and *Liberal Education for Everybody* (1932). He was a generous patron of the arts, with a special interest shown in the volume he edited on *Arts of West Africa* (1934).

Sadler's Wells. A theatre in Rosebery Avenue, London, originating from a pleasure resort established in 1683 by a Mr Sadler on whose property a medicinal spring had been found. It became a place of low repute and experienced many vicissitudes and sundry disasters, though in the nineteenth-century famous players performed in the theatre that had been built there in the 1760s, and for some years in the middle of the nineteenth century it ranked as one of London's leading theatres. It gradually sank back into disrepute and the building was virtually a ruin when it was taken over by Lilian *Baylis and rebuilt, opening in 1931 as a companion house to the *Old Vic, specializing after a few years as the centre for the opera and ballet companies of the joint organization. After World War II its senior company of dancers became the Covent Garden Ballet, and having won international fame under the direction of Ninette de Valois with Margot Fonteyn as prima ballerina it was eventually accorded the distinction of being named The Royal Ballet. The Coliseum in St Martin's Lane became the home of the Sadler's Wells Opera Company in 1968.

Saga. An Old Norse word for a prose narrative of heroic life. Popularized in modern English through the title of *The *Forsyte Saga* (1922) by John Galsworthy, it has become attached accurately or inaccurately to any prolonged family history or tedious verbal story.

Sagan, Françoise (pseudonym of Françoise Quoirez, 1935-). Born in France; educated privately and at a convent school. *Bonjour Tristesse* (1954) a naïve and brittle adolescent novel which accorded with the mood of the time and brought her popularity in England as well as France, was followed by *Un Certain Sourire* (1956), *Aimez-vous Brahms . . . ?* (1959), and others.

Sagittarius (pseudonym of Olga Katzin, 1896-). Born in London; educated privately. Wrote weekly satirical verses on current topics and public figures in the *New Statesman*. Author of *Sagittarius Rhyming* (1940), *Let Cowards Flinch* (1947), *Up the Poll* (1950).

Sagittarius Rising. See Cecil *Lewis.

Saint, The. Nickname given by Leslie *Charteris to Simon Templar in his series of crime novels.

Saint-Exupéry, Antoine de (Antoine Marie Reger de Saint-Exupéry, 1900-44). Born at Lyons; educated in France at Catholic schools and in Switzerland at the Collège de Fribourg. Having failed for the merchant navy, he trained as an aviator and was a civil air pilot from 1926 until the beginning of World War II, when he began service with the French air force, and after many flights was lost in July 1944, having previously narrowly escaped death on several occasions. His books, which express the humanistic ideals of a complex personality, one who was pilot-poet-philosopher, made a deep impression both in their own language and in English translations: *Night Flight* (1932), *Southern Mail* (1933), *Wind, Sand, and Stars* (1939), *Flight to Arras* (1942), *The Little Prince* (1943), *Wisdom of the Sands* (from the unfinished *La Citadelle;* posthumously, in French, 1948; in English, 1950).

Saint Joan: A Chronicle play in six scenes and an epilogue by Bernard *Shaw written in 1923; performed in New York 1923, in London 1924; published in 1924. Robert de Baudricourt threatens to punish his Steward because he procures no eggs or milk. The Steward insists that the failure of the hens to lay and the cows to give milk is due to his master's refusal to admit The Maid, Joan, a girl from Lorraine who has been waiting two days. When at last she is called in, she asks for a horse and armour and a few soldiers so that she can ride to the Dauphin, who, she says, will give her all she needs to raise the Siege of Orleans, which the voices of St Catherine and St Margaret tell her daily she is to do. When Robert has reluctantly agreèd, the Steward runs in to say 'the hens are laying like mad'. In the throne room of the castle at Chinon the Archbishop of Rheims and the Lord Chamberlain hear that Joan has got through with a letter of introduction from De Baudricourt to the Dauphin who, though indolent and 'a poor creature physically', defies his bullying advisers and agrees to receive Joan if she identifies him from among the courtiers. She does so, and promises to put courage into him and turn him into a real king to be crowned at Rheims. Given command of the army, she joins Dunois, the Bastard of Orleans, whose crossing of the river Loire is held up by an unfavourable wind. Joan takes him to the church to pray; the wind changes and makes possible a successful assault on the English besieging Orleans. In a tent in the English camp after the defeat at Orleans, the Earl of Warwick and John de Stogumber, Chaplain to the Cardinal of Winchester, are discussing the military situation and 'the witch' (Joan) while awaiting Cauchon, the Bishop of Beauvais, with whom the discussion of Joan's influence and fate is continued: the Bishop regarding her as a heretic dangerous to the Church but with a soul to be saved if possible; Warwick concerned only to consider her as an enemy of England with a body to be burned. After the victory at Orleans and the crowning of the Dauphin, Joan, captured by the Burgundians and sold to Warwick, who delivers her up to the Church, is brought to trial for heresy before the deputy Chief Inquisitor. Terrified by the threat of burning, she signs the form of recantation, but tears it up when sentenced to perpetual imprisonment, preferring immediate death by fire. The Epilogue is dated 1456, twenty-five years after Joan's martyrdom. As Charles VII lies in bed, the chief persons in the story of Joan's life and condemnation and also Joan herself appear. Time is transcended when an emissary appears to read the Vatican document of 1920 nullifying the Church's verdict of 1431 and canonizing Joan of Arc as Saint Joan.

St John, Christopher Marie (pseudonym of Christabel Marshall, died 1960). After leaving Oxford she worked temporarily as part-time secretary to Winston *Churchill and his mother, until her enthusiasm for Ellen *Terry introduced her to the great actress's household and to Edith Craig (Ellen Terry's daughter) with whom she formed a close friendship lasting until Edith Craig's death in 1947. She published in 1915 an anonymous novel *Hungerheart*, having previously cooperated, also anonymously, in Ellen Terry's autobiography *My Life* (1908), an enlarged edition of which appeared in 1933 as *Ellen Terry's Memoirs*, 'with Preface, Notes and Additional Biographical Chapters by Edith Craig and Christopher St John'. She edited the famous *Ellen Terry and Bernard Shaw: A Correspondence* (1931), wrote a few plays, in one of which (*Erikkson's Wife*) Ellen Terry played, a novel (*The Crimson Weed*, 1900), made English translations of the tenth-century plays of Roswitha (1923) and of ̩a Dutch play *The Rising Sun* (1925), and wrote a biography of Ethel *Smyth the composer (1959).

Saintsbury, George (George Edward Bateman Saintsbury, 1845-1933). Born in Southampton; educated in London and at Oxford. Taught at schools in Manchester and Guernsey; then worked for many years as a journalist, contributing to the *Manchester Guardian,* the *Saturday Review* and other periodicals. For ten years from 1895 he was Professor of Rhetoric and English Literature in the University of Edinburgh. From 1880, when his *Primer of French Literature* was published, until the closing years of his life he was a leading literary historian and scholar-critic, immensely widely and deeply read but lacking grace of style in his own writing. Many of his books were published in the last century; those issued from 1900 onward include *A History of Criticism* (3 vols, 1900, 1902, 1904), *The Earlier Renaissance* (1901), *A History of English Prosody* (3 vols, 1906, 1908, 1910), *The English Novel* (1913). Most readable among his literary studies is *The Peace of the Augustans* (1915), on eighteenth-century writers. His *Collected Essays and Papers* were published (4 vols) in 1924. *Notes on a Cellar Book* (1920) was an outcome of his pleasure in wine.

Saki (pseudonym of Hector Hugh Munro, 1870-1916). Born at Akyab, Burma, son of the Inspector-General of the Burma Police;

educated in England at Exmouth and at Bedford Grammar School. After spending some time on the Continent he returned to Burma in 1893 to join the Military Police there, but recurrent illness compelled him to resign after little more than a year and in 1896 he settled in London, writing political satires for the *Westminster Gazette*, collected in *The Westminster Alice*, with illustrations by a *Punch* artist, Carruthers Gould. His only serious book, *The Rise of the Russian Empire* (1900), was followed by a period as correspondent of the *Morning Post* in the Balkans, Poland, and Russia, and he was in St Petersburg at the time of the 1905 revolt. He found his true bent with the short stories published in *Reginald* (1904), *Reginald in Russia* (1910), *The Chronicles of Clovis* (1911) and *Beasts and Super-Beasts* (1914). He joined the Royal Fusiliers when war started in 1914 and was killed in France in November 1916. Other volumes of his stories were published posthumously: *The Toys of Peace* (1923), *The Square Egg* (1924). Although he also wrote novels, *The Unbearable Bassington* (1912) and others, it is by his short stories that he is remembered for his humour, wit, penetrating yet urbane satire and well-mannered malice. He took his pseudonym from the Rubáiyát of Omar Khayyam.

Salinger, J. D. (Jerome David Salinger, 1919-). Born in New York; educated in Manhattan and Pennsylvania. Served with the American army in Europe in World War II. Attracted widespread attention with his first novel, *The *Catcher in the Rye* (1951), which was followed by *For Esme—with Love and Squalor* (1953), *Franny and Zooey* (1962).

Salk, Jonas Edward (1914-). Born in New York; studied there at the University College of Medicine. Professor of Experimental Medicine, University of Pittsburg, from 1957. Specialized in poliomyelitis research and in 1954 developed the vaccine since used as an immunizing agent.

Salkey, Andrew (1928-). Born in Panama of Jamaican parents; educated in Jamaica and at the University of London. Became a teacher of English in London schools and settled in London. Author of *A Quality of Violence* (1959), *Escape to an Autumn Pavement* (1960); children's fiction: *Hurricane* (1964), *Earthquake* (1965), *Drought* (1966), *The Shark Hunters* (1966), *Riot* (1967).

Salt, Henry S. (Henry Stephens Salt, 1851-

1939). Born in India; educated at Eton and Cambridge. Assistant master at Eton, 1875-84. A believer in the simple life and holding socialist views, he planned to settle in a farm-worker's cottage. He was an early member of the *Fabian Society, and one of the two witnesses at Bernard Shaw's wedding in 1898. Among his several score of publications were writings against slavery, corporal punishment and vivisection, and in support of socialism, vegetarianism, and the protection of wild flowers; editions of Lucretius, Virgil, Shelley, Thoreau, and of novels by Herman Melville; biographies of *Henry David Thoreau* (1887), *James Thomson ('B.V.')* (1889; new edn 1914), *Percy Bysshe Shelley* (1896; new edn 1924); as well as poems, *Memories of Bygone Eton* (1928), *Company I Have Kept* (1930). *See* Stephen Winsten: *Salt and His Circle* (1951).

Salten, Felix (pseudonym of Felix Salzmann, 1869-1945). Born in Budapest; lived in Vienna until the Nazi invasion; travelled widely in Europe, America, and Palestine. Settled and died in Switzerland. Worked as a journalist and theatre critic. Achieved international repute with his story of a forest deer, *Bambi* (1923; Eng. trans. 1925). Other animal books: *Florian* (1935), *Bambi's Children* (1940), *Forest World* (1942), *Jibby the Cat* (1948).

Salter, Sir Arthur (James Arthur Salter, 1881- ; 1st Baron Salter of Kidlington, 1953). Born at Oxford; educated there at High School and University. Independent M.P. for Oxford University, 1937-50; Conservative member for Ormskirk, 1951-53. Held numerous official appointments, including that of Minister of State for Economic Affairs, 1951-52. Author of *The Framework of an Ordered Society* (1933), *The United States of Europe* (1933), *Security* (1939), *Personality in Politics* (1947), *Memoirs of a Public Servant* (1961).

Saltire Society, The. Founded in 1936 for the 'preservation of Scottish cultural traditions', and the encouragement of contemporary Scottish artists, writers, architects, craftsmen, etc. It published a quarterly, the *New Satire,* and books and pamphlets.

Salve. The second volume of the autobiographical trilogy *Hail and Farewell* (1911-14) by George Moore. The individual titles of the first and third volumes are *Ave* and *Vale.*

Sampson, George (1873-1950). Born in London; educated in Southwark Pupil Teachers' School and at Winchester Training College. He became an exceptionally successful teacher with a scrupulous regard for the use of the English language and a love for its literature. He was for years a London County Council Inspector of Schools. His writings include *English for the English* (1921), *The Concise Cambridge History of English Literature* (1941), *Seven Essays* (1947). ·

Sampson, John (1862-1931). Born in Ireland; had little schooling and at fourteen was apprenticed to an engraver in Liverpool. By intensive reading he widened and deepened his education and developed a passion for scholarly accuracy. As the fruit of this self-education he was appointed in 1892 librarian of University College, Liverpool (now Liverpool University), and held the post until 1928. Influenced by the writings of George Borrow, he devoted much time to contacts with gypsies and the mastery of their language, writing for the Gypsy Lore Society and publishing *The Dialect of the Gypsies of Wales* (1926), etc. He also produced an edition of William Blake's *Poetical Works* (1905) which was superior to any published before that date.

Sampson, Richard Henry. *See* Richard *Hull.

Samuel, A. M. *See* Lord *Mancroft.

Samuel, Viscount (Herbert Louis Samuel, 1870-1963; 1st Viscount Samuel, 1937). Born in Liverpool; educated in London and Oxford. Liberal M.P. for the Cleveland (Yorkshire) constituency, 1902-18, and for Darwen (Lancashire), 1929-35. Home Secretary, 1916 and 1931-32, and held other ministerial appointments. Though prominent in the Liberal Party, and its Leader in Parliament from 1931 to 1935, he was more statesman than party politician and was also eminent as a philosopher. His writings include *Liberalism: its Principles and Proposals* (1902), *Philosophy and the Ordinary Man* (1932), *The Tree of Good and Evil* (1933), *Practical Ethics* (1935), *Belief and Action: An Everyday Philosophy* (1937; new edn 1953), *Memoirs* (1945), *Essay in Physics* (1951), *In Search of Reality* (1957).

Samurai Press. *See* Harold *Monro.

Sandburg, Carl (Carl August Sandburg, 1878-1967). Born in Galesburg, Illinois, the son of Swedish immigrants. He left school at the beginning of his teens and worked in various menial jobs before serving in the Spanish-American war, after which he attended college in his home town and then turned to journalism in Chicago. Meanwhile he had begun to publish poems, often in Whitman-esque free verse and usually concerned with both the rural and the urban life of the Middle West. Some of his most impressive poems are confined to a single brief stanza and all are marked by democratic fervour. In 1926 he published the first two volumes of the vast biography of President Lincoln to which he devoted a large part of his own life. These first volumes—*Abraham Lincoln: The Prairie Years*—were followed in 1939 by the completing four volumes of the work—*Abraham Lincoln: The War Years*. He wrote other prose books, but it is as a poet that he is remembered: *Chicago Poems* (1915), *Cornhuskers* (1918), *Smoke and Steel* (1920), *Good Morning America* (1928), *The People, Yes* (1936); *Selected Poems* (1926), *Complete Poems* (1950). *The American Songbag* (1927) which he collected and edited, was an outcome of his practice of undertaking annual tours during which he gave recitals of folk-songs, besides readings of his own poems. Autobiography: *Always the Young Strangers* (1952).

Sanderson, F. W. (Frederick William Sanderson, 1857-1922). Born at Brancepeth, Durham; educated at the village school and, after working as a pupil teacher, went to Durham University and then to Cambridge. He taught at Girton College there until he became a master at Dulwich College from 1885 to 1892. In 1892 he was appointed headmaster of Oundle, in Northants, a Grocers' Company school then in decline. Sanderson not only increased the enrolment from 92 to 500 by 1920, but also started science laboratories and engineering workshops for boys with less aptitude for classics and other subjects in the traditional curriculum. He also introduced a system of cooperative study, dividing the pupils into small groups each dealing with a particular aspect of a given subject, the results of each group's work being combined to give a complete view of the whole. As a consequence of Sanderson's pioneer methods, Oundle became a model for other schools in Britain and overseas. H. G. Wells's *Story of a Great Schoolmaster* (1924) is a descriptive tribute by a warm admirer.

Sanger, Charles Percy (1871-1930). Educated at Cambridge; barrister; Lecturer in Statistics, London School of Economics. Author of *The Structure of 'Wuthering Heights'* (1926), a valuable brief study of Emily Brontë's novel.

Sanger, Margaret (*née* Margaret Higgins, 1883-1966). American pioneer of birth control at a time when advocacy of family planning aroused embittered prejudice and often persecution. Author of *Happiness in Marriage* (1927), *My Fight for Birth Control* (1931), *Margaret Sanger* (autobiography; 1938).

Sanger's Circus. Nickname of the Sanger family in Margaret Kennedy's *The *Constant Nymph* (1924). It comprises the celebrated opera-composer Albert Sanger, his seven children (Kate and Caryl by his first wife; Antonia, Tessa, Paulina, and Sebastian by his second; and Susan by his current mistress). They are undisciplined and noisy and run wild in the part of the Austrian Tyrol where they have a chalet.

Sankey, Ira D. (Ira David Sankey, 1840-1908). Born in Pennsylvania. Associated for nearly thirty years with the evangelist D. L. Moody, travelling with him as hymn-writer, vocalist, and musical director at the evangelical mission meetings which attracted large audiences in America, England, and elsewhere. He compiled *Sacred Songs and Solos* which continued to sell in very large numbers long after his death. He also compiled other hymn books and wrote *My Life and Sacred Song* (1906).

Sansom, William (1912-   ). Educated at Uppingham and abroad. Author of short stories collected in *Fireman Flower* (1944), *Three* (1946), *Something Terrible, Something Lovely* (1948), *A Touch of the Sun* (1952), *Pleasures Strange and Simple* (1953), *Blue Skies, Brown Studies* (1960). Novels: *The Body* (1949), *The Face of Innocence* (1951), *A Bed of Roses* (1954), *The Cautious Heart* (1958), *Goodbye* (1966).

Santayana, George (1863-1952). Born in Madrid; taken to the U.S. in childhood; educated there in Boston and at Harvard, and in Germany at Berlin. Professor of Philosophy at Harvard, 1889-1911, and occasional lecturer at Oxford and Cambridge and in Paris. He lived in England during World War I and his many works are written in English. Though mainly a philosopher,

the range of his interests and the lucidity and cool charm of his literary style attracted a large body of readers beyond philosophical circles. His unique contribution to literature is *The Last Puritan: A Memoir in the Form of a Novel* (1935), set partly in the neighbourhood of Oxford and displaying, in a quietly absorbing narrative, various aspects of the author's cultured mind. Other works: *The Sense of Beauty* (on aesthetic theory; 1896), *The Life of Reason, or the Phases of Human Progress* (5 vols, 1905-06), *Winds of Doctrine* (1913), *Little Essays* (1920), *Dialogues in Limbo* (1925), *Platonism and the Spiritual Life* (1927), *The Realm of Essence* (1928), *The Realm of Matter* (1930), *The Realm of Truth* (1937), *The Realm of Being* (1942). *Poems* (1923). Autobiography: *Persons and Places* (1944), *The Background of My Life* (1944), *The Middle Span* (1945), *My Host the World* (1953).

Sapper (pseudonym of Herman Cyril McNeile, 1888-1937). Educated at Cheltenham and the Royal Military Academy, Woolwich. From 1907 to 1919 he served in the Royal Engineers, rising to Lieutenant Colonel, and adopting as his pen-name the army word for a military engineer. He had published a few books which made no marked effect before *Bulldog Drummond* (1920), which he subtitled 'The Adventures of a Demobilized Officer Who Found Peace Dull'. With this character—tough, romantically fearless, chivalrous, and not immune to sentiment—he found a hero who retained his popularity in later books—*The Dinner Club* (1923), *Bulldog Drummond's Third Round* (1924), *Bulldog Drummond Strikes Back* (1933)—and survived his creator.

Sara Monday. Chief character in Joyce Cary's *Herself Surprised* (1941); mentioned in *To Be a Pilgrim* (1942) and prominent in *The *Horse's Mouth* (1944).

Sarajevo. The town in Serbia (now Yugoslavia) where the Archduke Francis Ferdinand of Austria was assassinated in June 1914, an event which led to World War I.

Sardou, Victorien (1831-1908). Born in Paris; educated there at the Collège Henri IV. In the second half of the nineteenth century his plays and those of Eugène Scribe (1791-1861) dominated the French stage, and in translations were almost equally popular in England. Both were skilled craftsmen and from their example the 'well-made play' degenerated into what the newer English dramatists condemned as lifeless pieces of stage-carpentry constructed from shoddy melodramatic material—the resulting product being named by Bernard Shaw 'Sardoodledom' (*Our Theatres in the Nineties*, i, 140 ff). Sarah Bernhardt performed in his *Fédora, Théodora*, and (among others) *La Tosca*, upon which Puccini's opera was later based. In London Ellen Terry appeared in his *Madame Sans-Gêne*.

Sargent, John Singer (1856-1925). Born in Florence, son of an American physician; studied painting in Italy and Paris; worked mainly in England and was elected R.A. in 1897. He was *par excellence* the portrait-painter of the Edwardian Age, his flamboyant style matching appropriately the opulence of the beauties and the arrogance of the financiers of the period. The Tate Gallery in London has expressive examples of his work.

Sargeson, Frank (1903-). Born in New Zealand. He has been described as a founding father of the literature of his country, and one of the earliest to secure an international reputation without leaving his homeland. In the short stories which form the bulk of his work he frequently makes the narrator a semi-educated, semi-illiterate person using the authentic vocabulary and verbal style of his class, thus bringing into literature, as it were at firsthand, character-types not to be found in bookish circles. His aim has been 'to open New Zealand eyes and ears: the undiscovered country was to leap not into the eyes of the Old World but into the eyes of those who lived in it' (*T.L.S.*, 17 June 1965). Author of *A Man and his Wife* (1940), *That Summer* (1946), *I Saw in My Dream* (1949), *Collected Stories* (1965), *Joy of the Worm* (novel; 1969). Plays: *A Time for Sowing, The Cradle and the Egg.*

Saroyan, William (1908-). Born in California of Armenian parentage; after brief and meagre schooling, he passed through a bewildering succession of jobs before achieving modest success as a writer in 1933. A year later a volume of short stories, *The Daring Young Man on a Flying Trapeze* (1934) made him the literary celebrity he continued to be, as author of stories, novels and plays distinguished by idiosyncrasy of style and by a generalized affection for humanity at large. His outstanding novel is

The Human Comedy (1943). Shorter fiction: *The Gay and Melancholy Flux* (1937), *The Trouble with Tigers* (1938), etc. Among his plays are *The Time of Your Life* (1939), *Love's Old Sweet Song* (1941), *The Cave Dwellers* (1959). Autobiography: *The Bicycle Rider in Beverly Hills* (1952). See Sirak *Goryan.

Sartorius, Mr and **Blanche,** his daughter. Characters in **Widowers' Houses** (1892) by Bernard Shaw. He is a 'self-made' man who has acquired wealth from rents of dilapidated slum property; Blanche is an ill-tempered shrew, living idly on money from the same tainted source.

Sartre, Jean-Paul (1905-). Born and educated in Paris, mainly as a student of philosophy, the subject he taught in Paris and elsewhere during the 1930s. Taken prisoner by the Germans in 1940 but released in the next year, for the rest of the war he was active in the French Resistance movement. Before the war he had gathered around him a number of the café-haunting students in Paris and, influenced by the theories and beliefs of *Heidegger and *Kierkegaard, developed the philosophy of *Existentialism with which his name is mainly associated. Before the war he published an autobiographical novel *La Nausée* (1937) and a volume of short stories *Le Mur* (1938). His plays include *Les Mouches, Huis-Clos* (both 1943), *Les Mains sâles* (1952), and *Nekrassov* (produced at the Edinburgh Festival, 1957). The philosophical and political attitudes which penetrate all his imaginative writings are directly and fully stated in *L'Être et néant* (1943; English trans. by H. E. Barnes, *Being and Nothingness*, 1957).

Sassoon, Siegfried (Siegfried Lorraine Sassoon, 1886-1967). Born in London; educated at Marlborough and Cambridge. He served in France from the beginning of World War I, but before it ended issued a volume of bitter antiwar poems *Counter-attack* (1918), the first published expression of the horrors of war by one who fought in it. He had won the Military Cross for bravery before, but in a period of hospital treatment for wounds, he declared himself a pacifist and hoped to be court-martialled for refusing to take any further part in the conflict. When the authorities refused to charge him he returned to the front, was promoted and again wounded. Though *Counter-attack* did nothing to shorten the war, it made a profound impression as a pacifist protest and endures as a human document of world tragedy. Sassoon had published poems at intervals from 1911 and continued to write, his *Collected Poems, 1908-56* appearing in 1961. He made a further reputation with the autobiographical prose volumes in which he named himself Sherston: *Memoirs of a Fox-Hunting Man* (1928), *Memoirs of an Infantry Officer* (1930), *Sherston's Progress* (1936), and others. He also wrote *Meredith* (1948), a biography of the Victorian novelist.

Satchell, William (1860-1942). Born in London; educated in Sussex and at Heidelberg; settled in New Zealand. Author of *The Land of the Lost* (1902), *The Toll of the Bush* (1905), *The Elixir of Life* (1907), *The Greenstone Door* (1914). *See* *New Zealand Writers.

Satire. In the dictionary definition: 'use of ridicule, irony, sarcasm, etc. in speech or writing for the ostensible purpose of exposing and discouraging vice and folly'. It flourished in ancient Greece in the comedies of Aristophanes, and in Rome bitterly in the poems of Juvenal and urbanely in those of Horace. In England John Skelton (*c.* 1460-1529) had a thundering gift of invective, but only in the seventeenth and eighteenth centuries did English satire come to its peak, in Dryden, Swift, and Pope. Later, Byron and (in *Erewhon*) Samuel *Butler continued the tradition. Satire, if it is not to be degraded, requires knowledge, wit, and understanding. Satirical exercises in journalism and broadcasting in the decades after World War II might not seldom have been stigmatized by Dryden as 'the slovenly butchering of a man' (see his essay on 'The Origin and Progress of Satire').

Saul Kane. *See* Kane, Saul.

Saunders, Hilary St George (Hilary Aidan St George Saunders, 1898-1951). Born at Brighton; educated at Downside and Oxford; librarian of the House of Commons, 1946-50. As historian to the Air Ministry in World War II he wrote *The Battle of Britain* (1941) and other pamphlets on various phases of the air war. In collaboration with John L. *Palmer he produced a series of thrillers under the pseudonym Francis Beeding (*The Seven Sleepers,* 1925; *The Six Proud Walkers,* 1928; *The Five Flamboys,* 1929; *The Four Armourers,* 1930; *The Three Fishers,* 1931;

The Two Undertakers, 1933, *The One Sane Man,* 1934; etc.), and, with the same collaborator, others (*So Great a Man,* 1938, etc) under the pseudonym David Pilgrim.

Saurat, Denis (1890-1958). Born at Toulouse; educated at Lille, London, and Paris. Held professorships in the University of Bordeaux before appointment as Professor of French Language and Literature, 1926-50. In addition to works on the literature of his own country, he wrote *Blake and Milton* (1920), *Milton: Man and Thinker* (1925; new edn 1944), *Blake and Modern Thought* (1929), *Literature and Occult Tradition* (1930), *Death and the Dreamer* (1946), *Gods of the People* (1947).

Sauser-Hall, Frédéric. *See* Blaise *Cendrars.

Sava, George (pseudonym of George Alexis Milkomanovich Milkomane, 1903-   ). Born in Russia; attended schools there and in Bulgaria, and studied at the Russian Imperial Naval Academy. After the Bolshevik Revolution he studied medicine in France, Italy and Germany before settling in Britain in 1932 (naturalized 1938) and continuing his medical studies in England and Scotland. His best known writings draw upon his personal life within the framework of professional experience: *The Healing Knife* (1937), *A Surgeon's Destiny* (1939), *Donkey's Serenade* (1940), *A Ring at the Door* (1941), *A Doctor's Odyssey* (1951), *All This and Surgery Too* (1958). Other works: *Rasputin Speaks* (1941), *Valley of Forgotten People* (1942), *A Tale of Ten Cities* (1944), *War Without Guns* (1944), and various novels.

Savi, E. W. (*née* Ethel Winifred Bryning, died 1954; Mrs J. A. Savi). Born in India; educated privately. After her marriage in 1884 she lived in rural India until 1896 and contributed short stories to journals, Indian and English. After settling in England in 1909 she wrote many popular romantic novels, now mostly forgotten: *The Reproof of Chance* (1910), *Banked Fires* (1919), *The Power of Love* (1929), *The Laughter of Courage* (1940), *The Unvarnished Truth* (1950), *The Ewe Lamb* (1955).

'Savonarola' Brown. In the story so entitled in Max Beerbohm's *Seven Men* (1919), Ladbroke Brown wanted to write a play about Savonarola. The fragment left when he died, and incorporated in the story, is a brilliant comic parody of minor Elizabethan tragedies.

Sayer, Rose. Missionary who inspires the perilous voyage with Charlie Allnutt in C. S. Forester's The *African Queen (1935).

Sayers, Dorothy L. (Dorothy Leigh Sayers, 1893-1957; Mrs Atherton Fleming). Born and educated in Oxford. She had some experience as an advertisement copy writer (reflected in one of the most entertaining of her novels, Murder Must Advertise, 1933), before settling into success as a writer of crime novels, with the quotation-packed Lord Peter Wimsey as amateur detective. She began to tire of the genre almost simultaneously with her readers' tiring of Wimsey, and Gaudy Night (1935), more novel than thriller, virtually ended a period of her career in which religion had been gradually ousting fictional mystery. The Zeal of Thy House (1937) was written for performance at the Canterbury Cathedral Festival, and her twelve-part radio play The Man Born to be King (1941) was given repeatedly by the B.B.C. in the weeks preceding Easter. She wrote miscellaneous prose volumes and embarked upon an English verse translation of Dante's Divine Comedy of which only the Inferno (1949) and the Purgatorio (1955) appeared. Besides those named above, her detective novels included Strong Poison (1930), The Five Red Herrings (1931), Have His Carcase (1932), Hangman's Holiday (1933). The Nine Tailors (1934), which depends upon a knowledge of campanology, shows her veering towards self-conscious erudition. She also edited three series of Great Short Stories of Detection, Mystery and Horror (1928, 1929, 1934).

SBN. See *Standard Book Numbering.

Scales, Gerald. Commercial traveller in Arnold Bennett's The *Old Wives' Tale (1908); elopes with Sophia Baines; deserts her in Paris; many years later dies penniless in Manchester.

Scarlet Pimpernel, The. Novel by Baroness *Orczy published in 1905. Sir Percy Blakeney and a group of friends smuggle aristocrats to England during the French Revolution, outwitting the sinister Chauvelin, and leaving each time their sign, representing a little English wild flower, the scarlet pimpernel. Both as a book and as a play it was tremendously popular, and has been long remembered, in so far as its theme of rescue operations carried out with nonchalant daring and ingenuity in circumstances of great peril, led during World War II to the naming of a film character Pimpernel Smith.

Schiff, Sydney. See Stephen *Hudson.

Schlegel, Margaret and **Helen.** Elder and younger sisters in E. M. Forster's *Howards End (1910). Margaret becomes Henry Wilcox's second wife, Helen the mother of a child by Leonard Bast.

Schnitzler, Arthur (1862-1931). Austrian playwright and novelist who previously practised as a physician. Though he wrote more serious works, he became known chiefly by his cynical comedies on amorous themes: e.g. *Anatol.

Scholes, Percy A. (Percy Alfred Scholes, 1877-1958). Born in Leeds. Did much to encourage informed appreciation of classical music through his frequent radio talks in the early years of the B.B.C. and as Music Editor of the Radio Times. He wrote The Great Doctor Burney (1948), The Life and Activities of Sir John Hawkins, Musician, Magistrate, and Friend of Johnson (1953), God Save the Queen: The History and Romance of the World's First National Anthem (1954). His compilations include The Listener's History of Music (3 vols, 1923-29; one-vol edn 1955) and The Oxford Companion to Music (1938 and successive editions).

Schomberg. Malicious Teutonic hotel-keeper, enemy of Axel Heyst in Joseph Conrad's *Victory (1915).

Schreiner, Olive (Olive Emily Albertina Schreiner, 1855-1920). Born in Basutoland of German-English parentage; self-educated. Became nursery-governess in a Boer family until she moved to England in 1881 and remained there for eight years. Before she left South Africa she had written The Story of an African Farm which has made her lastingly celebrated since it was first published in London in 1883. Though she wrote several other books, that first novel proved her to be essentially a one-book woman. Since it was feminist and anti-Christian, unwomanly characteristics at that time, it was first published under the pseudonym Ralph Iron, and the storm it aroused became fiercer when the sex of its author was known. See also Havelock *Ellis.

Schulberg, Budd (Budd Wilson Schulberg, 1914-   ). Born in New York; spent years of his early life in Hollywood, where his father was a script writer; educated in Los Angeles and in New Hampshire at Dartmouth College. His first novel *What Makes Sammy Run?* (1941) is a comic satire on the film industry in Hollywood. *The Disenchanted* (1950) is a grimmer story in the same setting.

Schwartz, Poorten-. *See* Maarten *Maartens.

Schweitzer, Albert (1875-1965). Born in Alsace; educated in Strasbourg, Paris and Berlin, studying theology, philosophy, and music. Became Principal of the Theological College of St Thomas, Strasbourg, in 1903 but resigned three years later to prepare himself for the life of a medical missionary to which he pledged himself years earlier. He qualified as a physician and surgeon in 1913, and in the same year founded the mission hospital at Lambaréné, in central Africa, supporting it by money he earned by his skill as an organist when visiting Europe to give recitals. An expert musicologist, he wrote two important books on J. S. Bach. Among other numerous writings, in addition to theological works are: *On the Edge of the Primeval Forest* (1922), *The Decay and Restoration of Civilisation* (1923), *Memoirs of Childhood and Youth* (1924), *My Life and Thought* (1933), *A Declaration of Conscience* (1957).

Science Fiction. With precursors in Jules *Verne (1828-1905) and H. G. *Wells, novels and stories exploiting the remoter possibilities of scientific discovery and invention appeared in profusion in America and England from the 1940s onward. Beginning mainly as fiction for juveniles, and pabulum for *pulp magazines, with sensational improbabilities in control, the genre progressed to a regard for quasi-science based on what, in the light of existing knowledge, might be deemed possible or probable. In this later development, fostered by its becoming a cult, science fiction was admitted to the fold of literature.

Scientific Revolution. The worldwide changes effected from *c.* the 1940s by nuclear physics, electronics, automation, computerization, plastics, antibiotics, etc.

Scots Quair, A. Trilogy of novels by Lewis Grassic *Gibbon published together in 1946, comprising *Sunset Song* (1932), *Cloud Howe* (1933), *Grey Granite* (1934).
Daughter of a crofter in the Mearns (Kincardineshire), Christine Guthrie ends her college education, which was to lead to an Aberdeen degree and a teaching career, when her mother poisons herself and her twin babies rather than go through another pregnancy. Chris nurses her brutal and sensual father when he becomes paralysed, and after he dies she marries Ewan Tavendale, foreman at a neighbouring farm, and they settle down to work their own land. Chris's love of the country is expressed through the many nature descriptions which are a notably attractive part of the trilogy. She bears a son, Ewan, and the small family live happily until World War I stretches its recruiting tentacles over them. When Chris's husband comes home on leave from the training camp after a long interval, he is changed into an obscene drunkard. He is drafted to the western front and before long Chris is informed of his death, afterwards learning from one of his comrades that he was shot for desertion. At the end of the war, the new minister of the parish chooses an ancient Standing Stone on the brae as a war memorial, on which the names of the four local men killed are carved. Chris marries the minister, Robert Colquohoun, a moody man prone to silent and solitary withdrawals, which chequer their lives together. Young Ewan develops an interest in archaeology and finds ancient implements and other remains. The minister's sermons are variously received by his congregation, for he has strong sympathies with the poor and with the miners during the General Strike of 1926. His outspokenness on behalf of the unemployed and needy are regarded by some as too political and radical. Chris's religious views are unorthodox, and she is unable to follow Robert in his mystical flights when he dwells upon having seen the Figure of Christ pass him bodily on the road. Robert's health breaks down and he falls into a galloping consumption; but he insists on getting from his bed to preach, and dies in the pulpit. Chris and her son move from the country to live in Duncairn, where she goes into partnership in a boarding house. Ewan abandons his study of prehistory and goes to work at a smelters and steel manufacturers, where he has to resort to fistfighting to get himself accepted by the other young men. He becomes an out-and-out Communist, organizes a strike, and is arrested and assaulted by the police. Finally he departs to lead a hunger march of the unemployed to London. Having made a mistaken third marriage, which ends with her

new husband emigrating to Canada, Chris goes back alone to cultivate the croft where she was born. The livingness of the trilogy is due in a large measure to the numerous company of lesser characters, who are often unflatteringly presented by the author as lewd scandalmongers blackening the names of those around them. There is an unusually high proportion of narrative, dialogue being kept to a minimum. In both narrative and dialogue there is free use of the Mearns dialect.

Scott, C. P. (Charles Prestwich Scott, 1846-1932). Born in Bath; educated privately and at Oxford. At the age of twenty-six he became editor of the *Manchester Guardian* and from 1905 its owner also and retained editorial control until 1929. He made it one of the world's great newspapers, maintaining standards of integrity throughout a period when the Press was declining into commercialization and triviality. He was Liberal M.P. for the Leigh division of Lancashire, 1895-1906.

Scott, Clement (Clement William Scott, 1841-1904). Born in London; educated at Marlborough. Became a War Office clerk, 1860-77. Dramatic critic of the *Daily Telegraph* from 1872, and is remembered chiefly by his intemperate attacks on plays by Ibsen (particularly *Ghosts*) when they were performed in London.

Scott, Duncan Campbell (1862-1947). Born in Ottawa; educated there and in Quebec; entered the Civil Service and became Deputy Superintendent of Indian Affairs, 1923-32. Author of *New World Lyrics and Ballads* (1905), *Beauty and Life* (1921), *The Green Cloister* (1935), *The Circle of Affection* (1947); a collected edition of his poems up to that date was published in 1926 as *The Poems of Duncan Campbell Scott*. His short stories were collected in *In the Village of Viger* (1896) and *The Witching of Elspie* (1923).

Scott, Geoffrey (1885-1929). Nephew of C. P. *Scott. Educated at Rugby and Oxford. He became librarian and secretary to Bernard *Berenson, and for a while practised as an architect in Florence. When the American financier Ralph Heyward Isham (1890-1965) bought the *Boswell Papers in 1927, Geoffrey Scott was commissioned to edit them for a privately published edition, but he died after preparing material for only a few volumes of the immense collection. His own writings comprised *The Architecture of Humanism: A Study in the Literature of Taste* (1914; revised edn 1924), *The Portrait of Zélide* (1925. Zélide was the pseudonym of Isabelle de Charrière, a friend of Boswell), and two books of verse—*A Box of Paints* (1923) and *Poems* (1931).

Scott, J. W. Robertson (John William Robertson Scott, 1866-1962). Born at Wigton, Cumberland; 'educated at Grammar and Quaker Schools'. Worked as a journalist on Birmingham and London newspapers. Spent four years in Japan, and on his return to England in 1910 became increasingly occupied with the study of the conditions of rural life. Wrote many books on farming and country affairs, notably *England's Green and Pleasant Land* (1925), but made his greatest success as founder in 1927 of *The Countryman*, which he edited from his home in an Oxfordshire village until 1947. Though the prospects for such a quarterly publication seemed unhopeful, it flourished from the beginning, mainly through Robertson Scott's unflagging energy in all directions, even in securing manifold advertisements by personal canvassing. After relinquishing control of *The Countryman* he wrote *Faith and Works in Fleet Street* (1947); *The Story of the 'Pall Mall Gazette'* (1950), the paper on which he had worked from 1887 to 1893; *The Day Before Yesterday* (1951), and other reminiscences.

Scott, Peter (Peter Markham Scott, 1909-). Born in London, son of Captain Robert Falcon Scott; educated at Oundle and Cambridge; studied art at Munich State Academy and in London at the Royal Academy Schools. Celebrated for his paintings of bird life and for broadcasts on nature programmes. Led ornithological expeditions in the Arctic and elsewhere. Founder and Director of the Wild Fowl Trust, Slimbridge, Gloucestershire. Served in the navy in World War II; represented Great Britain in the single-handed sailing event at the 1936 Olympic Games, winning the bronze medal. Author of *Morning Flight* (1935), *Wild Chorus* (1938), *The Battle of the Narrow Seas* (1945), *Wild Geese and Eskimos* (1951), *The Eye of the Wind* (autobiography; 1961).

Scott, Captain (Sir Robert Falcon Scott, 1868-1912; knighted posthumously). Born at Devonport. Entered the Royal Navy at the age of fourteen and rose to Captain's rank in 1904. He led national expeditions to the Antarctic from 1901 onward, and reached the South Pole on 18 January 1912, only to find evidence that he had been forestalled by the Norwegian Roald Amundsen on 14 December 1911. On the return journey he and his companions all died. He wrote *The Voyage of the Discovery* (1905), and his diaries, found beside his body by the search party after eight months, were published in 1913 as *Scott's Last Expedition*.

Scott-James, R. A. (Rolfe Arnold Scott-James, 1878-1959). Born at Stratford-on-Avon; educated at Mill Hill and Oxford. Literary Editor of the *Daily News* (1906-12); Leader-writer, *Daily Chronicle* (1919-30); Leader-writer and Assistant Editor of *The Spectator* (1933-35; 1939-45). Author of *Modernism and Romance* (1908), *Personality in Literature* (1913), *The Influence of the Press* (1913), *The Making of Literature* (1928), *Personality in Literature, 1913-31* (1931), *Fifty Years of English Literature 1900-1950* (1951), *Thomas Hardy* (1951), *Lytton Strachey* (1955).

Scott-Moncrieff, C. K. (Charles Kenneth Michael Scott-Moncrieff, 1889-1930). Born in Scotland; educated at Inverness, Winchester, and Edinburgh. For two years from 1921 he was on the staff of *The Times*, but thereafter became celebrated as a translator excelling with his classic translation (1922-30) of Marcel *Proust's *A la recherche du temps perdu*, though his early death left the final volume to be translated by Stephen *Hudson. Scott-Moncrieff also translated *The Song of Roland* (1919), *The Satyricon of Petronius* (1923), *The Letters of Abelard and Heloise* (1925), *Shoot!* (1925) and *The Old and the Young* (1928) by Luigi *Pirandello; *The Charterhouse of Parma* (1925) and *The Red and the Black* (1926) by Stendhal (pseudonym of Marie Henri Beyle, 1783-1842). Scott-Moncrieff's *Memories and Letters* were published in 1931.

Scott Thomson, Gladys (died 1966). Educated at City of London School, and at Stuttgart and Oxford. University history tutor in Nottingham and Oxford; Archivist at Woburn Abbey, 1927-40. Author of *Lords Lieutenant in the Sixteenth Century* (1923), which long remained of scholarly value, and in a vein of wider interest *Life in a Noble Household* (1937), *Russells in Bloomsbury* (1940),

Letters of a Grandmother (1943), *A Pioneer Family* (1953).

Screwtape Letters, The. A satirical sequence of imaginary letters passing between Screwtape, an elderly devil, and his nephew, Wormwood, on the most effective way of securing eternal damnation for another. Written by C. S. *Lewis and published in 1942 during World War II, its popular success coincided with the revival of interest in religion that war inspires.

Scrutator. Pseudonym used by R. C. K. *Ensor for weekly articles on foreign affairs in the *Sunday Times*, 1940-53.

Scrutiny. A quarterly critical review founded in Cambridge and edited by F. R. *Leavis from 1932 to 1953. It was reprinted as a whole in twenty volumes in 1963.

Sea and Sardinia. Travel book by D. H. *Lawrence, published in 1923, and treating of places and people encountered by the author and his wife (referred to in the book as 'the q-b', i.e. 'queen bee') in a voyage from Palermo in Sicily to Cagliari, thence journeying overland through Sardinia via Mandas, Sorgono, and Nuoro to Terranova, and by sea across to the Italian mainland at Civitavecchia and back to Palermo, where a visit to a marionette theatre brings the book to a characteristic Lawrence close: 'I loved them all in the theatre: the generous, hot southern blood, so subtle and spontaneous, that asks for blood contact, not for mental communion or spirit sympathy.'

Seaman, Sir Owen (1861-1936; knighted 1914; baronet 1933). Born in London; educated at Shrewsbury and Cambridge. He worked for some years as a schoolmaster at Rossall and as Professor of Literature at Durham College of Science, Newcastle, and became a barrister in 1897. In that year he joined the staff of *Punch*, became its Assistant Editor in 1902, and Editor from 1906 to 1932, giving it the dignity of a national institution without impairing its attraction as a source of civilized entertainment. He contributed parodies and much neatly contrived light verse to the paper, his skill as a commentator on topical matters making him something of an unofficial poet laureate. His published volumes include *The Battle of the Bays* (1896), *In Cap and Bells* (1899), *Borrowed Plumes* (1902), *A Harvest of Chaff* (1904), *Interludes of an Editor* (1929).

Seccombe, Thomas (1866-1923). Born in Norfolk; educated at Felsted and Oxford. Assistant Editor, *Dictionary of National Biography*, 1891-1900. Professor of English, Royal Military College, Sandhurst, 1912-19; Professor of English Literature, Queen's University, Kingston, Ontario, 1921-23. Author of *Twelve Bad Men* (1894), *The Age of Johnson* (1900), *George Meredith* (1913), and editor of various English classics.

Secret Agent, The: A Simple Tale. Novel by Joseph *Conrad published in 1907. Mr (Adolf) Verloc, a double agent working for and against an international anarchist organization, keeps a sleazy stationery and paper shop in Soho as a cover for his political activities. With him live his wife, Winnie, and her young half-idiot brother Stevie, to whom she is protectively devoted. Vladimir, a foreign anti-anarchist diplomat, incites Verloc to blow up Greenwich Observatory with a homemade bomb, calculating that the outrage will be attributed to anarchists and rouse the police against them. Verloc takes Stevie with him to carry the time bomb in a harmless-looking container, but before it can be planted by the boy he stumbles in Greenwich Park and is blown to pieces. The only clue found by the police is a fragment of cloth with the Soho address on it. Winnie recognizes this as a tag from Stevie's coat. While Verloc tries to convince her that he 'didn't mean any harm to come to the boy', Winnie sits absolutely silent and motionless in her grief, but afterwards stabs him to death while he is lying on the sofa. Horrified by what she has done, she starts for the Continent with Ossipon, one of Verloc's associates who has been in love with her and now supposes it is Verloc who has been killed in the explosion. When he discovers the truth, Ossipon deserts her on the boat-train, and that night Winnie jumps overboard from the cross-Channel steamer.

Secret Sharer, The: An Episode from the Coast. Story by Joseph *Conrad published in *'Twixt Land and Sea* in 1912. Appointed unexpectedly to the command of his present ship while she is loading at an Eastern river port, the narrator watches the tug which has brought them to their anchorage at the head of the Gulf of Siam returning up the river. As the sun is setting he sees that another ship is anchored behind a ridge inside the islands, and is informed by his second mate that she is the *Sephora* with a cargo of coal from Cardiff. Since his crew have been extra hard-worked lately, the narrator undertakes the first watch himself until 1 a.m. While he is walking along the deck after dark, he notices that the rope side-ladder put over for the master of the tug has not been pulled up. When he goes to haul it in himself, he finds it is being held below by a naked man who calls up that his name is Leggatt and asks whether he is to go on swimming until he sinks from exhaustion or come on board. He climbs the ladder while the Captain fetches a sleeping suit. In the cabin he explains that he is the mate of the *Sephora*, and that some weeks ago in a furious and seemingly endless gale a troublesome member of the crew was insolent and hesitant when given an order on which the survival of the ship depended. Leggatt knocked him down and during the fight that followed a great sea crashed on the *Sephora* and jammed them together in another part of the ship, where they were picked up with Leggatt's hands still round the throat of the strangled man. After being under arrest and locked in his cabin for almost two months, Leggatt took a sudden chance to escape and jumped overboard hoping to swim to land, until he saw the ship he had now boarded was nearer. For several days following he is kept hidden in the Captain's cabin, which, being L-shaped, with an adjoining bathroom, makes it just possible for him to avoid being seen. The strain of guarding Leggatt in silence as an 'other self' causes the Captain's behaviour to appear demented to his officers and crew, and they are terrified that the ship is being run aground when it is brought perilously close inshore—near enough for the still undetected 'secret sharer' to swim to land.

Sedgwick, Anne Douglas (1873-1935). Born in New Jersey; educated privately; studied painting in Paris. Settled in England and married Basil de Selincourt in 1908. Author of *The Dull Miss Archinard* (1898), *The Little French Girl* (1924), *The Old Countess* (1927), *Dark Hester* (1929), and other novels, the most successful being *Tante* (1911). She also wrote short stories collected in *The Nest* (1913) and *Autumn Crocuses* (1920). *A Portrait in Letters*, edited by her husband, was published in the year after her death.

Seeger, Alan (1888-1916). Born in New York; educated at various schools and at Harvard. Lived in Paris from 1912 until the beginning of World War I, when he joined the French Foreign Legion and served with distinction in France; killed in action. William *Archer wrote an introduction to Seeger's *Collected Poems* (1916), which contained 'I Have a Rendezvous with Death', by which he is best known. His *Letters and Diary* were published in 1917.

Sellar, W. C. (Walter Carruthers Sellar, 1898-1951). *See* R. J. *Yeatman.

Selvon, Samuel (1923-   ). Born and educated in Trinidad; settled in England in 1950. Author of novels—*A Brighter Sun* (1952), *An Island is a World* (1955), *Turn Again Tiger* (1958), *I Hear Thunder* (1963), *The Housing Lark* (1965); short stories—*The Lonely Londoners* (1956), *Ways of Sunlight* (1957).

Semantics. The science of meaning as a branch of *linguistics.

Senhouse, John. Scholar-gipsy in a trilogy of novels by Maurice *Hewlett: *Halfway House* (1908), *Open Country* (1909), *Rest Harrow* (1910). The son of a rich colliery-owner and educated at Cambridge in the early 1880s, he walks away in his third year there and takes to a wandering life, sleeping in a tent which he carries in a horse-drawn cart: 'He paints, he scribbles, he tinkers, he sawders—just as he damn pleases', says a friend. Senhouse, when thirty, falls in love with twenty-year-old Sanchia-Josepha Percival, the youngest of five daughters of a prosperous City merchant with a snobbish Society-conscious wife. In a series of letters to Sanchia from various places on his travels, Senhouse keeps love on a platonic level, and inculcates his philosophy of personal freedom and the pursuit of 'Poverty, Temperance, and Simplicity, these three. But the greatest of these is Poverty.' Sanchia, though half-consciously loving Senhouse, becomes attracted by Nevile Ingram, 'of Wanless Park, Felsboro'', whose wife has deserted him. Sanchia comes to feel it a duty to compensate his enforced loneliness and goes to live at Wanless. She is ostracized by her mother and sisters, guardians of the old morality and social propriety, and is able to maintain contact with her less-censorious father only by subterfuge. Senhouse meanwhile continues with his project of naturalizing exotic plants to grow wild in all parts of England: 'So he turns the Land's End into a rockery and stuffs the cracks with

things from the Alps. . . . And irises on Dartmoor from the Caucasus! And peonies growing wild in South Wales.' A young widow, Mary Germain, is drawn into association with him through interest in his planting, and they go together to the Continent, where he has a five-year collecting and gardening commission for a German grand duke. When he returns to England, Mary having already broken away to marry, Senhouse learns that Sanchia has left Wanless after eight years there, revolted by Ingram's long absences and neglect. But as his wife has now died, Sanchia's family convince her that she must 'put herself right with Society' by marrying him. She reluctantly acquiesces and the engagement is announced, but on the eve of the wedding she rebels and goes to join Senhouse in his free life, their love at last openly realized.

Sensibility. Unconnected with sensibleness, the operative factor in sensibility is emotionalism and susceptibility to the tender social graces and conventional artistic tastes. It had its heyday from the mid-seventeenth century to the mid-nineteenth, when young ladies were prone to tears and fainting, modesty and blushing, and devoted to the pianoforte and watercolour sketching. Jane Austen's *Sense and Sensibility* (1811) distinguishes thought from feeling.

Serendipity. The knack of making lucky discoveries; from a fairy tale, 'The Three Princes of Serendip'. In the 1920s an antiquarian bookseller's near the British Museum kept by Everard *Meynell was called The Serendipity Shop.

Service, R. W. (Robert William Service, 1876-1958). Born at Preston; educated in Glasgow and worked in a bank there until he emigrated to Canada in 1897. After farming on Vancouver Island and roaming up and down the Pacific coast often 'living rough', he joined the staff of a Canadian bank in 1905 and was sent to a branch in the Yukon where he lived for eight years. Then changed his occupation again, becoming a correspondent in Europe for a Toronto paper at the time of the Balkan War. In World War I he was for two years an ambulance driver with the Canadian army in France. Influenced by the work of Rudyard *Kipling and drawing on material from his wander years, he wrote verses which brought him great popularity and prosperity, though their want of literary sophistication caused them to be treated with severity by the critics: *Songs of a Sourdough* (1907; by 1940 two million copies were bought), *Rhymes of a Rolling Stone* (1912), *Rhymes of a Red Cross Man* (1916), *Ballads of a Bohemian* (1920), *Bar-Room Ballads* (1940), *Rhymes of a Roughneck* (1950), *Lyrics of a Lowbrow* (1951), *Rhymes of a Rebel* (1952). Novels: *The Trail of '98* (1910), *The Pretender* (1915), *The Roughneck* (1923), *The House of Fear* (1927). Autobiography: *Ploughman of the Moon* (1945), *Harper of Heaven* (1948).

Seton, Anya (Anya Seton Chase, 1916-   ). Born a British subject in New York, the daughter of the following; educated at school in New York and privately in England. Author of historical and biographical novels based on careful research which has not limited their popularity: *My Theodosia* (1941), *Dragonwyck* (1944), *The Turquoise* (1946), *Foxfire* (1951), *Katherine* (1954), *The Winthrop Woman* (1958), *Devil Water* (1962), *Green Darkness* (1972).

Seton, Ernest Thompson (originally Ernest Evan Seton Thompson, 1860-1946). Born at South Shields, Durham; taken to Canada as a child and educated in Toronto; studied art at the Royal Academy Schools in London, and wild life in Manitoba, where he became Government Naturalist. Founded the Boy Scouts of America and the Woodcraft League. Among his vast output of books on animals (illustrated by himself) are: *Wild Animals I Have Known* (1898), *Biography of a Grizzly* (1900), *Lives of the Hunted* (1901), *Biography of a Silver Fox* (1909), *The Arctic Prairies* (1911), *Wild Animals at Home* (1913), *Woodland Tales* (1921). Autobiography: *The Trail of an Artist-Naturalist* (1940). He also wrote books for boys on scouting and woodcraft.

Seton, Sally. Friend of Clarissa Dalloway and later becomes Lady Rosseter in Virginia Woolf's *Mrs Dalloway* (1925).

Seven Deadly Sins, The. In medieval belief, Pride, Covetousness, Lechery, Anger, Envy, Gluttony, Sloth; or Pride, Wrath, Envy, Lust, Gluttony, Avarice, Sloth.

Seven Men. Volume of imaginary portraits by Max *Beerbohm, published in 1919. An edition entitled *Seven Men and Two Others* (1949) included 'Felix Argallo and Walter Ledgett', first published in the *London Mercury* (May 1927) as 'Not That I Would Boast' and reprinted in the limited edition of *A Variety of Things* (1928).

In the first of the portraits, 'Enoch Soames', the utterly ignored author of three small books sells his soul to the devil in exchange for a visit to the British Museum Reading Room a hundred years in the future, hoping to enjoy in books written about him after his death the fame he is certain posterity will have conferred on him. He finds no mention of himself, however, except a paragraph in a work on nineteenth-century literature citing a story by Max Beerbohm about an imaginary character called Enoch Soames, 'a third-rate poet who believes himself a great genius and makes a bargain with the devil in order to know what posterity thinks of him' (the phonetic spelling of the 1992 book is normalized here). The paragraph is prophetic. for although Beerbohm's story was written in 1912, before the arrival of modern totalitarian States, it proceeds: 'Now that the literary profession has been organized as a department of public service, our writers have found their level and have learnt to do their duty without thought of the morrow.' The most brilliant of the other portraits is the last in the book *' "Savonarola" Brown'. Max himself appears as a character throughout, and is the seventh man.

Seven Pillars of Wisdom, The: A Triumph. T. E. *Lawrence's full account of his experiences as a leader in Arabia during World War I. Issued by the author in a lavishly illustrated limited edition in 1926, it was published for general circulation in 1935. Lawrence's abridged edition, *Revolt in the Desert*, came out in 1927.

Seven Wonders of the World, The. The Pyramids in Egypt, the Hanging Gardens of Babylon, the Tomb of Mausolus at Halicarnassus (part now in the British Museum), the Temple of Diana at Ephesus, the Colossus at Rhodes, the Statue of Zeus by Phidias at Olympia, the Pharos (lighthouse) at Alexandria. Alternatively, the Coliseum in Rome, the Catacombs at Alexandria, the Great Wall of China, Stonehenge, the Leaning Tower at Pisa, the Porcelain Tower at Nanking, the Mosque of St Sophia at Constantinople (now Istanbul).

Sewanee Review. A literary and critical quarterly published by the University of the South, Sewanee, Tennessee. Founded in 1892 by Professor W. P. *Trent, it is mainly devoted to the intellectual and cultural interests of the Southern States, and from the middle 1940s, under the editorship of Allen *Tate, has given much attention to modern poetry and prose.

Seymour, Beatrice Kean (*née* Beatrice Mary Stapleton; died 1955; Mrs William Kean Seymour). Born in London; educated there at a co-educational school and King's College. Before her marriage she worked in the office of Horatio *Bottomley. Author of *Intrusion* (1921), *The Romantic Tradition* (1925), *The Chronicles of Sally* (*Maids and Mistresses*, 1932; *Interlude for Sally*, 1934); *Summer of Life*, (1936), *Joy as it Flies* (1944), *The Wine is Poured* (1953). Her *Jane Austen* (1937) is a study based on her belief that the conventional view of Miss Austen is misconceived.

Seymour, William Kean (1887-1975). Born and educated in London. Worked as bank clerk and manager. Married Beatrice Stapleton (see the preceding) and afterwards Rosalind Wade. *Collected Poems* (1946), plays in verse (*The First Childermas*, 1959, etc), parodies (*A Jackdaw in Georgia*, 1925; *Parrot Pie*, 1927), *The Little Cages* (1944), *Names and Faces* (1956), and other fiction.

S.F. *See* Science Fiction.

Shackleton, Sir Ernest (Ernest Henry Shackleton, 1874-1922; knighted 1909). Born in Ireland; educated in England at Dulwich; apprenticed in the merchant navy; served under Captain Robert *Scott in the *Discovery* Antarctic Expedition (1901-03). Later led expeditions under his own command, that of 1915 in the *Endeavour* (1915) being an especially perilous experience involving a sledge journey of several hundred miles after the ship had been crushed in the ice. He died in the Antarctic on a further expedition. His *The Heart of the Antarctic* (1909) and *South* (1919) are classics of polar exploration.

Shakespeare & Company. *Avante-garde* bookshop in Paris run by Sylvia *Beach. It was a rendezvous for many celebrated English, American, and French writers. James Joyce's *Ulysses* was first published from there. An account of its history and associations is given in *Shakespeare and Company* by Sylvia Beach (1960).

Shakespeare Studies. The widespread extension of English literary study in schools and colleges in the present century has produced an outpouring of books on Shakespeare that threatens to impose a barrier hindering students and others from direct independent-minded approach to the plays. During the century the emphasis in Shakespeare scholarship passed from the biographical and humanistic to the bibliographical and linguistic one and to concentration on intensive textual analysis. The progress or regress from the earlier to the later mode can be traced chronologically through the following brief list of works of more than academic interest. The innumerable specialist studies of individual plays and isolated themes are perforce excluded.

Though first published in 1898, the long continued demand for Sidney Lee's *Life of Shakespeare* maintained it as the standard biography in immediately following decades. A. C. Bradley's *Shakespearean Tragedy* (1904), a classic study of the characters as 'real' people, has survived harsh and some facetious comment from critics of a later generation. The humanistic bent continued to prevail in the shorter studies by Walter Raleigh (*Shakespeare*, 1907) and John Masefield (*Shakespeare*, 1911). In *Shakespeare's England: An Account of the Life and Manners of his Age* (1916) various authors depict the environment in which the playwright worked. The documentary approach was pioneered by A. W. Pollard's bibliographical study *Shakespeare's Folios and Quartos* (1909), followed in 1917 by his *Shakespeare's Fight with the Pirates*, i.e. with the thievish printer-publishers' unauthorized editions. E. K. Chambers's *William Shakespeare: A Study of Facts and Problems* (2 vols, 1930), a corrective to fanciful biographical speculation, is no less indispensable than his great works on *The Medieval Stage* (2 vols, 1903) and *The Elizabethan Stage* (4 vols, 1923). Granville Barker's *Prefaces to Shakespeare* (5 series 1927-48) are unique in viewing the plays from the angle of a stage producer and actor. He also wrote, in collaboration with G. B. Harrison, *A Companion to Shakespeare Studies* (1934). Caroline Spurgeon's *Shakespeare's Imagery and What it Tells Us* (1935) brought the analysis of poetic imagery into fashion. *The Essential Shakespeare: A Biographical Adventure* (1932) and *What Happens in Hamlet* (1935) are two of the more popular of J. Dover Wilson's numerous writings on

Shakespeare. A. L. Rowse's *William Shakespeare: A Biography* (1963) made a confident but not generally accepted claim to have solved a number of long outstanding problems. Much scholarly labour continues to be given to the endeavour to establish once for all 'what Shakespeare actually wrote', preparatory to producing a final edition cleared of scribes' and compositors' and editors' errors and guesses and corruptions. Some of the inherent difficulties are discussed in W. W. Greg's *The Editorial Problems in Shakespeare* (1942, 1954); and an invaluable contribution is made by Charlton Hinman's recondite yet fascinating work *The Printing and Proof-reading of the First Folio Shakespeare* (2 vols, 1963) which identifies the several compositors and their idiosyncrasies, and shows that certain textual puzzles yield not to editorial ingenuity but to knowledge of Elizabethan printing-house practice. A vast amount of the produce of recent Shakespeare discovery and invention is scattered in learned periodicals. *Shakespeare Survey* (annually from 1948) is a review of Shakespearean scholarship, criticism and production. For general reading the one-volume *Oxford Shakespeare* is well-established, though specialists would suggest some textual emendations. Critical editions of the plays, each in a separate volume, are provided in the *New Cambridge Shakespeare* and in the *New Arden Shakespeare*. The theory that the plays were written by Francis Bacon or another using Shakespeare as cover has considerable support. H. N. Gibson's *The Shakespeare Claimants* (1962) subjects the theory to critical inquiry and includes a comprehensive bibliography of the literature of the subject from 1857 onward.

Shand, John, M.P. in J. M. Barrie's **What Every Woman Knows* (1908); marries Maggie Wylie.

Shangri-La. Name given in James *Hilton's novel *Lost Horizon* (1933) to an imaginary land isolated in the heart of Asia where the inhabitants are free from the turmoil of the world and the common disabilities of life. The term has since been used of any such supposed place of withdrawal from the distresses of ordinary life, a lotus land.

Shanks, Edward (Edward Richard Buxton Shanks, 1892-1953). Born in London; educated at Merchant Taylors' School and Cambridge. Assistant Editor, **London*

Mercury (1919-22); Chief leader-writer, *Evening Standard* (1928-35). Author of *The Queen of China and other poems* (1919), *Collected Poems* (1926), *Poems, 1912-32* (1933), *Poems, 1939-52* (1953). *First Essays on Literature* (1923; second series, 1927), *Bernard Shaw* (1924), *Rudyard Kipling* (1939).

Shanties. Sailors' traditional work songs while hauling on ropes, anchor chains, etc. They were annexed, inappropriately, as public concert items and sung with popular success by John Goss (1894-1953) among others.

Sharp, Evelyn (Evelyn Adelaide Sharp, 1903-55; Mrs H. W. *Nevinson). Born in London; educated privately. Was active in the militant women's suffrage campaign before World War I and twice imprisoned. Contributed to various papers and periodicals; on the staff of the *Daily Herald* 1915-23. Author of fairy stories and other books for children, including *The Youngest Girl in the School* (1901). She also wrote *Nicolete* (1907) and other novels; *Rebel Woman* (1910), *Unfinished Adventure* (autobiography, 1933), and edited her husband's *Visions and Memories* (1944).

Sharp, Margery (1905-   ). Born in London and educated there at Streatham and University of London. Contributed to various magazines in England and America. Her humorous novels display an original and refreshing gift for fun supported by an acute sense of character: *Fanfare for Tin Trumpets* (1932), *The Nutmeg Tree* (1937), *The Stone of Chastity* (1940), *Cluny Brown* (1944), *Britannia Mews* (1946), *The Foolish Gentlewoman* (1948), *Lise Lillywhite* (1951), *The Gipsy in the Parlour* (1953) etc.

Sharp, William. *See* Fiona *Macleod.

Shaw, Bernard (George Bernard Shaw, 1856-1950). Born in Dublin, third and youngest child and only son of George Carr Shaw and Lucinda Elizabeth Shaw. His father was the eighth of fifteen children of another Bernard Shaw, and second cousin of Sir Robert Shaw, Bart. His mother (*née* Gurly), daughter of a bankrupt landed gentleman, married George Carr Shaw when she was twenty-one and he thirty-eight, his alcoholism becoming evident immediately after. Two years before, he had been compulsorily retired from a sinecure in the Dublin Law Courts and had sold his pension of £60 a year for a lump sum of £500, which he put into partnership in a corn mill. Meanwhile his wife, who displayed no affection for husband or children, took voice-training lessons with George Vandaleur Lee. The Shaws set up a joint household with the Lees; and there, from the age of about ten, young Bernard began to acquire that knowledge and love of music (mainly operatic and Mozartian) which qualified him as a music critic in later years and had a marked technical influence on his plays, for which he said the actors should be chosen with attention to voice contrast, the four principals being soprano, alto, tenor, and bass. His formal education was conducted in turn by a governess and a clergyman uncle, and then at the Wesleyan Connexional School, a rural private school, the Central Model Boys' School and the Dublin English Scientific and Commercial Day School. At fifteen he became a clerk in an estate agents' office in Dublin, rising from eighteen shillings a month to £1 a week when he was promoted to cashier in about a year. His mother, with his two sisters, went to live in London in 1875. Bernard Shaw followed in the next year, with a testimonial from his Dublin employers certifying that he was 'a young man of great business capacity, strict accuracy, and thoroughly reliable and trustworthy'. He settled in London with £1 a week allowance from his father in Dublin, who died there in 1885. Mrs Shaw became a successful teacher of singing, and retained her own exceptional singing voice until she died aged eighty-three in 1913. Bernard Shaw had had to rely on his mother to supplement the allowance from his father, since from writing he made only £6 in nine years. Nevertheless he determined to live by writing, after working for eight months with the Edison Telephone Company. Between 1879 and 1883 he wrote five novels, which brought him neither profit nor fame. He devoted much of his energy to public speaking in the interest of socialism, and in the British Museum Reading Room combined the reading of Karl Marx's Das Kapital in French with close study of the score of Wagner's Tristan and Isolde. This unusual combination was noticed by a neighbouring reader, William *Archer, and began a lifelong friendship. Archer passed over to Shaw some of his own journalistic work, as book-reviewer on the Pall Mall Gazette, 1885-88; and from 1886 to 1889 he was art critic on The World, and wrote music criticism in The Star, as Corno di Bassetto, 1888-90. By then Shaw was making an income from journalism, a phase of his

career which had its culmination in his articles as theatre critic for the Saturday Review, 1895-98, reprinted as Our Theatres in the Nineties (3 vols, 1931). He joined the *Fabian Society in 1884, becoming one of its most influential members, both as speaker and as pamphleteer (see his reprinted Essays in Fabian Socialism, 1932). Sometime in 1885 Archer suggested to Shaw that they should collaborate in a play, and provided (as Shaw wrote later) a 'thoroughly planned scheme for a sympathetically romantic "well made play" of the Parisian type then in vogue'. The project lapsed, but the notion of a play revived in Shaw's *Widowers' Houses, put on for two performances by the Independent Theatre Society in December 1892. Archer's attention at this time was concentrated on the first English edition of *Ibsen's plays which he and other members of his family were bringing out in translation, while in 1891 Shaw published The Quintessence of Ibsenism, a study of Ibsen's ideas and writings. Widowers' Houses, published by itself in 1893, was the first of Shaw's plays to appear in print, and it was also included with the seven Plays: Pleasant and Unpleasant, published in two volumes (1898) each with a Preface. Thus began the series of Prefaces which were to be a distinctive feature of Shaw's volumes of plays from that time. Though not always directly relevant to the plays they precede, the Prefaces are a repository of the author's fecund opinions and convictions as well as a masterly body of plain but eloquent English prose. Dealing controversially with social, political, and metaphysical topics, Shaw's plays excited hostile comment, and though among the then young generation they found enthusiastic admirers, it was long before Shaw had the 'pit full of philosophers' he aimed at in *Man and Superman (1903), first performed at the *Court Theatre season (1905-07), when Shaw's position as the leading playwright of his time was established. He married Charlotte Payne-Townshend in 1898, a childless marriage of companionship and mutual respect rather than of romantic love or passion. He was attractive to women and much pursued by them, but he was resistant to emotional entanglements. His friendship with Mrs Patrick Campbell (the actress who first played Eliza Doolittle in Shaw's Pygmalion in England in 1914) is reflected in the Interlude to The *Apple Cart (1929), but his ideal of a devoted relationship between a man and a woman is exemplified in the letters that passed between him and Ellen *Terry, for whom he wrote the part of Lady Cicely Waynflete in *Captain Brassbound's Conversion (1900). Shaw considered Ellen Terry a great actress kept in chains by her manager and leading man, Henry Irving. Shaw's baiting of Irving in his Saturday Review articles and in Ellen Terry and Bernard Shaw: A Correspondence (1930) was on two counts: that he did nothing to help the New Drama of Ibsen and his English disciples; and that he discredited Shakespeare by mutilating the text of the plays and ignoring the poetry, in the interests of stage spectacle and of Irving's own idiosyncrasies as a character actor. There was in Shaw's lifetime and after, much misrepresentation of his attitude to Shakespeare, largely due to the section headed 'Better than Shakespeare?' in the Preface to Three Plays for Puritans (1901), where comparison is made of *Caesar and Cleopatra (one of the three plays) and Antony and Cleopatra. This section of the Preface, often quoted as a statement instead of as a question, is a complaint against the adulation of Shakespeare which he called 'Bardolatry'. Both in regard to his comments on Shakespeare and on other grounds, Shaw was often accused of unbridled personal vanity. But although, as he said himself, he was not addicted to 'the modest cough of a minor poet', nor was he self-inflated. He had genius, and also the rare gift of seeing his own qualities objectively. While among his friends there were many who dissented from his political opinions, all who knew the man behind the public mask bore witness to his abundant kindness, courtesy, and generosity. (See G.B.S. 90: Aspects of Bernard Shaw's Life and Work to which twenty-seven notable contemporaries contributed for his ninetieth birthday in 1946.) The Order of Merit was offered to him more than once, but he declined on the plea that determination of his merit must be left to posterity: 'Either I shall be remembered as a playwright as long as Aristophanes and rank with Shakespeare and Molière, or I shall be a forgotten clown before the end of the century.' He left £367,000, and willed the main part of it to finance the introduction and furthering of an enlarged English alphabet with a separate symbol for each vocal sound. If this project foundered, the residue was to be shared by the National Gallery of Ireland, the British Museum, and the Royal Academy of Dram-

atic Art. An edition of Androcles and the Lion was published in an enlarged alphabet in 1962, after the provision in Shaw's will had been ruled inoperative by the Courts. Meanwhile the fortune he left has greatly increased by royalties from books and performances. The film rights of My Fair Lady (adapted as a musical play from Pygmalion) were bought in 1962 for nearly two million pounds sterling, some proportion of which would accrue to the Shaw estate, for which the Public Trustee acts. While it is certain that many more words went into Shaw's political and other prose writings than into his plays, it is by his plays that he will be remembered. The nondramatic publications include The Perfect Wagnerite (1898), The Intelligent Woman's Guide to Socialism and Capitalism (1928), Everybody's Political What's What (1944). The *Adventures of the Black Girl in her Search for God (1932).

Shaw's principal plays, in addition to those named above, are (with dates of first English production): *Arms and the Man (1894), *Candida (1895), *You Never Can Tell (1899), *John Bull's Other Island (1904), *Major Barbara (1905), The *Doctor's Dilemma (1906), Getting Married (1908), The *Shewing-up of Blanco Posnet (1909), Misalliance (1910), *Fanny's First Play (1911), *Heartbreak House (1921), *Back to Methuselah (1923), *Saint Joan (1924), Too True to be Good (1932), In 'Good King Charles's Golden Days' (1939).

The publication of his Collected Letters began in 1965 with the 1874-97 volume, edited by Dan H. Laurence. As it is estimated that Shaw wrote at least a quarter of a million letters and postcards, and his own expectation was that a complete edition would run to twenty volumes, there will need to be a rigorous winnowing for the four-volume edition which is projected. And see under E. L. *Voynich.

Shaw, Mrs Bernard (née Charlotte Frances Townsend, 1857-1943). Born in Derry, Ireland. Her mother, socially ambitious, caused the family's name to be changed first to Payne-Townsend and then to Payne-Townshend when Charlotte was seventeen. Though the girl was contemptuous of the change, it was as Charlotte Frances Payne-Townshend that she was known thenceforward. Three years later the family moved to London in response to the mother's hankering for more exalted society than she found in Cork or Dublin. Their house in Derry was retained, and though Charlotte was not averse to the social round in London and formed a number of friendships with men, she took an active interest in Irish affairs and refused several proposals of marriage. After her parents' death she was a wealthy woman of thirty-four with a liking for travel. She visited India and Egypt, and in Rome in 1894 was introduced to Dr Axel *Munthe, whom she consulted professionally. A warm friendship developed, but Charlotte's expectation that he would ask her to marry was unfulfilled. Returning to London, she was drawn into the Beatrice and Sidney *Webb circle and was induced by Mrs Webb to contribute £1000 to the library of the London School of Economics. On 29 January 1896 she met Bernard Shaw at that institution and on 1 June 1898 they married. Charlotte's life thereafter merged with that of her husband, whose devoted helpmeet she became until her death forty-five years later. Their marriage was based first on economic convenience—she wished him to benefit by her wealth—and throughout on mutual respect and, on her part, on constant admiration of his genius. Passion was absent on both sides. She suffered at times from the interior loneliness which besets the wives of all men of genius, and late in life her correspondence with T. E. *Lawrence showed how deeply she needed mental and emotional release. *Three Plays by *Brieux* (1911) contains her translation of *Maternité;* in 1912 her *Selected Passages from the Works of Bernard Shaw* was published; and in *Knowledge in the Door: a Forerunner* (1914) she displayed something of her religious gropings, unsatisfied by any orthodox faith.

Shaw, Irwin (1913-   ). Born in New York; educated in Brooklyn. Worked in many jobs; wrote radio and film scripts and short stories in various magazines. Author of *Bury the Dead* (1936), *The Gentle People* (1939), *Quiet City* (1939), *The Assassin* (1945) and other plays; volumes of short stories— *Sailor Off the Bremen* (1940), *Mixed Company* (1950); novels—*The Young Lions* (1948), *The Troubled Air* (1951), *Lucy Crown* (1956), *Two Weeks in Another Town* (1960), *Evening in Byzantium* (1973).

Shaw, T. E. *See* T. E. *Lawrence.

Shearing, Joseph. One of several pseudonyms

used by Mrs A. L. Long (*née* Gabrielle Margaret Vere Campbell) who wrote mainly as Marjorie *Bowen.

Sheldon, C. M. (Charles Monroe Sheldon, 1857-1946). Born in New York; educated in Massachusetts and Rhode Island; studied theology and entered the Congregational ministry, becoming a pastor in Kansas. Editor of the American *Christian Herald* (1920-25). He wrote several novels before *In His Steps* (1896), the story of a minister who based his life on that of Christ, which had an unparalleled success, was translated into more than a score of languages and was said to have outstripped all other best-sellers. He continued to write for the next forty years but produced nothing as remarkable. Autobiography: *Charles M. Sheldon: His Life and Story* (1925).

Sheldon, Edward (Edward Brewster Sheldon, 1886-1946). Born in Chicago; educated in Pennsylvania and at Harvard, where he studied at the *47 Workshop under G. P. *Baker, having success with his first play *Salvation Nell* (1908). *Romance* (1913)—in which an elderly bishop relates the story of his early love for an opera singer, in an effort to dissuade his grandson from marrying an actress—made him internationally celebrated. Other plays: *The Nigger* (1900), *The Boss* (1911), *The High Road* (1912), *The Song of Songs* (1914) from a novel by Sudermann, *The Garden of Paradise* (1914) from Hans Andersen's *The Little Mermaid*.

Shepherd's Life, A: Impressions of the South Wiltshire Downs by W. H. *Hudson published in 1910. Written before the motor age, while Wiltshire was still 'little favoured by tourists' and many of the villages and hamlets were remote from main traffic routes, this account of the people and the animal and bird life on and around Salisbury Plain preserves an otherwise vanished picture of rural England emerging from the pastoral into the mechanical age. Its many anecdotes of the times are drawn mainly from the spoken recollections of Caleb Bawcombe, who from early boyhood to old age tended with devotion his employers' flocks on the downlands, with no company other than one of the sheepdogs he trained to the point where animal instinct seemed developed into almost human intelligence. Like the rest of farm workers at that period, he kept a wife and family on a normal wage of seven shillings a week and, at most, thirteen shillings.

In his eighties, after working for more than half a century 'on the downs and fields, day and night, seven days a week', he said that if his life could be offered to him over again 'and I was told to choose my work, I'd say, Give me my Wiltsheer Downs again and let me be a shepherd there all my life long'. The country lore in the book comprises much about flowers and birds and the small creatures—adders, shrews, hedgehogs, rabbits, hares, foxes—besides numerous stories of dogs. The human aspect embraces employers good and bad, villagers kindly and tyrannical, poachers and deer-stealers, machine-wreckers, gipsies, ghosts, and game-keepers whose indifference to all country things but the pheasants they rear only for wholesale destruction arouses the author's anger and contempt.

Sheridan, Clare (*née* Clare Consuelo Frewen, 1885-1970). Born in London; educated in Paris and Darmstadt. As a sculptor she produced portrait busts of notable British and foreign politicians, travelling widely for these and other purposes and gathering material for her books: *Russian Portraits* (1921), *My American Diary* (1922), *In Many Places* (1923), *Across Europe with Satanella* (1925), *A Turkish Kaleidoscope* (1926), *Arab Interlude* (1936), *Redskin Interlude* (1938). Other writings: *Nuda Veritas* (1927), *Genetrix* (1935), *My Crowded Sanctuary* (1943), *To the Four Winds* (1954).

Sheridan Jones. See Mrs Cecil *Chesterton (*née* Ada Elizabeth Jones).

Sherlock Holmes. See Conan *Doyle.

Sherriff, R. C. (Robert Cedric Sherriff, 1896-). Born at Kingston-on-Thames and went to school there. Served and was wounded in Flanders in World War I. Before and for some ten years after the war he worked as an insurance clerk, but the enormous success of his war play *Journey's End* (1929) enabled him to abandon office life and supplement his éducation at Oxford. He then spent some time in Hollywood as a script writer. His later plays and novels had the misfortune to be compared unfavourably with *Journey's End*, though their merit might have been more fairly appreciated without that inappropriate comparison, for the war play had inevitable emotional crises while Sherriff's inate temperament led to his subsequent works being pitched in a lower key. Plays: *Badger's Green* (1930), *Windfall*

(1933), *Miss Mabel* (1948), *Home at Seven* (1950), *The White Carnation* (1953), *The Long Sunset* (1955), *A Shred of Evidence* (1960). Novels: *The Fortnight in September* (1931), *Greengates* (1936), *The Hopkins Manuscript* (1939), *Another Year* (1946), *King John's Treasure* (1954), *The Wells of St Mary's* (1961). Autobiography: *No Leading Lady* (1968).

Sherwood, R. E. (Robert Emmett Sherwood, 1896-1955). Born at New Rochelle, New York; educated in Massachusetts and at Harvard. He joined the Canadian army in World War I and was severely wounded in France. Editor of *Life*, 1924-28. In World War II he worked for the U.S. government in the Office of War Information and was a valued friend of President F. D. *Roosevelt. After the war he devoted much time to preparing *Roosevelt and Hopkins: An Intimate History* (1948), Harry Hopkins having been a close associate of the President before and during the war and his personal commissioner on visits to Europe. Sherwood's book was received, as an important contribution to contemporary history, but he had a wider reputation as a playwright with *The Road to Rome* (1927), *The Queen's Husband* (1928), *Waterloo Bridge* (1930), *Reunion in Vienna* (1931), *The Petrified Forest* (1935), *Idiot's Delight* (1936), *Abe Lincoln in Illinois* (1938), *There Shall Be No Night* (1940).

Shewing-up of Blanco Posnet, The: A Sermon in Crude Melodrama. One-act play by Bernard *Shaw written and performed in 1909; published in *The Doctor's Dilemma* volume in 1911. A group of women are shelling nuts and arguing about whether stealing a horse is a worse crime than killing a man, in a room that serves as town hall and court house of an American town in pioneer days. Elder Daniels (alias of 'Boozy Posnet') comes in to say that the room is wanted for the trial of a man who has stolen a horse belonging to the Sheriff, thinking that it was Daniels's property. The thief, Blanco Posnet, is brought in, and when alone together it emerges that the Elder is his brother, a drunkard and drink-seller, and hypocritically pious. Though Blanco has been caught, the horse has not been found, and the trial cannot start with-out a witness who saw him with the horse. The local prostitute, Feemy Evans, comes forward to give evidence against him, but is interrupted by news that an unnamed woman has been found with the horse, and with a dead child. The woman tells the court that a man gave her the horse so that she could get the sick child to a doctor. Blanco is freed, but before leaving he jumps on to the table to preach a sermon on how he 'started in to be a bad man' but was made to 'go soft' by the Lord: 'He made me because He had a job for me. He let me run loose til the job was ready; and then I had to come along and do it.'

Shiel, M. P. (Matthew Phipps Shiel, 1865-1947). Born in the West Indies; educated there and in London at King's College; studied medicine at St Bartholomew's Hospital but did not proceed with it. He mixed with the men of the 1880s and 1890s in London and Paris. He became Interpreter to the International Congress of Hygiene and Demography, and described himself as teacher, journalist, author and inventor. He wrote novels in an entirely personal, per-fervid, and curiously opaque prose. They had only limited success, though between the World Wars some of the early ones (e.g. *The Purple Cloud*, first published 1901) were reissued and variously received—as, on the one hand, impenetrable and, on the other hand, as works of superb genius. In 1938 he received a Civil List pension for 'services to literature'. A volume of *Poems* appeared in 1936 and among the novels are *The Yellow Danger* (1898), *Unto the Third Generation* (1903), *The White Wedding* (1907), *The Dragon* (1913), *Dr Krasinski's Secret* (1930), *The Black Box* (1930), *The Invisible Voices* (1936), *The Young Men are Coming* (1937), *Above All Else* (1943).

Shimerda, Ántonia. See *Ántonia Shimerda.

Sholokhov, Mikhail Aleksandrovich (1905-). Born in a Cossack village on the river Don; educated in Moscow and Voronezh. Author of *Tales of the Don* (1925), *And Quiet Flows the Don* (1928-38) and its sequel *The Don Flows Home to the Sea* (1941); *Virgin Soil Upturned* (1935). His novels won worldwide esteem and Soviet approval, but his claim to be author of *Quiet Flows* and its sequel has been questioned. See *Solzhenitsyn.

Shorter, Clement, K. (Clement King Shorter, 1858-1926). Born in London; educated in Norfolk. Civil Service clerk (1877-90). Married Dora *Sigerson, 1896. Editor of the *Illustrated London News*, 1891-1900; founded

The Sketch (1893), *The Sphere* (1900), *The Tatler* (1903). He was a critic with some influence in his time and a pioneer in the revival of interest in the Brontës: *Charlotte Brontë and her Circle* (1896), *Charlotte Brontë and Her Sisters* (1905), *The Brontës: Life and Letters* (2 vols, 1907), *The Complete Poems of Emily Brontë* (1911). He also wrote books on Napoleon and George Borrow, edited an enlarged edition of Mrs Gaskell's *Life of Charlotte Brontë* and published his memoirs as *C.K.S.: An Autobiography* (1926).

Shotover, Captain. The ancient prophet-like sea-captain in *Heartbreak House* (1917) by Bernard Shaw. His last remaining ambition is to attain 'the seventh degree of concentra-tion' and thus reach ultimate interior wisdom free from the follies and evils of the world.

Shropshire Lad, A. See A. E. *Housman.

Shushions, Mr. Sunday-school teacher and superintendent in Arnold Bennett's *Clay-hanger* (1910). He rescues Darius and his parents from the workhouse. As a destitute old man 'whose sole crime against society was that he had forgotten to die' he loses his platform ticket at the Sunday-schools Centenary celebrations, and is jeered at by louts. Her kindly protection of the outcast 'oldest Sunday-school teacher' at the Centenary gives Edwin a new vision of Hilda Lessways.

Shute, Nevil (pseudonym of Nevil Shute Norway, 1899-1960). Educated at Shrews-bury and Oxford. After World War I, in which he served as an infantryman, he became almost exclusively interested in aeronautics, was closely concerned in the construction of airships, and as Deputy Chief Engineer of the R100 flew the Atlantic in 1930. He founded an aeroplane con-struction firm in 1931 and was its Joint Managing Director in 1938, by which time he had published several novels: *Marazan* (1926), *So Disdained* (1928), *Lonely Road* (1932), *Ruined City* (1938). In World War II he joined the Royal Naval Volunteer Reserve but continued to write. *What Happened to the Corbetts* (1939) foreshadowed the effects of bombing on a family; *Pied Piper* (1942) concerned the rescue of a collection of children from invading Nazis. Among his later novels *No Highway* (1948) utilized the theme of metal fatigue in aircraft before it became a matter of common discussion. *A Town Like Alice* (1949) is set in Alice Springs in central Australia, the continent to which the author emigrated, to register his dissatisfaction with the condition of England as a Welfare State. At his best Shute was a gripping storyteller with a rare gift of weaving technical knowledge into the fabric of fictional narrative, but he became less compelling in the novels of his last period. These included *The Far Country* (1952), *On the Beach* (1957), *The Trustee from the Toolroom* (posthumously, 1960). Autobiography: *Slide Rule* (1954).

Shy, Timothy. *See* D. B. Wyndham *Lewis.

Sichel, Walter (1855-1933). Educated at Harrow and Oxford. Contributed to *Punch* and other periodicals. Wrote historical biographies of Bolingbroke, Disraeli, Lady Hamilton, Sheridan, Sterne. *Recollections and Reflections* (1923), *Types and Characters* (1925).

Sick humour. Jokes, songs, verses, etc. in which the comic intention is exercised through a facetious attitude towards pain, misfortune, physical and mental handicap, or disaster. In its wittier form it appears in the *Ruthless Rhymes* and other verses of Harry *Graham (1874-1936); among comedians and others after World War II it took a harsher and sometimes crude turn.

Sickert, Walter Richard (1860-1942). Born in Munich. He took up acting, but after a few years on the stage, studied at the Slade School in London and under James McNeill Whistler. He spent much time visiting Paris and became a devotee of Degas's paintings. He helped to establish English art clubs having the aim to encourage Impressionism and later styles in painting. In 1934 he was elected R.A. but quickly resigned in protest against its attitude towards the younger painters. He was one of the few modern English artists of genius, with a technique all his own; his interiors (particularly of the old music-halls) are among the best of his works. He was also a forceful and influential writer: *A Free House! or, the Artist as Craftsman: Being the Writings of Walter Richard Sickert*, edited by Osbert Sitwell (1947).

Sidgwick, Ethel (1877-1970). Born in Rugby; educated in Oxford. Her novels have been compared with those of Henry James, though they are less subtly intellectualized:

Promise (1910), *Herself* (1912), *The Accolade* (1915), *Restoration* (1923), *The Bells of Shoreditch* (1928), *Dorothy's Wedding* (1931), Her uncle was Henry Sidgwick the philosopher, and her *Mrs Henry Sidgwick: A Memoir* (1938) was about her aunt, the Principal of Newnham College, Cambridge, from 1892-1910.

Siegfried, André (1875-1959). Born at Le Havre; educated in Paris. Became Professor of Economic Geography at the Collège de France. Author of *Democracy in New Zealand* (1904), *Post-War Britain* (1924), *America Comes of Age* (1927), *England's Crisis* (1931), *Europe's Crisis* (1931), and other works translated into English.

Sienkiewicz, Henryk (1846-1916). Born in Russian Poland; educated in Warsaw. Lived in America from 1876 to 1878. His trilogy of historical novels on his nation's struggle for independence in the 17th century made him a national hero and Poland's representative novelist: English titles: *With Fire and Sword* (1890), *The Deluge* (1891), *Pan Michael* (1893). His great popular success, however, was *Quo Vadis?*, a story of Rome in the time of Nero, which had worldwide circulation as a book and was rediscovered by Hollywood in the 1950s and made into a grandiose money-spinning film.

Sierra, Gregorio Martínez. *See* Gregorio *Martínez Sierra.

Sieveking, Lance (Lancelot de Giberne Sieveking, 1896-1972). Born at Harrow; educated in Switzerland and at Cambridge. Became an aviator in World War I; afterwards toured as an actor; joined the B.B.C. in 1924; produced and wrote many radio plays. His books include *The Psychology of Flying* (1919), *Stampede* (1924; illustrated by G. K. Chesterton), *The Stuff of Radio* (1934), *The Eye of the Beholder* (1957).

Sigerson, Dora (1866-1918). Born in Dublin; educated at home; married Clement K. *Shorter. Her poems were highly praised by George Meredith and other writers: *Ballads and Poems* (1898). *Collected Poems* (1907), *New Poems* (1912), *Love of Ireland: Poems and Ballads* (1916), *Sixteen Dead Men and other Poems of Easter Week* (1919).

Silberrad, Una L. (Una Lucy Silberrad, 1872-1955). Born in Essex. Author of many novels, including *The Lady of Dreams* (1901), *Simon Rideout, Quaker* (1911), *Rachel and her*

Relations (1921), *In the Course of Years* (1929), *Sun in November* (1937).

Silent Spring. *See* Rachel L. *Carson.

Sillitoe, Alan (1928-   ). Educated at elementary schools in Nottingham; worked in a bicycle factory. Author of *Saturday Night and Sunday Morning* (1958), *The Loneliness of the Long Distance Runner* (1959), *The General* (1960), *The Rats and other Poems* (1960), *The Fire of Life* (1974).

Silone, Ignazio (pseudonym of Secondo Tranquilli, 1900-   ). Born at Pescina; educated there and elsewhere in Italy. Engaged in political activities and worked against the Fascist régime. Author of *Fontamara* (1934), *Bread and Wine* (1936), and other novels; *Mr Aristotle* (1935), short stories.

Silver Box, The. Play in three acts by John *Galsworthy performed in 1906; published in 1909. Drunk on Easter Monday night, Jack Barthwick, son of John Barthwick, M.P., is helped to open the street-door of the family home by a boozy hangabout whom he then invites into the dining-room for a drink. The man, giving his name, says he is the husband of Mrs Jones, the Barthwick's charwoman. When Jack falls asleep on the sofa, after boasting that the woman's handbag he is carrying has been taken by him 'to score her off', Jones helps himself freely to whisky and leaves with a purse from the handbag and a silver cigarette-box. Jack is still asleep when Mrs Jones and the housemaid start their work in the dining-room next morning, but he goes off to bed before Marlow, the butler, misses the cigarette-box. At breakfast Mr and Mrs Barthwick discuss Jack's planting a worthless cheque on his Oxford tailor. His father has since given him the money to pay the bill, but he has spent it all. Jack's companion of the night before calls to demand the return of her purse, and, Jack being penniless, Mr Barthwick refunds £8 to her and stigmatizes his son as 'a nuisance to the community'. When the loss of the silver box is discovered, suspicion falls on Mrs Jones, a quiet-spoken hardworking woman persistently ill-used by her worthless husband. When she is arrested in their one-room lodging, Jones attacks the detective and confesses to the theft. The Barthwicks try unsuccessfully to avoid Jack's being called in court. The evidence he gives is evasive, beyond admitting that he drank too

much champagne and cannot remember what happened on the bank-holiday night. Mr Barthwick withdraws the theft charge, Mrs Jones is discharged, and Jones is given a month's hard labour for assault, and is told by the magistrate that he is 'a nuisance to the community'—the same words as Barthwick had used of his son, who goes scot free though the trouble originated with him. Jones protests from the dock: 'It's *'is money* got 'im off'.

Silver, Miss. Detective in crime novels by Patricia *Wentworth.

Simenon, Georges (1903-   ). Born in Liège, where he became a newspaper reporter at the age of sixteen. Settled in Paris. Though his first novel, *Aboard the Ark* was published in 1920, it was not till 1932 that he produced *The Crime of Inspector Maigret* (the first of the almost innumerable Maigret detective stories which gave him international fame). He stated that he also wrote under seventeen pen-names, one being Georges Sim. In addition to the Maigret series he wrote straight novels.

Simon, André (André Louis Simon, 1877-1970). Born and educated in Paris. President of the Wine and Food Society and Editor of the *Wine and Food Quarterly*. Author of a large number of books on the history of the wine trade in England and other works on wine and food, including *The Art of Good Living* (1929), *A Dictionary of Wine* (1936), *A Dictionary of Gastronomy* (1949), *The Gourmet's Week-end Book* (1952), *By Request: An Autobiography* (1957).

Simpson, Helen (Helen de Guerry Simpson, 1897-1940). Born in Sydney, Australia; educated at a convent school there and in France and Oxford. Author of *Boomerang* (1932), *Saraband for Dead Lovers* (1935), *Under Capricorn* (1937), *Maid No More* (1940). Collaborated with Clemence *Dane in other novels.

Sims, George R. (George Robert Sims, 1847-1922). Educated at Hanwell and Bonn. Best known for the miscellany he contributed under the heading 'Mustard and Cress' to the (Sunday) *Referee* from the beginning of the paper in 1877. For this he used the pen-name Dagonet. His books, on divers subjects, include *The Dagonet and other Poems* (1903), *In London's Heart* (1900) and other novels; *London by Night* (1906) and other books on London; *My Life: Sixty Years' Recollections of Bohemian London* (1916).

Sinclair, May (1870-1946). Born in Cheshire; educated at Cheltenham Ladies' College. Her first important novel *The *Divine Fire* (1904)—the sixth she published—is a detailed study of a poetic genius, Savage Keith Rickman, described as having 'the soul of a young Sophocles battling with that of a junior journalist in the body of a dissipated young Cockney'. In this and *The Combined Maze* (1913) she displayed considerable understanding of the lives of men and women in cramped circumstances. In later novels she experimented with Freudian themes and the 'stream of consciousness' technique which Dorothy *Richardson was exploring with more particularity. Among May Sinclair's novels in that period are *Mary Olivier* (1919), *The Life and Death of Harriet Frean* (1922), *Ann Severn and the Fieldings* (1922). She wrote a study of *The Three Brontës* (1912) and a Brontësque novel *The Three Sisters* (1914).

Sinclair, Upton (Upton Beall Sinclair, 1878-1968). Born in Baltimore; educated in New York at the City College and Columbia University. After writing stories for cheap magazines while still a boy, he determined to aim higher and lived for some years in poverty while producing five unsuccessful novels (*Springtime and Harvest*, 1901, to *Manassas*, 1904). Privations endured during that period led him to embrace socialism and to engage in investigations of commercial practices such as he exposed in *The *Jungle* (1906), which relates the ill-usage suffered by a poor immigrant employed in the Chicago stockyards and the generally deplorable conditions prevailing there. This novel was one of the most disturbing and influential indictments produced during the reform campaign of the so-called *muck-rakers. In the following decades Sinclair wrote numerous other novels exposing abuses in powerful organizations: *King Coal* (1917) deals with labour relations and the coal magnates' political and social stranglehold in Colorado; *Oil!* (1927) is an attack on private monopoly; *Boston* (1928)—which arraigns class privilege, false patriotism, police brutality, and a further range of social injustices and political misdeeds—is pivoted on the Sacco and Vanzetti case. Others were concerned with the Churches (*The Profits of Religion*, 1918), education

(*The Goose-step*, 1923; *The Goslings*, 1924), film finance (*Upton Sinclair Presents William Fox*, 1933), the motor industry (*The Flivver King*, 1937). The border-line at which fiction passes into fact in Sinclair's novels is shadowy. Though he was averse to prejudice and conscious falsification, his socialist fervour was unlikely to give the benefit of any doubt to those he crusaded against. With *World's End* (1940) he started a series of semi-novels in which the chief character Lanny Budd acts as a kind of international reporter-at-large moving through contemporary events and rubbing shoulders with the men, good and bad, who made the history of the period. These and Sinclair's other novels are saved from being little more than animated newspapers by his skill as a narrator. He made several attempts to secure election to Congress and to become Governor of California. He wrote more than a hundred books and used several pseudonyms.

Sinister Street. Novel by Compton *Mackenzie published in two volumes (1913, 1914). Volume one details the childhood of Michael Fane and his sister Stella in their West Kensington home, where their much-loved mother is seen only occasionally on brief visits. The children are left in charge of an unsympathetic Nanny until they come under the care of Miss Carthew, a governess adored by Michael, whose distressing night-fears now diminish. After passing through a preparatory school he goes on to St James's (= St Paul's) School. Stella, meanwhile, is showing signs of uncommon talent as a pianist. Alan Merivale, Michael's chief school-friend, is the nephew of Captain Ross, who marries Miss Carthew and is killed in the Boer War. On a single occasion Michael is taken by his mother on a visit to the Earl of Saxby, and after Saxby dies of enteric fever in South Africa Michael and Stella learn that he is their father, his wife having refused to divorce him. While still at school Michael develops a religious enthusiasm and spends a while at Clere Abbey, where he becomes acquainted with a dubious character, Henry Meats, known passingly as Brother Aloysius. When seventeen Michael falls in love with Lily Haden, a girl he first saw in Kensington Gardens, and remains devoted to her until he sees her and another boy kissing amorously. Stella has a thorough musical training on the Continent, and gives a successful first recital as a concert pianist shortly before Michael goes up to Oxford. Volume two gives a close account of undergraduate life at the university, where Michael is at St Mary's (= Magdalen) College, leaving at the end of four years with a first in history. His mother and sister now live in Cheyne Walk, where he joins them. Having been told that Lily Haden has been seen at the Orient Promenade, a notorious resort of prostitutes, he convinces himself that he must find and reclaim her by marriage. He takes lodgings in slum quarters where, after fruitless searches in the West End, he thinks he may see her. He encounters Henry Meats, now using the name of Barnes, takes a room in the same house in Pimlico, and undertakes to give Barnes a generous weekly allowance to help in the search for Lily, which brings Michael in contact with much of the underside of London life and leads to his being fined for alleged disorderly conduct in Leicester Square. He eventually sees Lily at a Carnival Ball in Fulham, and finds that she and a possessive friend, Sylvia Scarlett, have rooms in that district in the house of Mrs Gainsborough, an enormous, amoral, amusing old woman whom Michael gets to like. Against the strenuous opposition of Stella (now married to Alan Merivale) and his friends, and the jealous disapproval of Sylvia Scarlett, he makes immediate plans to marry Lily. Installing her with a housekeeper in a large flat they are to occupy after the wedding, he reluctantly yields to his mother's entreaties to wait three months. When he visits the flat unexpectedly one afternoon, Lily is entertaining a man in the bedroom. He goes to the Pimlico house to tell Barnes that he must vacate the room he has been occupying at Michael's expense. Soon after, Barnes is arrested for murder. Freed from his infatuation for Lily, Michael sets out for Rome, 'thinking very seriously of becoming a priest'.

Sinjohn, John. Pseudonym under which John *Galsworthy published his earliest books: *Four Winds* (1897), *Jocelyn* (1898), *The Villa Rubein* (1900), and *A Man of Devon* (1901).

Sisson, C. J. (Charles Jasper Sisson, 1885-1966). Born in County Durham; educated at Rutherford College and the University of Edinburgh; held university appointments in Dijon, Cairo, Bombay, and London. Lord Northcliffe Professor of Modern English

Literature, University of London, 1928-51. Editor of the *Modern Language Review,* 1927-55. Author of books on Shakespeare and other Elizabethans.

Sitwell, Dame Edith (1887-1964; D.B.E., 1954). Born at Scarborough; sister of Osbert Sitwell and Sacheverell Sitwell; educated at home. Though her father showed little affection for her as his eldest child, she inherited from him the eccentricity which expressed itself in various ways throughout life and no doubt led her to write the prose volume *The English Eccentrics* (1933). Though like her brothers she was in personal relationships a model of courtesy and good breeding, she could be aggressive and waspish in paper controversy and rarely failed to react vigorously to slighting criticism. Her literary career began in 1916 when she edited an anthology of contemporary verse *Wheels,* which marked the beginning of a new trend in English poetry. In her own independent early collections—*The Mother and other Poems* (1915), *Clowns' Houses* (1918), *The Wooden Pegasus* (1920), **Façade* (1922), and others, she employed original imagery which at times appeared wantonly freakish but often had the attraction of a fairy-tale and toyland world. She spoke of verbal 'texture' as being a feature in her verse, while in **Façade* (made widely familiar when set to music by William Walton) she used rhythms belonging to jazz and other popular music. Poetry of a more serious kind came in later years as the world scene darkened and her religious sense deepened, and in her closing years she was generally regarded as one of the most accomplished women poets that England has produced. *Gold Coast Customs* (1929), *The Song of the Cold* (1946), and *The Canticle of the Rose* (1949) contain much of her best poetry. She was the over-prolific author of prose volumes which at times appeared to be hardly more than hack-work for the publishers, but she had a genuine feeling for the Tudor period, displayed both in the style of dress she favoured as appropriate to her unmodern cast of countenance and in such books as *Fanfare for Elizabeth* (1946).

Sitwell, Sir George (George Reresby Sitwell, 1860-1943; succeeded his father as 4th baronet, 1862). Born in London, father of the preceding and the two following; educated at Eton and Oxford. Conservative M.P. for Scarborough, 1885-86 and 1892-95. His remarkable character and eccentricities appear in the superb account by his son Osbert in *Left Hand, Right Hand* (1945). He claimed to have 'captured a spirit at the headquarters of the Spiritualists, London, 1880'. He wrote *The First Whig* (1894), *Country Life in the 17th Century* (1901), *An Essay on the Making of Gardens* (1909), *Tales of My Native Village* (1934), *Idle Fancies in Prose and Verse* (1938). He also appears in Osbert Sitwell's *Tales My Father Taught Me* (1962).

Sitwell, Sir Osbert (1892-1969; succeeded his father as 5th baronet 1943). Born in London; educated at Eton. Spent much of his youth at the family home, Renishaw, near Sheffield. Served in World War I until he was invalided in 1916. He and his sister Edith and brother Sacheverell played leading parts in the literary and social life of England from 1919 onward, fighting all that they regarded as philistinism and national indifference to the arts. By temperament natural aristocrats, they nevertheless hungered for a 'true democracy', which Osbert declared required 'the rationing of brains' and 'compulsory Freedom everywhere'—statements characteristic of his inclination to flouting and paradox. He wrote poems, short stories, and novels, but excelled in the five-volume autobiography which is a literary masterpiece as well as a matchless record of the Sitwell family and cultured life in their wide circle: *Left Hand, Right Hand* (1945), *The Scarlet Tree* (1946), *Great Morning* (1948), *Laughter in the Next Room* (1949), *Noble Essences* (1950). His *Collected Poems and Satires* were published in 1931, followed by several later volumes of verse, including *Wrack at Tidesend* (1952); *Collected Short Stories* appeared in 1953; novels—*Before the Bombardment* (1927), *Miracle on Sinai* (1933). *Queen Mary and Others* (essays; 1974).

Sitwell, Sir Sacheverell (1897-   ; succeeded his brother as 6th baronet, 1969). Born at Scarborough; educated at Eton. He was less in the public eye than his brother (Osbert) and sister, though Edith did not hesitate to proclaim him openly, with sisterly devotion and some exaggeration, as a very great poet. He wrote fifteen books of verse, sampled in *Selected Poems* (1945), but his chief writings are on art and architecture: *Southern Baroque Art* (1924), *The Gothick North* (1929), *Conversation Pieces* (1936), *Narrative Pictures* (1937), *British Architects and Craftsmen* (1945). His extensive travels produced

Roumanian Journey (1938), *Mauretania* (1939), *Spain* (1950), *Portugal and Madeira* (1954), *Denmark* (1956), *Malta* (1958), etc. Other books include *Poltergeists* (1940), *Primitive Scenes and Festivals* (1942), *Splendours and Miseries* (1943), *Morning, Noon, and Night in London* (1948), *Arabesque and Honeycomb* (1957).

Skeat, W. W. (Rev. Walter William Skeat, 1834-1912). Born in London; educated at Highgate and Cambridge. Served as a curate in Essex and Surrey. Founded the English Dialect Society, 1873 and was its President until 1896. Edited Langland's *Piers Plowman* and other medieval texts, as well as poems by Chaucer and later works. He was eminent chiefly as a philologist, among his works in that field being *An Etymological Dictionary of the English Language* (1879-82), *A Concise Dictionary of Middle English* (1888), books on the place-names of several English counties, *The Proverbs of Alfred* (1907), *Early English Proverbs* (1910).

Skin Game, The. Play in three acts by John *Galsworthy performed and published in 1920. Hillcrist, a country gentleman, has sold Longmeadow, a part of his estate, to Hornblower, a pushing selfmade pottery manufacturer, on the understanding that the tenants occupying the cottages shall not be evicted, but he has given the Jackmans a week's notice to leave the cottage they have lived in for thirty years. Hornblower, who is aggrieved because Mrs Hillcrest has never called on his daughter-in-law Chloe or recognized her socially, not only refuses to keep his promise not to change the tenancies but threatens to surround the whole of the Hillcrists' property with his factories and lorry-roads, beginning with the Centry, an adjoining estate he is about to buy and build works on with tall chimneys which will spoil the Hillcrists' view. Hillcrist frustrates Hornblower's immediate plans by contriving that the owner of the Centry shall put it up to auction, hoping that he will be able to outbid Hornblower, who nevertheless by a trick secures the property, though at a price double that he had anticipated. Hillcrist scruples to abet his wife in using 'skin game' methods against Hornblower, and their daughter Jill finds young Rolf Hornblower 'a jolly good companion'. Mrs Hillcrist, nevertheless, unearths evidence about Chloe's past which dismays Hornblower and his son Charles, her husband. To prevent public disclosure Hornblower sells back Longmeadow and the Centry at a lower price. Chloe attempts unsuccessfully to commit suicide. Hillcrist remarks, finally, 'When we began this fight, we had clean hands—are they clean now? What's gentility worth if it can't stand fire?'

Skin of Our Teeth, The. Play in three acts by Thornton *Wilder performed and published in the U.S. in 1942. Originally described as 'a history of the world in comic strip', it shows the Antrobus family and their maid Lily Sabina 'living both in prehistoric times and in a New Jersey commuters' suburb today'. Intermingling farcical comedy, satire, and near-tragedy, the play begins when an ice age is threatening George Antrobus (Adam), his wife Maggie (Eve), their son Henry (Cain), Gladys their daughter, and Sabina, hilariously compounded of Lilith, the Serpent, and a *soubrette*. Henry has already killed his brother (Abel) with a stone. Mr Antrobus, inventor of the lever, the wheel, and the alphabet, returns from his office in a boisterously facetious mood, though annihilation approaches with the advancing icecap. He opens the door to a crowd of refugees who include Moses, Homer, and the Muses. Chairs and beds are broken up to keep the fire burning. The second act at Atlantic City combines the annual convocation of 'the Ancient and Honourable Order of Mammals, Subdivision Humans' (President: George Antrobus) with the threat of the Flood, Sabina intervening as winner of a Beauty Contest determined to steal Antrobus from his wife. The last act returns to the Antrobus home, now shattered in a seven-year war during which Mrs Antrobus and Gladys with a baby have existed 'like moles, like rats', and Sabina has lived all the time around camp. When Antrobus comes back from the war he finds Henry a snarling enemy whom he has to treat as 'a representation of strong unreconciled evil'. Antrobus himself admits to his wife that he has lost 'the most important thing of all: the desire to begin again'; but having recovered his books, he finds anew in them 'voices to guide us' and turns up inspiring passages from Spinoza, Plato, Aristotle, and Genesis which are then spoken by actors passing across the stage.

Skinner, Cornelia Otis (1901-   ). Born in Chicago, educated at Bryn Mawr and in Paris. Studied for the stage, following the profession of her parents, the celebrated Otis Skinner and his wife. Cornelia acted in numerous plays but made her name mainly in one-woman performances of monologues written by herself and requiring her to impersonate several characters, as in e.g. 'The Wives of Henry VIII'. As a writer she produced humorous books: *Tiny Garments* (1931), *Excuse It, Please* (1936), *Popcorn* (1943; entitled in America *Soap Behind the Ears*), *Happy Family* (1948; in America *Family Circle*). The most successful and the funniest *Our Hearts Were Young and Gay* (1942) was written in collaboration with a friend, Emily Kimbrough.

Skipps, Matthew. Rag-and-bone man in Christopher Fry's *The *Lady's Not for Burning* (1948). Thomas Mendip claims to have killed him; Jennet Jourdemayne is accused of turning him into a dog.

Skrebensky, Anton. In D. H. Lawrence's *The *Rainbow* (1915), the son of a Polish baron in exile who becomes an Anglican clergyman in Yorkshire; Anton joins the Royal Engineers as a sapper (afterwards an officer); lover and would-be husband of Ursula Brangwen, who declines to marry him; he marries another girl, who goes with him to India.

Slade Schools. The three Slade Schools of art— at the Universities of Oxford, Cambridge, and London—were established under the will of Felix Slade (1790-1868) who left £35,000 to provide for Professorships of Art at the universities named. He also bequeathed his valuable collections of glass, pottery, engravings and other objects to the British Museum.

Sladen, Douglas (Douglas Brooke Wheelton Sladen, 1856-1947). Born in London; educated at Cheltenham and Oxford. Became the first Professor of History in the University of Sydney. He wrote *Australian Ballads and Rhymes* (1888) and other verses, *The Japs at Home* (1892), *Carthage and Tunis* (1906), *The Tragedy of the Pyramids* (1909), popular historical studies, novels, books on the Australian poet Adam Lindsay *Gordon, to whose writings he was devoted. Autobiographies: *Twenty Years of My Life* (1915), *My Long Life: Anecdotes and Adventures* (1939).

Slater, Francis Carey (1876-1958). Born in South Africa (at Alice, Cape Province); on the staff of a Port Elizabeth bank, 1899-1930. Wrote *Footpaths Thro' the Veld* (1905), *Calls Across the Sea* (1917), *The Karroo* (1924), *Dark Folk* (1935), *The Trek* (1938), and other collections of verse; also novels— *The Shining River* (1925), *The Secret Veld* (1931), *See also* Jan *Van Avond.

Slater, Humphrey (1906-   ). Educated at Sedbergh and Tonbridge; studied art at the Slade School in London. Travelled in Russia and Germany and was a leader in the International Brigade during the Spanish Civil War of 1936-38. Served in the British forces in World War II. Author of *The Heretics* (1946), *The Conspirators* (1948), *Calypso* (1953); *Who Rules Russia?* (1955).

Slaughter, Frank (Frank Gill Slaughter, 1908-   ). Born in Washington, D.C.; educated in North Carolina at High School and Duke University; studied medicine and surgery and practised in Florida. Author of popular novels dealing variously with his profession (which he changed for that of a writer after World War II), the American Civil War, and biblical themes: *That None Should Die* (1941) *Spencer Brade, M.D.* (1942), *Air Surgeon* (1943), *Battle Surgeon* (1944); *In a Dark Garden* (1946), *Storm Haven* (1953); *The Galileans* (1953), *The Song of Ruth* (1954). He also wrote novels under the pseudonym C. V. Terry.

Slessor, Kenneth. *See* *Australian Writers.

Slocombe, George (George Edward Slocombe, 1894-1963). Journalist specializing in foreign affairs as correspondent in Paris, America, and India for English newspapers. In addition to his political writings he was the author of poems—*Gaucheries* (1922); novels —*Dictator* (1932), *Escape into the Past* (1943); historical biographies—*Henry of Navarre* (1931), *Don John of Austria* (1935); and an autobiography—*The Tumult and the Shouting* (1936).

Slocum, Joshua (1844-c. 1910). Born in Nova Scotia. Famous as the author of *Sailing Alone Around the World* (1900), a feat he was the first to achieve, starting in a small sailing vessel from Boston in 1895 and returning to Newport, Rhode Island, in 1898. He had had hazardous earlier voyages, and late in 1909 began another, from which he did not return, the manner of his end being unknown.

Smallways, Bert. Principal character in H. G. Wells's *The *War in the Air* (1908); described

as 'a vulgar little creature, the sort of pert, limited soul that the old civilization of the early twentieth century produced by the million. . . . He had lived all his life in narrow streets. . . . He thought the whole duty of man was to be smarter than his fellows . . . and have a good time.'

Smith, Alfred Aloysius. *See* Alfred Aloysius *Horn.

Smith, A. J. M. (Arthur James Marshall Smith, 1902-   ). Born in Montreal; educated there and in Edinburgh. Became a teacher and lecturer in English at U.S. colleges and Michigan State University. Author of *News of the Phoenix* (1943), *A Sort of Ecstasy* (1954), *Collected Poems* (1962). Sometime editor of literary periodicals and of anthologies (several with critical introductions) including *The Oxford Book of Canadian Verse* (1960).

Smith, Betty (*née* Betty Wehner, 1904-1972). Born in Brooklyn; her early schooling ended at fourteen, when she started a series of miscellaneous jobs until her marriage. Later she took university courses, including a period at Professor G. P. *Baker's *47 Workshop drama department at Yale, and was for a while an actress. Her novel *A Tree Grows in Brooklyn* (1943), internationally successful, is a poignant narrative of a girl's upbringing in a slum area of New York.

Smith, Dodie (*née* Dorothy Gladys Smith,   -   ). Born in Lancashire; educated in London (St Paul's School and Royal Academy of Dramatic Art). After some years as an actress in London and the provinces, she became buyer in a London store until the popularity of her play *Autumn Crocus* (1930; produced in London, 1931) led her to give up business. Other successful plays followed: *Service* (1932), *Touch Wood* (1933), and *Theatre Royal* (1934): these (and *Autumn Crocus*) were staged and published pseudonymously as by C. L. Anthony. Under her name as Dodie Smith she had further successes in the theatre with *Call it a Day* (1935), *Bonnet over the Windmill* (1937), *Dear Octopus* (1938), as well as with a novel *I Capture the Castle* (1949) and a children's book *The Hundred and One Dalmatians* (1956). *Look Back with Love* (autobiography, 1974).

Smith, Dorothy Gladys. *See* Dodie *Smith.

Smith, Lady Eleanor (Eleanor Furneaux Smith,

1902-45). Born in Birkenhead, daughter of F. E. Smith, 1st Earl of Birkenhead; educated privately and at schools in England and France. Worked on London papers and periodicals and in the publicity department of a circus, from which she gathered background knowledge for her novels and short stories: *Red Wagon* (1930), *Flamenco* (1931), *Satan's Circus and other Stories* (1932). She was of remote gypsy descent and found satisfaction in sharing the life of gypsies, learning their language, studying their customs, and devoting a novel *Tzigane* (1935) to them. Among her other books are *Ballerina* (1932), *Portrait of a Lady* (1936), *The Man in Grey* (1941), *Caravan* (1943), *British Circus Life* (1948). Autobiography: *Life's a Circus* (1939).

Smith, Emma (1923-   ). Author of *Maiden's Trip* (1948), *The Far Cry* (1949), *Emily* (1959), *No Way of Telling* (1972).

Smith, Ernest Bramah. See Ernest *Bramah.

Smith, Goldwin (1823-1910). Born at Reading; educated at Eton and Oxford. Became Regius Professor of Modern History in the University of Oxford, 1858-66, and in 1868 was made honorary Professor of English and Constitutional History in the newly founded Cornell University, New York, to which he subsequently left the residue of his large fortune. He settled in Canada and died there. In addition to much polemical writing on political, religious, educational, and pacifist topics, he was the author of books on William Cowper, Jane Austen, Specimens of Greek Tragedy; *Reminiscences* (posthumously, 1911). His unorthodox and uncompromisingly expressed opinions were unpopular, though as a person he was widely liked and admired; but in Disraeli's novel *Lothair* (1870) he was scathingly attacked.

Smith, H. Allen (Harry Allen Smith, 1907-   ). Born in Illinois. Went to work at an early age, and after a series of menial jobs became a reporter, graduating to New York in 1929. The typically American humour of his books is suggested by some of their titles: *Low Man on a Totem Pole* (1941), *Life in a Putty Knife Factory* (1943), *Larks in the Popcorn* (1948).

Smith, Janet Adam. See Janet *Adam Smith.

Smith, Lillian (Lillian Eugenia Smith, 1897-1966). Born in Florida. Worked for many years in support of racial equality, but opposed violence in support of civil rights. She had great success with her novel, *Strange Fruit* (1944), a tragic story of white intolerance of love between a young white man and an educated coloured girl.

Smith, Logan Pearsall (Lloyd Logan Pearsall Smith, 1865-1946). Born in New Jersey; educated at Harvard and Oxford; settled in England. His Quaker ancestry allied with his own fastidious mind and scholarly—even dilettante—temperament, made him a somewhat remote though far from friendless figure, and *Trivia,* a unique addition to the literature of his time, is expressive of a unique personality. Sometimes extending to no more than three, four or five lines, these essays-in-little reflect the moods of a man who enjoyed life ironically as a curious spectacle in which he took no active part; whose ambition, he wrote, was to live on after his funeral 'in a perfect phrase'. *Trivia* (1902), *More Trivia* (1921) and *Afterthoughts* (1931) are collected (with *Last Words* added) in *All Trivia* (1933). His other writings include *Songs and Sonnets* (1909), *The English Language* (1912), *Words and Idioms* (1925), *On Reading Shakespeare* (1933), *Milton and his Modern Critics* (1940). Autobiography: *Unforgotten Years* (1938).

Smith, Sheila Kaye. See Sheila *Kaye Smith.

Smith, Stevie (Florence Margaret Smith, died 1971). Born in Hull; educated in London. In addition to fiction (*Novel on Yellow Paper*, 1936; *Over the Frontier*, 1938; *The Holiday*, 1949) she published much poetry of a strongly individual kind in which opposing moods frequently jostle in the same poem. She sometimes used metrical forms which are amusingly odd, and the spirit of her poetry has been described as 'a combination of tenderness, humour, and a sort of sustained running battle with Christianity'. *Selected Poems* (1962).

Smith, Thorne (1893-1934). Born in Maryland; educated in Virginia and Pennsylvania and at Dartmouth College. Worked in advertising in New York before serving in the U.S. Navy in World War I. Author of broadly humorous novels: *The Night Life of the Gods* (1931), *Topper Takes a Trip* (1932), *The Bishop's Jaegers* (1932), *Skin and Bones* (1933).

Smuts, Jan Christiaan (1870-1950). Born in

Cape Province; educated in England at Cambridge. He fought with the Boers in the South African War of 1899-1902 and afterwards became a member of the House of Assembly and Prime Minister of the Union of South Africa, 1919-24, 1939-48. Member of the British War Cabinet in World War I and in World War II was made a Field-Marshal. He was highly regarded as a statesman, though not universally, and he stated his 'philosophy of the whole' in *Holism and Evolution* (1926).

Smyth, Dame Ethel (1858-1944; D.B.E. 1922). Born in London; studied music in Leipzig; composer of orchestral and chamber music, choral works, operas, etc. Took part in the militant women's suffrage campaign and composed their 'battle song', *The March of the Women*; imprisoned in 1911. Author of lively autobiographical reminiscences— *Impressions that Remained* (2 vols, 1919), *As Time Went On* (1935), *What Happened Next* (1940)—and other books.

Snaith, J. C. (John Collis Snaith, 1876-1936). Author of *Broke of Covenden* (1904), *William Jordan, Junior* (1908), *The Great Age* (1915), *The Unforeseen* (1930), and other novels, the two first mentioned receiving high praise.

Snake Pit, The. *See* Mary Jane *Ward.

Snobby Price. Nickname of Bronterre O'Brien Price, unemployed painter, 'sharp enough to be capable of anything . . . except honesty', in Bernard Shaw's *Major Barbara* (1905); poses as a convert at the Salvation Army's West Ham shelter.

Snow, C. P. (Charles Percy Snow, 1905- ; knighted 1957; 1st Baron Snow, 1964). Born in Leicester; educated there and at Cambridge, where he became a science tutor from 1935 to 1945; Civil Service Commissioner, 1945-60. When the Labour Government took office in 1964 was appointed Parliamentary Secretary to the Ministry of Science and Technology, with a seat in the House of Lords. He was previously noted as a novelist, his *Death Under Sail* (1932), a detective story, preceding the first of the ambitiously conceived sequence of novels with the general title *Strangers and Brothers*, a sort of conspectus of contemporary life seen from university, scientific, and political angles with a central character named Lewis Eliot. These were received with respect and critical praise, though Snow's style is inclined to be ponderous. The first volume, with the sequence title, came 'out in 1940, followed by *The Light and the Dark* (1947), *Time of Hope* (1949), *The *Masters* (1951), *The New Men* (1954), *Homecomings* (1956), *The Conscience of the Rich* (1958), *The *Affair* (1960), *Corridors of Power* (1964), etc. Much interest was stirred by his Rede Lecture at Cambridge, *The Two Cultures and the Scientific Revolution* (1959) in which he deplored the failure of the traditional arts culture to adjust itself to the requirements of an age in which science and technology were transforming civilization. He married Pamela Hansford *Johnson in 1950.

Soap opera. An American term for sponsored radio and television programmes which combined advertising for brands of soap (or other domestic necessities) with naïve sentimental serial entertainment.

Sob sister. Slang term for an earlier type of woman journalist addicted to maudlin sentimentality.

Social Credit. A proposed economic system whereby the state should provide every citizen with currency additional to wages and other normal sources of income; thus increasing the purchasing power and currency circulation on which it was held that economic stability depended. The originator of the theory was Clifford Hugh *Douglas (1879-1952), a distinguished Scottish engineer. Though Social Credit was considered a wild-cat scheme by orthodox economists, a Social Credit Party in Alberta, Canada, won state elections there in 1935 and after. Their endeavours to operate the scheme were for the most part frustrated by the Dominion government and legal action.

Solomon Eagle. Pseudonym used by J. C. *Squire for literary articles in the *New Statesman*.

Solzhenitsyn, Alexander Isayevich (1918-). Born in Russia at Rostov and educated at the university there; wounded in World War II; from 1945 until Stalin's death in 1953 he was imprisoned in labour camps; after a further period as an exile in Siberia, he became a school teacher. His short novel *One Day in the Life of Ivan Denisovich* (1962) was well received in Russia, as were other writings until 1968, when he was accused of anti-Sovietism and officially ostracized, being arrested and deported in 1974 after his victimization had provoked widespread protest abroad. His literary repute was sustained in western Europe (where he settled after deportation) and in America. He had been awarded the Nobel Prize in 1973. His novels include *Cancer Ward* (1968), *August 1914* (1971), *The Gulag Archipelago* (1974). Plays: *The Love Girl and the Innocent* (1969), *The Victors' Feast* (1971), *Candle in the Wind* (1973). In *D's Book: The Mainstream of the 'Quiet Don'* (Russian Edition, Paris 1974) he questioned *Sholokhov's claim to authorship of the 'Don' novels.

Somervell, D. C. (David Churchill Somervell, 1885-1965). Son of the Bursar of Harrow School; educated there and at Oxford. Taught at Repton and Tonbridge Schools, as History Master at the latter from 1919 until his retirement in 1950. He wrote *A History of Tonbridge School* (1947) and was also the successful author of *English Thought in the Nineteenth Century* (1928), *The British Empire* (1930), *A History of the United States* (1942), *British Politics since 1900* (1950). *Robert Somervell of Harrow* (1935) was a biography of his father, to whom both G. M. Trevelyan and Sir Winston Churchill, his pupils, acknowledged a debt. D. C. Somervell's most praised and widely circulated publication was his condensation of *A Study of History* by A. J. *Toynbee.

Somerville and Ross. Joint pen-name of Edith Anna Oenone Somerville (1858-1949) and Violet Florence Martin (1862-1915). Edith Somerville was born in County Cork, educated at home, and studied in Paris and London, having one-man shows of her drawings in London and New York at intervals from 1920 to 1938. Violet Martin was born in County Galway and educated in Dublin. The two women were cousins and in 1889 they began the collaboration which produced *An Irish Cousin* (1889), *Naboth's Vineyard* (1891), *The Real Charlotte* (1895), *The Silver Fox* (1897), *All on the Irish Shore* (1903), *Dan Russell the Fox* (1911) and (non-fiction) *Through Connemara in a Governess Cart* (1893), *Beggars on Horseback* (1895), *Some Irish Yesterdays* (1906). Their most popular books, however, were *Some Experiences of an Irish R.M.* (1899) and *Further Experiences of an Irish R.M.* (1908)—R.M. indicating Resident Magistrate. Edith Somerville continued to write after her cousin's death and still published the books as by Somerville and Ross: *In Mr Knox's*

Country (1915), *Mount Music* (1919), *The Big House of Inver* (1925), *Irish Memories* (1918).

Sondra Finchley. Rich society girl Clyde Griffiths plans to marry in Theodore Dreiser's *An *American Tragedy* (1925) after he has drowned his pregnant mistress Roberta Alden.

Sons and Lovers. Novel by D. H. *Lawrence published in 1913. Gertrude Coppard, daughter of an overbearing, harsh and ironic marine engineer, becomes a teacher in a private school. Though her interests are intellectual, she finds herself fascinated by Walter Morel, a Nottinghamshire miner, whose joyous, animated, non-intellectual manner is in warming contrast to the stern puritanism of her home. She marries Morel and is blissfully happy until she finds that he is unscrupulous with money, a liar, and a heavy drinker with intermittently brutal outbursts. Mentally isolated, and bitter against her husband, she concentrates her interests and love on her children—William, Annie, Paul and Arthur—with occasional outside relief from reading papers on social questions to the Co-operative Women's Guild. The family's poverty is alleviated slightly when William brings home 14s a week from his first job; and when, later, he goes to work in London, he helps more until he becomes engaged to a flighty 'weasel-brained' girl on whom he wastes his money. He falls ill with pneumonia and erysipelas and dies soon after his mother goes to him in London. Mrs Morel remains dumb with grief and 'could only brood on her dead son' until her life becomes rooted in Paul as she nurses him through a long illness. Annie marries; Arthur enlists in the army, being later bought out by his mother. Paul begins in business as a junior clerk in a surgical appliance manufacturer's premises in Nottingham and continues there. In his leisure time he has some encouraging success as a painter, winning money prizes at exhibitions. His mother is resentful of the girl when he falls in love with Miriam Leivers, a farmer's daughter, 'romantic in her soul . . . and inclined to be mystical'. Feeling her egocentric love intolerable, Paul reproaches her: 'Can you never like things without clutching them as if you wanted to pull the heart out of them? . . . You don't want to love—your eternal and abnormal craving is to be loved. You aren't positive, you're negative.' He turns from her to Clara Dawes, a woman living apart from her husband, but soon finds her passion stifling. His mother suffers a slow and painful death, and towards her lingering end he gives her an excessive dose of morphia. He makes an unavailing attempt to re-establish relations with Miriam and suggests marriage, but they recognize that it would bring them no peace. He is left thinking only of his dead mother: 'His soul could not leave her, wherever she was. Now she was gone abroad into the night, and he was with her still.'

Sorel, Georges (1847-1922). Born at Cherbourg; received a technical education and worked as an engineer until 1892, when he turned wholly to the consideration of social and political questions and formulated the theory that only through violence can a regenerated society be born; whether it was the product of the working class or of the middle class was relatively unimportant—the regenerative factor was in the conflict itself. From time to time he appeared to veer from Communism to Fascism and back again, finding political virtue in both Lenin and Mussolini. His chief written work is *Reflections on Violence* (1912, Eng. trans. of the 1908 French original).

Sorley, Charles Hamilton (1895-1915). Born in Scotland; educated at Marlborough and Oxford. He was killed in World War I. The antiwar poems in his posthumously published *Marlborough and other Poems* (1916) are memorable. A biographical preface (by his brother) is in his *Letters* (1919).

South African and Rhodesian writers. *See* Roy *Campbell, Doris *Lessing, H. F. *Maltby, Sarah Gertrude *Millin, Alan *Paton, Olive *Schreiner, Francis Carey *Slater, Laurens *Van der Post.

South Wind. Novel by Norman *Douglas published in 1917. Thomas Heard, D.D., Bishop of Bambopo, visiting his cousin Mrs Meadows in the Mediterranean island of Nepenthe at the season of the sirocco, is subject to the common effect of this south wind as an enervating influence on intellect and moral standards. He comes into contact, more or less, with the island's chief residents: among them the Duchess of San Martino, hovering on the brink of conversion to the Roman Catholic Church; Don Francesco, a popular ecclesiastic, 'worldly wise, indolent, good-natured', an unrivalled preacher, and

'a thoroughgoing pagan'; Mr Keith, a wealthy eccentric, who imparts educational heresies to the bishop; Ernest Eames, a classical scholar long engaged on a proposed annotated edition of a seventeenth-century Latin work on the *Antiquities of Nepenthe*; Muhlen, a disreputable hotel keeper; Freddy Parker, the Commissioner, who is also President of the Alpha and Omega Club, made prosperous by the labours of his step-sister of 'barn-like proportions', who distils whisky ('Parker's poison) in the basement when not inventing preposterous scandal; Count Caloveglia, 'an attractive and courteous old aristocrat' who collects curios, among which is a wonderful antique Greek bronze, the Locri Faun. From these and others the bishop learns much of the legends and curious topography of the island; while in his conversations with them, and in theirs with one another, a great many unorthodox and amoral opinions are propagated in prose which is often erudite, sometimes Rabelaisian, and consistently ironic and satiric. Though mainly a discussion novel, it also has a number of descriptive set-pieces, such as the procession of the patron saint Dodekanus, and the rain of ash from the volcano on the neighbouring mainland. In the denouement the Locri Faun (actually a fabrication by the Count, himself an amateur sculptor) is bought for 350,000 francs by an American collector, Cornelius van Koppen; and the bishop finds himself condoning a murder by his cousin, Mrs Meadows, which he had witnessed from a distance.

Southouse-Cheney, Reginald Evelyn Peter. *See* Peter *Cheney.

Southwold, Stephen. *See* Neil *Bell.

Soyinka, Wole (1934-   ). *See* *African Writers.

Spade, Mark. *See* Nigel *Balchin.

Spain, Nancy (1917-64). Born at Newcastle; educated at Roedean. An ebullient journalist and broadcaster, her abilities as a writer were shown in *Thank You, Nelson* (1945), an account of her wartime service in the W.R.N.S., and in *Mrs Beeton and Her Husband* (1948), Mrs Beeton having been her great-aunt.

Spark, Muriel (*née* Muriel Sarah Camberg, -   ). Born and educated in Edinburgh.

Author of *The Go-Away Bird* (1958), *Memento Mori* (1959), *The Ballad of Peckham Rye* (1960), *The Prime of Miss Jean Brodie* (1961), *The Girls of Slender Means* (1963), *The Mandelbaum Gate* (1965), and other novels. *Collected Stories I* (1967), *Collected Poems I* (1967). Also biographical and literary studies.

Speaight, Robert (Robert William Speaight, 1904-   ). Born in Kent; educated at Haileybury and Oxford. Became an actor and played many parts in England and abroad, being particularly successful as Becket in T. S. Eliot's *Murder in the Cathedral* at Canterbury in 1935 and elsewhere later. Author of the standard biographies of *Hilaire Belloc* (1957) and *Eric Gill* (1966), and books on *George Eliot* (1954), *William *Poel* (1954). Other works: *Acting* (1939), *Nature in Shakespearean Tragedy* (1955), *The Christian Theatre* (1960).

Spender, Harold (Edward Harold Spender, 1864-1926). Born at Bath, brother of the following; educated there and at Oxford. On the staff of various London newspapers from 1891 to 1914 and on the *Manchester Guardian*. He was prominent as a political journalist and as a biographer of *Herbert Henry Asquith* (1915), *General Botha* (1916), *David Lloyd George* (1920).

Spender, J. A. (John Alfred Spender, 1862-1942). Born at Bath, brother of the preceding; educated there and at Oxford. Editor of the *Westminster Gazette*, 1896-1922, a paper of high repute while under his control. Author of the standard *Life of Sir Henry Campbell-Bannerman* (1923)—Prime Minister, 1905-08—and other biographies; *The Comments of Bagshot* (1907), *The Public Life* (1925), *Life, Journalism and Politics* (1927), *A Short History of Our Times* (1934), *Men and Things* (1937), *New Lamps and Ancient Lights* (1940).

Spender, Stephen (Stephen Harold Spender, 1909-   ). Born in London, son of Harold Spender (see above); educated there and at Oxford. Travelled much on the Continent and lived at intervals in Germany. In the 1930s he was among the group of younger writers (including W. H. *Auden, Day *Lewis, and Louis *MacNeice) whose poems and political enthusiasms stirred much interest, and he was one of those who

supported the republican government in the Spanish Civil War. He was co-editor of *Horizon* (with Cyril *Connolly) 1939-41 and co-editor of *Encounter* 1953-67. His poems were written mostly before World War II though *Collected Poems* appeared much later (1954). *Trial of a Judge* (1938), described as 'A Tragedy in Five Acts', was typical of the anti-totalitarian feeling in England at the time. His later work included literary criticism—*The Destructive Element* (1935), *The Creative Element* (1953); short stories—*The Burning Cactus* (1936); a novel —*The Backward Son* (1940); and the autobiographical *World Within World* (1951).

Spengler, Oswald (1880-1936). Born in Germany at Blankenburg; studied mathematics and natural science at the University of Halle; worked as a schoolmaster until a legacy enabled him to embark upon the writing of *The Decline of the West* (*Der Untergang des Abendlandes* (1918-23; Eng. trans. 2 vols, 1926-29; one vol. edn 1933), which advanced the theory that all civilizations pass through a life-cycle and that Western civilization has passed the climacteric and must inevitably dwindle to its death. Though attacked by many scholars, Spengler's book was widely influential and encouraged the mood of pessimism which prevailed in some European and American circles in the post-World War periods.

Speranza. Pseudonym under which Lady Wilde (*née* Jane Francisca Speranza Elgee, 1826-96) published her *Poems* (1864). She wrote much else under her own name. Oscar Wilde was her son.

Spielmann, M. H. (Marion Harry Alexander Spielmann, 1858-1948). Born in London; educated there and in France. Contributed extensively on art and literature to periodicals, biographical dictionaries, and encyclopaedias. Author of *A History of Punch* (1895) and of books on *Ruskin* (1900), *Charles Keene, Etcher* (1903), *British Portrait Painting* (2 vols, 1910).

Spillane, Mickey (Frank Morrison Spillane, 1918-   ). Author of numerous detective novels, featuring sex and sadism.

Spilsbury, Sir Bernard (Bernard Henry Spilsbury, 1877-1947; knighted 1923). Born at Leamington; educated at Oxford and in London at St Mary's Hospital Medical School. He became eminent in forensic medicine, lecturing on the subject at St Thomas's and other London hospitals, and utilizing his specialized knowledge during many years as Honorary Pathologist to the Home Office. In that capacity he was called as expert witness at many murder trials, impressing by the assurance and imperturbability of his manner. He was supposed to have been often taken as a model by detective novel writers in court scenes.

Spintho. A Christian prisoner in *Androcles and the Lion* (1912) by Bernard Shaw; he is eager for martyrdom because he thinks it will save him from damnation for his sins, but his death is accidental and ignoble.

Spooner, William Archibald (1844-1930). Born in Staffordshire; educated at Oswestry and Oxford; ordained 1862; held various ecclesiastical appointments and was lecturer and tutor at Oxford, before becoming Warden of New College there from 1903 to 1924. Author of *Bishop Butler, his Life and Writings* (1901) and other writings, but was more widely reputed for his originally unconscious transposition of consonants in speech (e.g. 'kinkering congs' for 'conquering kings') which gave the word 'spoonerism' to the English language.

Spoonerism. See William Archibald *Spooner.

Sprigg, Christopher St John. See Christopher *Caudwell.

Spring, Howard (1889-1965). Born at Cardiff; educated at the local elementary school until family needs compelled him to start work at the age of twelve in menial jobs. He furthered his education in evening school, working at shorthand and languages, and was promoted from messenger boy to reporter on a South Wales newspaper. From 1911 to 1931 (with an interval of service in France during World War I) he was successively on the staff of the *Yorkshire Post* and the *Manchester Guardian*, and in the latter year succeeded Arnold *Bennett as book critic on the London *Evening Standard*. A book for children *Darkie and Co* (1932) preceded the beginning of his career as a novelist with *Shabby Tiger* (1934). Of the dozen novels that followed, his chief success, both literary and financial, was *Fame is the Spur* (1940), others of particular note being *My Son, My Son!* (1938) and *The Houses in Between* (1951). His fiction, solidly traditional, drew its strength from his understanding of human character in the provincial environ-

ment with which he was most familiar. Other works include *Sampson's Circus* (1936), *Tumbledown Dick* (1939)—both for children —and three autobiographical volumes, *Heaven Lies About Us* (1939), *In the Meantime* (1942), *And Another Thing* (1946). He was one of the two non-military men chosen by Winston Churchill to accompany him on the 1941 voyage to meet President Roosevelt which resulted in the *Atlantic Charter.

Sprung rhythm. A complex prosodic device which resists brief definition but was explained at length by Gerard Manley *Hopkins, its inventor, in the Author's Preface (to the MS. of his poems) which is included in current editions.

Spurgeon, Caroline F. E. (1869-1942). Born in Norfolk; educated at Cheltenham College and at Dresden, Paris, and the University of London. Held numerous university appointments, becoming Head of the Department of English Literature at Bedford College for Women, London, 1913-29. Author of literary studies, chiefly *Mysticism in English Literature* (1913), a small but enlightening book, and *Shakespeare's Imagery and What it Tells Us* (1935).

Spy (pseudonym of Sir Leslie Ward, 1851-1922; knighted 1918). His coloured portrait-caricatures in *Vanity Fair* from 1873 to 1900 constitute a remarkable and still valued gallery of legal and other notables of the period.

Squire, J. C. (Sir John Collings Squire, 1884–1958; knighted 1933). Born in Plymouth; educated at Blundell's School in Devon and at Cambridge. From 1913 Literary Editor of the *New Statesman* (in which he wrote under the pseudonym Solomon Eagle) and its Acting Editor, 1917–18. In 1919 he founded the monthly *London Mercury* and was its Editor until 1934. He was poet, essayist, short-story writer, anthologist, and parodist —in the last-named category being surpassed among contemporaries only by Max *Beerbohm. His *Collected Parodies* appeared in 1921, *Poems in One Volume* in 1926; some later poems are included in *Selected Poems* (1948). He collected many of his literary articles—in *Books in General* (3 series, 1918, 1920, 1921) and other volumes. *The Grub Street Nights Entertainments* (1924) and *Outside Eden* (1933) are volumes of short stories. He collaborated with J. L. *Balderston in

Berkeley Square (1929), a play suggested by Henry James's *A Sense of the Past*. Squire was a liberal humanist with wide interests, a cricket enthusiast, and a generous encourager of young writers whose work came under his editorial eye. Autobiography: *The Honeysuckle and the Bee* (1937).

Stage censorship. Until censorship of plays was abolished by the Theatres Act 1968 stage performances in Great Britain had been subject to some form of censorship from the late fifteenth century. The system in operation up to 1968 dated basically from an Act of 1737, more precisely formulated in the Theatre Regulation Act of 1843, which imposed upon managers the obligation to submit to the Lord Chamberlain of Her/His Majesty's Household 'one copy of every new stage play, and of every new act, scene, or other part added to an old stage play, and of every new prologue or epilogue, and of every new part added to an old prologue or epilogue, intended to be produced and acted for hire at any theatre in Great Britain . . . and in case the Lord Chamberlain shall disallow any play, or any act, scene, or part thereof, . . . it shall not be lawful for any person to act or present the same. . . .' Strong exception had been taken by playwrights to the powers conferred on the Lord Chamberlain, but theatre managers were on the whole content. From time to time agitation against the system came to a head, as in 1909 when a Joint Committee of the Lords and Commons heard evidence from playwrights and others and made recommendations for reform; but no government action was taken. The Committee's report is a valuable literary document containing in full the evidence given by J. M. Barrie, John Galsworthy, Gilbert Murray, A. W. Pinero, G. K. Chesterton, and Granville Barker among the authors, by Beerbohm Tree, George Alexander, and Forbes Robertson among the actors, and by theatre managers and dramatic critics. The most important literary representative whose evidence appears in the report (Bluebook No. 214) was Bernard Shaw, whose *Mrs Warren's Profession* was banned by the censor from 1898 till 1935 and his *Shewing-up of Blanco Posnet* from 1909 to 1916. In addition to his oral evidence, Shaw handed to the Committee a printed Statement which, following precedent, he wished to read to the members. They refused to allow this, and rejected the Statement for reasons described comically by Shaw in his Preface (including

the Statement verbatim) to *The Shewing-up of Blanco Posnet*. The functions of the Lord Chamberlain remained legally intact, though after 1909 the censorship was in practice liberalized in conformity with broadening standards of public morality. Agitation for the abolition of stage censorship was renewed in the 1960s, and a further parliamentary inquiry led to the 1968 Act.

Stamp, Sir Dudley (Laurence Dudley Stamp, 1898–1966; knighted 1965). Born at Catford; educated at home and at King's College, London, where he joined the geology staff. Professor of Geology and Geography, University of Rangoon, 1923–26; Reader in Economic Geography, London School of Economics, 1926–45; Professor there, 1945–58. Author of numerous works on geography and allied subjects; *The Face of Britain* (1940), *Britain's Structure and Scenery* (1945), *Our Undeveloped World* (1953), *Man and the Land* (1955), etc.

Standard Book Numbering. A numerical coding system (necessitated by computerization) adopted in the late 1960s by publishers and others concerned with the distribution and ordering of books, whereby the publisher and the title of every book in his list is identified by eight grouped digits to which is added a 'check digit': e.g. 19 180003 1 is the SBN of the Oxford University Press Standard Edition of the New English Bible (1970) without Apocrypha; 19 180004 X indicates the Standard Edition with Apocrypha. In these instances the first two digits (19) identify the publisher as Oxford University Press and none other; the following six digits identify the particular title and particular edition and none other; the final figure or letter (the 'check digit') enables the computer to guard against human error. SBN operates on a nine-digit system. The book-identification group of digits therefore varies in number according to the identification code allotted to the particular publisher. Thus, the Library Association, which publishes many fewer books than the large commercial publishers, needs fewer digits in the second group, and is allotted five digits in group one. The check digit is always single. SBN 85365 121 3 = *British Government Publications: An Index to Chairmen and Authors 1941–1966* published by the Library Association in 1969. The saving of time and labour is plainly apparent when lengthy information of this kind can be reduced to nine digits. The prefix SBN is changed to ISBN when the system operates internationally and a preliminary digit is added signifying the country of origin. Information can be had from the Standard Book Numbering Agency in London.

Stanhope, Captain. Company commander in R. C. Sherriff's *Journey's End* (1928).

Stanislavsky (pseudonym of Konstantin Sergeivitch Alexeyev, 1865-1938). Born in Moscow where, after experience as actor, producer, and teacher, he became in 1898 the controller of the Moscow Art Theatre. His autobiographical *My Life in Art* (1924) has been regarded internationally as an inspired book by many actors and others connected with the theatre. His advocacy of intensive psychological study of the characters became the basis of 'The *Method' school of acting and production in Britain and America in the period after World War II, influenced by Stanislavsky's *An Actor Prepares* (1926). Posthumously published works: *Stanislavsky Rehearses Othello* (1948) and *Building a Character* (1950).

Stanley, Ann Veronica. See *Ann Veronica* (1909) by H. G. Wells.

Stannard, Mrs Arthur (*née* Henrietta Eliza Vaughan Palmer). *See* John Strange *Winter.

Stapledon, Olaf (William Olaf Stapledon, 1886-1950). Born near Liverpool, but spent much of his childhood in the Suez Canal region of Egypt; educated at Oxford, and at Liverpool where he took his Ph.D. and afterwards lectured extramurally on English Literature and Industrial History. Author of *A Modern Theory of Ethics* (1929), *Philosophy and Living* (1938), *Saints and Revolutionaries* (1939) and several novels mainly speculating about the future of mankind: *Last and First Men* (1931), *Last Men in London* (1932), *Waking World* (1934), *Star Maker* (1937).

Stark, Dame Freya (Freya Madeline Stark, 1893-   ; Mrs Stewart Perowne). D.B.E. 1972. Educated in Italy and in London at Bedford College and the School of Oriental Studies. At an early age she was fired with an impassioned interest in eastern lands by an aunt's gift of *The Arabian Nights*, and in her early thirties she began the explorations in Arabia and Persia which resulted in a sequence of travel books which are among the best in the English language: *The Valleys of the Assassins* (1934), *The Southern Gates of Arabia* (1936), *A Winter in Arabia* (1940). *Traveller's*

Prelude (1950), *Beyond Euphrates* (1951), and *The Coast of Incense* (1953) are autobiographical. *Ionia: a Quest* (1954), *Riding to the Tigris* (1959), *Rome on the Euphrates* (1966), *Turkey: a sketch of Turkish History* (1971).

Starkadder family. Eccentrics in Stella Gibbons's *Cold Comfort Farm* (1932). *See* Elfine.

Starkey, James Sullivan. *See* Seumas *O'Sullivan.

Starkie, Enid (Enid Mary Starkie, died 1970). Born in Dublin; educated there and at Oxford and Paris. Reader in French Literature in the University of Oxford. Author of studies of *Emile Verhaeren* (1929), *Baudelaire* (1933; 1957), *Arthur Rimbaud* (1938; 1947; 1954; 1961), *André Gide* (1953); *From Gautier to Eliot* (1960). *A Lady's Child* (autobiographical; 1941).

Starkie, Walter (Walter Fitzwilliam Starkie, 1894-   ). Born in Dublin, brother of the preceding; educated at Shrewsbury and Dublin. Professor of Spanish, Dublin University, and Lecturer in Italian Literature there, 1926-47. Settled in Madrid. His special interest in gypsies is shown in *Raggle-Taggle* (1933), *Spanish Raggle-Taggle* (1934), *Don Gypsy* (1936). Other works: *Jacinto Benavente* (1924), *Luigi Pirandello* (1937), *The Waveless Plain* (1938), *Grand Inquisitor* (1940), *In Sara's Tents* (1953), *A Musician's Journey Through Time and Space* (1958), *The Dukes of Alba* (1961).

Status symbols. A term, of American origin, used colloquially to denote articles, goods, and habits acquired by persons, families, and firms for the ostentatious demonstration of social or commercial equality or superiority. Thus, cars, labour-saving domestic appliances, television sets, and (in commerce) 'prestige' buildings, 'prestige' advertising, computers and other business machines are regarded as status symbols as well as practical possessions. Among social aspirants on varying levels, parties for children, lavish dances for 'debutantes', and cocktail parties on any occasion, serve similarly. In the Civil Service and commercial firms the grading of officials is denoted by such symbols as the size and material of desks, curtains, carpets, pictures, etc., in offices. In the 1950s and after status symbols were a psychological phenomenon indicative of encroaching snobbery among all social classes.

Stead, Christina (Christina Ellen Stead, 1902- ; Mrs. W. J. Blake). Born in New South Wales; educated at Sydney University. Author of *Seven Poor Men of Sydney* (1935), *The Man Who Loved Children* (1940), *For Love Alone* (1944), *The People With the Dogs* (1951), *The Little Hotel* (1974).

Stead, W. Force (William Force Stead, 1884-1967). Born in Washington; educated at University of Virginia and at Oxford. Ordained, he became chaplain of Worcester College, Oxford; later joined the Roman Catholic Church. He was the intimate friend of T. S. Eliot, W. B. Yeats and other leading writers, and wrote much verse himself, including *Holy Innocents* (1917), *The Sweet Miracle* (1922), *Festival in Tuscany* (1927), *The House on the Wold* (1930). His edition of the *Jubilate Agno* of Christopher Smart (1722-71), which Stead published in 1939 as *Rejoice in the Lamb*, rescued that masterpiece from the confusion in which Smart's manuscript left it.

Stead, W. T. (William Thomas Stead, 1849-1912). Born in Northumberland; educated at Wakefield; apprenticed to a merchant in Newcastle upon Tyne but turned to journalism. Editor of the *Northern Echo*, Darlington, 1871-80; Assistant Editor of the *Pall Mall Gazette*, 1880-83; Editor, 1883-89. Among his innovations as a journalist was the printing of interviews with prominent people, and in several ways he stimulated and modernized the presentation of news and political comment. Fearless in exposing abuses, attacking vested interests, and espousing unpopular causes, he was sentenced in 1885 to three months' imprisonment arising from his campaign against the procurement of young girls for immoral purposes. To provide supporting evidence for articles in the *Pall Mall Gazette* under the title 'The Maiden Tribute of Modern Babylon' he took steps which proved his case but involved committing an indictable offence. Nevertheless his action led to further protection for women in the Criminal Law Amendment Act of 1885. He founded the *Review of Reviews* in 1890, while his Masterpiece Library of Penny Poets, Novels and Prose Classics was an invaluable boon to children and the poor and entitles him to be considered the pioneer of low-priced paperbacks. He wrote numerous books, mostly on subjects of now faded interest, though his prescience is evident in *The United States of Europe* (1899) and *The Americanisation of the World* (1902).

Steed, Wickham (Henry Wickham Steed, 1871-1956). Born in Suffolk; educated there and at the universities of Jena, Berlin, and Paris. Foreign correspondent of *The Times* in Berlin, Rome, and Vienna from 1896 to 1913; then became its Foreign Editor, 1914-19, and Editor, 1919-22. Lecturer on Central European History, King's College, University of London, 1925-38. In 1923 he bought the *Review of Reviews* (founded by W. T. *Stead in 1890) and edited it until 1930. He wrote books on the Hapsburg dynasty and other Central European topics; *The Real Stanley Baldwin* (1930); *Journalism* (1928); in the Penguin series a well-informed volume on *The Press* (1938); and *Through Thirty Years* (autobiographical, 1924).

Steel, Flora Annie (*née* Flora Annie Webster, 1847-1929). Born at Harrow; educated at home and in Brussels; married Henry William Steel of the Indian Civil Service in 1867 and until his retirement in 1889 lived in India. She was active in educational work there and served as an Inspector of Girls' Schools. Her novels and other books on Indian life are based on knowledge and accurate observation, the most popular being *On the Face of the Waters* (1896), a tale of the Indian Mutiny. Autobiography: *The Garden of Fidelity* (1929).

Steen, Marguerite (1894-). Born in Liverpool; educated there and at Kendal; became a schoolmistress and teacher of dancing before going on the stage from 1921 to 1926, when she gave up acting and devoted herself to the production of novels: *Gilt Cage* (1927), *The Wise and the Foolish Virgins* (1932), *Matador* (1934), *The Sun is My Undoing* (1941), and others. Non-fiction: *Hugh Walpole: A Study* (1933), *William Nicholson: A Biography* (1943), *A Pride of Terrys* (on Ellen Terry and other members of the family; 1962).

Steevens, G. W. (George Warrington Steevens, 1869-1900). Born in London; educated at the City of London School and Oxford. He was on the staff of the *Pall Mall Gazette* from 1893 until Harmsworth founded the *Daily Mail* in 1896. For that paper Steevens reported the Dreyfus trial and served as special correspondent in the U.S., Greece and Germany, the Middle and Far East, and as war correspondent in South Africa, where he died of enteric fever during the Boer War. A writer of great ability, his name has become legendary in press annals as a journalist of rare genius. Many of his articles are reprinted in *The Land of the Dollar* (1897), *With Kitchener to Khartoum* (1898), *The Tragedy of Dreyfus* (1899), and *From Capetown to Ladysmith* (1900). A fuller claim to remembrance is made by the striking originality and literary attraction of *Monologues of the Dead* (1895).

Steffens, Lincoln (Joseph Lincoln Steffens, 1866-1936). Born in San Francisco; graduated at the University of California before studying at universities in Europe. He worked on New York papers from 1892 to 1901, and then joined the staff of *McClure's Magazine*, to which he contributed the articles on rampant social abuses and political corruption which made him prominent among the reformers abused as *muckrakers. He reprinted these writings in *The Shame of the Cities* (1904) and *Upbuilders* (1909). Searching in later years for a panacea, he turned to Communism and hailed the Soviet Union. His *Autobiography* (1931) is an illuminating contemporary document.

Stein, Gertrude (1874-1946). Born in Pennsylvania; educated at Radcliffe College (an offshoot of Harvard) and at Johns Hopkins Medical School; settled in Paris in 1903 and became a supporter and publicizer of artists and writers of the several *avant-garde* movements born in her lifetime. She gained both fame and notoriety, adulation and derision, by the verbal eccentricities present in her writings, in which she sought to bring language back to its basic elements, though in the search for fundamental clarity she appeared to many readers to lapse from time to time into confusion and nonsense—as in her favourite device of repetition, usually mocked in the hypothetical specimen, 'a rose is a rose is a rose'. As a pupil of William *James the psychologist, and as a student of cerebral anatomy at medical school, her amalgam of pulverized language and esoteric learning was meaningful only to initiates and literary fashion-mongers, among whom she had an extensive contemporary following. She wrote two autobiographical volumes: the first, veiled as that of her lifelong companion, *The Autobiography of Alice B. Toklas* (1933), the other, *Everybody's Autobiography* (1937). Among her other writings, not all in 'experimental' prose, are: *Three Lives* (1909), *Tender Buttons* (1915), *Composition as Explanation* (1926), *How to Write* (1931), *Matisse, Picasso and Gertrude Stein* (1933),

Lectures in America (1935), *Picasso* (1938), *Brewsie and Willie* (1946). Her opera *Four Saints in Three Acts* (1934) has music by the American, Virgil Thomson, and her ballet, *Wedding Bouquet*, music by Lord *Berners.

Steinbeck, John (John Ernst Steinbeck, 1902-68). Born in California; educated there at High School and Stanford University. Began as a newspaper reporter in New York, was deemed unsuitable and then worked through a miscellaneous sequence of odd jobs before publishing a first novel, *Cup of Gold* (1929), concerning Sir Henry Morgan, the 17th-century buccaneer. His subsequent novels and short stories were, largely, sympathetic studies of the unhappy lot of California farm workers, *The Grapes of Wrath* (1939) being the most notable. He was charged with diluting the realistic tone of his fiction with sentimentality and dubious romanticism, which may have gained him a larger and more attentive public than would have heeded a more ruthless presentation. Other fiction: *The Pastures of Heaven* (1932), *Tortilla Flat* (1935), *Of Mice and Men* (1937), *The Moon is Down* (1942), *Cannery Row* (1944), *The Wayward Bus* (1947), *Winter of Our Discontent* (1961).

Steiner, Rudolf (1861-1925). Born in Austria; studied science in Vienna. Engaged from 1890 to 1897 in preparing Goethe's scientific writings for the Weimar edition of his works. Coming under the influence of Annie *Besant's teaching, he was for some years the leader of the German branch of the Theosophical Society, but broke away in 1913 to found his own Anthroposophical Society, with headquarters at the Goetheanum, a building designed in a plastic architectural style at Dornach, near Basle. He established schools for teaching his doctrines, which inculcated a system of education aiming at unified physical, mental, aesthetic, and spiritual development. The movement had a widespread influence in many lands.

Stenton, Lady (*née* Doris Mary Parsons, 1894-1971). Educated in Reading. Wife of Sir Frank *Stenton. Author of *English Society in the Middle Ages* (1951) and *The English Woman in History* (1957).

Stenton, Sir Frank (Frank Merry Stenton, 1880-1967; knighted 1948). Born at Southwell; educated there and at Reading and Oxford. Professor of Modern History at Reading, 1912-46. Author of *William the*

Conqueror (1908), *The Danes in England* (1927), *Norman London* (1934), *Anglo-Saxon England* (1943; 2nd edn 1947); editions of early Charters; studies of Place Names.

Step, Edward (1855-1931). Born in London; attended Holborn Estate Grammar School but was mainly self-educated through a lifelong addiction to nature study. He wrote copiously on plants, fungi, herbs, animals, insects, shells, etc., including *Wayside and Woodland Blossoms* (1895), and other Wayside and Woodland books on *Trees* (1904), *Ferns* (1908), *Orchids* (1929).

Stephen, Sir Leslie (1832-1904; knighted 1902). Born in London; educated at Eton and the Universities of London and Cambridge. Became a tutor at Cambridge but was compelled to resign when he became an agnostic. Editor of the *Cornhill Magazine*, 1871-82, and of the *Dictionary of National Biography* up to vol 26, 1885-91. He was renowned as a walker and mountaineer, was President of the Alpine Club, 1865-68, and collected some of his mountaineering essays in *The Playground of Europe* (1871). He was the model for the character of Vernon Whitford in George Meredith's novel *The Egoist*. By his second wife he had two daughters afterwards distinguished in literature and art— Virginia (Mrs Leonard *Woolf) and Vanessa (Mrs Clive *Bell). Leslie Stephen's numerous writings include: *Hours in a Library* (3 series, 1874, 1876, 1879), *History of English Thought in the Eighteenth Century* (1876), *Studies of a Biographer* (2 series, 1899, 1902), *English Literature and Society in the Eighteenth Century* (1904). He also published *Essays on Free Thinking and Plain Speaking* (1873), *An Agnostic's Apology* (1893), and studies of Hobbes, Pope, Swift, and George Eliot in the English Men of Letters series.

Stephen Wonham. Half-brother of Rickie Elliot in E. M. Forster's *The *Longest Journey* (1907). Rickie is fatally injured while rescuing him on a level crossing.

Stephens, James (1882-1950). Born in a poor district of Dublin; self-educated, he became an office-worker until early disappointments as a writer ended with marked success when *The *Crock of Gold* was published in 1912. *The Charwoman's Daughter*, his first novel, was published separately in 1912, having appeared previously in the *Irish Review* (1911). Later prose works include *The Demigods* (1914), *Deidre* (1923), *In the Land of*

Youth (1924), and volumes of short stories, *Here Are Ladies* (1913), *Etched in Moonlight* (1928). He also wrote much verse, beginning with *Insurrections* (1909); his *Collected Poems* were published in 1926 (enlarged edition 1954). Though an ardent supporter of the movement for Irish independence (see his *The Insurrection in Dublin*, 1916; reprint 1965) he supported the Allied cause in World War II in opposition to the official Irish neutrality. He played a practical part in the revival of interest in the Gaelic language and culture, and edited a collection of *Irish Fairy Tales* (1920).

Stern, G. B. (Gladys Bertha (Bronwyn) Stern, 1890-   ). Born in London; educated there and in Germany and Switzerland. She achieved considerable popularity with a family chronicle series of novels dominated by the Matriarch who, like other leading characters, was based upon one of her Jewish relatives. This series began with *Children of No Man's Land* (1919) and continued with *A Deputy Was King* (1926), *Mosaic* (1930), *The Young Matriarch* (1942), and others. In collaboration with Sheila *Kaye-Smith she wrote *Talking of Jane Austen* (1943) and *More Talk of Jane Austen* (1950). Autobiography: *Monogram* (1936), *Another Part of the Forest* (1941).

Stet. *See* T. Earle *Welby.

Stevens, Wallace (1879-1955). Born in Pennsylvania; educated at Harvard and New York Law School; practised as a lawyer, became Vice-President of an insurance company, and though one of America's leading modern poets he regarded verse writing as a leisuretime pursuit. His *Collected Poems* (1954) embody work appearing in numerous earlier volumes, from *Harmonium* (1923) to *Auroras of Autumn* (1950).

Stewart, Alfred Walter. *See* J. J. *Connington.

Stewart, J. I. M. (John Innes Mackintosh Stewart, 1906-   ). Born in Edinburgh, educated there and at Oxford; Reader in English Literature, Oxford, from 1969. Author of *Eight Modern Writers* (1963), *Rudyard Kipling* (1966), *Joseph Conrad* (1968), *Thomas Hardy* (1971); novels (under his own name) *Mark Lambert's Supper* (1954), *A Use of Riches* (1957), *An Acre of Grass* (1965), *Avery's Mission* (1971), *Mungo's Dream* (1973), and others. Also many detective novels as Michael *Innes.

Stewart, Mary (*née* Mary Florence Elinor Rainbow, 1916-   ; wife of Dr Frederick H. Stewart, Professor of Geology, Edinburgh University). Educated at Penrith and Ripon; and at Durham University, where she was subsequently Lecturer in English, 1948–56. Her novels, combining romance and suspense, and mostly involving a young Englishwoman in stirring experiences during a summer holiday, have been received with enthusiasm by readers of various ages, classes, and attainments: *Madam, Will You Talk?* (1954), *Wildfire at Midnight* (1956), *My Brother Michael* (1959), *The Moonspinners* (1962), *Airs Above the Ground* (1965), *The Gabriel Hounds* (1967), and others.

Still Glides the Stream. Autobiography by Flora *Thompson published in 1948, supplementing her *Lark Rise* trilogy.

Stirling, Mrs A. M. W. (*née* Anna Maria Wilhelmina Diana Pickering, 1865-1965). Born and brought up in the north of England where her father, Percival Pickering, Q.C., was Attorney-General for the County Palatine of Lancaster. She was the sister-in-law of William *De Morgan, potter and novelist, and wrote the biography of him and her sister Evelyn (a lesser Pre-Raphaelite painter) as *William De Morgan and his Wife* (1922). As early as 1881 she published two books of fairy tales and from 1893 to 1904 four novels under her father's name. She then turned from fiction to biographical works under her own (married) name, beginning with *Coke of Norfolk and his Friends* (1908; Sir Edward Coke, 1552–1634, famous jurist, was her ancestor); others were *The Life of the 1st Earl of Leicester* (1908) and *Macdonald of the Isles* (1913). Her miscellaneous writings included *Life's Little Day* (1924), *Life's Mosaic: Memories Canny and Uncanny* (1934), *The Merry Wives of Battersea* (1956). From 1931 she lived at Old Battersea House, in which she exhibited her collection of De Morgan's pottery and her sister's paintings. She died a few days before her hundredth birthday, a year after the publication of *Why?*, the last of her more than thirty books.

Stitch, Wilhelmina. Pseudonym of Ruth Collie, immensely popular author of innumerable sentimentally consoling and neighbourly rhyming verses in publications for women; they were usually printed as prose (i.e. run on, without line divisions). In the 1920s and 1930s more than twenty collections of them appeared in book form.

Stockton, F. R. (Francis Richard Stockton, 1834-1902). Born in Philadelphia. Though with the exception of *A Bicycle of Cathay* (1901) all his books were published in the 19th century, the novel *Rudder Grange* (1879) and the short story 'The Lady or the Tiger' (1884) continue to attract.

Stoker, Bram (Abraham Stoker, 1847-1912). Born and educated in Dublin. In the Irish Civil Service from 1866 to 1878, then became secretary and manager to Sir Henry Irving, of whom he published *Personal Reminiscences* (1906; 1907). His other writings range from *The Duties of Petty Sessions in Ireland* (1878) to the macabre *Dracula* (1897), which has received renewed attention and popularity in the present century as a fictional masterpiece of the horror genre.

Stone, Christopher (Christopher Reynolds Stone, 1882-1965). Born at Eton, son of a master at the College; educated there and at Oxford; served with distinction in World War I. He wrote several novels—*Scars* (1907), *Valley of Indecision* (1920), *The Rigour of the Game* (1922), and others—which made little impression, and his later considerable repute and popularity came from his interest in recorded music. With his brother-in-law Compton *Mackenzie he founded *The Gramophone* in 1923, and four years later began a long series of highly successful broadcasts of gramophone records accompanied by an informative and entertaining unscripted commentary. He was thus the first, as he was also the most cultured and best, of those to whom the slang name 'disc jockeys' was later applied. *Christopher Stone Speaking* (1933) gives autobiographical reminiscences. In early years, as C.R.S., he published *Lusus Pueriles* (poems; 1901) and *Eton Idylls* (1902); and he edited *The Poems of William Collins* (1907 and later).

Stone, Grace Zaring. See Ethel *Vance.

Stone, Irving (1903-   ). Born in San Francisco as Irving Tennenbaum, his name being changed to Stone when he was young. He worked his way through school and the University of California. After some two years as a teacher of economics he turned to writing, and had his first popular success with *Lust for Life* (1934), a biography in heightened style of the Dutch painter Vincent Van Gogh. He continued with biographies of Jack *London—*Sailor on Horseback* (1938)—and other notable American men and women.

Stopes, Marie (Marie Carmichael Stopes, 1880-1958). Born in Surrey; educated in London and Munich. Became the first woman science lecturer at the University of Manchester and, later, Lecturer in Palaeobotany in the University of London. A period in Tokyo devoted to the study of fossils had also a literary outcome, *The Nō Plays of Old Japan* (1913), written in collaboration with Professor Sakurai. Her many preceding and subsequent writings ranged over a wide variety of subjects, from *Ancient Plants* and *The Constitution of Coal* to *Love Songs for Young Lovers* (1939), and other collections of poems. But her name is indelibly associated with pioneering books on marital relationships: *Married Love* (1918), *Wise Parenthood* (1918), *Radiant Motherhood* (1920), *Enduring Passion* (1928), which, though attacked by the conventional, had an enormous circulation and opened the way for the flood of writings on sex technique which the next half-century was to bring. She also wrote copiously on contraception, and with her second husband, H. V. Roe (pioneer aviator and aircraft builder), founded in London in 1921 the world's first birth control clinic.

Storey, David (David Malcolm Storey, 1933-   ). Educated in Wakefield; studied art at the Slade School in London; played Rugby League football as a part-time professional. Author of *This Sporting Life* (1960), *Flight into Camden* (1960), *Radcliffe* (1963), etc.

Stout, Rex (Rex Todhunter Stout, 1886-   ). Born in Indiana of Quaker parents; brought up and educated in Kansas. After two years (1904-06) in the navy he took various jobs in a number of widely separated towns, wrote magazine stories, and in 1934 published *Fer-de-Lance*, the first of his crime novels with Nero Wolfe—the mountainously fat and apparently lethargic gourmet, beer-lover, and devoted orchid-grower—as private detective, and his sprightly and irreverent assistant, Archie Goodwin, as narrator. The many Nero Wolfe books that followed include *Some Buried Caesar* (1939), *Black Orchids* (1942), *Too Many Women* (1942), *The Golden Spiders* (1953), *The Black Mountain* (1954), *Gambit* (1963).

Strachey, Lady Jane (*née* Jane Maria Grant; died 1928). Mother of Lytton *Strachey, who lived with her until she died. Her house in Gordon Square was a meeting-place of the *Bloomsbury Group. She wrote *Nursery Lyrics* (1893); edited *Poets on Poets* (1894) and *Memoirs of a Highland Lady* (1898); and compiled *Lay Texts for the Young* (1887)..

Strachey, John (Evelyn John St Loe Strachey, 1901-63). Son of John St Loe *Strachey. Educated at Eton and Oxford. Member of Parliament, with intervals, from 1929. Minister in Labour Government, 1945-51. Author of *The Coming Struggle for Power* (1932), *The Menace of Fascism* (1933), *The Theory and Practice of Socialism* (1936), *The End of Empire* (1959), *On the Prevention of War* (1962).

Strachey, Lytton (Giles Lytton Strachey, 1880-1932). Born in London, the son of Sir Richard Strachey (soldier and civil-engineer in India) and Lady Jane *Strachey; educated at Liverpool, and at Cambridge where he was one of the brilliant circle who continued their friendship into later years and became known as the *Bloomsbury Group. He started his writing career as a reviewer on *The Spectator*, and in 1912 wrote a small masterpiece of criticism, *Landmarks in French Literature*, in the Home University Library. Though the quality of that book was appreciated by a limited public, his remarkable stylistic gifts and power of irony did not receive wide recognition until the publication of *Eminent Victorians* (1918), a group of essays in iconoclasm which earned considerable disfavour yet shook the whole fabric of English biographical writing and is now an established classic. He next directed a disillusioned eye towards the monarch and royal matriarch, but in *Queen Victoria* (1921) sympathy and a measure of admiration outweighed his mordant irony and desire to explode bubble reputations. *Elizabeth and Essex* (1928) was a less sparkling work, but *Pope* (1925) and the collections of articles in *Books and Characters* (1922), *Portraits in Miniature* (1931), and *Characters and Commentaries* (posthumously; 1933) contain much penetrating observation and notable prose. Though he has often been accused of wanton denigration of the eminent people he portrayed, he claimed that his judgments were based upon fair assessments of the available evidence.

Strachey, Marjorie (1882-1963). Sister of Lytton *Strachey. Became a primary-school teacher and later a private tutor. Author of *The Nightingale* (a biography of Chopin; 1925), *The Counterfeits* (a novel; 1927), and two religious works, *The Fathers Without Theology* (1957) and *Saints and Sinners in the Fourth Century* (1958).

Strachey, St Loe (John St Loe Strachey, 1860-1927). Born in Somerset; educated privately and at Oxford. Editor of the *Cornhill Magazine*, 1896–97; then Editor and proprietor of *The Spectator* until 1925, making it one of the most influential political (Conservative) and literary journals of the period. Author of *From Grave to Gay* (1897), *The Problems and Perils of Socialism* (1908); two autobiographical volumes, *The Adventure of Living* (1922) and *The River of Life* (1924); a novel, *The Madonna of the Barricades* (1925); and other works.

Strang, Herbert (pseudonym of George Herbert Ely, 1866-1958, and Charles James L'Estrange, died 1947). These two collaborated in many long-popular storybooks for children. L'Estrange contrived the plots, Ely supplied the literary workmanship.

Strangers and Brothers. Sequence of novels by C. P. *Snow in various settings and concerned with university life, politics, etc. They are linked together by Lewis Eliot, the narrator. The individual titles are: *Strangers and Brothers* (1940), *The Light and the Dark* (1947), *Time of Hope* (1949), *The Masters* (1951), *The New Men* (1954), *Homecomings* (1956), *The Conscience of the Rich* (1958), *The Affair* (1960), *Corridors of Power* (1964), *The Sleep of Reason* (1968).

Strangeways, Nigel. Detective in crime novels by Nicholas *Blake.

Strauss, Ralph (Ralph Sidney Albert Strauss, 1882-1950). Born in Manchester; educated at Harrow and Cambridge. Author of *The Scandalous Mr Waldo* (1909), *The Orley Tradition* (1914), *Married Alive* (1925), and other novels. Non-fiction: *Robert Dodsley, Poet, Publisher, and Playwright* (1910), *The Unspeakable Curll* (1927), *Dickens: A Portrait in Pencil* (1928), *Lloyd's: A Historical Sketch* (1937), *Sala: The Portrait of an Eminent Victorian* (1942).

Strawson, Peter (Peter Frederick Strawson 1919-). Born in north London; educated at Christ's College, Finchley, and at Oxford. Professor of Philosophy in the University of Oxford from 1968. Author of *Introduction to Logical Theory* (1952), *Individuals* (1959).

Stream of consciousness. A term first used by William *James in *Principles of Psychology* (1890) to indicate the flux of conscious and sub-conscious thoughts and impressions moving in the mind at any given time independently of the person's will. This concept led to the *'interior monologue', a literary device Edouard *Dujardin claimed to have originated and which has been employed in novels by James *Joyce, Dorothy *Richardson and others.

Streatfield, Noel (-). Born at St Leonards, where her father was vicar (he subsequently became Bishop of Lewes). After attending schools at Eastbourne, she studied for the stage and later had considerable experience acting in straight plays, pantomime and revue in Britain, South Africa, and Australia. She then turned to writing, being successful with her first novel *The Whicharts* (1931) and even more so when she began writing children's books, first with *Ballet Shoes* (1936) and then with a long succession of both adult and young people's novels, besides a biography of Edith *Nesbit, *Magic and the Magician* (1958). Autobiography: *A Vicarage Family* (1963), *Away from the Vicarage* (1966).

Street, A. G. (Arthur George Street, 1892-1966). Born and educated in Wiltshire. He came of farming stock and worked on the family farm until he emigrated to Canada in 1911, but returned in 1914 and took over the farm in 1918 after his father's death. Although he started to write only as a hobby, from 1932 (when *Farmer's Glory* was published with great success) he became widely known as author, lecturer, and broadcaster. His numerous books, which are among the best on English country life, include *Strawberry Roan* (1932), *Land Everlasting* (1934), *To Be a Farmer's Boy* (1935), *A Crook in the Furrow* (1940), *Ditchampton Farm* (1946; he was born there), *Sweetacres* (1956). He also wrote as James Brian, *Fair Enough* (1962).

Street, Cecil John Charles. See John *Rhode for detective novels written under that pseudonym and for non-fiction written under his birth name.

Street, G. S. (George Slythe Street, 1867-1936). Born at Wimbledon, near London; educated at Charterhouse and Oxford. Wrote *The Autobiography of a Boy* (1894, a satire on the aestheticism of the 1890s), and *The Ghosts of Piccadilly* (1907). Examiner of Plays in the Lord Chamberlain's Department (the censorship office) from 1913. He is the subject of one of the parodies in *A *Christmas Garland* by Max *Beerbohm, who was his contemporary at school and university.

Streetcar Named Desire, A. Play in eleven scenes by Tennessee *Williams performed and published in the U.S. in 1947; performed in London 1949. Stella Kowalski, living with Stanley her husband in Elysian Fields, a poor quarter of New Orleans, is visited by her sister, Blanche DuBois, who is shocked to find Stella with only a two-room apartment in a down-at-heel area. She says she is on leave of absence from the school in which she teaches, in order to recover from severe nervous exhaustion, but Stanley believes from the first that she is lying and suspects that she has dishonestly disposed of Belle Reve, the family property in Mississippi. He overhears Blanche expressing to Stella, who loves his animality and primitive sensuality, her low opinion of him: 'he's common! . . . sub-human . . . ape-like . . . survivor of the Stone Age!' He inquires into her past and finds that she had been dismissed from her school and has since lived as a prostitute. He passes this information to his friend Mitch, who had fallen in love with Blanche and intended to marry her. The misery of losing him leads her to heavier drinking, and while they are alone in the apartment when Stella has gone to the maternity hospital, Stanley rapes her. Blanche's degradation dated from the calamitous end to her girlhood marriage, when she found that her young husband was a homosexual and she shot himself. After Stanley's assault she becomes mentally deranged and is taken to an asylum. The title, used symbolically, is from the public-service vehicle in which Blanche travelled the last stage of the journey to her sister's place.

Stretton, Hesba (pseudonym of Sarah Smith, 1832-1911). Her earliest stories appeared in Charles Dickens's periodicals, *Household Words* and *All the Year Round*, and her 'religious and philanthropic' novels had a wide circulation in many languages. The most popular was *Jessica's First Prayer* (1866), and the title of another is preserved in that of Bernard Shaw's play, *The Doctor's Dilemma*.

Stribling, T. S. (Thomas Sigmund Stribling, 1881-1965). Born in Tennessee; educated in Alabama; qualified as a lawyer but practised only for a short time. Then worked as a journalist and story writer for popular fiction and religious magazines. From 1922 he wrote novels, mainly concerned with life in the southern states, the best known being *Fombombo* (1923), *Red Sand* (1924), *Teeftallow* (1926), and a historical trilogy, *The Forge*

(1931), *The Store* (1932), *Unfinished Cathedral* (1934).

Strickland, Charles. The stockbroker in *The *Moon and Sixpence* by W. *Somerset Maugham. He deserts his London home and his wife, in order to paint in Paris. From there he goes to settle in the South Seas and lives as a native, painting incessantly and at length dying from leprosy. With differences, the character is based on that of Paul Gauguin, the French Post-Impressionist painter.

Strife. A Drama in Three Acts by John Galsworthy performed and published in 1909. The Board of Directors of the Trenartha Tin Plate Works gather in the house of the Manager, Francis Underwood, on a February afternoon, having come from London to meet Simon Harness, the Trade Union representative, and a deputation of the men, who have been on strike throughout the winter. The Union has withdrawn its original support of the strike on the ground that some of the demands are in excess of current wage-rates. The men are led by 'a fanatical firebrand', David Roberts, who refuses to moderate the demands, although the men and their wives and families are near to starvation, and Roberts's own wife is dying. Old John Anthony, Chairman of the Directors, is no less inflexible, insisting 'No surrender! . . . No compromise! . . . No caving in!' Enid Underwood, the Manager's wife and Chairman's daughter, tries without success to exercise a humane and moderating influence. She fails to move her father, and her gifts of nourishment for Mrs Roberts (formerly her maid, Annie) are rejected by Roberts. At the meeting there are signs of a break in the unanimity of the Board, and Roberts, sensing this, urges the men to hold out. But at an open-air meeting when both Roberts and Harness address the strikers, Roberts is called away by the death of his wife and the men turn to acceptance of terms approved by the Union. These are also accepted by the Board, though the Chairman remains in opposition and resigns. At the end of the play the Secretary of the Company exclaims to Harness: 'These terms, they're the *very same* we drew up together, you and I, and put to both sides before the fight began.'

Strindberg, August (Johan August Strindberg, 1849-1912). Born in Stockholm, Sweden. An unhappy childhood stricken by poverty and family dissensions preceded his education at the Lyceum in Stockholm, followed by study at the University of Uppsala and a succession of attempts to find a career. He was drawn to science, but tried teaching, acting, and other occupations before becoming an assistant in the Royal Library, Stockholm, from 1874 to 1882. He married disastrously in 1877, and the miseries of that relationship discoloured much of his written work (see, e.g., his play *The Father*, 1887; translated 1907), aggravating the mental instability which had been evident from early years and resulted in periods of insanity. His literary output—plays, novels, short stories, satires, essays, poems—was enormous but, apart from plays, little has been translated into English. Next to Ibsen he was the outstanding European playwright of the period, and Bernard Shaw endeavoured to make Strindberg's plays more widely known in Britain by donating his Nobel Prize money to an Anglo-Swedish Literary Foundation for financing the publication of translations. In addition to *The Father*, among his well-known plays in English versions are *Master Olof* (1872; trans. 1915), *Miss Julie* (1888; trans. 1911), *The Stronger* (1890; trans. 1912), *The Dance of Death* (1901; trans. 1912), *The Spook Sonata* (1907; trans. 1916). His collected works in Swedish fill fifty-five volumes.

Strode, Edward David Chetham. *See* E. D. **Chetham-Strode.

Stroeve, Dirk. In Somerset Maugham's *The *Moon and Sixpence* (1919), the Dutch painter who befriends Strickland and is robbed by him of his wife.

Strong, Austin (1881-1952). Born in San Francisco; educated in Vailima and New Zealand. Author of many plays, including *The Drums of Oude* (1906), *The Toymaker of Nuremburg* (1907), *Three Wise Fools* (1918), *Seventh Heaven* (1922).

Strong, L. A. G. (Leonard Alfred George Strong, 1896-1958). Born near Plymouth; spent much of his childhood alternating between England and Ireland, his mother being Irish and his father Anglo-Irish; educated at Brighton and Oxford. From 1920 to 1930 he was a school teacher in Oxford, an occupation he was able to abandon when *Dewer Rides* (1929) started him as a successful novelist and was followed by *The Jealous Ghost* (1930), *The Brothers* (1932), *The Last Enemy* (1936), *The Bay* (1941), *The Hill of Howth* (1953) and many others. He also wrote verse (*Selected Poems*, 1931), short stories (*Don Juan and the Wheelbarrow*, 1932, and other collections), detective novels (*Othello's Occupation*, 1945, etc.), books for children (*Patricia Comes Home*, 1929 etc.), a study of James Joyce (*The Sacred River*, 1959) and other critical works.

Struther, Jan (pseudonym of Joyce Anstruther, 1901-53). Educated privately. Contributed poems, articles, and short stories to *Punch* for many years from 1917, and also wrote for several other periodicals. Her outstanding success was with *Mrs Miniver* (1939) sketches of an English family, which embodied a spirit of cheerful endurance attuned to the country's mood at the outset of World War II. Adapted for the screen they provided Greer Garson with an ideal part. Jan Struther's verses were issued in several volumes, including *Betsinda Dances* (1931), *Sycamore Square* (1932), *The Glassblower* (1940).

Stuart, D. M. (*née* Dorothy Margaret Browne, 1889-1963; adopted her mother's surname, Stuart, by deed-poll in 1933). Born in Yorkshire; educated at home. Author of many books both in prose and in verse, among them *Beasts Royal and Other Poems* (1923), *Sword Songs* (1925); studies of Horace Walpole (1927) and *Christina Rossetti* (1930) in the English Men of Letters series; *King George VI* (1937), *The Mother of Victoria* (1942), *The Story of William the Conqueror* (1952); *Regency Roundabout* (1943) and *Portrait of the Prince Regent* (1953).

Stuart, Francis (1902-). Born in Queensland, Australia, of Northern Irish parents. Educated in England at Rugby; took part in the Irish Civil War, 1922-3; lecturer at Berlin University, 1939-44. Author of *Women and God* (1930), *Pigeon Irish* (1932), *The Pillar of Cloud* (1948), *Good Friday's Daughter* (1951), *Angels of Providence* (1959), and other novels; *We Have Kept the Faith* (poems, 1923); *Things to Live For* (autobiography, 1935).

Sturgis, H. O. (Howard Overing Sturgis, 1855-1920). Born in London, son of Russell Sturgis, American architect and banker, and brother of Julian Sturgis, novelist; educated at Eton and Cambridge. Of his three novels—*Tim* (1891), *All That Was Possible* (1895), and *Belchamber* (1904), only the last has been revived (in 1935) and praised for its irony and grasp of character in a study of the London social scene at the end of the 19th century.

Sturt, George. *See* George **Bourne.

Subjective. As applied to literature, that which is coloured or modulated by the personality or individual bias of the author, as differentiated from *Objective.

Subtopia. A term coined by architectural and town-planning critics in contempt of sprawling ill-planned urban development, whether by commercial or by municipal bodies, mainly in the invasion of the countryside by new suburbs, satellite towns, and 'overspill' population areas after World War II.

Suckow, Ruth (1892-   ). Born in Iowa; educated there and at Denver University. Author of *Country People* (1924), *The Odyssey of a Nice Girl* (1925), *The Bonney Family* (1928), *The Kramer Girls* (1930), *New Hope* (1941), and other novels of the Middle West, several dealing with German-American settlers.

Suddaby, Donald (1901-64). Author of, mainly, stories for boys in the science-fiction mode: *The Death of Metal* (1952), *The Star Raiders* (1950), *The Moon of Snowshoes* (1956), etc.

Sudermann, Hermann (1857-1928). Born in East Prussia; educated at the Universities of Konigsberg and Berlin. A prolific and onetime popular playwright and novelist, little of his work is now read or remembered, though *Magda* (1896; in the original German, *Heimat*, 1893) was a popular stage drama with a chief role played in London by Mrs Patrick Campbell and also by Sarah Bernhardt and Eleanor Duse, giving Bernard Shaw during his years as a theatre critic opportunities of comparing the art of the great French and Italian actresses with the lesser talent of their English competitors, and also of claiming Sudermann's play as a serious contribution to the new drama.

Sullivan, Frank (1892-   ). Born in New York State; educated at Cornell University. One of America's outstanding contemporary humorists, he wrote frequently for the *New Yorker* and collected his contributions to that and other periodicals in several volumes, including *The Life and Times of Martha Hepplethwaite* (1926), *Broccoli and Old Lace* (1931), *Sullivan at Bay* (1939), *A Rock in Every Snowball* (1946).

Summers, Montague (Alphonsus Joseph-Mary Augustus Montague Summers, 1880–1948). Born near Bristol; educated at Clifton College and Oxford; founded the Phoenix Society which, from 1919, staged a series of rarely-seen plays by sixteenth- and seventeenth-century dramatists. He was an ordained Roman Catholic priest with a profound interest in witchcraft and other occult studies, among his writings being *The History of Witchcraft* (1926), *Horrid Mysteries* (1927), *The Vampire in Europe* (1929), *The Werewolf* (1933), *Witchcraft and Black Magic* (1946). He also wrote on Gothic novels, the Restoration Theatre, mysticism, and ghost stories, and edited scholarly editions of the plays of Congreve, Wycherley, and Dryden.

Sunday, Billy (William Ashley Sunday, 1862-1935). Born in Iowa. From 1883 to 1891 he was a member of leading baseball teams, but later became celebrated as a popular though naïve preacher of evangelical religion in saloons and elsewhere.

Sunday heavies. Slighting term applied to certain English Sunday papers, such as the *Sunday Times* and the *Observer*, which appear to cater for the intellectualist middle classes, particularly through their type of book reviews.

Super Tramp. *See* W. H. *Davies.

Surfaceman. Pseudonym of Alexander *Anderson.

Surrealism. A movement started by André *Breton in Paris in the early 1920s aiming to denude poetry and prose writing of conscious mental control and aesthetic technique, allowing the subconscious and all irrational impulses the freedom to express without reference to sense, logic, morals, or other traditional principles or standards. Its aesthetic anarchism tended to link it with types of political extremism. Though seeming to be on the wane in the later 1930s, it revived in the 'anti-art' crazes after World War II. Surrealism found its chief practitioners in André Breton, Louis Aragon, and other contemporary French poets, and it appears in the later prose of James *Joyce, in the writings of Gertrude *Stein, and sporadically in recent verse and prose when sense is either in abeyance or suppressed. The playwrights of The *Theatre of the Absurd are also surrealists, with whatever individual diversity. *And see* Dada.

Susan Deddington. The Lincolns' servant-maid in Drinkwater's *Abraham Lincoln* (1918).

Susan Brown. Daughter of the wealthy owner of an engineering works in John Braine's *Room at the Top* (1957). Marries Joe Lampton.

Sussex. Poem by Rudyard *Kipling, written in

SUSSEX

SWINNERTON

Africa in 1902. Kipling settled in the southern
English county of Sussex, and in the same
year bought an estate at Burwash which was
his home for the rest of his life. *Sussex* is both
one of the finest of Kipling's English poems
and also one of the best about England by
any poet.

Sutro, Alfred (1863-1933). Born in London;
educated there and in Brussels. He abandoned a business career and devoted himself
to playwriting, becoming a lesser contemporary of A. W. *Pinero and Henry Arthur
*Jones. Among his numerous plays the most
successful were *The Walls of Jericho* (1904),
A Marriage has been Arranged (1904), *Mollentrave on Women* (1905), *The Fascinating
Mr Vanderveldt* (1906), *John Glayde's
Honour* (1907), *The Builder of Bridges* (1908).
Autobiography: *Celebrities and Simple Souls*
(1933).

Sutton-Vane, V. H. (Vane Hunt Sutton-Vane,
1888-1963). Playwright and actor. Of his
many plays only *Outward Bound* (1923) was
notably successful. Its characters are passengers on a ship who realize at length that they
are the souls of their dead selves and are
voyaging to an undeclared place of judgment.

Svevo, Italo (pseudonym of Ettore Schmitz,
1861-1928). Born in Trieste and mainly educated there. He spent his working life in
banking and industry. He was taught English
by James *Joyce, who called the attention of
influential people to Svevo's talents as a
writer. He produced a small number of short
stories and three novels, including *The Confessions of Zeno* (1923; English trans. 1930).
Svevo's style is realistic, but his heroes are
ineffectual little men who have been likened
to Charlie Chaplin characters.

Swan, Annie S. (Annie Shepherd Swan, 1860-
1943; Mrs Burnett Smith). Born in Scotland
at Gorebridge; educated at the Ladies' College, Edinburgh. She wrote a vast number of
novels, beginning with *Ups and Downs* (1878);
her first success was *Aldersyde* (1883). Among
those published in the present century are:
Prairie Fires (1913), *The Stepmother* (1915),
The Pendulum (1928), *The Marching Feet*
(1931). Autobiography: *My Life* (1934). She
used the pseudonym David Lyall for many
novels.

Swann, Charles. See *Remembrance of Things
Past.*

Sweet, Henry (1845-1912). Born in London;
educated there and at Heidelberg and Oxford,
but also self-educated. He became the outstanding philologist of his time, and as a
pioneer in phonetics is ardently commemorated in the preface to Bernard Shaw's
*Pygmalion. The character of Professor
Higgins in that play is modelled on Sweet and
reproduces some of his characteristics and
personal quirks. Although he was given no
higher academic post than that of Reader in
Phonetics in the University of Oxford from
1901, his writings had an immeasurable educational impact. Among them are: *A History
of English Sounds from the Earliest Period*
(1874; enlarged edn 1880), *An Anglo-Saxon
Reader* (1876), *A Handbook of Phonetics*
(1877), *The History of Language* (1900), *The
Sounds of English* (1908).

Swing, Raymond Gram (1887-1968). Born in
New York; educated at Oberlin College,
Ohio. Worked on various American papers,
for some years as correspondent in Berlin.
He became well known in Britain before and
during World War II, while he was B.B.C.
commentator on American affairs 1935-45.
Author of *How War Came* (1940), *Preview of
History* (1943), *In the Name of Sanity* (1946).

Swinnerton, Frank (Frank Arthur Swinnerton,
1884-   ). Born in north London; began
work in a newspaper office in his early teens
after a boyhood of ill-health. From 1900 for
over twenty years he was a publishers' reader
and editor, meanwhile writing novels and
literary biographies, beginning with *The
Merry Heart* (1909). He came into prominence with the short novel *Nocturne* (1917),
and was for a while regarded by critics as a
major novelist. His many later novels—including *Shops and Houses* (1918), *Coquette*
(1921), *Young Felix* (1923), *The Elder Sister*
(1925), *Harvest Comedy* (1937), *A Flower for
Catherine* (1951), *Master Jim Probity* (1952),
Death of a Highbrow (1961)—received less
critical acclaim in a period when tradition
and careful craftsmanship were out of favour.
Among Swinnerton's non-fictional writings
are critical studies of *George Gissing* (1912;
new edn 1923), *R. L. Stevenson* (1914); essays,
Tokefield Papers (1927), *A London Bookman*
(1928), *The Reviewing and Criticism of Books*
(1939); surveys of authors and writings of the
period, *The Georgian Literary Scene* (1935)
and *Figures in the Foreground* (1963); autobiographical—*Swinnerton* (1937) and *Reflections from a Village* (1969).

Swinton, E. D. (Sir Ernest Dunlop Swinton, 1868–1951; knighted 1923). Born in India; educated at Rugby and Cheltenham; served in the army from 1888, rising to Major-General. Professor of Military History in the University of Oxford, 1925–39. He was one of the inventors of the self-propelling armoured gun-carrying tracked vehicles and originated the name 'tanks' for them. He wrote *The Study of War* (1926) and other military works, but under the pseudonym Ole-Luk-Oie became more widely known as the author of *The Green Curve* (1909), a volume of short stories.

Sykes, Christopher (Christopher Hugh Sykes, 1907-   ). Born in Yorkshire; educated at Downside, Oxford, and in Paris and at the School of Oriental Studies in London. Served in the British Legation in Tehran, Persia, and as a press correspondent; from 1948 was for a time Deputy Controller of the B.B.C. Third Programme. Author of *Answer to Question 33* (1948) and other novels; *Four Studies in Loyalty* (1946); *Character and Situation* (short stories, 1949); *Two Studies in Virtue* (1953); *Nancy, the life of Lady Astor* (1972).

Sylva, Carmen. See *Carmen Sylva.

Sylvan, Urbanus. See H. C. *Beeching.

Symbolism. The use of symbols, often to communicate extrasensory meaning or significance, is as old as literature itself. It abounds in the Bible and in the Greek and Latin classics. But whereas in earlier times symbolism arose as spontaneous illustration (cf. the New Testament parables), modern symbolism, dating from the French Symbolistes (*c.* 1880 onward), chiefly Mallarmé, Verlaine, Rimbaud, Villiers de l'Isle Adam, led to the growth of a cult of symbolism among lesser poets and prose writers—many of them English or American—in which the symbol takes command and promotes obscurity, not clarity. On a more justifiable level, symbolist elements appear in the writings of T. S. *Eliot and James *Joyce among the moderns.

Symonds, Emily Morse. See George *Paston.

Symons, A. J. A. (Alphonse James Albert Symons, 1900-41; in *Who's Who* he changed his given names to Albert James Alroy). Born in London; left school when fourteen and spent three years as a fur-dealer's apprentice. A period of joint management of his father's auction rooms ended in 1921, and he then became co-founder of the First Edition Club

and remained its Secretary and Director until its financial collapse in the early 1930s. Meanwhile he had begun the project which resulted in the production of a unique biography of Frederick Rolfe, the self-styled Baron *Corvo. *The Quest for Corvo* (1934), a masterpiece of biographical detective work, guarantees Symons a place in English literature which would probably have been confirmed and perhaps enhanced by the Life of Oscar Wilde which he did not live to complete. He was a fine conversationalist with an uncommon spontaneous narrative gift, but his literary talents were dissipated by his social aspirations and gastronomical activities in connection with the Wine and Food Society which he helped to found in 1933. Among his other distractions was an interest in African exploration which produced two small books, *Emin, Governor of Equatoria* (1928) and *H.M. Stanley* (1933). His plans for a grandiose bibliography of books of the 1890s remained unfulfilled, though *An Anthology of Nineties Verse* (1930) was a by-product. *The Nonesuch Century* (1936), a bibliography of a hundred books published by the Nonesuch Press, has an introductory essay by him.

Symons, Arthur (1865-1945). Born in Wales of Cornish parentage; educated privately, mainly in France and Italy. From 1891 he contributed voluminously to the *Athenaeum* and the *Saturday Review*, and in 1896 was editor of *The Savoy*. Overwork and a naturally unstable temperament led to a complete breakdown in 1908 and he spent two years in asylums. He told the painful story of that period in *Confessions: A Study in Pathology* (1930). He was an exceptionally accomplished critic and his *Symbolist Movement in Literature* (1899) was a pioneer work in attracting English attention to Baudelaire, Verlaine, and other modern French poets. He wrote a considerable amount of verse, mostly in the manner of the eighteen-nineties: *Poems* (2 vols 1902) and other collections. He wrote studies of Browning (1886), Aubrey Beardsley (1898), William Blake (1907), Baudelaire (1920), Hardy (1927), Oscar Wilde (1930), Walter Pater (1932), and numerous books on poetry, art, and travel. His *Collected Works* were published in sixteen volumes (1924-5).

Symons, Julian (Julian Gustave Symons, 1912-   ). Born in London, brother of A. J. A. *Symons. After some experience in business and advertising he turned to journalism and then to writing biographical and historical studies: *Charles Dickens* (1951), *Thomas Carlyle* (1952), *Horatio *Bottomley* (1955); *The General Strike* (1957), *The Thirties* (1960).

His detective novels are more widely read: *The Immaterial Murder Case* (1945), *The 31st of February* (1950), *The Narrowing Circle* (1954), *The Colour of Murder* (1957), *The Progress of a Crime* (1960), and others. His best book, *A. J. A. Symons: His Life and Speculations* (1950), equals in interest his brother's *Quest for Corvo*. *Bloody Murder* (a history of crime and detective fiction, 1972).

Synge, J. M. (John Millington Synge, 1871-1909). Born at Rathfarnham, near Dublin; educated at private schools and Trinity College, Dublin. Abandoning his early intention to become a professional musician, he spent some years on the Continent, mainly in Paris after periods in Germany and Italy. In 1899 W. B. *Yeats encountered him in Paris and persuaded him to return to Ireland and settle on the Aran Islands. There he lived among and with the peasants, familiarizing himself with their folk tales and with the colloquial speech which was to become the notable feature in the plays written in the few remaining years of his life for the Irish Literary Theatre (from 1904 at the *Abbey Theatre, Dublin): *In the Shadow of the Glen* (1903), **Riders to the Sea* (1904), *The Well of the Saints* (1905), *The *Playboy of the Western World* (1907), *The Tinker's Wedding* (1908). In all these he dealt with modern themes, his sole venture into legend being the unfinished *Deirdre of the Sorrows* (published in 1910). His only non-dramatic prose work is *The Aran Islands* (1907). Though the plays were at first badly received by audiences who found his characters incompatible with Irishmen's romantic and self-flattering view of themselves (*The Playboy* provoked a week of nightly riots in the theatre), his genius could not long be denied, and he stands first among the playwrights who made the Abbey Theatre and the *Irish Players famous in the period before World War I.

T. Signature of Joseph *Thorp for his dramatic criticisms in *Punch*, 1916-34.

Tabloid. Descriptive term, often derogatory, applied to a newspaper giving a minimum of plain news, using flaring 'banner' headlines and specializing in sensation and triviality. Though derided by thoughtful people who see them as a debasing influence 'tabloids' have captured the mass public in several countries.

Taffrail (pseudonym of Captain Henry Taprell Dorling, 1883-1968). Born in Berwickshire; educated on H.M.S. *Britannia*. Served in the Royal Navy in various parts of the world from 1900 and in both World Wars. Was for a period naval correspondent of the *Observer*, and active for the B.B.C. as broadcaster and script writer. His numerous books on the sea and naval affairs include *Pincher Martin, O.D.* (1915), *Sea Venturers of Britain* (1929), *Endless Story,* (1931), *Seventy North* (1934); *Mid-Atlantic* (1936), *The Navy in Action* (1940), *Battle of the Atlantic* (1946), *Eurydice* (1953), *Arctic Convoy* (1956).

Tagore, Sir Rabindranath (1861-1941; knighted 1915). Born in Calcutta of a wealthy Indian family; educated privately; studied law for a short time in London. He began writing at an early age and published the first of his poetical works (*A Poet's Tale*) in 1878. He lectured in the U.S., England, and other countries, and in 1901 founded in Bengal a school which developed into an international institution for synthesizing Eastern and European cultures. He became world-famous as a poet, writing in Bengali but translating several of his works into English, of which he had an impressive command. Best known of these is *Gitanjali* (1912), but his output included plays—*Chitra* (1913), *The Post Office* (1914), *The Cycle of Spring* (1917); novels—*The Home and the World* (1919), *The Wreck* (1921); autobiography—*My Reminiscences* (1917); and miscellaneous prose works—*Creative Unity* (1922) and others. His *Collected Poems and Plays* was published in 1936.

Tanks. See E. D. *Swinton.

Tanner, John. Leading character in Bernard Shaw's *Man and Superman* (1903). Made a guardian of Ann Whitefield in her father's will, he finds himself in the grip of the Life Force and, against his will, impelled to succumb to her in love and marriage. He is the reputed author of *The Revolutionist's Handbook* and *Maxims for Revolutionists* appended by Shaw to the printed text of *Man and Superman*.

Tarkington, Booth (Newton Booth Tarkington, 1869-1946). Born in Indianapolis; educated at Exeter Academy (New Hampshire) and Princeton. After flirtations with art and politics he settled to writing and was for many years one of America's most popular novelists, having his first success with *Monsieur Beaucaire* (1900), set in eighteenth-century England, which also had long life as a romantic play. More critical approval was given to his novels of life in Indiana, notably *The Magnificent Ambersons* (1918) and *Alice Adams* (1921). *Penrod* (1914), a book for and about boys, in the Mark Twain 'Tom Sawyer' tradition, was followed by *Penrod and Sam* (1916), and *Penrod Jashber* (1929).

Tate, Allen (Allen John Orley Tate, 1899-   ). Born in Kentucky; educated privately and at Vanderbilt University. A brief, unwilling and unsuccessful attempt at a business career preceded a series of academic appointments as lecturer and Professor of English, Resident Fellow in Poetry at Princeton, 1939-42, Professor of English at the University of Minnesota from 1951, and Editor of the *Sewanee Review*. As a metaphysical poet much influenced by T. S. *Eliot and as a leader in the 'New Criticism' movement, he had a prominent place among the contemporary intellectuals of American literature. He wrote biographies of *Stonewall Jackson* (1928) and *Jefferson Davis* (1929); his verse includes *Mr Pope and Other Poems* (1928), *Poems, 1928-31* (1932), *The Mediterranean and Other Poems* (1936), *Winter Sea* (1945); critical prose—*Reactionary Essays on Poetry and Ideas* (1936), *Reason in Madness* (1941), *On the Limits of Poetry* (1948), *The Forlorn Demon* (1952); novel—*The Fathers* (1938).

Tawney, R. H. (Richard Henry Tawney, 1880-1962). Born in Calcutta; educated in England at Rugby and Oxford. Professor of Economic History in the University of London, 1931-49. He had a leading part in the adult education movement as a member for more than forty years of the executive of the Workers' Educational Association and as its President from 1928 to 1944. Served on various Commissions and other official bodies. Author of *The Agrarian Problem in the Sixteenth Century* (1912), *The Acquisitive Society* (1920), *The British Labour Movement* (1925), *Religion and the Rise of Capitalism* (1926), *Equality* (1931), *Business and Politics under James I* (1958). Editor (with others) of collections of Tudor and later Economic Documents.

Taylor, A. J. P. (Alan John Percivale Taylor, 1906-   ). Born in Lancashire; educated at Bootham School in York and at Oxford. Became Lecturer in Modern History at Manchester and then Tutor in Modern History, Oxford. A successful university teacher, he was also popular as a television lecturer, his series on *The Russian Revolution of 1917* (1958) being the first delivered through that medium. Among his books on modern European history are *The Hapsburg Monarchy 1815-1918* (1941; new edn 1948), *From Napoleon to Stalin* (1950), *Bismarck* (1955). His interpretations of events and their causes were sometimes unorthodox, though his exposition was brilliant. Particular dissent was occasioned by *The Origins of the Second World War* (1961). His *English History, 1914-1945* (1965) is the concluding volume of the Oxford History of England. Director of the Beaverbrook Library and wrote *Beaverbrook* (biography, 1972).

Taylor, Elizabeth (*née* Elizabeth Coles, 1912-   ). Born and educated at Reading. After experience as teacher, librarian, and housewife, she published her first novel, *At Mrs Lippincote's* in 1946, followed by *Palladian* (1947), *A View of the Harbour* (1949), *A Wreath of Roses* (1950), *The Sleeping Beauty* (1953), *In a Summer Season* (1961), *The Soul of Kindness* (1964), *A Dedicated Man* (1965). Her uneventful novels attract readers who appreciate precision of language and avoidance of over-emphasis in style. Mrs Taylor's works also include *Hester Lilly and Other Stories* (1954), and *The Blush and Other Stories* (1958), *The Devastating Boys* (1972).

Taylor, Rachel Annand (*née* Rachel Annand, 1876-1960). Born in Aberdeen; educated at schools and the University there. Author of several books of verse—*Poems* (1904), *Rose and Vine* (1908), *The Hours of Fiametta: A Sonnet Sequence* (1909), *The End of Fiametta* (1923). Her poems were enthusiastically praised by eminent contemporaries, among them Gilbert *Murray, who wrote an Introduction to her *Leonardo the Florentine*

(1927). She also wrote *Aspects of the Renaissance* (1923), *Renaissance France* (1939) and a study of the 15th-16th century Scottish. poet William Dunbar.

Tchekhov, Anton (Anton Pavlovich Tchekhov, 1860-1904). Born in Russia at Taganrog, grandson of a freed serf; while a medical student in Moscow he began to contribute to the press and adopted writing as his profession after the successful publication of *Motley Stories* (1886). He had qualified as a doctor but had no regular practice. Though continuing to produce the short stories upon which one part of his world-fame is built, he also began to write for the theatre, but *Ivanov* (1887) and *The Seagull* (1896) were failures, until *Stanislavsky revived the latter at the Moscow Art Theatre in 1898. From that occasion Tchekhov acquired a second fame and sustained it with his other plays, *Uncle Vanya* (1900), *The Three Sisters* (1901), and *The Cherry Orchard* (1904). Though he has had imitators and disciples, Tchekhov's work remains unique. The characters in his plays are created with boundless sympathy and understanding even when they are comic or even absurd, and a deep sense of pity lifts the frustrated, the emotionally starved and barren up to a plane of intensely moving subdued tragedy. On the stage the plays call for a sensitive style of production which gives full effect to the almost dreamlike atmosphere in which the characters live. As a prophet of approaching social disintegration Tchekhov achieved his masterpiece in *The Cherry Orchard*, where the sound of the axe as the final curtain descends seems a portent of universal destruction. It would be no exaggeration to suggest that as a literary form the short story was never the same once Tchekhov's stories had worked as a ferment in the literature of the West, with effects shown, typically, in the stories of Katherine *Mansfield.

Teasdale, Sara (1884-1933). Born in St Louis; educated privately. She travelled extensively in Europe and the Middle East, before living in Chicago, where Vachel *Lindsay courted her without success. She greatly admired the writings of Christina Rossetti, though her own poems have little of the colour and ornamentation characteristic of the English poet's work, and are for the most part simple and sensuous. *Collected Poems* (1937).

Teixeira de Mattos, Alexander Louis (1865-

1921). Born in Amsterdam; educated in England at Roman Catholic schools. Translator into English of *Maeterlinck's works and those of J. H. *Fabre, Gaston *Leroux and others.

Tebrick, Richard. His wife, Silvia, is the subject of the title of David Garnett's *Lady into Fox* (1922).

Teilhard de Chardin, Pierre (1881-1955). Born in Auvergne. Professor of Geology at the Institut Catholique, Paris, from 1918. As a Jesuit he was not permitted during his lifetime to publish philosophical writings based on scientific research. These became influential when published posthumously: *The Phenomenon of Man* (Eng. trans. 1959) and *Le Milieu divin* (1960) in which he argues with originality concerning the existence of God.

Television Act 1954. After considerable controversy, this Act introduced commercial television into Britain in competition with the non-commercial but previously monopolistic B.B.C. A complicated system of programme contracting was set up under the nominal control of the newly formed Independent Television Authority, and contracts for various regional areas were allotted to companies mainly composed of entertainment and newspaper interests. The latter by entering the television field extended their power of mass communication and persuasion, and protected themselves against financial loss that might have been incurred by diversion of advertising revenue from print to television. In addition to providing programmes designed for the entertainment of the aesthetically and mentally uncritical millions whose spending capacity was the main target of commercial television, the programme contractors sought also to attract a more selective audience by discussions on current affairs, by talks on literature and art, and by commissioning original plays which in a number of instances created for authors a reputation which led to later success in the theatre. In such ways television, from the commercial companies and from the B.'3.C. alike, contributed, even if only indirectly, to the literature of the period. Those who had consistently opposed the introduction of commercial television—and, in the issue, many who had previously been neutral—found cause to criticize the nature and quality of programmes which habituated viewers (among whom were

innumerable children) to scenes of brutality and sexual licence and to entertainment which fostered the extreme of triviality. The intention of the euphemism 'Independent' was evident from the beginning. The mountainous profits which accrued to the promoters demonstrated that commercial advertisers were in effective control and that cultural programmes could be introduced only in so far as they did not divert viewers' attention from spending on goods and articles pictured and vocally commended. Whatever opinions might be expressed on either side, for the present generation television superseded other means of mass influence. The methods by which the plan for commercial television was made acceptable to Parliament were analysed by Professor H. H. Wilson in *Pressure Group* (London, 1961).

Templar, Simon. The 'gentleman burglar' known as The Saint in the series of crime novels by Leslie *Charteris.

Ten Days that Shook the World. A firsthand account of events in Petrograd at the time of the Bolshevik revolution in 1917 by John *Reed, an American socialist newspaper correspondent. It was published in America in 1919, and in England with an Introduction by Lenin in 1926.

Tenniel, Sir John (1820-1914; knighted 1893). Born in London; studied at the Royal Academy Schools. On the staff of *Punch* from 1851 to 1901 and was its chief cartoonist from 1864. He also illustrated *Aesop's Fables*, *The Ingoldsby Legends* and other books, achieving lasting fame with his drawings for Lewis Carroll's *Alice in Wonderland* and *Alice Through the Looking Glass*

Terry, C. V. *See* Frank *Slaughter.

Terry, Dame Ellen (Ellen Alice Terry, 1848-1928; G.B.E. 1925). Born at Coventry of a family of actors and made her own first stage appearance at the age of eight, as Mamillius in *The Winter's Tale*. In 1864 she married G. F. Watts, the painter, but a wide disparity in age and temperament led soon to separation and divorce, after which she lived for several years with E. W. Godwin (1833-86), architect and stage-designer, and bore two children who both became eminent in the theatre as Edward Gordon *Craig and Edith Craig. Returning to the stage, Ellen Terry became the outstanding English actress of her time as leading lady in Henry Irving's company from

1878 to 1902, excelling in the major Shakespearean parts. A woman of fascinating personality and fine intelligence, she has a place in English literature through the letters published in 1931 as *Ellen Terry and Bernard Shaw: A Correspondence*. Her autobiographical volumes *The Story of My Life* (1908) and *Memoirs of Ellen Terry* (edited by Edith Craig and Christopher St John, 1933) are valuable contributions to contemporary stage history.

Tessier, Ernest Maurice. *See* Maurice *Dekobra.

Tessimond, A. S. J. (Arthur Seymour John Tessimond, died 1962). Born at Birkenhead; educated there and at Charterhouse and, after a period as journalist in London, at Liverpool University. He then ranged through various occupations—as accountant, teacher, bookseller— before settling as an advertisement copy writer. In the 1930s he achieved some repute among the newer poets and a number of his poems had wider popularity in anthologies. The contributor of an obituary notice in *The Times* spoke of his indifference to nature and the countryside and his preference for dealing in verse with urban themes and human types. His collections of poems include *The Walls of Glass* (1934) and *Voices in a Giant City* (1947).

Testament of Beauty, The. Philosophical poem by Robert *Bridges published in 1929. Technically it was the culmination of the poet's years of experimentation with 'loose alexandrines', attempts to naturalize the classical iambic hexameter line in English. The more than 4000 lines of the poem are grouped in four Books: I. Introduction; II. Selfhood; III. Breed; IV. Ethick. In incidental subject matter it ranges over numerous aspects of contemporary life and thought, with occasional touches of scholarly humour and some discreet dipping into reformed spelling. Its immediate popularity and enormous sales, supported by much serious critical acclaim, was followed in subsequent years by equivalent denigration and neglect.

Textual analysis. An anti-romantic, philosophical and scientific method of academic study of poetry and imaginative prose, concentrating on linguistics, symbolism, imagery and the mechanics of composition, rather than on characterization and the variety of humane interests embraced in 'the pleasures of literature'. The method is associated with, particularly, the *New Criticism in America, and in

England with the Cambridge school of English studies (*vide* I. A. Richards: *Principles of Literary Criticism*, 1924; the writings of F. R. Leavis, William Empson, etc.) and its offshoots in the newer universities in Britain and elsewhere.

Tey, Josephine. Pseudonym under which Elizabeth Mackintosh wrote detective novels including *The Singing Sands* (1952). *See* Gordon *Daviot.

Thanet, Octave (pseudonym of Alice French, 1850-1934). Born in Massachusetts. Author of *Knitters in the Sun* (1887), *The Man of the Hour* (1905), *A Step on the Stair* (1913), and other novels; and of *Stories of a Western Town* (1893), *Stories that End Well* (1911) and other collections. Her books are set in the Middle West and display her interest in social and industrial problems.

Theale, Milly. *See* *Milly Theale.

Theatre criticism. *See* *Dramatic criticism.

Theatre of the Absurd. A study of contemporary drama under this title by Martin Esslin, published in 1962, surveys the writings of Samuel *Beckett, *Ionesco, and other playwrights whose main thesis is that human life, being without 'meaning' or coherence, is essentially chaotic; that consequently, human beings have no channel of 'meaningful' communication; and that plays aiming to give a genuine reflection of life must do so through a medium which suggests the full range of absurdity—meaninglessness, nonsense, non-communication. The idea was carried to the extreme by those who advocated that plays should be wordless, allowing the 'absurdity' to be conveyed by gesture and physical antics.

Theatre of Cruelty. Generic term for stage plays presenting as entertainment psychotic subjects, characters, and behaviour. Current in the period following World War II, they were written and defended by *avant-garde* authors and producers. Supporting critics suggested that the influence on the audience was cathartic (*see* Catharsis), while others regarded them as wholly emetic. Questions about their possible calamitous effect are put by Pamela Hansford *Johnson in *On Iniquity* (1967). The genre is studied in detail in *The Dark Comedy* by J. L. Styan (1962; revised edn 1968).

Theatres Act 1968. It abolished the system of censorship exercised by the Lord Chamberlain under the Theatre Regulation Act of

1843, and put stage plays on equal footing with books and other publications with respect to obscenity, libel, and other offences. See *Stage censorship.

These Twain. Novel by Arnold *Bennett published in 1916, completing the trilogy begun with *Clayhanger (1910) and continued with *Hilda Lessways (1911). The author's aim was to present an average successful marriage, which becomes in the experience of Edwin and Hilda 'the great passionate war of marriage' intermittently pacified by 'their solid but tarnished love'. Criticizing openly yet often comprehending silently, Edwin is exasperated by Hilda's attempts to divert him from determined courses, as when he negotiates for a site on which to build a larger printing works, spacious enough to accommodate a lithography department, which she prophesies (mistakenly as events prove) will ruin them. Their daily lives are punctuated and punctured by the thousand and one irritations common to those living in an inseparable relationship. Around the central couple swirl their relatives—Auntie Hamps; Edwin's sisters—patient Maggie, unwed and endlessly 'put upon'; Clara and Albert Benbow and their brood—and their friends, notably Janet Orgreave, fading from enchanting youth into hopeless spinsterhood, and her younger sister Alicia, prosperously married in a country mansion which Hilda envies. First among their new friends, Tertius Ingpen, though a bachelor with cynical views about women, gives sage though mostly unheeded matrimonial advice to both Hilda and Edwin, and is nearly killed when a fly-wheel breaks loose in Benbow's works, which Ingpen is visiting in his capacity as Factory Inspector. Most important in the Clayhanger household is the growing-up George, son of Hilda and George Cannon, loved by Edwin as well as by his mother.

Thesiger, Wilfred (Wilfred Patrick Thesiger, 1910-   ). Born in Addis Ababa, Abyssinia; educated at Eton and Oxford. Traversed the mountainous region of Abyssinia while on vacation, and after graduating joined the Sudan Political Service. With the Sudan Defence Force he served in Syria, Abyssinia and the Western Desert through World War II. In 1946-48, with only Arab companions he crossed the Empty Quarter of Arabia and described the journey in Arabian Sands (1959), an outstanding desert-travel book. Also wrote The Marsh Arabs (1964).

They Were Defeated. Historical novel by Rose *Macaulay published in 1932. In a preliminary note the author stated that she had endeavoured not to make any of the characters 'use in conversation any words, phrases, or idioms that were not demonstrably used at the time in which they lived'—the middle of the seventeenth century. The first of the novel's three parts, headed 'Bucolick', is set in the Devonshire village of Dean Prior, where Robert Herrick the poet was vicar from 1629 until he was ejected by the Puritans under the Commonwealth in 1647 (restored after the Restoration). He is introduced in the story in the autumn, when his church is decorated for the first time with fruits and vegetables, wheatsheaves and loaves and flowers for the rejoicings at harvest home, an innovation disfavoured by the ecclesiastical authorities as savouring of pagan rites. Herrick, a staunch Anglican 'of the cheerful middle English way', hates Puritans and Papists equally, and preaches robustly at his congregation, pointing from the pulpit at individual parishioners as he chastises their personal faults in his sermons. His heart is given more to poetry and to Julia and (as his friend Sir John Suckling says) to 'his lovely Corinnas, Sapphos, Lesbias, Antheas and the rest' than to his pastoral duties, and he escapes at intervals to rollick in London. He has as a pupil in his parish Julian (July) Conybeare, the fifteen-year-old pretty daughter of the neighbouring physician Dr Michael Conybeare, who expresses atheistical convictions and abhors the superstitious frenzies of the villagers. He shelters a harmless destitute old woman who is the victim of a witch hunt (led by an imported professional witch-finder), and when she is discovered hidden between floor and ceiling in his house he gives her a poisonous draught to save her from torture and burning. Prudently removing from local suspicion, he goes with July to Cambridge, where his son Christopher (Kit) has John Cleveland the metaphysical poet and political satirist as his tutor. In this 'Academick' environment July finds opportunities to cultivate her love of poetry and learning. She converses with Abraham Cowley, the precocious young poet whom she has hero-worshipped from a distance while at home, and attends philosophical lectures given for ladies by Henry More, one of the *Cambridge Platonists. In the third part of the novel—'Antiplatonick'—July falls in love with Cleveland, who scoffs at her leanings to poetry and philosophy, saying that a maid is 'formed for sweetness and love and not for learning'. He makes havoc of her life before tiring of her. July's elder brother Francis learns of her seduction and attacks Cleveland. While attempting to part them July is accidentally struck down and dies from a blow against the corner of a table as she falls.

Thirkell, Mrs Angela (*née* Angela Margaret Mackail, 1890-1961). Born in London, daughter of J. W. *Mackail; educated at St Paul's School; married (1) J. Campbell McInnes, (2) G. L. Thirkell with whom she settled in Australia for several years and began to write. Her first book, published in 1930 after she returned to England, was *Three Houses*, an attractive and historically valuable account of her childhood in contact with such older relatives as Burne-Jones the painter (her grandfather) and Rudyard Kipling (a cousin). Thereafter she produced a long series of urbane novels of cultured English life, often set in Barsetshire, the imaginary county invented in the previous century by Anthony Trollope. Among her novels are *Ankle Deep* (1932), *Coronation Summer* (1937), *The Brandons* (1939), *Marling Hall* (1942), *County Chronicle* (1950), *Happy Returns* (1952), *Enter Sir Robert* (1955). *See also* Colin *McInnes (her son) and Denis *Mackail (her brother).

This Side of Paradise. Novel by F. Scott *Fitzgerald published in 1920. Cosseted by his rich, beautiful, hard-drinking, lapsed-Catholic, Irish-American mother, Amory Blaine, born in 1896, grows up partly on her European estate in Geneva and partly with an aunt and uncle in Minneapolis. As a youth he is handsome, with 'personality charm, magnetism, poise, the power of dominating all contemporary males, the gift of fascinating all women', and is a confirmed egotist convinced of his complete, unquestioned mental superiority, a characteristic responsible for his unpopularity with boys and masters at boarding-school until he is accepted and imitated as an eccentric. In his first terms at Princeton he resents the glittering caste system, but forms friendships which gain him membership of exclusive undergraduate clubs. He goes on a Christmas vacation tour with a Triangle Club musical-comedy production, and comes into contact with 'that great current American phenomenon', the 'petting party', leading only to an abortive flirtation with Isabelle Borge. Cutting classes

in his second year, he goes on a three-day party to the coast in a stolen car with several Princetonians. They eat well at hotels and restaurants but cheat on the bills. A later drinking party, in New York, ends with a car smash in which one of the young men is killed. In his senior year at the university Amory develops a friendship with Burne Holiday, who leads a radical revolt against the clubs 'injurious to Princeton democracy' and influences Amory a good deal during prolonged talks on varied subjects, 'from biology to organized religion'. He contemplates marriage with his young widowed cousin, Clara Page, but she declines to marry again. Amory is caught up in World War I and becomes an officer with the American infantry in France. Afterwards he and Rosalind Connage, sister of a Princeton friend, fall deeply in love, but she turns to a richer man, leaving Amory to seek oblivion in a prolonged alcoholic bout, ended by the coming of Prohibition. A later idyllic affair with Eleanor Savage ends in an exchange of poems. Amory embarks on a long walk to revisit Princeton, where he reflects that 'the waters of disillusion had left a deposit on his soul, responsibility and a love of life, the faint stirring of old ambitions and unrealized dreams,' but 'It's all a poor substitute' for Rosalind.

Thomas, Brandon (1849-1914). Born in Liverpool; educated privately. Began as an actor and wrote a dozen or so plays between *Comrades* (1882) and *A Judge's Memory* (1906) but only *Charley's Aunt* (1892) survived his death, to become accepted, through successive revivals, as a classic farce.

Thomas, Dylan (Dylan Marlais Thomas, 1914-53). Born in Swansea and educated there. Worked for a short time as a reporter in Wales before his *Eighteen Poems* appeared in 1934, followed by *Twenty-five Poems* (1936), *The Map of Love* (1939), *Deaths and Entrances* (1946), *Collected Poems* (1952). His prose works include the partially autobiographical *Portrait of the Artist as a Young Dog* (1940) and the posthumously published *Adventures in the Skin Trade* (unfinished novel; 1955), *Quite Early One Morning* (broadcast talks; 1954), and *A Prospect of the Sea* (1955). Until the last few years of his life Thomas's poetry had only a limited audience, for it was found baffling by many and was praised mainly by fellow poets and intellectualist critics. His radio broadcasts in the 1940s and early 1950s introduced him to millions who were captivated by the incantatory manner and the Welsh intonation in readings of his own poems: the sound was found irresistible even when the sense remained elusive. His greatest success was with the radio play *Under Milk Wood*, first broadcast by the B.B.C., later staged for a short run and published in 1954. He died in New York, after a period of convivial as well as critical adulation in the United States. Though he received unmeasured praise on both sides of the Atlantic towards the end of his life, and was acclaimed the greatest English poet of his time by some influential writers, it is probable that there will be some diminishing revaluation of his poetry by future critics not under the spell of his personality and verbal exuberance, nor of the literary fashions of his time. He was much written about, often hastily and intemperately. *Left-Over Life to Kill* (1957) is an emotional testament by his wife Caitlin Thomas (*née* Macnamara) whom he married in 1936.

The most straightforwardly informative biography is *The Life of Dylan Thomas* by Constantine Fitzgibbon (1965). An illuminating letter by a friend of long standing, J. H. Martin, contributed to *The Times Literary Supplement* (19 March 1964, p. 235) describes Thomas's serio-comic and sceptical attitude towards his own reputation as an *avant-garde* poet, and gives an account of his methods of composition. *See also* J. Maclaren Ross: *Memoirs of the Forties* (1965).

Thomas, Edward (Philip Edward Thomas, 1878-1917). Born in London of Welsh parents; educated at St Paul's School and Oxford. Describing himself later as 'always a writer', he resisted attempts to direct him into the Civil Service, and he and his wife (whom he had married while still at Oxford) lived in straitened circumstances for years while he worked as a freelance journalist and author of nature books and biographies which gave little scope to his dormant genius, unawakened until the beginning of his friendship in 1912 with the American poet Robert *Frost, who had recently settled in England. Thomas then began to contribute poems to periodicals, disguising himself under the pseudonym Edward Eastaway, since he was known only as a hack writer under his own name. A small privately printed book of *Six Poems* came out in 1916, and a larger volume, *Poems* (1917), was preceded by his death. He had joined the army in the early days of World

War I and was killed in France in April 1917. He was then recognized as a poet of high stature with an original voice and unaffected clarity of vision which keep his simple-seeming lyrics free from conscious artifice. His *Collected Poems* were published in 1920 with a Foreword by Walter de la Mare, who wrote of Thomas's delight in simple and natural things, his 'fine, lucid, grave and sensitive mind', and of his poetry as ennobling by simplification. (New edns of the *Collected Poems* appeared in 1928 and 1949.) Though most of his other works were written to order and are mostly now unread, his prose is above the commonplace level and his genuinely personal love of nature is evident in *The Woodland Life* (1897), *The Heart of England* (1906), *The South Country* (1909), *In Pursuit of Spring* (1915). A number of his essays are collected in *Horae Solitaire* (1902), *Rose Acre Papers* (1904), *Rest and Unrest* (1910), *Cloud Castle and Other Papers* (1922). He wrote biographical studies of *Richard Jefferies* (1909), *Maeterlinck* (1911), *Swinburne* (1912), *George Borrow* (1912), and others. *The Happy-Go-Lucky Morgans* (1913) is a novel.

Thomas, Gwyn (1913-). Born in the Rhondda; educated at elementary and intermediate schools there and then at Oxford. Spent some months in Madrid; taught in Welsh schools until 1962. Described as 'a proletarian novelist of outstanding gifts', writing with gusto, humour, compassion and profound humanity (Glyn Jones: *The Dragon has Two Tongues*, 1968). His novels include: *The Dark Philosophers* (1946), *All Things Betray Thee* (1949), *A Frost on My Frolic* (1953), *The Love Man* (1958). Short stories: *Where Did I put My Pity* (1946), *Gazooka* (1957), etc. Essays: *A Welsh Eye* (1964), *A Hatful of Humours* (1965). Also plays.

Thomas Mendip. The discharged soldier and central character in Christopher Fry's *The *Lady's Not for Burning* (1948). Claiming to be a murderer, and suspected of being the Devil, he vainly demands to be hanged.

Thomas, R. S. (Ronald Stuart Thomas, 1913-). Born and educated in Wales; ordained 1936 and held several church appointments. Author of *Song at the Year's Turning* (1955), *Poetry for Supper* (1958), and other books of verse. His attitude may be seen in the opening lines of 'Poetry for Supper': '. . . verse should be as natural / As the small tuber that feeds on muck / And grows slowly from obtuse soil / To the white flower of immortal beauty'—though this is put into the mouth of only one of 'two old poets' arguing in an inn parlour.

Thompson, Edward (Edward John Thompson, 1886-1946). Educated in Bath; entered the Wesleyan Methodist ministry in 1909 and served as an educational missionary in Bengal from 1910 to 1923, with an interval as chaplain to the forces in Mesopotamia and Palestine in World War I. Lecturer in Bengali at Oxford, 1923-33, and Research Fellow in Indian History there, 1936-46. Author of *The Knight Mystic* (1907) and later books of verse, *Collected Poems* (1930); *These Men Thy Friends* (1927) and other novels; *A History of India* (1927) and several books in support of independence for India; **Tagore: Poet and Dramatist* (1926), *Sir Walter Raleigh* (1935), *Robert *Bridges* (1944).

Thompson, Flora (*née* Flora Jane Timms, 1876-1947). Born at Juniper Hill, Northamptonshire, and educated there at the village school, leaving to start work in a neighbouring post-office and later in the postal service in Surrey. In Bournemouth, after her marriage to a postmaster, she furthered her education by extensive reading, contributed to a periodical issued by a small organization, the Peveril Society, and published some poems; but her ambitions as a writer remained unfulfilled until 1939, when **Lark Rise* was recognized as an important as well as delightful addition to the authentic records of English country life and the annals of the rural poor in the last decades of the 19th century. It was followed by *Over to Candleford* (1941) and *Candleford Green* (1943), the three books being united in the trilogy *Lark Rise to Candleford* (1945). *Still Glides the Stream* (1948), in a similar vein but set in a different locality, appeared shortly after her death. *See* Margaret Lane: 'Flora Thompson' in *Purely for Pleasure* (1966).

Thompson, Francis (1859-1907). Born at Preston; educated at Ushaw College in preparation for the Roman Catholic priesthood, but was physically and psychologically unfitted; then studied medicine with no better success at Owen's College, Manchester. He moved to London in 1885, becoming a homeless wanderer and opium addict, and living in abject poverty until he was rescued by Wilfrid *Meynell to whom Thompson had sent a sheaf of his poems. The Meynells took him into their home for the rest of his life and fostered his remarkable talent as poet and prose writer. He contributed poems and essays to Meynell's paper, *Merry England*, and published *Poems* (1893), *Sister Songs* (1895), *New Poems* (1897). A treatise on *Health and Holiness* (1905), *Essay on Shelley*, and a *Life of St Ignatius Loyola* (both published posthumously in 1909) are his chief prose work. Though subsequently less esteemed than in the early decades of the present century, for his opulent language and religious fervour became less generally approved, Francis Thompson holds a place among English poets with 'The Hound of Heaven', included in his first volume.

Thompson, Sylvia (Sylvia Elizabeth Thompson, 1902-68; Mrs Peter Luling). Born in Scotland; educated at Cheltenham and Oxford. Author of *The Rough Crossing* (1918) and other novels, among which *The Hounds of Spring* (1925) was her outstanding success.

Thomson, A. A. (Arthur Alexander Thomson, 1894-1968). Born at Harrogate; educated there and in London. Best known as a writer on cricket: *Cricket My Pleasure* (1953); *The Great Cricketer* (1957), a biography of W. G. Grace; but he wrote numerous other books—novels, verse, humour, travel, etc. To intimates he was usually 'A.A.'

Thomson, Sir Arthur (John Arthur Thomson, 1861-1933; knighted 1930). Born in Scotland; educated in Edinburgh, Jena, and Berlin. Regius Professor of Natural History in the University of Aberdeen, 1899-1930. Author of *The Science of Life* (1904), *The Bible of Nature* (1909), *Secrets of Animal Life* (1919), *What is Man?* (1923), *The Biology of Birds* (1923), *Modern Science* (1929), *The Outline of Natural History* (1932), *Scientific Riddles* (1932), and numerous other authoritative works written for general reading.

Thomson, David Landsborough (1901-64). Born at Aberdeen; educated there and at Grenoble and Cambridge. Professor of Biochemistry, McGill University, Montreal, from 1937. Author of *The Life of the Cell* (1928), and of detective stories under an undisclosed pseudonym.

Thomson, Sir George (George Paget Thomson, 1892-   ; knighted 1943). Born at Cambridge, son of Sir J. J. Thomson; educated there at the Perse School and University.

Professor of Physics in the University of London, 1930-52. Took a leading part in research on atomic energy. Author of *Applied Aerodynamics* (1919), *The Atom* (1937 and later editions), and other scientific works.

Thomson, Gladys Scott. See Gladys *Scott Thomson.

Thomson, J. A. K. (James Alexander Kerr Thomson, 1879-1959). Born in Scotland. Professor of Classics in the University of London. Author of *The Greek Tradition* (1916), *Greeks and Barbarians* (1921), *Irony* (1926), *The Classical Background of English Literature* (1948), *Shakespeare and the Classics* (1952), *Classical Influences on English Prose* (1955).

Thorndike, Russell (Arthur Russell Thorndike, 1885-1972). Born at Rochester, brother of the actress Dame Sybil Thorndike; educated at Windsor and Rochester. Trained for the stage and played many parts in England, America, and other countries. He was also the prolific author of many novels, including a long and popular series centred on a sinister Dr Syn, who first appeared in *Doctor Syn: A Tale of the Romney Marsh* (1915), and was enacted by his creator on the stage in *Dr Syn* (1925). He wrote *Saul: An Historical Tragedy* (1906), and a biography of his sister *Sybil Thorndike* (1929; new edn 1950). Other novels include *The Slype* (1927), *The Vandekkers* (1929), *The Water Witch* (1932), *The First Englishman* (1949). Early experiences are related in *Children of the Garter: Being the Memoirs of a Windsor Castle Choir-boy during the last years of Queen Victoria* (1937), his father being Canon Arthur John Webster Thorndike.

Thorndyke, Dr. Forensic medicine expert in crime stories by R. Austin *Freeman.

Thorp, Joseph (Joseph Peter Thorp, 1873-1962). Educated at Stonyhurst and Oscott Roman Catholic Colleges. Entered the Society of Jesus (Jesuits) in 1891 but left after ten years. Then became a printers' traveller and adviser on typography. Dramatic critic for *Punch*, as 'T', 1916-34. Author of *Printing for Business* (1919), *Broken Bridges, or The Bolshevist: An Industrial Play* (1930), *Eric Gill* (1929), *Friends and Adventures* (autobiography; 1931), *Bernard Newdigate: Scholar-Printer* (1950).

Thorpe family. In William De Morgan's *Joseph Vance* (1906): Dr **Randall** Thorpe, benefactor of Joe Vance; **Violet** and **Lucilla** (*Lossie), his daughters. Joseph (**Beppino**) Thorpe, his son, masquerades in Italy under the name of Vance, and his child by an Italian girl is adopted by Joe Vance, who is later rumoured to be its father.

Thorpe, James (James H. Thorpe, 1876-1949). Mainly an illustrator, contributing to *Punch* from 1909 to 1938, but was also the author of *A Cricket Bag* (1929), *Phil May: Master Draughtsman and Humorist, 1864-1903* (1932), *Happy Days: Recollections of an Unrepentant Victorian* (1933), *English Illustration: The Nineties* (1935), *Come for a Walk: A Book for Motorists and Others* (1940).

Throssel, Susan and Phoebe. Sisters in J. M. Barrie's *Quality Street* (1902).

Thrums. Name under which the town of Kirriemuir, Forfarshire, Scotland, appears in *A Window in Thrums* and other books by J. M. *Barrie.

Thurber, James (James Grover Thurber, 1894-1961). Born in Ohio; educated at the State University there. Worked as a government clerk in Washington and at the Embassy in Paris, then as a journalist for a Chicago newspaper's Paris edition. Having returned to New York in 1926 he joined the staff of the *New Yorker* until 1933, and continued as a contributor for the rest of his life. He was a remarkable humorist both in words and in pictures; his drawings produce a richly comic effect with a bare economy of line. The 'Thurber dog' is a famous creation and, like the artist's men and women, achieves individuality with a minimum of anatomy (*Men, Women, and Dogs*, 1942). His humorous prose is a unique compound of craziness, fantasy, and supersanity: *The Owl in the Attic, and other Perplexities* (1932), *The Seal in My Bedroom, and other Predicaments* (1932), *My Life and Hard Times* (autobiography; 1933), *Let Your Mind Alone* (1937), *My World—and Welcome To It!* (1942), *The Beast in Me, and other Animals* (1948), *The Thirteen Clocks* (1950). In collaboration with E. B. *White he wrote *Is Sex Really Necessary?* (1929), and in collaboration with Elliott Nugent a play, *The Male Animal* (1940). He wrote of his experiences on the *New Yorker* in *The Years With Ross* (1959).

Thurston, E. Temple (Ernest Charles Temple Thurston, 1879-1933). After publishing two unremarkable books of verse when he was sixteen, he began a long and successful career as a novelist with *The Apple of Eden* (1905). From among the many novels that came after it, *The City of Beautiful Nonsense* (1909) and *The Greatest Wish in the World* (1910) are outstanding for humour and romance with a shrewd undercurrent of disillusioned observation of the human scene which were characteristic of Thurston's writing. He also wrote plays, including dramatizations of his own novels and of his first wife, Katherine Cecil Thurston's *John Chilcote, M.P. The Wandering Jew* (1920) ran for nearly five hundred performances with Matheson Lang in the title part and was several times revived.

Thurston, Katherine Cecil (*née* Katherine Cecil Madden, 1875-1911). Born in Cork, educated privately. Wrote several novels and achieved international repute with *John Chilcote, M.P.* (1904), a story of impersonation and mistaken identity which her husband, E. Temple Thurston, dramatized in 1905. Other novels: *The Circle* (1903), *The Gambler* (1906), *The Fly on the Wheel* (1908).

Tietjens, Christopher. Chief character in Ford Madox Ford's *Parade's End*; marries Sylvia Satterthwaite a beautiful girl with a vampire nature who ruins his life.

Tillich, Paul (Paul Johannes Tillich, 1886-1965). Born in Prussia; educated in Berlin and other German universities; held Chairs in theology at Marburg and elsewhere, and became Professor of Philosophy at Frankfurt from 1929 until he was dismissed by the Hitler faction in 1933 and settled in America as Professor of Philosophical Theology at Union Seminary, New York. His influence as a Christian thinker was widely extended by his writings, which include *The Interpretation of History* (1936), *The Protestant Era* (1951), *The Shaking of the Foundations* (1951), *The Courage to Be* (1953), *Systematic Theology* (i, 1953; ii, 1957), *Love, Power, and Justice* (1954), *Theology of Culture* (1959).

Tillotson, Geoffrey (1905-69). Born at Bradford; educated at Keighley and Oxford. Professor of English Literature in the University of London from 1944. Author of books on Pope and editor of editions of his poems; *Essays in Criticism and Research* (1942), *Criticism and the Nineteenth Century* (1951), *Augustan Studies* (1961).

Tillotson, Kathleen M. (*née* Kathleen Mary Constable, 1906-   ; married Geoffrey Tillotson 1933). Educated at York and Ox-

ford. Professor of English in the University of London from 1958. Author of *Novels of the Eighteen-Forties* (1954), etc. Joint editor of the complete edition of Dickens's letters. General Editor of the Clarendon Dickens (definitive editions of the novels).

Tillyard, E. M. W. (Eustace Mandeville Wetenhall Tillyard, 1889-1962). Born at Cambridge; educated at Lausanne and Cambridge. Master of Jesus College, Cambridge, 1945-59. Author of works on Shakespeare and Milton and other literary subjects.

Time. See *Fourth Dimension.

Time and Tide. See Lady *Rhondda.

Time Machine, The. Short novel by H. G. *Wells published in 1895, the first of his works in the field of 'science fiction'. The Time Traveller, having discoursed to a group of friends on space and time as length, breadth, thickness, and duration—constituting the four dimensions in which creatures move, shows them in his laboratory the model of a machine he is constructing in full size to make it possible to travel either forward or backward in time by operating one or other of two levers. When he presses one of the levers the model vanishes, having passed into future Time. A week later the company gathers again, finding a note from their host telling them to start dinner at the usual hour if he is not present. He comes in soon after, dishevelled, ghastly pale, 'haggard and drawn, as by intense suffering'. On the Time Machine he has travelled into the future, landing in A.D. 802701 in the neighbourhood of the Thames valley, where the landscape is ruinously different from the present. The people are only about four feet high, graceful, gentle and frail, and evidently of low intellect; freed from the old pains and penalties of mankind—its struggles and privations and jealousies—they have reached, he thinks, an apparently idyllic state in which, however, 'security sets a premium on feebleness'. But he finds, after a while, that Man had differentiated into two distinct animals, these graceful people of the Upper World, the Eloi, while in a teeming underworld perpetually dark and reached only by descent into great airshafts, live the 'bleached, obscene, nocturnal' Morlocks, meat-eaters preying on the vegetarian Eloi. The Time Traveller describes his frightening experiences with the Morlocks, and their pursuit of him and Weena, an Eloi girl, through a burning forest. They try to trap him in the hollow pedestal of a great White Sphinx where they have hidden his Time Machine, on which he is able to escape, since walls cannot confine it, and to penetrate millions of years into the future before pressing the lever which conveys him back to the present and to his friends at the dinner party.

Tinker, C. B. (Chauncey Brewster Tinker, 1876-1963). Born in Maine; educated at Denver and Yale. Professor of English Literature, Yale University, 1903-46. His scholarly writings were mainly on James Boswell and Matthew Arnold: *Young Boswell* (1922), *The Letters of James Boswell* (2 vols, 1924); *The Poetry of Matthew Arnold: A Commentary* (1940), *The Complete Poetical Works of Matthew Arnold* (1950)—the last two in collaboration with H. F. Lowry. He was one of the first to inspect the great hoard of unpublished *Boswell Papers discovered in Ireland at Malahide Castle in the 1920s. Among his miscellaneous works are *Dr Johnson and Fanny Burney* (1908), *Good Estate of Poetry* (1929), and *Essays in Retrospect* (1948).

Titterton, W. R. (William Richard Titterton, 1876-1963). Born in London. Served as a clerk and artist's model, tramped on the Continent, and worked as a ship's stoker before entering journalism as contributor to various newspapers and periodicals, writing after 1931 as a Roman Catholic. Author of *River Music and other Poems* (1900), *An Afternoon Tea Philosophy* (1909), *From Theatre to Music Hall* (1912), *Have We Lost God?* (1933), *G. K. Chesterton: A Portrait* (1936).

T.L.S. *The Times Literary Supplement* is commonly reduced to initials in references by its readers, and the paper adopted the abbreviation as its main front-page heading at the beginning of 1969.

To Be a Pilgrim. Novel by Joyce *Cary published in 1942, the second in the trilogy begun with *Herself Surprised* (1941) and completed with *The *Horse's Mouth* (1944).
While the first of the sequence is an autobiographical statement by Sara Monday in which Mr Wilcher and Gulley Jimson are leading characters, the present book views the world of his time as Thomas Loftus Wilcher, a bachelor, recollects or perceives it in old age. 'The background is historical change seen through the eyes . . . of the man of political and religious intuition' knowing

that 'man is condemned to be a pilgrim in an unexplored wilderness' (author's preface to 1951 edition). Though a Christian and nominally a Liberal, he recognizes that 'all the schemes of politicians, . . . all the near paradises of the churches, are fraud or delusion'. After the imprisonment of Sara whom (in *Herself Surprised*) he had planned as an old man to marry, he now falls ill and is put in charge of his niece, Ann, at his beloved manor of Tolbrook, near Dartmoor. In the drift of memory, past and present overlap and intermingle, circling around the various members of his family: his sister Lucy, who joined an unorthodox religious sect, the Benjamites, married Brown, 'the Master', and lived in devout squalor; his eldest brother, Ann's father Edward, a prominent and brilliant politician unamenable to party discipline; his soldier brother Bill, Major Wilcher; his nephew, Robert Brown, Lucy's son, who marries Ann and farms Tolbrook; John, son of Bill, who ruins a promising legal career by marrying the corrupt Gladys and becoming a car salesman. Among other intermittently appearing characters, Julie Eeles, Edward's mistress and subsequently the narrator's, is outstanding. After Brown's defection to America, Lucy returns to Tolbrook and becomes central in Wilcher's consciousness, intensely loved and intensely hated, ever quarrelling, becoming daily estranged and daily reconciled until her death. Admitting at last that he is 'an old fossil', he regards it as silently understood between Ann and himself that 'whether I die today or tomorrow does not matter to anybody'.

To Sir, with Love. *See* E. R. *Braithwaite.

To the Finland Station. *See* Edmund *Wilson.

To the Lighthouse. Novel by Virginia *Woolf published in 1927. The father of eight children, James Ramsay, a writer and lecturer on philosophy, insists that his children 'should be aware from childhood that life is difficult', that it needs, above all, 'courage, truth, and the power to endure'. In this spirit he quenches the hope of his small son, James, that they will be able to cross tomorrow by boat to the lighthouse off the Isle of Skye where the family and invited friends are staying during the summer. James hates his father for insisting, correctly, that the weather won't be fine, while his mother attempts to console him with ill-founded words: 'But it may be fine—I expect it will be fine.' Years pass before the voyage to the lighthouse is at last achieved, by James and his sister Cam and their father, after the deaths of Mrs Ramsay and two of the older children—Andrew killed in the war and Prue in childbirth. Action in the novel is minimal. Interest is concentrated upon the thoughts and moods and mental impressions of the Ramsays and their guests: Charles Tansley, a self-centred prig aiming at a fellowship and a professorship; Lily Briscoe, spinster and painter, and her sympathetic friend, the elderly scientist, William Bankes; Augustus Carmichael, the poor unhappy old poet; the young lovers, Minta Doyle and Paul Rayley.

Tobermory. The embarrassingly frank English-speaking cat in the humorous short story with that title by *Saki, first included in *The Chronicles of Clovis* (1911), reprinted in the complete *Short Stories of Saki* (1930).

Tobias and the Angel. Play in three acts by James *Bridie performed in 1930, published in 1931. Described by the author as 'a plain-sailing dramatic transcription of the charming old tale told in the Book of Tobit in the Apocrypha', it avoids imitating biblical phraseology and uses a timeless form of speech 'that might equally have been used by a pupil of Swift or an apostle of Arnold Bennett'. The setting is Mesopotamia and northern Persia before the reign of Ahasuerus (5th century B.C.). The once-prosperous Tobit, old and blind, lives in a hovel at Nineveh, reduced to poverty by his good nature and generosity, for which he is scolded by Anna his wife, who now has to go out office-cleaning. While their son Tobias (a timid youth claiming to be temperamental and highly strung) is lamenting to his father that it doesn't look as though their Pentecost will be very lively, a Porter comes with a basket of roast quails, fruit, and wine, which Tobit supposes is a gift from his nephew, though the Porter denies it, saying 'Shall we pretend that Jahveh Himself sent it?' Tobias is afraid of bandits and demons when told to journey to Rages to collect a debt from Gabael, grown wealthy as a perfume manufacturer. The Porter, Azarias, goes with him as guide and companion. Made plucky by Azarias, Tobias catches a gigantic fish in the Tigris, and afterwards frightens off a bandit. At Ecbatana they call at the house of Raguel, a friend of old Tobit, and there Tobias falls in love with Sara, the daughter of Raguel, and proposes to marry her, though he is told that she has already been married seven times,

each husband being strangled on the wedding night by a demon, Asmoday, to whom Sara is 'an object of admiration'. Azarias gives Tobias a charm to drive off the demon, and the couple astonish Raguel next morning when they meet him returning from digging a grave for the latest husband. On the way back to Nineveh Sara tells Azarias she loves him, but he reveals himself (to her only) as the Archangel Raphael and lectures her on the art of being a wife. They get home after being away eighty-five days, bringing the loan with interest from Gabael. With the gall-bladder of the fish caught in the Tigris, Tobit is cured of his blindness; and when they offer payment to the supposed Porter he declares to them all his angelic identity and disappears in a flash of light.

Today. *See* Holbrook *Jackson.

Todd, Margaret. *See* Graham *Travers.

Todd, Ruthven (1914-   ). Born and educated in Edinburgh; studied painting there but decided not to become a professional artist. Worked for a while as a farm labourer, then held editorial posts in Edinburgh and London. Settled in the U.S. in 1948. Author of *Until Now* (1940), *The Planet in My Hand* (1947), and other books of verse; *Over the Mountain* (1939), *Loser's Choice* (1953), and other novels; *Space Cat* (1952) and other children's books; *The Laughing Mulatto*: *The Story of Alexandre Dumas* (1940), *Tracks in the Snow* (1946), *The Tropical Fish Book* (1953).

Todhunter, John (1839-1916). Born in Dublin; educated at Trinity College there; studied medicine in Vienna and Paris and practised in Dublin for some years. Professor of English Literature, Alexandra College, Dublin, 1870-74, then settled in London. From the 1870s onward he published poems and verse plays, several of which were performed. His *Sounds and Sweet Airs* was published in 1905.

Toklas, Alice B. (Alice Babette Toklas, 1878-1967). Born in San Francisco of Polish descent. Intended to be a concert pianist until, in Paris in 1907, she met Gertrude *Stein and became her companion for almost forty years. *The Autobiography of Alice B. Toklas* (1933) was in fact the life-story of Gertrude Stein, who wrote it. After her friend's death in 1946, Miss Toklas wrote her own memoirs, *What is Remembered* (1963); also *The Alice B. Toklas Cook Book* (1955), and *Aromas and Flavors of Past and Present* (1958).

Told by an Idiot. Novel by Rose *Macaulay published in 1923. Disturbed periodically by the news that 'Poor papa has lost his faith again', the family of (the sometime Rev.) Aubrey Garden are shuttled from place to place as his conscience moves him from Anglican clergyman to Roman Catholic layman and thence in turn to Dissent, Agnosticism, and ardent membership of the Ethical Church. His wife cooperates serenely in this spiritual pilgrimage until his giddying succession of faiths has worn her out by the time his second bout of Romanism begins. Their six children view the upheavals in the light of the effect on their own interests and pleasures, though the first names they are given make them lifelong witnesses to their father's vagaries: Victoria, named for his victory over unbelief in 1856; Maurice, for Frederick Denison Maurice, the Christian Socialist leader; Rome, the second daughter, for that Church; Stanley, the third daughter, for Dean Stanley; Irving, the younger son, for Edward Irving of the Catholic Apostolic community; Una, youngest of all, for the Unitarians. The novel relates the experiences of the individuals of the Garden family—their comedies and tragedies, marriages and divorces, joys and miseries, dreams and achievements—in the context of historical events and movements from 1879 to 1923. Throughout, the author maintains an attitude of scepticism and disillusion, observing that the more humanity believes itself changed the more it remains the same; that youth in revolt repeats itself from generation to generation; that 'New' as applied to ideas is no more than a catchword. The title is from *Macbeth* V. v. 27-8. *See also* Garden.

Tolkien, J. R. R. (John Ronald Reuel Tolkien, 1892-1973). Born at Birmingham; educated there and at Oxford. Professor of Anglo-Saxon in the University of Oxford, 1925-45; Professor of English Language and Literature there, 1945-59. Author of *Beowulf: The Monsters and the Critics* (1937), *Fairy Stories, A Critical Study* (1946). Best known by his fantasies: *The Hobbit* (1937), *The Lord of the Rings*: (I. *The Fellowship of the Ring*, 1954; II. *The Two Towers*, 1954; III. *The Return of the King*, 1955).

Toller, Ernst (1893-1939). Born in Prussia of Jewish parentage; educated in Bromberg; studied law at Grenoble. Joined the German army as a volunteer in 1914, but was invalided home in 1916, having in the meantime developed pacifist convictions. He became a communist and his revolutionary activities led to a five-year prison sentence. He left Germany in 1932 and went to the U.S. The triumphs of Fascism in Europe caused him great distress and he committed suicide in New York. His plays had a vogue in England in the 1920s comparable with that of *Brecht's in the 1950s, and among those translated into English the best-known were *Masses and Men* (1920; trans. 1924), and *The Machine Wreckers* (1922; trans. 1923). Autobiography; *I Was a German* (1933; trans. 1934).

Tolstoy, Alexandra (1884-). Born at Yasnaya Polyana, daughter of Leo Tolstoy; educated at home and in Moscow. She was her father's secretary from 1901 to 1910 and after his death was associated with the preparation and publication of the 91-volume complete Russian edition of his writings. She worked in her own country as nurse and educational and cultural organizer until Soviet anti-religious measures led her to go to Japan in 1929 and two years later to settle in the U.S., becoming an American citizen in 1941. She described herself as 'farmer, speaker, and writer' and was the author of *The Tragedy of Tolstoy* (Eng. trans. 1933), *I Worked for the Soviet* (Eng. trans. 1935), *Tolstoy: A Life of My Father* (Eng. trans. 1953).

Tolstoy, Alexey (Count Alexey Nikolayevich Tolstoy, 1882-1945). Born in the province of Samara, on the Volga; educated at St Petersburg (Leningrad) and in Germany at Dresden. He fought against the Bolsheviks and went into exile in Paris until 1922, when he returned to Russia, and after an early lack of enthusiasm for the Soviet régime he became at length its ardent supporter and was accepted as one of its leading novelists. A remote relative of Leo *Tolstoy and of Ivan Turgenev, he was by some critics ranked with those great predecessors. His chief novels are: *The Road to Calvary* (1923), *Darkness and Dawn* (1936), *Peter the Great* (1936), *Bread* (1938), *The Golden Key* (1947) is a play for children.

Tolstoy, Leo (Count Lev Nikolayevich Tolstoy, 1828-1910). Born at Yasnaya Polyana; educated privately and at Kazan University. He served with the Russian army in the Crimean war, after having led a gay and riotous life as a man-about-town. At the end of the war, which gave him material for *Tales of Army Life* and *Sevastopol*, he travelled widely in

Europe and visited England. He married in 1862 and settled on the estates he had inherited, but eventually renounced all his property after emancipating the serfs and lived as a peasant. His domestic life was tempestuous, and he finally left home, only to die in a railway siding. His pacifist creed, summed up in the phrase 'resist not evil', made him many disciples in other countries. While his rank as thinker and moralist has been questioned, there is general agreement concerning his majestic genius as a writer. *War and Peace* (1863-69) is considered the greatest of all novels, with *Anna Karenina* (1874-76) little below it. *The Kreutzer Sonata* (1889) displays a morbid aspect of Tolstoy's mind. His short stories are masterly. His unorthodox religious views led to his excommunication by the Church, and while as a literary artist he was supreme, his aesthetic theory—expressed in *What is Art* (1897-98)—that art is to be judged by the ease of its assimilation by the simplest is typical of a curious naïvety in his make-up.

Tomfooleries. See *Trifles and Tomfooleries.

Tomlinson, H. M. (Henry Major Tomlinson, 1873-1958). Born in east London and became intimately acquainted with the Thames-side dockland in his early years. At the age of twelve he began to work in a shipping office and endeavoured to escape the routine drudgery by study and writing. His first encouragement came from the *Morning Leader* and he joined the staff of that paper in 1904 until 1912, when he voyaged to South America and sailed up the Amazon on a tramp steamer, obtaining material for his first book, *The Sea and the Jungle* (1912). Rejoining his former newspaper, which was by then merged with the *Daily News*, he was a war correspondent in Flanders and France from 1914 to 1917. For the next six years he found congenial employment as Literary Editor of the *Nation and Athenaeum*, until he was able to live on the income from his books, which by that time included *Old Junk* (1918), *London River* (1921), and *Waiting for Daylight* (1922). His most successful books were *Gallions Reach* (1927)—the title is that of a stretch of the lower Thames, abutting on dockland—and *All Our Yesterdays* (1930), one of the outstanding novels of World War I. Other novels by him include *The Snows of Helicon* (1933), *All Hands* (1937), *Morning Light* (1946). *South to Cadiz* (1934) and *Malay Waters* (1950) are among his later

travel books. Autobiographical essays: *A Mingled Yarn* (1953).

Tommy Atkins. See Atkins.

Tono-Bungay. Novel by H. G. Wells published in 1909. George Ponderevo spends his school holidays at Bladesover House, where his mother has lived as housekeeper since the disappearance of her husband. Bladesover is ruled by Lady Drew, an elderly representative of the aristocratic class dominating 'the farming folk and the labouring folk' and the tradespeople of the locality. Among the visitors to the house are two child cousins of Lady Drew, the Honourable Beatrice Normandy and her half-brother Archie Garvell, with whom the 'low-born' George can only play surreptitiously. When he quarrels and fights with Archie he is forbidden further access to his mother's quarters at Bladesover, and is sent to his cousin Nicodemus Frapp, a baker living with his wife and children in an atmosphere of piety and squalor at Chatham. Finding life intolerable there, George tramps back to his mother at Bladesover and is then taken to his uncle Edward Ponderevo's chemist's shop at Wimblehurst, where he works as assistant and is affectionately looked after by his aunt Susan. Uncle Ponderevo's grandiose plans for escaping from 'dead-and-alive' Wimblehurst lead him into stock-market speculation and bankruptcy, in which he also dissipates George's moderate inheritance from his mother. The chemist's shop is sold and the uncle moves to London, leaving George with the new owner at Wimblehurst, until spare-time study enables him to matriculate and win a scholarship. As a science student in London he becomes negligent through devoting time to Marion Ramboat, with whom he later makes a disastrous marriage. He rejoins his uncle who is already successfully marketing a patent medicine (mainly distilled water) he names Tono-Bungay. Together they develop the business by adding subsidiary products, and through extensive advertising and mergers Uncle Ponderevo builds a financial empire which eventually crashes. George, meanwhile, has branched out as a pioneer in aeronautics and is eventually made F.R.S. He attempts to avert his uncle's ruination by undertaking an expedition to transport a load of commercially valuable radioactive substance ('quap') discovered on an island off the west African coast, but the ship, rotted by the quap, sinks on the return voyage. He then saves his uncle from arrest for forgery by flying him in an airship to France, where the old man dies. George meets again his boyhood playmate, Beatrice Normandy, with whom he has an abortive love affair. He finally achieves success as a builder of fast destroyers, and the book ends with a description of London as seen from the river during a destroyer's run from Hammersmith Bridge down to the open sea.

Tonson, Jacob. Pseudonym of Arnold *Bennett for his writings in the *New Age* after a famous 18th-century bookseller.

Tovey, Sir Donald (Donald Francis Tovey, 1873-1940; knighted 1935). Born at Eton; educated privately and at Oxford; studied music and appeared in 1900 as a concert pianist, but did not continue as a professional soloist. Professor of Music in the University of Edinburgh from 1914 until his death. He organized many concerts and composed much music, but had a more substantial reputation with his *Essays in Musical Analysis* (6 vols, 1935-39) covering symphonies, concertos, 'illustrative music', and vocal music.

Townshend, Charlotte Frances Payne. *See* Mrs Bernard *Shaw.

Toynbee, Arnold J. (Arnold Joseph Toynbee, 1889-   ). Born in London, nephew of Arnold Toynbee (1852-83) the historian and social reformer who wrote *The Industrial Revolution in England* (1884) and is commemorated in the name of Toynbee Hall, a fruitful University Settlement in Whitechapel, east London. Arnold J. Toynbee was educated at Winchester and Oxford, served in the Foreign Office, was Professor of Modern Greek and Byzantine Language, History, and Literature in the University of London, 1919-24; Director of Studies in the *Royal Institute of International Affairs, 1925-55. Author of *Greek Historical Thought* (1924), *Greek Civilization and Character* (1924), *Civilization on Trial* (1948), *Hellenism* (1959), and editor of numerous volumes on international affairs. It is with the multivolume *Study of History* (1934-61) that his name is indelibly associated. This vast work in twelve volumes is a philosophy of world history from the earliest times to the present century, with a somewhat changed outlook between the earlier and later parts and culminating in more or less religious interpretation. Immensely erudite and with an impressive narrative sweep, it sees human history as largely determined by the principle of 'challenge and response'. Its thesis and execution stirred considerable controversy among other historians, who found its messianic conclusions incompatible with sober historical study. A condensed version in two volumes by D. C. *Somervell (1946, 1957; one-volume edn 1960) became a best seller for the general reader, though its omission of Toynbee's multitudinous footnotes deprived it of much that is lively and entertainingly informative in the original. *An Historian's Approach to Religion* (1953-54) is a personal testament by Toynbee. Other works: *East to West: A Journey Round the World* (1958), *Between Oxus and Jumna* (1961), *Between Niger and Nile* (1965), *Acquaintances* (essays on contemporaries; 1967); *Experiences* (1969).

Toynbee, Philip (Theodore Philip Toynbee, 1916-   ). Born at Oxford, son of Arnold J. Toynbee and grandson on his mother's side of Gilbert *Murray; educated at Rugby and Oxford. Political, military, and Civil Service experience preceded contributions to periodicals and membership of the *Observer* staff. As a writer of 'experimental novels' he was found impressive by intellectualists and baffling by others: *The Savage Days* (1937), *School in Private* (1941), *The Barricades* (1943), *Tea With Mrs Goodman* (1947), *The Garden to the Sea* (1953), *Pantaloon* (1961). *Friends Apart* (1952) is a memoir of two of his friends in the 1930s. With his father he produced *Comparing Notes: A Dialogue Across a Generation* (1963).

T.P.'s Weekly. 'A penny literary paper of more than ordinary merit' (*D.N.B.*) founded in 1902 by T. P. *O'Connor and edited by him for many years with assistance from Wilfred *Whitten. It was a popular source of literary education through articles and reviews which were both informative and engaging. *See also* *John O'London's Weekly.

Trader Horn. *See* Alfred Aloysius *Horn.

Traherne, Thomas (1637?-1674). The son of a Hereford shoemaker, educated at Oxford, ordained and appointed chaplain to the Lord Keeper of the Great Seal, Traherne's only writings published in his lifetime were *Christian Ethics* (1675) and *Serious and Pathetical Contemplations* (1699). His major works as a poet and prose writer comparable with Crashaw, Vaughan, and George Herbert remained unknown until the present century, when Bertram *Dobell published the first editions of *Poetical Works* (1903) and *Centuries of Meditations* (1908) from manuscript found a few years before. A definitive text in two volumes edited by H. M. Margoliouth was published as *Centuries, Poems, and Thanksgiving* in 1958.

Trahison des Clercs, La. *See* Julien *Benda.

Traill, Peter (pseudonym of Guy Mainwaring Morton, 1896-1968). Educated at Rugby and Oxford. Author of many novels, including *Woman to Woman* (1924), *Here Lies Love* (1932), *Golden Oriole* (1940), *Mutation Mink* (1950).

transatlantic review. Founded and published in Paris by Ford Madox *Ford. James Joyce and Ernest Hemingway were among its contributors. It ran from January to December 1924.

Travels in Arabia Deserta. *See* *Arabia Deserta*.

Travers, Ben (1886-   ). Born at Hendon; educated in Beckenham and at Charterhouse. Author of a succession of popular plays, among them those known as the 'Aldwych farces' from the London theatre they filled for several years: *A Cuckoo in the Nest* (1925), *Rookery Nook* (1926), *Thark* (1927), *Plunder* (1928), *A Cup of Kindness* (1929), *A Night Like This* (1930), *Turkey Time* (1931). His later plays include: *O Mistress Mine* (1936), *Banana Ridge* (1938), *Nun's Veiling* (1956). Autobiography: *Vale of Laughter* (1957).

Travers, Graham (pseudonym of Margaret Todd, 1859-1918). Educated in Edinburgh, Glasgow, and Berlin; studied medicine in Edinburgh and was assistant physician to the Hospital for Women and Children there. As a novelist she wrote *Mona Maclean* (1892), *Fellow Travellers* (1896), *The Way of Escape* (1902), *Growth* (1906).

Travers, P. L. (Pamela Lyndon Travers, 1906-   ). Born in Queensland, Australia, of Irish-Scottish descent. Moved to England in 1924, where she worked for several years as an actress and during World War II served the Ministry of Information in the U.S. Her early verse writings were encouraged by publication in periodicals and anthologies, but she became best known by her 'Mary Poppins' children's books upon which a Walt Disney film was based in 1964. Beginning with *Mary Poppins* (1934), the series continued with *Mary Poppins Comes Back* (1935),

Mary Poppins Opens the Door (1943), *Mary Poppins in the Park* (1952). She also wrote *I Go by Sea, I Go by Land* (1941).

Treece, Henry (1911-66). Born at Wednesbury; educated there and in Birmingham. From schoolteaching he turned to historical fiction, combining scholarship with a sense of the adventure of history which commended his books to young people. Among his many historical novels are *The Eagles Have Flown* (1954), *Hounds of the King* (1955), *The Children's Crusade* (1958), *Horned Helmet* (1963). He also wrote verse: *Invitation and Warning* (1942), *The Haunted Garden* (1947), *The Exiles* (1952).

Trees. Poem by Joyce *Kilmer.

Trefusis, Violet (1894-1972). Daughter of Lt.-Col. Hon. George Keppel and Mrs Alice Keppel; married in 1919 Denys Trefusis (died 1929); lived much in France and Italy; wrote novels (*Sortie de Secours*, 1929; *Tandem*, 1933; *Hunt the Slipper*, 1937; *Pirates at Play*, 1950) and autobiographies (*Prelude to Misadventure*, 1942; *Don't Look Round*, 1952). An account of her intense emotional and physical involvement with Vita *Sackville-West appears in the latter's intimate diary, embodied in *Portrait of a Marriage* (1973) by Nigel Nicolson.

Trembling of a Leaf, The. Volume of six short stories by W. Somerset *Maugham published in 1921 and containing what became his best-known story, then entitled 'Miss Thompson' (afterwards renamed *'Rain'), as well as 'Red', considered by the author the best of his stories.

Trench, Dr Harry. A leading character in *Widowers' Houses* (1892) by Bernard Shaw; his private income is derived from a mortgage on slum property, a humiliating fact of which he had been unaware.

Trench, Herbert (Frederic Herbert Trench, 1865-1923). Born in Ireland; educated at Haileybury and Oxford. Held a senior appointment in the Board of Education, 1891-1908; travelled widely throughout Europe and in North Africa and the Middle East. He was a most successful Artistic Director of the Haymarket Theatre, 1909-11. Author of *Deirdre Wed and Other Poems* (1901), *Apollo and the Seaman* in *New Poems* (1907), *Lyric and Narrative Poems* (1911), *Napoleon* (a play, 1919).

Tressell, Robert (pseudonym of Robert Noonan,

1868-1911). The facts of his life were gathered with difficulty by Frederick C. Ball in *Tressell of Mugsborough* (1951). Three birthplaces were named by informants: Cleveland Street, west-central London; Dublin; and Liverpool. A certificate of baptism for a Robert Noonan born on 5 December 1868, traced at a London Catholic church, makes Dublin and Liverpool less probable. There is evidence that he worked as a signwriter in South Africa at the end of last century, and lived and worked from 1902 in Hastings, where his experiences apparently resembled those of Owen and the other house-painters in *The *Ragged Trousered Philanthropists* which he wrote *c.* 1906-10. Again like Owen, he was tubercular. He set out in 1910 to emigrate to Canada but died in a Liverpool hospital early in the next year. He left the manuscript of his novel with the daughter he had lived with in Hastings (the Mugsborough of the book). It remained in her trunk, unopened, for some two years until a chance remark led her to mention it in the London house in which she was a children's nurse. The MS. ran to about 400,000 words written on 1674 sheets. F. C. Ball prints in the biography some of the passages omitted from the much-reduced edition published in 1914, with Tressell spelt as Tressall on the titlepage. A full edition was published in 1955.

Trevelyan, G. M. (George Macaulay Trevelyan, 1876-1962). Born at Stratford-on-Avon, third son of Sir George Otto *Trevelyan; educated at Harrow and Cambridge. Regius Professor of Modern History in the University of Cambridge, 1927-40; Master of Trinity College, Cambridge, 1940-51. He was the leading English historian of his time, exact in scholarship, lucid in presentation, and distinguished in literary style. His writings on the history of England ranged from *England in the Age of Wycliffe* (1904), through *England Under the Stuarts* (1905), *England Under Queen Anne* (*Blenheim*, 1930; *Ramillies and the Union with Scotland*, 1932; *The Peace and the Protestant Succession*, 1934), to *The Seven Years of William IV* (1952) and *British History in the 19th Century* (1922). His most widely circulated book, though not perhaps his best, was *English Social History: A Survey of Six Centuries* (1944) which rode on a wave of wartime interest in social studies in the U.S. and Britain. His fine Italian trilogy gave him his first popular success: *Garibaldi's Defence of the Roman Republic* (1907), *Garibaldi and the Thousand* (1909), *Garibaldi and the Making of Italy* (1911). He also wrote *The Poetry and Philosophy of George Meredith* (1906), biographies of *John Bright* (1913), *Lord Grey of the Reform Bill* (1920), *Sir George Otto Trevelyan* (1932), *Grey of Fallodon* (1937); essays—*Clio, a Muse* (1913), *A Layman's Love of Letters* (1954); and a brief *Autobiography* (1949). His one-volume *History of England* was published in 1926 and a *Shortened History of England* in 1959.

Trevelyan, Sir George Otto (1838-1928). Born in Leicestershire, son of Sir Charles Trevelyan, 1st baronet; educated at Harrow and Cambridge. Liberal M.P. from 1865 and held various Ministerial offices. Author of *The Life and Letters of Lord Macaulay* (1876), his uncle, *The Early History of Charles James Fox* (1880), *The American Revolution* (4 vols, 1909), *Interludes in Prose and Verse* (1905), *George III and Charles Fox* (1912, 1914).

Trevelyan, Laura. *See* *Laura Trevelyan.

Trevor, Glen. Pseudonym used by James *Hilton for *Murder at School* (1931).

Trevor-Roper, H. R. (Hugh Redwald Trevor-Roper, 1914-   ). Born in Northumberland; educated at Charterhouse and Oxford. Regius Professor of Modern History in the University of Oxford from 1957. His historical writings began with *Archbishop Laud, 1573-1645* (1940), but with the published results of a process of inquiry in contemporary history —*The Last Days of Hitler* (1947)—he first became widely known, and later gained a larger audience as an accomplished broadcaster on historical subjects. Other books: *The Gentry, 1540-1640* (1953), *Historical Essays* (1957), *The Rise of Christian Europe* (1965), *Religion, The Reformation and Social Change* (1967), *The European Witch-Craze of the 16th and 17th centuries* (1970), *The Plunder of the Arts in the 17th Century* (1970).

Trifles and Tomfooleries. Collective title given by Bernard *Shaw to certain of his shorter plays: *The Admirable Bashville; or, Constancy Unrewarded* (1901); *Press Cuttings* (1909); *A Glimpse of Reality* (1909); *Passion, Poison, and Petrification; or, The Fatal Gazogene* (1905); *The Fascinating Foundling: A Disgrace to the Author* (1909); *The Music-Cure: A Piece of Utter Nonsense* (1913).

Trilling, Lionel (1905-   ). Born in New York; educated at Columbia University, where he became Professor of English from 1948. He established an international reputation as a penetrating literary critic with his studies of *Matthew Arnold* (1939), and *E. M. Forster* (1943) and his essays collected in *The Liberal Imagination* (1950), *The Opposing Self* (1955), and *A Gathering of Fugitives* (1956). His novel, *The Middle of the Journey* (1947), was a product of the human and political problems of contemporary America.

Triple Thinkers, The. *See* Edmund *Wilson.

Trivia. Observations and reflections in condensed and polished prose by Logan Pearsall *Smith, collected in *All Trivia* (1933; comprising *Trivia*, 1918, *More Trivia*, 1922, *Afterthoughts*, 1931, *Last Words*, 1933). They range in length from two-line aphorisms on 'Life and Human Nature', four-line pieces on 'Adjectives', 'Chairs', etc., to a five-page essay on 'The Vicar of Lynch'.

Trotsky, Leon (*né* Lev Davidovich Bronstein, 1879-1940). Born in the Ukraine: educated in Odessa. Sent to Siberia for revolutionary activities, escaped and joined Lenin in London. A leader in the Bolshevik revolution in 1917, he organized the Red Army. After Lenin's death in 1924, he opposed Stalin, was expelled from Russia, and took refuge in Mexico. There he was assassinated in 1940, presumably by a Stalin agent. His brilliance as a writer appears in *The History of the Russian Revolution* (1932), *The Revolution Betrayed* (1937), and (published posthumously) *Stalin* (1948) and *Diary in Exile* (trans. 1959).

Troubetzkoy, Princess. *See* Amélie *Rives.

Troubridge, Sir St Vincent (Sir Thomas St Vincent Wallace Troubridge, 5th baronet; 1895-1963). Educated at Wellington and Sandhurst. Served in the army, 1914-22; on General Staff, 1939-45. Examiner of Plays in Lord Chamberlain's Office from 1952. Contributed valuably to lexicography and theatre research.

Tschiffely, A. F. (Aimé Felix Tschiffely, 1895-1954). Born in Switzerland. Became a teacher at schools in England and Buenos Aires, but achieved fame as an adventurous and indefatigable traveller, his chief exploit being the journey of 10,000 miles on horseback from Buenos Aires to Washington, of which he gave an account in *From Southern Cross to Pole Star* (1933), better known under the title used for later editions, *Tschiffely's Ride.*

Bridle Paths (1936) is an account of a journey through England on horseback; *This Way Southward* (1940) of a journey through Patagonia and Tierra del Fuego. He was a friend of R. B. Cunninghame *Graham, whose biography he wrote as *Don Roberto* (1937). Tschiffely's autobiographical reminiscences were published as *Bohemia Junction* (1950).

Tuohy, Frank (John Francis Tuohy, 1925-   ). Educated at Stowe and Cambridge. Professor of English in Brazil, later in Poland, and then in Japan. Author of *The Animal Game* (1957), *The Warm Nights of January* (1960), *The Admiral and the Nuns* (1962), *The Ice Saints* (1964), *Fingers in the Door* (1970).

Turner, W. J. (Walter James Redfern Turner, 1889-1946). Born in Melbourne; travelled in Africa and Europe and settled in England, where he became music critic of the *New Statesman*, 1916-40, literary editor of the *Daily Herald*, 1920-23, dramatic critic of the *London Mercury*, 1919-23, and literary editor of the *Spectator* from 1942. He was one of the poets who came into prominence during World War I, but though sometimes linked with the *Georgian poets his work was highly individual and did not catch the popular ear. *The Hunter* (1916) and *The Dark Fire* (1918) were followed by *Paris and Helen* (1921), *Landscape of Cytherea* (1923), *New Poems* (1928), *Songs and Incantations* (1936)—and *The Man Who Ate the Popomack* (1922) and other novels. His numerous writings on music included studies of *Beethoven* (1927), *Wagner* (1933), *Berlioz* (1934), *Mozart* (1938).

Tutuola, Amos (1920-   ). *See* *African Writers.

Tuwhare, Hone (1922-   ). Born at Kaikohe, Northland, New Zealand. Worked as a welder and boiler-maker. The only modern Maori poet writing in Maori and English. Author of *No Ordinary Sun* (1964).

Tweedsmuir, Lord. *See* John *Buchan.

Tweedsmuir, Susan, Lady (*née* Susan Grosvenor). Married John Buchan (later 1st Baron Tweedsmuir) 1907. Author of novels, essays, short plays; an autobiography (*The Lilac and the Rose*, 1952); (in collaboration) *John Buchan by his Wife and Friends* (1947).

Tweeny, the kitchen-maid in *The *Admirable Crichton* (1902) by J. M. Barrie.

Two Cheers for Democracy. Collected miscellaneous essays by E. M. *Forster published in 1951. The seventeen essays in Part I are under the general heading *The Second Darkness* (mainly the 1930s); Part II begins with 'What I Believe', followed by groups of essays subtitled 'Art in General', 'The Arts in Action', and 'Places'. The Prefatory Note ends: 'We may still contrive to raise three cheers for democracy, although at present she only deserves two.'

Two Cultures, The. A lecture at Cambridge by C. P. *Snow which excited interest and stirred controversy in 1959. Its main theme is that the intellectual gap between Science and the Humanities in the present technological age is disastrous: that no one is properly educated who does not understand the Second Law of Thermodynamics as well as being able to read and appreciate Shakespeare. A counterblast was delivered in 1962 by F. R. *Leavis in another lecture at Cambridge, disapproving Snow's literary style.

Two Nations, The. Phrase used by Disraeli (Lord Beaconsfield) as subtitle of his novel *Sybil* (1845), meaning the rich and the poor. A century later it began to be differently applicable, to a division of the nation by a cult of youth and immaturity into the two communities of the adolescent and the adult.

Tynan, Katherine (1861-1931). Born in County Dublin; educated at Sienna Convent, Drogheda. She became a friend of leading Irish and English writers and public men and women, including W. B. *Yeats and others active in the *Celtic Revival. Her writings in verse and prose fill several scores of volumes but she is remembered only by a small number of lyrics. Her *Collected Poems* were published in 1930 and she wrote the autobiographical *Twenty-five Years* (1913), *The Middle Years* (1917), *The Years of the Shadow* (1919), *The Wandering Years* (1922).

Tynan, Kenneth (Kenneth Peacock Tynan, 1927-). Born in Birmingham; educated there and at Oxford. He was dramatic critic of the *Spectator*, the *Evening Standard*, and the *Daily Sketch*, in succession from 1951 to 1954, when he went to the *Observer* until 1963 with an interval (1958-60) as guest critic on the *New Yorker*. His enthusiasm for the new and experimental work of the younger playwrights and his combative style made him a controversial figure, and his appointment as Literary Manager of the National Theatre (1963-9) ran counter to conservative opinion. Author of *He That Plays the King* (1950), *Persona Grata* (1953), *Bull Fever* (1955), *Curtains* (1961), *Alec Guinness* (1954). His *Oh, Calcutta!* naturalized sex and nudity on the English-speaking stage (N.Y. 1969; London 1970).

Typhoon. Story by Joseph *Conrad published in 1903 in *Typhoon and other Stories*. The steamer *Nan-Shan*, on her way in the China seas to the port of Fu-chau, has on board two hundred Chinese coolies returning to their village homes with their belongings and savings after years of working abroad. Captain MacWhirr, in command of the *Nan-Shan* since she was built at Dumbarton, is an indomitable man by reason of qualities which make him a figure of fun to some of his intimates: he is 'simply ordinary, irresponsive, and unruffled', literal-minded, prosaic, and unimaginative, but with an acute sense of honesty and justice. On the voyage with the coolies the barometer falls rapidly, accompanied by oppressive heat which makes tempers rise among the officers and crew and is followed by a typhoon which for some thirty hours threatens to overwhelm the ship, causes the crew to take refuge in the dark alleyway, and tosses the captain and Jukes, the first mate, into a heap on the bridge. The boatswain struggles down to get one of the half-dozen lamps from the between-deck where the coolies have been put under hatches for safety in the storm. He finds the two hundred sliding in an almost solid fighting mass from side to side of the ship as she rolls with every blow of the tempest. He crawls to the bridge to report to the captain, who sends Jukes to investigate. The mate and the crew manage to fix lifelines for the coolies to grasp when they have been prised apart and stopped from fighting for the silver dollars which have been thrown from their smashed wooden chests. When the battered *Nan-Shan* at length reaches Fu-chau, Captain MacWhirr prevents further trouble with the coolies by distributing the dollars equally among them.

Ullman, James Ramsay (1907-   ). Born in New York; educated at Princeton; journalist and play-producer; ambulance driver in North Africa in World War II; author of novels—*The White Tower* (1945), etc. and travel books, including *The Other Side of the Mountain* (1938), *High Conquest* (1941).

Ultima Thule (1). Thule was the name given in antiquity to a more or less legendary northern land which was thought of as the end of the world; 'ultima Thule', in common usage, indicates, usually in a metaphorical sense, that the last extremity has been reached.

Ultima Thule (2). The final volume (published in 1929) of Henry Handel Richardson's trilogy *The *Fortunes of Richard Mahony* (1930).

Ulysses. Novel by James *Joyce exposing the unassorted contents of the principal characters' minds, accumulating through external contacts and impressions intermingled with simmerings from subconscious memory, on a single day (16 June 1904) in Dublin. The chief characters are Stephen Dedalus (brought forward from *A *Portrait of the Artist as a Young Man*), Leopold Bloom, advertisement canvasser, and his wife Molly, of some repute as a concert singer. Such physical action as there is centres on Bloom's wanderings in and about Dublin, sometimes in the company of Dedalus or other cronies, sometimes alone. Among the places visited are public houses, a newspaper office, the National Library, the shore; there is much about the difficult labour of a woman in childbirth, while a celebrated section in dramatic form placed in 'nighttown' has the demoniac quality of a combination of brothel orgy and witches' coven. Intimations of immense erudition emphasize the esoteric nature of the whole composition, ranging from the extreme naturalism of the scatalogical passages to the wild fantastification of the brothel scenes. Obscurity and obscenity are inherent in the purpose of revealing mental states neither simplified nor sanitated. *Ulysses* attracts the close interest of literary critics capable of valuing its technical complexity—e.g. that it is patterned on the episodes of Homer's *Odyssey*, with Bloom as Odysseus (latinized as Ulysses), Mrs Bloom as Penelope, Dedalus as Telemachus, etc.—and it offers material for consideration by psychiatrists and alienists. The publishing history of the book made it known to a wider public than it might otherwise have reached. Published in Paris in 1922, impounded by the Customs in Britain, burned by U.S. postal authorities; charged as obscene in the district court of New York in 1933, it was cleared by the judge's ruling in that action: he found it 'brilliant and dull, intelligible and obscure by turns', in many places 'disgusting', but not pornographic. Since then it has circulated uncensored. Popular attention has concentrated on Molly Bloom's unpunctuated 'stream of consciousness' meditation of over 20,000 words in bed, mainly on sexual themes.

Unamuno y Jugo, Miguel de (1864-1936). Born in Bilbao; educated there and at the University of Madrid, where he obtained a doctorate in philosophy. He became Professor of Greek in the University of Salamanca in 1892 and Rector in 1901. Though independent of any political party, he was outspoken on public affairs and from 1924 to 1930 was in exile, mainly in France. His iconoclasm led to extreme scepticism in every field and to a view of life akin to that of *Kierkegaard, whose writings he studied in the original Danish. Intensely patriotic without partisanship, he became a Spanish author with a high European reputation. His works included novels, poems, essays, and studies in history and religion. Among those translated into English are: *The Tragic Sense of Life in Men and Peoples* (1921; in Spanish 1913), *Essays and Soliloquies* (1925), *The Agony of Christianity* (1928); and, in fiction, *Mist* (1928; Spanish 1914), *Three Exemplary Novels* (1930; Spanish 1920).

Under Milk Wood. 'A Play for Voices' by Dylan *Thomas broadcast by the B.B.C. in 1954 and published in the same year. True to the medium for which it was written, the play is essentially for hearing and is ineffective on the printed page unless the reader, by his inner ear, can recreate the text aurally.

The First Voice and Second Voice have a narrative function, opening with the description of a Welsh small coastal town, Llaregyb, on a moonless night in Spring. The narrative line is interrupted by voices of dreaming inhabitants and of the dead, and by the Voice of a Guide Book providing topographical detail. Morning comes, with the rising of blind Captain Cat and the opening of the front door of Bethesda House by the Rev. Eli Jenkins, the local bard, who speaks an invocatory poem to his country's natural beauty. Thereafter, throughout the day, the business and gossip and memories of men and women in the town are projected in speech and song by Lily Smalls, a domestic servant; Mr Pugh, the schoolmaster, who contemplates poisoning his wife; Dai Bread, the baker with two wives; Mary Ann Sailors of the Sailor's Arms; Polly Garters, the town's light o' love; Willy Nilly the postman; Evans the Death, undertaker, and numerous others, Captain Cat intervening as additional narrator identifying his neighbours by their footsteps. The hours pass until the town sleeps again at 'the second dark time' of 'this one Spring day'.

Under Western Eyes. Novel by Joseph *Conrad published in 1911. Mainly from the diary of Kirylo Sidorovitch Razumov, a student, an elderly English teacher of languages familiar with those living in the Little Russia quarter in Geneva learns and relates the story there told. Having thrown the bomb which kills a minister of state in St Petersburg, Victor Haldin, a fellow student, takes refuge in the apartment of Razumov while he is out. Although Razumov detests all revolutionary beliefs and action, he agrees to take a message to Ziemianitch, a town-peasant with horses for hire, to make arrangements for Haldin to be moved to safety that night. He finds the peasant dead-drunk in a stable, and fails to rouse him even by a beating with a pitchfork. On the way back, Razumov decides to denounce the fugitive to the police. Haldin is arrested, interrogated, and hanged. His mother and sister Nathalie (Natalia), living in Geneva, only learn of his fate through a paragraph by an English reporter in a London newspaper. When Razumov is interviewed by a police chief, Mikulin, in St Petersburg, he thinks he may himself be under suspicion and, as a personal safeguard, undertakes to go to Geneva and report on the plans of the revolutionary conspirators there. Among them, he feels himself safe from any charge of treachery against Haldin, but a revolutionary agent in St Petersburg sends news that Haldin's betrayer is assumed to be Ziemianitch, who has been found hanged. Razumov and Natalia meet and are so drawn to one another that, seeing in her the embodiment of truth, he can no longer hide the truth about his denunciation of her brother and he confesses to her. When he also confesses at a meeting of the conspirators, he is set upon and. both his eardrums are deliberately crushed. He is thrown into the street and, unable to hear an approaching tramcar, is

knocked down and permanently crippled.

Underhill, Evelyn (1875-1941). Born at Wolverhampton; educated privately and in London at King's College for Women; Lecturer on the Philosophy of Religion, Manchester College, Oxford, 1921-22. She wrote much on religious subjects and produced some poems, *Immanence* (1912), *Theophanes* (1916). Her best known books are on mysticism, of which she was a profound and influential expositor: *Mysticism: A Study in the Nature and Development of Man's Spiritual Consciousness* (1911; 13th edn 1940), *The Mystic Way* (1913), *Practical Mysticism* (1914), *The Essentials of Mysticism* (1920). She also wrote a few novels, including *The Grey World* (1904) and *The Column of Dust* (1909); and she was a notable letter-writer, *Letters* (1943).

Undershaft, Andrew. Head of the armaments firm of Undershaft and Lazarus, a position he inherited through the long-established tradition that it must always pass to an adopted foundling; married Lady Britomart, daughter of the Earl of Stevenage; father of Stephen, Barbara, and Sarah in Bernard Shaw's *Major Barbara* (1905). He is 'stoutish, easy-going, elderly', with kindly manners, simplicity of character, but also 'formidable reserves of power'.

Undertones of War. An account of his experiences as an infantry subaltern in France and Flanders during World War I by Edmund *Blunden, published in 1928. Enlisting in 1916 after leaving school, the author took part in the disastrous battles of the Somme, Ypres, and Passchendaele. He tells of the many evidences of endurance and heroism among the officers and men of his battalion in prose which is distinguished and compassionate but free from heroics. With the eyes and ears of a poet he observes the beauties of nature against the miseries and horrors of men at war, as in 'I heard an evening robin in a hawthorn, and in trampled gardens among the luggage of war, as Milton calls it, there was the fairy, affectionate immortality of the yellow rose and blue-grey crocus', opposed by such scenes as 'The water below, foul yellow and brown, was strewn with full-sized eels, bream, and jack, seething and bulged in death'; or 'a column of artillery waggons, noiseless, smashed, capsized, the remains of mules and drivers sprawling among the wreckage'. In manner and in style Blunden's book ranks as the established classic of the 1914-18 war.

Undset, Sigrid (1882-1949). Born in Denmark, at Kallundborg, but her parents settled in Norway while she was still an infant; educated in Christiania (now Oslo), she declined a university career and worked in an engineer's office for ten years, meanwhile beginning from 1907 to publish novels. The first to receive wide attention, *Jenny,* appeared in 1921, but it was with the trilogy *Kristin Lavransdatter* (1929, bringing together *The Garland*, 1923, *The Mistress of Husaby*, 1925, and *The Cross*, 1927) that she found an extensive and enthusiastic international public. Though set in 13th-14th century Norway, the historical factor in this and in the hardly less fine *Master of Hestviken* (1932; a collection of four novels) is subordinate to their quality as penetrating creations of human character. She wrote numerous other novels, mostly governed by her religious outlook as a devout Catholic convert.

U.N.E.S.C.O. United Nations Educational, Scientific and Cultural Organization, founded in 1946. Usually spoken as a single word: Unesco.

Unger, Gladys (Gladys Buchanan Unger, died 1940). Born in San Francisco; educated in London and Paris; studied art and had some success as a painter at the Paris Salon in 1900 before devoting herself to playwriting. Of her twenty or so plays the most successful was *Our Mr Hepplewhite* (1919); others are *Mr Sheridan* (1907), *Henry of Lancaster* (1908), *The Son and Heir* (1913).

Unities, The. In his treatise the *Poetics*, Aristotle deduced from the practice of the Greek dramatists the *Unity of Action* (that there should be a single plot, from which nothing could be deleted without damage to the whole, and allowing no sub-plot), and the *Unity of Time* (that the action be supposed to transpire within a single day or little more). A third Unity, the *Unity of Place* (that the action be confined to one site) was added by Renaissance critics. The three unities were strictly observed by the 17th-century French classical dramatists, Racine in chief. Shakespeare and most English playwrights ignored them, except when for occasional technical convenience in writing or staging, a play fitted within the compass of the unities.

University of London publications. *See* Athlone Press.

Unquiet Grave, The. 'A Word Cycle' by Palinurus (pseudonym of Cyril *Connolly) published in 1945. Described by the author as 'the doubts and reflections of a year, a word-cycle in three or four rhythms: art, love, nature and religion'. Palinurus was the pilot of Aeneas's ship in Virgil's *Aeneid* (Books v and vi).

Untermeyer, Louis (1885-   ). Born in New York; educated 'privately and abroad'. Consultant in Poetry at the Library of Congress in Washington, 1961-63. Author of numerous books of verse, including *Selected Poems and Parodies* (1935); a biography of *Heine* (2 vols, 1937), and a novel, *Moses* (1928); but best known for his anthologies, principally *Modern American Poetry* (1919 and later editions). Autobiography: *From Another World* (1939).

Unwin, Sir Stanley (1884-1968; knighted 1946). Started in publishing after he left school (Abbotsholme, Staffs.), working with his uncle T. Fisher Unwin; later took control of the firm of Allen & Unwin. For many years and until his death he was the Grand Old Man of British publishing, travelling far and wide in the interests of the book trade. His manual *The Truth About Publishing* (1926 and later editions) became essential reading for everyone concerned with the writing or production or selling of books. Other writings: *Two Young Men See the World* (1934); *The Truth About a Publisher* (1960), his personal record.

Upfield, Arthur (Arthur William Upfield, 1888-1964). Born in England at Gosport. Articled to a surveyor and estate agent, but having failed his examinations he was sent to Australia, where he did little but drift from job to job until the acceptance of articles by an English magazine and of a novel by a London publisher started his successful career as an author. He proceeded to write mystery novels of a unique kind in which the detective, Inspector Napoleon Bonaparte, is drawn from a half-caste tracker with whom Upfield was friendly. Though 'Bony' is an ingenious and attractive character, a greater merit of the books in which he appears is the Australian setting, frequently in desert or other areas remote from cities and towns. Among the best of these novels are *The Widows of Broome* (1950), *Death of a Lake* (1954), *Man of Two Tribes* (1956), *The Bachelors of Broken Hill* (1958), *Bony and the Kelly Gang* (1960).

Upton, Florence (died 1922). Born in New York of English parents; educated there; studied art in France and Holland; exhibited at Royal Academy, Paris Salon, etc. Published children's books, making a lasting impression with the Golliwog series (1895 onward) she illustrated with a grotesque large-headed black doll; its name added to the language a word still in common use.

Uspensky, P. D. (Petr Dem'yanovich Uspenskii, 1878-1947). Born in Moscow. He revolted against formal education and in boyhood and youth ranged widely over literature, science, psychology and the occult, travelling extensively in the East and leaving Russia finally when the Bolsheviks prevailed. He came under the influence of *Gurdjieff, whose doctrine he propagated in England, settling there from 1921 until he died, with an interlude in the United States in World War II. His writings include *Tertium Organum* (1920), *A New Model of the Universe* (1931), and a posthumously-published novel, *The Strange Life of Ivan Osokin* (1947). His theory of recurrence in time had some influence on plays by J. B. Priestley, e.g. *Time and the Conways* (1937), *I Have Been Here Before* (1937).

Ustinov, Peter (Peter Alexander Ustinov, 1921-   ). Born in London of Russian parents; educated at Westminster School. A prolific dramatist, his plays are generally original in form, frequently satirical and comic yet serious. They include *The Banbury Nose* (1943), *The Tragedy of Good Intentions* (1944), *The Love of Four Colonels* (1951), *The Moment of Truth* (1951), *Romanoff and Juliet* (1956). He acted in his own plays, wrote, directed and acted in films, and had considerable success as a broadcaster. Other works: *Add a Dash of Pity* (short stories, 1959); *The Loser* (novel, 1961).

Uttley, Alison (*née* Alison Dickens, Mrs J. A. Uttley). Born in Derbyshire; educated at Bakewell Grammar School and Manchester University. Author of numerous books for children and of recollections of her own early years: *The Country Child* (1931), *Ambush of Young Days* (1937), *Moonshine and Magic* (1932), *Candlelight Tales* (1936), *Adventures of Sam Pig* (1940), and other Sam Pig books. Among her collections of essays on rural and other topics are *Country Hoard* (1943), *A Year in the Country* (1957), *A Peck of Gold* (1966), *The Button-Box* (1968), *Secret Places* (1972).

Vachell, Horace Annesley (1861-1955). Born in Kent; educated at Harrow and Sandhurst; was briefly an army officer until he settled and married in California, returning to England in 1889 and spending the later years of his life in Bath. From 1894 he was a prolific novelist, succeeding especially with *The Hill* (1905), a story of Harrow School, and *Quinneys* (1914), a whimsical novel about an antique dealer who appears again in later books and in a successful dramatization. He also wrote several autobiographical volumes: *Fellow Travellers* (1923), *Methuselah's Diary* (1950), and others.

Vale. The last volume of the autobiographical trilogy **Hail and Farewell* (1911-14) by George Moore. The individual titles of the first and second volumes are *Ave* and *Salve*.

Valentine. The 'five-shilling dentist' in love with Gloria Clandon in Bernard Shaw's **You Never Can Tell* (1895).

Valentine Wannop. Christopher Tietjens's friend in Ford Madox Ford's **Parade's End*. Her mother, a protégée of Christopher's father, achieves success as a novelist. Valentine is by turns a militant suffragette, a domestic servant, and (during Tietjens's war service in France) physical training mistress at a minor public school, where her Armistice Day interview with the Head, Miss Wanostrocht, provides a comic interlude.

Valéry, Paul (1871-1945). Born, of French and Italian parentage, at Cette, near Montpellier, where he was educated and studied law at the University there. After military service he interested himself for years in philosophy and mathematics, worked for a while in London, but from 1892 spent much time in Paris, with André *Gide, Stephané Mallarmé and other Symbolist poets among his friends. His own writings were done slowly and with long intervals of silence, but though a good deal of his poetry is obscure and his prose highly metaphysical, both had a marked international influence—in England on T. S. Eliot among others. The poetical works include *La Jeune Parque* (1917) and *Les Charmes* (1922). *Variété* (1924-44) collected in five volumes most of his miscellaneous prose.

Van Avond, Jan. Pseudonym used by Francis Carey *Slater for *Drought: A South African Parable* (verse; 1929).

Vance, Christopher. In William De Morgan's **Joseph Vance* (1906) the drink-addicted father of Joseph; a secondhand signboard starts him on the way to affluence as a master-builder.

Vance, Ethel (pseudonym of Grace Zaring Stone, 1896-). American novelist who used her own name of Stone for *The Heaven and Earth of Doña Elena* (1929), *The Bitter Tea of General Yen* (1930) and other popular novels, but acquired a more serious reputation with *Escape* (1939) and *Reprisal* (1942), for which she adopted the pseudonym to avoid danger to a member of her family living under the Nazi régime she stigmatized in these novels.

Vance, Louis Joseph (1879-1933). Born in New York; educated at Brooklyn Polytechnic. Becoming a fiction writer while still holding an office job, the most popular of his many books were *The Lone Wolf* (1914) and a succession of others dealing with the adventures of a gentlemanly criminal.

Vance, Philo. Amateur detective in crime novels by S. S. *Van Dine.

Van der Post, Laurens (Laurens Jan Van Der Post, 1906-). Born in South Africa. Served with British forces on several fronts during World War II and from 1949 undertook various expeditions in Africa, notably those described in *The Lost World of the Kalahari* (1959) and *The Heart of the Hunter* (1961). Other writings: *Venture to the Interior* (1952), *Flamingo Feather* (1955), *The Seed and the Sower* (1963), *Journey into Russia* (1964), *A Portrait of Japan* (1968).

Van Dine, S. S. (pseudonym of Willard Huntington Wright, 1888-1939). Born in Virginia; educated in California and at Harvard; studied art in Paris. Worked as a journalist in Los Angeles; as Editor of the *Smart Set* in New York (1912-14) he published work by D. H. Lawrence, James Joyce, etc.; for other papers and periodicals he wrote much literary, music and art criticism. Under his birth name he also wrote *Songs of Youth* (1913), *What Nietzsche Taught* (1914), *Modern Painting* (1915), *The Man of Promise* (a novel, 1916) and other books, but had little success until, adopting the Van Dine nom-de-plume, he produced *The Benson Murder Case* (1926), the first of a dozen best-selling detective novels—with the sophisticated investigator Philo Vance as the central character—which also included *The 'Canary' Murder Case* (1927), *The Scarab Murder Case* (1930), *The Kidnap*

Murder Case (1936).

Van Doren, Carl (Carl Clinton Van Doren, 1885-1950). Born in Illinois; educated at the University of Illinois and at Columbia University, teaching later at both institutions. He married Irita Bradford in 1912 (see next entry). Best known as a critic and literary historian, he wrote biographical studies of *Thomas Love Peacock* (1911), *Swift* (1930), *Sinclair Lewis* (1933), *Benjamin Franklin* (1938), and among other activities was managing editor of the *Cambridge History of American Literature*, 1917-20, Literary Editor of the (New York) *Nation*, 1919-22, and of the *Century Magazine*, 1922-25. Historical works: *Secret History of the American Revolution* (1941), *The Great Rehearsal* (1948); autobiography: *Three Worlds* (1936).

Van Doren, Irita (*née* Irita Bradford, 1891-1966). Born in Alabama; educated in Florida and at Columbia University; married Carl Van Doren in 1912 and was his research assistant until she began to work on the *Nation* in 1919; from 1926 until her retirement in 1963 she was Editor of the *New York Herald-Tribune Sunday Literary Supplement*.

Van Doren, Mark (Mark Albert Van Doren, 1894-1972). Born in Illinois, brother of Carl Van Doren and educated at the same universities. Professor of English at Columbia University, 1920-59; Editor of the *Nation*, 1924-28. Author of *Collected and New Poems* (1964), *Collected Stories* (1962); novels: *The Transients* (1935); critical studies: *Henry David Thoreau* (1916), *Dryden* (1920), *Shakespeare* (1939), *Hawthorne* (1949); *The Last Days of Lincoln* (a play, 1959); *Autobiography* (1958).

Van Druten, John (John William Van Druten, 1901-57). Born in London of Dutch and English parentage; educated at University College School and at the University of London where he qualified in law and then became Lecturer in English Law and Legal History in the University of Wales, 1923-26. In 1924 his play *Young Woodley* was refused a licence by the British censor but was staged in New York in 1925 and privately in London in 1927, a year before the ban was removed and it had a long run of public performances; in 1929 he published a novel based on the play. Among his later successful plays are *There's Always Juliet* (1931), *The Voice of the Turtle* (1944), *Bell, Book and Candle* (1951), *I Am a Camera* (1952; based on stories

by Christopher *Isherwood); autobiographical: *Playwright at Work* (1953).

Van Dyke, Henry (1852-1933). Born in Pennsylvania; educated at Princeton; Presbyterian minister and popular preacher in New York, 1883-99, then Professor of English Literature at Princeton, 1900-1913; 1919-23; U.S. Minister to the Netherlands (1913-16). A popular lecturer and writer, his books of essays (often based on his sermons) are coloured by sentiment and piety: *The Story of the other Wise Man* (1896), *The First Christmas Tree* (1897). He also wrote a good deal of verse and a number of travel books, fishing stories, and literary studies.

Van Loon, Hendrik Willem (1882-1944). Born in Rotterdam; educated at schools in Holland and at American and German Universities. Settled in the U.S.; became a press correspondent in Washington and in European countries; history lecturer in American universities and visiting lecturer in Australasia and South Africa. Author of many immediately popular histories and biographies for non-academic readers: *The Story of Mankind* (1921); *R.v.R., The Life and Times of Rembrandt* (1931), *The Life and Times of Johann Sebastian Bach* (1940, *Van Loon's Lives* (1942), etc.

Van Vechten, Carl (1880-1964). Born in Iowa; educated at the University of Chicago; Paris correspondent and later dramatic critic of the *New York Times*; also wrote music criticism for other publications until 1920, when he turned novelist: *Peter Whiffle* (1922), *The Tattooed Countess* (1924), *Nigger Heaven* (1926). Other books include *Music and Bad Manners* (1916), *The Music of Spain* (1918); about cats, *The Tiger in the House* (1920); autobiographical: *Sacred and Profane Memories* (1932).

Vane, Sutton (Henry Vane Sutton Vane, 1888-1963). Actor and playwright who attracted much notice with *Outward Bound* (1923), in which a shipload of passengers find they are all dead and voyaging to judgment.

Variety of Things, A. Volume of essays etc. by Max *Beerbohm, published in 1928, and containing *The *Dreadful Dragon of Hay Hill*, 'Not That I would Boast', 'The Guerdon', 'T. Fenning Dodworth', 'A Note on the Einstein Theory', 'A Stranger in Venice', 'The Spirit of Caricature', 'Aubrey Beardsley', 'A Social Success' (text of a one-act play produced at the Palace Theatre, London, in 1913), 'The Story of the Small Boy and the Barley Sugar' (written in 1897 for a children's gift-book), 'Yai and the Moon', and The *Happy Hypocrite. 'Not That I Would Boast' was added to *Seven Men as 'Felix Argallo and Walter Ledgett' in a new edition Seven Men and Two Others (1949).

Vaughan, Hilda (1892-   ). Born in Wales; educated privately; married Charles *Morgan. As a novelist she wrote much about the Welsh borderland in which she spent her childhood, and also wrote a few plays in collaboration. The novels include The Battle to the Weak (1925), Here Are Lovers (1926), Her Father's House (1930), Harvest Home (1937), Pardon and Peace (1943).

Veblen, Thorstein (Thorstein Bunde Veblen, 1857-1929). Born in Wisconsin of a Norwegian family; educated at Carlton College and at Johns Hopkins, Yale and Cornell Universities. On the staff of the University of Chicago from 1892, becoming a Professor of Economics there until he transferred to Stanford University and then to the University of Missouri, 1909-18. The publication of his Theory of the Leisure Class (1899) with its attack on what he called 'conspicuous waste' as the distinguishing characteristic of that class, gained him the ready ear of radical thinkers and his contemporary influence was considerable among those who were not put off by turgid prose. Later works: The Theory of Business Enterprise (1904), The Instinct of Workmanship (1914), The Place of Science in Modern Civilization (1919), The Engineers and the Price System (1921). Selected writings: What Veblen Taught (1936).

Vedrenne-Barker Season. The season of plays at the Royal Court Theatre beginning in 1904 under the financial management of J. E. Vedrenne and with Granville *Barker as producer, was a brilliant chapter in the history of the modern theatre. It established Bernard *Shaw and John *Galsworthy among others, and Barker's own best produced play The *Voysey Inheritance was first produced there.

Vercors (pseudonym of Jean Bruller, 1902-   ). Born and educated in Paris. Trained and worked as a designer-engraver; illustrated many books. He adopted the penname Vercors from the Alpine plateau which was one of the centres of the French Resistance during the German occupation in World War II, and used it for his secretly distributed Le Silence de la Mer (1942), 'a tale of the conflict between patriotism and personal sentiment', which made a deep impression both in the original and in translation. The story of how the book came to be written and his thoughts about the Resistance and its post-war effects, are given in La Bataille du Silence (1968; Eng. trans. by his wife Rita Barisse, The Battle of Silence).

Verga, Giovanni (1840-1922). Born in Catania, Sicily; educated privately. In his middle twenties he settled in the northern part of the Italian mainland writing popular novels of no marked literary merit. Later he returned to Sicily and in the 1880s began to produce novels and stories portraying with realism Sicilian people and their lives. His international reputation, however, did not develop until the 1920s when D. H. *Lawrence translated Mastro Don Gesualdo (1923), Little Novels of Sicily (1925), and Cavalleria Rusticana and other Tales of Sicilian Peasant Life (1928), Mascagni's still popular opera (1890) being based on Verga's Cavalleria Rusticana.

Verhaeren, Émile 1855-1916). Born near Antwerp; educated in Brussels and Ghent before studying law in the University of Louvain; then worked in a Brussels lawyer's office until bad health compelled him to travel abroad for several years. Becoming a socialist, he worked and wrote for the Labour movement in Belgium, but was little known abroad until he earned wider appreciation for his courageous patriotism during the German occupation of his country in World War I. His works include Poems (1899), Belgium's Agony (1915). Plays: The Dawn, The Cloister, Philip II, Helen of Sparta (collected 1916, but of varying dates from 1898).

Verloc, Adolf. Double agent and police-informer in Joseph Conrad's The *Secret Agent (1907); killed by his wife, Winnie, after her half-idiot brother Stevie has been killed by a bomb Verloc gave him to carry.

Verne, Jules (1828-1905). Born at Nantes; studied law but turned to the writing of a new kind of adventure stories for boys which at the time seemed fantastically improbable but have since been mostly outstripped by modern inventions. He influenced the early novels of H. G. *Wells and can be regarded as the founding father of *science fiction.

Verrall, A. W. (Arthur Woollgar Verrall, 1851-1912). Born at Brighton; educated at Wellington and Cambridge. Professor of English Literature in the University of Cambridge from 1911. Produced editions and translations of Aeschylus and Euripides; author of *Euripides the Rationalist* (1895). His annotated editions of Shakespeare's plays had a long currency as school texts.

Verver, Maggie. In Henry James's *The *Golden Bowl* (1904), daughter of Adam Verver, American millionaire and connoisseur; she marries the impoverished Italian Prince Amerigo; her father marries Charlotte Stant, Maggie's friend and Amerigo's secret mistress.

Vickers, Ann. *See* *Ann Vickers.

Vicky (pseudonym of Victor Weisz, 1913-1966). Born in Berlin; worked as a cartoonist in Germany until he settled in England as a refugee from the Nazi régime in 1935. Though his knowledge of English politicians was then small, he quickly became a leading political cartoonist, on the London *News Chronicle* from 1941-55 and later, from 1958 until he died, on the *Evening Standard*.

Vico, Giovanni Battista (1668-1744). Italian philosopher; Professor of Rhetoric at Naples from 1697. Author of *Scienza Nuova* (1725; 1730) which has had a renewed influence in the present century through James *Joyce and historians (e.g. Arnold J. *Toynbee) who endorse his theory of cycles of civilizations. The *Autobiography of Giambattista Vico* appeared in an English translation by M. H. Frisch and T. G. Bergin in 1963.

Victoria History of the Counties of England, The. Started in 1899 and named after Queen Victoria. Still in progress, with new volumes and facsimile reprints forthcoming, it will constitute an historical encyclopedia of the English counties in more than 150 volumes. The *History* is now under the control of the University of London Institute of Historical Research.

Victory. Novel by Joseph *Conrad published in 1915. Adopting his father's philosophy of detachment from the affairs of mankind— 'Look on—make no sound'—Axel Heyst leads a wandering life as an unconcerned spectator 'determined to remain free from absurdities of existence', until a casual encounter in the Indonesian island of Timor with what he afterwards describes as 'a cornered man', breaks through his shell of non-involvement. The cornered man, Morrison, owner and captain of the trading brig *Capricorn*, has had his vessel 'arrested' by the Portuguese authorities 'on some pretence of irregularity in his papers' and is unable to pay the fine required to recover it. He is saved by Heyst's immediately lending him the large sum needed. In gratitude, Morrison offers Heyst a share in his trading ventures, which at length develop into the formation of the Tropical Belt Coal Company with Heyst as area manager. On a visit to his home in England Morrison dies. The Coal Company fails, but Heyst remains at the deserted mining station on the remote island of Samburan, alone except for Wang, a Chinese servant. Unawares, he has excited the hatred of the owner of a hotel in Sourabaya, Schomberg, who spreads malicious lies about him, alleging that he stole a lot of money from Morrison and murdered him. The hotelkeeper's enmity is increased when Heyst, while visiting Sourabaya, rescues from Schomberg's persecuting attentions an English girl member of Zangiacomo's Ladies Orchestra, which travels the islands. Heyst elopes with the girl to his bungalow on Samburan. Their solitude is invaded by a criminal trio—'plain Mr Jones' (a card-sharper), his bodyguard Ricardo ('evil intelligence, instinctive savagery' is Heyst's summing up of the two), and a semi-human Caliban-like creature, Pedro. The three had been resident at the hotel on Sourabaya, and to free himself from their detested company Schomberg leads them to believe that, at Samburan, Heyst has a fortune hidden. Heyst tries to keep the girl, Lena, isolated from them, but Ricardo finds and attacks her lustfully. She defends herself successfully, but, aware that Heyst is defenceless (his only weapon, a revolver, having been stolen by Wang), she pretends that she will 'stand in' with Ricardo in robbing Heyst of the (non-existent) 'hidden money'. Knowing that his master, Jones, has a pathological dread and hatred of women, Ricardo keeps him for a while in ignorance of Lena's existence. When Jones sees him and the girl together, he fires at Ricardo, only wounding him but hitting the girl fatally. A second bullet kills Ricardo, who has previously murdered Pedro. While attempting to reach the boat which brought them, Jones is drowned. Heyst immolates himself in the destruction by fire of the bungalow in which Lena died.

Vidal, Gore (1925-   ). Born at West Point, New York; educated in New Hampshire; served on an army transport vessel in the Aleutians in World War II, an experience reflected in his first novel *Williwaw* (1946). Later novels include *The City and the Pillar* (1948), *Dark Green, Bright Red* (1950), *Messiah* (1954), *Burr* (1973); plays: *Visit to a Small Planet* (1957), *The Best Man* (1960).

Villiers, Alan (Alan John Villiers, 1903-   ). Born in Australia at Melbourne and educated there before spending several years in sailing ships and in a whaling vessel. An interval on a Tasmanian paper preceded his return to the sea, when he sailed twice in the grain race from Australia to England in the early 1930s, and then bought his own vessel which he named the 'Joseph Conrad'. He became well known as a writer with *Falmouth for Orders* (1929), *Grain Race* (1932), *The Cruise of the 'Conrad'* (1937), *The Making of a Sailor* (1938), *Pioneers of the Seven Seas* (1956), *The New Mayflower* (1959), and many others.

Viola family. In Joseph Conrad's **Nostromo* (1904): **Giorgio,** once a follower of Garibaldi, now hotel-keeper in Sulaco; **Teresa,** his wife; **Linda** and **Giselle,** daughters. He shoots and kills his best friend and fellow Genoese, Nostromo, mistaking him for a rejected suitor of Giselle's he expects will attack her.

Vision and Design. Essays and lectures by Roger *Fry published in 1920. The most influential and also one of the most readable books of its time on aesthetic principles, it expounds the modern movement in art as 'a return to the ideas of formal design which had been almost lost sight of in the fervid pursuit of naturalistic representation'.

Vitrac, Roger (1899-1952). Co-founder with Antonin *Artaud of the Théâtre Alfred *Jarry in Paris in 1927. Author of plays with surrealist characteristics linking them with the *Theatre of the Absurd.

Vladimir. First Secretary of the foreign embassy in London which employs Verloc as a spy in Joseph Conrad's novel, *The *Secret Agent* (1907).

Vladimir. One of the two tramps in Samuel Becket's **Waiting for Godot* (1954). Nicknamed Didi.

Vortex, The. Play in three acts by Noel *Coward performed in 1923; published in 1925. Florence Lancaster, forty, a society woman of great beauty now fading, tries desperately to preserve the illusion that she remains young, and has Tom Veryan as the latest of her youthful lovers. Her son, twenty-four-year-old Nicky, returns from studying as a pianist in Paris and announces that he is engaged to Bunty Mainwaring, a girl he met there. It transpires that she and Tom Veryan 'used to know each other awfully well', and at a weekend party at the Lancasters' country house she breaks off her engagement. Florence goes into an hysterical rage when she finds Tom embracing and kissing Bunty. In Florence's bedroom the same night Helen Saville, her closest friend, tells Florence that she is battering herself against cast-iron delusions and attempts with small success to keep her from getting back to her 'usual worthless attitude of mind'. Nicky comes in and asks Helen to leave him alone with his mother, whom he compels to admit that Tom is her lover. In turn he confesses that he has become a drug-taker, and condemns her for giving him nothing all his life, letting him grow up all wrong and 'swirl about in a vortex of beastliness'. It was Noel Coward's first success.

Voss. Novel by Patrick *White published in 1957. Sponsored by Edmund Bonner, a Sydney merchant-draper and others, Johann Ulrich Voss, German explorer, plans to lead an expedition across the Australian continent through unknown territory. While assembling stores for the journey in Sydney, he is entertained by the Bonners in their suburban home, though they are not favourably impressed either by his company manners or by his physical appearance as 'a bit of a scarecrow'. Laura Trevelyan, Mrs Bonner's niece, is, however, fascinated by some strange quality she senses in Voss, and in the course of a metaphysical conversation in the Bonners' garden he calls her 'an Apostle of Love masquerading as an atheist' after she has expressed heretical convictions. Having travelled part of the way by ship, Voss sets out on the main overland journey with six white companions, two aborigines joining them as guides. At an early stage he has sent back to Laura a letter requesting permission to write to her uncle, Mr Bonner, 'with necessary formality', asking for her hand in marriage. Laura's reply, in guarded terms satisfies Voss and also forges between them a mystical bond uniting them spiritually as husband and wife. The expedition encounters a sequence of misfortunes: their store-animals are reduced by theft and death; a revolt splits the party—half, led by Judd, the most practical member, turn back, while Voss goes on with two others after Palfreyman the ornithologist has been killed by a black man's spear. Voss, the last of his trio to survive, is stabbed and decapitated when slowly dying by Jackie, the younger of the two native guides who joined the expedition. Disaster also overtakes the breakaway party: left alone, Judd at the last lies down in the shadow of a rock, muttering 'let me die now' During the later stages of the journey, Voss has believed Laura to be with him as a spiritual presence. She is taken seriously ill in Sydney with what Mrs Bonner calls 'brain fever', though the specialist fails to give it a name. The patient's condition is desperate until, after a paroxysm in which she cries out 'O God! It is over. It is over'—inferentially at the identical moment of Voss's death—and the fever breaks. She recovers, finds interest and comfort in the illegitimate orphaned girl-child of a house servant that she has cared for since birth, becomes a respected teacher, and eventually headmistress of an Academy for Young Ladies. Years after the cessation of news of Voss's expedition, a search-party returns to Sydney with an aged man believed to be Judd. At the unveiling ceremony of a memorial to Voss, Laura talks to Judd. Though she has no knowledge of the facts of Voss's end and cannot judge that Judd's claim to have closed his eyes when he died is false, she recognizes aspects of Voss's character in Judd's account of him.

The narrative of Voss's expedition is based on the three journeys of Ludwig Leichhardt in the same territory, 1844-48, on the last of which the whole party disappeared. No evidence of their fate has been discovered.

Voynich, E. L. (*née* Ethel Lilian Boole, 1864-1960). Born in Cambridge; studied music. She married Wilfrid Michael Voynich (1865-1930), born in Lithuania of aristocratic Polish parents; he was imprisoned by the Russians for political activities, escaped from Siberia, reached England in 1890, and became a British citizen. In London he set up in the antiquarian book trade and became internationally famed in that field. His novelist wife was best known for *The Gadfly* (1897), but also wrote *Jack Raymond* (1901), *Olive Latham* (1904), *An Interrupted Friendship* (1910), *Put Off Thy Shoes* (1946), etc. Made translations from the Russian, and of *Chopin's Letters* (1931). Bernard Shaw made a dramatization of *The Gadfly* (copyright performance only, 1898). Printed in vol. VII of *The Bodley Head Bernard Shaw* (1974).

The Voyniches are amusingly portrayed in *Rare People and Rare Books* (1967) by E. Millicent Sowerby, who worked in Voynich's business. See also *Adventures of a Bookseller* (1937) by Giuseppe Orioli.

Voynich, Wilfrid Michael. *See* E. L. *Voynich.

Voysey Inheritance, The. Play in five acts by Granville *Barker performed in 1905; published in 1909, revised in 1913 and 1934. In the Lincoln's Inn office of Voysey & Son, solicitors, Mr Voysey, 'sixty or more and masterful', reveals to his son Edward that securities, trust funds, and other properties of their clients have been misappropriated during many years and applied to speculative investments. Those yielding large dividends have made it possible to pay their normal income to the unsuspecting clients and have also kept the Voysey family in comfort. But the failure of other speculations has resulted in heavy capital losses. Voysey declares that these defalcations began in his father's time and were inherited by him; and Edward is shattered by the prospect that the inheritance will in due course become his. A few months later old Voysey dies. Edward has to break the news to the family that their father's legacies to them cannot be paid. He carries on the firm, risking the likelihood of exposure and imprisonment, and resisting the chief clerk's blackmailing threats. Edward succeeds in righting some of the worst cases, but his hope of slow further improvement seems vain when their chief client, George Booth, an old friend of his father, decides to withdraw his securities from the custody of the firm. Told that only half of his property remains, Booth suggests a settlement which Edward declines as detrimental to other clients. Alice Maitland, to whom Edward has repeatedly proposed, now accepts him and they consider the possibility that Edward may escape prison by inducing all the clients to syndicate themselves and keep him 'slaving at it'. The play is notable for its skilful characterization of the various members of the Voysey family.

Vulliamy, Anastasia. *See* *Anastasia Vulliamy.

Vyse, Cecil. Fiancé of Lucy Honeychurch, until she breaks the engagement in E. M. Forster's *A* *Room With a View (1908).

Waddell, Helen (Helen Jane Waddell, 1889-1965). Born in Tokyo, daughter of an Anglo-Irish professor at the University there; educated in Belfast and at Oxford, where she was awarded a research fellowship which led to *The *Wandering Scholars* (1927), a fine work of medieval scholarship which also attracted a large body of non-scholarly readers. She followed it with a no less attractive anthology of *Mediaeval Latin Lyrics* (1929) translated by herself, and in 1933 by *Peter Abelard*, a historical novel on the Heloise and Abelard love tragedy. Her other books include *The Abbé Prévost* (1933), *Beasts and Saints* (1934), *The Desert Fathers* (1936). Though her verse translations and her novel did not receive wholehearted academic approval, they nevertheless brought the Middle Ages to life for many thousands to whom medievalism was otherwise a dead study.

Waddell, Samuel J. *See* Rutherford *Mayne.

Wain, John (John Barrington Wain, 1925-   ). Born at Stoke-on-Trent; educated at Newcastle-under-Lyme and Oxford. Lecturer in English Literature, University of Reading, 1947-55. His first novel **Hurry on Down* (1953) put him among the iconoclastic young writers of the post-war period, alongside Kingsley *Amis, John *Osborne and others. Later novels include *Living in the Present* (1955), *A Travelling Woman* (1959). Poetry: *A Word Carved on a Sill* (1956), *Weep Before God* (1961). *Preliminary Essays* (1957). Autobiography: *Sprightly Running* (1962).

Wait, James. Negro from St Kitts in Conrad's *The *Nigger of the 'Narcissus'* (1897). Lying in his bunk throughout the voyage from Bombay he dominates the ship and causes dissension among the crew; dies and is buried at sea.

Waite, A. E. (Arthur Edward Waite, 1857-1942). Born in Brooklyn; taken to England in infancy after his father's death and educated in London. Spent several years as a clerk, then turned to poetry, first with *Israfel* (1886); *Collected Poems* (1914). From the early years of this century he was absorbed by magic, freemasonry, and the whole range of occult studies, on which he wrote many volumes.

Waiting for Godot. Tragicomedy in two acts by Samuel *Beckett. Originally written in French as *En attendant Godot* (1952), the English version by the author was published in New York in 1954; performed in London in 1955. Classed as an early and leading contribution to what came to be named the *Theatre of the Absurd, and dedicated to the proposition that human life is meaningless, the play has no plot, coherent action, or characterization that can be summarized. It is nonsensical or it is profound, according to how individual hearers or readers react to it. Two tramps, Estragon (Gogo) and Vladimir (Didi), are 'waiting for Godot' by a tree on a country road. There is comic business with boots and bowler hats, and the knockabout music-hall comedians' effect is sustained in the cross-talk dialogue between the two men, though seriousness keeps breaking in, as when Vladimir introduces and speculates about the story of the two thieves crucified with Jesus. Two other characters, Pozzo and Lucky, come along, slave-master and slave, Pozzo being momentarily thought to be Godot, whose nature or identity is totally unknown to Vladimir and Estragon. Pozzo abuses and ill-treats Lucky, who is tethered at the end of a rope, and orders him to dance, and also to 'think', which he does in a long incoherent tirade. After Lucky and Pozzo leave, a timid boy comes with a message to Gogo and Didi: 'Mr Godot told me to tell you he won't come this evening but surely tomorrow.' Next day the two visitors return, Pozzo now blind and Lucky dumb. They pass on, and the boy comes with the same message as yesterday. At each critical stage the two tramps contemplate suicide, and in the end Vladimir says: 'We'll hang ourselves tomorrow.—Unless Godot comes.' When asked who Godot was meant to be, Beckett is said to have replied: 'If I knew, I would have said so in the play.'

Wakeman, Frederic (1909-   ). Born in Kansas; educated in Parkville, Missouri; worked in advertising and as a film-script writer before turning novelist. *Shore Leave* (1944), a product of his naval service in World War II, preceded the popularity of *The Hucksters* (1946), a satirical fictional probe into advertisers' methods.

Walcott, Derek (1930-   ). Born in St Lucia; educated there and at the University of the West Indies; worked as a teacher and journalist. Regarded as the leading Caribbean poet: *Twenty-five Poems* (1948), *In a Green Night* (1962), *The Castaway and other Poems* (1965); also plays—*The Sea at Dauphin* (1954) and others.

Wales, Hubert (pseudonym of William Pigott,

1870-1943). Born in Linconshire; educated at Oundle and Harrow; articled as a solicitor but turned to literature, mainly as a novelist, but also wrote on psychical research. Author of *Mr and Mrs Villiers* (1906), *The Yoke* (1907), *The Wife of Colônel Hughes* (1910), and other novels; *The Purpose: Reflections and Digressions* (1914), etc.

Waley, Arthur (Arthur David Schloss, 1889-1966; he adopted his mother's surname in 1914). Born in London; educated at Rugby and Cambridge, and at the School of Oriental Studies, London. Assistant Keeper, Department of Prints and Drawings, British Museum, 1913-30. His adopted studies in Chinese and Japanese gave him the knowledge and understanding of oriental thought and expression shown in the many translations or renderings which made him famous from 1918 onward. Though the standard of his work is uniformly high, he was especially praised for *One Hundred and Seventy Chinese Poems* (1918), *The Tale of Genji* (6 vols. 1925-33; translation of the Lady Murasaki's 10th-11th century classic Japanese novel), and *Monkey* (1942; a Chinese allegorical fairy tale).

Walker, Bill. A 'tough customer of about twenty-five' in Bernard Shaw's **Major Barbara* (1905). He blusters up to the West Ham shelter of the Salvation Army demanding his 'girl', Mog Habbijam, who has been converted. He hits Jenny Hill and Rummy Mitchens, but is talked down by Major Barbara. Told that Mog is at the Canning Town barracks he goes to fetch her, but returns after being knocked down and prayed over by her new 'bloke'. Barbara makes him uneasy by harping on the state of his soul, and he tries to atone for hitting the women by an offering of £1. It is refused, but when a donation of £10,000 is accepted from a whisky magnate and Undershaft (betokening 'drunkenness and murder'), Bill taunts Barbara with 'Wot prawce selvytion nah?' (his cockney for 'What price salvation now?').

Walker, David (David Harry Walker, 1911-). Educated at Shrewsbury and Sandhurst; in the army 1931-47. Aide-de-camp to Lord Tweedsmuir (John *Buchan), Governor-General of Canada (1938-39); prisoner of war (1940-45); Comptroller to the Viceroy of India (1946-47); settled in Canada. Author of novels: *Geordie* (1950), *Digby* (1953), *Harry Black* (1956); short stories; and children's books.

Walker, Kenneth (Kenneth Macfarlane Walker, 1882-1966). Born in London; educated at Cambridge; qualified as a physician and surgeon. In addition to numerous medical and surgical works, he wrote *The Physiology of Sex* and *Sex and Society* (both 1940) in the Pelican paperback series. His contacts with *Uspensky and *Gurdjieff led to *Venture with Ideas* (1951) and *A Study of Gurdjieff's Teaching* (1957). Autobiographical: *I Talk of Dreams* (1946), *Life's Long Journey* (1959).

Walkley, A. B. (Arthur Bingham Walkley, 1855-1926). Born near Bristol; educated at Warminster and Oxford; civil servant from 1887 until his retirement in 1919. Meanwhile he had become dramatic critic for the *Star*, 1888-90, the *Speaker*, 1890-99, finally *The Times* from 1900. He published several collections of his articles and essays—including *Drama and Life* (1907), *Pastiche and Prejudice* (1921), *More Prejudice* (1923)—but is best known through the 'Epistle Dedicatory to Arthur Bingham Walkley' which precedes Bernard Shaw's *Man and Superman* (1903).

Wallace, Doreen (1897- ; Mrs D. E. A. Rash). Educated at Malvern and Oxford. Author of *A Little Learning* (1931), *The Gentle Heart* (1932), *Barnham Rectory* (1934), *Green Acres* (1941), *The Noble Savage* (1945), *Root of Evil* (1952), *Mayland Hall* (1960), and other novels.

Wallace, Edgar (1875-1932). Born at Greenwich, the illegitimate son of an actor and actress and registered as Richard Horatio Edgar Wallace; brought up in a fish-porter's family; educated at London elementary schools. After various odd jobs, he had six years as a private soldier, but while in South Africa he induced Reuters to engage him as war correspondent and was afterwards on the *Daily Mail*. He published *Songs* (1895) and some miscellaneous volumes before *The Four Just Men* (1905) and the *Sanders of the River* (1911) stories started him on the remarkable career which made him one of the most prolific, prosperous and spendthrift fiction writers of the century. Though his mystery stories were often preposterously improbable, their narrative drive overcame even the intellectuals who frowned but could not resist. In twenty-seven years he wrote 150 novels, among them *The Clue of the Twisted Candle* (1918), *The Crimson Circle* (1922), *The Clue of the New Pin* (1923), *The Mind of Mr J. G.*

Reeder (1925), *The Flying Squad* (1928), *When the Gangs came to London* (1932). Wallace had made unsuccessful attempts at playwriting before, with *The Ringer* in 1926 and *On the Spot* in 1930, he established himself as a money-maker on the stage, with seventeen plays in London in six years, though they were not uniformly successful. He earned as much as £50,000 a year, but died £140,000 in debt. Through films, broadcasting, and paperback editions of his thrillers, the debt was cleared, and thirty years after his death his books were still selling over a million copies annually. His daughter-in-law, Margaret *Lane, wrote *Edgar Wallace: The Biography of a Phenomenon* (1938).

Wallas, Graham (1858-1932). Born at Sunderland; educated at Shrewsbury and Oxford; became Classics master at Highgate School, and from 1895 to 1923 lecturer on political science at the London School of Economics, with intervals as a visiting lecturer at Yale and other American universities. He was an early and active member of the *Fabian Society in company with Bernard Shaw, Sidney Webb, and others. As a member of the London County Council and of the University of London Senate he played a useful part in municipal and educational affairs, and had a wider influence through his writings: *Human Nature in Politics* (1908), *The Great Society* (1914), *The Art of Thought* (1926).

Waller, M. E. (Mary Ella Waller, 1855-1938). Born in Boston; educated there and in Europe; taught in New York before starting a girls' school in Chicago. She wrote novels and books of essays, *The Wood-Carver of 'Lympus* (1904) having a very large and long-lasting sale.

Walling, R. A. J. (Robert Alfred John Walling, 1869-1949). Born at Exeter of a family of journalists. He began to work on newspapers in his early teens and became managing editor of a West Country daily. With *The Strong Room* (1926) he began a long sequence of mystery stories, including *Murder at the Keyhole* (1929), *The Corpse in the Crimson Slippers* (1936), etc. He also wrote lives of Sir John Hawkins (1907) and George Borrow (1908) and topographical volumes including *The West Country* (1935) and *The Green Hills of England* (1938).

Walmsley, Leo (1892-1966). Born at Shipley,

Yorkshire. He had a distinguished career in the Royal Flying Corps in World War I, and afterwards wrote *Flying and Sport in East Africa* (1920). He produced novels dealing mainly with the lives of fishermen on the Yorkshire coast—*Three Fevers* (1932), *Foreigners* (1935), *Sally Lunn* (1937), *Love in the Sun* (1939), etc.—and an autobiography, *So Many Loves* (1944).

Waln, Nora (1895-1964). Born in Pennsylvania; educated at the Quaker Swarthmore College there; foreign correspondent in Japan and Germany for American publications. She had considerable success with *The House of Exile* (1933), a product of living with a Chinese family for two years in their country, and *Reaching for the Stars* (1939), after several years in Nazi Germany.

Walpole, Sir Hugh (Hugh Seymour Walpole, 1884-1941; knighted 1937). Born at Auckland, New Zealand, son of an Anglican canon who became Bishop of Edinburgh in 1910. Educated at King's School, Canterbury, and Emmanuel College, Cambridge. Service with the Russian Red Cross, 1914-16 in World War I gave him knowledge of that country utilized in *The Dark Forest* (1916) and *The Secret City* (1919), two of his novels. Before the war he was for a time an Anglican lay reader and a school teacher, but found both occupations uncongenial. Nevertheless the inside knowledge of schools he obtained enabled him to produce in the story of two schoolmasters *Mr Perrin and Mr Traill* (1911) what is still ranked by many as his most durable novel. He had previously published *The Wooden Horse* (1909) and *Maradick at Forty* (1910), though it was with *Fortitude* (1913) that he first secured a large public, which grew steadily larger in following years, attracted particularly by his three novels of boyhood, *Jeremy* (1919), *Jeremy and Hamlet* (1923), and *Jeremy at Crale* (1927). In these and in *The Cathedral* (1922) he drew to some extent on autobiography. In the postwar decade he enjoyed as an author both prosperity and social success; but, appearing to undergo some weakening of intellectual fibre and to develop some self-distrust beneath the buoyant exterior, the earlier intimations of genius faded into over-productive competence and anxiety to ingratiate himself. This last trait is mercilessly exposed in the character of Alroy Kear in Somerset Maugham's *Cakes and Ale*. Though Maugham declared that he had not

Walpole in mind, the disclaimer was not found convincing and Walpole was deeply hurt. In perspective the author himself seems more enigmatic than most of his novels are impressive. That some darkness ran below the surface is indicated by his ability to horrify, as in *The Old Ladies* (1924) and *The Man with Red Hair* (1925). In his ecclesiastical vein he appeared a disciple of Trollope, as in *The Cathedral* and its successors set in Polchester. He also wrote a study of *Anthony Trollope* (1928). His most ambitious fictional venture was *The Herries Chronicle* (1942) which brought together *Rogue Herries* (1930), *Judith Paris* (1931), *The Fortress* (1932), and *Vanessa* (1933), tracing the history of a Lake District family from the 18th century to the present. In addition to the novels, Walpole published *Joseph Conrad* (1916), *The English Novel* (1925), *Four Reminiscences* (1933), and other miscellaneous writings.

Walsh, Maurice (1879-1964). Born in Kerry, Ireland; educated at Ballybunion and Listowel. Served in the Customs and Excise (first in British, afterwards in Irish, service). Among his numerous novels *The Key Above the Door* (1923) was outstandingly successful.

Walsh, Peter. Unsuccessful lover of Clarissa in Virginia Woolf's *Mrs Dalloway* (1925).

Wandering Scholars, The. A study by Helen *Waddell of medieval Latin secular poetry and its makers, published in 1927. As well as being a scholarly work on a fascinating aspect of life in the Middle Ages, it embodies the author's translations which made many readers aware for the first time of the beauty and manifold human interest of the Latin lyrics of the period.

War in the Air, The, and Particularly how Mr Bert Smallways Fared while it Lasted. Novel by H. G. *Wells published in 1908. In the early years of the mechanical age, while ballooning was still the weekend pastime of the Aero Clubs, England is startled by a sudden flight from London to Glasgow and back in a heavier-than-air machine built and piloted by a Mr Alfred Butteridge. His is the first stable and practicable aeroplane, but negotiations for the purchase of his invention by Britain fall through. Among those alarmed by the failure of the government to acquire this vital secret is Bert Smallways, an almost illiterate Cockney youth who is in partnership in an unprosperous bicycle-hiring business. Bert has recently bought a motor cycle, which breaks down and is destroyed by fire on a Sunday excursion with Edna, his girl friend. When, soon after, their business fails, Bert and his partner attempt to earn their living as entertainers at seaside resorts. While singing on Dymchurch sands, Bert grasps the trailing rope of a drifting balloon occupied by Butteridge and his woman companion. By mischance Bert is swept away alone in the basket of the balloon, and finds in it the secret plans of Butteridge's aeroplane. The balloon is carried into Germany and lands at an aeronautical park in Franconia, where a great fleet of huge airships is ready to attack the United States without warning. Bert's attempt to impersonate Butteridge fails, and he is used 'as ballast' in the *Vaterland*, the flagship leading the flight of the air-armada under the command of Prince Karl Albert, the German War Lord. From the *Vaterland* Bert watches the destruction of the American North Atlantic squadron, the chief part of their navy being in the Pacific. The airships bomb New York and other cities into official surrender, though resistance is mounted by citizen forces. In an aerial battle the *Vaterland* is disabled and comes to earth in Labrador. Meanwhile the war has spread all over the world, which is soon dominated by immense fleets of Chino-Japanese aircraft. The war continues by its own momentum, the powers that brought it about being unable to bring it to a final cessation. Bert passes Butteridge's plans to the Americans, and has numerous frightening experiences and witnesses many horrors before he gets back to England and is united to Edna. By that time, the welter of conflict has led mankind into anarchy, famine, pestilence, and universal social collapse. The novel is an enthralling story of adventure and also a forceful antiwar book.

War of the Worlds, The. Novel by H. G. *Wells published in 1898. Astronomers see vast jets of gas flaming out from Mars, not suspecting that missiles are approaching earthward at many miles a second. The first of what are mistaken for meteorites, great cylindrical canisters, embeds itself in a deep pit on a common near Woking in Surrey. Too hot to approach, it is viewed from a distance by the curious and by an expert group including the Astronomer Royal. When the cylinder cools, the top revolves as it is unscrewed from within, and unhuman shapes with coiling tentacles emerge. A deputation including the Astronomer Royal approaches, but a 'humped shape' rising from the pit ejects a beam of light which instantly incinerates them and, beyond them, destroys trees and houses and everything else in its path. The Martians encase themselves in 'walking engines of glittering metal' mounted on jointed tripod legs a hundred feet high. As further cylinders land, the invaders mass and move towards London, killing and burning with their Heat-Ray and laying a heavy Black Smoke which chokes and poisons all who breathe it. A panic evacuation towards the north and the coast fills the roads with millions of refugees on foot, on bicycles, and in horse-drawn vehicles (no motors were yet in use). A further affliction comes from a rapidly proliferating red weed which blocks the rivers and encroaches on the land until it is eliminated by an unknown disease. The Martians conquer the country, making London a dead city; civilization is ended, human survivors are scattered and reduced to animal habits. A saving reversal comes when the Martians, creatures of a germ-free planet, are annihilated by mankind's diseases, to which they have no resistance. Humanity creeps back over the land to rebuild civilization, and to speculate on methods of defence if another invasion from Mars should befall.

Ward, Arthur Sarsfield. *See* Sax *Rohmer.

Ward, Mrs Humphry (*née* Mary Augusta Arnold, 1851-1920). Born in Tasmania, where her father Thomas Arnold (brother of Matthew Arnold) was then an Inspector of Schools. She was brought to England in 1856 and educated at boarding schools. The family settled in Oxford from 1865, and there she was for a short time Secretary to Somerville College. In 1872 she married Thomas Humphry Ward, a Brasenose tutor, with whom she moved to London in 1881 when he joined *The Times* staff. From that year, when she published *Milly and Olly,* she became a well-known writer and the appearance of *Robert Elsmere* (1888) made her a popular though often controversial novelist, appealing to an audience interested in ethical problems and religious doubt. None of her later novels aroused the same religious concern as *Robert Elsmere,* but she continued for the next thirty years to write well-received novels, among them *The History of David Grieve* (1892), *Helbeck of Bannisdale* (1898), *The*

Marriage of William Ashe (1905), *The Case of Richard Meynell* (1911). She also wrote a considerable amount of non-fiction, and was active in social and educational work, founding the Mary Ward Settlement in London.

Ward, Leslie. *See* Spy.

Ward, Mary Jane (1905-). Born in Indiana; educated at High School there and at Northwestern University; studied art and music. Author of *The Tree Has Roots* (1937), *It's Different for a Woman* (1952) and other novels, among which *The Snake Pit* (1946) claimed most attention as a moving study of mental illness based on personal knowledge.

Ward, Mrs Elizabeth. *See* Fay *Inchfawn.

Ward, R. H. (Richard Heron Ward, 1910-69). Born in Buckinghamshire; educated at Stowe; worked as an actor and playwright, founding the Adelphi Players which performed in camps and factories during World War II. As a dramatist he concentrated on religious and related subjects—*Holy Family* (1942), *The Prodigal Son* (1944, 1952), *Faust in Hell* (1944), *The Builders* (1959), etc.—for church functions in Britain and the U.S. Among other writings: novels—*The Compelled Hero* (1931), *The Leap in the Dark* (1954), *The Conspiracy* (1964); verse—*The Encounter* (1948), *Twenty-three Poems* (1952); literary studies—*The Powys Brothers* (1935), *William Somerset Maugham* (1937); early memories—*A Gallery of Mirrors* (1956). *Names and Natures* (1968), subtitled 'Memories of Ten Men', includes sharply etched impressions of Maurice *Browne, and Charles *Williams.

Wardour Street. Term applied disapprovingly to a literary style (prevalent at the end of the nineteenth century) using a plethora of archaic words. Wardour Street in west London was at that time a centre of the antiques business.

Warner, Oliver (1903-). Educated in Staffordshire and at Cambridge. Many years a publishers' reader; worked at the Admiralty in World War II and until 1947. Deputy Director of Publications, British Council, 1947-63. Specialized in naval history and biography: *Captain Marryat* (1953), *A Portrait of Lord Nelson* (1958), *The Battle of the Nile* (1960), *Portsmouth and the Royal Navy* (1965), *Nelson's Battles* (1965). Other books: *A Secret of the Marsh* (1927), *Uncle Lawrence* (1939), *Joseph Conrad* (1951), *The Crown*

Jewels (1951), etc.

Warner, Rex (1905-). Born in Birmingham; educated at Harpenden and Oxford. Worked as a school teacher in England and Egypt; Director, British Institute, Athens, 1945-47. Novels: *The Wild Goose Chase* (1937), *The Professor* (1938), *The Aerodrome* (1941), *Escapade* (1953), *The Vengeance of the Gods* (1954), etc. *Poems* (1937). Numerous translations of Greek and other classics. Other works: *The Young Caesar* (1958), *Imperial Caesar* (1960), *Pericles the Athenian* (1963).

Warner, Sylvia Townsend (1893-). Born at Harrow; educated privately; studied music and became a leading authority on English Tudor Church Music. Her novel *Lolly Willowes* (1926) is one of the most distinguished of its period, while *The Corner That Held Them* (1948), though less praised, is a memorable story of medieval convent life. Other novels: *Mr Fortune's Maggot* (1927), *Elinor Barley* (1930), *The Flint Anchor* (1954), etc. Poetry: *The Espalier* (1925), *Time Importuned* (1928). Short stories: *A Garland of Straw* (1943), *The Museum of Cheats* (1947), and other collections. *The Cat's Cradle Book* (1960). Later works: *A Spirit Rises* (1962), *A Stranger with a Bag* (1966).

Warren, C. Henry (Clarence Henry Warren 1895-1966). Born in Kent; educated at Maidstone and the University of London. Taught English at Newport and then became an official lecturer at the National Portrait Gallery, afterwards working for the B.B.C., 1929-33. His writings, apart from book reviews, were almost wholly on country themes: *A Cotswold Year* (1936), *A Boy in Kent* (1937), *The Happy Countryman* (1939), *Corn Country* (1940), *England is a Village* (1940), *The Land is Yours* (1943), *The Scythe in the Apple Tree* (1953).

Warren, Mrs. The name character in *Mrs Warren's Profession* (1893-94) by Bernard Shaw. She directs an international chain of brothels.

Warren, Robert Penn (1905-). Born in Kentucky; educated there and at Vanderbilt University, Yale, and Oxford (Rhodes Scholar). Held several university appointments, including those of Professor of Drama at Yale, 1951-56, and Professor of English there from 1961. Author of *Night Rider* (1938), *At Heaven's Gate* (1943), *All the King's Men* (1946), *World Enough and Time* (1950), *Band of Angels* (1955), *Flood* (1964) and other novels, most with an historical, political, and moral background, *All the King's Men* having resemblances to the career and fate of Huey *Long. Warren's poetry is sampled in *Selected Poems* (1944), and he has also written critical essays and the biographical *John Brown: The Making of a Martyr* (1929).

Warren, Vivie. Daughter of Mrs Warren in *Mrs Warren's Profession* (1893-94) by Bernard Shaw. She has been well educated, and when she learns the source of the money provided by her mother, she determines to earn her own living forthwith and sets up successfully with a friend in a City business partnership.

Washington, Booker T. (Booker Taliaferro Washington, 1856-1915). Born in Virginia of a slave mother and a white father. He studied while working and graduated at Hampton Institute, where he later had charge of the night school. Made Principal of a newly founded Negro school at Tuskegee, Alabama, in 1881, he devoted the rest of his life to industrial education. He was opposed to political agitation for Negro rights and was consequently out of favour with the next generation of his people. His reputation rests upon his autobiographical *Up From Slavery* (1901).

Waste Land, The. Poem by T. S. *Eliot in 433 lines, mainly free verse with occasional snatches of rhyme, and quoted lines in German, French, Italian, and numerous references and allusions to English writers—Shakespeare, Webster, Milton, Middleton, Spenser, Marvell, John Day, Goldsmith, Kyd, and others. Published in 1922, derided by many but praised by a few, it is now seen in retrospect as a landmark in English poetry ending the romantic period nominally dated from 1798, and opening a period of predominantly intellectual verse in which classical elements met on common ground with such contemporary phenomena as crowds flowing over London Bridge (*The Waste Land*, 60-68), jazz (128-30), women's pub talk (139-70), the seduction of a bored typist in her squalid room (220-56). But these are incidental living aspects of the waste land of contemporary civilization where 'the dead tree gives no shelter' (23), where 'we are in rat's alley' (115) and women seek abortion (159), and dry bones and dirty finger-nails are appropriate images. Eliot appended elaborate source-notes to the poem but, acknowledging that 'Not only the title, but the plan and a good deal of the incidental symbolism of the poem' were suggested by Jessie L. Weston's *From Ritual to Romance*, he added that her book 'will elucidate the difficulties of the poem much better than my notes can do'.

The original manuscript of the poem was for many years thought to have been destroyed, but it was found in an American collection in 1968, with deletions and annotations by Ezra *Pound, to whom Eliot and submitted it for comment.

Waterhouse, Keith (Keith Spencer Waterhouse, 1929-). Educated in Leeds; worked as a journalist there and in London. Author of *Billy Liar* (1959) in collaboration with Willis *Hall, his collaborator also in other plays and films.

Watkins, A. T. L. (Arthur Thomas Levi Watkins, 1907-65). Born at Aberystwyth; educated at Tonbridge and Oxford. Worked in the Home Office before becoming Secretary to the British Board of Film Censors. Author of *Cavalier* (1932), *Muted Strings* (1936), *For Better, for Worse . . .* (1952), *Not in the Book* (1958), *Out of Bounds* (1962), and other plays.

Watkins, Vernon (Vernon Phillips Watkins, 1906-67). Born at Maesteg, South Wales; educated at Swansea, Repton, and Cambridge, studying French and German and developing his love and knowledge of poetry in Continental languages as well as in English and Welsh. While working as a bank clerk he met and was influenced by Dylan *Thomas, to whom he attributed the clearing from his poetry of imitative elements. *The Ballad of the Mari Lwyd and Other Poems* (1941), *The Lady with the Unicorn* (1948), *The Death Bell: Poems and Ballads* (1954), *Cypress and Acacia* (1959). *Letters to Vernon Watkins by Dylan Thomas* (1957).

Watson, Dr. Sherlock Holmes's confidant and foil in the detective stories by Conan *Doyle.

Watson, H. B. Marriott (Henry Brereton Marriott Watson, 1863-1921). Born and educated in New Zealand; settled in England in 1885; became Assistant Editor of the *Pall Mall Gazette*. Wrote nearly fifty novels and books of short stories from 1888 to 1919.

Watson, John. See Ian *Maclaren.

Watson, John B. (John Broadus Watson, 1878-1958). Professor of Psychology at Johns Hopkins University, Baltimore (1908-20). He came into prominence with his theory of Behaviorism, which postulated that all human behaviour is exclusively a product of response to external stimuli, not of immaterial mental processes.

Watson, Sir William (John William Watson, 1858-1935; knighted 1917). Born in Yorkshire; educated at Southport. He began to publish poetry in 1880 with *The Prince's Quest*, followed by *Epigrams of Art, Life, and Nature* (1884). *Wordsworth's Grave* (1890), greatly acclaimed, made it appear that he would inevitably succeed to the Laureateship on the death of Tennyson (1892), upon whom he wrote the elegy *Lachrymae Musarum*. No successor was appointed until 1896, when political considerations led to the preference of Alfred *Austin. Watson's not unjustified disappointment and indignation distempered the rest of his life, and though he continued to write and publish poetry, he saw himself as a forgotten genius. The belated grant of a knighthood when he had passed sixty did nothing to lessen his sense of injustice. Though not a major poet, his work has form and dignity and his *Ode on the Coronation of Edward VII* showed his quality as a ceremonial poet. *A Hundred Poems* (1922), *Selected Poems* (1928), and *I Was an English Poet* (a selection by his widow, 1941) provide a fair view.

Watts-Dunton, Theodore (Walter Theodore Watts-Dunton, 1832-1914). Born in Huntingdonshire as Walter Theodore Watts, he added his mother's name in 1897. Trained and practised as a solicitor, but turned to literary journalism, contributing critical articles to the *Athenaeum* for more than twenty years until 1898, and, later, articles on poets, dramatists, prose writers, and on poetic technique and verse-forms, for the Encyclopaedia Britannica and other publications. A particular interest in gipsy lore led him to write much on George Borrow, and also a celebrated novel of gipsy life, *Aylwin* (1898); similar themes had also produced a verse narrative, *The Coming of Love: Rhona Boswell's Story* (1897). A treatise on the Romantic movement, *The Renascence of Wonder* (1903), was his outstanding critical work. Although a remarkably prolific writer on a wide variety of subjects, and of high repute in his lifetime, he is chiefly remembered as Swinburne's house-mate and virtual guardian for thirty years from *c*. 1880 until the poet's death. A fascinating glimpse of their Putney ménage is given in Max *Beerbohm's 'No. 2. The Pines'.

Waugh, Alec (Alexander Raban Waugh, 1898-). Born at Hampstead; educated at Sherborne and Sandhurst; captured and held as a prisoner in World War I. His first novel *The Loom of Youth* (1917) was regarded as a libel on his old school, which ostracized him and obliterated his name from the roll. It nevertheless established him as a writer. His many later novels include: *The Lonely Unicorn* (1922), *Card Castle* (1924), *So Lovers Dream* (1931), *The Balliols* (1934), *No Truce With Time* (1941), *Island in the Sun* (1956). Travel books: *The Coloured Countries* (1930), *The Sunlit Caribbean* (1948). Autobiography: *Myself When Young* (1923), *Thirteen Such Years* (1932), *The Early Years of Alec Waugh* (1962). Also *My Brother Evelyn and other Profiles* (1967).

Waugh, Arthur (1866-1943). Born in Somerset; educated at Sherborne and Oxford. Father of Alec and Evelyn Waugh. Experience as journalist and literary adviser led to his becoming Managing Director of Chapman & Hall, publishers, from 1902 to 1930. He wrote on Tennyson, Browning and others, edited a collected edition of Dickens, and was author of a book of essays *Reticence in Literature* (1915) and the autobiographical *One Man's Road* (1931).

Waugh, Evelyn (Evelyn Arthur St John Waugh, 1903-1966). Born in London; educated at Lancing and Oxford; studied art, worked on the *Daily Express* and mixed with high society. Having written a critical biography of *Rossetti* (1928), he published in the same year *Decline and Fall*, which immediately gave him the position he retained to the end of his life as England's leading satirical novelist: *Vile Bodies* (1930), *Black Mischief* (1932), *A Handful of Dust* (1934), *Scoop* (1938), *The Loved One* (1948), etc. He joined the Roman Catholic Church in 1930, a conversion which paved the way for his biography of *Edmund Campion* (1935). Service in World War II led to the trilogy of novels beginning with *Men at Arms* (1952). *Brideshead Revisited* (1945) has been considered the best of his non-satirical novels, a complex story of the varying responses to religion of an Old Catholic family. Though his books were largely immune from serious informed criticism, and though they have many brilliantly comic passages, his satire was frequently directed at too-obvious targets, such as the press lord in *Scoop*, while in *The Loved One* (on American commercialization of bereavement) the satirical point is overworked and soon exhausted. His non-fiction books include *The Life of Ronald Knox* (1959), a particular friend, and *A Tourist in Africa* (1960).

Waves, The. Novel by Virginia *Woolf published in 1931. In a key passage towards the end of the book, Bernard reflects: 'How tired I am of stories . . . how I distrust neat designs of life. . . . Of story, of design, I see no trace.' Though not neglectful of literary design, this novel has, purposively, no connected story. Interspersed with descriptive nature passages covering a day from dawn to dark, the lives of Bernard, Susan, Rhoda, Neville, Jinny, and Louis are glimpsed in a succession of interior monologues taking them from childhood to old age. Brought together as young children, their lives diverge, their main later gatherings being at a dinner in a French restaurant in London to mark the departure to India of their common friend, Percival, whose death soon after, due to being thrown from his horse, is a shock to them all, but especially to Jinny. Years afterwards they dine together again at Hampton Court. Meanwhile Bernard marries outside the circle, Susan settles as a farmer's wife, Rhoda and Louis become lovers. Bernard, a confirmed note-taker and phrase-maker, comments on the individual lives of the group in a prolonged concluding monologue.

Way Home, The. The second volume (published in 1925) of Henry Handel Richardson's *The *Fortunes of Richard Mahony* (1930).

Way of All Flesh, The. Novel by Samuel *Butler published posthumously in 1903. Opening with a brief account of 'old Mr Pontifex', who was about eighty in 1807 and had been a carpenter, parish clerk, and organ-builder before attaining 'solid comfort' as owner of a farm, the narrative turns to the career of his son, George Pontifex, born about 1765. George goes into his uncle's London publishing business, and in his middle twenties is taken into partnership, several years before he marries. By the time his wife dies in 1805, there are five children, of whom the youngest two, Theobald (born in 1802) and Alethea, become important in the novel. George makes a large fortune as publisher of religious books, and, as a typical parent in that generation, imposes habits of strict obedience on his children. Theobald is destined from early years to become a clergyman; and, after failing while at Cambridge to persuade his father to allow him to adopt some other calling, he is ordained in 1825. Engaged to assist Mr Allaby, rector of a village near Cambridge, Theobald is marked down by Mrs Allaby as a husband for one of her five daughters—who play at cards to decide which. Christina, having won, softens up Theobald by her 'winning manners', and they marry after five years, a delay due to George Pontifex's refusal to encourage his son to venture into a penniless marriage. This objection is overcome by Theobald's securing the well-paid village living of Battersby-on-the-Hill. In the rectory there, a first child, Ernest, is born in 1835. Though regarding themselves as loving parents, Theobald and Christina's ruthlessly religious upbringing of Ernest, which involves much whipping and crushing of spirit by his father, destroys all filial affection. Sent to boarding school, Ernest finds the headmaster, Dr Skinner, 'much too like his father', and the undermining effect on his character is unrelieved until his aunt, Alethea Pontifex, comes to live near the school and, learning of his love of music, encourages him by providing him with a workshop beside her house in which to emulate his great-grandfather by building an organ. Alethea dies during a typhoid epidemic, leaving a fortune in trust to accumulate for Ernest until his twenty-eighth birthday. The trustee is a friend of Alethea's, Mr Overton, who knows the history of the family and is sympathetic to Ernest, his godson. Overton is also the narrator throughout the book. Ernest falls into disgrace after his aunt's death, which cuts him off from the interests she fostered. He does badly at school, and at home is baselessly suspected of responsibility for the pregnancy of Ellen, one of the servant maids, to whom he gives his watch and knife and pocket-money in compassion when she is turned from the house. After leaving school he goes up to Cambridge, in due course takes his degree, is ordained and appointed to a curacy in London. In his lodging near Drury Lane he resolves to convert other lodgers. He calls on one of them, Miss Maitland, supposing her a prostitute whose soul he must save. Frightened, she rushes from the house, having mistaken her visitor's purpose. Ernest

is charged with immoral intentions and sent to prison for six months. After his release he encounters Ellen, the ex-servant, in London and marries her. They set up in a secondhand clothes shop, and prosper until Ellen relapses into the drunkenness from which marriage had rescued her. He finds that she married him bigamously, being already the wife of his father's old coachman, who was her lover while she worked for the Pontifexes. After Ellen goes off to America with another man, Ernest settles the two children she bore him with foster parents. They grow up happily and marry suitably. On his twenty-eighth birthday Ernest had received from Mr Overton the legacy (accumulated to £70,000) left in trust by his aunt Alethea. After a Continental tour with his godfather, Ernest turns to the writing of provocative books on controversial subjects.

The Way of All Flesh was written between 1873 and 1884. Two chapters missing from the manuscript were supplied from the author's notes by his literary executor, R. A. Streatfield, who published the complete book in 1903. The account of Ernest's upbringing is based on Butler's own. His father and mother are portrayed as Theobald and Christina Pontifex; Ernest's aunt Alethea is drawn from Butler's wise and lovable friend Mary Ann Savage (1836-85).

Weaver, Harriet Shaw (1876-1961). Born in Cheshire. She became closely associated with *The Egoist*, through which she was able to give encouragement to such young writers as James *Joyce whose first novel *A *Portrait of the Artist as a Young Man*, was serialized in that periodical when she was assistant to the editor, T. S. *Eliot. The financial support she provided enabled Joyce to continue and finish *Ulysses* in Zurich, and, failing to find an English firm willing to print the book, she imported copies of the Paris edition and distributed them to London bookshops. Joyce appointed her his executor of his will, and she left her James Joyce Collection to the *National Book League.

Webb, Beatrice (*née* Beatrice Potter, 1858-1943; Mrs Sidney Webb). Born in London; educated privately. Her early and strongly developed social conscience caused her to begin while still a girl those inquiries into the condition of the poor which she continued with redoubled zeal after her marriage to Sidney Webb in 1892. Together they produced a series of economic and political masterpieces of minute investigation which greatly furthered the cause of Socialism and underpinned the Labour Party in its early years. They were among the architects of the Welfare State, though Mrs Webb died at its threshold. Her published *Diaries 1912-24* and *1924-32* and other evidence suggest that in her concern with mass welfare she tended to lose sight of men and women as individuals with innumerable differing foibles and needs, while for some at least of her political colleagues she had little but contempt. In addition to the jointly produced works named in the Sidney Webb entry, she published under her own name: *The Co-operative Movement in Great Britain* (1891), *Men's and Women's Wages: Should they be Equal?* (1919), *My Apprenticeship* (1926); *Our Partnership* (1948) and her *Diaries* were published posthumously.

Webb, Mrs Mary (*née* Mary Gladys Meredith, 1881-1927). Born in Shropshire; educated at home and at Southport. She had published four novels—*The Golden Arrow* (1916), *Gone to Earth* (1917), *The House in Dormer Forest* (1920), *Seven for a Secret* (1922)—with only little success until her books were swept into immediate celebrity when the Prime Minister, Stanley Baldwin, praised her *Precious Bane* (1924) in a public address. Her descriptions of the Shropshire countryside and rural life are impressive, though the characters are stereotypes and her lack of a counterbalancing sense of humour loaded her novels with a grim starkness which can be satirically parodied and exploded into farce (as in, for example, Stella *Gibbons's *Cold Comfort Farm*). Two books published after Mary Webb's death are an unfinished novel, *Armour Wherein He Trusted*, and a collection of poems and essays, *The Spring of Joy* (both 1929).

Webb, Sidney (Sidney James Webb, 1859-1947; 1st Baron Passfield 1929). Born in London; educated there privately and in Switzerland, Germany, and at Birkbeck and City of London Colleges. From 1878 he was a civil servant, until he retired in 1891 on his election to the London County Council. With Bernard Shaw and others he played a leading part in the propaganda work of the *Fabian Society, in the foundation of the London School of Economics (where he was honorary Professor of Public Administration from 1912 to 1927), and in launching the *New Statesman* in 1913. He became an M.P. in

1922 and went to the House of Lords in 1929 as Baron Passfield (though he preferred not to use the title) and held ministerial office under the Labour government. He wrote books on Socialism and education as well as collaborating with his wife in *The History of Trade Unionism* (1894), *English Local Government* (15 vols, 1906-27), *English Poor Law Policy* (1910), *The State and the Doctor* (1910), *The Prevention of Destitution* (1911), *The Decay of Capitalist Civilisation* (1923), *English Poor Law History* (3 vols., 1927-29), *Soviet Communism: A New Civilisation?* (1935), *The Truth about Soviet Russia* (1942), and other works.

Webber, Barbara K. See Elizabeth *Cambridge.

Webster, Jean (Alice Jane Chandler Webster, 1876-1916). Born in New York; educated there and at Vassar. Among her half-dozen or so novels, *Daddy Long Legs* (1912) became internationally popular and was also dramatized and filmed.

Wedekind, Frank (Benjamin Franklin Wedekind, 1864-1918). Born in Hanover; studied law at the University of Zurich, but spent the succeeding years in a wandering life which took him to Paris, London, and German cities, including Leipzig and Berlin. In 1899 he was imprisoned on a charge of *lèse-majesté* on account of political poems published in the German comic paper *Simplicissimus*. He wrote short stories and a large number of plays, including *The Awakening of Spring* (German 1891; English trans. 1909), *Earth Spirit* (1895; 1914), *Pandora's Box* (1903; 1918). His work is powerfully erotic and was condemned as pornographic, though its main purpose was to put the case for rational sex education.

Wedgwood, Dame C. V. (Cicely Veronica Wedgwood, 1910-). D.B.E., 1968. Born in Northumberland of the Wedgwood pottery family; educated at Oxford and in France and Germany. She had published *Strafford* (1935), *The Thirty Years War* (1938), and *Oliver Cromwell* (1939) before *William the Silent* (1944) made her widely recognized as a writer whose books brought history and literature into brilliant conjunction, a reputation maintained by her volumes on the English Civil War—*The King's Peace* (1955) and *The King's War* (1958). *Velvet Studies* (1946) is a collection of essays, and she has also written *Truth and Opinion* (1960) and *Poetry and Politics* (1960). O.M. 1969.

Weekley, Ernest (1865-1954). Born in London; educated in France, Germany, Switzerland, and at Cambridge. Professor of French, University of Nottingham, from 1898 and later Head of the Modern Language Department there until he retired in 1938. His wife (née Frieda von *Richtofen) married D. H. *Lawrence after she was divorced in 1914. Weekley devoted his life to the study of words and published many books on lexicography and etymology, among them *The Romance of Words* (1912), *The Romance of Names* (1914), *Surnames* (1916), *Words Ancient and Modern* (1926; 1927), *Jack and Jill, a Study of Our Christian Names* (1939).

Weidman, Jerome (1913-). Born in New York; educated there; studied law but did not practise. His awareness of contemporary materialism and commercialization is fictionally expressed with bitter humour in *I Can Get it for You Wholesale* (1937) and *What's in it for Me?* (1938).

Weigall, Arthur (Arthur Edward Pearse Brome Weigall, 1880-1934). Educated at Malvern, Wellington, and Oxford. Joined the staff of the Egypt Exploration Fund and became Inspector-General of Antiquities to the Egyptian Government from 1905 till his retirement in 1914. He published scholarly works on various aspects of Egyptology, and biographies of *Akhnaton, Pharaoh of Egypt* (1910), *Cleopatra, Queen of Egypt* (1914), *Nero* (1930), *Sappho of Lesbos* (1932), and *Alexander the Great* (1933). In a lighter vein he wrote novels—*Madeline of the Desert* (1920), *The Dweller in the Desert* (1921), *Bedouin Love* (1922), *Saturnalia in Room 23* (1927), etc.—lyrics for revues, and the comic *Laura was My Camel* (1933).

Weil, Simone (1909-1943). Born and educated in Paris. Intellectually precocious and abnormally sensitive to the poverty and sufferings of others, she combined the study of philosophy with personal deprivation, and leftward politics with mystical intensity. She left school-teaching in order to work in a Paris motor factory, and went to Spain to join the republicans in the civil war. After returning to France in 1940 and working as a farm hand, she visited America and then came to England where, after vainly hoping to join the Resistance and be parachuted into France, she virtually killed herself by declining adequate food. A modern voluntary martyr, her posthumous influence has been considerable and widespread through her writings: *L'Enracinement* (1949; English translation, *The Need for Roots*, 1951), *L'Attente de Dieu* (1950; *Waiting for God*, 1951), *La Pesanteur et la Grâce* (1947; *Gravity and Grace*, 1952), *Oppression et Liberté* (1955; *Oppression and Liberty*, 1958), *The Notebooks of Simone Weil* (Eng. trans. 1956).

Weinstein, Nathan Wallenstein. See Nathanael *West.

Welby, T. Earle (Thomas Earle Welby, 1881-1933). Born and educated in India, where he worked as a journalist until he settled in England in 1920 and joined the staff of the *Saturday Review* until 1930, when he transferred to the newly-founded *Week-end Review*, using the pseudonym 'Stet'. He wrote two books on Swinburne (1914; 1926), *A Popular History of English Poetry* (1923), *The Victorian Romantics* (1929); he described his essays and reviews as 'table-talk', collected in *Back Numbers* (by 'Stet' 1929) and *Second Impressions* (1933).

Welch, Denton (1915-1948). Author of *Maiden Voyage* (1943), *In Youth is Pleasure* (1945), *Journals* (1952).

Weldon, John. See Brinsley *Macamara.

Well-made plays. Stage plays obeying conventional technical rules of construction but unlifelike in plot and in presentation of human character. The intellectual and realistic dramatists of the post-1890 period—Bernard *Shaw and others— derided them as mere pieces of 'stage carpentry'. Their popularity, due in the first place to the manifold pieces by Eugène Scribe (1791-1861), lasted down to about 1910, when the later plays of Sir Arthur *Pinero (1855-1934) failed to attract the large public he had held for some twenty-five years. See also Victorien *Sardou.

Well of Loneliness, The. Novel by Radclyffe *Hall published in 1928; banned in Britain soon after publication on account of its lesbian theme, but later circulated without restriction.

Wells, H. G. (Herbert George Wells, 1866-1946). Born at Bromley, Kent, the son of a gardener, county cricketer and small shopkeeper who married a lady's maid in 1853. The boy was taught by his mother before starting at a cottage school whence, after lying up following an accident which fractured a leg, he continued elementary education at a Commercial Academy in Bromley High Street until he was thirteen and began work as a draper's assistant in Windsor. After two miserable months which failed to fit him for apprenticeship, he taught briefly in a Somerset school where his uncle was headmaster. When fifteen he was employed by a chemist in Midhurst, Sussex, but had to leave after a month because his mother (now working as housekeeper at Up Park, the Sussex mansion where she had previously been a lady's maid) could not afford the fees for his training. He had in the meantime taken Latin lessons from the headmaster of Midhurst Grammar School and became a boarder there for a few weeks before returning to the drapery business, now as an apprentice in Southsea. After two of the four years for which the indenture bound him, he went back to Midhurst Grammar School as a student-teacher in charge of a class of small boys, and in the evenings studied for examinations which passed him in 1884 to a free place at the Normal School of Science (since renamed the Imperial College of Science and Technology) in London. There he studied biology under Professor T. H. Huxley, whom he found inspiring, and physics and geology under other professors to whom, as he wrote in after years, he misbehaved as 'a detestable hobbledehoy'. But he took his B.Sc. in 1890 (when he was twenty-four) with first-class honours in zoology and second-class in geology. By that time he had left the Normal School and become a teacher and games master at Holt Academy, Wrexham. While on the football field there, he sustained a severe internal injury which compelled several months of invalidism with his mother at Up Park. This prostration, like the earlier one, enabled him to read abundantly, and he had also begun to write, winning a guinea while he was at Wrexham for a 'sloppy, sentimental, dishonest' story (his own later description) accepted by the Family Herald. He went back to teaching, this time at Henley House School in north-west London, undertaking science, English, and drawing. Concurrently he tutored in biology for a Correspondence College, and produced a Textbook of Biology, published in 1893, when he was twenty-seven, supplementing these activities by conducting laboratory classes of up to thirty-two students. His health again broke down and while convalescing at Eastbourne in 1893 he sent an article 'On Staying at the Seaside' to the Pall Mall Gazette which

started him on regular journalism. Two years before, the Fortnightly Review had printed an article by him, 'The Rediscovery of the Unique', a title which, however puzzling, was more in line with the books he was soon to write than the conventionally-named seaside essay. The *Time Machine, The Wonderful Visit, and a volume of short stories The Stolen Bacillus and Other Incidents, all three published in 1895, brought something new into English literature and made Wells the pioneer of science fiction half a century before it came into vogue after World War II. With The Wheels of Chance in the next year, Love and Mr Lewisham in 1900, and *Kipps in 1905 Wells became the originator of another type in contemporary literature, the 'Little Man' or 'Common Man' who was to be designated later as the key figure of the democratic twentieth century. In these and in The *History of Mr Polly (1910) Wells was at his most humorous and human, drawing considerably upon his own young manhood in schoolmastering and the drapery, even as in *Tono-Bungay (1909) he drew upon Up Park and the Midhurst chemist's shop. His interest in politics and sociology had led him into the *Fabian Society in its early years, but he left it on failing to dominate its policy, though in 1907 he published with the Society his most striking pamphlet This Misery of Boots. Up to 1910 his novels had been divided between those controlled by his powerful scientific and technological imagination and those in which his Dickensian fascination by human character was uppermost. In the former category, among those not already named, The Invisible Man (1897), The *War of the Worlds (1898), The *First Men in the Moon (1901), and The *War in the Air (1908) are outstanding. *Ann Veronica (1909) typified the emancipated woman. From The *New Machiavelli (1911) onward, human character was subordinate to his political and social preoccupations. Waning interest in his novels was compensated by the vast new audience he found with The Outline of History (1920). More and more he pursued his vision of mankind united, the lion with the lamb, in the One World State, but hope receded when World War II came. His final years found him increasingly in despair, with Mind at the End of its Tether (1945) as a sad swan song. Some of his best work is in the Collected Short Stories (1927), with 'The *Country of the Blind' outstanding, and the stories of wonder and humour uniquely entertaining. The account of his own life, *Experiment in Autobiography* (2 vols) came out in 1934.

Welty, Eudora (1909-   ). Born in Mississippi; educated at the State College there and at Wisconsin and Columbia Universities. Author of short stories and novels: *A Curtain of Green* (1941), *The Golden Apples* (1929), *Delta Wedding* (1946), *The Ponder Heart* (1954), *The Optimist's Daughter* (1972).

Wentworth, Patricia (pseudonym of Dora Amy Elles, died 1961). Author of well over fifty crime novels with the elderly Miss Maud Silver ('retired governess of rigid manners and morals but wide charity') as a chief character, knitting endlessly while detecting intermittently.

Werfel, Franz (1890-1945). Born in Prague; educated there and in Vienna. He served with the Austrian army in World War I, but was strongly anti-militarist. After the war he became prominent among the *Expressionist writers with plays—*Goat Song* (1926), *The Eternal Road* (1936)—and novels— *Death of a Poor Man* (1927) and (best known abroad) *The Song of Bernadette* (1942).

Wescott, Glenway (1901-   ). Born in Wisconsin; educated at the University of Chicago. Author of novels: *The Apple of the Eye* (1924), *The Grandmothers* (1912; English edition, *A Family Portrait*), *The Pilgrim Hawk* (1940), *Apartment in Athens* (1945); short stories: *Like a Lover* (1926), *Goodbye, Wisconsin* (1928); essays: *Fear and Trembling* (1932), *Images of Truth* (1962); poems: *The Bitterns* (1920).

Wesker, Arnold (1932-   ). Born in the east-end of London of a Russian refugee father and a Hungarian mother; educated at state schools; first apprenticed to a furniture maker, he became in turn a bookseller's assistant, a farm labourer, a kitchen porter, and a pastry cook, with a spell in the R.A.F. before turning to playwriting while attending a school of film technique. His early plays, *Chicken Soup with Barley* (1957), *Roots* (1959), and *I'm Talking about Jerusalem* (1960) were first performed at the Belgrade Theatre, Coventry, later in London, and published together as *The Wesker Trilogy* (1960). Other plays include *The Kitchen* (1959), *Chips with Everything* (1962), *The Four Seasons* (1965), *Their Very Own and Golden City* (1966), *The Wedding Feast* (1973). He was one of the founders of *Centre 42.

West African Writers. *See* *African Writers.

West, Anthony (1914-   ). Born in England, son of H. G. *Wells and Rebecca *West; worked on the *New Statesman* from 1937 and for the B.B.C. until 1946. Settled in America and became naturalized there. Author of novels—*On a Dark Night* (1949), *Another Kind* (1951)—and a study of D. H. Lawrence (1951).

West Indian Writers. *See* *Caribbean Writers.

West, Nathanael (pseudonym of Nathan Weinstein, 1903-1940). Born in New York; studied philosophy at Brown University, Rhode Island. Spent two years in Paris, then returned to America and published two novels—*The Dream Life of Balso Snell* (1931) and *Miss Lonelyhearts* (1933)—before going in 1935 as a screen writer to Hollywood, which he satirized scathingly in *The Day of the Locust* (1939). He and his wife (sister of Ruth *McKenney the wife of S. J. *Perelman) were killed in a motor accident in California.

West, Dame Rebecca (pseudonym of Cicily Isobel Fairfield, 1892-   ; D.B.E. 1959). Mrs Henry Maxwell Andrews. Born in County Kerry, Ireland; educated in Edinburgh; studied in London for the stage, but acted only for a short time, adopting her pseudonym from Ibsen's *Rosmersholm*. Turning to journalism, she reviewed for the *Freewoman* in 1911 and in 1912 joined the staff of the *Clarion*, writing on politics. While still in her early twenties she gained the reputation of displaying one of the acutest minds and sharpest wit among contemporary writers on literature and politics, and she contributed to numerous papers and periodicals in both Britain and America. She wrote a brief study of *Henry James* (1916), then two novels, *The Return of the Soldier* (1918) and *The Judge* (1922). *The Strange Necessity* (1928) presented an illuminating discussion of James *Joyce together with a selection of her shorter essays. In *Lions and Lambs* (1928), using the pseudonym Lynx, she provided literary sketches to accompany David Low's portrait caricatures of living celebrities, and collaborated again with Low in *The Rake's Progress* (1934), after publishing another novel, *Harriet Hume* (1929). Her most substantial work, *Black Lamb and Grey Falcon* (2 vols, 1942), the product of a journey in Yugoslavia several years before, is a many-

faceted book in which travel, history, and contemporary problems merge. At the end of World War II she became interested in the prevalence of offences against patriotism, and analysed the problem and those concerned in *The Meaning of Treason* (1949) and *A Train of Powder* (1955). *The Harsh Voice* (a group of short novels, 1935), *The Thinking Reed* (1936), *The Fountain Overflows* (1957), and *The Birds Fall Down* (1966) increased her reputation as a creative writer.
And see *H. G. Wells and Rebecca West* by Gordon N. Ray (1974).

West, Victoria Sackville-. *See* V. *Sackville-West.

Westmacott, Mary. *See* Agatha *Christie.

Westermarck, Edvard Alexander (1862-1939). Born in Helsingfors; educated at the University of Finland. Professor of Sociology in the University of London, 1907-30. Author of *The History of Human Marriage* (1891; 5th edn, rewritten, 3 vols, 1921), *The Origin and Development of the Moral Ideas* (2 vols, 1906 and later edns), *Memories of My Life* (Swedish, 1927; English, 1929), *Ethical Relativity* (1932), *Three Essays on Sex and Marriage* (1934), *The Future of Marriage in Western Civilisation* (1936), *Christianity and Morals* (1939).

Westray, Edward. Sent to superintend the restoration work at Cullerne Minster in J. Meade Falkner's *The *Nebuly Coat* (1903), he discovers the truth about the rightful succession to the Blandamer peerage.

Weyman, Stanley (Stanley John Weyman, 1855-1928). Born in Shropshire; educated at Shrewsbury and Oxford. After briefly acting as a history teacher, he studied law and was called to the Bar, practising unsuccessfully for several years. He then began (with *The House of the Wolf*, 1890) the series of robust historical novels which brought him a large fortune. Among them are *A Gentleman of France* (1893), *Under the Red Robe* (1894; dramatized 1896; musical version 1897).

Wharton, Edith (*née* Edith Newbold Jones, 1862-1937). Born in New York; educated at home. Her family was wealthy and both as a girl and after her marriage in 1885 she spent a considerable amount of time in Europe, and from 1906 lived mainly in France. She began her long and distinguished literary career as a short-story writer, but turned to full-length novels with *The Valley of Decision* (1902). *The House of Mirth* (1905), *The Fruit of the Tree* (1907), *The Custom of the Country* (1914), and *The Age of Innocence* (1920) are the most notable of her novels, though more famous is the tragic long short-story **Ethan Frome* (1911). She was permanently influenced by the work of Henry *James, for many years a personal friend. Like him, her preoccupations as a writer of fiction were with social, ethical, cultural and moral interrelationships. In addition to novels and short stories she published *The Writing of Fiction* (1925), *Twelve Poems* (1926), and the autobiographical *A Backward Glance* (1934) which includes entertaining glimpses of Henry James.

What Every Woman Knows. Play in four acts by J. M. *Barrie performed in 1908. Disappointed in their hopes that 'the minister of Galashiels' would marry her, the father and brothers of plain Maggie Wylie determine to find her 'what her heart is set on'—a husband. The police report that a man has been seen climbing into the house after midnight, and when the Wylies keep watch the intruder appears as John Shand, the local railway ticket-collector. He explains that he is desperate for want of books and has been breaking in to use the Wylies' to help him continue the studies he had started at Glasgow University but can no longer afford. Maggie's menfolk strike a bargain to lay out £300 on his education if he signs an undertaking that in five years' time Maggie will have the right to marry him if she so wishes. Shand agrees. Six years later he gets into parliament, marries Maggie, and soon makes a reputation with his speeches after a bad beginning in 'the most atrocious bow-wow public-park manner'. Now his speeches are so witty and humorous that they convulse the House, though Shand himself is entirely humourless. When he falls in love with Lady Sybil Tenterden, Maggie contrives an invitation for both to the country cottage of a mutual friend, telling John that Sybil will 'help and inspire' him. Her hidden expectation that the besotted lovers will bore each other is quickly fulfilled, and Shand at last realizes that it is Maggie as his confidante and typist who has transformed his speeches. She says 'Every man who is high up loves to think that he has done it all himself; and the wife smiles, and lets it go at that. It's our only joke. Every woman knows that.'

Wheatley, H. B. (Henry Benjamin Wheatley, 1838-1917). Born in Chelsea; educated privately. Clerk to the Royal Society, 1861-79; Assistant Secretary to the Society of Arts, 1879-1908. A founder of the *Early English Text Society and its Hon. Secretary, 1864-72. Author of bibliographical works, and of *London Past and Present* (1891), *Hogarth's London* (1909), but best known by his edition of *Pepys's Diary* in several volumes (1894-99), a fuller transcript than any previously published.

Wheeler, Sir Mortimer (Robert Eric Mortimer Wheeler, 1890-   ; knighted 1952). Born in Glasgow, Lecturer in Archaeology, University of Wales, 1920-24; Director, National Museum of Wales, 1924-26; Keeper and Secretary, London Museum, 1926-44; Director-General of Archaeology, India, 1944-48; Secretary of the British Academy from 1949. Directed many archaeological expeditions in Britain, India, Pakistan, and elsewhere. As a broadcaster he stimulated wide public interest in archaeology. Author of many books on Roman and other remains, and of an autobiography *Still Digging* (1955).

Wheeler-Bennett, Sir John (John Wheeler Wheeler-Bennett, 1902-   ; knighted 1959). Born in Kent; educated there and at Malvern. Lecturer in International Law, University of Virginia, 1938-39. Head of the British Political Warfare Mission, New York, 1942-44. Lecturer in International Politics, Oxford, 1946-50; Historical Adviser, Royal Archives, 1959; British Editor-in-Chief of captured German Foreign Ministry archives. Author of *Hindenberg, the Wooden Titan* (1936); *Nemesis of Power: The German Army in Politics 1918-45* (1953), *King George VI: His Life and Reign* (1958); Editor of *Action This Day: Working With Churchill* (1968).

Wheelwright's Shop, The. A classic of craftsmanship by George *Bourne (pseudonym of George Sturt) published in 1923. It begins with the history of the shop at Farnham in Surrey from 1706. The author gave up schoolteaching in 1884 to take over the business when his father died, and his book details the stages in the construction of farm-waggons before tractors displaced horses. 'Farm-waggons' he says 'had been adapted, through ages, so very closely to their own environment that, to understanding eyes, they really looked almost like living organisms. They were so exact . . . the provincial wheelwright could hardly help reading, from the waggon-lines, tales of haymaking and upland fields, of hilly roads and lonely woods and noble horses.'

Where Angels Fear to Tread. Novel by E. M. *Forster published in 1905. Despised by her mother-in-law and sister-in-law as foolish and vulgar, Lilia Herriton, a widow in her early thirties, is encouraged to go for a year's travel in Italy as companion to a younger neighbour, Caroline Abbott, Philip Herriton, Lilia's brother-in-law, much enamoured of Italy, believes that it 'really purifies and ennobles all who visit her'. The letters Lilia writes to the Herritons and to her own nine-year-old daughter Irma encourage the hope that she is 'improving', until they hear that she intends to marry again. Mrs Herriton sends Philip to prevent the marriage, on the ground that it would be an insult to Lilia's husband's memory and to his relatives. Philip learns on reaching the little mountain town of Monteriano that Lilia is already married to Gino Carella, a dentist's son younger than herself. Philip returns to England with Caroline Abbott, who comes to think herself responsible when the marriage turns out badly and Lilia dies in childbirth. Mrs Herriton and her intolerant spinster daughter Harriet, after first declaring that they will have nothing to do with the baby or its Italian father, decide that it is their duty to adopt it, to save it from being badly brought up by Gino. Again Philip is sent to Monteriano, this time with Harriet, to fetch the child. Caroline Abbott also goes independently, with the same purpose. A comic account of an evening at the local opera house, where *Lucia di Lammermoor* is wildly acclaimed by the audience, precedes fruitless interviews with Gino. Caroline finds that he is devoted to his infant son, whom he baths in her presence, and with her help. Refusing to recognize that their mission has failed, Harriett steals the child, but it is killed when the carriage she and Philip are in collides and overturns. The title is from the proverb 'Fools rush in where angels fear to tread'.

Whibley, Charles (1859-1930). Born in Kent; educated at Cambridge; assisted W. E. *Henley on the *Scots Observer* and the *National Observer*, and with him started the Tudor Translations series of reprints. Joined the staff of the *Pall Mall Gazette*; contributed 'Musings Without Method' to *Blackwood's Magazine* monthly for a quarter of a century from 1897. Author of *The Book of Scoundrels*

(1897), *Studies in Frankness* (1910), *Essays in Biography* (1913), *Letters of an Englishman* (1915), *Political Portraits* (1917).

Whipple, Dorothy (died 1966). Educated at English and French convent schools; married A. H. Whipple, a Director of Education. Author of *Young Anne* (1927), *Greenbanks* (1932), *They Knew Mr Knight* (1934), *Because of the Lockwoods* (1949), *Someone at a Distance* (1953), and other novels; short stories: *On Approval* (1935), *After Tea* (1941), *Wednesday* (1961); autobiography: *The Other Day* (1936).

White, Antonia (*née* Antonia Botting, 1899-   ). Educated at a convent school and at St Paul's Girls' School; copywriter, journalist, fashion editor; on staff of the B.B.C. Author of novels and short stories: *Frost in May* (1933), *The Lost Traveller* (1950), *The Sugar House* (1952), *Strangers* (1954), *The Hound and the Falcon* (1966). Made many translations of French books.

White, E. B. (Elwyn Brooks White, 1899-   ). Born in New York; educated at Cornell University. Worked as a reporter and in advertising before joining the *New Yorker*, contributing 'Talk of the Town' for many years. Often described as a serious humorist, he is also a distinguished essayist (*The Second Tree from the Corner*, 1954), a successful writer of children's stories (*Stuart Little*, 1945; *Charlotte's Web*, 1952), a poet (*The Lady is Cold*, 1929), and in collaboration with James *Thurber inquired *Is Sex Necessary?* (1929).

White Fang. Novel by Jack London published in 1905. Two men, Bill and Henry, struggling through the frozen Canadian north with a sled and four dogs, are followed every day by a starving wolf-pack. A she-wolf among them serves as a decoy to lure the dogs at night, and one by one they are killed and devoured. Bill goes out to shoot the decoy but is himself pulled down. Henry, left alone without dogs, is saved when the wolves make off on the trail of other meat. The she-wolf mates with an elder of the pack, One Eye, who outlasts his rivals, and during a famine only one of her five cubs survives. As he grows, some instinct inherited from his mother, who is the offspring of a dog and a wolf, leads him to seek human company and attach himself to a tribe of Indians and accept the chief, Grey Beaver, as a master to be obeyed. Among them he is called White Fang, and he be-

comes increasingly savage as he learns to defend himself from attacks by other dogs. Grey Beaver eventually sells him for whisky to a misshapen scullion in the Yukon, sardonically nicknamed Beauty Smith, whom White Fang defies and hates. Smith beats him into submission and cages him as a fighting-dog to be matched in contests against other animals. White Fang overcomes them all until he is opposed by a bulldog, whose grip on his throat he is unable to shake off. The spectacle is ended by the angry intervention of two newcomers—Matt, a dog-musher (i.e. leader of a sled team) and Weedon-Scott, a mining expert—who prise open the bulldog's jaws. White Fang, nearly dead, is bought from Smith and nursed back to health, but his savage ways persist until Scott gradually wins his devotion by kind treatment, and in his new master's home in California he learns by slow degrees to tolerate other creatures. He finally establishes himself in the family by saving Weedon Scott's father, Judge Scott, from an escaped prisoner who breaks into the house with intent to kill.

White, Patrick (Patrick Victor Martindale White, 1912-   ). Born in London of Australian parents; grew up partly in England, partly in Australia; educated at Cheltenham and Oxford; after service with the R.A.F. in World War II he settled in Australia. From the publication of *Voss* (1957), which won a large annual literary award in 1959, his reputation as a novelist soared and he received much critical attention and praise from reviewers and scholars in English-speaking and other countries. Before *Voss* he had published *Happy Valley* (1939), *The Living and the Dead* (1941), *The Aunt's Story* (1946), *The Tree of Man* (1954), and later *Riders in the Chariot* (1961), *The Eye of the Storm* (1973).

White, Stanford (1853-1906). American architect whose work included buildings in New York and other cities. His name became more widely known on account of his murder by the millionaire playboy Harry K. Thaw, whose wife (Evelyn Nesbit Thaw, former artist's model and showgirl) had been White's mistress. The prolonged series of trials and retrials that followed made the case one of the most notorious in American legal history.

White, Stewart Edward (1873-1946). Born in Michigan; educated there and at Columbia

University Law School. From boyhood he led an adventurous life—gold prospecting, sailing, working as a lumberman, and in Africa at the time of Theodore Roosevelt's hunting expedition there. These varied experiences are reflected in his many novels and travel books, such as *The Westerners* (1901), *The Blazed Trail* (1902), *The Silent Races* (1904), *The Leopard Woman* (1916), *Back of Beyond* (1927), *Wild Geese Calling* (1940); non-fiction: *The Forest* (1903), *African Camp Fires* (1913), *The Forty-Niners* (1918), *Daniel Boone* (1922).

White, T. H. (Terence Hanbury White, 1906-1964). Born in India; educated in England at Cheltenham and Cambridge. After teaching for some years at Stowe School he resigned and chose a solitary life in isolated country places and wrote a succession of highly original books, several derived from Malory's *Morte d'Arthur: The Sword in the Stone* (1939), *The Witch in the Wood* (1940), *The Ill-Made Knight* (1941)—rewritten for a one-volume edition *The Once and Future King* (1958), which became the basis of an American musical play: *Camelot*. White's other outstanding successes were *Mistress Masham's Repose* (1946), a fantasy about descendants of Gulliver's Lilliputians in England and *The Goshawk* (1951), an account of his training of a hawk. He also wrote *Farewell Victoria* (1933), *England Have My Bones* (1936), *The Book of Beasts* (1954), *The Godstone and the Blackymor* (1959). Earlier he published poems, *Loved Helen* (1926), and a novel *They Winter Abroad* (1932) under the pseudonym James Aston.

White, William Allen (1868-1944). Born and educated in Kansas; began as a reporter in his teens. In 1895 he bought a small newspaper published in his home town, the Emporia (Kansas) *Gazette*, being its owner and editor for the rest of his life and gaining nationwide repute and respect by the forceful expression of his independent views, though he was also a stalwart Republican. He republished a number of his *Gazette* articles in *The Editor and His People* (1924) and *Forty Years on Main Street* (1937), and also wrote novels—*A Certain Rich Man* (1909), *In the Heart of a Fool* (1918); short stories: *Stratagems and Spoils* (1901), *In Our Town* (1906); biographies: *Woodrow Wilson* (1924), *Calvin Coolidge* (1925). His *Autobiography* was published anonymously (1946).

White, William Hale. *See* Mark *Rutherford.

Whitefield, Ann. Under her father's will she has John Tanner and Roebuck Ramsden as joint guardians in Bernard Shaw's *Man and Superman* (1903). Indomitably self-willed, she achieves her purposes by subterfuge, laying the responsibility on others, and by such means ensnares John Tanner, who feels himself impelled by the Life Force to marry her.

Whitehead, Alfred North (1861-1947). Born in Ramsgate; educated at Sherborne and Cambridge. Professor of Applied Mathematics, Imperial College of Science, 1914-24; Professor of Philosophy, Harvard University, 1924-37. He was internationally esteemed as one of the foremost mathematical philosophers of his time. His writings, in which he aimed at clarity, were often found obscure, since the abstruse nature of his thinking debarred easy communication. Nevertheless, *Adventures of Ideas* (1933) reached a large audience. In collaboration with Bertrand *Russell he wrote *Principia Mathematica* (3 vols, 1910-13), and among his other books are *Science and the Modern World* (1925), *Symbolism* (1927), *The Aims of Education* (1929), *Nature and Life* (1934), *Modes of Thought* (1938). He evolved a system of philosophy which sought to harmonize religion and mysticism with knowledge and reason.

Whiteheaded boy. A favourite; usually applied to a doting mother's over-indulged son, but sometimes also to a teacher's or employer's pet. There is a play with that title by Lennox *Robinson.

Whiteing, Richard (1840-1928). Born in London; educated privately. After apprenticeship to an engraver of seals and medals he turned to journalism, working for London papers and for the *Manchester Guardian*, whose Paris correspondent he became. While abroad he travelled widely before returning to London to join the staff of the *Daily News*, 1886-99. He wrote several novels, including one by which he is remembered among the pioneers of naturalistic fiction, *No. 5 John Street* (1899), a grim story of life in a London slum.

Whiteoaks. *See* Mazo *de la Roche.

Whiting, John (1917-1963). Born at Salisbury; educated at Taunton and at the R.A.D.A. He worked as an actor before his *Penny for a Song* (1951) was performed after his more serious plays had failed to arouse interest. *Marching Song* (1954) and *The Gates of Summer* (1956), praised by actors and critics, were coldly received by audiences mystified by symbolism and by his 'personal vision of a dark world'. Nevertheless, he succeeded with *The Devils* (1961), based on *The Devils of Loudôn* by Aldous *Huxley, despite its harrowing subject—the martyrdom of a priest during an outbreak of mass hysteria in a French convent in the seventeenth century.

Whitten, Wilfred (died 1942). Best known under his pseudonym John O'London. Assistant editor of *The Academy* 1896-1902; acting editor of *T.P.'s Weekly* 1902-11; founder-editor of *John O' London's Weekly* 1919-36. Author of *Daniel Defoe* (1900), *A Londoner's London* (1913).

Whizz kids. Young people with hastily progressive ideas and contemptuous of established methods.

Wickham, Anna (born 1884). Born in Surrey; taken to Australia in infancy and educated in Sydney; returned to England in 1905 and then studied for a while in Paris as an opera singer. Author of *Songs of John Oland* (U.S. 1918), *The Contemplative Quarry* (1915), *The Man with a Hammer* (1916), *The Little Old House* (1921) and other books of verse.

Wide Sargasso Sea. Novel by Jean *Rhys published in 1966. Designed as an imaginative reconstruction of the earlier life of Mr Rochester's mad wife up to the time she appears in Charlotte Brontë's *Jane Eyre*, it introduces her in girlhood as Antoinette Cosway, a Creole (i.e. born in the Caribbean of English parentage) living in Jamaica in the 1830s. She and her widowed mother, who came as a girl from Martinique, exist in loneliness on an estate fallen into decay after the Emancipation Act of 1833 which freed the slaves, who then reacted with 'No more slavery—why should *anyone* work?' Antoinette, with her mother and her afflicted brother Pierre, live amidst coloured people who in their new freedom despise all Creoles and Europeans, taunting them as 'white niggers' or 'white cockroaches', and poisoning Mrs Cosway's horse. After she remarries, becoming Mrs Mason, their house is attacked and burned down; the helpless Pierre, badly hurt, dies soon after he is rescued from the blazing building, and his mother succumbs to the family taint of insanity. Antoinette is sent to a convent school and is afterwards quickly married to a newly-arrived Englishman not named but inferentially Mr Rochester. Their relationship alternates between passion and estrangement, and is ruptured when he receives blackmailing letters making charges against Antoinette. Robbed of marital comfort, she turns to hatred of her husband, who takes a half-caste mistress, and induces Christophine, an old native servant and reputed witch, to sell her poison to put in his drink, but it fails to kill him. After the death of his father and brother he inherits their wealth and brings Antoinette to England where she is put in charge of Grace Poole and confined in rooms apart, as in *Jane Eyre*.

Widow in the Bye Street, The. Narrative poem in seven-line stanzas rhyming a b a b b c c (rhyme royal) by John *Masefield published in 1912. With something of the naivety of a folk tale and a traditional ballad, it tells how in a little Shropshire town Widow Gurney stitches shrouds to earn a bare living for her child Jimmy and herself until he begins to work on the railway and brings home his wages. He falls in love with a wanton young widow, Anna, who has many lovers, among them Shepherd Ern, though she leads Jimmy to believe that they can be no more than friends for 'my love ended when my husband died'. Nevertheless, Jimmy takes to spending money on her and neglects his mother, who fails to convince him that Anna is a harlot. Later he watches Anna's house and, seeing her and Ern embracing, drinks himself into a murderous frenzy and kills Ern. After he is hanged his mother becomes a crazy wanderer.

The frequent simplicity of phraseology tends towards bathos and was parodied in J. C. *Squire's verses beginning 'Down Lupus Street there is a little pub', travestying Masefield's opening line, 'Down Bye Street, in a little Shropshire town'.

Widowers' Houses. 'An Original Didactic Realistic Play' by Bernard *Shaw. Begun in 1885 on material suggested by William *Archer but not completed (on different lines) until 1892, being performed in that year, the first of Shaw's plays; published in *Plays Unpleasant*, 1898.

While touring on the Continent, Dr Henry Trench, recently qualified, and his middle-aged friend William de Burgh Cokane become acquainted with Mr Sartorius and his daughter Blanche. Trench and Blanche fall in love and Sartorius agrees to their marrying if Trench produces evidence that his aristocratic relatives will receive Blanche into the family. A month later, at their 'handsomely appointed villa in Surbiton', while father and daughter are expecting Trench with favourable evidence, Sartorius's servile Cockney rent-collector, Lickcheese, calls with money, and is abused and summarily dismissed for spending small sums on essential minor repairs to Sartorius's dilapidated slum tenements. Trench and Cokane arrive before Lickcheese goes, and while Sartorius is out of the room the rent-collector asks them to intercede. Trench is so aghast at Lickcheese's account of how he extorts rents from virtually destitute tenants, that he refuses to agree to Blanche's accepting any income from her father, and the engagement is broken off. Enraged by this, Sartorius deflates Trench by demonstrating that he is equally culpable since his own income is from high interest on a mortgage on the same slum property. Some time later Lickcheese returns, now prosperous, having devised a crooked means of making large sums from compensation on buildings scheduled for demolition. Trench is induced to stand in with this scheme when Sartorius threatens to borrow money elsewhere and pay off the mortgage, thus depriving him of the main part of his income. His capitulation is completed by Blanche's subtle amorous wheedling, although he had previously had experience of her shrewish temper, of which her devoted maid is the principal victim.

Wiggin, Kate Douglas (*née* Kate Douglas Smith, 1856-1923). Born in Philadelphia; educated in Massachusetts; after training as a teacher, started a kindergarten school in San Francisco. Visiting the British Isles a number of times, she produced the long-popular *Penelope's English Experiences* (1900) and *Penelope's Irish Experiences* (1901), outstripped in popularity by *Rebecca of Sunnybrook Farm* (1903) and *New Chronicles of Rebecca* (1907). Her autobiography *My Garden of Memory* (1923) was completed shortly before she died. *See also* Jane Helen *Findlater.

Wilcher, Thomas Loftus. Sara Monday's bachelor employer and elderly lover in Joyce Cary's *Herself Surprised* (1941), and the narrator in *To be a Pilgrim* (1942). His plan to marry Sara is frustrated by his family, who doubt his sanity and commit him to the care of a niece.

Wilcox, Ella Wheeler (*née* Ella Wheeler, 1850-1919). Born in Wisconsin and educated at the University there. She began to write copiously while still a child, and from 1872, when her first book, *Drops of Water*, a collection of temperance verses was published, she was for the rest of her life the most widely read and quotable poet of her generation, though to sophisticated readers her 'homely philosophy', naïve eroticism, sentimentality, and metrical jog-trot, made her a figure of fun. That *Poems of Passion* (1883) was regarded as immoral when published is a measure of the subsequent changes of attitude in regard to morals. She published many other volumes of verse and prose, including *The Story of a Literary Career* (1905) and *The Worlds and I* (1918).

Wilcox family. In E. M. Forster's *Howards End* (1910): **Mrs Wilcox,** owner of Howards End; her dying wish to give the house to Margaret Schlegel is ignored. Her husband, **Henry,** a prosperous City merchant, whose second wife Margaret becomes. **Charles,** the elder son, partner in his father's business; later receives a three-year sentence for the manslaughter of Leonard Bast. **Paul,** the younger son, whose flirtatious evening with Helen Schlegel leaves an indelible emotional impression on her.

Wilde, Oscar (Oscar Fingal O'Flahertie Wills Wilde, 1854-1900). Born in Dublin; educated there and at Oxford; won the Newdigate Prize for Poetry at the University with *Ravenna*. He became a leader in the aesthetic movement with its principle of art for art's sake, and paraded its extravagances in dress and demeanour. He published *Poems* in 1881, *The Happy Prince* (fairy tales, 1888), *Lord Arthur Savile's Crime* (short stories, 1891), *The Picture of Dorian Grey* (a novel, 1891), *Intentions* (essays, 1891). He visited the United States for a lecture tour in 1882, and had a play, *Vera*, produced unsuccessfully in New York. Back in London, in the next year the first of his successful comedies, *Lady Windermere's Fan* (1892), was staged, followed by *A Woman of No Importance* (1893), *An Ideal Husband* (1895), and his masterpiece *The Importance of Being Earnest* (also 1895). The brilliance of his conversation, his mastery of epigram, and the audacity and polish of his wit had given him an outstanding place in society, and the same qualities made permanent in his plays ensured him a unique reputation in the theatre. He was, however, provoked into bringing a libel action against the Marquess of Queensbury, who objected to Wilde's association with his son, Lord Alfred Douglas. When the action was dismissed, Wilde was arrested and, having been convicted of homosexual practices, received a sentence of two years' imprisonment with hard labour. After his release in 1897, *The Ballad of Reading Gaol* (1898) was published, and after his death *De Profundis* (1905), abbreviated from a withheld letter to Lord Alfred Douglas written in prison (published in full, 1950). Wilde's plays disappeared from the stage and his books were ostracized after his conviction, but his literary reputation was gradually restored in the new century and by the mid-century, when the moral climate had undergone a fundamental change, Wilde the man was widely regarded as a martyr. But fair judgment, uncoloured by hero-worship, has put *The Importance of Being Earnest* on no lower level than the best of Sheridan, while his other plays, as late as the 1960s, were being revived successfully. His *Salome*, first written in French (1893), survives in German adaptation as the libretto for Richard Strauss's opera (1905).

Wilde, Percival (1887-1953). Born in New York; graduated at Columbia. From book reviewing he progressed to short stories and one-act plays, the latter finding an outlet in variety programmes and more importantly in the smaller repertory theatres. Among published collections are *Dawn and other One-Act Plays of Life Today* (1915), *Eight Comedies for Little Theatres* (1922), *Three-Minute Plays* (1927), etc. and several volumes of fiction. He also wrote *The Craftsmanship of the One-Act Play* (1923).

Wilder, Robert (1901-   ). Born of Scottish-Spanish parentage in Virginia; educated in Florida and at Columbia University. After a dozen years or so in publicity, he went into journalism in New York and on to Hollywood as a script writer, having meanwhile had two plays produced in New York with results which did not encourage him to continue as a dramatist, though a few years later his second novel *Flamingo Road* (1942) was adapted both for stage and film. Other novels: *God Has a Long Face* (1940), *Out of the Blue* (1943), *Written on the Wind* (1946), *Wait for Tomorrow* (1950), *And Ride a Tiger* (1951), *The Wine of Youth* (1955).

Wilder, Thornton (Thornton Niven Wilder, 1897-   ). Born in Wisconsin; taken to China in early boyhood, he began his schooling there; educated later at American universities and then in Rome. For several years from 1921 he was a schoolmaster in New Jersey, becoming subsequently Professor of English at the University of Chicago, 1930-36. Having turned to creative writing, he had a distinguished though limited success with his first novel, *The Cabala* (1926). A year later *The *Bridge of San Luis Rey* brought him both critical acclaim and wide popularity. *The Woman of Andros* (1930) and *Heaven's My Destination* (1934) are lesser novels than *The *Ides of March* (1948), a brilliantly imaginative endeavour at historical re-creation. In 1928 *The Angel That Troubled the Waters* introduced him as a dramatist, this and a second volume of one-act plays, *The Long Christmas Dinner* (1931), paving the way for the high success of the full-length plays *Our Town* (1938), *The Matchmaker* (1954), and *The *Skin of Our Teeth* (1942). Though the last named play exhibited Wilder's readiness to experiment, he was in essence a traditionalist whose inventive skill did not outpace his attention to style. Other novels: *The Eighth Day* (1967), *Theophilus North* (1974).

Wilkins, Vaughan (William Vaughan Wilkins, 1890-1959). Born in London. Worked as a journalist, becoming Editor of the short-lived London morning *Daily Call* and then Assistant Editor of the *Daily Express*, before the success of his first published novel *And So—Victoria* (1937) led him to abandon journalism. He continued to deal imaginatively with, mainly, the eighteenth and early nineteenth centuries, later novels including *Fanfare for a Witch* (1954).

Wilkinson, Iris Guiver. *See* Robin *Hyde.

Wilkinson, Louis (Louis Umfreville Wilkinson, 1881-1966). Born at Aldeburgh; educated there and at Radley and Oxford, whence, on account of an anti-Christian outburst, he and three companions were sent down; later he was admitted at Cambridge, where his intellectual gifts gave him eminence among a group which included J. C. *Squire and others who were later to become better known than himself. He was a great though in some ways reluctant admirer of J. C. *Powys and his books, and wrote a biographical study of the three Powys brothers, *Welsh Ambassadors*

(1936). After leaving Cambridge he lectured intermittently in America from 1905 to 1919 and was a University Extension lecturer in England from 1909 to 1945. He used the pseudonym Louis *Marlow for certain novels, but under his own name wrote *The Buffoon* (1916) and *A Chaste Man* (1917).

Wilkinson, Miss. Daughter of a clergyman and a friend of Philip Carey's uncle and aunt in Somerset Maugham's *Of Human Bondage* (1915). Though twice Philip's age she seduces him.

Willey, Basil (1897-   ). Born in London; educated at University College School and Cambridge. Professor of English Literature in the University of Cambridge (1946-64). Author of *The Seventeenth Century Background* (1934), *The Eighteenth Century Background* (1940), *Nineteenth Century Studies* (1949), *Darwin and Butler: Two Versions of Evolution* (1959), *The English Moralists* (1964), *Cambridge and other Memories 1920-1953* (1968).

Williams, Charles (Charles Walter Stansby Williams, 1886-1945). Born in London; educated at St Albans and University College, London. On the editorial staff of the Oxford University Press for many years and until his death, while also lecturing in London County Council evening institutes and during World War II in Oxford, where the University made him an honorary M.A. in 1944. As a writer he began with *The Silver Stair* (1912), a book of verse in the early Yeats mode. His later poems drew increasingly close to changing contemporary tendencies as he came personally within the orbit of the T. S. Eliot circle. In 1936 his Canterbury Festival play, *Thomas Cranmer of Canterbury*, followed in the wake of the new religious drama stemming from Eliot's *Murder in the Cathedral*, though Williams in all his writings displayed originality which tended towards eccentricity and caused many to find him obscure. From *Taliessin in Logres* (1938) he was immersed in the Arthurian legends, culminating in *The Arthurian Torso*, finished by C. S. *Lewis, his close friend and admirer, and published in 1948. He also wrote several novels which he described as 'metaphysical thrillers'—*War in Heaven* (1930), *Many Dimensions* (1931), *The Place of the Lion* (1931), *The Greater Trumps* (1932), *Descent into Hell* (1937) among them. These display his ranging preoccupations with religion, mysticism, sin, and the occult,

shown outside fiction in his theological books, *He Came Down from Heaven* (1937), *Descent of the Dove* (1939), *The Forgiveness of Sins* (1942). He also wrote *Witchcraft* (1941), several biographies—*James I* (1934), *Elizabeth* (1936), *Henry VII* (1937)—and criticism, including *The English Poetic Mind* (1932) and *The Figure of Beatrice* (1943), a product of his interest in Dante. See also Gerard Manley *Hopkins.

Williams, Emlyn (1905-   ). Born in Flintshire of a Welsh-speaking family; educated in Dorset and Geneva and at Oxford. Rejecting school-teaching, he turned to the stage and from 1927 acted in many plays in England and America. His own early plays were eclipsed by *A Murder Has Been Arranged* (1930), but his most spectacular success as author and actor was with *Night Must Fall* (1935). Among numerous other plays *The Corn is Green* (1938) and *The Light of Heart* (1940) are outstanding. From 1951 he gave Readings from Dickens in period costume and following Dickens's own programmes; and from 1955 presented *A Boy Growing Up*, another one-man show, based on the life and writings of Dylan *Thomas. Autobiography: *George* (1961), *Emlyn* (1973).

Williams, Sir Harold (Harold Herbert Williams, 1880-1964; knighted 1951). Born in Tokyo; educated privately and at Cambridge. After writing *Two Centuries of the English Novel* (1911) and *Modern English Writers* (1918; 3rd edn, 1942) he devoted himself mainly to exact textual scholarship, specializing in 18th-century literature and producing critical editions of *Gulliver's Travels* (1926), *The Poems of Jonathan Swift* (1937), *The Journal to Stella* (1948) and *The Correspondence of Jonathan Swift* (3 vols, 1963). He was President of the Bibliographical Society from 1938 to 1944.

Williams, Sir Ifor (1881-1965; knighted 1947). Born near Bangor; educated there and at the University of Wales. After holding appointments in the University College of North Wales from 1906, he became Professor of Welsh Language and Literature there in 1929 and until his retirement in 1947. He published many works in Welsh and as well as being an eminent scholar he was a brilliant interpreter of the national literature.

Williams, Iolo Aneurin (1890-1962). Born in Middlesbrough; educated at Rugby and Cambridge. Brother of the following. In bibliography his *Points in Eighteenth-Century Verse* (1934) became a standard reference work.

Williams, Orlo (Orlando Cyprian Williams, 1883-1967). Educated at Eton and Oxford. Beginning his career as a Clerk in the House of Commons he retired in 1948 as Clerk of Committees there. Contributed literary criticism to leading periodicals; published *Contemporary Criticism* (1924), *Some Great English Novels* (1926), etc. and several historical volumes on the procedure, topography, and clerical organization of the House of Commons.

Williams, Oscar (1900-1964). Born and educated in Brooklyn, by his own account, though another version suggests that he was born in Russia and taken to America in childhood. After publishing two volumes of poems, *The Golden Darkness* (1921) and *In Gossamer Grey* (1921), he went into advertising and produced no more poetry until *Hibernalia* (1938), followed by *The Man Coming Towards You* (1940) and *That's All That Matters* (1945) and *Selected Poems* (1947). He also compiled many anthologies of poetry, English and American, beginning with *The War Poets* (1945).

Williams, Tennessee (Thomas Lanier Williams, 1911-   ). Born in Columbus, Mississippi; educated in St Louis, and at Missouri, Iowa, and Washington Universities after working for some time as a clerk. He was awarded a Rockefeller Fellowship in 1940, and, having passed through various occupations, took employment in Hollywood and there wrote *The Glass Menagerie* (1945) which lofted him into the celebrity which blazed into immediate contemporary fame when *A *Streetcar Named Desire* followed in 1947 and made him one of America's most applauded playwrights. The momentum of success on stage and screen carried him above the critical and moral doubts occasionally expressed about his plays, and *The Rose Tattoo* (1951), *Camino Real* (1953), **Cat on a Hot Tin Roof* (1955), *The Night of the Iguana* (1961) found a welcoming public, as did his films—*Baby Doll* (1957) and others—and a novel, *The Roman Spring of Mrs Stone* (1950).

Williams, Valentine (George Valentine Williams, 1883-1946). Born in London; educated at Downside and in Germany. Became a foreign correspondent for, in turn, Reuters and the *Daily Mail*, reporting in 1923, as a 'scoop',

the discovery of Tutankhamen's tomb at Luxor. Author of numerous mystery novels— *The Man With the Clubfoot* (1918) and other 'Clubfoot' books, *The Yellow Streak* (1922), *The Crouching Beast* (1928), *Death Answers the Bell* (1932), *The Clue of the Rising Moon* (1935), *The Fox Growls* (1939). Autobiography: *The World of Action* (1938).

Williams, William Carlos (1883-1963). Born in New Jersey; educated in Geneva; studied medicine at the University of Pennsylvania and in Leipzig; practised as a physician. As a poet he first associated with the *Imagists but later evolved what he called Objectivism, in which form and meaning are single and identical. Though his poetry is essentially intellectual and therefore restricted in appeal, critics accord him high rank among the American *avant-garde* poets: *Collected Later Poems* (1950), *Collected Earlier Poems* (1951); *Selected Essays* (1954); *Autobiography* (1951).

Williams-Ellis, Amabel (*née* Amabel Strachey, 1894-   ). Born in Surrey, daughter of J. St Loe *Strachey and sister of Lytton *Strachey; educated privately; married Clough Williams-Ellis, architect. Author of *An Anatomy of Poetry* (1922); *Noah's Ark* (1926), *Volcano* (1931), *To Tell the Truth* (1933), *Learn to Love First* (1939) and other novels; children's books; *Exquisite Tragedy: An Intimate Life of John Ruskin* (1928).

Williams-Ellis, Sir Clough (1883-   ). Educated at Oundle and Cambridge. Carried out many architectural works; owned, designed, and built the model village resort of Portmeirion, North Wales. Author of numerous books on architecture, town and country planning, and related subjects. Knighted 1972.

Williamson, A. M. (*née* Alice Muriel Livingston, 1869-1933; Mrs C. N. Williamson). Born in New York; educated privately. Settled in England from 1893; married C. N. Williamson in 1895, and wrote the novels published jointly under their names. The best of these—*The Lightning Conductor* (1902), *Scarlet Runner* (1908), and others—utilized engagingly and usually excitingly the then-new and rapidly developing interest in motor travel.

Williamson, C. N. (Charles Norris Williamson, 1859-1920). Born at Exeter; educated in London at University College; studied science and engineering but turned to journalism. In 1891 founded and edited a weekly periodical, *Black and White*. Wrote many articles largely concerned with motor travel, and his name appeared as collaborator with his wife on novels of which she was said to be sole author (see above). Before they met he wrote a *Life of Thomas Carlyle* (2 vols, 1881).

Williamson, Henry (1895-   ). Born in Bedfordshire. Active service on the Western front throughout World War I had a shattering effect, and after the war he struggled for a while as a journalist, living a hard and friendless life until he left London and, tramping to the West Country, settled on Exmoor; later lived in Devon and ultimately farmed in Norfolk. Beginning with *The Beautiful Years* (1921), the first of a sequence of four novels collectively entitled *The Flax of Dream* and including *Dandelion Days* (1922), *The Dream of Fair Women* (1924), and *The Pathway* (1928), he gathered a gradually increasing audience, which was enlarged into a popular and enduring one when *Tarka the Otter* (1927) was published. This and *Salar the Salmon* (1935) demonstrated his unique ability to write sympathetically and movingly yet unsentimentally about non-human creatures. Though a lifelong admirer of the works of Richard Jefferies and often regarded mainly as his disciple, Williamson's books are not confined to natural-history themes. *The Wet Flanders Plain* (1929) is among the most impressive firsthand records of the miseries of war. His many other volumes include *The Patriot's Progress* (1930), *Life in a Devon Village* (1932), *T. E. Lawrence: Genius of Friendship* (1941), *The Story of a Norfolk Farm* (1941), *Tales of Moorland and Estuary* (1953), *The Innocent Moon* (1961). His most ambitious undertaking was the fifteen-novel sequence *Chronicle of Ancient Sunlight* begun with *The Dark Lantern* (1951) and completed with *The Gale of the World* (1969).

Williamson, Hugh Ross (1901-   ). Anglican clergyman from 1943 until he joined the Roman Catholic Church in 1955, having previously been Assistant Editor of the *Yorkshire Post*, 1925-30, and Editor of *The Bookman*, 1930-34. Author of many books, including *John Hampden* (1933), *King James I* (1936), *The Gunpowder Plot* (1951), *Enigmas of History* (1957) and plays.

Williamson, J. A. (James Alexander Williamson,

1886-1964). Educated at Watford Grammar School and the University of London. Assistant master at Westminster City School, 1910-37. Author of numerous studies of mainly maritime history including *Maritime Enterprise 1485-1558* (1913), *The Voyages of the Cabots* (1929), *The Age of Drake* (1938), *The Ocean in English History* (1941), *Great Britain and the Empire* (1944), *The Tudor Age* (1953), *The English Channel: a History* (1959).

Willis, George Anthony Armstrong. *See* Anthony *Armstrong.

Willowes, Laura Erminia. Central character in Sylvia Townsend Warner's *Lolly Willowes* (1926). She settles in the Chilterns and has uncommon experiences in the hamlet of Great Mop.

Wilson, Angus (Angus Frank Johnstone Wilson, 1913-   ). Born at Bexhill; educated at Westminster School and Oxford. Worked in the Foreign Office, 1942-46, following a period on the British Museum staff, to which he returned after the war, becoming Deputy Superintendent of the Reading Room from 1949 until he retired in 1955, having had considerable success with two volumes of short stories—*The Wrong Set* (1949) and *Such Darling Dodos* (1950), in which a compellingly readable style more than compensated a determination to exhibit human character without gloss. Turning then to novels, he exercised an equally corrosive view of humanity at greater length if with less effect in *Hemlock and After* (1952), *Anglo-Saxon Attitudes* (1956), *The Middle Age of Mrs Eliot* (1958), *The Old Men at the Zoo* (1961), *As If By Magic* (1973). His other writings include a study of *Emile Zola* (1950); a play, *The Mulberry Bush* (1955); *The World of Charles Dickens* (1970). Professor of English Literature, University of East Anglia, from 1966. Chairman, National Book League from 1971.

Wilson, Sir Arnold (Arnold Talbot Wilson, 1884-1940). Educated at Clifton and Sandhurst; served in the army and in the political department in India, and later held official and commercial appointments in Persia. Although in his middle fifties when World War II started, he joined the R.A.F. as a rear-gunner and was shot down a few months later. Author of *The Persian Gulf* (1928), *The Suez Canal* (1933), *Walks and Talks* (1934), *Thoughts and Talks* (1938), *Gallantry* (1939).

Wilson, Colin (Colin Henry Wilson, 1931-
). Educated in Leicester; spent several
years in various occupations until his philosophical volume, *The Outsider* (1956)—
highly praised by reviewers, some of whom
had cooler second thoughts—started his
career as a writer on miscellaneous subjects—
metaphysics, religion, music, murder, sex,
etc.

Wilson, Edmund (1895-1972). Born in New
Jersey; educated in Pennsylvania and at
Princeton. Worked on New York journals,
including *Vanity Fair* and the *New Republic*,
later becoming book reviewer and contributor of other articles to the **New Yorker*.
Though his standing as a literary critic and
political writer has been variously assessed
by others similarly engaged, his essays
reached an uncommonly wide and attentive
public, both in periodicals and when republished in *Axel's Castle* (1931), *The Triple
Thinkers* (1938), *To the Finland Station* (1940),
The Wound and the Bow (1941), and other
volumes. He wrote a few plays and some
poems, and the novels *I Thought of Daisy*
(1929) and *Memoirs of Hecate County* (1946),
the latter receiving much publicity on account
of charges of obscenity, which did not restrict
its circulation.

Wilson, F. P. (Frank Percy Wilson, 1889-1963).
Born in Birmingham; educated there at King
Edward's School and the University and at
Oxford, where he was eventually appointed
Merton Professor of English Literature,
1947-57, after holding university appoint-
ments elsewhere. He accumulated a know-
ledge of Elizabethan literature almost un-
rivalled in his time, producing editions of
contemporary plague pamphlets by Dekker
and others. Author of *Elizabethan and
Jacobean* (1945), *Shakespeare and the New
Bibliography* (1945), *Marlowe and the Early
Shakespeare* (1953), *Seventeenth Century
Prose* (1960).

Wilson, Harry Leon (1867-1939). Born in
Oregon; worked as a boy in his father's news-
paper office; from 1896-1902 was editor of a
humorous periodical, *Puck*. Author of *Zig
Zag Tales* (1896) and of novels including
Ruggles of Red Gap (1915) and *Merton of the
Movies* (1922) which became popular films.

Wilson, J. Dover (John Dover Wilson, 1881-
1969). Born in London; educated at Lancing
and Cambridge. In his career as an educationist he was, in turn, assistant master at Whit-

gift Grammar School, lecturer in English at
Goldsmith's College, Board of Education
Inspector for Adult Education, 1912-24,
Professor of Education, University of
London, 1924-35, Professor of Rhetoric and
English Literature, University of Edinburgh,
1935-45. His wider contemporary repute,
however, was based on his books on Shakes-
peare, which included *Life in Shakespeare's
England* (1911), *The Essential Shakespeare*
(1932), *What Happens in Hamlet* (1935), *The
Fortunes of Falstaff* (1943), *Shakespeare's
Happy Comedies* (1962), and erudite textual
studies, reflected in his editing of the New
Cambridge Shakespeare (1921-66) for which
**Quiller-Couch was co-editor until his death
in 1944. *Milestones on the Dover Road*
(autobiography, 1969).

Wilson, J. G. (John Gideon Wilson, 1876-
1963). Born and educated in Glasgow, where
his parents were bookbinders. Before he was
thirteen he became a booksellers' apprentice
in Glasgow and remained in Scotland until
1908, when he migrated to London and two
years later became manager of Jones &
Evans's bookshop in the City, to which many
well-known writers gravitated for talk with
Wilson and among themselves. After some
years there he went to manage Bumpus's
famous bookshop in Oxford Street, moved
with it to other quarters and became chairman and managing director of the firm. He
loved as well as sold books; they were his life,
and until his last years he was daily visible or
semi-hidden among them in the shop that he
always made more than a shop. His eminence
in the trade made Wilson the ideal author for
The Business of Bookselling (1930).

Wilson, Philip Whitwell (1875-1956). Born in
Westmorland; educated at Kendal and Cambridge. Liberal M.P., 1906-10; then parliamentary reporter and later American correspondent for the *Daily News*. Author of
William Pitt the Younger (1930), *The Romance
of the Calendar* (1938), novels and religious
books; edited an abridged version of *The
Greville Diary* (1927).

Wilson, Romer (*née* Florence Roma Muir
Wilson, 1891-1930; Mrs Edward J. **O'Brien).
Born in Sheffield; educated at Richmond
(Surrey) and studied law at Cambridge;
worked in the Ministry of Agriculture; after
marriage lived in Italy and settled in
Switzerland. Her early death cut short a
literary career of fine achievement and

greater promise. Author of *Martin Schüler* (1918), *All These Young Men* (1919), *The Death of Society* (1921), *Latter-Day Symphony* (1927), *Tender Advice* (1935), and other novels; a play, *The Social Climbers* (1927); and a biography of Emily Brontë, *All Alone* (1928).

Wilson, Woodrow (Thomas Woodrow Wilson, 1856-1924). Born in Virginia; educated privately and at Princeton, Virginia and Johns Hopkins Universities; practised law before accepting university appointments and becoming from 1890 to 1910 Professor of Jurisprudence and Politics at Princeton University and President of the University, 1902-10. He was Governor of New Jersey, 1911-13, and 28th President of the United States, 1913-20. Declared war on Germany in 1917, and having advocated a League of Nations he attended the Versailles Peace Conference in 1919, but afterwards, failing to win American support for the League Covenant, never fully recovered from his consequent complete breakdown in health. He wrote *Congressional Government* (1885), *An Old Master and Other Political Essays* (1893), *Mere Literature and Other Essays* (1896), *George Washington* (1896), *A History of the American People* (1902), *The New Freedom* (1916).

Wimsey, Lord Peter. Amateur detective in crime stories by Dorothy L. *Sayers.

Winch, John. *See* Marjorie *Bowen.

Wind in the Willows, The. Nature fantasy by Kenneth *Grahame published in 1908. Though written for young readers and long established as a children's classic, it is enjoyable by adults also through its open-air atmosphere and delicate word-painting of country and river scenes. The adventures of Water Rat, Mole, Toad, and Badger are humanized on a lilliputian scale, while retaining their animal perceptions and responses, and there is a delightful and occasionally touching sense of comradeship between the four. Mr Toad is a brilliant comic creation, mad about motor cars, a passion that leads to imprisonment in a medieval-type castle, from which he escapes disguised as a washerwoman and finds his imposing residence, Toad Hall, taken over by the stoats and weasels. His three friends restore him to his home by defeating the invaders in a fierce battle; after which Toad, not for the first time, promises to turn over a new leaf. They resume their peaceful summer evening strolls in the Wild Wood, and Water Rat no doubt resumes his beloved pastime of 'messing about in boats'.

Wine, Water and Song. The poems from G. K. Chesterton's novel *The *Flying Inn* (1914), published separately in 1915.

Wings of the Dove, The. Novel by Henry *James published in 1902. When her mother dies, Kate Croy goes to live with her rich widowed Aunt Maud (Mrs Lowder), who then offers to adopt her on condition that she breaks entirely with her handsome but disreputable father. Kate, finding Aunt Maud overbearing, proposes to reject the offer and live with Mr Croy, but he declines and she settles in the aunt's house at Lancaster Gate in west London. The girl has meanwhile fallen in love with Merton Densher, a Fleet Street journalist, and engages herself to him without consulting her aunt, who plans to marry Kate to Lord Mark or some other 'great' man. Densher is sent by his paper to America for six months to write a series of articles. While he is away, an old school friend of Mrs Lowder's, Mrs Susan Shepherd Stringham, comes to London from America (via the Continent) with a very wealthy girl, Milly Theale, to whom she is acting as companion. Milly and her friend are taken up enthusiastically by Mrs Lowder's Society acquaintances, and an intimate friendship develops between Milly and Kate. After Densher's return, it quietly emerges that he and Milly have met in New York and been mutually attracted. Having undisclosed reasons to consult Sir Luke Strett, an eminent surgeon, Milly is advised by him to rest happily in sunshine. She and Mrs Stringham, with Mrs Lowder and Kate, go to Venice, where Densher and Lord Mark visit them. It has become apparent that Milly is desperately ill and is also deeply in love with Densher, of whose secret engagement to Kate she is unaware. Recognizing that the girl is dying, Kate urges Densher to propose to Milly. As her husband he would inherit money and so make the way clear for Kate to marry him. The plan is wrecked by Lord Mark who, also fortune-hunting, proposes to Milly. Rejected, he maliciously informs her of Densher's engagement to Kate. After Milly's death, Densher receives a sealed envelope she left for him. Certain that it contains a bequest, he takes it, still sealed, to Kate, who burns it unopened. He also leaves her to choose whether or not to open the communication he receives later from Milly's executors. Her reply is ambiguous, though her knowledge of the facts can be deduced from her saying 'She did it *for* us. . . . I used to call her . . . a dove. Well, she stretched out her wings. . . . They cover us.'

Winslow Boy, The. Play in four acts by Terence *Rattigan performed and published in 1946. Ronnie Winslow, a fourteen-year-old cadet, is expelled from the Royal Naval College at Osborne on a charge of stealing a five-shilling postal order and forging the signature of a fellow cadet. He denies the accusation and convinces his family that he is innocent. His father, determined to fight to the end what he considers manifest injustice, applies to the Admiralty for a Court Martial but is fobbed off with an 'independent inquiry', at which the boy is not represented by counsel, solicitors, or friends. The charge is upheld. Pursuing the case, Mr Winslow instructs his solicitors to offer the brief to the best procurable advocate, Sir Robert Morton, who questions Ronnie in the presence of his parents and sister Catherine, and appears to be antagonistic. The boy continues to deny the theft but is made hysterical by the seemingly brutal questioning, whereupon Morton astonishes the hearers by declaring 'The boy is plainly innocent. I accept the brief.' A civil trial having been refused by the Admiralty, it is proposed to sue the Crown by Petition of Right, which needs endorsement by the Attorney-General; or to get the Director of Public Prosecutions to act. The Admiralty continue their refusal to reopen the case, until the First Lord, finding himself under attack from all sides in a Commons debate, consents that the Petition shall be endorsed. Bearing the heavy expense of the case makes it impossible for Mr Winslow to maintain his elder son Dickie at Oxford, while a clash of opinions with her fiancé about the ethics of continuing the proceedings has broken Catherine's engagement. The trial lasts for several days and appears to give the family little cause for optimism, until the postmistress's evidence of identity and that of the handwriting expert are discredited and the Admiralty acknowledge in Court that the boy is innocent. It then appears that Sir Robert Morton has in the meantime refused appointment as Lord Chief Justice in order to remain with the case and 'Let Right be done'.
The main theme of the play was suggested by

the facts of the Archer-Shee case, which excited national indignation and finally successful protest in 1910. The defending Counsel was Sir Edward Carson (1854-1935), who spent ten days in Court for a nominal fee, declining a far more profitable brief.

Winsor, Kathleen (1919-   ). Born in Minnesota; educated at the University of California. Author of *Forever Amber* (1944), *Star Money* (1950), *The Lovers* (1942), *America, With Love* (1957).

Winter, John Strange (pseudonym of Henrietta Eliza Vaughan Palmer, 1856-1911; Mrs Arthur Stannard). Born and educated in York. A prolific writer, her first novel, *Bootle's Baby* (1885), is most remembered by its title, though Ruskin commended her books as providing 'the most finished and faithful rendering ever yet given of the character of the British soldier'.

Winter, Keith (John Keith Winter, 1906-   ). Born in North Wales; son of the Professor of Agriculture at Bangor University College; educated at Berkhamsted, and at Oxford after working for a few months in the London offices of the American Express and as a schoolmaster. Best known for *The Rats of Norway* (1933), dramatized from his novel with the same title published in 1932, and *The Shining Hour* (performed 1934). Other works include: plays— *Ringmaster* (1936), *Old Music* (1937), *Weights and Measures* (1938); novels— *Other Man's Saucer* (1930), *Impassioned Pygmies* (1936).

Winters, Yvor (Arthur Yvor Winters, 1900-1968). Born in Chicago; educated at Chicago, Colorado, and Stanford Universities. Assistant Professor of English at Stanford from 1928; Professor from 1949. Though a distinguished poet (*Collected Poems*, 1960), he was more celebrated for the critical writings collected in *In Defence of Reason* (1947) and *The Function of Criticism* (1957).

Wise, Thomas James (1859-1937). Book collector and forger of 'rare editions'. He was first in business as a wine merchant, but in early years acquired a habit of book-buying which enabled him to build up the famous *Ashley Library consisting mainly of genuine and rare first editions of English poets and playwrights from Ben Jonson to later times. He also acted as agent for wealthy Americans whose desiderata he sought for and sold to them when found at prices which do not appear to have netted him any exorbitant profit. Until 1934 his reputation as a collector and bibliographer ranked him with the greatest in that field, more especially as he had 'discovered' a number of poems by 19th-century authors in editions which pre-dated any hitherto known and were therefore of unexampled rarity. In 1934 two younger bibliographers, John Carter and Graham Pollard produced *An Enquiry into the Nature of Certain Nineteenth Century Pamphlets*, in which they advanced evidence based upon the chemical analysis of paper and upon the history of printing types showing that certain editions of, for example, Mrs Browning's *Sonnets from the Portuguese*, and Tennyson's *Morte d'Arthur*, among others, which had been brought to notice by Wise, could not have been printed and published as early as the dates appearing on them and which Wise as an accepted expert had vouched for. The uniquely skilled detective work carried out by Carter and Pollard pointed to only one possible conclusion: namely that Wise had been the prime mover in forging a considerable number of 'first editions' and in foisting them on the rare-book market. Wise made no defence, excusing himself from doing so on the plea of illness. Many of his friends found it next to impossible to believe him guilty of a grave deception; but though Carter and Pollard bought no overt charge, their printed evidence was deployed with escape-proof exactitude and skill. In subsequent years other enquiries carried the investigation further, and aspersions were cast upon friends and associates of Wise, since he could not have proceeded single-handed. As secretary of the Shelley Society he had access to printers who legitimately produced type facsimiles of certain poems, and Wise used this channel for the discredited items. The exposure did not answer the question to which no sure answer has yet been found: 'Why did Wise, admired and trusted, commit the forgeries?' The profit he made from selling copies of the forged pamphlets to American collectors and others was no more than he could have made by honest trading as their agent, a source from which indeed he made a fair income. It was suggested by some that vanity was Wise's animating motive, since he was able to win kudos for finding 'rarities' that had escaped discovery by others. The mystery remains; but if as a forger his actions might be charged to some psychological quirk, the fact that he was in addition an arrant thief was undis-

covered until some years after his death. As a trusted reader in the British Museum Library he was allowed to use in the Library such rare books as he required for bibliographical research, and there could be no reason to suppose that any exceptional watch needed to be kept. It was in due course discovered, *post mortem*, that he had abstracted pages from valuable British Museum copies to insert into incomplete copies in his own possession. Such made-up copies were either included in his own Ashley collection or sold to Americans. Among the ironies of the Wise affair is that his forgeries of non-existent rarities have acquired their own, criminal, rarity value.

Wister, Owen (1860-1938). Born in Philadelphia; educated in New Hampshire and in England and Switzerland before graduating at Harvard, where he studied music. He then continued his musical education in Paris, but on returning to America became a clerk in New York until a breakdown compelled him to recuperate on a Wyoming ranch. An interval in law practice was followed by other periods in Wyoming and in 1902 the enormous success of *The Virginian: A Horseman of the Plains* established him as an author. His other books, fiction and non-fiction, which did not equal *The Virginian*, include *Lady Baltimore* (1906), *The Pentecost of Calamity* (1915), *When West was West* (1928), *Theodore Roosevelt* (1930).

Withers, Percy (1867-1945). Born in Cheshire; educated in Manchester at the Grammar School and University. Studied and practised as a surgeon; Oxford Extension Lecturer in English Literature. Author of *Egypt of Yesterday and Today* (1909), *The Garland of Childhood* (1910); *In a Cumberland Dale* (1914) and *Friends in Solitude* (1923) give an attractive account of the people and region of the Lake District, where he lived for some years. *A Buried Life* (1940) records personal memories of his friend A. E. *Housman.

Wittgenstein, Ludwig Josef Johann (1889-1951). Born in Vienna; educated privately; worked in Berlin and Manchester as an engineer; and later studied mathematical logic at Cambridge, where he was Professor of Philosophy from 1939 to 1948, having become a British citizen in 1938. His *Tractatus Logico Philosophicus* (1921; Eng. trans. 1922) was a key work for the *Logical Positivism school of thought.

Wodehouse, P. G. (Sir Pelham Grenville Wodehouse, 1881-   ). Knighted 1975. Educated at Dulwich College. Began writing while a London bank-clerk and turned to journalism in 1903. School stories serialized in a monthly magazine for boys, *The Captain*, introduced Psmith and other characters who reappeared in later books, but it was with the creation of Bertie Wooster and his valet Jeeves that the Wodehouse humorous mythology was born. Unsurpassed both in verbal ingenuity and in mastery of comic situations, he was Britain's chief literary laughter-maker for more than half a century, and though he incurred some obloquy for an ingenuous broadcast from Berlin in 1941 his post-war books recovered his popularity and restored the early ones to favour. His audience embraced all classes and all levels of intellect, and though he made no claim to be more than an entertainer, few eyebrows were raised disapprovingly when the University of Oxford made him an honorary Doctor of Literature. He also collaborated in numerous stage successes. Author of *The White Feather* (1907), *Enter Psmith* (1909), *Leave It to Psmith* (1923), *The Inimitable Jeeves* (1924), *Summer Lightning* (1929), *Blandings Castle* (1935), *The Code of the Woosters* (1938), *The Mating Season* (1949), *Something Fishy* (1956), *Ice in the Bedroom* (1961) and very many other novels and collections of short stories. Autobiography: *Performing Flea* (1953), *Over Seventy* (1957).

Wolfe, Humbert (1885-1940). Born in Italy; brought to England and educated at Bradford and Oxford; entered the Civil Service and rose to the position of Deputy Secretary in the Ministry of Labour. His early books of poems attracted little attention—*London Sonnets* (1919), *Circular Saws* (1922)—but he had a considerable though temporary vogue with *Kensington Gardens* (1923), *Requiem* (1927), *Humoresque* (1926) and *News of the Devil* (1926). *Dialogues and Monologues* (1929) is a collection of critical essays.

Wolfe, Nero. Detective in crime stories by Rex *Stout.

Wolfe, Thomas (Thomas Clayton Wolfe, 1900-1938). Born in North Carolina; educated at the University there; studied playwriting at Harvard. Taught English for a while at New York University; made several trips to Europe and lived briefly in London. Acclamation and condemnation were equally distributed when his first novel *Look Homeward,*

Angel (1929) appeared. Though still overlong, it had been hewn from a larger verbal mass by the publishers, and retained much of the strained verbosity and incompletely assimilated autobiography of the original manuscript. *Of Time and the River* (1935) was marked by similar characteristics, as were the posthumously published *The Web and the Rock* (1939) and *You Can't Go Home Again* (1940). Written by a man of undoubted genius, his books are robbed of greatness through lack of literary discipline and verbal control.

Women in Love. Novel by D. H. *Lawrence published in 1920. At the end of Lawrence's *The *Rainbow* Ursula Brangwen, having lost her lover and failed to get her degree, is left with the limited prospect of teaching in a local school in the Midland mining region. At the beginning of the present book, several years later, she is a class-teacher at Willey Green Grammar School, and her younger sister Gudrun is art mistress there after training in London, where she also has some repute as a carver and modeller. The sisters are brought into personal relationships with prominent men and women in neighbouring society, particularly with two close friends—Gerald Crich, son of the local mine-owner, and Rupert Birkin, school inspector. Gerald's father, who is slowly dying, had controlled the mine benevolently: 'he wanted his industry to be run on love'; but the son believes in position and authority, and by skilled organization and by establishing 'the perfect, inhuman machine' he restores the prosperity which had been fading from both owners and miners. During a water-party given by the Crich family, one of their young daughters, Diana, and her would-be rescuer are drowned; while the youngest, Winifred, a difficult but talented child, later receives tuition in art from Gudrun Brangwen, whose friendship with Gerald Crich is furthered when an attic studio is fitted up for Winifred and her teacher at Shortlands, the Crich residence. The two men are torn between attraction and repulsion in their bearing towards women, and the love between Birkin and Ursula and that between Crich and Gudrun intermingles passion and hatred. Although this highly complex metaphysical conflict appears to be resolved when Ursula and Birkin marry and the other pair cohabit, the development is tragic for Gerald Crich. The two couples go abroad together, and in a hotel at Innsbruck Gudrun shows particular interest in Loerke, a German sculptor, after her sister and Birkin have left for Verona. While she and Loerke are on a tobogganing excursion, Crich follows them, attacks the German and half-throttles Gudrun. He then goes off into the mountains and is found next day dead in the snow.

Wonham. *See* *Stephen Wonham.

Woodham-Smith, Cecil (*née* Cecil Blanche Fitzgerald, 1896- ; Mrs G. I. Woodham-Smith). Born in Wales; educated at Oxford. Author of *Florence Nightingale* (1950), *The Reason Why* (1953), *Lady in Chief* (1953), *The Great Hunger* (1962). Under the pseudonym Janet Gordon she published *April Sky* (1938), *Tennis Star* (1940), *Just Off Bond Street* (1940).

Woods, Margaret L. (*née* Margaret Louisa Bradford, 1856-1945). Born at Rugby; educated privately and at Leamington; married Rev. H. G. Woods, President of Trinity College, Oxford, and later Master of the Temple. Her *Collected Poems* appeared in 1913, *The Return and other Poems* in 1921. She also wrote novels, among which *A Village Tragedy* (1887) is her masterpiece; *A Poet's Youth* (1923).

Woolf, Leonard (Leonard Sidney Woolf, 1880-1969). Born in London; educated at St Paul's School and Cambridge. Served in the Ceylon Civil Service, 1904-11. On returning to England he wrote for the *Nation* and *New Statesman and took a prominent part in *Fabian Society and Labour Party politics. Married Virginia Stephen, 1912 (see below). Wrote novels—*The Village in the Jungle* (1913), *The Wise Virgins* (1914)—and *Stories of the East* (1915), but afterwards confined his writing mainly to politics and international affairs: *International Government* (1916), a foreshadowing of the League of Nations, *Principia Politica* (1953), etc. His autobiography began in *Sowing* (1960), and continued in *Growing* (1961) and *Beginning Again* (1964). His third volume, covering the years 1911 to 1918 is a valuable record of the early stages of the *Bloomsbury Group and for its individual portraits of eminent contemporaries—Beatrice and Sidney *Webb, Bernard *Shaw, Desmond *MacCarthy, Katherine *Mansfield—and with much about his wife. The autobiography continued in *Downhill All the Way* (1967) and concluded with *The Journey not the Arrival Matters* (published posthumously, 1969).

Woolf, Virginia (*née* Adeline Virginia Stephen, 1882-1941; Mrs Leonard Woolf). Born in London, daughter of Sir Leslie *Stephen; educated at home, where she was in frequent contact with her father's eminent literary and political friends. After his death in 1904, she and her brother settled in Gordon Square, which was to become the centre for the *Bloomsbury Group, and in that company she met Leonard Woolf and married him in 1912. In 1917 they started the Hogarth Press, named from Hogarth House in Richmond to which they moved in 1915. From childhood she suffered from recurrent conditions of nervous stress which led on several occasions to mental collapse and attempts at suicide, the last of these ending in her drowning. She began to write her first novel, *The Voyage Out*, before marriage and finished it in 1913, a breakdown delaying publication until 1915. Though she was to become the most celebrated woman writer of the period in the 1920s and after, the first edition (2000 copies) of her first novel lasted for fifteen years. In order that she might have some normal occupation with a therapeutic value, she and her husband taught themselves typesetting and printing with a hand press installed in the dining-room and produced *Two Stories* by L. and V. Woolf as Publication No 1 of the Hogarth Press in 1917. Katherine Mansfield's *Prelude* (1918) and T. S. Eliot's *Poems* (1919) followed, and by the time they printed and issued Eliot's *The Waste Land* in 1923 they were established publishers able to handle Virginia's novels: **Jacob's Room* (1922), *Mrs Dalloway* (1925), **To the Lighthouse* (1927), *Orlando (1928), *The* *Waves (1931), *The Years* (1938), *Between the Acts* (1941). Her genius was of a nature that was caged by the form of the novel, and genius has to be granted without confidence that she was well equipped as a writer of fiction. Her characters are for the most part made in her own image or in that of others in her own introspective intellectual circle of intimates: they are deficient in flesh and blood and bone and insufficiently differentiated one from another. The mental tension which, as her husband reports, set her mind 'racing' and, in conversation, might suddenly make her seem to 'leave the ground' and soar into some ecstatic region, would have found a more accordant outlet in verse. Her novels are, indeed, in spirit and atmosphere, more attuned to the poetic mode than to prose fiction. When she turned to literary criticism, ment and in other essays, she was able to shed the confining bonds of an inappropriate medium, and she may be longest remembered by *The Common Reader* volumes (1st series 1925, 2nd series 1932), to which could be added, by selection from her novels, some entrancing passages with no strict dependence upon story or characterization which establish her among the modern masters of English prose. Her several volumes of essays were reprinted as *Collected Essays of Virginia Woolf* (4 vols, 1966-67).

Woollcott, Alexander (Alexander Humphreys Woollcott, 1887-1943). Born in New Jersey; went on the stage in childhood before continuing his education at Hamilton College, New York, and Columbia University. Dramatic critic of the *New York Times*, 1914-22, and of the *World*, 1925-28. He capitalized his own exuberant personality and was not unrecognizably portrayed in the Kaufman and Hart comedy *The Man Who Came to Dinner* (1939), in which Woollcott himself acted. *While Rome Burns* (1934), a collection of mixed essays, made him best-known in England.

Woolley, Sir Leonard (Charles Leonard Woolley, 1880-1960; knighted 1935). Born in London; educated at Leatherhead and Oxford. Eminent as an archaeologist, his most important excavations were in Mesopotamia, where at the biblical Ur of the Chaldees (Genesis 11:28; 15:7) his important discoveries disclosed the royal cemetery. His various findings are attractively recorded in *The Sumerians* (1928), *Digging up the Past* (1930), *Ur of the Chaldees* (1929), *A Forgotten Kingdom* (1952).

Works of Max Beerbohm, The. The author's first volume of essays, published in 1896, containing 'Dandies and Dandies', 'A Good Prince', '1880', 'King George the Fourth', 'The Pervasion of Rouge', 'Poor Romeo!', 'Diminuendo'. It already showed a remarkable gift of irony and satire expressed in urbane and precociously mature prose.

Wouk, Herman (1915-). Born in New York; educated at Columbia. World War II service in the U. S. navy led to his widely acclaimed novel *The Caine Mutiny* (1951) which had further success as play and film. Other novels: *Aurora Dawn* (1947), *The City Boy* (1948), *Marjorie Morningstar* (1955). *The Traitor* (a play, 1949).

Wren, P. C. (Percival Christopher Wren, 1885-1941). Born in Devon; educated at Oxford; travelled widely and worked at many jobs before becoming a prolific novelist whose *Beau Geste* (1924) was for many years a popular favourite. Other novels include *The Wages of Virtue* (1916), *Valiant Dust* (1932), *The Fort in the Jungle* (1936).

Wrench, Sir Evelyn (John Evelyn Leslie Wrench, 1882-1966; knighted 1932). Born in Ireland; educated near Oxford and at Eton. When eighteen started a picture-postcard business which flourished for several years; then worked for the Northcliffe press at home and abroad. Founded the English-Speaking Union in 1918. Author of *Immortal Years* (1945), *Geoffrey Dawson and our Times* (1955), *Alfred Milner, the Man of no Illusions* (1958), etc.

Wright, Frank Lloyd (1869-1959). Born and educated in Wisconsin; apprenticed as an architect, and in his own practice from 1893 became internationally renowned for buildings in several countries which combined originality of design with structural strength and aesthetic merit. He wrote numerous books including *An Interpretation of Japanese Prints* (1912), *Experimenting with Human Lives* (1923), *Modern Architecture* (1931), *The Nature of Materials* (1932), *The Disappearing City* (1932), *An Autobiography— Frank Lloyd Wright* (1932; 1943).

Wright, Harold Bell (1872-1944). Born in New York. Losing his parents while still a small boy, he was educated at a county school and had further education terminated by ill-health. Without theological training he started to preach and was a pastor for several years. From 1907, when *The Shepherd of the Hills* was published, he was an immensely popular novelist, though his later books did not rival the more than a million sales of *The Winning of Barbara Worth* (1911), since his unimpeachable morality and outdoor healthiness ceased to be in tune with the tendencies of the new age.

Wright, Judith (Judith Arundell Wright, 1915-). Born in New South Wales; educated at Sydney University; lectured at universities on Australian literature. Author of several volumes of poetry including *The Moving Image* (1946), *Woman to Man* (1949), *The Two Fires* (1955), *A Book of Birds* (1962), *The Other Half* (1966). *Collected Poems* (1971).

Wright, Richard (1909-1960). Born on a plantation in Mississippi. The father having left the family, the boy was placed in an orphanage until he went to school, afterwards becoming a post-office clerk. Determined to be a writer, he published a volume of stories, *Uncle Tom's Children* (1938) and in 1940 *Native Son* (a novel about a Negro boy brought up in Chicago slums who ends as a murderer and is executed), which gave the author an assured place in contemporary literature. From having been a devout Communist, he wrote, in *The Outsider* (1953), a novel depicting the destruction wrought in a Negro's life by political extremism. His other books include *Black Power* (1954), *The Color Curtain* (1956), *The Long Dream* (1958), and his autobiography, *Black Boy* (1945).

Wright, Sydney Fowler. *See* Sydney *Fowler.

Wright, Willard Huntington. *See* S. S. *Van Dine.

Wycherley, Richard Newman. *See* Gilbert *Murray (2).

Wylie, Alick, his sons **David** and **James** and daughter **Maggie** in J. M. Barrie's *What Every Woman Knows* (1908).

Wylie, Elinor (*née* Elinor Hoyt, 1885-1928). Born in New Jersey; educated at private schools. She married William Rose *Benét, her third husband, in 1923. She was one of the most distinguished American poets and novelists of her time, intensity of expression being matched by delicacy and felicity of style. After an anonymous book of poems published privately in England, *Incidental Numbers* (1912), she was silent until *Nets to Catch the Wind* came out in 1921 and at once made her reputation as a poet. *Black Armour* (1923), *Angels and Earthly Creatures* (1929),

and *Trivial Breath* (1928) followed, and, after her death, *Collected Poems* (1932) and *Last Poems* (1943). The fragile beauty of her prose is displayed in the novels: *Jennifer Lorn* (1923), *The Venetian Glass Nephew* (1925), *Mortal Image* (1927), and *Mr Hodge and Mr Hazard* (1928). *Collected Prose* (1933).

Wylie, I. A. R. (Ida Alexa Ross Wylie, 1885-). Born in Australia; educated in Brussels, at Cheltenham, and in Germany. She travelled widely and spent lengthy periods writing in Germany, England, and America, buying and living on a farm in New Jersey. Had much success with her numerous short stories, collected in *Happy Endings* (1915), *All Sorts* (1919), *Storm in April* (1946). Novels: *Towards Morning* (1920), *The Silver Virgin* (1929), *Furious Young Man* (1935), *The Young in Heart* (1939). Autobiography: *My Life With George* (1940).

Wyndham, John (pseudonym of John Benyon Harris, 1903-1969). Son of a barrister; brought up in Birmingham; educated in Derbyshire and at Bedales. Worked in various occupations, from farming to advertising. As a short-story writer he contributed to American *pulp magazines from the mid-1920s until he had a more substantial success after World War II with *The Day of the Triffids* (1951), the first of the novels which made him outstanding among the writers of *Science Fiction, a kind which attracted him from boyhood through reading H. G. *Wells and Jules Verne. He preferred to call his own books 'logical fantasies'. They include *The Kraken Wakes* (1953), *The Chrysalids* (1955), *The Midwich Cuckoos* (1957), *Trouble With Lichen* (1960); and collections of short stories: *The Seeds of Time* (1956), *Consider Her Ways* (1961).

Xanadu. 'In Xanadu did Kubla Khan / A stately pleasure dome decree'. The opening lines of Coleridge's *Kubla Khan* were the starting point for *The Road to Xanadu* (1927) by the American scholar John Livingston *Lowes. It set an academic fashion in searching out the sources behind works of imagination.

Xerography. A method of reproducing printed or manuscript documents and books by a photographic process in which the sensitized image on the dry plate or paper is rendered permanent by being automatically coated in the machine with an electrically charged powder. The patented Xerox process enables copies to be made instantaneously on any ordinary (i.e. unprepared) paper.

Yates, Dornford (pseudonym of Cecil William Mercer, 1885-1960). Born in London; educated at Harrow and Oxford; studied law but turned to writing. Author of *Berry and Co.* (1921) and other novels about Berry; *Jonah and Co.* (1922), *Maiden Stakes* (1929), *Wife Apparent* (1956) are among numerous other novels. Autobiographical: *As Berry and I Were Saying* (1952), *Berry and I Look Back* (1958).

Yates, Marion. Senior assistant in the costume department of Roberts & Huxtable's drapery store in Granville Barker's *The *Madras House* (1910); seduced by Constantine Madras, she admits 'I knew what I was about. I wanted to have my fling.'

Yeatman, R. J. (Robert Julian Yeatman, 1898-1968). In collaboration with W. S. Sellar (1898-1951) he wrote one of the most popular humorous books of the century, *1066 and All That* (1930), 'a subtle mixture of schoolboy howlers, witty distortions and artful puns'. They also collaborated in *And Now All This* (1932), *Horse Nonsense* (1933), *Garden Rubbish* (1936). Both authors were educated at Oxford: Sellar became a schoolmaster, Yeatman a copywriter and advertising manager.

Yeats, W. B. (William Butler Yeats, 1865-1939). Born in Dublin; educated in London at Hammersmith and in Dublin. His father John Butler Yeats forsook law for painting, and his brother Jack B. Yeats (1871-1957) became the best-known Irish painter of his time. In conformity with this, W. B. became an art student until he was twenty-one, but on settling in London from 1887 he was attracted into literary circles and formed friendships with the leading 1890s writers. He also developed the interest in occultism and Eastern mysticism which for a time strongly influenced his outlook and was never entirely outlived. But his chief attraction was to Celtic myths and the Irish literary rebirth, of which he was one of the most active promoters. Having established in London the Irish Literary Society he went back to Dublin in 1891 and founded a similar movement leading in 1899 to the *Irish Literary Theatre, with Lady *Gregory as a principal associate. Meanwhile Yeats had already become a celebrated poet and poetic dramatist with *The Wanderings of Oisin* (1889), *The Countess Cathleen* (1892), *The Land of Heart's Desire* (1894), *The Wind among the*

Reeds (1899), and the two volumes *Poems* (1895 and 1899). He had also published prose works, *The Celtic Twilight* (1893), *The Secret Rose* (1897), *Tables of the Law* (1897), and *The Adoration of the Magi* (1897), besides a collection of *Irish Fairy Tales* (1892) and (in collaboration with E. J. Ellis) an edition of William Blake's writings (1893) which pioneered the many Blake studies undertaken by scholars in the next half century and more. *The Countess Cathleen* was part of the programme for the first performance by the Irish Literary Theatre in Dublin in 1899, and for many years Yeats continued to be prominent there as a playwright and in management, helping the *Abbey Theatre and its *Irish Players company on their road to worldwide fame. The first issue of his *Collected Works* appeared in 1908, by which time he was renowned as a lyrical and romantic poet and dramatist steeped in Irish mythology and the Irish scene. By the majority of readers he was still admired for such poems as 'The Lake Isle of Innisfree', 'Down by the Salley Gardens', 'When You are Old', 'The Fiddler of Dooney' and others which a later generation was inclined to belittle as mere 'anthology pieces'. Although World War I and the Irish troubles which burst into flame in the Easter 1916 rebellion left an indelible impression on his mind, a new Yeats was already evident in the poem headed 'September 1913' (included in *Responsibilities*, the volume published in 1914) with its refrain 'Romantic Ireland's dead and gone, / It's with O'Leary in the grave'. In *The Wild Swans at Coole* (1919) two poems in particular stood out, 'In Memory of Major Robert Gregory' and 'An Irish Airman Foresees His Death'; in *Michael Robartes and the Dancer* (1921), 'Easter 1916' and 'The Second Coming'; in *The Tower* (1928), 'Sailing to Byzantium'; in *The Winding Stair* (1933), 'Byzantium'. Ireland did not cease to preoccupy him, but it was modern political Ireland, not ancient legendary Ireland. And from being a romantic lyrical poet he became a poet in the new mode which dominated poetry in English from 1917 (the date of T. S. Eliot's *Prufrock*) onward. 'Difficulty' was in the air, and Yeats's poetry had become more difficult; despair was rampant, and Yeats was not wanting in despair, and even disgust, as he aged. In 'The Tower' he asked: 'What shall I do with this absurdity— / . . . this caricature, / Decrepit age that has been tied to me / As to a dog's tail?' He was approaching his middle sixties when the volume containing that poem was published. In 'The Spur', included with *Last Poems* written in his early seventies, he wrote that 'lust and rage . . . dance attention [*sic*] upon my old age'. He had become in the eyes of the generation into which he lived the revered patriarch of modern poetry, but in his last poem ('Under Ben Bulben') dated four months before he died at the age of seventy-three, he urged, 'Irish poets, learn your trade, / Sing whatever is well made, / Scorn the sort now growing up / All out of shape from toe to top'. The main bulk of his writings is contained in *Collected Poems* (complete edn, 1950), *Collected Plays* (complete edn, 1952), *Autobiographies* (1955).

Yeats-Brown, F. C. (Francis Charles Claypon Yeats-Brown, 1886-1944). Born in Italy; educated in England at Harrow and Sandhurst. Served as an army officer, 1906-25, in India, France and Mesopotamia; captured by the Turks in 1915, escaped 1918. After retirement from the army he was assistant editor of the *Spectator*, 1926-28. He had an immediate literary success with *Bengal Lancer* (1930), an autobiography which with many alterations in Hollywood became a popular film. Later books: *Golden Horn* (1932), *Lancer at Large* (1936), *Yoga Explained* (1937), *European Jungle* (1939), *Pageant of India* (1942).

Yellow Book, The. A literary and art quarterly, in yellow bindings decorated by Aubrey Beardsley which ran from 1894 to 1897, edited by Henry Harland. Though it was considered a 'decadent' publication, its contents did little or nothing to support that judgment, though Beardsley's drawings were thought shocking by many. The contributors included Henry *James, Max *Beerbohm, H. G. *Wells, W. B. *Yeats, and other 'classics' of the next generation.

Yerby, Frank (Frank Garvin Yerby, 1916-   ). Born in Georgia of Negro descent; educated there and in Tennessee and at the University of Chicago; worked in motor and aircraft factories. His historical novels, which sold many millions, include *The Foxes of Harrow* (1946), *The Golden Hawk* (1948), *The Saracen Blade* (1952), *The Girl from Storyville* (1972).

Yet Again. Volume of twenty-two essays by Max *Beerbohm, published in 1909, and including 'The Decline of the Graces' (originally subtitled 'With Advice on Deportment for Young Ladies'), 'The Ragged Regiment' (on the wax effigies in Westminster

Abbey), and pieces less characteristic than most of his writings.

York, Jeremy. *See* John *Creasey.

Yorke, Henry Vincent. *See* Henry *Green.

You Never Can Tell. Play in four acts by Bernard *Shaw, written 1895-96, performed in 1899; published in *Plays Pleasant*, 1898. In the dentist's surgery in a Devonshire seaside town, Mr Valentine has just made his first extraction. The pretty eighteen-year-old patient is soon joined by her twin brother, both irrepressibly and boisterously talkative in a humorously unconventional way. They invite Valentine to lunch at their hotel before introducing themselves as Dolly and Philip Clandon, children of Mrs Lanfrey Clandon, feminist author of a popular series of Twentieth Century Treatises, and all long-resident in Madeira. Their mother has persistently declined to give them the name of their father, a harsh-tempered violent man from whom she separated years ago, adopting her present name. Mrs Clandon and her elder daughter Gloria join Dolly and Philip at the dentist's, and Valentine immediately falls in love with Gloria. When his landlord, Fergus Crampton, is announced, Valentine fears he will demand the rent, six weeks overdue, but it is only an extraction he has come for. The young Clandons invite him, too, to join them at lunch. Mrs Clandon had previously left to meet an old solicitor friend, Finch M'Comas, at the hotel. She asks him to tell her daughters and son the story of her marriage, he being also a friend of her husband, who turns out to be the Crampton her children have recently met. The somewhat uncomfortable lunch party is soothed by the remarkable old waiter, William, who speaks 'with the sweetest propriety' in 'a quiet voice, with a gentle melody in it that gives sympathetic interest to his most commonplace remark'. When asked by Dolly if his son is also a waiter, William replies, 'He's at the Bar . . . a Q.C.', while his favourite saying is 'You never can tell'. Crampton informs M'Comas that he wants the deed of separation altered to give him custody of the twins, who are under age. Mrs Clandon having refused, M'Comas proposes that they take the opinion of an eminent Q.C. of his acquaintance whom he has just met near the hotel. At a fancy-dress ball that night Bohun Q.C.—William's son—persuades the disputants to come to a friendly arrangement. Gloria, brought up by her mother to be 'advanced' and unemotional, is at first disgusted when she feels herself mastered by Valentine, but says later 'I must fulfil my destiny, I suppose'—by marrying him.

Young, Andrew (Andrew John Young, 1885-1971). Born in Scotland at Elgin; educated in Edinburgh; entered the Anglican Church; after holding a living in Sussex he became Canon of Chichester Cathedral in 1948. His lyrical nature poems are gathered in *The Collected Poems of Andrew Young* (1960). *Into Hades* (1952) is a longer and more ambitious poem. Prose essays: *A Prospect of Flowers* (1945), *A Retrospect of Flowers* (1950).

Young, Edward Hilton (1879-1960; Baron Kennet 1960). Born in Surrey; educated at Eton and Cambridge; practised as a barrister; M.P., 1915-35. Served in the navy in World War I. Minister of Health, 1931-35. Member of numerous Royal Commissions. President of the Poetry Society and author of *A Muse at Sea* (1919), *Verses* (1935), *A Bird in the Bush* (1937). Father of Wayland *Young.

Young, E. H. (Emily Hilda Young, 1880-1949). Born in Northumberland. Author of distinguished novels in a plain style about plain people, among them *A Corn of Wheat* (1910), *Moor Fires* (1916), *William* (1925), *Jenny Wren* (1932), *Chatterton Square* (1947).

Young, Francis Brett (1884-1954). Born in Worcestershire; educated at Epsom School; studied medicine at the University of Birmingham; practised as a physician in England and then as a ship's surgeon until he went to East Africa in the Medical Corps throughout World War I, afterwards writing the best book dealing with the campaign there: *Marching on Tanga* (1918). Before the war he was regarded as one of the most promising of the young novelists, with *Deep Sea* (1914) and *The Dark Tower* (1914), followed by *The Iron Age* (1916). In the post-war years he wrote many novels which, though more popular than his early ones, disappointed critical expectations. *Portrait of Clare* (1927) had a popular reception, as did *My Brother Jonathan* (1928) and *The House under the Water* (1932). *The City of Gold* (1939) is set in South Africa where he settled some time before his death there. *The Island* (1944) is a long narrative poem in various styles and metres surveying English history.

Young, G. M. (George Malcolm Young, 1882-1959). Educated at St Paul's and Oxford. Author of *Gibbon* (1932), *Charles I and Cromwell* (1932), *Victorian England: Portrait of an Age* (1936), *Daylight and Champaign* (essays; 1937), *To-day and Yesterday* (1948), *Last Essays* (1950), *Stanley Baldwin* (biography; 1952).

Young, Stark (1881-1963). Born in Mississippi; educated at the University there and at Columbia University. Held professorships in the University of Texas and at Amherst College but retired in 1921 to devote his time to writing. Author of poems, plays in verse and prose, and novels, among which *So Red the Rose* (1934) received most attention. He also wrote dramatic criticism for the *New York Times* among other papers and translated plays by Tchekov.

Young, Wayland (Wayland Hilton Young, 1923- ; succeeded his father as 2nd Baron Kennet in 1960, but preferred not to use the title). Born in London; educated at Stowe, Cambridge, and Harvard. After naval service in World War II, worked in the Foreign Office and then as a journalist contributing to English, American and Italian publications. Author of *The Italian Left* (1949); *Old London Churches* (1956), *The Socialist Imagination* (1960)—both in collaboration with his wife, Elizabeth Young (née Elizabeth Ann Adams); *Eros Denied* (1965), and several novels, including *The Deadweight* (1952) and *Now or Never* (1953). His father was Edward Hilton *Young, 1st Baron Kennet.

Youth: A Narrative. Story by Joseph *Conrad published in *Youth and Two Other Stories* in 1902. Drinking in company with a 'man of finance', a 'man of accounts', 'a man of law', and another, *Marlowe tells of his first voyage to the East, which was also his first as second mate. He was twenty. His ship, the *Judea*, old, grimy, and rusty, 'left London in ballast—sand ballast—to load a cargo of coal in a northern port for Bangkok'. Caught in a gale off Yarmouth, the ship is damaged and the ballast shifts and has to be shovelled level again. Docking late in the Tyne, she has to wait a month to be loaded, is struck by a steamer when ready to leave dock and delayed three weeks for repairs. In a later gale the crew have to pump to keep afloat, and before the voyage proper begins they put in to Falmouth three times and ship a new crew at Liverpool. 'Then, on a fine moonlight night, all the rats left the ship.' In the Indian Ocean the cargo of coal is found to be on fire and eventually explodes before bursting into flame. The crew have to take to the boats, and after watching the *Judea* sink they row for nights and days before reaching land. 'And this is how I see the East. . . . I see it always from a small boat. . . . for me all the East is contained in that vision of my youth.'

Yutang, Lin. *See* *Lin Yutang.

Zangwill, Israel (1864-1926). Born in London of Russian-Jewish descent; from early education in elementary schools he went to London University; became in turn a teacher and a journalist, editing *Ariel*, a humorous periodical. His first novel came out in 1881 and several others followed before with *Children of the Ghetto* (1892), *The King of Schnorrers* (1894), *The Mantle of Elijah* (1900), and much other writing in prose, verse, and drama made him the most notable Jewish author of his time and a leader in various Jewish cultural organizations. Among his plays *The Melting Pot* (1908) attracted most attention, being concerned with the process of assimilating immigrants of various nationalities in the U.S.

Zionism. The movement started by Theodor Herzl in 1896 aiming to establish a Jewish state in Palestine with Jerusalem ('the city of Zion') as its capital. With Chaim Weizmann as its leader during World War I, it was encouraged by the *Balfour Declaration from the British Government in 1917; but it was not until 1948 that the independent State of Israel was proclaimed.

Zinsser, Hans (1878-1940). Born in New York of German parentage; after varied schooling, studied medicine at Columbia, where (after hospital and teaching experience) he was appointed Professor of Bacteriology from 1913. Service on medical commissions in Serbia, Russia, and Mexico led to his remarkable *Rats, Lice, and History* (1935), a work, which, though written for popular reading, is also a serious and well-founded study of the catastrophic effects of epidemics, especially typhus, on the course of world history. His autobiography appeared as *As I Remember Him* (1941) and, also posthumously, his poems *Spring, Summer, and Autumn* (1942).

Zuleika Dobson or an Oxford Love Story. Novel by Max *Beerbohm published in 1911. With sustained irony it narrates the history of the irruption into Oxford undergraduate society of the beautiful granddaughter of the Warden of Judas during Eights Week. Parodying the mythological dealings of Zeus with Clio the Muse of History, the author conceives that, made invisible, he is indued with the power to keep under surveillance Zuleika Dobson from the moment she steps out of the London train at Oxford station. While driving with her grandfather to his College, a very splendid youth goes spurring by on a polo-pony without a second glance at Zuleika, whose loveliness causes even the time-worn busts of Roman Emperors outside the Sheldonian Theatre to glisten with beads of perspiration. Zuleika is piqued by the apparent inattention of the splendid youth, who is the Duke of Dorset, an undergraduate of Jesus. She supposes that she has at last found a young man 'who would not bow down to her; whom, looking up to him, she could adore'. When she discovers that he is on the contrary infatuated, she spurns him, but is triumphant and encouraging when he swears he will die for her. This he does by drowning himself in the river from the Judas barge while the races are in progress. Having similarly sworn, the whole of the undergraduates of the University, except one who subsequently leaps from his window, plunge into the river. Zuleika looks up the next train to Cambridge.

Zweig, Arnold (1887-1968). Born in Prussia; educated at German universities. Author of many novels, short stories, plays, and essays. His novel, *The Case of Sergeant Grischa* (1928), made him internationally celebrated. It stands high among the books of World War I, a humane, ironic, and tragic glimpse of the fatal idiocies of war.

Zweig, Stefan (1881-1942). Born in Vienna and educated at school and university there. Travelled widely, eventually settling in England and becoming a naturalized British citizen, though he later went to America and, in despair at the state of war-ruined Europe, committed suicide. He wrote biographical and critical studies of *Verlaine* (1913), *Verhaeren* (1914), *Rolland* (1921), *Erasmus* and others, *Jeremiah* (a play, 1922), and novels among which *Beware of Pity* (1939) attracted most attention.

Appendix

Literature and its Transmission

Few readers, probably, give more than a passing glance at that part of a book known to printers and publishers as 'prelims' – the pages that come before the beginning of the author's own words. Print-addicted readers, however, who cannot bear to miss a single word, will notice with more or less incomprehension a warning in the prelims of many present-day books (including this one): 'All rights reserved. No part of this publication may be reproduced, stored in a retrieval system, or transmitted in any form or by any means, electronic, mechanical, photocopying, recording, or otherwise, without the prior permission of the Copyright owner.' That is modern legalise for 'Thou shalt not steal.' Piracy of books has been endemic for centuries, if not precisely from China to Peru, certainly from the far East to the far West. *Shakespeare's Fight with the Pirates* by A. W. Pollard is but one reminder that the English were once as active in stealing literary property as any other nation.

Copyright owners are alert to take legal proceedings against pirates when detected, but the words 'electronic, mechanical, photocopying, recording' in the current warning notice, indicate the greater difficulty of safeguarding nowadays against thievery, for none of those newer means of unauthorized reproduction comes easily to the notice of copyright owners. Culprits, when detected, may claim that they are benefactors spreading knowledge, but theft is theft; and products of an author's mental skill belong to him as much as a craftsman's handiwork belongs to the craftsman.

But it is not the purpose of this Appendix to dwell upon the ethics of piracy; it is to consider the possibility that the warning notice presages the death of the printed book.

If the printed book were to become a casualty of the scientific and technological revolution, would literature itself die? Or would it mean what some might regard as a lesser evil: the putting back of the clock some thirty centuries or more and returning to an age of oral transmission which might produce another Homer? Already, poets young and old are favouring oral transmission, delivering their verses by voice at poetry recitals and in pubs and other places where the audience is not a literary one. A good deal of what is thus transmitted may already have appeared or will later appear in print. Or it may be that no true transmission is thus effected, for a man with a pint is capable of profound inattention, though perhaps not more so than those in an overt literary audience at a poetry recital, or even readers of a book of printed verse.

The printed book is little more than five hundred years old. If the poets of antiquity produced what is accepted as 'literature', then literature existed for not less than five times as many centuries before the printed book was invented.

What print achieved uniquely was transmission by multiplication. It became possible for more to read than could hear when the poet had a numerically limited audience. It has to be assumed that an unlimited number of readers is preferable to a few score of hearers. Or at any rate it had to be so assumed until the 1920s when radio began to talk to millions; and, further, until the 1940s when television started the audio-visual revolution in the home and soon steered it into the schools, where children who had previously been readers became lookers and hearers. The positive gain in education from the roots cannot at this early stage be forecast. Publishers are expanding in the audio-visual field, and a permanent development there could hardly fail to check a child's desire · or willingness to read or to possess books. It is not universally lamented that a proportion of English-speaking children reach the school leaving age while still unable to read. (See page 336; entry on McLuhan.) Future historians, however, may view the growth of illiteracy, even among university graduates, as calamitous.

In the poetry revival thought to be in progress through the spoken delivery of (sometimes improvised) verse, the poet, like the oldtime bard, has musical support, though not now from a harp of his own plucking, but from a pop group with electric guitar and microphone. Whether by mass means it will be possible and socially beneficial to establish 'poetry for the millions' is open to doubt. The poetry-for-the-workers movement in the 1930s did not utter in terms understandable by its intended audience.

Before the demise of the book under neo-cultural and financial pressure is taken to be inevitable in the long run, it is not unbecoming to speak an ante-mortem word in praise of those, the publishers, who through the centuries have been transmitters of literature. Though it has been assumed, here and there and now and then, that publishers and authors are natural enemies, the gibe 'Barabbas was a publisher' is slanderous of all but the submerged few 'vanity publishers' who con the writers of manuscripts unpublishable except by raiding the unwary authors' pockets.

The history of publishing gives a host of instances of honest mutual advantage between authors and publishers, far outweighing such past penny-pinching as Samuel Simmons's contract with Milton for *Paradise Lost*. (It has been pointed out in extenuation that the down payment of £5 in 1667 would appear astronomically more in equivalent modern currency.) Charlotte Brontë and George Smith (later Smith, Elder and Company, who also published Thackeray, Browning, George Eliot, Trollope, Matthew Arnold, among others eminent in English literature); Byron and John Murray, leading to a salon of great writers at Murray's famous 50 Albemarle Street (still occupied by the firm more than a century and a half later); Longmans and Wordsworth, Scott, Macaulay, Newman, Disraeli, Stevenson; Macmillan and Hardy, Kipling, Yeats: these are but a very few of the fruitful and (on both sides) mostly profitable dealings between authors and their publishers. Authors invest their time, publishers their money; they are mutually dependent, though the publisher could find other outlets for his money. Authors have attempted to be their own publishers, but few have the business skill to succeed. Bernard Shaw already had his wife's fortune to buttress him before he engaged printers (R. & R. Clark of Edinburgh) to produce his books and publishers (Constable & Company) to distribute them to booksellers. This exceptional arrangement worked well for an exceptional man able to pay the bills and with an acute business instinct.

The service publishers can render to literature in the normal way is not limited to their output of new books. Since World War II the rocketing of production costs and consequently of the prices of books, has put almost all except paperbacks beyond the means of even the most dedicated bookbuyer. This has made it the more desirable to keep in remembrance those who have made it possible for the poor man (who is now as often in the upper and middle classes as among the historic 'poor') to acquire books. Though the beginning of Penguin Books in 1935 started a publishing revolution and put a myriad of readers in debt to Allen Lane the founder of the series, some older readers remember with gratitude among earlier paperbound series Cassell's National Library at 3d a volume (or 6d in cloth binding). Between 1886 and 1890 some two hundred titles were issued at the rate of one a week. Printing was not then the fine art it had become by the Penguins' day, nor did Cassell's National Library include recent books. It was confined to standard works of earlier literature, but was nevertheless immensely serviceable, whether to students or to those who read solely for pleasure. On a still more modest level were the publications of W. T. Stead, who combined a love of literature with a crusade against the white slave traffic. His Penny Poets and other series at the turn of the century made no pretension to scholarship, but they were wonderful pennorths and were often thumbed to final disintegration. Dent's Everyman's Library of 1000 classics was (at 1/– each until 1914) an incomparable extender of knowledge; Nelson's red cloth Sevenpennies a cherishable collection of modern novels, still good to snap up at secondhand. Penguins at 6d were an innovation to marvel at in 1935, and even now at variable higher prices they compare advantageously with new books in the £10 plus range, but the glamour is tarnished.

The 'economic crisis' to which all present woes are apt to be attributed, can certainly be held responsible for the shrinkage of channels of literary transmission owing to the merging of individual publishing houses into financially supportable agglomerations. Several long-established houses have come under American control or under that of British based concerns committed to diversification. This has led to the adoption of certain transatlantic procedures in the relations between author and publisher. In this connection there is point in the remark of an English publisher's working colleague who remarked that 'he supposed he was not an ideal editor because he thought that authors should write their own books'.*

* Quoted in *Publishing and Bookselling* (5th edn by F. A. Mumby and Ian Norrie, 1974), p.513

While most authors are glad to benefit from editorial aid kept within acceptable limits, the aim of an experienced, skilful and tactful English editor is to allow scope to the author's individuality while safeguarding him from inaccuracy or inconsistency. The editor should be scrupulous to ensure that what leaves his hands on the way to the printer is still the author's book and has not become transmogrified into the editor's book.

An American 'copy editor' is accustomed to exercise a larger function which need not be detailed here. It may extend as far as ensuring that the author's vocabulary is confined to the wordage in the *College Dictionary*. This practice might conceivably be viewed as a recrudescence of the old 'classical *versus* romantic' controversy which raged in the first Elizabethan age and has broken out periodically since. Though 'classical' and 'romantic' in the past sense are perhaps no longer usable, 'formality' and 'freedom of expression' could be substituted. The English tradition is (or was) to say what one thinks in the way one wants to say it. Americans, with their roots in the formal eighteenth century, may be more readily conditioned to say what they think in the way a teacher (or editor) decrees they shall say it.

Of course, whether in England or in America, a publisher who commissions a book expects to get the book he requires in the form he requires it, free from authorial meanderings, quirks and eccentricities. But when an English author 'does his own thing' and offers it to a publisher, he is unlikely to agree to his book being shackled. It seems, though, that the days when a writer *could* offer a book to a publisher may be passing, for at least one London house bearing a famous name is said to have declared that no unsolicited manuscript will be read. . . . No future *Jane Eyre*s!

A.C.W.